Logic, Argumentation & Reasoning

Interdisciplinary Perspectives from the Humanities and Social Sciences

Volume 9

Series editor
Shahid Rahman

Logic, Argumentation & Reasoning (LAR) explores links between the Humanities and Social Sciences, with theories (including decision and action theory) drawn from the cognitive sciences, economics, sociology, law, logic, and the philosophy of science. Its main ambitions are to develop a theoretical framework that will encourage and enable interaction between disciplines, and to integrate the Humanities and Social Sciences around their main contributions to public life, using informed debate, lucid decision-making, and action based on reflection.

The series welcomes research from the analytic and continental traditions, placing emphasis on four main focal areas:

- Argumentation models and studies
- Communication, language and techniques of argumentation
- Reception of arguments, persuasion and the impact of power
- Diachronic transformations of argumentative practices

LAR is developed in partnership with the Maison Européenne des Sciences de l'Homme et de la Société (MESHS) at Nord - Pas de Calais and the UMR-STL: 8163 (CNRS).

Proposals should include :

- A short synopsis of the work, or the introduction chapter
- The proposed Table of Contents
- The CV of the lead author(s)
- If available: one sample chapter

We aim to make a first decision within 1 month of submission. In case of a positive first decision, the work will be provisionally contracted—the final decision about publication will depend upon the result of an anonymous peer review of the complete manuscript. The complete work is usually peer-reviewed within 3 months of submission.

LAR discourages the submission of manuscripts containing reprints of previously published material, and/or manuscripts that are less than 150 pages / 85,000 words.

For inquiries and proposal submissions, authors may contact the editor-in-chief Shahid Rahman at: shahid.rahman@univ-lille3.fr, or the managing editor, Laurent Keiff, at: laurent.keiff@gmail.com.

More information about this series may be found at http://www.springer.com/series/11547

Walter Edward Young

The Dialectical Forge

Juridical Disputation and the Evolution of Islamic Law

Springer

Walter Edward Young
Alexander von Humboldt Kolleg
for Islamicate Intellectual History
Universität Bonn
Bonn, Nordrhein-Westfalen
Germany

ISSN 2214-9120 ISSN 2214-9139 (electronic)
Logic, Argumentation & Reasoning
ISBN 978-3-319-25520-0 ISBN 978-3-319-25522-4 (eBook)
DOI 10.1007/978-3-319-25522-4

Library of Congress Control Number: 2016958574

Printed on acid-free paper

This Springer imprint is published by Springer Nature
The registered company is Springer International Publishing AG
The registered company address is: Gewerbestrasse 11, 6330 Cham, Switzerland

To My Mother and Father
Nancy Louise Bird Young and *Courtney Denton Young, Jr.*
with loving gratitude for their
inspiration, encouragement,
and ceaseless giving

Acknowledgments

The present monograph would never have seen completion without the generous and patient support of mentors, family, and friends. My heartfelt thanks go to all who have provided me the space, the means, and the motivation to see this project through. Professor Robert Wisnovsky has been a constant, kind, and unstinting pillar of encouragement and support; and Professor Wael Hallaq has been an unflagging source of inspiration, strength, and bounteous good cheer. Both of these friends and mentors deserve more gratitude than I can properly express. A special word of thanks is owed to Professor Stephen Menn of McGill University and Professor Joseph Lowry of the University of Pennsylvania for their sound counsel and suggestions on numerous issues. It goes without saying that such faults as persist in the following pages are a measure of my falling away from the sound advice of all these benevolent teachers.

I would also thank my alma mater, the Institute of Islamic Studies at McGill University: its brilliant faculty, friendly staff, and kind-hearted librarians, with particular thanks to Professor Jamil Ragep and Professor Rula Abisaab. The greater part of my research was undertaken at this venerable institution, and I am grateful to all who have made it, and continue to make it, a congenial stronghold of pure scholarship. I also owe much to the generous support of the Islamic Legal Studies Program at Harvard University; a portion of this project was researched during my very beneficial time there as a Visiting Fellow in 2013, and I am particularly grateful to Dr. S. Nazim Ali and Ceallaigh Reddy. My special gratitude goes also to Professor Shahab Ahmed of Harvard for his warmhearted friendship, advocacy, and scholarly example. Your untimely passing is an unfathomable loss to us all. The latter stages of editing this volume were undertaken during my time on the IMPAcT project at the Oriental Institute, University of Oxford, under the profitable tutelage of Prof. Dr. Judith Pfeiffer; partial funding for this book was thus made available by the European Research Council under the *European Union's Seventh Framework Programme* (*FP7/2007-2013*)/ERC Starting Grant 263557 IMPAcT. Finally, I would express my appreciation to Professor Shahid Rahman for his kindness and subsequent encouragement in nominating this work for publication, and to all the helpful editors and staff at Springer, who rendered the process not only painless but enjoyable.

No project of this kind can be realized without a great deal of assistance and advice from family and friends. I would like to express my love and indebtedness to the Young Family and to the Mandjee Family, to the invincible Leonard Wood and the indomitable Hasher Majoka, and, above all, to the eternally smiling and supportive light of my heart, Saïs Mandjee.

Contents

Chapter 1
The Current Project

1.1 Starting Points, Objectives, Procedure

Project Title

The primary title of this monograph is "The Dialectical Forge," and its individual terms provide a suitable launching point for discussing the current project as a whole. As for the first, the most common Arabic terms for "dialectic" are *jadal* and *munāẓara*, both denoting formal disputation between scholars in a given domain, with regard to a specific thesis. When one encounters the term "dialectical" in the present work, one should think foremost of procedure-guided debate and the logic inherent to this species of discourse. A dialectical confrontation occurs between two scholars, in question and answer format, with the ultimate aims of either proving a thesis, or destroying it and supplanting it with another. A proponent-respondent introduces and attempts to defend a thesis; a questioner-objector seeks (destructively) to test and undermine that thesis, and (constructively) to supplant it with a counter-thesis. Through progressive rounds of question and response the questioner endeavours to gain concession to premises which invalidate the proponent's thesis, justify its dismantling, and provide the logical basis from which a counter-thesis necessarily flows.

Ultimately, and most importantly, a truly dialectical exchange—though drawing energy from a sober spirit of competition—must nevertheless be guided by a cooperative ethic wherein truth is paramount and forever trumps the emotional motivations of disputants to "win" the debate. This truth-seeking code demands sincere avoidance of fallacies; it views with abhorrence contrariness and self-contradiction. This alone distinguishes dialectic from sophistical or eristic argument, and, in conjunction with its dialogical format, from persuasive argument and rhetoric. And to repeat: dialectic is formal—it is an ordered enterprise, with norms and rules, and with a mutually-committed aim of advancing knowledge.

W.E. Young, *The Dialectical Forge*, Logic, Argumentation & Reasoning 9,
DOI 10.1007/978-3-319-25522-4_1

As for the second term in our title: "forge" is meant to conjure a place where metals are combined and recombined, shaped, refined, and given an edge. Here, the ultimate contour, sharpness, and utility of an implement is determined by continued hammering and grinding in extremes of heat, and through the prolonged exertions of the blacksmith. In our case, it is a great collective of blacksmiths—for the "Dialectical Forge" is, of course, a metaphor. The metals are various epistemological, hermeneutical, rational-inferential, and argumentative axioms; the heat is provided by competitive—albeit truth-seeking—disputation; the implements being forged are intellectual tools: theories, methods, species of argument and objection; the blacksmiths are Muslim jurists; and the forge itself is the venue of dialectical disputation.

Thus, "the dialectical forge" aims to convey the intellectually-formative dynamic of dialectical debate, and, with specific regard to the current project: debate within the Islamic juridical domain. My argument throughout this monograph is that dialectical disputation was a vital dynamic in the evolution of Islamic law—not only with respect to doctrinal bodies of substantive rulings, but to Islamic legal theories, and to a continually-evolving set of dialectical theories as well. The exigencies of dialectical debate provided key motives and forged key structures, elements, principles, and concepts for what became known as the sciences (*ʿulūm*) of derived substantive law (*fiqh*), legal theory (*uṣūl al-fiqh*), and juridical dialectic (*jadal* or *munāẓara*), not to mention certain sub-genres of the juristic sciences—e.g., the arts of discovering *qiyās*-invalidating inter-case distinctions (*furūq*) and weaker and stronger analogues (*ashbāh wa naẓāʾir*).

Starting Points

As those familiar with the field acknowledge: Islamic dialectics, in general, is critically understudied. The most comprehensive and detailed contribution to date—Larry Miller's 1984 doctoral dissertation: "Islamic Disputation Theory"—is unpublished. This is lamentable, for it is a seminal contribution and remains the most ambitious attempt at defining an essential field of Islamicate intellectual history.[1] A work of such scope, however, can seldom avoid the occasional

---

[1] Although Miller's dissertation takes precedence in detail and scope, a number of important studies both precede and follow it. Among others we find works by Muḥammad Abū Zahra (*Tārīkh al-Jadal*); Josef van Ess—who was in fact the supervisor of Miller's dissertation ("Disputationspraxis in der Islamischen Theologie;" and "The Logical Structure of Islamic Theology"); George Makdisi (select chapters from *The Rise of Colleges*; and his edition of Ibn ʿAqīl's *K. al-Jadal ʿalā Ṭarīqat al-Fuqahāʾ*); Wael Hallaq ("A Tenth-Eleventh Century Treatise on Juridical Dialectic"); Masʿūd Fallūsī (*al-Jadal ʿinda al-Uṣūliyyīn*); Mehmet Karabela ("The Development of Dialectic and Argumentation Theory in Post-Classical Islamic Intellectual History"); and Abdessamad Belhaj (*Argumentation et Dialectique en Islam*). The contribution of critical editions, with sometimes quite helpful introductions and notes, must also be acknowledged. In the realm of juridical dialectical theory the work of ʿAbd al-Majīd Turkī is of particular import, with

problematic assumption—I cannot hope that even a micro-study such as this will succeed in avoiding them—and one such problem forms an important starting point for the current monograph. In brief, Miller's dissertation asserts that the early literature of juridical disagreement (*ikhtilāf* or *khilāf*) is not dialectical in nature; he argues instead that a distinctly theological dialectic developed first, found its literary manifestation, and was then taken over by jurists.

In fact, a formulaic, systematic, and sophisticated juridical dialectic is clearly evident in the early *ikhtilāf* literature; it is certainly unmistakable in the several *ikhtilāf* treatises attributed to Muḥammad b. Idrīs al-Shāfiʿī (d.204/820), as found in the *Kitāb al-Umm* (roughly: "Foundational Sourcebook")—and for that matter, throughout its many substantive chapters which do not center themselves on *ikhtilāf*. Nor does the *Umm* merely contain the odd dialectical argument—it is replete with dialectical sequences, with the formulae common to (1) dialectical instruction: "if one should say: X; it is said to him: Y (*fa-in qāla* X, *qīla lahu* Y);" and (2) dialectical narrative, e.g.: "one scholar said: X; so I said to him: Y (*fa-qāla baʿḍ al-nās* X, *fa-qultu lahu* Y)." Many of these sequences extend over several pages of printed text. To be clear, this is not the systematic elaboration of juridical-dialectical *theory*—what I will refer to as "full-system *jadal*-theory," arising in the early fourth/tenth century—but it is copious evidence of what I will call "proto-system *jadal* teaching and practice," already quite developed, it appears, by the latter half of the second/eighth century.

The *Kitāb al-Umm* is prominent among early compendia with regard to the magnitude of its dialectical content, but it is by no means alone. The *Aṣl* or *Mabsūṭ* ("Foundation" or "Extended Exposition") of Muḥammad b. al-Ḥasan al-Shaybānī (d.189/805) exhibits a fair number of dialectical exchanges, as does his *Kitāb al-Ḥujja ʿalā Ahl al-Madīna* ("Book of Decisive Argument against the Scholars of Medina"); and likewise the *Mudawwana al-Kubrā* ("Great Register") of Saḥnūn (d.240/855). For the current project, however, I restricted myself to the *Umm*. Then, finding the sheer volume of dialectical material impossible to analyze within a reasonable time and space, I restricted myself yet further to the set of nine *ikhtilāf* and legal-theoretical treatises which constitute the final chapters of the *Umm*.[2] When this also proved too ambitious, I selected the first *ikhtilāf* treatise of this group—known variously as the *Book of that upon which Abū Ḥanīfa and Ibn Abī Laylā Disagreed, on the Authority of Abū Yūsuf* (*Kitāb mā Ikhtalafa fīhi Abū Ḥanīfa wa Ibn Abī Laylā ʿan Abī Yūsuf*); the *Book of Disagreement of Abū Ḥanīfa and Ibn Abī Laylā* (*Kitāb*

editions of the *Maʿūna fi'l-Jadal* of Abū Isḥāq al-Shīrāzī and the *Minhāj fī Tartīb al-Ḥijāj* of Abū al-Walīd al-Bājī, among other important works.

[2] These are the "*Treatises I-IX*" frequently referenced by Schacht in his *Origins*. See his bibliography (p. 338) for a listing, and Appendix I (p. 330) for a proposed chronology. See also Ḥassūn's introduction to his edition of the *Umm* (*Mawsūʿat al-Imām al-Shāfiʿī*, vol. 1, pp. 93–103), where each of these treatises is summarized in some detail.

Ikhtilāf Abī Ḥanīfa wa Ibn Abī Laylā); and the *Book of Disagreement of the (Two) Iraqis* (*Kitāb Ikhtilāf al-ʿIrāqiyyīn / al-ʿIrāqiyyayn*)—for argumentative analysis.[3]

Though the *Umm* offers more in terms of dialectical content, my selection of the *Disagreement of the (Two) Iraqis* proved fortuitous: its copious dialectical material is just manageable for the current project (hopefully the first of several micro-studies on the dialectic of the *Umm*), it transmits a great deal of earlier argumentative material (i.e., from before al-Shāfiʿī as well as from him), and it exhibits a rich spectrum of dialectical moves. On the whole, the *Book of Disagreement of the (Two) Iraqis*—which, for the sake of convenience, I will refer to as the "subject-text"—opens an excellent first window onto the proto-system dialectic of Islam's early jurists. At the same time, it must be acknowledged that a great deal of exploration and analysis awaits.

Having selected my subject-text, I proceeded to a first phase or surface analysis—through methodical translation of the entire treatise. I then progressed to a deeper analysis of the subject-text's proto-system dialectic, through the lens—i.e., using the analytical categories, concepts, and terms—of full-system *jadal* theory (the treatises employed in this endeavor will be called "lens-texts"). My first objective was to understand the argumentative character of an early juridical dialectic which, according to the most detailed narrative in the field, ought not to have existed.

[3] Whether the Iraqis of this last title are dual (*ʿIrāqiyyayn*) or plural (*ʿIrāqiyyīn*) remains a debatable question—though, perhaps, not a terribly pressing one. Both interpretations of عراقيين (which, unvowelled, could be either dual or plural) may be reasonably supported, and it may be that both interpretations were understood by different groups at different times, or even that the dual (recognizing only two Iraqis: Abū Ḥanīfa and Ibn Abī Laylā) gave way to the plural (in recognition of the additional Iraqi voices found in the text, *viz.* Abū Yūsuf and Muḥammad b. al-Ḥasan al-Shaybānī). It is for this latter reason that I interpreted the title as plural (*ʿIrāqiyyīn*) in my dissertation, but I have attempted to allow for both interpretations in the present work by transliterating "*Ikhtilāf al-ʿIrāqiyyīn / al-ʿIrāqiyyayn*" and translating "*Disagreement of the (Two) Iraqis*". Notably, al-Nawawī (Shāfiʿī; d.676/1277), in his *Tahdhīb al-Asmāʾ waʾl-Lughāt* (Munīriyya ed., vol. 2, p. 280, §912), asserts that the title is in the dual (*ʿIrāqiyyayn*), and that he is pointing this out to prevent a mistaken reading (presumably, in the plural). He proceeds, however, to ascribe the original composition to al-Shāfiʿī (*wa hādhā kitāb ṣannafahu al-Shāfiʿī*), making no mention whatsoever of Abū Yūsuf or al-Shaybānī, and saying that al-Shāfiʿī "stated in it the problem cases which they [dual] disagreed upon [meaning: Abū Ḥanīfa and Ibn Abī Laylā], sometimes preferring this or that [opinion], and sometimes degrading them both and preferring a third." This is more a description of Abū Yūsuf's program in the subject-text, and al-Nawawī's account, overall, does no justice to the layers of *ikhtilāf* which are evident in the text as it is found in the *Umm*. As a final note, ʿAbd al-Muṭṭalib—editor of a respected critical edition of the *Umm*—prefers the plural (*ʿIrāqiyyīn*); describing his manuscripts in the introduction to his critical edition, he provides—and perhaps this is the only time—partial vowelling for the title: اختلاف العراقِيِّين (vol. 1, p. 33, last line). In the end, it seems safest to assume that Abū Yūsuf—if he ever referred to his book by this title, and it is not only a later appellation—would have intended the dual (*ʿIrāqiyyayn*). After al-Shaybānī's additions, however, most later authors—perceiving the voices of four Iraqis in the text—would have preferred the plural (*ʿIrāqiyyīn*).

Questions and Objectives

Guiding questions were exploratory, calling in the first instance for comparative analysis. The dialogue sequences of the subject-text are dialectical in style and content, but what kind of dialectic is it—how do we qualify it? What are its elements, and what dialectical moves and strategies do we find? Importantly: how does it compare to the dialectical system propounded in Aristotle's *Topics* and *Sophistical Elenchi*—how "Aristotelian" is it? Equally important: how does it compare to the classical, full-system *jadal* theory elaborated by jurists in the fifth/eleventh century?

In the second instance were questions of an intellectual-evolutionary bent. Here is a distinctly Islamic juridical dialectic, with the formulaic marks of systematization, a century and more before the first specialized treatises on *jadal*-theory were said to be writ. Moreover, it quickly proved both similar and different to later *jadal*-theory in form and content—justifying a distinction between "proto-system *jadal* teaching and practice" and "full-system *jadal*-theory." What can the proto-system, once better understood, teach us about the evolution of Islamic legal dialectic? How will this affect current narratives?

Consequent to an exploratory drive, more questions arose as analyses progressed. As mentioned above, the first phase of analysis was achieved through translation. The juristic idiom of the subject-text is terse and difficult, presupposing a thorough knowledge of the debated substantive rulings and the indicants (*adilla*) from which they are derived. It was only through methodical translation, and a good deal of supplementary research, that I could hope to acquire a grasp of its contents and style.[4] Happily, this process yielded interesting discoveries which, in turn, helped to fine-tune procedures for subsequent stages of analysis. Most important was the clear and relatively common usage of *legal-theoretical premises* in dialectical exchange. What is more, these were sometimes themselves the *object* of debate, not merely tools of justification and critique. The revelation here is that—even at this early stage—disputation centered not only on substantive rulings, but on legal theory and method. So, besides asking what proto-system *jadal* can teach us with regard to the evolution of Islamic legal dialectic, we can ask: what can it teach us with regard to the evolution of Islamic legal theory (*uṣūl al-fiqh*)? And, again, how will this affect current narratives?

Ideally, the subject-text's argumentative material would be examined through a spectrum of approaches and an accompanying variety of analytical lenses. First is the lens of later, full-system *jadal* theory, exposing all dialectical features which could then be (1) identified in terms of the most appropriate full-system categories, or (2) provided new appellations whenever discordant with those categories.

[4] We are somewhat advantaged with regard to the dialectical sequences forming the focus of this study: the intent of the disputants is to explain and justify—a great aid to one who is nowhere near as immersed in the theoretical and substantive realms of Islamic law as were the studied jurists. Unfortunately, this explanatory quality is absent outside of dialectical sequences—i.e., from the bulk of the subject-text's material.

The subject-text would then be examined through the lens of later *uṣūl al-fiqh* literature, then through the lens of Arabic grammar theory, then through the lens of later logic traditions, and so forth and so on through multiple lenses. The current study, though acknowledging and indeed calling for additional approaches, is restricted in the main to the first: examination through the lens of classical, full-system *jadal* theory. In fact, this approach produced such a remarkable number of parallels and distinctions that other analytical projects may comfortably be left—for the time being—as open doors for future study. The point here is that questions have also arisen with regard to the relation of the subject-text's dialectic to grammar theory, later legal-theory and logic traditions, etc. Some will receive tentative answers in this study, others mere suggestions, and many more left to future exploration.

The questions which both kindled and arose through exploration gave shape to the primary aims of this study. They may be divided into two larger objectives. The first is to open a window on proto-system juridical dialectic—to bring our subject-text's fascinating and sophisticated dialectic to light, and to the attention of interested scholars. The second derives from numerous indicants of a larger, formative dynamic—the "Dialectical Forge" of our title—discovered while exploring the subject-text. The goal is to account for the complex workings of this dynamic, and to fashion a preliminary theoretical model for use and refinement in future studies. The first objective is the focus of Chaps. 5 and 6 (analyses of dialectical sequences), and of Chap. 7 (assessment of findings). The second objective is the focus of Chaps. 8 and 9. Here, I hope to have introduced a model of some utility, while recognizing it will very likely require future reworking.

Subsidiary aims include: (1) to amend evolutionary narratives which do not account for the sophistication and formulaic consistency of proto-system *jadal* as we find it in the subject-text; (2) to integrate the Dialectical Forge model into current narratives for the evolution of *uṣūl al-fiqh*, highlighting what I believe are critical intellectual dynamics and motives; (3) to present a more complete exposition on the organizing principles and contents of classical, full-system *jadal* treatises; and (4) to test a new analytical method, as will be further described below, and to assess its utility.

Procedure and Presentation

Focusing attention on the arguments of the *Kitāb mā Ikhtalafa fīhi Abū Ḥanīfa wa Ibn Abī Laylā ʿan Abī Yūsuf*, as it has come down to us in the *Kitāb al-Umm* of al-Shāfiʿī,[5] presents two problems: (1) how best to analyze its arguments—i.e., by which

[5] Our subject-text will be more fully designated "the *Umm* Version," thus distinguishing it from "the Shaybānī Version" (compiled by Abū Yūsuf and transmitted through Muḥammad b. al-Ḥasan al-Shaybānī) upon which al-Shāfiʿī commented (thus producing the expanded *Umm* Version), and to which he appended his own arguments—including all the dialectical sequences

categories of analysis; and (2) how best to select arguments for analysis, as it is plain that even this relatively small treatise (139 pages in Ḥassūn's edition of the *Umm*, but only 63 in the Būlāq edition) contains far too many arguments for full analysis and exposition in a single monograph.

As regards the first problem, I have employed the analytical categories devised (or inherited) by certain theorists of juridical *jadal* belonging to the fifth/eleventh century: the authors of our earliest extant full-system *jadal* theory lens-texts; and this decision is easily justified. In short, the many categories for argument from authoritative indicants (*istidlāl*) and objection (*iʿtirāḍ*), systematically arranged and explained in these treatises, are at once the most comprehensive, most detailed, most refined, and most *appropriate* set of analytical tools for the project at hand. Their appropriateness stems not only from being born of and tailor-made for the very species of dialectic with which we are most concerned, but from their chronological proximity to the proto-system era of the *Kitāb al-Umm*.[6] Importantly, with such a comprehensive and relevant set of analytical categories in Arabic, the need for imposing English or Latin near-equivalents can be much reduced; an earlier Islamic dialectical tradition can, to a large extent, be explained in the terms of later Muslim theorists.

Accordingly, I have selected from among the earliest extant theory-treatises of juridical *jadal*, and fashioned my lens for analysis primarily (though not exclusively) from them. In particular, I have relied upon the *Kitāb al-Qiyās al-Sharʿī* ("Book of Correlational Inference Consonant to God's Law") of Abū al-Ḥusayn al-Baṣrī (Muʿtazilī-Ḥanafī; d.436/1044), the *Maʿūna fi'l-Jadal* ("Disputation Aid") of Abū Isḥāq al-Shīrāzī (Shāfiʿī; d.476/1083), and the *Minhāj fī Tartīb al-Ḥijāj* ("Method for Ordering Dispute") of Abū al-Walīd al-Bājī (Mālikī; d.474/1081). I have also made occasional reference to the *Kāfiya fi'l-Jadal* ("Sufficient [Manual] for Disputation") of Imām al-Ḥaramayn Abū Maʿālī al-Juwaynī (Shāfiʿī; d.478/1085) and the *Kitāb al-Jadal ʿalā Ṭarīqat al-Fuqahā'* ("Book of Disputation According to the Method of the Jurists") of Abū al-Wafā' ʿAlī b. ʿAqīl (Ḥanbalī; d.513/1119). The many and refined genera, species, and subtypes of arguments from authoritative indicants (*istidlālāt*), objections (*iʿtirāḍāt*), and modes of bringing one indicant to preponderate over another (*tarjīḥāt*), as defined in these texts, comprise the primary analytical categories of my *jadal*-theory lens.[7]

---

treated in this study. Abū Yūsuf's original text, without the material added by al-Shāfiʿī, appears to have survived and been edited (from a single, unidentified manuscript) by Abū al-Wafā' al-Afghānī. Questions with regard to the authorship and transmission of both versions are addressed in Chap. 3.

[6] There may be even more refined and comprehensive *jadal*-theory treatises from later eras, but my selection reflects the "state of the theoretical field" close to its first inception sometime in the early fourth/tenth century. Examining the proto-system through these texts thus brings an additional benefit: providing indicants for continuity and change from older *jadal* teaching and practice.

[7] Some may mistake this as back-projecting; it is not. Nowhere will I argue that our proto-system jurist-dialecticians articulated the categories and terms under which we subsume their arguments. Though we classify a dialectical move executed by al-Shāfiʿī as *muʿāraḍat al-ʿilla bi'l-ʿilla*

With regard to the second problem: how best to select material for analysis from the subject-text, I settled upon a division of arguments according to "presentation categories." This method will be fully described in Chap. 5, but suffice it to say that inclusion in one category or the other depends upon how overtly dialectical an individual argument, or group of arguments, appears. Presentation categories are labelled A through G, ranging from transcript-like, extended question and answer sequences (category A) to plain statements of substantive rulings supported by neither transmission of textual support from a prior authority (*naql*) nor self-made rational inference (*ʿaql*) (category G). In fact, all of the arguments of the subject-text may be considered "dialectical" simply by virtue of being located in a work of *ikhtilāf*—it being understood that juridical disagreements were visited and revisited in disputational venues. In the main, however, my analyses focus only upon the most overtly dialectical material: twelve sets of problem-cases (*masāʾil*) concluding with category A extended dialectical sequences, and ten category B short dialectical sequences.

The monograph itself consists of three distinct parts. The first (Chaps. 1, 2, 3 and 4) aims to introduce project, procedure, current narratives and contexts, subject-text, lens-texts, and jurist-dialecticians. The second (Chaps. 5, 6 and 7) is the heart of the enterprise: analyzing the dialectic of the subject-text and cataloging the findings. The third (Chaps. 8 and 9) aims to explore the larger implications of this micro-study, and to develop the Dialectical Forge model.

In Part I, Chap. 1, I will proceed from this present section to a summary of findings and theories, and a brief discussion of key terms and definitions. In Chap. 2, I will outline and critique current developmental narratives for Islamic juridical dialectical theory, refuting the portrayal of juridical *jadal* as a late (fifth/eleventh century) offshoot of theological theory, pointing to copious evidence of a proto-system (second/eighth century) juridical dialectic, and proposing a new narrative for variant dialectical theory systems (stressing common origins, parallel development, and continuous cross-germination). Chapter 3 introduces the subject-text, its redactional history, and the history of its genre of "juridical disagreement" (*ikhtilāf*), explaining the relation of such works to other legal-theoretical and dialectical genres. Chapter 4 then introduces the analytical lens-texts; i.e., the classical *jadal*-theory texts (of al-Shīrāzī, al-Bājī, et al.) whose concepts and categories provide the "lens" through which the subject-text will be analyzed. A brief exposition on the categories and sub-categories of these texts (for dialectical questions, rule-derivation, epistemic-justification, and dialectical objection) follows, and the chapter closes with an overview of parallels and divergences between

(supplanting one occasioning factor with another), it cannot be claimed this technical formulation ever passed his lips, much less with the systematic objective of cataloging a dialectical move. Of course certain terms (e.g., *qiyās*) have an ancient pedigree, but even these were likely to have been understood differently in the second/eighth century. Though sophisticated in their own right, proto-systems of dialectic and legal theory were nowhere near as refined as those which emerged in the fifth/eleventh century and after. This is the very reason I insist on calling the juridical dialectic of al-Shāfiʿī, et al., a "proto-system."

jadal-theory and more ancient systems (especially Aristotle's dialectical method in the *Topics* and *Sophistical Elenchi*).

Part II comprises the core experiment—the analytical workspace—of the monograph. Chapter 5 analyzes twelve extended Q&A disputation sequences, presented in parallel translation, followed by full explanations. Chapter 6 analyzes ten shorter sequences in the same manner, then proceeds to survey and analyze key dialectical formulae and the contexts in which they occur throughout the subject-text—especially *a-ra'ayta* ("Have you considered..."); and *a-lā tarā* ("Don't you see, or do you not [yourself] opine..."). The findings from all preceding analyses and surveys are then gathered under categorical headings and summarized in Chap. 7, which places the whole of the subject-text's dialectical elements in contradistinction to those of the *jadal*-theory lens-texts surveyed in Chap. 4. An ordered exposition of the earlier dialectic's unique question and argument modes, and distinctive formulae of subsumption, extension, and objection, provides conclusive evidence for several of the monograph's major theses; among them: (1) there were, indeed, "proto-systems" of juridical dialectic and legal theory; (2) with proper analysis, a detailed portrait of the character of these proto-systems can emerge; (3) a genetic relationship is manifest between proto-system and full-system; and (4) successive surveys and analyses should allow more complete evolutionary narratives to be drawn for the domains of substantive law (*fiqh*), legal theory (*uṣūl al-fiqh*), and disputation theory (*jadal*).

Part III of the monograph attempts to induce more universal hypotheses and theories from the particular findings catalogued in Part II. Chapter 8 first introduces the bare, structural outline of the Dialectical Forge model—meant, as I have mentioned, to explain the mechanics by which dialectical disputation powered the evolution and refinement of theory-systems. Individual components of this model are drawn forth and attached to the general outline, first by turning attention to Islamic legal theory, and then to Islamic disputation theory. The differences between proto- and full-systems (i.e., proto-system legal theory vs. full-system *uṣūl al-fiqh*; and proto-system juridical dialectic vs. full-system *jadal*-theory) are more deeply explored; examples of legal-theoretical and dialectical premises "forged" in disputation are revisited; and certain current evolutionary paradigms for *uṣūl al-fiqh* are tested for consonance / dissonance with the Dialectical Forge model.

After an overall summary of the Dialectical Forge model, with all of its legal-theoretical and dialectical components in place, Chap. 9 proceeds to a few broader hypotheses. First, and acknowledging the vast compass of pending research, I take the first steps towards an abstracted "background narrative" for Islamic legal-theoretical evolution. More particular developmental narratives, though still wanting further survey and analysis, may nevertheless be someday laid over a matrix of constantly evolving "argumentation epistemes." It is an early confluence of such epistemes, infused by new Islamic axioms and driven by the exigencies of dialectical disputation, which lies behind the development of epistemic justification in Islamic sciences. Second, a brief outline is sketched for a paradigm explaining how the exigencies of dialectical disputation may actually shape theory-systems at an individual level. A "motive model" is proposed, wherein dialectical axioms are bequeathed to theory-systems through pressures of avoiding thesis-destroying critiques—anticipating, in other words, critical objections to (1) epistemic insufficiency of premises and indicants, (2) intensional and semantic misinterpretation, (3) invalid inference, and (4) intra-argument or doctrinal inconsistency. Finally, I proceed to a few closing statements and a general appeal that the study of Islamic dialectical disputation be recognized as vitally important—not only for what it may contribute to a better understanding of Islamicate intellectual history, but for what it can impart to disciplines outside of Islamic studies, and to the broader intellectual history of the world.

1.2 Summary of Findings, Arguments, and Theories

The individual conclusions (whether firm or tentative) of this study are manifold; here I will list only the larger groupings into which they fall. Even this, however, cannot be attempted without first providing a short introduction to the larger categories of analysis—the categories of justification and critique found in our *jadal*-theory lens-texts.

Our *jadal*-theorists always treat, in an opening chapter and in hierarchical order, the full gamut of authoritative indicants (*adilla*) from which a proponent may derive his/her argument or epistemic justification (which activity is called *istidlāl*). These indicants are grouped under the highest-order categories of *aṣl* (divinely-sanctioned source-case), *maʿqūl aṣl* (what is rationally understood from an *aṣl*), and *istiṣḥāb ḥāl* (presumption of continuity of a legal *status quo ante*). In turn, *aṣl* is comprised of *Kitāb* ("the Book," i.e., the Qur'ān), *Sunna* (the Prophet's instruction and example), *Ijmāʿ* (communal and/or scholarly consensus), and, more controversially, *qawl al-wāḥid min al-Ṣaḥāba* (asserted doctrine of one of the Companions of the Prophet). *Maʿqūl aṣl* is comprised of *laḥn al-khiṭāb* (implication of [what is unspoken but understood in] the instruction), *faḥwā al-khiṭāb* (the *a fortiori* signification of the instruction), *dalīl al-khiṭāb* ([restrictive] indication of the instruction) or *al-ḥaṣr* (restriction [of the instruction to a particular object]), and *maʿnā al-khiṭāb* (intension-property of the instruction) which is synonymous with *qiyās* (correlational inference). Having reviewed these domains of indicants (*adilla*) and modes of drawing them forth in support of argument (*istidlālāt*), our *jadal*-theorists proceed, in very precise and orderly fashion, to detail a comprehensive range of objections/critiques (*iʿtirāḍāt*) for each of these domains, along with appropriate responses (*ajwiba*) to each and every objection, all amply illustrated with sample problem-cases (*masāʾil*).[8] Finally, all of our *jadal*-theorists fol-

[8] Should one's opponent justify his/her solution to the contended case by drawing a supporting indicant from the Qur'ān (*istidlāl biʾl-Kitāb*), for instance, al-Shīrāzī lists some eight dialectical objections which may be of use to the questioner in testing or undermining that mode of argu-

low their discussions of *iʿtirāḍāt* with a listing of *tarjīḥāt*—that is, hierarchical principles for determining which Sunnaic *dalīl* (indicant) preponderates over another, or which *maʿnā* (intension-property) or *ʿilla* (occasioning factor) preponderates over another.[9]

What I found by peering through the analytical lens of *jadal*-theory was quite surprising. The relatively small amount of dialectical material selected from the subject-text produced nearly the full gamut of *istidlālāt* treated by our *jadal*-theorists, and a fairly large sampling of *iʿtirāḍāt* and *tarjīḥāt*. However, I also found much more than our *jadal*-theorists discuss. There are a considerable number of dialectical moves and strategies which do not conform to the categories of our later theorists, or which can be described only by making alterations to *jadal*-theory categories.

The material well-matched to our lens-texts included plentiful examples of (1) prescribed dialectical questions; (2) moves pertaining to reasoning from the Qur'ān, from the Prophet's Sunna (both pronouncement [*qawl*] and act [*fiʿl*]), from subtypes of *ijmāʿ*, and from *qawl al-wāḥid min al-Ṣaḥāba*; (3) *faḥwā al-khiṭāb* and *dalīl al-khiṭāb*; and (4) *qiyās*-related *istidlālāt*, *iʿtirāḍāt*, and *tarjīḥāt*. The material which did not match well with our lens-texts may be considered in three larger sets. First were *istidlālāt*, *iʿtirāḍāt*, and *tarjīḥāt* that fell outside the usual scope of application prescribed in the lens-texts.[10] Second were question strategies which fell outside the categories of our lens-texts.[11] Third were modes of justification and objection which fell completely outside the discussions of our lens-texts.

These latter instances proved quite numerous, in fact, and included, among many other things: (1) appeals to the asserted doctrine (*qawl*) of a Successor (and objections against it); (2) charges of what I have called method-*naqḍ*; (3) a strategy I have called "*naqḍ* dilemma"; (4) a strategy which might be termed "argument to the *maʿqūl*"; and (5) arguments to custom or convention. Additionally, there were genera of formulaic arguments evincing a marked concern for doctrinal consistency—this was a family of "super-*qiyās*," and I have called these arguments *manzila*-subsumption (with such formulae as "X is in the status [*manzila*] of Y for

---

ment. And for the very important domain of *maʿnā al-khiṭāb* (or *qiyās*) we find no less than fifteen dialectical objections, with very specific (and consistent) designations (e.g., *manʿ*; *ʿadam al-ta'thīr*; *naqḍ*; *kasr*; *muʿāraḍa*; etc.), each comprising a different genus of dialectical move.

[9] All of these terms will be fully explained in Chap. 4. For now, this is the briefest possible overview of the analytical categories distilled from our *jadal*-theory lens-texts. And please bear in mind that these are merely first-tier categories: for every genus of *istidlāl* and *iʿtirāḍ* there are species, types, and subtypes, resulting in hundreds of dialectical justifications, critiques, and responses. Our lens-texts are indeed very thorough and comprehensive treatments of juridical-dialectical theory.

[10] For example, I found *naqḍ*-like charges outside the domain of *qiyās al-ʿilla*; *manʿ*-like objections in the domain of *istidlāl bi'l-Sunna*; and both transmission-oriented objections and *tarjīḥ* in the domain of *qawl al-wāḥid min al-Ṣaḥāba*.

[11] These included objection-oriented (as opposed to *istidlāl*-oriented) questions and evidential demands (*muṭālabāt*); a *Topics*-reminiscent method of procuring premise after premise for *elenchus*; and other features.

all Z"); *taswiya*-subsumption ("the same obtains [*wa sawā'un*] in X and Y"); and *farq*-extension (whereby a critical difference [*farq*] between particular species of cases is extended to their genera). Most intriguing of all were certain species of argument which generally exhibited an ancient tenor. There were, for example, charges of intra-argument contradiction (*tanāquḍ*), such as "what you say is contradictory (*fa qawluka mutanāqiḍ*)"; various modes of *reductio* arguments; arguments *ad verecundiam*; objections to affirming the consequent, to *petitio principii*, and to mistaken cause; *a fortiori* arguments outside the domain of *faḥwā al-khiṭāb*; charges of complete arbitrariness (*taḥakkum*); etc.

Patterns emerged from these findings; and these (along with my hypotheses regarding them) came to form the components of the Dialectical Forge: a theoretical model of the dynamic engine powering the evolution of both *uṣūl al-fiqh* and *jadal*-theory. In other words, the apparatus of the Dialectical Forge model was derived and assembled from an investigation into (1) what proto-system dialectic had in common with full-system *jadal*-theory, (2) what proto-system legal theory had in common with full-system *uṣūl al-fiqh*, (3) where these systems diverged, (4) how legal-theoretical premises were employed in dialectical exchanges, and (5) how *jadal*-theory itself appears to have developed through its own practice.

Extending the engine metaphor, the resultant model may be considered to have two simultaneously-functioning "engine-compartments": one for dialectical exchange and legal theory, the other for dialectical exchange and *jadal*-theory. As for the first, a number of processes and considerations are at work: (1) what I have called the "three-stage cycle"; (2) dynamic symbiosis and co-evolution; (3) the bequeathing of dialectical axioms; (4) the *ijtihādic* anticipation of *jadal*; and (5) what I have called the "first principles parallel." As for the second, processes at work include: (1) the very phenomenon of *jadal* exchange itself shaping what *jadal*-theory was to become; (2) the processes of dialectic defining what is *endoxon*; and (3) the transmission and study of past *jadal*—i.e., the continuity of practice and the backwards-looking analyses of our *jadal*-theorists.[12] Together these comprise the components of the Dialectical Forge model: the engine (with its two compartments) powering the intertwined evolutions of *uṣūl al-fiqh* and *jadal*-theory.

Finally, I might summarize the evolutionary narrative proposed in this monograph for Islamic dialectical theory. In brief, rather than a linear trajectory of absolute priority (as current narratives entail), I have proffered a model of common origins, parallel development, and cross-germination. That is to say, rather than a narrative whereby jurists take over the systematized *jadal*-theory and practice of theologians, I propose a more complex, organic narrative marked by: (1) the emergence of a spectrum of dialectical "proto-systems" (e.g. grammatical, juridical, theological, etc.) from a common collective of argumentation epistemes, in the first century of Islam; (2) the subsequent parallel and divergent development of these proto-systems according to the dictates of their variant (e.g., specu-

[12] All of these components are introduced throughout the course of Chaps. 5, 6 and 7, and then developed more fully in Chaps. 8 and 9.

lative vs. normative) agendas; (3) the simultaneous elaboration of "full-system" theory treatises during that great literary fluorescence of the fourth/tenth century—the culmination of a systematizing impetus recognizable across all scholarly projects; and (4) cross-germination between scholarly projects at every stage of development—due to the close proximities and interactions between epistemic communities, and the many hats worn by our polymath theorists—throughout the breadth and length of Islam's formative period.

At the very least, the juridical dialectic manifest in such works as the *Kitāb al-Umm* problematizes any notion of an absolute priority for fourth/tenth century theological *jadal* theory. This, in combination with other indicants discovered throughout my research and recorded in the following chapters, leads me to conclude that a model of common origins, parallel development, and cross-germination best accounts for both the similarities and dissimilarities of theological, philosophical, and juridical *jadal*.

As mentioned above, the two larger aims of this project are: (1) to open a window onto proto-system juridical dialectic—to provide as thorough an analysis as I may of the second/eighth century disputation found in the *Disagreement of the (Two) Iraqis*: its dialectical moves, strategies, formulae, and principles; and (2) to account for the complex workings of the Dialectical Forge—to provide a preliminary model for use (and subsequent refinement) in future studies of legal theory and *jadal*. In pursuit of these aims, I hope also to have contributed a more thorough exposition on the organizing principles and contents of our earliest extant (fifth/eleventh century) juridical *jadal*-theory treatises, and the same with regard to crossovers, parallels, and differences between Aristotelian dialectic and Islamic *jadal*-theory. It is equally my hope that the new paradigm offered for the evolution of Islamic dialectical systems, and for the natural, symbiotic co-evolution of dialectical and legal-theoretical systems may—with the necessary adjustments—come to supplant narratives which do not account for the sophistication or formative dynamic of proto-system *jadal*. As for my analytical approach to the dialectical material of the subject-text, I hope it may—again, with the necessary adjustments—serve as a procedural model for the analysis of early juridical argumentation. And one final aim and most sincere hope is that this monograph—having shed some light on both proto-system and full-system *jadal*—not only earns the approval of scholars knowledgeable in these areas, but entices others to join us in exploring the rich but understudied domains of Islamic dialectical disputation.

1.3 Recurrent Terms and Definitions

Certain terms will appear with frequency throughout this monograph. I have already made regular reference to the "subject-text;" this will always refer to the *Ikhtilāf al-ʿIrāqiyyīn / al-ʿIrāqiyyayn*, the subject of argumentative analysis in Chaps. 5, 6 and 7. "Lens-texts," on the other hand, will always refer to the full-system *jadal*-theory treatises discussed in Chap. 4, constituting the analytical lens through which we peer at the subject-text. The "*Umm* Version" will always refer to the subject-text as we find it in the *Kitāb al-Umm*, with the additional layers of argument and commentary provided by al-Shāfiʿī. This is in contrast to the older "Shaybānī Version"—the original *Ikhtilāf Abī Ḥanīfa wa Ibn Abī Laylā* compiled by Abū Yūsuf and transmitted to Muḥammad b. al-Ḥasan al-Shaybānī (and through him, quite possibly, to al-Shāfiʿī)—containing only the argument material and opinions of the Iraqi jurists.

I have also introduced the term "proto-system;" and this will continue to underscore an important distinction. With regard to disputation, I will apply "proto-system" only to *jadal* teaching and practice before the appearance of the first, comprehensive *jadal*-theory treatises in the fourth/tenth century—i.e., before the appearance of "full-system" *jadal*-theory. The dialectic of our subject-text jurists belongs to a proto-system milieu, while that of our lens-text authors belongs to a full-system milieu. I will also maintain this distinction between proto-system legal-theory and full-system *uṣūl al-fiqh*. "Proto-system" will reference discrete legal-theoretical phenomena and less choate systems prior to the first, "full-system" treatises on the science of *uṣūl al-fiqh*. These latter—far from coincidentally—also first appeared in the fourth/tenth century. The legal theory of our subject-text jurists—including al-Shāfiʿī's famed *Risāla*—belongs to a proto-system milieu, while that of our lens-text authors (all of whom authored *uṣūl al-fiqh* treatises) belongs to a full-system milieu.

"*Endoxon*" (pl. *endoxa*) is an important term I will use with great frequency. It is borrowed from Aristotle's dialectical theory, and will serve in a very similar sense. I intend it to capture the connected meanings of: (1) a premise, method, ruling, etc., which is accepted as valid or true by an authoritative community, group, or individual; and (2) a premise, method, ruling, etc., which one's dialectical opponent is expected to concede.[13] For example, the Respondent (R) might consider the method of arguing from the indicant of an instruction's implicit restriction (*al-istidlāl bi-dalīl al-khiṭāb*), as regards an unambiguous directive (*qawl*) of the Prophet, to be an *endoxon* method for both himself and the Questioner (Q). Now, being that the Prophet said: «Regarding such as are pasturing (*sā'ima*) of the sheep/goats, there is an alms-tax (*zakāt*)», R might claim: "there is *no zakāt* for sheep/goats which are *not* pasturing." This is *dalīl al-khiṭāb*, in a broader form.[14] However, Q might not consider *dalīl al-khiṭāb* to be *endoxon* unless the authoritative source-case (*aṣl*)—in this instance, the Prophet's aforementioned *zakāt* direc-

[13] Robin Smith lucidly discusses the meaning of *endoxon* in his "Aristotle on the Uses of Dialectic." The same article serves as an excellent introduction to Aristotle's dialectical theory, in general. Importantly, I will employ the term *endoxon* purely as a descriptor, not as an identification. That is to say, when I use "*endoxon*" to describe a dialectical phenomenon in the subject-text or lens-texts, I am not claiming an identity with Aristotle's method, nor am I implying a genetic relationship with the *Topics*. *Endoxon* is a very useful analytical category, but—unless otherwise stated—it implies no intellectual-historical linkages in this study.

[14] The Prophet, by his formulation, is understood to have singled out only pasturing sheep/goats for *zakāt*, and excluded other categories of sheep/goats.

tive—is formulated as a conditional.[15] On the other hand, if R's broader *dalīl al-khiṭāb* happens to be condoned by Q's doctrinal *madhhab*, then R is right in expecting Q to concede it as *endoxon*. But if Q stolidly rejects R's broader *dalīl al-khiṭāb*, then the disputation must shift from the substantive to the methodological—from the *zakāt* question to an examination of the argumentative conclusiveness (*ḥujjiyya*) of R's broader *dalīl al-khiṭāb* method.

Istidlāl, *iʿtirāḍ*, and *tarjīḥ* are three particularly important technical terms of juridical *jadal*. *Istidlāl* (pl. *istidlālāt*) is the process of drawing forth an indicant (*dalīl*) from authoritative or *endoxic* sources—and via authoritative or *endoxic* methods—in support of an argued solution to the *problēma* (*mas'ala*; pl. *masā'il*) at hand; it is primarily the proponent-respondent's activity. *Iʿtirāḍ* (pl. *iʿtirāḍāt*), on the other hand, is the objection to an opposing argument and its *istidlāl*—thus the primary activity of the questioner-objector. *Tarjīḥ* refers to the weighing of seemingly equivalent indicants (*adilla*) against each other, with an eye to discovering which has more epistemic mass. It is applied when conflicts occur between reports (*akhbār*), and between intension-properties (*maʿānī*); and it is an important means for determining which occasioning factor (*ʿilla*) preponderates over another.

A final set of terms I will employ deals with the givens or motives of argumentation as assumed—or studied and developed—within particular epistemic communities, in different regions and at different times, and according to the dictates of different intellectual projects. "Episteme" is the first in this set; I will use it in a sense similar to what Michel Foucault appears to have intended.[16] From this I have constructed "argumentation episteme" to denote an inclusive set of foundational principles—all of which are concerned with what constitutes knowledge or proof, what justifies an assertion or advances one probability over another, etc. These principles may or may not be studied or articulated by practitioners, but analysis will reveal them operating at the foundations of individual arguments and methods of argument.

An argumentation episteme is thus a collection of epistemological and inferential *axioms*—be they studied, assumed, or even subconscious—which constitute the building blocks of argumentation for a particular individual or community. And, though not necessarily true in and of themselves (like geometry's axioms), such "argumentation axioms," as I will call them, are nevertheless the starting points for any number of intellectual projects.[17] As discrete epistemic units,

---

[15] For this, he might cite the authority of Ibn Surayj (d.306/918), a founding figure in both *uṣūl al-fiqh* and *jadal*-theory; see al-Shīrāzī, *Lumaʿ*, Mustū ed., 106.

[16] In the course of a multi-party discussion, Foucault says (*Power/Knowledge*, p.197): "If you like, I would define the *episteme* retrospectively as the strategic apparatus which permits of separating out from among all the statements which are possible those that will be acceptable within, I won't say a scientific theory, but a field of scientificity, and, which it is possible to say are true or false. The *episteme* is the 'apparatus' which makes possible the separation, not of the true from the false, but of what may from what may not be characterised as scientific."

[17] The "problem of induction" is a case in point. Even though recognized—axiomatically—as problematic in certain epistemes, the utility of induction and the great effects which may be achieved through controlled inductive reasoning ensure that induction is a "given" axiom in

axioms may belong only to a particular argumentation episteme, or be shared between several; and they may be further categorized as either "givens" or "motives." An axiom of the "given" variety, by way of example, is the law of non-contradiction. Whether articulated or not, developed in theoretical discourse or not, this particular axiom plays a role in most argumentation epistemes, be they empirical, speculative, normative, or what have you—it is simply a "given". Axioms of the "motive" variety, on the other hand, are of a more normative character; corollaries to the "given" of non-contradiction might be phrased negatively: "One must not contradict oneself;" or positively: "One must argue consistently." As such, "motive" axioms tend to subsist at a more conscious level; I may feel compelled to argue consistently and avoid contradiction without ever having read or understood a theoretical explanation as to why.

Importantly, it is while building upon, refining, and reformulating such argumentation axioms that different schools of thought may emerge within the same intellectual project-domain; different theological and philosophical schools will develop within the same speculative project, and different legal schools within the same normative project. These in turn may develop and defend unique and variant argument systems, emerging as distinct argumentative entities from within the older, shared, argumentation episteme (or collective of epistemes) in which the larger intellectual project has its roots.

Any one argumentation episteme may be peculiar to a certain region or era, or to a specific epistemic community among other epistemic communities in the same region and era. And to underscore how axioms may differ between argumentation epistemes, one could cite, in normative projects: (1) "*a fortiori* reasoning, in general, is valid;" versus (2) "*a fortiori* reasoning is valid only when based on a clear, revelatory indicant." Whereas #1 is shared by a great many normative projects across numerous epistemes (modern and pre-modern, religious, secular, and otherwise), #2 is not even shared by all argumentation epistemes within the superset of Islamic normative projects—much less outside of it.[18] Similarly, the "motive" axiom "one must not assert legal solutions which plainly contradict the Qur'ān" is not to be found outside of Islamic argumentation epistemes, and in fact is not to be found in a number of modern Islamic argumentation epistemes.[19]

A final note on the term "argumentation episteme": it is markedly distinct from the term "system." A "system" of argument is the product of concentrated analytical effort. It is a singularly conscious organizing of argumentative elements into a theoretical or practical pattern—or series of patterns, such as

almost all argumentation epistemes. That is to say, even though axiomatically recognized as flawed in episteme X, we may still find the axiom "induction yields valid conclusions" to be a "given" within that same episteme X—just as we find it in epistemes which do not problematize induction.

[18] Axioms of this sort may also appear in certain developmental stages of a project, and not others.

[19] For example, such as incorporate the axiom "some Qur'ānic injunctions are specific to the time (and audience) of revelation, and are not applicable to modern situations."

Aristotle contributed (*viz.* demonstration, dialectic, and rhetoric). An argumentation episteme, on the other hand, may consist entirely of unexamined assumptions, motives, and modes of reasoning—elements which were never scrutinized and organized by anyone participating in that episteme. Or it may contain, along with unexamined elements, axioms belonging to a "system" of argument—or even entire systems themselves. For example, the argumentation episteme of a fifth century CE Nestorian community in Iraq might contain—along with relatively unexamined modes of reasoning (e.g., induction), and givens or motives peculiar to a Christian scheme of salvation—various axioms consciously integrated from the "systems" of Aristotelian and Stoic logic. In short, the argumentation episteme of that Nestorian community is every mode of reasoning and every argumentative element upon which a member of that community might draw in the course of argument—including such systems (or parts thereof) which have been inherited, studied, or self-devised.

References

Abū Yūsuf, Yaʿqūb b. Ibrāhīm. *Ikhtilāf Abī Ḥanīfa wa Ibn Abī Laylā* [= Shaybānī Version]. Ed. Abū al-Wafāʾ al-Afghānī. Cairo: Maṭbaʿat al-Wafāʾ, 1357/1939.

Abū Zahra, Muḥammad. *Tārīkh al-Jadal*. Cairo: Dār al-Fikr al-ʿArabī, 1934.

al-Bājī, Abū al-Walīd Sulaymān. *Kitāb al-Minhāj fī Tartīb al-Ḥijāj (L'art de la Polémique: Édition Critique d'al-Minhāǧ de Bāǧī)*. Ed. ʿAbd al-Majīd Turkī. Paris: Maisonneuve et Larose, 1978.

al-Baṣrī, Abū al-Ḥusayn Muḥammad. *Kitāb al-Qiyās al-Sharʿī*. In *idem*, *Kitāb al-Muʿtamad fī Uṣūl al-Fiqh*. Ed. Muḥammad Ḥamīd Allāh, Muḥammad Bakīr, and Ḥasan Ḥanafī. Damascus: al-Maʿhad al-ʿIlmī al-Faransī li'l-Dirāsāt al-ʿArabiyya bi-Dimashq, 1964–1965, vol. 2, pp. 1029–1050.

al-Baṣrī, Abū al-Ḥusayn Muḥammad. *Kitāb al-Qiyās al-Sharʿī*. In *idem*, *al-Muʿtamad fī Uṣūl al-Fiqh*. Ed. Khalīl al-Mays. Beirut: Dār al-Kutub al-ʿIlmiyya, 1983, vol. 2, pp. 443–62.

Belhaj, Abdessamad. *Argumentation et Dialectique en Islam: Formes et Séquences de la Munāẓara*. Bruxelles: Presses Universitaires de Louvain, 2010.

Fallūsī, Masʿūd. *Al-Jadal ʿinda al-Uṣūliyyīn: bayna al-Naẓariyya wa'l-Taṭbīq*. Riyadh: Maktabat al-Rushd Nāshirūn, 2003.

Foucault, Michel. *Power/Knowledge: Selected Interviews and Other Writings, 1972–1977*. Ed. and Trans. Colin Gordon. New York: Pantheon Books, 1980.

Hallaq, Wael B. "A Tenth-Eleventh Century Treatise on Juridical Dialectic." *Muslim World* 77 (1987): 197–228.

Ibn ʿAqīl, Abū al-Wafāʾ ʿAlī. *Kitāb al-Jadal ʿalā Ṭarīqat al-Fuqahāʾ* (*Le Livre de la Dialectique d'Ibn ʿAqīl*). Ed. George Makdisi. *Bulletin d'Études Orientale* 20 (1967): 119–206.

Ibn ʿAqīl, Abū al-Wafāʾ ʿAlī. *Kitāb al-Jadal ʿalā Ṭarīqat al-Fuqahāʾ*. Al-Ẓāhir [Cairo]: Maktabat al-Thaqāfa al-Dīniyya, 1980. [An unattributed reproduction of George Makdisi, ed., *Le Livre de la Dialectique d'Ibn ʿAqīl*, minus his introduction and critical apparatus].

al-Juwaynī, Imām al-Ḥaramayn. *Al-Kāfiya fi'l-Jadal*. Ed. Fawqiya Ḥusayn Maḥmūd. Cairo: Maṭbaʿat ʿĪsā al-Bābī al-Ḥalabī, 1979.

Karabela, Mehmet Kadri. "The Development of Dialectic and Argumentation Theory in Post-Classical Islamic Intellectual History." PhD diss., McGill University, Montréal, 2010.

Makdisi, George. *The Rise of Colleges: Institutions of Learning in Islam and the West*. Edinburgh: Edinburgh University Press, 1981.

Miller, Larry Benjamin. "Islamic Disputation Theory: A Study of the Development of Dialectic in Islam from the Tenth Through Fourteenth Centuries." PhD diss., Princeton University, 1984.

al-Nawawī, Muḥyī al-Dīn Abū Zakarīyā' Yaḥyā. *Tahdhīb al-Asmā' wa'l-Lughāt*. 4 vols. in 2. Cairo: Idārat al-Ṭibā'a al-Munīriyya, [1927?].

Schacht, Joseph. *The Origins of Muhammadan Jurisprudence*. Oxford: Oxford University Press, 1950.

al-Shāfi'ī, Muḥammad b. Idrīs. *Hādhā Kitāb mā Ikhtalafa fīhi Abū Ḥanīfa wa Ibn Abī Laylā 'an Abī Yūsuf... wa huwa Kitāb Ikhtilāf al-'Irāqiyyīn* (or *al-'Irāqiyyayn*) [= *Umm* Version]. In *idem, al-Umm*. Ed. Maḥmūd Maṭrajī. Beirut: Dār al-Kutub al-'Ilmiyya, 1993, pt. 7, pp. 161–250.

al-Shāfi'ī, Muḥammad b. Idrīs. *Kitāb Ikhtilāf Abī Ḥanīfa wa Ibn Abī Laylā* [= *Umm* Version]. In *idem, Mawsū'at al-Imām al-Shāfi'ī: al-Kitāb al-Umm* (2nd ed.) Ed. Aḥmad Badr al-Dīn Ḥassūn. Beirut: Dār Qutayba, 2003, vol. 9, pt. 14, pp. 7–235.

al-Shāfi'ī, Muḥammad b. Idrīs. *Kitāb Ikhtilāf al-'Irāqiyyīn* (or *al-'Irāqiyyayn*). In *idem, al-Umm*. Ed. Rif'at Fawzī 'Abd al-Muṭṭalib. al-Manṣūra: Dār al-Wafā' li'l-Ṭibā'a wa'l-Nashr wa'l-Tawzī', 2001, pt. 8, pp. 217–390.

al-Shāfi'ī, Muḥammad b. Idrīs. *Kitāb mā Ikhtalafa fīhi Abū Ḥanīfa wa Ibn Abī Laylā 'an Abī Yūsuf wa huwa Kitāb Ikhtilāf al-'Irāqiyyīn* (or *al-'Irāqiyyayn*)... [= *Umm* Version]. In *idem, al-Umm*. Cairo: al-Hay'a al-Miṣriyya al-'Āmma li'l-Kitāb, 1407/1987 [= reprint of the 1321/1903 Būlāq ed.], pt. 7, pp. 87–150.

al-Shāfi'ī, Muḥammad b. Idrīs. *Al-Umm*. 11 Pts. in 11 Vols. Ed. Rif'at Fawzī 'Abd al-Muṭṭalib. al-Manṣūra: Dār al-Wafā' li'l-Ṭibā'a wa'l-Nashr wa'l-Tawzī', 2001.

al-Shīrāzī, Abū Isḥāq Ibrāhīm. *Kitāb al-Luma' fī Uṣūl al-Fiqh* (*Traité de Théorie Légale Musulmane*). Introduction, traduction annotée et index par Éric Chaumont. Berkeley, CA: Robbins Collection, 1999.

al-Shīrāzī, Abū Isḥāq Ibrāhīm. *Kitāb al-Ma'ūna fi'l-Jadal*. Ed. 'Abd al-Majīd Turkī. Beirut: Dār al-Gharb al-Islāmī, 1988.

al-Shīrāzī, Abū Isḥāq Ibrāhīm. *Al-Luma' fī Uṣūl al-Fiqh*. Ed. Muḥyī al-Dīn Dīb Mustū and Yūsuf 'Alī Badīwī. Damascus: Dār al-Kalam al-Ṭayyib; Dār Ibn Kathīr, 1995.

al-Shīrāzī, Abū Isḥāq Ibrāhīm. *Al-Ma'ūna fi'l-Jadal*. Ed. 'Alī b. 'Abd al-'Azīz al-'Umayrīnī. Al-Ṣafāh, Kuwait: Manshūrāt Markaz al-Makhṭūṭāt wa'l-Turāth, 1987.

Smith, Robin. "Aristotle on the Uses of Dialectic." *Synthese* 96:3 (1993): pp. 335–58.

van Ess, Josef. "Disputationspraxis in der Islamischen Theologie. Eine Vorläufige Skizze." *Revue des Études Islamiques* 44 (1976): 23–60.

van Ess, Josef. "The Logical Structure of Islamic Theology." In *Logic in Classical Islamic Culture*, Ed. G. von Grunebaum (Wiesbaden: Otto Harrassowitz, 1970): 21–50.

Young, Walter Edward. "The Dialectical Forge: Proto-System Juridical Disputation in the Kitāb Ikhtilāf al-'Irāqiyyīn." 2 vols. PhD diss., McGill University, Montréal, 2012.

Chapter 2
Evolutionary Narratives

2.1 Current Narratives for the Evolution of Juridical Dialectical Theory in Islam

On the Dialectical World of Early Islam

It cannot be claimed that dialectical disputation was the only dynamic powering the intellectual history of early Islamicate civilization; what I claim is that it was the most present and influential of dynamics.[1] Vast bodies of literature attest to this; in works of history, biography, religion, philosophy, natural sciences, and law—from late antiquity and onwards—there is clear testimony that developments across all intellectual disciplines were advanced by formal disputations in a variety of dialectical styles. These may have occurred within or between confessional communities, epistemic communities, and schools of thought; before the prince's court, in private salons, in academy and library, or in temple, church, or mosque; on themes of theology, philosophy, grammar, jurisprudence, *belles lettres*, science, or politics; and with opponents standing face to face, or trading argument and counter-argument through a literary medium.[2] If one feature above all

[1] The current project does not delve into social history, despite the proven and fruitful application of its methods in the study of Islamic Law. Important social and scholarly dynamics of relevance to the current project are revealed in a critical study by Ahmed El Shamsy, *The Canonization of Early Islamic Law*.

[2] See, among other works, the articles in Lazarus-Yafeh, et al., eds. *The Majlis*; Ḥasan, *Manhaj al-Jadal*; Abū Zahra, *Tārīkh al-Jadal*; Griffith, *The Beginnings of Christian Theology*; Cook, *Early Muslim Dogma*; Soffer, "The Theological *Majlis*"; Karabela, "Development"; and Tahiri, "The Birth of Scientific Controversies."

W.E. Young, *The Dialectical Forge*, Logic, Argumentation & Reasoning 9,
DOI 10.1007/978-3-319-25522-4_2

others marks the intellectual landscape of the Near East in Late Antiquity and early Islam, it is dialectical debate.[3]

It is vital that this intellectual setting be recognized, for the jurists of our subject-text were born into the truly dialectical world of Islam's second and third centuries; and, as we shall see, the earliest Arabic treatises dedicated specifically to the theory of a distinctly Islamic dialectic did not surface until a century or more later. Our proto-system jurists were practiced dialecticians nevertheless, immersed in a cultural milieu permeated with debate. Islamic disputation praxis and theories—in any of their thematic domains—did not emerge suddenly and startlingly systematized from a three-century vacuum, and only then begin to take hold in Islam's many and already sophisticated sciences. Rather, they grew forth from a synthetic mixture of prior and early Islamic argumentation epistemes, guided by the dictates of various intellectual projects and variant agendas; and, throughout all stages, they provided a primary dynamic for the refinement and systematization of such sciences with which they were intertwined. The world of our subject-text—composed and expanded in the heartland of Islamicate civilization in the second and third Islamic centuries—was exactly as other sources tell us it was: overflowing with prolifically debating epistemic communities, alive with intellectual competition, driven by the agendas of variant speculative and normative projects, drawing upon complex, interwoven, and continually evolving sets of epistemes, and guided overall by the truth-seeking imperative of dialectical disputation and its accompanying modes of epistemic justification and critique.

[3]To further situate the subject of this monograph in broader intellectual history, dialectical disputation must first be recognized as a phenomenon common to multiple societies in the premodern world. For a broad overview, see the articles in Cabezón, ed. *Scholasticism: Cross-Cultural and Comparative Perspectives.* For the influence and development of dialectic in ancient and late antique Hellenic thought, see, among other works, Baltussen, *Theophrastus against the Presocratics and Plato*; idem., "Dialectic in Dialogue"; Rubinelli, *Ars Topica*; Marion, "Remarks on Syllogistic"; and select articles in Sorabji, ed., *The Philosophy of the Commentators.* For dialectic in Judaism and Christianity, see Neusner and Chilton, *The Intellectual Foundations.* For the influence of dialectic in medieval European intellectual history, see Stump, *Dialectic and its Place*; Makdisi, "Scholastic Method"; idem. *Rise of Colleges* [both works with special focus on the contribution of Islamic dialectic]; Angelelli, "Techniques of Disputation"; and Hohmann, "Logic and Rhetoric." And for Hindu and Buddhist contexts, see Dreyfus, *The Sound of Two Hands Clapping*; and Cabezón, *Buddhism and Language.*

Evolutionary Narratives for Juridical Dialectic[4]

Only a handful of modern scholars have treated juridical *jadal* to any considerable extent; and, in the main, their contributions have been superseded—and at times corrected—by those of Larry Miller and Wael Hallaq. There are other reasons why I will give these two scholars the last word on juridical *jadal* evolution. George Makdisi's accounts, for example, though on the whole very informative and at times even entertaining (citing many anecdotes of dialectical disputations gone wrong), are chronologically inconsistent. On more than one occasion, he implies that jurists had no interest in *jadal* until the fourth century (citing al-Qaffāl al-Shāshī [d.365/976] and Abū ʿAlī al-Ṭabarī [d.350/961] as first authors),[5] but elsewhere relates anecdotes and in other ways makes reference to formal juridical disputations from as early as the start of the second century H.[6] Importantly, however, we should note that he recognizes the central role of juridical dialectic

---

[4] In the current project, focus will remain strictly upon evolution of dialectic in the juridical domain. Developmental trajectories of dialectical theory and practice in Islamic theology, philosophy, and other domains (and their relation to parallel developments in law) are critical areas of study in which important work has been done but much more remains. In the domain of Philosophy and Arabic-Aristotelian logical traditions, see, among others, the contributions of Tony Street (e.g., "Logic," and "Arabic Logic"), Fehmi Jadaane (*L'Influence du Stoïcisme sur la Pensée Musulmane*), Ibrāhīm Madkūr (*L'Organon d'Aristote dans le Monde Arabe*), and David DiPasquale ("Alfarabi and the Starting Point of Islamic Philosophy"). In theology, see Josef van Ess, especially his "Disputationspraxis in der Islamischen Theologie" and "Logical Structure of Islamic Theology." For an exposition on the nature and evolution of the post-classical dialectical theory known as the "proper guidelines of dialectical inquiry" (*ādāb al-baḥth*), with brief forays into classical dialectical systems of theology, poetry, grammar, philosophy, and law, see Mehmet Karabela's dissertation, "The Development of Dialectic and Argumentation Theory in Post-Classical Islamic Intellectual History;" and for later developments in the *ādāb al-baḥth* in the Ottoman context see the second chapter of Khaled El-Rouayheb, *Islamic Intellectual History in the Seventeenth Century*. A useful overview of terminology, genres, and select problems from the domains of *jadal*, *munāẓara*, and *ādāb al-baḥth* may be found in Abdessamad Belhaj, *Argumentation et Dialectique en Islam*. In the realms of early Islamic theology and philosophy, however, the most comprehensive treatment of dialectical theory remains Larry Miller's dissertation, "Islamic Disputation Theory," pp. 1–86. See a review and partial critique of these chapters in my own dissertation ("Dialectical Forge," pt.1, pp. 22–44).

[5] "By the first half of the fourth/tenth century, the jurisconsults became interested in the study of dialectic, adapting it to their own purpose..." (*Colleges*, p. 108; and again on p. 147, citing the same early authors: al-Qaffāl al-Shāshī and Abū ʿAlī al-Ṭabarī). And: "After the first works on dialectic had adapted it to the needs of legal studies, jurisconsults, becoming fully cognizant of its value to their work, began to study it in earnest" (ibid., p. 109).

[6] "Disputation is usually connected with theology; but some of the earliest disputations were in the fields of law and grammar." He cites a juridical disputational *majlis* held before the Umayyad Caliph ʿUmar b. ʿAbd al-ʿAzīz, and then presents a fascinating overview of early disputations in the domain of grammar studies (ibid., pp. 123 ff.) Importantly, Makdisi presents a listing of "regular sessions of legal disputation"—his first example being the court of Hārūn al-Rashīd, where a student of Mālik would dispute Abū Yūsuf (p. 133 ff.) Of interest, too, are two anecdotes of Ibn Surayj's humour in disputation (ibid., p. 134). Indeed, Makdisi even relates the famed session in Egypt which supposedly resulted in al-Shāfiʿī's death (ibid., p. 136), and elsewhere references juridical disputation's "long period of development" (ibid., p. 139).

in the legal-pedagogical enterprise and the elaboration of law,[7] the relationship between the study of juridical disagreement (*khilāf*) and *jadal*,[8] and the connection between *jadal* and legal theory (*uṣūl al-fiqh*).[9] The general introduction to *jadal* one finds in his *Rise of Colleges* is an important contribution, but there is no coherent evolutionary trajectory to be found, and his discussions in no way account for the sophisticated dialectic we find in al-Shāfiʿī's *Kitāb al-Umm*.

As for the important contributions of ʿAbd al-Majīd Turkī with regard to *jadal* evolution, they are, in the main, echoed in and surpassed—in terms of scope and detail—by Miller's dissertation,[10] and in other ways covered by the accounts of Muḥammad Abū Zahra[11] and Khalīl al-Mays.[12] The same may be said for the important discussions of Wolfhart Heinrichs.[13] This in no way subtracts from the signifi-

[7] "So important was dialectic for the development of law and legal studies in Islam that it became a sine qua non of these studies in the colleges of law, both masjids and madrasas" (ibid., p. 109 f.)

[8] "To deal with khilaf, one had to be skilled in jadal, dialectic, and in munazara, nazar, disputation" (ibid., p. 109).

[9] "With the rise of dialectic, jadal, as applied to the study of legal theory and methodology, usul al-fiqh, the literary arts were relegated to the background" (ibid., p. 76). And: "[jurisconsults, after "adapt[ing *jadal*] to the needs of legal studies"] devoted individual works to it; and more significantly, they incorporated the subject, in more or less detail, in their works on legal theory and methodology" (ibid., p. 109). I will of course argue that *jadal* and legal theory were inseparably intertwined from the very beginning of the Islamic jurisprudential enterprise; this "dynamic symbiosis" and co-evolution is a core element of the Dialectical Forge theory, and, among other things, accounts for the inclusion of *jadal*-oriented chapters in early *uṣūl al-fiqh* works.

[10] See Turkī's introductions to al-Bājī's *Minhāj* (pp. 7–11); and his *Polémiques* (especially at pp. 27–45 [= pp. 31–52 of the Arabic version]). Importantly, however, Turkī underscores certain phenomena which Miller either neglects or implicitly denies. Among them, the following are of great significance to the current project: (1) that the Prophet's Companions engaged in *jadal* (*Polémiques*, p. 9); and (2) that there is «une évolution parallèle du *ǧadal* dans le *kalām* et le *fiqh*» (ibid., p. 29; compare this statement with the "common source, parallel development, and cross-germination" model I propose in chapter 4, section 4.6, fig. 4.2). Turkī also goes some way towards explaining the relationship between the genres of juridical disagreement (*khilāf*), guidelines for dialectical investigation (*ādāb al-baḥth*), legal theory (*uṣūl al-fiqh*), and *jadal* (ibid., pp. 32 ff.) Finally, although I would disagree with him regarding al-Shāfiʿī's role as "founder," Turkī yet acknowledges an early history—potentially, even a priority—for the study and technical practice of juridical *jadal*: «En effet, on est en droit de considérer Šāfiʿī... comme le véritable fondateur de la science des *uṣūl al-fiqh*..., et, par là-même de la science et de la technique du *ǧadal* et du *ẖilāf* que l'historien maghrébin [Ibn Khaldūn] fait dépendre de l'autre science; toutefois, on peut se demander si, en un certain sens et dans une mesure limitée, le mouvement dogmatique muʿtazilite qui imprégnait tout le deuxième siècle de l'Hégire et précédait donc notre imam de quelques décennies, ne fut pas susceptible d'une influence quelconque sur une pensée juridique contemporaine ou légèrement postérieure» (ibid., pp. 29–30).

[11] See his *History of Disputation* (*Tārīkh al-Jadal*) and his *Legal Theory* (*Uṣūl al-Fiqh*).

[12] See the introduction to his edition of al-Dabbūsī's *Ta'sīs al-Naẓar*.

[13] See his Arabic introduction (the German intro. deals mostly with MSS descriptions) of al-Ṭūfī's *ʿAlam al-Jadhal* (especially at يط - يح). Importantly, Heinrichs tells us: "I have chosen to edit and publish al-Ṭūfī's book on *jadal* for two reasons: First, the infrequency with which the *kutub al-jadaliyya* are printed, and what is printed of them as a specialized science; and that is despite the fact that there is no understanding the systematic program (*manhaj*) of the science of legal

cance of the works of these scholars, all of whom—especially through their contributions of critical editions—are founding figures in this understudied field (and this goes for Makdisi, too).[14] I mean only to say that their historical trajectories for the evolution of juridical *jadal* (which is our focus here) have generally been supplanted by Miller's far more comprehensive treatment.[15]

A more recent contribution, with a focus particularly relevant to this current project, deserves special notice here: *al-Jadal ʿinda al-Uṣūliyyīn: bayna al-Naẓariyya wa'l-Taṭbīq* (*Dialectic According to the Legal Theorists: Between Theory and Practice*), by Masʿūd b. Mūsā Fallūsī. Besides an encyclopedic transmission of dialectical objections culled from the pages of our lens-texts and other sources, the author contributes a broad developmental narrative. This narrative is interesting in its own right, exhibiting doctrinal commitments which might be categorized as "modern, Muslim-Traditionalist."[16] Fallūsī's narrative may be outlined as follows: (1) a capacity for dialectic was created in man by God, who thus employs dialectic in the Qur'ān to appeal to that innate faculty, and the Prophet also employed dialectic to that end;[17] (2) the Companions inherited dialectic from the Prophet, and practiced it to similar ends, but especially with regard to the disagreements which arose between them, then the Successors followed suit, and so it continued straight through to the first Imām Mujtahids; (3) "legal-theoretical dialectic" (*al-jadal al-uṣūlī*) first appeared in its applied form (*fī ṣūratihi al-taṭbīqiyya*) with al-Shāfiʿī, especially in his *Risāla* and *Jimāʿ al-ʿIlm*; (4) research in *al-jadal al-uṣūlī* grew after al-Shāfiʿī, and the fourth century H marks the start of a second phase: the maturation and perfection of the system of *jadal* in both its applied and theoretical manifestations—Abū Bakr al-Bāqillānī (Mālikī; d.403/1013), famed dialectician, built the foundations; (5) this phase witnessed the greatest activity of *jadal*-influenced *uṣūl al-fiqh* writing and *jadal* theory texts, by many greats including al-Juwaynī, al-Shīrāzī, al-Bājī, et al.; (6) a period of decline followed, marked by abridgements and commentaries and lack of innovation, though with a few independent exceptions such as al-Ṭūfī; (7) legal studies in general mortified after the 10th c. H, including *al-jadal al-uṣūlī*.

---

theory (*ʿilm uṣūl al-fiqh*)—the most important of the theoretical sciences (*ʿulūm al-naẓariyya*) in Islam—nor the intellectual style to which this *ʿilm* conforms, except from the likes of these treatises...." (ibid., يح).

[14] I refer to his edition of Ibn ʿAqīl's *Kitāb al-Jadal ʿalā Ṭarīqat al-Fuqahā'*: *Le Livre de la Dialectique d'Ibn ʿAqīl.*

[15] The same may be said with regard to E. Wagner's entry for *Munāẓara* in the *EI*², which cites both Makdisi and Miller. Importantly, Wagner also speaks of *munāẓara* in its poetic forms, and highlights links to pre-Islamic genres.

[16] In much the same way as certain works sharing the title *Ta'rīkh al-Tashrīʿ al-Islāmī* (*History of Islamic Legislation*). Like these, Fallūsī's narrative, though embracing pre-modern sources, "[does] not eschew modern frameworks, terms, and concepts—nor [is it] untouched by Orientalist conclusions" (see my entry "Origins of Islamic Law" in the *Oxford Encyclopedia of Islam and Law*).

[17] NB: Fallūsī does not entirely neglect non-Islamic dialectical traditions; he briefly raises Greek dialectic and its potential influence, but only as an unexplored area for future research (*al-Jadal ʿinda al-Uṣūliyyīn*, p. 501).

Wael Hallaq on the History of Juridical Jadal

In the introduction to his translation of al-Baṣrī's *Kitāb al-Qiyās al-Sharʿī*, Hallaq observes: "with the emergence of *uṣūl al-fiqh* as an independent 'science' towards the end of the third/ninth century, the art of dialectic (*jadal* or *munāẓara*) had become an important ingredient in legal education and legal theoretical formulations."[18] This is significant, and in line with the evidence of the *Umm* compendium; it not only implies a role for dialectic in legal pedagogy, but it leaves the way open for a formative dynamic with regard to *uṣūl* principles and methods before the appearance of specialized genres. Following this, we get an idea of Hallaq's evolutionary narrative for juridical dialectic.

In sum, Hallaq presents a trajectory in which: (1) Greek works on dialectic were translated into Arabic (in the first half of the third century H); (2) "Immediately afterwards dialectic was studied and rapidly assimilated in the Muslim religious sciences;" and (3) specialized (Sunnī) juridical-*jadal* treatises, "totally Islamicized and, like juridical logic, [their] link to the 'ancient sciences'... dissipated," were being composed by the mid-fourth century H.[19] There is no doubt that this narrative holds true in the main; what I would suggest is that what occurred after the translation of Greek dialectic is best understood as a *re*-invigoration—a new systematization along more strictly Aristotelian lines, in certain quarters and among certain theorists. From the evidence of the *Umm* compendium and pre-Translation Movement disputation practice on juridical and theological themes, I would make the claim that a tradition—or traditions—of dialectical disputation preceded this infusion of Aristotelian dialectical method resulting from the Translation Movement.[20] If, however, this suggested trajectory (pre-Translation Movement *jadal* tradition[s] → Translation Movement → assimilation of Greek dialectic → systematized juridical-*jadal* genre) is to be tested, it must be done so by: (1) analyzing the argumentation method (and associated concepts, terms, categorizations, and orderings) employed in disputations on juridical and theological themes through to the early stages of the Translation Movement; (2) analyzing the same as formulated in Arabic after translation from systematic works of Greek dialectic; and (3) analyzing the same in the earliest extant works of *jadal*/*munāẓara*.[21]

It is by examining in detail the argumentation, dialectical moves, and associated terms and formulae, that we can come to determine something of the grammar and lexicon of juridical dialectic before, during, and after the Translation Movement; and it is by comparing these with the grammar and lexicon of system-

---

[18] "Treatise," p. 197.

[19] Ibid., pp. 197–8.

[20] With regard to the Translation Movement as a whole, the most diligent and comprehensive study of this prolonged and far-reaching intellectual-historical event remains *Greek thought, Arabic culture*, by Dimitri Gutas.

[21] Miller's dissertation goes some distance with respect to these last two priorities, but neglects the first.

atic Greek dialectic in translation that we can assess the impact of the Translation Movement on the systematization of Islamic juridical *jadal* tradition(s). This passage from Hallaq's introduction thus serves as another starting point for the current project. So far as can be seen by comparison with dialectical arguments from our subject-text, the *jadal* theory of our lens-texts show a strong connection to pre-Translation Movement disputation—while certain terms, formulae, and structures may bear the marks of a post-Movement influence.

Hallaq's contribution to the study of juridical dialectic continues to some degree in his *History of Islamic Legal Theories*. Here, the important role of *jadal* with regard to the *ijtihādic* elaboration of substantive rulings is roundly asserted:

> In one sense, dialectic constituted the final stage in the process of legal reasoning, in which two conflicting opinions on a case of law were set against each other in the course of a disciplined session of argumentation with the purpose of establishing the truthfulness of one of them. The aim of this exercise, among other things, was to reduce disagreement (*ikhtilāf*) among legists by demonstrating that one opinion was more acceptable or more valid than another. Minimizing differences of opinion on a particular legal question was of the utmost importance, the implication being that truth is one, and for each case there exists only one true solution.[22]

Especially important for the current project, Hallaq not only asserts the "essential" role of dialectic in legal theory, but also implies a *formative dynamic*, while indicating the variety of argument types which may arise during the course of a question and answer debate:

> This function of narrowing down disagreements by establishing where truth resides rendered the art of disputation... essential to legal theory, although one can find numerous treatises that do not devote any space to a discussion of this art. *The systematic effect of dialectic on the modes of exposition of legal theories is readily obvious, reflecting the background against which this theory grew to maturity*. The most common method of exposition—though exceptions are many—is that of the question-answer: 'If someone says such and such, we reply with such and such.' But this method is versatile, and an analysis of the logical structure of questions, and especially answers, shows that theorists adopted for their use the entire gamut of arguments we nowadays subsume under logic and rhetoric.[23]

The italicized sentence is of singular import. It a starting point; and the current project aims to bring consideration of this "background" to the forefront of Islamic legal-theoretical studies, to demonstrate its dynamism in the evolution of *jadal* and *uṣūl* systems since their earliest stages, and to formulate a general theory explaining it.

Returning to Hallaq's exposition, we also gain insight into his narrative for juridical *jadal* evolution from a preceding discussion:

> In the initial stages of its development, legal theory seems to have incurred another debt to *kalām*,[24] namely, dialectic (*jadal* or *munāẓara*) which occupied a prominent place in the overall structure of this theory. Defining the precise extent of this debt is not an easy

---

[22] Hallaq, *History*, pp. 136–7.

[23] Ibid., p. 137; italics are mine.

[24] Meaning Islamic dialectical theology.

> task, for *kalām* itself was influenced in this respect by the new Greek ideas that infiltrated Muslim religious sciences. Whether the dialectical method entered legal theory via *kalām* or was directly borrowed from Greek translations is a question that must await further research. But that the Muslim art of dialectic was significantly influenced by the Greek sources seems beyond dispute. And here, as elsewhere, borrowing was highly selective, as suggested by the distinction drawn between the dialectic of the philosophers—who in the view of the orthodox, are not far removed from heresy—and the "good dialectic" (*al-jadal al-ḥasan*) which was harmonious with the spirit of law and legal theory.[25]

Again, we see here more than one starting point. I would argue that whether or not juridical *jadal* at its earliest stage (and afterwards) owes a "debt to *kalām*" (or, for that matter, Greek dialectic) remains to be seen. I will, in later chapters, claim the similarity between *kalām* method and juridical dialectic is most likely the result of the origins of both in a common pot of prior argumentation epistemes—including, but not exclusively so, the Aristotelian and Stoic—and infused with newer Islamic epistemes, then followed by parallel development (as directed by variant normative vs. speculative agendas), and accompanied at every stage by mutual cross-germination. The evidence provided by dialectical sequences in the *Umm* however, demonstrates that one thing is certain: a distinctly *juridical* dialectic had already acquired a high level of sophistication by al-Shāfiʿī's day.[26] Finally, Hallaq summarizes the advent and subsequent history of full-system *jadal* theory, as follows:

> By the middle of the fourth/tenth century, entire treatises on juridical dialectic appear to have come into existence, and the name of al-Qaffāl al-Shāshī is associated with the first composition on 'good dialectic.' Writings on the subject grew steadily, culminating in such imposing and recondite contributions as Juwaynī's *al-Kāfiya fī al-Jadal*. Beginning with the fifth/eleventh century, dialectic as a method of argumentation was incorporated into works of legal theory, a practice that became increasingly popular in the following centuries.[27]

In his translation of al-Baṣrī, Hallaq lists a number of references for the earliest works in juridical dialectic;[28] importantly, he cites al-Shīrāzī's claim (in the *Ṭabaqāt al-Fuqahā'*)[29] that Abū Bakr Muḥammad b. ʿAlī b. Ismāʿīl al-Qaffāl al-Shāshī (d.336/947, a student of Ibn Surayj [d.306/918]) was the first among jurists (*fuqahā'*) to compose a work on "the good dialectic" (*al-jadal al-ḥasan*). According to al-Shīrāzī, he composed a book on legal theory (*uṣūl al-fiqh*), a commentary (*sharḥ*) on al-Shāfiʿī's *Risāla* (our oldest surviving treatise on legal theory), and he is credited with spreading the legal doctrine (*fiqh*) of al-Shāfiʿī in Transoxiana.

[25] *History*, p. 136.

[26] That is, by the end of the second/eighth century.

[27] *History*, p. 136.

[28] "Treatise," p. 198, n. 6.

[29] Khalīl al-Mays ed., p. 120.

Larry Miller on the History of Juridical Jadal

In briefest summation, Miller constructs a four-century trajectory for the evolution of Islamic dialectics along the following stages: (1) the Q&A objection dialectic of the theologians; (2) the juristic take over of *jadal*, the development of good vs. bad *jadal*, and the reformulation of old teachings with logic; and (3) the *ādāb al-baḥth* as a final stage and synthesis of all that came before.[30] His narrative is one in which juridical *jadal* blossomed from theological *jadal*, took root and became an essential part of jurisprudence. He subsequently treats the evolution of juridical *jadal* in three periods: (1) earliest works; (2) a century later when logic is first applied; and (3) a final period before the transition from the strictly legal to the universal dialectic of al-Samarqandī.[31] This trajectory, especially the earlier stages, is problematic not only in light of the *Umm* compendium and its overtly dialectical character, but in the juridical *jadal* of al-Baṣrī.[32]

Miller also speaks of two genres—appearing in the 4th/10th c.—resulting from "the incursion of jadal in jurisprudence." He mentions: (1) "works with the jadal method devoted to uṣūl al-fiqh," and which "usually had the word jadal somewhere in their title;" and (2) "works devoted to the furūʿ,"[33] and which "were generally called ṭarīqa."[34] This description parallels the two functions (prescriptive vs. descriptive) of *uṣūl al-fiqh*—and the variant-objective "Shāfiʿī/Mutakallimūn" vs. "Ḥanafī/Fuqahā'" methodologies—as described by Ibn Khaldūn and others.[35] Certainly Ibn Khaldūn mentions two juridical-*jadal* "*ṭarīqas*", but he describes them thus: (1) the *ṭarīqa* of the first to write on the subject, al-ʿAmīdī (Ḥanafī, d.615/1218)—in his *Irshād*—which is "general, for any indicant (*dalīl*) which may provide indication, as pertains to any science (*ʿilm*) which may be"; and (2) that of al-Bazdawī (Ḥanafī, d.482/1089), which is "specifically according to indicants consonant with God's Law (*al-adilla al-sharʿiyya*)."[36]

---

[30] "Islamic Disputation Theory," pp. 1–4.

[31] Ibid., pp. 87–8.

[32] Miller considers the earliest "direct source" to be the *Maʿūna* of al-Shīrāzī, who died 40 years after al-Baṣrī (ibid., p. 88). He also suggests that a "long and close association between theology and jurisprudence from the very beginning of Islamic thought" makes the jurists' later take over unsurprising (ibid., p. 87).

[33] That is, to derived substantive rulings. *Furūʿ* (s. *farʿ*, literally: "branches") were metaphorically cultivated from *uṣūl* (s. *aṣl*, literally: "roots," technically: authoritative source materials and methods) through the efforts of the qualified jurist (*mujtahid*).

[34] Meaning, "method." Unfortunately, Miller provides no list of titles for each genre, and proceeds only by noting that his focus will be upon "works written on juristic jadal," according to his tripartite periodization ("Islamic Disputation Theory," p. 87).

[35] See my entry "Uṣūl al-Fiqh" in *Oxford Islamic Studies Online*.

[36] *Muqaddima*, Shaḥāda ed., p. 579 [trans. is mine; see: *Faṣl* 9, "*Fī Uṣūl al-Fiqh wa mā yataʿallaqu bihi min al-Jadal wa'l-Khilāfiyyāt*," pp. 573–9]; Rosenthal transl., vol. 3, §13, pp. 33–4 (see: "The science of the principles of jurisprudence and its subdivisions, dialectics and controversial questions;" vol. 3, §13, pp. 23–34).

Miller's "Early Period" of Juridical Dialectic[37]

Miller consults works by the following *jadal*-theorists: (1) Abū Isḥāq Ibrāhīm al-Shīrāzī (Shāfiʿī, d.476/1083); (2) Abū al-Walīd al-Bājī (Mālikī, d.474/1081); (3) Abū al-Wafāʾ b. ʿAqīl (Ḥanbalī, d.513/1119); and (4) Imām al-Ḥaramayn al-Juwaynī (Shāfiʿī, d.478/1085).[38] Importantly, he notes that both al-Bājī and Ibn ʿAqīl were students of al-Shīrāzī. With regard to Ibn ʿAqīl, Miller finds him more dependent upon al-Shīrāzī, and al-Bājī less so, as the latter "will occasionally profess a different opinion or explicitly criticize al-Shīrāzī." As for al-Juwaynī, however, Miller notes he "comes from the Islamic east, and from an apparently different tradition." Moreover, he makes the claim—although al-Juwaynī "often refers in his work to al-Ustādh Abū Isḥāq" (which *kunya* belongs to al-Shīrāzī)—that he is "referring most probably to the Ashʿarite theologian al-Isfarāʾinī (d.1027)."[39]

Finally, Miller observes that al-Juwaynī, al-Bājī, and Ibn ʿAqīl all cite other *jadal*-authors, from both theological and juridical realms. He adds that this should not surprise us, as "our authors were writing a good century after b. al-Rīwandī's opus on jadal and about a half century after the first attempts at making jadal a part of jurisprudence were carried out, if we can believe our sources, by the likes of b. al-Suraij, A. ʿAlī al-Ṭabarī, and others."[40] I would argue that such a narrative,

---

[37] Miller's discussions of the nature and content of "early period" juridical dialectic are important; for a review and partial critique, see my dissertation ("Dialectical Forge," pt. 1, pp. 120 ff.) The focus now is on his historical narrative.

[38] He does not include al-Baṣrī's *K. al-Qiyās al-Sharʿī*, nor makes reference to *jadal*-oriented discussions in his *Muʿtamad*. As for the focal sources, the earliest cited is the Princeton MS of al-Shīrāzī's *Maʿūna*. We may note he depends upon ʿAbd al-Majīd Turkī's 1978 ed. of al-Bājī's *Minhāj fī Tartīb al-Ḥijāj*; G. Makdisi's publication of Ibn ʿAqīl's *K. al-Jadal ʿalā Ṭarīqat al-Fuqahā'* in the 1967 *Bulletin d'Études Orientales*; and the 1979 Ḥusayn Maḥmūd ed. of al-Juwaynī's *Kāfiya fī'l-Jadal* ("Islamic Disputation Theory," pp. 88–9, and nn. 1–3).

[39] "Islamic Disputation Theory," pp. 89. The basis for this assumption is unclear. Many factors tie al-Shīrāzī not only to the east and its traditions, but to the person of al-Juwaynī himself. From al-Subkī's *Ṭabaqāt* (and E. Chaumont's rendering of much of its detail in his *EI*[2] article on al-Shīrāzī), we learn that: (1) Abū Isḥāq al-Fīrūzābādī al-Shīrāzī (note the *nisbas*) studied with Shāfiʿīs in Fīrūzābād and Shīrāz, as well as in Baṣra and Baghdād (where his teachers also bear many an eastern *nisba*); (2) the Niẓāmiyya *madrasa* in Baghdad—where he was to teach for nearly 20 years—was constructed in his honour; and (3) late in life he journeyed to Nīshāpūr and met al-Juwaynī (there directing the *madrasa* also built in his honour by Niẓām al-Mulk), "with whom he conducted several sessions of judicial controversy (the text of these *disputatios* is preserved in al-Subkī [*Ṭabaqāt*])" (Chaumont, "al-Shīrāzī," *EI*[2]). Considering the interrelationships of Miller's "early period" authors—all of whom composed lens-texts used in this current project—I believe we may consider each of their extant works, however similar or distinct, as emanating from a larger body of *jadal*-theory discourse. The hotspots of this discourse were in Iraq, Persia, and Khurāsān, and it was eventually disseminated through Niẓām al-Mulk's *madrasa* system—by teachers such as al-Shīrāzī and al-Juwaynī.

[40] "Islamic Disputation Theory," pp. 89–90, and nn. 5–6. I should point out that Ibn al-Rāwandī may have been a contemporary of Ibn Surayj—even of his students. The apparent gap in *jadal*-theory compositions is by no means certain; nor is it certain that priority would belong to Ibn al-Rāwandī in anything more than the composition of a treatise. The century preceding Ibn Surayj—himself a master dialectician—is replete with master jurist-dialecticians, stretching all the way back to al-Shāfiʿī's time (himself included), and before.

if accurate, would pertain only to the literary enterprise of producing *jadal*-theory treatises. As for the actual practice and teaching of juridical *jadal*, it stretches back to the very dawn of Islamic jurisprudence, and certainly at least to the first half of the second century H.

Miller's "Middle Period" of Juridical Dialectic[41]

An exposition on the "middle period" of juristic *jadal* opens by turning to Ibn Khaldūn's (d.808/1406) account in the *Muqaddima*. Miller presents the great historian's observation "that in his time there were two important methods (tarīqa) one of Abū Yusr Muḥammad al-Pazdawī and another of Rukn al-Dīn al-ʿAmīdī," then notes: "The 'method' of al Pazdawī has not been preserved; but that of al-ʿAmīdī has."[42] He continues his review of "middle period" *jadal* works by noting: "there exist other 'methods' from an earlier period [i.e., prior to al-ʿAmīdī], one of al-Marwazī [Shāfiʿī, d.461/1069];[43] and another of Raḍī al-Dīn al-Sarakhsī [Ḥanafī, d.544/1149]."[44] Miller then proceeds to compare these three methods.[45] I would contend that al-Marwazī should be considered along with his "early period" contemporaries, rather than "middle period" successors—for he predeceased al-Bājī by 13 years, al-Shīrāzī by 15, al-Juwaynī by 17, and Ibn ʿAqīl by 52. This is no small matter; it pushes back a parallel literary tradition of juridical *jadal*—which, after all, is quite different from that of al-Shīrāzī, et al.—so that two simultaneous literary traditions are apparent by the first half of the fifth century H.[46] Miller may not have proceeded to a new period so much as shifted to a parallel juridical-dialectical genre whose first writings extend back to the "early period".

He nevertheless succeeds in demonstrating how very different these works are from those of al-Shīrāzī et al., opening a detailed comparison of the *ṭarīqa* manuscripts of al-Marwazī, al-Sarakhsī/Nisabūrī, and al-ʿAmīdī by noting: "If we examine these three 'methods' as members of a genre of juristic literature, we find several shared characteristics in form and style." They are, in brief: (1) each work's arguments support the author's *madhhab* against another; (2) the familiar dialectical arguments are employed, "but their theoretical foundations are ignored;" (3) they are more practice than theory oriented; (4) their contents are

---

[41] I will not pursue Miller's narrative past this period as, chronologically speaking, it moves far beyond our primary concerns.

[42] "Islamic Disputation Theory," pp. 143. We are fortunate, however, that al-Bazdawī's *Kitāb fīhi Maʿrifat al-Ḥujaj al-Sharʿiyya* did survive, and has been recently edited (2003) by Marie Bernand and Eric Chaumont.

[43] In a footnote, Miller identifies him as al-Ḥasan b. Shuʿayb.

[44] Identified in footnote and bibliography as Raḍī al-Dīn al-Nisabūrī.

[45] "Islamic Disputation Theory," pp. 143–8.

[46] We should note that al-Bazdawī, too, was a contemporary of al-Bājī, al-Shīrāzī, and al-Juwaynī.

arranged by substantive legal category, beginning with purification (*ṭahāra*), etc.; and (5) "there is a uniformity of method employed" in the three works.[47]

I would consider, along with these observations, the full titles of Miller's manuscripts; they are, in chronological order of author's death-date: al-Marwazī's "Method of Disagreement between the Shāfiʿīs and the Ḥanafīs, with Mention of the Indicants of Each" (*Ṭarīqat al-Khilāf bayn al-Shāfiʿiyya wa'l-Ḥanafiyya maʿa Dhikr al-Adilla li-kull minhumā*);" al-Sarakhsī/Nisabūrī's "Raḍawī Method" (*al-Ṭarīqa al-Raḍawiyya*;) and al-ʿAmīdī's "ʿAmīdī Method for Disagreement and Disputation" (*al-Ṭarīqa al-ʿAmīdiyya fi'l-Khilāf wa'l-Jadal.*)[48] Not only is *ṭarīqa* the primary element for all three, but two also incorporate the term "disagreement" (*khilāf*). Note also that all but one of the *ṭarīqa* authors Miller has introduced for his "middle period"—including Abū al-Yusr al-Pazdawī—are Ḥanafīs, with al-Marwazī being the sole exception—whereas not a single one of the "early period" authors belonged to that doctrinal *madhhab*. Again, this does not fit a pattern of developmental stages so much as parallel subgenres within a larger and competitive endeavor—subprojects within a larger argumentation episteme of juridical *jadal*.

Besides other notes of interest, Miller's comparison of his three *ṭarīqa* manuscripts reveals that for all three: "the basic method is to state the problem, the evidence, the objections and their solutions."[49] Inherent to Raḍī al-Dīn al-Sarakhsī/Nisabūrī's presentation, moreover, is a "kalām-style" sequencing of objection and response, replete with formulaic patterns—"as for his saying X, we say we don't concede" (*ammā qawluhu* X *qulnā lā nusallim*), or "even if what you stated of the *dalīl*-indicant provides indication of X, nevertheless here is another *dalīl*-indicant providing indication for Y" (*mā dhakartum min al-dalīl wa in dalla ʿalā* X *wa lākin hāhunā dalīl ākhar yadullu ʿalā* Y), etc.—nothing less than an abstraction and abridgment of disputational sequences, and for didactic purposes. This corresponds well with what we find throughout the *Umm* compendium, although there is undoubtedly a higher level of sophistication in Miller's "kalām-style;" it is quite obviously structured according to the dictates of a fully-systematized juridical *jadal*, separated by centuries of development.

Miller now returns to the question of a developmental narrative for juridical dialectic, beginning by stating a problem in George Makdisi's narrative:

> This is the method that Makdisi discovered in the Wāḍiḥ of b. ʿAqīl and that he claimed derived from (juristic) sources prior to al-Qirqisānī.[50] This was a method which he said b. ʿAqīl applied 'to any field' of investigation. His argument is implausible on several counts.

Miller's counter-argument is this: (1) juridical *jadal* is indeed "indebted" to older *khilāf* works, but "we have shown that this earlier literature was not dialectical in character;" (2) the first works of juridical dialectic were written "a good

[47] "Islamic Disputation Theory," pp. 143–4.

[48] Ibid., p. 143 nn. 147–8, p. 145 n. 153.

[49] Ibid., pp. 143–6.

[50] Citing Makdisi's "Scholastic Method," p. 650; and his *Rise of Colleges*, pp. 117 ff.

generation or two after al-Qirqisānī and long after b. al-Rīwandī's heyday;" (3) the jurists' development of "praise-worthy" vs. "blameworthy" dialectic "is another sign of the transfer of dialectics from the controversy-steeped books of the theologians;" (4) the continued attempts by jurists to order objections "is a continuation of the dialectical tradition first found in b. al-Rīwandī's book;" (5) terminology provides "indication of the 'theological' origins of juristic dialectic"—the first "question" for both theological and juridical *jadal* is 'about the *madhhab*'—"But in jurisprudence, the term madhhab usually has the meaning of 'school of law'"; (6) Makdisi says: "...a *su'āl* is not a question, it is an objection...,"[51] but (Miller responds) for theologians, philosophers, and jurists, "jadal was question and answer," and "the objections were understood primarily as questions, and secondarily as objections"; and (7) "In the face of such evidence, Makdisi's position is no longer tenable."[52]

I would respond drawing from and defending the findings of the current project—to each of the above points in their listed order, as follows: (1) the *ikhtilāf* treatises found in al-Shāfiʿī's *Umm* compendium—indeed the entirety of the *Umm* itself—are alone sufficient to invalidate any claim that earlier *khilāf* literature was not dialectical in character; (2) Ibn al-Rāwandī was either a contemporary of Ibn Surayj or of his students, al-Qirqisānī was a contemporary of Ibn Surayj's students, and it is a student of Ibn Surayj who is credited with writing the first work of juridical *jadal*;[53] (3) the notion of "praiseworthy" vs. "blameworthy" dialectic may easily be discerned in Aristotle's *Topics* and *Sophistical Elenchi*, and did not require a juridical response to "theological" *jadal* for conception, and, even if it did, juridical *jadal* might better be described as a "reaction against" rather than a "take over from" theologically-themed *jadal*; (4) attempts by theologians and jurists alike to develop a strict ordering for questions and objections was driven by the common principle that Q cannot retract something he has conceded to, and so must take special care in the dissection of R's argument step-by-step, without jumping ahead and mistakenly conceding something he later finds problematic; (5) that both theologically and juridically-themed *jadal* open with 'the question about the *madhhab*' proves little in the way of chronological considerations; moreover, the term *madhhab* bore no less than four common meanings in

---

[51] Citing "Scholastic Method," p. 653.

[52] "Islamic Disputation Theory," pp. 146–8.

[53] All sources I have encountered place Ibn Surayj's death at 306/918 (not 336, as Miller has it), and all acknowledge that he was a master dialectician. As for Ibn al-Rāwandī, van Ess estimates his death at 298/910, but nothing is known with certainty about either his birth or death dates (*EIr*, s.v. "Ebn Rāvandī"); the latter has been placed as late as the middle or end of the 4th/10th c. (See *EI²*, s.v. "Ibn al-Rāwandī or al-Rēwendī"). This would mean he was either a contemporary of Ibn Surayj, or of his students, or of both. What is not disputed, however, is that the first juridical-*jadal* authors (and *uṣūl al-fiqh* authors) were the students of Ibn Surayj, the master dialectician, and themselves master dialecticians.

the juridical literature of the time, including the *mujtahid*'s '*madhhab*-opinion';[54] and (6) though I agree with Miller's interpretation of how *su'āl* was conceived, it is nevertheless a matter of semantics without clear bearing on the question of chronological development.

These and other arguments point to the presence of a juridical-dialectical practice and teaching which either predates or is contemporary to Ibn al-Rāwandī, and certainly to al-Qirqisānī, who died after 325/937. Miller's early developmental trajectories and juridical take over paradigm prove, in the end, untenable when faced with the overtly juridical-dialectical practices of al-Shāfiʿī, his contemporaries, and his predecessors, as evident throughout the *Umm*. A more tenable model in light of the evidence is that *jadal* practice and teaching developed in numerous streams, side-by-side, with juridical and theological themes, driven by variant normative and speculative agendas, sometimes through the teachings of master dialecticians who were both jurist and theologian, with perhaps regional variants, and in full flow by the time of al-Shāfiʿī. To be certain, *jadal* was employed differently, and evolved differently, in different projects—theological, philosophical, juridical, and others—and its different practices forged different sciences (e.g., *kalām* vs. *uṣūl al-fiqh*). Different sects and schools crystallized along the way as variant first principles were hammered out in disputation, and divergent bodies of doctrine branched off from contested starting points.

2.2 Dialectical Qualities of the Subject-Text and its Jurists

Al-Shāfiʿī and the Kitāb al-Umm

Our subject-text will speak for itself in following chapters; at this point it suffices to say that its dialectical qualities are manifest and marked by a particular style and sophistication. But the *Umm* Version of the *Ikhtilāf al-ʿIrāqiyyayn/ʿIrāqiyyīn* is only one treatise of many in the *Umm* compendium's treasure-trove of proto-system argument; and I am certainly not the first to notice the abundance and refinement of the *Umm*'s overall dialectical features, nor the particular qualities of its author and master dialectician, Muḥammad b. Idrīs al-Shāfiʿī.[55] By way of example, I will present a number of observations made by the editor of the *Umm*—Aḥmad Badr al-Dīn Ḥassūn—upon whose edition I have most relied, paraphrasing and quoting from his introduction, and collecting these into the table below. The overall assessment, if enthusiastic, is nonetheless accurate, and in the main uncontested.

[54] See Hallaq, *Sharīʿa*, 61 ff. I would also argue Miller's reference to *madhhab* as "school of law" is counter-productive; if he is implying that the first question of juridical *jadal* was "Are you a Ḥanafī, Shāfiʿī, etc.?" he has argued a difference, not a commonality, with "theological" *jadal*.

[55] Among other sources, see Kecia Ali's *Imam Shafiʿi: Scholar and Saint*, Mohyddin Yahia's *Šāfiʿī et les Deux Sources de la Loi Islamique*, and Joseph Lowry's *Early Islamic Legal Theory: the Risāla of Muḥammad ibn Idrīs al-Shāfiʿī*, for significant insights into al-Shāfiʿī's dialectical prowess, his legal theory and method, and his life, works, and comportment as a jurist.

- The *Umm* is one of a kind; singular in its era and what came after it. Ḥassūn extols its argumentative and dialectical virtues, and those of al-Shāfiʿī:
  - "potent dialectical investigation (*munāẓara qawiyya*), [al-Shāfiʿī] does not merely present the problem case (*mas'ala*), but, much more, he encompasses it in a solid enclosure of transmitted and rational indicants (*adilla al-naqliyya wa'l-ʿaqliyya*), deep research, constructive criticism (*al-naqd al-bannāʾ*), and a sound drawing of conclusions."[56]
  - "The *Kitāb al-Umm* is dominated by debate (*ḥiwār*): 'He said such and such, so I said: Have you considered (*a-ra'ayta*) if such-and-such is claimed? And if a speaker says such and such, I would respond to him with such and such. One of them said such and such to me, so I said to him...'—this sort of thing, which predominates in *jadal*, *munāẓara*, and *ḥiwār*. And how frequently [the *Umm*] presents an opposing opinion, and notes its proof (*ḥujja*), then refutes it with its own argument, while disposing one towards the determination of general legal principles (*qawāʿid*), and their derivation and attestation."[57]
  - "In the *Umm*, the power of al-Imām al-Shāfiʿī in *jadal* is made manifest, for the style of the book—almost all of it—is a dialectical (*jadalī*) style, to the extent that he even postulates [the position of] a dialectical opponent debating him, then rebuts him, then brings a counter-argument and responds: 'if one should profess such and such we rebut him with such and such' (*fa-in qāla qā'il kadhā raddadnā ʿalayhi kadhā*); [and] 'He said: the two parties to a contract of commutation have option (*khiyār*) regarding what they did not verbally apportion. So I said: That which you've opined is absurd (*muḥāl*), not permitted on the tongue. He said: And what is its absurdity (*iḥāla*), and how does the tongue not tolerate it? I said: [etc.]' And thus he proceeds in many subjects, in this style of debate which was influenced by the method (*namaṭ*) of the Iraqis, their argumentation (*ḥijāj*), and their invariable use of 'have you considered...' (*a-ra'ayta*)."[58]
- Ḥassūn reminds us that al-Shāfiʿī was a student and proponent of Mālik's doctrinal circle until his second coming to Iraq, where he benefited from the books of Muḥammad b. al-Ḥasan al-Shaybānī (supposed transmitter

(continued)

[56] [Ḥassūn], *Mawsūʿat al-Imām* (Intro.), vol. 1, p. 83.

[57] Ibid., vol. 1, p. 84.

[58] Ibid., vol. 1, pp. 84–5. Re: "absurdity" (*iḥāla*) and "absurd" (*muḥāl*): The term *muḥāl* occurs some twenty-five times in the *Umm*, in the same sense as we see it here, and quite often in reference to an opponent's argument. It would be a worthwhile project to collate all occurrences, compare their contexts, and determine the consistency of its use. Does *muḥāl* reference a specific type of fallacy? Or is it simply a general charge of untenable consequence, subsumed by the class of *reductio* arguments?

of the Shaybānī Version of our subject-text) and others. In what follows, we gain an overview of the argumentative and dialectical qualities of the Scholars of Iraq, that group to which most other key jurists of our subject-text belonged.

  - Ḥassūn observes that al-Shāfiʿī benefited from "his knowledge of the method (*ṭarīqa*) of the Scholars of Iraq (*Ahl al-ʿIrāq*), since he opined with regard to their method and procedure (*manhaj*) that no good would come from taking it up completely, nor in abandoning it completely; for they had *qiyās*, which is a valid (*ṣaḥīḥ*) procedure, but, in his view, not absolutely. Rather, it must necessarily be subservient to valid Prophetic reports (*aḥādīth al-ṣaḥīḥa*)—even such as are of solitary transmission (*khabar āḥād*). And they [also] had a method for cultivating (*tafrīʿ*) many problem cases (*masāʾil*) from their authoritative source materials (*uṣūl*), and for division (*taftīt*) of intension-properties (*maʿānī*)—with a method for their elaboration—and [methods] for dialectic (*jadal*), and for drawing indication (*istidlāl*) by way of equity (*ʿadāla*), public welfare considerations (*maṣlaḥa*), rationalized juristic preference (*istiḥsān*), and the appending of like to like (*ilḥāq al-shabīh bi'l-shabīh*); and [they had] other [methods] for complementarity and invalidating differences (*furūq*), ardent engagement in dialectical investigation (*munāẓara*), and composition of decisive arguments (*ḥujaj*), proofs (*barāhīn*) and indicants (*adilla*)."[59]

- Ḥassūn tells us that al-Shāfiʿī took the best of this Iraqi method, and added it to the wealth of the Scholars of the Ḥijāz, namely: the refinement of language and comportment (*adab*), the priority of Prophetic reports (*ḥadīth*), the consensus of the Medinese (*ijmāʿ Ahl al-Madīna*), and the Ḥijāzī method of rational inference (*istinbāṭ*). All of this—Iraqi and Ḥijāzī methods both—was combined in al-Shāfiʿī's *madhhab*-doctrine, and broadcast in Iraq. There it attracted some of his companions (*aṣḥāb*), like al-Karābīsī (d.256/869), who was a famed scholar in his own right in Iraq; and Abū Thawr al-Kalbī (d.240/854), who wrote on the disagreement (*ikhtilāf*) of al-Shāfiʿī and Mālik, leaning towards al-Shāfiʿī in his books; and al-Zaʿfarānī (d.260/874), who recited al-Shāfiʿī's ("Old Doctrine") books, from before his coming to Egypt.[60]

[59] Ibid., vol. 1, pp. 85–6. Note well the major role Ḥassūn reserves for al-Shaybānī and Iraqi scholars in general, as providing bases for the science of legal theory. Al-Shāfiʿī was an early systematizer of legal theory; and it was the Meccan, Medinan, and Iraqi scholars who supplied the raw material for his manner of dialectic, epistemic-justification, etc.

[60] Ibid., vol. 1, p. 86.

Ḥassūn is not alone in his unreserved praise of al-Shāfiʿī as master dialectician. Aḥmad Shākir, a respected editor of al-Shāfiʿī's early legal-theoretical tractate, the *Risāla*, suggests he had no equal "in the *fiqh* of the Qur'ān and Sunna, and the penetration of his analytical insight (*naẓar*) with regard to them, and in the refinement of rational inference (*diqqat al-istinbāṭ*); with eloquence, perspicacity, a singular ability in the establishing of proof (*ḥujja*) and the silencing of his dialectical opponent (*ifḥām munāẓirihi*); [he was] perfectly articulate, clear in explication (*bayān*), and at the very apex of eloquence (*balāgha*)." Speaking of al-Shāfiʿī's career in general, Shākir also gives us a sense of the dialectical milieu in which our proto-system jurists thrived:

> He was well-educated in the desert Bedouin's refinement of language and comportment (*adab*); he took up the sciences (*al-ʿulūm al-maʿārif*) of civilized folk, until he towered above every scholar before and after him; he distinguished himself in the Ḥijāz, and was an authoritative source (*marjiʿ*) of transmission (*riwāya*) and Sunna to its scholars, while they were authoritative masters (*asāṭīn*) of knowledge regarding the *fiqh* of the Qur'ān. But not many of them were folk of eloquence and *jadal*, and they were close to being incapable of dialectical disputation (*munāẓara*) with the Scholars Championing Considered Opinion (*Ahl al-Ra'y*). Then along came this youth, debating and defending, knowing how to establish his proof (*ḥujja*), how to enjoin upon the *Ahl al-Ra'y* the obligation of following the Sunna, how to establish proof for them in a solitary report (*khabar al-wāḥid*), how to set forth in detail for the people the methods of understanding the Qur'ān—by what he knew of the explanatory capability (*bayān*) of the Arabs and their linguistic fluency—and how to provide them indication by way of the abrogator (*nāsikh*) and the abrogated (*mansūkh*) of Qur'ān and Sunna, and by integration of what appears contradictory between them, or in one of them—until the folk of Mecca named him 'Vindicator of the Prophetic Report' (*nāṣir al-ḥadīth*); and his reports (*akhbār*) spread via unbroken, consistent transmissions with multiple transmitters at every stage (*tawātarat*) to the scholars of Islam of his era. They travelled to Mecca for the Ḥajj, debating him (*yunāẓirūnahu*), and acquiring knowledge from him [even] in the lifetime of his *shaykhs*—even to the point that Aḥmad b. Ḥanbal[61] once sat at his teaching-session (*jalasa... maʿahu*), and one of his brothers came to him, scolding him for leaving the teaching-session (*majlis*) of Ibn ʿUyayna[62]—the *shaykh* of al-Shāfiʿī—and attending the *majlis* of 'this Bedouin,' so Aḥmad said to him: 'Be silent! Verily, if a *ḥadīth* should escape you on the way up, you will find it on the way down. But if the rational-intellection (*ʿaql*) of this one eludes you, I fear you will never find it. I have seen no one more deeply understanding of the Book of God than this young man.'[63]

Of course, there are eulogies (*manāqib*) and biographical dictionaries (*ṭabaqāt*) filled with praise for al-Shāfiʿī, and it is upon these that Ḥassūn draws when he speaks of his qualities, as in the following passage regarding al-Shāfiʿī's career:

> Al-Imām al-Shāfiʿī continued teaching people the Sunna, and the *fiqh* of the Qur'ān and Sunna, and he engaged in dialectic those who differed from him and disputed them. Most of them were among the followers of his *shaykh* Mālik b. Anas—zealots (*mutaʿaṣṣibīn*) of his *madhhab*-doctrine—but al-Shāfiʿī dazzled them with his knowledge, his guidance, and

[61] Famed eponym of the Ḥanbalī doctrinal *madhhab*, d.241/855.

[62] Famed Meccan scholar and transmitter of *ḥadīth*, d.198/814.

[63] From Shākir's introduction to his edition of the *Risāla*, pp. 5–6; also quoted in full by Ḥassūn, *Mawsūʿat al-Imām* (Intro.), vol. 1, pp. 9–10.

> his intellect. They saw a man the likes of whom the eye had never beheld, and they adhered to his teaching-session (*majlis*), acquiring from him the sciences of Qur'ān and *ḥadīth*, and learning language, genealogy, and poetry from him, and with some of his time he provided them the benefits of his medicine. They learned from him the proper guidelines of dialectical debate and investigation (*adab al-jadal wa'l-munāẓara*). He composed books in his hand, then they would recite to him what they had copied down from them; or he would dictate to them some of [his books]. Most of them turned away from what they had zealously adhered to; they learned *ijtihād* from him, and the rejection of *taqlīd*, and al-Shāfiʿī filled the strata of the earth with knowledge.[64]

Of particular import to the current project is Ḥassūn's observation: "they learned from him the *adab* of *jadal* and *munāẓara*." This is more than effusive praise for a beloved master; our subject-text is filled with signs of the didactic intent inherent to al-Shāfiʿī's dialectical sequences. Juridical dialectic was not only systematic to an appreciable extent in al-Shāfiʿī's day, but its method and procedure was transmitted from teacher to student. In the end, rather than continue quoting in this vein from the inexhaustible body of material on al-Shāfiʿī and his scholarly qualities,[65] I will let him speak for himself—and for the sophistication of proto-system juridical dialectic—in subsequent chapters.

Jurist Dialecticians and the Truth Seeking Ethic

I will say the same for other key jurists of the *Ikhtilāf al-ʿIrāqiyyayn/ʿIrāqiyyīn*: their voices will be heard in its dialectical sequences. Biographical materials abound for Abū Ḥanīfa, Abū Yūsuf, Muḥammad b. al-Ḥasan—and, to a lesser extent, Ibn Abī Laylā and al-Rabīʿ—and the reader may begin an acquaintance with them in respective entries of the *Encyclopaedia of Islam* (2nd ed.) There one will find further evidence that these scholars, all of them, were masters of dialectic in their own right; and one will also find listings of biographical and historical materials replete with descriptions of scholarly and dialectical prowess, and numerous anecdotes of purportedly historical disputation sessions. The evidence is plentiful; our proto-system jurists, all of them, were leading dialecticians in their day.

As for the full-system theorists of our fifth/eleventh century lens-texts, the question hardly needs to be asked. Nevertheless, I would first direct the reader to the introductions of the editions I have employed for biographical information. All of our *jadal*-theorists were engaged in the intellectual debates of their day—and not only regarding difficult problem cases (*masāʾil*) in the substantive realm of *fiqh*. The very premises of *uṣūl al-fiqh* were debated (I will call this *uṣūl*-oriented *jadal*), as were the very procedural and argumentative premises of *jadal*-theory

[64] Ḥassūn, *Mawsūʿat al-Imām* (Intro.), vol. 1, p. 10.

[65] See the useful bibliography in Kecia Ali's *Imam Shafiʿi*, and the "Further Reading" section (pp. 117–19).

itself (which I will call *jadal*-oriented *jadal*).[66] The modern editors of our lens-texts provide plentiful background on al-Baṣrī, al-Shīrāzī, al-Bājī, al-Juwaynī, and Ibn ʿAqīl, and an initial acquaintance with these scholars and biographical sources may again be obtained from the *Encyclopaedia of Islam*.

Other important jurists will surface in following discussions—notably Ibn Surayj and his students—and most of these were leading dialecticians as well. In sum, the primary *mujtahids* (the eponyms of the juridical doctrinal *madhāhib*, and their prominent companions and opponents), the most eminent contributors to *uṣūl al-fiqh* (Ibn Surayj and students, al-Jaṣṣāṣ, al-Baṣrī, et al.), and of course, our lens-text *jadal*-theorists themselves, were all chief dialecticians. It is not surprising that systematic genres of *uṣūl* and *jadal* theory appeared at the same time, and—in the case of al-Qaffāl al-Shāshī and others—by the same hand.[67] Key jurists in the evolution of Islamic legal theory and dialectic, from proto-system to full-system and after, were born into a dialectical world; they thrived in it, excelled in it, and through them the legal sciences of Islam flourished.

It is of paramount importance, however, that we also bear in mind certain aspects of the social and communal fabric by which respected scholars were bound, and to which they leant considerable support; for our jurists also thrived in a world of tangible, pious morality. Despite the untoward events which are bound to—and no doubt did—occur in heated discussion, there was yet a permeating truth-seeking ethic which guided the often intense debates on juridical problems. In other words, whether or not individual jurists were always capable of toeing the ethical line, there was a prominent and well-circulated ideal of the "good dialectic" (*al-jadal al-ḥasan*)—and our subject-text and lens-texts are saturated with signs that this ideal was honoured to an extent that would surprise many a modern cynic.

It is this evident truth-seeking ethic, in fact, which allows us to identify Islamic juridical disputation as dialectical, rather than sophistical. This is a critical distinction, with wider implications for the systematic construction of legal sciences. Hallaq in particular has recognized this:

> In the Islamic context, juridical dialectic was viewed as an efficient means to reach the truth about a particular legal question. It constituted the final stage in the process of legal reasoning, a stage whereby two conflicting views on one question were set against each other through a disciplined session of argumentation with the purpose of establishing the truthfulness of one of them. In the tradition of Aristotle, Muslim scholars reckoned that success is achieved when one secures the agreement of his opponent on a view which one advocates. Minimizing differences of opinion on a particular legal question was of utmost importance, the implication being that truth is one, and for each case there is only one true solution. At least on the theoretical level—and presumably in practice—dialectic served to minimize legal pluralism in Islam.[68]

[66] Importantly, these orientations hold just as true for proto-system juridical *jadal*. This will be made plain in subsequent chapters.

[67] This, along with countless other indicants, supports Hallaq's observation that the genesis of both genres may be found in the circle of Ibn Surayj.

[68] "Treatise," p. 198; citing al-Juwaynī's *Kāfiya*; and Evans, *Aristotle's Concept of Dialectic*.

He also explains the role of dialectic in curbing juridical disagreement (*ikhtilāf*), highlighting certain important moral imperatives along the way:

> Dialectic was instrumental in narrowing down the volume of *ẓannī*[69] legal judgments, and consequently responsible for enlarging the base of consensus. Normally, two compatible jurists who represent their school in a certain geographical area would meet with the intent of convincing one another of the validity of their opinion on a *ẓannī* case of law. Should one of the disputants be successful in establishing that his adversary's legal reasoning is erroneous with regard to the disputed case and should he also persuade him that his own reasoning and conclusion are sound, the adversary is morally, if not legally, bound to abandon his views on that case and adopt those of the other. Once this is done, the number of legal opinions on that case is minimized, and it may be that the disputation is pursued until there remains only one *qaṭʿī*[70] and irrevocable legal opinion.[71]

This constitutes another starting point for the current project; my aim is simply to broaden the vision of dialectic's role to include not only the ordered and truth-oriented resolution of variant juridical opinions, but the formation and refinement of their guiding science itself—*uṣūl al-fiqh*—in arriving at and justifying those opinions. Juridical dialectic, as is evident from the earliest recorded arguments and debates, is a contest of argument/proof (*ḥujja*); its points of contention and attack, inevitably, are concerns of epistemology, hermeneutics, and rational-inference.

In the context of truth-seeking dialectic, where disputants must acknowledge the *endoxa*—the broadly accepted premises and principles which cannot be easily circumvented without charges of inconsistency or contentiousness—it is easy to see how the following must come about: (1) textual source-material proven to be of higher epistemic value must win out in the end; (2) interpretations of source-material proven to be most probably accurate must win out in the end; and (3) rational-inference making from source to case-at-hand proven most probably accurate must win out in the end. And the concerns of legal epistemology, hermeneutics, and rational-inference making are nothing less than the primary domains of *uṣūl al-fiqh*.[72] No matter the *uṣūl*-tradition or doctrinal affiliation of the disputant-jurist, it is dialectical disputation which provided the intense focus and heat required to forge elaborations and refinements in these domains.[73]

As a further note on the truth-seeking motivation inherent to juridical dialectic, we should mark Hallaq's following observation well—it not only highlights a patent concern for mutual arrival at a (singular) truth on a given *mas'ala*, but underscores that such a concern is as pietistic as it is philosophical:

---

[69] Meaning merely probable, as opposed to certain, and thus still open to disagreement on the basis of stronger proofs.

[70] Meaning certain.

[71] "Treatise," p. 199.

[72] See my entry on "Uṣūl al-Fiqh" in *Oxford Islamic Studies Online*.

[73] Hallaq ("Treatise," 199–200) was well aware of the critical relationship between dialectic and *uṣūl al-fiqh*—in many ways presaging the larger conclusions of this monograph.

> The religious implication of reaching a single legal judgment, which through the process of elimination proves to be the 'truest' judgment, is highly significant; it not only confirms that the Muslim community has come closest to the law decreed by God, but also that the much sought after certainty and consistency in law have been achieved.[74]

Not only al-Baṣrī and contemporaries, but our proto-system jurists, too, thrived in an intellectual milieu interwoven with such pious and moral imperatives. Signs are everywhere to be found—not the least of which, with regard to al-Shāfiʿī specifically, is the very fact that he has an "Old" and "New" Doctrine. Al-Shāfiʿī, in other words, did not spend his career doggedly insisting upon older opinions in the face of superior *ḥujja*.[75] Ḥassūn notes, with regard to the problem case of one who sleeps during prayer: "Thus we observe the evolution (*taṭawwur*) of the considered opinion (*ra'y*) of al-Imām al-Shāfiʿī, may God be pleased with him, in this *mas'ala*, for he wasn't long in developing and meticulously refining it before he arrived at the best of it—in his 'New' (*Jadīd*) *madhhab*-doctrine."[76]

A better illustration appears in the problem case of ablution (*wuḍū'*) after eating meat from a slaughter camel (*laḥm al-jazūr*). Ḥassūn notes that al-Shāfiʿī's opinion before his "Old (*Qadīm*) Doctrine" mirrored that of Mālik, Abū Ḥanīfa, et al. Then al-Shāfiʿī changed his opinion in his Old Doctrine; and then, in Egypt—where the "New (*Jadīd*) Doctrine" was formulated—he reverted to what he held before the Old Doctrine—thus his New Doctrine position actually reflects his pre-Old-Doctrine position, and all due to his continuous (and conscientious) assessment of the strength of supporting *ḥadīth*. What, asks Ḥassūn, could have motivated al-Shāfiʿī to take what looks like a step backward? He hypothesizes that perhaps "it occurred to him that what he opined (*dhahaba ilayhi*) before his Old Doctrine was more in synch from the perspective of practicability, and more in step with the political exigencies (*siyāsa*) of law-making (*tashrīʿ*) and the binding spirit of the *Sharīʿa*...." Ḥassūn also mentions avoidance of undo hardship (*ḥaraj*) as a factor;[77] and speaks of the practice of the Companions, especially the Rāshidūn,[78] since:

> the actions of the Companions (*Ṣaḥāba*) and their doctrines (*aqwāl*), and especially the Rightly Guided Caliphs (*Khulafā' al-Rāshidūn*), were considered by al-Shāfiʿī as among the preponderance-giving proofs (*murajjiḥāt*);[79] it is likely that one of the *ḥadīths* was

---

[74] "Treatise," p. 199.

[75] Ḥassūn also stresses that al-Shāfiʿī would not solidly commit to any opinion unless confirmation (*thubūt*) of its source had been realized; he reminds us once again of al-Shāfiʿī's dedication to confronting "legislative problems" (*al-masā'il al-tashrīʿiyya*); and, as a consequence of his publishing these problems, many unresolved *masā'il* were left to his followers to investigate more deeply (*Mawsūʿat al-Imām* (Intro.), vol. 1, p. 168).

[76] *Mawsūʿat al-Imām* (Intro.), vol. 1, p. 181.

[77] Ibid., pp. 185–6.

[78] That is, those who were to become the first, "Rightly Guided" Caliphs: Abū Bakr, ʿUmar, ʿUthmān, and ʿAlī.

[79] We will see that the *aqwāl* of the Ṣaḥāba are just as Ḥassūn describes them, and for all the jurists of the subject-text. I have likened them to glass weights—adding to the epistemic mass of a *dalīl*-indicant, and tipping the balance in favour of one solution over another.

abrogating (*nāsikh*), the other abrogated (*mansūkh*)—and all of this supported the decision of al-Shāfiʿī to revert, in his New Doctrine, to his pre-Old Doctrine.[80]

With regard to our subject-text, al-Shāfiʿī is not alone in exhibiting this "follow the *ḥujja*," truth-seeking ethic. A number of indications from other jurists are produced in the table below, many another will be made plain in subsequent chapters, and—were it not for the terse quality of the subject-text with regard to the opinions of al-Shāfiʿī's predecessors—a great many more would probably be evident. For the present, I would submit the following as signs that the "good dialectic" was practiced by the jurists of our subject-text:[81]

- in §464, Abū Yūsuf reports Abū Ḥanīfa's retreat from an old opinion, and proposal of a new opinion: "then he withdrew from that, and said..." (*thumma rajaʿa ʿan dhālika fa-qāla...*)[82]
- the example of Abū Yūsuf throughout the entire treatise—sometimes adhering to Ibn Abī Laylā's opinion (*qawl*), sometimes to Abū Ḥanīfa's, and sometimes expressing his own, variant *ijtihād*ic solution—he is clearly "following the *ḥujja*," not polemically defending a regional or doctrinal loyalty
- Abū Yūsuf adheres to Ibn Abī Laylā's opinion in §1068, but supplies a supporting transmission and explanation (§§1069-70) for Abū Ḥanīfa's position (in §1067)
- in §§1250-1, Abū Yūsuf conveys a supporting transmission for Ibn Abī Laylā's position, even though he adheres to the opinion of Abū Ḥanīfa
- an excellent example of Abū Yūsuf "following the *ḥujja*" by way of collecting opinions:

(continued)

[80] *Mawsūʿat al-Imām* (Intro.), vol. 1, p. 186. Ḥassūn notes that for some *masāʾil* there may be as many as five doctrines (*aqwāl*) attributed to al-Shāfiʿī; the later is considered an abrogator (*nāsikh*) of the earlier. If that can't be determined, then one considers the one that al-Shāfiʿī himself seems to have preponderated. And if one can do neither (this only occurs with 15–16 *masāʾil* according to al-Nawawī), one must preponderate for oneself, "and here the gate of preponderance (*bāb al-tarjīḥ*) is opened before the companions (*aṣḥāb*) [of the Shāfiʿī *madhhab*]" (ibid., p. 190).

[81] NB: here, and throughout, I will identify passages by way of Ḥassūn's numbering system.

[82] With regard to Abū Ḥanīfa's dialectical ethic, I should draw attention to a particular contribution from Oussama Arabi; mainly, a chapter entitled "The Law and the Truth: Abu Hanifa's Critical Constructivism" (in his *Early Muslim Legal Philosophy*, pp. 58 ff.) Specifically, he relates a certain anecdote in which Abū Ḥanīfa says to Abū Yūsuf: "Yaʿqūb! Don't write what you hear from me. I might hold an opinion today and abandon it tomorrow! And I might hold an opinion tomorrow and abandon it the day after!" (p. 60, and n. 18; the referenced anecdote is in al-Khaṭīb al-Baghdādī's *Taʾrīkh Baghdād* [1931 Cairo ed.] vol. 13, p. 402.)

- in §1040 he asks Abū Ḥanīfa for his opinion
- in §1041 he audits Ibn Abī Laylā's conveyance of a supporting transmission
- in §1042 he relates the conveyance of an anonymous *shaykh*'s transmission (supporting Abū Ḥanīfa's ruling in §1040, to which he eventually adheres)

- another example of Abū Yūsuf "following the *ḥujja*" by way of collecting opinions:
  - in §1036 he asks Abū Ḥanīfa for his opinion
  - in §1037 he asks Ibn Abī Laylā for his opinion
  - in §1038 he asks al-Ḥajjāj b. Arṭāt for his opinion, and this latter relates that he himself sought after the opinion of ʿAṭāʾ b. Abī Rabāḥ (to which Abū Yūsuf eventually adheres)
- in §1412 al-Rabīʿ reports that Muḥammad b. al-Ḥasan al-Shaybānī changed his own opinion to correspond with al-Shāfiʿī's (possibly as the result of a dialectical encounter); al-Rabīʿ closes his discussion with "and God knows best" (*wa Allāhu aʿlam*)[83]
- in §640-1 al-Shāfiʿī first brings traditions (*āthār*) of three Companions in support of his own opinion, then adds another to make four, then reports another five traditions for the contradictory of his opinion and in support of Abū Ḥanīfa's—thus bringing opposing traditions to outnumber his own.
- in §1119 al-Shāfiʿī concludes with "and God Most High knows best" (*Allāhu Taʿālā Aʿlam*), mitigating what is, in effect, an *e silentio* assumption on his part.

Beyond all else, the evolution of systematic *jadal*-theory and *uṣūl al-fiqh* is itself the greatest indication of a real, palpable truth-seeking ethic in the juridical disputation of early Islam. How, after all, did these intertwined enterprises continue to develop and refine their argumentation epistemes—establishing and building upon bodies of *endoxa* premises and principles—if disputants did not concede

[83] Such pious expressions, following upon expressed solutions which are still merely probable (*ẓannī*) in terms of epistemic quality, are often overlooked or discounted by modern scholarship as irrelevant. This is an error, for they are consciously and systematically applied, and provide strong indication of a truth-seeking ethic—they are not random outbursts of piety. Other examples in our subject text are numerous, and include the following: al-Shāfiʿī concludes his argument with "and God is the Giver of Success" (*wa-Allāhu... al-Muwaffiq*) in §607; "and God knows best" (*Allāhu aʿlam*) in §§135, 929, 1035, 1044; and "and from God comes success" (*wa bi-Allāh... al-tawfīq*) in §1124. Abū Yūsuf or Muḥammad b. al-Ḥasan, reporting the opinions of Abū Ḥanīfa and Ibn Abī Laylā, concludes with "if God Most High wills it" (*in shāʾ Allāh Taʿālā*) in §1353. Either Abū Ḥanīfa, Abū Yūsuf, or Muḥammad b. al-Ḥasan concludes with "and God knows best" (*Allāhu aʿlam*) in §1431. And Ibn Abī Laylā concludes with the same in §131.

when faced with epistemically-superior arguments and proofs? Sophistry and eristic argument simply do not produce functioning systems—they allow no stable base of *endoxa* to build on. If practiced on a large enough scale, they militate against systematic, universal formulations, and lead towards relativism. As we shall see, however, the full-system *jadal*-theory of our lens-texts was anything but relativistic. To be certain, Islamicate civilization is rich with variant and competing schools of thought, but this pluralism is not a mark of relativism; there has always remained a core of authoritative *endoxa*, and disputants who contravened—without epistemic justification—the more foundational premises and principles, simultaneously contravened the pietistic imperatives and ethical norms of their scholarly communities.

2.3 Towards a New Narrative

I would reiterate here: the dialectical qualities and elements of our subject-text are more than sufficient to render linear take over narratives untenable.[84] This evidence is compounded a hundredfold by the remaining material of the *Umm*-compendium, and yet more by the dialectical material of other extant proto-system texts. The new evolutionary narrative I propose will be developed in subsequent chapters, and has already been outlined in Chap. 1. In fact, it is more abstract than most narratives, and more closely resembles a paradigm into which new findings can be integrated—or which can be altered to accommodate them—or by way of which particular known elements and individuals can be located. It is a model of common origins, parallel development, and cross-germination: a spectrum of "proto-systems" emerging from a common pool of epistemes, with individual systems developing in parallel or diverging thereafter—according to the exigencies of variant subject matters and their requisite argumentative approaches, and with every stage of development marked by cross-germination between scholarly projects. It is meant to supplant models of absolute priority and linear trajectory, and to better account for (1) the evidence found in surviving, early texts; and (2) the complex interactions of scholars across disciplinary boundaries—boundaries which may never have existed in the minds of many early period polymaths to begin with. In concert with this paradigm-narrative, the Dialectical Forge model is meant to account for the high degree of systematization attained by Islamic legal and dialectical theory, the reason these disciplines are so inseparably intertwined, and the intellectual dynamic powering their symbiotic evolution.

---

[84] That Miller proposed such a paradigm in no way subtracts from the overall importance of his contribution to the study of Islamic Disputation. The scope and analytical depth of his dissertation have yet, in my opinion, to be surpassed.

If these models remain rather abstract, it is nothing more than a sign of how much more research remains to be done with regard to proto-system dialectic and legal theory. This much, however, is certain: juridically-themed *jadal* theory was not taken over from theologically-themed *jadal* theory sometime in the fourth or fifth centuries of Islam. The practice and teaching of a distinctly juridical dialectic had been refining itself since long before even al-Shāfiʿī appeared on the scene—he is at the middle, in fact, of our proto-system—and the first formulators of juridical *jadal*-theory (which honour appears to belong to the circle of Ibn Surayj) were participants in a much-evolved teaching and practice of juridical dialectic whose roots are as old as Islam itself.

References

Abū Zahra, Muḥammad. *Tārīkh al-Jadal*. Cairo: Dār al-Fikr al-ʿArabī, 1934.

Abū Zahra, Muḥammad. *Uṣūl al-Fiqh*. Cairo: Dār al-Fikr al-ʿArabī, 1424/2004.

Ali, Kecia. *Imam Shafiʿi: Scholar and Saint*. Oxford: Oneworld, 2011.

Angelelli, Ignacio. "The Techniques of Disputation in the History of Logic." *The Journal of Philosophy* 67 (October, 1970): pp. 800–815.

Arabi, Oussama. *Early Muslim Legal Philosophy: Identity and Difference in Islamic Jurisprudence*. Los Angeles: CNES Publications, UCLA, 1999.

al-Bājī, Abū al-Walīd Sulaymān. *Kitāb al-Minhāj fī Tartīb al-Ḥijāj* (*L'art de la Polémique: Édition Critique d'al-Minhāǧ de Bāǧī*). Ed. ʿAbd al-Majīd Turkī. Paris: Maisonneuve et Larose, 1978.

Baltussen, H. "Dialectic in Dialogue: The Message of Plato's *Protagoras* and Aristotle's *Topics*." In E. Anne Mackay, ed., *Orality, Literacy, Memory in the Ancient Greek and Roman World*. Leiden; Boston: Brill, 2008, pp. 203–25.

Baltussen, H. *Theophrastus against the Presocratics and Plato: Peripatetic Dialectic in the De Sensibus*. Boston: Brill, 2000.

al-Bazdawī, Abū al-Yusr. *Kitāb fīhi Maʿrifat al-Ḥujaj al-Sharʿiyya*. Ed. Marie Bernand and Eric Chaumont. Cairo: al-Maʿhad al-ʿIlmī al-Faransī li'l-Āthār al-Sharqiyya, 2003.

Belhaj, Abdessamad. *Argumentation et Dialectique en Islam: Formes et Séquences de la Munāẓara*. Bruxelles: Presses Universitaires de Louvain, 2010.

Cabezón, José Ignacio, ed. *Scholasticism: Cross-Cultural and Comparative Perspectives*. Albany: State University of New York Press, 1998.

Cabezón, José Ignacio. *Buddhism and Language: a Study of Indo-Tibetan Scholasticism*. Albany: State University of New York Press, 1994.

Cook, Michael. *Early Muslim Dogma*. Cambridge: Cambridge University Press, 1981.

al-Dabbūsī, Abū Zayd. *Kitāb Taʾsīs al-Naẓar*; with the *Risālat Abī al-Ḥasan al-Karkhī fī'l-Uṣūl allatī ʿalayhā Madār Furūʿ al-Ḥanafiyya; maʿa Shawāhidihā wa-Naẓāʾirihā li-Abī Ḥafṣ ʿUmar al-Nasafī*. Ed. Khalīl al-Mays. Beirut: Dār al-Fikr, 1979.

DiPasquale, David Michael. "Alfarabi and the Starting Point of Islamic Philosophy: A Study of the *Kitāb Al-Jadal* (*Book of Dialectic*)." PhD diss., Harvard University, 2002.

Dreyfus, Georges. *The Sound of Two Hands Clapping: the Education of a Tibetan Buddhist Monk*. Berkeley, CA: University of California Press, 2003.

EI[2] = *Encyclopaedia of Islam, Second Edition*. Ed. P. Bearman; Th. Bianquis; C.E. Bosworth; E. van Donzel; and W.P. Heinrichs. Brill Online, 2014 <http://referenceworks.brillonline.com/entries/encyclopaedia-of-islam-2>

EIr = *Encyclopaedia Iranica*. Ed. Ehsan Yarshater, et al. Online Edition. http://www.iranicaonline.org/

El-Rouayheb, Khaled. *Islamic Intellectual History in the Seventeenth Century: Scholarly Currents in the Ottoman Empire and the Maghreb*. Cambridge; New York: Cambridge University Press, 2015.
El Shamsy, Ahmed. *The Canonization of Early Islamic Law: a Social and Intellectual History*. New York: Cambridge University Press, 2013.
Fallūsī, Masʿūd. *Al-Jadal ʿinda al-Uṣūliyyīn: bayna al-Naẓariyya wa'l-Taṭbīq*. Riyadh: Maktabat al-Rushd Nāshirūn, 2003.
Griffith, Sidney. *The Beginnings of Christian Theology in Arabic: Muslim-Christian Encounters in the Early Islamic Period*. (Variorum Collected Studies Series). Aldershot: Ashgate, 2002.
Gutas, Dimitri. *Greek Thought, Arabic Culture : the Graeco-Arabic Translation Movement in Baghdad and Early ʿAbbāsid Society (2nd-4th/8th-10th Centuries)*. London; New York: Routledge, 1998.
Hallaq, Wael. *A History of Islamic Legal Theories: An Introduction to Sunnī Uṣūl al-Fiqh*. Cambridge; New York: Cambridge University Press, 1997.
Hallaq, Wael. *Sharīʿa: Theory, Practice, Transformations*. Cambridge; New York: Cambridge University Press, 2009.
Hallaq, Wael. "A Tenth-Eleventh Century Treatise on Juridical Dialectic." *Muslim World* 77 (1987): 197–228.
Ḥasan, ʿUthmān ʿAlī. *Manhaj al-Jadal wa'l-Munāẓara fī Taqrīr Masā'il al-Iʿtiqād*. 2 vols. Riyadh: Dār Ishbiliyā, 1420/1999.
Hohmann, Hans. "Logic and Rhetoric in Legal Argumentation: Some Medieval Perspectives." *Argumentation* 12:1 (February, 1998): pp. 39–55.
Ibn ʿAqīl, Abū al-Wafā' ʿAlī. *Kitāb al-Jadal ʿalā Ṭarīqat al-Fuqahā' (Le Livre de la Dialectique d'Ibn ʿAqīl)*. Ed. George Makdisi. *Bulletin d'Études Orientale* 20 (1967): 119–206.
Ibn Khaldūn. *Muqaddima*. Ed. Khalīl Shaḥāda. Beirut: Dār al-Fikr, 2001. [Translation by Franz Rosenthal: *The Muqaddimah : an Introduction to History*. 2nd Ed. 3 vols. London: Routledge & Kegan Paul, 1967].
Jadaane, Fehmi. *L'influence du Stoïcisme sur la Pensée Musulmane*. Beirut: Dar el-Machreq, 1968.
al-Juwaynī, Imām al-Ḥaramayn. *Al-Kāfiya fi'l-Jadal*. Ed. Fawqiya Ḥusayn Maḥmūd. Cairo: Maṭbaʿat ʿĪsā al-Bābī al-Ḥalabī, 1979.
Karabela, Mehmet Kadri. "The Development of Dialectic and Argumentation Theory in Post-Classical Islamic Intellectual History." PhD diss., McGill University, 2010.
Lazarus-Yafeh, Hava, et al., eds. *The Majlis: Interreligious Encounters in Medieval Islam*. Wiesbaden: Harrassowitz, 1999.
Lowry, Joseph. *Early Islamic Legal Theory : the Risāla of Muḥammad ibn Idrīs al-Shāfiʿī*. Leiden; Boston: Brill, 2007.
Madkūr, Ibrāhīm. *L'Organon d'Aristote dans le Monde Arabe, ses Traductions, son Étude et ses Applications*. Paris: Vrin, 1934 [2nd. Ed., 1969].
Makdisi, George. *The Rise of Colleges: Institutions of Learning in Islam and the West*. Edinburgh: Edinburgh University Press, 1981.
Makdisi, George. "The Scholastic Method in Medieval Education: An Inquiry into Its Origins in Law and Theology." *Speculum* 49:4 (Oct., 1974): pp. 640–661.
Marion, Mathieu. "Some Remarks on Syllogistic, Dialectic, and the Study of Their History." *al-Mukhāṭabāt* 08 (2013): pp. 9–36.
Miller, Larry Benjamin. "Islamic Disputation Theory: A Study of the Development of Dialectic in Islam from the Tenth Through Fourteenth Centuries." PhD diss., Princeton University, 1984.
Neusner, Jacob and Bruce Chilton. *The Intellectual Foundations of Christian and Jewish Discourse: the Philosophy of Religious Argument*. London; New York: Routledge, 1997.
Rubinelli, Sara. *Ars Topica: The Classical Technique of Constructing Arguments from Aristotle to Cicero*. Dordrecht: Springer, 2009.
al-Shāfiʿī, Muḥammad b. Idrīs. *Mawsūʿat al-Imām al-Shāfiʿī: al-Kitāb al-Umm*. 2nd ed. Ed. Aḥmad Badr al-Dīn Ḥassūn. 16 Pts. in 10 Vols. Beirut: Dār Qutayba, 2003.
al-Shāfiʿī, Muḥammad b. Idrīs. *Kitāb Ikhtilāf Abī Ḥanīfa wa Ibn Abī Laylā* [= *Umm* Version]. In *idem*, *Mawsūʿat al-Imām al-Shāfiʿī: al-Kitāb al-Umm* (2nd ed.) Ed. Aḥmad Badr al-Dīn Ḥassūn. Beirut: Dār Qutayba, 2003, vol. 9, pt. 14, pp. 7–235.

al-Shāfiʿī, Muḥammad b. Idrīs. *Al-Risāla*. Ed. Aḥmad Muḥammad Shākir. Cairo: Maṭbaʿat Muṣṭafā al-Bābī al-Ḥalabī, 1940.

al-Shīrāzī, Abū Isḥāq Ibrāhīm. *Ṭabaqāt al-Fuqahā'*. Ed. Khalīl al-Mays. Beirut: Dār al-Qalam, n.d.

al-Shīrāzī, Abū Isḥāq Ibrāhīm. *Al-Maʿūna*. MS Princeton, Princeton University Library, MS. 867, Garrett no. 447H. Available at: http://pudl.princeton.edu/objects/2f75r807h

Soffer, Yossef. "The Theological *Majlis* and Religious Otherness in Medieval Islam." In Katell Berthelot and Matthias Morgenstern, eds., *The Quest for a Common Humanity: Human Dignity and Otherness in the Religious Traditions of the Mediterranean*. Leiden; Boston: Brill, 2011, pp. 219–35.

Sorabji, Richard, ed. *The Philosophy of the Commentators, 200–600 AD: A Sourcebook*. Ithaca, N.Y.: Cornell University Press, 2005.

Street, Tony. "Arabic Logic." In J. Woods and D. Gabbay, eds., *Handbook of the History and Philosophy of Logic, Vol. I* (Amsterdam: Elsevier, 2004): pp. 523–96.

Street, Tony. "Logic." In P. Adamson and R.C. Taylor, eds., *The Cambridge Companion to Arabic Philosophy* (Cambridge, UK: Cambridge University Press, 2005): pp. 247–65.

Stump, Eleonore. *Dialectic and its Place in the Development of Medieval Logic*. Ithaca, N.Y.: Cornell University Press, 1989.

Tahiri, Hassan. "The Birth of Scientific Controversies, The Dynamics of the Arabic Tradition and Its Impact on the Development of Science: Ibn al-Haytham's Challenge of Ptolemy's *Almagest*." In Shahid Rahman, Tony Street, and Hassan Tahiri, eds. *The Unity of Science in the Arabic Tradition: Science, Logic, Epistemology and Their Interactions*. [Dordrecht]: Springer, 2008, pp. 183–225.

al-Ṭūfī, Sulaymān b. ʿAbd al-Qawī. *ʿAlam al-Jadhal fī ʿIlm al-Jadal*. Ed. Wolfhart Heinrichs. Wiesbaden: F. Steiner Verlag, 1987.

Turkī, ʿAbd al-Majīd. *Polémiques entre Ibn Ḥazm et Bāǧī sur les Principes de la Loi Musulmane: Essai sur la Littéralisme Zahirite et la Finalité Malikite*. Alger: Société Nationale d'Édition et de Diffusion, 1975. [Translation by ʿAbd al-Ṣabūr Shāhīn: *Munāẓarāt fī Uṣūl al-Sharīʿa al-Islāmiyya bayna Ibn Ḥazm wa'l-Bājī*. Beirut: Dār al-Gharb al-Islāmī, 1986.]

van Ess, Josef. "Disputationspraxis in der Islamischen Theologie. Eine Vorläufige Skizze." *Revue des Études Islamiques* 44 (1976): 23–60.

van Ess, Josef. "The Logical Structure of Islamic Theology." In *Logic in Classical Islamic Culture*, Ed. G. von Grunebaum (Wiesbaden: Otto Harrassowitz, 1970): 21–50.

Yahia, Mohyddin. *Šāfiʿī et les Deux Sources de la Loi Islamique*. Turnhout: Brepols, 2009.

Young, Walter Edward. "The Dialectical Forge: Proto-System Juridical Disputation in the Kitāb Ikhtilāf al-ʿIrāqiyyīn." 2 vols. PhD diss., McGill University, 2012.

Young, Walter Edward. "Origins of Islamic Law." In *The [Oxford] Encyclopedia of Islam and Law. Oxford Islamic Studies Online*, http://www.oxfordislamicstudies.com/article/opr/t349/e0106

Young, Walter Edward. "Uṣūl al-Fiqh." In *Oxford Islamic Studies Online. Oxford Islamic Studies Online*, http://www.oxfordislamicstudies.com/article/opr/t343/e0152

Chapter 3
The Subject-Text and Its Genre

3.1 Introducing the Subject-Text

The subject treatise, which I have labelled the *Umm* Version, is designated in various extant manuscripts of the *Kitāb al-Umm* as either the *Book of that upon which Abū Ḥanīfa and Ibn Abī Laylā Disagreed, on the Authority of Abū Yūsuf* (*Kitāb mā Ikhtalafa fīhi Abū Ḥanīfa wa Ibn Abī Laylā ʿan Abī Yūsuf*); the *Book of Disagreement of Abū Ḥanīfa and Ibn Abī Laylā* (*Kitāb Ikhtilāf Abī Ḥanīfa wa Ibn Abī Laylā*); or the *Book of Disagreement of the (Two) Iraqis* (*Kitāb Ikhtilāf al-ʿIrāqiyyīn / al-ʿIrāqiyyayn*). As for the older source-text—our subject-text constituting a commentary on it, partial refutation of it, and general expansion of it in terms of argument, justification, and refinement—I have labelled it the Shaybānī Version (after its purported transmitter from Abū Yūsuf: Muḥammad b. al-Ḥasan al-Shaybānī). This has been edited by Abū al-Wafā' al-Afghānī, from a single manuscript,[1] and I will assume this manuscript bore, at least in part, the title of his edition: *The Disagreement of Abū Ḥanīfa and Ibn Abī Laylā [Attributed to] the Imām Abū Yūsuf [etc.]* (*Ikhtilāf Abī Ḥanīfa wa Ibn Abī Laylā li'l-Imām Abī Yūsuf Yaʿqūb b. Ibrāhīm al-Anṣārī*).[2] My aim in recounting these titles is to underscore that our subject-text, whatever its appellation, is a work of 'juridical disagreement' (*ikhtilāf*) from start to finish, with all that this implies.

[1] "And the Lajnat Iḥyā' al-Maʿārif al-Nuʿmāniyya desired to publish it, and we found of it naught but a single manuscript in India, and the Lajna was of the opinion that I should attempt a revision (*taṣḥīḥ*) of it..." (from al-Afghānī's intro. to the *Ikhtilāf Abī Ḥanīfa wa Ibn Abī Laylā*, pp. 5–6).

[2] Al-Afghānī does not tell us the title of his manuscript, nor does he describe it in any way, nor inform us as to its precise location. Brockelmann has missed the title, and Sezgin appears also to have neglected its mention entirely, although noting al-Afghānī's editions of Abū Yūsuf's *K. al-Āthār* and *K. al-Radd ʿalā Siyar al-Awzāʿī* (*Tārīkh al-Turāth al-ʿArabī*, vol. 1, p. 3, 54). I have yet to locate a record of the manuscript.

W.E. Young, *The Dialectical Forge*, Logic, Argumentation & Reasoning 9,
DOI 10.1007/978-3-319-25522-4_3

On the Layers of Ikhtilāf *in the Subject-Text*

The *Umm* Version is a layered work of *ikhtilāf*. That is to say, a first layer of juridical argument is apparent in the problem cases (*masā'il*) and variant opinions of Abū Ḥanīfa and Ibn Abī Laylā as recorded by Abū Yūsuf in his initial composition. Abū Yūsuf was sure to indicate either his adherence to one opinion or another, or his refinement, supporting arguments, or objections to one of these opinions, or even the results of his own *ijtihād*[3]—the voice of Abū Yūsuf, wherever it may be discerned, constitutes another layer of *ikhtilāf*.[4] On top of this, wherever we may detect it—and it is not an easy task, once the repetition of "he said" (*qāla*) becomes untraceable—is another layer consisting of the rare comments, arguments, or objections of the transmitter of the Shaybānī Version, i.e., al-Shaybānī himself, Muḥammad b. al-Ḥasan.[5]

The most significant layer of *ikhtilāf* for the purposes of this current project—wherein no less than 22 transcript-like sequences of Q&A dialectical disputation occur—is that added by al-Shāfiʿī. The additions of al-Shāfiʿī to the Shaybānī Version, in fact, more than double the size of the work; and they constitute not only a refined and detailed exposition of his rulings for each of the problem cases raised in the Shaybānī Version, but his arguments, objections, and renditions of both "historical" and "instructional" debates. Finally, on top of all this is an additional layer consisting of the comments and occasional expositions and arguments of al-Shāfiʿī's student, al-Rabīʿ b. Sulaymān, to whom we owe the transmission and preservation of the *Umm* Version (not to mention the compilation and preservation of all the treatises and books of the *Umm* itself).[6] Thus, though the bulk of arguments and objections belong to Abū Ḥanīfa, Ibn Abī Laylā, and al-Shāfiʿī, we must nevertheless bear in mind that the *Umm* Version consists of no less than five layers of *ikhtilāf*:

[3] Whether Abū Yūsuf himself recorded his opinions in his original composition is impossible to determine; it may be that al-Shaybānī introduced them to the text, which was then transmitted to, or acquired by, al-Shāfiʿī.

[4] It is important to bear in mind that even the support of a jurist, whether through a statement of adherence, or the contribution of a supporting transmission, or argument, or explanation, constitutes an instance of *ikhtilāf*. By supporting or arguing a prior ruling, that jurist is not only contributing to its defence, but to the arsenal of proofs which may be levelled against the opposing ruling.

[5] See §§33-4 (Ḥassūn ed., vol. 9, pt. 14, p. 13; and my translation and attached note: "Dialectical Forge," pt. 2, p. 10) for a particularly illuminating example of what appears an editorial objection (against an opinion of Ibn Abī Laylā), by al-Shaybānī himself. Doubtless there are a number of other instances which represent the voice of Muḥammad b. al-Ḥasan, but it is impossible—and this holds for most of the treatise in both Shaybānī and *Umm* Versions—to distinguish what may be his voice from that of Abū Yūsuf.

[6] This is what I have termed the "traditional status quo" of compilation and transmission of the *Umm* corpus.

Original Layers of the Shaybānī Version

- [1] Abū Ḥanīfa vs. Ibn Abī Laylā
- [2] Abū Yūsuf vs. either of his teachers
- [3] Muḥammad b. al-Ḥasan vs. various preceding opinions of Abū Yūsuf's transmitted compilation

Additional Layers of the *Umm* Version

- [4] al-Shāfiʿī vs. various of the positions of the Shaybānī version, or vs. an anonymous opponent professing one of these opinions, or vs. an anonymous opponent professing the opinion of an epistemic community—e.g., the "Dialectical Theologians" (Ahl al-Kalām), or "Scholars of Basra" (Ahl al-Baṣra), or "Easterners" (Mashriqiyyūn)
- [5] al-Rabīʿ vs. various of the opinions which preceded al-Shāfiʿī

Additionally, the individual layers of *ikhtilāf* within a given set of problem cases of the *Umm* Version, though not often easily distinguished, may be said to follow a rough pattern of accretion. That is to say, though rarely if ever including all of these layers, the presentation of a given *mas'ala* will typically follow this format:[7]

- Abū Ḥanīfa's ruling(s) on the *mas'ala* at hand
  - supporting transmission (*naql*), argument, or explanation of Abū Ḥanīfa's position, or rhetorical objection to the opposing position
    - [Abū Yūsuf's adherence, if he follows Abū Ḥanīfa, or his reversion to the *qawl* of Ibn Abī Laylā, or his independent revision of Abū Ḥanīfa's ruling]
- Ibn Abī Laylā's counter-ruling(s) for the *mas'ala* at hand
  - supporting *naql*, argument, or explanation of Ibn Abī Laylā's position, or rhetorical objection to the opposing position
    - [Abū Yūsuf's adherence, if he follows Ibn Abī Laylā, or his reversion to the *qawl* of Abū Ḥanīfa, or his independent revision of Ibn Abī Laylā's ruling]
- [Abū Yūsuf's independent *ijtihād*, if he does not follow or revise a *qawl* of one of his teachers]
  - [supporting *naql*, argument, or explanation of Abū Yūsuf's position, or rhetorical objection to the opposing position(s)]

(continued)

[7] Bear in mind that al-Shaybānī's voice, for the most part, cannot be easily distinguished from Abū Yūsuf's.

- al-Shāfiʿī's (usually more detailed) ruling(s) for the *mas'ala* at hand
  - supporting *naql*, argument (often extended), or explanation of his position, or rhetorical objection to the opposing position, or appended dialectical sequence elaborating on the core of *ikhtilāf* (terminating with al-Shāfiʿī's *elenchus* or successful defence of his own position)
    - [occasional reference to another *kitāb*, to which al-Shāfiʿī directs the reader for a more complete rendering of arguments and proofs]
- [al-Rabīʿ's commentary, explanation, or additional argument with respect to al-Shāfiʿī's position (rare)]

Again, the most significant of these layers for the current project is al-Shāfiʿī's. All of the dialectical sequences—the focal points of analysis—occur between al-Shāfiʿī and an anonymous opponent (usually championing a position professed by Abū Ḥanīfa, Ibn Abī Laylā, or Abū Yūsuf), although dialectical formulae and other overt signatures of past and recurrent dialectical disputation are common throughout all layers. This (fifth) layer of al-Shāfiʿī is by far the richest in terms of overtly dialectical material, and boasts twelve extended sequences of Q&A disputation, and another ten short sequences.[8] These may be roughly categorized as either "historical" or "instructional" dialectical sequences. The "historical" is usually initiated by al-Shāfiʿī with a telltale formula such as "'one of the people' contradicted us in this, saying [X]" (*wa khālafanā baʿḍ al-nās fī hādhā, wa qāla*: [X]), followed by "so I said to him: [Y]" (*fa-qultu lahu*: [Y]), and so on. The ensuing dialectic is thus introduced as a narrative, a real occurrence, even if abstracted or in other ways reduced to a more abbreviated form. The "instructional" variety, on the other hand, is usually initiated by al-Shāfiʿī with the hallmark "and if one should say [X]" (*fa-in qāla qā'il*: [X]), followed by "it is said to him [Y]" (*qīla lahu*: [Y]), and so on. The didactic intent of these formulae is self-evident. Finally, it should be noted that any one sequence may incorporate qualities or intentions of both categories.[9]

Taking all these features into account, our subject-text—a literary project spanning several generations—would fit squarely in that genre of legal literature eventually known as "points of disagreement" (*khilāfiyyāt*) or "the science of disagreement" (*ʿilm al-khilāf*), even had the term *ikhtilāf* been absent from its title.

[8] These twenty two sequences are scattered throughout the treatise, extending from al-Shāfiʿī's arguments re: the *mas'ala* at hand, as appendages, wherever he saw fit.

[9] It is likely that sequences which appear purely of the "instructional" variety were motivated by al-Shāfiʿī's previous dialectical encounters. On the other hand, those of a purely "historical" appearance have been related by al-Shāfiʿī for a purpose: to instruct the reader how to defend this position—and/or refute the opposing position—in any future dialectical encounter centering upon the same *mas'ala*.

What is more, the contents and arrangement of the *Umm* Version suggest a purpose fully in consonance with the general aims of the *ʿilm al-khilāf* as they would later be described: exploring the best methods of drawing indication (*istidlāl*) and rational inference (*istinbāṭ*), and building the faculties of confirmation (*al-ibrām*) and refutation-by-inconsistency (*al-naqḍ*), all with an eye towards dialectical disputation.[10] In other words, the *ikhtilāf* treatises of the *Umm*—our subject-text prominent among them—not only contain examples of *jadal*, but were composed and elaborated with an eye towards practical application in *jadal*. This intention is evident through the preservation and transmission of these texts alone, and all the more so through an examination of their contents.

This adds an important dimension to what we can already discern as a rather sophisticated "proto-system" of juridical *jadal*. The *Umm* treatises are accounts of *ikhtilāf*, certainly, but to what end were they preserved, transmitted, and studied—simply as histories of disagreement? Certainly not. They are as much handbooks as histories, and their ultimate objective is far more than providing a record of who held what opinion. Rather, the larger objective of the *ikhtilāf* treatises in the *Umm* compendium is to preserve and transmit a knowledge of the *masāʾil* of *ikhtilāf* along with the argument styles and strategies of master jurist-dialecticians—to the extent that whole sequences of dialectic are frequently transcribed. The jurist in training needed to learn more than what the contended *masāʾil* were—he needed to learn how to argue them;[11] and *ikhtilāf* treatises were as vital a component to proto-system *jadal* teaching and practice as systematic *jadal*-theory treatises were to the disputation of later eras.

A final note: in addition to layers of *ikhtilāf*, categories of dialectical sequence, and didactic intentions, there are a number of other qualities and features of import in the *Umm* Version with regard to the window it opens on proto-system *jadal*. Primary among these is a marked formulaic consistency—not only in the sequential "transcription" of dialectical debates, but in the very presentation of substantive rulings, statements of adherence to one ruling or another, extensions and subsumptions of rulings with reference to legal genera, etc. These will become apparent as we proceed through our analyses in Chaps. 5 and 6, and will be summarized and discussed in Chap. 7. The sum total of their effect, however, may be stated now: Though far less refined than the systems elaborated by al-Shīrāzī and other authors of our lens-texts, proto-system *jadal* was still—to a considerable extent—a *system*, and a sophisticated system at that.

---

[10] See our following discussion re: al-Dabbūsī's *Taʾsīs al-Naẓar*, from which this definition is extracted.

[11] An illuminating example of a student employing one of al-Shāfiʿī's treatises to trump a contemporary, and apparent acquaintance, of al-Shāfiʿī: the famed Murjiʾī *faqīh* Bishr al-Marīsī (d.218/833), may be found in an anecdote related in the note attached to §53, in Chap. 6 of this monograph.

3.2 Authenticity and Transmission of the Subject-Text

General Approach

My position with regard to questions of authenticity—whether pertaining to authorship or transmission and redaction, for the *Umm* compendium as a whole, or for the *Kitāb Ikhtilāf al-ʿIrāqiyyīn / al-ʿIrāqiyyayn* in particular—may be stated plainly: the onus of proof lies with those who challenge the "traditional status quo" of how and by whom these texts were composed, compiled, and transmitted. I have yet to see creditable proof brought forward that would compel me to question the *Umm* and its treatises are anything other than what—by their very structure, internal consistency, and intra-*kitāb* references—they claim themselves to be. In other words, I believe the texts argue their own authenticity, even without the supporting narratives of *madhhab* historians and bio-bibliographers which they enjoy; and, in the end, I have mostly allowed the subject-text to speak for itself (if not on behalf of the entire *Umm*).[12]

In discussions of the text, a neutral stance has nevertheless been attempted, allowing for the possibility that authorship and transmission is not always as traditional narratives (the "status quo") would have us believe. But the indicants of authenticity in our subject-text far outweigh the more arbitrary "proofs" for re-ascription and post-dating that I have, so far, encountered. The more conspiratorial of theses appear to stand on shaky legs indeed. We will first turn our attention to traditional narratives of authorship and transmission, and then to the arguments of scholars who have questioned them.[13]

The "Traditional Status Quo" for the Shaybānī Version

In order to provide a sense of the "Traditional" narrative for the authorship and early transmission of the Shaybānī Version, I will turn to the editor of our first edition: Abū al-Wafāʾ al-Afghānī. His remarks are summarized in the following table:

---

[12] Notes drawing attention to editorial clues and intra-*kitāb* references may be found throughout my translation of the subject-text ("Dialectical Forge," pt. 2, *passim*); with an appendix dedicated entirely to linked treatises and chapters (ibid., 350–5).

[13] Importantly, Ahmad El Shamsy has recently contributed an article entitled "Al-Shāfiʿī's Written Corpus: A source-Critical Study;" in this, he very effectively vindicates the traditional accounts of the *Umm*'s composition and transmission, refuting the revisionist arguments of Norman Calder (and others). Mohyddin Yahia, in his *Šāfiʿī et les Deux Sources de la Loi Islamique*, dedicates a section to refuting Calder on this very same question (pp. 170 ff.; « Réfutation de la thèse de N. Calder »). The arguments of El Shamsy and Yahia both supersede and vindicate my own arguments in following sections.

- Abū Yūsuf (d.182/798) was a student of both Abū Ḥanīfa (d.150/767) and Ibn Abī Laylā (d.148/765). In this book, Abū Yūsuf gathers together what they, specifically, disagreed about, and pays no attention to the *ikhtilāf* of others (like Sufyān al-Thawrī, Ḥasan b. Ṣāliḥ, Sharīk b. ʿAbd Allāh, Ibn Shubruma, et al.), "because he took *fiqh* from the two (*tafaqqaha ʿalayhimā*), and his desire was to compile what he derived from them, from what they disagreed upon, to make clear his opinion with [regard to] them—agreeing with this one and differing with that one at one time, and the opposite another time—so that it be a treasure-store and recollection for those who came after him."[14]
- Muḥammad b. al-Ḥasan [al-Shaybānī; d.189/804] transmitted the *K. Ikhtilāf Abī Ḥanīfa wa Ibn Abī Laylā* on the authority of Abū Yūsuf.[15]
- After this, "al-Ḥākim Abū al-Faḍl Muḥammad b. Muḥammad b. Aḥmad al-Marwazī al-Shahīd [d.334/945] abridged it along with all that he abridged of [al-Shaybānī's] books;[16] and al-Sarakhsī [d.483/1090] provided commentary upon it in his *Mabsūṭ*, with the rest of [al-Shaybānī's] books."[17]
- Al-Afghānī determines from al-Sarakhsī's account that the *K. Ikhtilāf Abī Ḥanīfa wa Ibn Abī Laylā* was originally among the parts of al-Shaybānī's *Aṣl* (else why would al-Ḥākim have abridged it?) Yet it does not seem to appear as an integral volume, as it does here; and, at least in one manuscript, parts of it appear in related chapters of the *Aṣl*, preceded by headings such as *Bāb Ikhtilāf Abī Ḥanīfa wa Ibn Abī Laylā fi'l-Wadīʿa*. Al-Afghānī hypothesizes that it may appear piece-meal in other copies.[18]

The "Traditional Status Quo" for the Umm *Version*

As for the *Umm* Version, I will again turn to an editor for his overview of the "traditional status quo" for composition and transmission. Ḥassūn provides brief overviews for all the treatises of the *Umm* compendium, among them our

[14] Afghānī, pp. 3–4.

[15] Ibid., p. 4.

[16] The well-famed abridgment of al-Ḥākim al-Shahīd is his *Kāfī fi'l-Fiqh*.

[17] Afghānī, p. 4. Al-Sarakhsī, in his *Mabsūṭ*, says that Abū Yūsuf "desired to compile the *masā'il* in which there was *ikhtilāf* from his two professors, so he gathered together this composition (*taṣnīf*); and Muḥammad [al-Shaybānī], may God have mercy on him, learned it from him, and transmitted it on his authority—except that he added a little of what he heard from others. The original (*aṣl*) composition (*taṣnīf*) belongs to Abū Yūsuf, and the compilation (*ta'līf*) belongs to Muḥammad, God's mercy on them both; but such is considered as the composition (*taṣnīf*) of Muḥammad. And due to this al-Ḥākim, may God have mercy upon him, mentioned him in the *Mukhtaṣar*." (*Mabsūṭ*, vol. 30, p. 129; quoted in Afghānī, p. 5).

[18] Afghānī, p. 5.

subject-treatise. There, however, we find his narrative under the heading "*Kitāb Ikhtilāf al-ʿIrāqiyyīn*, or *Kitāb Ikhtilāf Abī Ḥanīfa wa Ibn Abī Laylā*" is—for the most part—a verbatim repeat of al-Afghānī's narrative summarized above.[19] I would conclude that Ḥassūn, like al-Afghānī, derived his narrative from al-Sarakhsī's *Mabsūṭ*, or borrowed it wholesale from al-Afghānī's edition of the Shaybānī Version.[20] The little we may add from Ḥassūn is in the table below; what remains of relevance to the authorship and transmission of the *Umm* Version will be treated in subsequent discussions and summaries of the *Umm* compendium as a whole.

- "it contains the notes (*mulāḥaẓāt*) of al-Imām al-Shāfiʿī on the book of Abū Yūsuf: the *Ikhtilāf Abī Ḥanīfa wa Ibn Abī Laylā*..."[21]
- "... al-Shāfiʿī came along and [re]stated what Abū Ḥanīfa and Ibn Abī Laylā disagreed about according to Abū Yūsuf, and added to this his notes, supported by Prophetic reports (*aḥādīth*) and traditions (*āthār*)."[22]

The "Traditional Status Quo" for the Kitāb al-Umm

As for the authorship and transmission of the *Umm* compendium as a whole, Ḥassūn provides a far more detailed narrative. This terminates in a lengthy argument against a certain scholar (Dr. Zakī Mubārak) who has attempted to attribute authorship of the entire *Umm* corpus to one of al-Shāfiʿī's famed students, al-Buwayṭī (d.231/846). Before turning to this, however, I will summarize Ḥassūn's narrative, as representative of the "traditional status quo:"

- The *Book of Proof* (*K. al-Ḥujja*; al-Shāfiʿī's 'Old Doctrine' compendium of *fiqh* and *furūʿ*, transmitted on his authority by his Baghdādī companions) is the *vorlage* (*aṣl*) of the *K. al-Umm*; the most well-known transmitters of the *Ḥujja* are al-Zaʿfarānī [d.260/874] and al-Karābīsī [d.245/859 or 248/862], and it was a massive tome.[23]

(continued)

[19] Ḥassūn, vol. 1 (Intro.), pp. 93–4.

[20] The only citation he provides is the same that al-Afghānī provides for his passage from the *Mabsūṭ*.

[21] Ḥassūn, vol. 1 (Intro.), p. 93.

[22] Ibid., p. 94. This is a vast understatement of what al-Shāfiʿī contributed to the *Umm* Version, as will be made plain in subsequent chapters.

[23] Ḥassūn, vol. 1 (Intro.), p. 79.

- "Al-Buwayṭī said: 'al-Shāfiʿī said: The Traditionists (Aṣḥāb al-Ḥadīth) met with me and requested that I compose something on the book of Abū Ḥanīfa, so I said: "I won't know their doctrine (*qawlahum*) until I research their books. Then I issued an order, and the books of Muḥammad b. al-Ḥasan were written for me, and I perused them for a year until I committed them to memory, then I composed the Baghdad book (*al-Kitāb al-Baghdādī*)."' Al-Buwayṭī said: 'He means *The [Book of] Proof* (*al-Ḥujja*).'"[24]
- Other sources attest to the Old Doctrine contents of the *Ḥujja*, and its composition in Iraq.[25]
- Ḥassūn quotes the following passage from the *Fihrist* of Ibn al-Nadīm [d. ca. 385/995]: "There belonged to [al-Shāfiʿī] of books (*kutub*): a *Kitāb al-Mabsūṭ fi'l-Fiqh*, transmitted on his authority by al-Rabīʿ b. Sulaymān [d.270/883] and al-Zaʿfarānī; and this book (*kitāb*) contained a *Kitāb al-Ṭahāra, Kitāb al-Ṣalāt, Kitāb al-Zakāt, Kitāb al-Ṣiyām, Kitāb al-Ḥajj, Kitāb al-Iʿtikāf, Kitāb al-...*"[26]
- Ḥassūn posits the probability there wasn't much disagreement between the *Mabsūṭ*, the *Ḥujja*, and the *Umm*; except for time, place, and argumentative power; additions and subtractions. The New *madhhab*, he says, was an extension of the Old—a natural development—not entirely different from the Old, except that al-Shāfiʿī recanted (*rajaʿa ʿan*) some of the doctrines he stated in Iraq.[27]
- Ḥassūn speculates with regard to these different titles: "Why is it that al-Rabīʿ is famed for transmitting the *K. al-Umm* from al-Shāfiʿī, may God be pleased with him, and al-Zaʿfarānī for transmitting the *K. al-Ḥujja* from

(continued)

[24] Citing Ibn Ḥajar al-ʿAsqalānī's *Tawālī al-Ta'sīs*; Ḥassūn, vol. 1 (Intro.), p. 79 and n. 1.

[25] Ḥassūn cites the *Tawālī al-Ta'sīs* and the *Kashf al-Ẓunūn*. He interprets this to mean that al-Shāfiʿī's old doctrine in Baghdad was, for the most part, a response (*radd*) to the *madhhab* of the Scholars Championing Considered Opinion (*Ahl al-Ra'y*), and that it was close to the *madhhab* of the Scholars Championing Prophetic Reports (*Ahl al-Ḥadīth*).

[26] Ḥassūn, vol. 1 (Intro.), pp. 79–80. Which is to say, it contained all the chapters of a work on substantive rulings. Ḥassūn continues to quote al-Nadīm with regard to the slight discrepancies in al-Zaʿfarānī's transmission; the jurists don't request, and don't practice, the recension of al-Zaʿfarānī, only that of al-Rabīʿ. He then turns to al-Subkī [*Ṭabaqāt al-Shāfiʿiyya al-Kubrā*, al-Ḥusayniyya ed., p. 275], who mentions that the famed *Mukhtaṣar* of al-Buwayṭī was, according to Abū ʿĀṣim, systematically arranged according to the chapters of this *Mabsūṭ* (Ḥassūn, vol. 1 [Intro.], p. 80). Elsewhere, Ḥassūn notes a (relatively) early reference to the *Umm* and its many "books" (*kutub*): "Al-Bayhaqī [fl. ca. 402/1011; some 20 years after the death of al-Nadīm] mentioned *al-Kitāb al-Umm* [in his *Manāqib*], and that it was a composition on derived substantive rulings (*muṣannaf fi'l-furūʿ*), and that its books (*kutub*) amounted to 128 in number" (ibid., p. 93).

[27] Ibid. I have already noted this as an indication of a sincere dialectician "following the evidence" according to the truth-seeking ethic of dialectic. Ḥassūn says: "The foundation of al-Shāfiʿī's Old *madhhab* was the *K. al-Ḥujja*; so, too, is it the foundation of the New *madhhab*, after a few improvements, and the changing of its name from *al-Ḥujja* to *al-Umm*" (ibid.)

al-Shāfiʿī...; then Ibn al-Nadīm claims that the *Mabsūṭ* transmitted by al-Zaʿfarānī was arranged like the *Mabsūṭ* transmitted by al-Rabīʿ, with slight discrepancies, and that the people don't practice al-Zaʿfarānī's *Mabsūṭ*, but only practice the *K. al-Ḥujja* and the *K. al-Umm*; unless the *Mabsūṭ* of al-Zaʿfarānī, which is the *Ḥujja*, is the *Mabsūṭ* of al-Rabīʿ? That indicates that the *K. al-Mabsūṭ* does not differ much from the *K. al-Ḥujja*, which itself is the *vorlage* (*aṣl*) of the *K. al-Umm*; and if the *Mabsūṭ* of al-Zaʿfarānī—which is the *Ḥujja*—originated in Baghdad before the coming of al-Shāfiʿī to Egypt, and the *Mabsūṭ* of al-Rabīʿ—which is the *Umm*—originated in Egypt, then [the latter] is the more powerful [in epistemic terms], and the one that is indeed practiced, as it represents al-Shāfiʿī's New *madhhab*."[28]

- The *K. al-Umm* is among the most important and comprehensive of the books of al-Shāfiʿī. It was transmitted on his authority, as his New *madhhab* regarding the categories of *fiqh*, by four of his students: al-Muzanī (d.264/877), al-Buwayṭī (d.231/846), al-Rabīʿ al-Jīzī (d.256/870 or 257/871), and al-Rabīʿ b. Sulaymān al-Murādī (d.270/883).[29]

---

[28] Ibid., pp. 80–1. He continues in this vein, noting that it is probable that al-Shāfiʿī did not label his "Old" or "New" books with a specific name, but was satisfied to mention the "Baghdādī" if he meant the Old. Some of his companions called his Old book *al-Ḥujja*, as he composed it as a decisive proof/argument (*ḥujja*) against the Scholars Championing Considered Opinion (*Ahl al-Ra'y*), and some of them called it the *Mabsūṭ*; and his new book was called *al-Umm* because it is a collection of al-Shāfiʿī's *fiqh* works, but some of them called it the *Mabsūṭ*; and the *K. al-Umm* was also known as the *Kitāb al-Rabīʿ* (he cites the *Ṭabaqāt* of al-Nawawī, as quoted in the *Tamhīd li-Tārīkh al-Falsafa al-Islāmiyya* of Professor Mustafā ʿAbd al-Razzāq). Ḥassūn then quotes Aḥmad Muḥammad Shākir's introduction to his edition of the *Risāla*, to the effect that it was al-Rabīʿ who called the new book *al-Umm*, having gathered in it some of the books of al-Shāfiʿī (ibid., p. 82; cf. Shākir, p. 9).

[29] Ḥassūn, vol. 1 (Intro.), p. 82. Ḥassūn notes that the [Shāfiʿī] *fatwā* should be based on what is in the New [doctrine], excluding the Old, as al-Shāfiʿī had recanted it, and said: "I make no allowance for he who transmits it from me (*lā ajʿalu fī ḥillin man rawāhu ʿannī*);" except with regard to uncomplicated *masā'il*, like the 'seventeen'—one bases *fatwās* for them on the Old Doctrine, except when the Old is supported by a valid Prophetic report (*ḥadīth ṣaḥīḥ*) having no opposition (*muʿāriḍ*). For if it is supported by a *dalīl*-indicant, then it is the *madhhab* of al-Shāfiʿī—it is true that he said: 'If the *ḥadīth* is valid (*ṣaḥīḥ*), then it is my *madhhab*; don't give a hoot about my professed doctrine (*qawl*)'" (ibid., p. 82, and again on p. 88). Note this as another indication of the truth-seeking dialectical ethic. Stronger yet are provided by Ḥassūn, who later says that in the *Umm* we have the greatest legacy (*athar*) of al-Shāfiʿī, "and within it we find reports (*akhbār*) of al-Shāfiʿī's renunciation of some of his opinions, and sections on *uṣūl al-fiqh*." We are reminded that his doctrine is split into Old (Iraqi) and New (Egyptian), "which is to say that when he came to Egypt he renounced some of his opinions which he used, before, to affirm; and the reason is that he mixed with the scholars of Egypt, and heard what was valid of their *ḥadīth*, and heard the pupils of al-Layth b. Saʿd [d.175/791] transmit his opinions and his *fiqh*, and saw that some of the social conditions in Egypt differed from those he had seen in the Ḥijāz and in Iraq. And so the *fiqh* of al-Shāfiʿī, to the extent of some of his opinions, was changed, and it was called 'The New Doctrine' (*al-madhhab al-jadīd*)" (ibid., p. 88).

Perhaps the most eloquent of Ḥassūn's narratives, however, is to be found some pages after his refutation of the re-ascription claims to which I will shortly turn. Because Ḥassūn presents a detailed picture with regard to stages of authorship, compilation, and editing; and because we will see so many signs of these stages—just as Ḥassūn describes them—in our own subject-treatise; I will here translate passages from Ḥassūn's discussion in full:

- "Al-Shāfiʿī composed many books, some of which he wrote by himself and recited to the people, or they recited to him, and some of them he delivered as dictations; and many of his books have been lost. That is to say that he composed in Mecca, and composed in Baghdad, and composed in Egypt; and what he composed in Mecca and Baghdad have been lost, and what of his books remain in the hands of the *ʿulamā'*, now, are those he composed in Egypt. And it is this book, *al-Umm*, in which al-Rabīʿ gathered together (*jamaʿa fīhi*) some of the books of al-Shāfiʿī, and called it by this name, after having audited these books from him. And what eluded his audition, he makes clear; and what he found in al-Shāfiʿī's script, but didn't audit from him, he also makes clear. Just as the scholars among those who recite this *K. al-Umm* know.[30] And [the same goes for] the *K. Ikhtilāf al-Ḥadīth*, and the *K. al-Risāla*—they are among what al-Rabīʿ transmitted on the authority of al-Shāfiʿī separately, and didn't enter into the *K. al-Umm*."[31]
- "From a thorough examination of the books of al-Shāfiʿī, it is made clear that he renewed the compilation of his books in Egypt from his memory, and his books were not all with him. Observe as he says, in the *Risāla*, §1184: 'And every *ḥadīth* I wrote is interrupted (*munqaṭiʿan*), for I had heard it uninterrupted (*muttaṣilan*), or widespread (*mashhūran*) on the authority of the one from whom it was transmitted, by collective conveyance (*bi-naqli ʿāmmatin*) from the Scholars (*Ahl al-ʿIlm*), who know it from a collectivity (*min ʿāmmatin*). But I disliked putting down a *ḥadīth* I had not mastered by memory (*lā utqinuhu ḥifẓan*), and some of my books were absent from me. So I verified—by means of what the Ahl al-ʿIlm knew—what I had memorized. Then I abbreviated, fearing lengthy

(continued)

[30] Cf. my "final word on the authorship question," below. In a footnote attached to his refutation of re-ascription claims, Ḥassūn quotes from Abū Zahra's biography. Here we find further details with regard to al-Rabīʿ's caution in detailing sources, and whether he heard it from al-Shāfiʿī, or merely knows that al-Shāfiʿī said it, etc.; correcting and explaining errors of transmission, and changes in al-Shāfiʿī's sayings—i.e., "He also used to say such-and-such..." (Ḥassūn, vol. 1 (Intro.), p. 91). There is more than one expression of the same editorial caution in our subject-text.

[31] Ibid., pp. 121–2.

writing, and arrived at what is sufficient for some of it, without a thorough examination (*taqaṣṣī*) of the knowledge (*ʿilm*) on every issue."[32]

- "It is most apparent that he renewed the compilation of the *Risāla* after compiling most of the books in the *Umm*, because he points often in the *Risāla* to subjects which are written therein, and he says, for example [§1173]: 'I have explained the exegesis (*qad fassartu*) for this *ḥadīth* before this passage (*mawḍiʿ*).' And this is an allusion to what is in the *Umm*."[33]

Scholars Questioning the Authorship and Transmission of the Kitāb al-Umm

Before turning to Norman Calder's attempt to post-date the composition and compilation of the *Umm* corpus past the era of al-Rabīʿ b. Sulaymān, I will quickly review another modern scholar's attempt at re-ascription—more accurately, I will present the arguments of Ḥassūn and Shākir *against* this re-ascription attempt. The well-known Egyptian academic Dr. Zakī Mubārak (d.1952),[34] apparently expanding upon a claim by the fourth century Ṣūfī *shaykh* Abū Ṭālib al-Makkī (d.386/996), then echoed by the famed Abū Ḥāmid Muḥammad al-Ghazālī (d.505/1111) in his *Iḥyāʾ ʿUlūm al-Dīn*, put forward an argument that it was al-Shāfiʿī's student al-Buwayṭī—*not* al-Shāfiʿī himself—who authored the *Umm*, and that al-Rabīʿ, in effect, plagiarized it from him. This argument extends to the *Risāla* as well, and I will review Shākir's refutation of Mubārak[35] after Ḥassūn's. As for Ḥassūn, his rebuttal (mostly against al-Makkī and al-Ghazālī) may be found in a massive footnote—spawning in turn its own footnotes—extending for more than four pages of the introduction to his edition of the *Umm*.[36] He first presents an overview of the claims, then launches into his own argument:

---

[32] Ibid., p. 122. Unless forged by a Shāfiʿī detractor, it is difficult to conceive of a finer show of truth-seeking sincerity and scholarly caution than this explanation provides. Another is provided in a subsequent quote: "And [al-Shāfiʿī] says in the *K. Ikhtilāf al-Ḥadīth*: A trustworthy transmitter (*thiqa*) related to me (*ḥaddathanī*) that al-Ḥasan used to insert—between himself and ʿUbāda—Ḥiṭṭān al-Raqqāshī. And I don't know whether or not ʿAbd al-Wahhāb inserted him between them; it vanished from my book when I transferred it from the *vorlage* (*aṣl*). And the *aṣl*, on the day this book was written, was absent from me" (ibid.)

[33] Ibid., pp. 122–3 (citing vol. 6, p. 77 of the Būlāq edition). A key feature of our subject-text, which I explored in numerous footnotes and an appendix in my dissertation (part 2), is the frequency with which al-Shāfiʿī says, e.g., "and we have set this down in the *Kitāb al-Aqḍiya*" (§53); or "and this is written in the *Kitāb al-Rahn*" (§388); or "and the *aṣl* of this is written in the *Kitāb al-ʿItq*" (§681); etc. There are well over twenty such "intra-*Umm* / *Ḥujja* / *Mabsūṭ*" references in our subject-text alone.

[34] Presumably in his *Iṣlāḥ Ashnaʿ Khaṭaʾ fī Tārīkh al-Tashrīʿ al-Islāmī: Kitāb al-Umm : lam Yuʾallifhu al-Shāfiʿī wa-innamā Allafahu al-Būwayṭī wa-Taṣarrafa fīhi al-Rabīʿ b. Sulaymān*.

[35] Shākir, (Intro.) pp. 9–10.

[36] Ḥassūn, vol. 1 (Intro.), p. 88 (n. 1) – p. 92 (with 15 dependent footnotes).

- there is *ijmāʿ* of the scholars (*ʿulamāʾ*) that the *Umm* is, all of it, "composed by (*min taṣnīf*) al-Shāfiʿī," and transmitted by al-Rabīʿ al-Murādī
- there was no claim to the contrary until the end of the fourth century H; this claim was that it was not the composition (*taṣnīf*) of al-Shāfiʿī, but the compilation (*taʾlīf*) of al-Buwayṭī, taken by al-Rabīʿ, who added to it, then promoted it, and that this is what the people audited
- this claim first appeared in the *K. Quwwat al-Qulūb* of Abū Ṭālib al-Makkī, a Ṣūfī; and it was repeated, almost verbatim, by al-Ghazālī in his *Iḥyāʾ* [37]
- the claim was then taken up by Dr. Zakī Mubārak (with no convincing support or cogent argument), who asserts that there are words in the *Umm* which indicate it could not have been written by al-Shāfiʿī
- Ḥassūn next reproduces the relevant text from the referenced works of both al Makkī and al-Ghazālī; then he makes his case, as follows:
  - 1) there was *ijmāʿ* that the *Umm* was the compilation (*taʾlīf*) of al-Shāfiʿī for a century and a half—al-Makkī's claim flew in the face of it, and was neither considered, nor discussed
  - 2) if [al-Makkī] meant *taʾlīf* when he said *taṣnīf*, then there is more than enough in the *Umm* to refute his claim. But if he meant by *taṣnīf*: assembling (*al-tajmīʿ*) and arranging (*al-tartīb*), which is indicated by his saying "indeed it is merely the assemblage of al-Buwayṭī (*wa innamā huwa jamʿu al-Buwayṭī*);" then, Ḥassūn claims, the *Umm* is merely a continuation of the *K. al-Ḥujja*. Their arrangement (*tartīb*), in other words, was the same; the only difference is that al-Shāfiʿī recanted some of his earlier doctrines.[38]
  - 3) all of this indicates that the *Umm* was the compilation (*taʾlīf*), assemblage (*jamʿ*), and arrangement (*tartīb*) of al-Shāfiʿī, that his role with regard to the *Umm* was the same as his role regarding the *K. al-Ḥujja*, and that his companions were nothing but transmitters from him. The claim that al-Buwayṭī composed it is nullified.
- Ḥassūn then proceeds to a set of interlinked arguments which, not surprisingly, resemble the "hypothetical" argument style of al-Shāfiʿī himself:
  - Suppose, for the sake of argument, that the *Umm* was indeed first compiled by al-Buwayṭī. This means either:
    - a) al-Rabīʿ propagated the *Umm* with the permission of al-Buwayṭī, and ought to be praised, not belittled; or...

(continued)

[37] Ḥassūn cites Muḥammad Abū Zahra's biography of al-Shāfiʿī, and the introduction to Shākir's edition of the *Risāla*.

[38] Here, Ḥassūn reiterates most of his earlier discussion regarding the *Ḥujja*, *Mabsūṭ*, and *Umm*, as summarized in the previous table.

- b) al-Rabīʿ misappropriated it—a dangerous accusation against one of the great scholars whose trustworthiness is sanctioned by consensus
  - Ḥassūn then brings certain premodern criticisms of al-Makkī, which claim that he muddled his words, and that people lost faith in him and abandoned him—i.e., that he was in no position to claim untrustworthiness, and that he was not one of the scholars entrusted to verify the qualifications of narrators (*Ahl al-Jarḥ wa'l-Taʿdīl*). Al-Makkī's book has also been criticized for employing faulty *ḥadīth*.
  - Based on all of this, al-Makkī's downgrading of (*tajrīḥ*), and accusation against, al-Rabīʿ must be rejected. Al-Ghazālī's repeating of it is therefore rendered meaningless, as he provides no additional evidence in its support.
- Again, Ḥassūn brings a "hypothetical" argument in the style of al-Shāfiʿī
  - Suppose, for the sake of argument, that al-Rabīʿ took the *Umm* from the assemblage (*jamʿ*) of al-Buwayṭī...
  - Why would he need to do so, when he is famed for transmitting it in its entirety straight from al-Shāfiʿī (like all the other greats of his companions), and praised specifically by al-Shāfiʿī for just that?
  - There is no need whatsoever for him to take from al-Buwayṭī, even if al-Buwayṭī was more knowledgeable in *fiqh* (*afqah*). This is a matter of transmission (*naql*) and narration (*riwāya*), not superiority in *fiqh*.
- Finally, Ḥassūn turns to the arguments of Dr. Zakī Mubārak, but he does so by reproducing Shākir's refutation (see the following table)

Shākir's refutation of Mubārak stresses that certain of his claims lead to consequences which are quite difficult to account for. More importantly, he indicates that the writings attributed to al-Shāfiʿī are themselves replete with proofs of authenticity. This, in my opinion, is the strongest of arguments which may be levelled against claims of re-ascription. Mubārak, it would seem, like Calder after him, took no account of the multitudinous indicants for authenticity within the larger corpus—the consistency of editorial remarks, the frequency of "intra-references" to other *kutub* in the corpus, etc. These scholars, instead, have hinged their arguments upon a handful of "proofs" which are, in the end, only "proofs" by way of a very particular and pre-committed interpretation. Shākir's refutation may be summarized as follows:[39]

[39] From Shākir, (Intro.) pp. 9–10.

- Dr. Zakī Mubārak claims that the *Umm* was not authored by al-Shāfiʿī, but is the compilation (*taʾlīf*) of al-Buwayṭī, and was taken from him after his death by al-Rabīʿ, who then attributed it to himself. He rests his claim on that of al-Makkī, and al-Ghazālī's transmission of it.
- With regard to Mubārak's pamphlet Shākir says "the best of what is in it, is that it was written by the pen of an eloquent author; but the proofs (*ḥujaj*) for the refutation of his writing are plentiful throughout the books of al-Shāfiʿī themselves."
- Shākir then points out the following:
    - Mubārak's claim entails questioning the whole community of *ʿulamāʾ* and their methods, by whom *ʿilm* and Sunna have come down to us
    - al-Rabīʿ was highly regarded for his transmission-trustworthiness (*thiqa*)
    - the charge that al-Rabīʿ stole it from al-Buwayṭī and claimed it for his own entails that al-Rabīʿ lies every time he attributes something to al-Shāfiʿī in the text
- Shākir reproduces later claims that refute this misattribution, then relates how al-Buwayṭī used to say: "al-Rabīʿ is more firmly established (*athbat*) with regard to al-Shāfiʿī than I am," and that Abū Zurʿa al-Rāzī audited all of the books of al-Shāfiʿī from al-Rabīʿ 4 years before the death of al-Buwayṭī[40]
- In defense of being so critical of Mubārak's claims, Shākir admits that he has no choice—even though Mubārak is a respected friend; for the consequences of such claims left unrefuted are enormous, and must lead to absurdities. Shākir then details one of those claims, as follows:
    - the expression "he reported to us (*akhbaranā*)" does not indicate the auditing of a narration (*riwāya*), but 'report' (*ikhbār*) sometimes means transmission and considered opinion (*al-naql waʾl-raʾy*); Mubārak gives the example of where al-Shāfiʿī said "*akhbaranā Hashīm*," yet could never have met Hashīm, who died before al-Shāfiʿī came to Baghdad
    - Shākir, however, protests that nowhere does al-Shāfiʿī say "*akhbaranā Hashīm*," only "*Hashīm*"–Mubārak, moreover, excludes the explanation of al-Bulqīnī for all of this, although Bulqīnī is his source; and he is guilty of adding the word "*akhbaranā*" where it never existed, in order to further his argument[41]

Now we will turn to Calder, who, to my knowledge, nowhere references Mubārak's re-ascription claim. Instead, Calder pursues a course of literary analysis—"an emphatically secular exercise in historical reconstruction"—on the

[40] Shākir, pp. 9–10; quoted in full in Ḥassūn, vol. 1 (Intro.), pp. 91–2.

[41] Shākir, p. 10; quoted in full in Ḥassūn, vol. 1 (Intro.), p. 92.

model, among others, of John Wansbrough and Jacob Neusner.[42] I have found Calder's arguments baffling. On the whole, conclusions are based upon unexplained assumptions of what must belong to what era, and what portion of his textual sample is more or less sophisticated than another portion. This problem is compounded by an analysis restricted to less than two pages of text from a single chapter from the entire *Umm* compendium, which, as we have seen it described, is a collection of some 120 and more different *kutub*.[43] Nevertheless, I will present a portion of his discussion, then explain and critique it:

- "The attribution of two items (Paras. 3 and 4) to Rabīʿ would seem to imply that these are late additions interpolated into a text which is otherwise fully attributed to Shāfiʿī. This conclusion, however, presents problems. Paragraph 3 gives expression to a number of juristic rules regarding the sweat of humans and animals, and the *su'r* of animals, all of which are formally related on the authority of Rabīʿ. But the sweat of animals is explicitly also the subject matter of Paragraph 6 (anonymous, but read as from Shāfiʿī), and is raised again at Paragraph 15.2. The *su'r* of animals is the subject-matter of 5.2 (to be understood as from Shāfiʿī) and remains the main subject-matter from Paragraph 9 to the end of the passage. The problem is this: if Rabīʿ had before him a text including all the material that is now before us, why should he have introduced his own opinion—with miserably rudimentary arguments—into a passage by Shāfiʿī in which the questions he, Rabīʿ, raised were more circumstantially dealt with by his acknowledged master? The answer I would propose is that there was no such text by Shāfiʿī, not even in the time of Rabīʿ."[44]

---

[42] Calder, *Studies*, pp. ix-x. Again, see El Shamsy, "Al-Shāfiʿī's Written Corpus," for his assessment and refutation of Calder's argument; and Yahia, *Šāfiʿī et les Deux Sources de la Loi Islamique*, pp.170 ff., for the same.

[43] My point is that whatever one "discovers" in one *kitāb* insofar as post-dating indicants are concerned, need not apply outside that *kitāb*. If Calder's analyses prove anything, they do so only for that section of text he selected, not for the rest of the *kutub* and treatises in the *Umm*. His analyses, for example, could not apply to our subject-text, nor does our subject-text provide material of the sort Calder examines in his sample text.

[44] Calder, *Studies*, p. 74.

The paragraphs 3 and 4 referenced by Calder read as follows, in his own translation:[45]

- 3.1. Rabīʿ said: The sweat of a Christian woman, of a ritually impure [woman], and of a menstruating woman is pure *(ṭāhir).*
- 3.2. Likewise the Magian [person].
- 3.3. The sweat of all animals *(dābba)* is pure.
- 3.4. The *su'r* of animals *(dābba)* and predatory animals *(sibāʿ),* all of them, is pure; except the dog and the pig.
- 4. Rabīʿ said: That is Shāfiʿī's view.

Calder's "problem" simply vanishes upon closer inspection, as I will explain: First, if we read 3 and 4 as they appear in the text, then al-Rabīʿ has not "introduced his own opinion—with miserably rudimentary arguments." Rather, he has listed a series of plain substantive rulings, *with no arguments*, and attributed them to al-Shāfiʿī. This is a simple function of commentary, and not an argumentative intrusion.

If I understand Calder correctly, another part of the "problem" is that this listing of rulings repeats what al-Shāfiʿī argues in subsequent paragraphs. In the whole of Calder's sample, however, al-Shāfiʿī nowhere mentions the sweat of a Christian woman, a ritually impure woman, a menstruating woman, or a Magian (3.1-2). Each of these is a specific *mas'ala* which either has been, or might be, raised in a debate;[46] and this is something Calder recognizes in a subsequent but largely tangential discussion.[47] In my estimation, the worst textual "problem" thus far is that al-Rabīʿ has introduced four *masā'il* of *ikhtilāf* which might be subsumed by al-Shāfiʿī's more general ruling in paragraph 6.[48] However, this is not Calder's interpretation. Rather, it is a "gradual expansion" of the passage, one *mas'ala* at a time—an "organic growth." This is supported by an unexplained assumption: the placement of a gender-specific "Christian woman" (*al-naṣrāniyya*) next to a gender-neutral "Magian" (*al-majūsī*) is "illogical".[49]

With regard to 3.3 and 3.4, however, we do in fact see al-Shāfiʿī (in 6 and 5.2, respectively) directly address the sweat of the *dābba*, and *su'r* of *dābba* and *sibāʿ*; and in both (al-Rabīʿ's) 3.4 and (al-Shāfiʿī's) 5.2, dog and pig are exceptions. We will note, however, that al-Rabīʿ merely states that sweat and *su'r* are *ṭāhir*; while al-Shāfiʿī discusses them in the context of sweat dripping into water, and saliva mixing with water. Al-Rabīʿ's statements, in other words, are more general. Still,

[45] Ibid., p. 70.

[46] Note that Calder's sample text contains no less than three short dialectical Q&A sequences of the type I have labelled "instructional" (*fa-in qāla qā'il*... etc.) He makes no reference to dialectic, however.

[47] Ibid., pp. 74–5.

[48] "the sweat of men and animals (*ʿaraq al-insān wa-'l-dābba*) is not impure, no matter where the sweat comes from..." (ibid., p. 74).

[49] *Studies*, p. 75.

in my estimation the worst "problem" posed by paragraphs 3 and 4 is that al-Rabīʿ initiates a transmission of al-Shāfiʿī's arguments and "instructional" dialectical sequences—of which there are three—by listing some of al-Shāfiʿī's rulings relating to the problem cases at hand. Some are more specific, and some are more general; some are dealt with by al-Shāfiʿī in subsequent sections, and some are not. The "problem" remains ambiguous, nor is it clear how these features constitute proof "there was no such text by Shāfiʿī, not even in the time of Rabīʿ."

Calder, however, interprets paragraphs 3 and 4 as *pre*-dating 5.2, 6, 9 ff., and 15.2. Thus, if I understand correctly from the quoted passage above, "rudimentary" and repetitive are markers of "older." But: "Longer passages incorporating a coherent and consistent rational argument, as at Paragraphs 7 and 8, or a lengthy, subtle, and nuanced exegetical argument, as at Paragraphs 9–15, are probably to be understood as later developments."[50] Then: "this is consistent with the supposition that these materials were added to the 'Rabīʿ said' passage rather than that the Rabīʿ material was interpolated into a previously existent text by Shāfiʿī."[51] And then: "the content of the Rabīʿ passage (unnecessarily repeating material also presented, and in a superior manner, under a *qāla al-Shāfiʿī* rubric) and the form (rudimentary in argument, and archaic and incoherent in its formal development) suggest that the material attributed to Rabīʿ here is older than the material attributed to Shāfiʿī."[52]

In the end, unexplained assertions have fused with assumptions, and a circle has become complete: (1) al-Rabīʿ's list of substantive rulings is deemed an argument; (2) this in turn is deemed rudimentary, archaic, and incoherent; (3) one of the reasons stated for this assessment is that the list is "unnecessarily repeating material also presented, and in a superior manner, under a *qāla al-Shāfiʿī* rubric;" and (4) somehow, this material which the list (in inferior manner) repeats, post-dates the list. Paragraphs 3 and 4 are older because they are cruder; cruder, in part, by their repetition of what is more sophisticated; while what is more sophisticated is more recent; all of which hinges on an original, and unexplained, assessment of a simple listing of substantive rulings as rudimentary, archaic, and incoherent. Assumptions are built upon complementary assumptions; *circulus in probando*.[53]

---

[50] Ibid.

[51] Ibid.

[52] Ibid. Parentheses are Calder's. I have already noted that al-Rabīʿ's listing of substantive rulings in no way constitutes an argument. Note, however, it is now not only "rudimentary in argument," but "archaic and incoherent in its formal development." Returning to paragraphs 3 and 4, I remain perplexed as to how any of these descriptors apply. They have been asserted—and strongly—but not explained.

[53] Calder's argument continues over several more pages, but the quality of proofs is similar. Moreover, his selected paragraphs 3–4, above, may be compared with the following sections of our subject-text: §§20, 74, 199, 309, 350, 439, 499, 510, 843, 955–6, 1004, 1154, 1179, and 1329 (by Ḥassūn's numbering system). All of these feature al-Rabīʿ's arguments or editorial comments; and all are stated in a manner which defies Calder's assessment that the Rabīʿ layer is the oldest. These sections of our subject-text, and additional presentations featuring al-Rabīʿ's voice, may be read in my dissertation ("Dialectical Forge," pt. 2, *passim*, and appendices).

In further defence of my critique, I will only add that I am not alone in finding Calder's post-dating attempts problematic. Ahmed El Shamsy has provided solid support for the authentic ascription of both *Umm* and *Risāla* to al-Shāfiʿī;[54] Mohyddin Yahia has also vindicated the authenticity of the *Umm* against Calder's arguments;[55] Joseph Lowry has problematized Calder's post-dating of the *Risāla*;[56] and Wael Hallaq has refuted Calder's post-dating of Mālik's *Muwaṭṭa'* and Saḥnūn's *Mudawwana*.[57] In the end, Calder's assessment of the *Umm* is surprisingly inconclusive in formulation. After having pinned further arguments on another unexplained assumption ("hermeneutic material [is] clearly secondary to established law");[58] he concludes:

> Providing a date for this kind of material is almost pointless. Conceding a (surely limited) impetus from Rabīʿ himself, the growth of the text can be placed in the second half of the third century, with most of the material and all of the most sophisticated argument entering the text towards the end of that period. Stabilization of the text was slow, and, as in the case of the *Aṣl*, scarcely achieved in medieval times. There are obvious (and probably minor) interpolations from much later than the third century and no evidence of any major redaction achieved before the decisive intervention of Sirāj al-Dīn Bulqīnī (d. 805 [H]).[59]

Ultimately, Calder's arguments and narrative find neither application nor relevance to the *Umm* Version of our subject-text. "Sophisticated" arguments are attributed to al-Rabīʿ—as well as the plain commentary material—and numerous intra-*kitāb* references and other indicants point towards authenticity.

3.3 The Genres of Juridical Disagreement and Their Relationship to *Uṣūl al-Fiqh* and *Jadal*-Theory

All of the literary genres of pre-modern Islamic law have been touched by the practice and/or theory of juridical *jadal*. That is not to say that all legal works may be subsumed under a super-category of *jadal* literature, but that treatises and their authors across all juridical projects were participants—from the very beginning—in a larger Islamic legal episteme, or set of epistemes, marked by *ikhtilāf* and disciplined debate, whether in face-to-face Q&A disputation, or in refutational,

[54] See "Al-Shāfiʿī's Written Corpus."

[55] See *Šāfiʿī et les Deux Sources de la Loi Islamique*, pp.170 ff.

[56] See "Legal Hermeneutics."

[57] See "On Dating Mâlik's *Muwaṭṭa'*."

[58] Calder, *Studies*, 82. See my discussion of Calder's evolutionary narrative for *uṣūl al-fiqh* in Chap. 8. This is a common theme, linked to the supposed primary function of *uṣūl al-fiqh* as "descriptive."

[59] Ibid., p. 83.

treatise-vs.-treatise "literary encounters." Such works as are related to, or subsumed by, the larger genre of *uṣūl al-fiqh*, are particularly marked by the argument epistemes of juridical dialectical disputation. Primary among these is the subgenre of *jadal*-theory itself—whether it appears as chapters in *uṣūl al-fiqh* works or as specialized, systematic treatises—and these latter are the focus of Chap. 4, where select early works will be reviewed in order to fashion our *jadal*-theory lens.

But also marked by *jadal* are the subgenres of "*qiyās*-invalidating inter-case distinctions" (*furūq*), "weaker and stronger analogues" (*ashbāh wa naẓā'ir*), "induced objectives of God's Law" (*maqāṣid al-Sharīʿa*), "induced general principles of derived law" (*qawāʿid fiqhiyya*), and "juridical disagreement" (*ikhtilāf*) or "the science of juridical disagreement" (*ʿilm al-khilāf*). These were not only born and refined in dialectical encounter, but provided critical material and method for the jurist engaged in the complementary processes of private *ijtihād* and public disputation. With regard to these latter subgenres, the most important in terms of the current project are the categories of *ikhtilāf* and *ʿilm al-khilāf*; our subject-treatise may be said to belong to both. The purpose now is to briefly explore the genre(s) of *ikhtilāf* and *ʿilm al-khilāf* for later comparison with the *jadal*-theory treatises comprising our lens for analysis. In so doing, the kinship between the genre of our subject-text and the genre of our lens-texts will be manifest.

The ʿIlm al-Khilāf: *Definition and Introduction*

Schacht provides a brief definition of *ikhtilāf*, as follows:

> difference, also inconsistency; as a technical term, the differences of opinion amongst the authorities of religious law, both between the several schools and within each of them; opp. *idjmāʿ*..., *ittifāḳ*.[60]

Our current concern is the science of *ikhtilāf*, or the *ʿilm al-khilāf*, and its literature; in particular I have chosen a specific (and relatively early) treatise as exemplar of this genre in a *systematized* stage:[61] *The Founding of Investigation* (*Ta'sīs al-Naẓar*) commonly attributed to Abū Zayd ʿAbd Allāh b. ʿUmar b. ʿĪsā al-Dabbūsī (Ḥanafī; d.430/1038).[62] I have emphasized "systematized" in the preceding sentence to

---

[60] *EI*², s.v. "*Ikhtilāf.*"

[61] There is quite some difference between the *Ta'sīs al-Naẓar* and our proto-system subject-text, even though they both properly belong to the genre of *ikhtilāf*. The intent for which these two works were composed is of course different, but markedly different is the organizing principle of the later work: a mark of the refinements and systematic approaches developed over the intervening two hundred years.

[62] Note that the very title of this work provides indication for the overlapping concerns of *khilāf* and *jadal*-theory, with the latter referring often to "investigation" (*naẓar*) and "dialectical investigation" (*munāẓara*).

highlight the fact that the "science of juridical disagreement" (*ʿilm al-khilāf*), just like the "sciences" (*ʿulūm*) of *jadal* and *uṣūl al-fiqh*, appears to have developed in stages from a less choate proto-system—inherent to the early *ikhtilāf* treatises—to a period of fully-systematized *ʿilm al-khilāf* treatises.[63]

An editor of the *Ta'sīs al-Naẓar*, the prolific Khalīl al-Mays, opens his introduction with an instructive overview of the *ʿilm al-khilāf*.[64] He begins with a pair of definitions from the *Abjad al-ʿUlūm* of Muḥammad Ṣiddīq Ḥasan: (1) "It is the science (*ʿilm*) by way of which is known/defined the means of producing decisive arguments in consonance with God's Law (*kayfiyyat īrād al-ḥujaj al-sharʿiyya*), and rebuttal of sophisms (*dafʿ al-shubah*), and critiques (*qawādiḥ*) of the contended primary indicants (*al-adilla al-khilāfiyya*), via the production of certain [or, "categorical"] proofs (*īrād al-barāhīn al-qaṭʿiyya*);" and (2) "*ʿIlm al-khilāf* is the science (*ʿilm*) which investigates the various modes of rational inference (*istinbāṭāt*) from the general or particular primary indicants (*al-adilla al-ijmāliyya aw al-tafṣīliyya*)."[65] Al-Mays then quotes the larger part of Ibn Khaldūn's description of the "points of disagreement" (*khilāfiyyāt*) in his *Muqaddima*,[66] ending with the fact that most writers in this genre are Shāfiʿīs and Ḥanafī's—the latter because so much of their substantive rulings (*furūʿ*) are derived via *qiyās*, and due to which they are "The Scholars of Intellectual Investigation and Inquiry" (*Ahl al-Naẓar wa'l-Baḥth*)."[67]

On the Relationship between the ʿIlm al-Khilāf, Jadal, *and* Uṣūl al-Fiqh

Al-Mays ties the *ʿilm al-khilāf* to the *ʿilm al-jadal*—both directly and indirectly—a number of times. He quotes from the *Madīnat al-ʿUlūm*, as conveyed in the *Abjad al-ʿUlūm*, the following points: (1) "the best and most exemplary of *ʿulamā'* in the *technē* (*fann*) of *khilāf* are Abū Ḥanīfa, and his companions Abū Yūsuf, Muḥammad, and Zufar; and al-Shāfiʿī, Mālik, and Aḥmad b. Ḥanbal";[68] (2) "inquiry (*baḥth*) into [the modes of rational inference (*wujūh al-istinbāṭāt*)] is by way of confirmation and refutation-by-inconsistency (*al-ibrām wa'l-naqḍ*)[69] for any thesis (*waḍʿ*)

---

[63] Importantly, and also like the *ʿulūm* of *jadal* and *uṣūl al-fiqh*, the first appearance of systematized *ʿilm al-khilāf* works appears to belong to the fourth/tenth century. See the discussion on the Ḥanafī Abū al-Layth al-Samarqandī (d.373/983) in section 4.3, below.

[64] *Ta'sīs al-Naẓar*, al-Mays ed., pp. 3 ff.

[65] Ibid., p. 3. The latter definition is quoted in the *Abjad* from the *Madīnat al-ʿUlūm*.

[66] Corresponding to pp. 577–8 of the Shaḥāda ed.; and vol. 3, vi.13, pp. 30–2 of Rosenthal's translation.

[67] *Ta'sīs al-Naẓar*, al-Mays ed., pp. 3–4.

[68] Note that four of these figures are key jurists of our subject-treatise.

[69] *Naqḍ* ("inconsistency") is a category of objection of primary import to both proto-system and full-system *jadal*. See the section on *naqḍ* in Chap. 4, and its frequent occurrence in Chaps. 5 and 6.

intended in these modes"; (3) "first principles (*mabādi'*) [of the *'ilm al-khilāf*] are derived from the *'ilm al-jadal*, and *jadal* has the status of material (*bi-manzilat al-mādda*), while *khilāf* has the status of form (*bi-manzilat al-ṣūra*)";[70] (4) "[*'ilm al-khilāf*] is derived from the Arabic and legal sciences (*'ulūm al-'Arabiyya wa'l-Shar'iyya*)"; (5) "its goal is the attainment of a faculty for confirmation and refutation-by-inconsistency (*malkat al-ibrām wa'l-naqḍ*)"; (6) "its utility (*fā'ida*) is in the repulsion of doubts (*shukūk*) from the doctrinal *madhhab*, and causing them to fall on the doctrinal *madhhab* of the opponent."[71]

Al-Mays further highlights the relationship between the *'ilm al-jadal* and the *'ilm al-khilāf* through the person of the latter's (purportedly) first systematizer (*awwal man akhraja 'ilm al-khilāf*): al-Dabbūsī himself, a dialectician of repute. Regarding him, al-Mays quotes from the *Jawāhir al-Muḍī'a* of al-Qurashī, the *Ansāb* of al-Sam'ānī, and the *Fikr* of al-Sāmī:[72]

> [al-Dabbūsī] is the first to set down (*waḍa'a*) the *'ilm al-khilāf*, and to bring it into being; and he is one of those for whom proverbs were struck: for investigation (*naẓar*) and the systemizing of proofs (*ḥujaj*) and rational opinion (*ra'y*). In Samarqand and Bukhārā he held dialectical disputations (*munāẓarāt*) with luminaries; and he was the *shaykh* of those parts. It is narrated that he disputed (*nāẓara*) a certain jurist, and every time Abū Zayd [al-Dabbūsī] refuted him (*alzamahu*),[73] [the jurist] smiled or laughed. So Abū Zayd heartened himself with a poem:
>
> 'Why is it, when I refute him with *ḥujja*,
> He opposes me by chuckling and laughing?
> If the laughter of man comes from his *fiqh*,
> How much more *fiqh* has the desert hyena!'[74]

---

[70] Note this artful rendering of the *jadal-khilāf* relationship twice employs the formula "*bi-manzila* X." As we shall see in our analyses, this formula enjoyed great currency in juridical dialectic from the earliest times.

[71] *Ta'sīs al-Naẓar*, al-Mays ed., pp. 4–5. Al-Mays closes this section with a particular mention of the *K. al-Ma'ālim* (and other unnamed treatises and commentaries) of Fakhr al-Dīn al-Rāzī (Shāfi'ī, d.606/1209), as having special import to the *'ilm al-khilāf wa'l-jadal*.

[72] *Ta'sīs al-Naẓar*, al-Mays ed., p. 7. It is difficult to determine where one citation ends and the other begins.

[73] That is, brought him to a point where he must either concede or explain his way out of a contradiction.

[74] *Ta'sīs al-Naẓar*, al-Mays ed., p. 7. I have assumed the "*dubb fi'l-ṣaḥrā*" to be a hyena, partly due to context, and partly due to Lane's listing of *dabāb* as "a call to a female hyena" (*Lexicon*, s.v. دباب). Importantly, al-Mays notes al-Dabbūsī authored respected *uṣūl al-fiqh* works, mainly the *Asrār* and the *Taqwīm al-Adilla*. See Sezgin, *Tārīkh*, vol. 1, pt. 3, pp. 125 f. re: manuscripts and materials for the *Taqwīm al-Adilla fī Uṣūl al-Fiqh* and the *Kitāb al-Asrār* (*wa'l-Taqdīm li'l-Adilla*) *fi'l-Furū'* of al-Dabbūsī.

On the Historical Development of Ikhtilāf *Literature*

Al-Mays has claimed al-Dabbūsī the first "in the world" to extract (*akhraja*)—that is, to systematize—the *ʿilm al-khilāf*. He proceeds to list all the *fiqh* works which fall into this *technē* (*fann*), as both precede and follow al-Dabbūsī (*min al-salaf wa'l-khalaf*):[75]

- [1] The *Ikhtilāf Abī Ḥanīfa wa Ibn Abī Laylā*;[76] the *Ikhtilāf Abī Ḥanīfa wa'l-Awzāʿī* (known as *al-Radd ʿalā Siyar al-Awzāʿī*), the *Ikhtilāf al-Shāfiʿī maʿa Muḥammad b. al-Ḥasan*, the *Ikhtilāf al-Shāfiʿī maʿa Mālik*, and the *Ḥujja* of Muḥammad b. al-Ḥasan[77]
- [2] the *Ikhtilāf al-Fuqahā' of Abū Jaʿfar al-Ṭaḥāwī* (d.321 H)
- [3] the *Tajrīd* of al-Qudūrī al-Ḥanafī (d.428 H)
- [4] [al-Dabbūsī and the *Ta'sīs al-Naẓar* would appear here]
- [5] the *Khilāfiyyāt* of al-Bayhaqī al-Shāfiʿī (d.458 H)
- [6] the *Wasā'il fī Furūq al-Masā'il* of Ibn Jamāʿa al-Shāfiʿī (d.480 H)
- [7] the *Mukhtaṣar al-Kifāya* of al-ʿAbdurī al-Shāfiʿī (d.493 H)
- [8] the *Ḥilyat al-ʿUlamā' fī Ikhtilāf al-Fuqahā'* of Abū Bakr Muḥammad b. Aḥmad al-Shāshī al-Mustaẓharī al-Shāfiʿī (d.507 H)
- [9] the *Manẓūmat al-Nasafī* of al-Nasafī al-Ḥanafī (d.537 H)
- [10] the *Ṭarīqat al-Raḍawiyya* of Raḍī al-Dīn al-Sarakhsī al-Ḥanafī (d.544 H)[78]
- [11] the *Mukhtalif al-Riwāya* of ʿAlā' al-Dīn Muḥammad b. ʿAbd al-Ḥamīd al-Samarqandī al-Ḥanafī (d.552 H)
- [12] the *Ishrāf ʿalā Madhāhib al-Ashrāf* of Ibn Hubayra al-Ḥanbalī (d.555 or 560 H)
- [13] the *Taqwīm al-Naẓar* of al-Dahhān al-Shāfiʿī (d.589 H)

With special regard to early works of *ikhtilāf*, another, somewhat more abbreviated, literary history is presented by al-Afghānī, editor of the Shaybānī Version of our subject-text. He opens his introduction to the *Ikhtilāf Abī Ḥanīfa wa Ibn Abī Laylā* with the following points: (1) the *ikhtilāf* of the Imams over derived rulings (*furūʿ*) is a mercy to the Muslim community (*raḥma li'l-Umma*); (2) the Companions differed among themselves, and the jurists after them—yet, had there not been *ikhtilāf*, decrees would have become too narrow, and hardship would have reigned; and (3) *ikhtilāf* works have been written since opposing traditions (*āthār*)

[75] *Ta'sīs al-Naẓar*, al-Mays ed., 5–6.

[76] It is significant that the very first compilation is our subject-text.

[77] With the exception of al-Shaybānī's *Ḥujja*, all of these works are found in the *Umm*.

[78] NB: this is the very same treatise Miller includes among the *jadal* texts of his "middle period."

were first collected. He then provides his brief history of *ikhtilāf* works, beginning with the oldest:[79]

- [1] the *K. Ikhtilāf al-Ṣaḥāba* of Abū Ḥanīfa [d.150/767]
- [2] the *K. Ikhtilāf Abī Ḥanīfa wa Ibn Abī Laylā* of the Qāḍī Abū Yūsuf [d.182/798][80]
- [3] the *Ikhtilāf Ya'qūb wa Zufar* of Abū 'Abd Allāh Muḥammad b. Shujā' al-Thaljī [d.267/880]
- [4] the general compilation: *Ikhtilāf al-Fuqahā'* of al-Ṭaḥāwī [d.321/933]
- [5] the *Ishrāf fi'l-Khilāf* of Ibn al-Mundhir [d.319/856]
- [6] the *Ikhtilāf al-Fuqahā'* of Ibn Jarīr [al-Ṭabarī; d.310/923][81]

Note that, with the exception of the last two independents,[82] these are all authors affiliated with the Ḥanafī *madhhab*. Note also the early termination of this list; what al-Afghānī means by the literature of *ikhtilāf* may not be precisely the same as what al-Mays means by the literature of *'ilm al-khilāf*. Again, it would seem best to presume a multi-stage development of *ikhtilāf* literature, with a less choate proto-system building towards the first fully-systematized treatises of *'ilm al-khilāf.*

Joseph Schacht also compiled a history of *ikhtilāf* and its literature. He opens his *ikhtilāf* entry in the *Encyclopaedia of Islam* with a summary of his well known paradigms for the formation of legal schools, the rise of Prophetic Sunna, the role of al-Shāfi'ī, etc. Schacht's assessments bear upon the subject-matter of this monograph, so I will reproduce his account in full:[83]

> [1] The ancient schools of law, on the one hand, accepted geographical differences of doctrines as natural; on the other hand, they voiced strong objections to disagreement within each school, an opinion which was mitigated by their acceptance as legitimate of different opinions if based on *idjtihād*.... [2] The rising tide of traditions from the Prophet,

---

[79] Afghānī, p. 3.

[80] Our Shaybānī Version, the text of al-Afghānī's edition.

[81] Al-Afghānī claims al-Ṭabarī denuded his work of indicants (*dalā'il*); and Miller, relying solely upon al-Ṭabarī's *Ikhtilāf al-Fuqahā'* as his model, found it "totally free of the jadal technique," and concluded that in the whole of *ikhtilāf* literature "the techniques of argumentation are ignored" ("Islamic Disputation Theory," pp. 102–3), and that the genre "was not dialectical in character" (ibid., p.146). I have employed what survives of al-Ṭabarī's *Ikhtilāf al-Fuqahā'* frequently in translating and analyzing the subject-text, and do not understand al-Afghānī's complaint; al-Ṭabarī indeed supplies indicants supporting either side of a contended *mas'ala*. As for Miller, it is understandable he would reach his conclusion on the basis of al-Ṭabarī's *Ikhtilāf* alone, but he erred in interpolating from it to the whole of the genre, and so missed the patently dialectical character of the *Umm* compendium and its treatises.

[82] Ibn al-Mundhir is both independent (*mustaqill*) and claimed by the Shāfi'īs; Ibn Jarīr al-Ṭabarī is the eponym of his own short-lived *madhhab*.

[83] *EI*², s.v. "*Ikhtilāf.*" I have inserted numbers to divide the text's themes for brief re-assessment.

> in particular, threatened the continuity and uniformity of doctrine in the ancient schools, and reinforced their aversion to disagreement. [3] The opportunity for disagreements on questions of principle arose only from the time of S̲h̲āfiʿī... and his systematic innovation. [4] But the several schools arrived at a compromise, and the consensus (*id̲j̲māʿ*), which acted as the integrating principle of Islam, succeeded in making innocuous those differences of opinion which it could not eliminate. [5] The four schools, then, are equally covered by *id̲j̲māʿ*, their alternative interpretations of Ḳurʾān and *sunna* are equally legitimate, they are all equally orthodox. [6] This view has found expression in a saying which occurs first in the *Fiḳh al-akbar* of Abū Ḥanīfa... and was later attributed to the Prophet, to the effect that "difference of opinion in the community of Muslims is a concession (*raḥma*) on the part of Allāh".[84] The work of S̲h̲aʿrānī... expresses the attitude underlying this tradition with monotonous regularity.

Most of these assertions have been problematized and supplanted by more recent scholarship.[85] I will only contend certain of them. As for #1, the abhorance of *ikhtilāf* within a "school" in a period before the formation of doctrinal *madhāhib* is problematic, and impossible to reconcile with the spirit of *ikhtilāf* we find in our subject-text. Abū Ḥanīfa and Ibn Abī Laylā were both Kūfans, and the behaviour of Abū Yūsuf, best described as "following the *ḥujja*"—whether it supported Ibn Abī Laylā, Abū Ḥanīfa, or required a new, independent formulation—suggests a far different ethic at work than an obsession with regional or "school" consistency.

As for #2 and #4, I would propose that the roles Prophetic Sunna and *ijmāʿ* came to play were determined by a natural interaction of prior and developing argumentation epistemes with new (and epistemically hierarchical) Islamic axioms.[86] That is to say, I would supplant, with a different conception, (A) the linear dynamic of #2, whereby a "rising tide of traditions" served to bolster an "aversion to disagreement" between "schools;" and (B) the assertion, in #4, of a "compromise" of schools with the role of *ijmāʿ* "making innocuous those differences of opinion which it could not eliminate." Instead, I would claim that the refinement and ranking of epistemically-authoritative *uṣūl* (Prophetic Sunna and *ijmāʿ* among them), the techniques of verifying, interpreting, preponderating, and arguing from these *uṣūl* (the nascent sciences of *uṣūl al-fiqh*), and the formation of doctrinal *madhāhib* were all resultant of a singular, powerful, intellectual dynamic: the evolution of argumentation epistemes powered by proto-system juridical dialectic, and guided throughout by a general truth-seeking ethic of "following the *ḥujja*."

Finally, as regards #3: the evidence in our subject-text—with which Schacht was intimately familiar[87]—alone disproves this assertion. Taken together with other treatises from the *Umm*, the evidence is overwhelming: "questions of principle" were debated before al-Shāfiʿī arrived on the scene, and the history of

---

[84] Cf. al-Afghānī's repetition of this proverb in the opening of his introduction, above.

[85] See, in particular, Hallaq, *Origins*.

[86] See the discussion near the end of Chap. 4, where the ranking of primary *uṣūl* is portrayed, in part, as an hierarchical reformulation of the old Aristotelian episteme of *endoxa* premises.

[87] See his *Origins*, *passim*.

Islamic legal theory neither begins nor culminates in this nevertheless remarkable jurist.

Returning to Schacht's brief history of *ikhtilāf*, he next turns attention towards the literature itself, saying:

> The recording of these differences of opinion has produced a considerable literature since the beginnings of the study of *fiḳh*. The earlier works reflect the discussions between the several schools, the later ones are simply handbooks.

To this I would add the following: (1) the "discussions" of earlier works, as we shall see, often included detailed arguments in which sources, proofs, and modes of inference were all laid bare; (2) such arguments are frequently supported by lengthy, transcript-like sequences of dialectical debate; and (3) these earlier works exhibit a patently didactic intent. Not merely records of disagreement, they (too) were "handbooks"—manuals for the jurist-dialectician taking up the defence and critique of variant opinions, in the spirit of *jadal*.

Schacht then introduces a series of works in roughly chronological order, distinguishing an earlier and later period;[88] the detailing of later period works was not meant to be comprehensive, and we may allow that his early period discussion is in the same spirit. I have outlined the works with some of his notes in the following table:

Early Period

- the *Radd ʿalā Siyar al-Awzāʿī* and the *Ikhtilāf Abī Ḥanīfa wa Ibn Abī Laylā* of Abū Yūsuf
  - both appear in the *Umm* with al-Shāfiʿī's commentary
- the *Kitāb al-Ḥujaj* of al-Shaybānī
  - part of which appears in the *Umm*, with al-Shāfiʿī's commentary[89]
- the *Kitāb Ikhtilāf Mālik wa'l-Shāfiʿī* of al-Shāfiʿī (in the *Umm*)
- the *Kitāb Ikhtilāf ʿAlī wa-ʿAbd Allāh b. Masʿūd* of al-Shāfiʿī (in the *Umm*)
- the *Kitāb Ikhtilāf al-Ḥadīth* of al-Shāfiʿī
- the *Jāmiʿ* of al-Tirmidhī[90]
- the *Kitāb Mukhtalif al-Ḥadīth* of Ibn Qutayba[91]

(continued)

[88] *EI*², s.v. "*Ikhtilāf.*"

[89] Presumably Schacht is referring to al-Shāfiʿī's *Kitāb al-Radd ʿalā Muḥammad b. al-Ḥasan.*

[90] Schacht includes this canonical *ḥadīth* work, as al-Tirmidhī "indicates for which doctrine each tradition serves as authority, so that his work is an important source for the comparative study of early *ikhtilāf.*"

[91] Schacht notes Ibn Qutayba "tries to reconcile the contradictions of traditions."

- the *Kitāb Ikhtilāf al-Fuqahā'* of al-Ṭabarī[92]
- the *Sharḥ Ma'ānī al-Āthār* of al-Ṭaḥāwī[93]

Later Handbooks

- the *Ishrāf 'alā Masā'il al-Khilāf* of 'Abd al-Wahhāb al-Baghdādī (d.422/1031)
- the *Bidāyat al-Mujtahid* of Ibn Rushd (d.595/1198)
- the *Ishrāf* of Ibn Hubayra (d.560/1165)
  - [derivation] the *Raḥmat al-Umma* of Muḥammad b. 'Abd al-Raḥmān al-Dimashqī (wr. 780/1378)
  - [derivation] the *Mīzān al-Kubrā* of al-Sha'rānī (d.973/1565)
- the (modern) *Kitāb al-Fiqh 'alā al-Madhāhib al-Arba'a* [of al-Jazīrī, d.1360/1941]

3.4 A Key Text of the *'Ilm al-Khilāf*: The *Ta'sīs al-Naẓar*

I would turn now to what may be the first—certainly a very early—attempt at systematizing the *'ilm al-khilāf*: the *Ta'sīs al-Naẓar* attributed to Abū Zayd 'Abd Allāh al-Dabbūsī. The importance of this work for the current project stems from its contents and its relatively early date (al-Dabbūsī died in 430/1038). As for the contents, the *Ta'sīs* provides an excellent illustration of the intertwining and mutually-contributive dynamics of the sciences (*'ulūm*) of *jadal*, *uṣūl al-fiqh*, and *khilāf*. Al-Dabbūsī was also a contemporary of his fellow Ḥanafī, Abū al-Ḥusayn al-Baṣrī (d.436/1044), whose treatise on *qiyās*-oriented *jadal* is among the earliest extant *jadal*-theory material,[94] and will form a component of our analytical lens. Moreover, it is likely a considerable amount of material in the *Ta'sīs* can be pushed further back in time; mainly, to the *Ta'sīs al-Naẓā'ir* of the Ḥanafī Abū al-Layth al-Samarqandī (d.373/983).

In his *Madkhal al-Mufaṣṣal li-Madhhab al-Imām Aḥmad*,[95] Bakr b. 'Abd Allāh Abū Zayd claims it is more correct to think of al-Samarqandī's *Ta'sīs al-Naẓā'ir* as the first *uṣūl* composition in the Ḥanafī method (*ṭarīqa*), since "the book of al-Dabbūsī

[92] Schacht comments that al-Ṭabarī composed this work "as a kind of systematic justification of his own *madhhab*." He also notes: "it consists mostly of extracts from the works of his predecessors and, as many of them have been lost, is very valuable as a source, but unfortunately only two fragments of this very extensive work have survived."

[93] Schacht concludes: "The early period of the works on *ikhtilāf* comes to an end with the *Sharḥ ma'ānī 'l-āthār* of Ṭaḥāwī...; the author argues from the Ḥanafī point of view but unfortunately does not mention the adherents of the numerous divisions of doctrine which he discusses."

[94] With the exception of what might be culled from the *Fuṣūl fi'l-Uṣūl* of al-Jaṣṣāṣ (d.370/981).

[95] Vol. 2, p. 940.

is extracted from it (*mustall minhu*), with additions to it."[96] He then cites a modern tractate by Shāmil Shāhīn entitled "*al-Taḥqīq al-Muʿtabar fī Nisbat Kitāb Ta'sīs al-Naẓar*," in which the author argues attribution of the *Ta'sīs* to al-Dabbūsī is wrong, and the correct attribution is to al-Samarqandī. If this is true, then the composition of much of the contents of the *Ta'sīs* may be placed in the latter half of the fourth/tenth century—i.e., at the heart of a period of system-fluorescence which saw the birth of *uṣūl al-fiqh* and *jadal/munāẓara* theory literature.

Whatever the case may be, the author of the *Ta'sīs* begins by explaining why—and by which organizing principles—he composed it. This provides valuable insight, and I have attempted a partial translation of the author's introduction with the hope of making it more accessible. First, his goal in composition:[97]

> When I observed the difficulty of the matter, as regards the memorization of contended problem questions (*masā'il al-khilāf*) for aspiring jurists... and the hardship inherent to the methods of rational inference (*istinbāṭ*) [for the *masā'il*], and their insufficiency of knowledge in examining the true sources/methods [of the *masā'il*], and [their] uncertainty of the topoi (*mawāḍiʿ*) of argument, during disputation (*tanāẓur*) about [the *masā'il*], I gathered together in this, my book, such words as the disputant (*nāẓir*)—when he contemplates and meditates upon them—will know, during the disputation-contest (*takhāṣum*), the loci of contention (*maḥāll al-tanāzuʿ*), and the pivotal theme of controversy (*madār al-tanāṭuḥ*). And he will devote his particular care to the proper ordering of argument (*tartīb al-kalām*), and to the strengthening of proofs (*ḥujaj*) for the topoi he knows to constitute the hinge of the stated solution (*madār al-qawl*), and the loci of contention in the topos of dispute (*mawḍiʿ al-nizāʿ*). And, so, memorization [of the *masā'il*] will be made easy for them, and the means of attaining knowledge of the sources/methods [of the *masā'il*] will be facilitated for them, and they will find it possible to make correlational inference (*qiyās*) from [the *masā'il*] to other matters.

A number of features in this manifesto are of immediate import. Most striking of all is the repeated mention of *mawāḍiʿ*, *maḥāll*, and *madār*—three terms which, in the context of debate, parallel Aristotle's *topoi* in one way or another.[98] One is reminded, moreover, that the purpose behind memorizing *masā'il* of *khilāf*, and becoming conversant in the methods of *istinbāṭ* employed by the venerated exemplar *mujtahid*s who disputed them, is not a function of preserving legal history. Rather, it is a critical study by means of which the aspiring jurist perfects his skills as a dialectician (and, perhaps, as a *mujtahid*, which is suggested by the author's final aim of extending the student's range of *qiyās*). Specifically, the author aims to facilitate a student's ability to: (1) isolate, in the heat of disputation, the core point(s) of contention; and (2) arrange his arguments and fortify his *ḥujja* with

[96] The Arabic text reads "فإن كتاب الدبوسي مستل منه مع زيادات عليه" and I am interpreting "مستل" as the passive participle of form VIII *istalla*. This verb carries the sense of "to extract gently" and "to steal a. th." (Hava, *al-Farā'id*, 329, s.v. "سَلّ"), from which I infer the more neutral "extracted" for *mustall*.

[97] *Ta'sīs al-Naẓar*, al-Mays ed., p. 11.

[98] This is not to say that the author necessarily employed these as technical terms, as has been pointed out to me. Their synonymous repetition may simply reflect a rhetorical design. Still, a didactic intention: preparing aspiring jurists for debate, is manifest. And when memorization is specifically promoted, a parallel to the *topoi* seems all the more likely.

regard to the *mawāḍiʿ*—this being one of the more common terms used to translate *topoi*—upon which his opponent's thesis is hinged. This identifies very closely with Aristotelian dialectical method.

A better measure of the disputation teaching and practice informing the author's project may be acquired by examining his organizing principle. Does it reflect in any way the organizing principles of Aristotle's *Topics*?[99] In fact, our author—be it al-Dabbūsī or al-Samarqandī—forthrightly explains the principle by which he organized the *Taʾsīs*:[100]

> ... when I examined the *masāʾil* over which the jurists disagree, I found them to be divided into eight divisions (*aqsām*):
>
> [1] a division [of *masāʾil*] being the *khilāf* between Abū Ḥanīfa [on one side]... and his two companions, Muḥammad b. al-Ḥasan and Abū Yūsuf [on the other]...
> [2] ... the *khilāf* between Abū Ḥanīfa and Abū Yūsuf [on one side], and Muḥammad b. al-Ḥasan [on the other]...
> [3] ... the *khilāf* between Abū Ḥanīfa and Muḥammad [on one side], and Abū Yūsuf [on the other]...
> [4] ... the *khilāf* between Abū Yūsuf and Muḥammad...
> [5] ... the *khilāf* between our three *ʿulamāʾ* Muḥammad b. al-Ḥasan and al-Ḥasan b. Ziyād [on one side], and Zufar [on the other]...
> [6] ... the *khilāf* between our *ʿulamāʾ* [on one side], and the oldest Imām Mālik b. Anas [on the other]...
> [7] ... the *khilāf* between our three *ʿulamāʾ* Muḥammad b. al-Ḥasan, al-Ḥasan b. Ziyād, and Zufar [on one side], and Ibn Abī Laylā [on the other]...
> [8] [and] a division of them being the *khilāf* between our three *ʿulamāʾ* [on one side], and Abū ʿAbd Allāh al-Imām al-Qurashī Muḥammad b. Idrīs al-Shāfiʿī [on the other].
>
> Then I made for each of these eight divisions a chapter (*bāb*), and mentioned in each chapter such authoritative premise-principles (*uṣūl*) as pertain to it, setting forth—for each premise-principle (*aṣl*)—a paradigm (*ḍarb*) from among model cases (*amthila*) and parallel cases (*naẓāʾir*). And I placed, at the end of these eight divisions, another in which I mentioned the *uṣūl* for which each *aṣl* comprises a variety of contended cases (*masāʾil khilāfiyya*). And as for what these eight divisions pass over of doctrinal opinions (*aqwāl*) from [other] opponents (*mukhālifīn*)—such as the opinion of Ibrāhīm al-Nakhaʿī, Sufyān al-Thawrī, al-Awzāʿī, al-Shaʿbī, and others? I avoided mentioning them, and setting forth their *uṣūl* for their own solutions, out of distaste for prolonging the discussion. Nor did I occupy myself with commentary (*sharḥ*) on those model cases I did set forth, except to a measure by which their connection to the mentioned *uṣūl* is clarified....

The organizing principle of the *Taʾsīs* is thus patently different from that of the Aristotelian *topoi*, which are organized by categories of predicable. Nevertheless, combined with the author's plainly-stated objectives, there is remarkable convergence with the organizational aims of the *Topics*.

Equally importantly, from this manifesto of the *Taʾsīs* we gain new insight into the nature and function of the "principles" (*uṣūl* / *qawāʿid*) of the famed jurist Abū al-Ḥasan al-Karkhī (Ḥanafī; d.340/952), and others, and the pivotal role they play in dialectical disputation. In brief, an *aṣl*—in this genre of *khilāf*—is one from

---

[99] See Smith's intro. to *Topics I and VIII*, pp. xxx ff.

[100] *Taʾsīs al-Naẓar*, al-Mays ed., pp. 11–12.

among a collection of *endoxa* juridical premise-principles, organized according to who employed which against whom, and in which *mas'ala*, and in such a manner as echoes the Aristotelian objective of "location."

The *Ta'sīs*, like the *Topics*, is thus very evidently a handbook for the dialectician. Its primary difference is the following: whereas the *Topics* relies upon predicables and argument form to aid in locating such premises which—if the opponent concedes—commit him to the contradictory (*naqīḍ*) of his own thesis, the *Ta'sīs* relies upon a historical catalogue of *ikhtilāf*—categorized by its exemplary disputants—to do the same. And the objective of both "location" systems is indeed the same: to produce whatever might commit R to the *naqīḍ* of his position. But how might we envisage the location system of the *Ta'sīs* in practice?

Remember that the contended problem cases (*masā'il al-khilāf*) are, like the categories of *topoi*, meant to be memorized—and with the explicit, practical intent of providing Q with a readily-accessible structure for locating the propositions suitable for nullifying R's thesis, via impossibility, inconsistency, absurdity, or some other untenable consequence. The *Ta'sīs* is written for a Ḥanafī disputant; and the only conceivable motive for disputation is that an opponent holds a juristic opinion contrary or contradictory to a Ḥanafī disputant's stance. This is the starting point of the *Ta'sīs*, and it is organized to provide greatest utility for the Hanafī. Note that one "side" of each of the eight divisions (*aqsām*) always contains a figure or group with whom a Ḥanafī might comfortably align, even when his opponent upholds a variant Ḥanafī stance.

In fact, no less than five of the eight *aqsām* of the *Ta'sīs al-Naẓar* comprise competing Ḥanafī opinions. This speaks volumes with regard to the role of juridical dialectic *within* doctrinal *madhāhib*, as well as between them. That is to say, it is plain that *jadal* was a significant dynamic in the internal, doctrinal development of the Ḥanafī *madhhab*—not merely "defense of the *madhhab*" polemic.

This is how the "location" system might have worked: First, although the *masā'il* of *ikhtilāf* are legion, there are still only so many variant opinions for each *mas'ala*, and the history of *ikhtilāf* has provided us with a stockpile of such variants and who held to them. So the first task of the Ḥanafī Q, once the *mas'ala* of the dispute is established, is to locate both his own, and his opponent's, stances from among what most resembles them from past opinions. For example, let us say that the *mas'ala* at hand considers the *mutayammim*[101] whose gaze, at the end of his prayer-cycle (*ṣalāt*), before the utterance of salaams (*taslīm*), falls upon a source of water he might have used for ablution (*wuḍū'*) had he seen it earlier. Is his *tayammum*-initiated prayer invalidated, or not? R says "No, his prayer is not invalid (*fāsid*)." Now Q—having a great storehouse of *masā'il* readily at hand, neatly memorized in the eight distinct compartments of the *Ta'sīs*—immediately accesses the proposition he requires for *elenchus*. For he recognizes R's stance to

[101] One performing pre-prayer ablutions with sand or earth. The verbal noun for this procedure is *tayammum*.

be that of both Abū Yūsuf and Muḥammad b. al-Ḥasan, and his own to be that of Abū Ḥanīfa.

In other words, once Q has obtained R's thesis, he will go immediately to compartment #1 of his storehouse of *masāʾil al-khilāf* and extract the key premise which, combined with the particulars of the case at hand, necessarily produces the contradictory (*naqīḍ*) of his opponent's stance. This key premise is called an *aṣl*, and, in this case, it is: "whatever alters a textually-fixed obligation (*farḍ*) at its initial stage of performance, also alters it at its concluding stage (*mā ghayyara al-farḍ fī awwalihi, ghayyarahu fī ākhirihi*)."[102]

Now Q must embark upon the more difficult task of getting R to concede to this *aṣl*, and he might follow any of a number of paths to assure this. For example, he might ask R's opinion regarding a parallel case of fasting (*ṣawm*): Does drinking water at the beginning of the fast not invalidate it? Does drinking water near the end of the fast not invalidate it? Would you not agree, then, that what invalidates the fast at its beginning also invalidates it at its end? Whatever path Q decides to take, once he obtains R's concession to his *aṣl*-premise, he need only announce his *elenchus* in a form composed of elements conceded by R.

So what is an *aṣl*, as per the *Uṣūl* of al-Karkhī, the *Taʾsīs al-Naẓar* of al-Dabbūsī / al-Samarqandī, and like sources? It is nothing less than an *endoxon* legal premise which (1) the Ḥanafī disputant believes he might get his opponent to concede to; and which (2) produces—in juxtaposition with other professed or conceded premises—a ruling contradictory to that of his opponent, yet comfortably consistent with a Ḥanafī disputant's corpus of *fiqh*. In a simplified (and idealized) dialectical sequence, our example *masʾala* might appear as follows:

- **R [states his thesis]**: If a *mutayammim* does not see water until near the end of his prayer, his prayer suffices him—it is not invalid.
- **Q [having "located" his *aṣl*, elicits a component premise]**: But do you not opine (*a-lā tarā*) that, if he sees water at the beginning of his prayer, his prayer is invalid?
- **R**: Yes.
- **Q [introduces parallel case, in order to "veil" his *aṣl*]**: And do you not also opine that drinking water at the beginning of the fast invalidates it?
- **R**: Yes.
- **Q**: And would you not also say that drinking water near the end of the fast invalidates it?
- **R**: Yes.

(continued)

[102] *Taʾsīs al-Naẓar*, al-Mays ed., p. 13.

- **Q [elicits his *aṣl*]**: Would you not agree, then, that whatever alters a textually-fixed obligation (*farḍ*) at its initial stage of performance, also alters it at its concluding stage?
- **R**: Yes.
- **Q**: Then, in the case of the *mutayammim* who does not see water until near the end of his prayer, you are wrong to say his prayer is not invalid. Because if—as you concede—for any *mutayammim* who sees water at the beginning of his prayer, his prayer is invalid; and if–as you concede—whatever makes a textually-fixed obligation invalid at its initial stage of performance, also makes it invalid at its concluding stage; then, in this case, since the *mutayammim* sees water at the concluding stage of his prayer, you must also say that his prayer is invalid.

The nature of the *Ta'sīs*, in conjunction with what we know of Aristotelian dialectic, raises important possibilities which ought to be pursued.[103] Among questions for further investigation are the following: To what extent, after deeper analyses, can we claim a shared conception between the *uṣūl* of al-Karkhī, the *uṣūl* of the author(s) of the *Ta'sīs* and like works, and the *topoi* of Aristotle's *Topics*? And if these "*uṣūl*" works may in fact be considered the first of the Ḥanafī method (*ṭarīqa*) of *uṣūl al-fiqh*, then to what extent may we claim this tradition to have incorporated a patently Aristotelian dialectical episteme? Are the parallels we observe resultant of a direct application of the *Topics* to juridical argumentation, or simply a natural convergence of dialectical objectives? How do these convergences bear upon the developmental history of the term *aṣl/uṣūl*; and what other terms—besides *waḍʿ*, *mawḍiʿ*, and *ḥujja*—are shared by these early Ḥanafī "*uṣūl*" works and the Arabic translations of Aristotle?

What can be said at this point, and without hesitation, is that the *uṣūl* of al-Karkhī and of the author(s) of the *Ta'sīs* were recognized critical components of juridical dialectic. *Jadal*, in fact, is both the birthplace and raison d'être of these early Ḥanafī *uṣūl*. The authors themselves make this plain in their manifestos, organizing principles, and selection of *khilāf* material.

[103] Although he says nothing about dialectic *per se*, an important analysis of the "logic" of the *Ta'sīs al-Naẓar* may be found in Brannon Wheeler's *Applying the Canon in Islam* (pp. 132–50, "Logical Structure of the Opinions").

3.5 Premise-Principles of Legal Theory and Dialectic: The *Uṣūl al-Karkhī*

"Uṣūl" *as* Qawāʿid Fiqhiyya

As the *mutayammim* example shows, these early "*uṣūl*" were in fact the "induced general principles of derived law" (*qawāʿid fiqhiyya*) of later times.[104] Wolfhart Heinrichs noted this, and I would reproduce a few of his observations before proceeding to a brief review of relevant *uṣūl* put down by al-Karkhī. Discussing the origins of the *qawāʿid* literary genre, Heinrichs says:

> Historically, general rules can be found already strewn throughout early *furūʿ* works. They were first collected by Ḥanafīs like Abu'l-Ḥasan al-Karkhī (d. 340/952), but under the title of *uṣūl* rather than *ḳawāʿid*. (As a result, the term *aṣl* acquires, minimally, a fourfold meaning: (1) an act that has already been legally determined and now serves as a "model" for similar cases; (2) a scriptural pronouncement (Ḳurʾān or Ḥadīth) that is considered decisive for the legal determination of a given act; (3) a legal principle, under which several individual cases are subsumed; (4) a source of the law, such as the Ḳurʾān.) But this early start hardly bore fruit, and it is only around the 7th/13th century that all the legal schools began to produce books on *ḳawāʿid* (predominantly with this term in the title of their books), except (!) the Ḥanafīs.[105]

With regard to the practice of later jurists in their *qawāʿid* works, Heinrichs offers another important observation:

> The school-specific *ḳawāʿid* were collected from the *furūʿ* works or, where the imāms and other earlier authorities had not been explicit about their principles, were arrived at by induction from their *furūʿ* decisions (*ḳawāʿid istiḳrāʾiyya*). Ibn al-Wakīl (d. 716/1317) and Abū ʿAbd Allāh al-Maḳḳarī (d. 758/1357) are said to have done their own *istiḳrāʾ* of the major Shāfiʿī and Mālikī sources respectively...

Although this latter observation has less bearing on the current discussion, a parallel concern will surface in the course of analyzing our subject-text. In short: as with induction of unspoken *qawāʿid* from the corpus of an early *mujtahid*'s doctrine, so too with the extraction of unrecorded argumentation behind an early *mujtahid*'s substantive rulings. That is to say, we are sometimes confronted in our analyses of the subject-text with plain substantive solutions unaccompanied by the arguments which produced them; although, in the main, I have only selected "overtly dialectical" material in which supporting arguments are laid bare. A jurist

---

104 Importantly, another sense of the term "*uṣūl*" in earlier legal literature has been noted by Hallaq ("Master Architect," pp. 588 ff.) In short, works of *uṣūl* ascribed to the third/ninth century were, in the main (if not entirely), works of derived law (*furūʿ*) and points of disagreement (*khilāfiyyāt*)–not legal theory (in the way of *uṣūl al-fiqh*).

105 Heinrichs continues: "This strange gap in the latter's record is probably not to be attributed to a loss of their works, because the Ḥanafī scholar, Ibn Nudjaym (d. 970/1562), complains about the fact that his school has nothing to compete with against the Shāfiʿīs in this respect—a situation that he tries to redress by writing a *ḳawāʿid* book on the model of the Shāfiʿī Tādj al-Dīn al-Subkī's (d. 771/1370) work." (*EI*^{2}, s.v. "*Ḳawāʿid Fiḳhiyya*"; parentheses are Heinrichs'; references have been ommited).

thoroughly trained in the *fiqh* of venerated exemplar *mujtahids* might be able to accurately reconstruct the arguments of such predecessors when they do not appear in our text. We have recourse—when faced with plain solution-statements—to the works of later jurists like al-Ṭabarī (*Ikhtilāf al-Fuqahā'*) and al-Sarakhsī (*Mabsūṭ*), which sometimes supply the arguments missing from our subject-text. It is possible these arguments were supplied through a process of extraction—similar to the induction of later *qawāʿid* works; but it is also possible that al-Ṭabarī and al-Sarakhsī had recourse to sources which are no longer extant.[106]

Relevant Premise-Principles from the Uṣūl al-Karkhī

The entirety of al-Karkhī's *uṣūl* were patently meant to play a role in *ijtihād*; thus, they are all principles belonging to the science of *ijtihād*: the developing *ʿilm uṣūl al-fiqh*, which, in al-Karkhī's day, attained its first full-system phase. A certain number of these *uṣūl* are of special note, for they are explicitly oriented towards step-by-step procedures for "drawing indication" (*istidlāl*) and "objection" (*iʿtirāḍ*)—in other words, they are dialectical-procedural *uṣūl*. Moreover, there is at least one *aṣl*—noted by Miller[107]—which is unambiguously oriented to the Q&A procedure of juridical *jadal*. These are important, for they predate the bulk of our extant *jadal* and *uṣūl* theory treatises by a 100 years, and provide a glimpse at early fourth/tenth century developments.

Whatever the exact thrust of a particular *aṣl*, they are, all of them, useful premises for the Ḥanafī dialectician. It is quite obvious that al-Karkhī—like al-Dabbūsī after him—did not intend his collection of *uṣūl* only for the jurist labouring in private; al-Karkhī's *uṣūl* are also—and sometimes explicitly—for the jurist engaged in dialectical disputation. I have extracted such *uṣūl* as appear most relevant to *ijtihād*ic and dialectical concerns in the following table, that we might assess something of the flavour of dialectic in al-Karkhī's time:[108]

[106] I have been asked why we would not assume later authors invented arguments to fill in unexplained lacunae in a founding *mujtahid*'s earlier doctrine. In answer, I would stress the likelihood that—whatever the motive—arguments and proofs would nevertheless have been back-projected by jurists who were themselves *engaged in dialectic*. That is to say: if the argument was not in fact drawn from an older text (lost to us, but known to the citing jurist's dialectical opponent), and if it was not in consonance with the (largely consistent) methods and principles of legal reasoning known to have been practiced by the founding *mujtahid* to whom it was attributed (thus opening the way to charges of inconsistency), then the attribution itself would not likely have survived the heat of subsequent dialectical encounter—whether within or between doctrinal *madhāhib*. A jurist, in other words, could not simply invent an argument dissonant with the accepted methodology of a founding *mujtahid*, and then expect to attribute the same to that *mujtahid*; it is most likely the arguments which al-Ṭabarī, al-Sarakhsī, et al., conveyed from older authorities were either carefully reconstructed / extracted "in the way of" such authorities, or simply transmitted from older materials or teachings still available to them (and to their dialectical opponents).

[107] "Islamic Disputation Theory," p. 95 and n. 18.

[108] al-Karkhī, *Uṣūl*, ʿInāyat Allāh ed., pp. 314–17; cf. al-Mays ed., pp. 152–6.

Explicitly *Uṣūl al-Fiqh* and *Jadal*-Oriented *Uṣūl* from the *Uṣūl al-Karkhī*	
28—Principle: every [Qur'ānic] verse contradicting the doctrine of our [Ḥanafī] companions is made to bear abrogation [by another verse] or preponderance [of intension]. And the superior solution is that it be made to bear preponderating exegesis, with regard to bringing them into conformity.[109]	28- الْأَصْلُ أَنَّ كُلَّ آيَةٍ تُخَالِفُ قَوْلَ أَصْحَابِنَا فَإِنَّهَا تُحْمَلُ عَلَى النَّسْخِ أَوْ عَلَى التَّرْجِيْحِ وَالْأَوْلَى أَنْ تُحْمَلَ عَلَى التَّأْوِيْلِ مِن جِهَةِ التَّوْفِيْقِ
29—Principle: every *khabar*-report coming in contradiction to the doctrine of our [Ḥanafī] companions is made to bear abrogation or being opposed by its like [in epistemic valuation]; then one proceeds to another *dalīl*-indicant, or a [mode of] preponderance for it—by what our companions draw argumentative support from among the modes of preponderance. Or it is made to bear harmonizing [exegesis]. And [all] that is only performed in accordance with establishing the *dalīl*-indicant. If indication of abrogation is established, it is made to bear it; and if indication is established for something else, we proceed to that.	29- الْأَصْلُ أَنَّ كُلَّ خَبَرٍ يَجِيْءُ بِخِلَافِ قَوْلِ أَصْحَابِنَا فَإِنَّهُ يُحْمَلُ عَلَى النَّسْخِ أَوْ عَلَى أَنَّهُ مُعَارَضٌ بِمِثْلِهِ ثُمَّ يُصَارُ إِلَى دَلِيْلٍ آخَرَ أَوْ تَرْجِيْحٍ فِيْهِ بِمَا يَحْتَجُّ بِهِ أَصْحَابُنَا مِن وُجُوْهِ التَّرْجِيْحِ أَوْ يُحْمَلُ عَلَى التَّوْفِيْقِ وَإِنَّمَا يُفْعَلُ ذَلِكَ عَلَى حَسَبِ قِيَامِ الدَّلِيْلِ فَإِنْ قَامَتْ دَلَالَةُ النَّسْخِ يُحْمَلُ عَلَيْهِ وَإِنْ قَامَتِ الدَّلَالَةُ عَلَى غَيْرِهِ صِرْنَا إِلَيْهِ
30—Principle: when a *ḥadīth* is cited on the authority of a Companion in contradiction to the doctrine of our [Ḥanafī] companions... If it is not in fact valid, we are sufficed by providing its proper rebuttal. But if it is valid in its citation, mention of its [relevant principles] has preceded [in our discussions]—but the best of modes and most distant from sophisms is: when a *ḥadīth* of a Companion is cited for something besides a locus of consensus, it is made to bear preponderating exegesis, or counter-indication between him and a Companion of his like [in epistemic authority].	30- الْأَصْلُ أَنَّ الْحَدِيْثَ إِذَا وَرَدَ عَنِ الصَّحَابِيِّ مُخَالِفًا لِقَوْلِ أَصْحَابِنَا فَإِنْ كَانَ لَا يَصِحُّ فِي الْأَصْلِ كُفِيْنَا مُؤْنَةَ جَوَابِهِ وَإِنْ كَانَ صَحِيْحًا فِيْ مَوْرِدِهِ فَقَدْ سَبَقَ ذِكْرُ أَقْسَامِهِ إِلَّا أَنَّ أَحْسَنَ الْوُجُوْهِ وَأَبْعَدَهَا عَنِ الشُّبَهِ أَنَّه إِذَا وَرَدَ حَدِيْثُ الصَّحَابِيِّ فِيْ غَيْرِ مَوْضِعِ الْإِجْمَاعِ أَنْ يُحْمَلَ عَلَى التَّأْوِيْلِ أَوْ الْمُعَارَضَةِ بَيْنَهُ وَبَيْنَ صَحَابِيٍّ مِثْلِهِ
31—Principle: when [the case] concludes by way of *ijtihād*, it is not cancelled by *ijtihād* of its like [in epistemic valuation], but it is cancelled by way of univocal text [from Qur'ān, Sunna, or Consensus].	31- الْأَصْلُ أَنَّه إِذَا مَضَى بِالِاجْتِهَادِ لَا يُفْسَخُ بِاجْتِهَادٍ مِثْلِهِ وَيُفْسَخُ بِالنَّصِّ
32—Principle: univocal text requires determination of occasioning factor by way of the ruling of another [text], not by way of its own ruling.	32-الْأَصْلُ أَنَّ النَّصَّ يَحْتَاجُ إِلَى التَّعْلِيْلِ بِحُكْمِ غَيْرِهِ لَا بِحُكْمِ نَفْسِهِ
33—Principle: one draws distinction between the occasioning factor of the ruling and its rationale; for indeed its occasioning factor is a compelling agency, while its rationale is not a compelling agency.	33- الْأَصْلُ أَنَّه يُفَرَّقُ بَيْنَ عِلَّةِ الْحُكْمِ وَحِكْمَتِهِ فَإِنَّ عِلَّتَهُ مُوْجِبَةٌ وَحِكْمَتَهُ غَيْرُ مُوْجِبَةٍ

(continued)

[109] A fitting definition for *tawfīq* is found in Sānū's *Muʿjam* (s.v. التوفيق): "Binding together (*al-tarābuṭ*) and combination (*al-jamʿ*); making two opposing indicants (*al-dalīlayn al-mutaʿāriḍayn*) to be in conformity with one another (*mutawāfiqayn*). And such is through rejecting their mutual incompatibility (*dafʿ taʿāriḍihimā*), and the elimination of the *ikhtilāf* between them by some mode of preponderating exegesis (*taʾwīl*), such as limiting the unrestricted (*taqyīd al-muṭlaq*), and particularizing the general (*takhṣīṣ al-ʿāmm*); and this *tawfīq* is [also] called *jamʿ* (combination)."

35—Principle: when a novel case occurs, and the interpreter finds neither proper answer nor parallel case in the books of our [Ḥanafī] companions, he must rationally infer its answer from something else: whether from the Qur'ān, or from the Sunna, or something else from what is strongest [in epistemic valuation]—then he will not transgress the ruling of these *uṣūl*.	35- الْأَصْلُ أَنَّ الْحَادِثَةَ إِذَا وَقَعَتْ وَلَمْ يَجِدِ الْمُؤَوِّلُ فِيْهَا جَوَابًا وَنَظِيْرًا فِيْ كُتُبِ أَصْحَابِنَا فَإِنَّهُ يَنْبَغِيْ لَهُ أَنْ يَسْتَنْبِطَ جَوَابَهَا مِن غَيْرِهَا إِمَّا مِنَ الْكِتَابِ أَوْ مِنَ السُّنَّةِ أَوْ غَيْرَ ذَلِكَ مِمَّا هُوَ أَقْوَى فَالْأَقْوَى فَإِنَّهُ لَا يَعْدُوْ حُكْمَ هَذِهِ الْأُصُوْلِ
36—Principle: when the expression conveys two intensions, one of which is more perspicuous than the other, and the other more concealed; the perspicuous is more authoritative than the concealed.	36- الْأَصْلُ أَنَّ اللَّفْظَ إِذَا تَعَدَّى مَعْنَيَيْنِ أَحَدُهُمَا أَجْلَى مِنَ الْآخَرِ وَالآخَرُ أَخْفَى فَإِنَّ الْأَجْلَى أَمْلَكُ مِنَ الْأَخْفَى
37—Principle: it is allowed that the first part of the [Qur'ānic] verse be taken as general in scope and the latter part as particular.	37- الْأَصْلُ أَنَّهُ يَجُوزُ أَنْ يَكُونَ أَوَّل الآيَة عَلَى العُمُومِ وآخِرُهَا عَلَى الخُصُوصِ
38—Principle: when two attempts at harmonizing exegesis meet and mutually oppose, but one of them leaves the two expressions in the originally-coined intension, it is superior.	38- الْأَصْلُ أَنَّ التَّوْفِيْقَيْنِ إِذَا تَلَاقَيَا وَتَعَارَضَا وَفِيْ أَحَدِهِمَا تَرْكُ اللَّفْظَيْنِ عَلَى الْحَقِيْقَةِ فَهُوَ أَوْلَى

An *Aṣl* from the *Uṣūl al-Karkhī* Explicitly Oriented to *Jadal*-Procedure

34—Principle: when [Q] asks a question, [R] should not respond unreservedly and with full conveyance [of premises], but should examine [the question] and consider it divided into a single division, or two divisions, or [multiple] divisions. Then he should confront word after word, for each division; then array his rebuttal according to what the question yields to him. The benefits of this principle are many; because when he unreservedly delivers up his speech, it may be swiftly undone—for how infrequently does the expression run the course of its general scope!	34- الْأَصْلُ أَنَّ السَّائِلَ إِذَا سَأَلَ سُؤَالًا يَنْبَغِيْ لِلْمَسْئُوْلِ أَنْ لَا يُجِيْبَ عَلَى الْإِطْلَاقِ وَالْإِرْسَالِ لَكِنْ يَنْظُرُ فِيْهِ وَيَتَفَكَّرُ أَنَّهُ يَنْقَسِمُ إِلَى قِسْمٍ وَاحِدٍ أَوْ إِلَى قِسْمَيْنِ أَوْ أَقْسَامٍ ثُمَّ يُقَابِلُ فِيْ كُلِّ قِسْمٍ حَرْفًا فَحَرْفًا ثُمَّ يُعَدِّلُ جَوَابَهُ عَلَى مَا يَخْرُجُ إِلَيْهِ السُّؤَالُ وَهَذَا الْأَصْلُ تَكْثُرُ مَنْفَعَتُهُ لِأَنَّهُ إِذَا أَطْلَقَ الْكَلَامَ فَرُبَّمَا كَانَ سَرِيْعَ الِانْتِقَاضِ لِأَنَّ اللَّفْظَ قَلَّمَا يَجْرِيْ عَلَى عُمُوْمِهِ

These *uṣūl* appear all the more remarkable when compared with the domains of drawing indication (*istidlāl*) and objection (*iʿtirāḍ*) of our lens-text authors. The first four *uṣūl* above (28–31) conform to concerns of *istidlāl* and *iʿtirāḍ* in four domains of our *jadal*-theory texts, in precisely the same order of appearance: Qur'ān (*Kitāb*); Sunna; Decree of a Solitary Companion (*Qawl al-Wāḥid min al-Ṣaḥāba*); and *Qiyās* (here: *ijtihād*).[110] Each of these in turn contain references to methods and techniques specifically related in our lens-texts for these domains: for *Kitāb*: abrogation (*naskh*), preponderance (*tarjīḥ*), and preponderating exegesis (*ta'wīl*); for Sunna: *naskh*, counter-indication (*muʿāraḍa*), and *tarjīḥ*; for *Qawl al-Wāḥid min al-Ṣaḥāba*: *ta'wīl* and *muʿāraḍa* (by conveyance of *khilāf* from another Companion); and for *Ijtihād*/*Qiyās*: "counter-indication by way of divinely-

[110] NB: al-Shāfiʿī refers to *ijtihād* and *qiyās* as "two names for a single *maʿnā*-intension" (*Risāla*, Shākir ed., p. 477, §1323-4).

sanctioned decree" (*muʿāraḍa bi'l-nuṭq*; here: cancellation by way of *naṣṣ*). Although simplistic in comparison with the extraordinary refinement of our lens-texts, there is a remarkable consonance between these *uṣūl* of al-Karkhī and the techniques of *istidlāl* and *iʿtirāḍ* of al-Shīrāzī, al-Bājī, et al. Moreover, these four *uṣūl* reflect procedural considerations of dialectic; i.e., step by step instructions for responding to an opposing *dalīl*-indicant brought by an opponent.

Al-Karkhī's *uṣūl* 32–3 and 35–8 are of equal use in the procedures of private *ijtihād* and in the real-time *istidlāl* of disputation; and they reflect a variety of techniques from the nascent systematization of *uṣūl al-fiqh*. Al-Karkhī's *uṣūl* appear to be on the threshold between proto-system legal theory and full systematization, and were compiled by an author living at the time the first full systems were said to be developed (al-Karkhī is a contemporary of the students of Ibn Surayj). His *aṣl* #34, however, is of greatest interest for the current project. The procedural guidelines provided by this *aṣl* find a number of parallels in our lens-texts wherever R's economy in response is cautioned. The motive for this is made plain in the *aṣl* itself, and suggests, among other things, that a respondent might avoid falling victim to a questioner's sophistical *elenchus* via the "many questions" fallacy.[111]

Overall, al-Karkhī's *uṣūl* provide testimony to a nascent (early fourth/tenth century) systematization of juridical *jadal* which again—in combination with my analyses in Chaps. 5 and 6—makes a fifth/eleventh century juridical take over from theologians untenable. The picture of a far more organic continuity of juridical *jadal* teaching and practice—from the earliest proto-systems (as observed in the *Umm*), to the earliest extant procedural systematizing (as in the *uṣūl* of al-Karkhī), and onwards to the earliest extant full-system treatises (al-Baṣrī, al-Shīrāzī, et al.)—is beginning to emerge. This natural evolution unfolded in tandem with the evolution of theological *jadal*; and the two branches—heavy laden with prior argumentation epistemes and newer Islamic axioms—enjoyed cross-germination throughout every stage of their respective evolutions.

References

Abū Zayd, Bakr b. ʿAbd Allāh. *Madkhal al-Mufaṣṣal li-Madhhab al-Imām Aḥmad*. 2 vols. Riyadh: Dār al-ʿĀṣima, 1997.

Afghānī = Abū Yūsuf, Yaʿqūb b. Ibrāhīm. *Ikhtilāf Abī Ḥanīfa wa Ibn Abī Laylā* [= Shaybānī Version]. Ed. Abū l-Wafāʾ al-Afghānī. Cairo: Maṭbaʿat al-Wafāʾ, 1357/1939.

Aristotle. *Topics. Books I and VIII, with Excerpts from Related Texts*. Trans., Intro. and Commentary by Robin Smith. Oxford: Clarendon Press, 1997.

Calder, Norman. *Studies in Early Muslim Jurisprudence*. Oxford: Clarendon Press, 1993.

al-Dabbūsī, Abū Zayd. *Kitāb Ta'sīs al-Naẓar*; with the *Risālat Abī al-Ḥasan al-Karkhī fī'l-Uṣūl allatī ʿalayhā Madār Furūʿ al-Ḥanafiyya; maʿa Shawāhidihā wa-Naẓāʾirihā li-Abī Ḥafṣ ʿUmar al-Nasafī*. Ed. Khalīl al-Mays. Beirut: Dār al-Fikr, 1979.

[111] See the discussion of this fallacy at the end of the following chapter.

EI^2 = *Encyclopaedia of Islam, Second Edition*. Ed. P. Bearman; Th. Bianquis; C.E. Bosworth; E. van Donzel; and W.P. Heinrichs. Brill Online, 2014 <http://referenceworks.brillonline.com/entries/encyclopaedia-of-islam-2>

El Shamsy, Ahmed. "Al-Shāfiʿī's Written Corpus: A source-Critical Study." *Journal of the American Oriental Society* 132.2 (2012), pp. 199–220.

Hallaq, Wael. "On Dating Mâlik's Muwaṭṭa'." *UCLA Journal of Islamic and Near Eastern Law* 1:1 (2001–02): pp. 47–65.

Hallaq, Wael. *The Origins and Evolution of Islamic Law*. Cambridge; New York: Cambridge University Press, 2005.

Hallaq, Wael. "Was al-Shāfiʿī the Master Architect of Islamic Jurisprudence?" *International Journal of Middle East Studies* 25 (1993), pp. 587–605.

Ḥassūn = al-Shāfiʿī, Muḥammad b. Idrīs. *Mawsūʿat al-Imām al-Shāfiʿī: al-Kitāb al-Umm*. 2nd ed. Ed. Aḥmad Badr al-Dīn Ḥassūn. 16 Pts. in 10 Vols. Beirut: Dār Qutayba, 2003.

Hava, J.G. *Al-Farā'id Arabic English Dictionary*, 5th ed. Beirut: Dār al-Mashriq, 1982.

Ibn Khaldūn. *Muqaddima*. Ed. Khalīl Shaḥāda. Beirut: Dār al-Fikr, 2001. [Translation by Franz Rosenthal: *The Muqaddimah : an Introduction to History*. 2nd Ed. 3 vols. London: Routledge & Kegan Paul, 1967].

al-Karkhī, Abū al-Ḥasan. *Uṣūl al-Karkhī maʿa Dhikr Amthilatihā wa Naẓā'irihā wa Shawāhidihā min al-Imām Najm al-Dīn Abī Ḥafṣ ʿUmar b. Aḥmad al-Nasafī*. [Printed in al-Bazdawī, ʿAlī b. Muḥammad. *Uṣūl al-Bazdawī: Kanz al-Wuṣūl ilā Maʿrifat al-Uṣūl*. Ed. ʿIṣmat Allāh ʿInāyat Allāh. Karachi: Maṭbaʿat Jāwīd Barīs, n.d.: pp. 308–17.]

al-Karkhī, Abū al-Ḥasan. *Risālat Abī al-Ḥasan al-Karkhī fi'l-Uṣūl allatī ʿalayhā Madār Furūʿ al-Ḥanafiyya; maʿa Shawāhidihā wa-Naẓā'irihā li-Abī Ḥafṣ ʿUmar al-Nasafī*. [Printed in al-Dabbūsī, Abū Zayd. *K. Ta'sīs al-Naẓar*. Ed. Khalīl al-Mays. Beirut: Dār al-Fikr, 1979: pp. 143–57.]

Lane, Edward William. *An Arabic-English Lexicon*. 8 vols. Beirut: Librarie du Liban, 1968.

Lowry, Joseph. "The Legal Hermeneutics of al-Shāfiʿī and Ibn Qutayba." *Islamic Law and Society* 11:1 (2004): pp. 1–41.

Sānū, Quṭb Muṣṭafā. *Muʿjam Muṣṭalaḥāt Uṣūl al-Fiqh, ʿArabī-Inkilīzī*. Beirut: Dār al-Fikr al-Muʿāṣir, 2000.

Schacht, Joseph. *The Origins of Muhammadan Jurisprudence*. Oxford: Oxford University Press, 1950.

Sezgin, Fuat. *Tārīkh al-Turāth al-ʿArabī*. [Vol. I, Pt. 3: "*al-Fiqh*"]. Trans. Maḥmūd Fahmī Ḥijāzī. Qum: Maktabat Āyat Allāh al-ʿUẓmā al-Marʿashī al-Najafī al-ʿĀmma, 1983-. [An Arabic translation of Sezgin's *Geschichte des Arabischen Schrifttums*, 12 vols. Leiden: E :J. Brill, 1967-].

al-Shāfiʿī, Muḥammad b. Idrīs. *Kitāb Ikhtilāf Abī Ḥanīfa wa Ibn Abī Laylā* [= *Umm* Version]. In *idem, Mawsūʿat al-Imām al-Shāfiʿī: al-Kitāb al-Umm* (2nd ed.) Ed. Aḥmad Badr al-Dīn Ḥassūn. Beirut: Dār Qutayba, 2003, vol. 9, pt. 14, pp. 7–235.

Shākir = al-Shāfiʿī, Muḥammad b. Idrīs. *Al-Risāla*. Ed. Aḥmad Muḥammad Shākir. Cairo: Maṭbaʿat Muṣṭafā al-Bābī al-Ḥalabī, 1940.

Wheeler, Brannon M. *Applying the Canon in Islam: The Authorization and Maintenance of Interpretive Reasoning in Ḥanafī Scholarship*. Albany: State University of New York Press, 1996.

Yahia, Mohyddin. *Šāfiʿī et les Deux Sources de la Loi Islamique*. Turnhout: Brepols, 2009.

Young, Walter Edward. "The Dialectical Forge: Proto-System Juridical Disputation in the Kitāb Ikhtilāf al-ʿIrāqiyyīn." 2 vols. PhD diss., McGill University, 2012.

Chapter 4
The Full-System *Jadal* Theory of the Lens-Texts

4.1 Selecting the Lens-Texts: A Brief Justification

The greater part of our lens for analyzing the dialectical material of the subject-text will be fashioned from the following primary treatises: (1) the *Book of Correlational Inference Consonant to God's Law* (*Kitāb al-Qiyās al-Sharʿī*) of Abū al-Ḥusayn Muḥammad al-Baṣrī (Muʿtazilī-Ḥanafī; d.436/1044); (2) the *Disputation Aid* (*Maʿūna fi'l-Jadal*) of Abū Isḥāq Ibrāhīm al-Shīrāzī (Shāfiʿī; d.476/1083); and (3) the *Method for Ordering Dispute* (*Minhāj fī Tartīb al-Ḥijāj*) of Abū al-Walīd Sulaymān al-Bājī (Mālikī; d.474/1081). I will briefly survey the contents and organizing principles of these texts in the following sections; my present task is to relate my reasons for relying chiefly upon them. My primary motive stems from the provenance and relatively early date of these treatises: they represent juridical *jadal* theories taught at the geographical heart of Islamicate civilization in the first half of the fifth/eleventh century.[1] These three works are among the earliest extant treatises dedicated specifically to juridical *jadal*-theory which have been edited and published.[2]

These are not the only relevant texts to survive from the classical period, however, which brings me to the secondary motives prompting my primary reliance upon al-Baṣrī, al-Shīrāzī, and al-Bājī: their well-ordered arrangement, concision

[1] And not only in the heartlands, but in Andalusia, due to al-Bājī's return to his homeland and subsequent 40 years of scholarship there.

[2] See the references at the end of this section for a list of editions. Notably, the *Epitome on Dialectical Disputation* (*Mulakhkhaṣ fi'l-Jadal*) of al-Shīrāzī has also survived, but—though edited by Muḥammad Yūsuf Ākhund Jān Niyāzī in his 1986 MA thesis (Umm al-Qura University)—it remains unprinted. Fortunately, al-ʿUmayrīnī makes frequent reference to a manuscript witness of the *Mulakhkhaṣ* found in the collection of the Great Mosque at Ṣanʿāʾ; he supplemented the *Maʿūna* from its passages wherever he deemed it lacking. I have, moreover, recently acquired the first volume of Niyāzī's thesis, and will make frequent reference to it with regard to al-Shīrāzī's exposition on *qiyās*.

W.E. Young, *The Dialectical Forge*, Logic, Argumentation & Reasoning 9,
DOI 10.1007/978-3-319-25522-4_4

of presentation, and clarity of explanation—in a word: their accessibility. The *Sufficient [Manual] for Disputation* (*Kāfiya fi'l-Jadal*) of Abū al-Ma'ālī 'Abd al-Malik al-Juwaynī, Imām al-Ḥaramayn (Shāfi'ī; d.478/1085) is a thorough tome representing an "Eastern" teaching of juridical dialectic.[3] I have, however, found it more challenging to navigate and interpret.[4] The *Book of Disputation According to*

[3] It must be acknowledged that attribution of the *Kāfiya* to al-Juwaynī has been contested by Daniel Gimaret. His argument (*La doctrine d'al-Ash'arī*, p. 183, n. 2.) is brief, and may be presented in full: « Qui n'est probablement pas Ǧuwaynī, contrairement à ce qu'assure l'éditeur [Fawqiya Ḥusayn Maḥmūd]. J'en vois pour preuves—outre le fait que ce titre n'apparaît nullement dans les bibliographies de l'Imam—les deux définitions de *naẓar* (§44) et de *'ilm* (§64), totalement différentes de celles du *Šāmil* pour l'un (éd. Frank 4,5), de l'*Iršād* pour l'autre (7,4). Dans l'*Iršād* (7,6-7 et 11-14), Ǧuwaynī rejette explicitement la définition aš'arienne du *'ilm* reprise dans la *Kāfiya*. Un autre indice dans le même sens me paraît être l'absence, dans la *Kāfiya*, de toute mention de Bāqillānī, si souvent cité tant dans le *Šāmil* que dans le *Burhān*. » On the whole, though Gimaret has certainly sustained the possibility of a different author through these indicants, I do not believe they amount to a probability. With regard to the absence of mention of the *Kāfiya* in bio-bibliographical works: this is no proof at all, especially when we consider that al-Juwaynī is supposed to have authored so many works that al-Subkī (in his *Ṭabaqāt*) proclaimed: "the abundance of his literary production could be explained only by a miracle" (cited in the *EI*[2], s.v. "al-Djuwaynī"). The same applies for the absence of mention of al-Bāqillānī in the *Kāfiya*: it does not constitute, in my opinion, a pointer in either direction. And as for the differing definitions cited by Gimaret, I would note the following: (1) variant definitions are not proofs of different authorship, as we must allow that a scholar will rethink and reformulate his/her opinions over time (see Fischer, *Historians' Fallacies*, pp. 199f., where the author discusses a variant of the "Idealist Fallacy," concluding: "Surely many thinkers have been *in*consistent within their own limits... presumption of logical consistency is as unjustified as a presumption of the opposite"); (2) the *Irshād* and the *Shāmil* are theological works, while the *Kāfiya* is a work of distinctly juridical *jadal*, and we will soon see proofs that al-Juwaynī understood variant epistemological first principles for theology and law (acknowledging, *inter alia*, a difference between "rational causes" [*'ilal 'aqliyya*] and "legal causes" [*'ilal shar'iyya*]); (3) al-Juwaynī's definition for "intellectual investigation" (*al-naẓar*) in his *Waraqāt fī Uṣūl al-Fiqh* (al-Qāsimī and al-Balkhī ed., p. 46)—"it is thinking about the condition of the object of investigation" (*huwa al-fikr fī ḥāl al-manẓūr fīhi*)—is in full consonance with the definition and arguments in the *Kāfiya*—indeed, in the *Kāfiya* the author argues *against* two opinions which seek to distinguish *naẓar* from "thinking" (*fikr*) (pp. 16–18, §§44–46); and (4) al-Juwaynī's definition for "knowledge" (*al-'ilm*) in his *Waraqāt* (op. cit.)—"cognition of the object of knowledge according to what it, in reality, *is*" (*ma'rifat al-ma'lūm 'alā mā huwa bihi fi'l-wāqi'*)—is, again, in full consonance with his definition and arguments in the *Kāfiya*—in the latter, he in fact links *'ilm* and "cognition" (*ma'rifa*) more than once in his arguments against opposing positions (pp. 25–7, §§64–5). With regard to points (3) and (4), Gimaret does not treat the author's full discussions with their arguments; and, adding to these points the various inter-textual references in the *Kāfiya* (which, in the main, seem to point to al-Juwaynī's *Burhān*), I stand by the editor of the *Kāfiya* (Maḥmūd) in attributing this work to al-Juwaynī.

[4] For this reason I have largely abandoned the *Kāfiya* in favour of my three primary treatises. The *Kāfiya* is referenced more frequently in my dissertation, though primarily in reviewing Miller's observations and assessments. Notably, al-Juwaynī also composed a detailed *Burhān fī Uṣūl al-Fiqh*. Tāj al-Dīn al-Subkī (d.771/1369) apparently found it so difficult to work with that he gave it the appellation "*Laghz al-Umma*" ("Riddle of the Muslim Community;" see the entry on al-Juwaynī in the *EI*[2]). If this renowned Shāfi'ī scholar found the *Burhān* inaccessible, then my own difficulties in navigating al-Juwaynī's *Kāfiya fi'l-Jadal* may be thrown into a new light; Miller, too, appears to have concentrated his efforts in just a few of the more clearly organized pages of the *Kāfiya*.

the Method of the Jurists (*Kitāb al-Jadal fī Ṭarīqat al-Fuqahā'*) of Abū al-Wafā' ʿAlī b. ʿAqīl (Ḥanbalī; d.513/1119), although more accessible than al-Juwaynī's *Kāfiya*, is less so than my primary treatises; it is less organized, often terse in presentation, and tends to duplicate a significant amount of material (definitions, explanations, and example-*masā'il*) found in the *Maʿūna* of al-Shīrāzī (one of Ibn ʿAqīl's teachers).[5] Finally, all of the *jadal*-theorists mentioned thus far were—in addition to master dialecticians in their own right and not merely theorists—the authors of seminal works in legal theory (*uṣūl al-fiqh*). The dynamic symbiosis of juridical dialectic and legal theory will only become clearer as we proceed, and nowhere is this more evident than in the persons of the theorists themselves.

It should also be clear that the above do not constitute the earliest systematization of juridical dialectic; they represent, rather, what is extant of early texts dedicated solely to *jadal* theory and procedure. There are reports of earlier works (e.g., the early fourth/tenth century *jadal* treatise of Abū Bakr Muḥammad al-Shāshī)[6] which appear to be lost. Moreover, and as we have seen in the *Uṣūl* of al-Karkhī and the *Ta'sīs al-Naẓar* of al-Samarqandī/al-Dabbūsī, systematic material for *jadal*-theory may be found in works predating those of our lens-texts by as much as a century and more. In particular, one would expect to find chapters relevant to juridical *jadal* in the earliest full-system treatises on legal theory—just as we find them in al-Baṣrī's *Muʿtamad* and many later works on *uṣūl al-fiqh*. Again, there are reports of earlier, lost works (e.g., the *uṣūl* treatises of the students of Ibn Surayj, al-Shāshī among them). Two extant and published works, however, have arisen as candidates for the extraction of systematic *jadal* material predating al-Baṣrī.

The first is the fourth/tenth century *Fuṣūl fi'l-Uṣūl* of Abū Bakr Aḥmad al-Rāzī al-Jaṣṣāṣ (Ḥanafī and student of al-Karkhī; d.370/981). It is a compendious and thorough tome of *uṣūl al-fiqh* from a mere generation or two after the first full-system treatises are reported to have been written, and from a generation or two before al-Baṣrī wrote his *Muʿtamad*. Moreover, it is extant, has been published in more than one edition, and contains material directly relevant to the concerns of juridical dialectic. Isolating and analyzing this material, however, constitutes another—though very worthwhile—project on its own. As for the second candidate, it is the so-called *Uṣūl al-Shāshī* which some attribute—mistakenly, I believe—to another student of al-Karkhī: Abū ʿAlī al-Shāshī (Ḥanafī; d.344/955). In fact, this appears to be a much later work; and, although rich in *jadal*-theory—especially

[5] For these reasons, Ibn ʿAqīl has mostly been relegated to footnotes in the following discussions and analyses. A brief disclaimer: my primary reliance upon the three works of al-Baṣrī, al-Shīrāzī, and al-Bājī in no way suggests that those of al-Juwaynī, Ibn ʿAqīl, et al., are less important or inferior—they exhibit every quality of sophistication and erudition, and are fully deserving of detailed study.

[6] Known as al-Qaffāl al-Kabīr (d.336/947), he was a Shāfiʿī and student of Ibn Surayj.

with regard to disputation in the domain of *qiyās*—I have abandoned it as a source with regard to the current study.[7]

Thus, and for all the reasons cited above, this chapter will deal mostly with the specialized *jadal*-theory treatises of al-Baṣrī, al-Shīrāzī, and al-Bājī. My objective is to fashion an analytical lens composed from the terms and categories employed by *jadal* theorists from the early era of *jadal* systematization. It will soon be apparent that these three works are well-suited to the task.

4.2 Categories of Epistemic Justification: Drawing Indication (*Istidlāl*)

At the center of any juridical-dialectical disputation lies the opposing position's legal solution, as reached—normatively—through the most vigorous of inquiries (*ijtihād*). It is no surprise, therefore, that the more complete *jadal* theory texts of al-Shīrāzī, al-Bājī, et al., first present systematic overviews of the various domains of epistemic justification by which the products of *ijtihād* are both presented and defended in disputation: the categories of "drawing indication," or *istidlāl*.[8] These opening chapters are essentially primers in applied legal theory (*uṣūl al-fiqh*), and follow the hierarchical ordering of the authoritative source materials (*uṣūl*) themselves. By way of illustration I will outline the presentations of al-Shīrāzī and al-Bājī.

---

[7] A full argument, drawing largely upon the anachronistic references noted by Muḥammad Akram al-Nadwī in his edition of the *Uṣūl al-Shāshī*, may be read in my dissertation (pt. 1, pp. 93–7). My reasoning there serves as part of my argument against Calder's post-dating of the *Umm* corpus. In short, the text of the *Uṣūl al-Shāshī* contains unambiguous anachronisms providing clear indicants that it cannot be ascribed to Abū ʿAlī al-Shāshī (or at least not in its entirety). Calder's arguments, on the other hand, rest on no such unambiguous bases—they rely upon textual features which are equivocal of interpretation and not at all self-evident. His arguments therefore produce no more than a possibility, whereas the anachronisms of the *Uṣūl al-Shāshī* (the equal of which are not found in the *Umm*) make its ascription to a later generation probable.

[8] See al-Shīrāzī, *Maʿūna*, al-ʿUmayrīnī ed., pp. 26–39; al-Bājī, *Minhāj*, Turkī ed., pp. 15–33, §§19–63; Ibn ʿAqīl, *K. al-Jadal*, pp. 3–13, §§10–65. Al-Juwaynī's approach varies significantly from that of al-Shīrāzī and his students, and appears to be based upon a variant organizing principle. He begins with a protracted discussion of definitions—beginning with the definition of "definition" (*ḥadd*) itself—for terms one is likely to encounter in discourse on legal theory and disputation (*Kāfiya*, pp. 1–73, §§4–176); the ordering principle is quite difficult to determine at times, and he even includes definitions for substantive legal categories (e.g., for ritual purity). He proceeds to an exposition on *jadal* and its types of dialectical questions, with yet more definitions (pp. 73–87, §§177–94), and eventually reaches the various means of deriving rulings (*aḥkām*). After this, discussions are wide ranging and interspersed with species of objection (*iʿtirāḍ*)—with special focus on *qiyās*-oriented dialectical moves. Although al-Shīrāzī (in his *Mulakhkhaṣ*, not his *Maʿūna*) and al-Bājī in his *Minhāj* both open with definitions and the dialectical questions, they are at once far more concise, clear, and orderly.

Before doing so, I must draw attention to the centrality of *ijtihād*—of its epistemic justification via *istidlāl*, and the larger science of *uṣūl al-fiqh* which underpins them both—to the overall enterprise of juridical dialectic. The hierarchic domains for "drawing indication" constitute the very organizing principle for all systematic elaborations of dialectical theory; and, considering that these very domains for the right-derivation of legal solutions were developed and refined in dialectical venues from the start, we should not be surprised. The dynamic symbiosis shared by *jadal* and *uṣūl al-fiqh* is writ large in the composition and contents of our lens-texts.

Al-Shīrāzī's Hierarchy of Modes for Drawing Indication (Istidlāl)

The *Chapter on Explaining the Modes of Indicants of God's Law* (*Bāb Bayān Wujūh Adillat al-Sharʿ*) of al-Shīrāzī's *Maʿūna fi'l-Jadal* is logically organized by domains for *istidlāl*, and each category and sub-category is accompanied by definitions, examples, and procedural norms. The whole is outlined in the following table, according to al-Shīrāzī's first-tier ordering of the Indicants of God's Law (*Adillat al-Sharʿ*), by *Aṣl* (divinely-sanctioned source-case), *Maʿqūl Aṣl* (what is rationally understood from an *aṣl*), and *Istiṣḥāb Ḥāl* (presumption of continuity of a legal *status quo ante*).

Aṣl (Divinely-Sanctioned Source-Case)

***Kitāb* ("the Book," i.e., the Qur'ān)**[9]

- *al-Naṣṣ* (the Univocal Text): "the expression (*lafẓ*, pl. *alfāẓ*) which bears no more than a single intension (*maʿnā*)"
  - its methodological norm (*ḥukm*): "It is brought to bear, and not abandoned except for such *naṣṣ*-text as counter-indicates it (*yuʿāriḍuhu*)"
- *al-Ẓāhir* (the Apparent): "every *lafẓ*-expression which may possibly bear two injunctions (*amrayn*), but is, regarding one of them, more apparent (*aẓhar*)"
  - *Ẓāhir bi-Waḍʿ al-Lugha* (Apparent by Way of the Posited Intension of the [Arabic] Language)[10]

(continued)

[9] al-Shīrāzī, *Maʿūna*, al-ʿUmayrīnī ed., pp. 27–9. Only al-Shīrāzī's categories, definitions, and procedural norms will be presented in this table, though many of the *istidlāl*-relevant concepts and terms playing a role in subsequent analyses are adequately explained in this manner. For the most part, his examples, additional explanations, and discourses on variant opinions are not provided here.

[10] Examples include (1) the injunction (*amr*) which may possibly bear obligation (*ījāb*) or recommendation (*nadb*), but is "more apparent" (*aẓhar*) as regards obligation; and (2) the proscription (*nahy*) which may possibly bear prohibition (*taḥrīm*) or reprehension (*karāha*) and abstention (*tanzīh*), but is "more apparent" as regards prohibition.

- its methodological norm (*ḥukm*): "It is linked with the more apparent (*aẓhar*) of the two *maʿnā*-intensions, and is not linked with something else—except by way of an indicant (*dalīl*)"
  - *Ẓāhir bi-Waḍʿ al-Sharʿ* (Apparent by Way of the Posited Intension of God's Law)[11]
    - its *ḥukm*: "It is linked with such as has been transferred to it in God's Law, and is not linked with something else—except by way of a *dalīl*-indicant"
- *al-ʿUmūm* (the General): "every *lafẓ*-expression which subsumes (*ʿamma*) two things or more in a singular mode (*ʿalā wajh wāḥid*), there being no priority for one of them over the other"[12]
  - its *ḥukm*: "Such *alfāẓ*-expressions are linked to the general (*al-ʿumūm*), and nothing of [the general] is particularized—except by way of a *dalīl*-indicant"

Sunna (The Prophet's Instruction and Exemplary Conduct)[13]

- *Qawl* (Saying [of the Prophet])
  - *Mubtadaʾ* (Self-Initiated; Unprompted)[14]
    - *al-Naṣṣ*: [as with the Qurʾān, and bearing the same methodological norm]
    - *al-Ẓāhir*: [as with the Qurʾān, and bearing the same methodological norm]
    - *al-ʿUmūm*: [as with the Qurʾān, and bearing the same methodological norm]
  - *Khārij ʿalā Sabab* (Proceeding from a Reason; Prompted)[15]
    - Type 1: *Mustaqill dūna al-Sabab* (Standing Alone Without the Reason)[16]
      - [as with the modes of unprompted saying, and bearing the same methodological norms]

(continued)

[11] Examples include such nouns as acquire a more technical legal meaning than that of their origins in common language, such as prayer (*ṣalāt*) and pilgrimage (*ḥajj*).

[12] The four *alfāẓ*-expressions of this category are listed as: (1) plural nouns; (2) definite singular nouns; (3) demonstrative pronouns; and (4) negative constructions with indefinite nouns.

[13] al-Shīrāzī, *Maʿūna*, al-ʿUmayrīnī ed., pp. 29–33.

[14] Meaning, the Prophet's utterance did not come about due to a particular incident (e.g., the petitioning of a Companion).

[15] Meaning, the Prophet's utterance was in response to some external factor, and addresses it.

[16] al-Shīrāzī's example is a *qawl* of the Prophet who, having been informed he had performed ablutions (*wuḍūʾ*) from a polluted well, said: "Water is pure (*ṭahūr*), nothing pollutes it."

- Type 2: *Lā Yastaqillu dūna al-Sabab* (Not Standing Alone Without the Reason)[17]
  - [no methodological norm is mentioned]
- *Fi'l* (Deed [of the Prophet])
  - Type 1: "What he did in something besides a 'pious mode' (*'alā ghayr wajh al-qurba*), like walking and eating and other things"[18]
    - its methodological norm (*ḥukm*): "It indicates allowance (*al-jawāz*)"
  - Type 2: "What he did in a 'pious mode' (*'alā wajh al-qurba*)"
    - Type 1: "It is obeying a command (*amr*) [of God]"
      - its *ḥukm*: "So it is considered in the light of that command; if it was obligatory (*wājib*), then [the action] is obligatory; and if it was recommended (*nadb*), then it is recommended"
    - Type 2: "It is a clarification (*bayān*) of something ambiguous (*mujmal*)"
      - its *ḥukm*: "So it is considered according to the thing clarified (*mubayyan*); if it was obligatory (*wājib*), then [the action] is obligatory; and if it was recommended (*nadb*), then it is recommended"
    - Type 3: "It is self-initiated (*mubtada'*)"
      - Mode 1: "It necessitates obligation (*al-wujūb*)"
        - its *ḥukm*: "It is not directed at anything else—except by way of a *dalīl*-indicant"
      - Mode 2: "It necessitates recommendation (*al-nadb*)"
        - its *ḥukm*: "It is not directed at anything else—except by way of a *dalīl*-indicant"
      - Mode 3: "It is in the manner of suspension (*'alā al-waqf*) [between obligation and recommendation]"
        - its *ḥukm*: "It is not linked with either one of the two—except by way of a *dalīl*"
- *Iqrār* (Acknowledgement [of the Prophet])
  - Type 1: "[The Prophet] hears a saying and acknowledges it"
    - its *ḥukm*: "Its methodological norm is the [same as] the methodological norm of [the Prophet's] saying (*qawl*)"
  - Type 2: "[The Prophet] sees a man doing something and acknowledges it"

(continued)

[17] The example is a *qawl* of the Prophet who, when a Bedouin confessed to daytime sexual intercourse during Ramaḍān, replied: "Manumit a slave." Al-Shīrāzī explains: "And so the *qawl* of the Messenger becomes, along with the reason (*sabab*), like a single sentence: as though he said—upon him be peace—'When you have sexual intercourse; manumit.'"

[18] By the phrase *'alā ghayr wajh al-qurba*, we understand such acts as have no moral or religious significance; the aim of the act was not "nearness to God" (*qurba*).

  - its *ḥukm*: "Its methodological norm is the [same as] the methodological norm of [the Prophet's] deed (*fiʿl*)"

Ijmāʿ (Consensus)[19]

- [Definition]: "It is the agreement (*ittifāq*) of the scholars of the age (*ʿulamāʾ al-ʿaṣr*) on the ruling of the case (*ʿalā ḥukm al-ḥāditha*)"
  - Type 1: "What their *ijmāʿ* established by way of their all professing it"[20]
    - its *ḥukm*: "It is brought to bear, and practiced, and abandoning it is not allowed in any circumstance"
  - Type 2: "What was established by way of the saying (*qawl*) or deed (*fiʿl*) of one/some of them, and the silence (*sukūt*) of the remainder, despite the wide dissemination (*intishār*) of such [sayings or deeds] among them"
    - its *ḥukm*: "Such is an authoritative proof (*ḥujja*)"

***Qawl al-Wāḥid min al-Ṣaḥāba, idhā lam yantashir* (The Saying of a Solitary Companion when Not Widely Disseminated)**[21]

- Doctrine 1: "[Al-Shāfiʿī] professed, in his New Doctrine (*fiʾl-jadīd*), that such is not an authoritative proof (*ḥujja*)"
  - its *ḥukm*: "So according to this, [R] does not base an argument on it, but uses it to make one indicant preponderate over another (*yurajjaḥu bihi*)"[22]
- Doctrine 2: "[Al-Shāfiʿī] professed, in his Old Doctrine (*fiʾl-qadīm*): It is an authoritative proof (*ḥujja*)"
  - its *ḥukm*: "So according to this, [R] bases an argument on it, and it is advanced over correlational inference (*qiyās*)"[23]

---

[19] al-Shīrāzī, *Maʿūna*, al-ʿUmayrīnī ed., pp. 33–4.

[20] Examples include: "their *ijmāʿ* upon the allowance (*jawāz*) of commutation (*bayʿ*), partnership (*mushāraka*), speculative partnership (*muḍāraba*), etc."

[21] al-Shīrāzī, *Maʿūna*, al-ʿUmayrīnī ed., p. 34. Al-Shīrāzī earlier points out (pp. 26–7) that al-Shāfiʿī added this to the *uṣūl* in his Old Doctrine (*fiʾl-qadīm*). This is here confirmed.

[22] al-Shīrāzī notes: "One of our [Shāfiʿī] companions said: "[R] bases an argument upon it with a weak *qiyās*. But this is not correct."

[23] al-Shīrāzī asks: "But is the general (*ʿumūm*) to be particularized by way of [the saying of a solitary Companion]? Regarding this there are two approaches." He does not elaborate further here, but al-ʿUmayrīnī (p. 34, n. 5) fills in the gap from al-Shīrāzī's *Lumaʿ*: "One of [the two approaches] is that [the general] is indeed particularized by way of [the saying of a solitary Companion]—because if it is advanced over correlational inference (*qiyās*), then particularization of the general (*takhṣīṣ al-ʿumūm*) is all the more appropriate (*awlā*). [Note this as an *a fortiori* argument employed in a problem of legal theory]. And the second [approach]: [The general] is *not* particularized by way of [the saying of a solitary Companion], because [the Companions] used to return to the general (*ʿumūm*) and abandon what they were doing."

Maʿqūl Aṣl/Adillat al-Maʿqūl (What is Rationally Understood of the _Aṣl_/ The Indicants of What is Rationally Understood)[24]

Faḥwā al-Khiṭāb (the _A Fortiori_ Signification of the Instruction)[25]

- [Definition]: "[God, or the Prophet] clearly designates the greater (*aʿlā*) and [thus] draws attention to the lesser (*adnā*) [*a maiore ad minus*]. Or he cites the lesser and [thus] draws attention to the greater [*a minore ad maius*]"
  - its *ḥukm*: "And the ruling for this is the ruling of the textual designation"[26]

Dalīl al-Khiṭāb (the [Restrictive] Indicant of the Instruction)[27]

- [Definition]: "[God, or the Prophet] makes the ruling (*ḥukm*) contingent upon one of the properties of a thing, indicating that what goes beyond it is [to be judged by] its contradictory (*khilāf*)"[28]

(continued)

[24] Al-Shīrāzī begins by stating "the indicants of what is rationally understood [of the divinely-sanctioned source-cases] (*adillat al-maʿqūl*) are three," and he then lists the second-tier categories of *A Fortiori* Signification of the Instruction (*faḥwā al-khiṭāb*), [Restrictive] Indicant of the Instruction (*dalīl al-khiṭāb*), and Intension-Property of the Instruction (*maʿnā al-khiṭāb*). As al-ʿUmayrīnī notes (p. 35, n. 1), however, al-Shīrāzī—in his *Mulakhkhaṣ fi'l-Jadal*—states that the *adillat al-maʿqūl* are four, and among them lists *laḥn al-khiṭāb*. This he defines as "the unspoken element (*ḍamīr*) without which the discourse (*kalām*) is not completed." In other words, it refers to such a locution from which an element has been omitted, but which is arguably understood to include that element. A common example is when God says, in Q.12:82: «Ask the village (*wa is'al al-qaryata*),» meaning: "the folk of the village (*ahl al-qarya*)" (see al-Shīrāzī, *al-Lumaʿ*, Mustū ed., pp. 104–5, §114). As we shall see, al-Bājī treats *laḥn al-khiṭāb* as a category of *maʿqūl al-aṣl*.

[25] al-Shīrāzī, *Maʿūna*, al-ʿUmayrīnī ed., p. 35. Note that al-Bājī also calls *faḥwā al-khiṭāb* by the following: "what is understood of the instruction" (*mafhūm al-khiṭāb*), and "self-evident appeal" (*al-tanbīh*); and that he says: "This is what al-Shāfiʿī calls 'clearly-disclosed correlational inference' (*al-qiyās al-jalī*)" (*Minhāj*, Turkī ed., p. 24, §45). Cf. Hallaq on *a fortiori* arguments in general, and *al-qiyās al-jalī* in particular (*History*, pp. 96–9, 102–3, 105).

[26] Meaning, the ruling for the greater is transferred to the lesser in the *a maiore ad minus* case; and from the lesser to the greater in the *a minore ad maius* case.

[27] al-Shīrāzī, *Maʿūna*, Turkī ed., pp. 138–9, §18. Al-ʿUmayrīnī's diplomatic edition (p. 35) here suffers from a lacuna in the Gotha manuscript, observed and corrected in Turkī's critical edition (p. 136, and n. 1 for §18).

[28] Examples include God's decree, in Q.65:6: «And if they are pregnant, then pay maintenance (*nafaqa*) for them;» and the Prophet's decree: «Regarding such as are pasturing (*sāʾima*) of the sheep/goats there is alms tax (*zakāt*).» As for the first, it "provides indication that there belongs no maintenance to the one who is *not* pregnant;" and as for the second, it provides indication that "there is no alms tax for *other than* the pasturing sheep/goat." This matches well with al-Shīrāzī's definition; God makes His *ḥukm* contingent upon the property (*waṣf*) of "pregnant," and thus indicates that what goes beyond this ("not pregnant") occasions the opposite *ḥukm*; and the Prophet makes his *ḥukm* contingent upon the property of "pasturing," and thus indi-

Maʿnā al-Khiṭāb, fa-huwa al-Qiyās (Intension-Property of the Instruction—meaning Correlational Inference)[29]

- [Definition]: "It is the linking of a branch-case (*farʿ*) with a source-case (*aṣl*) by way of an occasioning factor (*ʿilla*) uniting them (*jāmiʿa baynahumā*), and the application (*ijrā'*) of the ruling (*ḥukm*) of the source-case to the branch-case"
  - Type 1: *Qiyās al-ʿIlla* (Correlational Inference of the Occasioning Factor)
    - [Definition]: "The branch-case (*farʿ*) is linked with the source-case (*aṣl*) by way of the intension-property (*maʿnā*) upon which the ruling (*ḥukm*) is made contingent in God's Law (*Sharʿ*)"
  - Type 2: *Qiyās al-Dalāla* (Correlational Inference of Indication)
    - [Type I *Qiyās al-Dalāla*]
      - [Definition]: "[R] draws indication[30] for [the contended case] by way of one of the special characteristics of a thing (*bi-khaṣīṣa min khaṣā'iṣ al-shay'*)"[31]

(continued)

cates that what goes beyond this ("not pasturing") occasions the opposite *ḥukm*. Importantly, al-Shīrāzī cites Abū al-ʿAbbās b. Surayj—a most important figure in the early systematization of both *uṣūl al-fiqh* and *jadal*—reporting his saying: "What goes beyond the mentioned thing (*mā ʿadā al-madhkūr*) does *not* provide indication for a *ḥukm*." This sounds as though Ibn Surayj denied the argumentative conclusiveness of *dalīl al-khiṭāb*; and al-Shīrāzī makes his disagreement plain, saying: "And the *madhhab*-doctrine is the first" (i.e., al-Shīrāzī's methodological norm is correct). However, when we read al-Shīrāzī's citation of Ibn Surayj in the *Lumaʿ*, we find that Ibn Surayj denied the argumentative conclusiveness of *dalīl al-khiṭāb* only when the *khiṭāb* (instruction) does not include a "conditional expression" (*lafẓ al-sharṭ*) (Mustū ed., p. 106). It would appear from the examples in the *Maʿūna* that the first ("*if* they are pregnant, *then* pay maintenance") would have enjoyed Ibn Surayj's sanction, but not the second.

[29] al-Shīrāzī, *Maʿūna*, Turkī ed., pp. 139–40, §19. The various modes of *qiyās* will be explored fully in a following section.

[30] The verb is استدل. The most literal (yet still idiomatic) rendering of this important technical term would be "to draw forth an indicant (*dalīl*)"—i.e., with regard to the legal problem at hand, and in order to derive or further support a solution.

[31] Al-Shīrāzī's example—along with al-Bājī's explanation and examples—confirms that "special characteristics" (*khaṣā'iṣ*) can include, among other things, an established *ḥukm* shared by *aṣl* and *farʿ*. This indicates that the *farʿ* shares the *ʿilla* which occasions that *ḥukm* in the *aṣl*. Sānū's definition of *qiyās al-dalāla* (*Muʿjam*, s.v. "قياس الدلالة") underlines three categories of uniting element (*jāmiʿ*), all of which provide indication (hence: "*dalāla*") that the *farʿ* shares the same *ʿilla* as the *aṣl*. First is when the uniting element is one of the properties inseparable from the *ʿilla* (*waṣf lāzim min lawāzim al-ʿilla*), e.g., the smell shared by grape-wine (*khamr*) and date-wine (*nabīdh*), providing indicant that date-wine shares the same *ʿilla*—namely, "it is an intoxicant." Note that "smell" is not efficient in occasioning the *ḥukm*, even though it is inseparable from the *ʿilla*. Second is when the uniting element is one of the effects of the *ʿilla* (*athar min āthār al-ʿilla*); e.g., the effect of "he commits a sin" shared between killing with a blunt instrument and killing with a cutting instrument—this provides indication that these cases share the same *ʿilla* occasioning the *ḥukm* of retaliation (*qiṣāṣ*). Note once again that "he commits a sin" is not efficient in the *ʿilla*

- [Type II *Qiyās al-Dalāla*]
  - [Definition]: "[R] draws indication for a parallel (*naẓīr*) by way of [its] parallel"[32]
- [Type III *Qiyās al-Dalāla*] = *Qiyās al-Shabah* (Correlational Inference of Resemblance)
  - [Definition]: "[R] draws indication by way of a type of resemblance (*ḍarb min al-shabah*)"[33]

Istiṣḥāb al-Ḥāl (Presumption of Continuity of the Legal *Status Quo Ante*)[34]

Istiṣḥāb Ḥāl al-ʿAql fī Barāʾat al-Dhimma (Presumption of Continuity of a *Status Quo Ante* of Rational Intellection for Absolution from Obligation)

- [Examples]: "Like our doctrine regarding the elimination of the [obligation for] blood-money (*diya*), for the Muslim when he is killed in non-Muslim enemy territory (*Dār al-Ḥarb*); or the elimination of what exceeds a third of the blood-money for the killing of a Jew: the *status quo ante* (*al-aṣl*) is exemption from obligation (*barāʾat al-dhimma*), and a clean slate, and a path [cleared] of God's Law being involved with it (*farāgh*

(continued)

---

itself, but is merely one of its effects. Third is when the uniting element is one of the norms occasioned by the *ʿilla* (*ḥukm min aḥkām al-ʿilla*), e.g., the *ḥukm* of "blood-money (*diya*) is obliged (*wājib*) for it," shared by both the cutting of one hand (*aṣl*) and the cutting of both hands (*farʿ*); this provides indication that the *farʿ* shares the same *ʿilla* occasioning the *ḥukm* of retaliation (*qiṣāṣ*) in the *aṣl*. In other words, in this third case the "special characteristic" (*khaṣīṣa*) is the ruling "blood-money is obliged for it;" and the fact that the branch-case (cutting both hands) shares this ruling with the source-case (cutting one hand) provides a *dalīl*-indicant that it also shares the branch-case's (unidentified) *ʿilla*, which occasions the sought-after ruling obliging retaliation in the source-case, and thus—presumably—in the branch-case.

[32] As will be explained, al-Shīrāzī's examples make clear that "parallels" (*naẓāʾir*, s. *naẓīr*) are a special category of rulings, with regard to certain subjects, which appear to be twinned in God's Law. If we wish to determine whether ruling Y is obliged for subject B, we might reason: since, for subject A, whenever ruling X is obliged, ruling Y is also obliged, it is reasonable—knowing that X is obliged for subject B—that ruling Y should also be obliged for subject B.

[33] Meaning, by way of shared properties which may or may not be efficient, but—being shared—indicate a shared *ʿilla*. Al-Shīrāzī notes: "Among our [Shāfiʿī] companions are those who say: 'It is a *dalīl*-indicant.' And among them are those who say: 'It is not a *dalīl*-indicant, but indeed something else may be given preponderance by means of it' (*yurajjaḥu bihi ghayruhu*). And [this latter opinion] is the more correct (*al-aṣaḥḥ*)." As al-ʿUmayrīnī notes (p. 38, n. 3), al-Shīrāzī seems to have been more decisive elsewhere, claiming that *qiyās al-shabah* is not valid. Sānū (*Muʿjam*, s.v. "قياس الشبه") defines *qiyās al-shabah* as follows: "The joining (*ilḥāq*) of a *farʿ* to an *aṣl* due to the abundance of its resemblance (*li-kathrat shabahihi*) to the *aṣl* in terms of properties (*awṣāf*), without believing that the properties by which the *farʿ* resembles the *aṣl* constitute the *ʿilla* for the *ḥukm* of the *aṣl*."

[34] al-Shīrāzī, *Maʿūna*, Turkī ed., p. 141, §20.

*al-sāḥa wa ṭarīq ishtighālihā al-Shar*ʿ). For nothing is found in God's Law which provides indication of a concern for the killing of a Muslim in the *Dār al-Ḥarb*, nor of a concern for what exceeds a third [of the *diya*] for the killing of a Jew."
- its *ḥukm*: "So [the contended ruling] remains in the *status quo ante* (*fa-baqiya ʿalā al-aṣl*) [of exemption from obligation]. And this is a *dalīl*-indicant in which the qualified jurisprudent (*mujtahid*) takes refuge when there is a lack of [other] *adilla*-indicants."

Istiṣḥāb Ḥāl al-Ijmāʿ (Presumption of Continuity of a *Status Quo Ante* of Consensus)

- [Example]: "That is like [R's] saying, regarding one who did ablutions with sand/earth (*mutayammim*), when he [afterwards] sees water during his prayer-cycle (*ṣalāt*): 'Verily he proceeds with his prayer, because his prayer was legally effected (*inʿaqadat*), by authority of *Ijmāʿ*.'"
  - its *ḥukm*: "So one does not abandon that [*status quo ante* of consensus]—except by way of a *dalīl*-indicant. But regarding this there are two opinions..."
  - "Among our [Shāfiʿī] companions are those who say: It is a *dalīl*-indicant."
  - "But among them are those who say: It is not a *dalīl*-indicant. And [this latter opinion] is the more valid (*al-aṣaḥḥ*)."

I earlier described al-Shīrāzī's brief introduction to the domains of *istidlāl* as a primer in applied *uṣūl al-fiqh*. Rather, I should say (as al-Shīrāzī's chapter heading suggests) it is a primer in the *adilla*—the body of authoritative indicants confirmed, with some debate, in the Shāfiʿī *madhhab*[35]—with the more detailed epistemological, hermeneutical, rational-inferential, and practical concerns of *uṣūl al-fiqh* texts omitted. Most importantly, it illustrates al-Shīrāzī's organizing principle. Subsequent discussions of *iʿtirāḍ* (objection/critique) and *jawāb* (rebuttal/response) are arranged according to these domains of *istidlāl* in precisely the same order; and it is not difficult to ascertain the utility of such an arrangement to the dialectician in training. The domains of *istidlāl* thus presented constitute a parallel to Aristotle's *topoi*, and we may assume a parallel intention is at work.[36] In theory, the domains of *istidlāl* might act as a first rank of *topoi*: once Q has ascertained the domain of *istidlāl* by which R derived his solution to the legal problem (*mas'ala*) at

[35] As we shall see, al-Bājī's hierarchy of *istidlāl* treats additional categories current to the Mālikī *madhhab*—e.g., "the Consensus of the Medinese" (*Ijmāʿ Ahl al-Madīna*)—and problematizes other categories supported by his contemporaries and predecessors—including certain doctrines of his teacher, al-Shīrāzī.

[36] Acknowledging, of course, that the *topoi* are quite differently organized according to types of predicable.

hand, he may first "locate" the set of objections relevant to that domain. Having done so, he may proceed to further questions (all the while bearing in mind the premises necessary to his own solution), until he "locates" that specific species of objection by which he might attain *elenchus*. Whether Q's aim is problematizing and deconstructing R's solution, or forcing R's concession to his own solution, or first one then the other, the obvious starting place is identification of the domain—the *topos*—of R's *istidlāl*. Al-Shīrāzī's introductory *Chapter on Explaining the Modes of Indicants of God's Law* provides a logically-structured—and easily memorized—outline of starting points for the questioner in a dialectical investigation.

Al-Bājī's Hierarchy of Modes for Drawing Indication (Istidlāl)

Al-Bājī's *Minhāj fī Tartīb al-Ḥijāj* opens with a short justification for the work's composition—and for the study of *jadal*-theory in general[37]—before proceeding to a brief introduction to the comportment (*adab*) of the dialectician.[38] He then continues with a useful chapter on definitions, including most of the terms of *istidlāl* and *iʿtirāḍ* one is likely to encounter in juridical disputation: the *Chapter on Explanation of Definitions for Expressions Current Among Disputationists* (*Bāb Bayān Ḥudūd al-Alfāẓ al-Dāʾira bayn al-Mutanāẓirīn*).[39] After this we find his *Chapter on Divisions of the Indicants of God's Law* (*Bāb Aqsām Adillat al-Sharʿ*), which illustrates—like the *Bāb Bayān Wujūh Adillat al-Sharʿ* of his teacher—the organizing principle by which later chapters of objection and response are arranged.[40] A notable characteristic of the *Minhāj*, setting it apart from the *Maʿūna*, is its greater refinement of categories, more extended discussions of objection and response, and more thorough treatment of variant theories. In other words, the *Minhāj* is more in the way of a detailed exposition (*mabsūṭ*) than an abridgment (*mukhtaṣar*), and in this sense more comparable to al-Shīrāzī's *Mulakhkhaṣ fiʾl-Jadal* than to his *Maʿūna*.[41] This more detailed approach is just as apparent in al-Bājī's introduction to the

[37] *Minhāj*, Turkī ed., pp. 7–9, §§1–7.

[38] Ibid., pp. 9–10, §§8–13.

[39] Ibid., pp. 10–14, §§14–18. Notably, these definitions are roughly grouped in the order we usually find them in *uṣūl al-fiqh* treatises. Epistemological terms are first (e.g., *ḥadd*, *ʿilm*, *shakk*, etc.), followed by hermeneutical terms for Kitāb and Sunna (e.g., *naṣṣ*, *ẓāhir*, *naskh*, etc.), then definitions of norms (*wājib*, *jāʾiz*, *fāsid*, etc.), then *ḥadīth* transmission terms (*tawātur*, *āḥād*, *mursal*, etc.), then terms for *ijmāʿ*, *qiyās*, and various genera of *iʿtirāḍ*.

[40] Ibid., pp. 15–33, §§19–63.

[41] Al-Shīrāzī, in the opening section justifying his composing of the *Maʿūna* (al-ʿUmayrīnī ed., p. 26), describes his prior work, the *Mulakhkhaṣ fiʾl-Jadal*, as a *mabsūṭ*. This is why he composed the *Maʿūna*, as a primer for beginners, and a review for initiates. We will note that it is a far more abbreviated work than the *Minhāj*, not just in terms of the contents of chapters, but in the absence of chapters themselves. The *Maʿūna*, for example, treats neither proper comportment (*adab*), nor definitions, nor dialectical questions, but plunges straight into the domains of *istidlāl* outlined above, before proceeding directly to the identically-ordered domains of objections (*iʿtirāḍāt*).

aqsām adillat al-Sharʿ as it is in his later chapters on objections and responses. Still, his organizing principle is the same as al-Shīrāzī's, and we may assume the same intention—a first rank ordering of *topoi*—to be at work. Like his teacher, al-Bājī states his largest categories of Indicants of God's Law as *Aṣl* (divinely-sanctioned source-case), *Maʿqūl Aṣl* (what is rationally understood from an *aṣl*), and *Istiṣḥāb Ḥāl* (presumption of continuity of a legal *status quo ante*); a brief outline of these domains, however, will reveal the greater detail and refinements of the *Minhāj*.[42]

Aṣl (Divinely-Sanctioned Source-Case)

***Kitāb* ("the Book," i.e., the Qur'ān)**[43]

- Type 1: *Mufaṣṣal* (Unambiguous)[44]
  - *Ghayr Muḥtamal* (Unequivocal)[45]
    - *al-Naṣṣ* (the Univocal Text): "What is elevated in its explication (*bayān*) to the utmost of its intentions (*ilā abʿad ghāyātihi*)."
  - *Muḥtamal* (Equivocal)
    - Type 1: *al-Ẓāhir* (the Apparent): "Such as whose intension (*maʿnā*) arrives first, from its *lafẓ*-expression, to the understanding of one who hears it; and no obstacle (*māniʿ*), with reference to the *lafẓ*-expression, prevents him from knowledge/understanding (*ʿilm/fahm*) of it."[46]

(continued)

[42] For the most part, we will dispense with such definitions as have appeared in our outline of the *Maʿūna*, except where they differ from al-Shīrāzī's. Al-Bājī's examples, extended explanations, and reporting/refuting of variant opinions are also omitted from our outline, except where deemed necessary. Finally, a number of terms which have already appeared in the previous outline will not be translated here, but remain in transliteration.

[43] al-Bājī, *Minhāj*, Turkī ed., pp. 15–18, §§20–7.

[44] Al-Bājī provides no definition for *mufaṣṣal*—neither here, nor in his opening chapter on definitions. It is evident from his presentation, however, that *mufaṣṣal* is to be understood in contradistinction to "ambiguous" (*mujmal*). In other words, it is more or less synonymous with "explained" (*mufassar*), which he earlier defines (p. 12, §15) as: "Such as whose intended meaning (*al-murād bihi*) is understood from its *lafẓ*-expression, and does not require anything else for its explanation (*bayān*)." Moreover, the Ẓāhirī Ibn Ḥazm (d.456/1064), an Andalusian contemporary and frequent dialectical opponent of al-Bājī, provides a definition of *mufaṣṣal* in his *Precision in the Authoritative Source-Materials of Rulings* (*Iḥkām fī Uṣūl al-Aḥkām*) (Shākir ed., vol. 1, p. 48). It is: "Such as whose divisions (*aqsām*) are clarified (*buyyinat*); and it is, in original linguistic usage (*aṣl al-lugha*), such as part of which has been separated (*furriqa*) from another part—you say: I cut apart (*faṣṣaltu*) the garment, or the meat, etc." As the passive participle of Form II *faṣṣala*, *mufaṣṣal* also bears the sense of "that which is exposited in detail."

[45] Again, al-Bājī provides no definition for *muḥtamal*, but the meaning of "possibly bearing X" is easily inferred. That which may be classified as "univocal" (*naṣṣ*) does not "possibly bear" more than one interpretation, hence: "not possibly bearing" (*ghayr muḥtamal*). In contradistinction, that which is "apparent" (*ẓāhir*) or "general" (*ʿāmm*) may "possibly bear" more than one interpretation (hence: *muḥtamal*), but a primary meaning can be made to preponderate over others.

[46] Al-Bājī's definition for *ẓāhir* in §15 (with *fahm*) differs slightly from his definition here in §22 (with *ʿilm*).

- Type 1: *Ẓāhir bi'l-Waḍʿ* (Apparent by Way of the Posited Intension): "Every *lafẓ*-expression posited/coined (*wuḍiʿa*) in the [Arabic] language (*lugha*) with an intension (*maʿnā*), and employed according to what it was posited/coined for; like the injunctions and proscriptions of God's Law."
- Type 2: *Ẓāhir bi'l-ʿUrf* (Apparent by Way of Customary Usage)
  - Type 1: *Ẓāhir bi-ʿUrf al-Sharʿ* (Apparent by Way of the Customary Usage of God's Law): "Such *alfāẓ*-expressions as were posited/coined (*mawḍūʿa*) in the original linguistic sense (*aṣl al-lugha*) for a genus among genera, then were revealed in God's Law for a [more particular] *maʿnā*-intension from that very same genus"
  - Type 2: *Ẓāhir bi-ʿUrf al-Lugha wa'l-Istiʿmāl* (Apparent by Way of the Customary Linguistic and Practical Usage of the [Arabic] Language)[47]
- Type 3: *Ẓāhir bi'l-Dalāla* (Apparent by Way of Indication): "The *lafẓ*-expression is posited/coined (*mawḍūʿ*) for a *maʿnā*-intension, except the *dalīl*-indicant has established that some other *maʿnā*-intension is meant by it"

  - Type 2: *ʿĀmm; Lafẓ al-ʿUmūm* (General; Expression of the General): "every *lafẓ*-expression which subsumes (*ʿamma*) two things or more, there being no priority for one of them over the other"
    - *Lafẓ al-Jamʿ* (Expression of the Plural)[48]
    - *Lafẓ al-Jins* (Expression of the Genus)[49]
    - *al-Alfāẓ al-Mubhama* (Indeterminate Expressions)[50]
    - *al-Ism al-Mufrad idhā dakhala ʿalayhi al-alif wa'l-lām* (Definite Singular Nouns)[51]
    - *Alfāẓ al-Nafy* (Expressions of the Negative)[52]

(continued)

[47] Al-Bājī's example, "excrement" (*al-ghāʾiṭ*)—originally meaning "low ground used as a latrine" (see Lane, *Lexicon*, s.v. "غائط")—makes clear that this category comprises words which acquired a different meaning through customary usage. He concludes: "and it is obliged that one link it with [the acquired meaning], unless the *dalīl*-indicant provides indication that something else is intended by it."

[48] Examples are: "believers" (*al-muʾminīn*), "Muslims" (*al-Muslimīn*), etc.

[49] Examples are: "animal" (*al-ḥayawān*), "camel" (*al-ibil*), etc.

[50] Examples are: "who" (*man*), "what" (*mā*), "which" (*ayy*), "where" (*ayna*), and "when" (*matā*).

[51] Examples are: «*wa'l-sāriq wa'l-sāriqa*» (Q.5:38), "the male and female thief."

[52] Example: "There is no man in the house" (*lā rajul fi'l-dār*).

- *al-Muḍāf ilayhi* (Noun Governed by Genitive Construction)[53]
- Type 2: *Mujmal* (Ambiguous)[54] [not to be used for drawing indication]

Sunna (The Prophet's Instruction and Exemplary Conduct)[55]

- Type 1: *Aqwāl* (Sayings [of the Prophet])
  - Type 1: *Mubtada'* (Self-Initiated; Unprompted): "It is divided into that which the Qur'ān is divided into..."
    - *al-Naṣṣ*
    - *al-Ẓāhir*
      - *Ẓāhir bi'l-Waḍ'*
      - *Ẓāhir bi'l-'Urf*
        - *Ẓāhir bi-'Urf al-Shar'*
        - *Ẓāhir bi-'Urf al-Isti'māl fi'l-Lugha*
      - *Ẓāhir bi'l-Dalāla*
    - *al-'Umūm; al-'Āmm*
    - *al-Mujmal*
  - Type 2: *Khārij 'alā Sabab* (Proceeding from a Reason; Prompted)
    - Type 1: "It does not stand alone by itself without the reason (*sabab*), and so is restricted to its reason"[56]
    - Type 2: "What stands alone by itself, and has no need for a reason (*sabab*)"[57]

(continued)

[53] Examples include: "there is alms tax for the property of the Muslim" (*fī māl al-Muslim al-zakāt*). Al-Bājī concludes: "And these *alfāẓ*-expressions, when cited, are inked with their general sense (*'umūm*), and their rulings are applied to all that falls under them, unless a particularization (*takhṣīṣ*) is revealed by way of divinely-sanctioned decree (*nuṭq*) or rational inference (*istinbāṭ*)."

[54] Al-Bājī defines *mujmal* in his introductory chapter on definitions (p. 12, §15): "Such as whose *ma'nā*-intension is not understood from its *lafẓ*-expression, and so requires something else for its explanation." Here in this current section (p. 18, §27), he notes: "And as pertains to the Qur'ān there is a fourth type [i.e., after *naṣṣ*, *ẓāhir*, and *'āmm*] by which drawing indication (*istidlāl*) does not occur, but the Scholars of Dialectic (*Ahl al-Jadal*) have appended it to these three types. It is the "ambiguous" (*mujmal*), like His decree, Most High: «And render [unto him] his due (*ḥaqq*), on the day of his harvest» [Q.6:141]. For this is *mujmal*—there is understood from the apparent meaning (*ẓāhir*) of the *lafẓ*-expression neither the genus of the *ḥaqq*, nor its measure—so compliance with it is not possible, nor usage of it, except by means of something which ties it to something else explaining it."

[55] al-Bājī, *Minhāj*, Turkī ed., pp. 18–21, §§28–36.

[56] Having provided an example, al-Bājī concludes: "Thus, for this and what resembles it, there is no disagreement (*khilāf*) among our [Mālikī] companions that it is restricted to its reason (*sabab*), and no [*ḥukm*] is extended by way of it to anything else [besides its reason]."

[57] Al-Bājī reports: "And regarding this our [Mālikī] companions disagreed; for some of them said: 'It is restricted to its reason;' while [al-Qāḍī] Ismā'īl [Abū Isḥāq (Mālikī; d.282/895)] said: 'It is linked with its general sense (*'umūm*), and not restricted to its reason. And [this latter opinion] is the valid one (*al-ṣaḥīḥ*)." Turkī's footnote (p. 20, n.2) explains that the Qāḍī Ismā'īl is here being referenced.

- Type 2: *Afʿāl* (Deeds [of the Prophet])
  - Type 1: "It is a clarification (*bayān*) for something else"[58]
  - Type 2: "What appears self-initiated of his deed"
    - "such [of his deeds] as was in a 'pious mode' (*min al-qurb*)"[59]
    - "such [of his deeds] as was not in a 'pious mode'"[60]
- Type 3: *Iqrār* (Acknowledgement [of the Prophet]):
  - Type 1: "The Messenger of God... saw and acknowledged it"
    - "[the acknowledged] was a saying (*qawl*)"
    - "[the acknowledged] was a deed (*fiʿl*)"
  - Type 2: "What was done in his era, and was widespread to the extent that it was not possibly hidden from him"
  - [Fallacious Type]: "What was done in his time but most likely was not visible to him"[61]

***Ijmāʿ* (Consensus)**[62]

- [Definition]: "It is the consensus (*ijmāʿ*) of the folk of the age (*ahl al-ʿaṣr*) on the ruling of the case (*ʿalā ḥukm al-ḥāditha*)"[63]
- Type 1: "It is known by way of agreement (*ittifāq*)"
  - "Like when the scholar (*ʿālim*) professes a doctrine (*maqāla*), and it appears and is publicized to the extent that neither its appearance nor publication is hidden from us; moreover, there is no known disagreement (*khilāf*), or critique (*ṭaʿn*), or rebuttal (*radd*) from anyone

(continued)

---

[58] Al-Bājī explains: "Like his deeds (*afʿāl*) regarding prayer (*ṣalāt*), pilgrimage (*ḥajj*), etc., from among ritual observances (*ʿibādāt*) for which the revealed *lafẓ*-expression is ambiguous (*mujmal*)—according to the one who claims such. And what is of this species runs the same course with regard to obligation (*wujūb*) and recommendation (*nadb*) and permission/normative neutrality (*ibāḥa*) as that which was an explanation (*bayān*) for it."

[59] Al-Bājī notes disagreement: The predominant [Mālikī] opinion (*ẓāhir al-madhhab*) is that such a deed be linked with obligation (*wujūb*); "But among our [Mālikī] companions are those who say: 'It is [linked] with recommendation (*nadb*);' and among them are those who say: 'It is [linked] with suspension (*al-waqf*).'"

[60] Al-Bājī's examples are eating, drinking, and *bayʿ*-commutation. He concludes: "And this provides indication for permission/normative neutrality (*al-ibāḥa*)."

[61] Al-Bājī provides an example, then concludes: "And this provides indication for permission, but drawing argumentative support from it is not valid—because it is of the hidden matters (*umūr al-khafiyya*), and it is possible that the Prophet did not know of it."

[62] al-Bājī, *Minhāj*, Turkī ed., pp. 21–3, §§37–41. NB: at the start of his discussion of the *adillat al-Sharʿ*, al-Bājī lists this third *aṣl* as "Consensus of the Muslim Community" (*Ijmāʿ al-Umma*).

[63] Cf. al-Shīrāzī's definition, and note that al-Bājī states *Ahl al-ʿAṣr*, and not *ʿUlamāʾ al-ʿAṣr*. Although "folk" may have commonly referred to scholars—e.g., the "Ḥadīth Folk" (*Ahl al-Ḥadīth*)—perhaps this broader term facilitates al-Bājī's incorporation, as a subcategory, of the Mālikī "Consensus of the Medinese" (*ijmāʿ Ahl al-Madīna*).

regarding it. This is an *ijmāʿ* of the folk (*ahl*) of that era (*ʿaṣr*) upon the validity (*ṣiḥḥa*) of what he professed, and a contentment with it."[64]

- Type 2: "It is known by way of disagreement (*ikhtilāf*)"
  - "It is that the Companions were divided on two doctrines, there being no third, and no one else can invent a third doctrine"[65]
- Type 3: *Ijmāʿ Ahl al-Madīna ʿalā mā Ṭarīquhu al-Naql* (The Consensus of the Medinese on What was Conveyed by a Sound Transmission)"[66]
- [Problematic Type]: "Connected to this is the doctrine (*qawl*) of a [solitary] Companion when no opposing doctrine (*mukhālif*) is known; it is narrated on Mālik that it is an authoritative proof (*ḥujja*). But some of our [Mālikī] companions said: It is not a proof. And Abū Ḥanīfa said: When it goes against *qiyās*, it acts as a suspension (*tawqīf*)."

---

[64] Al-Bājī notes two opposing opinions: (1) that of Dāwūd (the famed *imām* of the Ẓāhirī school; d.270/883), who claimed *ijmāʿ* "is not a proof (*ḥujja*) except for the *ijmāʿ* of the jurists (*fuqahāʾ*) of the Age of the Companions, specifically, with the condition that the doctrine of all of them be manifest;" and (2) that of the Shāfiʿī jurist Ibn Abī Hurayra (a disciple of Ibn Surayj; d.345/956), who claimed that if the original doctrine gaining the sanction of *ijmāʿ* was uttered by an *imām* (in the sense of community leader), then it is not a proof (*ḥujja*), because it is possible that rebuttals were abandoned from fear of treason (*iftiyāt*) against him. Al-Bājī concludes by referring us to his work on *uṣūl al-fiqh* (Turkī, p. 22, n. 6, cites the *Iḥkām al-Fuṣūl*), wherein: "We have provided indicant for the nullification (*ibṭāl*) of that, all of it."

[65] Any third doctrine would be against their *ijmāʿ*, and would be null and void. Al-Bājī reports the variant opinion of the Ẓāhirīs and some Ḥanafīs—that bringing a third doctrine is allowed—and that he has explained its nullification (*ibṭāl*) in his *Kitāb al-Uṣūl* (meaning, his *Iḥkām*).

[66] Importantly, one of al-Bājī's examples reads: "Like that by which Mālik drew argumentative support against Abū Yūsuf in the disputation session (*majlis*) of [Hārūn] al-Rashīd, with regard to the 'problem (*mas'ala*) of the *ṣāʿ*-measure'. Abū Yūsuf recanted and submitted to the validity of the *ijmāʿ* of the Ahl al-Madīna for such as enjoys this manner of conveyance." He concludes, after a second example: "And this is a proof (*ḥujja*) obliging adherence to it, and performance (*ʿamal*) by way of it." Whether or not such a *majlis* took place—and, in the absence of evidence to the contrary, there is no reason to believe it did not—is irrelevant. Either way, it (1) supports a notion that early *jadal* theory (and in this case, *uṣūl* theory) was developed in part from an analysis of past juridical disputation; and (2) shows that, at least in this instance, dialectic was recognized by later theorists as fine-honing the argumentative conclusiveness of certain *uṣūl*. That is to say, Abū Yūsuf may first have generally rejected the argumentative conclusiveness of Consensus of the Medinese; but when confronted by Mālik, in dialectical disputation at the court of Hārūn al-Rashīd, he was unable to refute that subtype of Consensus of the Medinese whose method (*ṭarīq*) of conveyance was sound transmission (*naql*). Abū Yūsuf's concession is a prime illustration of a legal theory—an *aṣl*, in fact—gaining conclusiveness through dialectic. Whether or not such an event actually occurred, it is nevertheless important that al-Bājī references it in his *jadal*-theory treatise.

Maʿqūl al-Aṣl/Adillat al-Maʿqūl* (What is Rationally Understood of the *Aṣl*/The Indicants of What is Rationally Understood)

***Laḥn al-Khiṭāb* (the Unspoken Implication of the Instruction)[67]**

- [Definition]: "It is the implication of the omitted (*taqdīr al-maḥdhūf*)"[68]
  - Type 1: "The discourse (*kalām*) is not completed except by means of it"
    - Type 1: "The omission (*ḥadhf*) of the response (*jawāb*) when there is, in the discourse, what provides indication for it"[69]
    - Type 2: " The omission (*ḥadhf*) of the governing noun (*muḍāf*) and the standing of the governed noun (*muḍāf ilayhi*) in its place"[70]
  - Type 2: "The discourse (*kalām*) is completed without it"[71]

***Faḥwā al-Khiṭāb* (the *A Fortiori* Signification of the Instruction); *Mafhūm al-Khiṭāb* (What is Understood of the Instruction); *al-Tanbīh* (Self-Evident Appeal)[72]**

- [Definition]: "It is what the instruction (*khiṭāb*) indicates by way of self-evident appeal (*tanbīh*); that is, [God, or the Prophet] clearly designates the lesser (*adnā*) and [thus] draws attention to the greater (*aʿlā*) [*a minore ad maius*]. Or he cites the greater and [thus] draws attention to the lesser [*a maiore ad minus*]."

(continued)

[67] al-Bājī, *Minhāj*, Turkī ed., p. 24, §§43–4.

[68] The *Hans Wehr Dictionary of Modern Written Arabic* (4th ed., s.v. "تقدير") accurately locates *taqdīr* as a technical term of grammar, meaning: "implication of a missing syntactical part."

[69] Al-Bājī's first example is from Q.26:63: «[We revealed to Moses]: 'Strike the sea with your staff;' and it was split.» Al-Bājī explains: "So [Moses] struck, and it was split." The omission in the original is "so he struck;" God's discourse is thus incomplete without our assuming the unspoken response (*jawāb*) of Moses' action. We can, however, supply the omission for ourselves thanks to the indicants provided by the discourse (God's command to strike, coupled with the result of striking), and this is the nature of *laḥn al-khiṭāb*.

[70] Al-Bājī employs the same example as al-Shīrāzī (Q.12:82) in his *Mulakhkhaṣ fi'l-Jadal* (see the above note for al-Shīrāzī's hierarchy of *istidlāl*). Having confirmed that the *maʿnā*-intension of «Ask the village (*wa is'al al-qaryata*),» is in fact, "ask the folk of the village (*ahl al-qarya*)" al-Bājī concludes: "And this obliges its implication (*taqdīr*) in the instruction, so it is in the status of something spoken (*bi-manzilat al-manṭūq bihi*)." As a quick aside, note the formula "X is in the *manzila* of Y"; this is a very common expression in the *Umm* compendium, and I will draw attention to it in the analyses of the subject-text. In the realm of legal argument, I have termed it "*manzila*-subsumption."

[71] Al-Bājī's procedural norm: "the implication (*taqdīr*) of this [omission] is not allowed without a supporting *dalīl*-indicant [...] because the discourse is independent without the implication of an omission."

[72] al-Bājī, *Minhāj*, Turkī ed., p. 24, §45. Al-Bājī considers these terms synonymous. As noted above, he concludes: "And this is what al-Shāfiʿī calls *al-qiyās al-jalī*."

***al-Ḥaṣr* (Restriction)**[73]

- [Definition]: "It is a single *lafẓ*-expression: 'only' (*innamā*)"[74]

***Maʿnā al-Khiṭāb, fa-huwa al-Qiyās* (Intension-Property of the Instruction—meaning Correlational Inference)**[75]

- Type 1: *Qiyās al-ʿIlla* (Correlational Inference of the Occasioning Factor): "The branch-case (*farʿ*) is linked with the source-case (*aṣl*) by way of an occasioning factor established in God's Law (*ʿilla sharʿiyya*)"
  - Type 1: *Jalī* (Clearly-Disclosed)
    - "the *ʿilla* is made known by way of univocal source-text (*naṣṣ*)"
    - "the *ʿilla* is made known by way of consensus (*ijmāʿ*)"
  - Type 2: *Wāḍiḥ* (Plainly-Evident)
    - "established by a type of apparent meaning (*ẓāhir*) which is an attribute (*ṣifa*)"[76]
    - "established by a type of apparent meaning (*ẓāhir*) which is of general scope (*ʿumūm*)"
  - Type 3: *Khafī* (Latent)
    - "its *ʿilla* is known by way of rational inference (*istinbāṭ*)"[77]

(continued)

[73] al-Bājī, *Minhāj*, Turkī ed., pp. 25–6, §46.

[74] Al-Bājī's first example is the Prophet's saying: "Works are *only* by way of intentions (*innamā al-aʿmāl bi'l-niyyāt*)." He concludes: "And it is understood from this that it is not 'work' (*ʿamal*) when it is devoid of intention (*niyya*)." Importantly, he lists the *alfāẓ*-expressions which "Our Shaykh" Abū Isḥāq al-Shīrāzī considered to belong to the category of *al-ḥaṣr*: (1) "only" (*innamā*); (2) the definite article *alif* and *lām*; (3) "that" (*dhālika*); and (4) the genitive construction (*al-iḍāfa*). Al-Bājī disagrees, however, accepting only *innamā*, and directs us to his *uṣūl* work for a full explanation. He also cites an indication that Mālik held the *lām kay* (in the sense of "due to") to be a *lafẓ*-expression in this category of *Ḥaṣr*. Al-Bājī's referring the reader to another of his treatises for a more complete exposition, or argument, is also a frequent practice of al-Shāfiʿī in our subject-text. Such editorial comments are noteworthy; they reveal an intra-doctrinal consistency, and provide support for the "traditional status quo" of authorship and compilation.

[75] al-Bājī, *Minhāj*, Turkī ed., pp. 26–7, §§47–8.

[76] NB: al-Bājī's example is a variant of the Prophetic saying employed by al-Shāfiʿī in one of the dialectical sequences (§§248ff.) we will explore. This is an important indicant of continuity in *jadal* teaching and practice, from proto-system to full-system theory.

[77] Al-Bājī's example: "Like our doctrine, regarding the *ʿilla* for the proscription of grape-wine (*taḥrīm al-khamr*), that [the *ʿilla*] is 'euphoric intensity' (*al-shidda al-muṭriba*); and this is known by [the method of] 'negation and presence' (*al-salb wa'l-wujūd*). Which is to say that when 'euphoric intensity' is present in the grape-wine, proscription (*taḥrīm*) is established, and when it is absent proscription is absent; so the most apparent interpretation (*ẓāhir*) is that ['euphoric intensity'] is an *ʿilla* for [proscription]."

- Type 2: *Qiyās al-Dalāla* (Correlational Inference of Indication)
  - Type 1: "[R] draws indication, by way of confirming one of the rulings (*aḥkām*) of the *aṣl* in the *far*ʿ, for their equivalence (*tasāwīhimā*) regarding the contended norm (*al-ḥukm al-mukhtalaf fīhi*)"[78]
  - Type 2: "[R] draws indication, by way of confirming the parallel (*naẓīr*) of the contended ruling in the *far*ʿ, for [that ruling's] confirmation in the *far*ʿ"[79]
  - Type 3: *Qiyās al-Shabah* (Correlational Inference of Resemblance)[80]

"What is Connected to *Qiyās* in Terms of Modes of Drawing Indication (*Wujūh al-Istidlālāt*)"[81]

- Mode 1: *al-Istidlāl bi'l-Awlā* (Drawing Indication by way of *A Fortiori* Valuation): "[R] clarifies in the *far*ʿ the *ma*ʿ*nā*-intension upon which the *ḥukm* is made contingent in the *aṣl*, and an augmentation [of that *ma*ʿ*nā*-intension, in the *far*ʿ]"[82]

(continued)

[78] This definition not only confirms that shared rulings (*aḥkām*) may be among the *khaṣā'iṣ* of al-Shīrāzī's definition for Type I *qiyās al-dalāla* (see above), but that it might in fact be the prominent focus of this type of *qiyās*. Al-Bājī's definition, read in isolation, would bring one to infer the distinctive marker of this species of *qiyās* is the indicant provided by a shared *ḥukm*.

[79] Meaning, as *naẓā'ir* (parallels), a pair of rulings (*aḥkām*) preserve the same relationship for certain subjects in God's Law. See the note for al-Shīrāzī's Type II *qiyās al-dalāla*, above.

[80] See the note for al-Shīrāzī's Type III *qiyās al-shabah*, above.

[81] al-Bājī, *Minhāj*, Turkī ed., pp. 27–9, §§49–53. The importance of this appendix to al-Bājī's *qiyās* typology is self-evident. There is a patent overlap with the various modes of ʿ*illa*-justification outlined in *uṣūl al-fiqh* works, which are here presented as R's *istidlāl* in dialectical debate. This supports a theory of this monograph; mainly, that methods developed for private *ijtihād* were shaped in part by an anticipation of dialectical confrontation. The epistemes of *jadal*, in other words, show themselves a primary dynamic in shaping the epistemes of *uṣūl al-fiqh*. Al-Bājī notes: "The modes of drawing indication (*wujūh al-istidlālāt*) are many, but five modes are repeated and are most frequent among disputants." These he lists as above. Notably, al-Shīrāzī also discusses such species of *istidlāl* in his *Luma*ʿ, in the *Chapter on Categories of Correlational Inference* (*Bāb Aqsām al-Qiyās*). He begins by stating (Mustū ed., p. 210, §261): "And as for *istidlāl*, it branches out from what we have mentioned of the categories of *qiyās*. And it is according to types...." He then discusses: (1) *al-istidlāl bi-bayān al-*ʿ*illa* (two types; cf. al-Bājī above); 2) *al-istidlāl bi'l-taqsīm* (two types; cf. al-Bājī); and 3) *al-istidlāl bi'l-*ʿ*aks* (cf. al-Bājī). There is a more thorough treatment in al-Shīrāzī's *Mulakhkhaṣ*, which will be presented in Sect. 4.3.

[82] As the term *awlā* would indicate, al-Bājī's example reveals this species of *qiyās*-related *istidlāl* as an *a fortiori* argument. The rejection of the testimony (*shahāda*) of non-Muslim subjects (*Ahl al-Dhimma*) is justified in that: (1) the testimony of a profligate Muslim (*fāsiq*) is rejected due to his depravity (*fisq*); (2) it is known that the depravity of the non-Muslim (*kāfir*) is greater than the depravity of the Muslim [as it includes unbelief]; thus (3) it is confirmed that not accepting the testimony of the non-Muslim is both *awlā* (more fitting) and *aḥrā* (more appropriate). With the latter term (*aḥrā*), one might also define this species of *istidlāl* as an *a potiori* argument.

- Mode 2: *al-Istidlāl bi'l-Taqsīm* (Drawing Indication by way of Analytical Disjunction)[83]
  - Type 1: "[R] states the divisions (*aqsām*) of things upon which the opponent (*khaṣm*) can possibly make the *ḥukm* contingent, then clarifies the invalidity of all of them, and so establishes that truth (*ḥaqq*) lies in their contradictory (*khilāf*)"
  - Type 2: "[R] states the divisions (*aqsām*) of things upon which contingency (*taʿlīq*) of the *ḥukm* is possible, then clarifies the invalidity of all but one, and so establishes that truth (*ḥaqq*) lies in that one"
- Mode 3: *al-Istidlāl bi-Bayān al-ʿIlla* (Drawing Indication by way of Clarifying the Occasioning Factor)
  - Type 1: "[R] clarifies the *ʿilla* of the *ḥukm*, then draws indication—from its presence in the locus of disagreement (*mawḍiʿ al-khilāf*)—for confirmation of the *ḥukm* [therein]"
  - Type 2: "[R] clarifies the *ʿilla*, and draws indication from its absence [in the locus of disagreement] for the negation of the *ḥukm* [therein]"
- Mode 4: *al-Istidlāl bi-Shahādat al-Uṣūl* (Drawing Indication by way of Testimony of the Authoritative Source-Cases)[84]
- Mode 5: *al-Istidlāl bi'l-ʿAks* (Drawing Indication by way of the Opposite)[85]
- [Fallacious Categories of *Adillat al-Maʿqūl*][86]

[83] NB: this mirrors the *ijtihād*ic procedure of "examination and division" (*al-sabr wa'l-taqsīm*), as it appears in full-system *uṣūl al-fiqh* treatises. See Hallaq, *History*, p. 92.

[84] Al-Bājī's example clarifies this species of *istidlāl*: "It is like the *istidlāl* of the Mālikī against the Ḥanafī—with regard to the one who falsely accuses (*qadhafa*) his wife [of adultery], then irrevocably separates from her (*abānahā*), [and ought to] do the *liʿān*-procedure—that what Abū Ḥanīfa opined for this is the contradictory (*khilāf*) of the *uṣūl*. For [Abū Ḥanīfa] voided [the husband's] false accusation (*qadhf*), and obliged neither *ḥadd*-punishment nor *liʿān*-procedure for it. And this is the contradictory of the *uṣūl* because the *uṣūl* are clear (*mubayyana*) that there must be either the *ḥadd*-punishment or the *liʿān*-procedure for whomever falsely accuses a free, chaste woman."

[85] Al-Bājī's example does not at first shed much light on this mode of *istidlāl*. He says: "It is like the *istidlāl* of the Mālikī for [the ruling] that hair (*al-shaʿr*) does not become impure (*najas*) by way of death; indeed, if it became impure by death, then taking it while alive would not have been permitted, like the meat and the bones." The problem is that this example does not tell us the *ʿilla*. Reviewing another explanation from al-Bājī's *Iḥkām* (Turkī ed., vol. 2, p. 679, §736) renders the current example clear: "When [R] clarifies (*bayyana*) that the *ʿilla* for the prevention (*manʿ*) of the taking of an organ from an animal while alive is that the soul (*rūḥ*) is resident in that organ, and he provides indication of the contingency (*taʿalluq*) of that *ḥukm* on this *ʿilla*; it is permitted that he draw indication by means of that for the soul's *not* being resident in the hair—because if the soul was resident in it, then taking it while alive would have been forbidden, like [taking] the meat. And if it is allowed that the soul be resident in the hair, while taking it while alive is allowed, then the *ʿilla* which he appointed for the prevention of that would be destroyed (*intaqaḍat*)." Cf. Hallaq, *History*, p. 100, where he reviews the very same explanation from al-Bājī's *Iḥkām* in his discussion of *reductio ad absurdum* arguments under the rubric of *qiyās*.

[86] al-Bājī, *Minhāj*, Turkī ed., pp. 29–31, §§54–7. Al-Bājī explains: "What preceded was discourse regarding the types of valid indicants (*al-adilla al-ṣaḥīḥa*) from among the *adillat al-maʿqūl*.

Istiṣḥāb al-Ḥāl (Presumption of Continuity of the Legal _Status Quo Ante_)

Istiṣḥāb Ḥāl al-ʿAql (Presumption of Continuity of a _Status Quo Ante_ of Rational Intellection)[87]

- Type 1: "Presumption of continuity of a *status quo ante* for absolution from obligation (*barā'at al-dhimma*), and a clean slate (*khuluww al-sāḥa*), and a lack of God's Law compelling involvement of obligation (*ʿadam al-Sharʿ al-mūjib li-ishtighāl al-dhimma*)"
- Type 2: "Agreement (*ittifāq*) upon the measure of a right (*ḥaqq*) confirmed for obligation (*dhimma*), but disagreement (*ikhtilāf*) as to what exceeds that; the object of agreement is the *status quo ante* (*aṣl*), and the object of disagreement is a *farʿ* requiring a *dalīl*-indicant."[88]
- [Fallacious Categories of *Istiṣḥāb Ḥāl*][89]
  - *Istiṣḥāb Ḥāl al-Ijmāʿ* (Presumption of Continuity of a *Status Quo Ante* of Consensus)[90]
  - [other modes][91]

Discourse will now concern what is connected to them, but not of them." He then treats (and repudiates) a number of fallacious modes, *dalīl al-khiṭāb* among them (cf. al-Shīrāzī's hierarchy, in which *dalīl al-khiṭāb* is valid).

[87] al-Bājī, *Minhāj*, Turkī ed., p. 31, §§58. NB: at the start of his discussion of the *adillat al-Sharʿ*, al-Bājī lists this third domain as "Presumption of Continuity of a *Status Quo Ante* of Absolution from Obligation" (*Istiṣḥāb Ḥāl Barā'at al-Dhimma*).

[88] Al-Bājī's example *mas'ala* is the disagreement between the Mālikī (blood-money [*diya*] for a Zoroastrian is 800 dirhams) and the Ḥanafī (it is the same as the blood-money for a Muslim). The former argues: "What I have asserted is an object of agreement (*muttafaq ʿalayhi*), but what you have asserted is an augmentation (*ziyāda*); and the *status quo ante* (*aṣl*) for this is exemption from obligation (*barā'at al-dhimma*), so involving [obligation] requires a *dalīl*-indicant from God's Law." Al-Bājī concludes: "And the Disputation Theorists (*Ahl al-Jadal*) call this: 'That the *ḥukm* be determined by way of the lesser of what is professed (*an al-ḥukm bi-aqalla mā qīla*)."

[89] al-Bājī, *Minhāj*, Turkī ed., pp. 31–33, §§59–62.

[90] Al-Bājī provides no definition, but his example *mas'ala* is the same as al-Shīrāzī's, above. Al-Shīrāzī, as we have seen, was not a Shāfiʿī who subscribed to the validity of this species of *istiṣḥāb*.

[91] These include (1) the "Presumption of Continuity of a *Status Quo Ante* of Generality" (*Istiṣḥāb Ḥāl al-ʿUmūm*) professed by some Shāfiʿīs and Abū Bakr al-Bāqillānī (Mālikī, d.403/1013); (2) a mode of "*istidlāl* for the negation of something by way of the absence of a *dalīl*-indicant for it" attributed to al-Shāfiʿī himself; and (3) a mode attributed to some Ẓāhirīs, who claim "I am negating (*anā nāfin*), so furnishing a *dalīl*-indicant is not enjoined upon me; rather, the *dalīl* is only enjoined upon the one affirming (*al-muthbit*)."

This outline shows, more or less, the same hierarchy of authoritative indicants as al-Shīrāzī in his *Maʿūna* and elsewhere. Considering al-Shīrāzī was a teacher of al-Bājī's, we ought not be surprised. We may note, however, that such differences as do occur reflect not only al-Bājī's continued research and elaboration of theory-oriented argument—e.g., his disagreement with al-Shīrāzī regarding the *alfāẓ*-expressions of *istidlāl bi'l-ḥaṣr*—but "first principle" *madhhab*ic differences (Mālikī vs. Shāfiʿī) regarding primary *uṣūl*—e.g., al-Bājī's inclusion of Consensus of the Medinese as a subtype of *ijmāʿ*. Commonalities of presentation, structurally and content-wise, reveal a common intent, however; these summary chapters on the domains of *istidlāl* should serve as (1) a primer or review of relevant *uṣūl al-fiqh* discussions, so the dialectician in training may better present his *istidlāl* in debate; and (2) an ordering of first-rank *topoi*, that he—in the role of Q—might "locate" the relevant objections for testing and critiquing his opponent's *istidlāl*. Some of these aims are expressed by al-Bājī himself, in his conclusion to this chapter:

> We have mentioned, in abridged format, definitions and subdivisions of *uṣūl* in the domain of dialectical disputation, which the dialectician must learn in order to [1] know what he can draw indication from, then [2] turn towards the method of drawing indication (*kayfiyyat al-istidlāl*). And we have omitted indicants (*adilla*), and many problem cases (*masā'il*) of the *uṣūl*, in aversion to long-windedness; and we have obliged those who seek after more [to reference] our *Kitāb fī Uṣūl al-Fiqh*. And now we will begin stating the categories of question and response (*aqsām al-su'āl wa'l-jawāb*) and their method. Then, after that, we will turn to the rest of the 'chapters' of dialectic (*abwāb al-jadal*)—and through God comes success![92]

This conclusion is followed, as al-Bājī promised, by a *Chapter on the Categories of Question and Response* (*Bāb Aqsām al-Su'āl wa'l-Jawāb*).[93] This is followed in turn by a series of chapters on "modes of objection" (*wujūh al-iʿtirāḍ*), exactly arranged according to the domains of *istidlāl* and their subcategories, as outlined above. All of this taken together reveals a highly precise and systematic organizing principle which can only have been of great benefit to the dialectician in training; and the same of course obtains in al-Shīrāzī's *Maʿūna*. The utility of these works—the relative ease with which one may navigate the astounding plurality of objections—is again of great benefit in fashioning a *jadal*-theory lens. Like the fifth/eleventh century dialecticians in training who first used these manuals, we will benefit greatly from the logical organization of the *Maʿūna* and *Minhāj*.

4.3 Representative Typologies of *Qiyās*

Qiyās and its components—source-case (*aṣl*), branch-case (*farʿ*), occasioning factor (*ʿilla*), and ruling (*ḥukm*)—are key foci of juridical dialectic. In the following section, I will outline—in some detail—a representative typology from classical *jadal*

[92] *Minhāj*, Turkī ed., p. 33, §63.

[93] Ibid., 34–41, §§64–79.

theory: that of al-Shīrāzī in his *Mulakhkhaṣ fi'l-Jadal*. To a large extent, al-Shīrāzī will be allowed to speak for himself. His definitions and examples illustrate widely understood conceptions, and—as we have come to expect—they are presented in a systematic and accessible manner. Before proceeding to al-Shīrāzī, however, I will briefly diagram the two types of *qiyās* al-Baṣrī deals with in his *Muʿtamad* and *Kitāb al-Qiyās al-Sharʿī*: "correlational inference of co-presence" (*qiyās al-ṭard*) and "correlational inference of the opposite" (*qiyās al-ʿaks*).

Al-Baṣrī's Typology of Qiyās

Qiyās al-Ṭard (Correlational Inference of Co-Presence):[94]

Source-Case (*Aṣl*) X		Branch-Case (*Farʿ*) Y
Occasioning Factor (*ʿIlla*) A	← SAME →	Occasioning Factor (*ʿIlla*) A
Ruling (*Hukm*) B	← THUS, ALSO SAME →	Ruling (*Hukm*) B

Qiyās al-ʿAks (Correlational Inference of The Opposite):[95]

Aṣl X		*Farʿ* Y
ʿIlla A	OPPOSITE/CONTRADICTORY ← (*NAQĪḌ*) →	*ʿIlla* ¬A
Hukm B	THEREFORE ALSO OPPOSITE/CONTRADICTORY ← (*NAQĪḌ*) →	*Hukm* ¬B

[94] See al-Baṣrī, *Muʿtamad*, Ḥamīd Allāh ed., vol. 2, pp. 697ff.; and *K. al-Qiyās al-Sharʿī*, pp. 1031–3 (trans. of the latter in Hallaq, "Treatise," pp. 207–9). Note that *qiyās al-ṭard*, according to the definition of al-Baṣrī, matches the definitions of al-Shīrāzī, al-Bājī, et al. for *qiyās al-ʿilla*.

[95] See al-Baṣrī, *Muʿtamad*, Ḥamīd Allāh ed., vol. 2, pp. 698–9; and *K. al-Qiyās al-Sharʿī*, pp. 1031–2 (trans. of the latter in Hallaq, "Treatise," pp. 207–8). His definitions there match well with Sānū's (*Muʿjam*, s.v. "قياس العكس"): "The confirmation (*ithbāt*) of the contradictory (*naqīḍ*) [¬B] of a *ḥukm* [B] of a known thing (*maʿlūm*) [X], in another known thing [Y], due to the presence of the contradictory (*naqīḍ*) [¬A] of [X's] *ʿilla* [A] in [Y]."

Al-Shīrāzī's Typology of Qiyās

Qiyās (Correlational Inference)

- Definition:[96]

"*Qiyās* is the linking of a branch-case with a source-case by way of an occasioning factor, and the application of the ruling of the source-case to the branch-case."	والقياس حمل فرع على أصل بعلة واجراء حكم الأصل على الفرع.

Qiyās al-'Illa (Correlational Inference of the Occasioning Factor)

- Definition:[97]

"As for *Qiyās al-'Illa*, it is that one link the branch-case with the source-case by way of the occasioning factor upon which the ruling is made contingent in God's Law; and that is according to three types: clearly-disclosed, plainly-evident, and latent."	فأما قياس العلة فهو أن يحمل الفرع على الأصل بالعلة التي علق الحكم عليها في الشرع وذلك على ثلاثة أضرب جلي وواضح وخفي.

After reviewing al-Shīrāzī's various types and subtypes of *qiyās al-'illa*, it will become clear they are all a function of "how do we come to know the *'illa* in the *aṣl*?" Either we know it because God or the Prophet clearly told us what it is ("clearly-disclosed" [*jalī*], type 1); or because its identity is sanctioned by *ijmā'* ("clearly-disclosed" [*jalī*], type 2); or because God or the Prophet, though not specifically naming it, nevertheless formulated the decree in such a way as leaves us with little doubt as to what the *'illa* in fact is ("plainly-evident" [*wāḍiḥ*], type 1); or because the reported context-cause for which the ruling was decreed leaves us with little doubt as to what the *'illa* is ("plainly-evident" [*wāḍiḥ*], type 2); or because demonstrated efficiency (*ta'thīr*) allows us to rationally infer it ("latent" [*khafī*]). And, as with all the modes of indicants (*wujūh al-adilla*) in our *jadal*-theory texts, the types and subtypes of *qiyās al-'illa* are ranked; they are discussed in order of epistemic strength (strongest = *jalī* 1; weakest = *khafī*). Bear in mind this is all with regard to the category *qiyās al-'illa*, which itself (including all subtypes) is ranked higher than the second high-order category of *qiyās*: *qiyās al-dalāla*. As we shall see, this category also has three types—and subtype(s)—introduced and treated in order of epistemic strength. The overall effect is an *hierarchy of qiyās*.[98]

[96] al-Shīrāzī, *Mulakhkhaṣ*, Niyāzī MA ed., vol. 1b, p. 22.

[97] Ibid., vol. 1b, p. 76.

[98] Again, individual modes are ranked from strongest to weakest in terms of epistemic strength—i.e., in terms of the certainty or probability with which they may be understood to convey the correct solution, the true articulation of God's Law. The most certain (and least controversial) mode is that *qiyās al-'illa* which is *jalī bi'l-naṣṣ*; the least certain (and most controversial) is that *qiyās al-dalāla* which is known as *qiyās al-shabah*. This is systematization at its most evident extent, and a stark illustration of the difference between "full-system" and "proto-system" legal

Qiyās al-ʿIlla, Type I: *Jalī* (Clearly-Disclosed)

- Definition:[99]

"As for the clearly-disclosed, it is such as whose occasioning factor is known with definite certainty, either by way of univocal formulation in authoritative source-text, or by way of consensus."	فأما الجلي فما عرفت علته قطعا إما بالنص أو إما بالإجماع.

Qiyās al-ʿIlla, Type I.1: *Jalī bi'l-Naṣṣ* (Clearly-Disclosed by way of Univocal Formulation)

- Example:[100]
  Al-Shīrāzī's *aṣl* is from the Sunna: a *ḥadīth* in which the Prophet forbade the storage (*iddikhār*) of sacrifice remains for more than three nights. The *ʿilla* may be formulated as: "[the storage] is at a time when there is a pressing need for charity." We know that *ʿilla* because the Prophet later clearly explained his proscription:

"I only forbade you [from doing that] for the sake of the *Dāffa*."[101]	إنما نهيتكم لأجل الدّافّة

Al-Shīrāzī explains: "Thus [the Prophet] explicitly announced the occasioning factor (*ṣarraḥa bi'l-ʿilla*), and clearly formulated it (*wa naṣṣa ʿalayhā*)."[102] He then states the methodological norm for *qiyās* based on this species of occasioning factor: "Whatever has an *ʿilla* established by *naṣṣ*, its *ḥukm* is the *ḥukm* of that *naṣṣ*."[103]

Qiyās al-ʿIlla, Type I.2: *Jalī bi'l-Ijmāʿ* (Clearly-Disclosed by way of Consensus)

- Example:[104]
  Al-Shīrāzī's *aṣl* is from the Qur'ān: «don't say 'uff!' to them» (Q.17:23). The *ḥukm* in this *aṣl* is plain: "the forbidding (*manʿ*) of saying 'uff' (*ta'fīf*) is among the rights of parents." The explanation of the *ʿilla*, sanctioned by *ijmāʿ*, is: "due to

---

and disputational theory. Although an early work such as al-Shāfiʿī's *Risāla* is clearly representative of a systematizing effort (hence: proto-*system*), it boasts nothing close to this detailed hierarchy of *qiyās*, with its specialized terms and epistemological valuations, simply and definitively arranged in logical order.

[99] Shīrāzī, *Mulakhkhaṣ*, Niyāzī MA ed., vol. 1b, p. 76. See, by way of contrast, the definition for *qiyās al-khafī*, below.

[100] Ibid., vol. 1b, pp. 76–7.

[101] See *MF*, s.v. "أضحية", vol. 5, p. 102, §59, for an explanation. Briefly, the *Dāffa* were a poverty-stricken group who settled at Medina; the Prophet wanted to hasten the charity of the Medinans by forbidding them to store the remains of their sacrifices for more than three nights.

[102] al-Shīrāzī, *Mulakhkhaṣ*, Niyāzī MA ed., vol. 1b, p. 77.

[103] Ibid., vol. 1b, p. 78.

[104] Ibid., vol. 1b, p. 77.

the harm or insult it causes" (*li-ajli al-adhā*). *Qiyās* in the legal problem of striking one's parents may thus be presented as follows:

Mas'ala: what is the ruling re: striking one's parents?		
Aṣl «don't say "uff!" to them» (Q.17:23)		**Farʿ** striking them
ʿIlla (Ijmāʿ-sanctioned) it causes them harm/insult	*awlā* →	**ʿIlla** it causes them [a greater degree of] harm/insult
Ḥukm it is forbidden	therefore, also *awlā* →	**Ḥukm** [it is (more strongly) forbidden]

Note this example considers the same cases by which al-Shīrāzī illustrates *faḥwā al-khiṭāb*, noting:[105] "And al-Shāfiʿī, may God have mercy upon him, calls this *al-qiyās al-jalī*." Here, however—in the domain of *qiyās al-ʿilla*, type I.2—emphasis is upon the aspect of an *ijmāʿ*-sanctioned-*ʿilla*. In the *faḥwā al-khiṭāb* illustration, occasioning factors are not discussed at all—the proscription of striking is rationally understood as a purely linguistic entailment of the Qur'ānic *lafẓ*-expression.[106] It is interesting that the same example cases are used to illustrate two separate modes of "indicants of what is rationally understood" (*adillat al-maʿqūl*): for *faḥwā al-khiṭāb* they illustrate an *a fortiori* linguistic entailment, but for *qiyās al-ʿilla*, type I.2, they illustrate the amplified occasioning power of an augmented, *ijmāʿ*-sanctioned *ʿilla*. Al-Shīrāzī follows the current example *mas'ala* with the methodological norm for *qiyās* based on this species of occasioning factor: "Whatever has an *ʿilla* established by *ijmāʿ*, its *ḥukm* is the *ḥukm* of that *ijmāʿ*."[107]

Qiyās al-ʿIlla, Type II: *Wāḍiḥ* (Plainly-Evident)

- Definition:[108]

"And as for the plainly-evident, it is such as whose occasioning factor is established by way of a type of apparent formulation; and such might be a divinely-sanctioned decree, or such might be a reason transmitted along with the ruling."	وأما الواضح فما ثبتت علته بضرب من الظاهر وقد يكون نطقا وقد يكون سببا ينقل مع الحكم.

[105] Ibid., vol. 1b, pp. 64–5.

[106] See also the notes on *al-istidlāl bi'l-awlā*, below.

[107] *Mulakhkhaṣ*, Niyāzī MA ed., vol. 1b, p. 78.

[108] Ibid.

Qiyās al-ʿIlla, Type II.1: *Wāḍiḥ bi'l-Nuṭq* (Plainly-Evident by way of Divinely-Sanctioned Decree)

- Example:[109]
  Al-Shīrāzī's *aṣl* is from the Sunna: the Prophet forbade the *bayʿ*-commutation of 'food for food' (*ṭaʿām bi-ṭaʿām*), except 'like for like' (*mithl bi-mithl*). For questions of usury (*ribā*), then, the *ʿilla* understood to occasion proscription is: "it is a foodstuff of [the same] genus" (*maṭʿūm jins*). Al-Shīrāzī explains: "So the most apparent interpretation (*ẓāhir*) is that the *ḥukm* was made contingent upon that [*ʿilla*] when [the Prophet] made proscription contingent upon ['food for food']." Note that in this case, the Prophet did not specifically point out the *ʿilla* by saying "I ruled X due to Y" or the like, as in *al-jalī bi'l-naṣṣ*. The form of his decree (*nuṭq*), however, plainly evinces an occasioning factor—in other words, he proclaimed his ruling in such a way as makes the *ʿilla* apparent (*ẓāhir*), and thus: plainly-evident by way of divinely-sanctioned decree (*wāḍiḥ bi'l-nuṭq*).

Qiyās al-ʿIlla, Type II.2: *Wāḍiḥ bi'l-Sabab* (Plainly-Evident by way of [Reported] Reason)

- Example[110]
  Al-Shīrāzī's *aṣl* is from the Sunna: ʿĀ'isha reported that Barīra was manumitted while her husband was a slave, so the Prophet granted her *khiyār*-option (with regard to preserving the marriage). The *ḥukm* of this *ḥadīth* is plain: when the female slave (*ama*) is manumitted while the wife of a slave, she has the right to *khiyār*-option. The *ʿilla*, too, is plain: "she is the wife of a slave (*taḥta ʿabdin*) at the time of her manumission." Al-Shīrāzī explains: "So the most apparent interpretation (*ẓāhir*) is that she was granted *khiyār*-option due to this intension-property (*maʿnā*)."[111] Note that (1) the *maʿnā*-quality efficient in occasioning the *ḥukm* is "she is the wife of a slave" (*taḥta ʿabdin*), and (2) the Prophet never said anything in this *ḥadīth* for us to interpret—this is not, in other words, *naṣṣ* or *nuṭq*. Rather, the *ʿilla* is made plain to us by the *reported reason* for which the Prophet's ruling was delivered. This is in consonance with al-Shīrāzī's definition for Type II *Qiyās al-ʿIlla*: "it is such as whose *ʿilla* is established by way of a type of an apparent formulation (*ẓāhir*); and such might be [...] a reason (*sabab*) transmitted along with the ruling." Thus: "plainly-evident by way of [reported] reason" (*wāḍiḥ bi'l-sabab*).

Qiyās al-ʿIlla, Type III: *Khafī* (Latent/Concealed)

- Definition:[112]

"And as for the latent, it is such as whose occasioning factor is known by way of rational-inferential discovery; it is that for which efficiency provides indication."	وأما الخفي فما عرفت علته بالاستنباط وهو ما دل عليه التأثير.

---

[109] Ibid.

[110] Ibid., pp. 78–9.

[111] Note that *maʿnā* and *ʿilla* occur here as near-synonyms, and we are granted an insight into the type of "intension-property" a *maʿnā* can engender.

Niyāzī cites Ibn al-Ḥājib (Mālikī; d.646/1249), who compares and contrasts the "latent" type (*qiyās al-khafī*) with the "clearly-disclosed" type (*qiyās al-jalī*), saying: "*al-qiyās al-khafī* is that in which the thing disallowing invalidating distinction (*nafy al-fāriq*) [between *aṣl* and *far*ʿ] is probable (*maẓnūn*)—like the *qiyās* of date-wine (*nabīdh*) on the basis of grape-wine (*khamr*), with regard to [the *ḥukm* of] proscription; while [*qiyās*] *al-jalī* is that in which the thing disallowing distinction between the *aṣl* and the *far*ʿ is known with definite certainty—like the *qiyās* of the female slave (*ama*) on the basis of the male slave (ʿ*abd*), with regard to the normative rulings of manumission (*aḥkām al-*ʿ*itq*)."[113]

- Example:[114]
  Al-Shīrāzī's *aṣl* is the case of grape-wine (*khamr*). The ʿ*illa* occasioning its proscription is: "it is a beverage (*sharāb*) in which there is a 'euphoric intensity' (*shidda muṭriba*)." He explains: "...and we know that [ʿ*illa*] by way of demonstrated efficiency (*ta'thīr*), which is the presence of the *ḥukm* due to the presence of the ʿ*illa*, and [the *ḥukm*'s] cessation (*zawāl*) due to [the ʿ*illa*'s] cessation; and one draws indication by means of that for [the ʿ*illa*'s] validity (*ṣiḥḥa*)." Note that this is the lowest in the hierarchy of *qiyās al-*ʿ*illa*, for the ʿ*illa* is determined entirely via rational inference (*istinbāṭ*), and only of a specific mode: concomitance of ʿ*illa* and *ḥukm*. Demonstration of this efficiency (*ta'thīr*) is our only guide—there is neither authoritative designation, nor consensual sanction, nor compelling formulation or reported reason.

Summary of al-Shīrāzī's Qiyās al-ʿIlla

For all their variant particulars, the modes of *qiyās* outlined above are all subsumed by al-Shīrāzī's general definition for "correlational inference of the occasioning factor" (*qiyās al-*ʿ*illa*): "that one link the branch-case (*far*ʿ) with the source-case (*aṣl*) by way of the occasioning factor (ʿ*illa*) upon which the ruling (*ḥukm*) is made contingent in God's Law." Note that all types focus on how we come to know the ʿ*illa* in the *aṣl*; and, by this general formulation, all of the above may be diagramed as follows:

[112] *Mulakhkhaṣ*, Niyāzī MA ed., vol. 1b, p. 79.

[113] Ibid., vol. 1b, pp. 79–80, n. 11. At the end of this footnote, Niyāzī says: "According to the Ḥanafīs, *al-qiyās al-khafī* is one of the types of *istiḥsān*." We should note this as another example of how *jadal* shaped legal theory: the broadly untenable category of *istiḥsān* was either reduced to only those components which proved *endoxa* in the long run, or it was redefined in such a way as to parallel or subsume certain *endoxa* inference methods to which other schools applied different technical terms.

Aṣl A *ʿIlla* (Established) I *Hukm* (Established) H	 (same) ←→ (therefore, should also be the same) →	*Farʿ* F *ʿIlla* (Claimed) [I] *Hukm* (Transferred) [H]

Qiyās al-Dalāla (Correlational Inference of Indication)

- Definition:[115]

"As for *Qiyās al-Dalāla*, it is that one link the branch-case with the source-case by way of a type of resemblance other than the occasioning factor upon which the ruling is made contingent in God's Law. The validity of this type of correlational inference is not known except by way of drawing indication from the authoritative source-cases; and it is [also] of three types."	وأما قياس الدلالة فهو أن يحمل الفرع على الأصل بضرب من الشبه غير العلة التي علق الحكم عليها في الشرع. وهذا ضرب من القياس لا تعرف صحته إلا بالاستدلال بالأصول وهو على ثلاثة أضرب.

Implied by al-Shīrāzī's definition is that one resorts to *qiyās al-dalāla* when the modes of *qiyās al-ʿilla* cannot be practiced; lacking knowledge of the *ʿilla*, one must draw forth an indicant (*dalīl*) from some other relational "resemblance" (*shabah*)—exhibited by authoritatively established source-cases (*uṣūl*)—to justify one's correlational inference.

Qiyās al-Dalāla, Type I

- Definition:[116]

"The first [type] is that one draws indication for confirmation of the branch-case by way of confirmation of one of the branch-case's [other] rulings; then one refers that back to a source-case."	أحدها أن يستدل بثبوت حكم من أحكام الفرع على ثبوت الفرع ثم يرد ذلك إلى أصل.

[114] Ibid., vol. 1b, p. 79.

[115] al-Shīrāzī, *Mulakhkhaṣ*, Niyāzī MA ed., vol. 1b, p. 80.

[116] Ibid.

- Example:[117]

Mas'ala: is the prostration of Qur'ān recital (*sujūd al-tilāwa*) obligatory?		
Aṣl prostration of supererogatory prayer (*sujūd al-nafl*)		**Far'** prostration of Qur'ān recital (*sujūd al-tilāwa*)
Ḥukm Y_A (sanctioned by *ijmā'*) it is allowed (to be mimed) while mounted on a travelling camel, without validating excuse (*'udhr*)	(same) ← →	**Ḥukm Y_F (also sanctioned by *ijmā'*)** it is allowed (to be mimed) while mounted on a travelling camel, without validating excuse (*'udhr*)
Ḥukm X_A (by definition) not *wājib*	(therefore, should also be the same) →	**Ḥukm X_F** [not *wājib*]

The procedure for Type I *qiyās al-dalāla* may be described as follows. (1) We wish to discover *ḥukm* $\mathbf{X}_F$ (the normative status of *sujūd al-tilāwa*), but no *'illa* can be learned, so we review the relevant, established rulings of the *far'* (*sujūd al-tilāwa*) and find *ḥukm* $\mathbf{Y}_F$ (*sujūd al-tilāwa* is allowed while mounted on a travelling camel, without validating excuse). (2) Among the *uṣūl*, we know of an *aṣl* (*sujūd al-nafl*) with the relevant pair of established rulings: $\mathbf{Y}_A$ (*sujūd al-nafl* is allowed while mounted on a travelling camel, without validating excuse), and $\mathbf{X}_A$ (the normative status of *sujūd al-nafl* = not *wājib*). (3) Because of the resemblance (*shabah*) of *aṣl* and *far'*, and because of the identity of their rulings $\mathbf{Y}_A$ and $\mathbf{Y}_F$, we can reasonably assume an identity between their rulings $\mathbf{X}_A$ and $\mathbf{X}_F$ (thus solving the *mas'ala* without real knowledge of the *'illa*).

Note that both $\mathbf{Y}_F$ and $\mathbf{X}_F$ belong to the same *far'* (*sujūd al-tilāwa*); thus the initial stage of reasoning is purely internal to the *far'*—i.e., one first looks at other rulings of the same *far'* before referring the resulting pair of rulings back to an *aṣl*.[118] Al-Shīrāzī's explanation reads: "And [Type I *qiyās al-dalāla*] is like the *istidlāl* of our [Shāfi'ī] companions for the non-obligatory status of the prostration of Qur'ān recital (*sujūd al-tilāwa*) because it is a prostration whose performance is allowed mounted on a travelling camel without a validating excuse; so it is not obligatory (*wājib*), like the prostration of supererogatory prayer (*sujūd al-nafl*). Thus they draw indication, by way of its performance being allowed while mounted on a travelling camel, for the fact that it is not *wājib*, because performances of obligatory duties (*wājibāt*) are not permitted while mounted on a travelling camel except due to a validating excuse. And when the performance of this is allowed (*jāza*)[119] while mounted on a travelling camel without an excuse, it provides indication that it is not *wājib*."[120]

[117] Ibid. See *MF*, s.v. "الصلاة على الراحلة (أو الدابة)", vol. 27, pp. 227ff., for details on this *mas'ala*.

[118] Compare this to Type II *qiyās al-dalāla*, below, where one first goes outside of the *far'* (*ẓihār* of the *dhimmī*) to something which is highly analogous to it (*ṭalāq* of the *dhimmī*), before tracing that *naẓīr*-relationship back to a *naẓīr*-pair in the *uṣūl* (*ṭalāq* and *ẓihār* of the Muslim).

[119] The word جاز is missing from Niyāzī's transcription. I have supplied the omitted word from the Ṣan'ā' manuscript, fol.5b, end of line 12.

[120] al-Shīrāzī, *Mulakhkhaṣ*, Niyāzī MA ed., vol. 1b, pp. 80–1. NB: in the second part of his explanation, al-Shīrāzī explains the example in quite a different light: as a type I *qiyās al-dalāla* from

Qiyās al-Dalāla, Type II

- Definition:[121]

"The second type is that one draws indication for the ruling of the branch-case by way of a ruling which closely resembles the ruling of the branch-case and proceeds in the same manner; then one correlates that with a source-case."	والضرب الثاني أن يستدل بحكم يشاكل حكم الفرع ويجري مجراه على حكم الفرع ثم يقيس ذلك على أصل.

- Example:[122]

<table>
<tr><th colspan="7">Mas'ala: is the ẓihār-divorce of the non-Muslim subject (dhimmī) valid?</th></tr>
<tr><td>Naẓīr al-Aṣl[a]
ṭalāq of Muslim

Ḥukm X_{NA}
it is valid</td><td>←→</td><td>Aṣl
ẓihār of Muslim

Ḥukm X_{A}
it is valid</td><td rowspan="2">(same naẓīr-pairs should have same rulings)
←→</td><td>Farʿ
ẓihār of Dhimmī

Ḥukm X_{F}
[it is valid]</td><td>←</td><td>Naẓīr al-Farʿ
ṭalāq of Dhimmī

Ḥukm X_{NF}
it is valid</td></tr>
<tr><td colspan="3">Normative Analogues
(identical aḥkām)</td><td colspan="3">Normative Analogues
(aḥkām should be identical)</td></tr>
</table>

[a]NB: al-Shīrāzī does not employ the term *naẓīr* ("parallel") in his discussion of Type II *qiyās al-dalāla* in the *Mulakhkhaṣ*. He does use it, however, in the *Maʿūna*—as does al-Bājī in his *Minhāj*—for explaining this type of *qiyās*. Moreover, even though he does not use it in this current exposition, his discussion constitutes the most complete definition of *naẓīr* I have yet encountered: the *naẓīr* of X is its close analogue in both form and function—it "closely resembles [ruling X] and runs the same course" (*yushākilu* [*ḥukm* X] *wa yajrī majrāhu*)—so closely that associated rulings are likely to be identical.

The procedure for Type II *qiyās al-dalāla* may be described as follows. (1) We wish to discover or justify *ḥukm* X_F (validity of the *dhimmī*'s *ẓihār*), but no *ʿilla* can be learned, so we review relevant, established rulings—*beyond other rulings of the farʿ* (unlike Type I *qiyās al-dalāla*)—in search of an analogue which resembles the *farʿ* in form and function. (2) *Ṭalāq*-divorce is the obvious choice: an analogue in form and function; and its *ḥukm* X_{NF} (*ṭalāq*-divorce of the *dhimmī* is valid) being known, we presume to transfer X_{NF} to X_F. (3) We must now justify this presumption that a *dhimmī*'s *ẓihār*-divorce and a *dhimmī*'s *ṭalāq*-divorce are normative analogues by linking the pair back to the *uṣūl*—where, of course we find the *naẓīr*-pair of a Muslim's *ẓihār*-divorce and a Muslim's *ṭalāq*-divorce, with identical rulings.

Thus Type II *qiyās al-dalāla* appears as a sort of double-*qiyās*, with two, distinct correlational actions. The first correlation is between *farʿ* and the *naẓīr*-parallel of the *farʿ*, and presumes (on the basis of analogue forms and functions) the transfer of *ḥukm* X_{NF} to *ḥukm* X_F. The second correlation is between *naẓīr*-pairs: our assuming the identity of *ḥukm* X_{NF} and *ḥukm* X_F in the *naẓīr*-pair of our *farʿ* is justified by

the whole category of *uṣūl* known as *wājibāt*, but with the *ʿaks* element of *qiyās al-ʿaks*. The whole category of *wājibāt* shares the *ḥukm* of "not permitted while mounted on a traveling camel, without validating excuse." Thus, since the opposite *ḥukm* (permitted) is established for *sujūd al-tilāwa*, it must *not* belong to the category of *wājibāt*.

[121] Ibid., 81.

[122] Ibid.

linking it to the same *ḥukm*-identity (**X**$_{NA}$ and **X**$_A$) in an authoritatively-established *naẓīr*-pair of the *uṣūl*. Al-Shīrāzī's explanation reads: "And [Type II *qiyās al-dalāla*] is like the doctrine (*qawl*) of our [Shāfiʿī] companions for the *ẓihār*-divorce of the *dhimmī*: his *ṭalāq*-divorce is valid, so his *ẓihār*-divorce is valid; as with Muslims. Thus have we drawn indication, by way of the validity of *ṭalāq*-divorce, for the validity of *ẓihār*-divorce, because they both function in the same manner (*yajriyān majrā wāḥidan*: lit., 'they both run a single course'). Don't you see/opine (*a-lā tarā*) that they are both contingent upon declaration (*qawl*), and they are both peculiar to the domain of matrimony? So when one of the two is valid, it provides a *dalīl*-indicant for the validity of the other."[123]

Qiyās al-Dalāla, Type III = *Qiyās al-Shabah* (Correlational Inference of Resemblance)

- Definition:[124]

"The third type is that one links the branch-case with a source-case, by way of a type of [shared-property] resemblance."	والضرب الثالث هو أن يحمل الفرع على أصل بضرب من الشبه.

- Example:[125]

Mas'ala: is a slave legally permitted to own anything?		
Aṣl the free person		**Far'** the slave
Property X$_A$[a] he is a human being to whom instructive communication is addressed (*mukhāṭab*)...	(same) ←→	**Property X$_F$** he is a human being to whom instructive communication is addressed (*mukhāṭab*)...
Property Y$_A$ ... who is rewarded (*muthāb*)...	(same) ←→	**Property Y$_F$** ... who is rewarded (*muthāb*)...
Property Z$_A$ ... and punished (*muʿāqab*).	(same) ←→	**Property Z$_F$** ... and punished (*muʿāqab*).
Ḥukm A he is legally permitted to own	(therefore, should also be the same) →	**Ḥukm A** [he is legally permitted to own]

[a]NB: al-Shīrāzī does not mention "properties" in his exposition on *qiyās al-shabah* in the *Mulakhkhaṣ*, nor does he separate them as I have in his example.

Al-Shīrāzī explains: "this and its like are called *qiyās al-shabah*, and there are two views regarding its validity." Those who maintain its validity argue by: (1) linking *qiyās al-shabah* to certain instructions in the famed letter of ʿUmar b.

[123] Note the use of the formula *a-lā tarā* in a justification of *qiyās* method. This staple formula of dialectic will be treated at the end of Chap. 6.

[124] Al-Shīrāzī, *Mulakhkhaṣ*, Niyāzī MA ed., vol. 1b, p. 81.

[125] Ibid.

al-Khaṭṭāb to Abū Mūsā al-Ash'arī, part of which al-Shīrāzī quotes; and (2) stating: "the close-resemblance (*mushābaha*) of the *far'* to the *aṣl* necessitates that it be alike unto it, so it must be that its *ḥukm* is its *ḥukm*."[126] As for the view that it is not valid, it is argued that: (1) allowing *qiyās al-shabah* is equivalent to conceding that every *qiyās* is valid; (2) no *far'* resembles an *aṣl* regarding one quality without differing from it in another—and if resemblance obliges a union between them, then difference equally obliges a dividing distinction.[127] Al-Shīrāzī favors the argument against, saying: "and in this is a *dalīl* for the nullification (*ibṭāl*) of *qiyās al-shabah*."[128]

Al-Shīrāzī on the Modes of *Qiyās*-Based *Istidlāl* Most Commonly Employed in Dialectical Argumentation

- Explanation:[129]
  "Section: On the mention of what is appended to *qiyās*, and branches out from it in terms of modes of *istidlāl*. Know that *istidlāl* is of many types, and strongly resists restrictive inventorying (*ḥaṣr*), but I will explain that by which argument is most frequently made in intellectual investigation (*naẓar*). In general, *istidlāl* might be by way of an *a fortiori* valuation (*bi'l-awlā*), by way of analytical disjunction (*bi'l-taqsīm*), by way of the opposite (*bi'l-'aks*), by way of clarifying the occasioning factor (*bi-bayān al-'illa*), and by way of [the testimony of] the divinely-sanctioned source-cases (*bi'l-uṣūl*)."

al-Istidlāl bi'l-Awlā (Drawing Indication by way of *A Fortiori* Valuation)

- Definition:[130]

"And as for *al-istidlāl bi'l-awlā*, it is that one clarify, in the branch-case, the intension-property upon which the ruling is made contingent in the source-case, and an augmentation [of that property, in the branch-case]."	فأما الاستدلال بالأولى فهو أن يبين في الفرع المعنى الذي تعلق الحكم به في الأصل وزيادة.

- Example 1:[131]
  The first example is a Shāfi'ī argument regarding ritual atonement (*kaffāra*) for intentional homicide (*qatl al-'amd*): "ritual atonement was only posited, originally, for the remission of [intentional] sin (*raf' al-ma'tham*) and the expiation

[126] Ibid., pp. 82–4.

[127] Ibid., p. 84.

[128] This view is confirmed in his *Ma'ūna* (Turkī ed., p. 140). Al-Shīrāzī notes that this section on *qiyās* has been according to his choice of categorization; there are other Shāfi'īs who do it differently, with four types: *jalī*, *wāḍiḥ*, *khafī*, and *shabah*. These he illustrates with short examples, then closes the section by expressing his hope that his own categorization is clearer and more beneficial (*Mulakhkhaṣ*, Niyāzī MA ed., vol. 1b, pp. 84–5).

[129] Ibid., p. 85.

[130] Ibid., p. 86.

[131] Ibid.

of [intentional or unintentional] transgressions (*takfīr al-dhunūb*);[132] so when it is obliged for unintentional homicide (*qatl al-khaṭa'*), with absence of intentional sin (*ma'a 'adam al-ma'tham*), then it is all the more appropriate (*awlā*) for intentional homicide, with presence of intentional sin (*ma'a wujūd al-ma'tham*)." Note that unintentional homicide still entails a sin, though not an intentional one (*ma'tham*); thus, intentional homicide, which entails a *ma'tham*, may be properly considered as containing an augmentation of the (unintentional) sin entailed by unintentional homicide. The example is thus accurate, for the branch-case (intentional homicide) contains an augmentation of the efficient property (sin)—the intension-property (*ma'nā*) of the source-case—thus making the obligation of *kaffāra* "all the more appropriate" (*awlā*) for the branch-case. This may be diagramed as follows:

Mas'ala: is ritual atonement obliged for intentional homicide?		
Aṣl unintentional homicide		**Far'** intentional homicide
'Illa X_A it is an unintentional sin	(*awlā*) →	**'Illa X_F** it is an intentional sin
Ḥukm A ritual atonement is obliged	(therefore, also *awlā*) →	**Ḥukm A** [ritual atonement is (all the more) obliged]

- Example 2:[133]
  The second example is a Ḥanafī argument regarding ritual atonement (*kaffāra*) for breaking one's fast by eating, as opposed to breaking it via sexual intercourse: "*kaffāra* was only made obligatory for sexual intercourse due to intentional sin (*ma'tham*), and the intentional sin of eating is greater than the intentional sin of intercourse, by the indicant that the reward for abstaining from eating is greater than the reward for abstaining from intercourse. So if breaking fast by intercourse obliges *kaffāra*, then it is all the more [obliged for breaking it] by eating (*fa-bi'l-akl awlā*)."

Mas'ala: is ritual atonement obliged for breaking the fast by eating?		
Aṣl breaking fast by sexual intercourse		**Far'** breaking fast by eating
'Illa X_A it is an intentional sin	(*awlā*) →	**'Illa X_F** it is a greater intentional sin
Ḥukm A ritual atonement is obliged	(therefore, also *awlā*) →	**Ḥukm A** [ritual atonement is (all the more) obliged]

[132] See Lane, *Lexicon*, s.v. إثم and ذنب. Here we learn that *ma'tham* is synonymous with *ithm*, which is in turn a synonym of *dhanb* (pl. *dhunūb*)—except that *dhanb* refers to both intentional and inadvertent transgression, whereas *ithm* refers only to intentional sin.

Note this illustration involves a *secondary* indicant, required to support the claim that breaking fast by eating is a greater sin than breaking it by sexual intercourse (which premise describes the augmented *ʿilla*): "the reward for abstaining from eating is greater than the reward for abstaining from intercourse." In a disputation, this premise would first have to be conceded by the opponent. We may also ask what distinguishes *al-istidlāl bi'l-awlā* from that "indicant of the rationally-understood" called *faḥwā al-khiṭāb*? The latter—though termed *al-qiyās al-jalī* by al-Shāfiʿī—is a purely linguistic entailment. The proscription of the minor act of saying "uff!" to one's parents (*ta'fīf*) is automatically, rationally understood—from the *lafẓ*-expression itself—to entail the proscription of the major act of striking one's parents.[134] In this case, there is no *aṣl* and *far*ʿ being compared for a common, augmented *ʿilla* (as in *al-istidlāl bi'l-awlā*); the *lafẓ*-expression of the *aṣl* (*ta'fīf*) is rationally understood to entail a proscription of striking, just as thc proscription of the flesh of the pig is understood by most to include wild boar.[135] In short, there is no *ʿilla* under consideration in *faḥwā al-khiṭāb*; we do not discuss what efficient property occasions the proscription of *ta'fīf*, but we rationally understand that the *lafẓ*-expression of this "instruction" (*khiṭāb*) entails a proscription of striking. If we were to argue the above two examples in terms of *faḥwā al-khiṭāb*, we would have to somehow show that the *lafẓ*-expression prescribing *kaffāra* for unintentional homicide linguistically entails a prescription of *kaffāra* for intentional homicide, and that the *lafẓ*-expression prescribing *kaffāra* for sexual intercourse linguistically entails a prescription of *kaffāra* for eating—*without* discussing the augmented efficient property of sin. In short, *al-istidlāl bi'l-awlā* discusses *ʿilal* and *faḥwā al-khiṭāb* does not; and understanding this helps us to further grasp the distinction between *maʿnā al-khiṭāb* (*qiyās*)—which involves a matching of efficient properties (or the indicants of such), between *aṣl* and *far*ʿ—from the other species of *maʿqūl aṣl*. These latter appear to hinge on purely linguistic entailments.

---

133 *Mulakhkhaṣ*, Niyāzī MA ed., vol. 1b, p. 86.

134 See ibid., vol. 1b, pp. 64–5.

135 Note, however, that the same example of *ta'fīf* is used to illustrate *al-qiyās al-jalī*—only this time, the *ʿilla* of harm/insult is discussed, and shown to be amplified in the branch-case of striking (*Mulakhkhaṣ*, Niyāzī MA ed., vol. 1b, p. 77).

al-Istidlāl bi'l-Taqsīm (Drawing Indication by way of Analytical Disjunction)

- Definition:[136]

"And as for *al-istidlāl bi'l-taqsīm*, it is of two types. [1] One is that [R] states the divisions of things upon which the ruling is allowed to be made contingent—from a contradicting opponent's [Q's] perspective—then nullifies all of them, thus nullifying [Q's] [opposing] opinion.[137] [2] The second is that [R] states the divisions of things upon which the ruling is allowed to be made contingent, then nullifies all of them—except that upon which [R's] response-solution is contingent, from [R's] own perspective—thus validating his own opinion."	فأما الاستدلال بالتقسيم فضربان. أحدهما أن يذكر الأقسام التي يجوز أن يتعلق بها الحكم من جهة المخالف فيبطل جميعها فيبطل بذلك قوله. والثاني أن يذكر الأقسام التي يجوز أن يتعلق الحكم بها فيبطل جميعها الا الذي يتعلق به الجواب من جهته فيصح قوله.

- Example 1:[138]
  The example for the first type is a Shāfiʿī argument regarding the oath of abstention from sexual intercourse (*īlā'*):[139] "It does not lead inevitably to *ṭalāq*-divorce, being that (1) *ṭalāq*-divorce does not come about except by way of either direct statement (*ṣarīḥ*) or indirect declaration of intent (*kināya*); (2) the *īlā'*-oath must be either *ṣarīḥ* or *kināya*; (3) it cannot be *ṣarīḥ*, because such is, according to us, three particular utterances, and, according to them, but one, and the *īlā'*-oath is none of these; (4) it cannot be *kināya*, because if it was *kināya*, divorce would not come about except with intent (*niyya*) or an eyewitness (*shāhid ḥāl*), according to them, and because if it was *kināya*, divorce would have come about immediately [at the time the *īlā'*-oath was pronounced]; and (5) if it is nullified that it be *ṣarīḥ*, and nullified that it be *kināya*, then it is impossible that *ṭalāq*-divorce occur by means of it." Note this example depends upon a logical disjunction which, applied to the opposing position, entails a contradiction—it is a species of *reductio* argument.[140]

---

[136] Ibid., 87.

[137] Although this first procedure resembles objection and refutation, it is recognizably a true mode of *istidlāl* once the following is born in mind: the opponent is the *mukhālif*—his opinion is *contradictory* to that of the one doing *istidlāl* (*mustadill*). By eliminating all of the opponent's possible justifications for "X is not the case", one simultaneously proves one's contradictory solution "X is the case." Eliminating all possible support for not-X serves as a proof for X, and vice versa.

[138] *Mulakhkhaṣ*, Niyāzī MA ed., vol. 1b, pp. 87–8.

[139] Niyāzī explains (p. 86, n. 6): if the husband refrains from approaching his wife after such an oath for 4 months, irrevocable divorce ensues, according to the Ḥanafīs. According to the Shāfiʿī's, however, he is given two options: return to the marriage through the sexual act, or divorce; if he refuses both, the *qāḍī* considers it a single divorce.

[140] Hallaq references the same example—as argued by al-Ghazālī in his *Shifā'*—in his discussion of non-analogical modes of *qiyās*, and subsumes this argument under *reductio ad absurdum* (*History*, pp. 100–101; I have borrowed his translations of *ṣarīḥ* and *kināya*). As Hallaq shows us, al-Ghazālī presents this example in syllogistic form (I have modified it to better match al-Shīrāzī's formulation): if Īlā' is Ṭalāq, then Īlā' is EITHER Ṣarīḥ OR Kināya; Īlā' is not Ṣarīḥ AND Īlā' is not Kināya; therefore, Īlā' is not Ṭalāq. Thus, as Hallaq says: "In al-Ghazālī's view then, the *reductio* argument as presented in this case seems to manifest the characteristics of the conditional hypothetical syllogism in the *modus tollens*."

Mas'ala: does the oath of abstention from sex, fulfilled, result in divorce?		
Aṣl pronouncement of *ṭalāq*		**Farʿ** pronouncement of *īlāʾ*
Logical Disjunction of Efficient Properties EITHER it is *ṣarīḥ* OR it is *kināya*	(contradictory) ← →	**Comprehensive Exclusion of Efficient Properties** it cannot be *ṣarīḥ* AND it cannot be *kināya*
Ḥukm A *ṭalāq*-divorce occurs	(therefore, also contradictory) →	**Ḥukm ¬A** [*ṭalāq*-divorce does not occur]

- Example 2:
  The example for the second type is a Shāfiʿī argument regarding the efficiency of false accusation of illicit sexual activity (*qadhf*) in refusing a perpetrator's testimony (*shahāda*): "When the divinely-sanctioned punishment (*ḥadd*) [for the crime of *qadhf*] is administered, [the perpetrator's] testimony is refused; and that can be occasioned by the false accusation (*qadhf*), or by the punishment (*ḥadd*), or by them both. But it cannot be that the refusal is occasioned by the *ḥadd*-punishment, because the *ḥadd* is a mode of purification (*taṭhīr*), so it is not allowed to be a reason (*sabab*) with regard to the refusal of testimony. And it cannot be that the refusal is occasioned by [the *ḥadd*] and by the false accusation (*qadhf*) [both], because if [the *ḥadd*] is not by itself a cause for the refusal of testimony, it is not allowed to be—in conjunction with something else—a cause for the refusal of testimony. So it is established that [refusal of testimony] is contingent only upon the false accusation of illicit sexual activity—and when this is established, our doctrinal opinion (*madhhab*) is validated." Note that this example does not appear to be a *qiyās* argument for the discovery of a substantive rule, but for the justification of an occasioning factor (*ithbāt al-ʿilla*) on which a *madhhab*-opinion rests—it is *qadhf* alone (not the *ḥadd*, and not both *ḥadd* and *qadhf* together) which occasions the *ḥukm* of refusal of testimony. In this respect, this second type of *al-istidlāl bi'l-taqsīm* seems identical to that *ijtihādic* method for verifying the *ʿilla* known as *al-sabr wa'l-taqsīm*.[141]

al-Istidlāl bi'l-ʿAks (Drawing Indication by way of the Opposite)

- Example:[142]
  The example is al-Shāfiʿī's argument against Abū Ḥanīfa, nullifying the latter's *ʿilla* for usury (*ribā*) with regard to "prices" (*athmān*): "If a single *ʿilla* united

[141] As described by Hallaq (*History*, p. 92).

[142] Shīrāzī, *Mulakhkhaṣ*, Niyāzī MA ed., vol. 1b, pp. 89–90. NB: Shīrāzī provides no definition in his *Mulakhkhaṣ*, but starts right in with an example. Niyāzī (p. 89, n. 1) instead supplies the following observations in a footnote: (1) this species of *istidlāl* is mentioned by al-Juwaynī, Abū Yaʿlā [al-Qāḍī, Ḥanbalī; d.458/1066], al-Bājī, and Ibn ʿAqīl; (2) most jurists call it *qiyās al-ʿaks*, including Abū al-Ḥusayn al-Baṣrī, al-Āmidī, Ibn al-Ḥājib, et al.; (3) al-Rāzī (Fakhr al-Dīn) and al-Bayḍāwī said it is "drawing indication by way of implication" (*istidlāl bi'l-talāzum*); (4) most Ḥanafīs—like al-Sarakhsī, al-Bazdawī, al-Samarqandī, and al-Nasafī—call it "drawing indication by way of denial" (*al-istidlāl bi'l-nafy*) and "justifying the occasioning factor by way of denial and absence"

silver and iron with regard to usury, the handing over of one for the other would not be allowed; don't you see/opine (*a-lā tarā*) that, due to gold and silver being united by a single *ʿilla* for usury, handing over one for the other is not allowed? And when the handing over of silver for iron is allowed by consensus (*ijmāʿ*), it provides indication that a single *ʿilla* does not unite them." Note that, once again, this example is not a *qiyās* argument for the discovery of a substantive rule, but for justification of an occasioning factor (*ithbāt al-ʿilla*)—or, rather, for the denial of an opponent's *ʿilla*. There are still, however, two cases being brought into comparison (though we would not refer to them as *aṣl* and *farʿ*): the contradictory reference case (gold and silver) introduced by *a-lā tarā* (in conformity with the function of *a-lā tarā* in introducing an *endoxon* premise the denial of which would lead to untenable consequences);[143] and the disputed-*ʿilla* case (silver and iron), whose *ḥukm* is already sanctioned by *ijmāʿ*. Both cases, in other words, are already solved—the purpose in bringing them together is to highlight their "opposite" (*ʿaks*) relationship (working from the *ʿaks* of their *ḥukms* to the *ʿaks* of their *ʿillas*). In fact, this example shows a reverse procedure to *qiyās al-ʿaks*, which proceeds from the *ʿaks* of the *ʿillas* to the *ʿaks* of the *ḥukms*.[144]

Mas'ala: do silver and iron have the same occasioning factor with regard to usury?		
Contradictory Reference Case gold and silver		**Disputed-*ʿilla* Case** silver and iron
Ḥukm A handing over one for the other is not allowed	(contradictory) ← →	**Ḥukm ¬A (sanctioned by *ijmāʿ*)** handing over one for the other is allowed
ʿIlla Relationship they are united by a single *ʿilla*	(therefore, also contradictory) →	**ʿIlla Relationship** they are not united by a single *ʿilla*

Note that, as above in the *taqsīm* example, this may also be rendered as a syllogism in the *modus tollens* (if P then Q; not-Q; therefore not-P). In fact, al-Shīrāzī's

(*al-taʿlīl biʾl-nafy waʾl-ʿadam*); (5) al-Baṣrī defines it (as we see in his *Kitāb al-Qiyās al-Sharʿī*) as: "obtaining the contradictory (*naqīḍ*) of something's ruling, for something else, due to their divergence with regard to the occasioning factor (*ʿilla*) of the ruling." [Niyāzī cites numerous *uṣūl* and *jadal* works]. Note that al-Bājī also provides no definition, but turns immediately to the familiar hair, meat, and bones example (*Minhāj*, Turkī ed., p. 29, §53).

[143] See the discussion in Sect. 6.2 of Chap. 6.

[144] Perhaps, thanks to the reverse order of al-Shīrāzī's example vis-à-vis *qiyās al-ʿaks*, we might make a distinction between *al-istidlāl biʾl-ʿaks* and *qiyās al-ʿaks* (or at least acknowledge that the former has two modes). We might define *al-istidlāl biʾl-ʿaks* (or its first mode) as the bringing together, in a context of *ithbāt al-ʿilla*, of two cases with contradictory *ḥukms*, for the purpose of providing indication that they must have contradictory *ʿillas*. *Qiyās al-ʿaks* (or the second mode of *al-istidlāl biʾl-ʿaks*) is the procedure in reverse: bringing, in a context of discovering a substantive ruling, an established source-case with a contradictory *ʿilla*, for the purpose of providing indication that *aṣl* and *farʿ* must also have contradictory *ḥukms*.

formulation of the example nearly does so. We might render it thus: If the usury-*ʿilla* for silver is the same as the usury-*ʿilla* for iron, then handing over silver for iron is not allowed [like the *endoxon* case of gold and silver]; but handing over silver for iron is allowed [by *ijmāʿ*]; therefore, the usury-*ʿilla* for silver is not the same as the usury-*ʿilla* for iron.

Al-Shīrāzī[145] proceeds to describe the disagreement among Shāfiʿīs with regard to the validity of this mode of *istidlāl*—some say it is not valid (including al-Juwaynī and al-Bāqillānī);[146] but the *madhhab*-opinion is that it is valid, and al-Shāfiʿī himself is said to have relied upon it in a number of places. Al-Shīrāzī's proof for the validity of *al-istidlāl bi'l-ʿaks* is an interesting *a fortiori* argument from the fact that it enjoys authoritative indication: "The indicant (*dalīl*) for the validity of *al-istidlāl bi'l-ʿaks* is that *al-istidlāl bi'l-ʿaks* is an *istidlāl* by way of a *qiyās* whose validity is authoritatively-indicated (*madlūl ʿalā ṣiḥḥatihi*); and when *qiyās* regarding co-presence (*ṭard*) is valid—though its validity is *not* authoritatively-indicated—then the validity of *al-istidlāl bi'l-ʿaks*, while it is a *qiyās* whose validity *is* authoritatively-indicated, is all the more appropriate (*awlā*)." As for the authoritative indicants for the validity of *al-istidlāl bi'l-ʿaks*, al-Shīrāzī notes that God Himself indicates His Unity (*tawḥīd*) by way of *al-ʿaks* in Q.21:22 («Were there, in [heaven and earth], deities besides God, then [heaven and earth] would have been corrupted»), and that He is the source of the Qur'ān in Q.4:82 («Were it from another besides God, they would have found in it a great deal of divergence (*ikhtilāf*)»). In such a way, al-Shīrāzī argues, God indicates that *al-istidlāl bi'l-ʿaks* is a method for discovering norms (*ṭarīq li'l-aḥkām*).[147]

al-Istidlāl bi-Bayān al-ʿIlla (Drawing Indication by way of Clarifying The Occasioning Factor)

- Definition:[148]

"And as for *al-istidlāl bi-bayān al-ʿilla* , it is of two modes. One is that one clearly identifies the occasioning factor of the ruling, then draws indication by its presence in the locus of disagreement [i.e., the contended case] that the ruling is [also] present in it. The second is that one clearly identifies the occasioning factor, then draws indication by its absence in the locus of disagreement that the ruling is [also] absent, due to [the occasioning factor's] absence."	وأما الاستدلال ببيان العلة فمن وجهين. أحدهما أن يبين علة الحكم ثم يستدل بوجودها في موضع الخلاف ليوجد بها الحكم. والثاني أن يبين العلة ثم يستدل بعدمها في موضع الخلاف ليعدم الحكم بعدمها.

---

[145] *Mulakhkhaṣ*, Niyāzī MA ed., vol. 1b, pp. 91–3.

[146] Ibid., p. 91, n. 1.

[147] Niyāzī also provides the Ḥanafī opinion (drawing on Sarakhsī, Samarqandī, Bazdawī, et al.), in n. 3 on p. 91: "If the *ḥukm* is established by a specifically-assigned occasioning factor (*ʿilla mutaʿayyana*), and has no other *ʿilla*, then *istidlāl* by way of [the *ʿaks*] is valid. But if not, it is not valid, due to the allowance that the *ḥukm* be contingent upon some other property (*waṣf*) besides it."

[148] Ibid., vol. 1b, p. 92–3.

- Example 1:[149]
  The example for the first mode is a Shāfiʿī argument regarding the obligation of amputating the hand of the grave robber (*nabbāsh*): "Cutting is only (*innamā*) obliged for the sake of deterrence and suppression of the taking of property, so that a covetous eye be not cast upon people's property. Thus it is not obliged for that with regard to which deterrence and suppression are not needed, and the taking of which the eye does not covet, it being a small amount of property. But this *ʿilla* is present with regard to the burial shroud; so cutting is obliged for it."[150] Note this is not a mode of *qiyās*, but merely the identification of a clarified *ʿilla* in the contended case. It may be formulated as a syllogism in the *modus ponens* (if P then Q; P; therefore Q). If the object of theft is a significant amount of property calling for deterrence, then cutting is obliged for its theft; a burial shroud is a significant amount of property calling for deterrence; therefore, cutting is obliged for its theft. Note also that the arguer appears first to demonstrate concomitance (*dawarān*) of *ʿilla* and *ḥukm* (when deterrence factor is present, cutting is present, when deterrence factor is not present, cutting is not present) before confirming that the *ʿilla* is present.
- Example 2:
  The example for the second mode is a Shāfiʿī argument for the discontinuance of maintenance (*nafaqa*) for the irrevocably divorced wife (*mabtūta*): "Maintenance in the marriage (*nikāḥ*) is only (*innamā*) obliged in recompense for sexual availability. Thus, if she is available, maintenance for her is enjoined; but when she is recalcitrant in marital duties, her maintenance is discontinued. And this *ʿilla* is not present with regard to the irrevocably divorced wife, because [sexual] availability on her part is not valid; so it is obliged that her maintenance be discontinued." Note that, again, this is not a mode of *qiyās*, but a confirmation of the absence of a clarified *ʿilla* from the contended case. Observe, however, that when formulated as a syllogism, it appears to be in the fallacious mode of denying the antecedent (if P then Q; not-P; therefore not-Q)—unless sexual availability is understood as a *necessary condition* (rather than a sufficient condition) for *nafaqa*. Or perhaps it must first be confirmed that *only* R (sexual availability) can give rise to Q (*nafaqa* is obliged)—that nothing but R can occasion Q. We might understand this as the function of "only" (*innamā*) in both this and the previous example; and note that for both it is at the opening of the argument: [القطع إنما وجب للردع والزجر...] and [النفقة في النكاح إنما تجب في مقابلة التمكين...]. And perhaps the power of *innamā* here can be understood from the discussions of that mode of "indicant of the rationally-understood" known as *al-Ḥaṣr*[151]—which is to say: "Y is only (*innamā*) obliged

[149] Ibid., p. 93.

[150] See *MF*, s.v. نباش, vol. 40, pp. 18–23, where this ruling is confirmed.

[151] Al-Bājī, *Minhāj*, Turkī ed., p. 25, §46 [he restricts *ḥaṣr* to *innamā* alone]; al-Shīrāzī, *Mulakhkhaṣ*, Niyāzī MA ed., vol. 1b, pp. 70ff. [with *ḥaṣr* as *innamā* on p. 75]).

due to X" means "nothing but X can occasion the obligation of Y". Finally, note that once again the arguer appears first to demonstrate concomitance (*dawarān*) of *ʿilla* and *ḥukm* (when sexual availability is present, maintenance is present, when sexual availability is not present, maintenance is not present) before confirming that the *ʿilla* is *not* present.

al-Istidlāl biʾl-Uṣūl (Drawing Indication by way of [(inductive?) Testimony of] Divinely-Sanctioned Source-Cases)

- Definition:
  As with *al-istidlāl biʾl-ʿaks*, Shīrāzī gives no definition in his *Mulakhkhaṣ*, but starts right in with an example. Niyāzī, however, supplies the following observations in a footnote: (1) this mode of *istidlāl* is covered by both al-Shīrāzī and al-Bājī, but both only mention examples (no definitions); (2) nevertheless it is evident from the examples that it is an *istidlāl* by way of a type of *qiyās al-dalāla* whose *ʿilla* is confirmed via the testimony of divinely-sanctioned source-cases (*bi-shahādat al-uṣūl*); (3) Niyāzī quotes al-Shīrāzī later in this section ("Contingency upon this [mode of *istidlāl*], and its like in function, is valid; because it is, in truth, a *qiyās* whose validity is authoritatively indicated (*madlūl*) by an abundance of *uṣūl*"), then he explains: "the meaning of that is that this type of *istidlāl* is in reality a *qiyās* in which the *ʿilla* is established via testimony of the *uṣūl*, even if the *ʿilla* is not clearly stated in it;" (4) he quotes al-Shīrāzī from his *Lumaʿ* on *shahādat al-uṣūl* and its specific application in *qiyās al-dalāla*; (5) he quotes definitions of *qiyās al-dalāla* from al-Shīrāzī and Ibn al-Himām; and (6) he concludes: "Perhaps we can say that *qiyās al-dalāla* is more general than *al-istidlāl biʾl-uṣūl*—because it includes *al-istidlāl biʾl-uṣūl* insofar as the *ʿilla* is not stated in it, but also includes something else because the *ʿilla* in *qiyās al-dalāla* might be established by a single *aṣl*. This, and *al-istidlāl biʾl-uṣūl* also enjoys a connection with the issue of 'giving preponderance to the occasioning factor via abundance of divinely-sanctioned source-cases' (*tarjīḥ al-ʿilla bi-kathrat al-uṣūl*), in the modes of giving preponderance to (potentially-efficient) intension-properties (*tarjīḥāt al-maʿānī*)."[152]
- Example 1:[153]
  Al-Shīrāzī's first example is a Shāfiʿī argument regarding the consideration of proxyship (*niyāba*) in the greater pilgrimage (*ḥajj*), and that Abū Ḥanīfa's opinion in this regard contradicts the *uṣūl*: "He claims that—when one pays the one who attributes the '*labbayka*, etc.' (*talbiyya*) to him, and intends the state of ritual sanctity (*iḥrām*) for him—this is the commissioning of a lie without urgent need (*amr biʾl-kidhb min ghayr ḥāja*), and that such is not allowed in any one of the *uṣūl*."[154]

---

[152] Ibid., vol. 1b, p. 94, n. 1.

[153] Ibid., vol. 1b, pp. 94–5.

[154] Niyāzī (p. 94, n. 2) notes that both Shāfiʿī's and Ḥanafīs permit proxyship for one incapable of undertaking the *ḥajj*, and whose lack of ability looks never to be reversed, nor do they disagree on the allowance of the proxy to take maintenance costs (*nafaqa*) from him. Disagreement concerns only the allowance of the proxy's taking a hiring fee (*ijāra*); Shāfiʿīs but not Ḥanafīs allow this.

- Example 2:
  Al-Shīrāzī's second example is a Shāfiʿī argument that one who slanders his wife with adultery then irrevocably divorces her must perform the mutual oath-cursing (*liʿān*), and that Abū Ḥanīfa's opinion in this regard contradicts the *uṣūl*: "For he voids his accusation of adultery (*qadhf*), and does not oblige for it the divinely-sanctioned punishment (*ḥadd*) or the mutual oath-cursing (*liʿān*), and this is in contradiction to the *uṣūl*." Al-Shīrāzī further explains: "Contingency upon this [mode of *istidlāl*], and its like in function, is valid; because it is, in truth, a *qiyās* whose validity is authoritatively indicated (*madlūl*) by an abundance of *uṣūl*. And the assessment of that in the first example is that such is a commissioning of a lie without urgent need (*amr bi'l-kidhb min ghayr ḥāja*) so is not allowed, like in the rest of the *uṣūl*; and in the second example that such is an unsupported accusation of adultery (*qadhf*) so ignoring it is not allowed, like in the rest of the *uṣūl*."[155] Note that, although promoted as a valid form of *istidlāl*, al-Shīrāzī's examples show this mode being used in a way that much more resembles an objection (charge: Abū Ḥanīfa's solution contradicts the collective of relevant *uṣūl* on this matter). Of course, this can be equally constructive if the opponent's position is the real contradictory of the *mustadill*'s position (R simultaneously proves his solution X to be true when he proves his opponent Q's contradictory solution not-X to be false).

Importantly, there is not only an analogical aspect to this species of *istidlāl*, but it resembles the same sort of analogical basis underpinning induction. As in the most general formulation of scientific method, when we take experiment A_1 with elements 1,2,3, and see it produces result X; then take experiment A_2 with the same elements 1,2,3, and see it produces result X; then take experiment A_3 with the same elements 1,2,3, and see it produces result X; etc.—we induce that, should we perform experiment A_N with the same elements 1,2,3, it will produce the same result X. Likewise, if we know relevant *aṣl* A_1 has properties 1,2,3, and *ḥukm* X; and relevant *aṣl* A_2 has the same properties 1,2,3, and the same *ḥukm* X; and relevant *aṣl* A_3 has the same properties 1,2,3, and the same *ḥukm* X; etc.—we induce that any *farʿ* A_N with the same properties 1,2,3 will also have the same *ḥukm* X. Reasoning from the shared properties (demonstrably or potentially efficient) of a single, relevant *aṣl*, as in the various modes of *maʿnā al-khiṭāb* (*qiyās*), is an analogical enterprise. Perhaps we might say that reasoning from the shared properties of a significant *collective* of relevant *uṣūl*—the method of *shahādat al-uṣūl*—is an inductive enterprise.

[155] Ibid., p. 95. In a following section (pp. 95–6), al-Shīrāzī describes another mode which opponents incorrectly link to *al-istidlāl bi'l-uṣūl*: that one draw indication by way of one/some of the *uṣūl* for the locus of disagreement (while the remainder of the relevant *uṣūl* indicate otherwise). He supplies a Ḥanafī argument by way of illustration, then refutes it. Finally, al-Shīrāzī closes his discussion of the *adillat al-maʿqūl* in his *Mulakhkhaṣ* by pointing out additional modes which are invalid and incorrectly placed under this rubric: (1) *al-istidlāl bi'l-qarā'in* (pp. 97–100); and (2) *ḥaml al-muṭlaq ʿalā al-muqayyad min jihat al-lafẓ* (pp. 101–3). Both are illustrated and refuted.

4.4 Categories of Dialectical Inquiry: Question (*Su'āl*) and Response (*Jawāb*)

It is the question and answer procedure of dialectic, more than any other feature, which sets it apart from other argumentative modes.[156] Accordingly, most of the *jadal* works constituting our analytical lens treat the proper modes of dialectical question to some extent or another.[157] A particularly useful summary may be found in al-Bājī's *Minhāj*, and the remainder of this section will consist of an outline of his *Chapter on the Categories of Question and Response* (*Bāb Aqsām al-Su'āl wa'l-Jawāb*). Like al-Shīrāzī in the preceding section, al-Bājī will, in the main, be allowed to speak for himself. As will be seen, he was every bit as concise, systematic, and lucid as his teacher.

Al-Bājī's Typology of Question (*Su'āl*) and Response (*Jawāb*)[158]

Question #1: "about the confirmation (*ithbāt*) of the doctrinal opinion (*madhhab*) of the respondent (*mas'ūl*)."[159]

- "The question: Does [R] have a *madhhab*-opinion regarding the case-at-hand (*al-ḥāditha*), or not?"
  - Type 1: "[Q] asks: Does [R] have a *madhhab*-opinion for this problem (*mas'ala*)?"

(continued)

[156] Miller treats the questions of classical juridical dialectic in detail ("Islamic Disputation Theory," pp. 90–113). For a summary and partial critique, see my dissertation (pt. 1, pp. 124–35).

[157] A notable exception is al-Shīrāzī in his *Ma'ūna*. He affords the topic full treatment, however, in his *Mulakhkhaṣ*.

[158] *Minhāj*, Turkī ed., pp. 34–41, §§64–79. Al-Bājī begins by listing his five types of question (*su'āl*) in the precise order he will discuss them (as will be outlined above). Having done so, he adds: "And according to the *madhhab*-opinion of the one who allows adherence to a qualified jurisprudent (*taqlīd*), the questions are six. For the third question ["the question about the indicant for the opinion" (*al-su'āl 'an dalīl al-madhhab*), see above] becomes: "Does he have a *dalīl*-indicant for the problem (*mas'ala*), or does he practice adherence (*taqlīd*) regarding it?" Importantly, al-Bājī then notes: "And belonging to every type of *su'āl* is a type of response (*jawāb*) specifically associated with it." He concludes his introduction, saying: "I will explain that, and put it into order (*urattibuhu*), if God wills, in such a manner as will draw understanding close, and clarify its normative procedure (*ḥukm*). And from God comes success!"

[159] Ibid., pp. 34–5, §§65–6. As with previous outlines, al-Bājī's examples and discussions will mostly be omitted.

- Type 2: "[Q] conveys two opinions belonging to the one whose *madhhab*-doctrine [R] follows (*yataqalladu*), and then asks: Does [R] prefer one of the two?"[160]
- [Section: al-Bājī discusses the proper comportment of R, and the procedural norms of response (*jawāb*) relevant to Question #1]

Question #2: "about the quiddity (*māhiyya*) of the *madhhab*-opinion."[161]

- "The question falls sometimes on the ruling (*ḥukm*), and other times on the method (*ṭarīq*) [leading to] the *ḥukm*:"
  - [1] "The question about the *ḥukm*: [Q] says: 'Is date-wine (*nabīdh*) lawful (*ḥalāl*) or forbidden (*ḥarām*)?' And: 'Does usury (*ribā*) obtain for fruits, or not?' and such as resembles [these questions], from among the rulings which the jurists (*fuqahā'*) disagree about (*ikhtalafa fīhi*)."[162]
  - [2] "The question about the method (*ṭarīq*) [leading to] the *ḥukm*, which may be..."
    - about an associated name (*ism*)...[163]
    - about an attribute (*ṣifa*) upon which the *ḥukm* is made contingent (*yataʿallaqu bihā*)...[164]
    - about an occasioning factor (*ʿilla*)...[165]
    - about a report (*khabar*)...[166]

(continued)

[160] In al-Bājī's example, Q brings two narrated rulings of Mālik b. Anas [eponym of the Mālikī *madhhab*], then asks R whether he prefers one, or whether the two *dalīl*-indicants are equal according to him. Following this, al-Bājī notes: "All of these are valid questions in intellectual investigation (*naẓar*), and calculated methods (*ṭuruq maqṣūda*)."

[161] *Minhāj*, Turkī ed., pp. 35–6, §§67–9.

[162] The relationship between the legal literary genres of "the Science of Juridical Disagreement" (*ʿilm al-khilāf*) and "the Science of Dialectical Disputation" (*ʿilm al-jadal*)—with the former providing material and past practice, and the latter providing theory and systematic method—is brought into sharp focus here.

[163] Among al-Bājī's examples is: "[Q] asks about date-wine (*nabīdh*): 'Is it called (*yusammā*) "wine" (*khamr*)?'" Cf. al-Baṣrī's objections to "justifying the occasioning factor by way of the name" (*al-taʿlīl bi'l-ism*), in the following section and Appendix I.

[164] Al-Bājī says: "For one may disagree (*yakhtalifu*) about the attribute (*ṣifa*), like the disagreement regarding hair: 'Does the soul reside in it?' And about bone: 'Does the soul reside in it?'" A typical mark of al-Bājī's consistency, we have already encountered this *mas'ala* in the outline of his *Aqsām Adillat al-Sharʿ* (see the section and attached notes for *al-istidlāl bi'l-ʿaks*).

[165] Al-Bājī's examples: "[Q] says to [R]: 'What is the *ʿilla* for the proscription (*taḥrīm*) of disparity of exchange (*al-tafāḍul*) for wheat?' And: 'What is the *ʿilla* for the proscription of grape-wine (*khamr*)?'"

[166] Al-Bājī says (among other examples): "Like the question about the conquest of Mecca: Was it by peaceable surrender (*ṣulḥan*), or by force (*ʿanwatan*)?" He concludes his subtypes and examples by saying: "And the question about all of these [methods] is valid, because confirming [the

- [Section: al-Bājī warns [Q] against: (1) asking open-ended questions which may cause him to make retractions; and (2) asking ambiguous questions which may forestall a response.]
- [Section: al-Bājī discusses the proper comportment of R, and the procedural norms of response (*jawāb*) relevant to Question #2][167]

Question #3: "about the indicant (*dalīl*) [of the *madhhab*-opinion]"[168]

- "[Q] says to [R], after the response (*jawāb*) about the *madhhab*-opinion: 'What is the *dalīl*-indicant for that?' Thus he confronts [R] with [the task of] furnishing the *dalīl*."
- [al-Bājī outlines a step-by-step procedure for R's response, depending on whether he knows Q's *madhhab*-opinion,[169] or does not[170]]
- [Section: al-Bājī outlines three methods (*ṭuruq*) of indication (*dalāla*) for R]:
    - Method 1: "[R] provides indication for the *mas'ala* as it is (*bi-ʿaynihā*)"
        - [procedure and examples]
    - Method 2: "[R] allocates the indication (*dalāla*) to some of its parts (*shuʿab*) and sections (*fuṣūl*)"
        - [permissible and impermissible procedures with examples]
    - Method 3: "[R] constructs [his approach to] the *mas'ala* on the basis of another"[171]

(continued)

---

method] leads to confirmation of the *ḥukm*—so the question about [the method] is like the question about the *ḥukm*."

[167] Importantly, al-Bājī recommends that both R and Q be guardedly conservative (*yataḥarrazu*) in both question and response. The danger, of course, lies in accidentally conceding something which cannot be retracted. As will be seen in the analyses of the subject-text, al-Shāfiʿī—in the role of R—is often parsimonious in response. The same is true when he is questioner; at times his questions appear so carefully crafted as to elicit precisely the response necessary for *elenchus*.

[168] *Minhāj*, Turkī ed., pp. 36–9, §§70–5.

[169] If R knows Q's *madhhab*-opinion, he indicates this, and is then allowed two choices: (1) he may provide indication for the validity (*ṣiḥḥa*) of his own doctrine; or (2) he may provide indication for the invalidity (*fasād*) of the doctrine of his opponent (*khaṣm*).

[170] In this case, if "the *mas'ala* has variant doctrines and various opinions, and the *dalīl*-indicant differs due to disagreement of the *madhhab*-doctrine of the one professing it, [R] asks [Q] about his *madhhab*-doctrine so that the *dalīl*-indicant may be in accordance with it."

[171] Al-Bājī justifies the permissibility of this method, saying: "the construction is an explanation (*bayān*) for one of the methods of the *mas'ala*; it is in the status (*manzila*) of the rest of the methods of the *mas'ala*." Importantly, what al-Bājī is suggesting here is a kind of methodological "*manzila*-subsumption." (What I have termed *manzila*-subsumption will be discussed in the forthcoming analyses of the subject-text.) Besides this, we will see several demonstrations of an obvious crossover between *fiqh*-oriented charges of inconsistency (*naqḍ*) and method-oriented charges of inconsistency (what I have termed method-*naqḍ*). Al-Bājī's allowance for a kind of methodological *manzila*-subsumption is indicative of the same phenomenon: crossovers—in the

- Type 1: "[R] constructs [his indication (*dalāla*)] upon a *mas'ala* of the primary source-materials (*uṣūl*)"[172]
- Type 2: "[R] constructs [his indication (*dalāla*)] upon one of the *masā'il* of the derived branch-cases (*furūʿ*)"[173]
- [Section: al-Bājī explains two types of constructing a *mas'ala* upon a *mas'ala*][174]

Question #4: "about the mode (*wajh*) of the *dalīl*-indicant"[175]

- "[R] draws indication by way of a Qur'ānic verse (*āya*) or a report (*khabar*), and his *dalīl*-indicant from it is not clear, so [Q] demands (*yuṭālibu*) the mode (*wajh*) of the *dalīl*-indicant—and, in general, the mode of the *dalīl*-indicant must be either clear (*wāḍiḥ*) or unclear (*ghāmiḍ*)."[176]

(continued)

realm of *jadal*-theory—between *fiqh*-oriented justifications (substantive *manzila*-subsumption) and critiques (*naqḍ*), and method-oriented justifications (methodological *manzila*-subsumption) and critiques (method-*naqḍ*). The significance is that *jadal*, whether from the perspective of *istidlāl* or *iʿtirāḍ*, comprised justifications and critiques at two levels: (1) the substantive legal level (justifying or critiquing a ruling); and (2) the legal-theoretical level (justifying or critiquing a method). Based upon my analyses, this was just as true in al-Shāfiʿī's day as it was in al-Bājī's—perhaps we may consider it natural, or even unavoidable, as dialectical systems evolve.

[172] In al-Bājī's example, a Mālikī R constructs his *dalāla*-indication on the basis of *qiyās*, and informs the Ẓāhirī Q that (1) if he accepts *qiyās* as valid, he will construct his *dalāla* for the *mas'ala* on its basis; and (2) if he does not accept *qiyās*, he will first provide indication that *qiyās* is valid.

[173] Al-Bājī's example is important, for he once again refers to the *mas'ala* of hair we encountered in his exposition on *al-istidlāl bi'l-ʿaks*. Here, he explains: "It is like when the Mālikī is asked about hair: Does it become impure (*najas*) through death? So [the Mālikī R] says: This *mas'ala*, according to me, is constructed upon the fact that hair is something in which the soul does not reside. So if you concede [that] to me [I will build on it]; and if not, I will shift the debate to it [i.e., to this more primary *mas'ala*]." Al-Bājī explains this can only be done when the methods of the two *mas'ala*s are one and the same (as with the impurity and soul *masā'il* for hair).

[174] There is no disagreement as to the permissibility of the first, which is that R constructs *mas'ala* upon *mas'ala* before commencing his *istidlāl*. As for the second, when he begins his *dalāla*-indication but does not mention he intends construction, al-Bājī provides two sets of procedures. In the first case, if R builds on a *mas'ala* of *uṣūl*-principles particular to his *madhhab*-doctrine, the debate shifts to that *mas'ala* if Q does not accept it. In the second case, if R builds on a *mas'ala* of derived branch-cases—and Q objects, requesting a shift to debating that *mas'ala*—al-Bājī records two opinions: (1) Abū ʿAlī al-Ṭabarī (Shāfiʿī; d.350/961, a noted dialectician and *uṣūl*ist, and author of works in both genres) said: "That right does not belong to him, because it is shifting ground (*intiqāl*)." Abū Isḥāq al-Shīrāzī, on the other hand, said (2): "That right belongs to him." Al-Bājī agrees with his teacher, so long as it is constructed upon one of the unambiguous *uṣūl*-principles (*al-uṣūl al-ẓāhira*).

[175] *Minhāj*, Turkī ed., pp. 39–40, §§76–7.

[176] Al-Bājī explains that if the mode (*wajh*) of the *dalīl*-indicant is clear (*wāḍiḥ*), then Q's requesting an explanation (*bayān*) is disapproved of. Qualification as "clear" means that the *dalīl*-indicant is either *naṣṣ*, or *ẓāhir*, or *ʿāmm*; and al-Bājī provides examples for each. "Unclear" (*ghāmiḍ*), of course, is none of these, and "demand for an explanation (*al-muṭālaba bi'l-bayān*) for

- [Section: al-Bājī clarifies that all questions up to this point are presented in the order they must be asked][177]

Question #5: "according to the mode of critique (*'alā wajh al-qadḥ*) [against the *dalīl*-indicant]"[178]

- **Type 1: *al-Muṭālaba* (Demand):** "It is [Q's] demand (*muṭālaba*) for the validation (*taṣḥīḥ*) of the *akhbār*-reports, and for the confirmation (*ithbāt*) of their chains of transmission (*asānīd*); and [Q's] demand (*muṭālaba*) for the validation (*taṣḥīḥ*) of *ijmā'* and for its confirmation (*ithbāt*); and the production (*ījād*) of the *'illa* and its validation (*taṣḥīḥ*); and for other things from among the modes (*wujūh*) of demands (*muṭālabāt*)."[179]

(continued)

---

its like" is deemed appropriate. The import of this question is obvious to the objectives of the questioner, for R—proceeding cautiously as al-Bājī recommends—may merely cite an authoritative *dalīl*-indicant as a proof for his solution to the *mas'ala* at hand. If the relationship between that *dalīl*-indicant and the *mas'ala* at hand is not obvious, however, and Q does not demand clarification of their correlation, then R's solution might slip past on the authority of the *dalīl*-indicant alone. In this manner an error of correlation, by which the *dalīl*-indicant itself ought to be rejected as irrelevant, might be overlooked.

[177] He says: "And these questions are arranged according to the order in which we arranged them, so that one depart from the first to the second, and from the second to third, and so on to the last of them. And it is not allowed that one begin with the question about the *madhhab*-opinion, then follow it with the question about the mode of the *dalīl*-indicant which has not been presented, and yet ask about its mode. Likewise, it is not allowed for [Q] to begin with a critique against the *madhhab*-opinion until he asks about the *dalīl*-indicant, and about its mode if it is not clear. But some of the Theorists of Intellectual Investigation (*Ahl al-Naẓar*) have allowed objection (*al-i'tirāḍ*) by way of critique (*qadḥ*) before the question about the *dalīl*-indicant and its mode. And this is erroneous, because [Q] (*sā'il*) at such a time becomes [R] (*mas'ūl*), and he has no right to such."

[178] *Minhāj*, Turkī ed., pp. 40–1, §§78–9.

[179] It is important to recognize that—with al-Bājī's fifth question—we are shifting from a phase of information-gathering to a phase of objection, critique, rebuttal, and refutation. Although distinct from the categories of "objections" (*i'tirāḍāt*) and "counter-indications" (*mu'āraḍāt*), the "demands"(*muṭālabāt*) still qualify as objections insofar as Q is initiating the problematizing of R's solution to the *mas'ala* at hand through his demand for the validation (*taṣḥīḥ*) of X, Y, or Z. In some ways, this is a shadowy area between the question about the mode of the *dalīl*-indicant (the final phase of information-gathering) and outright objection (the *i'tirāḍāt*). As we shall see in the analyses of the subject-text, it is often difficult to identify the dialectical questions we encounter by the *muṭālabāt* which al-Bājī defines here, and in later discussions; such an identification relies upon indication of the questioner's intentions, which are not always evident in the

- **Type 2: *al-I'tirāḍ* (Objection):** "It is [Q's] objection (*iʿtirāḍ*) against the selfsame *dalīl*-indicant [proffered by R], by way of what nullifies it (*bimā yubṭiluhu*). And this is like the contestation of (*al-ṭaʿn fī*) the chains of transmission (*asānīd*) of the *ḥadīth* by way of proving the weakness (*taḍʿīf*) of its transmitter, or the contestation of *ijmāʿ* by way of the clarification (*bayān*) of disagreement [in the community] (*khilāf*), or the contestation of the *ʿilla* by way of 'inconsistency' (*al-naqḍ*) and 'breaking apart' (*al-kasr*), etc."[180]
- **Type 3: *al-Muʿāraḍa* (Counter-Indication):** "It is that [Q] opposes (*yuqābila*) [R's] *dalīl*-indicant by way of its like, or by what is stronger than it; and [R] responds to him by way of all that [Q] puts forth against the *dalīl*-indicant of [R],[181] from among the demands (*muṭālabāt*) and objections (*iʿtirāḍāt*); or [R] gives preponderance (*yurajjiḥu*) to his formulation of the *dalīl*-indicant over that which is opposed to it."[182]
- [Section: al-Bājī explains further procedural considerations for the number of questions, and the order in which they must be asked]

presentations of the subject-text. This may also be a general quality of proto-system *jadal*—i.e., a less systematic practice of question order and formulation—for we also find questions which are oriented towards an opponent's objections (a category we do not find in the *jadal*-theory works), along with the standard questions oriented towards his *istidlāl*. Returning to the *muṭālabāt*, al-Bājī concludes: "So [R] is confronted with the validation (*taṣḥīḥ*) of all this, according to what we will explain in its proper place." As we are able to observe in subsequent chapters of the *Minhāj*: such objections as are designated "*al-muṭālaba bi*-X"—or which are, in other ways, linked to *muṭālabāt*—constitute the first set among the ordered objections pertaining to each mode of *istidlāl*.

[180] Al-Bājī concludes: "[R] is obliged to eliminate the question, and to repel it, by way of what arrests it, so that [Q] concedes the *dalīl*-indicant to him."

[181] Meaning, R takes on the role of Q.

[182] It is important to note that the last chapters of both al-Shīrāzī's *Maʿūna* and al-Bājī's *Minhāj* are dedicated to ordered listings of "modes of preponderance" (*tarjīḥāt*). The above description of *muʿāraḍa* makes clear why this is so—for among R's responses to Q's *muʿāraḍa* is that he trump the opposing *dalīl*-indicant by way of "giving preponderance" (*tarjīḥ*) to his own. It is also important to recognize some of the hallmarks of *muʿāraḍa*. The first is that the modality of Q's role has become "constructive" as opposed to merely "destructive." That is to say, he has moved from undermining and in other ways invalidating R's solution to the *mas'ala* at hand, to supplanting that solution with one of his own. Q's opposing R's *dalīl*-indicant with another *dalīl*-indicant initiates the process by which R may eventually be forced to concede Q's solution. And this in

On the Prescribed Ordering of Questions and Objections

The precision and systematic approach of full-system *jadal* theory should be more than plain at this point. This extended to matters of procedure, with sections and chapters of our lens-texts devoted to the proper order of disputation. This has been duly noted by the few scholars who have contributed to the field of Islamic dialectics in recent times: Miller dedicates three short sections of his dissertation to "The Order of the Objections", "The Signs of Defeat", and "The Adab al-Jadal ['Proper Comportment of Disputation']" with regard to the classical juridical dialectic of our lens-text authors;[183] and Hallaq contributes a concise discussion on the procedure of disputation in the introduction to his translation of al-Baṣrī's *Kitāb al-Qiyās al-Sharʿī*. In treating this same matter of "ordering" (*tartīb*), Hallaq draws upon al-Juwaynī's *Kāfiya*, al-Khaṭīb al-Baghdādī's *al-Faqīh wa'l-Mutafaqqih*, and Ibn ʿAqīl's *K. al-Jadal* in order to present a general portrait of the sequence and procedural concerns of juridical disputation.[184] The following outline is drawn from his prose description, and will serve to illustrate the procedural norms common to our lens-texts:

- (1) Q asks R's opinion regarding the ruling (*ḥukm*) for the problem at hand (*mas'ala*)
- (2) Q asks R "to adduce the evidence and proof" justifying his *ḥukm*
- (3) Q "casts doubt" on R's evidence and proof, pushing R to validate them
  - If R fails at any stage, he must either adopt Q's opinion, or another which he is capable of defending
  - If R succeeds at all stages, then Q proceeds to #4
- (4) Q raises objections to R's indicants

(continued)

turn brings about another hallmark characteristic of *muʿāraḍa*: the switching of roles. For as Q is now himself *proposing* a solution, rather than merely undermining R's, he must *defend* his solution against all that R may bring against it by way of demand (*muṭālaba*) and objection (*iʿtirāḍ*). Thus, the original questioner becomes the new respondent, and the original respondent the new questioner. Al-Bājī closes his description of the dialectical questions by saying: "And this is the whole collective of modes of critique (*qadḥ*) and response (*jawāb*). And as for the details, I will mention them according to the ordering (*tartīb*) of the *adilla*-indicants, one by one, and I will explain the responses for them, if God wills." Thus, we are again reminded of the organizing principle of this (and al-Shīrāzī's) *jadal*-theory. The questions, objections, and responses are all ordered according to the hierarchy of *istidlāl*, and a parallel objective to Aristotle's ordering of *topoi* is easy to discern.

183 "Islamic Disputation Theory," pp. 134–41. See my summary review and partial critique ("Dialectical Forge," pt. 1, pp. 135, 190–6).

184 "Treatise," pp. 203ff.

- If R's indicant is Qur'ānic
  - Q makes the charge that it is equivocal or abrogated
  - Or, Q objects to the interpretation, and suggests another
  - Or, Q discredits the indicant, and produces a stronger one
- If R's indicant is Sunnaic
  - Q makes charges against the chain of transmission, or against the transmitted text
  - Q may charge (as with Qur'ānic evidence) abrogation, or produce a more reliable, or univocal, *ḥadīth*
- If R's indicant is established by consensus
  - Q demands that R confirm such a consensus has taken place
  - Q attempts to prove "the existence of a dissenting voice"
- If R's *ḥukm* is derived through *qiyās*
  - Q objects to R's *qiyās*, in that:
    - R's *ḥukm* contradicts text or consensus
    - R's derivation of the *ḥukm* from the *aṣl* is not precise (thus the *ḥukm* of the *far*ʿ is compromised)
    - R's *aṣl* is itself a *far*ʿ based on another *aṣl* (R must therefore prove that the *ʿilla* of both the first and second *aṣl* occasion the same *ḥukm*)
    - R's *far*ʿ does not have all the properties comprised by the *ʿilla* of his *aṣl*, or vice versa
    - R's *ʿilla* is not efficient as a whole, or its properties are not efficient in particular
      - co-absence and co-presence must be proven for all properties of the *ʿilla*

Hallaq's description of juridical *jadal* procedure covers most of the domains of *istidlāl*, though not to the full extent presented in the works of al-Shīrāzī, al-Bājī, et al. Nevertheless, we gain further insight into the organizing principle behind our *jadal*-theory works, and a portrait of how this principle plays out in the course of disputation. In other words, we can clearly see how the ordering of questions and the hierarchical approach to the domains of *istidlāl* mesh together into a seamless and efficient *jadal* procedure, designed to provide a systematic truth-seeking program with maximum utility. The components of objection (*iʿtirāḍ*) and response (*jawāb*) directed to each domain of *istidlāl* go far beyond this summary outline, as we shall see below; nevertheless it more than adequately shows the cohesiveness of systems put forward by early *jadal* theorists.[185]

[185] Hallaq closes his description by noting the systematic checking and "methodical interrogation" of dialectic. He then concludes: "It is precisely this question-and-answer method which characterizes juridical dialectic in general and al-Baṣrī's treatise in particular" ("Treatise," p. 205).

4.5 Categories of Critique: Demand (*Muṭālaba*), Objection (*Iʿtirāḍ*), and Counter-Indication (*Muʿāraḍa*)

On the Higher Order Categories of Objection

A review of the numerous categories of objection found in our lens-texts will at once provide (1) further insight into the sophistication of classical, full-system *jadal*, and (2) the core focal material of the analytical lens by which the subject-text will be examined. From this point forward, the appendices I have provided at the end of the monograph—outlining the many modes of demand (*muṭālaba*), objection (*iʿtirāḍ*), counter-indication (*muʿāraḍa*), and preponderance (*tarjīḥ*) treated by al-Shīrāzī and al-Bājī—should prove useful references, while providing a larger picture of these startlingly complex but orderly systems. By way of introduction, I have compressed both systems into a general outline consisting only of the higher categories of dialectical objection, in order to bring broader organizational features to light.[186]

Al-Shīrāzī	Al-Bājī
[Disputing the Authoritative Source-Case (*Aṣl*)]	
Modes of Objection against Drawing Indication from the Qur'ān (*al-Iʿtirāḍ ʿalā al-Istidlāl bi'l-Kitāb*)	
• 1) "you, yourself, do not advocate it" (*annaka lā taqūlu bihi*) • 2) [Q] professes [the verse's] compelling agency (*mūjibihā*) • 3) the ambiguity (*ijmāl*) of the verse is claimed, by measure of either God's decrees (*Sharʿ*) or the customary usage (*al-lugha*) • 4) Sharing the Indicant (*al-mushāraka fi'l-dalīl*) • 5) Variant Reading [of the Qur'ān] (*ikhtilāf al-qirā'a*) • 6) Abrogation (*naskh*) • 7) Preponderating Exegesis (*Ta'wīl*) • 8) Counter-Indication (*Muʿāraḍa*)	• 1) [Objection] that [R] does not advocate it (*lā yaqūlu bihi*) • 2) Profession of the compelling agency of the indicant (*al-qawl bi-mūjib al-dalīl*) from the Qur'ān, and contestation (*munāzaʿa*) regarding what the *lafẓ*-expression necessitates • 3) Claim of Sharing [R's] Drawing of Indication from the Qur'ān (*daʿwā al-mushāraka bi'l-istidlāl bi'l-Kitāb*) • 4) Variant Readings [of the Qur'ān] (*ikhtilāf al-qirā'āt*) • 5) Claim of Abrogation (*daʿwā al-naskh*) • 6) [Objection] with reference to Preponderating Exegesis (*min jihat al-ta'wīl*) • 7) Counter-Indication (*Muʿāraḍa*) • 8) [related but fallacious modes]

(continued)

[186] This outline, like the second and third appendices, is distilled from the *Maʿūna* and *Minhāj*, in the precise chapter order of treatment. Bear in mind that these are only the higher order categories; a multitude of subtypes have been omitted, along with categories deemed by the authors to be problematic or fallacious, systematic responses to objections, and other elements. The responses (*ajwiba*, s. *jawāb*) are of particular importance; nearly every type and subtype of objection is twinned with one. In our lens-texts, one will find not only how to object (as Q) to the various domains of *istidlāl*, but how to defend (as R) against such objections. Our treatises are not manuals only for the questioner; they offer a complete, systematic structure for both positions in a dialectical disputation.

Modes of Objection against Drawing Indication from the Sunna (*al-I'tirāḍ ʿalā al-Istidlāl bi'l-Sunna*)	
• **(A) *I'tirāḍ* against the Sunna as Outright Rejection (*Radd*) [on the basis of legal-theoretical principles]** ○ 1) the rejection of the Shīʿa (*Rāfiḍa*) [of solitary reports (*akhbār āḥād*)] ○ 2) the rejection of the Ḥanafīs [of solitary reports, when they go against] common knowledge (*mā yaʿummu bihi al-balwā*) ○ 3) the rejection of the Mālikīs [of reports] which contradict (*khālafa*) the *qiyās* ○ 4) the rejection of the Ḥanafīs [of reports] which contradict *qiyās* of the *uṣūl* ○ 5) the rejection of the Ḥanafīs [of reports] necessitating addition to the unambiguous text (*naṣṣ*) of the Qur'ān, and that such constitutes abrogation	[....]
• **(B) *I'tirāḍ* against the Sunna with reference to the Chain of Transmission (*Isnād*)** ○ 1) Demand for [the *isnād*'s] Confirmation (*al-Muṭālaba bi-ithbātihi*); for *akhbār*-reports which are not consistent with the exemplary traditions (*sunan*), and are not audited except by dissenters (*mukhālifīn*) ○ 2) Degrading the Chain of Transmission (*al-Qadḥ fi'l-Isnād*) ○ 3) Other Modes of the Ḥanafīs	• **1) [Objection] with reference to the Chain of Transmission (*min jihat al-isnād*)** ○ 1.1) [an opponent to the category of "unbroken, multiple-party transmission of a *maʿnā*-intension" (*al-tawātur ʿalā al-maʿnā*) says]: "these are solitary reports (*akhbār āḥād*) and we don't profess such" ○ 1.2) Objection to the Chains of Transmission for Reports Relied upon for Argument ■ 1.2.1) with reference to Demand and Validation (*al-muṭālaba wa'l-taṣḥīḥ*) ■ 1.2.2) with reference to Degrading and Defaming (*min jihat al-qadḥ wa'l-tajrīḥ*)
• **(C) *I'tirāḍ* against the Sunna with reference to the transmitted text (*matn*) [as a self-initiated saying of the Prophet (*qawl mubtada'*)]** ○ 1) [R] draws indication by way of something he does not profess ○ 2) [Q] professes [the transmitted text's] compelling agency (*yaqūlu bi-mūjibihi*) ○ 3) [Q] claims ambiguity (*ijmāl*), by measure of either God's decrees (*Sharʿ*) or the customary usage (*al-lugha*) ○ 4) Sharing the Indicant (*al-mushāraka fi'l-dalīl*) ○ 5) Variant Narration (*ikhtilāf al-riwāya*) ○ 6) Abrogation (*naskh*) ○ 7) Preponderating Exegesis (*Ta'wīl*) ○ 8) Counter-Indication (*Muʿāraḍa*)	• **2) Modes of Objection to the Transmitted Text of the Sunna (*wujūh al-i'tirāḍ ʿalā matn al-Sunna*); [for Sunna which came about for no particular individual (*wārida fī ghayr mu'ayyan*)]** ○ 2.1) Because [R] does not profess it (*al-mustadill lā yaqūlu bihi*) ○ 2.2) Contestation regarding what the *lafẓ*-expression of the Sunna necessitates, and profession of its compelling agency (*al-munāzaʿa fī muqtaḍā lafẓ al-Sunna wa'l-qawl bi-mūjibihā*) ○ 2.3) Sharing [R's] Drawing of Indication from the Sunna (*al-mushāraka fi'l-istidlāl bi'l-Sunna*) ○ 2.4) Variant Narration (*ikhtilāf al-riwāya*) ○ 2.5) Claim of Abrogation (*daʿwā al-naskh*) ○ 2.6) [Objection] with reference to Preponderating Exegesis (*min jihat al-ta'wīl*) ○ 2.7) Counter-Indication (*Muʿāraḍa*)

(continued)

• **(D) *Iʿtirāḍ* against the Sunna with reference to the transmitted text (*matn*) [as a prompted Prophetic decree (*qawl khārij ʿalā sabab*)]:** ○ 1) The *lafẓ*-expression stands alone, by itself (*bi-nafsihi*), without the reason (*sabab*) [which prompted it], and argument against it (*al-kalām ʿalayhi*) is like arguing against the self-initiated (*mubtadaʾ*) Sunna ○ 2) What does not stand alone, by itself, without the reason [which prompted it]; and what distinguishes it from the [other] *iʿtirāḍ* is a claim of ambiguity (*daʿwā al-ijmāl*)	• **3) Objection against Drawing Indication from Prompted Sunna (*al-iʿtirāḍ ʿalā al-istidlāl bi'l-Sunna al-wārida ʿalā al-sabab*)** ○ 3.1) Sunna which came about for a particular individual (*wārida fī muʿayyan*); the ruling of the Prophet may be transmitted with respect to a particular individual (*qad yunqal ḥukm al-Nabī fī ʿayn*) ▪ 3.1.1) no reason (*sabab*) is conveyed with the ruling (*ḥukm*) ▪ 3.1.2) a reason (*sabab*) is conveyed with the ruling (*ḥukm*); the *ḥukm* came with regard to a particular individual for a specific reason (*muʿayyan bi-sabab*)
• **(E) *Iʿtirāḍ* against the Sunna with reference to the transmitted text (*matn*) [as the Prophet's deed (*fiʿl*)]** ○ 1) [R] does not profess it (*lā yaqūlu bihi*) ○ 2) [Q] disputes with [R] (*yunāziʿuhu*) regarding [the deed's] obligation (*muqtaḍāhu*) ○ 3) Claim of Ambiguity (*Daʿwā al-Ijmāl*) ○ 4) Sharing the Indicant (*al-Mushāraka fi'l-Dalīl*) ○ 5) Variant Narration (*Ikhtilāf al-Riwāya*) ○ 6) Claim of Abrogation (*Daʿwā al-Naskh*) ○ 7) Preponderating Exegesis (*Taʾwīl*) ○ 8) Counter-Indication (*Muʿāraḍa*)	• **4) Objection against Drawing Indication from the Deeds of the Prophet (*al-iʿtirāḍ ʿalā al-istidlāl bi-afʿāl al-Nabī*)** ○ 4.1) Denial that one can draw argumentative support by way of it (*al-manʿ min al-iḥtijāj bihi*) ○ 4.2) that [R] does not profess it ○ 4.3) Contestation regarding [the deed's] obligation (*munāzaʿa fī muqtaḍāhi*) ○ 4.4) Claim of Ambiguity (*Daʿwā al-Ijmāl*) ○ 4.5) Sharing the Indicant (*al-Mushāraka fi'l-Dalīl*) ○ 4.6) Variant Narration (*Ikhtilāf al-Riwāya*) ○ 4.7) Claim of Abrogation (*Daʿwā al-Naskh*) ○ 4.8) Preponderating Exegesis (*Taʾwīl*) ○ 4.9) Counter-Indication (*Muʿāraḍa*) ○ 4.10) [related but fallacious objections]

(continued)

• **(F) *Iʿtirāḍ* against the Sunna with reference to the transmitted text (*matn*) [as the Prophet's acknowledgment (*iqrār*)]** ○ 1) [the Prophet's] acknowledgment of [another's] saying (*iqrār ʿalā al-qawl*) ○ 2) [the Prophet's] acknowledgment of [another's] deed (*iqrār ʿalā al-fiʿl*)	• **5) Objection against Drawing Indication from the Acknowledgment of the Prophet (*al-iʿtirāḍ ʿalā al-istidlāl bi'l-iqrār*)** ○ 5.1) [the Prophet] saw something and acknowledged it ○ 5.2) something was done in [the Prophet's] time in such a manner as could not be hidden from him
Modes of Objection against Drawing Indication from Consensus (*al-Iʿtirāḍ ʿalā al-Istidlāl bi'l-Ijmāʿ*)	
• 1) Outright Rejection (*Radd*) [on the basis of legal-theoretical principles] • 2) Demand for Validation of the Consensus (*al-muṭālaba bi-taṣḥīḥ al-ijmāʿ*) • 3) [Q] conveys disagreement (*khilāf*) from one of [the Companions] • 4) [Q] debates it as he does the transmitted text (*matn*) of the Sunna	• 1) Drawing indication from Consensus of a type known by agreement (*ittifāq*) ○ 1.1) Demand for Validation of the Consensus and its Conspicuousness (*al-muṭālaba bi-taṣḥīḥ al-ijmāʿ wa ẓuhūrihi*) ○ 1.2) Conveyance of Disagreement (*naql al-khilāf*) ○ 1.3) [Q] discusses what is conveyed [of the consensus], of decree (*qawl*), deed (*fiʿl*), and acknowledgment (*iqrār*); just as with Sunna • 2) Drawing indication from Consensus of a type known by disagreement (*ikhtilāf*); [when disagreement is split evenly in two camps, disallowing a third opinion] • 3) [related but fallacious modes]
Modes of Objection against Drawing Indication from the Consensus of the Folk of Medina (*al-Iʿtirāḍ ʿalā al-Istidlāl bi-Ijmāʿ Ahl al-Madīna*)	
[....]	• 1) Medinese consensus that attains the degree of unbroken, consistent transmission with multiple transmitters at every stage (*Tawātur*) • 2) [Medinese consensus that] falls short of *Tawātur* • 3) what enjoys consensus with respect to considered opinion and correlational inference (*min jihat al-ra'y wa'l-qiyās*)
Modes of Objection against Drawing Indication from the Saying of a Solitary Companion (*al-Iʿtirāḍ ʿalā al-Istidlāl bi-Qawl al-Wāḥid min al-Ṣaḥāba*)	
• 1) [Q] says: the saying of a solitary Companion is not a proof (*ḥujja*) • 2) [Q] counter-indicates it (*yuʿāriḍuhu*) with the unambiguous text (*naṣṣ*) of Qur'ān or Sunna • 3) [Q] conveys disagreement (*khilāf*) from another Companion, in order to make of the *mas'ala* a disagreement (*khilāf*) between the Companions	• 1) [Q] says: "This is the saying of a solitary Companion, so *qiyās* is advanced over it." • 2) [Q] conveys disagreement (*khilāf*) [among the Companions] as regards the contended case (*mas'ala*) • 3) [Q] debates the transmitted material (*manqūl*) in the same way he debates [R's supporting] Sunna

Al-Shīrāzī	Al-Bājī
[Disputing What is Rationally Understood from the Authoritative Source-Case (*Maʿqūl al-Aṣl*)]	
Modes of Objection against Drawing Indication from the Unspoken Implication of the Instruction (*al-Iʿtirāḍ ʿalā al-Istidlāl bi-Laḥn al-Khiṭāb*)	
[....]	• 1) [objection when] the unspoken implication is added to the words so that they be completed by it • 2) [objection when] the unspoken implication is added so that its preponderating exegesis (*ta'wīl*) be validated
Modes of Objection against Drawing Indication from the *A Fortiori* Signification of the Instruction (*al-Iʿtirāḍ ʿalā al-Istidlāl bi-Faḥwā al-Khiṭāb*)	
• 1) [Q] demands validation (*taṣḥīḥ*) of the *maʿnā*-intension which necessitates intensification (*ta'kīd*) of the *far*ʿ over the *aṣl* • 2) [Q] professes the compelling agency of the intensification (*mūjib al-ta'kīd*) • 3) Nullification (*ibṭāl*) • 4) [Q] demands [R's] ruling for the intensification (*ḥukm al-ta'kīd*) • 5) [Q] makes the intensification (*ta'kīd*) into a proof against [R] • 6) [Q] opposes the intensification with what eliminates it (*bimā yusqiṭuhu*)	• 1) [objection when] the *a fortiori* signification of the instruction is clearly-disclosed (*jalī*)—it being in the *maʿna*-intension of what is authoritatively and textually fixed (*manṣūṣ ʿalayhi*) • 2) [objection when] the *a fortiori* signification is latent (*khafī*) ○ 2.1) [Q] denies the object of agreement's sharing (*mushāraka*) with the object of disagreement in the occasioning factor of the ruling (*ʿillat al-ḥukm*) ○ 2.2) [Q] makes the *ḥukm* contingent upon another *ʿilla* besides that upon which [R] made it contingent
Modes of Objection against Drawing Indication from the [Restrictive] Indicant of the Instruction (*al-Iʿtirāḍ ʿalā al-Istidlāl bi-Dalīl al-Khiṭāb*)	
• 1) Outright Rejection (*Radd*) [of the method itself] • 2) [Q] counter-indicates it with a divinely-sanctioned decree (*nuṭq*) or by the *a fortiori* signification of a divinely-sanctioned decree (*faḥwā al-nuṭq*)—which is [also called] "self-evident appeal" (*tanbīh*)—or with correlational inference (*qiyās*) • 3) [Q] debates it by way of preponderating exegesis (*ta'wīl*), explaining the lesson inherent to the singling out [of the object of the decree] (*fā'idat al-takhṣīṣ*)	[....]

(continued)

<table>
<tr><th colspan="2">Modes of Objection against Drawing Indication by way of Restriction (al-I'tirāḍ 'alā al-Istidlāl bi'l-Ḥaṣr)</th></tr>
<tr><td>[....]</td><td>• 1) [Q] says: "this is drawing indication by way of the [restrictive] indicant of the instruction (dalīl al-khiṭāb), and you do not advocate [this method]."
• 2) Counter-Indication (mu'āraḍa) of his dalīl-indicant by way of divinely-sanctioned decree (nuṭq)</td></tr>
<tr><th colspan="2">Modes of Objection against Drawing Indication by way of the Intension-Property of the Instruction, that is, against Correlational Inference (al-I'tirāḍ 'alā al-Istidlāl bi-Ma'nā al-Khiṭāb, wa huwa al-Qiyās)</th></tr>
<tr><td>• 1) Outright Rejection (Radd) [on the basis of legal-theoretical principles]
• 2) [Q] says: "You don't advocate qiyās for this ruling"
• 3) Denial (man') of the ḥukm in the aṣl
• 4) Denial (man') of the property (waṣf) in the aṣl, or in the far', or in both
• 5) Demand for Validation of the Occasioning Factor (al-Muṭālaba bi-taṣḥīḥ al-'illa)
• 6) Lack of Efficiency ('Adam al-ta'thīr), which is the presence of the ḥukm with the absence of the 'illa</td><td>[Muṭālabāt (Demands)][187]
• 1) Objection that the object of disagreement is not allowed to be confirmed by way of qiyās (al-mukhtalaf fīhi lā yajūzu ithbātihi bi'l-qiyās)
• 2) Objection that what serves as a basis for [R's] qiyās is not allowed to be made an aṣl
• 3) Objection that what he made an occasioning factor ('illa) is not allowed to be an 'illa
• 4) Objection that what he made a ruling (ḥukm) is not allowed to be a ḥukm
• 5) Denying the Source-Case (man' al-aṣl); Objection by Denial regarding the Ruling of the Source-Case (mumāna'a fī ḥukm al-aṣl)</td></tr>
</table>

(continued)

[187] Importantly, al-Bājī begins his section on *qiyās*-oriented objections with an explanation of their logical sequence (see the appendix). All fifteen higher categories are grouped under more general headings: "demands" (*muṭālabāt*; categories 1–7, above), "objections" (*i'tirāḍāt*; categories 8–14), and "counter-indications" (*mu'āraḍāt*; category 15). Although al-Bājī's choice of terms does not always correspond with his opening tripartite division, it must nevertheless be considered a first-rank of *topoi* for this particular subset of *qiyās*-oriented dialectical moves; and it is noteworthy that al-Bājī's detailed discussions for each category follow it to the letter, despite his references to all fifteen categories as *al-i'tirāḍ bi*-X, *al-i'tirāḍ bi*-Y, and so on.

<table>
<tr>
<td>
• 7) Inconsistency (Naqḍ); which is the presence of the ʿilla, but not the ḥukm, according to the doctrine of one who does not opine (lā yarā) [the theory of] "particularization of the occasioning factor" (takhṣīṣ al-ʿilla)[188]
• 8) Breaking Apart (Kasr); which is the presence of a maʿnā-quality of the ʿilla, but not the ḥukm
• 9) Professing the compelling agency of the occasioning factor (al-Qawl bi-mūjib al-ʿilla)
• 10) The ʿilla does not oblige its rulings (aḥkām); which is that [R's] ʿilla obliges two rulings, but [R only] makes one of them conditional upon it, without the other
• 11) Invalidity of Occasioned Status (Fasād al-waḍʿ); which is that [R] makes conditional upon the ʿilla the opposite (ḍidd) of what it necessitates
• 12) Invalid Compatibility-Comparison (Fasād al-iʿtibār)
• 13) [R's] ʿilla is opposed to its aṣl
• 14) Reversal (Qalb)
• 15) Counter-Indication (Muʿāraḍa)
</td>
<td>
• 6) Denying the Property (manʿ al-waṣf/ mumānaʿa fiʾl-waṣf)
• 7) Demand for Validation of the Occasioning Factor (al-muṭālaba bi-taṣḥīḥ al-ʿilla)
[Iʿtirāḍāt (Objections/Critiques)]
• 8) Professing the compelling agency of the occasioning factor (al-Qawl bi-mūjib al-ʿilla)
• 9) Reversal (Qalb)
• 10) Invalidity of Occasioned Status (Fasād al-Waḍʿ)
  ○ 10.1) when [R] makes conditional upon the ʿilla the opposite (ḍidd) of what it necessitates
  ○ 10.2) Invalid Compatibility-Comparison (Fasād al-iʿtibār)
• 11) Inconsistency (Naqḍ)
• 12) Breaking Apart (Kasr); which is called inconsistency (naqḍ) with respect to the intension-property (min jihat al-maʿnā)
• 13) Demand for Concomitance of the Occasioning Factor in What it Occasions (al-muṭālaba bi-ijrāʾ al-ʿilla fī maʿlūlātihā)
• 14) Lack of Efficiency (ʿAdam al-taʾthīr), meaning the ḥukm is not absent when the ʿilla is absent in some locus or another
[Muʿāraḍāt (Counter-Indications)]
15) Counter-Indication (Muʿāraḍa)
</td>
</tr>
<tr>
<td colspan="2">Modes of Objection against Drawing Indication by Various Qiyās-Related Methods (al-Iʿtirāḍ ʿalā al-Istidlāl biʾl-Awlā; biʾl-Taqsīm; biʾl-ʿAks; bi-Bayān al-ʿIlla; bi-Shahādat al-Uṣūl)</td>
</tr>
<tr>
<td>[....]</td>
<td>
Arguing Against Drawing Indication by way of A Fortiori Valuation (al-Kalām ʿalā al-Istidlāl biʾl-Awlā)
• 1) by way of demand (muṭālaba) of validation (taṣḥīḥ) for the maʿnā-quality necessitating intensification (taʾkīd) of the ḥukm of the farʿ over the ḥukm of the aṣl
• 2) by way of inconsistency (naqḍ)
• 3) by way of breaking apart (kasr)
• 4) by way of [Q's] making the intensification (taʾkīd) into a decisive argument (ḥujja) against [R]
• 5) by way of opposition (muqābala) of the intensification (taʾkīd) of the farʿ with a maʿnā-quality which eliminates it
• 6) by way of invalidating distinction (farq)
</td>
</tr>
</table>

(continued)

[188] "Particularization of the occasioning factor" (*takhṣīṣ al-ʿilla*) is the much-problematized theory that an *ʿilla* occasioning *ḥukm* X, in general circumstances, can be "particularized" by a certain preventative factor (*māniʿ*) in order to occasion *ḥukm* Y, in a particular circumstance.

	Arguing Against Drawing Indication by way of Analytical Disjunction (*al-Kalām ʿalā al-Istidlāl bi'l-Taqsīm*)
	• 1) Against Type 1, in which "[R] states the divisions (*aqsām*) of things upon which the opponent (*khaṣm*) can possibly make the *ḥukm* contingent, then clarifies the invalidity of all of them, and so establishes that truth (*ḥaqq*) lies in their contradictory (*khilāf*)"
	  ○ 1.1) [Q objects] by way of inconsistency (*naqḍ*)
	  ○ 1.2) [Q objects] by way of breaking apart (*kasr*)
	  ○ 1.3) [Q] clarifies another division (*qism*) which [R] neglected, then makes the *ḥukm* contingent upon it
	  ○ 1.4) [Q] claims the contingency (*taʿlīq*) of the *ḥukm* upon one of the aspects for which [R] has provided indication of its nullification (*ibṭāl*), then he validates it
	• 2) Against Type 2, in which "[R] states the divisions (*aqsām*) of things upon which contingency (*taʿlīq*) of the *ḥukm* is possible, then clarifies the invalidity of all but one, and so establishes that truth (*ḥaqq*) lies in that one"
	  ○ 2.1) [Q] makes the *ḥukm* contingent upon one of the divisions for which [R] has provided indication of its nullification (*ibṭāl*), then he validates it

	Arguing Against Drawing Indication by way of the Opposite (*al-Kalām ʿalā al-Istidlāl bi'l-ʿAks*) • 1) by way of inconsistency (*naqḍ*) • 2) by way of breaking apart (*kasr*) • 3) by way of invalidating distinction (*farq*)

	Arguing Against Drawing Indication by way of Clarifying the Occasioning Factor (*al-Kalām ʿalā al-Istidlāl bi-Bayān al-ʿIlla*)
	• 1) Against Type 1, in which "[R] clarifies the *ʿilla* of the *ḥukm*, then draws indication—from its presence in the locus of disagreement (*mawḍiʿ al-khilāf*)—for confirmation of the *ḥukm* [therein]"
	  ○ 1.1) [Q objects by way of] Denial (*Manʿ*); when [R] has begun his *istidlāl*
	  ○ 1.2) [Q objects by way of] Inconsistency (*Naqḍ*); when [R] has begun his *istidlāl*
	• 2) Against Type 2, in which "[R] clarifies the *ʿilla*, and draws indication from its absence [in the locus of disagreement] for the negation of the *ḥukm* [therein]"
	  ○ 2.1) [same as 1.1]
	  ○ 2.2) [same as 1.2]

(continued)

	Arguing Against Drawing Indication by way of Testimony of the Authoritative Source-Cases (*al-Kalām ʿalā al-Istidlāl bi-[Shahādat] al-Uṣūl*) • 1) Inconsistency (*Naqḍ*): [Q] clarifies for [R], in the *uṣūl*, the contradictory (*khilāf*) of what [R] claims; and such constitutes a denial (*manʿ*) of what [R] claims of the *uṣūl*, and a destruction [by inconsistency] (*naqḍ*) of what [R] brings in terms of a *dalīl*-indicant • 2) Invalidating Distinction (*Farq*): [Q] clarifies that this locus (*mawḍiʿ*) is contradictory (*mukhālif*) to the rest of the *uṣūl* with respect to the *maʿnā*-quality, and due to this it contradicts them with regard to the *ḥukm*

Al-Shīrāzī	**Al-Bājī**
[Disputing Presumption of Continuity (*Istiṣḥāb Ḥāl*)]	
Modes of Objection against Drawing Indication by Presumption of Continuity of the Legal *Status Quo Ante* (*al-Iʿtirāḍ ʿalā al-Istidlāl bi-Istiṣḥāb al-Ḥāl*)	

• [1] [Against] Presumption of Continuity of a *Status Quo Ante* of Rational Intellection for Absolution from Obligation (*Istiṣḥāb Ḥāl al-ʿAql fī Barāʾat al-Dhimma*)
  ○ 1) Counter-Indication by way of its Like (*al-Muʿāraḍa bi-mithlihā*)
  ○ 2) [Q] conveys [the ruling] away from the original state (*aṣl*) [i.e., away from the *status quo ante*] by way of a *dalīl*-indicant
• [2] [Against] Presumption of Continuity of a *Status Quo Ante* of Consensus (*Istiṣḥāb Ḥāl al-Ijmāʿ*)
	• 1) [Against] Presumption of Continuity of a *Status Quo Ante* of Rational Intellection (*Istiṣḥāb Ḥāl al-ʿAql*)
	  ○ 1.1) Counter-Indication (*Muʿāraḍa*); [Q] counter-indicates it with its like [in epistemic strength]
	  ○ 1.2) Conveyance by way of Indicant (*al-naql biʾl-dalīl*); [Q] conveys [the ruling] away from the *status quo ante* by way of a *dalīl*-indicant, saying: "Indeed, the original state (*aṣl*) is absolution from obligation by way of rational intellection (*barāʾat al-dhimma biʾl-ʿaql*); however, God's Law (*al-Sharʿ*) has provided an indicant for the involvement of his obligation (*ishtighāl dhimmatihi*)."
	• 2) [Against] [Fallacious Mode] Presumption of Continuity of a *Status Quo Ante* of Consensus (*Istiṣḥāb Ḥāl al-Ijmāʿ*)
	  ○ 2.1) Comprehensive denial (*manʿ*) that one may draw indication by this mode of presumption
	  ○ 2.2) Counter-Indication (*Muʿāraḍa*) [as in 1.1]
	  ○ 2.3) Conveyance by way of Indicant (*al-naql biʾl-dalīl*) [as in 1.2]

Al-Shīrāzī	Al-Bājī
[Modes of Preponderance (Tarjīḥāt)]	
Preponderance of Expressions whose Intensions are Most Apparent (*Tarjīḥ al-Ẓawāhir*) • [1]: Regarding the Chain of Transmission (*Isnād*); specifically concerned are solitary reports (*akhbār al-āḥād*) ○ [twelve modes] • [2]: Regarding the Transmitted Text (*Matn*) ○ [thirteen modes] **Preponderance of (Potentially-Efficient) Intension-Properties (*Tarjīḥ al-Ma'ānī*)** • [sixteen modes]	**Preponderance of Expressions whose Intensions are Most Apparent (*Tarjīḥ al-Ẓawāhir*)** • [1]: Regarding the Chain of Transmission (*Isnād*) ○ [twelve modes] • [2]: Regarding the Transmitted Text (*Matn*) ○ [thirteen modes] **Preponderance of (Potentially-Efficient) Intension-Properties (*Tarjīḥ al-Ma'ānī*)** • [fifteen modes]

Though I have listed only the higher categories, the systems of al-Shīrāzī and al-Bājī—even in barest outline—appear sophisticated and skilfully organized. There is a systematic genius at work here, and a penetrating thoroughness, for a structured method with a wide scope of application. Notably, the *qiyās*-oriented objections—though of critical import—represent only a fraction of the overall number: fifteen higher categories out of some sixty-five or so *iʿtirāḍāt* (and some forty *tarjīḥāt*); the scope of classical juridical *jadal* goes far beyond what most contemporary *qiyās*-oriented studies have shown us. One should also take note, despite the close resemblance of al-Bājī's system to that of his teacher, that there are points of difference—especially with regard to *ijmāʿ* and the categories of *maʿqūl al-aṣl*. These divergences are substantive as well as organizational, and reflect not only the requirements of different doctrinal schools (Mālikī vs. Shāfiʿī), but the truth-seeking ethic which our jurists embraced; al-Bājī was not slavish in adherence to the system of al-Shīrāzī.[189]

Most importantly, the objections are presented according to the domains of *istidlāl* in precisely the same hierarchy found in introductory chapters on the "indicants of God's Law" (*adillat al-Sharʿ*). Thus the domains of *istidlāl* very likely served as the first tier of *topoi* by which a disputant could "locate" the proper arguments for critique or defence. In all of our early *jadal*-theory texts the aspiring dialectician would also find an illustrative example at each "location," for nearly every subtype of objection and response. Every objection and matching response is shown *in practice*—these texts exhibit a high order of pragmatic pedagogy. A final note: there are a number of *iʿtirāḍ* categories which appear in more than one domain of *istidlāl*. "Counter-Indication" (*muʿāraḍa*) is prominent among these multi-domain objection types, but we also find "professing the compelling agency of X" (*al-qawl bi-mūjib* X); "sharing the indicant" (*al-mushāraka fi'l-dalīl*); "claiming abrogation" (*daʿwā al-naskh*); "preponderating exegesis" (*al-ta'wīl*);

[189] The significance of divergent theory is even more plain when further comparisons are drawn with Ibn ʿAqīl (al-Shīrāzī's famed Ḥanbalī student), and al-Juwaynī (al-Shīrāzī's distant Shāfiʿī colleague and sometime opponent in disputation).

"claiming ambiguity" (*da'wā al-ijmāl*); and "demand for validation of X" (*al-muṭālaba bi-taṣḥīḥ* X) in multiple domains. This is important, showing not only a terminological consistency, but a meta-logical consciousness of argument form and application.

Considering the complexity I hope this bare outline has conveyed, this monograph is not the place for a detailed exposition on each and every type and subtype of objection.[190] The appendices I have provided will serve as catalogs for assessing similar objections in the dialectical sequences of the subject-text. Related discussions in this chapter will focus only upon certain *qiyās*-oriented objections which have already been the object of previous studies—beginning, most appropriately, with al-Baṣrī's *Kitāb al-Qiyās al-Shar'ī* and Hallaq's translation and companion study. Other details regarding the various categories of our lens-texts will surface in the analyses of Chaps. 5 and 6.

A Brief Outline of the K. al-Qiyās al-Shar'ī

Al-Baṣrī's treatise on *qiyās*, like the *jadal* works of following generations, is marked by a high degree of organization, precision of detail, and systematic approach. He begins with definitions for "correlational inference of co-presence" (*qiyās al-ṭard*) and of the "opposite" (*qiyās al-'aks*), formulates a more general definition of *qiyās* incorporating both types, fully details the components necessary to *qiyās*, and then launches directly into a logically ordered series of discussions on *qiyās* in the context of dialectical debate. Having concluded that debate about *qiyās* invariably focuses on either the *ḥukm* or the *'illa*,[191] he first develops an ordered sequence of questions by which one might examine one's own, or one's opponent's, *qiyās*—first with regard to the *ḥukm*,[192] then with regard to the *'illa*.[193]

One might characterize these questions as occurring on two levels: (1) internally, insofar as R/Q asks himself: "Is the presence of the *ḥukm* possible in the *far'*, or not?" etc.; and (2) externally, insofar as these internal questions prompt dialectical questions, objections, and defences in real venues of disputation. For every internal question, al-Baṣrī provides both the reason for asking it, and the sort of dialectical question or objection which might ensue. Overall, it is an ordered

[190] I am presently compiling an expository *Primer in Classical Islamic Juridical Dialectic* which will explore and illustrate the systems of al-Shīrāzī, al-Bājī, et al. in full detail.

[191] This, and all topics mentioned so far, are in the "Section: On the Definition (*ḥadd*) of *Qiyās*" (al-Baṣrī, *K. al-Qiyās al-Shar'ī*, Ḥamīd Allāh ed., pp. 1032–3; Hallaq, "Treatise," pp. 207–9).

[192] The "Section: On Arguments Regarding the *Ḥukm*" (Ḥamīd Allāh ed., pp. 1033–5; Hallaq, "Treatise," pp. 209–12). For the ordered questions suggested by al-Baṣrī, please see my Appendix I.

[193] The "Section: On Arguments Regarding the *'Illa*" (Ḥamīd Allāh ed., p. 1035; Hallaq, "Treatise," pp. 212–13).

approach by which R/Q might examine the particulars of the contended *qiyās* and construct his defence/critique.[194] Al-Baṣrī next proceeds to outline the methods by which R might validate his *ʿilla*, again providing an ordered apparatus—this time for Q's assessment of R's "validation of the occasioning factor" (*taṣḥīḥ al-ʿilla*);[195] and, finally, he presents a set of discussions covering the familiar *qiyās*-oriented dialectical objections[196] and modes of preponderance,[197] concluding with an appended mini-treatise on the dialectical move of "reversal" (*qalb al-qiyās*).[198]

The Focal Point of Dialectic: Hallaq on al-Baṣrī's Qiyās

Al-Baṣrī's twofold typology of *qiyās* is outlined by Hallaq as follows: (1) *qiyās al-ṭard*, the familiar analogical archetype, *argumentum a simile*, wherein the *ḥukm* is transferred from *aṣl* to *farʿ* via shared *ʿilla*; and (2) *qiyās al-ʿaks*, *reductio ad absurdum*, wherein the solution is achieved "by demonstrating the falsehood or invalidity of its converse".[199] Although both of these types appear frequently in the argument and debate of the *Umm* compendium and other early sources, we should note in particular the many areas of overlap between the *ijtihādic* method of *qiyās al-ʿaks* and the dialectical use of *reductio* arguments, whether of the more strictly logical variety (*tanāquḍ*), of general doctrinal inconsistency (*naqḍ*), or of broader notions of untenable consequence. This relationship has its parallel in the philosophical dialectic described by Aristotle, al-Fārābī, et al.

Ultimately, there is no understating the central role of *qiyās* in the *mujtahid*'s "discovery of God's Law," nor of the arsenal of *qiyās*-related dialectical moves which come into play once his *ijtihād* is scrutinized in disputation. Hallaq asserts:

---

[194] Again, this parallels the function of *topoi*, insofar as Q begins through this process to "locate" any problematic elements of R's *qiyās*-reasoning upon which to focus his dialectical questions and objections. Already at this stage, the dialectical move of *al-qawl bi-mūjib al-ʿilla* and the charge of *ikhtilāf mawḍūʿ al-aṣl wa'l-farʿ* (i.e., *fasād al-waḍʿ*), among others, may become open possibilities for Q (see Appendix I).

[195] The "Section: On what Provides Indication for the Validity (*ṣiḥḥa*) of the *ʿIlla*" (Ḥamīd Allāh ed., pp. 1036–8; Hallaq, "Treatise," p. 213–16).

[196] The "Section: On what Distinguishes the *ʿIlla* as pertains to Modes which Invalidate it" (Ḥamīd Allāh ed., pp. 1039–45; Hallaq, "Treatise," pp. 216–23).

[197] Two Sections: "On *Tarjīḥ* of the *ʿIlla* of the *Aṣl* over another *ʿIlla*, and *Tarjīḥ* of a *Qiyās* over a *Qiyās*" (Ḥamīd Allāh ed., p. 1046; Hallaq, "Treatise," pp. 223–4). These are followed by a fascinating section in which al-Baṣrī discusses a meta-logical concern; mainly, the manner in which the familiar *qiyās*-oriented dialectical moves (*muʿāraḍa*, *naqḍ*, etc.) all belong to the domain of *tarjīḥāt* (Ḥamīd Allāh ed., p. 1047; Hallaq, "Treatise," pp. 224). I have labelled this simply "Additional *Tarjīḥ*-related Discussion" in the appendix.

[198] The "Supplement (*ḍamīma*) on *Qalb*" (Ḥamīd Allāh ed., pp. 1048–50; Hallaq, "Treatise," pp. 224–8).

[199] "Treatise," p. 200.

"*Qiyās*, the primary method of legal reasoning in Islamic law, is indeed the focal point of dialectic;" and: "Equally important are the methods by which the textual premises of *qiyās* are extracted and verified."[200] In asserting the centrality of determining the *ʿilla* to the project of legal reasoning as a whole, Hallaq reminds us that "the nature of the process of discerning the *ʿilla* entails the verification of both the text encompassing the *ʿilla* and the *ʿilla* qua *ʿilla*."[201] This is a matter of determining efficiency, and Hallaq next defines *ta'thīr*: "By efficiency it is meant that the judgments in both the original and the assimilated cases are effected by the property (*waṣf*) present in the *ʿilla*.... Any irrelevant, that is, inefficient property joined to the *ʿilla* may cause that *ʿilla* to be invalid."[202] Describing how we come to know the *ʿilla* in a text, Hallaq relates the distinction between *dalāla* ("textual indicant") and *amāra* ("textual sign"). As for the former, it "represents an unambiguous statement of the cause of judgment revealed in the sources [and] may also be found in a matter upon which the entire Muslim community had agreed to be authoritative;" and as for the latter, it is "merely a sign alluding to the cause for which a judgment was decreed."[203]

Hallaq highlights al-Baṣrī's promotion of the 'method of co-presence and co-absence' for "extract[ing the *ʿilla*] from its textual context, while ensuring that extraneous elements are not attached to it"; and discusses other methods of determining the *ʿilla* and weighing potentially-efficient intension-properties against each other, including: immediacy of effect, subjection of an *ʿilla* to *ijmāʿ* of the *mujtahids*, and the practice of grouping together and then methodically eliminating all but one from a set of occasioning factors.[204] Finally, and continuing to draw from elsewhere in the *Muʿtamad*, Hallaq reviews al-Baṣrī's solutions to other *ʿilla*-justification problems, including: (1) when the *aṣl* has multiple *ʿilla*s, but the *farʿ* shares only one of them (*qiyās* is based on that single, common *ʿilla*); and (2) a list of *tarjīḥ* considerations, applicable to *aṣl* or *farʿ*, for deciding between *ʿilla*s with equally strong indicants and/or signs.[205]

---

[200] Ibid. As we have seen, there were in fact several focal points of juridical dialectic—critical areas of testing and contention spanned the full gamut of *istidlālāt*—as listed above and in the appendices, and, presumably, including whatever other principles and sources (e.g., *istiḥsān*, *maṣlaḥa*, *ʿurf*, etc.) to which a jurist-dialectician might subscribe.

[201] Ibid.

[202] Ibid., citing earlier discussions in al-Baṣrī's *Muʿtamad*.

[203] Ibid., 201; citing the *Muʿtamad*.

[204] Ibid., 201–2; from the *Muʿtamad*.

[205] Ibid., 202–3.

Higher Categories of al-Baṣrī's Qiyās*-Oriented Objections*

Most of al-Baṣrī's categories will appear familiar following our review of al-Shīrāzī and al-Bājī, and will be discussed in more detail in subsequent sections. The objective now is to present them for comparison with what we have seen of later theory systems; and, although no strong claims should be made on the basis of this comparison, one is tempted to see al-Baṣrī's treatment as intermediate—in terms of detail, scope of application, and overall complexity—to what following generations of theorists produced. Al-Baṣrī's quite different doctrinal background (Muʿtazilī and Ḥanafī) is also worthy of consideration, although the implications of this must be explored in another study. Whatever the reason, a review and extraction from al-Baṣrī's "Section On what Distinguishes the *ʿIlla* as pertains to Modes which Invalidate it" (*Faṣl fīmā Yakhtaṣṣu al-ʿIlla min al-Wujūh al-Mufsida lahā*) yields only the following higher categories of *qiyās*-oriented objections:

- Mode 1: "*ʿIlla*-Justification by way of the Name" (*al-Taʿlīl bi'l-Ism*)
- Mode 2: "Divergence of Occasioned Status" (*Ikhtilāf al-Waḍʿ*)
- Mode 3: "Lack of Efficiency" (*ʿAdam al-Ta'thīr*)
- Mode 4: "Reversal of the Correlational Inference" (*Qalb al-Qiyās*)
- Mode 5: "Inconsistency" (*al-Naqḍ*)[206]
- Mode 6: "Breaking Apart" (*al-Kasr*)
- Mode 7: "Counter-Indication by way of an Occasioning Factor" (*al-Muʿāraḍa bi-ʿIlla*)

Of note is the first mode, which finds no parallel in the systems of al-Shīrāzī and al-Bājī; the second mode, with its terminological variant (cf. "invalidity of occasioned status" [*fasād al-waḍʿ*]); the remaining modes, and their substantive and terminological identity with modes of al-Shīrāzī and al-Bājī; and the absence of some seven or eight additional modes treated by these latter systems.

Further on al-Baṣrī's K. al-Qiyās al-Sharʿī

There are a number of features in al-Baṣrī's treatise which are worth highlighting. Al-Baṣrī's organizing principle is different from others we have seen. Nevertheless, it is clearly oriented (like the *Topics*, *Ta'sīs al-Naẓar*, *Maʿūna*, and *Minhāj*) towards

[206] Note that *naqḍ* also bears the sense of "destruction." Quite possibly this nuance was intended throughout the period in which the term gained its fixed technical sense as a species of objection. *Naqḍ*, after all, is a purely "destructive" critique by which the opponent's *qiyās* is demolished—it does not have the "constructive" aspect of *muʿāraḍa*, by which R's *qiyās* is not only opposed, but supplanted with something epistemically superior.

providing a *manual*—a step-by-step, structured guide for the disputant. Al-Baṣrī's methodical approach is most concerned with examining one's own, or one's opponent's, *qiyās* from a number of different angles. These, as noted, are first outlined, then systematically discussed in sequential assessments—i.e., first, Q must examine aspect X; and if it holds, he must then examine aspect Y; and if that holds... etc. Again, this may also work as a "location" device for Q to achieve *elenchus*—working from larger to more specific observations of R's *qiyās*, until a problematic point is discovered and exploited.

Notably, al-Baṣrī sets forth his question sequences in a manner allowing a student to memorize them in groups—specifically, there are four groups, depending upon the *ḥukm* and its relation to *aṣl* and *far'*. Once memorized, they may have functioned in two ways: (1) as a rigorous plan for examination-testing (such as might occur between companion-scholars of the same *madhhab*), whereby a *mujtahid*'s proposed *qiyās* is thoroughly examined from every angle; and (2) as a set of *topoi* for the experienced dialectician. In the latter case, a trained disputant, rather than asking question after question to search out problem points, might: (1) first consider them inwardly; (2) discover the problem-*topos* for attack; then (3) carefully plan the delivery of his juridical premises, so as to (4) trap R in an impossibility, absurdity, or more general inconsistency.

Returning to the categories of objection, al-Baṣrī's treatment of inconsistency (*naqḍ*) and counter-indication (*mu'āraḍa*) highlights that difference I would label "destructive" vs. "constructive" critique. With *naqḍ*, Q brings forward a case where R's *'illa* is present and ought to produce the same *ḥukm*, but doesn't—Q's charge merely "destroys" R's *'illa*, but does not supplant it with anything superior. In *mu'āraḍa*, however, Q appears not to destroy R's *'illa* (at first), but he brings another *'illa* claimed to be superior or more appropriate in some fashion. Rather than a mere, invalidating critique, Q contributes a more valid solution. Thus *mu'āraḍa* prompts a change of roles for the disputants; R must now probe and test Q's counter-*'illa* before conceding or rejecting it.

That portion of al-Baṣrī's treatise opening with "*Tarjīḥ* and *ifsād* of the *'illa* do not go outside of the categories we have discussed"[207] is both fascinating and important to our understanding of early *jadal*-theory. Al-Baṣrī's exposition reveals the inner consistency belonging to his systematic rendering of *qiyās*-related *jadal*. In fact, he has produced another organizing principle—one which is *tarjīḥ*-related, rather than sequential-*jadal*-related, but which contains all of the same methods and moves. The advantages of this are twofold: (1) it highlights essential features of these moves and methods; (2) it provides us another hierarchy by which to memorize them. Moreover, it is made very clear that a large part of what goes on in *qiyās*-related *jadal* is, in fact, a manner of cooperative *tarjīḥ*.[208]

---

[207] Ḥamīd Allāh ed., p. 1047; Hallaq, "Treatise," pp. 224.

[208] This meta-logical concern is echoed in the works of al-Shīrāzī, al-Bājī, et al. They are not only concerned to list the numerous modes of *tarjīḥ*, but several of these find parallels among their modes of objection.

As for al-Baṣrī's appended *qalb* "supplement:" a summary of his discussions (see Appendix I) will make his objective quite clear. In response to objections against the move of *qalb*, some of which may have arisen between stages of treatise composition, al-Baṣrī: (1) reviews these objections, (2) concludes (with arguments provided) that *qalb* is valid in three disputation scenarios, and (3) summarizes these scenarios.[209] Finally, I would direct attention to two other features: (1) as in other texts, designations for the disputants change according to their dialectical activities: R may be "the one doing *qiyās*" (*qā'is*) or "the one justifying the *ʿilla*" (*muʿallil*) or simply "the questioned one" (*mas'ūl*), depending upon his particular project; and (2) there are two instances where al-Baṣrī's paradigm argument is introduced by the dialectical formula "don't you see/opine?" (*a-lā tarā*).[210]

I will now turn to certain of the more important *qiyās*-oriented *iʿtirāḍāt*, with the following objectives in mind: first is to tighten our grasp of their various forms and functions; second is to examine what has been claimed of these modes in previous studies; and third is to take note of certain concerns which will arise in the course of this review, and which have larger implications for the current project as a whole.

On "Denial" (Manʿ/Mumānaʿa)

In the category of *manʿ* or *mumānaʿa* we find two terms denoting the same sense of prevention, blocking, opposition, forbidding, and denial—al-Shīrāzī tends to use *manʿ*, while al-Bājī tends to favour *mumānaʿa*.[211] We might also note that al-Bājī has grouped his two instances under his larger category of "demands" (*muṭālabāt*). Importantly, in discussing *manʿ/mumānaʿa*, Miller translates al-Juwaynī's definition of the latter, having first recounted something of its originally fluid association with related terms: "the word mumānaʿa has become a terminus technicus among the jurists denoting the disallowance of the characteristic (waṣf) peculiar to the principal case (aṣl) or to the test case (farʿ) or to both together, or to the juristic qualification (ḥukm) of the principal case (aṣl)."[212] This matches well with what might be observed in our outlines.

[209] Ḥamīd Allāh ed., pp. 1048–50; Hallaq, "Treatise," pp. 224–8.

[210] First, in his *naqḍ* discussion (Ḥamīd Allāh ed., near the end of p. 1041); and second, in his *qalb* supplement (early on p. 1049).

[211] See Shīr.VII.3-4 and Bāj.IX.B.5-6 in the appendices. In al-Bājī's mode #5, there is evidence he saw the terms as synonymous, or nearly so.

[212] "Islamic Disputation Theory," pp. 113–15; mistakenly citing al-Juwaynī's *Burhān*, p. 131, lines 10–12 (these numbers correspond to the *Kāfiya*, Maḥmūd ed.)

Miller proceeds to comment on an illustrative example belonging to al-Juwaynī;[213] and it is from this discussion that a significant starting point for the current project was culled. He first presents al-Juwaynī's example meant to illustrate *mumāna'a* at work.[214] Reduced to its key components, this example of R's *qiyās* and Q's *man'* may be diagramed as follows:

***Mas'ala*: Is the *ijāra*-contract[a] nullified by the death of one of the contracting parties, or not?**		
R's *Qiyās*		Q's *Man'*
Aṣl contract of marriage (*nikāḥ*) *'Illa* it is a "contract for a benefit" (*'aqd 'alā manfa'a*) *Ḥukm* it is cancelled (*infasakhat*) by death	*Far'* contract of hire (*ijāra*) *'Illa* it is a "contract for a benefit" (*'aqd 'alā manfa'a*) *Ḥukm* [should be the same]	*Man'* of the *Aṣl* the *nikāḥ*-contract is not cancelled by death; it merely concludes. Likewise with the *ijāra*-contract: it merely concludes with the completion of the term (*mudda*). Thus, *nikāḥ* cannot be used as an *aṣl* for conveying a *ḥukm* of cancellation (*faskh*) due to death.[b]

[a]For the most part, I will not provide detailed explanations of substantive legal categories in this section unless they impinge upon our understanding of the dialectical move being discussed. In the present example, *ijāra* is a contract of hire.
[b]Note that Q says nothing about R's proposed *'illa*. Rather, his point of critique is R's interpretation of the conclusion of *nikāḥ* by death as constituting *faskh*. In other words, Q has objected to what R claims as the *ḥukm* for the *aṣl*; and this in turn serves as a denial (*man'*) to that *aṣl*'s use for conveying R's solution to the *mas'ala* at hand. This illustrates perfectly al-Juwaynī's category of "denial relevant to the source-case" (*al-man' al-mukhtaṣṣ bi'l-aṣl*).

The example is indeed illustrative of *man'*/*mumāna'a*; Q has "denied" or "prevented" R's use of the *nikāḥ*-contract as an *aṣl* for *qiyās* in the *mas'ala* at hand. Importantly, however, Miller next observes that al-Juwaynī, al-Shīrāzī, al-Bājī, and Ibn 'Aqīl all share this same *ijāra-nikāḥ* example as their illustrative problem case (*mas'ala*):

> The role of R is filled by a Ḥanbalite [*sic*],[215] while the role of Q is filled by a Shāfi'ite in al-Shīrāzī,[216] a Mālikite in al-Bājī,[217] and a Ḥanbalite in b. 'Aqīl.[218] There are other instances where common examples are used. This coincidence reveals the topos character of the examples. They are without a doubt gleaned from the earlier literature on the divergence of the jurists (ikhtilāf al-fuqahā').[219]

---

[213] Ibid., pp. 115–17.

[214] *Kāfiya*, Maḥmūd ed., p. 140, §235. In fact, the example was intended by al-Juwaynī to illustrate a specific type of *man'* which he terms "denial relevant to the source-case" (*al-man' al-mukhtaṣṣ bi'l-aṣl*).

[215] In fact, R is a Ḥanafī in al-Juwaynī's example.

[216] *Ma'ūna*, al-'Umayrīnī ed., p. 93.

[217] *Minhāj*, Turkī ed., p. 163, §349.

[218] *K. al-Jadal*, 1980 Cairo ed., 48

[219] "Islamic Disputation Theory," pp. 115–17.

The significance of this statement for the current project is immediately apparent. Miller brings no citations in support of the *ikhtilāf* literature claim, but is more than vindicated by the *Umm* compendium alone. Nor would I contend his interpretation of these shared examples as having a "*topos* character." The authors of our earliest extant *jadal* works have indeed researched back—or, more properly, transmitted forward—the arguments of earlier, venerated, exemplar *mujtahids*. In this case, al-Māwardī (d.450/1058; a Baṣran and Baghdādian contemporary of al-Baṣrī and al-Khaṭīb al-Baghdādī) has examined this *mas'ala* in great detail,[220] attributing R's stance to Abū Ḥanīfa, Sufyān al-Thawrī, and al-Layth b. Saʿd. And as for al-Shāfiʿī: we find his argument against death-induced cancellation of *ijāra*-contracts produced in detailed and extended dialectical format in the *Chapter on Contracts of Hire* (*Bāb al-Ijārāt*) of the *Umm* compendium.[221]

Based on this observation—and similar examples are manifold in the literature of *fiqh* and *uṣūl al-fiqh*—I will make a general claim that the systematization of juridical *jadal* in specialized treatises comprised, to a large extent, the study of an older disputation praxis—it was not only rulings and supporting arguments which were studied. Much as I attempt in the current project, al-Shīrāzī, al-Juwaynī, et al. (or their teachers, and teacher's teachers before them) analyzed proto-system juridical dialectic. This should seem obvious, but is nevertheless important to mark: it links the literary activities of our lens-text authors to the practice and teaching of proto-system *mujtahids*. There is a continuity, and if the literary systemization of juridical *jadal* occurred relatively late, it did not do so *ex nihilo*, nor via a restructuring and take over of fourth/tenth century theological *jadal*. Neither did it impose itself, post-creation, upon the arguments of centuries-dead jurists. Rather, its systematizers derived their schemes from the transmitted corpus of *ikhtilāf*—replete with dialectical narratives—through argument analysis, categorization, and transmitted procedure—as well as from current teachings (which were themselves part of continuum harking back to the proto-system era). I will also claim that this analytical process was intertwined from the start with the production of systematized literature in the domain of *uṣūl al-fiqh*. Both *jadal* and *uṣūl* theory genres are part and parcel of the same analytical and systematizing dynamic.

[220] *al-Ḥāwī al-Kabīr*, Maʿʿūd ed., vol. 7, pp. 401ff.

[221] Ḥassūn ed., vol. 4, pt. 8, pp. 73ff., §§11132ff. In the end, although his dialectical opponent does not appear to draw upon *nikāḥ* as an *aṣl*, al-Shāfiʿī's multi-directional deconstruction of the "*faskh*-due-to-death" thesis is a sure model for later jurists.

On "Professing the Compelling Agency of the Occasioning Factor" (al-Qawl bi-Mūjib al-'Illa)

In his treatment of al-Baṣrī, Hallaq translates *al-qawl bi-mūjib al-'illa* as: "the acceptance of the cause while excluding its application to the case in point."[222] He further notes: "In dialectics this expression is used to indicate that the disputant approves of the cause but excludes its application to the disputed point;" and then directs us to al-Juwaynī's *Kāfiya*.[223] Miller, on the other hand, translates *al-qawl bi-mūjib al-'illa* as: "limited acceptance;" he then presents translations of the definitions of al-Bājī and al-Juwaynī, and a translated example illustrating the latter.[224] I would render al-Bājī's definition thus: "It is a valid question (*su'āl ṣaḥīḥ*) by means of which the *'illa* is excluded from being a *dalīl*-indicant in the locus of contention (*mawḍi' al-khilāf*)."[225] Notably, al-Bājī further subdivides this *i'tirāḍ* according to whether R's *qiyās* is: (1) of a type posited for obligation (*wuḍi'a li'l-wujūb*); or (2) of a type posited for permission (*wuḍi'a li'l-jawāz*). As for al-Juwaynī, I would render his definition of *al-qawl bi-mūjib al-'illa* thus: "It is an agreement (*muwāfaqa*) of the opponent regarding [the *'illa*'s] *ḥukm*, while excluding it from the locus of contention (*mawḍi' al-nizā'*)."[226]

The *i'tirāḍāt*—for all juridical *jadal* authors—were never confined merely to the realm of *istidlāl* by way of *qiyās*; moreover, certain genera such as *mu'āraḍa* had specialized applications in more than one domain of *istidlāl*. "Professing the compelling agency of X" (*al-qawl bi-mūjib* X) is one such genus. Al-Shīrāzī catalogues the following: two types of "professing the compelling agency of the verse" (*al-qawl bi-mūjib al-āya*), for *istidlāl bi'l-Kitāb*;[227] two types of "professing the compelling agency of the transmitted text" (*al-qawl bi-mūjib al-matn*), for a subcategory of *istidlāl bi'l-Sunna*;[228] one type of "professing the compelling agency of the intensification" (*al-qawl bi-mūjib al-ta'kīd*), for *istidlāl bi-Faḥwā al-Khiṭāb*;[229] and two types of "professing the compelling agency of the occasioning factor" (*al-qawl bi-mūjib al-'illa*), for *istidlāl bi-Ma'nā al-Khiṭāb*.[230] If, from all of this, we were to isolate that

---

[222] "Treatise," p. 211.

[223] Ibid., n. 20.

[224] "Islamic Disputation Theory," pp. 129–30.

[225] *Minhāj*, Turkī ed., p. 173, §381. Miller (op. cit.) renders: "Q's accepting the ratio legis while excluding its application to the disputed point."

[226] *Kāfiya*, Maḥmūd ed., p. 69, §166. Miller renders: "Q's agreeing with R's argument as to the juristic quality of the ratio legis, while excluding its application to the point of dispute" ("Islamic Disputation Theory," p. 129).

[227] *Ma'ūna*, al-'Umayrīnī ed., pp. 41–2.

[228] Ibid., pp. 57–9.

[229] Ibid., p. 85.

[230] Ibid., pp. 108–11.

characteristic common to all species of genus "*al-qawl bi-mūjib* X," it would be the following: Q concedes that a premise of R's is indeed necessary/effective to the production of a *ḥukm* in a particular *mas'ala*, but not in the manner which R has proposed. Taking al-Shīrāzī's two types of *al-qawl bi-mūjib al-ʿilla* as examples, we find that application of this *iʿtirāḍ* is dependent upon whether: (1) Q uses the *ʿilla* to provide indication for the nullification (*ibṭāl*) of the reason (*sabab*) of R's *ḥukm*; or (2) Q uses some element of R's *qiyās* to provide indication for the same *ḥukm* as R. In either case, Q is conceding, at least in part, to the exigencies of R's premise; Hallaq's "acceptance of the cause while excluding its application to the case in point" and Miller's "limited acceptance" appear apt translations for the broader genus of "*al-qawl bi-mūjib* X."

Miller, as mentioned, also translates one of al-Juwaynī's examples of *al-qawl bi-mūjib al-ʿilla.*[231] Rather than return to it, I will instead diagram one of al-Shīrāzī's examples. First, a review of al-Shīrāzī's typology of *al-qawl bi-mūjib al-ʿilla*, which appears thus:

- *Iʿtirāḍ* 9: Professing the compelling agency of the occasioning factor (*al-Qawl bi-mūjib al-ʿilla*)
  - Type 1: regarding an *ʿilla* by which [Q] provides indication for the nullification (*ibṭāl*) of the reason (*sabab*) of the *ḥukm*
  - Type 2: regarding an *ʿilla* by which [Q] provides indication for nominating the [same] *ḥukm*
    - Response 1: [R] explains that its general scope (*ʿumūm*) prevents [Q's] *qawl bi-mūjibihi*
    - Response 2: [R] explains that its most apparent meaning (*ẓāhir*) prevents [Q's] *qawl bi-mūjibihi*
    - Response 3: [R] explains that its exegesis (*tafsīr*) prevents [Q's] *qawl bi-mūjibihi*

The following example-*mas'ala* was intended by al-Shīrāzī to illustrate Type 2, Response 2, of the above, and should serve to elucidate the general mode of *al-qawl bi-mūjib al-ʿilla.*[232]

[231] "Islamic Disputation Theory," pp. 129–30.

[232] *Maʿūna*, al-ʿUmayrīnī ed., p. 110; Turkī ed., p. 248.

Mas'ala: Determining categories of jewellery subject to alms tax (*zakāt*)		
Shāfiʿī R's *Qiyās*		Opponent Q's *Qawl bi-Mūjib al-ʿIlla*
Aṣl *zakāt* for cattle *ʿIlla* it is property for which yearly alms tax on the minimum measure is obliged *Ḥukm* division into two types is obliged: (1) that for which *zakāt* is enjoined; and (2) that for which *zakāt* is not enjoined	*Farʿ* *zakāt* for jewellery *ʿIlla* it is [also] property for which yearly alms tax on the minimum measure is obliged *Ḥukm* [thus] division into two types is [also] obliged: (1) that for which *zakāt* is enjoined; and (2) that for which *zakāt* is not enjoined	*Qawl bi-Mūjib al-ʿIlla* "I myself profess its compelling agency (*anā aqūlu bi-mūjibihi*); for according to me [jewellery] is divided into two types: (1) *zakāt* is enjoined for it—being what belongs to the major (*bāligh*); and (2) *zakāt* is not enjoined for it—being what belongs to the minor (*ṣabī*)"

Note that Q has conceded to nearly the whole of R's *qiyās*, up to and including the "compelling agency" of the *ʿilla* to occasion the *ḥukm*: obliged subdivision into two types. He then redefines the application of the *ḥukm* to support his own solution for the *mas'ala* at hand: that *zakāt* is obliged for *all types* of jewelry, when it is obliged at all (the division concerning who pays and who doesn't). This objection entails a subtle change of principle with regard to division, however: R's division falls on the property (*māl*), while Q's new division falls on the owner (*mālik*). This is precisely what the Shāfiʿī R objects to in his follow-up response (*jawāb*): "The most apparent meaning (*ẓāhir*) of the *ʿilla*-justification (*taʿlīl*) requires that it be type-divided *in itself* (*fī nafsihi*); but in what you have stated, the property (*māl*) is not type-divided in itself. Rather, only the owner (*mālik*) is type-divided: (1) an owner upon whom it is enjoined; and (2) an owner upon whom it is not enjoined." Thus, al-Shīrāzī's example *mas'ala* serves as a perfect illustration of: (1) Q's objection by "professing the compelling agency of the occasioning factor" (*al-qawl bi-mūjib al-ʿilla*), "regarding an *ʿilla* by which he provides indication for nominating the [same] *ḥukm*;" and (2) R's response by which he "explains that its most apparent meaning (*ẓāhir*) prevents [Q's] profession of its compelling agency."

On Objection to "Justifying the Occasioning Factor by way of the Name" (al-Taʿlīl bi'l-Ism)

This is al-Baṣrī's first of the modes for invalidating the *ʿilla*, and I have yet to locate its equivalent in the theory texts of al-Shīrāzī and al-Bājī. His division into subtypes is as follows:

- Mode 1: "Justifying the Occasioning Factor by way of the Name" (*al-Taʿlīl bi'l-Ism*)
    - Type 1: [the name has no efficiency]
    - Type 2: the *ʿilla* is established by genus

Al-Baṣrī's example problems are lucid. In the first *mas'ala*, for type 1 *taʿlīl bi'l-ism*, R fixes the *ʿilla* for proscription of grape-wine (*taḥrīm al-khamr*) on the fact that the Arabs called it *khamr*; and Q simply objects that this is invalid (*fāsid*), because the Arab designation has no efficiency (*ta'thīr*). In the second *mas'ala*, for type 2 *taʿlīl bi'l-ism*, R's *ʿilla* is that a beverage is "of the genus of grape-wine (*khamr*)," and this is made to occasion the *ḥukm* of proscription (*taḥrīm*). In this case, al-Baṣrī tells us, it is *not* invalid; "being of the genus" has efficiency, and Q can make no objection to it. Al-Baṣrī proceeds to explain that the following, related modes of justifying the occasioning factor (*taʿlīl*) are also allowed: (1) by way of an attribute (*ṣifa*) among attributes; and (2) by way of a ruling (*ḥukm*) among rulings. Note that the first mode corresponds well to al-Shīrāzī's *qiyās al-shabah*, and the second to his Types I and II *qiyās al-dalāla*.

On "Divergence of Occasioned Status" (Ikhtilāf al-Waḍʿ), *or "Invalidity of Occasioned Status"* (Fasād al-Waḍʿ), *and "Invalid Compatibility-Comparison "* (Fasād al-Iʿtibār)

Note the following: (1) al-Baṣrī's "Divergence of Occasioned Status" (*ikhtilāf al-waḍʿ*) appears to correspond to the "Invalidity of Occasioned Status" (*fasād al-waḍʿ*) of al-Shīrāzī and al-Bājī; (2) al-Shīrāzī treats *fasād al-waḍʿ* and "Invalid Compatibility-Comparison" (*fasād al-iʿtibār*) as separate categories; and (3) al-Bājī presents the latter as a subtype of the former. Miller translates *fasād al-waḍʿ* as "false construction," and presents the definitions of al-Juwaynī, al-Shīrāzī, and al-Bājī.[233] For al-Juwaynī, it is the rather cryptic "*ʿawd al-waḍʿ bi-mā yaqtaḍī fasād al-mawḍūʿ*,"[234] which Miller translates: "turning back the construction by means of that which necessitates the falsification of the constructed." As for al-Shīrāzī, it is *an yuʿalliqa ʿalā al-ʿilla ḍidd mā yaqtaḍīhi*;[235] and for al-Bājī: *an yuʿalliqa ʿalā al-ʿilla ḍidd muqtaḍāhā.*[236] Miller translates both of these as "the attachment to the ratio legis (ʿilla) to the contrary of what it

[233] "Islamic Disputation Theory," p. 118.

[234] *Kāfiya*, Maḥmūd ed., p. 68, §162; Maḥmūd (n. 1) informs us that his lead manuscript reads "claim" (*daʿwā*) rather than "return/reversion" (*ʿawd*).

[235] *Maʿūna*, al-ʿUmayrīnī ed., p. 111.

[236] *Minhāj*, Turkī ed., 178, §391; NB: for al-Bājī this is the first mode of two, the second being *fasād al-iʿtibār*.

requires." As an alternative, I would render al-Bājī as: "[R] makes contingent upon the occasioning factor the opposite (*ḍidd*) of what it necessitates."

Miller then summarizes one of al-Shīrāzī's illustrations of *fasād al-waḍʿ* at work, but—by a slight misreading of the example—he incorrectly concludes that the dialectical moves of *fasād al-waḍʿ* and "reversal" (*qalb*) are one and the same. To rectify this, we must first review al-Shīrāzī's example *mas'ala*, which may be diagramed as follows:[237]

Mas'ala: Does the saliva (*su'r*) of beasts of prey (*sibāʿ*) constitute an impurity (*najas*)?		
Ḥanafī R's *Qiyās*		Shāfiʿī Q's charge of *Fasād al-Waḍʿ*
Aṣl the saliva of the pig[a] *ʿIlla* it is a possessor of canine teeth (*dhū nābin*) *Ḥukm* it qualifies as impurity (*najāsa*)	*Farʿ* the saliva of the beast of prey *ʿIlla* it is a possessor of canine teeth (*dhū nābin*) *Ḥukm* [should be the same]	*Fasād al-Waḍʿ* God's Law makes being a beast of prey an *ʿilla* for purity (*ṭahāra*). The *dalīl*-indicant is a *ḥadīth* wherein the Prophet accepts an invitation from a cat-owner, but declines one from a dog-owner, 'because the cat is a beast of prey (*sabuʿ*). The cat's being a beast of prey was thus made an *ʿilla* for purity, so it is not allowed to be made an *ʿilla* for impurity.

[a]The Princeton MS (fol. 15b), and both al-ʿUmayrīnī's and Turkī's editions, read "like the pig" (*ka'l-khinzīr*); but Miller has the *Ḥanafī* R link his *farʿ* to the *aṣl* of dogs.

Miller concludes: "by stating what the real juristic quality should be, Q has turned the argument around using R's principal case to bring about the contrary of his thesis."[238] In the example, however, we can see that Q has made no use of R's *aṣl* (saliva of the pig). Nor has Q mentioned R's *ʿilla* (possession of canine teeth). Q's argument, drawn from a Sunnaic *dalīl*-indicant, is that 'being a beast of prey' (*sabuʿ*)—that property which defines the *farʿ*—is itself an efficient property for occasioning the quality of purity (*ṭahāra*). Q's argument thus corresponds to both al-Shīrāzī's and al-Bājī's definitions for "invalidity of occasioned status" (*fasād al-waḍʿ*), for Q has indeed charged R with "making contingent upon the [true] *ʿilla* (being a beast of prey) the opposite (impurity) of what it necessitates (purity)." This is a different operation from that of "reversal" (*qalb*).[239] Definitions of *qalb* are consistent in that they require Q's use of R's components for *qiyās*—the only difference, in fact, between R's *qiyās* and Q's *qalb*, is that Q makes R's *ʿilla* occasion a *ḥukm* contrary to that which R made it occasion. In other words, Q concedes to R's

[237] *Maʿūna*, al-ʿUmayrīnī ed., p. 112.

[238] "Islamic Disputation Theory," pp. 119. This is a fair description of "reversal" (*qalb*), but not, as we shall see, of "invalidity of occasioned status" (*fasād al-waḍʿ*). Again, Miller's conclusion appears to hinge on supplanting "pig" with "dog."

[239] Miller first links *fasād al-waḍʿ* to the "*methodos kata peritropēn*" of the Greek rhetoricians ("Islamic Disputation Theory," p. 119; but in an earlier footnote [p. 38, n. 83] we learn that van Ess compares the "*methodos kata peritropēn*" to *muʿāraḍa*). He then concludes: "the usual technical term for this ancient method was qalb, reversal. It would appear that, at this stage, some of the technical terms of juristic dialectics had not yet been given their permanent technical meaning."

aṣl and *ʿilla* both, rejecting only R's *ḥukm*;[240] and this is not the case in the beast of prey example, where Q clearly avoids R's *aṣl* and *ʿilla* both.

As for "Invalid Compatibility-Comparison" (*fasād al-iʿtibār*), Miller—rendering it as "false perspective"—also notes that al-Shīrāzī treats it as a stand-alone category of *iʿtirāḍ*, while al-Bājī considers it a subtype of *fasād al-waḍʿ*.[241] To this I would add that both authors treat *fasād al-iʿtibār* according to two sub-categories, both of which they define in the same way. The first category, according to al-Shīrāzī, is "for what is known by way of unambiguous text (*naṣṣ*) [from Qur'ān and Sunna]; which is that [R] considers (*an yaʿtabira*) a *ḥukm* on the basis of another *ḥukm*, although *naṣṣ*-text has revealed the dividing difference (*tafriqa*) between them."[242] Al-Bājī's definition of this subtype is practically identical;[243] and in their different examples, we find Q declaring—on the basis of a *dalīl*-indicant with the epistemic strength of *naṣṣ*—that "[the *naṣṣ*] has made a distinction (*farraqa*) between them [i.e., between the two *ḥukm*s considered by R]." As for the second category, it is when R's *fasād al-iʿtibār* is known to Q "by way of the authoritative source-cases (*uṣūl*)," collectively. Both al-Shīrāzī and al-Bājī consider various subtypes, but the common characteristic of R's *fasād al-iʿtibār*, as known to Q by way of the *uṣūl*, is that R has tried to relate two *ḥukm*s which each exhibit a non-compatible general quality.[244] For example, one may have an expanding (*tawsiʿa*) and the other a restricting (*taḍyīq*) effect; or one may embody the easing (*takhfīf*) of some hardship, while the other aims at making one more severe (*taghlīẓ*); etc. Such general qualities of rulings, it would seem, are learned inductively from the collective *uṣūl* in which they are manifest.

On "Lack of Efficiency" (ʿAdam al-Ta'thīr)

Al-Baṣrī's definition for this category is that: "the one justifying the *ʿilla* (*muʿallil*) mentions, among the collective properties of the *ʿilla*, such a property that, if it is absent in the *aṣl*, the *ḥukm* yet remains."[245] Miller translates *ʿadam al-ta'thīr* as "ineffective ratio legis;" and claims there are "conflicting accounts about the meaning of this 'question'" among his authors. In support of this, he brings

[240] See, e.g., al-Bājī, *Minhāj*, Turkī ed., p. 14, §18; and pp. 174ff., §§385ff.; al-Baṣrī, *K. al-Qiyās al-Sharʿī*, Ḥamīd Allāh ed., pp. 1040f., 1048ff.; and al-Juwaynī, *al-Kāfiya*, Maḥmūd ed., p. 68, §159.

[241] "Islamic Disputation Theory," pp. 119–20.

[242] *Maʿūna*, al-ʿUmayrīnī ed., p. 113.

[243] *Minhāj*, Turkī ed., p. 179, §398.

[244] al-Shīrāzī, *Maʿūna*, al-ʿUmayrīnī ed., pp. 114ff.; al-Bājī, *Minhāj*, Turkī ed., pp. 180ff., §400ff.

[245] *K. al-Qiyās al-Sharʿī*, Ḥamīd Allāh ed., p. 1040; Hallaq, "Treatise," p. 217.

definitions from al-Juwaynī, al-Shīrāzī, and al-Bājī, along with one of al-Shīrāzī's examples.[246] I would render al-Juwaynī's definition as follows:[247]

163 – As for efficiency: It is the appearance of the contingency of the ruling upon the *ma'nā*-quality. And the loss of the efficiency and its absence: That the contingency of the ruling does not appear to be upon that which [R] claims it to be contingent upon. And the required condition for efficiency is not the loss of the ruling due to loss of the occasioning factor; indeed, this is the condition of co-absence—and such is obliged only for rational-intellectual 'causes'. Loss of efficiency for the 'occasioning factors' of God's Law might be for all the properties of the occasioning factor, or for some of them, according to what will be explained, if God Most High wishes it.	163 – وأما التأثير: فظهور تعلق الحكم بالمعنى. وفقدُ التأثير وعدمهُ: ألاّ يظهر تعلق الحكم بما يدّعيه متعلّقاً به؛ وليس شرط التأثير فَقْدَ الحكم بفقد العلة؛ فإن هذا شرطُ العكس – ولا يجب ذلك إلا في علل العقل، وفقْدُ التأثير في علل الشرع قد يكون في كل أوصاف العلة وفي بعضها، على ما يرد بيانه، إن شاء الله تعالى.

Al-Shīrāzī's definition of *'adam al-ta'thīr*, on the other hand, is simply: "the presence of the ruling despite the absence of the occasioning factor" (*wujūd al-ḥukm ma'a 'adam al-'illa*).[248] We may understand much from this, and from al-Shīrāzī's subsequent subdivisions and examples. In brief: (1) Q's focus is upon the components of R's *aṣl*—particularly its *'illa*; (2) Q objects to R's proposed *'illa*, claiming it cannot occasion the *ḥukm* in that *aṣl*; (3) Q demonstrates this to R by mentioning an established case where the very same *ḥukm* is present, but R's proposed *'illa* is not, thus suggesting a lack of *ta'thīr*-efficiency between R's proposed *'illa* and the *ḥukm* of R's *aṣl*. However, al-Shīrāzī is of course also cognizant that occasioning factors may consist of more than one efficient property. That is why he immediately subdivides the *i'tirāḍ* of *'adam al-ta'thīr* into two types: (1) "lack of efficiency for a property (*waṣf*), which, when it is removed from the *'illa*, the *'illa* is destroyed"; and (2) "lack of efficiency for such as which the *'illa* is not destroyed by its removal".[249] This more narrow focus upon individual properties brings the definitions of al-Shīrāzī and al-Juwaynī into close correspondence.

---

[246] "Islamic Disputation Theory," pp. 120–2.

[247] *Kāfiya*, Maḥmūd ed., p. 68, §163. Miller renders only part of the Arabic, as follows: "...when R claims a connection between a juristic qualification (ḥukm) and a certain thing (ma'nā) and this claim is not apparent" (ellipsis is his). I would suggest that *ma'nā* be interpreted in the sense which al-Shāfi'ī seems to have intended, something like: "(potentially-shared, potentially-efficient) intension-property"—or "common characteristic," as Miller, with reference to Brunschvig, himself earlier renders *ma'nā* ("Islamic Disputation Theory," p. 98, n. 25). If I am correct, al-Juwaynī's definition and discussion correspond well with those of al-Shīrāzī and al-Bājī.

[248] *Ma'ūna*, al-'Umayrīnī ed., p. 100.

[249] Importantly, al-Shīrāzī's first mode of response (*jawāb*) against the first type of *'adam al-ta'thīr* includes an example debate wherein the difference between *qiyās al-'illa* and *qiyās al-dalāla* is laid bare (*Ma'ūna*, al-'Umayrīnī ed., pp. 100–101). This is an excellent explanation of the key differences between *qiyās* categories, and it receives an even better explanation from Ibn 'Aqīl (*K. al-Jadal*, p. 56, §275). Most importantly, however, it provides indication of how distinctions between

After translating al-Shīrāzī's definition of *ʿadam al-taʾthīr*, Miller states: "This question is a form of the old fourth theological question, then called jarayān al-ʿilla fī maʿlūlātihā, applying the cause to its causata;" he then suggests that al-Juwaynī "is being rather cautious in his definition" (presumably in comparison with al-Shīrāzī).[250] To be certain there are some concepts shared between al-Qirqisānī's fourth question: "accepting the compelling agency by way of demonstrating the concomitance of its occasioning factor with what it occasions" (*akhdh al-mūjib bi-ijrāʾ ʿillatihi fī maʿlūlātihā*), al-Maqdisī's fourth question "validation of the occasioning factor" (*taṣḥīḥ al-ʿilla*), and the juridical *iʿtirāḍ* of "lack of efficiency" (*ʿadam al-taʾthīr*); and before continuing I will clarify the meanings of relevant terms as I have come to understand them:

- *ṭard*: co-presence of *ʿilla* and *ḥukm* in the same locus
- *ʿaks*: co-absence of *ʿilla* and *ḥukm* from the same locus
- *jarayān*: when both *ṭard* and *ʿaks* are established for various loci, confirming the concomitance of *ʿilla* and *ḥukm*
- *ijrāʾ*: the demonstration of *jarayān*
- *taʾthīr*: when *ʿaks* is established for various loci
- *ʿadam al-taʾthīr*: the charge that *ʿaks* is decidedly not the case for various loci

From this I would deduce that the dialectical charge of "lack of efficiency" (*ʿadam al-taʾthīr*) is not the same as the dialectical demand for evidence of "concomitance of the occasioning factor with what it occasions" (*jarayān al-ʿilla fī maʿlūlātihā*); the former constitutes a claim that R's *ʿilla-ḥukm* relationship is not confirmed by *ʿaks*—Q shows that *ʿaks* is not the case, while the latter constitutes Q's request that R confirm his *ʿilla-ḥukm* relationship by demonstrating both *ṭard* and *ʿaks* (*jarayān*). Not surprisingly, we see that al-Bājī has treated these dialectical moves as separate categories—his thirteenth and fourteenth modes of *qiyās*-oriented objection:

- 13) Demand for Demonstrating Concomitance of the Occasioning Factor with What it Occasions (*al-muṭālaba bi-ijrāʾ al-ʿilla fī maʿlūlātihā*)[251]
- 14) Lack of Efficiency (*ʿAdam al-taʾthīr*), meaning the *ḥukm* is not absent when the *ʿilla* is absent in some locus or another

---

these categories of *qiyās* arose through the medium of dialectical debate. The key consideration between them, in fact, can *only* arise in a disputation, as it revolves around what a proponent-respondent *claims*. This is a prime example of *uṣūl al-fiqh* concepts and definitions refined in the forge of juridical dialectic.

[250] "Islamic Disputation Theory," pp. 120–1.

[251] Al-Bājī notes this mode of objection is very similar to the preceding mode: *kasr*.

Thus, the "theological" demand for *jarayān al-ʿilla fī maʿlūlātihā* is a precise match for al-Bājī's thirteenth mode, but no match for *ʿadam al-ta'thīr*.[252]

As for al-Bājī's definition of *ʿadam al-ta'thīr*, it may be rendered: "the *ḥukm* is not absent when the *ʿilla* is absent in some locus or another."[253] Miller provides a complete translation of this definition and al-Bājī's subsequent comments.[254] In sum, al-Bājī opines: (1) *ta'thīr* is indeed a *dalīl*-indicant for validity of the occasioning factor (*ṣiḥḥat al-ʿilla*); but (2) *ʿadam al-ta'thīr* is not a *dalīl*-indicant for invalidity of the occasioning factor (*fasād al-ʿilla*), when another *dalīl* provides indication for its validity. Thus, he would have been happier to include *ʿadam al-ta'thīr* in the category of "demand for validation of the occasioning factor" (*al-muṭālaba bi-taṣḥīḥ al-ʿilla*), but "our *shaykhs*" consider it as compelling the invalidity of the occasioning factor (*mūjib li-fasād al-ʿilla*), so he discusses it here among the *iʿtirāḍāt*.[255]

Moreover, after making his own opinion plain, but continuing along the path of "our *shaykhs*," al-Bājī not only follows his teacher al-Shīrāzī in subdividing *ʿadam al-ta'thīr* on the basis of the two types of properties (*awṣāf*), but adds to our understanding of how objections to them were valued. For the first type of *waṣf* (when eliminated, the *ʿilla* is destroyed), he adds: "and this is the one which damages the *ʿilla* through its *ʿadam al-ta'thīr*, according to the one who professes such;" and for the second type of *waṣf* (when eliminated, the *ʿilla* is not destroyed), he adds: "and for this one, [the *ʿilla*'s] *ʿadam al-ta'thīr* does not damage it, according to [he who professes such]." So it becomes clear that even among those who professed *ʿadam al-ta'thīr* as a clear sign of *fasād al-ʿilla*, there was a recognition that its "destructive" value lay only within this first category of properties (*awṣāf*).

Miller also explores a potential connection between al-Bājī's call for *ʿadam al-ta'thīr* to be subsumed by "demand for validation of the occasioning factor" (*al-muṭālaba bi-taṣḥīḥ al-ʿilla*) and al-Shīrāzī's consecutive treatment of the two

---

[252] Miller himself, continuing on the theme of al-Juwaynī's caution in defining *ʿadam al-ta'thīr*, notes: "[al-Juwaynī] tells us more than once, the ʿillа of the law are unlike the ʿilla of the intellect for the latter are correlative while the former are not" ("Islamic Disputation Theory," p. 121; citing *Kāfiya*, p. 9, lines 5ff.) This corresponds with the last section of al-Juwaynī's definition, above: "And the required condition for efficiency is not the loss of the ruling due to loss of the occasioning factor (*faqd al-ḥukm bi-faqd al-ʿilla*); indeed, this is the condition of co-absence—and such is obliged only for rational-intellectual 'causes' (*ʿilal al-ʿaql*). Loss of efficiency for the 'occasioning factors' of God's Law (*ʿilal al-Sharʿ*) might be for all the properties (*awṣāf*) of the occasioning factor, or for some of them." As a whole, then, al-Juwaynī's definition makes two clear distinctions regarding occasioning factors of God's Law (*ʿilal al-Sharʿ*): (1) co-absence of *ʿilla* and *ḥukm* (*al-ʿaks*) is not a necessary condition of *ta'thīr*-efficiency; and (2) the charge of *ʿadam al-ta'thīr* may apply to the *ʿilla* as a whole, or to only some of its properties (*awṣāf*).

[253] *Minhāj*, Turkī ed., p. 195, §443. In his introductory chapter on definitions, al-Bājī also supplies a definition of *al-ta'thīr*, as follows: "the cessation (*zawāl*) of the *ḥukm* due to the cessation of the *ʿilla* in some locus (*mawḍiʿ*)" (p. 14, §18).

[254] "Islamic Disputation Theory," p. 121.

[255] Although I would disagree with Miller's assessment of al-Bājī as "also very wary about the value of this objection," it is indeed plainly evident that he does not find *ʿadam al-ta'thīr* to be categorically *mūjib li-fasād al-ʿilla*. However, he is also sure to qualify this lack of *fasād*-conviction with "when another *dalīl* provides indication for [the *ʿilla*'s] validity."

(*muṭālaba bi-taṣḥīḥ al-ʿilla* as *iʿtirāḍ* #5, and *ʿadam al-taʾthīr* as *iʿtirāḍ* #6). Importantly, however, and evidenced by the illustrative example problem selected by Miller,[256] is that the Shāfiʿī R defending the efficiency of his *ʿilla* cites *both* co-presence and co-absence of *ʿilla* and *ḥukm*. This example from the *Maʿūna* was intended by al-Shīrāzī to illustrate a specific subcategory of response (*jawāb*); mainly, response method 2, type 1 from the below hierarchy:[257]

- *Iʿtirāḍ* 5: Demand for Validation of the Occasioning Factor (*al-Muṭālaba bi-taṣḥīḥ al-ʿilla*)
  - [response with methods (*ṭuruq*)]
    - [1] Method of its Validation: context of the *lafẓ*-expressions (*siyāq al-alfāẓ*)
      - its indication is from the mode of univocal text (*dalālatuhā min wajh al-naṣṣ*)
      - its indication is from the mode of most apparent meaning (*dalālatuhā min wajh al-ẓāhir*)
        - The most apparent meaning (*ẓāhir*) is a divinely-sanctioned decree (*nuṭq*)
        - The most apparent meaning (*ẓāhir*) is a reason (*sabab*) conveyed with the *ḥukm*
    - [2] Method of its Validation: rational inference (*istinbāṭ*)
      - Type 1: efficiency (*taʾthīr*)
      - Type 2: testimony of the authoritative source-cases (*shahādat al-uṣūl*)

It is al-Shīrāzī's example for R's response to Q's *muṭālaba bi-taṣḥīḥ al-ʿilla*, via the inferential (as opposed to contextual) method of showing *taʾthīr*-efficiency, and I would render it as follows:[258]

- **Shāfiʿī R:** "[Date-wine (*nabīdh*)] is forbidden (*ḥarām*) because it is a drink in which there is a 'euphoric intensity' (*shiddat muṭriba*); so it is *ḥarām*, like grape-wine (*khamr*)."
- **Ḥanafī Q:** "What is the *dalīl*-indicant for the validity of this *ʿilla* [of 'euphoric intensity']?"

(continued)

[256] "Islamic Disputation Theory," p. 122.
[257] *Maʿūna*, al-ʿUmayrīnī ed., pp. 97–100.
[258] *Maʿūna*, al-ʿUmayrīnī ed., p. 99.

- **Shāfiʿī R:** "The *dalīl*-indicant for it is efficiency (*ta'thīr*), which is: 'the presence of the *ḥukm* due to the presence of the *ʿilla*, and the absence of the *ḥukm* due to its absence (*wujūd al-ḥukm li-wujūd al-ʿilla, wa ʿadamuhu li-ʿadamihi*).' Don't you see/opine (*a-lā tarā*) that—before the occurrence of the [euphoric] intensity—the lawfulness of pressed-juice is the object of consensus? Then, after the intensity occurs [i.e., it becomes wine]—and nothing else occurs—they form consensus as to its proscription? Then, its intensity falls away [i.e., it becomes vinegar]—and nothing else falls away—so they form consensus as to its lawfulness? And if we evaluate the force of the intensity, then we have evaluated the intensity of the proscription. Thus did God say: «and if they were brought back, they would return to what was forbidden» [Q.6:28]. And this provides indication that ['euphoric intensity'] is the *ʿilla*."

Note that the Shāfiʿī R responds to the Ḥanafī Q's demand (*muṭālaba*) by detailing the steps of an inferential process by which co-presence and co-absence of *ʿilla* and *ḥukm* (and thus, the *ta'thīr* of the *ʿilla*) is confirmed. We have seen, however, that *ʿadam al-ta'thīr* consists of a charge by Q that R's *ḥukm* is present in a case where R's *ʿilla* is not present (thus *ʿaks* is shown to be lacking). Such a charge, in this example, could only be made by Q *after* his current *muṭālaba*. This justifies al-Shīrāzī's separate and sequential treatment of *muṭālaba bi-taṣḥīḥ al-ʿilla* (as *iʿtirāḍ* 5) and *ʿadam al-ta'thīr* (as *iʿtirāḍ* 6). Most importantly, we should recognize the differences between al-Juwaynī, al-Shīrāzī, and al-Bājī as regards *ʿadam al-ta'thīr* represent an ongoing debate among *jadal* and *uṣūl* theorists as to the destructive power of this charge, and whether or not showing the absence of *ʿaks* is enough to demonstrate invalidity of the occasioning factor.[259]

On "Reversal" (Qalb)

Al-Baṣrī twice treats *qalb*, once along with the other modes of invalidating the *ʿilla*, and once in a specially designated appendix. He first defines *qalb* as when "the contradictory (*naqīḍ*) of the *ḥukm* stated in the *qiyās* [of R] is made conditional upon the *ʿilla* [by Q], and the *farʿ* is referred, by means of that *ʿilla*, to the [same] *aṣl* to which the *farʿ* of [R's] *qiyās* is referred."[260] In his second definition (from the

[259] We might also note that the Shāfiʿī respondent in al-Shīrāzī's example *mas'ala* employs the formula *a-lā tarā* as a means of introducing his inferential proof of *ta'thīr*. This same function of defense is apparent in the formula's proto-system use, as we shall see in Sect. 6.2.

[260] *K. al-Qiyās al-Sharʿī*, Ḥamīd Allāh ed., p. 1040; Hallaq, "Treatise," p. 217.

ḍamīma-supplement): "the one doing *qalb* (*qālib*) to the *qiyās* makes the contradictory (*naqīḍ*) of the *ḥukm* stated in the *qiyās* dependent upon the *ʿilla*, and he refers the *farʿ* back to that same, exact *aṣl*. In terms of conditional dependence upon the *ʿilla*, one of the two *ḥukm*s is not superior (*awlā*) to the other; nor is it valid that they both, together, be dependent upon it, due to their mutual negation (*tanāfīhimā*)."[261] In short, then, *qalb* is when Q counters with the same *qiyās*-components as R, except with the contradictory (*naqīḍ*) of R's *ḥukm*. I would diagram this as follows, with al-Baṣrī's example *masʾala* included:

Qiyās of R		*Qalb* of Q	
Aṣl A *ʿIlla* efficient property Z *Ḥukm* X is the case	*Farʿ* B *ʿIlla* efficient property Z *Ḥukm* X is [also] the case	*Aṣl* A *ʿIlla* efficient property Z *Ḥukm* ¬X is the case	*Farʿ* B *ʿIlla* efficient property Z *Ḥukm* ¬X is [also] the case
Argument: In *aṣl* A, the *ʿilla* of efficient property Z occasions *ḥukm* X. Thus, in *farʿ* B, because it shares the *ʿilla* of efficient property Z, *ḥukm* X is also occasioned.		Argument: In *aṣl* A, the *ʿilla* of efficient property Z occasions *ḥukm* ¬X. Thus, in *farʿ* B, because it shares the *ʿilla* of efficient property Z, *ḥukm* ¬X is also occasioned.	
Example: For the standing (*wuqūf*) at ʿArafa,[a] the *ʿilla* of tarrying at a specific place occasions the *ḥukm* that fasting is a required condition (*sharṭ*). Thus, for seclusion in a mosque (*iʿtikāf*),[b] because it shares the *ʿilla* of tarrying at a specific place, the *ḥukm* that fasting is a condition (*sharṭ*) is also occasioned.		Example: For the standing at ʿArafa, the *ʿilla* of tarrying at a specific place occasions the *ḥukm* that fasting is NOT a required condition. Thus, for seclusion in a mosque, because it shares the *ʿilla* of tarrying at a specific place, the *ḥukm* that fasting is NOT a required condition is also occasioned.	

[a] One of several ritual components of the pilgrimage (*ḥajj*).
[b] Obliged after taking a vow, and especially recommended during the latter part of Ramaḍān.

Note that Q is "turning over, inverting, reversing" the *qiyās* of R—the very meaning of *qalb*; in so many words, Q is saying "Au contraire. In *aṣl* A—due to *ʿilla* Z—*not*-X is the case; thus, in *farʿ* B—which also has *ʿilla* Z—*not*-X must also be the case."[262]

Al-Juwaynī illustrates a specific mode of "reversal and oppositeness" (*al-qalb waʾl-ʿaks*) with the following example:[263]

> It is like what they profess, regarding the saliva (*suʾr*) of the beasts of prey (*sibāʿ*), that it is an animal (*ḥayawān*) whose meat is not eaten, so its saliva is impure (*najas*); like the dog. And the one 'reversing' [the *qiyās*] (*qālib*) says: 'The saliva of an animal whose meat is not eaten is pure (*ṭāhir*); like the cat.' So the *ʿilla* is one *ʿilla*, but has two opposite rulings

---

[261] *K. al-Qiyās al-Sharʿī*, Ḥamīd Allāh ed., p. 1048; Hallaq, "Treatise," pp. 224–5.

[262] Miller treats "reversal" (*qalb*) and "sharing the indication" (*ishtirāk al-dalāla*) as identical dialectical objections, and offers certain other observations which I consider problematic ("Islamic Disputation Theory," pp. 122ff.) See my dissertation (pt. 1, pp. 166ff.) for a review and critique. The other subtypes and example problems of *qalb* which I will discuss in this section are those selected by Miller; my justifications for reinterpreting them may be found in the same section of my dissertation.

[263] *Kāfiya*, Maḥmūd ed., p. 233.

(*ḥukmān mutaḍāddān*), by reference to two *aṣl*s of contradictory ruling (*mutanāqiḍay al-ḥukm*). And it is as if the purity of saliva of the cat is a case exposing inconsistency (*naqḍ*) with regard to the *ʿilla* of impurity of saliva of the beasts of prey (*sibāʿ*), and the impurity of saliva of the dog is a case exposing inconsistency (*naqḍ*) with regard to the *ʿilla* of purity of saliva of the beasts of prey (*sibāʿ*). And by this clarification is drawn that its 'being something whose meat is not eaten' does not allow its being an *ʿilla* for purity of saliva, nor for its impurity; and drawing argumentative support (*iḥtijāj*) by means of it is eliminated.[264]

I would diagram this example as follows:

Mas'ala: Is the saliva of the beasts of prey (*sibāʿ*) impure (*najas*)?			
R's Qiyās		Q's Qalb	
Aṣl saliva of the dog (*kalb*) *ʿIlla* it is an animal whose meat is not eaten *Ḥukm* its saliva is impure (*najas*)	Farʿ saliva of beasts of prey (*sibāʿ*) *ʿIlla* it is an animal whose meat is not eaten *Ḥukm* [thus] its saliva is [also] impure (*najas*)	Aṣl saliva of the cat (*hirr*) *ʿIlla* it is an animal whose meat is not eaten *Ḥukm* its saliva is pure (*ṭāhir*)	Farʿ saliva of beasts of prey (*sibāʿ*) *ʿIlla* it is an animal whose meat is not eaten *Ḥukm* [thus] its saliva is [also] pure (*ṭāhir*)

Note that Q, in searching among the indicants of God's Law, finds R's *ʿilla* among the properties of the cat, but occasioning the opposite *ḥukm*. This is in the way of a charge of inconsistency (*naqḍ*), precisely as al-Juwaynī says, and it invalidates use of the *ʿilla* of "being an animal whose meat is not eaten" for occasioning a *ḥukm* of either purity or impurity of saliva. But the features of *qalb* are most prominent here, as Q has "reversed" R's *qiyās*, causing R's *ʿilla* of R's *aṣl* to occasion the opposite *ḥukm*.

Al-Shīrāzī illustrates his second type of *qalb*—Reversal of Equalization (*Qalb al-Taswiya*)—with an example which I would diagram as follows:[265]

Mas'ala: Does ablution (*wuḍūʾ*) require intent (*niyya*)?		
Ḥanafī R's *Qiyās*		Shāfiʿī Q's *Qalb al-Taswiya*
Aṣl removal of impurity (*izālat al-najāsa*) *ʿIlla* it is a purification with a liquid (*ṭahāra bi-māʾiʿ*) *Ḥukm* it does not require intent (*niyya*)	Farʿ ablution (*wuḍūʾ*) *ʿIlla* it is a purification with a liquid (*ṭahāra bi-māʾiʿ*) *Ḥukm* [thus] it [also] does not require intent (*niyya*)	*Qalb al-Taswiya* Regarding removal of impurity (*izālat al-najāsa*), there is an equalization (*taswiya*) between purification with a liquid (*ṭahāra bi-māʾiʿ*) and purification with dry matter (*ṭahāra bi-jāmid*). But we know that ablution with earth/sand (*tayammum*) requires intent. So there must be an equalization (*taswiya*) between liquid and dry matter regarding ablution [in that both require intent], just as there is an equalization between them in removal of impurity [in which neither requires intent].

[264] Note this is not the same example employed by al-Shīrāzī to illustrate a type of *fasād al-waḍʿ*; conflation of the two may have led to some of Miller's problematic observations.

[265] *Maʿūna*, Turkī ed., p. 260, §144.

Note that Q retains R's *aṣl* along with his *ʿilla* in this example. He argues, however, that: (1) removal of impurity (*izālat al-najāsa*) may also be a purification with dry matter (*ṭahāra bi-jāmid*); (2) whether as purification with a liquid (*bi-māʾiʿ*) or with dry matter (*bi-jāmid*), removal of impurity does not require intent (*niyya*)—establishing an equalization (*taswiya*) of the two *ʿilla*'s; (3) this equalization must be maintained for ablution (*wuḍūʾ*), where the *ʿilla* of purification with dry matter (*ṭahāra bi-jāmid*) requires intent; and, therefore, (4) ablution as purification with a liquid must also require intent. It is evident why this constitutes a type of *qalb*: Q has taken both R's *aṣl* and R's *ʿilla* and, by maintaining the *taswiya*-equalization of that *ʿilla* (purification with a liquid) with its sister *ʿilla* (purification with dry matter), occasioned the opposite *ḥukm* in the *farʿ*—Q has "reversed" R's *qiyās*, by way of maintaining a *taswiya*-equalization, hence: "Reversal of Equalization" (*Qalb al-Taswiya*).

Miller, discussing al-Shīrāzī's first type of *qalb*: "Reversal by way of an intended ruling" (*Qalb bi-Ḥukm Maqṣūd*)[266] observes that al-Juwaynī treats the very same species of objection but calls it by the different term "explicit reversal" (*al-qalb al-ṣarīḥ*). Miller then relates al-Juwaynī's explanation and example.[267] I would diagram al-Juwaynī's example as follows:

Masʾala: Does seclusion in a mosque (*iʿtikāf*) require fasting (*ṣawm*)?		
R's *Qiyās*		Q's *Qalb al-Ṣarīḥ*
Aṣl the standing (*wuqūf*) at ʿArafa *ʿIlla* it is a sojourn in a specific place which does not become a pious act (*qurba*) except by way of a sign (*qarīna*) *Ḥukm* it requires fasting (*ṣawm*)	*Farʿ* seclusion in a mosque (*iʿtikāf*) *ʿIlla* it is a sojourn in a specific place which does not become a pious act (*qurba*) except by way of a sign (*qarīna*) *Ḥukm* [thus] it [also] requires fasting (*ṣawm*)	*Qalb al-Ṣarīḥ* By way of this same *ʿilla*, it is obliged that fasting NOT be stipulated for the validity of seclusion in a mosque; just like [it is not obliged for] the standing at ʿArafa

Note that Q simply claims—by way of the same *aṣl* and *ʿilla* as R—the opposite *ḥukm*. It is not terribly clear in this, or other examples, by what justification Q makes this claim. I would surmise, however, that it stems from: (1) an established difference between the doctrinal schools of R and Q for the rulings of the *aṣl*; and (2) established differences regarding the perceived aim (*maqṣid*) of God with regard to that *aṣl*. In other words, it may be that according to R's *madhhab* sojourn-

[266] Miller renders this "the reversal of the intended juristic qualification."

[267] "Islamic Disputation Theory," pp. 126–7. Miller also records (pp. 125–6) al-Juwaynī's discussion of *qalb al-taswiya* in his *Kāfiya* (239ff.), at some length. Al-Juwaynī notes variant terms (*qalb al-tafriqa, qalb al-iʿtibār*), and various contentions for and against its validity as an argument. In the end, he argues that *qalb al-taswiya* is indeed valid.

ing in a specific place only becomes a pious act (*qurba*) by an additional sign of pious intent: fasting (*ṣawm*); while for Q's *madhhab* God's original aim with regard to sojourning is, in fact, that it be itself a pious act (*qurba*). This interpretation would make sense of al-Shīrāzī's appellation of "Reversal by way of an intended ruling" (*qalb bi-ḥukm maqṣūd*)—meaning that Q "reverses" R's *qiyās* by asserting a variant interpretation of God's original aim (*maqṣid*).

As a final note, observe that al-Juwaynī's example *mas'ala* is precisely the same that al-Baṣrī employs in his *Kitāb al-Qiyās al-Shar'ī*. It does not appear among any of al-Shīrāzī's examples for *qalb*, however, nor is it among al-Bājī's examples, nor among Ibn 'Aqīl's. This may have significance with regard to the transmission of variant *jadal*-theory traditions, as the different organizing principle of al-Juwaynī's *Kāfiya* from that of these other jurists would also suggest. Certainly, Miller considers al-Juwaynī to represent a different "eastern" tradition,[268] and indicants such as these lend support to his assessment.

On "Inconsistency" (Naqḍ)

Al-Baṣrī defines *naqḍ* as "the presence of the *'illa* in a locus (*mawḍi'*) from which its *ḥukm* is absent."[269] He further explains the difference between invalid and valid charges of *naqḍ*, as follows:

- Invalid *naqḍ*: "When the one justifying the *'illa* (*mu'allil*) establishes his *'illa* for the general (*jumla*), then it is "contradicted" by particularization (*tafṣīl*); it is not *naqḍ*, because the *ḥukm* of the *'illa* itself is general, and this is not absent from the locus in which the *'illa* is found. Rather, only the particularized *ḥukm* is absent, and the particularized *ḥukm* is not that which is made conditional upon [the *'illa*]."
- Valid *naqḍ*: "If the *mu'allil* establishes his *'illa* for the particularized, then he is contradicted by the general; this is valid *naqḍ*."

The difference between the valid and invalid forms of *naqḍ* may be diagramed as follows, with al-Baṣrī's examples:

[268] "Islamic Disputation Theory," pp. 89–90.

[269] *K. al-Qiyās al-Shar'ī*, Ḥamīd Allāh ed., p. 1041; Hallaq, "Treatise," p. 218.

Valid: Inconsistency by way of the General (*al-Naqḍ bi'l-Jumla*)[a]		
Qiyās of R		*Naqḍ* of Q
Aṣl killing a Muslim with intent	*Far'* killing a non-Muslim subject (*dhimmī*) with intent	*Mas'alat al-Naqḍ* killing a non-Muslim residing in a non-Muslim polity (*ḥarbī*)
'Illa victim is free and legally capacitated (*ḥurr mukallaf*)	*'Illa* victim is free and legally capacitated (*ḥurr mukallaf*)	*'Illa* victim is free and legally capacitated (*ḥurr mukallaf*)
Ḥukm there is retaliation (*qiṣāṣ*)	*Ḥukm* [thus] there is [also] retaliation (*qiṣāṣ*)	*Ḥukm* there is no retaliation (*qiṣāṣ*)

[a] NB: al-Baṣrī introduces his example with "don't you see/opine" (*a-lā tarā*); cf. relevant discussions in Sect. 6.2, below.

Note that R's *aṣl* and *far'* are more particular (killing with intent), while Q's *mas'alat-al-naqḍ* (an *endoxon* parallel case brought to expose R's inconsistency) is more general (killing)—that is, killing both with and without intent are included in the *mas'alat-al-naqḍ*. R's *ḥukm* is shown to be absent from the more general locus (*mawḍi'*) of the *mas'alat-al-naqḍ*, even though his *'illa* is present. Because of this inconsistency, the efficiency of R's *'illa* for occasioning his *ḥukm* in the more particular case at hand is destroyed—if it were truly efficient, then the *ḥukm* for the *mas'alat al-naqḍ* would have to be for retaliation, but it is not.

Invalid: Inconsistency by way of Particularization (*al-Naqḍ bi'l-Tafṣīl*)		
Qiyās of R		*Naqḍ* of Q
Aṣl killing of a Muslim by a Muslim	*Far'* killing of a Muslim by a non-Muslim subject (*dhimmī*)	*Mas'alat al-Naqḍ* killing of a *dhimmī* by a Muslim, without intent
'Illa they are both free, legally capacitated, and their blood is not lawfully shed (*ḥurr mukallaf maḥqūn al-dam*)	*'Illa* they are both free, legally capacitated, and their blood is not lawfully shed (*ḥurr mukallaf maḥqūn al-dam*)	*'Illa* they are both free, legally capacitated, and their blood is not lawfully shed (*ḥurr mukallaf maḥqūn al-dam*)
Ḥukm there is retaliation (*qiṣāṣ*)	*Ḥukm* [thus] there is [also] retaliation (*qiṣāṣ*)	*Ḥukm* there is no retaliation (*qiṣāṣ*)

Note that R's *aṣl* and *far'* are more general (killing), while Q's *mas'alat-al-naqḍ* is more particular (killing without intent)—that is, killing both with and without intent are included in R's *aṣl* and *far'*, but only without intent in Q's *mas'alat-al-naqḍ*. R's *ḥukm* is thus only shown to be absent from the more particular locus (*mawḍi'*) of the *mas'alat-al-naqḍ*; it has not been shown absent from the more general locus of killing with and without intent. The efficiency of R's *'illa*, therefore, has not been validly destroyed.

Drawing from al-Baṣrī, Hallaq notes: "The inability of [an] *ʿilla* to produce a judgment leads to its refutation (*naqḍ*). According to al-Baṣrī, *naqḍ* and *kasr* constitute particularization (*takhṣīṣ*), a deficiency which prevents the *ʿilla* from resulting in a judgment."[270] Note also al-Shīrāzī's extensive treatment of *naqḍ* in his *Maʿūna* (*Iʿtirāḍ* 7), where he defines it as "the presence of the *ʿilla*, but not a *ḥukm*, according to the doctrine of one who does not opine (*lā yarā*) [the theory of] particularization of the occasioning factor (*takhṣīṣ al-ʿilla*)." There is a logical overlap between the concepts of *naqḍ*, "contradictory" (*naqīḍ*), "refutation" (*tabkīt*), "counter-indication" (*muʿāraḍa*), etc., and what might be understood by "refutation." Al-Shīrāzī's *naqḍ*—like al-Baṣrī's—refers to a specific type of charge, made by Q, that R's *ʿilla* exists in another case, without R's *ḥukm*, and which—if R does not subscribe to the problematic theory of *takhṣīṣ al-ʿilla*—ought to lead to Q's *elenchus*.[271] Miller translates *naqḍ/munāqaḍa* as "inconsistency;"[272] then adds "al-Juwainī offers two definitions of <u>naqd</u>."[273] In fact, al-Juwaynī offers three consecutive definitions.[274] They are: (1) "the absence (*intifāʾ*) of the *ḥukm* from what its *ʿilla* was claimed to be;"[275] (2) "the presence of the *ʿilla* despite the absence (*faqd*) of what its *ḥukm* was claimed to be;"[276] and (3) "the application (*ijrāʾ*) of the *ʿilla* where there is no *ḥukm*."[277]

Miller also considers *naqḍ* an example of a juridical expansion upon "theological" dialectic, saying: "Together with the ineffective cause [*ʿadam al-taʾthīr*], [*naqḍ*] comprises the old category of applying the cause to its causata."[278] Although I must disagree that *naqḍ* is a later juridical take over—it is ubiquitous throughout our subject-text, as we will see—it is easier now to understand Miller's earlier claim that *ʿadam al-taʾthīr* is a form of the dialectical demand for *jarayān al-ʿilla fī maʿlūlātihā*, which in turn was equated to "applying the cause to its causata." It will help to chart the relationships between different species of justifying the *ʿilla-ḥukm* relationship (*taʿlīl*) and their corresponding species of objections:

[270] "Treatise," p. 202.

[271] al-ʿUmayrīnī ed., pp. 104ff.; cf. Ibn ʿAqīl, *K. al-Jadal*, pp. 56ff. Al-Shīrāzī focuses his following discussion upon a set of possible replies to a charge of *naqḍ*—three for the Shāfiʿī so charged, and an additional three responses propounded by the Ḥanafīs.

[272] "Islamic Disputation Theory," pp. 127ff., *passim*.

[273] "Islamic Disputation Theory," p. 127.

[274] *Kāfiya*, Maḥmūd ed., p. 69, §165.

[275] Miller translates: "it is the denial that the juristic qualification has the alleged <u>ratio legis.</u>"

[276] Miller: "The existence of the <u>ratio legis</u> with the absence of its alleged juristic qualification"

[277] Reading (إجراء) rather than the (إبراء) of Maḥmūd's edition.

[278] "Islamic Disputation Theory," pp. 128 and n. 101.

Justifying the *'Illa-Ḥukm* Relationship (*Taʿlīl*)	Objecting to the *'Illa-Ḥukm* Relationship
• *ṭard*: presence of the *ḥukm* due to presence of the *ʿilla*	• *naqḍ*: absence of the *ḥukm* despite presence of the *ʿilla* (objection: *ṭard* is not the case)
• *ʿaks*: absence of the *ḥukm* due to absence of the *ʿilla* • *ta'thīr*: disappearance of the *ḥukm* due to disappearance of the *ʿilla* in some context/locus	• *ʿadam al-ta'thīr*: presence of the *ḥukm* despite absence of the *ʿilla* (objection: *ʿaks* is not the case)
• *jarayān*: the *ḥukm* is present upon presence of the *ʿilla*, and the *ḥukm* disappears upon disappearance of the *ʿilla* (there is both *ṭard* and *ʿaks*)	• *al-iʿtirāḍ ʿalā al-ʿilla bi-annahā lā tajrī fī maʿlūlātihā*: objection that *jarayān* is not the case • *al-muṭālaba bi-ijrā' al-ʿilla fī maʿlūlātihā*: demand that *jarayān* be demonstrated

Miller's claims are clearer now; for just as *ṭard* and *ʿaks* appear as complementary halves to a complete *jarayān*, so too *naqḍ* and *ʿadam al-ta'thīr* appear as complementary halves for a complete *iʿtirāḍ ʿalā al-ʿilla bi-annahā lā tajrī fī maʿlūlātihā* (al-Bājī's thirteenth mode).

Finally, Miller relates al-Juwaynī's mention of "another category of objection, munāqaḍa, contradiction or self-contradiction."[279] In fact al-Juwaynī appears to treat *naqḍ* and *munāqaḍa*, for the most part, as synonyms. On the other hand, both the first and third form *maṣdars* of *n-q-ḍ* bear the connotation of "contradiction;" and this is indeed the essence of the objection of *naqḍ*, made clear by the examples of our lens-text authors: by bringing R to concede to a case where his *ʿilla* is present but does not occasion his *ḥukm*, Q shows that R has contradicted himself with regard to that *ʿilla*'s efficiency in the *mas'ala* at hand. Because the contradiction is intra-doctrinal (between R's *aṣl* and *farʿ* and the *endoxon mas'alat al-naqḍ* brought by Q), and not more strictly intra-argument (as in *tanāquḍ*, an internal logical contradiction), I have followed Miller in preferring "inconsistency" over "contradiction" as a translation of *naqḍ*. Miller may be correct, however, in considering *munāqaḍa* a variant dialectical move; it may very well be that al-Juwaynī intended *munāqaḍa* as a more strictly logical form of *naqḍ*—where the *ḥukm* of the *mas'alat al-naqḍ* is the true contradictory of R's *ḥukm*.[280]

On "Inconsistency" (Naqḍ) *and "Particularization of the Occasioning Factor"* (Takhṣīṣ al-ʿIlla)

Al-Shīrāzī has drawn our attention to the relationship between *naqḍ* and the much-contended theory of *takhṣīṣ al-ʿilla*; mainly, should one deny the theory of *takhṣīṣ al-ʿilla*, yet maintain (in practice) an inconsistent doctrine wherein the

[279] "Islamic Disputation Theory," p. 128 and n. 103. He laments that al-Juwaynī is "somewhat careless in his use of these terms," using sometimes one, sometimes the other.

[280] See the discussion on al-Juwaynī's conception of *muʿāraḍa* below. This may explain why he appears to place *munāqaḍa* under the rubric of *muʿāraḍa*.

same *ʿilla* does not always occasion the same *ḥukm*, then one may be charged with *naqḍ* whenever such inconsistent *ʿilla*s are pointed out in the course of debate. Subscription to the theory, on the other hand, would explain one's apparently inconsistent practice. Disputation must then shift focus to R's defence of *takhṣīṣ al-ʿilla*. Hallaq reproduces and explains al-Baṣrī's argument against *takhṣīṣ al-ʿilla*; from this we gain insight into the form such a disputation might take.[281] Al-Baṣrī's argument is a species of *reductio*, and provides a fine example of how this genus was employed:

- Given that, for Gold:
  - *ḥukm*: sale of smaller for larger quantities is forbidden
  - *ʿilla*: (because of) its measurability by weight
- Should we say that, for Lead:
  - *ḥukm*: sale of smaller for larger quantities is allowed
  - *ʿilla*: (because of) its whiteness of color [NB: measurability by weight has been "particularized" by the added consideration of color]
- Then we are faced with the following impossibility, for Iron:
  - *ḥukm*: sale of smaller for larger quantity is at once forbidden and allowed
  - *ʿilla*: (because of) its measurability by weight and its whiteness of color

Among other things, this argument shows how the same dialectical techniques which were employed in disputations regarding substantive legal doctrine were also employed in disputations regarding legal theory: in this case, the theory of *takhṣīṣ al-ʿilla* has been refuted by the raising of a case (corresponding to the *mas'alat al-naqḍ* of *fiqh*-oriented *jadal*) wherein that theory would result in an impossibility (the *ḥukm* for iron is both X and ¬X). Many similar instances appear in the subject-text, and I have given them the general label of "method-*naqḍ*." Most importantly for the current project, arguments such as al-Baṣrī's provide patent examples of legal theory crafted through dialectic; the theoretical insistence upon *ʿilla*-consistency (and the denial of *takhṣīṣ al-ʿilla*) is here gaining the edge of argumentative conclusiveness (*ḥujjiyya*) in the dialectical forge.

On "Breaking Apart" (Kasr)

Al-Baṣrī defines *kasr* simply as "*naqḍ* of the *ʿilla* on account of its *maʿnā*-quality, not its *lafẓ*-expression."[282] Hallaq, citing earlier material in al-Baṣrī's *Muʿtamad*, relates another description of *kasr*, which occurs to an *ʿilla* "when one of the *ʿilla*'s

[281] "Treatise," p. 202; citing from *Muʿtamad*, Ḥamīd Allāh ed., vol. 2, p. 824.

[282] *K. al-Qiyās al-Sharʿī*, Ḥamīd Allāh ed., p. 1043; Hallaq, "Treatise," p. 220.

properties is cancelled due to inefficiency, and when it becomes clear that the remaining properties cannot induce a judgment…."[283] Miller introduces *kasr* as "a special case of naqd," while observing that al-Shīrāzī, al-Bājī, and Ibn ʿAqīl all treat it as an independent category.[284] In his *Maʿūna*, al-Shīrāzī treats *kasr* (*iʿtirāḍ* 8) immediately after *naqḍ* (*iʿtirāḍ* 7);[285] so, too, does al-Bājī. Tellingly, al-Bājī names his eleventh *qiyās*-oriented objection: "objection to the *ʿilla* by way of inconsistency" (*al-iʿtirāḍ ʿalā al-ʿilla biʾl-naqḍ*), and his twelfth: "objection to the correlational inference by way of breaking apart" (*al-iʿtirāḍ ʿalā al-qiyās biʾl-kasr*), or "inconsistency with respect to the *maʿnā*-quality" (*al-naqḍ min jihat al-maʿnā*).[286] As for al-Shīrāzī, he simply defines *kasr* as: "the presence of the *maʿnā*-quality of the *ʿilla*, and not a *ḥukm*."[287]

After praising this *iʿtirāḍ* as "one of the most refined (*adaqq*) and most *fiqh*-inducing (*afqah*)," al-Bājī subdivides *kasr* into two categories: (1) "[Q] replaces one of the properties (*awṣāf*) of the *ʿilla* by something in its [same] *maʿnā*-intension;" and (2) "[Q] eliminates one of the properties (*awṣāf*) of the *ʿilla*."[288] Miller's definition for *kasr*—"the existence of the meaning (maʿnā) of the ratio legis without the existence of the corresponding juristic qualification"—is drawn from al-Shīrāzī, al-Bājī, and Ibn ʿAqīl.[289] Returning to al-Shīrāzī, light may be shed on the dialectical move of *kasr* by diagraming his example *masʾala*:

Masʾala: Is the *bayʿ*-commutation of what the buyer has not seen valid?		
Shāfiʿī R's *Qiyās*		Opponent Q's *Kasr*
Aṣl *bayʿ*-commutation when the seller merely says: 'I sell you a garment'	*Farʿ* *bayʿ*-commutation of what the buyer has not seen	*Masʾalat al-Kasr* marriage (*nikāḥ*) of a woman the groom has not seen
ʿIlla it is an object of sale of unknown attribute to the contracting party at the time of contract (*mabīʿ majhūl al-ṣifa ʿinda al-ʿāqid ḥāl al-ʿaqd*)	*ʿIlla* it is an object of sale of unknown attribute to the contracting party at the time of contract (*mabīʿ majhūl al-ṣifa ʿinda al-ʿāqid ḥāl al-ʿaqd*)	*ʿIlla* she is unknown to the contracting party at the time of contract (*majhūla ʿinda al-ʿāqid ḥāl al-ʿaqd*)
Ḥukm it is not valid	*Ḥukm* [thus] it is [also] not valid	*Ḥukm* it is valid

[283] "Treatise," 201–2. Cf. al-Shīrāzī (*Maʿūna*, al-ʿUmayrīnī ed., pp. 107–8), and Ibn ʿAqīl, *K. al-Jadal*, 65.

[284] "Islamic Disputation Theory," p. 128.

[285] al-ʿUmayrīnī ed., pp. 104ff.

[286] *Minhāj*, Turkī ed., pp. 185ff., §§412ff.

[287] *Maʿūna*, al-ʿUmayrīnī ed., p. 107.

[288] *Minhāj*, Turkī ed., p. 191, §432. In his earlier chapter on definitions, al-Bājī defines *kasr* as "presence of a *maʿnā*-quality of the *ʿilla*, despite absence of the *ḥukm*" (p. 14, §18), thus tying it closely to *naqḍ* ("presence of the *ʿilla* despite absence of the *ḥukm*").

[289] "Islamic Disputation Theory," pp. 128–9.

The relationship between *naqḍ* and *kasr* is plain: Q has attempted to show inconsistency in R's doctrine by confronting him with a case which he ought to concede, but where a similar set of properties do not yield the same *ḥukm*. The difference from *naqḍ* is also plain, however, for a woman in a *nikāḥ*-contract is not a *mabīʿ* (object of sale)—we notice that *mabīʿ* is missing from the properties (*awṣāf*) of Q's *ʿilla*.[290] So Q, in his supporting *mas'ala* for *kasr*, does not use the self-same *ʿilla* as R; whereas he would have to use R's exact *ʿilla* in a *mas'alat al-naqḍ*. Rather, Q is employing only that shared *maʿnā*-quality, or potentially-efficient intension-property, of "unknown to the contracting party at the time of contract" (*majhūl ʿinda al-ʿāqid ḥāl al-ʿaqd*). Confirmation of this is evident in al-Shīrāzī's suggested response (*jawāb*) for the Shāfiʿī R:

> He says: 'Marriage (*nikāḥ*) is not like *bayʿ*-commutation regarding this *ḥukm*, because, in terms of efficiency (*ta'thīr*), there belongs to being-uninformed (*jahāla*) in the category of *bayʿ*-commutation, what does not belong to [being uninformed] in marriage. Due to this, if he marries a woman he has not seen, then he sees her, option (*khiyār*) is confirmed for him. So it is permitted that lack of seeing (*ʿadam al-ru'ya*) in the marriage contract be no impediment to validity, but in the *bayʿ*-contract it impedes.

The suggested response to *kasr* is thus also related to the suggested response to *naqḍ*; after Q's attempted *kasr*, R finds the means to reject Q's supporting *mas'ala* for *kasr*, whereas after Q's *naqḍ*, R would find the means to reject Q's *mas'alat al-naqḍ*.

Miller observes that al-Juwaynī also discusses *kasr* in his larger treatment of *naqḍ/munāqaḍa*, with special attention to arguments against its validity.[291] Those who support *kasr* as a valid move call it "refuting R by referring to the 'spirit of the law' (ilzām ʿalā al-maʿnā)." I have attempted to adhere to a different translation for *maʿnā*, closer to what I have come to believe was al-Shāfiʿī's usage: a potentially-shared and potentially-efficient "property" or "quality" or "intension."[292] Support for this meaning, and for the interpretation of al-Shīrāzī's *kasr* example, may be found in a brief statement belonging to al-Juwaynī: "And because of what is claimed that [this sort of *naqḍ*] refutes the *maʿnā* and not the *lafẓ*-expression,[293] the jurists call it: "breaking apart" (*kasr*); and such cannot ever come about except by omission (*tark*) of one/some of the properties (*awṣāf*) of the *ʿilla*, and obliging concession (*ilzām*) to the remainder...."[294] Not only does this statement clarify the link between *maʿnā* and *waṣf* (property), but it describes precisely what Q attempts against the Shāfiʿī R's *qiyās* in al-Shīrāzī's illustration of *kasr*. Q "breaks apart" R's *ʿilla* into its component *maʿnā*-qualities (object of sale + of unknown attribute to

---

[290] We may also note she is merely "unknown" (*majhūla*), and not "of unknown attribute" (*majhūl al-ṣifa*).

[291] "Islamic Disputation Theory," p. 129.

[292] In the main, I will prefer "intension-property" and the hybrids "*maʿnā*-intension" and "*maʿnā*-quality".

[293] Cf. al-Baṣrī's definition, above.

[294] *Kāfiya*, bottom of p. 212.

the contracting party at the time of contract), omits certain of them, and then locates the reduced *ʿilla* (unknown to the contracting party at the time of contract) in an *aṣl* which R is expected to concede (marriage of the unseen bride).

On Qiyās-*Oriented "Counter-Indication"* (Muʿāraḍa) *and "Invalidating Distinction"* (Farq)

It is evident from al-Juwaynī's definition, and from the *iʿtirāḍ*-hierarchies of al-Shīrāzī and al-Bājī, that all three authors considered "invalidating distinction" (*farq*) a subcategory of "counter-indication" (*muʿāraḍa*).[295] As for al-Juwaynī's definition of *farq*, I would render it thus: "It is comprehensive counter-indication due to [or consisting of] the branch-case's divergence from the source-case with regard to the occasioning factor of the ruling" (*al-muʿāraḍa al-mutaḍammina li-mukhālafat al-farʿ al-aṣl fī ʿillat al-ḥukm*).[296] A better idea of how *farq* and *muʿāraḍa* intertwine may be acquired through first re-examining an outline of al-Shīrāzī's *qiyās*-related modes of *muʿāraḍa* culled from his *Maʿūna*:[297]

- *Iʿtirāḍ* 15: Counter-Indication (*Muʿāraḍa*)
  - (1) Counter-Indication with a Divinely-Sanctioned Decree (*al-Muʿāraḍa bi'l-Nuṭq*); [*al-Nuṭq*] being Qur'ān, Sunna, and Ijmāʿ [298]
  - (2) Counter-Indication with the Occasioning Factor (*al-Muʿāraḍa bi'l-ʿIlla*)
    - Type 1: Counter-Indication with a Self-Initiated Occasioning Factor (*al-Muʿāraḍa bi-ʿIlla Mubtada'a*)
    - Type 2: Counter-Indication regarding the *Aṣl*, which is Invalidating Distinction (*Farq*)

(continued)

[295] See Miller, "Islamic Disputation Theory," p. 130. Observing that *farq* was considered a subcategory of *muʿāraḍa*, Miller treats it under a separate subheading before moving on to his section on *muʿāraḍa*. Translating *farq* as "distinction," he provides al-Juwaynī's definition from the *Kāfiya* (Maḥmūd ed., p. 69, §167), and follows up with a translated discussion from al-Bājī's *Minhāj* (Turkī ed., p. 201, §456).

[296] Miller: "a type of counter-objection (<u>muʿāraḍa</u>) which contains an objection that the case at hand (<u>farʿ</u>) and the principal case (<u>aṣl</u>) differ with respect to the <u>ratio legis</u> of the juristic qualification."

[297] Turkī ed., pp. 262ff., §146ff. The first half of this material is missing from al-ʿUmayrīnī's ed.

[298] A definition of *nuṭq* may be found in Rafīq al-ʿAjam's *Mawsūʿat Muṣṭalaḥāt Uṣūl al-Fiqh ʿinda al-Muslimīn* (vol. 2, pp. 1636f.; s.v. نطق): "It is the *lafẓ*-expression which is found in the Qur'ān or the Sunna, by which indicants are drawn (*al-mustadall bihi*) for the *ḥukm* of things; it is the most apparent meaning (*ẓāhir*) itself, and might be designated as 'all the discourse (*kalām*) cited, as unambiguous text (*naṣṣan*), just as it was said (*kamā qālahu*) by he who spoke it (*al-mutakallim bihi*).'"

- [2.1] Invalidating Distinction by way of Correlational Inference of the Occasioning Factor (*al-Farq bi-Qiyās al-'Illa*)[299]
- [2.2] Invalidating Distinction by way of Correlational Inference of Indication (*al-Farq bi-Qiyās al-Dalāla*)
  - Type 1: [Q] makes distinction by way of one of the rulings of the branch-case (*ḥukm min aḥkām al-far'*)[300]
  - Type 2: [Q] makes distinction by way of one of the parallel cases of the ruling (*naẓīr min naẓā'ir al-ḥukm*)
- [2.3] Invalidating Distinction by way of Correlational Inference of Resemblance (*al-Farq bi-Qiyās al-Shabah*)

Farq occupies a similar position in al-Bājī's ordering of *qiyās*-related *mu'āraḍāt*, as may be seen by revisiting the more detailed outline drawn from his *Minhāj*:[301]

- 15) Counter-Indication (*Mu'āraḍa*)
  - 15.1) Counter-Indication of the Occasioning Factor with Divinely-Sanctioned Decree (*mu'āraḍat al-'illa bi'l-nuṭq*)
  - 15.2) Counter-Indication of the Occasioning Factor with [another] Occasioning Factor (*mu'āraḍat al-'illa bi'l-'illa*)
    - 15.2.1) Counter-Indication with a Self-Initiated Occasioning Factor (*al-mu'āraḍa bi-'illa mubtada'a*)
    - 15.2.2) Counter-Indication with the Occasioning Factor of the Source-Case—which is Invalidating Distinction (*al-mu'āraḍa bi-'illat al-aṣl wa huwa al-farq*)
      - 15.2.2.1) Invalidating Distinction by way of the Occasioning Factor of the Ruling (*farq bi-'illat al-ḥukm*); the *ma'nā*-quality upon which the *ḥukm* is made contingent in God's Law (*fi'l-Shar'*) is in the *aṣl*, but the opposite (*'aks*) is true of the *far'*
        - 15.2.2.1.1) the *ma'nā*-quality is an object of agreement (*muttafaq 'alayhi*)

(continued)

[299] Turkī ed., pp. 262–3, §149. It is in this section that al-'Umayrīnī's edition resumes after a preceding lacuna.

[300] I have followed Turkī here; al-'Umayrīnī renders "one of the rulings of God's Law" (*ḥukm min aḥkām al-Shar'*).

[301] Turkī ed., pp. 201ff., §456ff.

  - 15.2.2.1.2) the *maʿnā*-quality is an object of disagreement (*mukhtalaf ʿalayhi*)
- 15.2.2.2) Invalidating Distinction by way of Indication of the Ruling (*farq bi-dalālat al-ḥukm*)
  - 15.2.2.2.1) [Q] makes distinction between the *farʿ* and the *aṣl* by way of a *ḥukm* peculiar to the *farʿ*, without leaving [the example of the *farʿ*]
  - 15.2.2.2.2) [Q] makes distinction by way of the same *ḥukm*, in other loci of disagreement (*mawāḍiʿ al-khilāf*)
  - 15.2.2.2.3) [Q] makes distinction by way of *ḥukm* which resembles the contended *ḥukm*
  - 15.2.2.2.4) [Q] makes distinction by way of a type of property resemblance (*shabah*)

Miller provides a translation of al-Bājī's opening discussion on *farq*; and within the first paragraph we find al-Bājī's definition of *al-muʿāraḍa bi-ʿillat al-aṣl wa huwa al-farq*: "It consists in mentioning something which necessitates a difference between the test case (farʿ) and the principal case. That is, to mention something (maʿnā [in the sense of the ḥukm of the ʿilla]) and its contrary (ʿaks) in the point of dispute."[302] Alternately, I would render al-Bājī's definition: "it is that [Q] states what obliges invalidating distinction (*farq*) between the branch-case and the source-case; which is to say that he mentions a (potentially-efficient) *maʿnā*-quality in the source-case, but shows its absence/opposite (*yaʿkisuhu*) in the branch-case."

General characteristics of the *iʿtirāḍ* of *farq* found in the definitions of our lens-text authors are illustrated by example *masāʾil* for each and every subtype. The following example from al-Bājī's *Minhāj*, meant to illustrate 15.2.2.1.2 in the above outline, is instructive:[303]

[302] "Islamic Disputation Theory," p. 130; translating from al-Bājī, *Minhāj*, Turkī ed., p. 201, §456 (parentheses and brackets are Miller's).

[303] Turkī ed., p. 203, §460.

***Mas'ala*: Does retaliation (*qiṣāṣ*) apply to one who has killed with a blunt object (*muthaqqal*)?**		
Mālikī R's *Qiyās*		Ḥanafī Q's charge of *Farq*
Aṣl the one who kills with a sharp object (*muḥaddad*) *ʿIlla* he kills, iniquitously (*ẓulman*), one who is equal in status to him (*man yukāfiʾuhu*), by means of what most probably will result in his death *Ḥukm* retaliation is obliged against him	*Farʿ* the one who kills with a blunt object (*muthaqqal*) *ʿIlla* he kills, iniquitously (*ẓulman*), one who is equal in status to him (*man yukāfiʾuhu*), by means of what most probably will result in his death *Ḥukm* [thus] retaliation is [also] obliged against him	Invalidating Distinction by way of the Occasioning Factor of the Ruling (*farq bi-ʿillat al-ḥukm*); where the *maʿnā*-quality is an object of disagreement (*mukhtalaf ʿalayhi*) The *maʿnā*-quality for "sharp object" (*muḥaddad*) is that prescribed slaughter (*dhakāt*) occurs by means of it; due to that we say: "Retaliation is indeed confirmed by way of it." But it is not so for our *mas'ala*—for prescribed slaughter does not occur by means of [a blunt object], so retaliation is not confirmed by way of it;[a] like [killing with] the small cane/stick (*al-ʿaṣā al-ṣaghīra*).

[a] That is, an intention to kill is best substantiated by use of an object which meets the requirements for killing swiftly and surely. See *MF*, s.v. "ذبائح" (vol. 21, pp. 171–204; at p. 196, §42): the tool for ritual slaughter should be sharp iron/steel, like a sharp knife or sword, not a non-iron or blunt object.

Note that Q has focused entirely upon a particular *maʿnā*-quality of R's *aṣl*: "by means of what most probably will result in his death," and then exposed its opposite (*ʿaks*) in the *farʿ*: "prescribed slaughter does not occur by means of it"—meaning: a blunt object (*muthaqqal*) is elsewhere acknowledged as unsuitable for killing swiftly and surely; it is not "what most probably will result in death." Note also that this example clarifies why our *jadal*-theory authors place *farq* under the rubric of *muʿāraḍa*: in establishing his charge of *farq*, Q claims an opposing *ʿilla* ("prescribed slaughter does not occur by means of it"), which he then links to a different *aṣl* ("like [killing with] the small cane/stick"), in which Q's counter-*ʿilla* occasions the opposite ("retaliation is not confirmed by way of it") to R's *ḥukm*.[304] In sum, the Ḥanafī Q has exposed an invalidating distinction (*farq*) in the Mālikī R's *qiyās*, then counter-indicated R's *qiyās* with a new *qiyās* (being the essence of *muʿāraḍa*); and this new *qiyās* may be diagramed as follows:

Aṣl the one who kills with a small cane/stick (*al-ʿaṣā al-ṣaghīra*) *ʿIlla* he kills with an object by which prescribed slaughter does not occur *Ḥukm* retaliation is not obliged	(same) ←→ (therefore, should also be the same) →	*Farʿ* the one who kills with a blunt object (*muthaqqal*) *ʿIlla* he kills with an object by which prescribed slaughter does not occur *Ḥukm* [thus] retaliation is [also] not obliged

[304] Miller notes, as regards al-Bājī's first type of *farq*: "Q is in effect bringing a counter-claim with respect to both the test case and the principal one. The association with counter-objection [*muʿāraḍa*]... is transparent" ("Islamic Disputation Theory," p. 132).

Notably, Q's *farq*-resultant *muʿāraḍa-qiyās* is of the familiar species *qiyās al-ʿilla*; hence, al-Bājī's category (for which this example *mas'ala* illustrates a subtype) is termed: "Invalidating Distinction by way of the Occasioning Factor of the Ruling" (*farq bi-ʿillat al-ḥukm*). This, in turn, corresponds to al-Shīrāzī's "Invalidating Distinction by way of Correlational Inference of the Occasioning Factor" (*farq bi-qiyās al-ʿilla*), which a comparison of the two hierarchies will show. Notably, al-Bājī's subtype illustrated above is labeled "[when] the *maʿnā*-quality is an object of disagreement (*mukhtalaf ʿalayhi*)." This is exactly the case in the example, as R contends the blunt object "most probably will result in his death," while Q contends it does not meet the requirements for killing swiftly and surely.

Miller reminds us that the dialectical move of *farq* is found among the *jadal* works of theologians, and then notes: "It also seems to have been used as early as the tenth century [CE] as a technical term in jurisprudence."[305] To this I will add that its use, as a dialectical move employing verbs and nouns of root *f-r-q*, is ubiquitous throughout the *Umm* compendium; and several instances are evident in our subject-text. Whatever date we consider *farq* to have crystallized as a uniform technical term, its practice and teaching as a dialectical move in juridical disputation stretch back at least to the latter half of the second/eighth century.

Returning to the larger category of "counter-indications" (*muʿāraḍāt*), we may note that Miller translates *muʿāraḍa* as "counter-objection," and opens his exposition on (*qiyās*-oriented) *muʿāraḍa* with a translation of al-Juwaynī's technical definition, and a short definition of al-Bājī's.[306] Al-Juwaynī begins with the term's linguistic usage, saying: "it pertains, in ordinary linguistic usage, to 'prevention/blocking/denial' (*wa hiya, fi'l-lugha, min al-mumānaʿa*)." He then proceeds to the customary usage of jurists (*fī ʿurf al-fuqahā'*): "[it is] the opponent's 'prevention/blocking/denial' (*mumānaʿa*) by way of claiming something equal [in epistemic valuation] (*bi-daʿwā al-musāwāt*), or the equal [epistemic valuation] of the opponent (*musāwāt al-khaṣm*) in claiming indication (*fī daʿwā al-dalāla*)."[307] As for al-Bājī, *muʿāraḍa* is: "the questioner's confronting (*muqābala*) the one drawing indication (*mustadill*) with the like of his *dalīl*-indicant [in epistemic valuation], or what is stronger than it."[308]

With regard to al-Juwaynī's definition, Miller complains that "al-Juwainī's account of counter-objection is confusing. It seems at times that he understands it as a species of munāqaḍa... and at other times as another entirely different species of objection."[309] I stand with Miller on the recurrent opaqueness of al-Juwaynī's style. In this case, however, I would argue his treatment is consistent, and that the

[305] "Islamic Disputation Theory," p. 131; citing van Ess's 1966 monograph on ʿAḍud al-Dīn al-Ījī.

[306] "Islamic Disputation Theory," p. 133; citing *Kāfiya*, p. 69, §168; and *Minhāj*, Turkī ed., p. 14.

[307] Miller translates: "preventing one's opponent ('s argument from prevailing) by making an equal and opposing claim; or it is matching the opponent's claim to prove his thesis (with another opposed to it)" (parentheses are his).

[308] Miller: "Q's opposing... R with a proof of equal weight or weightier."

[309] "Islamic Disputation Theory," p. 133; citing *Kāfiya*, p. 213, §343 and p. 418, §604.

confusion is instead caused by an enigmatic inversion made by the editor of the *Kāfiya fi'l-Jadal*. Note that Maḥmūd's was a difficult task; he was forced to rely upon a single manuscript in the collection of al-Azhar, supplemented by images taken of the same manuscript some point before it had lost a significant number of folia.[310] Maḥmūd's is thus a diplomatic edition; his source manuscript was not collated with other extant manuscript witnesses of the *Kāfiya*, and perhaps he would not otherwise have inverted a portion of al-Juwaynī's definition, as illustrated below. At the start of al-Juwaynī's full treatment of *mu'āraḍa*, the text of Maḥmūd's edition reads:[311]

604 – اعلم (1 أن المعارضة: ضرب من المناقضة 1) وهي أقوى أنواع المعارضات...

Following Maḥmūd's footnote, we read:

(1-1) في الأصل: « أن المناقضة ضرب من المعارضة »

Though diligently recording the editorial change, Maḥmūd does not explain why he inverted this critical phrase.[312] Whatever the impetus, the inversion would certainly bring one to evaluate al-Juwaynī's conception of *mu'āraḍa* as confusing. Once reverted to the formulation as found in the Azharī manuscript witness, however, it is both clear and consistent: "Know that inconsistency/contradiction (*munāqaḍa*) is a type of counter-indication (*mu'āraḍa*), and that it is the strongest of the types of counter-indications (*mu'āraḍāt*); and that every *munāqaḍa* is a *mu'āraḍa*, even though not every *mu'āraḍa* is a *munāqaḍa*." If this is the correct reading, al-Juwaynī clearly considers *munāqaḍa* as a subset of the greater set of *mu'āraḍāt*, and he proceeds at some length to show this relationship between the two categories of *i'tirāḍ*:

> Whenever one of the opponents [Q] compels the other [R] to apply his *'illa* in a locus for which its application is impossible,[313] though [R] applies it in its parallel (*wa huwa yajrīhā fī naẓīrihi*);[314] then [Q] has contradicted [that parallel (meaning R's *aṣl*)] from one perspective, and counter-indicated it from another.[315] But when [Q] counter-indicates [R's] *dalīl*-

[310] See editor's intro, *Kāfiya*, pp. 136–7.

[311] *Kāfiya*, p. 418, §604.

[312] As noted, the "*aṣl*" was not collated with other manuscript witnesses; why one would invert the phrase is all the more unclear, unless it simply seemed odd the "Section on Norms of Counter-Indication" (*Faṣl fī Aḥkām al-Mu'āraḍa*) should open with mention of a different dialectical move: "Know that *al-munāqaḍa* is a type of *al-mu'āraḍa*...."

[313] This being the *mas'alat al-naqḍ*.

[314] This being R's *aṣl*, which enjoys a "parallel" (*naẓīr*) relationship with Q's *mas'alat al-naqḍ*, and thus should have the same *ḥukm*, but does not. Which is to say, Q has brought, as *mas'alat al-naqḍ*, the *naẓīr* of R's *aṣl*, in which R's purported *'illa* is present, but R's *ḥukm* is not.

[315] In other words, the *naẓīr* of R's aṣl which Q brings as his *mas'alat al-naqḍ* accomplishes two tasks at once. First, since its *ḥukm* contradicts that of R's *aṣl*, but should not (as its *naẓīr*, with R's *'illa* present in it), this means that R must either concede to inconsistency with regard to what

indicant with another, or counter-indicates [R's] claim with its contradictory (*naqīḍ*), or [counter-indicates] [R's] *dalīl*-indicant by way of his reversal (*qalb*) of it—in drawing indication from it in a mode different from that which [R] is claiming for it—then such is *muʿāraḍa*, not *munāqaḍa*.[316]

A final note on *muʿāraḍa*: al-Baṣrī relates there are only three escapes, when confronted with *muʿāraḍa*, for the respondent whose *qiyās* is being supplanted: (1) "[R] validates his *ʿilla*, and clarifies that it is superior (*awlā*) to the *ʿilla* of [Q]; or he validates his *ʿilla*, and professes the *ʿilla* of [Q] along with it—if it is, according to [R], valid;"[317] (2) "[R] invalidates the *ʿilla* of [Q] by means of the modes we have mentioned;" and (3) preponderance (*tarjīḥ*) [of R's *ʿilla* over Q's].[318] Note this sheds light on why, for all our lens-text authors, *muʿāraḍa* is treated last among *qiyās*-oriented *iʿtirāḍāt*; if Q engages in *muʿāraḍa*, R may then use the full range of dialectical moves which precede it in the hierarchy, in order to critique Q's supplanting *qiyās*. The roles now switch, and R becomes Q. We are also provided insight as to why, for most of our early *jadal* theorists, treatises close with chapters on the modes of preponderance (*tarjīḥ*). As al-Baṣrī has shown us, *tarjīḥ* constitutes the third refuge of the *qiyās*-builder (*qā'is*) faced with *muʿāraḍa*; and with al-Shīrāzī and al-Bājī, their closing sections on "preponderance of *maʿnā*-qualities" (*tarjīḥ al-maʿānī*) would come to his aid.[319]

---

his *ʿilla* occasions, or he must abandon his *aṣl* as not actually having that *ʿilla* in it—and this is *naqḍ/munāqaḍa*. Second, since the *ʿilla* claimed by R actually does exist in both the *farʿ* under consideration and Q's *mas'alat al-naqḍ*, the latter also serves as the *aṣl* for Q's counter-*qiyās*, supplanting R's *aṣl* and transferring the opposite of R's *ḥukm* to the *farʿ*—and this is *muʿāraḍa*.

316 *Kāfiya*, op. cit. Note that all of Q's activities are more general forms of counter-indication, and none of them need rest on R's inconsistency or self-contradiction. Complaining of al-Juwaynī's inconsistency, Miller has also cited *Kāfiya*, p. 213, §343, where al-Juwaynī purportedly treats *muʿāraḍa* "as another entirely different species of objection" from *munāqaḍa*. The cited passage, however, occurs in the context of a disputant incorrectly claiming *munāqaḍa* where in fact some other type of *muʿāraḍa* has occurred. Al-Juwaynī says: "And there belongs to *muʿāraḍa* another degree (*daraja ukhrā*) besides what he claims, and its place (*maḥalluhā*) is not that of *al-munāqaḍa*...." This is fully consistent with al-Juwaynī's conception of *munāqaḍāt* as a subset of *muʿāraḍāt*; every *munāqaḍa* is a *muʿāraḍa*, but not every *muʿāraḍa* is a *munāqaḍa*.

317 Note this latter path constitutes a counter-*qawl bi-mūjib al-ʿilla*, as R confirms the compelling agency of Q's occasioning factor along with his own.

318 *K. al-Qiyās al-Sharʿī*, Ḥamīd Allāh ed., pp. 1044–5; Hallaq, "Treatise," pp. 222–3.

319 See the ends of appendices II and III for translated lists of all modes of preponderance.

4.6 Procedural Norms: Inexorable Concession (*Ilzām*), Termination of the *Jadal* Session (*Inqiṭāʿ*), and Proper Comportment in Dialectic (*Ādāb al-Jadal*)

On Inexorable Concession (Ilzām)

Miller closes his discussion of "early period" *qiyās*-related objections by introducing *ilzām* as "one other 'technique'... [which] al-Juwainī defines... in passing."[320] I would posit that *ilzām*—meaning "compulsion"—is not so much a technique of argumentation as the result of a successful refutation: R is "compelled" by the epistemic qualities of Q's objections and proofs to abandon his own thesis and accept Q's counter-thesis. First note that al-Juwaynī's definition for *ilzām* (in the *Kāfiya*) occurs after he has completed his definitions of *iʿtirāḍāt* (the last being *muʿāraḍa*), and is separated from them by the definitions of "preponderance" (*tarjīḥ*), "question" (*su'āl*), "response" (*jawāb*), and "seeking supporting testimony" (*istishhād*); and his definition itself seems to lean more towards my interpretation. Al-Juwaynī says: "as for *ilzām*, it is the repudiation of the opponent's argument (*dafʿ kalām al-khaṣm*) by means of what imposes a severance (*bi-mā yūjibu faṣlan*) between him and what comprises his support (*baynahu wa bayna mā taḍammana nuṣratahu*)."[321]

On Termination of the Jadal *Session* (Inqiṭāʿ)

Our primary lens-texts do not contain chapters dedicated to disputation procedure *per se*.[322] Miller, however, has located pertinent discussions in other texts.[323] As regards "the signs of defeat" discussed by al-Khaṭīb al-Baghdādī, Ibn Ḥazm, Ibn ʿAqīl, and al-Juwaynī, he remarks: "The vocabulary of their accounts is fairly

---

[320] "Islamic Disputation Theory," p. 134.

[321] *Kāfiya*, p. 70, §173. Miller's translation has a different cast to it: "It is rejecting (daf) R's discussion by showing something which brings about a difference (fasl) between what R says and what R was entrusted to defend" ("Islamic Disputation Theory," p. 134). In such a light, *ilzām* would indeed appear to be a dialectical objection—specifically, that of *ignoratio elenchi*, or the charge that an opponent has indeed proven something, but not his original claim as to the issue at stake. If my interpretation above is correct, however, it is questionable that al-Juwaynī intended this by *ilzām*. Moreover, Miller provides a later interpretation of *ilzām* which supports my interpretation, when translating a passage from al-Samarqandī's *Qusṭās*: "The debate continues until R is silenced (ifḥām) or Q is forced to accept his argument (ilzām)" (ibid., p. 211).

[322] Al-Bājī is a slight exception, with, as we will see, a few brief paragraphs on the prescribed comportment of the disputant.

[323] See also Fallūsī, *al-Jadal ʿinda al-Uṣūliyyīn*, pp. 254–67, where he delivers a full exposition on the conclusion of debate, citing a number of sources (al-Juwaynī and Ibn ʿAqīl among them).

standard and their authors' debt to the dialectic of the theologians is obvious."[324] I would of course disagree with this indebtedness for reasons already stated, and which will only become more apparent in following chapters. Importantly, however, Miller locates among the "signs of defeat" what he terms "self-contradiction (munāqaḍa)" and "R's rejection of a priori knowledge or his being forced to say something absurd"—and I would add that these both have clear predecessors in the dialectic of the *Umm*-compendium.[325] He cites al-Khaṭīb al-Baghdādī, al-Juwaynī, and Ibn Ḥazm for the first. I do not find "*munāqaḍa*" *per se* as a "sign of defeat" in these, and one suspects the term—a cognate and possible synonym of *naqḍ*—would be reserved for Q's dialectical charge leading to R's defeat via contradiction or inconsistency.

Among al-Khaṭīb al-Baghdādī's "kinds of termination [of debate] (*aqsām al-inqiṭā'*)" we find: "that some of his arguments contradict each other (*an yanquḍa bi-ba'ḍ kalāmihi ba'ḍan*)."[326] More importantly, among al-Juwaynī's "modes of shifting [topic] and termination [of the debate] (*wujūh al-intiqāl wa'l-inqiṭā'*)" we find: "there is, in what casts doubt upon him as pertains to his argument, incoherence and contradiction (*tahāfut wa tanāquḍ*), part of it repudiating some other part."[327] The term *tanāquḍ* is of great import to my analyses of the subject-text. For the present, I will mention: (1) the phrase "self-contradicting statement" (*qawl mutanāqiḍ*) renders final judgment upon an opponent's argument some 26 times in the *Kitāb al-Umm*; (2) if the term *tanāquḍ* is added, then both *tanāquḍ* and *mutanāqiḍ* enjoy some 40 occurrences in the *Umm*, all in dialectical contexts; and (3) al-Shāfi'ī thrice reduces the opposing opinion to a *qawl mutanāqiḍ* in our subject-text. Finally, in Ibn Ḥazm's "description of the one conclusively blocked [in debate]" (*ṣifat al-munqaṭi'*), we find: "he produces a ruling, then contradicts it (*thumma yanquḍuhu*)," along with two further references to *tanāquḍ*.[328] Contradiction as a cause terminating debate appears thus to be described in terms of *tanāquḍ* and "*an yanquḍa* X;" and I will assume that *munāqaḍa* was reserved for the species of *i'tirāḍ* associated most closely with *naqḍ*.

Also important to the current project is what Miller noted of the opponent's "being forced to say something absurd"—this being the patent objective of myriad *reductio* arguments recorded for several of the jurists in our subject-text. Miller cites Ibn 'Aqīl and Ibn Ḥazm for this "sign of defeat,"[329] but I have found

---

[324] "Islamic Disputation Theory," p. 139.

[325] "Islamic Disputation Theory," pp. 140. Note the following: (1) these are among the primary objectives of dialectic in general; (2) the primary functions of the ubiquitous formulae *a-ra'ayta* and *a-lā tarā* in our subject-text are to push the opponent to concede an untenable consequence (contradiction, absurdity, etc.); and (3) these formulae are more ancient even than Abū Ḥanīfa, who makes plentiful use of them.

[326] *al-Faqīh wa'l-Mutafaqqih*, 'Azzāzī ed., vol. 2, p. 111.

[327] *Kāfiya*, 551ff., §§820ff.; at 553, line 15.

[328] *Taqrīb*, 'Abbās ed., p. 197.

[329] *K. al-Jadal*, p. 72, §335; and *Taqrīb*, 'Abbās ed., p. 188.

al-Khaṭīb al-Baghdādī's presentation of "Kinds of Termination [of Debate] (*Aqsām al-Inqiṭā'*)" in *al-Faqīh wa'l-Mutafaqqih* more accessible:[330]

- [1] Silence in response, due to inability to answer (*al-sukūt 'an al-jawāb li'l-'ajz*)
- [2] That he determine the *'illa* to no avail (*an yu'allila wa lā yujdī*)
- [3] That some of his arguments contradict each other (*an yanquḍa bi-ba'ḍi kalāmihi ba'ḍan*)
- [4] That his argument leads to an absurdity/impossibility (*an yu'addiya kalāmuhu ilā al-muḥāl*)
- [5] That he shift ground from indicant to indicant (*an yantaqila min dalīlin ilā dalīlin*)
- [6] That he be asked about one thing, but respond about another (*an yus'ala 'an al-shay' fa yujību 'an ghayrihi*)
- [7] That he deny necessary truths (*an yajḥada al-ḍarūrāt*), and reject what is empirical (*wa yadfa'a al-mushāhadāt*), and engage in obstinate contentiousness and lies in the disputation (*wa yasta'mila al-mukābara wa'l-buht fi'l-munāẓara*)

Importantly, Miller also observes that "Ibn 'Aqīl brings in several signs connected with the failure of R or Q to fulfill their duties as required by the 'four questions'...." Having listed them,[331] however, he concludes: "The relation of these signs to the four questions is so obvious that it requires no comment other than to note how the jurists on the whole took over elements of the theologians' teaching on disputation. But as in the case of questions of juristic dialectic, there were new developments...."[332] I agree with Miller that some portion of the "signs of defeat"—in all cases, not just Ibn 'Aqīl—is closely tied to the approved questions of dialectic, and deem it only natural in a dialectical exchange: Q's ultimate object in asking these questions is to compel R to abandon his thesis, and his inability to defend it further would naturally terminate the *jadal* session. I would again disagree, however, that this constitutes evidence of a juristic take over from the theologians. Cross-germination between dialectical traditions stretching back at least to the second/eighth century—especially considering the many hats worn by polymath theorists—makes more sense of later overlaps and parallels than an absolute priority of theological *jadal*-theory. Further, the idea that "new developments" took place after a take over is a circular assessment of the *distinctiveness* of juridical *jadal*. I would note this as a common problem of genetic projects in the study of early Islam: what is similar in the subject system is presumed to have

[330] *al-Faqīh wa'l-Mutafaqqih*, 'Azzāzī ed., vol. 2, p. 111.

[331] From *K. al-Jadal*, pp. 71–2, §§331 and 336.

[332] "Islamic Disputation Theory," pp. 140–1.

been borrowed or taken over from what is (or is deemed to be) an older system, while what is dissimilar in the subject system is presumed to constitute an expansion upon—or, in more extreme examples, a "denaturalization" of—the borrowed or taken over predecessor system. Formulators of the subject system are largely deprived of originative or creative agency. With regard to the evolution of dialectical systems, I would again argue that a common collective of argument epistemes at the dawn of Islam—with subsequent parallel and divergent development, and cross-germination at every stage—best accounts for both the similarities and dissimilarities of theological and juridical *jadal*.

Miller also introduces us to al-Juwaynī's discussion of *jadal* termination.[333] I have returned to the *Kāfiya fi'l-Jadal* and attempted to render the larger part of al-Juwaynī's exposition on the reasons for which debate concludes:[334]

- "[The disputant's] incapability (*ʿajz*)—such as is in fact a cause for termination (*inqiṭāʿ*)[335]—may be due to a gap (*nuqṣān*) in his knowledge of the regulations of dialectic (*rusūm al-jadal*) and its principles (*uṣūl*)..."
    - "... because he doesn't know: the manner of positing indicants in their loci (*kayfiyyat waḍʿ al-adilla mawāḍiʿhā*); or the manner of memorizing/preserving them; or the manner of ordering them; or the manner of [?] as pertains to the modes of inexorable concession (*wujūh al-ilzāmāt*)"[336]
- "Or he may be skilled in the regulations of dialectic (*rusūm al-jadal*), but lack knowledge of the modes of authoritative indicants (*wujūh al-adilla*) and correlational inferences made from them; so he is blocked due to his insufficiency of knowledge of the indicants"
- "Or he may be perfectly conversant in the regulations of dialectic, and the authoritative indicants, yet be brought to a stop (*yanqaṭiʿu*) by an invalidity (*fasād*) inherent to the very thesis (*maqāla*) whose vindication is his goal"

(continued)

[333] Ibid., p. 141. Intriguingly, he claims: "al-Juwainī's account is also influenced by Aristotle. Thus, he gives four of Aristotle's five criticisms of an argument…." Although I agree that elements of Aristotle's dialectic are present, I have been unable to locate the "five criticisms" in al-Juwaynī. See my dissertation ("Dialectical Forge," pt. 1, pp. 192–4) for a critique.

[334] Maḥmūd ed., pp. 556–7.

[335] Following his definition of *inqiṭāʿ*, al-Juwaynī notes that "every terminating cause (*inqiṭāʿ*) is an inability (*ʿajz*), but not every inability is a cause for termination" (ibid., 556).

[336] Maḥmūd records that two words are obliterated or illegible (where I have placed [?] above), but I cannot make sense of his reconstruction: كيفية [ما يرد] عليه من وجوه الإلزامات (p. 557, n. 1_1).

- "Or he may be perfectly conversant in all that, but will not refrain from subjecting the general to particularization (*raf' al-jumla bi'l-tafṣīl*), [hoping] his cutting off (*inqiṭā'*) should never materialize..."
  - "but when he shifts (*intaqala*) from one rank [in the hierarchy of questions and objections] to what precedes it, he is stopped (*munqaṭi'*)" [examples are shifting from *naqḍ* to *man'*; or from *mu'āraḍa* to *naqḍ* or *man'*; etc.]
  - "and when he claims a question or response is in a certain mode, but it isn't so... he is stopped (*munqaṭi'*)" [examples include wrongly claimed *farq*, *qawl bi-mūjib al-'illa*, *qalb*, etc.]

Perhaps the most striking cause for termination is al-Juwaynī's first: "a gap in his knowledge of the regulations of dialectic and its principles" (*nuqṣān 'ilmihi bi-rusūm al-jadal wa uṣūlihi*); this ties his *Kāfiya* to Aristotle's *Topics*, and his list of examples of insufficiency even more so. As for not knowing "the manner of positing indicants in their loci" (*kayfiyyat waḍ' al-adilla mawāḍi'hā*), there is some resemblance, terminologically at least, to the theory of *topoi*. As for not knowing "the manner of memorizing/preserving them" (*kayfiyyat ḥifẓihā*); if memorizing is intended, I have already suggested the listings of *adilla* in our lens-texts were arranged in hierarchical order (in terms of epistemic strength) partly with the aim of aiding in memorization, and we have seen concerns for memorization elsewhere. Of course, this a primary goal of the *topoi*: to provide a logically-structured, internally maintained store house of *endoxa* premises and arguments. And as for "the manner of ordering them" (*kayfiyyat tartībihā*), this again resembles a chief function of the *topoi*. If my interpretations are correct, a significant parallel to Aristotelian dialectic emerges in al-Juwaynī's first cause for terminating the *jadal* session. However, it is another question entirely as to whether this parallel constitutes an indication of direct influence from the Aristotelian tradition, and, if so, positing when, where, and how such an influence came to be.[337]

[337] To say that al-Juwaynī is "influenced by Aristotle" does not contribute much in light of the far more numerous differences between his method and that of the Aristotelian tradition. Even less so when one considers that the greater Islamic corpus of argumentation epistemes (to which al-Juwaynī's *Kāfiya* was a relatively late contribution) had long been woven with innumerable and untraceable threads. Some of these threads were doubtless Aristotelian in the fullest sense of the word, straight from the *Organon*, and its ancient and late antique commentaries, through a variety of languages, and across several eras and far-flung teaching centers. But other threads were parallels of non-Aristotelian inspiration, both Islamic and pre-Islamic; and some of these latter were so ancient as to have potentially inspired the flowering of "Hellenic" philosophy itself (see, among other works, Walter Burkert's *Orientalizing Revolution: Near Eastern Influence on Greek Culture in the Early Archaic Age*). Moreover, there were doubtless threads whose distant origins were Aristotelian, but whose long periods of development in different regions, and according to the dictates of different intellectual projects, transformed them into something unique unto themselves.

On Proper Comportment in Dialectic (Ādāb al-Jadal)

Al-Bājī provides a short chapter on the prescribed comportment of the disputant in his *Minhāj*.[338] Among other things, he tells us the dialectician must approach *jadal* in full piety, fearing God and calling on his assistance, etc.; maintain a dignified bearing; and act deferentially towards his opponent, treating him with respect, showing patience, and not interrupting him. He must not discourse on what he doesn't know, or on something besides the focus of disputation, and he must not employ indicants which he is uncertain of. He must not engage in disputation while hungry, tired, afraid, or angry; nor should he continue disputing the incompetent, but disengage from them once their ineptitude becomes clear, with kindness and tact. Al-Bājī concludes: "For verily the aim of intellectual investigation (*naẓar*) is getting to the truth (*iṣābat al-ḥaqq*); and when the dialectician (*munāẓir*) takes upon himself what we have described, and comports himself properly according to what we have mentioned, he will derive benefit from his *jadal*, and be blessed for his *naẓar*, if God wills."[339]

4.7 Aristotle's Dialectic and Full-System *Jadal* Theory: Parallels and Divergences

There is a vital distinction to be made between: (A) an argument which is reducible to syllogistic form; and (B) an argument which is formulated syllogistically. The former might include practically any rational argument, so long as sufficient analysis can convert it into component premises, which might then be connected and arranged in a familiar syllogistic pattern—whether productive or otherwise. An (A) argument might, therefore, provide little or no indication as to whether the arguer was familiar with a studied system of syllogistic logic; neither, on this basis of form alone, can we rule out the possibility the arguer was *not* familiar with—or even highly trained in—such a logical system. On the other hand, a (B) argument will have been initially presented by the arguer in a familiar syllogistic form. Thus, if coincidence of form can be ruled out (or at least minimalized), we might take this form as an indication that the arguer is familiar with—and attempting to formulate arguments in consonance with—a studied system of syllogistic logic.

---

[338] Turkī ed., pp. 9–10, §§8–13. See Fallūsī, *al-Jadal ʿinda al-Uṣūliyyīn*, pp. 278–321, for a full exposition on this topic as drawn from texts by al-Bājī, al-Juwaynī, Ibn ʿAqīl, and others.

[339] Miller dedicates a short section to this topic as well ("Islamic Disputation Theory," pp. 141–2). Among other things, he maintains the take over paradigm: "These basic rules of conduct during the debate were taken over by the jurists from theological jadal" (ibid., 141); briefly mentions that Ibn Ḥazm discusses the topic (citing the *Taqrīb*, ʿAbbās ed., p. 196); and provides an informative translation of al-Juwaynī's review of the responsibilities of questioner and respondent (p. 142; citing *Kāfiya*, p. 558, line -3 ff.)

Accepting this, and turning to the arguments, real and illustrative, of both our subject-text and lens-texts, it is true that, through prolonged analytical effort, one might reduce most or all of them to the syllogistic forms of the Aristotelian and Stoic traditions. However, they are, to my knowledge at least, *never* originally formulated in the patterns familiar to these systems. This is not to say they are not formulaic and systematic; the opposite is true. Rather, and acknowledging we can never claim, on the basis of form alone, that our jurists were not familiar with or trained in Aristotle, we can nevertheless say that if they were, they were not terribly concerned to formulate their arguments in consonance with the shapes familiar to those systems.[340] Had they been so, we would expect to see argument after argument in the style presented by Ibn Ḥazm (Ẓāhirī, d.456/1063) in his *Approach to the Border of Logic and its Entryway, in Common Language and Legal Paradigms* (*Taqrīb li-Ḥadd al-Manṭiq wa'l-Madkhal ilayhi bi'l-Alfāẓ al-ʿĀmmiyya wa'l-Amthila al-Fiqhiyya*).[341]

By way of illustrating what a consciously, syllogistically-formulated legal argument might look like, I need only present a few examples from the *Taqrīb*. In the *Book on Demonstration* (*Kitāb al-Burhān*), Ibn Ḥazm illustrates the familiar "Barbara" mood of the first figure, with: "every intoxicating drink is fermented expressed juice; and every fermented expressed juice is forbidden; therefore, every intoxicating drink is forbidden" (*kull muskir khamr; wa kull khamr ḥarām; fa-kull muskir ḥarām*).[342] And in the *Chapter on Demonstration which is Conditional of Expression, Categorical of Intention* (*Bāb min al-Burhān Sharṭī al-Lafẓ, Qāṭiʿ al-Maʿnā*), he illustrates the familiar *modus ponens*: "If 'intoxicating' is attributed to something then 'proscription is attributed to it; and 'intoxicating' is attributed to fig-wine when it exceeds in fermentation; therefore, 'proscription' is obliged for fig-wine when it exceeds in fermentation" (*in wuṣifa shay' bi'l-iskār wuṣifa bi'l-taḥrīm; wa nabīdh al-tīn idhā ghuliya wuṣifa bi'l-iskār; fa'l-taḥrīm wājib li-nabīdh al-tīn idhā ghuliya*).[343]

Again, formulae such as these simply do not appear in our subject-text and lens-texts, though it is difficult to perceive how their authors could not have been touched by Aristotelian tradition in some manner or form—certainly, al-Bājī was more than familiar with Ibn Ḥazm; and the famed Abū Ḥāmid al-Ghazālī (d.505/1111), student of al-Juwaynī, is often credited with the first serious attempt to incorporate logic into *uṣūl al-fiqh*.[344] At present, my objective is merely to take

[340] Needless to say, I have never encountered references to Aristotle or syllogistic figures and moods in the *Umm* compendium or lens-texts, either.

[341] The significance of this work for the developmental histories of fifth/eleventh century philosophical and/or juridical *jadal* theory is self-evident: the *Taqrīb* represents an early system for applying Aristotelian and Stoic logic to legal reasoning. Its author, the famed Andalusian Ẓāhirī Ibn Ḥazm (d.456/1063), not only predeceased al-Shīrāzī by two decades, but was a prominent dialectical opponent of al-Bājī (see Turkī, *Polémiques entre Ibn Ḥazm et Bāǧī*).

[342] *Taqrīb*, Mazīdī ed., p. 115.

[343] *Taqrīb*, Mazīdī ed., p. 128; reading واجب, instead of واجد.

[344] See Hallaq, *History*, pp. 137ff., for an exposition on al-Ghazālī's contribution; Hallaq notes that Ibn Ḥazm made the "first step" towards bring formal logic into legal theory (p. 137).

note of such Aristotelian parallels as occur in our subject-text and lens-texts, and to offer a developmental model which makes sense of systemic parallels and divergences both.

Developmental Schemas for Dialectical Traditions in Islam

I hope to have sufficiently problematized the origins and borrowing paradigms that have arisen in previous discussions, especially with regard to a 'take over' from theological *jadal* theory, and the direct influence of Aristotelian traditions. On the whole my stance is supported by the dialectical material of the *Kitāb al-Umm*, and the evidence which analyses of the subject-text provides. The general picture is that far more complex dynamics and relationships were at work in the proto-system teaching and practice of dialectic, across intellectual projects, than what simplistic, linear trajectories of absolute priority—as in Fig. 4.1—can explain.

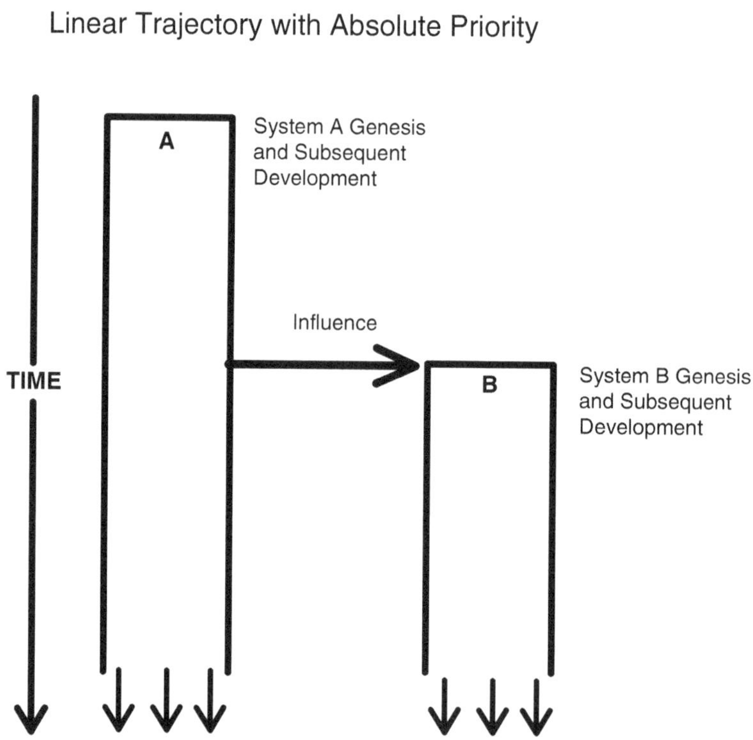

Fig. 4.1 In this schema: (1) System B has no real existence prior to the genesis and partial development of System A; (2) System B owes its genesis entirely to System A; and (3) no cross-germination occurs between systems subsequent to the unidirectional influence which generated System B. In terms of theological and juridical *jadal*, the arrow representing unidirectional influence occurs on the timeline subsequent to the appearance of systematic treatises for theological *jadal*-theory

In contrast to the above, I would propose another schema for the development of theological and juridical systems of *jadal*. Note the picture remains overly-simplistic—not taking into account, among other things, additional systems (in grammar, philosophy, etc.) developing in parallel, and systems within systems—but Fig. 4.2 is still sufficient to highlight the major themes of the developmental model.

In terms of "Greek" influence we are faced, as mentioned, with a number of difficulties. It is not doubted the teachings and literature of Hellenic logic, dialectic, and rhetoric were woven into the developmental stages of the second schema above, throughout the timeline, in various thicknesses. But it is impossible to identify distinct threads of influence unless the examined literary material distinctly references these teachings, or is formulated in plain consonance with, e.g.,

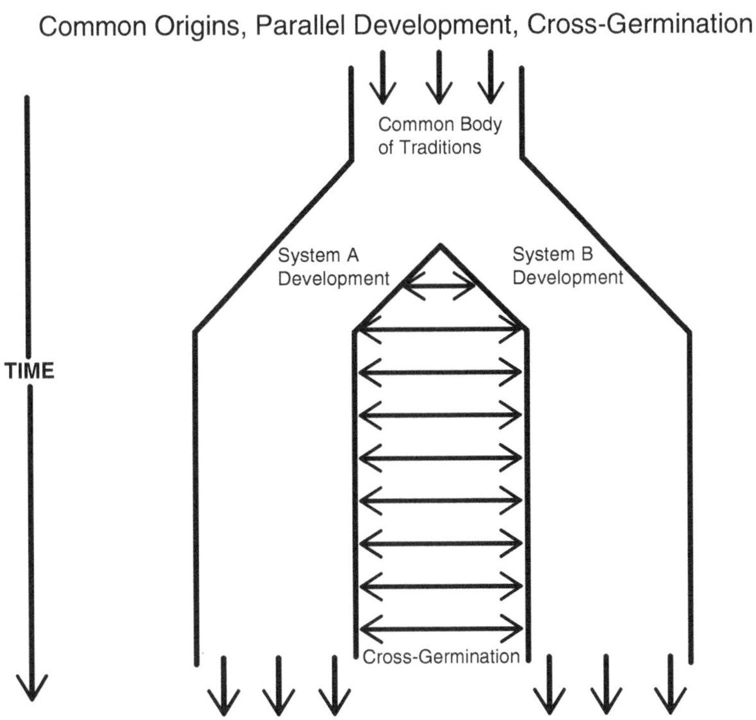

Fig. 4.2 This schema aims to portray the following: (1) absence of concrete points of genesis for either system; (2) continuity of both systems from a common body of traditions; (3) subsequent divergence and parallel development of both systems, according to the variant exigencies of different intellectual projects; and (4) bidirectional cross-germination between systems at every stage of development, reinforced by polymath scholars active in both. In terms of theological and juridical *jadal*, the singular stem and diagonal bases of the branches of the schema represent the proto-system period of development for both. The appearance of systematic theory-literature is understood to have occurred for both systems subsequent to this, at roughly the same time; i.e., at the start of the great literary fluorescence of the fourth/tenth centuries

a book of the *Organon* (as in the *Taqrīb*). Compounding this difficulty is another: parallels simply cannot be assumed to constitute evidence of influence, especially in the proto-system period with which we are most concerned.

A distinction must also be drawn between the practice of various species of reasoning and the elaboration of systematic theories of reasoning. Early Muslim intellectuals did not need to learn inductive, deductive, or analogical reasoning from the *Organon*, or from any other theory-system, in order to induce, deduce, and analogize. These are species of reasoning common to all human societies, with or without accompanying theory-systems. Their practice in early Islamic disputation, across thematic domains, does not presuppose dependence upon a systematized theory of argument—even though such systems were present in the broader intellectual landscape. At the same time, it should never be claimed that precursor argumentation epistemes were not drawn upon, or inherited, in early Islamic intellectual projects; I would merely suggest that hasty ascriptions of origins to specific epistemes (Hellenic, Judaic, Iranian, etc.), on the basis of parallels alone, be set aside until plain intra-textual ascriptions or thorough formal analyses lend them support.

At present I will refrain—in discussing both proto-system and full-system *jadal*—from labeling parallels anything more than "parallels." Positive assertions of Aristotelian or Stoic influence require indicants which, so far as I am aware, do not manifest themselves in our texts clearly enough to support assertions either way.[345] In the light of parallels, the possibility of influence will always be entertained—but the probability of influence will not, unless an adequate *dalīl*-indicant is raised in support. It is in this spirit that our lens-text parallels to the following Hellenic dialectical concerns will be discussed.

On Aristotelian Dialectic and Early Juridical Jadal-*Theory*

In his abstract, Miller states the following:

> Although the earliest writings on dialectic (from around the 10th century) are fairly free of direct Aristotelian influence, there are coincidences of theme and treatments. But after jurisprudence had assimilated the technique of theological dialectic, its own theory became increasingly influenced by logical terminology and techniques.[346]

With the exception of "jurisprudence... assimilated the technique of theological dialectic," I am in agreement with Miller regarding: (1) his cautious phrasing of

[345] Again, Ibn Ḥazm's *Taqrīb* might provide a standard of measure. Even so, our lens-texts do not belong to the sort of intellectual project in which he engaged in the *Taqrīb*. And if they do not bear the marks of consciously syllogistic argument engineering, they nevertheless bear the marks of other systems: prior *jadal* teachings, some of which are transmitted in a language and style older even than al-Shāfiʿī, and used by him.

[346] "Islamic Disputation Theory," pp. iii.

"coincidences of theme and treatments;" and (2) his assessment that juridical *jadal* theory "became increasingly influenced by logical terminology and techniques." This latter has also been asserted for the realm of legal theory in general.[347]

It is my aim now to briefly review a few of the more relevant discussions and chapter headings from Aristotle's *Organon*, in order to quickly highlight parallels in early juridical *jadal* theory as we have come to understand it in this chapter. Bear in mind that the greater part of Aristotle's argumentation episteme may be qualified as *formal, syllogistic logic*—much preoccupied with determining valid syllogistic moods. In the particular domain of dialectic, Aristotle's episteme—with its focus on predicables—will also appear very different from the episteme evident in our lens-texts. Such being the case, I will focus on more general themes and methods: in the main, material taken from the *Prior Analytics*, *Topics* and *Sophistical Elenchi*, with special attention to the domain of objection, the organizing principle of *topoi*, and the identification of fallacies. What follows, in other words, is not intended as a thorough comparative analysis of Aristotelian and *jadal*-theory argument forms.

Reduction ad impossibile *(εἰς τὸ ἀδύνατον; "[argument] to the impossible"); and Proof* per impossibile *(διὰ τοῦ ἀδυνάτου; "[argument] by means of the impossible")*

There are a number of parallels between these species of argument as described by Aristotle and certain species of *istidlāl* (e.g., *qiyās al-ʿaks*) and objection (e.g., *naqḍ*) in our *jadal*-theory treatises. The bulk of Aristotle's discussions occur in the *Prior Analytics*, and a few excerpts should suffice in bestowing the general disposition of his arguments by way of, or to, the impossible. As for *per impossibile*, we learn, among other things, that it is a kind of "hypothetical" proof:

> Now every demonstration and every syllogism must prove that some attribute does or does not apply to some subject, and that either universally or in a particular sense. Further, the proof must be either ostensive or hypothetical. One kind of hypothetical proof is proof *per impossibile*. First, then, let us deal with ostensive proofs; for when we have shown the conditions which govern these, the facts will also be made clear with regard to proofs by reduction *ad impossibile* and to hypothetical proofs in general.[348]

As for arguments *per/ad impossibile* and the "procedure of hypothetical proof," we learn:

> It is evident, then, that ostensive proofs are carried out by means of the figures already described. That proofs by reduction *ad impossibile* are also carried out by their means will be clearly shown by what follows. Everyone who carries out a proof *per impossibile* proves the false conclusion by syllogism and demonstrates the point at issue *ex hypothesi* when

[347] Again, see Hallaq, *History*, pp. 39–40, and 132ff.

[348] *An. Pr.* I.23, 40b17ff.; trans. Tredennick.

> an impossible conclusion follows from the assumption of the contradictory proposition. *E.g.*, one proves that the diagonal of a square is incommensurable with the sides by showing that if it is assumed to be commensurable, odd become equal to even numbers. Thus he argues to the conclusion that odd becomes equal to even, and proves *ex hypothesi* that the diagonal is incommensurable, since the contradictory proposition produces a false result. For we saw that to reach a logical conclusion *per impossibile* is to prove some conclusion impossible on account of the original assumption. Therefore since in reduction *ad impossibile* we obtain an ostensive syllogism of falsity (the point at issue being proved *ex hypothesi*), and we have stated above that ostensive syllogisms are effected by means of these figures, it is evident that *per impossible* syllogisms will also be obtained by means of these figures.[349]

The first translator of the *Prior Analytics* into Arabic,[350] according to the *Fihrist* of Ibn al-Nadīm,[351] was one Tidhārī, or Tiyādūrus (= Theodorus).[352] Transmissions of his translation show us the "proof *per impossibile*" of the above excerpts was rendered into Arabic as "*al-qiyās alladhī yakūnu bi-raf' al-kalām ilā al-muḥāl;*"[353] while "proofs by reduction *ad impossibile*" was rendered as "*al-maqāyīs allatī bi-raf' al-kalām ilā al-muḥāl.*"[354] Phrases such as "since the contradictory proposition produces a false result" appear as "*li-annahu yajibu 'an naqīḍihi hādhā al-qawl al-kidhb.*"[355] In addition to this, I would note Goichon's description of Ibn Sīnā's (d.428/1037) usage of the term "impossible" (*khulf*): « l'impossible, l'absurde, au sens donné par les expressions ἡ εἰς τὸ ἀδύνατον ἀπαγωγή, *Anal. Pr.* A 7, 29 b 5; et διὰ τοῦ ἀδυνάτου qui correspond à *bil-ḫulf* (le raisonnement, τὸ συλλογίσασθαι) par l'absurde, *Anal. Pr.* A 23, 41 a 31. »[356] Finally, note that an extensive discussion

---

[349] *An. Pr.* I.23, 41a20ff.; trans. Tredennick.

[350] A brief disclaimer: I do not suggest that Aristotle's works, or any other non-Arabic compositions, had to await translation into Arabic before they could be studied or learned by early Muslim scholars. Too often this has been assumed in modern scholarship, and often by scholars who have themselves mastered difficult foreign tongues for the sake of their own studies. Early Muslim scholars were more than capable of doing the same, and may have been privy to Aristotelian teachings—regardless of whether or not they commanded Greek or Syriac—via intermediary teachers and peers. That enormous and lengthy project known as the Translation Movement was without any doubt a seminal event in early Islamic scholarship, but access to the works translated did not hinge upon their translation; a variety of conduits for the teaching and study of these works preceded the Translation Movement. My objective in noting the early Arabic translations of certain terms and concepts is merely to highlight parallels or divergences in the Arabic formulations of our lens-texts.

[351] Ṭawīl ed., p. 405.

[352] Badawī (*Manṭiq Arisṭū*, vol. 1, [Introduction], p. 16) believes this cannot be Theodore Abū Qurra, Bishop of Ḥarrān [d.210/820; a contemporary of al-Shāfi'ī], because Ḥunayn b. Isḥāq would only have been 11 years old at the time the *Fihrist* tells us this Theodorus showed his translation to him and his companions. There is the possibility that this Theodore was the Bishop of Karkh, in Baghdād, but Badawī prefers to leave the question open.

[353] Ibid., vol. 1, p. 204, *passim*.

[354] Ibid., p. 207, *passim*.

[355] Ibid.

[356] *Vocabulaires Comparés*, p. 10, s.v. "*Ḫulf.*"

regarding "principles applying to syllogisms established *per impossibile*" occurs in *An. Pr.* I.29, and includes a brief reference to another hypothetical syllogism involving "a qualitative relation." Tredennick links this latter to "*A fortiori* or analogical arguments."[357]

Objection (*Ἐνστασις*), *or* Instantia, *or Instance*

Objection, or *Instantia*, is that single, contrary instance which destroys a universal claim, and thus finds a kind of general parallel in the dialectical move of *naqḍ*; i.e., when Q brings his *mas'alat al-naqḍ*, the universality of R's claimed *ʿilla-ḥukm* relationship is destroyed and his *qiyās* invalidated—unless he subscribes to "particularization of the occasioning factor" (*takhṣīṣ al-ʿilla*). *Instantia* is discussed to some length in *An. Pr.* II.26, where we find the following definition:[358]

> An objection [Ἐνστασις] is a premiss which is contrary to another premiss. It differs from the premiss in that it may be particular, whereas the premiss either cannot be particular at all, or at least not in universal syllogisms.

The parallel concern with universals and particulars is intriguing, especially considering al-Baṣrī's parameters for valid and invalid *naqḍ*. As we recall, he said: "When the one justifying the *ʿilla* (*muʿallil*) establishes his *ʿilla* for the general (*jumla*), then it is 'contradicted' by particularization (*tafṣīl*); it is not *naqḍ*..."and "If the *muʿallil* establishes his *ʿilla* for the particularized, then he is contradicted by the general; this is valid *naqḍ*." Note this is quite different from the parameters of Aristotle's *instantia*, however.[359] As for Tidhārī, he appears to have preferred a transliteration for this term, rendering it "الأنسطاسيس."[360] Importantly, Badawī equates this to "dialectical premise" (*al-muqaddima al-jadaliyya*) in his table of contents.[361]

---

[357] *Prior Analytics*, Loeb ed., p. 354, note b; citing Alexander 324. 19. For "proving results in the figures [*ad/per impossibile*]," see: *An. Pr.* I.5, 27a14, 28a7; I.6, 28a23, 29, 28b14, 17; I.7, 29a35; etc. (more references are in the Loeb ed. index, s.v. "Reduction; *ad impossibile*"); and for comparison of *per impossibile* and other methods, see *An. Pr.* II.11–14.

[358] *An. Pr.* II.26, 69a37-69b1; trans. Tredennick.

[359] In fact, instantia as objection appears most suited to dismantling an inductive argument, and seems to have little or nothing at all to do with *ʿillas* (whether "causes" or "occasioning factors").

[360] Badawī, *Manṭiq Arisṭū*, vol. 1, pp. 310ff.

[361] Ibid., p. 323.

Aristotle's Topics

My intention now is to highlight certain parallels between Aristotle's dialectical method and that of our lens-texts. The *Topics* and our *jadal*-theory treatises of course share a common project: systematizing the questions, methods, objectives, and procedures of dialectical disputation. Such being the case, parallel discussions abound throughout almost the entire work; and a brief overview of the structure and contents of the *Topics* is in order. Our guide to the *Topics* is a renowned scholar of Aristotle's logic, Robin Smith; a brief outline of its structure may be culled from the introduction to his translation and commentary for Books I and VIII:[362]

Books I and VIII
- "describe and discuss Aristotle's dialectical method"

Books II–VII
- "collections of individual argumentative locations"

As regards the organizing principle of the *Topics*, i.e. the "argumentative locations," or *topoi*, themselves, Smith makes the following important observations:[363]

> The predicables give a highest-level classification of problems or conclusions, and thus a highest level organization of *topoi*. This is explicitly reflected in the arrangement of Books II-VII, which give *topoi* first concerning accidents (II-III), then genera (IV), then unique properties (V), then definitions (VI-VII). When we look to each of these sections, principles of organization are less obvious.... But in fact, there are patterns, and they reveal other categories of classification of conclusions which are actually more important to the *topoi* themselves (and to Aristotle's implicit theory of logical form) than the predicables. In particular we find a number of closely related *topoi* in each of the four main divisions (i.e. for accidents, for genera, for unique properties, for definitions) which fall under three large classifications: *topoi* involving 'opposites' (*antikeimena*), *topoi* involving 'coordinates' and 'cases' [in the grammatical sense] (*sustoicha*, *ptōseis*), and *topoi* involving 'more and less equal'. Aristotle generally presents these three groups together and in the same fixed order.

Again, note that Aristotle's overall episteme is one of formal syllogistic, and his discussions regarding these *topoi* will be quite different from what we see in the various domains of *istidlāl* forming our lens-texts' organizing principle. Nevertheless, the idea of an organizing principle based on categories of potentially problematic argument components, with the objective of "locating" the proper material for critique and refutation, is one and the same. Moreover, note the predicable-categories of Aristotle's *Topics* have their parallels in similar cate-

---

[362] Smith, *Topics I and VIII*, p. xxxiv.

[363] Ibid., pp. xxx-xxxiii.

gories of concern to *uṣūl al-fiqh*, some of which surface with frequency throughout the subdivisions of *istidlālāt* and *iʿtirāḍāt*—specifically, such as occur through genus (*jins*), property (*waṣf*), and definition (*ḥadd*).

Location (τόπος) or Mawḍiʿ*, and the Dialectician's Method*

More with regard to the meaning and function of *topos*/*topoi* may be learned from Smith's introduction to Books I and VIII.[364] Importantly: "A *topos* is a point at which the answerer's position may be probed for attack."[365] Smith continues, however, to show two more "dimensions" to the meaning of *topos*: (1) "each *topos* serves as a location at which many arguments may be found by appropriate substitutions in the relevant form;" and (2) "the conclusion-form of the *topos* itself serves as a means of finding it when we need it." He then proceeds to the description of mnemonic devices, "rooms," etc., familiar to ancient treatises on debate and rhetoric. In sum: "An Aristotelian *topos* may then be described in two ways: as a point of attack in an adversary's position, and as a location under which to file arguments."[366] The very same two functions may be observed in the *istidlāl*-arrangement of our lens-texts, regardless of their variant criteria of categorization.

Perhaps the most significant parallels begin to surface once we become familiar with dialectical procedure as described by Aristotle. Of particular import is the comparison of the dialectician's method over and against that of the individual philosopher:[367]

> He who is about to ask questions must, first of all, choose the ground [τόπον] from which he must make his attack; secondly he must formulate his questions and arrange them separately in his own mind; thirdly and lastly, he must go on to address them to another person. As far as the choice of ground [τόπον] goes, the philosopher and the dialectician are making a similar inquiry, but the subsequent arrangement of material and the framing of questions are the peculiar province of the dialectician; for such a proceeding always involves a relation with another party.

With additional observations from Smith regarding dialectical procedure, a familiar pattern will become evident. Having briefly reviewed the argument method of Socrates, Plato, and Zeno, Smith then continues:[368]

---

[364] Ibid., pp. xxiv-xxviii. In addition to Smith, see Eleonore Stump's *Dialectic and its Place* (especially at pp. 11–30, "Dialectic and Aristotle's *Topics*") for an excellent introduction.

[365] *Topics I and VIII*, p. xxvii.

[366] Ibid., p. xxviii.

[367] *Top.* VIII.1, 155b3ff.; trans. Forster.

[368] *Topics I and VIII*, pp. xiv-xv.

> For the present, what is important is that all these kinds of dialectical argument involve a questioner who secures premisses from an answerer and then uses them to deduce—or at least try to deduce—some conclusion which actually follows from them. This is the fundamental purpose of dialectical argument. To show another that his expressed opinions lead to an absurdity, or at least to a proposition he rejects, is to show him something important about his views. But even if an answerer were only pretending to give sincere answers, the dialectical exercise could show that a certain set of opinions, if held by anyone, would be inconsistent. An examination of this sort of the opinions held by other thinkers, or people in general, would be a plausible first stage in a philosophical inquiry. As a variant of this, an answerer could undertake to impersonate some well-known sage and answer appropriately; the questioner's arguments then are an examination of that sage's philosophical position. By these and similar measures, dialectical argument becomes a general exploration of the consequences of a set of views, with special emphasis on the detection of inconsistencies.

With this focus on "examination" (cf. *naẓar/munāẓara/baḥth*) via the exposing of absurd or impossible consequences, rejected propositions, and inconsistency, Smith could just as easily be describing the dialectic of our lens-texts—or of al-Shāfiʿī himself, and other jurists whose voices are heard in the *Umm*. This excerpt provides a lucid, if general, overview of the function of dialectic across thematic domains, and holds particularly true for the "good" juridical dialectic of Islam.

Most important of all is the "special emphasis on the detection of inconsistencies." Juridical *jadal*, as we have seen, is much preoccupied with the exposing, and avoiding, of self-contradiction and larger doctrinal inconsistency. Considering this concern is most evident in Aristotle's dialectic, we might also consider whether the ultimate reference for a *topos* might not in fact be: "the locus wherein the contrary/contradictory of the opposing opinion may be found." Aristotle employs *topos* as "the ground from which [Q] must make his attack." It would seem likely this "ground" would consist, in many cases, of the contrary or contradictory of R's thesis; Q would aim at R's concession to such premises. Once accomplished, R's thesis would be invalidated (the "destructive" aim), and Q's counter-thesis would necessarily be confirmed (the "constructive" aim). Both of these aims are achieved time and again in the dialectical sequences of the *Ikhtilāf al-ʿIrāqiyyayn/ʿIrāqiyyīn*, via the dialectical moves of *naqḍ* ("destructive" for R's solution) and *muʿāraḍa* ("constructive" for Q's solution).

The greatest support for this conception of *topos* in Aristotle's dialectic comes from Aristotle himself. He opens a lengthy discussion on the use of contraries in *topoi* of accident with the following: "Seeing that contraries may be combined with one another in six ways, and four of these combinations make a contrariety, we must avail ourselves of contraries in whatever way may be useful both for destructive and constructive purposes."[369] He adds:

> Furthermore, if the accident of anything has a contrary, you must examine whether it belongs to that to which the accident has been said to belong. For, if the former belongs,

[369] *Top.* II.7, 112b27ff.; trans. Forster.

> the latter cannot belong; for it is impossible for two contraries to belong to the same thing at the same time.[370]

The language of "accident" is foreign to the discussions in our lens-texts. On the other hand, if a *ḥukm* constitutes an accident adherent to a thing, or to an action, on account of an *ʿilla* inherent to that thing or action, then this suggested examination for contraries resembles something like the dialectical move of *naqḍ*. Certainly, we might describe the charge of *naqḍ* as exposing R's attaching of contrary *ḥukms* to the same *ʿilla*.

Nor is the *topos* concern for contrariety the only parallel we find; arguably, the *a fortiori* argument itself constitutes a *topos*, as outlined in *Top*. II.10. A quick summary of the chapter (constituting the first line of the next chapter) reads: "Such then are the various ways in which you can argue from the greater and the less and the like degrees."[371] Smith recognizes the lines preceding this summation (*Top*. II.10, 115a15-24) as "the type of argument we call *a fortiori*... and several similar principles."[372] Such being the case, we might consider the *istidlāl* categories of "*A Fortiori* Signification of the Instruction" (*faḥwā al-khiṭāb*) and "Drawing Indication by way of *A Fortiori* Valuation" (*al-istidlāl bi'l-awlā*) to themselves constitute a parallel "*topos*."

We must remember, however, that despite the general and thematic resemblances between Aristotelian and *jadal*-theory parallels mentioned thus far, they are all quite different when it comes to particulars and substance. This is true of the many more parallels we might unearth, especially if we made reference to the early Arabic translations of the *Topics* and the Arabic terms employed. For example, note that *topos/topoi* is translated as *mawḍiʿ/mawāḍiʿ*; a term frequently encountered in our lens-texts. Sometimes, it strongly resembles Aristotle's dialectical *topos*, as in "locus of contention" (*mawḍiʿ al-khilāf*), and at others it seems merely to designate "place/locus."[373] Other terms are too numerous to mention here; not the least of them being *jadal* itself, and plentiful references to problem (*mas'ala*), disagreement (*ikhtilāf*), expressions (*alfāẓ*), etc.

Of particular import to the current project is a general convergence born, no doubt, of the common exigencies of dialectical debate no matter its thematic content or disputants' intellectual project: (1) the nature of the dialectical premise itself, and of its epistemic valuation; (2) the nature of dialectical problems; and (3) the nature of dialectical theses. The most important discussions with regard to these occurs in *Top*. I.10-11. I will reproduce a few excerpts from Smith's translation[374] to gauge the general tenor of Aristotle's discussions; and parallel concerns of juridical *jadal*-theory—and *uṣūl al-fiqh* in general—will be immediately evident.

---

[370] *Top*. II.7, 113a20–24; trans. Forster.

[371] *Top*. II.11, 115a25; trans. Forster.

[372] *Topics I and VIII*, p. xxxiii.

[373] See, e.g., al-Shīrāzī, *Maʿūna*, al-ʿUmayrīnī ed., pp. 40–1; 42; 57; 58–9; 88–9.

[374] *Topics I and VIII*, pp. 9–10. All parentheses, etc., belong to the translation.

***Top.* I.10, 104a9ff**

- "A *dialectical premiss* is the asking of something acceptable to everyone, most people, or the wise (that is, either all of them, most of them, or the most famous), provided it is not contrary to opinion (for anyone would concede what the wise think, so long as it is not contrary to the opinions of the many). Dialectical premisses also include: things which are similar to what is acceptable; the contraries of things which appear to be acceptable, put forward by negation; and such opinions as are derived from any established arts."

***Top.* I.10, 104a34f**

- "It is also clear that such opinions as are derived from arts are dialectical premisses. For anyone would concede what those who have examined these subjects think, e.g. what a doctor thinks about medical questions, or what a geometer thinks about geometrical questions, and likewise in other cases."

***Top.* I.10, 104b1ff**

- "A *dialectical problem* is a point of speculation, directed either to choice and avoidance or to truth and knowledge (either on its own or as working in conjunction with something else of this sort), about which people either have no opinion, or the public think the opposite of the wise, or the wise think the opposite of the public, or each of these groups have opposed opinions within itself."

***Top.* I.10, 104b13ff**

- "Those are also <dialectical> problems concerning which there are contrary deductions (for there is a puzzle whether it is so or not, because there are persuasive arguments about both sides), as well as those about which, because they are vast, we have no arguments, thinking that it is difficult to give the reason why (e.g. whether the universe is eternal or not). For one could also pursue an enquiry about such problems."

***Top.* I.10, 104b19ff**

- "A *thesis* is: a belief contrary to opinion held by someone famous for philosophy, e.g. that contradiction is impossible (as Antisthenes used to say), or that everything moves (according to Heraclitus), or that what is is one (as Melissus says). (For to take things contrary to our opinions seriously when just any person declares them is silly.) Or: something about which we possess an argument contrary to our opinions...."

As for *Top.* I.10, 104a9ff., this formulation of the dialectical premise rests upon a neatly-categorized conception of what is *endoxon*. I have borrowed this latter term throughout this monograph as a descriptor expressing not only Aristotle's *endoxa* sets as listed above, but its implications—i.e., what an opponent in disputation ought to accept, and what one expects one's opponent to accept. We must also understand that Aristotle's description of the dialectical premise represents a fully-comprehensive framework for premises which ought to be accepted. This is best conveyed as an inclusive universal set containing smaller subsets; collectively, I will call this "Aristotle's *Endoxa* Set." The most important feature the following diagram (Fig. 4.3) is meant to show is this: all of Aristotle's subsets (most of the people, all of the wise, most of the wise, and the most famous of the wise) are subsumed by the superset of everyone. Note this well, for when Aristotle says "everyone" he means just that: everyone, *including* all the wise. Thus, when something is *endoxon* by the superset of everyone, it is in consonance not only with the opinions of laypeople, but with the opinions of the most learned scholars and scientists.

Parallels should become evident when we consider Aristotle's *endoxa* set in conjunction with Islamic axioms inherent to—and partly forged by—the argument epistemes of juridical *jadal* and *uṣūl al-fiqh*. The primary domain of overlap is *istidlāl bi'l-ijmāʿ*, and becomes clear once we substitute terms such as *Umma* for "everyone" and *ʿulamā'*, *Ahl al-ʿIlm*, *Ahl al-Naẓar*, etc., for "the wise." Alternately, we might consider God as "the Most Wise;" with the Prophet's divinely-sanc-

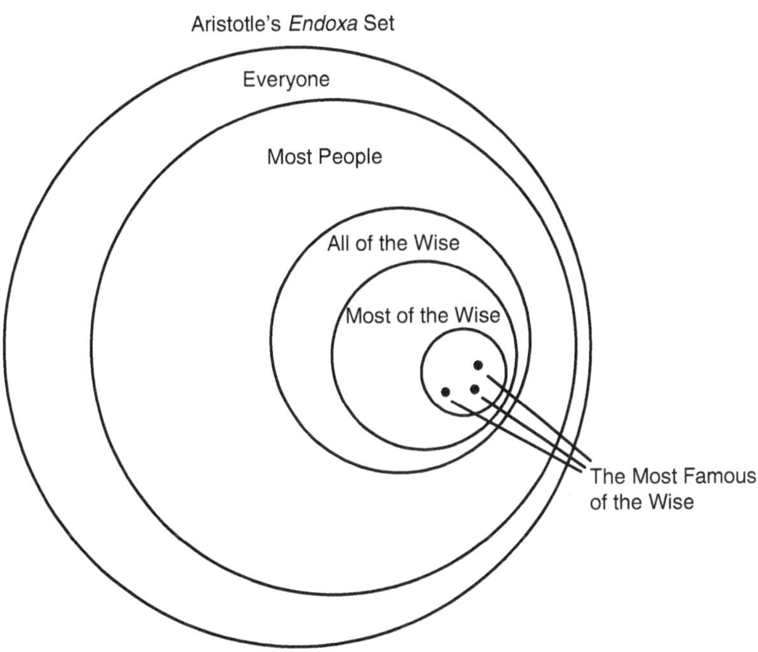

Fig. 4.3 Aristotle's *Endoxa* Set (NB: it is possible Aristotle would have placed the "All of the Wise" subset and its contents *outside* the domain of "Most People," but within the domain of "Everyone," as one kind reader has pointed out. In other words, it is possible Aristotle intended a distinction between "Most People" and "The Wise" (all, most, or select famous of them))

tioned decrees and conduct in a special subset, and Imāms and Companions among "the most famous of the wise." The difference is this: in Islamic argument epistemes the *endoxa* set has been further transformed into an hierarchy of epistemic authority: God (Qur'ān), His Prophet (Sunna), Companions and/or Imāms (*sunan*, *āthār*), and *ijmāʿ* (of *Umma*, *ʿulamā'*, and Ahl al-Madīna).[375]

Other parallels from *Top.* I.10, 104a9ff. are the inclusion among dialectical premises of: (1) "the contraries of things which appear to be acceptable, put forward by negation;" and (2) "such opinions as are derived from any established arts." As for the first, there are parallels in "Drawing Indication from the [Restrictive] Indicant of the Instruction" (*istidlāl bi-dalīl al-khiṭāb*) and "correlational inference of the opposite" (*qiyās al-ʿaks*); and as for the second there are further parallels in the legal-theoretical discussions of "consensus of the scholars" (*ijmāʿ al-ʿulamā'*) and "adherence to a qualified jurisprudent" (*taqlīd*). This second set of parallels is even more evident in *Top.* I.10, 104a34f.: "For anyone would concede what those who have examined these subjects think."

As for the "dialectical problem," in *Top.* I.10, 104b1ff., we are reminded of: (1) the truth-seeking ethic of juridical *jadal*; (2) the objective of *ijtihād* with regard to both novel cases ("about which people... have no opinion") and problems of disagreement (*masā'il al-khilāf*), where "the wise" set has "opposed opinions within itself." This latter type of "dialectical problem" constitutes the very substance of both the *ikhtilāf* and *jadal*-theory genres of legal literature. Again the parallel is bolstered in *Top.* I.10, 104b13ff., with the mention of "dialectical problems [read: *masā'il*] concerning which there are contrary deductions [the very domain of *ikhtilāf*]... because there are persuasive arguments about both sides." No finer collection of "dialectical problems," then, might we hope to find than those example-*masā'il* of our *jadal*-theory works, and the core *masā'il* of *ikhtilāf* in our subject-text. On the other hand, we also find a parallel—not to mention a mark of direct continuity—for theologically-themed *jadal*; mainly, those more speculative dialectical problems "about which, because they are vast, we have no arguments, thinking that it is difficult to give the reason why (e.g. whether the universe is eternal or not)." Finally, we may interpret Aristotle's "dialectical thesis," as introduced in *Top.* I.10, 104b19ff., as a fitting parallel-descriptor for such *ijtihād*ic solutions a proponent might bring in dialectical disputation, as either: (1) conflicting with the *ijtihād* of an authoritative *mujtahid* ("contrary to opinion held by someone famous for philosophy"); or (2) conflicting with the opponent's *ijtihād*.

As a final note before moving on to the *Sophistical Elenchi*, I would highlight one last important parallel. Earlier, we encountered Aristotle's distinction between the procedures of the independent philosopher and the dialectician. Recall that he said:

---

[375] Understanding Aristotle's dialectical premises as belonging to an *endoxa* set becomes particularly important for parallel conceptions of *ijmāʿ*. Some have seen conflict or inconsistent usage of *ijmāʿ al-Umma* over and against *ijmāʿ al-ʿulamā'*. But an *endoxa* set schema would show that *ijmāʿ al-Umma* includes *ijmāʿ al-ʿulamā'*, while the reverse need not necessarily be the case.

> As far as the choice of ground [τόπον] goes, the philosopher and the dialectician are making a similar inquiry, but the subsequent arrangement of material and the framing of questions are the peculiar province of the dialectician; for such a proceeding always involves a relation with another party.

To this I would add an observation of Smith's. Following his description of dialectic as "a general exploration of the consequences of a set of views, with special emphasis on the detection of inconsistencies," he continues:

> Carrying out such an exploration in a live exchange between questioner and answerer would have some advantages—for instance, two competitors could do a better job of presenting both sides of a case than one—but a skilled practitioner could dispense with the need for a partner and explore the consequences of a set of views alone. This recalls Aristotle's own practice of beginning his treatments of scientific subjects by first reviewing the 'puzzles,' i.e. the inconsistent conclusions which can be deduced from the received opinions on any subject.[376]

If we substitute *masāʾil* for "puzzles" and *ikhtilāf* for "inconsistent conclusions," we might be describing the starting points for many a juridical treatise in which—having first stated the problem (*masʾala*)—the author reviews the variant extant solutions (*ikhtilāf*) before supporting one, or arguing his own.[377] Moreover, we are reminded that a *mujtahid* must have a strong knowledge of juridical *ikhtilāf* with regard to substantive rulings. Most importantly, however, we see in both Aristotle's description of (independent) philosopher and (cooperative) dialectician, and Smith's description of a sort of internal dialectic, an important interplay between an individual's private philosophizing and the public procedure of dialectic.

This parallels a hypotheses put forward in the current project. The dynamic symbiosis of juridical dialectic and legal theory is not only a consequence of the latter being forged in—and in turn providing additional premises and structure for—the former. It may also be explained through the private activity of *ijtihād* as an *internal dialectic*, in anticipation of the argument epistemes which public disputation will bring to bear. In other words: (1) the argument epistemes of proto-system juridical dialectic forged the systematized epistemes of *uṣūl al-fiqh*; (2) these latter were meant to guide *mujtahids* towards right-*ijtihād*; and (3) the ultimate vindication—or deconstruction—of later *ijtihād* was achieved through fully-systematized juridical dialectical disputation praxis. Thus, whether at the start of one's private *ijtihādic* process, or in the final, public stages in which one's *ijtihādic* solution was tested, the master set of argument epistemes was that of dialectic.

---

[376] *Topics I and VIII*, p. xv.

[377] This is precisely the spirit in which Abū Yūsuf compiled the *K. Ikhtilāf Abī Ḥanīfa wa Ibn Abī Laylā*; and it is the same spirit in which al-Shāfiʿī expanded upon that work.

Aristotle's Sophistical Elenchi

The *Sophistical Elenchi*—as a continuation of the *Topics*—again shares a common project with our juridical *jadal*-theory treatises: this time, it is systematizing the identification and refutation of incorrect assumptions and flawed reasoning—our theorists' system for the dialectical *practice* which we find throughout the *K. al-Umm*. With this in mind, parallel concerns and methods between the *Sophistical Elenchi* and our lens-texts ought to be noted wherever they occur. Bear in mind that the *Sophistical Elenchi* is a critical part of Aristotle's overall theory of dialectic, and in fact represents the continuation and conclusion to what is discussed in the *Topics*. Miller considers the *Sophistical Elenchi* to be the ninth book of the *Topics*;[378] while Smith observes the *Sophistical Elenchi* is "a treatise which Aristotle intended as the last section of the *Topics*," and "is really Aristotle's closing chapter for the *Topics*, since it begins with a reference to the project laid out in its opening sentence; it gives Aristotle's own assessment of his achievement and its relationship to what came before."[379]

There is a great deal in the way of parallels which might be unearthed here. I will therefore only give the most cursory treatment to such parallels as I have found, beginning with a brief outline of problematic argument types discussed in the *Sophistical Elenchi*, providing insight as to the structure and ordering principle of the text. Our guide in this will be Scott Schreiber, an insightful scholar of Aristotelian dialectic.[380]

The Fallacy Scheme of the *Sophistical Elenchi*

- False Reasoning
  - Ignoratio Elenchi
    - Due to Language
      - Double Meaning
        - Homonymy
        - Amphiboly
        - Form of the Expression
      - Non-Double Meaning
        - Accent
        - Composition
        - Division

(continued)

[378] "Islamic Disputation Theory," p. 57.

[379] *Topics I and VIII*, pp. xxxiv, xxxv.

[380] *Aristotle on False Reasoning*, p. 4; the table has been reordered as an outline from Schreiber's diagram.

- Outside of Language
  - Begging the Question
  - Non-Cause As Cause
  - Accident
  - Consequent
  - Secundum Quid
  - Many Questions

In order to proceed quickly through these categories of fallacy, I have adopted the following abbreviated approach: (1) variant appellations for each category will be provided, in different English translations, preceded by their Greek formulae, and followed by early Arabic translations (the names of the translators will appear in brackets);[381] (2) Bekker numbers for relevant discussions will be footnoted; and (3) parallels with our lens-texts will be noted wherever immediately evident.[382]

παρὰ τὴν τοῦ ἐλέγχου ἄγνοιαν

- "ignorance of what refutation is" [Schreiber]
- "ignorance of the nature of refutation" [Forster]
- "*ignoratio elenchi*" [Schreiber; Forster]
- *min al-jahl bi'l-tabkītāt* [Yaḥyā b. ʿAdī]
- *min ʿadam al-ʿilm bi'l-tabkīt* [Ibn Zurʿa]
- *min qillat al-ʿilm bi'l-tabkīt* [*naql qadīm*]

Schreiber notes: "In *S.E.* 4 and 5, Aristotle cites *Ignoratio Elenchi* as one of the thirteen distinct sources, but in *S.E.* 6, he elevates it to the genus under which the other twelve fall."[383] Surprisingly, I have not yet located the term *tabkīt* in our

---

[381] The sources for all may be found in the list of references at the end of this chapter. Again, my intention with the Arabic translations is merely to highlight any parallels of terminology between the efforts of the translators and the technical jargon of our *jadal* theorists. Two of the translators edited by Badawī in his *Manṭiq Arisṭū* belong to the fourth/tenth century, i.e., the century in which the sciences of *jadal* and *uṣūl al-fiqh* were first systematized in literary treatises. They are: Yaḥyā b. ʿAdī (d.363/974); and ʿĪsā b. Isḥāḳ b. Zurʿa (d.398/1008). Badawī's third source is an "old transmission" (*naql qadīm*) attributed to al-Nāʿimī (d.?) For more on these translators, see Badawī's introduction to the *Manṭiq Arisṭū*.

[382] There is much more we might learn from a thorough, move-by-move, comparative analysis between the *Sophistical Elenchi* and our *jadal*-theory texts. What follows is merely a first foray.

[383] *False Reasoning*, p. 192, n. 13; see also pp. 87–8. For the description of *ignoratio elenchi* as an independent fallacy, see: *Soph. El.* 4, 166b24; 5, 167a21ff. As for its description as a genus of fallacies, see: *Soph. El.* 6, 168a18ff.; and Schreiber, *False Reasoning*, 87–93. And as for its resolution as an independent fallacy, see: *Soph. El.* 26.

lens-texts. On the other hand, we have seen Miller point out a description of *ilzām* which appears related in concept. We have also seen, in al-Juwaynī's hierarchy of causes for *inqiṭāʿ*, that a disputant's incapacity (*ʿajz*) "may be due to a gap in his knowledge of the *rusūm al-jadal* and its *uṣūl*;" Miller aptly paraphrases this as: "ignorance of dialectic."[384]

ὁμωνυμία	**ἀμφιβολία**
• "homonymy" [Schreiber][385] • "equivocation" [Forster] • *ittifāq al-ism* [Yaḥyā b. ʿAdī] • *al-ittifāq fiʾl-ism* [Ibn Zurʿa] • *ishtirāk al-asmāʾ* [*naql qadīm*]	"amphiboly" [Schreiber][386] "ambiguity" [Forster] *al-mirāʾ* [Yaḥyā b. ʿAdī; Ibn Zurʿa] *al-shakk fiʾl-kalām* [*naql qadīm*]
σχῆμα λέξεως	**προςῳδία**
• "form of the expression" [Schreiber; Forster][387] • *shakl al-lafẓa* [Yaḥyā b. ʿAdī] • *shakl al-qawl* [Ibn Zurʿa] • *ṣūrat al-kalām wa shaklihi* [*naql qadīm*]	• "accent" [Schreiber; Forster][388] • *al-taʿjīm* [Yaḥyā b. ʿAdī; Ibn Zurʿa] • *iʿrāb* [of the *Kalām*] *biʾl-ʿalāmāt waʾl-nuqaṭ* [*naql qadīm*]
σύνθεσις	**διαίρεσις**
• "composition" [Schreiber][389] • "combination [of words]" [Forster] • *al-tarkīb* [Yaḥyā b. ʿAdī; Ibn Zurʿa] • *tarkīb* [*al-kalām*] [*naql qadīm*]	• "division" [Schreiber][390] • "division [of words]" [Forster] • *al-qisma* [Yaḥyā b. ʿAdī; Ibn Zurʿa] • *tajziʾat* and *qismat* [of the *kalām*] [*naql qadīm*]

[384] "Islamic Disputation Theory," p. 141.

[385] Description: *Soph. El.* 4, 165b26, 30ff.; 6, 168a25; 7, 169a23ff.; and Schreiber, *False Reasoning*, pp. 21–5. Resolution, with examples: *Soph. El.* 17; 19, 177a10ff.; 22, 178a24ff.; 23, 179a17; and Schreiber, *False Reasoning*, pp. 31–6.

[386] Description: *Soph. El.* 4, 165b26, 166a7ff.; and Schreiber, *False Reasoning*, pp. 25–31. Resolution: *Soph. El.* 17; 19, 177a16ff.; 23, 179a20; and Schreiber, *False Reasoning*, pp. 31–6.

[387] Description: *Soph. El.* 4, 165b26, 166b10ff.; 7, 169a37ff.; and Schreiber, *False Reasoning*, pp. 37–54. As a category mistake: *Soph. El.* 6, 168a26; 7, 169a35; 22, 178a6ff., 178b24ff.; and Schreiber, *False Reasoning*, pp. 38–44. As other than a category mistake: Schreiber, *False Reasoning*, pp. 44–48. Form of the Expression and solecism: *Soph. El.* 3, 165b15; 14, 173b17ff.; and Schreiber, *False Reasoning*, pp. 48–51. As a linguistic fallacy of double-meaning: *Soph. El.* 6, 168a24ff.; Schreiber, *False Reasoning*, pp. 51–4.

[388] Description: *Soph. El.* 4, 165b27, 166b1ff.; 6, 168a27; 7, 169a29; and Schreiber, *False Reasoning*, pp. 58–60. Resolution: *Soph. El.* 20, 177b3; 21; 23, 179a15.

[389] Description: *Soph. El.* 4, 165b27, 166a23ff.; and Schreiber, *False Reasoning*, pp. 60–76. Resolution: *Soph. El.* 22.

[390] Description: *Soph. El.* 4, 165b27, 166a34ff.; and Schreiber, *False Reasoning*, pp. 60–76. Resolution: *Soph. El.* 22.

As for the larger set of properly linguistic fallacies, there are numerous parallels among the hermeneutical concerns of *uṣūl al-fiqh*, and among such subcategories of objections in the *jadal* literature as are directed against *lafẓ*-expressions. A properly detailed analysis is beyond the scope of the current project; I have preferred simply to list the six categories above, with their Arabic translations and accompanying references for further investigation. Some parallels are immediately obvious, however, and include, for "homonymy": such species of *istidlāl* and *iʿtirāḍ* as are preoccupied with determining the most apparent meaning (*ẓāhir*); for "amphiboly": such species of *istidlāl* and *iʿtirāḍ* as are preoccupied with generality/ambiguity (*ijmāl*) and ambiguous (*mujmal*) expressions; for "form of the expression"—that is, for its subtype: "other than a category mistake"—such species of *istidlāl* and *iʿtirāḍ* as are preoccupied with distinguishing between general (*ʿāmm*) and particular (*khāṣṣ*); and for "accent": that category of Qur'ān-oriented objection known as "variant readings" (*ikhtilāf al-qirā'āt*).

τὸ ἐν ἀρχῇ αἰτεῖσθαι/τὸ ἐν ἀρχῇ λαμβάνειν

- "asking the original point;" or "assuming the original point [to be proved];" or "begging the question" [Schreiber][391]
- "*petitio principii*" [Forster]
- *an ya'khudha alladhī min al-bad'* [Yaḥyā b. ʿAdī]
- *min al-umūr al-ma'khūdha bad'an* [Ibn Zurʿa]
- *min awwal al-mas'ala* [*naql qadīm*]

Although this fallacy is not readily apparent among the *istidlāl* and *iʿtirāḍ* considerations of our *jadal*-theorists, it could most certainly have occurred in juridical debate. That is to say, whenever R or Q supports a solution with evidence which itself rests upon the validity of that solution, this species of fallacy may be said to have occurred. This opens the way for parallels in certain *iʿtirāḍāt* against an opponent who appears to have "gotten it backwards;" e.g., the third type of al-Shīrāzī's *qalb*: "[Q] makes the occasioned effect (*maʿlūl*) an occasioning factor (*ʿilla*), and the occasioning factor an occasioned effect."[392] An interesting possibility occurs in our subject-text as well (in §284), where al-Shāfiʿī points out that the *aṣl* (*muḍāraba*-contract) upon which his opponent relies for *qiyās* to the *mas'ala* at hand (re: *muʿāmala*-contract) is in fact itself a *farʿ* confirmed via *qiyās* from the *aṣl* of the *muʿāmala*-contract. The opponent has inverted *aṣl* and *farʿ*, and thus, from a certain perspective, may be said to have provided evidence for the validity of his solution, which evidence itself rests upon the validity of that solution.[393]

---

[391] Description: *Soph. El.* 4, 166b25; 5, 167a37ff.; 6, 168b23ff.; 7, 169b13; Schreiber, *False Reasoning*, pp. 98–105. Resolution: *Soph. El.* 27; Schreiber, *False Reasoning*, pp. 106.

[392] Shīr.VII.14.3; and al-Bājī: "That he says: I make the *maʿlūl* an *ʿilla*, and the *ʿilla* a *maʿlūla*" (*Minhāj*, Turkī ed., pp. 177, §389). Al-Bājī relates *ikhtilāf* regarding this subspecies of *iʿtirāḍ*, and then rejects it.

[393] See the analysis for §284 in Chap. 5.

More intriguing is an argument of al-Baṣrī's identified by Hallaq as a *petitio principii*. In brief, al-Baṣrī is arguing against those who would claim the concomitance (*jarayān*) of the *ʿilla* in the *maʿlūl* provides indication for its validity. His retort consists of the following assertions: (1) efficiency (*ta'thīr*) of the *ʿilla* means R has made the *ḥukm* conditional upon it in each locus in which it is found; (2) this is R's act, and his act does not provide indication for the *ʿilla*'s validity; since (3) he must first establish its validity in the *aṣl* before attaching it to the *farʿ*. After further explanation, Hallaq explains this as a charge of *petitio principii*.[394] From this, we may assume that any *istidlāl* or *iʿtirāḍ* involving "concomitance of the occasioning factor with what it occasions" (*jarayān al-ʿilla fī maʿlūlātihā*) allowed the possibility of raising such a charge. As for al-Baṣrī, this fallacy type appears to have been well known to him; he again refutes an opposing position's *petitio principii* during a long discourse on the argumentative conclusiveness (*ḥujjiyya*) of *ijmāʿ*, in his *Muʿtamad*.[395]

παρὰ τὸ μὴ αἴτιον ὡς αἴτιον

- "non-cause as cause" [Schreiber][396]
- "mistaken cause" [Forster]
- *an yaḍaʿa lā ka-ʿilla ka-ʿilla* [Yaḥyā b. ʿAdī]
- *min waḍʿ mā laysa bi-ʿilla ʿalā annahu ʿilla* [Ibn Zurʿa]
- *bi-ithbāt ʿilla lā ka-ʿilla* [*naql qadīm*]

There are many parallel concerns for this particular category of fallacy in our *jadal*-theory texts, both in terms of the implications of the fallacy itself, and the manner in which it has been rendered into Arabic. Any one of the *qiyās*-oriented *iʿtirāḍāt* which attempt to destroy or supplant the opponent's *ʿilla* may be subsumed beneath this larger category of "mistaken cause." Even those which are less focused upon problematizing efficiency (*ta'thīr*) are worthy of note, if only for the similarity with which they are formulated in comparison to the Arabic translations in our header. First among these would be al-Bājī's third *qiyās*-oriented objection: "the objection that what [R] made an *ʿilla* is not allowed to be made an *ʿilla*."[397]

If we consider *ʿilla* as "cause"—in the sense that theologians and philosophers did—then any repudiation of the opponent's justification or establishing of the

---

[394] "Treatise," p. 216, n. 31. Elsewhere, Hallaq has noted that Orientalist Snouck Hurgronje assessed the entire institution of *ijmāʿ* as a singular *petitio principii* ("Authoritativeness of Sunni Consensus," p. 429). Building upon an earlier attempt by George Hourani, Hallaq shows in this article, among many other things, how jurists such as al-Ghazālī and al-Āmidī, among others, avoided what was termed *dawr*: "circularity."

[395] Ḥamīd Allāh ed., vol. 2, pp. 476–7. See Bernand's entry on *ijmāʿ* in the *EI*², to which I owe this reference. Among other things, al-Ghazālī's argument in his *Mustaṣfā* is also explained therein.

[396] Description: *Soph. El.* 4, 166b26; 5, 167b21ff.; 7, 169b14; Schreiber, *False Reasoning*, pp. 107–12.

[397] Bāj.IX.B.3.

occasioning factor (*taʿlīl* or *ithbāt al-ʿilla*) would plainly be subsumed by the charge of "mistaken cause." If, on the other hand, we acknowledge al-Juwaynī's warning that the *ʿilla*s of God's Law (*Sharʿ*) are not like those of rational intellection (*ʿaql*), then such charges as depend upon co-absence (*ʿaks*) would have to be reconsidered.[398] In normative domains of "correlational inference in consonance with God's Law" (*qiyās sharʿī*), then, we might consider a variant fallacy of "mistaken occasioning factor."

With regard to the role played by "mistaken cause" in Aristotle's dialectic, we may refer to *Soph. El.* 5, 167b21ff. Of special note in this passage is the following observation:

> Such a case [mistaken cause] occurs in reasonings leading up to an impossibility; for in these one is bound to destroy one of the premisses. If, therefore, what is not a cause is enumerated among the questions which are necessary for the production of the resultant impossibility, the refutation will often seem to come about as the result of it....[399]

"Mistaken cause" and *reductio ad impossibile* thus appear to be tied in dialectical disputation. We may observe the same phenomenon in juridical *jadal*; for a charge of *naqḍ* is at once a charge of "mistaken *ʿilla*" and a reduction to inconsistency or contradiction. By raising a *mas'alat al-naqḍ* Q attempts to show: (1) R has misidentified the *ʿilla* in the *mas'ala* at hand; and (2) R, by elsewhere attributing a contrary *ḥukm* to this same *ʿilla*, has contradicted himself with regard to the *mas'ala* at hand. Alternately, Q may extend R's *ʿilla* to a hypothetical situation wherein the *ʿilla* obtains, but the proposed *ḥukm* would be absurd, or contradictory, or impossible. Both of these objection methods enjoy great frequency in the dialectic of the *Umm*.

παρὰ τὸ συμβεβηκός

- "accident" [Schreiber; Forster][400]
- *min al-aʿrāḍ* [Yaḥyā b. ʿAdī; Ibn Zurʿa]
- *bi'l-ʿaraḍ* [*naql qadīm*]

---

[398] *Kāfiya*, Maḥmūd ed., p. 68, §163. Cf. the discussion of *ʿadam al-ta'thīr*, above.

[399] Trans. Forster.

[400] Description: *Soph. El.* 4, 166b22; 5, 166b28ff.; 6, 168a34ff., 168b27ff.; 7, 169b3ff.; Schreiber, *False Reasoning*, pp. 113–16, 126–30. Resolution: *Soph. El.* 24; Schreiber, *False Reasoning*, pp. 114–16. Note that Schreiber considers "accident" and "consequent" to be, in fact, "one single fallacy with one single resolution" (p. 113). He also points out that past approaches to the analysis of this fallacy via "appeal to linguistic ambiguity" challenge Aristotle's typology (whereby "accident" and "consequent" are fallacy-types "outside of language"). As for the formal analytical approach, with specific regard to the fallacy of consequent: "It was rechristened the 'fallacy of Affirming the Consequent' by John Neville Keynes in the nineteenth century and continues to thrive under that label in most introductions to modern propositional logic" (Schreiber, op. cit.)

Aristotle describes this fallacy, in *Soph. El.* 5, 166b28ff., as follows:

> Fallacies connected with Accident occur when it is claimed that some attribute belongs similarly to the thing and to its accident; for since the same thing has many accidents, it does not necessarily follow that all the same attributes belong to all the predicates of a thing and to that of which they are predicated.[401]

Aristotle's formulations and analyses still appear, on the whole, couched in a very different language than that of our early *jadal*-theorists. Nevertheless, we can see a parallel concern of guarding against this fallacy should certain alterations to the above quotation be made. We might consider a *ḥukm* a kind of attribute, and properties (*awṣāf*, s. *waṣf*) as divisible into two classes: such as are accidental, and such as are not (e.g., "red" and "intoxicating" with regard to wine).

If we proceed with a common example of invalid *ʿilla*-ascription, whereby the *ḥukm* of proscription is attributed to wine on account of its redness, something like Aristotle's fallacy of accident is clearly at work. In this case, "it is claimed that some attribute [proscription] belongs similarly to the thing [wine] and to its accident [redness];" for we have invested an accidental *waṣf* (redness) with the power of occasioning the *ḥukm* of proscription for its own substrate (wine). Of course, the truly efficient *waṣf* (intoxicant) is not at all accidental to wine, but integral to its quiddity. Among other things, the problem with a fallacious *ʿilla*-ascription to redness is that this accident-*waṣf* belongs to a great many other things. If we were to extend, by way of *qiyās*, what we have mistakenly attributed to it (the *ḥukm* of proscription), then we would have dangerously compounded our initial error.

This potential interplay between mis-ascribing the *ʿilla* and Aristotle's fallacy of accident should be further explored. At this point, however, it does seem that a parallel concern is found in such *iʿtirāḍāt*—like *kasr*—by which Q problematizes certain of the *awṣāf* of R's *ʿilla*. Moreover, as we have seen with al-Bājī's typology of *kasr*, Q might eliminate an efficient *waṣf* from R's *ʿilla*, or he might eliminate a non-efficient *waṣf*.[402] Conceivably, further investigation might reveal that the non-efficient variety of *awṣāf* tend to be more often accidental, but this remains to be seen.

παρὰ τὸ ἑπόμενον

- "consequent" [Schreiber; Forster][403]
- *min allatī talzamu/tulzimu* [Yaḥyā b. ʿAdī]
- *min al-lawāzim* [Ibn Zurʿa]
- *min lawāḥiq al-kalām wa min waḍʿ al-muqaddimāt* [*naql qadīm*]
- [*the* fallacy of affirming the consequent]

---

[401] Trans. Forster.

[402] Such being Bāj.IX.B.12.2.1-2.

[403] Description: *Soph. El.* 4, 166b25; 5, 167b1ff.; 6, 168b28ff.; 7, 169b7ff.; Schreiber, *False Reasoning*, pp. 130–9. Resolution: *Soph. El.* 28.

A concern for this fallacy should be obvious in any intellectual project whose premises and conclusions may be reduced to the forms of propositional logic (such as the discovery or formulation of substantive norms). In a previous footnote, I mentioned Schreiber's observation that Keynes's fallacy of Affirming the Consequent remains the most common appellation with regard to the formal analysis of Aristotle's "consequent." Aristotle's own description of this fallacy in *Soph. El.* 5, 167b1ff. makes it clear why this should be so:

> The refutation connected with the consequent is due to the idea that consequence is convertible. For whenever, if A is, B necessarily is, men also fancy that, if B is, A necessarily is. It is from this source that deceptions connected with opinion based on sense-perception arise. For men often take gall for honey because a yellow color accompanies honey; and since it happens that the earth becomes drenched when it has rained, if it is drenched, we think that it has rained, though this is not necessarily true. In rhetorical arguments proofs from signs are founded on consequences; for, when men wish to prove that a man is an adulterer, they seize upon the consequence of that character, namely, that the man dresses himself elaborately or is seen wandering abroad at night—facts that are true of many people, while the accusation is not true.[404]

There are a number of reasons this description should capture our attention, not the least of which is Aristotle's own forensic-rhetorical example. At the very least, we might say that *ikhtilāf* among the jurists with regard to circumstantial evidence is concerned with the fallacy of consequent. There may be more in the way of parallel concerns, however, especially within *qiyās*-related domains of *istidlāl* and *iʿtirāḍ*. The *istidlālāt* which concern themselves with *ṭard*, *ʿaks*, and *jarayān*—along with the *iʿtirāḍāt* directed against them—would likely constitute the launching point for a more complete investigation.

παρὰ τὸ πῇ καὶ ἁπλῶς

- "due to [something said] in some way and without qualification" = *secundum quid et simpliciter* [Schreiber][405]
- *min maʿnā fī shay'in aw ʿalā al-iṭlāq* [Yaḥyā b. ʿAdī]
- *min al-ḥaml min jihat aw ʿalā al-iṭlāq* [Ibn Zurʿa]
- *mimmā fī'l-shay' aw min al-mursal min al-qawl* [*naql qadīm*]

Schreiber nominates *secundum quid* "as a convenient label for this family of errors;"[406] while Forster captures its essence with the following header in his translation: "The confusion of absolute and qualified statements."[407] Although

[404] Trans. Forster.

[405] "which depend on whether a statement is made in a limited sense or absolutely" (*Soph. El.* 6, 168b11; trans. Forster). Description: *Soph. El.* 4, 166b23; 5, 166b37ff; 6, 168b11ff.; 7, 169b11ff.; Schreiber, *False Reasoning*, pp. 141–4, 145–51. Resolution: *Soph. El.* 25; Schreiber, *False Reasoning*, p. 144. False Resolutions: Schreiber, *False Reasoning*, p. 144.

[406] Schreiber, *False Reasoning*, p. 141.

[407] *Sophistical Refutations*, Loeb ed., margin of p. 85.

precise treatments of this fallacy in the *uṣūl* and *jadal*-theory literature are not readily apparent, Forster's heading and the early Arabic translations point us towards the hermeneutical categories of absolute (*muṭlaq*) and restricted (*muqayyad*) expressions. We might detect a concern for *secundum quid*, e.g., in one of the non-valid modes of reasoning discussed in al-Bājī's "Explanation of What is Connected to the *Adillat al-Maʿqūl*, but is Not of Them." Certain Mālikīs practice: "Correlating the Absolute (*Muṭlaq*) with the Restricted (Muqayyad) without an *ʿIlla*."[408] Again, this and other forms of *iʿtirāḍāt* focusing upon the *muṭlaq/muqayyad* distinction provide a point of embarkation in the hunt for parallels.

τὸ τὰ πλείω ἐρωτήματα ἓν ποιεῖν

- "the making of several questions into one;" many questions [Schreiber][409]
- plurality of questions [Forster]
- *an yajʿala masāʾil kathīra masʾala wāḥida* [Yaḥyā b. ʿAdī; *naql qadīm*]
- *an yajʿala al-suʾālāt al-kathīra suʾāl wāḥid* [Ibn Zurʿa]

Again, it is difficult to pinpoint precise domains of *istidlāl* or *iʿtirāḍ* in which the fallacy of many questions would most likely be treated. Schreiber offers a cogent explanation, however, which allows us some idea of how "many questions" might come about in a dialectical debate:

> Because questions in dialectic become the premises of arguments, this fallacy arises when one concedes a premise having multiple parts as though it were a simple proposition. The problem, then amounts to an inability to individuate premises. As such, these arguments fail to be true refutations, because they violate clause (2) of the definition of refutation: the conclusion does not follow necessarily from the premises. The reason for this is that what appears to be a premise is actually not one.[410]

We are reminded of our *jadal* authors' repeated warnings to be both specific in question and parsimonious in response. The disputant must avoid having to retract something he carelessly or accidentally conceded. Al-Bājī, as we have seen, also warns against asking "ambiguous" questions which may forestall a response. Here, especially, the fallacy of many questions might come into play. A modern, textbook example illustrates how this fallacy forestalls a response, and thus violates the objective of "good" dialectic. Q asks R: "Have you stopped beating your wife?" R is flustered, as he will be condemned by either a "Yes" or a "No." The fallacy occurs should we interpret R's hesitancy to provide a "yes" or "no" answer as a confirmation of his wife-beating (Q's sophistical *elenchus*). The prob-

408 *Minhāj*, Turkī ed., pp. 29–30, §55.

409 *Soph. El.* 5, 166b27; trans. Forster. Description: *Soph. El.* 4, 166b27; 5, 167b38ff.; 6, 169a6ff.; Schreiber, *False Reasoning*, pp. 153–9, 161–6. With disjunctive premises: Schreiber, *False Reasoning*, pp. 154, 155–6; and with conjunctive premises: *False Reasoning*, pp. 154, 156–9. Resolution: *Soph. El.* 17, 175b39ff.; 30, 181a36ff.; Schreiber, *False Reasoning*, pp. 159–60.

410 *False Reasoning*, p. 153.

lem, of course, is that two questions—[1] "Have you ever beaten your wife," and [2] "if you have, have you stopped?"—have been posed as a singular, "yes" or "no" question.[411]

Refutations "By seeking the contradictions between the views of your opponent and the school to which he belongs"[412]

In addition to the identification and dismantling of fallacies, Aristotle provides pragmatic advice to the dialectician in his *Sophistical Elenchi*, just as he does in the *Topics*. The following is of particular note for comparison to our *jadal*-theory texts:

> Moreover, as in rhetorical arguments, so likewise also in refutations, you ought to look for contradictions between the answerer's views and either [1] his own statements or [2] the views of those whose words and actions he admits to be right, or [3] of those who are generally held to bear a like character and to resemble them, or [4] of the majority, or [5] of all mankind.[413]

This reads almost as a catalogue of "Aristotelian *iʿtirāḍāt*." Among other things, there are parallels with *naqḍ*, the charge of intra-doctrinal inconsistency; with charges of contradicting Qur'ān, Sunna, and *ijmāʿ*; and with charges of contradicting the substantive law or method of one's own juristic *madhhab*.

Concluding Statement

If, after this lightning review of Aristotelian dialectical concerns, we are at all impressed by the number of parallels in our lens-texts, we ought to be equally impressed by all the differences. As I have argued earlier, this combination of likenesses and dissimilarities is best accounted for by: (1) more complex developmental models (Fig. 4.2); and (2) the infusion of prior Near Eastern argumentation epistemes (including the Hellenic) with new Islamic axioms, with the subsequent development of unique argument epistemes according to the dictates of variant intellectual projects.

It will never be easy to answer the question of how "Aristotelian" early Islamic juridical *jadal* is. That being said, we are now equipped with a sufficient lens for the analysis of proto-system juridical *jadal* as it appears in the dialectical sequences of our subject-text: the *Umm* Version of the *Kitāb Ikhtilāf al-ʿIrāqiyyayn/ʿIrāqiyyīn*. In this enterprise many similarities and differences will also surface—between

[411] See Pirie, *How to Win Every Argument*, p. 29: "The complex question (*plurium interrogationum*)."
[412] *Soph. El.*, Loeb ed., margin of p.85 (Forster's heading).
[413] *Soph. El.* 15, 174b19ff. (trans. Forster; brackets are mine).

proto-system disputation practice and fully-systematized *jadal*-theory—but now we are on somewhat firmer ground in terms of the transmission of ideas. I would argue that what we witness in the subject-text is an early stage in a continuous developmental process within a single intellectual project: the *ijtihādic* elaboration of norms consonant with God's Law within a nascent Sunnī juridical episteme, along with the justification and "testing" of this *ijtihād*.

My analyses and conclusions should hold little in the way of surprises. The window onto proto-system dialectic and legal theory opened by our subject-text illuminates only a small patch of a much larger intellectual scene; but that small patch appears much as one would expect. It is far less choate than later systems would become, yet, at the same time, it is sophisticated to an astonishing degree; and, overall, it is manifestly more ancient in tenor.

References

al-ʿAjam, Rafīq. *Mawsūʿat Muṣṭalaḥāt Uṣūl al-Fiqh ʿinda al-Muslimīn*. 2 vols. Beirut: Maktabat Lubnān, 1998.

Aristotle. *The Categories; On Interpretation* (Ed. and Transl. Harold P. Cooke); *Prior Analytics* (Ed. and Transl. Hugh Tredennick). Aristotle I; Loeb Classical Library #325. Cambridge, Mass: Harvard University Press, 1938.

Aristotle. *On Sophistical Refutations; On Coming-to-Be and Passing-Away* (Transl. E.S. Forster); *On the Cosmos* (Transl. D.J. Furley). Aristotle III; Loeb Classical Library #400. Cambridge, Mass: Harvard University Press, 1955.

Aristotle. *Posterior Analytics* (Ed. and Transl. Hugh Tredennick); *Topica* (Ed. and Transl. E.S. Forster). Aristotle II; Loeb Classical Library #391. Cambridge, Mass: Harvard University Press, 1960.

Aristotle. *Topics. Books I and VIII, with Excerpts from Related Texts*. Trans., Intro. and Commentary by Robin Smith. Oxford: Clarendon Press, 1997.

Badawī, ʿAbd al-Raḥmān, ed. *Manṭiq Arisṭū*. 3 Vols. Cairo: Maṭbaʿat Dār al-Kutub al-Miṣriyya, 1948.

al-Bājī, Abū al-Walīd Sulaymān. *Iḥkām al-Fuṣūl fī Aḥkām al-Uṣūl*. 2nd ed. Ed. ʿAbd al-Majīd Turkī. 2 vols. Beirut: Dār al-Gharb al-Islāmī, 1995.

al-Bājī, Abū al-Walīd Sulaymān. *Kitāb al-Minhāj fī Tartīb al-Ḥijāj* (*L'art de la Polémique: Édition Critique d'al-Minhāğ de Bāğī*). Ed. ʿAbd al-Majīd Turkī. Paris: Maisonneuve et Larose, 1978.

al-Bājī, Abū al-Walīd Sulaymān. *Al-Minhāj fī Tartīb al-Ḥijāj, ta'līf Abū al-Walīd al-Bājī; wa maʿahu al-Sirāj ʿalā al-Minhāj, li-Abī ʿAbd Allāh ʿAbd al-Salām b. Muḥammad b. ʿUmar ʿAllūsh*. Ed. ʿAbd al-Salām ʿAllūsh. Riyadh: Maktabat al-Rushd Nāshirūn, 2004.

al-Baṣrī, Abū al-Ḥusayn Muḥammad. *Kitāb al-Qiyās al-Sharʿī*. In *idem*, *Kitāb al-Muʿtamad fī Uṣūl al-Fiqh*. Ed. Muḥammad Ḥamīd Allāh, Muḥammad Bakīr, and Ḥasan Ḥanafī. Damascus: al-Maʿhad al-ʿIlmī al-Faransī li'l-Dirāsāt al-ʿArabiyya bi-Dimashq, 1964–1965, vol. 2, pp. 1029–1050.

al-Baṣrī, Abū al-Ḥusayn Muḥammad. *Kitāb al-Qiyās al-Sharʿī*. In *idem*, *al-Muʿtamad fī Uṣūl al-Fiqh*. Ed. Khalīl al-Mays. Beirut: Dār al-Kutub al-ʿIlmiyya, 1983, vol. 2, pp. 443–62.

Burkert, Walter. *The Orientalizing Revolution: Near Eastern Influence on Greek Culture in the Early Archaic Age*. Cambridge, Mass.: Harvard University Press, 1992.

EI[2] = *Encyclopaedia of Islam, Second Edition*. Ed. P. Bearman; Th. Bianquis; C.E. Bosworth; E. van Donzel; and W.P. Heinrichs. Brill Online, 2014 <http://referenceworks.brillonline.com/entries/encyclopaedia-of-islam-2>

Fallūsī, Masʿūd. *Al-Jadal ʿinda al-Uṣūliyyīn: bayna al-Naẓariyya wa'l-Taṭbīq*. Riyadh: Maktabat al-Rushd Nāshirūn, 2003.

Fischer, David Hackett. *Historians' Fallacies: Toward a Logic of Historical Thought*. New York: Harper and Row, 1970.

Gimaret, Daniel. *La doctrine d'al-Ashʿarī*. Paris : Cerf, 1990.

Goichon, A.-M. *Vocabulaires Comparés d'Aristote et d'Ibn Sīnā*. Paris: Desclée de Brouwer, 1939.

Hallaq, Wael. *A History of Islamic Legal Theories: An Introduction to Sunnī Uṣūl al-Fiqh*. Cambridge; New York: Cambridge University Press, 1997.

Hallaq, Wael. "On the Authoritativeness of Sunni Consensus." *The International Journal of Middle East Studies* 18/4 (1986): pp. 427–54.

Hallaq, Wael. "A Tenth-Eleventh Century Treatise on Juridical Dialectic." *Muslim World* 77 (1987): 197–228.

Ibn ʿAqīl, Abū al-Wafāʾ ʿAlī. *Kitāb al-Jadal ʿalā Ṭarīqat al-Fuqahāʾ* (*Le Livre de la Dialectique d'Ibn ʿAqīl*). Ed. George Makdisi. *Bulletin d'Études Orientale* 20 (1967): 119–206.

Ibn ʿAqīl, Abū al-Wafāʾ ʿAlī. *Kitāb al-Jadal ʿalā Ṭarīqat al-Fuqahāʾ*. Al-Ẓāhir [Cairo]: Maktabat al-Thaqāfa al-Dīniyya, 1980. [An unattributed reproduction of George Makdisi, ed., *Le Livre de la Dialectique d'Ibn ʿAqīl*, minus his introduction and critical apparatus].

Ibn Ḥazm, Abū Muḥammad ʿAlī. *Al-Taqrīb li-Ḥadd al-Manṭiq wa'l-Madkhal ilayhi bi'l-Alfāẓ al-ʿĀmmiyya wa'l-Amthila al-Fiqhiyya*. Ed. Aḥmad b. Farīd b. Aḥmad al-Mazīdī. Beirut: Manshūrāt Muḥammad ʿAlī Bayḍūn, Dār al-Kutub al-ʿIlmiyya, 2003.

Ibn Ḥazm, Abū Muḥammad ʿAlī. *Al-Taqrīb li-Ḥadd al-Manṭiq wa'l-Madkhal ilayhi bi'l-Alfāẓ al-ʿĀmmiyya wa'l-Amthila al-Fiqhiyya*. Ed. Iḥsān ʿAbbās. Beirut: Dār Maktabat al-Ḥayāh, 1959.

Ibn al-Nadīm, Abū al-Faraj Muḥammad. *Al-Fihrist*. Ed. Yūsuf ʿAlī Ṭawīl. Beirut: Dār al-Kutub al-ʿIlmiyya, 1996.

al-Jaṣṣāṣ, Aḥmad b. ʿAlī al-Rāzī. *Uṣūl al-Fiqh, al-Musammā bi'l-Fuṣūl fi'l-Uṣūl*. 2nd ed. Ed. ʿUjayl Jāsim al-Nashamī. 4 vols. Kuwait: Wizārat al-Awqāf wa'l-Shu'ūn al-Islāmiyya, 1994.

al-Juwaynī, Imām al-Ḥaramayn. *Al-Kāfiya fi'l-Jadal*. Ed. Fawqiya Ḥusayn Maḥmūd. Cairo: Maṭbaʿat ʿĪsā al-Bābī al-Ḥalabī, 1979.

al-Juwaynī, Imām al-Ḥaramayn. *Al-Waraqāt fī Uṣūl al-Fiqh*. In *Arbaʿa Mutūn fī Uṣūl al-Fiqh ʿalā al-Madhāhib al-Arbaʿa*. Eds. Jamāl al-Dīn al-Qāsimī and Usāma al-Balkhī. Damascus: Dār al-Balkhī, 2005.

al-Khaṭīb al-Baghdādī, Abū Bakr Aḥmad b. ʿAlī. *Kitāb al-Faqīh wa'l-Mutafaqqih*. 2nd ed. 2 Vols. Ed. Abū ʿAbd al-Raḥmān ʿĀdil b. Yūsuf al-ʿAzzāzī. Riyadh: Dār Ibn al-Jawzī, 1996.

Lane, Edward William. *An Arabic-English Lexicon*. 8 vols. Beirut: Librarie du Liban, 1968.

al-Māwardī, Abū al-Ḥasan ʿAlī b. Muḥammad. *Al-Ḥāwī al-Kabīr: fī Fiqh Madhhab al-Imām al-Shāfiʿī, wa huwa Sharḥ Mukhtaṣar al-Muzanī*. Ed. ʿAlī Muḥammad Maʿʿūd, et al. 20 vols. Beirut: Dār al-Kutub al-ʿIlmiyya, 1999.

Miller, Larry Benjamin. "Islamic Disputation Theory: A Study of the Development of Dialectic in Islam from the Tenth Through Fourteenth Centuries." PhD diss., Princeton University, 1984.

MF = *al-Mawsūʿa al-Fiqhiyya*. 45 Vols. Kuwait: Wizārat al-Awqāf wa'l-Shu'ūn al-Islāmiyya, 1990.

Pirie, Madsen. *How to Win Every Argument: The Use and Abuse of Logic*. London; New York: Continuum, 2006.

Sānū, Quṭb Muṣṭafā. *Muʿjam Muṣṭalaḥāt Uṣūl al-Fiqh, ʿArabī-Inkilīzī*. Beirut: Dār al-Fikr al-Muʿāṣir, 2000.

Schreiber, Scott G. *Aristotle on False Reasoning: Language and the World in the Sophistical Refutations*. Albany: State University of New York Press, 2003.

al-Shāshī [?]. *Uṣūl al-Shāshī: Mukhtaṣar fī Uṣūl al-Fiqh al-Islāmī, ta'līf Niẓām al-Dīn al-Shāshī, min Rijāl al-Qarn al-Sābiʿ al-Hijrī*. Ed. Muḥammad Akram al-Nadwī, with introduction by Yūsuf al-Qaraḍāwī. Beirut: Dār al-Gharb al-Islāmī, 2000.

al-Shāshī [?]. *Uṣūl al-Shāshī, li-Abī ʿAlī al-Shāshī; wa bi-Hāmishihi ʿUmdat al-Ḥawāshī li'l-Mawlā Muḥammad Fayḍ al-Ḥasan al-Kankūhī*. Ed. Khalīl al-Mays. Beirut: Dār al-Kitāb al-ʿArabī, 1982.

al-Shīrāzī, Abū Isḥāq Ibrāhīm. *Kitāb al-Maʿūna fi'l-Jadal*. Ed. ʿAbd al-Majīd Turkī. Beirut: Dār al-Gharb al-Islāmī, 1988.

al-Shīrāzī, Abū Isḥāq Ibrāhīm. *Al-Lumaʿ fī Uṣūl al-Fiqh*. Ed. Muḥyī al-Dīn Dīb Mustū and Yūsuf ʿAlī Badīwī. Damascus: Dār al-Kalam al-Ṭayyib; Dār Ibn Kathīr, 1995.

al-Shīrāzī, Abū Isḥāq Ibrāhīm. *Al-Maʿūna fi'l-Jadal*. Ed. ʿAlī b. ʿAbd al-ʿAzīz al-ʿUmayrīnī. Al-Ṣafāh, Kuwait: Manshūrāt Markaz al-Makhṭūṭāt wa-al-Turāth, 1987.

al-Shīrāzī, Abū Isḥāq Ibrāhīm. *Al-Mulakhkhaṣ fi'l-Jadal fī Uṣūl al-Fiqh*. MS Ṣanʿā', Maktabat al-Jāmiʿ al-Kabīr al-Gharbiyya bi-Ṣanʿā', No. 39 [أصول الفقه] (76 foll.; Dated: 688 H/1289 CE), [Film 25].

al-Shīrāzī, Abū Isḥāq Ibrāhīm. *Al-Mulakhkhaṣ fi'l-Jadal fī Uṣūl al-Fiqh li'l-Shaykh Abī Isḥāq Ibrāhīm b. ʿAlī b. Yūsuf al-Shīrāzī (393–476 H)*. Ed. Muḥammad Yūsuf Ākhund Jān Niyāzī. 2 vols. MA Thesis, Umm al-Qura University, 1407/1986.

Stump, Eleonore. *Dialectic and its Place in the Development of Medieval Logic*. Ithaca, N.Y.: Cornell University Press, 1989.

Turkī, ʿAbd al-Majīd. *Polémiques entre Ibn Ḥazm et Bāğī sur les Principes de la Loi Musulmane: Essai sur la Littéralisme Zahirite et la Finalité Malikite*. Alger: Société Nationale d'Édition et de Diffusion, 1975. [Translation by ʿAbd al-Ṣabūr Shāhīn: *Munāẓarāt fī Uṣūl al-Sharīʿa al-Islāmiyya bayna Ibn Ḥazm wa'l-Bājī*. Beirut: Dār al-Gharb al-Islāmī, 1986.]

Wehr, Hans. *A Dictionary of Modern Written Arabic: (Arabic-English)*. 4th Edition. Ed. J. Milton Cowan. Ithaca, N.Y.: Spoken Language Services, 1994.

Young, Walter Edward. "The Dialectical Forge: Proto-System Juridical Disputation in the Kitāb Ikhtilāf al-ʿIrāqiyyīn." 2 vols. PhD diss., McGill University, 2012.

Chapter 5
Extended Dialectical Sequences

5.1 Notes on Translation and Analysis

Materials for the Arabic Text

With regard to the Arabic text in Chaps. 5 and 6, I have, in the main, followed the *Kitāb Ikhtilāf Abī Ḥanīfa wa Ibn Abī Laylā* as found in Ḥassūn's edition of the *Kitāb al-Umm*.[1] In particular, his system of frequently dividing the text into numbered sections has proven of enormous utility.[2] Ḥassūn's edition of the *Umm* is also the only one which provides consistent—though partial—vowelling of the text. This was also of enormous utility. I have differed, however, on numerous occasions, and I have also attempted a full vowelling of the text. In sum, the Arabic text of my parallel translations is closest to Ḥassūn's edition, though with significant variants of transcription and vowelling.

---

[1] *Mawsūʿa*, vol. 9, pt. 14, pp. 7–235. Ḥassūn's edition, though lacking in extensive critical apparatus, is a praiseworthy contribution. For descriptions of the manuscripts and fragments he employed, his methods of collation, etc., see vol. 1 (Intro.), pp. 116–21, 125–6. ʿAbd al-Muṭṭalib's edition of the subject-text (*Umm*, pt. 8, pp. 217–390) boasts a much more detailed and refined critical apparatus, and has been relied upon particularly wherever interpretive difficulties arose. I have also relied on other scholarly editions, among them: Būlāq (pt. 7, pp. 87–150); and Maṭrajī (pt. 7, pp. 161–250). Ḥassūn points out numerous problems he encountered with the Būlāq edition, which he refers to by name of the Amīriyya press (*Mawsūʿa*, vol. 1 [Intro.], pp. 123–4).

[2] Schacht's numbering system—by which he made references to the subject-text and other treatises from the *Umm* in his *Origins*—was, unfortunately, unsuitable for the current project. The numbered sections by which he refers to our subject-text are more in the way of thematic groupings, and incorporate large swathes of text. Ḥassūn, on the other hand, has apportioned the text into much smaller, discrete units. Occasional errors in the sequence occur (e.g., the numbers §§880–889 were omitted, though without loss of text), but these will not effect us in the main. Rather than add yet another numbering system to the mix, I have followed Ḥassūn's.

W.E. Young, *The Dialectical Forge*, Logic, Argumentation & Reasoning 9,
DOI 10.1007/978-3-319-25522-4_5

I have also made frequent reference to the Shaybānī Version of the subject-text. Al-Afghānī's diplomatic edition,[3] with its frequent quotations from al-Sarakhsī's *Mabsūṭ*, has proven invaluable for solving some of the subject-text's more difficult passages.[4] Schacht deserves special mention here; he made frequent reference to our subject-text, and translated the occasional passage.[5] There remains, however, no readily accessible comprehensive study or commentary for our subject-text, or for the *Kitāb al-Umm* as a whole.[6]

A final note: an electronic version of the *Kitāb al-Umm*—transcribed from a Beirut edition (Dār al-Maʿrifa, 1990), and provided in the electronic library program *al-Maktaba al-Shāmila*—has been of tremendous utility in locating key terms throughout the larger *Umm* compendium.[7] Of course, this version also suffers many of the problems all too common to electronic libraries: occasional omissions, incorrect transcriptions, errors in vowelling, etc. However, cautiously employed as instantaneous indexing machines and textual databases—with results compared over and against printed editions of the text—it is impossible to conceive of a more convenient or thorough search tool than what *al-Maktaba al-Shāmila* provides. The electronic library, for all its potential failings, nevertheless constitutes a magnificent concordance.

Translation Approach

Why a parallel translation? First and foremost, none would question that translation is a hermeneutical exercise, but only to which degree; and when the subject-text was authored by one or more multiple-Others—separated from the translator by manifold removes of time, space, social and religious contexts, etc., as well as language—that degree of interpretation is presumably all the greater. There is no reason, however, that an adequate level of "accuracy" may not be attained, with proper attention paid to context, cross references to other texts, and referrals to

[3] *Ikhtilāf Abī Ḥanīfa wa Ibn Abī Laylā.*

[4] I have also directly consulted the *Mabsūṭ* myself, employing the same edition upon which al-Afghānī relied (al-Sarakhsī, *Kitāb al-Mabsūṭ*, Muḥammad Rāḍī, et al., eds.) Additional sources upon which I relied for solving difficult passages may be found in the list of references at the end of this chapter.

[5] *The Origins of Muhammadan Jurisprudence.*

[6] To my knowledge, there is only one extant commentary (*sharḥ*) for the *Kitāb al-Umm*, and it is a modern and incomplete "ordering according to the categories of derived rulings" (*tartīb ʿalā abwāb al-fiqh*) still in manuscript form at the Dār al-Kutub al-Miṣriyya, by Aḥmad Bek b. Yūsuf b. Aḥmad al-Ḥusaynī al-Muḥāmī (d.1332/1913), and titled *Murshid al-Imām li-Birr Umm al-Imām*. At 24 vols., the author had only dealt with the first books of ritual obligations (*ʿibādāt*) before his passing; I am uncertain as to whether he incorporated material from our subject-text. See Ḥibshī, *Jāmiʿ al-Shurūḥ*, vol. 1, pp. 270–1.

[7] Details regarding the program may be obtained from <http://shamela.ws/index.php/main>.

more learned scholars who have immersed themselves in the subject-text (and subject matter) to a level the translator may never attain. *Parallel* translation, nevertheless, was imperative to my aims in this particular project. Presentation of the Arabic alongside the English should prove valuable to reader and translator alike.

For the reader, it allows an opportunity to assess my translation in light of his/her own interpretation. Nothing will be hidden as in straight translation, which is oftentimes frustrating for one attempting to determine an original term or phrase with all its nuances. As for the translator, benefits were, and will be, at least two-fold: (1) parallel columns provided an easy layout for continual revision; and (2) the published translation, accompanied by the Arabic, may invite more comments and suggestions with regard to problematic passages and my interpretations of them.

I have attempted as literal a rendering as possible, in order to preserve the nuances of the Arabic text: its word order, terminology, terseness, etc. Many of my renderings into English, therefore, cannot be considered "good English;" turns of phrase are often unidiomatic, and intentionally so. I have also attempted to provide helpful markers and references; I have frequently added terms in brackets to assist the reader in grasping what I believe the textual voice intends, and made frequent recourse to Arabic-English hyphenations (e.g., *bay*ʿ-commutation rather than "sale"; *ʿitq*-manumission, *shufʿa*-preemption, *khiyār*-option, and the like). I have especially favoured Arabic-English hyphenations for technical terms and—for more important or well known terms such as *qiyās*—I have rendered them only in transliteration. Ultimately, this is a project of immersion: an attempt to put the reader into the text, and to facilitate an acquisition of our jurists' semantics and syntax. I would prefer the reader encounter—for معنى and قياس—the terms *maʿnā*-intension rather than "meaning," or *maʿnā*-quality rather than "property," and *qiyās* rather than "analogy." The Arabic terms are pregnant with technical nuances lost in straight English translation, which, consequently, has great potential to mislead.

Presentation Categories and Procedure

As I hope to have shown in Chap. 3, the whole of our subject-text constitutes dialectical material. I have therefore, of necessity, sifted through hundreds of rulings, arguments, and objections from the *Ikhtilāf al-ʿIrāqiyyayn* / *ʿIrāqiyyīn* in order to isolate an exemplary core. The material ultimately selected for deeper analysis was the most "overtly dialectical."[8] Bearing in mind the often terse and in other ways abbreviated argument presentations of our subject-text, materials requiring a greater amount of conjecture[9] received only a surface level analysis, then were

[8] Consisting, in the main, of presentation categories A, B, and C in the table following.

[9] Presentation categories D through G.

largely set aside for future study.[10] All of this will be made plain once we proceed to the analyses themselves, and the reader will gain a better sense of the principle behind my selections.

My procedure generated a set of "presentation categories"—derived from observations of the text as a whole—under which individual sections might be placed. A total of seven categories manifested themselves through this study, and a brief listing should adequately exhibit my determining criteria:

Presentations Which Are "Overtly Dialectical"

A. Extended dialectical sequences (sequence = "*in qāla* [X]; *fa-qīla lahu* [Y]", or the like), with several Q&A exchanges
B. Short dialectical sequences, with only one Q&A exchange
C. Non-sequence arguments employing dialectical formulae (e.g., "*a-ra'ayta*" and "*a-lā tarā*"), which plainly signify past or recurrent disputation

Presentations Which Are Not "Overtly Dialectical"

D. Extended arguments with no dialectical formulae
E. Short arguments with no dialectical formulae
F. Plainly-stated substantive rulings supported only by a brief reference to evidence (*naql*, *ʿaql*, or both)
G. Plainly-stated substantive rulings with no reference to evidence whatsoever

Again, I would stress that all of the material in the subject-text, whatever its presentation category, is "dialectical" insofar as it appears in a book of *ikhtilāf* and is understood to have formed the focus of past and recurring disputation. The above chart, however, should make clear the difference between material which is

[10] At the same time, none of the selected dialectical sequences are "complete" either—whether in the sense of whole from start to finish, or of preserving all the details and components of a real disputation. In consonance with the didactic aims of al-Shāfiʿī in this, and other, *ikhtilāf* treatises, the sequences of dialectic he presents are both abridged and abstracted, and, quite often, appear only as segments—singular facets of what can only have been multi-faceted and much longer debates. In terms of abridgment we are placed at a far greater disadvantage when confronted with arguments outside of Q&A sequences (presentation categories C, D, and E), and at even greater disadvantage by plain statements of substantive rulings, unaccompanied by full arguments (F and G). These latter require a significant amount of background research and conjecture—reconstituting the bases of *istidlāl* and *iʿtirāḍ* from later reports of a jurist's reasoning—in order to identify the components of such arguments, and the role they would have played in the dialectical encounters certain to have spawned them.

overtly dialectical—exhibiting the most direct, most accessible signs of past and ongoing disputation—and material which is otherwise. The focus of my analyses is the overt material of presentation categories A, B, and C.

Having isolated a core set of materials, I examined their arguments and proofs through the lens of the early *jadal*-theory texts described in Chap. 4. Note well that my *jadal*-theory analyses also constitute *uṣūl al-fiqh* analyses to some extent; the focal point of any juridical disputation is the opponent's *istidlāl*, the science of right-*istidlāl* is the science of *ijtihād*, and the science of *ijtihād* is the *ʿilm uṣūl al-fiqh*, with its systematized epistemological, hermeneutical, and rational-inferential concerns. Our jurists' *istidlāl* is often quite clearly stated, or at least indicated, in most of the presentations selected for analysis. Even when absent, however, identified *iʿtirāḍāt* presuppose a species of *istidlāl* employed by the opposing jurist whose ruling has come under critique, even if the abridged nature of the text does not present his reasoning in full, or at all. Thus, while peering through our subject-text's window onto proto-system *jadal*, we are also glimpsing the landscape of proto-system legal theory; and we will see several theories—the principles and methods of which bolster disputed *istidlāl*—become themselves the very subject of dispute.[11] This is the Dialectical Forge at work.

Analyses were first performed for presentation category A. Rather, my first analyses treated distinct *masāʾil*-sets—twelve in number—concluding in category A extended sequences. This was designed to better illustrate how *masāʾil* presentations in the subject-text unfold layer by layer, and how the various presentation categories interact. I examined the rulings, arguments, proofs, and objections from each section of each *masāʾil*-set, identifying species of *istidlāl* and *iʿtirāḍ* according to the categories of early *jadal*-theory, and to the extent which the abbreviated material allowed. I next analyzed the ten category B sequences of the subject-text—not as *masāʾil*-sets, but in isolation. Finally, rather than present full analyses for the fifty and more category C arguments, I distilled the functions of their distinctive dialectical formulae, and composed a brief exposition. As for categories D through G, I have recorded only the most obvious features revealing themselves during my categorical sifting process, and these will be summarized in the following chapter. Full analyses of these latter categories—a sampling of which proves them very rich indeed, if far less accessible—must await future study.

A final note: I have used abbreviated identification markers so that dialectical moves may be quickly referenced in the hierarchies of al-Shīrāzī and al-Bājī provided in Appendices II and III. The following table illustrates their use:

[11] The most prominent illustration of theory-oriented, as opposed to *fiqh*-oriented, dialectic is what I have labeled method-*naqḍ*. See, among other places, the analyses for §§288, 646–7, 766–7, and 1057 ff.

<table>
<tr><th>From al-Shīrāzī's Maʿūna fi'l-Jadal</th><th>From al-Bājī's Minhāj fī Tartīb al-Ḥijāj</th></tr>
<tr><td>Shīr.VII.15.2.2.3 = Invalidating Distinction by way of Correlational Inference of Resemblance (al-Farq bi-Qiyās al-Shabah)
• Shīr.VII [istidlāl domain of objection]
○ Argument Against the Intension-Property of the Instruction—meaning against Correlational Inference (al-Kalām ʿalā Maʿnā al-Khiṭāb wa huwa al-Qiyās)
• Shīr.VII.15 [genus of iʿtirāḍ]
○ Counter-Indication (Muʿāraḍa)
• Shīr.VII.15.2 [species of iʿtirāḍ]
○ Counter-Indication with the Occasioning Factor (al-Muʿāraḍa bi'l-ʿIlla)
• Shīr.VII.15.2.2 [type]
○ Counter-Indication regarding the Aṣl, which is Invalidating Distinction (Farq)
• Shīr.VII.15.2.2.3 [subtype]
○ Invalidating Distinction by way of Correlational Inference of Resemblance (al-Farq bi-Qiyās al-Shabah)</td><td>Bāj.IX.B.15.2.2.2.4 = [Q] makes distinction by way of a type of property resemblance (shabah)
• Bāj.IX [istidlāl domain of objection]
○ Objection against Drawing Indication by way of the Intension-Property of the Instruction—meaning against Correlational Inference (al-Iʿtirāḍ ʿalā al-Istidlāl bi-Maʿnā al-Khiṭāb, wa huwa al-Qiyās)
• Bāj.IX.B [full treatment of 15 modes]
• Bāj.IX.B.15 [genus of iʿtirāḍ]
○ Counter-Indication (Muʿāraḍa)
• Bāj.IX.B.15.2 [species of iʿtirāḍ]
○ Counter-Indication of the Occasioning Factor with [another] Occasioning Factor (muʿāraḍat al-ʿilla bi'l-ʿilla)
• Bāj.IX.B.15.2.2 [type]
○ Counter-Indication with the Occasioning Factor of the Source-Case—which is Invalidating Distinction (al-muʿāraḍa bi-ʿillat al-aṣl wa huwa al-farq)
• Bāj.IX.B.15.2.2.2 [subtype]
○ Invalidating Distinction by way of Indication of the Ruling (farq bi-dalālat al-ḥukm)
• Bāj.IX.B.15.2.2.2.4 [subtype of subtype]
○ [Q] makes distinction by way of a type of property resemblance (shabah)</td></tr>
</table>

5.2 *Masā'il*-Sets with Extended Dialectical Sequences

Prefatory Notes

There are twelve extended dialectical sequences (presentation category A) in the *Umm* Version of the *K. Ikhtilāf al-ʿIrāqiyyayn / ʿIrāqiyyīn*. In order to present a complete picture of the manner in which al-Shāfiʿī interacts with the past opinions of Abū Ḥanīfa, Abū Yūsuf, and Ibn Abī Laylā, I have chosen to treat category A sequences along with the rulings and opinions which precede them, as forming distinct "*masā'il*-sets." The primary analyses of this chapter are concerned with twelve *masā'il*-sets, each of which begins with a variety of presentation categories, but all of which conclude in a category A extended dialectical sequence. I will present the first five *masā'il*-sets in more detail, then revert to quicker play by play accounts for the latter seven, limiting additional observations to the footnotes.

Note also that all dialectical sequences in the subject-text (presentation categories A and B) involve a debate between al-Shāfiʿī and an anonymous opponent (R or Q)—the latter usually defending a position expressed in preceding sections by Abū Ḥanīfa, Abū Yūsuf, Ibn Abī Laylā, or a certain epistemic community (the Mashriqiyyūn, Ahl al-Baṣra, Ahl al-Kalām, et al.) No doubt owing to the presentation format of the original Shaybānī Version, we are invariably first presented with abbreviated opinions and arguments belonging to Abū Ḥanīfa, Abū Yūsuf, and Ibn Abī Laylā, followed by more detailed ones from al-Shāfiʿī. In our twelve *masā'il*-sets, these will in turn be followed by extended dialectical sequences featuring al-Shāfiʿī vs. his anonymous opponent.

Masā'il-Set #1

§§89–102 from the *Chapter on Disagreement Over Defects (Bāb al-Ikhtilāf fi'l-ʿAyb)*[12]

89 – When a man [X] contracts *bay*ʿ-commutation with a man [Y] [tied] to the *ʿaṭā'*-pension [i.e., pending distribution of X's portion of the pension];[13] then indeed Abū Ḥanīfa, may God Most High have mercy upon him, used to say regarding that: the *bay*ʿ-contract is invalid.[14]	89 - وَإِذَا بَاعَ الرَّجُلُ الرَّجُلَ بَيْعًا إِلَى الْعَطَاءِ فَإِنَّ أَبَا حَنِيفَةَ رَحِمَهُ اللهُ تَعَالَى كَانَ يَقُولُ فِي ذَلِكَ: الْبَيْعُ فَاسِدٌ.
90[a] – But Ibn Abī Laylā used to say: the *bay*ʿ-contract is permitted, but the payment-property is presently due.[15]	90[a] - وَكَانَ ابْنُ أَبِي لَيْلَى يَقُولُ: الْبَيْعُ جَائِزٌ وَالْمَالُ حَالٌّ.

(continued)

[12] Ḥassūn ed., vol. 9, pp. 25–7; ʿAbd al-Muṭṭalib ed., vol. 8, pp. 230–2.

[13] For expositions on *bay*ʿ-commutation and related rulings, see *MF*, s.v. "البيع" (vol. 9, pp. 5–42), and sub-topics (e.g., "البيع الفاسد", vol. 9, pp. 98–114); *EI*², s.v. "Bayʿ"; *DJP*, vol. 2, pp. 153–231; and Hallaq, *Sharīʿa*, pp. 247–50. See *EI*², s.v. "ʿAṭā'," for details regarding this historical pension/soldiers' pay; and also *MF*, s.v. "عطاء" (vol. 30, pp. 150–8) for a full treatment of different categories and associated substantive rulings.

[14] For §§89–90, see al-Sarakhsī, *Mabsūṭ*, vol. 13, pp. 26–7. The reasoning (*ʿaql*) and transmitted support (*naql*) for both Abū Ḥanīfa's and Ibn Abī Laylā's positions are there explained.

[15] See Lane, *Lexicon*, s.v. "دين حالّ": "A debt of which the appointed term, or period, is ended...; a debt falling due...; contr. of مُؤَجَّل...." Interestingly, though stating that Ibn Abī Laylā embraced the doctrine of ʿĀ'isha (who said that the distribution of the *ʿaṭā'* was something known by custom—early or late only rarely—and thus the contract is tied to a known term [*ajal maʿlūm*]), al-Sarakhsī's *Mabsūṭ* (vol. 13, pp. 26–7) explains his ruling (that the contract is allowed, but the property due) thus: "because when the contract is unsound due to the term which he mentioned, his mention of it is null." Rather than an argument that the *ʿaṭā'* constitutes a known term, this appears an automatic cancelling of invalid terms by operation of law. The *Mabsūṭ* thus presents us with two very different arguments for Ibn Abī Laylā: (1) ʿĀ'isha's declaration that the *ʿaṭā'* is a known term; and (2) the *ʿaṭā'* is an unknown term, but unknown terms—though by nature invalid—are auto-

90[b] – And likewise their doctrines regarding everything sold to an unknown term.[16]	90[b] - وَكَذَلِكَ قَوْلُهُمَا فِي كُلِّ مَبِيعٍ إِلَى أَجَلٍ لاَ يُعْرَفُ.
90[c] – And if the buyer [X] consumes it [i.e., what he bought from Y under invalid contract], then upon him is enjoined the value [paid to Y], according to the doctrine of Abū Ḥanīfa. And if a defect occurs in it [in X's possession, under invalid contract], he returns it, and what the defect devalued of it [to Y]. And if it remains exactly as it was,[17] and the buyer [X] says [after the invalid contract]: I don't want the [delayed] term, and I will pay you the payment-property [now]; such is permitted him as regards this, all of it, according to the doctrine of Abū Ḥanīfa.[18] And he [Abū Yūsuf] embraced it.	90[c] - فَإِنْ اسْتَهْلَكَهُ الْمُشْتَرِي فَعَلَيْهِ الْقِيمَةُ فِي قَوْلِ أَبِي حَنِيفَةَ، وَإِنْ حَدَثَ بِهِ عَيْبٌ رَدَّهُ وَرَدَّ مَا نَقَصَهُ الْعَيْبُ، وَإِنْ كَانَ قَائِمًا بِعَيْنِهِ فَقَالَ الْمُشْتَرِي: لاَ أُرِيدُ الأَجَلَ وَأَنَا أَنْقُدُ لَكَ الْمَالَ. جَازَ ذَلِكَ لَهُ فِي هَذَا كُلِّهِ فِي قَوْلِ أَبِي حَنِيفَةَ. وَبِهِ يَأْخُذُ.

(continued)

matically cancelled without invalidating the contract. Only the second argument makes sense with regard to his ruling (in §90[a]) that the contract is allowed, but the property presently due (thus cancelling the term).

[16] I.e., Abū Ḥanīfa and Ibn Abī Laylā maintain their variant solutions across all cases under the rubric "commutation tied to an unknown term." This signifies adherence to variant principles of contract: for Abū Ḥanīfa, an invalid stipulation invalidates the whole contract; but for Ibn Abī Laylā, an invalid stipulation is automatically annulled (in a way, simply ignored) and the remainder of the contract stands.

[17] The phrase is *qā'im bi-ʿaynihi*, meaning something like "existing in its (original) substance." If this is a correct interpretation, then use of the term *ʿayn* in the sense of "substance" may offer a tantalizing glimpse at the cross-fertilization of technical terms among disciplines. Van den Bergh (*EI*², s.v. "ʿAyn") notes that *ʿayn* "can also denote the effect of the function of sight, the aspect, the thing viewed, and especially in the plural, *aʿyān*, the particular things that are perceived in the exterior world." He continues: "It is therefore not astonishing when we read in K̲h̲ʷārizmī's *Mafātīḥ al-ʿUlūm*... that in an old translation of Aristotle's *Categories* which he ascribes to ʿAbd Allāh b. al-Muḳaffaʿ, the first category, οὐσία, substance, which signifies a particular concrete individual, e.g. a particular horse or a particular man, was rendered by *ʿayn*. However, in a later translation of the *Categories* by Isḥāḳ b. Ḥunayn the word *ʿayn* is replaced by the Persian word *d̲j̲awhar* and this word becomes the technical term in all later philosophy for all the meanings of οὐσία, substance." We also learn from Van den Bergh that Ibn Sīnā, in discussing the opening to Aristotle's *Hermeneutics*, "uses for the things in the exterior world (in Greek τὰ πράγματα) the term *aʿyān*." As for al-Khwārizmī's observation, it is confirmed by referencing an edition of Ibn al-Muqaffaʿ's *al-Manṭiq*, edited by Muḥammad Taqī Dānish'pazhūh and published in Tehran in 1978 (pp. 7 ff., *passim*). Abū Ḥanīfa, a contemporary of Ibn al-Muqaffaʿ, may well have understood *ʿayn* in the categorical sense of "substance."

[18] Abū Ḥanīfa thus allows party X to unilaterally 'rectify' the invalid contract after it has been concluded; al-Shāfiʿī will contest this ruling in the dialectical sequence of §§96–102.

91 – Al-Shāfiʿī, may God Most High have mercy upon him, said: And when a man [X] contracts *bay*ʿ-commutation with a man [Y] [tied] to the *ʿaṭāʾ*-pension; the *bay*ʿ-contract is invalid, due to the fact that God, to Him belong might and majesty, gave His permission for debt [tied] to a "designated" term,[19] and the "designated" is the time appointed by way of the new moons which God, to Him belong might and majesty, *designated*. For indeed He says: «They ask you about the new moons. Say: They are time-markers for the people, and for the *ḥajj*-pilgrimage» [Q.2:189]. And the new moons are well known among time-markers, along with what the intension of time-markers includes of fixed days—for verily He says: «On fixed days» [Q.22:28]—and of years, for indeed He says: «Two entire years» [Q.2:233]; and all of this is such as does not come early, or come late. But the *ʿaṭāʾ*-pension is never so, according to what I have known, and we don't opine that it will ever be anything but coming early and coming late. And even if the *imām* exercises *ijtihād* to the extremes of exertion, coming early or late would still enter into it.	91 - قَالَ الشَّافِعِيُّ رَحِمَهُ اللّٰهُ تَعَالَى: وَإِذَا بَاعَ الرَّجُلُ الرَّجُلَ بَيْعًا إِلَى الْعَطَاءِ فَالْبَيْعُ فَاسِدٌ مِن قِبَلِ أَنَّ اللّٰهُ عَزَّ وَجَلَّ أَذِنَ بِالدَّيْنِ إِلَى أَجَلٍ مُسَمًّى، وَالْمُسَمَّى الْمُوَقَّتُ بِالأَهِلَّةِ الَّتِي سَمَّى اللّٰهُ عَزَّ وَجَلَّ فَإِنَّهُ يَقُولُ: يَسْئَلُونَكَ عَنِ ٱلْأَهِلَّةِ قُلْ هِيَ مَوَٰقِيتُ لِلنَّاسِ وَٱلْحَجِّ» [البقرة: 189]. وَالأَهِلَّةُ مَعْرُوفَةُ الْمَوَاقِيتِ وَمَا كَانَ فِي مَعْنَاهَا مِنَ الأَيَّامِ الْمَعْلُومَاتِ فَإِنَّهُ يَقُولُ: «فِيٓ أَيَّامٍ مَّعْلُومَٰتٍ» [الحج: 28]. وَالسِّنِينَ فَإِنَّهُ يَقُولُ: «حَوْلَيْنِ كَامِلَيْنِ» [البقرة: 233]. وَكُلُّ هَذَا الَّذِي لاَ يَتَقَدَّمُ وَلاَ يَتَأَخَّرُ، وَالْعَطَاءُ لَمْ يَكُنْ قَطُّ فِيمَا عَلِمْتُ وَلاَ نَرَى أَنْ يَكُونَ أَبَدًا إِلاَّ يَتَقَدَّمُ وَيَتَأَخَّرُ، وَلَوِ اجْتَهَدَ الإِمَامُ غَايَةَ جَهْدِهِ لَدَخَلَهُ التَّقَدُّمُ وَالتَّأَخُّرُ.
92 – Al-Rabīʿ related to us: al-Shāfiʿī related to us, saying: Sufyān b. ʿUyayna related to us, on the authority of ʿAbd al-Karīm, on ʿIkrima, on Ibn ʿAbbās, saying: Don't contract *bay*ʿ-commutation to the *ʿaṭāʾ*-pension, nor to the [time of] threshing, nor to the [time of] pressing.	92 - أَخْبَرَنَا الرَّبِيعُ: أَخْبَرَنَا الشَّافِعِيُّ قَالَ: أَخْبَرَنَا سُفْيَانُ بْنُ عُيَيْنَةَ عَنْ عَبْدِ الْكَرِيمِ عَنْ عِكْرِمَةَ عَنِ ابْنِ عَبَّاسٍ قَالَ: لاَ تُبَايِعُوا إِلَى الْعَطَاءِ وَلاَ إِلَى الأَنْدَرِ وَلاَ إِلَى الْعَصِيرِ.
93 – Al-Shāfiʿī said: And this, all of it, is just as he [Ibn ʿAbbās] said, because it comes early or comes late.	93 - قَالَ الشَّافِعِيُّ: وَهَذَا كُلُّهُ كَمَا قَالَ؛ لأَنَّ هَذَا يَتَقَدَّمُ وَيَتَأَخَّرُ.
94 – And for every *bay*ʿ-contract [tied] to an unknown term: the *bay*ʿ-contract regarding it is invalid.[20]	94 - وَكُلُّ بَيْعٍ إِلَى أَجَلٍ غَيْرِ مَعْلُومٍ فَالْبَيْعُ فِيهِ فَاسِدٌ.
95 – Al-Shāfiʿī, may God Most High have mercy upon him, said: If a commodity, contracted for *bay*ʿ-commutation to an unknown term, is destroyed in the possession of the buyer [X], he returns the value [of that commodity, to the seller (Y)].[21] If it is devalued in his [X's] hands due to a defect, he returns it [to Y], along with whatever [amount] that defect devalued. But if the buyer [X] says: "I am content [to pay for] the commodity for a price presently due, and I nullify the condition of payment after a term"—he has no right to do such. For when the *bay*ʿ-commutation was invalidly contracted [i.e., with payment set to an unknown term], neither [X nor Y] has the right to rectify it independently of the other [i.e., unilaterally].	95 - قَالَ الشَّافِعِيُّ رَحِمَهُ اللّٰهُ تَعَالَى: فَإِنْ هَلَكَتِ السِّلْعَةُ الَّتِي أُبْتِيعَتْ إِلَى أَجَلٍ غَيْرِ مَعْلُومٍ فِي يَدَيْ الْمُشْتَرِي رَدَّ الْقِيمَةَ، وَإِنْ نَقَصَتْ فِي يَدَيْهِ بِعَيْبٍ رَدَّهَا وَمَا نَقَصَهَا الْعَيْبُ، فَإِنْ قَالَ الْمُشْتَرِي: أَنَا أَرْضَى السِّلْعَةَ بِثَمَنٍ حَالٍّ وَأَبْطَلُ الشَّرْطَ بِالأَجَلِ، لَمْ يَكُنْ ذَلِكَ لَهُ إِذَا انْعَقَدَ الْبَيْعُ فَاسِدًا لَمْ يَكُنْ لأَحَدِهِمَا أَنْ يُصْلِحَهُ دُونَ الآخَرِ.

(continued)

[19] See Q.2:282.

[20] For further reference, see *MF*, s.v. "البيع الفاسد" (vol. 9, pp. 98–114, esp. at §10), which summarizes the main points of this *masʾala*, in much the same terms, under the heading: "reasons of invalidity (*asbāb al-fasād*)" (pp. 100 ff., §§7–10).

[21] Bear in mind this is under an invalid contract—X must return the commodity. The question here is what happens if it is destroyed or damaged before he can do so.

96 – To one professing the doctrine of Abū Ḥanīfa [§90(c), third ruling], it is said: "Have you considered, having claimed that the *bay*ʿ-contract is invalid: at what point, precisely, would it become rectified?"	96 - وَيُقَالُ لِمَنْ قَالَ قَوْلَ أَبِي حَنِيفَةَ: أَرَأَيْت إِذَا زَعَمْتَ أَنَّ الْبَيْعَ فَاسِدٌ فَمَتَى صَلَحَ؟
97 – And if he says: "It would become rectified by so-and-so's [X's] nullification of his stipulation [of delayed payment to an unknown term]."	97 - فَإِنْ قَالَ: صَلَحَ بِإِبْطَالِ هَذَا شَرْطَهُ.
98 – It is said to him: "And does so-and-so [X] have the right to act as [both] seller [and] buyer, or does he merely remain the buyer, while the original owner of the commodity [Y] remains the seller?"	98 - قِيلَ لَهُ: فَلِهَذَا أَنْ يَكُونَ بَائِعًا مُشْتَرٍ، أَوْ إِنَّمَا هَذَا مُشْتَرٍ وَرَبُّ السِّلْعَةِ بَائِعٌ؟
99 – And if he says: "Well, of course the owner of the commodity [Y] remains the seller."	99 - فَإِنْ قَالَ: بَلْ رَبُّ السِّلْعَةِ بَائِعٌ.
100 – It is said to him: "And does the owner of the commodity [Y] occasion a *bay*ʿ-contract besides the first *bay*ʿ-contract?"	100 - قِيلَ لَهُ: فَهَلْ أَحْدَثَ رَبُّ السِّلْعَةِ بَيْعًا غَيْرَ الْبَيْعِ الْأَوَّلِ؟
101 – And if he says: "No."	101 - فَإِنْ قَالَ: لاَ.
102 – It is said: "Then your doctrine is contradictory. For you claim that an invalid *bay*ʿ-contract whose ruling is like that in which no *bay*ʿ-commutation came about, nevertheless becomes a [valid] *bay*ʿ-contract—without the proprietor in that contract [Y] having ever contracted it!"	102 - قِيلَ: فَقَوْلُكَ مُتَنَاقِضٌ تَزْعُمُ أَنَّ بَيْعًا فَاسِدًا حُكْمُهُ كَمَا لَمْ يَصِرْ فِيهِ بَيْعٌ يَصِيرُ بَيْعًا مِن غَيْرِ أَنْ يَبِيعَهُ مَالِكُهُ.

The abridged presentation of rulings for Abū Ḥanīfa and Ibn Abī Laylā in §§89–90a at first precludes any discussion of the arguments which lay behind them. With reference to the *Mabsūṭ*,[22] and later sections of this *mas'ala*, however, we can set the stage for the ensuing dialectic of al-Shāfiʿī vs. R in §§96–102, by noting the conflicting supporting traditions (*āthār*) and *ʿilla*-interpretations upon which Abū Ḥanīfa and Ibn Abī Laylā are reported to have based their opposing arguments. As for Abū Ḥanīfa, we are told in the *Mabsūṭ* that he followed an *athar*-tradition of Ibn ʿAbbās, who declared *bay*ʿ-commutation tied to distribution of the *ʿaṭā'*-pension (among other things) was invalid (*fāsid*; cf. al-Rabīʿ in §92 above); Ibn Abī Laylā, however, followed an *athar*-tradition of ʿĀ'isha, who allowed *bay*ʿ-commutation tied to distribution of the *ʿaṭā'*-pension. From the start, then, and from one perspective, we can identify the source of *ikhtilāf* between Abū Ḥanīfa and Ibn Abī Laylā as "opposition of indicants" (*taʿāruḍ al-adilla*)—in the broadest sense, the supporting *athar*-tradition of one represents a *muʿāraḍa* of the *athar*-tradition of the other.

By the fourth and fifth centuries H, reliance upon a decree of a solitary Companion (*qawl al-wāḥid min al-Ṣaḥāba*) for proof (*ḥujja*) had become a far more contentious practice. Still—were we to assume that Abū Ḥanīfa and Ibn Abī Laylā, or associates and students, actually engaged in disputation over this *mas'ala*—we

[22] Rāḍī, et al. eds., vol. 13, pp. 26–7.

can easily locate the broader dialectical objection which either side might have brought as an initial *i'tirāḍ*, in the *jadal* works of al-Shīrāzī, Ibn ʿAqīl, and al-Bājī.[23] For al-Shīrāzī, it is the third *iʿtirāḍ* of *al-Kalām ʿalā Qawl al-Wāḥid min al-Ṣaḥāba*, which he defines as: "[Q] conveys disagreement (*khilāf*) from another Companion, in order to make of the *mas'ala* a disagreement (*khilāf*) between the Companions" (Shīr.IV.3; Bāj.V.2). The definitions of Ibn ʿAqīl and al-Bājī for this *iʿtirāḍ* follow that of their teacher for the most part, with slight variations regarding methods of response.

It is immediately apparent—from the following section §90a, wherein the core property of the *mas'ala* in dispute is clearly indicated—that there is a deeper level to this Abū Ḥanīfa vs. Ibn Abī Laylā *ikhtilāf*. Simply put, the distribution of *ʿaṭā'* is deemed by all to constitute a term (*ajal*), but *ikhtilāf* centers upon precisely what species of *ajal* it is: Is it an *ajal* which is known (*maʿlūm*), or unknown (*ghayr maʿlūm*)? Reference to al-Sarakhsī's explanation in the *Mabsūṭ* brings us back to the respective *āthār*-traditions followed by Abū Ḥanīfa and Ibn Abī Laylā, but we also learn more as regards their purported interpretations and subsequent reasoning; i.e., we gain insight into the reasoned support (*ʿaql*) as well as the transmitted support (*naql*) of *ikhtilāf*. Ibn Abī Laylā reasoned that "the *bayʿ*-commutation is permitted (*jā'iz*) and the property is presently due; because when the contract (*ʿaqd*) is not sound due to the *ajal* he mentioned, his mention of it is null." Moreover, al-Sarakhsī informs us that "ʿĀ'isha used to say: The time of the distribution of the *ʿaṭā'* is known via custom (*maʿlūm bi'l-ʿurf*)—its distribution only rarely comes late—so this is commutation set to a known term (*bayʿ bi-ajal maʿlūm*)."

As for the Ḥanafī position reported by al-Sarakhsī, it is, in its base essentials, the same as that argued by al-Shāfiʿī in §§91–3 above. In brief: (1) the *ʿaṭā'* distribution is a human act (*fiʿl al-ʿibād*) which might come early or late; (2) terms are known by way of designated times (*awqāt*), not anticipated acts (*afʿāl*); (3) Q.2:189 confirms the "time-markers" (*mawāqīt*) as fixed times for terms; (4) Prophetic Sunna (re: the *salam*-contract) shows the stipulation (*sharṭ*) of advanced-payment contracts to be announcement of the term (for delivery)—a known term (*ajal maʿlūm*); (5) announcement of the term is by what does not come early or late; and (6) what comes early or late of human acts (*afʿāl al-ʿibād*) is unknown (*majhūl*).

Assuming the respective positions of Abū Ḥanīfa and Ibn Abī Laylā were debated in dialectical venues, much more would have followed subsequent to the opposition of opposing *āthār*-traditions. We will note that Ibn Abī Laylā's position appears to have rested upon two bases: (1) a supplementary explanation by ʿĀ'isha of her decree (*ʿaṭā'* is an *ajal maʿlūm*); and (2) his own considered opinion (*ra'y*) regarding the non-efficiency of an unknown term in occasioning a *ḥukm* of invalid commutation—it merely nullifies the *sharṭ*-stipulation, and the *bayʿ*-contract perseveres as

[23] al-Shīrāzī, *Maʿūna*, al-ʿUmayrīnī ed., pp. 82 f.; Ibn ʿAqīl, *K. al-Jadal*, pp. 39 f.; al-Bājī, *Minhāj*, Turkī ed., p. 144, §298.

that species whose payment/exchange is immediately due (no *dalīl*-indicant for this reasoning being given by al-Sarakhsī).

As we see in al-Sarakhsī's report, however, the Ḥanafī position appears much stronger, relying upon Qur'ānic and Sunnaic *adilla*-indicants to support a definition of *ajal maʿlūm* as a term fixed by the clockwork of the heavens, and divorced from the imprecise anticipation of human acts (such as *ʿaṭā'* distribution). Importantly, we are assured by al-Shāfiʿī's nearly identical argument in §§91–3 that these indicants and interpretations were employed by those arguing Abū Ḥanīfa's position as early as the late second century H. We will turn soon to al-Shāfiʿī's argument, in an attempt to identify his *istidlāl*, and to infer his *iʿtirāḍ* against Ibn Abī Laylā's position. Before we do so, however, I will attempt the same for Ibn Abī Laylā and Abū Ḥanīfa, benefiting from al-Sarakhsī's explanation.

We are limited by not knowing the *aṣl* of either Abū Ḥanīfa or Ibn Abī Laylā (although Q.2:282 presented by al-Shāfiʿī in §91 is a likely candidate for *istidlāl bi-dalīl al-khiṭāb*), but we have been provided the core focus of *ikhtilāf*: the precision of distribution of *ʿaṭā'* as an *ajal*-term. We have, in other words, been provided a proposed *ʿilla* and counter-*ʿilla* for the *farʿ* of *bayʿ*-commutation tied to the *ʿaṭā'*. For Abū Ḥanīfa, following the *athar*-tradition of Ibn ʿAbbās, the *ʿaṭā'*-distribution constitutes a property (*waṣf*)—it is an unknown term (*ajal ghayr maʿlūm*)—which is efficient in occasioning the *ḥukm* of invalid (*fāsid*) for the *bayʿ*-contract. For Ibn Abī Laylā, however, following the *athar*-tradition of ʿĀ'isha, it constitutes the opposite *waṣf*—it is a known term (*ajal maʿlūm*)—which is efficient in occasioning the *ḥukm* of permitted (*jā'iz*). The beginning of a dispute between proponents of these opposing properties, then, would be an objection to the opponent's proposed *waṣf* as existing in the *farʿ*, which is a subspecies of an *iʿtirāḍ*—denial of the property in the source-case (*manʿ al-waṣf fi'l-aṣl*)—we find in the *jadal* works of al-Shīrāzī, Ibn ʿAqīl, and al-Bājī (Shīr.VII.4; Bāj.IX.6.1.2).[24]

Of particular note is al-Bājī's discussion. After supplying an example of *manʿ al-waṣf fi'l-aṣl*, he proceeds to delineate three methods of response against such an *iʿtirāḍ*: (1) explanatory exegesis (*tafsīr*); (2) explaining the locus of concession (*bayān mawḍiʿ al-taslīm*); and (3) indication (*dalāla*). If we were to imagine a proponent of Abū Ḥanīfa's position (*ʿaṭā'* is an unknown term [*ajal ghayr maʿlūm*]) faced with a denial (*manʿ/mumānaʿa*) of the *waṣf*-property of *ajal ghayr maʿlūm* as existing in the *farʿ* of *bayʿ*-commutation tied to the *ʿaṭā'*, we can tentatively locate the Ḥanafī reasoning—as reported by al-Sarakhsī—in the first and third of al-Bājī's response-methods. In other words, al-Sarakhsī's reported Ḥanafī reasoning constitutes, in fact, two kinds of *jawāb* to an opponent's objection that *ʿaṭā'* is not an *ajal ghayr maʿlūm*: (1) *tafsīr* (the human act might come early or late; terms are known by way of fixed times, not anticipated acts); and (2) *dalāla* (Q.2:128; Prophetic Sunna for the *salam*-contract).

---

[24] al-Shīrāzī, *Maʿūna*, al-ʿUmayrīnī ed., p. 96; Ibn ʿAqīl, *K. al-Jadal*, p. 50, §251; al-Bājī, *Minhāj*, Turkī ed., p. 166, §§357 and 359.

Switching the roles, however, does not produce the same result, and we find that al-Sarakhsī's reported reasoning for Ibn Abī Laylā does not constitute a defence of ʿĀ'isha's *waṣf*-property (*ʿaṭā'* is a known term [*ajal maʿlūm*]). In fact, it points to a different line of reasoning altogether: Ibn Abī Laylā argues that any *sharṭ*-stipulation which ties the *bay*ʿ-contract to an unknown term is simply (and automatically) nullified; that is to say, the *waṣf* of *ajal ghayr maʿlūm* is efficient in occasioning the nullification (*ibṭāl*) of the *sharṭ*-condition—not the invalidity (*ifsād*) of the whole *bay*ʿ-contract, and the contract lives on as a valid *bay*ʿ-contract of immediate payment/exchange (the *māl* is *ḥāll*).[25] Note that Ibn Abī Laylā is now making a general argument for all *bay*ʿ-contracts tied to an unknown term, rather than a particular argument about the *ajal*-nature of *ʿaṭā'*.[26] Accordingly, there is a shift in focus from *ʿilla* in the *far*ʿ to *ʿilla* in the *aṣl* (although Ibn Abī Laylā's *dalīl*-indicant remains hidden from us). In essence, Ibn Abī Laylā has accepted the efficiency of the *ʿilla* in the *aṣl*, but objected to what Abū Ḥanīfa purports to be the effect—it is as though the same *ʿilla* occasions a different *ḥukm* for Ibn Abī Laylā (*ibṭāl al-sharṭ*) than it occasions for Abū Ḥanīfa (*ifsād al-bay*ʿ). Imagining an adherent to Ibn Abī Laylā's reported reasoning in the role of Q, we might conjecture as to the type of *iʿtirāḍ* he would level against a proponent of the Abū Ḥanīfa position. Not knowing the precise *istidlāl* of either position makes this difficult, but most likely it would be similar to that genus of *iʿtirāḍ* known as *al-qawl bi-mūjib al-ʿilla*.[27]

To this point my analyses have been marked by conjecture and the drawing of reported arguments from a significantly later source: the *Mabsūṭ* of al-Sarakhsī (d.483/1090). Due to the abridged form in which the positions and arguments of Abū Ḥanīfa, Ibn Abī Laylā, and Abū Yūsuf almost invariably occur in the *Kitāb Ikhtilāf al-ʿIrāqiyyīn* (presentation categories F-G), there is usually no alternative. This is far less often the case with al-Shāfiʿī, however, for although his rulings and supporting arguments are also abridged to some extent, we are more frequently presented with his *adilla*-indicants and rational explanations—not to mention the occasional Q&A dialectic against an anonymous opponent. Before approaching that dialectical sequence, however, I will conclude my analysis of the *mas'ala* of *bay*ʿ-commutation tied to an unknown term by reviewing al-Shāfiʿī's ruling (*bay*ʿ-commutation tied to the *ʿaṭā'* is invalid) and his accompanying argument.

---

[25] Support for this interpretation of Ibn Abī Laylā's argument is found in the early *ikhtilāf* work of al-Ṭabarī (d.310/923), wherein the famed polymath says: "And the *ʿilla* of one who says: The *bay*ʿ-contract is permitted when the terms are unknown: it is that the *bay*ʿ-contract is one *maʿnā*-quality, and the postponement (*taʾjīl*) another, so permissibility for the *bay*ʿ-contract is not nullified due to the invalidity (*fasād*) of the unknown term (*al-ajal al-majhūl*)—such being like an invalid stipulation (*al-sharṭ al-fāsid*). And the *ʿilla* of one who nullifies the *bay*ʿ-contract by way of a *sharṭ*-stipulation of invalid term (*al-ajal al-fāsid*) is like the one whose *ʿilla* nullifies the *bay*ʿ-contract by way of invalid stipulation (*al-sharṭ al-fāsid*)" (*Ikhtilāf al-Fuqahā'*, Kern ed., p. 54).

[26] Cf. §90[b], above, where the respective Abū Ḥanīfa and Ibn Abī Laylā positions are maintained across all *buyū*ʿ tied to an unknown *ajal*.

[27] (Shīr.VII.9 [especially type 2]; Bāj.IX.8) al-Shīrāzī, *Maʿūna*, al-ʿUmayrīnī ed., pp. 108 ff.; Ibn ʿAqīl, *K. al-Jadal*, pp. 60 f., §290 ff.; al-Bājī, *Minhāj*, Turkī ed., pp. 173 ff., §§381 ff.

Al-Shāfiʿī's *istidlāl* is clearly indicated in §91 by "due to the fact that God, to Him belong might and majesty, gave His permission for debt [tied] to a 'designated' term (*dayn ilā ajal musamman*)"—a reference to Q.2:282.[28] Although this looks like plain "Drawing Indication from the Qur'ān" (*al-istidlāl bi'l-Kitāb*) at first, we must remember that our *mas'ala* is one of unknown term (*ajal ghayr maʿlūm*)—the opposite, in fact, of designated term (*ajal musamman*). The *istidlāl* of al-Shāfiʿī in this instance thus resembles that species known as "[Restrictive] Indicant of the Instruction" (*dalīl al-khiṭāb*). In other words, when we know from the unambiguous *naṣṣ* of the Qur'ān that God allows debt tied to a designated term (*dayn ilā ajal musamman*), we can infer that God does *not* allow debt tied to an *un*designated term (*dayn ilā ajal ghayr musamman*).[29] Importantly, al-Shīrāzī (in his *Lumaʿ*) cites Ibn Surayj—a founding father of both *uṣūl al-fiqh* and juridical *jadal*—as saying: "If [the instruction] is by way of a conditional expression (*lafẓ al-sharṭ*), like His saying, Most High: «if a sinner should come to you (*in jā'akum fāsiqun*)...»,[30] it provides indicant that what is outside of [sinner] is [judged] by its contradictory (*khilāf*). And if it is not via a conditional expression, it does not provide indicant—and this is the doctrine of some Ḥanafīs."[31] The *istidlāl* of al-Shāfiʿī in §91 conforms very

---

[28] «يَا أَيُّهَا الَّذِينَ آمَنُوا إِذَا تَدَايَنْتُمْ بِدَيْنٍ إِلَى أَجَلٍ مُسَمًّى...» Al-Ṭabarī's juridical exegesis (*tafsīr*) of this verse sheds light upon its connection to *bay*ʿ-commutation tied to a known term (*al-Aḥkām al-Fiqhiyya*, Ismāʿīl ed., pp. 189–90). First, he interprets "when you contract debt" (*idhā tadāyantum*) as "when you contract commutation" (*idhā tabāyaʿtum*, or *ishtaraytum*) etc.; and "to a designated term" (*ilā ajal musamman*) as "to a known time (*waqt maʿlūm*) which you have fixed between yourselves." He then mentions the latter might include interest-free loan (*qarḍ*) and advanced-payment sale (*salam*), and implies the possibility of "commutation of lawfully sold, present property for term-specified payment" (*bayʿ al-ḥāḍir al-jā'iz bayʿahu min al-amlāk bi'l-athmān al-mu'ajjala*). All of these, he says, are "term-specified debts tied to a designated term (*al-duyūn al-mu'ajjala ilā ajal musamman*), when their terms are known to a precisely designated limit." Interestingly, he concludes by saying: "And Ibn ʿAbbās used to say: This verse was revealed regarding advanced-payment sale (*salam*), specifically (*khāṣṣatan*)." If such a "reason for revelation" (*sabab al-nuzūl*) was indeed attributed to Ibn ʿAbbās in al-Shāfiʿī's time, then we might conceive of another layer of complexity in al-Shāfiʿī's *istidlāl* from this verse—as supported by another saying of Ibn ʿAbbās. In other words, if Ibn ʿAbbās was thought to have considered this verse *salam*-specific, an opponent might have objected to al-Shāfiʿī's twinning his *bay*ʿ-oriented *athar*-tradition with his *istidlāl* from the Qur'ān.

[29] Cf. al-Shīrāzī's examples of *dalīl al-khiṭāb* (*Maʿūna*, al-ʿUmayrīnī ed., pp. 35–6). Note that al-Shāfiʿī's *istidlāl* above does not conform, however, to al-Bājī's *istidlāl bi'l-ḥaṣr*, which is restricted to ruling-pronouncements preceded by the *lafẓ*-expression of "only" (*innamā*); nor does it belong to the additional markers al-Bājī attributes to his teacher al-Shīrāzī (*alif lām*, *dhālika*, and *iḍāfa*)—with which al-Bājī disagrees (*Minhāj*, Turkī ed., pp. 25–6, §46; cf. al-Shīrāzī, *al-Lumaʿ*, Mustū ed., pp. 105–6, §115). Sānū's definitions, however (*Muʿjam*, s.v. "دليل الخطاب" and "مفهوم المخالفة"), are certainly broad enough to include al-Shāfiʿī's *istidlāl* above. Finally, I should note al-Shīrāzī reviews all of the variant opinions regarding *dalīl al-khiṭāb* and its restrictions in his *Tabṣira* (Hītū ed., pp. 218–39).

[30] Q.49:6.

[31] al-Shīrāzī, *Lumaʿ*, Mustū ed., p. 106.

well to these parameters, as God's *qawl* in Q.2:282 employs the conditional sign *idhā*. The association of this form of *dalīl al-khiṭāb* with "some Ḥanafīs" (*ba'ḍ Aṣḥāb Abī Ḥanīfa*) also provides indication that Abū Ḥanīfa's ruling of §89 may have depended upon the same *istidlāl* as al-Shāfiʿī in §91.

Al-Shāfiʿī proceeds to fine-tune his initial *istidlāl* by fixing a definition of designated term (*ajal musamman*)—based upon a number of Qur'ānic indicants—to the clockwork of the "new moons," never early or late, and divorcing it from human acts in much the same way as al-Sarakhsī ascribes to proponents of the Ḥanafī position. He then seals his *istidlāl* by assuring us that *ʿaṭā'*-distribution is of the very opposite nature, regardless of the Imam's most strident efforts in keeping on schedule. The Qur'ānic indicants, then, constitute a form of explanatory exegesis (*tafsīr*) via Qur'ānic indication (*dalāla*). As for al-Shāfiʿī's closing justification, however, it is difficult to identify by the categories of our *jadal*-theory lens-texts; I will simply consider "from what we have seen, the *ʿaṭā'* never comes but early or late" to be an empirical, inductive argument.

At this point we encounter an editorial comment from al-Rabīʿ who, in §92, relates an *athar*-tradition of Ibn ʿAbbās—narrated to him by al-Shāfiʿī himself, on the authority of his teacher Sufyān b. ʿUyayna—which is largely the same as that which al-Sarakhsī reports as a *dalīl*-indicant for the Ḥanafī ruling we find in §89 (minus a few human acts). Note that Ibn ʿAbbās proscribes *buyūʿ* tied to a number of human acts, and al-Rabīʿ reports al-Shāfiʿī's extraction of the *ʿilla* from this *athar*-tradition in §93: because all of this "comes early or comes late." Thus, with the help of al-Rabīʿ's comments, we gain a rounded picture of al-Shāfiʿī's argument: it is *istidlāl bi-dalīl al-khiṭāb*, refined by *tafsīr* from Qur'ānic *adilla*-indicants and supported by *istidlāl bi-qawl al-wāḥid min al-Ṣaḥāba*. With the general efficiency of his *ʿilla* thus confirmed, we learn in §94 that al-Shāfiʿī extended his ruling (the *bayʿ*-contract is invalid) to the entire genus of *bayʿ*-contracts tied to an unknown *ajal*-term.

We are approaching the first extended dialectical exchange of the *K. Ikhtilāf al-ʿIrāqiyyayn / ʿIrāqiyyīn*.[32] In §95 al-Shāfiʿī revisits the same subsidiary *masā'il* upon which Abū Ḥanīfa ruled in §90[c], agreeing with all but the last. As this disagreement marks the point of departure for the ensuing dialectic, I will briefly review it here, first noting: (1) it occurs within the larger *mas'ala* of a commutative contract (*bayʿ*) whose payment is tied to an unspecified term (*ajal*); and (2) Abū Ḥanīfa earlier ruled (in §90[c]) that—if the object of commutation "remains exactly as it was" (*qā'im bi-ʿaynihi*)—it is allowed that the buyer dismiss his condition (*sharṭ*) of payment tied to a term, and offer to pay in ready-property (*māl*). Al-Shāfiʿī, to the contrary, declares the buyer has no such right; rather, he claims: "when the *bayʿ*-commutation was invalidly contracted [i.e., with payment set to an unknown term] (*inʿaqada... fāsidan*), neither [X nor Y] has the right to rectify it (*yuṣliḥahu*)

[32] In terms of presentation types, §§96–102 is category A, while §§89–90 were both G, and §§91–4, collectively, category D.

independently of the other [i.e., unilaterally]." He then presents his supporting argument by way of a concise disputation-sequence—an "instructional" dialectic—with a proponent of Abū Ḥanīfa's ruling.[33]

Al-Shāfiʿī assumes the role of Q in §96, and clarifies the disposition of his opponent (which we are normally left to infer ourselves) by way of the introductory formula: "To one professing the doctrine of Abū Ḥanīfa, it is said... (*Yuqālu li-man qāla qawl Abī Ḥanīfa...*)," the referenced doctrine (*qawl*) being Abū Ḥanīfa's ruling in §90(c). He then launches his first dialectical question via one of the two staple formulae of proto-system dialectical practice, across both juridical and theological domains: *a-ra'ayta*—meaning, roughly, "Have you considered [the consequent problem that...?]"[34] We will see this question-formula put to a number of uses in following excerpts, but in this instance it serves to focus R's attention upon the problem of determining the precise moment at which the commutative contract—which R concedes is invalid (*fāsid*)—purportedly becomes rectified. In effect, al-Shāfiʿī's opening *a-ra'ayta* sets the stage for what progresses into a premise-by-premise unveiling of his opponent's self-contradiction—a classic species of *reductio*, in successive stages.[35]

R's first response, presented via the instructional formula "and if he says... (*fa-in qāla...*)," is a direct answer to al-Shāfiʿī's opening *a-ra'ayta*. R defines the precise moment of the claimed rectification: at party X's nullification (*ibṭāl*) of his condition (*sharṭ*)—i.e., the condition of tying his payment to an imprecise term (*ajal*). R thus delivers to al-Shāfiʿī the first two premises (of four), from which al-Shāfiʿī will eventually construct his charge of self-contradiction (*tanāquḍ*). For in this first response, R has conceded not only premise (#1): the precise moment of purported rectification (*iṣlāḥ*), when the invalid commutative contract becomes sound, but he has also conceded premise (#2): verifying the agency of contracting-party X.

Al-Shāfiʿī brings his second dialectical question, presented via the instructional formula "it is said to him... (*qīla lahu...*)," in §98. Here, he confronts his opponent with an absurdity (essentially, a non-*endoxon* situation), with regard to which only a denial can be expected. Is it possible, after all, for party X to embody both buyer and

---

[33] I label §§96–102 as "instructional" dialectic due to the didactic intent evinced by the formulae employed: "To one professing the doctrine of Abū Ḥanīfa, it is said: 'X.' And if he says: 'Y;' It is said to him: 'Z;' etc." The sequence reads as a script for the jurist who might find himself in the role of Q undermining a proponent with Abū Ḥanīfa's position. Note that I have attempted, throughout this study, to consistently refer to the proto-system juridical dialectic of the *Umm* as "*jadal* teaching and practice." This is intended to suggest a mode of *jadal*-tradition transmission from jurist to student across generations, and in lieu of specialized, systematic treatises. §§96–102, and all the many dialectical sequences preserved in the *Umm* for that matter, stand witness to a proto-system *jadal* teaching and practice. Some sequences have more of a "historical" character ("And one of the people [*baʿḍ al-nās*] said to me: 'X;' so I said to him: 'Y;' etc."); while others—such as that which presently concerns us—have a more "instructional" character; and yet others meld both intentions together.

[34] The other formula is *a-lā tarā*, meaning, roughly, "Do you not [yourself] see/opine...?"

[35] Whenever *ra'ā* formulae appear in analyzed sequences, I will identify them by categories which will be reviewed at the end of Chap. 6. Al-Shāfiʿī's *a-ra'ayta* in §96 is dialogical, and pushes concession to premises for a final charge of *tanāquḍ*.

seller? The aim is to elicit R's concession that party X can only ever be the buyer, and that the owner of the commodity (*rabb al-silʿa*) can only ever be the seller—thus confirming the buyer as acting unilaterally in his nullification (*ibṭāl*) of his own condition (*sharṭ*). As expected, in §99 R denies this absurdity, and, in conceding that the owner of the commodity can only be the seller, in effect confirms the seller's lack of agency, and the unilateral agency of the buyer. Thus, from his opponent, al-Shāfiʿī acquires premise (#3) for his charge of self-contradiction (*tanāquḍ*).

With his final question in §100, al-Shāfiʿī presses his opponent for one last concession; mainly, that the seller has nowhere introduced a new commutative contract (*bayʿ*). R concedes this in §101, thus delivering premise (#4) to al-Shāfiʿī. Now, in §102, we at last encounter al-Shāfiʿī's tersely formulated *elenchus*:

> Then your doctrine is contradictory. For you claim that an invalid *bayʿ*-contract whose ruling is like that in which no *bayʿ*-commutation came about, nevertheless becomes a [valid] *bayʿ*-contract without the proprietor in that contract [Y] having ever contracted it!

This *elenchus*-statement consists of two parts. First comes the charge of self-contradiction (*tanāquḍ*). Second comes a demonstration of that self-contradiction, by way of a succinct laying-out of R's conceded premises, in abbreviated form. Note that, to complete our understanding of this elenchus, we must acknowledge a premise which has been taken for granted by the disputants; mainly, that no commutation can be contracted without participation of the seller. Such a proposition is understandably lacking; stating it, in fact, is tautologous. Note also that al-Shāfiʿī leads off with a premise he never elicited from his opponent; being quintessential to the definition of an invalid commutative contract (*bayʿ fāsid*), however, we must accept it would be assumed, or pre-conceded, by an opponent. The components of al-Shāfiʿī's *elenchus*-statement thus appear as follows:

"...an invalid *bayʿ*-contract whose ruling is like that in which no *bayʿ*-commutation came about...	• [assumed premise: an *endoxon* description of an invalid commutative contract]
...nevertheless becomes a [valid] *bayʿ*-contract...	• [from conceded premise #1]
...without the proprietor in that contract [Y]...	• [from conceded premises ##1, 2, and 3]
...having ever contracted it!"	• [from conceded premise #4]

The results of this analysis may come as something of a surprise: for all that its premises contain substantive legal matter, the disputation of §§96–102 does not conform to the expectations instilled from a perusal of the lens-texts—neither with regard to question, nor to epistemic justification, nor to objection. There is some resemblance here to the *iʿtirāḍ* of *naqḍ*, but the hallmark of *naqḍ*—Q's bringing a parallel case wherein R's *ʿilla* produces a contradictory *ḥukm*, i.e., a *mas'alat al-naqḍ*—is missing. Missing, too, is any mention of *adilla*-indicants, or hermeneutic, or modes of *uṣūl*-associated reasoning. In short, the domain of juridical *jadal* as we have come to expect from the lens-texts should be the domain of *istidlāl* and the problematizing of an opponent's *istidlāl*. In §§96–102, however, we encounter the reduction of an opponent's professed solution (*qawl*) to an internal, logical contradiction. The *qawl*-solution is exposed as self-contradicting—a *qawl mutanāqiḍ*, which may be rendered as follows:

Opponent's Assumptions / Concessions:	**Universe:**
1. ¬(B without an S) 2. F = ¬B 3. claim: F becomes a B without an S **Contradiction:** ¬(B without an S) & (B without an S)	• B = a contract in which valid commutation (*bay'*) occurs • F = an invalid commutative contract (*bay' fāsid*) • S = a contracting seller

This analysis of the first extended disputation sequence in the subject-text reveals something much closer in appearance to an Aristotelian *elenchus* via *reductio ad impossibile*, than an *elenchus* via the objections (*i'tirāḍāt*) of the early *jadal*-theory texts. This is not usually the case with the remaining sequences, most of which—though roughly at times—correspond to later systems of *jadal*. The fact, however, that this particular example appears so Aristotelian—focusing upon an internal, logical contradiction, as opposed to a problem of *istidlāl*—provides an important insight into the character of proto-system juridical dialectic, and the more ancient argumentation epistemes still manifest in its teaching and practice.

Masā'il-Set #2

§§236–67 & 270–2 from the *Chapter on Preemption* (*Bāb al-Shuf'a*)[36]

236 – When the right to preemption involves an orphan [O];[37] then indeed Abū Ḥanīfa, may God Most High have mercy upon him, used to say: The preemption belongs to him [O]; and if he has a *waṣiyy*-guardian [G], then he [G] takes it [i.e., the property subject to preemption] via [O's] right to preemption. And if he doesn't have a *waṣiyy*-guardian, he comes into his right to preemption upon attaining legal maturity. And if the *waṣiyy*-guardian does not demand right to preemption after knowing it exists; then no right to preemption belongs to the orphan when he matures.[38]	236 - وَإِذَا كَانَتِ الشُّفْعَةُ لِلْيَتِيمِ فَإِنَّ أَبَا حَنِيفَةَ رَحِمَهُ اللَّهُ تَعَالَى كَانَ يَقُولُ: لَهُ الشُّفْعَةُ فَإِنْ كَانَ لَهُ وَصِيٌّ أَخَذَهَا بِالشُّفْعَةِ. وَإِنْ لَمْ يَكُنْ لَهُ وَصِيٌّ كَانَ عَلَى شُفْعَتِهِ إِذَا أَدْرَكَ، فَإِنْ لَمْ يَطْلُبِ الْوَصِيُّ الشُّفْعَةَ بَعْدَ عِلْمِهِ، فَلَيْسَ لِلْيَتِيمِ شُفْعَةٌ إِذَا أَدْرَكَ.

(continued)

[36] Ḥassūn ed., vol. 9, pp. 50–5; ʿAbd al-Muṭṭalib ed., vol. 8, pp. 246–53.

[37] For expositions on *shuf'a*-preemption and related rulings, see *MF*, s.v. "شفعة" (vol. 26, pp. 136–69); *EI*², s.v. "Shuf'a"; *DJP*, vol. 2, pp. 307–16; and Hallaq, *Sharī'a*, pp. 306–7.

[38] Ḥassūn (in *Umm*, vol. 9, p. 50, n. 2) notes that in his manuscript ك this section begins with "al-Rabīʿ reported to us, saying: al-Shāfiʿī said…" (أخبرنا الربيع قال: قال الشافعي). Al-Afghānī (in Abū Yūsuf, *Ikhtilāf*, p. 37, n. 2) quotes al-Sarakhsī (no page citation): "And according to the opinion (*qawl*) of Muḥammad and Zufar the right to preemption (*shuf'a*) belongs to him when he attains legal

237 – And likewise [with regard to] the boy, when his father is alive. And he [Abū Yūsuf] embraced it.	237 - وَكَذَلِكَ الْغُلاَمُ إِذَا كَانَ أَبُوهُ حَيًّا. وَبِهِ يَأْخُذُ.
238 – But Ibn Abī Laylā used to say: No right to preemption belongs to the minor.[39]	238 - وَكَانَ ابْنُ أَبِي لَيْلَى يَقُولُ: لاَ شُفْعَةَ لِلصَّغِيرِ.
239 – And Abū Ḥanīfa, may God Most High have mercy upon him, said: The right to preemption belongs to the partner who did not partition [his part of the shared room/house].[40] After him, it belongs to the partner who partitioned, so long as between them is [but] one passageway. And, after him, it belongs to the adjoining neighbour; and, when the neighbours are gathered about, and their adjacency is all equal, then they are partners in the preemption.[41]	239 - وَقَالَ أَبُو حَنِيفَةَ رَحِمَهُ اللهُ تَعَالَى: الشُّفْعَةُ لِلشَّرِيكِ الَّذِي لَمْ يُقَاسِمْ وَهِيَ بَعْدَهُ لِلشَّرِيكِ الَّذِي قَاسَمَ، وَالطَّرِيقُ وَاحِدَةٌ بَيْنَهُمَا، وَهِيَ بَعْدَهُ لِلْجَارِ الْمُلاَصِقِ، وَإِذَا اجْتَمَعَ الْجِيرَانُ وَكَانَ الْتِصَاقُهُمْ سَوَاءً فَهُمْ شُرَكَاءُ فِي الشُّفْعَةِ.

(continued)

maturity (*adraka*); and it is the opinion of Ibn Abī Laylā. We have explained it in the [book of] *shuf'a*-preemption."

[39] Schacht (*Origins*, pp. 271–2) finds the debate over this *mas'ala* (§48 by Schacht's system; §§236–8 by Ḥassūn's) symptomatic of his decline paradigm:

> On the exercise of a minor's right of preemption, Abū Ḥanīfa, followed by Abū Yūsuf, holds a reasonable and defensible opinion. Shaibānī, however, with complete disregard for the stability of real property, applies purely formal reasoning (see Sarakhsī, xiv. 155; xxx. 145); in this he is followed by Shāfi'ī. Both seem to lose sight of the purpose of preemption and to regard it as an institution existing for its own sake. This attitude heralds the end of the formative period of Muhammadan law.

[40] This is a reference to commixion; that is to say, "the *shuf'a*-preemption belongs to the partner in a partnership of commixion." Hallaq (*Origins*, p. 44, n. 47) defines this relationship as follows: "Partnership of commixion refers to a property owned by two or more persons without clear definition of their individual shares in it, such as a residential property inherited by two or more persons."

[41] Al-Afghānī (in Abū Yūsuf, *Ikhtilāf*, p. 37, n. 3) writes: "And it is the doctrine (*qawl*) of his two companions [i.e., Abū Yūsuf and al-Shaybānī]. And the *mas'ala* is in vol. 14, p. 94 of the *Mabsūṭ*. He [al-Sarakhsī] said: 'And this, i.e., the doctrine of 'Alī and Ibn 'Abbās [cf. §241], is the doctrine of the Ahl al-Madīna [the "Folk of Medina," meaning its legal scholars], but the Ahl al-Kūfa don't subscribe to it, except that Ibn Abī Laylā turned to it (etc.) But as for us, we embrace the doctrine of 'Umar.'" Schacht (*Origins*, pp. 219 f.) discusses this *mas'ala* and its implications in considerable detail:

> The following example, taken from the doctrine of pre-emption, will show how cross-references to other schools enter into the development of legal doctrine in the pre-literary period. The result of this development, as it affected pre-emption, was that two opposite doctrines prevailed in the Medinese and the Iraqian school respectively: the Medinese restricted the right of pre-emption to the owner of a share in undivided property, and the Iraqians extended it to the neighbor. [Here he cites (n.6) not only this section (§49 by his system), but two recensions of the *Muwaṭṭa'*, the *Āthār* works of both Abū Yūsuf and al-Shaybānī, the *K. Ikhtilāf Mālik wa'l-Shāfi'ī*, and the *K. Ikhtilāf al-Ḥadīth*.] The oldest Iraqian formula, however, was that 'the right of pre-emption goes by gates, and

240 – And Ibn Abī Laylā used to profess the doctrine of Abū Ḥanīfa, until Abū al-ʿAbbās, Amīr al-Mu'minīn[42] wrote to him, ordering that he not pass judgment for *shufʿa*-preemption except in favour of the partner who did not partition; so he embraced that [doctrine], and judged only in favour of the partner who did not partition—this being the doctrine of the Ahl al-Ḥijāz.[43]	240 - وَكَانَ ابْنُ أَبِي لَيْلَى يَقُولُ بِقَوْلِ أَبِي حَنِيفَةَ حَتَّى كَتَبَ إِلَيْهِ أَبُو الْعَبَّاسِ أَمِيرُ الْمُؤْمِنِينَ يَأْمُرُهُ أَنْ لاَ يَقْضِيَ بِالشُّفْعَةِ إِلاَّ لِلشَّرِيكِ الَّذِي لَمْ يُقَاسِمْ، فَأَخَذَ بِذَلِكَ وَكَانَ لاَ يَقْضِي إِلاَّ لِلشَّرِيكِ الَّذِي لَمْ يُقَاسِمْ. وَهَذَا قَوْلُ أَهْلِ الْحِجَازِ.

(continued)

the person whose gate is nearest has the best right to pre-emption'; it was projected back to Ibrāhīm Nakhaʿī as his alleged former opinion, and on the fictitious authority of Ibrāhīm back to Shuraiḥ. This formula, which reflects the social background of the institution of pre-emption in early Muhammadan law, seems to be the common starting-point of the Medinese and of the Iraqian doctrines. [fn.7: A tradition in Kindī... reflects the change in Egypt from the common ancient to the final Medinese doctrine, and the arguments adduced in favour of the latter.]

The Basrians, while essentially maintaining this opinion, justified it as against the Medinese restriction of the right of pre-emption by pointing out that the lane, on which the several adjoining plots abutted, remained undivided and constituted an interest common to them all. The earlier Kufians, on the other hand, extended the right of pre-emption to all owners of plots within a single block or section not traversed by a thoroughfare, irrespective of whether the plots adjoined or opened on the same lane. Final systematic consistency was achieved in Iraq only in the time of Abū Ḥanīfa and his companions who gave the right to pre-emption to the owner of a share in undivided property in the first place [fn.1: This distinction is perhaps the result of further reference to the Medinese doctrine], then to the owner of a separate plot who had, however, retained a common interest in the lane, and finally to the owner of an adjoining plot. [fn.2: This opinion was also projected back to Shuraiḥ (Sarakhsī, xiv. 92)].

[42] That is, the first ʿAbbāsid Caliph, al-Saffāḥ (r. 132–6/750–4).

[43] This allusion to a caliph's interference in a matter of substantive law may illustrate larger issues contested in modern scholarship. See, among others, Crone and Hinds, *God's Caliph*; Zaman, *Religion and Politics*; and a very relevant discussion in Hallaq, *Origins*, pp. 43 ff. An isolated occurrence in the subject-text, it may serve as indicant for variant claims. On the one hand, it may support a claim that early caliphs were legislators, or pressured jurists. Or it may be read as polemic—a slight against the integrity of Ibn Abī Laylā, bound by his judgeship (unlike Abū Ḥanīfa), and disallowed from administering the "right" doctrine. But it may also illustrate a caliph-*qāḍī*-jurist symbiosis. The issue, after all, begins with jurists' *ikhtilāf*, itself arising from the conflicting doctrines/practices of ʿAlī, Ibn ʿAbbās, and ʿUmar; and, in the end, al-Saffāḥ is not imposing a self-made, novel decree, but that of the Ahl al-Ḥijāz ("Folk of Hejaz"; meaning its legal scholars), and he applies it to the real practice of a *qāḍī* in his court. Nor should we be surprised—considering the nature of the ʿAbbāsid *daʿwā*—that its first caliph would lean on a *qāḍī* straddling the Umayyad-ʿAbbāsid divide to abandon the doctrine of ʿUmar and take up that of ʿAlī and Ibn ʿAbbās. Most interesting of all, however, is what Hallaq (*Origins*, p. 44) relates of an earlier caliph-*qāḍī* dialogue on very nearly the same subject:

> The *qāḍī*s' practice of writing letters seeking caliphal opinion on difficult cases confronting them in their courts was evidently a common one. So were caliphal letters to the *qāḍī*s, most of which appear to have been solicited, although some were written on the sole initiative of the caliph himself or—presumably—in his name, by his immediate advisors. Iyās [b. Muʿāwiya: *qāḍī* in Baṣra], for instance, used to grant neighbours—merely by

241 – And likewise it has reached us on the authority of ʿAlī and Ibn ʿAbbās, may God Most High be pleased with them both.	241 - وَكَذَلِكَ بَلَغَنا عَن عَلِيٍّ وَابْنِ عَبَّاسٍ رضي الله تعالى عنهما.
242 – Al-Shāfiʿī, may God Most High have mercy upon him, said, on the authority of ʿAbd Allāh b. Muḥammad b. ʿAbbād, on al-ʿAwwām, on Yaḥyā b. Saʿīd, on ʿAwn b. Abī Rāfiʿ, on ʿUbayd Allāh b. ʿAbd Allāh b. ʿUmar, who said: ʿUmar b. al-Khaṭṭāb said: When boundaries occur, there is no *shufʿa*-preemption.[44]	242 - قَالَ الشَّافعيُّ رَحِمَهُ اللهُ تعالى عَن عَبْدِ اللهِ بْنِ مُحَمَّدِ بْنِ عَبَّادٍ، عَنِ العَوَّامِ، عَن يَحْيَى بْنِ سَعِيدٍ، عَن عَوْنِ بْنِ أَبِي رَافِعٍ، عَن عُبَيْدِ اللهِ بْنِ عَبْدِ اللهِ بْنِ عُمَرِ، قَالَ: قَالَ عُمَرُ بْنُ الخَطَّابِ: إِذَا وَقَعَتِ الحُدُودُ فَلاَ شُفْعَةَ.
243 – Al-Shāfiʿī reported to us, on the authority of ʿAbd Allāh b. Idrīs, on Muḥammad b. ʿUmāra, on Abū Bakr b. Jarīr, on Abān b. ʿUthmān, who said: When alleyways occur, there is no *shufʿa*-preemption. And the alleyways are the boundaries.	243 - أَخْبَرَنَا الشَّافِعِيُّ عَن عَبْدِ اللهِ بْنِ إِدْرِيسَ، عَن مُحَمَّدِ بْنِ عُمَارَةَ، عَن أَبِي بَكْرِ بْنِ جَرِيرٍ، عَن أَبَانَ بْنِ عُثْمَانَ، قَالَ: إِذَا وَقَعَتِ الأَزِقَّةُ فَلاَ شُفْعَةَ. وَالأَزِقَّةُ الحُدُودُ.
244 – Al-Shāfiʿī, may God Most High have mercy upon him, said: Muʿallā b. Asad reported to us, he said: ʿAbd al-Wāḥid b. Ziyād transmitted to us, on the authority of al-Ḥajjāj, on al-Ḥakam, who said: [He said:] When boundaries occur, there is no *shufʿa*-preemption.	244 - قَالَ الشَّافعيُّ رَحمَه اللهُ تَعالى: أَخْبَرَنَا مُعَلَّى بْنُ أَسَدٍ، قَالَ: حَدَّثَنا عَبْدُ الوَاحِدِ بْنُ زِيَادٍ، عَنِ الحَجَّاجِ، عَنِ الحَكَمِ، قَالَ: [قال] إِذَا وَقَعَتِ الحُدُودُ فَلاَ شُفْعَةَ.

(continued)

virtue of being neighbours—the right of preemption (*shufʿa*), a practice that did not seem to accord, for some reason, with caliphal public policy. On hearing of Iyās' practice, ʿUmar II (99/717–101/720) wrote a letter ordering him to confine preemption rights to domiciles having a shared right of access (e.g., two houses sharing one gate) and to properties owned as partnerships of commixion [citing (n.47) the *Akhbār al-Quḍāt* of Wakīʿ]. The same caliph wrote to another *qāḍī* in Egypt imposing a similar, but even more restrictive decree, saying: 'We used to hear (*kunnā nasmaʿ*) that preemption rights can be enjoyed by the partner only, not by the neighbor' [citing (n.48) the *Akhbār Quḍāt Miṣr* of al-Kindī]. It seems reasonable to infer that many *qāḍī*s were in the habit of bestowing rights of preemption on the neighbor, and this caliph deemed it necessary to intervene.

44 Here in §§242–44 (and without notice) Ḥassūn includes text relegated to nearly identical footnotes in the Būlāq (vol. 7, p. 100, n. 1), Maṭrajī (vol. 7, p. 176), and ʿAbd al-Muṭṭalib (vol. 8, p. 247, n. 5) editions. These notes are all preceded by the phrase: "Here, in some of the copies, there is more; this is its text…" followed by nearly the same transcription as in Ḥassūn's edition. There are some very minor differences—in §244, Būlāq (but not Maṭrajī and ʿAbd al-Muṭṭalib) reads حجاج , rather than الحجاج ; and there are, in Būlāq and Maṭrajī (but not ʿAbd al-Muṭṭalib), two adjacent *qālas*.

245[a] – Al-Shāfiʿī, may God Most High be pleased with him, said: And when a portion from the house is sold, there belonging to an orphan the right of preemption for it, or to a boy under the protective-guardianship of his father; the guardian of the orphan, and the father, have the right to take [it]—on behalf of the one for whom they are guardian, by right of preemption—if it is felicitous [to do so]. And if they don't do so; then when the two [orphan and boy] attain the capacity to administer their own property, they have the right to take [it] by way of preemption. And when they find out after attainment of that capacity, and they proceed to forsake [it]—in such a way that if the *bay*ʿ-commutation occurs in that circumstance, and they forsake it, their *shufʿa*-preemption is terminated—then their *shufʿa*-preemption is indeed terminated.	245[a] - قَالَ الشَّافِعِيُّ رضي الله تعالى عنه: وَإِذَا بِيعَ الشِّقْصُ مِن الدَّارِ وَلِلْيَتِيمِ فِيهِ شُفْعَةٌ أَوْ الْغُلاَمِ فِي حِجْرِ أَبِيهِ، فَلِوَلِيِّ الْيَتِيمِ وَالأَبِ أَنْ يَأْخُذَا لِلَّذِي يَلِيَانِ بِالشُّفْعَةِ إنْ كَانَتْ غِبْطَةً، فَإِنْ لَمْ يَفْعَلاَ فَإِذَا بَلَغَا أَنْ يَلِيَا أَمْوَالَهُمَا كَانَ لَهُمَا الأَخْذُ بِالشُّفْعَةِ، فَإِذَا عَلِمَا بَعْدَ الْبُلُوغِ فَتَرَكَا التَّرْكَ الَّذِي لَوْ أَحْدَثَ الْبَيْعَ فِي تِلْكَ الْحَالِ فَتَرَكَاهُ انْقَطَعَتْ شُفْعَتُهُمَا فَقَدْ انْقَطَعَتْ شُفْعَتُهُمَا .
245[b] – And there is no preemption except for what is not partitioned; and when boundaries occur, there is no *shufʿa*-preemption.	245[b] - وَلاَ شُفْعَةَ إلاَّ فِيمَا لَمْ يُقْسَمْ فَإِذَا وَقَعَتِ الْحُدُودُ فَلاَ شُفْعَةَ.
246 – And likewise if they divide among themselves the house and land, leaving between them a passageway, or leaving between them a trough/fountain; there is no preemption. Nor do we oblige preemption for what is partitioned, in partnership, of passageway, nor of water.	246 - وَكَذَلِكَ لَوْ اقْتَسَمُوا الدَّارَ وَالأَرْضَ وَتَرَكُوا بَيْنَهُمْ طَرِيقًا أَوْ تَرَكُوا بَيْنَهُمْ مَشْرَبًا لَمْ تَكُنْ شُفْعَةٌ، وَلاَ نُوجِبُ الشُّفْعَةَ فِيمَا قُسِمَ بِشِرْكٍ فِي طَرِيقٍ وَلاَ مَاءٍ.
247 – And some of the Ahl al-Baṣra[45] have subscribed [only] to the general part of our doctrine, saying: There is no preemption except for what is between the partnership members; so, when there remains between the members a passageway—owned by them [jointly]—or a trough/fountain—owned by them [jointly]—then, though house and land are partitioned, there is [still] preemption regarding them, because they are [yet] partners in some property.[46] And they [the Ahl al-Baṣra] transmitted a *ḥadīth*—on the authority of ʿAbd al-Malik b. Abī Sulaymān, on ʿAṭāʾ, on Jābir, on the Prophet, may God bless and save him—resembling this *maʿnā*-intension, [but] which I regard to both possibly bear a resemblance to this *maʿnā*-intension, and to possibly bear its opposite: He [the Prophet] said: «The neighbour has the greater right due to his nearness when the [intervening] passageway is [but] one.»[47]	247 - وَقَدْ ذَهَبَ بَعْضُ أَهْلِ الْبَصْرَةِ إلَى جُمْلَةِ قَوْلِنَا فَقَالُوا: لاَ شُفْعَةَ إلاَّ فِيمَا بَيْنَ الْقَوْمِ الشُّرَكَاءِ، فَإِذَا بَقِيَتْ بَيْنَ الْقَوْمِ طَرِيقٌ مَمْلُوكَةٌ لَهُمْ أَوْ مَشْرَبٌ مَمْلُوكٌ لَهُمْ فَإِنْ كَانَتِ الدَّارُ وَالأَرْضُ مَقْسُومَةً فَفِيهَا شُفْعَةٌ؛ لأَنَّهُمْ شُرَكَاءُ فِي شَيْءٍ مِنَ الْمِلْكِ وَرَوَوْا حَدِيثًا عَن عَبْدِ الْمَلِكِ بْنِ أَبِي سُلَيْمَانَ، عَن عَطَاءٍ، عَن جَابِرٍ، عَن النَّبِيِّ - صَلَّى اللَّهُ عَلَيْهِ وَسَلَّمَ - شَبِيهًا بِهَذَا الْمَعْنَى أَحْسَبُهُ يَحْتَمِلُ شَبِيهًا بِهَذَا الْمَعْنَى وَيَحْتَمِلُ خِلاَفَهُ؛ قَالَ: «الْجَارُ أَحَقُّ بِسَقَبِهِ إذَا كَانَتِ الطَّرِيقُ وَاحِدَةً.»

(continued)

[45] The "Folk of Baṣra," meaning its scholars.

[46] That is, because they are partners in the (unpartitioned) passageway (*ṭarīq*) or trough/fountain (*mashrab*).

[47] Ḥassūn (*Umm*, vol. 9, p. 52, n. 1) and ʿAbd al-Muṭṭalib (*Umm*, vol. 8, p. 249, n. 1) define *saqab* as "nearness" (*qurb*). Ḥassūn further notes: "He who obliges the right to *shufʿa*-preemption for the neighbor (*jār*)—even if he is not a partner (*muqāsim*)—argues by way of this *ḥadīth* (*yaḥtaju bi-hādhā al-ḥadīth*)." I have followed ʿAbd al-Muṭṭalib insofar as the placement of quotation marks, as it seems likely the transmitted Prophetic statement included "when the passageway (*ṭarīq*) is but one" (Ḥassūn leaves that outside). In the *Ikhtilāf al-Ḥadīth* attributed to al-Shāfiʿī

248 – And the only thing that prevents us from professing this doctrine is that Abū Salama and Abū al-Zubayr audited Jābir; and that one of our Ḥijāzīs transmits—on the authority of ʿAṭāʾ, on Jābir, on the Prophet, may God bless and save him, regarding *shufʿa*-preemption—something which doesn't have this [*maʿnā*-intension of the Ahl al-Baṣra] in it, but has its contrary.[48] And two [transmitters]—when they concur on the transmission on Jābir's authority, while the third is in concordance with them—are superior in affirming the *ḥadīth*, to when it diverges from the third.[49] And the [efficient] property by which we prevent *shufʿa*-preemption for what is partitioned is conspicuously-existent in this partitioned thing.[50]	248 - وَإِنَّمَا مَنَعَنَا مِن الْقَوْلِ بِهَذَا أَنَّ أَبَا سَلَمَةَ وَأَبَا الزُّبَيْرِ سَمِعَا جَابِرًا، وَأَنَّ بَعْضَ حِجَازِيِّينَا يَرْوِي عَن عَطَاءٍ، عَن جَابِرٍ، عَن النَّبِيِّ - صَلَّى اللّٰهُ عَلَيْهِ وَسَلَّمَ - فِي الشُّفْعَةِ شَيْئًا لَيْسَ فِيهِ هَذَا وَفِيهِ خِلاَفُهُ، وَكَانَ اثْنَانِ إِذَا اجْتَمَعَا عَلَى الرِّوَايَةِ عَن جَابِرٍ وَكَانَ الثَّالِثُ يُوَافِقُهُمَا أَوْلَى بِالتَّثَبُّتِ فِي الْحَدِيثِ إِذَا اخْتَلَفَ عَن الثَّالِثِ، وَكَانَ الْمَعْنَى الَّذِي بِهِ مَنَعْنَا الشُّفْعَةَ فِيمَا قُسِمَ قَائِمًا فِي هَذَا الْمَقْسُومِ.
249 – Don't you see/opine that the *khabar*-report on the authority of the Prophet, may God bless and save him, is: «Verily *shufʿa*-preemption is for what was not partitioned, and when boundaries occur, there is no *shufʿa*-preemption»? Yet no one who professes this doctrine [of the Ahl al-Baṣra] finds a way out from having made *shufʿa*-preemption for that in which boundaries occur.	249 - أَلاَ تَرَى أَنَّ الْخَبَرَ عَن النَّبِيِّ - صَلَّى اللّٰهُ عَلَيْهِ وَسَلَّمَ -: «إِنَّ الشُّفْعَةَ فِيمَا لَمْ يُقَسَّمْ، فَإِذَا وَقَعَت الْحُدُودُ فَلاَ شُفْعَةَ» وَلاَ يَجِدُ أَحَدٌ قَالَ بِهَذَا الْقَوْلِ مَخْرَجًا مِن أَنْ يَكُونَ قَدْ جَعَلَ الشُّفْعَةَ فِيمَا وَقَعَتْ فِيهِ الْحُدُودُ.

(continued)

(and included in many editions of the *Umm*), the Jābir-ʿAbd al-Mālik transmission reads: [الجار أحق بشفعته ينتظر بها وإن كان غائبا إذا كانت الطريق واحدة]—that is, "the neighbour has the greater right to his *shufʿa*-preemption—because of it he is waited for, even if absent—when the passageway is but one" (ʿAbd al-Muṭṭalib [*Umm*, vol. 10, p. 215] and Najjār [*Umm*, vol. 8, p. 536] render this entire phrase in quotations; but Maṭrajī [*Umm*, vol. 9, p. 608] provides no quotation marks at all, and neither does the Būlāq edition [*Umm*, vol. 7, p. 264 (margin)]). As noted by Lane (*Lexicon*, s.v. "سقب"), it may also be that *saqab*—though bearing the connotation of "nearness"—was intended to mean *shufʿa*. Thus, the phrase *al-jār aḥaqq bi-saqabihi* might be rendered "the neighbour has the greater right to his *shufʿa*-preemption"—in consonance with the Jābir-ʿAbd al-Mālik transmission in the *Ikhtilāf al-Ḥadīth*. I have, however, preferred "... due to his nearness;" the dialectical sequence of §§252 ff. makes it plain that "nearness" was a key point of contention.

48 Schacht (*Origins*, p. 155) cites al-Shāfiʿī's *K. Ikhtilāf al-Ḥadīth* where the Ahl al-Baṣra's *ḥadīth* on Jābir is discussed, noting: "Shāfiʿī mentions that the specialists on traditions suspect it because of Jābir's doctrine to the contrary."

49 The first two transmissions are (1) Abū Salama – Jābir – Prophet; and (2) Abū al-Zubayr – Jābir – Prophet; and they accord with a third, which is (3a) Ḥijāzī – ʿAṭāʾ – Jābir – Prophet; but if we take the Ahl al-Baṣra *ḥadīth* as the third—(3b) ʿAbd al-Mālik b. Abī Sulaymān – ʿAṭāʾ – Jābir – Prophet—they are contrary in intension. Thus the first combination of 1, 2, and 3a is epistemically superior.

50 That is to say, the efficient property (*maʿnā*) which, for al-Shāfiʿī, occasions the ruling of no *shufʿa*-preemption, is present in the house or land separated by the passageway or fountain/trough in §247.

250 – So if he says: Indeed, I have only made [*shufʿa*-preemption] for that in which boundaries occur, because something of the property remains in which boundaries did *not* occur...[51]	250 - فَإِنْ قَالَ: فَإِنِّي إِنَّمَا جَعَلْتُهَا فِيمَا وَقَعَتْ فِيهِ الْحُدُودُ؛ لأَنَّهُ قَدْ بَقِيَ مِنَ الْمِلْكِ شَيْءٌ لَمْ تَقَعْ فِيهِ الْحُدُودُ.
251 – It is said: Then it is possible that one bring about *shufʿa*-preemption in that remaining thing. And if it is possible, then make [the *shufʿa*-preemption] for it [alone]; and don't make it for that in which boundaries occur, and you will have followed the [Prophetic] *khabar*-report.[52] But if it is not possible; don't bring about the *shufʿa*-preemption in something else!	251 - قِيلَ: فَيَحْتَمِلُ ذَلِكَ الْبَاقِي أَنْ يَجْعَلَ فِيهِ الشُّفْعَةَ. فَإِنْ احْتَمَلَ فَاجْعَلْهَا فِيهِ وَلاَ تَجْعَلْهَا فِيمَا وَقَعَتْ فِيهِ الْحُدُودُ فَتَكُونُ قَدِ اتَّبَعْتَ الْخَبَرَ، وَإِنْ لَمْ يَحْتَمِلْ فَلاَ تَجْعَلِ الشُّفْعَةَ فِي غَيْرِهِ.
252 – And some of the Easterners said:[53] The right to preemption belongs to the neighbour, and to the partner, when the neighbour is immediately adjacent, or when there exists—between the sold house and the house in which his right to preemption obtains—a court of some kind, so long as there is no open and public passageway in it. But if there is an open and public passageway in it—however narrow—the neighbour has no right to preemption.	252 - وَقَالَ بَعْضُ الْمَشْرِقِيِّينَ: الشُّفْعَةُ لِلْجَارِ وَلِلشَّرِيكِ إِذَا كَانَ الْجَارُ مُلاَصِقًا، أَوْ كَانَتْ بَيْنَ الدَّارِ الْمَبِيعَةِ وَالدَّارِ الَّتِي لَهُ فِيهَا الشُّفْعَةُ رَحْبَةٌ مَا كَانَتْ إِذَا لَمْ يَكُنْ فِيهَا طَرِيقٌ نَافِذَةٌ، وَإِنْ كَانَ فِيهَا طَرِيقٌ نَافِذَةٌ وَإِنْ ضَاقَتْ فَلاَ شُفْعَةَ لِلْجَارِ.

(continued)

[51] That being the intervening but jointly-owned passageway or fountain/trough in §247.

[52] In other words, if the lots are separated by a passageway or fountain/trough for which *shufʿa*-preemption is lawful, then the *shufʿa*-preemption applies only to that intervening passageway or fountain/trough—not to the lots separated by it.

[53] This reference to "The Easterners" (al-Mashriqiyyūn) provides an indicant for the intellectual groupings and trends, and geo-political diffusions, of al-Shāfiʿī's times. In fact, he refers to "al-Mashriqiyyūn," or to "Baʿḍ al-Mashriqiyyīn," or to the "Aṣḥāb al-Mashriqiyyīn," some thirty-six times throughout the *Umm*. An explanation is offered by al-Rabīʿ who, in the context of a chapter on juridical disagreement regarding apostates (*al-khilāf fiʾl-murtadd*), explains al-Shāfiʿī's references as follows (*Umm*, Ḥassūn ed., vol. 7, pt. 12, p. 627, §23834): "When he [al-Shāfiʿī] says: some of the people (*baʿḍ al-nās*); they are the Mashriqiyyūn. And when he says: one of our companions (*baʿḍ aṣḥābinā*), or one of the folk of our country (*baʿḍ ahl baladinā*); it is Mālik." Yet another clue surfaces in the dialectic of the *Kitāb Ikhtilāf Mālik waʾl-Shāfiʿī*, during a discussion of the *imām* who must remain seated throughout the duration of prayer due to illness (*Umm*, Ḥassūn ed., vol. 9, pt. 14, p. 368, §§178–9): "So I said to al-Shāfiʿī: And has any one of the Mashriqiyyūn professed your doctrine (*qawl*)? And he said: Yes, Abū Ḥanīfa professes our doctrine regarding it, but his two companions [i.e., Abū Yūsuf and al-Shaybānī] disagree with him (*yukhālifuhu ṣāḥibāhu*)." From these references, we gather that Abū Ḥanīfa was among the Mashriqiyyūn, but Mālik was not. We might conclude that the term was used in a similar way as "Iraqis"—a means of distinguishing such jurists who were not a part of, or did not subscribe to, the doctrines current in the Ḥijāz. Elsewhere in the *K. Ikhtilāf Mālik waʾl-Shāfiʿī* we learn that among the Mashriqiyyūn there are *ḥadīth* specialists (Ahl al-Ḥadīth; see *Umm*, Ḥassūn ed., vol. 9, pt. 14, p. 374, §§201–3). It is also significant that, for the most part, al-Shāfiʿī tends to call the Mashriqiyyūn by this name when the attributed doctrine conflicts with his own; it is certain that he does not include himself in this group. Moreover, the Mashriqiyyūn often appear in contrast with "Our Companions" (*aṣḥābunā*) (see, e.g., such references as occur in the *K. Ibṭāl al-Istiḥsān*, in *Umm*, Ḥassūn ed., vol. 10, pt. 15, p. 134, §§146 ff.) Significantly, so far as I have yet discovered, the only other reference to the Mashriqiyyūn among the books of the Shāfiʿī *madhhab* is that of al-Māwardī (d.450/1058), in his commentary on the *Mukhtaṣar al-Muzanī* (see *al-Ḥāwī al-Kabīr*, Maʿʿūd, et al., eds., vol. 5, pp. 307–8).

253 – We said to one who professes this doctrine: Upon which thing did you (pl.) rely [for proof]?	253 - قُلْنَا لِبَعْضِ مَنْ يَقُولُ هَذَا الْقَوْلَ: عَلَى أَيِّ شَيْءٍ اعْتَمَدْتُمْ؟
254 – He said: Upon the *athar*-tradition: Sufyān b. ʿUyayna reported to us, on the authority of Ibrāhīm b. Maysara, on ʿAmr b. al-Sharīd, on Abī Rāfiʿ, that the Messenger of God, may God bless and save him, said: «The neighbour has the greater right due to his nearness.»[54]	254 - قَالَ: عَلَى الأَثَرِ؛ أَخْبَرَنَا سُفْيَانُ بْنُ عُيَيْنَةَ، عَن إِبْرَاهِيمَ بْنِ مَيْسَرَةَ، عَن عَمْرِو بْنِ الشَّرِيدِ، عَن أَبِي رَافِعٍ أَنَّ رَسُولَ اللهِ - صَلَّى اللهُ عَلَيْهِ وَسَلَّمَ - قَالَ: «الْجَارُ أَحَقُّ بِسَقَبِهِ.»
255 – So it was said to him: This [tradition] does not contradict our *ḥadīth*, but is a general/non-specific type, while our *ḥadīth* is an interpreting type.[55]	255 - فَقِيلَ لَهُ: فَهَذَا لاَ يُخَالِفُ حَدِيثَنَا، وَلَكِنَّ هَذَا جُمْلَةٌ وَحَدِيثُنَا مُفَسِّرٌ.
256 – He said: And how does it not contradict your (pl.) *ḥadīth*?	256 - قَالَ: وَكَيْفَ لاَ يُخَالِفُ حَدِيثَكُمْ؟
257 – We said: The partner who did not partition is called "neighbour," and the one who partitions is [so] called, and the one for whom there are forty houses between you and him is [so] called; so there is not allowed, as regards this *ḥadīth*, except what we said: it pertains to some "neighbours" and not to others. But our saying this is not granted against [the opinions of] others except by way of indication, on the authority of the Messenger of God, may God bless and save him. For when the Messenger of God, may God bless and save him, said: «*shufʿa*-preemption is for what was not partitioned, and when boundaries occur, there is no *shufʿa*-preemption», this provides indicant that his saying in the general/non-specific [tradition]: «The neighbour has the greater right due to his nearness» pertains to some "neighbours" and not others, and that he [the intended] is the "neighbour" who did not partition.	257 - قُلْنَا: الشَّرِيكُ الَّذِي لَمْ يُقَاسِمْ يُسَمَّى جَارًا وَيُسَمَّى الْمُقَاسِمَ، وَيُسَمَّى مَنْ بَيْنَكَ وَبَيْنَهُ أَرْبَعُونَ دَارًا، فَلَمْ يَجُزْ فِي هَذَا الْحَدِيثِ إلاَّ مَا قُلْنَا مِن أَنَّهُ عَلَى بَعْضِ الْجِيرَانِ دُونَ بَعْضٍ. فَإِذَا قُلْنَاهُ لَمْ يَجُزْ ذَلِكَ لَنَا عَلَى غَيْرِنَا إلاَّ بِدَلاَلَةٍ عَن رَسُولِ اللهِ - صَلَّى اللهُ عَلَيْهِ وَسَلَّمَ - فَلَمَّا قَالَ رَسُولُ اللهِ - صَلَّى اللهُ عَلَيْهِ وَسَلَّمَ: «الشُّفْعَةُ فِيمَا لَمْ يُقْسَمْ، فَإِذَا وَقَعَتِ الْحُدُودُ فَلاَ شُفْعَةَ» دَلَّ هَذَا عَلَى أَنَّ قَوْلَهُ فِي الْجُمْلَةِ: «الْجَارُ أَحَقُّ بِسَقَبِهِ» عَلَى بَعْضِ الْجِيرَانِ دُونَ بَعْضٍ وَأَنَّهُ الْجَارُ الَّذِي لَمْ يُقَاسِمْ.
258 – And if he says: And the Arabs called the partner "neighbour"?	258 - فَإِنْ قَالَ: وَتُسَمِّي الْعَرَبُ الشَّرِيكَ جَارًا؟
259 – It is said: Yes. To all whose body is close to that of his companion, it is said: "Neighbour."	259 - قِيلَ: نَعَمْ، كُلُّ مَنْ قَارَبَ بَدَنُهُ بَدَنَ صَاحِبِهِ قِيلَ لَهُ: جَارٌ.
260 – He said: Provide me an indicant for this.	260 - قَالَ: فَادْلُلْنِي عَلَى هَذَا.
261 – It was said to him: Ḥamal b. Mālik b. al-Nābigha said: I was between two of my female "neighbours" when one of them struck the other with a tent pole, so that she gave birth to a dead foetus. And the Messenger of God, may God bless and save him, judged in this case for the best sort of slave [by way of compensation].	261 - قِيلَ لَهُ: قَالَ حَمَلُ بْنُ مَالِكِ بْنِ النَّابِغَةِ: «كُنْتُ بَيْنَ جَارَتَيْنِ لِي فَضَرَبَتْ إِحْدَاهُمَا الأُخْرَى بِمِسْطَحٍ، فَأَلْقَتْ جَنِينًا مَيِّتًا، فَقَضَى فِيهِ رَسُولُ اللهِ - صَلَّى اللهُ عَلَيْهِ وَسَلَّمَ - بِغُرَّةٍ.»

(continued)

[54] See Schacht (*Origins*, p. 164), who considers this a maxim of Iraqian doctrine (thus, for Schacht, Mashriqiyyūn = Iraqian).

[55] In other words, the specifics inherent to the Easterner's more general (*jumla*) tradition must be provided elsewhere, which is what al-Shāfiʿī believes his own interpreting (*mufassir*) *ḥadīth* to do.

262 – And al-Aʿshā said to his wife: «O "neighbour" of ours: part, for you are divorced.»[56]	262 - وَقَالَ الأَعْشَى لِامْرَأَتِهِ: «أَجَارَتَنَا بِينِي فَإِنَّكِ طَالِقَهْ».
263 – And it was said to him: But *you*, when you say it is specific to some "neighbours" and not others—you bring no indication for that from the Prophet, may God bless and save him. Nor do you apply it to whom rightly adheres "the label of proximity."[57] The *ḥadīth* of Ibrāhīm b. Maysara does not possibly carry but one of the two *maʿnā*-intensions,[58] and you have contradicted them both together. For you have claimed—of the house sold while between it and the house of a man there exists a courtyard of a thousand cubits and more—that, so long as it contains no open and public passageway, the right to preemption obtains; but even if between them lies an open passageway whose width is [but] one cubit, you effect no preemption for it. So you have made the *shufʿa*-preemption for the most distant of two "neighbours," and prevented it for the nearest of them! And you have claimed, of one who registers a bequest to his "neighbours," that you apportion his bequest on behalf of one whose house is forty houses away. So how is it you make no *shufʿa*-preemption for what you apportioned the bequest, when you have contradicted our *ḥadīth*—and the *ḥadīth* of Ibrāhīm b. Maysara, upon which you based your argument?[59]	263 - فَقِيلَ لَهُ: فَأَنْتَ إِذَا قُلْتَ: هُوَ خَاصٌّ عَلَى بَعْضِ الْجِيرَانِ دُونَ بَعْضٍ. لَمْ تَأْتِ فِيهِ بِدَلَالَةٍ عَلَى النَّبِيِّ - صَلَّى اللَّهُ عَلَيْهِ وَسَلَّمَ - وَلَمْ تَجْعَلْهُ عَلَى مَنْ لَزِمَهُ اسْمُ الْجِوَارِ، وَحَدِيثُ إِبْرَاهِيمَ بْنِ مَيْسَرَةَ لَا يَحْتَمِلُ إِلَّا أَحَدَ الْمَعْنَيَيْنِ وَقَدْ خَالَفْتَهُمَا مَعًا، ثُمَّ زَعَمْتَ أَنَّ الدَّارَ تُبَاعُ وَبَيْنَهَا وَبَيْنَ دَارِ الرَّجُلِ رَحْبَةٌ فِيهَا أَلْفُ ذِرَاعٍ فَأَكْثَرُ إِذَا لَمْ يَكُنْ فِيهَا طَرِيقٌ نَافِذَةٌ فَيَكُونُ فِيهَا الشُّفْعَةُ، وَإِنْ كَانَتْ بَيْنَهُمَا طَرِيقٌ نَافِذَةٌ عَرْضُهَا ذِرَاعٌ لَمْ تَجْعَلْ فِيهَا الشُّفْعَةَ، فَجَعَلْتَ الشُّفْعَةَ لِأَبْعَدِ الْجَارَيْنِ وَمَنَعْتَهَا أَقْرَبَهُمَا، وَزَعَمْتَ أَنَّ مَنْ أَوْصَى لِجِيرَانِهِ قَسَّمْتَ وَصِيَّتَهُ عَلَى مَنْ كَانَ بَيْنَ دَارِهِ وَدَارِهِ أَرْبَعُونَ دَارًا، فَكَيْفَ لَمْ تَجْعَلِ الشُّفْعَةَ عَلَى مَا قَسَّمْتَ عَلَيْهِ الْوَصِيَّةَ إِذَا خَالَفْتَ حَدِيثَنَا وَحَدِيثَ إِبْرَاهِيمَ بْنِ مَيْسَرَةَ الَّذِي احْتَجَجْتَ بِهِ؟
264 – He said: Did any one of the Companions of the Prophet, may God bless and save him, profess your opinion?	264 - قَالَ: فَهَلْ قَالَ بِقَوْلِكُمْ أَحَدٌ مِن أَصْحَابِ النَّبِيِّ - صَلَّى اللَّهُ عَلَيْهِ وَسَلَّمَ؟

(continued)

[56] This line is from a short *qaṣīda* attributed to the famed Maymūn b. Qays al-Aʿshā (d. ca. 629 CE). A variant may be found in the *Kitāb Ṣubḥ al-Munīr fī Shiʿr Abī Baṣīr* (Geyer ed., p.183, *qaṣīda* 41, line 1):

يَا جَارَتِي بِينِي فَإِنَّكِ طَالِقَهْ   كَذَاكِ أُمُورُ النَّاسِ غَادٍ وَطَارِقَهْ

The line as it appears in §262, however, is repeated in a number of *ḥadīth* commentaries, *fiqh* works, etc., most often employed, as it is here, to illustrate a connotation of "neighbour" (*jār*) and its effects on preemption rulings. By way of example, see Ibn Baṭṭāl's (d.449/1057) *Sharḥ Ṣaḥīḥ al-Bukhārī* (Ibrāhīm ed., vol. 6, p. 381).

[57] The *ism al-jiwār*, possibly in the sense of "the noun of vicinity/neighbourhood," and referring to the designation *jār*, "neighbour".

[58] That is, either (1) "neighbour" intending partner, or (2) "neighbour" intending one who is close.

[59] In other words, since the Easterner appears to have contradicted both possible connotations of "neighbour" (meaning either a partner, or one who is close)—and thus both al-Shāfiʿī's *ḥadīth* and his own—why wouldn't he extend the right to preemption to one whose house is forty houses distant: neither partner nor close?

265 – We said: Yes. Nor would it harm us, anyway—since it is confirmed on the authority of the Prophet, may God bless and save him—if no one at all professes it.	265 - قُلْنَا: نَعَمْ. وَلاَ يَضُرُّنَا بَعْدُ إِذْ ثَبَتَ عَنِ النَّبِيِّ -صَلَّى اللهُ عَلَيْهِ وَسَلَّمَ - أَنْ لاَ يَقُولَ بِهِ أَحَدٌ.
266 – He said: And who professed it?	266 - قَالَ: فَمَنْ قَالَ بِهِ؟
267 – It was said: ʿUmar b. al-Khaṭṭāb, may God Most High be pleased with him, and ʿUthmān, may God Most High be pleased with him. And of the Successors:[60] ʿUmar b. ʿAbd al-ʿAzīz professed it, may the mercy of God Most High be upon him, and others.	267 - قِيلَ: عُمَرُ بْنُ الْخَطَّابِ رضي الله تعالى عنه - وَعُثْمَانُ رضي الله تعالى عنه. وَقَالَ بِهِ مِنَ التَّابِعِينَ: عُمَرُ بْنُ عَبْدِ الْعَزِيزِ رَحْمَةُ اللهِ تَعَالَى عَلَيْهِ - وَغَيْرُهُ.

[§§268–9 introduce the opinions of Abū Ḥanīfa, Abū Yūsuf, and Ibn Abī Laylā on another *masʾala*; and al-Shāfiʿī treats the same *masʾala* in §273]

270 – Al-Ḥasan b. ʿUmāra reported to us, on the authority of al-Ḥakam, on Mujāhid, on Ibn ʿAbbās—and [alternately] on the authority of al-Ḥakam, on Yaḥyā, on ʿAlī—that both of them [i.e., both Ibn ʿAbbās and ʿAlī] said: There is no right to preemption except for the partner who did not partition.	270 - أَخْبَرَنَا الْحَسَنُ بْنُ عُمَارَةَ، عَنِ الْحَكَمِ، عَنْ مُجَاهِدٍ، عَنِ ابْنِ عَبَّاسٍ، وَعَنِ الْحَكَمِ، عَنْ يَحْيَى، عَنْ عَلِيٍّ أَنَّهُمَا قَالاَ: لاَ شُفْعَةَ إِلاَّ لِشَرِيكٍ لَمْ يُقَاسِمْ.
271 – Al-Ḥajjāj b. Arṭāt [reports], on the authority of ʿAmr b. Shuʿayb, on ʿAmr b. al-Sharīd, on his father, who said: The Messenger of God, may God bless and save him, said: «The neighbour has the greater right due to his nearness, whatever it may be.»[61]	271 - الْحَجَّاجُ بْنُ أَرْطَاةَ؛ عَنْ عَمْرِو بْنِ شُعَيْبٍ، عَنْ عَمْرِو بْنِ الشَّرِيدِ، عَنْ أَبِيهِ قَالَ: قَالَ رَسُولُ اللهِ - صَلَّى اللهُ عَلَيْهِ وَسَلَّمَ: «الْجَارُ أَحَقُّ بِسَقَبِهِ مَا كَانَ.»
272 – Abū Ḥanīfa [reports], on the authority of Abū Umayya, on al-Miswar b. Makhrama, or on Saʿd b. Mālik, who said: The Messenger of God, may God bless and save him, said: «The neighbour has the greater right due to his nearness.»[62]	272 - أَبُو حَنِيفَةَ، عَنْ أَبِي أُمَيَّةَ، عَنِ الْمِسْوَرِ بْنِ مَخْرَمَةَ، أَوْ عَنْ سَعْدِ بْنِ مَالِكٍ قَالَ: قَالَ رَسُولُ اللهِ -صَلَّى اللهُ عَلَيْهِ وَسَلَّمَ: «الْجَارُ أَحَقُّ بِسَقَبِهِ.»

[60] Here I follow ʿAbd al-Muṭṭalib (vol. 8, p. 252) and the Būlāq edition (vol. 7, p. 101), which have وقال به من التابعين, rather than وقال بعض من التابعين, as with Ḥassūn.

[61] Note the significant addition of "whatever it may be" (*mā kāna*) in this transmission.

[62] The *athar* and Prophetic *ḥadīth*s recorded in §§270–2—though very relevant to previous "neighbour" arguments—have no bearing on the intervening *masʾala* of §§268–9 (picked up again by al-Shāfiʿī in §273), which concerns the buyer of a house who subsequently contracts an unfairly priced advanced-payment sale (*salam*) to the pre-emptor (*shafīʿ*)—this being the last *masʾala* of the chapter on preemption in our subject-text. These reports appear to have been tacked on to the end of the Shaybānī Version's chapter on *shufʿa*—either as incorporated notes of al-Shaybānī, or additional proofs listed by Abū Yūsuf for the earlier "neighbour" *masāʾil*. Their disordered appearance here in the *Umm* Version—sandwiched between a non-related *masʾala*, and al-Shāfiʿī's evaluation of the same—provides another indicant for the authenticity of both the Shaybānī and *Umm* Versions. Notably, §§270–2 retain their tacked-on position at the end of the *shufʿa* chapter in al-Afghānī's edition of the *Ikhtilāf Abī Ḥanīfa wa Ibn Abī Laylā* (pp. 38–40). We might surmise that the version available to al-Shāfiʿī had the very same feature of tacked-on proofs; and these were faithfully reproduced, *in situ*, in his commentary, even though irrelevant to the immediate *masʾala*. The odd position of these reports in the *Umm* Version—and their lack of excision or relocation—suggests a strong redactional bond between the *Umm* and Shaybānī Versions as they have come down to us.

A brief review of this set of related *masā'il* by presentation category shows a typical layout of Abū Ḥanīfa, Abū Yūsuf, and Ibn Abī Laylā rulings for *masā'il* ##1–3 (the original Shaybānī Version material) in abridged F and G presentations (§§238–41), followed by a series of *adilla*-indicants and rulings for al-Shāfiʿī on the same *masā'il* (§§242–6; also F and G, if somewhat more detailed). These, however, are followed in turn by a rather extended dialectical sequence (category A) in two parts (§§247–51: al-Shāfiʿī vs. an anonymous opponent of the Ahl al-Baṣra; §§252–67: al-Shāfiʿī vs. an anonymous opponent of the Mashriqiyyūn), offering up a wealth of legal-theoretical and dialectical detail, and closing—though not before the introduction of a new *mas'ala* (§§268–9)—with three "tacked on" *akhbār*-reports (§§270–2) provided by Abū Yūsuf or al-Shaybānī to support the rulings of Abū Ḥanīfa and Ibn Abī Laylā back in §§239 and 241.[63] Before treating the core dialectical material of these sections, I will, as before, attempt a brief conjectural analysis of the G category rulings and arguments which precede it.

In §236 a set of Abū Ḥanīfa's rulings are presented as regards the orphan (*yatīm*)—who may or may not have a *waṣiyy*-guardian—and his right to *shufʿa*-preemption (*masā'il* #1–#1c); and the whole is extended to the parallel *mas'ala* (#2) of the boy (*ghulām*) with a living father—who, we are meant to assume, may or may not be guardian over his financial transactions. Although unstated as such, it is clear from the rulings—here, and in following sections—that Abū Ḥanīfa is dealing with a set of properties and their effects, collectively and in isolation. These properties are: (1) he is a *yatīm/ghulām* with a *waṣiyy*/living father; (2) he is a *yatīm/ghulām* without a *waṣiyy*/living father; (3) he is a minor; (4) the *waṣiyy*/living father did not make the demand; and (5) he reached the age of legal maturity (*adraka*).

It would appear, then, that Abū Ḥanīfa considered the property of being a "minor" (*ṣaghīr*) as efficient in occasioning a right to demand *shufʿa*-preemption only when combined with the property of "*yatīm/ghulām* with a *waṣiyy*/living father," upon whom the responsibility of making the demand could devolve. On the other hand, "*ṣaghīr*" in combination with "he is a *yatīm/ghulām* without a *waṣiyy*/living father" is no longer efficient in occasioning that right to *shufʿa*-preemption until such a time as "*ṣaghīr*" is replaced by "legal maturity." Moreover, in such cases where the combined properties of "*ṣaghīr*" and "*waṣiyy*/living father did not make the demand" precede the replacement of "*ṣaghīr*" with "legal maturity," we find that the "legal maturity" property is no longer efficient in occasioning the right to *shufʿa*-preemption. For Ibn Abī Laylā, however, as we see in §238, the property of "*ṣaghīr*" is efficient over all these other properties in occasioning a *ḥukm* of no right to *shufʿa*. We are left to assume that Ibn Abī Laylā considered only

[63] §§268–72 thus mark a return to the Shaybānī Version material, with the final rulings and arguments of al-Shāfiʿī (§273) closing the chapter. The *mas'ala* of §§268–9 and 273 will not be treated in the current analysis.

"legal maturity" to be efficient in occasioning the right to *shufʿa* in these cases, and for this we find confirmation in al-Sarakhsī's *Mabsūṭ*.[64]

In essence, we are confronted with a conflict of properties—or, more accurately: a conflict of conceptions as to which properties override which insofar as efficiency in producing a *ḥukm*. As we have seen with Abū Ḥanīfa, both "*ṣaghīr*" and "legal maturity" may be cancelled out by other properties; but with Ibn Abī Laylā, they override all else. Moreover, once we consider al-Shāfiʿī's rulings on these *masāʾil* (from §245), we find not only another property added to the mix (the *shufʿa*-preemption is "felicitous" [*ghibṭa*]), but another cancellation ("legal maturity" trumps "*waṣiyy*/living father did not make the demand"). In other words, al-Shāfiʿī sides with Abū Ḥanīfa ("*ṣaghīr*" + "*yatīm*/*ghulām* with a *waṣiyy*/living father" occasions right to *shufʿa*) only when these two properties are combined with "the *shufʿa*-preemption is *ghibṭa*", i.e., felicitous. He sides with Ibn Abī Laylā, however, in regard to "legal maturity" which, against Abū Ḥanīfa, overrides "*waṣiyy*/living father did not make the demand."

Unfortunately, not one of the rulings for our jurists on *masāʾil* ##1–2 are supported by reference to *adilla*-indicants; neither transmitted support (*naql*) nor rational support (*ʿaql*) is presented for any of them (i.e., they are all of presentation category G). Regardless, it is easy to see that in a disputation between proponents of the Abū Ḥanīfa, Ibn Abī Laylā, or al-Shāfiʿī positions—which we have every reason to believe would have occurred—the dialectical domain of concern is that of preponderance of properties, singly or in combination, one over the other. In other words, the opponents would be arguing which property or properties are superior (*awlā*); and specifically, in al-Shīrāzī's parlance, this is a matter of "Preponderance of [Potentially-Efficient] Intension-Properties" (*Tarjīḥ al-Maʿānī*). Al-Shīrāzī, as we have seen, dedicates a list of no less than sixteen modes to this dialectical domain; while al-Bājī lists twelve types and discusses three of the many others known to the Ahl al-Naẓar (Theorists of Intellectual Investigation) (Shīr.X.1–16; Bāj.XVI.2).[65] Without knowing the respective *adilla*-indicants for these *yatīm*/*ghulām* right to *shufʿa* rulings, however, this is as far as we can proceed insofar as identifying the relevant modes.

§§239–41 (with §§270–2) mark a shift in the original Shaybānī Version material to the core *masʾala* of this particular set: precisely which relationship to the seller occasions the right to demand *shufʿa*-preemption. The provision of *adilla*-indicants in connection with the rulings of Abū Ḥanīfa and Ibn Abī Laylā (though not always in sequence) allows us to locate §§239–41 in presentation category F, and it is easy enough to discern that we are faced once again with a conflict of conceptions as to

[64] Rāḍī, et al. ed., vol. 30, p. 145: "*lahu al-shufʿa idhā adraka*" is said to be the doctrine of Muḥammad [b. al-Ḥasan], Zufar, and Ibn Abī Laylā (the complete reference in the *Mabsūṭ* is quoted without page-citation by al-Afghānī, p. 37, n. 2).

[65] al-Shīrāzī, *Maʿūna*, al-ʿUmayrīnī ed., pp. 125–7; al-Bājī, *Minhāj*, Turkī ed., pp. 234–40, §§533–48. Please see the appendices for a full translation of each type; and cf. Ibn ʿAqīl, *K. al-Jadal*, pp. 21–5 for his discussion on *Tarājīḥ fiʾl-ʿIlal*, and pp. 26–7 for his *Masāʾil al-Khilāf fiʾl-ʿIlal*.

which properties are efficient in occasioning a *ḥukm* of right to *shufʿa*-preemption. For Abū Ḥanīfa (§239), drawing *ḥujja* from the Prophetic *ḥadīth*-decrees of §§271–2 (and, most likely, the *ḥadīth*-decree employed by the Ahl al-Baṣra in §247), it is evident that the following properties and combinations of properties are deemed efficient, in order of priority: (1) "partner of commixion;" (2) "partner who partitioned" + "only one passageway separating;" and (3) "adjoining neighbour (*jār mulāṣiq*)."

In an intriguing historical aside we are told by Abū Yūsuf or al-Shaybānī (§240) that Ibn Abī Laylā once also subscribed to this hierarchy of rulings but was commanded to alter his doctrine—by none other than the first ʿAbbāsid Caliph: Abū al-ʿAbbās (al-Saffāḥ)—to that of the Ḥijāzīs.[66] This Ḥijāzī counter-doctrine is supported by the *āthār*-decree of ʿAlī and Ibn ʿAbbās, alluded to in §241, and appearing with quoted transmitted text (*matn*) and chain of transmission (*isnād*) in §270: "There is no right to preemption except for the partner who did not partition" (*lā shufʿata illā li-sharīkin lam yuqāsim*)." In other words, the new conception to which Ibn Abī Laylā was compelled—as acting *qāḍī* of Kūfa—is one in which the property "partner of commixion" is alone efficient (against other relationship-properties) in occasioning the right to *shufʿa*-preemption. As we shall see, the same position was championed by al-Shāfiʿī against the Easterners (Mashriqiyyūn), and *ikhtilāf* on this *masʾala* indeed appears, in part, occasioned by regional adherences to different *adilla*-indicants.[67] Rather than engage in a conjectural recreation of a dialectic between the Abū Ḥanīfa vs. (new) Ibn Abī Laylā positions, I will rely instead upon an analysis of al-Shāfiʿī's dialectic against the Ahl al-Baṣra and the Mashriqiyyūn. These partially recorded sequences, by virtue of the time and place of their compilation, provide by far the best window on whatever disputations preceded them for this *masʾala*.

The voice of al-Shāfiʿī in this set of *masāʾil* is first presented as transmitting three *āthār*-decrees (§§242–4) in which the same property-efficiency is manifest: the occurrence of boundaries (*ḥudūd*) is efficient in cancelling the right to *shufʿa*-preemption. Insofar as these oppose the Sunnaic *adilla*-indicants attached to Abū Ḥanīfa's solution, and recognizing the epistemic inferiority of the decrees of Companions against an established *ḥadīth*-decree of the Prophet, we may interpret them as preparing the way for a forthcoming *iʿtirāḍ* (rather than constituting a full *iʿtirāḍ* in and of themselves). As we shall see in the dialectical sequence of §§255 ff., al-Shāfiʿī levels a "Claim of Ambiguity" (*daʿwā al-ijmāl*)—the opponent's *jumla* vs. his own *mufassir*—against the *istidlāl bi'l-Sunna* of the Abū Ḥanīfa / Easterner position. Here in §§242–4, this forthcoming *iʿtirāḍ*—as yet unmentioned—is supported by three *āthār*-tradition indicants.

[66] See the notes attached to §240 in the translation, above.

[67] The rulings of Abū Ḥanīfa and pre-compulsion Ibn Abī Laylā correspond to the position of al-Shāfiʿī's Mashriqiyyūn, and may be set over and against the position of al-Shāfiʿī and the Ahl al-Ḥijāz. See my note attached to §252 in the translation for a brief investigation into the meaning of Mashriqiyyūn.

In §245[a] al-Shāfiʿī proceeds to render judgments for the *yatīm/ghulām masāʾil* ##1–2 (discussed above), and in §245[b] we hear his first pair of related rulings as regards the *masʾala* at hand (#3): (1) there is *shufʿa*-preemption only for what is not partitioned (in consonance with the Ḥijāzī / "new" Ibn Abī Laylā position in §240); and (2) there is no *shufʿa*-preemption where boundaries occur (in consonance with his *āthār* transmissions of §§242–4). The property-efficiency considerations of these rulings have already been mentioned, and it is apparent that they constitute an objection to those which are implied in the Abū Ḥanīfa rulings of §239 and supporting *adilla*-indicants. Finally, in §246 we are presented with two of al-Shāfiʿī's subsidiary rulings: (#3a) there is no *shufʿa*-preemption regarding partitioned house/land separated by a passageway/trough/fountain; and (#3d) no *shufʿa*-preemption is obliged for what is partitioned of a partnership in passageway/water. These, taken together with the main rulings of §245[b], constitute the core positions for which al-Shāfiʿī achieves *elenchus* against proponents of the Ahl al-Baṣra and Mashriqiyyūn positions in the two ensuing sets of juridical disputation.

Al-Shāfiʿī begins the first dialectical sequence by relating the adherence of the Ahl al-Baṣra to "the general part of our doctrine" (*jumlati qawlinā*), as regards his ruling #3; that is to say, they profess the same general doctrine that *shufʿa*-preemption belongs only to "the partnership members" (*al-qawm al-shurakāʾ*)—against the Abū Ḥanīfa hierarchy of rulings which includes neighbours (*jīrān*). Their doctrine diverges, however, as regards *masʾala* #3a, for they claim the right to *shufʿa*-preemption for partitioned house/land, separated by a passageway (*ṭarīq*) or trough/fountain (*mashrab*) which is owned by the partners. This goes against al-Shāfiʿī's ruling #3a, and he supplies their reasoning in two parts. First is an *ʿaql* argument, introduced with "because" (*li-anna*)[68] and pinpointing an efficient property: "because they are [yet] partners in some property." In other words, the fact that they are partners, too, in the separating *ṭarīq/mashrab* is itself efficient in occasioning one partner's right to *shufʿa*-preemption. As a second part of the argument, al-Shāfiʿī relates the Prophetic *ḥadīth* which the Ahl al-Baṣra considered similar (*shabīhan*) to the *maʿnā*-intension of their doctrine "the neighbour has the greater right due to his nearness " (*al-jār aḥaqq bi-saqabihi*), along with their *isnād* (ʿAbd al-Mālik b. Abī Sulaymān – ʿAṭāʾ – Jābir – Prophet). Thus we may classify the base of their argument as *al-istidlāl biʾl-Sunna*, and it becomes clear that ensuing dialectical objections will belong to the corresponding genus of *iʿtirāḍāt*.

Al-Shāfiʿī does not leave off questioning "*shabīhan li-hādhā al-maʿnā*" before tackling other matters, for he promptly states his opinion (still in §247) that this *ḥadīth* is just as likely to bear the "opposite" (*khilāf*) of the Ahl al-Baṣra's *maʿnā*-intension, as it is to bear its *shabīh*-resemblance. From the start, then, al-Shāfiʿī gives voice to an *iʿtirāḍ* which we may easily identify in later *jadal* treatises as "Claim of Ambiguity" (*daʿwā al-ijmāl*). In al-Shīrāzī's "*Iʿtirāḍ* against the Sunna with

[68] "*li-anna*" is perhaps the most common marker for introducing an *ʿaql* argument/explanation in the subject-text; others include "*li-*", "*min qibali*", and "*fa-*".

reference to the transmitted text (*matn*) [as a self-initiated saying of the Prophet (*qawl mubtada'*)]", we find it as the third *i'tirāḍ*: "[Q] claims ambiguity (*ijmāl*), by measure of either God's decrees (*Shar'*) or the customary usage (*al-lugha*)" (Shīr. II.C.3).[69] As we shall see later, when al-Shāfi'ī revisits this *i'tirāḍ* against an opponent of the Mashriqiyyūn, it is a matter of *ijmāl* of the *lugha* (Shīr.II.C.3.2).[70] Finally, note that §247 contains a number of terms and verbs which may be considered of some legal-theoretical import; among them are: *jumla* (in the sense of "general/ ambiguous"), *ma'nā* (in the sense of [shared] efficient properties), *shabīh* (as a means of indicating that efficient properties may be shared—just as in *qiyās al-shabah*), *khilāf* (as contradictory, or opposite), *ḥasaba* (as conveying a considered opinion), and *iḥtamala* (as conveying the possibility a *lafẓ*-expression bears another *ma'nā*-intension).

In §248 al-Shāfi'ī launches straight into another objection, and perhaps tellingly he employs a verb which has great currency in the *jadal* treatises, saying: "The only thing that prevents us from professing this doctrine (*innamā mana'anā min al-qawl bi-hādhā*) is [X, Y, and Z]." The operative verb here is *mana'a*, and—as we have seen—*man'/mumāna'a* is a staple objection of the *jadal* literature. Al-Shāfi'ī has, in effect, announced *man'*—that he denies concession to this doctrine due to an objection which, as we shall see, stems in part from an epistemically-oriented theory of *ḥadīth* transmission. In brief, although much of his argument focuses upon respective chains of transmission, al-Shāfi'ī enacts a dialectical move of *mu'āraḍa*; he announces a Prophetic *ḥadīth* bearing the opposite (*khilāf*) of the Ahl al-Baṣra's *ma'nā*-intension, and then gives it preponderance over their *ḥadīth* on the basis of an epistemic principle of transmission. The argument takes a number of stages, as he mentions: (1) Abū Salama and Abū al-Zubayr (narrators of the al-Shāfi'ī counter-*ḥadīth*) also audited Jābir (the first narrator in the Ahl al-Baṣra *ḥadīth*); (2) "one of our Ḥijāzīs" also transmitted the al-Shāfi'ī counter-*ḥadīth* from 'Aṭā' on Jābir (the first two narrators in the Ahl al-Baṣra *ḥadīth*); (3) the fact that two narrators (Abū Salama and Abū al-Zubayr) concur on Jābir, and a third (Ḥijāzī on 'Aṭā' on Jābir) agrees, is "superior in affirming the [counter-] *ḥadīth* (*awlā bi'l-tathabbut fi'l-ḥadīth*)" than when a third (the Ahl al-Baṣra *ḥadīth* of 'Abd al-Mālik b. Abī Sulaymān on 'Aṭā' on Jābir) disagrees (with Abū Salama and Abū al-Zubayr on Jābir); and (4) the *ma'nā*-intension (from the counter-*ḥadīth*) by which he prevents (*mana'nā*) *shuf'a*-preemption for what is partitioned (the Ahl al-Baṣra ruling for *mas'ala* #3a) is existing (*qā'im*) in this "partitioned thing" (*maqsūm*)—i.e., in the house/land separated by a *ṭarīq/mashrab* owned by partners, the object of the *mas'ala*. In this fashion al-Shāfi'ī brings a counter-*ḥadīth*, explains why it is epistemically superior, and then establishes that the efficient property (*ma'nā*) of that

[69] al-Shīrāzī, *Ma'ūna*, al-'Umayrīnī ed., pp. 59–60. Cf. Ibn 'Aqīl, *K. al-Jadal*, p. 34, §§179–80, who employs the same typology and example-*masā'il* as his teacher al-Shīrāzī.

[70] al-Shīrāzī, op. cit. Al-Bājī's typology is somewhat more refined, and we find an *i'tirāḍ* even closer to al-Shāfi'ī's objection to the Mashriqiyyūn: "*al-Munāza'a fi'l-'Umūm bi-da'wā al-ijmāl*" (Bāj. II.2.2.3.2; *Minhāj*, Turkī ed., p. 102, §198).

ḥadīth—which occasions the *ḥukm* of no *shufʿa*-preemption—is "*qā'im*" in the *mas'ala* at hand. Although we are in the domain of *istidlāl bi'l-Sunna*, this constitutes a type of *manʿ/mumānaʿa* of the *ḥukm* in the *aṣl* (Shīr.VII.3; Bāj.IX.B.5),[71] as well as a *muʿāraḍa*.

This is an extraordinary argument from a number of perspectives, and there is again a wealth of legal-theoretical and dialectical concepts and terms put into practice. We find the verb *manaʿa* twice employed in a similar sense as that conveyed in the *jadal* literature (but not in the single domain it came to occupy); we find an instance of *muʿāraḍa* of Sunna by Sunna; we find an instance of *tarjīḥ* by which one *ḥadīth* is proven superior (*awlā*) to another by virtue of a legal-theoretical principle, and employing terms such as *ijtamaʿa*, *wāfaqa*, and *tathabbut*; and, significantly, we find a reference to a *maʿnā*-intension being *qā'im* in the *mas'ala* at hand—this constitutes a *muʿāraḍa* of the supposed *maʿnā*-intension of the Ahl al-Baṣra *ḥadīth*: "because they are partners in something of the property" is overruled, as we shall see, by "boundaries occur in it."

As for al-Shāfiʿī's use of *manaʿa*, the absence of *manʿ/mumānaʿa* among the Sunna-related *iʿtirāḍāt* of our lens-texts (it appears only among the *qiyās*-related *iʿtirāḍāt*) makes his usage here in a context of *al-istidlāl bi'l-Sunna* significant. Considering that this early Islamic practice and teaching of juridical dialectic represents a proto-system allows for the possibility that particular terms became restricted to particular domains over time. His introduction of a counter-*ḥadīth* to that of the Ahl al-Baṣra, however, would clearly be labelled a *muʿāraḍa* in later systems, and we may locate it easily in Shīrāzī's *Maʿūna*, in his treatment of "*Iʿtirāḍ* against the Sunna with reference to the transmitted text (*matn*) [as a self-initiated saying of the Prophet (*qawl mubtada'*)]": it is the first type: "counter-indication by way of divinely-sanctioned decree (*muʿāraḍa bi'l-nuṭq*)" of the eighth *iʿtirāḍ* of "Counter-Indication " (*Muʿāraḍa*) (Shīr.II.C.8.1).[72] Of note is the second mode of al-Shīrāzī's proposed response to this species of *muʿāraḍa*: "[R] gives preponderance (*yurajjiḥa*) to a *dalīl*-indicant over the *muʿāraḍa*, via what we will mention [in following chapters] of modes of preponderance (*wujūh al-tarjīḥāt*)."[73] As we see, al-Shāfiʿī pre-empts such a *jawāb* by doing his own *tarjīḥ* first.

Moreover, al-Shāfiʿī's *tarjīḥ* also finds a precise match in al-Shīrāzī's chapter on *Tarjīḥ al-Ẓawāhir*, as the fifth mode of the first focal-point (the *isnād*), which is

[71] Notably, this objection—like all *manʿ/mumānaʿa* objections—is confined to the domain of *istidlāl bi'l-qiyās* in the *jadal*-theory texts. I would mark this as an expanded application in proto-system *jadal*.

[72] al-Shīrāzī, *Maʿūna*, al-ʿUmayrīnī ed., p. 67. Cf. Ibn ʿAqīl, *K. al-Jadal*, p. 36, §190, who once again employs the same typology and example-*masā'il* as his teacher. Al-Bājī, however, has developed a more refined typology by which we can precisely identify al-Shāfiʿī's *muʿāraḍa* when he employs it again—with a shift in tactic—against the Mashriqiyyūn in §§255 ff. For now, we can locate his §248 *muʿāraḍa* more generally, under Bāj.II.2.7.1, or *al-iʿtirāḍ ʿalā al-istidlāl bi'l-Sunna min jihat al-muʿāraḍa bi-nuṭq* (*Minhāj*, Turkī ed., p. 119 ff., §§233 ff.)

[73] al-Shīrāzī, *Maʿūna*, al-ʿUmayrīnī ed., p. 67. The referenced treatments of *tarjīḥāt* begin on p. 121.

"specifically concerned with solitary reports." Al-Shīrāzī's explanation is important here:

> That one of the two [*khabar*-reports] is more narrated; it is superior (*awlā*), because the Law is better preserved (*aḥfaẓ*) in a group than it is among a small number. Due to this the Prophet said: «al-Shayṭān is with one, but he is further from two.» And among our [Shāfiʿī] companions are those who say: [the *khabar*-report] is not given preponderance [in terms of numbers] like testimony (*shahāda*). But the first [opinion] is more valid. (Shīr.IX.1.5)[74]

Not only does this conform well with al-Shāfiʿī's reasoning in §248 (that two supported by a third is superior to when the third disagrees), but the very fact that al-Shīrāzī references *ikhtilāf* over this type of preponderance by number[75] drives home a core thesis of the current study. In short, we are witness to a continued *ikhtilāf* over a *tarjīḥ* method dating back at least to the late second / early third century H, and which constitutes part of a staple chapter of *uṣūl al-fiqh* treatises: "conflict of indicants" (*taʿāruḍ al-adilla*). Moreover, this *tarjīḥ* method is just as plainly a dialectical tool of the al-Shāfiʿī vs. Ahl al-Baṣra dispute of §248 ff., as it is an object of dispute in later *jadal* literature. In other words, we have in both the *Umm* of al-Shāfiʿī and the *Maʿūna* of al-Shīrāzī a testimony to the forging of a critical *jadal/uṣūl* method in dialectical venues. Dialectic as a major dynamic in the development of both Islamic legal theory and disputation theory is illustrated here in bold relief.

Nor is this all that we might say, for al-Bājī opens his chapter on *Tarjīḥāt* with the following: "Know that *al-tarjīḥ* is a method (*ṭarīq*) for the advancing of one of the two *dalīl*-indicants over the other; and the ancients (Qudamā') used to make use of it in intellectual investigation (*al-naẓar*), and they did so frequently; but I will point out [only] that which is most necessary, in abbreviated manner (*bi-wajh al-ikhtiṣār*)."[76] We are thus provided some support for another theory the current study proposes; mainly, that the systematization of later *jadal* theory was accomplished, in part, by research and analysis of the dialectical argument and method of earlier jurists. In other words, the later systems were partially determined via analysis of the proto-systems.

Returning to the last part of al-Shāfiʿī's argument in §248, his establishing that the *maʿnā*-intension of his *ḥadīth* is "extant" (*qā'im*) in the *mas'ala* at hand may be registered as an early expression connoting efficient properties shared between

---

[74] al-Shīrāzī, *Maʿūna*, al-ʿUmayrīnī ed., 121–2. Cf. Ibn ʿAqīl, *K. al-Jadal*, 24, §128; and al-Bājī, *Minhāj*, Turkī ed., 223–4, §508. Al-Bājī accompanies his discussion with a Mālikī vs. Ḥanafī example which parallels the above *tarjīḥ* of al-Shāfiʿī in a number of ways.

[75] He discusses this *ikhtilāf* in more detail in his *Lumaʿ* (Mustū ed., p. 174), and in his *Tabṣira* (Hītū ed., p. 348). In the latter he mentions not only the above *ḥadīth* as *dalīl*-indicant, but a Qur'ānic indicant as well, in conjunction with the *shahāda* argument of opponents to this type of *tarjīḥ* and—significantly—the proper *jawāb* against it. It is evident throughout the *jadal* literature that dialectical disputation was as much the forge for systems of *jadal* as is it was for systems of *uṣūl al-fiqh*. The *Kāfiya* of al-Juwaynī is particularly rich in expositions on *jadal*-theory *ikhtilāf*.

[76] al-Bājī, *Minhāj*, Turkī ed., p. 221, §504.

source-case and case under consideration—a relationship which would be expressed in later *uṣūl* and *jadal* literature in terms of properties (*awṣāf*), occasioning factors (*ʿilal*), and efficiency (*taʾthīr*) as regards source-case (*aṣl*) and branch-case (*farʿ*). More importantly, it constitutes another species of *muʿāraḍa* on the part of al-Shāfiʿī. In effect, al-Shāfiʿī has overridden the efficiency of the supposed *maʿnā*-intension of the Ahl al-Baṣra's *ḥadīth* (they are partners in something of the property) by the efficiency of the *maʿnā*-intension of his own *tarjīḥ*-superior *ḥadīth* (no *shufʿa*-preemption where boundaries occur), as pertains to the *masʾala* at hand.[77]

Taking into account al-Shāfiʿī's *daʿwā al-ijmāl* against the *ḥadīth* of the Ahl al-Baṣra, his subsequent *muʿāraḍa*, and his *tarjīḥ* of that counter-*ḥadīth*, we can see that al-Shāfiʿī is now taking the argument to its logical conclusion: consideration of the *maʿnā*-intension which is supposedly derived from the ambiguous *ḥadīth* is to be supplanted—here, in the *masʾala* at hand—by consideration of the *maʿnā*-intension of the unambiguous, *tarjīḥ*-superior *ḥadīth*, for *muʿāraḍa*. This subsidiary act of *muʿāraḍa* also finds its place in the *jadal*-theory treatises. For al-Shīrāzī, it is the second type of *muʿāraḍa* against *istidlāl biʾl-Sunna* (with reference to the transmitted text [*matn*] as a self-initiated saying of the Prophet [*qawl mubtadaʾ*])—whereas the first, as we have seen, was "counter-indication by way of divinely-sanctioned decree (*muʿāraḍa biʾl-nuṭq*)," the second is "counter-indication by way of the occasioning factor (*muʿāraḍa biʾl-ʿilla*)." More specifically, it is that third subspecies of *muʿāraḍa biʾl-ʿilla* employed "When the Sunna is general (*ʿumūm*), allowing the possibility of particularization (*takhṣīṣ*)" (Shīr.II.C.8.2.3; Bāj.II.2.7.2.3).[78]

In §249 the first dialectical sequence begins, with al-Shāfiʿī assuming an "instructional" role of Q against an R of the Ahl al-Baṣra. He immediately launches an objection-question by way of *a-lā tarā*—that staple formula (along with *a-raʾayta*) of early *jadal* practice. It is a push for R to concede acceptance of the counter-*ḥadīth* (given preponderance in §248), which al-Shāfiʿī now quotes in his question: «Verily *shufʿa*-preemption is for what was not partitioned, and when boundaries occur, there is no *shufʿa*-preemption».[79] Additionally, al-Shāfiʿī clearly sets the stage for another *reductio* terminating in a charge of internal, logical self-

[77] That "no *shufʿa* where *boundaries* occur" is the *maʿnā*-intension which al-Shāfiʿī references here is immediately clarified by his following dialectical question (§249), in which he pushes the opponent to concede to it.

[78] al-Shīrāzī, *Maʿūna*, al-ʿUmayrīnī ed., pp. 67–8, n. 6. NB: this is reproduced from al-ʿUmayrīnī's manuscript of al-Shīrāzī's *Mulakhkhaṣ fiʾl-Jadal*. The anticipated "*muʿāraḍa biʾl-ʿilla*," listed at the start of this chapter of the *Maʿūna*, is missing from both *Maʿūna* MSS. Turkī also notes this in his edition of the *Maʿūna* (p. 184, n. 11), but he does not fill the lacuna from another source, as al-ʿUmayrīnī does. Intriguingly, the *K. al-Jadal* of Ibn ʿAqīl also indicates two types of *muʿāraḍa* (p. 36, §190), but proceeds only to name and treat one (*muʿāraḍa biʾl-nuṭq*). Al-Bājī, however, provides a full treatment of *muʿāraḍa biʾl-ʿilla*, using the same sub-categories as al-Shīrāzī (for when R's Sunnaic *dalīl* is *naṣṣ*, *ẓāhir*, or *ʿumūm*; see *Minhāj*, Turkī ed., pp. 123–5, §§244–7).

[79] Cf. the *āthār*-decrees transmitted by al-Shāfiʿī in §§242–4, and the *athar*-decree "tacked on" by Abū Yūsuf or al-Shaybānī in §270, all of which contain components of this *ḥadīth*-decree.

contradiction (*tanāquḍ*)—he right away states that no proponent of the Ahl al-Baṣra doctrine may find an evasion (*makhraj*) from having brought about *shufʿa*-preemption where boundaries occur. Al-Shāfiʿī has made his strategy clear: (1) his *a-lā tarā* presents an *endoxon* ruling (straight from the Prophet) which R is bound to concede;[80] (2) R will be shown to have ruled, in the *mas'ala* at hand, the opposite of the conceded *endoxon* ruling; thus (3) R will be shown to have contradicted himself—a charge for which he has no real *makhraj*.[81]

R's concession to al-Shāfiʿī's Prophetic *ḥadīth*-decree is evident in §250; he is now forced to defend his apparent contradiction in its light, and—despite al-Shāfiʿī's assurance of no *makhraj*—R nevertheless attempts an explanation. The sequence continues, then, in "instructional mode," with R's response (*fa-in qāla*) that he brought about *shufʿa*-preemption where boundaries occur (a concession to the *endoxon* ruling) only because there remains of the (jointly-owned) property something in which boundaries did *not* occur (i.e., the jointly-owned *ṭarīq/mashrab*). In other words, R concedes to the *maʿnā*-intension of al-Shāfiʿī's *ḥadīth*, while simultaneously maintaining that it does not obtain in a part of the *mas'ala* at hand: part of the property remains without boundaries. In effect, he is conceding that the greater part of the property (the land/house) is partitioned or divided by something which may be described as a boundary; and, at the same time, he is maintaining that the divider itself is also jointly owned, and is not itself partitioned or divided by boundaries. Thus, the *mas'ala* as a whole remains—for R—an exception to the expected *ḥukm* of no *shufʿa*-preemption.

Al-Shāfiʿī is quick to jump to *elenchus* at this point (§251); in effect he charges R with ignoring the procedures requisite to his own distinction of property with/without boundaries. First of all, if it is possible that the remaining property (*al-bāqī*; i.e., the *ṭarīq/mashrab* of the *mas'ala*) be the object of *shufʿa*-preemption, then R should rule the right to *shufʿa*-preemption for that remaining property, specifically (and not for the property marked by boundaries). In other words, only the referenced *ṭarīq/mashrab* may be the locus of *shufʿa*-preemption, not the partitioned land/house; and thus, al-Shāfiʿī says: "you will have followed the [Prophetic] *khabar*-report" (which embodies the conceded *endoxon* ruling). Secondly, if the *bāqī* may not be the object of *shufʿa*-preemption, al-Shāfiʿī declares: "don't bring about the *shufʿa*-preemption in something else!"

In my final analysis, then, it is clear that al-Shāfiʿī has once again reduced the position of his opponent to an internal, logical inconsistency. In other words, and despite the absence of a direct charge of *qawl mutanāqiḍ* (as we saw in §102 above), al-Shāfiʿī is nevertheless accusing R of *tanāquḍ*. Notably, notwithstanding the prefatory arguments of *muʿāraḍa* and *tarjīḥ* and *maʿnā*-intension, both al-Shāfiʿī and the

[80] Al-Shāfiʿī's *a-lā tarā* in §249: rhetorical, pushing concession to an endoxon *dalīl* which contradicts the opposing *qawl*; followed by a *tanāquḍ*-like charge.

[81] It is noteworthy that al-Shāfiʿī uses "*makhraj*" here in a sense similar to the "*jawāb*" of later *jadal* systems—this latter constitutes a study of response-method: R's means of overcoming Q's *iʿtirāḍ*. By claiming no *makhraj* al-Shāfiʿī assures that the opponent can have no real *jawāb* to the objection, and that *elenchus* will be sure to follow.

R of the Ahl al-Baṣra are arguing from the same *dalīl*-indicant in §§249–51, and no question of *istidlāl* is at stake. Rather, the charge is that R has: (1) conceded the *endoxon dalīl*-indicant; and (2) contradicted it in his ruling for the *mas'ala* at hand. We may attempt to represent his *tanāquḍ* thus:[82]

	Universe:
• R concedes: (x)[(Mx & Hx) → ¬Px][83]	• M = jointly-owned property (*milk*)
• R rules: (Ma & Ha) & (Mb & ¬Hb) ⊢ Pa & Pb[84]	• H = boundaries (*ḥudūd*) occur in it
al-Shāfiʿī's correction:	• P = right to pre-emption obtains in it
(Ma & Ha) & (Mb & ¬Hb) ⊢ ¬Pa & Pb[85]	• a , b = parts A and B of the property

R's *tanāquḍ* lies in that he at once concedes (x)[(Mx & Hx) → ¬Px], but rules (Ma & Ha) ⊢ Pa.[86] Al-Shāfiʿī underscores this *tanāquḍ* by showing what R ought to have concluded had he remained consistent to the logic of his concession. Thus, once again, we are faced with an *elenchus* which bears a much closer resemblance to the classical Aristotelian dialectical paradigm than to anything we find in the *jadal*-theory texts of al-Shīrāzī, et al. Although we might find some similarity in this case to *naqḍ*, we must again point out: (1) the hallmark move of bringing a parallel *endoxon* ruling in which the same *ʿilla* occasions a different *ḥukm* is missing; and (2) the above arguments unfold within the domain of *al-istidlāl bi'l-Sunna*, for which the *jadal*-theory texts do not speak of *naqḍ* (it is confined to *al-istidlāl bi'l-qiyās*). Certainly al-Shāfiʿī sees the solution of this *mas'ala* as a simple matter of *al-istidlāl bi'l-Sunna*, and would have been content had R restricted his *ḥukm* of *shufʿa*-preemption to that part of the property (*ṭarīq*/*mashrab*) in which the efficient property of the *ḥadīth* obtains—R would have "followed the *khabar*-report." What he objects to is that R has extended his *ḥukm* for that specific part of the property to another part of the property (land/houses) where the efficient property of the *ḥadīth* does not obtain.[87]

---

[82] For this analysis I utilize a basic set of symbols for predicate logic, as employed by Rodes and Pospesel in *Premises and Conclusions* (especially at pp. 113–206).

[83] Read: "For any x: if x is jointly-owned property, and x is something in which boundaries occur; then x is something in which the right to *shufʿa* does not obtain."

[84] Read: "Part A of the property is jointly owned and boundaries occur in it; and part B of the property is jointly owned but no boundaries occur in it; therefore the right to *shufʿa* obtains in part A of the property and in part B of the property."

[85] Read: "Part A of the property is jointly owned and boundaries occur in it; and part B of the property is jointly owned but no boundaries occur in it; therefore the right to *shufʿa* does not obtain in part A of the property, but the right to *shufʿa* does obtain in part B of the property."

[86] "Part A of the property is jointly owned and boundaries occur in it; therefore the right to *shufʿa* obtains in part A."

[87] Al-Shāfiʿī has divided the *mas'ala* into two: one part in which the *ʿilla* occasioning *shufʿa* obtains (and thus, the opponent's *ḥukm*—if restricted to it—is correct), and one part in which it does not (and thus, the opponent's *ḥukm*—extended to it—is wrong). Al-Shāfiʿī's solution thus requires two separate *ḥukm*s when the dividing (but not divided) portion of the property may itself be subject to *shufʿa*, whereas the opponent's problematic solution has but one *ḥukm*.

Having demonstrated how a disputant might achieve *elenchus* against a proponent of the Ahl al-Baṣra argument, al-Shāfiʿī immediately launches a new—and quite protracted—dialectical sequence, extending from §252 to §267. This sequence has a decidedly "historical" tenor, opening with "And some of the Easterners said: [X, Y, Z]" (*wa qāla baʿḍ al-Mashriqiyyīn*: [X, Y, Z]) (§252); followed by "We said to one who professes this doctrine" (*qulnā li-baʿḍ man yaqūlu hādhā al-qawl*) (§253); then "he said..." (*qāla*) and "so it was said to him..." (*fa-qīla lahu*) and so on. The sequence provides significant indication, in other words, that this is something like a transcript of a real debate between al-Shāfiʿī and "one of the Easterners." Even so, its very location in a work of *ikhtilāf* testifies to its didactic value, as do other indicants such as a temporary lapse to "and if he says... it is said to him..." (*fa-in qāla... qīla lahu...*) in §§258–9. That aside, we may immediately recognize this new R of the Mashriqiyyūn as the proponent of a variant on the Abū Ḥanīfa rulings in §239. Regarding these *masāʾil* he rules the right of *shufʿa*-preemption for partner (*sharīk*) and for neighbour (*jār*), when: (1) the neighbour is adjoining (*mulāṣiq*), or (2) the considered houses are separated by a court (*raḥba*) with no open and public passageway (*ṭarīq nāfidha*) in it. This latter he confirms by ruling no right to *shufʿa*-preemption for the neighbour when the court has an open and public passageway in it—even if narrow.

Al-Shāfiʿī, in the role of Q, opens the debate with a dialectical question we may instantly identify as the "question about the indicant" (*suʾāl ʿan al-dalīl*) of later *jadal* systems (*suʾāl* #3 of al-Bājī's question-schema); al-Shāfiʿī says: "Upon which thing did you (pl.) rely [for proof] (*ʿalā ayyi shayʾin iʿtamadtum*)?"[88] Accordingly, the Mashriqī R renders his *dalīl*-indicant in §254: an "*athar*," transmitted from Ibn ʿUyayna (a teacher of al-Shāfiʿī), which consists in fact of a Prophetic *ḥadīth*-decree: «The neighbour has the greater right due to his nearness (*al-jār aḥaqq bi-saqabihi*).»[89] Of course, we recognize this as the same *ḥadīth*-decree from which the Ahl al-Baṣra claimed to derive the *maʿnā*-intension for their ruling above. Al-Shāfiʿī now takes a different tack as regards this *ḥadīth*, however, saying in so many words (§255): Your *ḥadīth* does not conflict with ours; rather, yours is a general/non-specific type (*jumla*), while ours is an interpreting type (*mufassir*).[90] I cannot overstress that

[88] al-Bājī (*Minhāj*, Turkī ed., pp. 34, 36, §§64 and 70) calls it "the question about the indicant of the opinion" (*al-suʾāl ʿan dalīl al-madhhab*) and "the question about the indicant" (*al-suʾāl ʿan al-dalīl*); Q asks: "what is the indicant for that" (*mā al-dalīl ʿalā dhālika*)? In his short section on the "types of question" (*aqsām al-suʾāl*) Ibn ʿAqīl also refers to "the question about the indicant" (*al-suʾāl ʿan al-dalīl*); his Q asks: "what is your indicant for this opinion" (*mā dalīluka ʿalā hādhā al-madhhab*)? (*K. al-Jadal*, p. 42, §220).

[89] NB: although for the sake of consistency I maintain different usages for "*athar*" (as reported saying/act of Companions and Successors) and "*ḥadīth*" (as reported saying/act/acknowledgment of the Prophet), the ancient practice was far more fluid and interchangeable. In §254, for instance, we have *athar* followed by *akhbaranā* and terminating in a *qawl* of the Prophet.

[90] Joseph Lowry, in "The Legal Hermeneutics of al-Shāfiʿī and Ibn Qutayba" sheds considerable light on the terms here employed by al-Shāfiʿī. First (p. 22), he points to a discussion in the *Risāla* (Shākir ed., §§624–35) where al-Shāfiʿī utilizes a *jumla*/*mufassar* distinction, and he translates *jumal* as "non-specific." Further on (pp. 36–7), he supplies a definition of *jumla* as understood in

in §§255 ff. we have an exemplary model of al-Shāfiʿī's hermeneutic at work. Moreover, it is at work in a context of juridical dialectic born from *ikhtilāf* over the meaning of "*jār*" and the right to preemption. This is not to say, of course, that this particular *mas'ala* of *ikhtilāf* and ensuing debates gave birth to the *mufassir/mujmal* distinction. There can nevertheless be little doubt that such dialectical settings as this prompted both its introduction and its refinement of formulation over time. Certainly, whatever the case as to its origins, we cannot deny that a *mufassar/mubayyan* vs. *mujmal* distinction is a fundamental component of most *uṣūl al-fiqh* works, and no stronger evidence of the dynamic role of juridical dialectic in the formation of Islamic legal theory can be found than what we have in §§255 ff.

---

the *Risāla* ("a general rule the details of which are found elsewhere"), and he describes al-Shāfiʿī's use of *jumla* vs. *naṣṣ*: "Passages in the Qur'ān labelled *jumla* contain a general but undefined obligation (e.g., *aqīmū al-ṣalāṭ*!) the details of which are supplied by *ḥadīths*. Passages that do not require to be supplemented by another text (that is, are hermeneutically self-sufficient), are labelled *naṣṣ*." Finally, in a footnote (p. 37, n. 85), Lowry observes that *naṣṣ* and sometimes *mufassar* are opposed to *jumla/jumal*. To this I would add some additional notes. First, in the context of §255 it would seem that the active *mufassir* is more appropriate than the passive *mufassar*; this is borne out by the sense of the passage, and by a parallel distinction (in this case, *jumal/mufassira*) in the *Risāla* (Shākir ed., §314). There, al-Shāfiʿī explains the role of the Sunna as an exemplification of the *naṣṣ*, and an interpreter of the *jumal* of the Qur'ān:

314 – And God explained for them that He only abrogated what he abrogated of the Kitāb by means of the Kitāb, and that the Sunna is not a *nāsikha* (abrogator) to the Kitāb; rather, it only followed the Kitāb, representing what was revealed as *naṣṣ* (univocal), and a *mufassira* (interpreter) of the *maʿnā*-intension of what God revealed of it as *jumal* (equivocal).	314 – وأبان الله لهم أنه إنما نسخ ما نسخ من الكتاب بالكتاب، وأن السنةَ لا ناسخةٌ للكتاب، وإنما هي تَبَع للكتاب، يُمَثِّلُ ما نَزل نصاً، ومفسِّرةٌ معنى ما أنزل الله منه جُمَلاً.

The Sunna, we see, not only exemplifies (*yumaththilu*) what God sent down as univocal (*naṣṣan*), but is an [active] interpreter (*mufassira*) for the *maʿnā*-intension of such as God revealed as ambiguous/equivocal (*jumalan*). And it is this same sense of "active interpreter/specifier" and "equivocal/non-specific" which appears to be at work in §255 above. Certainly, elsewhere in the *Risāla* (§§418 and 698) we find the passive *mufassar*, and precisely in the sense which Lowry aptly describes as "hermeneutically self-sufficient." These distinctions, of course, all fall within the hermeneutical purview of most later *uṣūl al-fiqh* works, and are discussed under the headings of *mufassar/mubayyan* (clear) vs. *mujmal* (ambiguous; note that *jumla* and *mujmal* are cognates). See Hallaq, *History of Islamic Legal Theories*, pp. 43 ff., and note that he cites relevant chapters from a number of important *uṣūl* works. Finally, we might add that al-Muzanī—expounding on the same *mas'ala* of §255 above—confirms all of this in his *Mukhtaṣar* (Būlāq ed., vol.3, p. 48 [margin]; Maṭrajī ed., vol. 9, p. 130; Najjār ed., vol. 8, p. 119):

"And your *ḥadīth* does not contradict our *ḥadīth*—because it is equivocal, and our *ḥadīth* is an interpreter, and the interpreter clarifies the equivocal."	وَحَدِيثُكَ لاَ يُخَالِفُ حَدِيثَنَا – لأَنَّهُ مُجْمَلٌ وَحَدِيثُنَا مُفَسِّرٌ وَالْمُفَسِّرُ يُبَيِّنُ الْمُجْمَلَ.

What is more, we can once again easily identify al-Shāfiʿī's statement in §255 among the *iʿtirāḍāt* of later *jadal* works—we have, in fact, already seen it in §247. It is a claim of ambiguity (*daʿwā al-ijmāl*). More specifically—and this will be made clear in following sections)—it is a claim that the *language* of R's *ḥadīth*-decree is ambiguous (*mujmal*) (Shīr.II.C.3.2; Bāj.II.2.2.3.2).[91] We will also note here that such a *daʿwā* entails—as indicated by al-Shāfiʿī in §255—more than a mere claim and a linguistic explanation (which latter al-Shāfiʿī provides, at the behest of his opponent, in following sections), but it entails a kind of *muʿāraḍa*—that is to say, the "*mufassir*" *ḥadīth* of al-Shāfiʿī is brought in to particularize the "*jumla*" *ḥadīth* of the Mashriqī opponent. In so doing, the efficient properties which have been improperly drawn from the *jumla* are supplanted by those of the *mufassir* (see the end of §257).

Being that al-Shāfiʿī's *daʿwā al-ijmāl* of §255 is accompanied by a kind of *muʿāraḍa*, we are not surprised to see that hallmark of *muʿāraḍa* much mentioned by Miller in his dissertation: the switching of roles of R and Q. Perhaps al-Bājī describes this phenomenon best, when he explains the nature of *muʿāraḍa* as a dialectical question:

> [Q] opposes (*yuqābila*) [R's] indicant (*dalīl*) by its like, or by what is stronger than it; and [R] responds to him via all that [Q] puts forth against the *dalīl* of [R] [i.e., they switch roles] as pertains to *muṭālabāt* and *iʿtirāḍāt*, or he gives preponderance (*yurajjiḥu*) to his statement of the *dalīl*, over that by which it was opposed.[92]

This is precisely what happens in §256, as the Mashriqī opponent becomes a Q, and asks al-Shāfiʿī his first dialectical question of this sequence. With regard to his own *ḥadīth* (of §254), Q asks: "And how does it not contradict your (pl.) *ḥadīth* (*kayfa lā yukhālifu ḥadīthakum*)?" The *muʿāraḍa* of al-Shāfiʿī is now shown in bold relief, as his *mufassir ḥadīth* becomes the focus of attention. The new Q is aware that al-Shāfiʿī supports his ruling via *istidlāl* from another Sunnaic *dalīl*-indicant, but he is not aware of the exact nature of this *dalīl*-indicant—especially with regard to its role as *mufassir* to his own *ḥadīth*. Accordingly, we may identify Q's request with al-Bājī's fourth dialectical question: the question about the mode of the indicant (*al-suʾāl ʿan wajh al-dalīl*).[93]

Al-Shāfiʿī's *jawāb* in §257 consists of two parts. The first is an explanation of a particular *lafẓ*-expression: neighbour/neighbours (*jār/jīrān*). Recall that the *ḥadīth*-decree from which Q derives his ruling for *masʾala* #3a-b is: «"the neighbour has the greater right due to his nearness " (*al-jār aḥaqq bi-saqabihi*).» Al-Shāfiʿī now

[91] al-Shīrāzī, *Maʿūna*, al-ʿUmayrīnī ed., pp. 59–60; al-Bājī, *Minhāj*, Turkī ed., p. 102, §198; Ibn ʿAqīl, *K. al-Jadal*, p. 34, §180. Intriguingly, both al-Shīrāzī and Ibn ʿAqīl employ the same example of an ambiguous decree (*qawl mujmal*): the Prophet's maxim "the security is for what it was pledged for" (*al-rahn bimā fīhi*). This same maxim crops up in §378 of the subject-text, and a number of other places in the *Umm* (see the note attached to §378 in my dissertation: "Dialectical Forge," pt. 2, p. 106). Although occurring mostly in the midst of dialectical sequences, the issue at stake in §378 does not seem to be the *ijmāl* of this maxim, however.

[92] al-Bājī, *Minhāj*, Turkī ed., p. 41, §78.

[93] al-Bājī, *Minhāj*, Turkī ed., pp. 39–40, §76.

explains that *jār* may be used to designate a partner (*sharīk*) of commixion, or a partner who partitions (*muqāsim*), or even someone living forty houses away. The significance is that, necessarily, Q's *ḥadīth* must refer to some neighbours (*jīrān*) and not others. Importantly, al-Shāfiʿī follows this explanation by indicating his endorsement and adherence to a principle which belongs as much to *jadal*-theory as it does to legal theory in general: "But our saying this is not granted against [the opinions of] others except by way of indication (*dalāla*), on the authority of the Messenger of God, may God bless and save him...." This is clearly the statement of a restricting norm: a *daʿwā* of *ijmāl* regarding a *ḥadīth*-decree followed by a purely linguistic analysis does not alone constitute *ḥujja*—it must be supported by authoritative *dalāla*-indication. I would pause to mark this as another instance of proto-system *jadal/uṣūl* theory played out in a purely dialectical venue. If, for example, we search for the forge-marks of later *mujmal/mufassar* theory, it is in contexts such as §257 that we should first look.

In accordance with this self-imposed principle, al-Shāfiʿī now quotes his explanatory indication in full; it is the now familiar *ḥadīth*-decree: «*shufʿa*-preemption is for what was not partitioned, and when boundaries occur, there is no *shufʿa*-preemption (*al-shufʿa fīmā lam yuqsam, fa-idhā waqaʿat al-ḥudūd fa-lā shufʿata*).» Note we are dealing with the same *ḥadīth* vs. counter-*ḥadīth* as were raised in the previous dialectic against a proponent of the Ahl al-Baṣra's doctrine. The difference here is a shift in approach. Against the Ahl al-Baṣra, al-Shāfiʿī brought his "commixion/boundaries" counter-*ḥadīth* by way of *muʿāraḍa* against the *maʿnā*-intension which they attributed to their "*jār*" *ḥadīth*—it was a means of confirming the *khilāf* of their purported *maʿnā*-intension. Now al-Shāfiʿī brings his *ḥadīth*—also by way of *muʿāraḍa*—as an interpreter (*mufassir*) to the ambiguous (*jumla*) *ḥadīth* of the Easterners. Accordingly, he at last explains the mode of his *dalīl*-indicant (requested by Q in §256) as *mufassir*: "this [my *ḥadīth*-decree] provides indicant (*dalla... ʿalā*) that his saying in the general/non-specific (*jumla*) [tradition of Q]: «The neighbour has the greater right due to his nearness» pertains to some "neighbours" (*jīrān*) and not others, and that he [the intended] is the "neighbour" (*jār*) who did not partition (*lam yuqāsim*)." From this, it is immediately apparent what al-Shāfiʿī has done with his *dalīl*-indicant: he has particularized the general scope which Q attributed to the efficient property of "he is a *jār*" for occasioning the *ḥukm* of right to *shufʿa*-preemption—in effect, the efficiency of a plurality of types of "*jār*" has been supplanted by the singular efficiency of "*jār* as partner of commixion."

Once again, al-Shāfiʿī's explanation corresponds to that type of *matn*-oriented *muʿāraḍa* implied at the end of §248 and foreshadowed in §255: counter-indication by way of the occasioning factor (*al-muʿāraḍa bi'l-ʿilla*) (Shīr.II.C.8.2.3; Bāj.II.2.7.2.3). Q's general *ʿilla* (*jār* as "neighbour": adjoining/separated by a court) has indeed been supplanted by al-Shāfiʿī's particular *ʿilla* (partner of commixion), through the action of his *mufassir-ḥadīth*.[94] For both al-Shīrāzī and al-Bājī, this subspecies is to

---

[94] al-Shīrāzī, *Maʿūna*, al-ʿUmayrīnī ed., pp. 67–8, n. 6 [NB: this is part of the lacuna reproduced from the *Mulakhkhaṣ fi'l-Jadal*]; al-Bājī, *Minhāj*, Turkī ed., p. 125, §§247).

be employed "when the Sunna is general (*ʿumūm*), allowing the possibility of particularization (*takhṣīṣ*)." For both, as well, the recommended *jawāb* is that the one targeted by such a *muʿāraḍa* argue against the new R's *dalīl*-indicant in such a way as eliminates it, that he be allowed to persist in his *istidlāl* from the general. This is precisely what the new Q proceeds to do in §258, focusing upon al-Shāfiʿī's *tafsīr*-explanation of "*jār*."

Note that al-Shāfiʿī presented his argument in two parts: (1) his polysemous *tafsīr*-explanation of *jār* as applying to several types of individual; and (2) his explanation that his *muʿāraḍa-ḥadīth* pinpoints exactly which individual is intended (the partner of commixion). He has not, however, provided a *dalīl*-indicant supporting his initial *tafsīr*-explanation of *jār* in part one of the argument (part two merely assumes its polysemous nature). Q very prudently does not accept this *tafsīr*-explanation without a further *dalīl*-indicant, and his next question may be read in the spirit of both objection and request: "And the Arabs called the partner (*sharīk*) 'neighbour' (*jār*)?" This corresponds quite well with the general dialectical category of "demand" (*muṭālaba*), which Sānū defines as "[Q's] lack of acceptance for what [R] mentions of premises (*muqaddimāt*)—all of them, or some of them—without establishing the *dalīl*-indicant for them."[95] Q's question is of such a nature; he objects to the unsupported *tafsīr*-explanation, while simultaneously requesting proof from an authoritative domain: the language (*lugha*) of the Arabs. I would pause here to note that the manner of hermeneutic this represents constitutes one of the major domains of *uṣūl al-fiqh*—yet another illustration of *uṣūl*-theory developing in an early dialectic.

Note also that throughout this exchange, al-Shāfiʿī is somewhat parsimonious in his replies, never rendering up his argument in full detail, but doling it out premise-by-premise only at Q's behest. This matches well with the comportment of the respondent as we have seen it described in the *jadal* works, as does Q's practice of halting al-Shāfiʿī at every step and digging deeper for supporting proofs. Al-Shāfiʿī's response in §259 continues in this spirit, providing only a definition of *jār*: "all whose body is close to that of his companion" (*kullu man qāraba badanuhu badana ṣāḥibihi*), but not a source. Accordingly, Q cannot accept it without further support, so his next question (§260) is once again in the spirit of *muṭālaba*. He says: "Provide me an indicant for this (*fa-dlulnī ʿalā hādhā*)."[96] Al-Shāfiʿī immediately

---

[95] Sānū, *Muʿjam*, s.v. "المطالبة." The reference to "premises" doubtless marks this definition as emanating from a later source/sources. I have yet to find a more precise match in the early *jadal*-theory texts, although we might consider Q's *muṭālaba* as similar to al-Bājī's "demanding from [R] confirmation of the property in the source-case" (*al-muṭālaba lahu bi-ithbāt al-waṣf fi'l-aṣl*); Bāj. IX.A.1.5; *Minhāj*, Turkī ed., p. 151, §312), if we consider al-Shāfiʿī's *jār-sharīk* of commixion correspondence as critical to establishing the efficient property of his *aṣl-ḥadīth*.

[96] Due to the wording of Q's demand, we might be tempted to identify this as *al-muṭālaba bi'l-dalīl*. It would seem, however, that this particular species of *muṭālaba* is restricted to the domain of *qiyās*—specifically for demanding the *dalīl* by which R provides indicant that the *ḥukm* is occasioned by a certain *ʿilla* (Sānū, *Muʿjam*, s.v. "المطالبة بالدليل"). Al-Bājī's several *dalīl*-oriented *muṭālabāt* seem to bear this out (Bāj.IX.A.1.2–4; *Minhāj*, Turkī ed., pp. 149–50, §312).

replies with not one, but two such *dalīl*-indicants, citing: (§261) a Prophetic *ḥadīth* wherein the Prophet judges against one of the "two neighbours" (*jāratayn*) of Ḥamal b. Malik b. al-Nābigha, and in which the context allows us to interpret *jāra* as wife—or, perhaps, female slave (*jāriya* or *ama*)—and (§262) a verse from a short *qaṣīda* of Maymūn b. Qays al-Aʿshā (d. ca. 8/629) wherein *jāra* clearly means wife.[97]

Following this, al-Shāfiʿī launches (in §263) a multi-tiered *iʿtirāḍ* against Q's rulings for *mas'ala* #3a-b, whereby all of *tanāquḍ*, *reductio ad absurdum*, and the *iʿtirāḍ* of *naqḍ* come into play, and by which we would expect al-Shāfiʿī's *elenchus* to be sealed (Q, however, is not yet ready to concede). First, al-Shāfiʿī charges Q with not adhering to the very *jadal/uṣūl* principle which al-Shāfiʿī imposed upon himself back in §257: *tafsīr*-explanation of the *jumla* is not sufficient argument in and of itself, but must be supported by an authoritative *dalīl*-indicant. "But *you*, when you say it is specific to some 'neighbour'" and not others—you bring no indication for that from the Prophet, may God bless and save him. Nor do you apply it to whom rightly adheres 'the label of proximity.'" In other words, inherent to the very rulings of the Mashriqī opponent for *mas'ala* #3a-b is a conception that the *jār* of «the neighbour has the greater right due to his nearness (*al-jār aḥaqq bi-saqabihi*)» applies to some *jīrān*-neighbours and not others, but Q has not backed this conception with another Prophetic *dalīl*-indicant, as al-Shāfiʿī has done for his opposing

[97] As discussed in the note attached to §262, above, variants of this *bayt* appear in a number of *ḥadīth* commentaries, *fiqh* works, etc., usually for the purpose of interpreting *jār* in connection to preemption. Al-Muzanī, in a detailed discourse on *shufʿa* in his *Mukhtaṣar* (Būlāq ed., vol. 3, pp. 48–9 [margin]; Maṭrajī ed., vol. 9, p. 130; Najjār ed., vol. 8, p. 119), reproduces a number of lines from the poem, prefaced by the following "historical" dialectical Q&A (bear in mind that al-Muzanī was purportedly praised as a master dialectician by al-Shāfiʿī):

He said: And does the 'label of proximity' fall upon the partner?	قَالَ: وَهَلْ يَقَعُ اسْمُ الْجِوَارِ عَلَى الشَّرِيكِ؟
I said: Yes—is your wife closer to you, or your partner?	قُلْتُ: نَعَمْ – امْرَأَتُكَ أَقْرَبُ إِلَيْكَ أَمْ شَرِيكُكَ؟
He said: My wife, of course! Because she is my bed-fellow.	قَالَ: بَلْ امْرَأَتِي، لأَنَّهَا ضَجِيعَتِي.
I said: And so the Arabs say the wife of a man is his neighbor.	قُلْتُ: فَالْعَرَبُ تَقُولُ امْرَأَةُ الرَّجُلِ جَارَتُهُ.
He said: But where?	قَالَ: وَأَيْنَ؟
I said: Al-Aʿshā said: O *jāra* of ours: part, and you are indeed divorced [etc.]	قُلْتُ: قَالَ الأَعْشَى: أَجَارَتَنَا بِينِي فَإِنَّكِ طَالِقَهْ...[إلخ]

Note that the "the label of proximity" (*ism al-jiwār*) of this discussion also occurs in §263 above, and that al-Muzanī's dialectical sequence parallels that of al-Shāfiʿī vs. the Mashriqī Q quite closely. I would consider this an example of a proto-system transmission of *jadal* teaching and practice, from al-Shāfiʿī to al-Muzanī. If al-Muzanī did in fact engage in the above dialectic, and if he learned its basic structure and premises from the *Umm*, than the didactic role of *Umm* dialectical sequences would be illustrated here in bold relief.

conception. There is something important in this charge which we ought not overlook. If we conceive of the development of a science of methodology (such being *uṣūl al-fiqh* and *jadal*-theory) as a "pursuit of argumentative conclusiveness (*ḥujjiyya*)"—i.e., a gradual winning-out of proven epistemically-superior methods over those less productive in disputation —then we are witnessing here the very thing itself. Al-Shāfiʿī is chiding his opponent for not adhering to a principle of method whose epistemic superiority (within the greater superset of theological and legal-theoretical first principles) cannot be ignored.[98] Moreover, it is a principle which Q himself has pressed for by earlier demanding al-Shāfiʿī's *dalīl*-indicant.[99]

Al-Shāfiʿī's charge contains a second component (Q does not fix the *lafẓ*-expression of *jār* upon whom 'the label of proximity' rightly adheres), and we may understand this as a setting of the stage for another charge of internal, logical self-contradiction (*tanāquḍ*). The meaning of this first step becomes clear in the second, when al-Shāfiʿī develops his argument thus: (1) the *ḥadīth* of Ibn Maysara (i.e., Q's *ḥadīth* in §254)[100] permits only one of the two *maʿnā*-intensions which Q attributes to it—i.e., *jār* can only designate either an efficient property of (a) partner of commixion, or (b) neighbour separated by a court with no open passageway; and (2) "you have contradicted them both, together (*qad khālaftahumā maʿan*)." Thus is the cause of Q's *tanāquḍ* exposed, he never fixed the *maʿnā*-intension of *jār* in his source *ḥadīth* with any precision and, as a result, he ended up contradicting both possible *maʿnā*-intensions by allowing them all to occasion the same ruling. Recalling that his source *ḥadīth* (*al-jār aḥaqq bi-saqabihi*) bequeaths "the most right" to the "*jār*," I would represent Q's *tanāquḍ* thus:

• Q's source *ḥadīth*: $(x)(Jx \rightarrow Sx)$[101] • Q does not fix the meaning of *jār*, and thus mistakenly rules: $Jp \vee Jn \vdash Sp \ \& \ Sn$[102]	**Universe:** • J = neighbour (*jār*) • S = has most right to *shufʿa*-preemption • p = Partner of commixion • n = neighbour separated by a court with no open passageway

[98] One might claim, in fact, that al-Shāfiʿī's *Risāla* represents a distillation of these epistemically-superior methods as developed over time in al-Shāfiʿī's disputations, not to mention presented in a style of didactic dialectic. Here in §263 we find something in that spirit of the *Risāla*.

[99] In this sense, al-Shāfiʿī's charge could be read as one of hypocrisy. This is verging upon something we will encounter later, which I have labelled "method-*naqḍ*."

[100] Note that al-Shāfiʿī does not refer to it by its last narrator—his own teacher, Ibn ʿUyayna—but prefers to label it by the next narrator in the *isnād*.

[101] Read: "For any x, if x is a *jār*, then x has the most right to *shufʿa*."

[102] Read: "The partner of commixion is a *jār* OR the neighbour separated by a *raḥba* with no *ṭarīq nāfidha* is a *jār*; therefore, the partner of commixion has the most right to *shufʿa* AND the neighbour separated by a *raḥba* with no *ṭarīq nāfidha* has the most right to *shufʿa*.

Clearly, according to al-Shāfiʿī's argument, if the *lafẓ*-expression of *jār* can only designate one of two possible types of individual, then "the most right to *shufʿa*-preemption" can be granted only to one, and not to the other. By granting it to both, Q has contradicted both possible *maʿnā*-intensions of his own source *ḥadīth*. To a certain extent, this is similar to the *tanāquḍ* of §251, where al-Shāfiʿī shows how R contradicted the *maʿnā*-intension of the very *ḥadīth* which he conceded. Perhaps we might consider a family of *tanāquḍ*, then, in which an opponent's purported *istidlāl bi'l-Sunna* is shown to contradict the *maʿnā*-intension of the very Sunnaic *dalīl*-indicant which is the source of his *istidlāl*.

Al-Shāfiʿī does not stop here. Without hesitation, he shifts to a different angle of attack, initiating a three-stage *reductio* argument. We may read al-Shāfiʿī's argument as a set of premises (1–2) consequent to Q's rulings, followed by a conclusion (3) which, in combining premises 1–2, exposes an absurdity inherent to Q's reasoning: (1) Q would concede the right to *shufʿa* preemption for a house separated by a court of 1,000 cubits and more, so long as there is no open passageway in it; (2) Q would *not* concede the right to *shufʿa*-preemption when the properties are separated by an open passageway of only one cubit; (3) therefore, Q would concede the right to *shufʿa*-preemption for the most distant of *jīrān*-neighbours, while preventing it from the nearest. The absurdity lies, of course, in that this set of hypothetical rulings—consequent to those expressed by Q in §252 for *mas'ala* #3b—defy the conception of *jār* as implied in his own source-*ḥadīth* by "due to his nearness (*bi-saqabihi*)." We might, therefore, also classify al-Shāfiʿī's argument as another charge of *tanāquḍ*—for Q has once again contradicted the very *ḥadīth* from which he claims *istidlāl*—but the extremes of 1,000 cubits and 1 cubit seem to make *reductio ad absurdum* a more appropriate fit.

Still not satisfied with his critique, al-Shāfiʿī shifts to yet another tack, and we are finally exposed to what has seemed "missing" from previous charges of *tanāquḍ*, and which disallowed us from interpreting these past objections as *naqḍ*. Al-Shāfiʿī raises, near the end of §263, a parallel ruling of Q as regards another genus of substantive law, demonstrating clearly that—although the same purportedly efficient property obtains in this *mas'alat al-naqḍ*—Q does not cause it to occasion the same ruling as he does in the *mas'ala* at hand. These are the two "hallmarks" of the *iʿtirāḍ* of *naqḍ*: (1) the raising of a parallel *mas'ala* whose ruling is *endoxon*; and (2) that this *mas'alat al-naqḍ* exhibits, by the definition of the *jadal* works, "the presence of the occasioning factor despite the absence of the ruling (*wujūd al-ʿilla maʿa ʿadam al-ḥukm*)."[103] And these two hallmarks are evident in al-Shāfiʿī's charge: "And you have claimed, of one who registers a bequest (*awṣā*) to his 'neighbours' (*jīrān*),

[103] al-Bājī, *Minhāj*, Turkī ed., p. 14; and p. 185 (§142). Cf. the definitions of al-Shīrāzī and al-Baṣrī as discussed in Chap. 4. The opening (§276) of Ibn ʿAqīl's *Chapter on Inconsistency* (*Bāb al-Naqḍ*) begins: "*Naqḍ* is presence of the occasioning factor despite absence of the ruling (*wujūd al-ʿilla maʿa ʿadam al-ḥukm*), and that is the opposite (*ḍidd*) of efficiency (*ta'thīr*), because *ta'thīr* is presence of the ruling without the occasioning factor (*wujūd al-ḥukm bi-ghayr al-ʿilla*). And such is a valid question according to the doctrine of who does not profess particularization of the occasioning factor (*takhṣīṣ al-ʿilla*), and such are our Ḥanbalī companions" (*K. al-Jadal*, p. 56).

that you apportion his bequest (*qassamta waṣiyyatahu*) on behalf of one whose house is forty houses away (!)" This *waṣiyya*-bequest ruling is the *mas'alat al-naqḍ*; we can clearly see that the same pair of efficient properties (i.e., "he is a *jār*" and "he is separated by forty houses") as would occasion a *ḥukm* of "no right belongs to him" by Q's rulings on the *shufʿa*-preemption *mas'ala*, instead occasion the contrary *ḥukm* by Q's rulings on the *mas'alat al-naqḍ*. So not only are we witnessing an *iʿtirāḍ* of *naqḍ* some two hundred years or more before our first extant works of juridical *jadal* theory, but we are witnessing it in a most pristine form. Notably, however, we are also witnessing it in a domain (against *istidlāl bi'l-Sunna*) in which it does not appear in our *jadal*-theory texts (being confined there only to the realm of *qiyās*).[104]

Delving deeper for a more exact identification in later *jadal* theory, we find that al-Shīrāzī (Shīr.VII.7) does not break the category of *naqḍ* into subcategories; rather, he proceeds directly from his definition to the treatment of several modes of *jawāb*—i.e., of valid methods of responding to the *iʿtirāḍ* of *naqḍ*. Among these we find one (mode 3) which has some relevance to al-Shāfiʿī's *iʿtirāḍ* above, in that it describes a response-procedure which parallels the procedure undertaken by al-Shāfiʿī himself in his objection. Al-Shīrāzī prescribes: "That he repudiate (*an yadfaʿa*) the *naqḍ* by way of the *maʿnā*-intension of the *lafẓ*-expression, and that consists of two things: the obligation (*muqtaḍā*) of the *lafẓ*-expression, and the *tafsīr*-explanation of the *lafẓ*-expression."[105] As to this latter approach, he writes: "the *lafẓ*-expression may possibly bear two commands with a single likelihood (*iḥtimālan wāḥidan*), so he interprets (*yufassiru*) one of them in order to repudiate the *naqḍ*."[106] Thus, in describing a counter to *naqḍ*, al-Shīrāzī comes quite close to describing the procedure by which al-Shāfiʿī initiated his set of arguments, closing with an attack of *naqḍ*.[107]

Al-Bājī, on the other hand, subdivides *naqḍ* into two types dependent upon the nature of the *ʿilla* under debate—it is either: (1) "posited for the genus (*wuḍiʿa li'l-jins*), being in the position (*manzila*) of the definition (*ḥadd*);" or (2) "posited for the affirmation of rulings for individuals (*wuḍiʿa li-ithbāt al-aḥkām fi'l-aʿyān*)."[108] He explains the first type: "regarding it, co-presence and co-absence (*al-ṭard wa'l-ʿaks*) are taken into account; and if it is undone (*intaqaḍa*) in one of the two ways, then

[104] Again, note this expanded range for *naqḍ* as a feature of proto-system *jadal*.

[105] al-Shīrāzī, *Maʿūna*, al-ʿUmayrīnī ed., p. 105.

[106] al-Shīrāzī, *Maʿūna*, al-ʿUmayrīnī ed., 106.

[107] Clearly, if the *lafẓ*-expression may possibly bear two commands, then Q may base his *iʿtirāḍ* upon one and R his *jawāb* upon the other. The initial vehicle for both would be *tafsīr* of the *lafẓ*-expression.

[108] al-Bājī, *Minhāj*, Turkī ed., p. 185, §412.

it is undone in the other."[109] I would quickly note this as another instance of cross-over between two method-theory domains of *uṣūl al-fiqh* (*al-ṭard wa'l-ʿaks* as a method for *ithbāt al-ʿilla*) and *al-jadal al-fiqhī* (type #1 of the *iʿtirāḍ* of *naqḍ*). This provides evidence for another of the theories considered in this study; namely, that the private deliberations of *ijtihād* may in part attempt to anticipate the public critique of dialectical disputation. Hence the science of *ijtihād* (*uṣūl al-fiqh*) is geared in part towards an *internal dialectic*—which is to say, in this case, that when the *mujtahid* employs the procedure of *al-ṭard wa'l-ʿaks* privately, he is anticipating the *naqḍ* of his jurist-peers (who will "test" or critique his *ijtihād* through dialectic).

The *ʿilla* of al-Shāfiʿī's *mas'alat al-naqḍ* clearly does not stand up to the procedure of *al-ṭard wa'l-ʿaks*;[110] we may thus identify his *naqḍ* as the second type of al-Bājī's typology. This however, is again subdivided into two types: (1) for the *ʿilla* posited for obligation (*mawḍūʿa li'l-wujūb*); and (2) for the *ʿilla* posited for permission (*li'l-jawāz*). Considering the *ḥukm* for our *mas'alat al-naqḍ*, we would classify its *ʿilla* by the first type, of which al-Bājī writes: "when it is found without the *ḥukm*, such constitutes *naqḍ*." Thus, my final identification of al-Shāfiʿī's objection at the end of §263 is: *iʿtirāḍ* by way of the *naqḍ* of an *ʿilla* which was posited for a *ḥukm* of obligation regarding an individual, not a genus (Bāj.IX.B.11.2.1).[111]

Finally, we reach the end of §263, where al-Shāfiʿī drives home his charges of *naqḍ* and *tanāquḍ* with a rhetorical question which, normally, would mark the sealing of his *elenchus*: "So how is it you make no *shufʿa*-preemption for what you apportioned the bequest (*waṣiyya*), when you have contradicted (*khālafta*) our *ḥadīth*—and the ḥadīth of Ibrāhīm b. Maysara, upon which you based your argument (*iḥtajajta bihi*)?" Al-Shāfiʿī has drawn together the threads of his objection into a singular confounding question, and we can see from the remaining sections that Q is understood to have afterwards conceded the overthrow of his own *ḥujja*. Still, before committing to the "partner of commixion only" ruling of al-Shāfiʿī, Q has one more test.

---

[109] al-Bājī, *Minhāj*, Turkī ed., p. 185, §413. Of particular import here is an evident correspondence between the classical requirements of definition: "what subsumes" and "what excludes" (*jāmiʿ* and *māniʿ*), and of *jarayān* (*ṭard* and *ʿaks*). This is an idea worthy of further investigation in light of al-Bājī's twofold typology of the *ʿilla*, and that the first is "in the *manzila* of the *ḥadd*," while the second is for "individuals (*aʿyān*)."

[110] The *ʿilla* of his *mas'alat al-naqḍ* is composed of two efficient properties ("he is a *jār*" and "he is separated by forty houses"); together, these occasion a *ḥukm* of "he has the right to a portion of the *waṣiyya*." According to the procedure of *al-ṭard wa'l-ʿaks*, the *ḥukm* must be present wherever the *ʿilla* is present, and absent wherever it is absent. Clearly, however, in the *mas'ala* of the *waṣiyy* who bequeaths to his *jīrān*, the *ḥukm* of "he has the right to a portion of the *waṣiyya*" is not dependent solely upon the *ʿilla* "he is a *jār* separated by forty houses"—were he the *jār* next door he would have his portion.

[111] al-Bājī, *Minhāj*, Turkī ed., p. 185, §415. Cf. Ibn ʿAqīl's discussion on *naqḍ* (*K. al-Jadal*, pp. 56 ff., §§276 ff.); he follows the same typology as al-Bājī, and from this we might surmise that al-Shīrāzī's was the same (as the teacher of both).

In §264, and once more in the spirit of *muṭālaba*, Q asks: "Did any one of the Companions of the Prophet, may God bless and save him, profess your opinion?" Although I have yet to find an exact match for this question in the later *jadal* literature, it is obvious that Q's request is related to theories of abrogation (*naskh*) and, perhaps, consensus of the Companions (*ijmāʿ al-ṣaḥāba*). As for *naskh*, we find a relevant objection related to the transmitted text of the Sunna (as *qawl mubtadaʾ*) in al-Shīrāzī's *Maʿūna*; his sixth *iʿtirāḍ* (*naskh*) is divided into several modes, the third of which is "abrogation by way of the contradictory doings of the Companions (*al-naskh bi-ʿamal al-Ṣaḥāba bi-khilāfihi*)" which is that "[Q] conveys, about the Companions [of the Prophet], such doings as contradict [the *khabar*-report], in order to indicate its abrogation" (Shīr.II.C.6.3).[112] Although this *iʿtirāḍ* is directed towards the practice (*ʿamal*) of the Companions, not their decree (*qawl*) (as with Q), a parallel rationale may be discerned in Q's *muṭālaba*: if none of the Companions professed the same decree, this may serve as an indicant that such a Prophetic decree is abrogated (*mansūkh*). On the other hand, if a significant number of Companions professed this decree, without *khilāf*, then this might serve as indicant of consensus of the Companions (*ijmāʿ al-ṣaḥāba*). Either way, it is evident that Q's *muṭālaba* represents a demand for a certain kind of supporting transmission (*naql*) which—in addition to al-Shāfiʿī's rational arguments (*ʿaql*)—would elevate al-Shāfiʿī's *mufassir-ḥadīth* over all other possible *adilla*-indicants. As such, it is most related to a demand for *tarjīḥ*. Not surprisingly, the very first mode of al-Shīrāzī's *matn*-oriented *tarjīḥāt* (Shīr.IX.2.1) reads: "That one of the two *khabar*-reports is consistent (*muwāfiq*) with another *dalīl*-indicant, from an authoritative source-case (*aṣl*), or what is rationally understood from one (*maʿqūl aṣl*); it is given precedence, because it is accompanied by something which facilitates understanding of it."[113] We might interpret Q's question, then, as a *muṭālaba* for *tarjīḥ* based on a supporting decree from one or more Companions.

Al-Shāfiʿī, as frugal as ever with his *jawāb*, responds in §265 not with the requested source(s), but with a simple confirmation "yes" (*naʿam*) followed by the profession of a principle of transmission-related legal epistemology. This latter is meant to pre-empt any further objections, simply by pointing out the irrelevance of Q's *muṭālaba*; al-Shāfiʿī asserts: "Nor would it harm us, anyway—since it is confirmed on the authority of the Prophet, may God bless and save him—if no one at all professes it." Once again, we are witnessing the assertion of a proto-system legal theory within a dialectical context: a confirmed Prophetic *ḥadīth* may stand alone as an *aṣl*, unharmed by the silence of Companions (or Successors). From another perspective, we may read this response as the quashing of an *e silentio* argument in the bud—i.e., Q might intend to argue: "If the Prophet really pro-

---

[112] al-Shīrāzī, *Maʿūna*, al-ʿUmayrīnī ed., pp. 62, 63–4. Cf. Ibn ʿAqīl (*K. al-Jadal*, p. 35, §185) and al-Bājī (Bāj.II.2.5.3; *Minhāj*, Turkī ed., p. 112, §219), both of whom employ the same definition as their teacher, and the same *masʾala* example.

[113] al-Shīrāzī, *Maʿūna*, al-ʿUmayrīnī ed., p. 123.

fessed it, then so would one or more of the Companions, but we have no such *naql* from them." Either way, we have testimony here of a legal theory honed—gaining the edge of *ḥujjiyya*, in fact—in the forge of dialectic. Note also that, however briefly, legal-theory itself has become the *subject* of dialectic. In other words, al-Shāfiʿī's apparent dismissal of Q's grasping at the silence of the Companions is an instance of *uṣūl*-oriented *jadal*.

Q is persistent, however, and will not concede without the final confirmation which a decree from the Companions would lend to al-Shāfiʿī's already extensive argument; he repeats his *muṭālaba* in §266, asking: "And who professed it" (*fa-man qāla bihi*)? At last al-Shāfiʿī complies, and with an overwhelming response. In §266 he lists not only ʿUmar b. al-Khaṭṭāb and ʿUthmān, but "some of the Successors" including the highly regarded Umayyad Caliph ʿUmar b. ʿAbd al-ʿAzīz, and others. And with that the dialectical sequence comes to a close, as did—or so we must assume—the Mashriqī Q's resistance.

Masāʾil-Set #3

§§274–88 from the *Chapter on Sharecropping* (*Bāb al-Muzāraʿa*)[114]

274 – Al-Shāfiʿī, may God Most High have mercy upon him, said: And when a man gives over [tillable] land to a man for sharecropping, for a half, or a third, or a quarter [of the produce]; or he gives over date-palms or trees for cultivation, for half, or less than that, or more [of the produce]; then indeed Abū Ḥanīfa, may God Most High be pleased with him, used to say: This, all of it, is null and void, because he seeks to hire him in exchange for something unknown.[115]	274 - قَالَ الشَّافِعِيُّ رَحِمَهُ اللّٰهُ تَعَالَى: وَإِذَا أَعْطَى الرَّجُلُ الرَّجُلَ أَرْضًا مُزَارَعَةً بِالنِّصْفِ أَوْ الثُّلُثِ أَوْ الرُّبُعِ، أَوْ أَعْطَى نَخْلاً أَوْ شَجَرًا مُعَامَلَةً بِالنِّصْفِ أَوْ أَقَلَّ مِن ذَلِكَ أَوْ أَكْثَرَ فَإِنَّ أَبَا حَنِيفَةَ رضي الله تعالى عنه كَانَ يَقُولُ: هَذَا كُلُّهُ بَاطِلٌ؛ لأَنَّهُ اسْتَأْجَرَهُ بِشَيْءٍ مَجْهُولٍ.
275 – He [used to] say: Have you considered [what would happen] if no harvest comes of it; would not his work have been without wage?	275 - يَقُولُ: أَرَأَيْتَ لَوْ لَمْ يَخْرُجْ مِن ذَلِكَ شَيْءٌ، أَلَيْسَ كَانَ عَمَلُهُ ذَلِكَ بِغَيْرِ أَجْرٍ؟

(continued)

[114] Ḥassūn ed., vol. 9, pp. 57–9; ʿAbd al-Muṭṭalib ed., vol. 8, pp. 253–5.

[115] For expositions on sharecropping on tillable land (*muzāraʿa*) and related rulings, see *MF*, s.v. "مزارعة" (vol. 37, pp. 49–85); and *EI*², s.v. "Muzāraʿa." For sharecropping with trees/vines (*muʿāmala*/*musāqāt*) and related rulings, see *MF*, s.v. "مساقاة" (vol. 37, pp. 112–147); *EI*², s.v. "Musāḳāt"; and *DJP*, vol. 2, pp. 293–300. As noted by Lane (*Lexicon*, s.v. "عامله" [form 3 under "عمل"]), *muʿāmala* is synonymous with *musāqāt*—the first being the Iraqi term, and the second the Ḥijāzī—meaning: "The employing a man to take upon himself, or manage, the culture [or watering, etc.] of palm-trees or grape-vines [or the like] on the condition of his having a certain share of their produce."

276 – But Ibn Abī Laylā used to say: That, all of it, is lawful. It has reached us concerning the Messenger of God, may God bless and save him, that he gave over Khaybar for half [of the produce],[116] and so it was until he was taken up [i.e., passed away], and [during] the caliphate of Abū Bakr, may God Most High be pleased with him, and the greater part of the caliphate of ʿUmar. And he [Abū Yūsuf] embraced it.	276 - وَكَانَ ابْنُ أَبِي لَيْلَى يَقُولُ: ذَلِكَ كُلُّهُ جَائِزٌ، بَلَغَنَا عَن رَسُولِ اللهِ - صَلَّى اللهُ عَلَيْهِ وَسَلَّمَ - أَنَّهُ أَعْطَى خَيْبَرَ بِالنِّصْفِ، فَكَانَتْ كَذَلِكَ حَتَّى قُبِضَ، وَخِلاَفَةِ أَبِي بَكْرٍ رضي الله تعالى عنه وَعَامَّةِ خِلاَفَةِ عُمَرَ. وَبِهِ يَأْخُذُ.
277 – And indeed, according to us, the *qiyās* for this concurs with the *athar*-tradition. Don't you see/opine that a man may give over property to a man in a speculative partnership for half [the profit], and there is no harm in that?[117]	277 - وَإِنَّمَا قِيَاسُ هَذَا عِنْدَنَا مَعَ الأَثَرِ. أَلاَ تَرَى أَنَّ الرَّجُلَ يُعْطِي الرَّجُلَ مَالاً مُضَارَبَةً بِالنِّصْفِ وَلاَ بَأْسَ بِذَلِكَ.
278 – And it has reached us concerning ʿUmar b. al-Khaṭṭāb, may God Most High be pleased with him, and ʿAbd Allāh b. Masʿūd, and ʿUthmān b. ʿAffān, may God Most High be pleased with him, that they gave over property in speculative partnership.	278 - وَقَدْ بَلَغَنَا عَن عُمَرَ بْنِ الْخَطَّابِ رضي الله تعالى عنه وَعَن عَبْدِ اللهِ بْنِ مَسْعُودٍ وَعَن عُثْمَانَ بْنِ عَفَّانَ رضي الله تعالى عنه أَنَّهُمْ أَعْطُوا مَالاً مُضَارَبَةً.
279 – And it has reached us concerning Saʿd b. Abī Waqqāṣ, and Ibn Masʿūd, may God Most High be pleased with them both, that they used to give over their land for a quarter and a third [of the produce].	279 - وَبَلَغَنَا عَن سَعْدِ بْنِ أَبِي وَقَّاصٍ، وَعَن ابْنِ مَسْعُودٍ رضي الله تعالى عنهما أَنَّهُمَا كَانَا يُعْطِيَانِ أَرْضَهُمَا بِالرُّبُعِ وَالثُّلُثِ.
280 – Al-Shāfiʿī, may God Most High have mercy upon him, said: And when a man turns over to a man date-palms, or grape-vines, that he cultivate them with the understanding that half the fruit belongs to the worker—or a third, or whatever they mutually stipulate as a portion from it; this is the lawful sharecropping of trees/vines[118] which the Messenger of God, may God bless and save him, transacted with the Ahl Khaybar.[119]	280 - قَالَ الشَّافِعِيُّ رَحِمَهُ اللهُ تَعَالَى: وَإِذَا دَفَعَ الرَّجُلُ إِلَى الرَّجُلِ النَّخْلَ أَوْ الْعِنَبَ يَعْمَلُ فِيهِ عَلَى أَنَّ لِلْعَامِلِ نِصْفَ الثَّمَرَةِ أَوْ ثُلُثَهَا أَوْ مَا تَشَارَطَا عَلَيْهِ مِن جُزْءٍ مِنْهَا، فَهَذِهِ الْمُسَاقَاةُ الْحَلاَلُ الَّتِي عَامَلَ عَلَيْهَا رَسُولُ اللهِ -صَلَّى اللهُ عَلَيْهِ وَسَلَّمَ - أَهْلَ خَيْبَرَ.

(continued)

[116] See *EI*², s.v. "Khaybar," for a detailed exposition on this historically-important oasis, especially renowned for its date-palms.

[117] On the speculative or "sleeping" partnership (*muḍāraba/qirāḍ*) and related rulings, see *MF*, s.v. "مضاربة" (vol. 38, pp. 35–99); *EI*², s.v. "Muḍāraba" and "Ḳirāḍ"; *DJP*, vol. 2, pp. 284–92; and Hallaq, *Sharīʿa*, pp. 254–6.

[118] On *musāqāt*, see the note for §274, above.

[119] The "Folk of Khaybar," meaning the inhabitants of the conquered oasis.

281 – But when a man turns over to a man "white [i.e., uncultivated] land," with the understanding that the recipient will cultivate it, and [that] whatever God brings forth from it of anything, there belongs to him a portion of it; this is the sale of a green crop for a known portion before its wholesomeness becomes apparent,[120] and the renting of land for some of what is produced from it,[121] and the sharecropping of tillable land[122] which the Messenger of God, may God bless and save him, proscribed. So we have made lawful the sharecropping of date palms from *khabar*-reports on the Messenger of God, may God bless and save him; and we have made unlawful the sharecropping of "white land" from *khabar*-reports on the Messenger of God, may God bless and save him.	281 - وَإِذَا دَفَعَ الرَّجُلُ إِلَى الرَّجُلِ أَرْضًا بَيْضَاءَ عَلَى أَنْ يَزْرَعَهَا الْمَدْفُوعَةُ إِلَيْهِ، فَمَا أَخْرَجَ اللَّهُ مِنْهَا مِن شَيْءٍ فَلَهُ مِنْهُ جُزْءٌ مِنَ الأَجْزَاءِ؛ فَهَذِهِ الْمُحَاقَلَةُ وَالْمُخَابَرَةُ وَالْمُزَارَعَةُ الَّتِي نَهَى عَنْهَا رَسُولُ اللَّهِ - صَلَّى اللَّهُ عَلَيْهِ وَسَلَّمَ، فَأَحْلَلْنَا الْمُعَامَلَةَ فِي النَّخْلِ خَبَرًا عَن رَسُولِ اللَّهِ - صَلَّى اللَّهُ عَلَيْهِ وَسَلَّمَ، وَحَرَّمْنَا الْمُعَامَلَةَ فِي الأَرْضِ الْبَيْضَاءِ خَبَرًا عَن رَسُولِ اللَّهِ - صَلَّى اللَّهُ عَلَيْهِ وَسَلَّمَ.
282 – And we were no more compelled to proscribe what we made unlawful than to sanction what we made lawful; nor was it our right to discard one of [the Prophet's] exemplary practices on the basis of the other; nor that we proscribe—via what he proscribed—that which he sanctioned; just as we never sanction—via what he sanctioned—that which he proscribed. And I know not a single one of the people[123] saved from contradicting the Prophet, may God bless and save him, in either of the two matters—neither the one who sanctioned them both, together, nor the one who proscribed them both, together.[124]	282 - وَلَمْ يَكُنْ تَحْرِيمُ مَا حَرَّمْنَا بِأَوْجَبَ عَلَيْنَا مِن إِحْلاَلِ مَا أَحْلَلْنَا، وَلَمْ يَكُنْ لَنَا أَنْ نَطْرَحَ بِإِحْدَى سُنَّتَيْهِ الأُخْرَى، وَلاَ نُحَرِّمَ بِمَا حَرَّمَ مَا أَحَلَّ كَمَا لاَ نُحِلُّ بِمَا أَحَلَّ مَا حَرَّمَ، وَلَمْ أَرَ بَعْضَ النَّاسِ سَلِمَ مِن خِلاَفِ النَّبِيِّ - صَلَّى اللَّهُ عَلَيْهِ وَسَلَّمَ - مِن وَاحِدٍ مِنَ الأَمْرَيْنِ؛ لاَ الَّذِي أَحَلَّهُمَا جَمِيعًا وَلاَ الَّذِي حَرَّمَهُمَا جَمِيعًا.

(continued)

[120] For this forbidden transaction, known as *muḥāqala*, see *MF*, s.v. "بيع المحاقلة" (vol. 9, p. 138).

[121] On *mukhābara*—generally understood as synonymous with *muzāraʿa*—see *MF*, s.v. "مخابرة" (vol. 9, p. 138).

[122] On *muzāraʿa*, see the note for §274, above.

[123] See the note for §252, above, where al-Rabīʿ explains that *baʿḍ al-nās* refers to the "Easterners," meaning, most likely, the Iraqis. The attributed opinions in the latter part of the current §282 confirm this.

[124] That is, whoever sanctions both *muʿāmala* of palm/vine and *muzāraʿa* of tillable land (like Ibn Abī Laylā and Abū Yūsuf), has contradicted one of the Prophet's *sunnas* (the proscription on sharecropping "white land"); while whoever proscribes both *muʿāmala* of palm/vine and *muzāraʿa* of tillable land (like Abū Ḥanīfa), has contradicted the other *sunna* (the Prophet's sanctioning of sharecropping date palms).

283 – And as for what was narrated concerning Saʿd and Ibn Masʿūd, that they both turned over their land for *muzāraʿa*-sharecropping: it is neither confirmed by its like, nor by the Ahl al-Ḥadīth.[125] But if anything is confirmed regarding someone with the Prophet, may God bless and save him: [it is] authoritative proof.[126]	283 - فَأَمَّا مَا رُوِيَ عَن سَعْدٍ وَابْنِ مَسْعُودٍ أَنَّهُمَا دَفَعَا أَرْضَهُمَا مُزَارَعَةً فَمَا لاَ يُثْبِتُ هُوَ مِثْلُهُ وَلاَ أَهْلُ الْحَدِيثِ، وَلَوْ ثَبَتَ مَا كَانَ فِي أَحَدٍ مَعَ النَّبِيِّ - صَلَّى اللّٰهُ عَلَيْهِ وَسَلَّمَ – حُجَّةٌ.
284 – And as for his *qiyās*, and what it permits of date palms and land based on the *muḍāraba*-partnership;[127] we know of the Ahl al-Fiqh[128] that they weigh what has come down to us about those beneath the Prophet, may God bless and save him, against what has come down to us about the Prophet, may God bless and save him. But as for weighing the Sunna of the Prophet, may God bless and save him, against a *khabar*-report from one of the Companions—as though seeking to confirm [his Sunna] as concurring with the *khabar*-report about his Companions—this is ignorance. Indeed, God, to Him belong power and might, fixed for the people, all of them, only the need for the Prophet, may God bless and save him. And he [Abū Yūsuf] also errs in the *qiyās*: we ourselves have only permitted *muḍāraba*-partnership since it has come down to us about ʿUmar and ʿUthmān that it was a *qiyās* based on the sharecropping of date-palms! So it was following a *qiyās*, not followed as a basis for *qiyās*.[129]	284 - وَأَمَّا قِيَاسُهُ وَمَا أَجَازَ مِن النَّخْلِ وَالأَرْضِ عَلَى الْمُضَارَبَةِ فَعَهْدُنَا بِأَهْلِ الْفِقْهِ يَقِيسُونَ مَا جَاءَ عَمَّنْ دُونَ النَّبِيِّ - صَلَّى اللّٰهُ عَلَيْهِ وَسَلَّمَ - عَلَى مَا جَاءَ عَن النَّبِيِّ - صَلَّى اللّٰهُ عَلَيْهِ وَسَلَّمَ، وَأَمَّا أَنْ يُقَاسَ سُنَّةُ النَّبِيِّ - صَلَّى اللّٰهُ عَلَيْهِ وَسَلَّمَ - عَلَى خَبَرٍ وَاحِدٍ مِن الصَّحَابَةِ، كَأَنَّهُ يَلْتَمِسُ أَنْ يُثْبِتَهَا بِأَنْ تُوَافِقَ الْخَبَرَ عَن أَصْحَابِهِ فَهَذَا جَهْلٌ، إِنَّمَا جَعَلَ اللّٰهُ عَزَّ وَجَلَّ لِلْخَلْقِ كُلِّهِمْ الْحَاجَةَ إِلَى النَّبِيِّ - صَلَّى اللّٰهُ عَلَيْهِ وَسَلَّمَ، وَهُوَ أَيْضًا يَغْلَطُ فِي الْقِيَاسِ، إِنَّمَا أَجَزْنَا نَحْنُ الْمُضَارَبَةَ وَقَدْ جَاءَتْ عَن عُمَرَ وَعُثْمَانَ أَنَّهَا كَانَتْ قِيَاسًا عَلَى الْمُعَامَلَةِ فِي النَّخْلِ، فَكَانَتْ تَبَعًا قِيَاسًا لاَ مَتْبُوعَةً مَقِيسًا عَلَيْهَا.
285 – And if one should say: And how does *muḍāraba*-partnership resemble *musāqāt*-sharecropping?	285 - فَإِنْ قَالَ قَائِلٌ: فَكَيْفَ تُشْبِهُ الْمُضَارَبَةُ الْمُسَاقَاةَ؟

(continued)

[125] The "Ḥadīth Folk," meaning the traditionists and specialists in transmission. ʿAbd al-Muṭṭalib transcribes instead [فمما لا يثبت هو مثله ، ولا هذا الحديث] (vo. 8, p. 255). I have followed Ḥassūn's transcription, finding it easier to make sense of, and more consonant with other *ḥadīth* valuations in the subject-text.

[126] This is a critical illustration of al-Shāfiʿī's epistemology of authority in practice: Companion traditions confirmed neither by their like, nor by *ḥadīth* specialists, cannot stand as proof (*ḥujja*) unless supported by Prophetic Sunna.

[127] Referring to Abū Yūsuf in §277, and his use of the speculative partnership (*muḍāraba*) as an authoritative root-case (*aṣl*), for correlational inference (*qiyās*) in support of his adherence to Ibn Abī Laylā's ruling.

[128] The "Folk of Deep Understanding [of God's Law]," meaning the legal specialists.

[129] In other words, ʿUmar and ʿUthmān justified the *muḍāraba* contract by way of correlational inference from the Prophet's date-palm sharecropping. By justifying sharecropping by *qiyās* from *muḍāraba*, Abū Yūsuf has committed the fallacy of *circulus in probando*.

286 – It is said: The date-palms remain belonging to the principal;[130] he turns them over with the understanding that the cultivator will do to them such as by which the healthy growth of their fruit may be expected, [and] with the understanding that some of [the fruit] will belong to him. So when the turned-over property [in a *muḍāraba*-partnership] remains belonging to the principal, in the hands of [the agent] to whom he turned it over, who does to it such as by which he can expect a surplus; it is allowed that some of that surplus belong to him, according to what they mutually stipulated. It exhibits the like *maʿnā*-intension of the *musāqāt*-contract.	286 - قِيلَ: النَّخْلُ قَائِمَةٌ لِرَبِّ الْمَالِ؛ دَفَعَهَا عَلَى أَنْ يَعْمَلَ فِيهَا الْمُسَاقِي عَمَلاً يُرْجَى بِهِ صَلاَحُ ثَمَرِهَا عَلَى أَنَّ لَهُ بَعْضَهَا، فَلَمَّا كَانَ الْمَالُ الْمَدْفُوعُ قَائِمًا لِرَبِّ الْمَالِ فِي يَدَيْ مَنْ دَفَعَ إِلَيْهِ يَعْمَلُ فِيهِ عَمَلاً يَرْجُو بِهِ الْفَضْلَ جَازَ لَهُ أَنْ يَكُونَ لَهُ بَعْضُ ذَلِكَ الْفَضْلِ عَلَى مَا تَشَارَطَا عَلَيْهِ وَكَانَ فِي مِثْلِ مَعْنَى الْمُسَاقَاةِ.
287 – And if he says: So why isn't this [so] regarding [tillable] land?	287 - فَإِنْ قَالَ: فَلِمَ لاَ يَكُونُ هَذَا فِي الأَرْضِ؟
288 – It is said: The land is not what thrives and has surplus taken from it. Rather, there only thrives in it something else—and not something remaining as it originally was, which is sold and its surplus taken—like [the capital in] *muḍāraba*; nor something intensely productive and its fruit taken—like date-palms; but only something which occurs in [the land]—and, moreover, by way of a conduct which exhibits the *maʿnā*-quality of neither of these two.[131] So [that thing which thrives in the land] is not allowed to be a *qiyās* based upon [*musāqāt*-sharecropping], while it is divergent from it from start to finish. And even were it allowed to be a *qiyās*, it is not permitted that something proscribed by the Prophet be decided by *qiyās*—and that there be sanctioned by way of it something which he proscribed. Just as the Messenger of God, may God bless and save him, fixed [as penance], for one who invalidates his fast by sexual intercourse, [the manumission of] a slave; but no correlational inference is made from this for the one who invalidates his prayer by sexual intercourse, even though each invalidated a duty through sexual intercourse.	288 - قِيلَ: الأَرْضُ لَيْسَتْ بِالَّتِي تَصْلُحُ فَيُؤْخَذُ مِنْهُ الْفَضْلُ، إِنَّمَا يَصْلُحُ فِيهَا شَيْءٌ مِن غَيْرِهَا وَلَيْسَ بِشَيْءٍ قَائِمٍ يُبَاعُ وَيُؤْخَذُ فَضْلُهُ، كَالْمُضَارَبَةِ، وَلاَ شَيْءٍ مُثْمِرٍ بَالِغٍ فَيُؤْخَذُ ثَمَرُهُ كَالنَّخْلِ، وَإِنَّمَا هُوَ شَيْءٌ يَحْدُثُ فِيهَا، ثُمَّ بِتَصَرُّفٍ لاَ فِي مَعْنَى وَاحِدٍ مِن هَذَيْنِ، فَلاَ يَجُوزُ أَنْ يَكُونَ قِيَاسًا عَلَيْهَا وَهُوَ مُفَارِقٌ لَهَا فِي الْمُبْتَدَإِ وَالْمُتَعَقَّبِ، وَلَوْ جَازَ أَنْ يَكُونَ قِيَاسًا مَا جَازَ أَنْ يُقَاسَ شَيْءٌ نَهَى عَنْهُ النَّبِيُّ - صَلَّى اللهُ عَلَيْهِ وَسَلَّمَ - فَيَحِلُّ بِهِ شَيْءٌ حَرَّمَهُ؛ كَمَا جَعَلَ رَسُولُ اللهِ - صَلَّى اللهُ عَلَيْهِ وَسَلَّمَ - فِي الْمُفْسِدِ لِلصَّوْمِ بِالْجِمَاعِ رَقَبَةً، فَلَمْ يُقَسْ عَلَيْهَا الْمُفْسِدُ لِلصَّلاَةِ بِالْجِمَاعِ، وَكُلٌّ أَفْسَدَ فَرْضًا بِالْجِمَاعِ.

This *masāʾil*-set constitutes the whole of the subject-text's *Chapter on Sharecropping* (*Bāb al-Muzāraʿa*). Its presentation categories are as follows: §§274–5 (Abū Ḥanīfa, category C); §§276–9 (Ibn Abī Laylā & Abū Yūsuf, category C); §§280–1 (al-Shāfiʿī, category D); §§282–4 (al-Shāfiʿī, category C); §§285–8 (al-Shāfiʿī vs. anonymous opponent, category A). It is noteworthy that both the presentations of Abū Ḥanīfa's and of Ibn Abī Laylā's rulings bear formulaic signs of past dialectic (hence, category C)—in this case, the staple formulae of *a-raʾayta* and *a-lā tarā*. I would thus

[130] The principal is "the owner of the property" (*rabb al-māl*), which is also the term for the "sleeping partner" of a *muḍāraba* contract.

[131] That is to say, the activities by which crops are raised share no properties with such as bring trees to bear fruit, or capital to bear surplus.

claim of the entire chapter that it bears overt signs of past, and recurring, dialectical disputation. We begin with §274, where Abū Ḥanīfa's ruling for both *mas'ala* #1 (*muzāraʿa* of land for half, third, or quarter) and *mas'ala* #2 (*muʿāmala* of palms/trees for half, less, more) is presented: "This, all of it, is null and void (*bāṭil*)." This is followed by brief *ʿaql* support wherein "because (*li-anna*)" indicates the efficient property which, according to Abū Ḥanīfa, occasions this ruling: "he seeks to hire him in exchange for something unknown (*majhūl*)." Immediately following this (§275), a rhetorical *a-ra'ayta* is attributed to Abū Ḥanīfa, which introduces a *reductio* argument by which a hypothetical negative consequence might result from the contradictory of his ruling: perhaps nothing will be produced, leading to the untenable consequence of work without wage (*ajr*). This consequence of the opposing ruling is patently non-*endoxon*; R cannot maintain it and its potential consequence both. We thus gain insight into one of the major functions of *a-ra'ayta*: the formula is most often a vehicle for delivering *reductio* arguments of this type.[132]

With the help of later works such as al-Ṭabarī's *Ikhtilāf al-Fuqahā'*, we can also confirm that the non-*endoxon* consequence of Abū Ḥanīfa's *a-ra'ayta* would be deemed as such: "And the *ʿilla* of the one who professes the doctrine of Abū Ḥanīfa, as regards his distaste (*karāha*) for *muzāraʿa* and *musāqāt*, is the consensus of all (*ijmāʿ al-kull*) that wage (*ujra*) is not permitted unless known (*maʿlūma*). So when the cultivator (*ʿāmil fi'l-arḍ*) is merely one hiring the land (*musta'jir al-arḍ*) [with the conditions of the *mas'ala*, and the untenable consequence of no produce] then it is an 'unknown hire' (*ijāra majhūla*), and it is null and void (*bāṭila*) by way of *qiyās* with what they achieved consensus upon (*ajmaʿū ʿalayhi*)."[133] Al-Ṭabarī's explanation allows us to pinpoint the *aṣl* ('unknown hire' is null), sanctioned by *ijmāʿ*, on the basis of which Abū Ḥanīfa performs *qiyās* to both *muzāraʿa* and *musāqāt*.

Assuming the *dalīl*-indicant for the opposing position is the Sunnaic example of the Prophet at Khaybar (see Ibn Abī Laylā in §276), we may also understand Abū Ḥanīfa's *a-ra'ayta* as delivering a specific species of *muʿāraḍa*. In short, his *a-ra'ayta* serves to underscore the rationale (*ḥikma*)—"what if nothing is produced?"—behind the *ʿilla* ("it is for something unknown") in the *masā'il* at hand (*muzāraʿa* and *musāqāt*), which *ʿilla* is also present in the *aṣl*-ruling ('unknown hire' is null) made *endoxon* via "the consensus of all" (*ijmāʿ al-kull*). The whole thus represents a trumping, by way of *qiyās*, of the *istidlāl bi'l-Sunna* by which proponents of the opposing ruling of permission draw support; Abū Ḥanīfa's argument is *muʿāraḍa*, by way of *qiyās*, against *istidlāl bi'l-Sunna*. We might predict that al-Shāfiʿī would find this mode of reasoning problematic, and we would be correct; al-Shāfiʿī will soon take proponents of Abū Ḥanīfa's position to task.

---

[132] Abū Ḥanīfa's *a-ra'ayta* in §275: rhetorical, posing an untenable consequence: a derived case which is more logically necessary and immediate, and contingent-possible, supporting a ruling with an efficient property (identified); for an overall justification/objection of *istidlāl bi'l-qiyās/muʿāraḍa bi-ʿilla* of opposing *istidlāl bi'l-Sunna*.

[133] *Ikhtilāf al-Fuqahā'*, Kern ed., pp. 147–8.

Abū Ḥanīfa's type of *mu'āraḍa* may be identified with some precision in later *jadal* systems. The opposing opinion (Ibn Abī Laylā in §276) relies upon that species of *istidlāl bi'l-Sunna* drawing from the Prophet's deeds (*af'āl*)—specifically, his actions at Khaybar. Having thus located the corresponding domain of *i'tirāḍāt* (Shīr.II.E; Bāj.II.4), we may thus narrow focus to the *i'tirāḍ* of *mu'āraḍa* (Shīr.II.E.8; Bāj.II.4.9), and at last to *mu'āraḍa* by way of an *'illa* (Shīr.II.E.8.2; Bāj.II.4.9.3).[134] Al-Bājī further subdivides this species according to the nature of the Prophet's deed as either (1) "susceptible of interpretation" (*muḥtamal*), or (2) "not susceptible of interpretation" (*ghayr muḥtamal*)—i.e., R's supporting Sunnaic deed may either incorporate the new *'illa* brought by Q, or it may not. Abū Ḥanīfa's *mu'āraḍa bi-'illa* falls under the latter (Bāj.II.4.9.3.2), and al-Bājī's Mālikī (R) vs. Ḥanafī (Q) example is instructive; it shows Q attempting to overturn R's *istidlāl* from Sunnaic deed by way of introducing an *'illa-ḥukm* relationship established in another source (just as with Abū Ḥanīfa above). Accordingly, al-Bājī suggests a method for R's rebuttal to this *mu'āraḍa*, part of which includes "that it be said... *qiyās* may not counter-indicate (*lā yu'āriḍu*) unambiguous text (*naṣṣ*), and if [R] desires to instructively debate the *qiyās*, so that [Q] concede his *dalīl*-indicant, then such is his right."[135] This *jawāb* is a fair description of al-Shāfi'ī's counter-argument against Abū Ḥanīfa's position, as we will see.

Ibn Abī Laylā's ruling (in §276), for *mas'ala* #1 and #2, is the contrary of Abū Ḥanīfa's: "That, all of it, is lawful (*jā'iz*)."[136] This receives immediate *naql*-support in two parts: (1) the Prophetic deed: Khaybar was given over for half the produce; and (2) the tacit compliance of Abū Bakr and 'Umar, whereby the Prophet's deed at Khaybar remained in effect until near the end of 'Umar's reign. As for the first part, we may understand it simply as *istidlāl* by way of Sunnaic deed. In a dialectical context, however, and placing the proponent of Ibn Abī Laylā's position in the role of Q, we might also read it as a type of *mu'āraḍa* against the *qiyās* of Abū Ḥanīfa's position—the very converse of the *mu'āraḍa* suggested by Abū Ḥanīfa's *a-ra'ayta* in §275. Were such the case, we could also easily identify this objection: it

---

[134] al-Shīrāzī, *Ma'ūna*, al-'Umayrīnī ed., p. 77; al-Bājī, *Minhāj*, Turkī ed., pp. 134–5, §272 ff. Cf. Ibn 'Aqīl, *K. al-Jadal*, p. 38, §200, who mentions this species but provides neither discussion nor example nor response. Note my identification procedure above is meant to mimic a disputant employing the *istidlāl*-based organizing principle of al-Shīrāzī, Ibn 'Aqīl, and al-Bājī. This is the logic of *topoi* at work—the same as is propounded in the *Topics*. A practiced disputant who has memorized the many argument types according to larger sets and subsets may quickly "locate" the largest set of counter-arguments relevant to the opponent's argument, then proceed through subsets until locating the precise form of relevant counter-argument, and finally go about collecting from the opponent such premises by which that counter-argument will transform into *elenchus*.

[135] al-Bājī, *Minhāj*, Turkī ed., p. 135, §274.

[136] In the strict sense of contraries, both rulings may not be true, but both may be false. According to al-Shāfi'ī's rulings, such is the case here. Abū Ḥanīfa rules "*al-muzāra'a* and *al-musāqāt* are *bāṭil*;" Ibn Abī Laylā rules the contrary "*al-muzāra'a* and *al-musāqāt* are *jā'iz*;" while al-Shāfi'ī rules "*al-muzāra'a* is *bāṭil* and *al-musāqāt* is *jā'iz*."

is the first species of *qiyās*-oriented *muʿāraḍāt*—i.e., "Counter-Indication with a Divinely-Sanctioned Decree (*al-Muʿāraḍa bi'l-Nuṭq*)" (Shīr.VII.15.1; Bāj.IX.B.15.1)—with al-Shīrāzī describing *nuṭq* as Qur'ān, Sunna, and Ijmāʿ, and Ibn ʿAqīl noting: "When the *qiyās* counter-indicates (*ʿāraḍa*) the *naṣṣ* of Kitāb or Sunna, the *ḥukm* of the *qiyās* is eliminated."[137] As for the second part of Ibn Abī Laylā's *naql* in §276, it is presented as support for the Sunnaic deed. In a sense, it is giving more weight to Ibn Abī Laylā's *istidlāl bi'l-Sunna*, and thus interpreted constitutes a kind of preponderance (*tarjīḥ*). A suitable category of *tarjīḥ* is found among al-Shīrāzī's *matn*-oriented "Modes of Preponderance of Expressions whose Intensions are Most Apparent" (*tarjīḥāt al-ẓawāhir*), wherein the preponderant *khabar*-report "is consistent (*muwāfiq*) with another *dalīl*-indicant, from an authoritative source-case (*aṣl*), or what is rationally understood from one (*maʿqūl aṣl*)" (Shīr.IX.2.1).[138] In this case, the supporting *aṣl* is the tacit continuation of the Prophet's Khaybar transaction under the reigns of Abū Bakr and ʿUmar.

Abū Yūsuf embraces the ruling of Ibn Abī Laylā;[139] the position rendered in §§277–9 may thus emanate from either. In §277, a further argument is put forth: "And indeed, according to us, the *qiyās* for this concurs with the *athar*-tradition"—i.e., with the Sunnaic deed and its continuation under Abū Bakr and ʿUmar. This added support also constitutes a type of *tarjīḥ*, and may be found under the same category as above (Shīr.IX.2.1). This time, however, the *muwāfiq* is what is rationally understood from another authoritative source-case (*maʿqūl aṣl*)—being *maʿnā al-khiṭāb*, or *qiyās*—rather than an *aṣl* itself. The *qiyās*-support of Ibn Abī Laylā/Abū Yūsuf is followed by a rhetorical *a-lā tarā* by which the new *aṣl* of the proposed *athar*-supporting *qiyās* is introduced; in short, *muḍāraba* is contracted for half the profit, and "there is no harm in that" (*la ba'sa bi-dhālika*).[140] Note this as a general function of the *a-lā tarā* formula: the delivery of an *endoxon* ruling (indeed, one sanctioned by *ijmāʿ al-kull*) which is to serve as *aṣl* for *qiyās* in the *mas'ala* at hand.[141] Moreover, this *qiyās* is then supported from two different directions: (1) in §278 the *aṣl* for *qiyās* is supported by *āthār*-traditions of ʿUmar, Ibn Masʿūd, and ʿUthmān (who gave property for *muḍāraba*); and (2) in §279 the transferred *ḥukm* of permission is supported by *āthār*-traditions of Saʿd b. Abī Waqqāṣ and Ibn Masʿūd (who contracted the giving of land for a third and a quarter). Taken in its totality, then,

---

[137] al-Shīrāzī, *Maʿūna*, Turkī ed., p. 262, §147 [missing from al-ʿUmayrīnī ed.]; al-Bājī, *Minhāj*, Turkī ed., p. 201, §454; Ibn ʿAqīl, *K. al-Jadal*, p. 70, §327.

[138] al-Shīrāzī, *Maʿūna*, al-ʿUmayrīnī ed., p. 123.

[139] This is an act of frequent occurrence in the subject-text, and a clear sign that "following the *ḥujja*" held sway over teacher/school loyalties.

[140] Cf. al-Ṭabarī (*Ikhtilāf al-Fuqahā'*, Kern ed., p. 148): "And as for the *ʿilla* of the one who professes the doctrine of Abū Yūsuf and Muḥammad [b. al-Ḥasan al-Shaybānī], it is [in] the *qiyās* from the *ijmāʿ al-kull* for the allowance of *muqāraḍa*; etc." *Muqāraḍa* is synonymous with *muḍāraba*.

[141] Abū Yūsuf's *a-lā tarā* in §277: rhetorical, bringing supporting evidence as a parallel case with an established *ḥukm*, sharing elements of the *mas'ala* at hand, identified (or obviously intended) as an *aṣl* for *qiyās*; for an overall justification/objection of *istidlāl bi'l-qiyās* / *muʿāraḍa bi'l-qiyās* of the opposing *istidlāl bi'l-Sunna*; and as a *qiyās* in support of an *athar* (as a kind of *tarjīḥ*).

Ibn Abī Laylā's/Abū Yūsuf's ruling (*muʿāmala* of both land and trees for a portion of the produce is permitted) is derived/supported via: (1) *istidlāl bi'l-Sunna*; which is in turn given preponderance by (2) *āthār*-traditions of Abū Bakr and ʿUmar; then by (3) a corresponding *qiyās* from the *endoxon* ruling on *muḍāraba*; which is in turn supported by (4) *āthār*-traditions for both *muḍāraba* and *muʿāmala* of land.

The *aṣl* for Ibn Abī Laylā's/Abū Yūsuf's supporting *qiyās* is delivered via rhetorical *a-lā tarā*, we may thus interpret the production of *qiyās* from *muḍāraba* to *muʿāmala* as a dialectical move from past disputation. As such, it is identifiable not only as *qiyās* supporting Sunna—which, as we shall see, is highly problematic for al-Shāfiʿī—but as a species of *muʿāraḍa*. Moreover, and thanks once again to al-Ṭabarī, we may distinguish the *ʿilla* thought by Abū Yūsuf and al-Shaybānī to be efficient in both *muḍāraba* and *muzāraʿa/musāqāt*, and to have occasioned their *ḥukm* of permission: the labour is for something "which will come into existence, but is not in existence, and it is unknown (*majhūl*) before its existence, known (*maʿlūm*) upon its existence."[142] Against this is the *ʿilla* for Abū Ḥanīfa's *qiyās*, which occasioned the *ḥukm* of null and void: "it is for something unknown (*majhūl*)." In effect, the Ibn Abī Laylā/Abū Yūsuf *ʿilla* asserts a *qiyās*-invalidating distinction (*farq*) between the *ʿilla* of Abū Ḥanīfa's *aṣl* and the (true) *ʿilla* of the contended branch-cases (*furūʿ*) of *muzāraʿa* and *musāqāt*. Thus, a new *aṣl* (with a more appropriate, matching *ʿilla*) is brought to supplant Abū Ḥanīfa's *aṣl*. Equipped with a knowledge of the *uṣūl* and *ʿilal* of the opposing *qiyās*-sets, we can proceed to identify the most likely species of *qiyās*-oriented *muʿāraḍa* which proponents of the Abū Ḥanīfa vs. Ibn Abī Laylā/Abū Yūsuf positions might have employed in dialectical debate. Assuming Ibn Abī Laylā/Abū Yūsuf to be in the role of Q, a most precise identification may be found in al-Bājī's refined subdivisions. Bearing in mind that the *uṣūl* for both *qiyās*-sets are sanctioned by *ijmāʿ*, it is: "Counter-Indication with the Occasioning Factor of the Source-Case—which is Invalidating Distinction (*al-muʿāraḍa bi-ʿillat al-aṣl wa huwa al-farq*)," with "Invalidating Distinction by way of the Occasioning Factor of the Ruling (*farq bi-ʿillat al-ḥukm*)," when "the *maʿnā*-intension is an object of agreement (*muttafaq ʿalayhi*)" (Bāj.IX.B.15.2.2.1.1);[143] and this finds its corresponding match in al-Shīrāzī's hierarchy (Shīr.VII.15.2.2.1.1).[144]

In §280 al-Shāfiʿī rules, for the cultivation of vines/trees for a third, or whatever portion stipulated, that "this is the lawful sharecropping of trees/vines (*al-musāqāt al-ḥalāl*)"—supporting this immediately by reference to the now familiar Sunnaic deed: the Prophet's transaction with the Ahl al-Khaybar. In §281, however, he rules, for the cultivation of "white land" for whatever portion stipulated, that "this is the sale of a green crop for a known portion before its wholesomeness becomes apparent (*muḥāqala*), and the renting of land for some of what is produced from it (*mukhābara*), and the sharecropping of tillable land (*muzāraʿa*) which the

---

[142] *Ikhtilāf al-Fuqahā'*, Kern ed., p. 148.

[143] al-Bājī, *Minhāj*, Turkī ed., pp. 202–3, §459.

[144] al-Shīrāzī, *Maʿūna*, Turkī ed., pp. 262–3, §149.

Messenger of God, may God bless and save him, proscribed (*nahā ʿanhā*)"—in other words, the *muʿāmala* of land is proscribed by a different *istidlāl bi'l-Sunna*. Al-Shāfiʿī clarifies his reasoning in a succinct manner: *muʿāmala* of the date-palm (*mas'ala* #2) has been made lawful (*ḥalāl*) on the basis of a *khabar*-report about the Prophet; *muʿāmala* of "white land" (*mas'ala* #1) has been made unlawful (*ḥarām*) on the basis of another *khabar*-report about the Prophet. Already we can see that Abū Ḥanīfa and Ibn Abī Laylā/Abū Yūsuf will be taken to task for their respective *qiyās*-based arguments made in full light of contradicting, but established, Sunna. We may also measure this initial response as corresponding to that species of *muʿāraḍa*—Sunna over *qiyās*—already encountered in my analysis of Ibn Abī Laylā's argument in §276; the explanation of al-Shāfiʿī here constitutes a *muʿāraḍa bi'l-nuṭq* (Shīr. VII.15.1; Bāj.IX.B.15.1).

As we discover in §282, however, there is more at stake from al-Shāfiʿī's perspective. As we understand from his explanation, Abū Ḥanīfa and Ibn Abī Laylā are both in violation of a fundamental legal-theoretical principle. Consequently, we will witness a most illuminating illustration of proto-system legal theory acquiring the edge of argumentative conclusiveness (*ḥujjiyya*), in a dialectical context. Al-Shāfiʿī asserts his principle in three stages, which—by way of tedious repetition—are quite evidently designed to hammer the principle home. He says: (1) "we were no more compelled to proscribe what we made unlawful than to sanction what we made lawful;" (2) "nor was it our right to discard one of [the Prophet's] exemplary practices on the basis of [i.e., by way of *qiyās* from] the other;" and (3) "nor that we proscribe—via [*qiyās* from] what he proscribed—that which he sanctioned; just as we never sanction—via [*qiyās* from] what he sanctioned—that which he proscribed."

This is more than a mere statement of legal-theoretical principle, but itself constitutes a type of *iʿtirāḍ*—an "appeal to legal theory"—against reasoning from *qiyās* when the result is problematic, conflicting with established Sunna. Certain "appeals to legal theory" are found in lens-texts in opposition to the use of *qiyās* in certain instances (cf. Shīr.VII.1.1–2; Bāj.IX.B.1.1–2). There are stronger hints, however, that this particular principle of al-Shāfiʿī was well-understood. Ibn ʿAqīl says (while introducing *al-muʿāraḍa bi'l-nuṭq*): "When the *qiyās* counter-indicates (*ʿāraḍa*) the *naṣṣ* of Kitāb or Sunna, the *ḥukm* of the *qiyās* is eliminated;"[145] and I earlier foreshadowed al-Shāfiʿī's objection by quoting part of al-Bājī's *jawāb* to a charge of *muʿāraḍa bi-ʿilla*: "that it be said… *qiyās* may not counter-indicate (*lā yuʿāriḍu*) unambiguous text (*naṣṣ*), and if [R] desires to instructively debate the *qiyās*, so that [Q] concede his *dalīl*-indicant, then such is his right."[146] Finally, note that al-Bājī dedicates a set of *iʿtirāḍāt* (Bāj.IX.B.2–4) consisting of charges that R's *aṣl* is not allowed to be an *aṣl* for *qiyās*, or his *ʿilla* is not allowed to be an *ʿilla*, or his *ḥukm* is not allowed to be a *ḥukm*.[147] Notably, the fourth component of *qiyās* (the

[145] Ibn ʿAqīl, *K. al-Jadal*, p. 70, §327.

[146] al-Bājī, *Minhāj*, Turkī ed., p. 135, §274.

[147] al-Bājī, *Minhāj*, Turkī ed., pp. 155 ff., §326 ff.

*far*ʿ) is not treated here, and it is precisely the *far*ʿ with which al-Shāfiʿī is concerned. In other words, al-Shāfiʿī's objection consists, from a certain perspective, of a charge that R's *far*ʿ is not allowed to be a *far*ʿ for *qiyās*—because it is already established by Sunna. This is equivalent to the charge of *muʿāraḍa biʾl-nuṭq* (Shīr. VII.15.1; Bāj.IX.B.15.1).

Returning to §282, we now find that a more palpable dialectical element enters al-Shāfiʿī's argument, which I would label a "historical" objection. He laments: "I know not a single one of the people [meaning Easterners, or Iraqis] saved from contradicting the Prophet, may God bless and save him, in either of the two matters—neither the one who sanctioned them both, together [like Ibn Abī Laylā and Abū Yūsuf, re: both *muʿāmala* of trees/vines and 'white land'], nor the one who proscribed them both, together [like Abū Ḥanīfa]."[148] Read in the spirit of dialectical objection—and if we assume all of Abū Ḥanīfa, Ibn Abī Laylā, and Abū Yūsuf to have been cognizant of the Sunnaic *adilla*-indicants referenced by al-Shāfiʿī, and to have conceded their verification—I would consider al-Shāfiʿī's lament as a charge of *tanāquḍ*, reminiscent of those we have seen earlier. In other words, had Abū Ḥanīfa, Ibn Abī Laylā, and Abū Yūsuf all known of and conceded al-Shāfiʿī's Sunnaic *adilla* (which, by his reckoning, are certainly *endoxa*), then they would have been shown by al-Shāfiʿī to contradict their own concessions by generating contrary rulings. Alternately, we might, again, consider his statement as an expression of *qiyās*-oriented *muʿāraḍa biʾl-nuṭq*.

Al-Shāfiʿī turns to another appeal in §283, where he launches a two-part *iʿtirāḍ* against the *istidlāl* of Ibn Abī Laylā/Abū Yūsuf (in §279) from the *āthār*-traditions of Saʿd b. Abī Waqqāṣ and Ibn Masʿūd. First, he claims that their practice (*muzāraʿa* for a third and a quarter) is not confirmed by its like (*lā yuthbitu huwa mithluhu*); second, that it is not confirmed by the Ahl al-Ḥadīth. Again, we may read this in the spirit of a "historical" objection—a dialectic with jurists of the past—and two distinct types of *iʿtirāḍ* are at work. Recognize first that we have entered the *istidlāl*-domain of "the saying of a solitary companion" (*qawl al-wāḥid min al-Ṣaḥāba*), which was controversial from the start and only became more so over time. Importantly, al-Shāfiʿī closes his objection with a revealing hypothetical observation: had one of the above *athar* narrations been confirmed in accordance with the Prophetic Sunna, it would have constituted proof (*ḥujja*). This statement provides certain insights: (1) al-Shāfiʿī indicates that *qawl al-wāḥid min al-Ṣaḥāba* can, in fact, constitute *ḥujja* when certain conditions are met; (2) he sheds light on what he meant by "it is not confirmed by its like" (*lā yuthbitu huwa mithluhu*): it is not, as might first be expected, a call for additional supporting *āthār*-traditions (as a thrust towards *ijmāʿ* of the Companions); rather, it is a call for Sunnaic consonance. The confirming "*mithluhu*," in other words, must be found in the Prophet's Sunna, as he later argues.

[148] Note that all three are, as al-Shāfiʿī said, Easterners/Iraqis.

The evidence of such statements allows us to link the subject-text (as Schacht and Ḥassūn have) to al-Shāfiʿī's "Old Doctrine;" and no better confirmation might be found than what the *Maʿūna* provides. First among al-Shīrāzī's objections to *istidlāl* from *qawl al-wāḥid min al-Ṣaḥāba* (Shīr.IV.1) is: "[Q] says: the saying of a solitary Companion is not a proof (*ḥujja*)." The sole recorded *jawāb* to this, however, is: "[R] says: 'Verily, such according to me is *ḥujja*, in [al-Shāfiʿī's] Old Doctrine (*fī qawlihi al-qadīm*);' and if [Q] does not concede, [R] provides indication for this."[149] Note that "the saying of a solitary Companion when it is not conspicuous is not *ḥujja*" appears as the primary stance of al-Bājī (it is the dominant opinion [*ẓāhir*] of the Mālikī *madhhab*), as well as the first *iʿtirāḍ* of al-Shīrāzī and Ibn ʿAqīl.[150] That al-Shāfiʿī at all allows for the possibility that *qawl al-wāḥid min al-Ṣaḥāba* may stand as *ḥujja* provides a strong link to his Old Doctrine, although I would note he still insists it be in consonance with the Prophet's Sunna (as opposed to merely in consonance with *qiyās*).

Most important to the objectives of this study, we are once again provided insight as to how a legal-theoretical principle might be forged in a dialectical context. Al-Shāfiʿī's claim that the contents of these opposing *āthār*-traditions are not supported by their like (*mithl*), twinned with his critique that they are not consonant with Prophetic Sunna, constitutes another "appeal to legal theory." This, as we have seen, most closely resembles al-Bājī's objection to "the saying of a solitary Companion when it is not conspicuous" (*qawl al-wāḥid min al-Ṣaḥāba idhā lam yaẓhar*). But we have seen al-Shāfiʿī object via appeal to the non-confirmation of the Ahl al-Ḥadīth, which itself most closely resembles a transmission-oriented *iʿtirāḍ*. This again confirms that he considered the possibility that *qawl al-wāḥid min al-Ṣaḥāba* might constitute *ḥujja*, for our early *jadal*-theory texts do not even treat transmission-oriented objections for this controversial domain of *istidlāl*. Any similarity to al-Shāfiʿī's objection could only be found in the domain of "Objection against Drawing Indication from the Sunna, with reference to the Chain of Transmission" (*al-iʿtirāḍ ʿalā al-istidlāl bi'l-Sunna min jihat al-isnād*) (Shīr.II.B; Bāj. II.1).[151]

Al-Shāfiʿī is not through with appealing to such principles; in §284, expressly targeting the *qiyās* of Ibn Abī Laylā/Abū Yūsuf from *muḍāraba*, he makes a patently dialectical push towards the concession of yet another methodological norm. His formulation is important here, for it is as much an "appeal to the *endoxon*" as it is

[149] al-Shīrāzī, *Maʿūna*, al-ʿUmayrīnī ed., p. 82. Importantly, we may infer from this that both Q and R may belong to the Shāfiʿī *madhhab*. This reminds us that juridical dialectic was far more than an inter-*madhhab* contest, but a critical venue for testing the *ijtihād* of jurist-peers within one's own doctrinal school.

[150] al-Bājī, *Minhāj*, Turkī ed., pp. 134 ff., §296; al-Shīrāzī, (op. cit.); Ibn ʿAqīl, *K. al-Jadal*, p. 39, §207. All these authors discuss means by which R might attempt to support his *qawl al-wāḥid min al-Ṣaḥāba* as *ḥujja*.

[151] al-Shīrāzī, *Maʿūna*, al-ʿUmayrīnī ed., pp. 52 ff.; al-Bājī, *Minhāj*, Turkī ed., pp. 76 ff., §147 ff. Cf. Ibn ʿAqīl, *K. al-Jadal*, pp. 30 ff., §161 ff.

to principle: "we know of the Ahl al-Fiqh that they weigh what has come down to us about those beneath the Prophet, may God bless and save him, against what has come down to us about the Prophet, may God bless and save him. But as for weighing the Sunna of the Prophet, may God bless and save him, against a *khabar*-report from one of the Companions—as though seeking to confirm [his Sunna] as concurring with the *khabar*-report about his companions—this is ignorance." In other words, our knowledge of the legal specialists is that they follow method X, not the method of Ibn Abī Laylā/Abū Yūsuf, which is wrong. We may, of course, read this as an *argumentum ad verecundiam*, but in this setting of juridical dialectic it is much more. In fact, it is a claim by al-Shāfiʿī that his argument-method is in perfect consonance with the argument-method of that specialized subset which Aristotle labelled "the Wise." By positioning his reasoning thus, he at once exiles contrary reasoning from the domain of the Ahl al-Fiqh—a powerful critique of the Ibn Abī Laylā/Abū Yūsuf *qiyās*. As to the nature of this *endoxon* method: it is simply that *qiyās* is used to judge those who came after the Prophet, on the basis of what has been transmitted by the Prophet. As for the reverse, al-Shāfiʿī declares: "this is ignorance (*jahl*)."

Importantly, al-Shāfiʿī's stating of this *endoxon* method may also be read as an objection to the fallacy inherent to the Ibn Abī Laylā/Abū Yūsuf procedure. More specifically, we might locate this fallacy under "affirming the consequent" ($p \rightarrow q$; $q \vdash p$, where "p" is "Prophet ruled X for this *mas'ala*" and "q" is "Companions/Successors ruled X for this *mas'ala*). Al-Shāfiʿī does not stop there, but supports his Ahl al-Fiqh method by yet another appeal—this time to a patently theological principle: God only confirmed the need, of all people, for the Prophet (i.e., not for the Companions, Successors, et al.) With all the preceding appeals to theory, method, and principle, al-Shāfiʿī's arguments from §281–4 constitute by far one of the most brilliant examples of legal theory forged in dialectic which our subject-text has to offer.

These latter appeals all build to a final *iʿtirāḍ*, introduced in clearly dialectical language at the end of §284: "he [Abū Yūsuf] also errs (*yaghlaṭu*) in the *qiyās*."[152] Al-Shāfiʿī only allows *muḍāraba* in the first place because it represents the *qiyās* of ʿUmar and ʿUthmān from the *aṣl* of *muʿāmala* of date-palms. Thus, as he says, "[*muḍāraba*] was following a *qiyās*, not followed as a basis for *qiyās* (*kānat tabaʿan qiyāsan lā matbūʿan maqīs ʿalayhi*)." Schacht interpreted this as illustrating the principle "no further *qiyās* can be based on the result of a *qiyās*,"[153] but there is something different happening here. In fact, it is a charge of *aṣl-farʿ* inversion—the *muʿāmala* of date-palms served as the *aṣl* for two Companions' *qiyās* to the *farʿ* of *muḍāraba*. Ibn Abī Laylā/Abū Yūsuf have mistakenly taken this prior *qiyās*-ruled *farʿ* and made it the *aṣl* for a new *qiyās* which—as astonishes al-Shāfiʿī—purports to extend its *ḥukm* to nothing less than its own original *aṣl* (presumed a *farʿ* by Ibn Abī

[152] NB: Aristotle's σόφισμα (*Top.* VIII.11, 106a16–17) was most often translated as *mughāliṭ* or *mughālaṭa*. See, Badawī, *Manṭiq Arisṭū*, vol. 3, p. 758; and Goichon, *Vocabulaires Comparés*, p. 23.

[153] Schacht, *Origins*, p. 124.

Laylā/Abū Yūsuf). I have been unable to locate a parallel to this charge of *aṣl-farʿ* inversion in the lens-texts. We might even presume that inversions of this sort were of rare occurrence, and—with advancements in the sciences of *ḥadīth* and *uṣūl*—grew rarer yet as relevant theory-systems became more refined. Note again that among the first of al-Bājī's *qiyās*-oriented *iʿtirāḍāt* is a set of objections that R's *aṣl* can't be used as an *aṣl*, nor his *ʿilla* as an *ʿilla*, etc. (Bāj.IX.B.2–4).[154]

A final note: al-Shāfiʿī's charge against the Ibn Abī Laylā/Abū Yūsuf *qiyās* implies circularity. Were one to consider al-Shāfiʿī's usage of the verb *yaghlaṭu* as indicating a fallacy or sophism (*mughālaṭa*), in combination with his explanation, one might propose that his *iʿtirāḍ* consists, in fact, of a charge of *petitio principii* or *circulus in probando*.[155] On the other hand, one might interpret his argument as a charge of mistaken cause.[156] If either of these readings were supported by stronger indicants—something more than a mere paralleling of the *Organon*—one could indeed assert the strongly Aristotelian flavour of proto-system juridical dialectic. It may in fact be the case, but I would call for stronger proof than resemblance and the use of a cognate verb. There is, however, the appearance of terminological crossover with early *jadal* and *uṣūl* treatises, as the translators of the *Soph. El.* rendered Aristotle's παρὰ τὸ μὴ αἴτιον ὡς αἴτιον as: "*an yaḍaʿa lā ka-ʿilla ka-ʿilla*," and "*min waḍʿ mā laysa bi-ʿilla ʿalā annahu ʿilla*," and "*bi-ithbāt ʿilla lā ka-ʿilla*." Notably, there is a striking resemblance between these translations and al-Bājī's third *qiyās*-oriented objection: "that what he made an occasioning factor is not allowed to be an occasioning factor" (*al-iʿtirāḍ... bi-an mā jaʿalahu ʿillatan lā yajūzu an yujʿala ʿillatan*) (Bāj.IX.B.3).[157]

We have now reached the start of that brief dialectical sequence which closes the *Bāb al-Muzāraʿa*. In §285 al-Shāfiʿī (who will play the role of R) initiates an "instructional" dialectical sequence (with *fa-in qāla qāʾil*); Q opens with a dialectical question aimed at al-Shāfiʿī's claim that the ruling for *muḍāraba* was derived via *qiyās* from *musāqāt* (and not the reverse): "how does *muḍāraba*-partnership resemble *musāqāt*-sharecropping (*kayfa tushbihu al-muḍāraba al-musāqāt*)?" Being that the *aṣl* and *farʿ* components of al-Shāfiʿī's "historical" *qiyās* are already known to Q, we have mostly passed the point of information-gathering and may read this question as an objection. Q's use of the verb *tushbihu* is the key element here, as it connotes the focus of his demand: the *maʿnā*-intension purportedly shared by the *aṣl* and *farʿ* of this *qiyās*.[158] Accordingly, we may locate Q's question somewhere

---

[154] al-Bājī, *Minhāj*, Turkī ed., pp. 155 ff., §326 ff.

[155] See the discussion in Sect. 4.7, under "τὸ ἐν ἀρχῇ αἰτεῖσθαι" (asking the original point/*petitio principii*).

[156] Again, see the discussion in Sect. 4.7, under "παρὰ τὸ μὴ αἴτιον ὡς αἴτιον" (non-cause as cause). In this case, the "effect" (*muḍāraba* is *jāʾiz*) has been mistaken as the "cause" for what is, in fact, its own "cause" (*musāqāt* is *jāʾiz*).

[157] al-Bājī, *Minhāj*, Turkī ed., pp. 158 ff., §335 ff.

[158] As we shall soon see quite plainly, the term *maʿnā* for al-Shāfiʿī denotes the property (*waṣf*) or collective properties (*awṣāf*) which are efficient in occasioning the *ḥukm* in the *aṣl*, and which—in *qiyās* procedure—are claimed to be shared by the *farʿ*.

between al-Bājī's fourth dialectical question—"about the mode of the indicant" (*al-su'āl ʿan wajh al-dalīl*)[159]—and the initial stage of al-Bājī's sixth type of *qiyās*-oriented *muṭālabāt/mumānaʿāt*: "Demand for [R's] confirmation of the property in the contended branch-case" (*muṭālaba bi-ithbāt al-waṣf fi'l-farʿ*) (Bāj.IX.A.1.6), or "denying the property in the branch-case" (*manʿ al-waṣf fi'l-farʿ*) (Bāj.IX.B.6.1.2).[160] That is to say, Q knows al-Shāfiʿī's *aṣl* and *farʿ*, but the properties which are supposed to connect them have not been made clear to him; and, of course, he cannot object to the properties before he is absolutely certain as to how al-Shāfiʿī conceives of them—hence his question "about the mode of the indicant."

Al-Bājī's ordered hierarchy-outline of *muṭālaba*, *iʿtirāḍ*, and *muʿāraḍa* (Bāj.IX.A) is followed by the individual treatment of each individual objection in (roughly) the same order (Bāj.IX.B). Being that he employs *muṭālaba* for Bāj.IX.A.1.6 and *mumānaʿa/manʿ* for Bāj.IX.B.6.1–2, the overlapping intension of these terms is plain. This is true in other treatises as well, and confirmed by Sānū's cross-referencing *muṭālaba* with *mumānaʿa*.[161] Perhaps we may think of *muṭālaba* and *mumānaʿa/manʿ* not so much as synonymous, but as indicative of initial and subsequent stages of the same dialectical move. In other words, for confirming the *waṣf*-property in the *farʿ*, Q initiates by requesting that R explain how the *farʿ* shares the *waṣf*-property of the *aṣl* (this being *muṭālaba bi-ithbāt al-waṣf fi'l-farʿ*); then, when he has done so, Q objects to some aspect of R's explanation (this being *manʿ al-waṣf fi'l-farʿ*). What we witness in Q's question of §285 is that request-stage (*muṭālaba*) immediately prior to a planned objection-stage (*mumānaʿa/manʿ*).

Al-Shāfiʿī readily complies—in "instructional" mode, with "it is said" (*qīla*)—to Q's *muṭālaba* in §286, rendering the shared properties of *aṣl* and *farʿ*. The whole constitutes a *qiyās al-shabah*, which may be diagramed as follows:

Aṣl date-palms for *musāqāt*		**Farʿ** capital for *muḍāraba*
Property X_A they remain belonging to the principal (*qā'ima bi-rabb al-māl*)	(same) ←→	**Property X_F** it remains belonging to the principal (*qā'ima bi-rabb al-māl*)
Property Y_A it is understood the work is to procure the healthy growth (*ṣalāḥ*) of the fruit	(same) ←→	**Property Y_F** it is understood the work is to procure surplus (*faḍl*) on the capital
Ḥukm A it is permitted that some fruit belong to the worker [according to mutual stipulation]	(therefore, should also be the same) →	**Ḥukm A** [it is permitted that that some of the surplus belong to the worker (according to mutual stipulation)]

[159] al-Bājī, *Minhāj*, Turkī ed., 39 f., §76.

[160] al-Bājī, *Minhāj*, Turkī ed., p. 150, §312; and pp. 166–7, §359.

[161] *Muʿjam*, s.v. "المطالبة".

Al-Shāfiʿī closes by plainly stating: "It [*muḍāraba*] exhibits the like *maʿnā*-intension (*fī mithli maʿnā*) of the *musāqāt*-contract." We not only receive a succinct, step by step account of his *qiyās* (and, purportedly, that of ʿUmar and ʿUthmān), but we are afforded one of the best illustrations of what al-Shāfiʿī means by "*fī mithli maʿnā* X" as occurs in the subject-text. "*Maʿnā*," for al-Shāfiʿī, is here equivalent to the potentially-efficient property (*waṣf*) or properties (*awṣāf*)—i.e., the *ʿilla*—of later *uṣūl* and *jadal* theorists; "*fī mithli maʿnā*," for al-Shāfiʿī, is his formula for declaring that the case-at-hand shares the potentially-efficient *waṣf* or *awṣāf* of the authoritative source-ruling.

Q's following question in §287 is subsidiary to his *muṭālaba* of §285; and, although al-Shāfiʿī, as we shall see, in fact never allows him to reach the stage of openly-stated objection, we can still perceive the connection between *muṭālaba* and *mumānaʿa*/*manʿ*. Q asks: "So why isn't this [so] regarding [tillable] land (*lima lā yakūnu hādhā fiʾl-arḍ*)?" In other words: "Why doesn't this *maʿnā*-intension exist in *muzāraʿa*?" Exactly how we identify this question depends on whether or not we perceive Q as having conceded to al-Shāfiʿī's *qiyās*. This is not entirely clear from the presentation. Nevertheless, and regardless of Q's intention, I might still produce a label for this dialectical question—if not one which is found in the lens-texts. In essence, Q's question is a "demand for an invalidating distinction"—a *muṭālaba biʾl-farq*. Q clearly believes that—for consistency's sake—al-Shāfiʿī should extend his *qiyās*-reasoning to the *masʾala* of *muzāraʿa*. That al-Shāfiʿī does not do so indicates for Q that al-Shāfiʿī believes there is a *farq* between the *aṣl* of *musāqāt* and the *farʿ* of *muzāraʿa*. This *farq* is what he requests, and it is exactly what al-Shāfiʿī delivers in §288. Still, Q's real objective is uncertain, and two possibilities must be considered.

If we read Q as rejecting al-Shāfiʿī's *qiyās*, then his question in §287 may be understood as leading towards a charge of *naqḍ*. For if there is no *farq* between *musāqāt* and *muzāraʿa*, then clearly al-Shāfiʿī should extend the ruling from the former to the latter, but he does not. In other words, Q is employing *muzāraʿa* as the *masʾalat al-naqḍ*, arguing that al-Shāfiʿī's properties are present therein, but not his *ḥukm*—thus, his *musāqāt*-to-*muḍāraba qiyās* should be rendered void. Accordingly, al-Shāfiʿī may be read (in §288) as denying the presence of the properties in the *masʾalat al-naqḍ*.

On the other hand, if we read Q as having conceded to al-Shāfiʿī's rendering of *qiyās* from *musāqāt* to *muḍāraba*, then Q may be seen to have shifted tactics—abandoning the mistakenly inverted Ibn Abī Laylā/Abū Yūsuf *qiyās* in an attempt to rescue the Ibn Abī Laylā/Abū Yūsuf ruling for *muzāraʿa*. He thus proceeds by pushing al-Shāfiʿī to concede that the *maʿnā*-quality of *musāqāt* obtains as much in *muzāraʿa* as it does in *muḍāraba*—and, thus, the Ibn Abī Laylā/Abū Yūsuf ruling should be sound (by a new *qiyās*) regardless of having been improperly reasoned (by the inverted *qiyās*). If such is the case, then Q's question in §287 may be understood as leading towards that type of *muʿāraḍa* which is anathema to al-Shāfiʿī (and most later jurists): Q's *qiyās* (in this case: proposed from *musāqāt*-to-*muzāraʿa*) is made to supplant R's Sunnaic *dalīl*-indicant (in this case: the Prophet's transaction at Khaybar). If we furthermore consider that *jadal* theorists conceived of the charge of *farq* as a subset of *muʿāraḍat al-ʿilla bi-ʿilla*, then we can read the first part of al-Shāfiʿī's response in §288 as a counter-*muʿāraḍa* (of subspecies *farq*) against Q's proposed *qiyās*-over-Sunna *muʿāraḍa*. In the end, as we shall see, this seems the most satisfactory assessment.

One thing is certain: Q has requested a *farq* between *muzāraʿa* and *musāqāt*, and al-Shāfiʿī more than delivers in §288. In fact, he delineates no less than four *qiyās*-invalidating distinctions (*furūq*)—two with *musāqāt*, one with *muḍāraba*, and one with both—as follows: (1) "land is not what thrives and has surplus (*faḍl*) taken from it [like date-palms in *musāqāt*], rather, there only thrives in it something else;" (2) "[that something else is] not something remaining as it originally was, which is sold and its surplus taken—like [the capital in] *muḍāraba*;" (3) "nor [is that something else] intensely productive and its fruit taken—like date-palms [in *musāqāt*], but only something which occurs in [the land];" and (4) "[it occurs in the land] by way of a conduct (*taṣarruf*) which exhibits the *maʿnā*-quality of neither of these two [i.e., neither *musāqāt* nor *muḍāraba*]." Al-Shāfiʿī concludes by plainly stating his charge of *farq*: "So [that thing which thrives in the land] is not allowed to be a *qiyās* based upon [*musāqāt*-sharecropping], while it is divergent from it from start to finish (*mufāriq lahā fiʾl-mubtadaʾ waʾl-mutaʿaqqab*)."[162]

If we consider Q as having suggested a *muʿāraḍa* by which a *musāqāt*-to-*muzāraʿa* *qiyās* would supplant al-Shāfiʿī's Sunnaic *dalīl*-indicant, then this response would constitute al-Shāfiʿī's counter-*muʿāraḍa* against the properties of Q's proposed *aṣl*—bearing in mind that al-Shāfiʿī does not consider Q's *muʿāraḍa qiyās* to be valid in the first place, as it conflicts with the Sunna. Nevertheless, al-Shāfiʿī's reply is suggestive of a hypothetical counter-*qiyās* from an unstated *aṣl*, inasmuch as the void left by his *farq* (and the subsequent invalidation of Q's *aṣl*) would normally be filled by a new *aṣl* brought by al-Shāfiʿī. We must also point out that, although the *awṣāf*-properties of *musāqāt* and *muzāraʿa* are quite clear now, the efficiency of any of them has not been determined. It may well be that the *ʿilla* (as opposed to *waṣf/awṣāf*) of *musāqāt* and *muzāraʿa* are known by neither al-Shāfiʿī nor Q nor by anyone, and the language of Q (*tushbihu* in §285) followed by al-Shāfiʿī's rendering of shared *awṣāf* as a *qiyās al-shabah* (in §286, with no demonstration of efficiency), suggests that both al-Shāfiʿī's *musāqāt*-to-*muḍāraba qiyās* and Q's proposed *musāqāt*-*muzāraʿa qiyās* are based upon resemblance (*shabah*). In other words, we are entirely in the domain of *qiyās al-shabah*—where only shared properties are established—and not *qiyās al-ʿilla*—where the *ʿilla* is demonstrably efficient, and firmly indicated by *naṣṣ*, *ijmāʿ*, *ẓāhir*, or *istinbāṭ*.[163]

---

[162] Al-Shāfiʿī employs a similar expression in §1131: "*mukhālif... fiʾl-badʾi waʾl-mutaʿaqqabi*." It is obvious that these phrases are meant to convey a certain comprehensiveness of difference between two things which are claimed by an opponent to be similar. Neither phrase occurs elsewhere in the *Umm*, however.

[163] See al-Bājī's typology of *qiyās al-ʿilla*: *Minhāj*, Turkī ed., pp. 26–7, §47; and al-Shīrāzī's typology of *qiyās* in Sect. 4.3, above.

I would therefore propose that al-Shāfiʿī's counter-*muʿāraḍa* (suggested through his delineation of *furūq*) is the supplanting of Q's *qiyās al-shabah* with a hypothetical *qiyās al-shabah* (whose *aṣl* is never suggested, but would fill the void left by the elimination of the Ibn Abī Laylā/Abū Yūsuf *aṣl*). In other words: (1) it is clear that al-Shāfiʿī's objection constitutes *farq*; (2) as a subspecies of *muʿāraḍa*, *farq* normally entails (in the *jadal*-theory literature) the replacement of R's *aṣl* by another (constituting a counter-*qiyās*); but (3) perhaps not seeing the need to support his Sunnaic proscription of *muzāraʿa*, al-Shāfiʿī does not produce such a counter-*qiyās*; although (4) if he had, it would likely have been another *qiyās al-shabah* (being that only *awṣāf* not necessarily efficient in occasioning a *ḥukm* have been discussed). I would therefore locate this hypothetical counter-*qiyās* under al-Shīrāzī's *al-farq bi-qiyās al-shabah* (Shīr.VII.15.2.2.3), and al-Bājī's *al-farq bi-dalālat al-ḥukm*, subclass four: "[Q] makes distinction by way of a type of property resemblance (*shabah*)" (Bāj.IX.B.15.2.2.2.4).[164]

Hypotheses aside, al-Shāfiʿī continues with his concluding explanation, allowing that even if Q's *qiyās* were valid, one is simply not allowed to do *qiyās* regarding what the Prophet proscribed, nor allowed to make lawful (*ḥalāl*) by *qiyās* what the Prophet made unlawful (*ḥarām*). Again, we are reminded of al-Bājī's *jawāb* that "*qiyās* may not be raised against *naṣṣ*," and may read al-Shāfiʿī's critique as an *iʿtirāḍ* that what has been proposed as a *farʿ* is not allowed to be a *farʿ*, or as a *muʿāraḍa bi'l-nuṭq*.

Finally, al-Shāfiʿī closes this dialectical sequence (and the *Bāb al-Muzāraʿa*) with a fascinating illustration which ought to draw our attention in a number of ways. It is, in fact, a unique charge, in two parts, of method-theory *naqḍ*—a dialectical objection exposing Q's self-contradiction in ignoring, in the *mas'ala* at hand, a key method of proto-system legal theory. Al-Shāfiʿī asserts: (1) the Prophet fixed the manumission of a slave as penance for one who invalidates his fast through sex (*al-mufsid li'l-ṣawm bi'l-jimāʿ*); but (2) we don't do *qiyās* [i.e., we don't transfer that *ḥukm* of manumission] to one who invalidates his prayer through sex (*al-mufsid li'l-ṣalāt bi'l-jimāʿ*); despite (3) a common property shared by both: each invalidated a duty (*farḍ*) through sexual intercourse. This short argument speaks volumes for the nature of proto-system legal theory, juridical dialectic, and their dynamic symbiosis. From one perspective, we once again witness the honing of a legal theory in the dialectical forge; from another, we witness a higher register of dialectic. The subject matter of the current sequence up to this point—although necessarily utilizing tools of legal principle and theory in both *istidlāl* and *iʿtirāḍ*—has nevertheless remained derived law. In other words, the base-matter has remained *furūʿ*, as worked by the tools of proto-system legal theory in the dialectical forge. Now, however, the base-matter has become the tools themselves—the dialectic has shifted "up" one level—and we may thus begin to speak in terms of an *uṣūl*-method oriented dialectic as well as a *furūʿ*-oriented dialectic. Moreover, we recognize the same dialectical instrument of objection at work in both: *naqḍ*.

---

[164] al-Shīrāzī, *Maʿūna*, al-ʿUmayrīnī ed., pp. 117–8; al-Bājī, *Minhāj*, Turkī ed., p. 203, §461; pp. 205–6, §466 (using the same example-*mas'ala* as his teacher). Ibn ʿAqīl does not appear to discuss *muʿāraḍa* by way of *qiyās al-shabah* in his *K. al-Jadal*.

We have seen (in Chap. 2) that Miller speaks of two genres of juridical *jadal* appearing in the 4th/10th c. H: (1) "works with the jadal method devoted to uṣūl al-fiqh" (and which "usually had the word jadal somewhere in their title"); and (2) "works devoted to the furū" (which "were generally called ṭarīqa").[165] The distinction inherent to these genres, however, is plainly apparent in the practice of al-Shāfiʿī some two centuries or more before their introduction. This provides at least potential support to a theory that early *jadal*-systems were conceived, in part, through an analysis of past *jadal* practice and teaching. Whoever the authors of the "*jadal* method devoted to *uṣūl al-fiqh*" may have been, they may well have developed a category of *naqḍ* drawn from a study of practices such as that of al-Shāfiʿī in §288. Historical-developmental implications aside, I would label this unique application of a classical *iʿtirāḍ* "method-*naqḍ*." Whereas *fiqh*-oriented *naqḍ* has consisted in bringing an *endoxon* ruling in which R's *ʿilla* is present but his *ḥukm* is not, al-Shāfiʿī's method-*naqḍ* has instead brought an *endoxon* ruling in which R's method consideration (shared efficient properties) is present, but his method procedure (*qiyās*) is not. Perhaps the most lucid demonstration of a dynamic symbiosis between proto-system *jadal* and legal theory which our subject-text affords thus concludes with an illuminating instance of a method-oriented *iʿtirāḍ*.

Masāʾil-Set #4

§§634–667 from the *Chapter on Inheritances* (*Bāb al-Mawārīth*)[166]

634 – Al-Rabīʿ related to us, he said: Al-Shāfiʿī, may God Most High have mercy upon him, said: And when a man dies and leaves behind [only] his brother—by his father and his mother—and his grandfather; then indeed Abū Ḥanīfa, may God Most High have mercy upon him, used to say: The estate-property, all of it, belongs to the grandfather; he is in the *manzila*-status of the father with regard to every inheritance.[167]	634 - أَخْبَرَنَا الرَّبِيعُ قَالَ: قَالَ الشَّافِعِيُّ رَحِمَهُ اللهُ تَعَالَى: وَإِذَا مَاتَ الرَّجُلُ وَتَرَكَ أَخَاهُ لأَبِيهِ وَأُمِّهِ وَجَدَّهِ، فَإِنَّ أَبَا حَنِيفَةَ رَحِمَهُ اللهُ تَعَالَى كَانَ يَقُولُ: الْمَالُ كُلُّهُ لِلْجَدِّ، وَهُوَ بِمَنْزِلَةِ الأَبِ فِي كُلِّ مِيرَاثٍ.

(continued)

[165] Ibn Khaldūn, as we have seen, also speaks of two *ṭarīqas* of *jadal* known in his time: that of al-Bazdawī, and that of al-ʿAmīdī. The distinction between them, however, does not correspond to "*fiqh*-oriented" dialectic vs. "*uṣūl al-fiqh*-oriented" dialectic. Rather, as his exposition makes clear, al-Bazdawī's was a specialized *ṭarīqa* for juridical dialectic by way of *al-adilla al-sharʿiyya*, while al-ʿAmīdī's *ṭarīqa* was more general, treating *adilla* from any *ʿilm*, and with particular focus on *istidlāl* (*Muqaddima*, Shaḥāda ed., p. 579; Rosenthal trans., vol. 3, p. 33).

[166] Ḥassūn ed., vol. 9, pp. 117–20; ʿAbd al-Muṭṭalib ed., vol. 8, pp. 296–8.

[167] For expositions on inheritance (*mīrāth/irth*), inheritance shares (*farāʾiḍ*), and related rulings, see *MF*, s.v. "إرث" (vol. 3, pp. 17–80); *EI*², s.v. "Mīrāth"; *DJP*, vol. 2, pp. 411–42; and Hallaq, *Sharīʿa*, pp. 291–5.

635 – And likewise it has reached us concerning Abū Bakr al-Ṣiddīq, and ʿAbd Allāh b. ʿAbbās, and ʿĀʾisha Mother of Believers, and ʿAbd Allāh b. al-Zubayr, may God Most High be pleased with them, that they used to say: The grandfather is in the *manzila*-status of the father, when he [the deceased] has no [surviving] father.	635 - وَكَذَلِكَ بَلَغَنَا عَن أَبِي بَكْرٍ الصِّدِّيقِ، وَعَن عَبْدِ اللهِ بْنِ عَبَّاسٍ، وَعَن عَائِشَةَ أُمِّ الْمُؤْمِنِينَ، وَعَن عَبْدِ اللّٰهِ بْنِ الزُّبَيْرِ رضي الله تعالى عنهم أَنَّهُمْ كَانُوا يَقُولُونَ: الْجَدُّ بِمَنْزِلَةِ الأَبِ إذَا لَمْ يَكُنْ لَهُ أَبٌ.
636 – But Ibn Abī Laylā used to profess, regarding the grandfather, the pronouncement of ʿAlī b. Abī Ṭālib, may God be pleased with him: To the brother belongs half, and to the grandfather half.	636 - وَكَانَ ابْنُ أَبِي لَيْلَى يَقُولُ فِي الْجَدِّ بِقَوْلِ عَلِيِّ بْنِ أَبِي طَالِبٍ رضي اللّٰه عنه: لِلأَخِ النِّصْفُ وَلِلْجَدِّ النِّصْفُ.
637 – And likewise did Zayd b. Thābit and ʿAbd Allāh b. Masʿūd profess with regard to this *manzila*-status.	637 - وَكَذَلِكَ قَالَ زَيْدُ بْنُ ثَابِتٍ وَعَبْدُ اللّٰهِ بْنُ مَسْعُودٍ فِي هَذِهِ الْمَنْزِلَةِ.
638 – Al-Shāfiʿī, may God Most High have mercy upon him, said: And when a man dies and he leaves behind [only] his grandfather and his brother—by his father and his mother—the estate-property is [divided] between them both, in two halves.	638 - قَالَ الشَّافِعِيُّ رَحِمَهُ اللّٰهُ تَعَالَى: وَإِذَا هَلَكَ الرَّجُلُ وَتَرَكَ جَدَّهُ وَأَخَاهُ لأَبِيهِ وَأُمِّهِ، فَالْمَالُ بَيْنَهُمَا نِصْفَانِ.
639 – And likewise did Zayd b. Thābit, and ʿAlī, and ʿAbd Allāh b. Masʿūd profess.	639 - وَهَكَذَا قَالَ زَيْدُ بْنُ ثَابِتٍ وَعَلِيٌّ وَعَبْدُ اللّٰهِ بْنُ مَسْعُودٍ.
640 – And such is narrated concerning ʿUthmān, may God be pleased with them.[168] But Abū Bakr al-Ṣiddīq, may God be pleased with him, disagreed with them, and made the estate-property belong to the grandfather.	640 - وَرُوِيَ عَن عُثْمَان رضي اللّٰه عنهم؛ وَخَالَفَهُمْ أَبُو بَكْرٍ الصِّدِّيقُ رضي اللّٰه عنه فَجَعَلَ الْمَالَ لِلْجَدِّ.
641 – And ʿĀʾisha professed that along with him, and Ibn ʿAbbās, and Ibn al-Zubayr, and ʿAbd Allāh b. ʿUtba, may God be pleased with them.[169]	641 - وَقَالَتْهُ مَعَهُ عَائِشَةُ وَابْنُ عَبَّاسٍ وَابْنُ الزُّبَيْرِ وَعَبْدِ اللّٰهِ بْنِ عُتْبَةَ رضي اللّٰه عنهم.
642 – And that is the *madhhab*-opinion of the Ahl al-Kalām[170] regarding the shares of inheritance, which is to say they are under the delusion it is the *qiyās*—though neither of the two opinions is by way of *qiyās*, and, moreover, rejecting the brother for the grandfather is *farther* from the *qiyās* than confirming the brother along with him!	642 - وَهُوَ مَذْهَبُ أَهْلِ الْكَلَامِ فِي الْفَرَائِضِ، وَذَلِكَ أَنَّهُمْ يَتَوَهَّمُونَ أَنَّهُ الْقِيَاسُ، وَلَيْسَ وَاحِدٌ مِن الْقَوْلَيْنِ بِقِيَاسٍ غَيْرَ أَنَّ طَرْحَ الأَخِ بِالْجَدِّ أَبْعَدُ مِن الْقِيَاسِ مِن إثْبَاتِ الأَخِ مَعَهُ.

(continued)

[168] "Them," as the three Companions previously mentioned are included.

[169] Thus al-Shāfiʿī begins to explain the disagreement (*khilāf*) between these respected Companions by tracing the lineage of the two doctrines. The "wrong" doctrine (from his perspective) appears to have begun with Abū Bakr.

[170] The "Folk of Dialectical Theology," meaning rational theologians, and, quite possibly, early Muʿtazilites in particular.

643 – And one of those who subscribe to this *madhhab*-opinion has said: We have only rejected the brother for the grandfather due to three properties regarding which you yourselves agree with us: certainly you eclipse the sons of the mother by him [the grandfather]—likewise being the *manzila*-status of the father; and you do not diminish him from the sixth[-part of the estate]—likewise the *manzila*-status of the father; and, moreover, you actually call him "father!"	643 - وَقَدْ قَالَ بَعْضُ مَنْ يَذْهَبُ هَذَا الْمَذْهَبَ: إِنَّمَا طَرَحْنَا الأَخَ بِالْجَدِّ لِثَلاَثِ خِصَالٍ أَنْتُمْ مُجْتَمِعُونَ مَعَنَا عَلَيْهَا؛ إِنَّكُمْ تَحْجُبُونَ بِهِ بَنِي الأُمِّ، وَكَذَلِكَ مَنْزِلَةُ الأَبِ وَلاَ تُنْقِصُونَهُ مِن السُّدُسِ، وَكَذَلِكَ مَنْزِلَةُ الأَبِ وَأَنَّكُمْ تُسَمُّونَهُ أَبًا.
644 – Al-Shāfiʿī, may God Most High have mercy upon him, said: [so] I said: We only eclipsed the sons of the mother by [the grandfather] by way of a *khabar*-report, not by way of correlational inference from the father.	644 - قَالَ الشَّافِعِيُّ رَحِمَهُ اللّٰهُ تَعَالَى: قُلْتُ: إِنَّمَا حَجَبْنَا بِهِ بَنِي الأُمِّ خَبَرًا لاَ قِيَاسًا عَلَى الأَبِ.
645 – He [the opponent] said: And how is that?	645 – قَالَ: وَكَيْفَ ذَلِكَ؟
646 – I said: We, ourselves, [also] eclipse the sons of the mother by the daughter of the son of a son, however-so-low. But even if she corresponds to the *manzila*-status of the father in this situation, we would certainly never rule—neither we nor you—that she stands in place of the father anywhere else.	646 – قُلْتُ: نَحْنُ نَحْجُبُ بَنِي الأُمِّ بِبِنْتِ ابْنِ ابْنٍ مُتَسَفِّلَةٍ، وَهَذِهِ وَإِنْ وَافَقَتْ مَنْزِلَةَ الأَبِ فِي هَذَا الْمَوْضِعِ فَلَمْ نَحْكُمْ لَهَا نَحْنُ وَأَنْتَ بِأَنْ تَكُونَ تَقُومَ مَقَامَ الأَبِ فِي غَيْرِهِ.
647 – Thus [the grandfather] corresponds to [the father] in one *maʿnā*-quality, even as he diverges from him in another. And as for our not diminishing him from the sixth[-part of the estate]: it is by way of a *khabar*-report that we do not decrease him. Nor do we, ourselves, diminish the grandmother as pertains to the sixth. So do you think that we—and you—should stand her in place of the father, since she corresponds to him in a *maʿnā*-quality? And as for the "label of fatherhood":[171] we and you [both] attach the "label of fatherhood" to the one between us and Adam.	647 - وَإِذًا وَافَقَهُ فِي مَعْنًى وَإِنْ خَالَفَهُ فِي غَيْرِهِ، وَأَمَّا أَنْ لاَ نَنْقُصَهُ مِنَ السُّدُسِ فَإِنَّا لَمْ نَنْقُصْهُ خَبَرًا، وَنَحْنُ لاَ نَنْقُصُ الْجَدَّةَ مِن السُّدُسِ، أَفَرَأَيْتَنَا وَإِيَّاكَ أَقَمْنَاهَا مَقَامَ الأَبِ أَنْ وَافَقَتْهُ فِي مَعْنًى، وَأَمَّا اسْمُ الأُبُوَّةِ فَنَحْنُ وَأَنْتَ نُلْزِمُ مَنْ بَيْنَنَا وَبَيْنَ آدَمَ اسْمَ الأُبُوَّةِ.
648 – And when it is thus, and below any one of them is a "father" nearer [to the deceased] than him, he does not inherit.	648 - وَإِذَا كَانَ ذَلِكَ وَدُونَ أَحَدِهِمْ أَبٌ أَقْرَبُ مِنْهُ لَمْ يَرِثْ.
649 – And likewise, if he is a nonbeliever and the deceased a Muslim, or a murderer and the deceased murdered [by him], or the deceased was free but the father enslaved; if we had transferred inheritance through the "label of fatherhood" alone, we would have transferred inheritance to those whom we have forbidden—all of them. But we have only transmitted inheritance by way of a *khabar*-report, not based on the label [of fatherhood].	649 - وَكَذَلِكَ لَوْ كَانَ كَافِرًا وَالْمَوْرُوثُ مُسْلِمًا، أَوْ قَاتِلاً وَالْمَوْرُوثُ مَقْتُولاً، أَوْ كَانَ الْمَوْرُوثُ حُرًّا وَالأَبُ مَمْلُوكًا، فَلَوْ كَانَ إِنَّمَا وَرَّثْنَا بِاسْمِ الأُبُوَّةِ فَقَطْ وَرَّثْنَا هَؤُلاَءِ الَّذِينَ حَرَمْنَاهُمْ كُلَّهُمْ، وَلَكِنَّا إِنَّمَا وَرَّثْنَاهُمْ خَبَرًا لاَ بِالاِسْمِ.
650 – He said: Then which of the two doctrines most resembles the *qiyās*?	650 – قَالَ: فَأَيُّ الْقَوْلَيْنِ أَشْبَهُ بِالْقِيَاسِ؟

(continued)

[171] The *ism al-ubuwwa*, possibly in the sense of "the noun of fatherhood," and referring to the designation *ab*, "father".

651 – I said: There is no *qiyās* regarding either one, but the doctrine you have chosen is *farther* from *qiyās* and rational understanding.	651 – قُلْتُ: مَا فِيهِمَا قِيَاسٌ، وَالْقَوْلُ الَّذِي اخْتَرْتَ أَبْعَدُ مِن الْقِيَاسِ وَالْعَقْلِ.
652 – He said: How so?	652 – قَالَ: فَأَيْنَ ذَلِكَ؟
653 – I said: Have you considered [what would happen] when the grandfather and the brother both demand the inheritance of the deceased; would they be united [to the deceased][172] by their own proximate-kinship, or by the proximate-kinship of another?	653 – قُلْتُ: أَرَأَيْتَ الْجَدَّ وَالأَخَ إِذَا طَلَبَا مِيرَاثَ الْمَيِّتِ أَيُدْلِيَانِ بِقَرَابَةِ أَنْفُسِهِمَا أَمْ بِقَرَابَةِ غَيْرِهِمَا؟
654 – He said: What do you mean?	654 – قَالَ: وَمَا ذَلِكَ؟
655 – I said: Wouldn't the grandfather only say: "I am the father of the father of the deceased;" and the brother: "I am the son of the father of the deceased?"	655 – قُلْت: أَلَيْسَ إِنَّمَا يَقُولُ الْجَدُّ: أَنَا أَبُو أَبِي الْمَيِّتِ. وَيَقُولُ الأَخُ: أَنَا ابْنُ أَبِي الْمَيِّتِ؟
656 – He said: Of course.	656 – قَالَ: بَلَى.
657 – I said: Then by the proximate-kinship of the father of the deceased they are, together, united to the deceased.	657 – قُلْتُ: فَبِقَرَابَةِ أَبِي الْمَيِّتِ يُدْلِيَانِ مَعًا إِلَى الْمَيِّتِ.
658 – I said: Now make the father of the deceased to be [instead] the deceased one. Which of the two is foremost in terms of greater inheritance: his son, or his father?	658 – قُلْتُ: فَاجْعَلِ أَبَا الْمَيِّتِ هُوَ الْمَيِّتَ أَيُّهُمَا أَوْلَى بِكَثْرَةِ مِيرَاثِهِ، ابْنُهُ أَوْ أَبُوهُ؟
659 – He said: His son of course, because five sixths belong to him, but to his father [only] the [remaining] sixth.	659 – قَالَ: بَلِ ابْنُهُ؛ لأَنَّ لَهُ خَمْسَةَ أَسْدَاسٍ وَلأَبِيهِ السُّدُسُ.
660 – I said: So how is it you eclipsed the brother by the grandfather, while the brother—when the father dies—outranks the grandfather in terms of greater inheritance? If you must eclipse one by the other, you should eclipse the grandfather by the brother!	660 - قُلْتُ: فَكَيْفَ حَجَبْتَ الأَخَ بِالْجَدِّ، وَالأَخُ إِذَا مَاتَ الأَبُ أَوْلَى بِكَثْرَةِ مِيرَاثِهِ مِن الْجَدِّ، لَوْ كُنْتَ حَاجِبًا أَحَدَهُمَا بِالآخَرِ انْبَغَى أَنْ تَحْجُبَ الْجَدَّ بِالأَخِ.
661 – He said: But how is the *qiyās* regarding this?	661 – قَالَ: وَكَيْفَ يَكُونُ الْقِيَاسُ فِيهِ؟
662 – I said: No *maʿnā*-quality for *qiyās* is permitted, together, in either one. But if there was a *maʿnā*-quality for [*qiyās*], then we ought always to have made five sixths for the brother—when he [alone survives] with the grandfather—and the [remaining] sixth for the grandfather.	662 – قُلْتُ: لاَ مَعْنَى لِلْقِيَاسِ فِيهِمَا مَعًا يَجُوزُ. وَلَوْ كَانَ لَهُ مَعْنًى انْبَغَى أَنْ نَجْعَلَ لِلأَخِ أَبَدًا حَيْثُ كَانَ مَعَ الْجَدِّ خَمْسَةَ أَسْدَاسٍ وَلِلْجَدِّ السُّدُسَ.
663 – And I said: Have you considered the brothers: are they confirmed an inheritance-share in the Book of God?	663 – وَقُلْتُ: أَرَأَيْتَ الإِخْوَةَ أَمُثْبَتِي الْفَرْضِ فِي كِتَابِ اللّٰهِ؟
664 – He said: Yes.	664 – قَالَ: نَعَمْ.
665 – I said: And does the grandfather have, in the Book of God, an inheritance-share?	665 – قُلْتُ: فَهَلْ لِلْجَدِّ فِي كِتَابِ اللّٰهِ فَرْضٌ؟

(continued)

[172] See Lane, *Lexicon*, s.v. "دلو" (near the end of form 4. "ادلى").

666 – He said: No.	666 – قَالَ: لاَ.
667 – I said: And likewise the [Prophet's] *Sunna*. [The brothers] are confirmed in it; but I know of no inheritance-share belonging to the grandfather—except from a singular mode [of transmission] which the Ahl al-Ḥadīth do not grant full confirmation. And I don't know you to have done ought but discard the stronger of every mode for the weaker!	667 – قُلْتُ: وَكَذَلِكَ السُّنَّةُ. هُمْ مُثْبَتُونَ فِيهَا وَلاَ أَعْلَمُ لِلْجَدِّ فِي السُّنَّةِ فَرْضًا إلاَّ مِن وَجْهٍ وَاحِدٍ لاَ يُثْبِتُهُ أَهْلُ الْحَدِيثِ كُلَّ التَّثْبِيتِ، فَلاَ أَعْلَمُكَ إلاَّ طَرَحْتَ الأَقْوَى مِن كُلِّ وَجْهٍ بِالأَضْعَفِ.

This extended dialectical sequence is preceded by brief presentations of rulings, with supporting *naql*-transmissions, for Abū Ḥanīfa, Ibn Abī Laylā, and al-Shāfiʿī on a single *masʾala*; unusually, there is no mention of the adherence or revised ruling of Abū Yūsuf (in both *Umm* and Shaybānī versions).[173] In terms of presentation, the categories are: §§634–5 (Abū Ḥanīfa's ruling and *naql*; category F); §§636–7 (Ibn Abī Laylā's ruling and *naql*; category F); §§638–41 (al-Shāfiʿī's ruling and *naql* [mostly the same as Ibn Abī Laylā's, but followed by a "lineage" for Abū Ḥanīfa's counter-*naql*]; category F); and §§642–67 (extended "historical" dialectic between al-Shāfiʿī and an R/Q of the Ahl al-Kalām; category A). As we shall see, this latter sequence of dialectic provides an exceedingly rich illustration of early hermeneutic, rational inference, and objection. Before delving into it, however, I will once again engage in the more conjectural task of drawing out the species of argument and objection which might have been employed by proponents of the Abū Ḥanīfa and Ibn Abī Laylā positions (if not even by Abū Ḥanīfa and Ibn Abī Laylā themselves).[174]

The sole *masʾala* treated in these sections was a highly contentious one. In §634 we learn that Abū Ḥanīfa ruled all of the estate-property to the grandfather. This plain statement is followed by a brief *ʿaql* explanation: "[the grandfather] is in the *manzila*-status of the father with regard to every inheritance (*huwa bi-manzilat al-ab fī kull mīrāth*)." Note this formulaic statement as belonging to a general category of legal argument: due to a status consideration (usually expressed with *bi-manzila*) of an agent/object/action X of the *masʾala*-at-hand, the entire set of rulings-in-question as pertains to that agent/object/action X is subsumed by the appropriate set of rulings already established for agent/object/action Y, for that entire genus of *masāʾil*. In other words: X is in the *manzila* of Y for the whole of substantive genus A; thus, X will have the *ḥukm* of Y for the whole of substantive genus A. This particular mode of legal solution—which I have labeled "*manzila*-subsumption," with its accompanying formula of "X is in the *manzila* of Y," is of

[173] In his edition of the Shaybānī Version, al-Afghānī informs us that both Abū Yūsuf and al-Shaybānī sided with Ibn Abī Laylā and his *naql* support as regards the focus *masʾala* (p. 84, n. 2).

[174] Note later historical and biographical authors narrate a number of face-to-face disagreements and disputes between them. See the sources listed in *EI*², s.v. "Abū Ḥanīfa, al-Nuʿmān b. Thābit" and "Ibn Abī Laylā."

great frequency throughout our subject-text and the *Umm* as a whole.[175] Notably, this formula of subsumption appears older than Abū Ḥanīfa; his ruling is supported in §635 by *naql*: the *āthār*-traditions of Abū Bakr, Ibn ʿAbbās, ʿĀʾisha, and Ibn al-Zubayr, who are all reported to have said: "The grandfather is in the *manzila*-status of the father, when he [the deceased] has no [surviving] father" (*al-jadd bi-manzilat al-ab idhā lam yakun lahu ab*).

In §636–7, however, we learn that Ibn Abī Laylā's ruling on this *mas'ala* stems from a counter-set of *āthār*-traditions belonging to ʿAlī, Zayd b. Thābit, and Ibn Masʿūd: the inheritance is to be equally distributed between the surviving grandfather and full-brother (*li'l-akh al-niṣf wa li'l-jadd al-niṣf*). Thus the background to the Abū Ḥanīfa vs. Ibn Abī Laylā dispute becomes quite plain: our jurists adhere to opposing sets of Companion decrees (*aqwāl al-Ṣaḥāba*), each with a separate "lineage," and we may consider identifying the domain of *istidlāl* (or, perhaps more accurately, *taqlīd*) for both positions as "the saying of a solitary Companion" (*qawl al-wāḥid min al-Ṣaḥāba*)—despite the fact that one position is backed by four, and the other by three. Additionally, we may consider investigating the domain of "consensus of the Companions" (*ijmāʿ al-Ṣaḥāba*), insofar as the solution to this *mas'ala* appears split more or less evenly between two camps, and we might find relevant objection material therein. Finally, we might consider the domain of *tarjīḥ*, insofar as a numerical preponderance of *āthār*-traditions might be at work in the support of either position.

From the perspective of Abū Ḥanīfa in the role of Q, and assuming a dialectical confrontation with a proponent of the Ibn Abī Laylā position (R), we can envisage three or four potential species of *iʿtirāḍ* to be brought forth when the Ibn Abī Laylā proponent states the *āthār*-traditions which form the basis of his *istidlāl/taqlīd*. First, if the Ibn Abī Laylā proponent draws his *dalīl*-indicant via *qawl al-wāḥid min al-Ṣaḥāba*, thrice, the Abū Ḥanīfa-position Q might object by conveying the *khilāf* of another Companion, four times, "in order," as we have seen al-Shīrāzī say, "to make of the *mas'ala* a *khilāf* between the Companions" (Shīr.IV.3; Bāj.V.2).[176] Second, if the Ibn Abī Laylā-position R intends to establish his *dalīl*-indicant as *ijmāʿ al-Ṣaḥāba*, then the Abū Ḥanīfa proponent—like the "*mukhālif*" of al-Shīrāzī's example *mas'ala*—might object by saying "this is the decree of a group of Companions, and it is not *ijmāʿ*." This constitutes "Demand for Validation of the Consensus (*al-muṭālaba bi-taṣḥīḥ al-ijmāʿ*)," and is the second type of al-Shīrāzī's *iʿtirāḍāt* against *al-istidlāl bi-ijmāʿ* (Shīr.III.2; Bāj.III.1.1).[177] Alternately, Q might once

---

[175] Cf. instances of *manzila*-subsumption translated in part 2 of my dissertation (§§202, 346, 391 m, 474, 537, 752, 987, 1072, 1204, 1341, 1348, 1350–2, 1358–9). In the entirety of the *Umm* there are some 56 occurrences of the phrase "*bi-manzila.*"

[176] al-Shīrāzī, *Maʿūna*, al-ʿUmayrīnī ed., pp. 82 f.; al-Bājī, *Minhāj*, Turkī ed., p. 144, §298. Cf. Ibn ʿAqīl, *K. al-Jadal*, pp. 39 f.

[177] al-Shīrāzī, *Maʿūna*, al-ʿUmayrīnī ed., pp. 80–1. Cf. Ibn ʿAqīl, *K. al-Jadal*, p. 39, §204, employing the same example *mas'ala*. Al-Bājī's typology is somewhat more refined, and the Abū Ḥanīfa position Q would proceed according to one of the three types of *al-muṭālaba bi-taṣḥīḥ al-ijmāʿ wa ẓuhūrihi* (*Minhāj*, Turkī ed., pp. 139–40, §§281–4).

again simply "convey *khilāf* on the authority of one of them [i.e., of another Companion]" in order to cancel any claim of *ijmā'* (Shīr.III.3; Bāj.III.1.2).[178] Third, if R implies that he will support his *naql* by way of a numerical *tarjīḥ* (with three narrated *āthār*-traditions), then Q might pre-empt him by way of a counter-*tarjīḥ* (with four narrated *āthār*-traditions). We have earlier seen a weighing of narrators as al-Shīrāzī's, et al., *isnād*-oriented *Tarjīḥ al-Ẓawāhir* (Shīr.IX.1.5; Bāj.XVI.1.1.3).[179] The difference here is that both originator and transmitter of doctrine are of the Companions. Finally, were we to reverse the roles of R and Q, we would expect the same *i'tirāḍāt* from an Ibn Abī Laylā Q against the *istidlāl* of an Abū Ḥanīfa R—except for the *isnād*-oriented *tarjīḥ*, as the Ibn Abī Laylā position boasts one less *athar*-tradition than the Abū Ḥanīfa position.

Al-Shāfi'ī, as we see in §638, parallels the Ibn Abī Laylā position for this *mas'ala* "the estate-property is [divided] between them both, in two halves" (*al-māl baynahumā niṣfān*), and, at first, references the same *āthār*-traditions of Zayd b. Thābit, 'Alī, and Ibn Mas'ūd as supporting *naql*. We may thus—at first—hypothesize his objections to the Abū Ḥanīfa position as the same as our Ibn Abī Laylā proponent above. In §640, however, al-Shāfi'ī references an additional supporting *naql*: the *athar*-tradition of 'Uthmān. We may thus imagine that, were the *mas'ala* set in a venue of dialectical debate, and did the procedure of argument and defence devolve into a question of *tarjīḥ*—al-Shāfi'ī may well have stood ground against the Abū Ḥanīfa position by demonstrating an equal number of Companion adherents and transmitters. Moreover, al-Shāfi'ī marks Abū Bakr's ruling (estate-property only for the grandfather) as being in disagreement with his own referenced Companion; i.e., he not only raises the Ibn Abī Laylā supporting *āthār* (with the addition of 'Uthmān) to a numerical equivalence with those of the opposing Abū Ḥanīfa position, but he specifically points to this as an issue of "disagreement of the Companions" (*khilāf al-Ṣaḥāba*). Thus he conforms to the very definition of *i'tirāḍāt* against *istidlāl bi-ijmā' al-Ṣaḥāba* (Shīr.III.2; Bāj.III.1.1) and *istidlāl bi-qawl al-wāḥid min al-Ṣaḥāba* (Shīr.IV.3; Bāj.V.2) by way of conveying the *khilāf* of others from this same group.

Moreover, and despite adding (in §641) another *athar*-tradition in support of the Abū Ḥanīfa position (and thus upsetting the numerical balance in an Abū Ḥanīfa proponent's favour),[180] al-Shāfi'ī draws further attention to the underlying *khilāf* of the Ṣaḥāba by drawing a sort of "lineage" for the opposing doctrine. He claims that all of 'Ā'isha, Ibn 'Abbās, Ibn al-Zubayr, and 'Abd Allāh b. 'Utba professed the opposing doctrine along with Abū Bakr. Overall, then, al-Shāfi'ī has established this as a *mas'alat al-khilāf* split down the middle between two more or

---

[178] al-Shīrāzī, *Ma'ūna*, al-'Umayrīnī ed., p. 81; al-Bājī, *Minhāj*, Turkī ed., p. 140, §285. Cf. Ibn 'Aqīl, *K. al-Jadal*, p. 39, §205.

[179] al-Shīrāzī, *Ma'ūna*, al-'Umayrīnī ed., pp. 121–2; al-Bājī, *Minhāj*, Turkī ed., pp. 223–4, §508. Cf. Ibn 'Aqīl, *K. al-Jadal*, p. 24, §128.

[180] Again, I would consider this a clear sign of al-Shāfi'ī's sincere dialectical ethic. Mentioning additional *adilla*-indicants for the opposing position is a mark of "good" dialectic.

less equal groupings of important Companions. We may predict, too, that an additional *dalīl*-indicant might be sought by an opponent, in order to tip the evidence in favour of the Abū Ḥanīfa doctrine. This is precisely what happens in the ensuing dialectical sequence; and al-Shāfiʿī quite vehemently objects to the *qiyās* method by which his opponent seeks to strengthen the argumentative conclusiveness (*ḥujjiyya*) of the Abū Ḥanīfa doctrine.[181]

In §642, al-Shāfiʿī initiates a patently "historical" dialectic by informing his reader that the Abū Ḥanīfa/Abū Bakr ruling (all property to the grandfather) is also the opinion of the Dialectical Theologians on inheritance shares (*madhhab Ahl al-Kalām fi'l-farā'iḍ*). Note this is the only mention of the Ahl al-Kalām in the subject-text, and, as we shall see, it is accompanied with some spleen on the part of al-Shāfiʿī.[182] This selfsame debate appears in a variant form in the *Risāla*, although the Ahl al-Kalām are nowhere mentioned—neither as regards this *mas'ala*, nor elsewhere in the treatise.[183] Whether a specific reference to the Muʿtazila or otherwise, al-Shāfiʿī accuses the Ahl al-Kalām as deluded (*yatawahhamūna*) into thinking the doctrine of the Abū Ḥanīfa/Abū Bakr group is also the *qiyās*. Al-Shāfiʿī ardently denies that this could be so, saying: (1) neither doctrine is by way of *qiyās*; and (2) the doctrine of the Abū Ḥanīfa/Abū Bakr group is further from *qiyās* than the doctrine of the Ibn Abī Laylā/al-Shāfiʿī/ʿAlī group.[184]

Although we have not yet reached the particulars of the al-Shāfiʿī vs. Ahl al-Kalām arguments and objections, we may, from the perspective of early *jadal*-theory (and based upon what follows in §§643 ff.), interpret the overall aims of the opposing positions here. The project of the Ahl al-Kalām position—attempting *tarjīḥ* of opposing *āthār*-traditions via supporting *qiyās*—finds a match in al-Shīrāzī's first mode of *matn*-oriented *tarjīḥāt*: "That one of the two *khabar*-reports is consistent (*muwāfiq*) with another *dalīl*-indicant, from an authoritative source-case (*aṣl*), or what is rationally understood from one (*maʿqūl aṣl*)" (Shīr.IX.2.1).[185] As for

---

[181] Cf. this same dialectical debate as it plays out in the *Risāla* (Shākir ed., pp. 591 ff., §§1773 ff.)

[182] Including this instance, the Ahl al-Kalām are referenced eight times by al-Shāfiʿī in the *Umm*.

[183] Khadduri, in his translation (p. 347, n. 30) claims: "It is the Ḥanafī's opinion which the interlocutor supports." As we see here, however, al-Shāfiʿī attributes this attempted *qiyās*-support to the Ahl al-Kalām. This appellation is commonly understood to reference the Muʿtazila. See, e.g., Schacht, *Origins*, p. 128, where he references this very debate in our treatise under the heading "The Muʿtazila," observing: "Shāfiʿī, in *Tr. I*, 122, reports their analogical reasoning on a question of law and refutes it. They reject traditions on account of *naẓar* and reason, and use *qiyās* as a basis for criticizing traditions." In a footnote attached to this last sentence, he refers the reader to Ibn Qutayba's *Ta'wīl Mukhtalif al-Ḥadīth*. I would question Schacht on two counts: (1) in our dialectical sequence above (his *Tr. I*, 122), the opponent of the Ahl al-Kalām is attempting to use *qiyās* as a means of preponderating opposing sets of *āthār*—he is neither rejecting nor criticizing his own set, whatever Ibn Qutayba might accuse the Ahl al-Kalām of doing elsewhere; and (2) I see no objection to "Ahl al-Kalām" as applied in a broader sense, encompassing those who engage in dialectical theology, rather than a specific reference to the Muʿtazila.

[184] Schacht (*Origins*, p. 124) interprets this as follows: al-Shāfiʿī "recognizes its limits [i.e., the limits of *qiyās*], in opposition to the *ahl al-kalām*...."

[185] al-Shīrāzī, *Maʿūna*, al-ʿUmayrīnī ed., p. 123.

al-Shāfiʿī's two projects—confirming: [1] neither doctrine is by *qiyās*, and [2] the Abū Ḥanīfa/Abū Bakr doctrine is further from the *qiyās*—they may be interpreted as: (1) a range of *muṭālabāt* and *mumānaʿāt* against the components of the opposing position's purported *qiyās*; and (2) the reversal of the Ahl al-Kalām attempt at *tarjīḥ* by way of *qiyās*-agreement, which takes the form of a "hypothetical" *iʿtirāḍ* of *qalb*. By this latter move al-Shāfiʿī demonstrates that the same properties of the purported *qiyās*—were *qiyās* at all valid here—should produce a *ḥukm* closer to the al-Shāfiʿī/Ibn Abī Laylā/ʿAlī group doctrine than to that of the Ahl al-Kalām/Abū Ḥanīfa/Abū Bakr group. It is a reversal of the purported *qiyās*—hence "*qalb*"—but it is done only for the sake of argument—hence "hypothetical."

The dialectical sequence begins in §643, when al-Shāfiʿī introduces the doctrine of an R of the Ahl al-Kalām, saying: "And one of those who subscribe to this *madhhab*-opinion has said... (*qad qāla baʿḍ man yadhhabu hādhā al-madhhab...*)." We now hear the voice of this "historical" R, who has rejected brother for grandfather "due to three properties (*khiṣāl*) regarding which you yourselves agree with us (*antum mujtamiʿūna maʿanā ʿalayhā*):"

- [*endoxon ḥukm* A] "you eclipse the sons of the mother [i.e., the maternal half-brothers of the deceased] by [the grandfather]—likewise being the *manzila*-status of the father"
- [*endoxon ḥukm* B] "you do not diminish [the grandfather] from the sixth[-part of the estate]—likewise the *manzila*-status of the father"
- [*endoxon* "nominal" *waṣf*] "moreover, you actually call [the grandfather] 'father'"[186]

[186] There are a number of salient features in the summation of the opponent's stance in §643 alone; among them are: (1) the term *madhhab* in the sense of doctrinal opinion; (2) the term *khiṣāl* (s. *khaṣla*) in the sense of "quality, property"—cf. al-Shīrāzī's use of *khaṣīṣa* in discussing *qiyās al-dalāla*; (3) the acknowledgement of a doctrinal consensus as conveyed through the descriptor *mujtamiʿūna maʿanā ʿalayhā*; (4) a technical usage of *manzila*; and (5) a "nominal" hermeneutic—i.e., the semantic connecting of the common denomination of a thing ("father") to its legal status. A search for these elements and terms in early *kalām* works might help us to identify more precisely the theological affiliation of these Ahl al-Kalām—be they Muʿtazila or otherwise. Of greater import, however, is the fact that al-Shāfiʿī may here be engaged in disputation with a dialectical theologian on a point of law (as opposed to only a proponent of their *qiyās* for this *mas'ala*). If such is the case, it illustrates the "many hats" paradigm in conjunction with "cross-germination between epistemic communities." That is to say that dialectic marked the procedure—the form of disputation—whether an individual scholar was engaged in theological speculation, normative inference, or other projects. One might be a specialist in one field or another, but the origins of terms, concepts, and methods may not necessarily be attributable to one field over another. They are better linked to the individual projects of individual scholars across thematic domains. In other words, we need not interpret al-Shāfiʿī's dialectic as an absolute convergence of prior *Kalām*-method and nascent legal theory/dialectic, as some might claim it to be. Both al-Shāfiʿī and the opponent of the Ahl al-Kalām position appear to have "worn more than one hat."

This not only constitutes R's appeal to the *endoxa* properties (*khiṣāl*) supporting his *qiyās* from father to grandfather, but it provides indicants for the type of *qiyās* he proposes: Type I *qiyās al-dalāla*—via shared *ḥukm* A, shared *ḥukm* B, and a shared "nominal" *waṣf*—all of which R believes to be *endoxa*.[187] In fact, due to this "nominal *waṣf*," the *qiyās* has a pluralistic quality: it shares an aspect of *qiyās al-shabah* and al-Baṣrī's "Justifying the Occasioning Factor by way of the Name" (*al-taʿlīl bi'l-ism*).[188] Due to the predominance of indication from shared rulings, however, I will treat this as Type I *qiyās al-dalāla*, and diagram it as follows:

Aṣl Father		*Farʿ* Grandfather
Endoxon Ḥukm A he eclipses maternal half-brothers	← SAME →	*Endoxon Ḥukm* A he eclipses maternal half-brothers
Endoxon Ḥukm B he retains minimum 1/6	← SAME →	*Endoxon Ḥukm* B he retains minimum 1/6
Endoxon "Nominal" *Waṣf* he is called "father"	← SAME →	*Endoxon* "Nominal" *Waṣf* he is called "father"
Endoxon Ḥukm C he eclipses full-brothers	THEREFORE, SAME →	Contended *Ḥukm* C [he should also eclipse full-brothers]

From this illustration it is easy to see how the legal argument I have labelled *manzila*-subsumption may be supported by Type I *qiyās al-dalāla*. Due to the shared (and *endoxa*) rulings A and B, along with the shared (also *endoxon*) property "he is called 'father,'" one ought to be able to claim—according to R—that when the father of the deceased does not survive (or for some other reason cannot inherit), the grandfather should inherit in his place—his *manzila*—across the whole genus of *masā'il* having to do with inheritance shares.

Al-Shāfiʿī, as we have seen, is entirely opposed to allowing a *qiyās* to overrule established *khabar*-reports for the same *mas'ala*. In §644, attacking the first property (*khaṣla*) of R's *qiyās*—what I have labeled *endoxon ḥukm* A—he again makes this clear, saying: "We only eclipsed the sons of the mother by [the grandfather] by way of a *khabar*-report, not by way of *qiyās* from the father (*khabaran lā qiyāsan ʿalā al-ab*)." This objection constitutes—on one level—the now familiar *muʿāraḍa bi'l-nuṭq* (Shīr.VII.15.1; Bāj.IX.15.1)—although al-Shāfiʿī does not mention which Prophetic *ḥadīth* he relies upon in the case of grandfather vs. half-brother. On another level—and bearing in mind that al-Shāfiʿī's starting point for this objection is a principle of legal theory—implicit to his objection is a charge at the higher

[187] al-Shīrāzī, *Maʿūna*, al-ʿUmayrīnī ed., pp. 36, 116–17; Turkī ed., pp. 140, 263–4. al-Bājī, *Minhāj*, Turkī ed., p. 27, §48; pp. 203 f., §461 f. Ibn ʿAqīl, *K. al-Jadal*, p. 13, §62.

[188] This serves to illustrate what ties all subtypes of *qiyās al-dalāla* together: the *ʿilla* is not in fact known. Instead indication (*dalāla*) is drawn from shared rulings, qualities, etc., with the objective of demonstrating *aṣl* and *farʿ* likely share the same *ḥukm* (whatever the *ʿilla* may be).

register of method-oriented *jadal*. In so many words, al-Shāfiʿī has claimed: "You have violated a fundamental principle by attempting *qiyās* where there is established *khabar*; therefore I am supplanting your *istidlāl bi'l-qiyās* with my *istidlāl bi'l-khabar*." R's problematic method is trumped by Q's *endoxon* method. Previously, we encountered a method-oriented objection in the form of *naqḍ*, and I proposed a new label: method-*naqḍ*. Now we have encountered a method-oriented objection in the form of *muʿāraḍa*, and I will call it method-*muʿāraḍa*. However we assess al-Shāfiʿī's objection in §644, it constitutes a form of *muʿāraḍa*; we might predict a consequent change in roles, and this is precisely what occurs in §645: R becomes Q.

The new Q now launches his first dialectical question: "And how is that" (*wa kayfa dhālika*)? Again, we may interpret this on two levels, depending upon Q's understanding of al-Shāfiʿī's intention. At the substantive ruling register—and indicated by "how" (*kayfa*)—Q's question resembles al-Bājī's "question about the mode of the indicant" (*su'āl ʿan wajh al-dalīl*). Based on al Shāfiʿī's ensuing multi-tiered *jawāb* in §§646–9, however, I might better qualify Q's question as a method-oriented *su'āl*—a "question about the mode of the objection" (*su'āl ʿan wajh al-iʿtirāḍ*)—or, more specifically, a "question about the mode of counter-indication" (*su'āl ʿan wajh al-muʿāraḍa*). In essence, he appears to be asking: How is it that you supplant my *qiyās*? And he receives, in response, a very succinct and programmatic account. Al-Shāfiʿī proceeds step by step to *elenchus*; and note that he does little to vindicate his own *istidlāl bi'l-Sunna*; rather, he engages solely in the destruction of Q's *qiyās*.[189]

In §646 al-Shāfiʿī initiates a three-part *jawāb* by objecting to Q's first property (*khaṣla*) with an ordered set of *endoxa* premises: (1) "We, ourselves, [also] eclipse the sons of the mother [i.e., the maternal half-brothers of the deceased] by the daughter of the son of a son [i.e., the great-granddaughter of the deceased], however-so-low;" (2) "but even if she corresponds to the *manzila*-status of the father in this situation (*fī hādhā al-mawḍiʿ*);" (3) "we would certainly never rule—neither we nor you—that she stands in place of the father anywhere else." This is a specific attack against Q's employment of *endoxon ḥukm* A in his proposed *qiyās al-dalāla*, and the dialectical move employed by al-Shāfiʿī is a now familiar one: it is a species of *naqḍ*. In effect, al-Shāfiʿī has shown that the same *khaṣla*-property (*endoxon ḥukm* A) is present in the great-granddaughter *mas'alat al-naqḍ*, but Q would never extend it—by way of *qiyās al-dalāla*—to other *masā'il* in the genus of inheritance shares. Nor would Q ever claim "she stands in place of the father for all inheritance matters" (*wa hiya fī manzilat al-ab fī kull mīrāth*) simply because she is in the *manzila* of the father in a single instance.

As for identifying this species of *naqḍ* in the *jadal*-theory literature, we are at first struck with a conundrum: *naqḍ*, as we have seen, is defined in terms of "the

[189] Cf. the discussion near the end of Sect. 4.5, above, where al-Juwaynī compares *muʿāraḍa* and *munāqaḍa*, saying: "Know that inconsistency/contradiction (*munāqaḍa*) is a type of counter-indication (*muʿāraḍa*), and that it is the strongest of the types of counter-indications (*muʿāraḍāt*); and that every *munāqaḍa* is a *muʿāraḍa*, even though not every *muʿāraḍa* is a *munāqaḍa*."

presence of the *ʿilla*, and not the *ḥukm*." In other words, the *naqḍ* of the *jadal* texts is oriented specifically towards *qiyās al-ʿilla* (Shīr.VII.7; Bāj.IX.B.11.1–2), whereas al-Shāfiʿī's target is clearly *qiyās al-dalāla*. That his objection belongs to the genus of *naqḍ*, however, is self-evident: the hallmark of bringing a *mas'alat al-naqḍ* (the great-granddaughter case) is present; so, too, is the employing of that *mas'alat al-naqḍ* to show an opponent's inconsistency.

I would suggest two possible explanations: (1) the proto-system objections of genus *naqḍ* enjoyed a larger domain of application than existed in later times, when *qiyās*-procedure in general became more refined, and disputation centered more specifically on *istidlāl bi-qiyās al-ʿilla*; or (2) al-Shāfiʿī's objection may be targeted more at Q's overall method, than upon his particular usage of *endoxon ḥukm* A in his *qiyās al-dalāla*. As for the first explanation, we might simply conclude we are witnessing a species of *qiyās al-dalāla*-oriented *naqḍ* which was not discussed in the early *jadal*-system literature for some reason or another. As to the second, we might understand al-Shāfiʿī's objection as belonging to that higher register of method-oriented *iʿtirāḍāt*, and thus label it, once again, method-*naqḍ*—aimed, in this case, at Q's inconsistent practice of *manzila*-subsumption.

This latter explanation gains support when we consider al-Shāfiʿī's conclusion at the start of §647. Here he draws to a close his objection against Q's first *khaṣla*-property for *qiyās*, asserting: "Thus [the grandfather] corresponds to [the father] in one *maʿnā*-quality, even as he diverges from him in another." A principle of legal theory is implicit to this statement: whatever it is that allows the grandfather or great-granddaughter, in one instance, to stand in the *manzila* of father, is not necessarily transferable to other contexts (*mawāḍiʿ*). In other words, the *khaṣla*-property shared by X and Y in one case may not be shared in another—and thus the *khaṣla*-property itself cannot be trusted to indicate the *manzila*-subsumption "X is in the *manzila* of Y for the whole genus of *masā'il*." This implication of a more general legal principle at work supports an interpretation of al-Shāfiʿī as charging method-*naqḍ*; his objection is akin to saying: "This is the principle you adhere to in the great-granddaughter *mas'ala*, why do you ignore it here in the grandfather *mas'ala*, where it is just as relevant?" Q's practice of *manzila*-subsumption is exposed as inconsistent.

Al-Shāfiʿī's *jawāb* to Q's dialectical question in §645 was in three parts; al-Shāfiʿī now (still in §647) proceeds to attack Q's second *khaṣla*-property—what I have labeled *endoxon ḥukm* B. First, he reasserts that the grandfather retains his minimum of one-sixth due to a *khabar*-report (not *qiyās*). As before, we may classify this objection as *muʿāraḍa bi'l-nuṭq*, even though he does not identify the particular *ḥadīth* (Shīr.VII.15.1; Bāj.IX.15.1). Al-Shāfiʿī then proceeds to bring another *mas'alat al-naqḍ*: the *mas'ala* of the grandmother, who also retains a minimum of one-sixth. This time, however, he follows with a rhetorical *reductio* introduced by our familiar *a-ra'ayta* formula: "So do you think (*a-fa-ra'ayta*) that we—and you—should stand her in place of the father, since she corresponds to him in a *maʿnā*-quality?" Thus al-Shāfiʿī (rhetorically) pushes Q to concede, once more, to his own inconsistency.[190] This objection, in most ways, is a mirror of al-Shāfiʿī's objection to Q's first *khaṣla*-property, and we may interpret it in the same two ways: (1) as a specifically *qiyās al-dalāla*-oriented *naqḍ*, by which Q's employing of *endoxon ḥukm* B has been shown to be inconsistent; and (2) as a method-*naqḍ*, whereby Q's procedure of *manzila*-subsumption has once again been exposed as inconsistent.

Finally, al-Shāfiʿī proceeds to attack Q's third *khaṣla*-property (the shared "nominal" *waṣf*), and he does so in a series of stages with a devastating finish. First, at the end of §647, he puts forth a single premise: "And as for the 'label of fatherhood' (*ism al-ubuwwa*): we and you [both] attach the 'label of fatherhood' to the one between us and Adam." In short, this is something like an appeal to the (*endoxon*) "customary linguistic usage" (*ʿurf al-lugha*).[191] Second, in §648, al-Shāfiʿī brings another premise in the form of an appeal to a general (and *endoxon*) *ḥukm* consequent to this *endoxon* usage of the 'label of fatherhood' (*ism al-ubuwwa*): "And when it is thus," he says, "and below any one of them is a 'father' nearer [to the deceased] than him, he does not inherit." Third, in §649, al-Shāfiʿī introduces a series of three (*endoxa*) *masāʾil al-naqḍ*, for the *ism al-ubuwwa* also obtains when: (1) the 'father' is a nonbeliever (*kāfir*) and the deceased a Muslim; (2) the 'father' is a murderer (*qātil*) and the deceased murdered [by him] (*maqtūl*); and (3) the 'father' is enslaved (*mamlūk*) and the deceased is free (*ḥurr*).

The stage thus set, al-Shāfiʿī delivers a devastating *iʿtirāḍ*: "if we had transferred inheritance through the 'label of fatherhood' alone, we would have transferred inheritance to those whom we have forbidden [in these *masāʾil al-naqḍ*]—all of them." "But," he continues (at the end of §649), "we have only transmitted inheritance by way of a *khabar*-report, not based on the label (*ism*) [of fatherhood]." This objection once again corresponds well to the genus of *naqḍ*. In fact, it is a triple-*naqḍ*—for al-Shāfiʿī has shown Q to be thrice-inconsistent in his claims of the "nominal" *waṣf* for his *qiyās* in the *masʾala* at hand. Clearly, had this *waṣf*-property any link to an efficient *ʿilla* in the *farʿ* of the grandfather's inheritance, it would have shown it in these *masāʾil al-naqḍ*—but it has failed to be co-present with anything but the opposite *ḥukm*.

Moreover, this focus upon the *ism al-ubuwwa*—and the telltale objection "we have only transferred inheritance by *khabar*, not by *ism*"—points us towards another species of objection found in our oldest extant treatise on juridical *jadal*: the *Kitāb al-Qiyās al-Sharʿī* of al-Baṣrī. Al-Baṣrī's section "On what Distinguishes the *ʿIlla* as pertains to Modes which Invalidate It (*al-wujūh al-mufsida lahā*)" is initially divided into what provides indication for *fasād al-ʿilla* by way of (1) Muslim Communal Doctrine (*Qawl al-Umma*); and (2) Rational Inference (*Istinbāṭ*). This latter, he tells us, consists of modes, and the very first mode is entitled

[190] Al-Shāfiʿī's *a-raʾayta* in §647: rhetorical, soliciting a ruling for a parallel *masʾala*, constituting a charge of method-*naqḍ* or *qiyās al-dalāla*-oriented *naqḍ*.

[191] Cf. al-Shīrāzī's example *jawāb* as regards the first type of the second *iʿtirāḍ* against *al-istidlāl bi'l-Kitāb* (*Maʿūna*, al-ʿUmayrīnī ed., p. 42). The Ḥanafī R appeals to the *ʿurf* of the *lugha*, as "the *khiṭāb* [of the Qurʾān] is in the *lugha* of the Arabs."

"*ʿIlla*-Justification by way of the Name" (*al-Taʿlīl biʾl-Ism*). This mode in turn is subdivided into three types, which may be summarized as follows:[192]

- Type 1: [the name has no efficiency]
  - example: the one justifying the *ʿilla* (*muʿallil*) fixes the *ʿilla* for proscription of grape-wine (*taḥrīm al-khamr*) on the fact that the Arabs called it *khamr*. This is invalid (*fāsid*), because the Arab designation has no efficiency (*taʾthīr*).
- Type 2: the *ʿilla* is established by genus
  - example: the *ʿilla* that a beverage is of the genus of grape-wine (*khamr*) occasions the *ḥukm* of proscription (*taḥrīm*). This is *not* invalid; "being of the genus" may have efficiency.
- also allowed are: (1) *ʿilla*-justification (*taʿlīl*) by way of an attribute (*ṣifa*) among attributes; or (2) *taʿlīl* by way of a ruling (*ḥukm*) among rulings (i.e., one divinely-sanctioned *ḥukm* may be used to establish another).
  - NB: the first corresponds to the *qiyās al-shabah* of al-Shīrāzī, and the second corresponds to his Type I and II *qiyās al-dalāla*.

Q's appeal to an *endoxon* usage of the *ism al-ubuwwa* fits well within this general category of *al-taʿlīl biʾl-ism*—as does al-Shāfiʿī's objection, which seems to prove that the *ism al-ubuwwa* has no efficiency (Type 1). This is made all the more interesting when we consider Q was the proponent of an Ahl al-Kalām (possibly Muʿtazilī) position, while al-Baṣrī himself represented that rare combination of Muʿtazilī-Ḥanafī. There may be implications here, at least in terms of a continuity of proto-system teaching and practice of *jadal* in the Muʿtazilī camp. What is clear, however, is that we place al-Shāfiʿī's objection—the conclusion of his triple-*naqḍ*—within this domain-set, and note that shades of his overall critique bear upon all of al-Baṣrī's types.

I earlier suggested that al-Shāfiʿī's strategy was less concerned with defending his (unnamed) source *akhbār*-reports than with utterly destroying Q's *qiyās*. It is quite evident he has succeeded in this—Q ceases to pursue validating his *qiyās*, and we may read his shifting to new ground as conceding the invalidity of his *qiyās* and moving on. In §650, Q launches another dialectical challenge, and we are reminded of the overall Ahl al-Kalām project: *tarjīḥ* of their *āthār*-tradition group via consonance with *qiyās*. This was the motive which prompted Q to propose *qiyās* in the first place; that is, his *qiyās al-dalāla* rendered forth the very same *ḥukm* as the Abū Ḥanīfa/Abū Bakr group doctrine. But now Q has conceded to al-Shāfiʿī's *khaṣla* by *khaṣla* dismembering of his *qiyās*, so he retreats to a less perfect vantage. Whereas before he could claim his doctrine to *be* the *qiyās*, he now challenges al-Shāfiʿī with: "Then which of the two doctrines most resembles the *qiyās* (*fa-ayy al-qawlayn*

[192] al-Baṣrī, *K. al-Qiyās al-Sharʿī*, Ḥamīd Allāh ed., p. 1039; Hallaq, "Treatise," pp. 216–17.

ashbahu al-qiyās)?" His project has been reduced—from *āthār*-traditions in complete accordance with the *maʿnā al-khiṭāb*, he has retreated to *āthār*-traditions "most resembling" the *maʿnā al-khiṭāb*. His question must still be recognized as a challenge, however, and it contains a clever trap for al-Shāfiʿī. Were al-Shāfiʿī simply to pursue the question and argue his own set of *āthār*-traditions as closest to *qiyās*, he would have gone back on his afore-stated stance: "there is no *qiyās* regarding these two doctrines." Not surprisingly, the very first thing al-Shāfiʿī does in his *jawāb* (start of §651) is to reiterate his *muʿāraḍa bi'l-nuṭq*, saying: "There is no *qiyās* regarding either one, but the doctrine you have chosen is *farther* from *qiyās* and rational understanding."

Note that it has become very difficult to classify Q's questions at this point in the dialectical sequence. The discussions we have found in the *jadal*-theory texts as regards the defining and proper ordering of questions have been presented in an abstracted, and ideal, light. There we find a simple, logical ordering for Q, proceeding cautiously so as to never retract or accidentally concede. The reality of this particular dialectical sequence, however, has seen a number of twists whereby R has become Q, and wherein the new Q cannot proceed to dismantle his opponent's *istidlāl/taqlīd*, which is at least equal to his own; nor can he dismantle his opponent's *ʿaql* arguments—for al-Shāfiʿī denies *qiyās* in this *mas'ala*, and brings nothing to fill the void except his unnamed *khabar*-reports. In short, even as questioner, Q is constantly on the defensive, as al-Shāfiʿī does nothing positive—he does not assert his *ḥukm*—but instead contents himself with dismantling whatever Q brings forward. Thus, Q's questions continue in the vein of a "question about the mode of the objection" (*su'āl ʿan wajh al-iʿtirāḍ*) or "demand for validation of the objection" (*muṭālaba bi-taṣḥīḥ al-iʿtirāḍ*) or some such combination we do not find in the *jadal*-theory texts.[193]

One thing is clear: a number of the dialectical questions we have encountered thus far (including "which of the two doctrines most resembles the *qiyās*?") do not seem to fit the neatly-ordered question hierarchy of al-Bājī. The implications of this are not immediately clear. We might conjecture that, over time, juridical *jadal* in practice became more refined and strictly-ordered as *jadal*-theory itself became more and more systematized. Thus, the first fully-systematized treatises saw no need to address questions which fell outside of al-Bājī's (and others') hierarchy—for they simply would never have been asked in the first place, or at least not in

[193] We do find several relevant challenges among the *ajwiba*-responses suggested by our *jadal* authors, but they do not receive a separate classification or typology. As such, it is a more difficult task to "name" these *iʿtirāḍ*-oriented questions/objections, except by combining formulaic elements from the classified categories of *istidlāl*-oriented questions/objections, as I have attempted here. A disclaimer: my invention of such terms as "*su'āl ʿan wajh al-iʿtirāḍ*" is exactly that—an invention—and is not meant to suggest that *jadal* practitioners or theorists ever entertained such labels. I am merely attempting to describe, with an appropriate Arabic terminology, what I perceive Q intends with his questions. This is similar to my use of *endoxon*: unless otherwise stated, it is simply a descriptor, not a strict identification of the subject dialectician's source or "unspoken" classification.

the same way. Still, a category of "*iʿtirāḍ*-oriented" questions/objections—e.g., "how does your *qiyās* supplant my *qiyās*?" or "on what basis do you claim your *khabar*-report is superior (*awlā*) to my *khabar*-report?"—seems like something we ought to find in the lens-texts (in addition to the *jadal* authors' suggestions regarding appropriate responses).[194]

Returning to the current sequence, al-Shāfiʿī reinforces his "no *qiyās* for either" stance in the first part of his *jawāb* in §651. Parsimonious in response, he supplies only a short counter-challenge to Q, saying: "the doctrine you have chosen is *farther* from *qiyās* and rational understanding (*ʿaql*)." I would pause once again to examine this statement carefully; for it is heavy laden with significant implications. As we see time and again with *maʿqūl*—in §§402, 633, 929, 1056, 1061, and 1411,[195] and repeatedly throughout the *Umm*—rational understanding (*ʿaql*) is here presented as a measuring-stick—similar to the sources and guiding principles of the later "rational indicants" (*adilla ʿaqliyya*) and "method principles" (*uṣūl al-ʿamaliyya*) of Ithnā ʿAsharī Shīʿī tradition.[196] As I will do for *maʿqūl* in a later section, I will attempt now for *ʿaql*, although a preliminary electronic search for the term is made more difficult due to the common appearance of *ʿaql* as an object of various substantive concerns (e.g., when *compos mentis* is discussed), and due to its polysemous nature (e.g., *ʿaql* as referring to blood-money [*diya*]). However, a simple search pairing of *al-qiyās wa'l-ʿaql*, as above in §651, uncovers two more illustrative usages.

First, from a discussion of "the non-Muslim resident of an enemy polity, who converts to Islam in the Abode of War, whilst there belongs to him property therein (*al-ḥarbī yuslimu fī dār al-ḥarb wa lahu bihā māl*)" in the *Book on al-Awzāʿī's Laws of War* (*Kitāb Siyar al-Awzāʿī*):[197]

593 – [....] This doctrine is alien to *qiyās*, *ʿaql*, and Sunna.	593 - [...] هَذَا الْقَوْلُ خَارِجٌ مِنَ الْقِيَاسِ وَالْعَقْلِ وَالسُّنَّةِ.

Second, from a discussion "regarding the *ʿaql* [meaning: blood-money] of a woman (*fī ʿaql al-mar'a*)," in the *Book of Rebuttal against Muḥammad b. al-Ḥasan [al-Shaybānī]* (*Kitāb al-Radd ʿalā Muḥammad b. al-Ḥasan*):[198]

---

[194] It is quite likely, as one kind reader suggested to me, that even the most thorough of *jadal*-theory treatises would not have accounted for all of the questions and objections which might occur in an actual dialectical exchange. What is important here, however, is the great number of "unfamiliar" questions and objections (in terms of the later theory) we find in proto-system *jadal*, and their formulaic nature; this strongly suggests that earlier manifestations of juridical *jadal* were indeed quite different from later ones, and that the dialectic of our subject-text and lens-texts represent different phases in the evolution of a larger tradition.

[195] We will encounter *maʿqūl* when we analyze the dialectical sequences of §§1056, 1061, and 1411. A final interpretation as to precisely what al-Shāfiʿī means by *ʿaql* and *maʿqūl* will be presented in Sect. 8.2, below.

[196] See my entry on "Uṣūl al-Fiqh," in *Oxford Islamic Studies Online*.

[197] *Umm*, Ḥassūn ed., vol. 10, pt. 15, p. 346.

[198] *Umm*, Ḥassūn ed., vol. 10, pt. 15, p. 162. Note that both of these books are *ikhtilāf* treatises, replete with short and extended dialectical sequences.

151 – [...] nor is there in that which Saʿīd calls Sunna—[not] when it contradicts *qiyās* and *ʿaql*, unless on the strength of *ʿilm* according to what we opine. And God Most High knows best.	151 - [...] وَلاَ يَكُونُ فِيمَا قَالَ سَعِيدٌ: السُّنَّةُ. إِذَا كَانَتْ تُخَالِفُ الْقِيَاسَ وَالْعَقْلَ إِلاَّ عَنْ عِلْمِ اتِّبَاعٍ فِيمَا نَرَى وَاللَّهُ تَعَالَى أَعْلَمُ.

Note that: (1) in both of these examples, *ʿaql* appears ranked among authoritative "sources" alongside Sunna and *qiyās*; and (2) both instances occur at the concluding section of an overtly dialectical exchange.

Moreover, there is a very enlightening discussion in the *Book on Nullification of Juristic Preference* (*Kitāb Ibṭāl al-Istiḥsān*),[199] which bears heavily on al-Shāfiʿī's conception and usage of the term *ʿaql*. Al-Shāfiʿī, near the middle of the treatise, reviews a few relevant Qur'ānic indicants, relates the famed *ḥadīth* of the Prophet's discourse with Muʿādh [b. Jabal], and then the equally famed *ḥadīth* by which the accurate *mujtahid* receives two rewards and the mistaken *mujtahid* receives one.[200] He then proceeds to an "instructional" dialectic featuring the "Folk of Rational Intellection and Proper Comportment" (Ahl al-ʿUqūl wa'l-Adab).[201]

Additionally, the "Folk of Rational Intellection" (Ahl al-ʿUqūl) appear once in the *Risāla*,[202] and also during a refutation of "juristic preference" (*istiḥsān*):

1458 – And if the suspension/denial of *qiyās* were permitted; it would be permitted to the Ahl al-ʿUqūl—not the Ahl al-ʿIlm—that they profess [legal solutions], for what has no relevant *khabar*-report, on the basis of whatever comes to them of juristic preference.	1458 - ولو جاز تعطيلُ القياس جاز لأهلِ العقولِ من غيرِ أهل العلم أن يقولوا فيما ليس فيه خبرٌ بما يَحْضُرهم من الاستحسانِ.

Note that the ambiguity of *min ghayr* in this context makes it difficult to determine whether the Ahl al-ʿUqūl and the Ahl al-ʿIlm are exclusive to each other—one cannot belong to both sets—or otherwise.[203] We will return to this question in Chap. 8; but my conclusion, in brief, is that by *ʿaql* and *maʿqūl* al-Shāfiʿī means something like "that which may be rationally inferred from the textual *dalīl*-indicant (i.e., from Qur'ān and Sunna) when it is not directly stated therein." In

199 A treatise on legal theory which is every bit as important as the *Risāla*, but often overlooked.

200 *Umm*, Ḥassūn ed., vol. 10, pt. 15, p. 125, §89–90.

201 See my dissertation for a translation of this passage ("Dialectical Forge," pt. 2, pp. 358–9, appendix II.§651).

202 §1458, Shākir ed., 505. A kind reader has also pointed out to me the reference to an Ahl al-Murū'a wa'l-ʿAql in §1304 (Shākir ed., p. 470).

203 Remarkably, a search among a great many pre-modern sources of Shāfiʿī *fiqh* has revealed no other occurrence of the Ahl al-ʿUqūl, while among *Uṣūl al-Fiqh* literature in general, I have only found mention in: (1) the *Iḥkām fī Uṣūl al-Aḥkām* of the Ẓāhirī Ibn Ḥazm (whose *Taqrīb* has been mentioned) (Shākir ed., vol. 1, p. 28; vol. 5, pp. 146, 161; vol. 8, p. 96); (2) a line of verse quoted by al-Khaṭīb al-Baghdādī in his *Al-Faqīh wa'l-Mutafaqqih* (Al-ʿAzzāzī ed., vol. 2, p. 402); (3) the famed

other words, *ʿaql* and *maʿqūl* are used in practically the same way that al-Shīrāzī, al-Bājī, et al. speak of *maʿqūl aṣl*—i.e., *laḥn al-khiṭāb*, *faḥwā al-khiṭāb*, and *dalīl al-khiṭāb*—with the exception of *maʿnā al-khiṭāb* or *qiyās*, which al-Shāfiʿī always lists separately from *ʿaql* and *maʿqūl*.

Returning to our dialectical sequence, we find that Q's question "which of the two doctrines most resembles the *qiyās*" has again born no fruit—al-Shāfiʿī, again, avoids saying anything positive about his *akhbār*-reports. Nor does he say "mine is closer to *qiyās* than yours;" rather, he simply says "yours is farther from the *qiyās* and the *ʿaql*." The significance is that Q must remain on the defensive, still, despite the fact that he has been in the role of Q for some time now, because al-Shāfiʿī has given him nothing positive to critique. All that al-Shāfiʿī has done, in fact, is to suggest his own objections in such a way that Q is left with no option except to keep asking al-Shāfiʿī to reveal the particulars of his objection. Such is the case now, and Q meekly asks (§652): "How so (*fa-ayna dhālika*)?"

I will attempt to identify al-Shāfiʿī's *jawāb* and Q's follow-up question as follows: First of all, al-Shāfiʿī has—in pre-empting Q's *qiyās*-consonance *tarjīḥ* project, brought his own "counter-*tarjīḥ*." Moreover, *qiyās*-consonance has now been twinned with the measure of *ʿaql*. Of course, al-Shāfiʿī would have to say something positive regarding his reports in order to properly give them preponderance over Q's *āthār*-traditions on the basis of closer proximity to *qiyās* and *ʿaql*. However, al-Shāfiʿī does no such thing. What is more, his true intention is revealed in following sections: he will, in fact, turn Q's proposed *qiyās* on its head—via a move resembling the *iʿtirāḍ* of *qalb*;[204] and we might best understand al-Shāfiʿī's second claim in §651 as a setting of the stage for a "hypothetical" *qalb*. As for Q's question in §652, it is once again of a genus we don't find in the *jadal*-theory literature—a genus of *iʿtirāḍ*-oriented questions/objections. Here, he appears to be anticipating al-Shāfiʿī, and demands that he pinpoint the locus (hence: *ayna*?) of his own doctrine's failure to conform to *qiyās* and *ʿaql*. In other words, Q's dialectical question is something akin to a "demand for the mode of denial, or mode of counter-indication, or mode of reversal" (*muṭālaba bi wajh al-manʿ/wajh al-muʿāraḍa/wajh al-qalb*), etc. Again, Q is left asking al-Shāfiʿī "how does your objection work?"

In §§653 ff., al-Shāfiʿī more than answers the question; he commandeers the role of Q, then pushes R to concede a number of *endoxa* premises, then seals at last his *elenchus* via a move resembling *qalb*-reversal. The first stage of the process may be outlined thus: (1) in §653 al-Shāfiʿī asserts himself as Q with an opening *a-raʾayta* question: "Have you considered [what would happen] when the grandfather and the brother both demand the inheritance of the deceased; would they be united [to the deceased] by their own proximate-kinship, or by the proximate-kinship of

Muwāfaqāt of al-Shāṭibī (Āl Salmān ed., vol. 2, pp. 41, 214); and (4) the *Baḥr al-Muḥīṭ* of al-Zarkashī (Dār al-Kutubī ed., vol. 6, p. 493; and vol. 8, p. 96—in paraphrase of the *Risāla* passage [§1458, above]).

[204] In so many words, al-Shāfiʿī will say that—were *qiyās* valid here—the same properties should indicate a *ḥukm* closer to his own doctrine than that of the opponent.

another?"—this latter being the first premise he wants R to concede;[205] (2) R is uncertain as to the relevance and/or significance of this dichotomous choice thrust upon him, and is rightly hesitant to answer—his *jawāb* in §654 is thus itself a question seeking clarity/explanation: "What of it?" or "What do you mean?" (*wa mā dhālika*); (3) al-Shāfiʿī takes advantage of this request to fine-tune the premise he seeks, and to "feed" it to R in just the formula he requires it to be conceded in: "Wouldn't the grandfather only say: 'I am the father of the father of the deceased' (*anā abū abī al-mayyit*); and the brother: 'I am the son of the father of the deceased' (*anā ibnu abī al-mayyit*)?'" Al-Shāfiʿī's objective is that his opponent concede to a locus of inheritance claim in proximate-kinship (*qarāba*) with the father of the deceased. In §656, the opponent concedes "of course" (*balā*), and thus al-Shāfiʿī secures the first stage of his *qalb*-like move. He then confirms Q's concession to this axis of proximate-kinship by plainly stating it in §657: "Then by the proximate-kinship of the father of the deceased they are, together, united to the deceased."

In §658, al-Shāfiʿī proceeds to the next stage—introducing what I would call a *mas'alat al-qalb*—a parallel in which the opponent's backwards ruling should be made plain: "Now make the father of the deceased to be [instead] the deceased one," he enjoins of his opponent, "Which of the two is foremost (*awlā*) in terms of greater inheritance: his son [corresponding to the brother of the *mas'ala* at hand], or his father [corresponding to the grandfather of the *mas'ala* at hand]?" For the sake of clarity, I will diagram the *mas'ala* at hand and the *mas'alat al-qalb* as follows:

***Mas'ala* at Hand**	**Individual**	***Mas'alat al-Qalb***
• Grandfather of deceased (boxed)	← A →	• Father of deceased (boxed)
• Father of deceased	← B →	• DECEASED
• DECEASED • Brother of Deceased (boxed)	← C & D →	• Son of deceased • Son of deceased (boxed)
• Son of deceased	← E →	• Grandson of deceased
NB: The boxed "A" and "D" are the same individuals in both *mas'alas*.		

Al-Shāfiʿī, working from the conceded premise of the axis of proximate-kinship for the father of the deceased, now pushes his opponent (R) to concede the *endoxon* ruling for his *mas'alat al-qalb*—who is *awlā* in terms of inheritance, father or son? In §659, R has no choice but to rule appropriately: "His son of course, because five sixths belong to him, but to his father [only] the [remaining] sixth." Thus, he concedes to what I would call the "*qalb*-premise." And so, with both conceded premises in hand ("axis of proximate-kinship" and "*qalb*-premise"), al-Shāfiʿī (in §660)

[205] NB: thus we witness yet another usage of the *a-ra'ayta* formula: presenting R with a dichotomous choice, in this case: "kinship via X, or kinship via not-X?" Al-Shāfiʿī's *a-ra'ayta* in §653: dialogical, as part of a *reductio* sub-strategy: framing a disjunction of premises (have you considered: is it X or Y?); the endoxic choice (Y) serving as a premise justifying his choice of *aṣl* for a "hypothetical" *muʿāraḍa-qiyās*, which is itself a *reductio* sub-strategy within a larger, non-reductio argument scheme (a "real" *muʿāraḍa bi'l-nuṭq*).

springs his *elenchus* via a *qalb*-like move, in the form of a rhetorical question to which R is not expected to have a reply: "So how is it you eclipsed the brother by the grandfather, while the brother—when the father dies [as in the *mas'alat al-qalb*]—outranks the grandfather in terms of greater inheritance?" Al-Shāfiʿī now confirms that this move resembles *qalb*, by declaring the "reversal": "If you must eclipse one by the other,[206] you should eclipse the grandfather by the brother!"[207]

I would pause again to acknowledge two significant points. First of all, §§651 ff. is testimony to the use of something resembling *qalb*-reversal in juridical dialectic some two hundred years and more before our earliest extant *jadal*-theory treatises. As we have seen, al-Baṣrī dedicates both a regular overview and a separate subsection to the move, treating some of its peculiarities and the *ikhtilāf* regarding it;[208] while al-Shīrāzī, al-Bājī, Ibn ʿAqīl, et al., treat *qalb* as a staple of *qiyās*-oriented *iʿtirāḍāt*.[209] Second—and before placing al-Shāfiʿī's species of *qalb* in the *jadal*-theory hierarchies—we must remind ourselves that al-Shāfiʿī is engaged in—or has mostly been engaged in—a *hypothetical* enterprise. Simply put, he denies that *qiyās* obtains for either of the opposing doctrines, and however he dismantles his opponent's arguments—via *naqḍ*, *qalb*, *muʿāraḍa*, etc.—he is doing so 'for the sake of argument' only.

This is important to recognize, for *naqḍ*, *qalb*, *muʿāraḍa* and other *qiyās*-oriented objections entail the existence of, or potential for, a counter-*qiyās*—but al-Shāfiʿī has stalwartly refused to entertain the notion. We are witness to something which is at once in close conformity with the early *jadal*-theory literature, and at once unique to al-Shāfiʿī. This is a style of argumentation he employs time and again—a powerful genre of *reductio* arguments which invariably open with: "I deny that what you say can be the case, but let us, for the sake of argument, assume that it could be the case; X, Y, and Z would result, none of which you yourself accept, and thus do you contradict yourself / prove yourself inconsistent / etc." It is for this reason—due to the "unreal" mode of al-Shāfiʿī's argument style—that I must refer to his objections as "hypothetical." For *qalb* there has to be a real efficiency-proven *ʿilla* for Q to 'reverse'; but al-Shāfiʿī neither recognizes any *ʿilla* on the part of his opponent, nor introduces one of his own—he simply shows that his opponent's solution for the *mas'alat al-qalb* should bring him to rule the reverse of what he rules in the *mas'ala* at hand. This is *qalb* in general, but not in particulars—a consequence of al-Shāfiʿī's "hypothetical" argument style. It is important we bear this in mind while attempting to identify al-Shāfiʿī's *qalb*-like move in the *jadal* works, and it is important for what comes next in terms of his "hypothetical" *muʿāraḍa*.

As we have seen, al-Shīrāzī's first type of *qalb* (Shīr.VII.14.1) is called "Reversal by way of an intended ruling (*Qalb bi-Ḥukm Maqṣūd*)." This is a fair description of

[206] I.e., if *qiyās* actually obtained here, which it does not...

[207] Being the 'reverse' of the Abū Ḥanīfa/Abū Bakr *āthār*-traditions—hence '*qalb*'.

[208] *Kitāb al-Qiyās al-Sharʿī*, al-Mays ed., pp. 1040 f., 1048 ff.; Hallaq, "Treatise," pp. 217 f., 224 ff.

[209] al-Shīrāzī, *Maʿūna*, Turkī ed., pp. 259–61 [missing from al-ʿUmayrīnī ed.]; Ibn ʿAqīl, *K. al-Jadal*, pp. 62–3 §§295–301; al-Bājī, *Minhāj*, Turkī ed., pp. 174 ff., §385 ff.; al-Juwaynī, *Kāfiya*, pp. 217 ff.

al-Shāfiʿī's argument, and al-Shīrāzī's example *mas'ala* parallels it; for the focus is upon R's "aimed-at *ḥukm*" which—without changing a single component of his reasoning—can be shown to be the 'reverse' of what he should have concluded. R says: Due to components A-C, I rule that X is the case; Q objects: Due to components A-C, you *should* rule that X is *not* the case. The "aimed-at *ḥukm*" is reversed, hence: *qalb bi-ḥukm maqṣūd.*

Al-Bājī's typology, on the other hand, derives from a different ordering principle. Thus, the closest match to al-Shāfiʿī's "hypothetical" *qalb* might be "Reversal of one/some of the properties of the occasioning factor (*qalb bi-baʿḍ awṣāf al-ʿilla*)" (Bāj.IX.B.9.1.2). We remain unaware, of course, as to the complete *ʿilla* for the *mas'ala* at hand, but al-Shāfiʿī has shown us quite clearly that a part of it—the shared property of proximate-kinship (*qarāba*) through the father—ought to be efficient in occasioning the reverse of his opponent's ruling regarding the grandfather. Hence: *qalb* as regards "one of the properties (*awṣāf*)." Importantly, al-Bājī adds a note to this species of *qalb*, saying: "Indeed, it is of the category of counter-indication (*bāb al-muʿāraḍa*) according to what our *shaykh* Abū Isḥāq [al-Shīrāzī] stated, because there belongs to [R] the right to say: 'I only made the *ʿilla* the collectivity of the properties (*awṣāf*), so when you reversed some/one of them, you did not invalidate the *ʿilla*—rather, you have only obliged another.'"[210] Remarkably, although al-Shāfiʿī's opponent (returning again to the role of Q in §661) does not follow this formula directly, his next dialectical question shows precisely the same understanding of al-Shāfiʿī's *qalb*-like move as entailing a kind of *muʿāraḍa*: "but how," he asks, "*is* the *qiyās* regarding this?"

Al-Shāfiʿī's opponent has perceived the *qalb*-like move just as al-Shīrāzī—according to al-Bājī—said he ought to perceive it. We may thus read his question in §661 in the spirit of an *iʿtirāḍ*-oriented objection—something akin to a "question about the mode of counter-indication" (*su'āl ʿan wajh al-muʿāraḍa*), or a species of *muṭālaba*. The gist of his question is: "You have knocked down my *qiyās*, but you have never replaced it with something better—so how *should* the *qiyās* be for this *mas'ala*?" In essence, he is demanding that al-Shāfiʿī produce a counter-*qiyās*; and, as we shall see, al-Shāfiʿī at once obliges him and denies him full satisfaction—simply by sticking to his "unreal" style of argument. In other words, al-Shāfiʿī responds with a "hypothetical" counter-*qiyās* opposing the opponent's position; and what follows constitutes an "unreal" *muʿāraḍa* of *qiyās* by way of a "hypothetical" counter-*qiyās*.

In §§662 ff., al-Shāfiʿī develops this unique argument in three parts. He begins by reassuring us that he still finds true *qiyās* untenable, though he now formulates this message differently. He says: "No *maʿnā*-quality for *qiyās* is permitted, together, in either one." In other words, when brother and grandfather are brought together as contenders for a portion of inheritance, no *maʿnā*-quality can be extracted from the *mas'ala* and announced as efficient. I have noted this before: R's attempted *qiyās* was not the sort for which an *ʿilla* was known, and al-Shāfiʿī made short work

[210] al-Bājī, *Minhāj*, Turkī ed., pp. 175–6, §387.

of R's *qiyās al-dalāla*. If we were to attempt to identify this first objection on the part of al-Shāfiʿī, we might call it a form of "denial" (*mumānaʿa*) by which the *farʿ* is prevented from being a *farʿ* due to some set of considerations—among them, in this case, the impossibility of extracting a *maʿnā*-quality from the brother-grandfather *mas'ala*. That being said, al-Shāfiʿī makes the jump into "unreal" mode—saying: "*But if* there was a *maʿnā*-quality for [*qiyās*]..."—and thus initiating the anticipated "hypothetical" *muʿāraḍa qiyās* (which "hypothetically" supplants his opponent's *qiyās*, already discredited via a "hypothetical" *qalb*). The hypothetical *muʿāraḍa qiyās* is first stated in terms of its *ḥukm*-solution: "if there was a *maʿnā*-quality for [*qiyās*], then we ought always to have made five sixths for the brother—when he [alone survives] with the grandfather—and the [remaining] sixth for the grandfather." In other words, the result of this *muʿāraḍa qiyās* confirms the hypothetical *qalb* conclusion: the brother is still foremost (*awlā*), in terms of inheritance, over the grandfather.

But it is one thing to state the conclusion of one's hypothetical *muʿāraḍa qiyās*, and another to demonstrate the validity of one's *qiyās*-reasoning which achieved that result. Accordingly, al-Shāfiʿī immediately sets about demonstrating his *muʿāraḍa qiyās*—and, moreover, he does it in a properly dialectical fashion: by securing the premises requisite to his *muʿāraḍa* from the opponent himself. Al-Shāfiʿī accomplishes this through a two-part *a-ra'ayta* question, starting in §663, whose sole purpose is to introduce the *endoxa adilla*-indicants requisite to his hypothetical *muʿāraḍa*, and to which his opponent (once again R) cannot help but concede. First, the *a-ra'ayta* pushes R to concede the fact that brothers are confirmed an inheritance share (*farḍ*) in the Qur'ān; and R concedes with a simple "Yes" in §664. In §665, still governed by the *a-ra'ayta* of §663, R is pushed to concede another premise: that there does *not* belong to the grandfather an inheritance share in the Qur'ān. As he must, R concedes in §666 with a simple "No."[211]

With two questions, governed by the same *a-ra'ayta* formula, al-Shāfiʿī has secured from R the premises requisite to his hypothetical *muʿāraḍa*. Before proceeding to *elenchus*, however, he must make sure to have closed all doors to objection. Thus—and with firm assertion—he states that the same (confirmation of brother's *farḍ*-share; no confirmation for the grandfather's) is true of the Sunna—except for a single Sunnaic *dalīl*-indicant to which al-Shāfiʿī objects before it may even be raised as counter-*naql*.[212] His objection to the sole possible exception is stated in a patently transmission-oriented *iʿtirāḍ*: the Sunnaic *dalīl*-indicant in question is "a singular mode [of transmission] (*min wajhin wāḥidin*) which the Ahl al-Ḥadīth do not grant full confirmation (*lā yuthbituhu... kulla tathbīt*)." Finally, with all doors closed, al-Shāfiʿī announces his *elenchus* by way of a critique which at

[211] Al-Shāfiʿī's *a-ra'ayta* in §663: dialogical, as a *reductio* sub-strategy drawing attention to an *endoxon dalīl* (from Qur'ān) for a "hypothetical" *muʿāraḍa-qiyās*, which is itself a *reductio* sub-strategy within a larger, non-reductio argument scheme (a "real" *muʿāraḍa bi'l-nuṭq*).

[212] Note this again demonstrates the spirit of "good" dialectic; al-Shāfiʿī leaves no opposing stone unturned, even when his opponent has not mentioned it himself.

once asserts the superiority of his hypothetical *muʿāraḍa qiyās* and disparages his opponent's perpetual error: "And I don't know you to have done ought but discard the stronger of every mode for the weaker!" Implied here is that the conclusion of al-Shāfiʿī's *muʿāraḍa-qiyās* (brother is *awlā* in inheritance) is built upon—extended from—the epistemically stronger indicants of Qur'ān and Sunna. At the same time, he implies the conclusion of R's *qiyās* (grandfather is *awlā*) ignores these stronger indicants, and he chides his opponent for clinging to weaker stuff.

I must again reiterate this is a "hypothetical" *muʿāraḍa*—al-Shāfiʿī does not believe that *qiyās* obtains in this *mas'ala*. We may still, however, identify his "hypothetical" *muʿāraḍa qiyās*: it is a Type I *qiyās al-dalāla* whereby known rulings provide indicant for the brother being foremost in inheritance as regards the *mas'ala* at hand. To review: (1) al-Shāfiʿī—all the while in "unreal, for the sake of argument" mode—first reversed his opponent's *qiyās* via an *iʿtirāḍ* resembling *qalb*; which in turn (2) implied a kind of *muʿāraḍa*; which (3) Q induced al-Shāfiʿī to demonstrate; which (4) al-Shāfiʿī then did, in the form of a counter-*qiyās al-dalāla* from *endoxa* rulings of Qur'ān and Sunna. This final stage we may easily identify in the *jadal*-system treatises: it is "invalidating distinction by way of correlational inference of indication" (*al-farq bi-qiyās al-dalāla*) (Shīr.VII.15.2.2.2.1; Bāj.IX.B.15.2.2.2.1), and conforms perfectly with al-Shīrāzī's definition: "That [Q] make distinction by way of one of the rulings of the branch-case (*ḥukm min aḥkām al-farʿ*)."[213] Al-Bājī's definition for the relevant subspecies of "Invalidating Distinction by way of Indication of the Ruling (*farq bi-dalālat al-ḥukm*)" is also quite descriptive of al-Shāfiʿī's "hypothetical" *muʿāraḍa*: "[Q] makes distinction between the *farʿ* and the *aṣl* by way of a *ḥukm* peculiar to the *farʿ*, without leaving [the example of the *farʿ*]"

Before concluding this analysis, I would repeat that this hypothetical *muʿāraḍa qiyās* does not represent al-Shāfiʿī's solution to the *mas'ala* at hand. We have already seen what that is: strict adherence (*taqlīd*) to the *āthār*-traditions whereby grandfather and brother are guaranteed equal shares—half and half. All of these hypothetical arguments were meant only to show that his opponent's *qiyās* would be wrong, even if *qiyās* obtained for this *mas'ala*. This is a powerful argument style in the hands of al-Shāfiʿī, and he appears—at least in our subject-text—the unique master of it. Certainly, we do not find any Q putting al-Shāfiʿī through the same motions of "suppose what you say is true...;" and I have yet to discover in the *jadal*-theory texts discussions of this sort of extended "unreal" *iʿtirāḍāt*. I would be remiss, however, if I did not note a broad similarity with the Aristotelian arguments *per/ad impossibile* and the "procedure of hypothetical proof."[214]

---

[213] al-Shīrāzī, *Maʿūna*, al-ʿUmayrīnī ed., pp. 116–17; al-Bājī, *Minhāj*, Turkī ed., pp. 203–4, §461–2.

[214] See the relevant discussions in Sect. 4.7, above (under "Reduction *ad impossibile* [εἰς τὸ ἀδύνατον]" etc.), and note especially that "proof *per impossibile*" was rendered into Arabic as "the *qiyās* [meaning syllogism] which comes by way of bringing the [contradictory] argument to an impossibility" (*al-qiyās alladhī yakūnu bi-rafʿ al-kalām ilā al-muḥāl*).

Masā'il-Set #5

§§686–704 from the *Chapter on Inheritances* (*Bāb al-Mawārīth*)[215]

686 – And when a man dies, leaving his wife behind, and leaving behind [movable] goods in his house; then indeed Abū Ḥanīfa, may God be pleased with him, used to transmit on the authority of Ḥammād, on Ibrāhīm, who said: What is for men of the goods belongs to the husband; and what is for women belongs to the wife; and what is for [both] men and women belongs to whichever of the two remains, be it wife or husband.	686 - وَإِذَا تُوُفِّيَ الرَّجُلُ وَتَرَكَ امْرَأَتَهُ وَتَرَكَ فِي بَيْتِهِ مَتَاعًا، فَإِنَّ أَبَا حَنِيفَةَ رضي الله عنه كَانَ يُحَدِّثُ عَن حَمَّادٍ، عَن إِبْرَاهِيمَ أَنَّهُ قَالَ: مَا كَانَ لِلرِّجَالِ مِن الْمَتَاعِ فَهُوَ لِلرَّجُلِ، وَمَا كَانَ لِلنِّسَاءِ فَهُوَ لِلْمَرْأَةِ، وَمَا كَانَ لِلرِّجَالِ وَالنِّسَاءِ فَهُوَ لِلْبَاقِي مِنْهُمَا الْمَرْأَةُ كَانَتْ أَوْ الرَّجُلُ.
687 – And likewise [with regard to] the husband, when he unilaterally divorces [his wife], and the one remaining [in the house] after the divorce is the husband. And Abū Ḥanīfa and Abū Yūsuf used to embrace [this doctrine].[216]	687 - وَكَذَلِكَ الزَّوْجُ إِذَا طَلَّقَ؛ وَالْبَاقِي الزَّوْجُ فِي الطَّلاَقِ، وَبِهِ كَانَ يَأْخُذُ أَبُو حَنِيفَةَ وَأَبُو يُوسُفَ.
688 – Then, after that, he [Abū Yūsuf] said: There belongs to the woman, with regard to all of that, only what her like would be provided with [as trousseau]; because he might be a merchant—having women's goods from his mercantile dealings—or an artisan; or there [might] be pledged-articles in the keeping of a man.	688 - ثُمَّ قَالَ بَعْدَ ذَلِكَ: لاَ يَكُونُ لِلْمَرْأَةِ إلاَّ مَا يُجَهَّزُ بِهِ مِثْلُهَا فِي ذَلِكَ كُلِّهِ؛ لأَنَّهُ يَكُونُ رَجُلٌ تَاجِرٌ عِنْدَهُ مَتَاعُ النِّسَاءِ مِن تِجَارَتِهِ أَوْ صَانِعٌ أَوْ تَكُونُ رُهُونًا عِنْدَ رَجُلٍ.
689 – But Ibn Abī Laylā used to say: When the man dies or unilaterally divorces; the goods of the house, all of them, are the goods of the man—except for blouse and veil and the like—unless, for one of the two [disputants], *bayyina*-evidence is furnished in support of the claim.	689 - وَكَانَ ابْنُ أَبِي لَيْلَى يَقُولُ: إِذَا مَاتَ الرَّجُلُ أَوْ طَلَّقَ فَمَتَاعُ الْبَيْتِ كُلُّهُ مَتَاعُ الرَّجُلِ إلاَّ الدِّرْعَ وَالْخِمَارَ وَشِبْهَهُ، إلاَّ أَنْ تَقُومَ لأَحَدِهِمَا بَيِّنَةٌ عَلَى دَعْوَاهُ.
690 – And if he unilaterally divorces her in *her* house, their situation is just as I have described it for both their doctrines [i.e., Abū Ḥanīfa's and Ibn Abī Laylā's], together.	690 - وَلَوْ طَلَّقَهَا فِي دَارِهَا كَانَ أَمْرُهُمَا عَلَى مَا وَصَفْتُ فِي قَوْلِهِمَا جَمِيعًا.

(continued)

[215] Ḥassūn ed., vol. 9, pp. 123–6; ʿAbd al-Muṭṭalib ed., vol. 8, pp. 301–3.

[216] The context for both cases is one in which ownership is disputed. For the one whose spouse dies, ownership might be disputed by a third party linked to the deceased (heirs, pledgor-debtors, etc.); while the divorcée might dispute ownership with her former husband. For further details and rulings, see *MF*, s.v. "متاع" (vol. 36, pp. 63–4; esp. §3).

691 – Al-Shāfiʿī said: And when two spouses dispute the goods of the house in which they both dwell, before they are separated, or after they are separated, whether the house belongs to the woman or to the man; or after they both die, and the heirs of each dispute [the goods] after their death; or the heirs of the deceased [dispute] with the one who remains, be it husband or wife—that, all of it, is onc and the same. For whosoever furnishes *bayyina*-evidence for anything of such [goods]; it belongs to him. And whosoever does not furnish *bayyina*-evidence: the *qiyās*, based upon authoritative consensus—and no one, in my opinion, can ever be excused for neglecting it—is that these goods are in the possession of *both*, together, and are [divided] between them in two halves—just like two men disputing the goods in their collective possession, so that they are [divided] between them in two halves after the oaths [are taken].	691 - قَالَ الشَّافِعِيُّ: وَإِذَا اخْتَلَفَ الزَّوْجَانِ فِي مَتَاعِ الْبَيْتِ يَسْكُنَانِهِ قَبْلَ أَنْ يَتَفَرَّقَا أَوْ بَعْدَ مَا تَفَرَّقَا، كَانَ الْبَيْتُ لِلْمَرْأَةِ أَوْ الرَّجُلِ، أَوْ بَعْدَمَا يَمُوتَانِ وَاخْتَلَفَتْ فِي ذَلِكَ وَرَثَتُهُمَا بَعْدَ مَوْتِهِمَا أَوْ وَرَثَةُ الْمَيِّتِ مِنْهُمَا وَالْبَاقِي، كَانَ الْبَاقِي الزَّوْجَ أَوْ الزَّوْجَةَ فَسَوَاءٌ ذَلِكَ كُلُّهُ. فَمَنْ أَقَامَ الْبَيِّنَةَ عَلَى شَيْءٍ مِن ذَلِكَ فَهُوَ لَهُ، وَمَنْ لَمْ يُقِمْ بَيِّنَةً فَالْقِيَاسُ الَّذِي لاَ يُعْذَرُ أَحَدٌ عِنْدِي بِالْغَفْلَةِ عَنْهُ عَلَى الإِجْمَاعِ أَنَّ هَذَا الْمَتَاعَ فِي أَيْدِيهِمَا مَعًا فَهُوَ بَيْنَهُمَا نِصْفَانِ، كَمَا يَخْتَلِفُ الرَّجُلاَنِ فِي الْمَتَاعِ بِأَيْدِيهِمَا جَمِيعًا فَيَكُونُ بَيْنَهُمَا نِصْفَيْنِ بَعْدَ الأَيمَانِ.
692 – And if one should say: How can there belong to a man *naḍūḥ*-perfume, and saffron-perfume, and blouses, and veils; and [how can] there belong to a woman a sword, and a spear, and a coat of mail?	692 - فَإِنْ قَالَ قَائِلٌ: فَكَيْفَ يَكُونُ لِلرَّجُلِ النَّضُوحُ وَالْخَلُوقُ وَالدُّرُوعُ وَالْخُمُرُ، وَيَكُونُ لِلْمَرْأَةِ السَّيْفُ وَالرُّمْحُ وَالدِّرْعُ؟
693 – It is said: Men might own the goods of women, and women the goods of men.	693 – قِيلَ: قَدْ يَمْلِكُ الرِّجَالُ مَتَاعَ النِّسَاءِ وَالنِّسَاءُ مَتَاعَ الرِّجَالِ.
694 – Have you considered [what would happen] if a man furnishes *bayyina*-evidence for the goods of women, and a woman *bayyina*-evidence for the goods of men—would not each be judged favourably for what they furnished *bayyina*-evidence?	694 - أَرَأَيْتَ لَوْ أَقَامَ الرَّجُلُ الْبَيِّنَةَ عَلَى مَتَاعِ النِّسَاءِ، وَالْمَرْأَةُ الْبَيِّنَةَ عَلَى مَتَاعِ الرِّجَالِ، أَلَيْسَ يُقْضَى لِكُلٍّ بِمَا أَقَامَ عَلَيْهِ الْبَيِّنَةَ؟
695 – And when he says: Of course!	695 - فَإِذَا قَالَ: بَلَى.
696 – It is said: And have you not claimed—and the people claimed—that the existence of a thing in the possession of two contenders confirms half for each of them?[217]	696 – قِيلَ: أَفَلَيْسَ قَدْ زَعَمْتَ وَزَعَمَ النَّاسُ أَنَّ كَيْنُونَةَ الشَّيْءِ فِي يَدَيِ الْمُتَنَازِعَيْنِ تُثْبِتُ لِكُلٍّ النِّصْفَ؟
697 – And if he says: Of course!	697 - فَإِنْ قَالَ: بَلَى.
698 – It is said: Just as the *bayyina*-evidence confirms it for him?	698 – قِيلَ: كَمَا تَثْبُتُ لَهُ الْبَيِّنَةُ.
699 – And if he says: Of course!	699 - فَإِنْ قَالَ: بَلَى.

(continued)

[217] Again, "the people" (*al-nās*) may be understood as a reference to Iraqi jurists (see note for §252, above)—or, perhaps, as a general, Muslim-communal consensus (cf. the "majority doctrine" [*madhhab al-ʿāmma*] in §703, below).

700 – It is said: Then why don't you treat the two spouses like that, while it is in the possession of both? And if you make assumptions about them [all] and abandon what is manifest, it is said to you: Then what do you say as regards a perfume-maker and a tanner in whose [joint-] possession there is perfume and tanners' utensils, which they both, together, claim against each other?	700 – قِيلَ: فَلِمَ لَمْ تَجْعَلِ الزَّوْجَيْنِ هَكَذَا وَهِيَ فِي أَيْدِيهِمَا؟ فَإِنِ اسْتَعْمَلْتَ عَلَيْهِمْ الظُّنُونَ [وَتَرَكْتَ الظَّاهِرَ قِيلَ لَكَ]:[218] فَمَا تَقُولُ فِي عَطَّارٍ وَدَبَّاغٍ فِي أَيْدِيهِمَا عِطْرٌ وَمَتَاعُ الدَّبَّاغِ تَدَاعَيَاهُ مَعًا.
701 – And if you claim that you give the tanner the tanners' utensils, and the perfume-maker the perfume-makers' utensils…	701 - فَإِنْ زَعَمْتَ أَنَّكَ تُعْطِي الدَّبَّاغَ مَتَاعَ الدَّبَّاغِينَ وَالْعَطَّارَ مَتَاعَ الْعَطَّارِينَ.
702 – It is said: Then what do you say as regards an insolvent man and a solvent man, who each claim against the other a ruby and a pearl?	702 – قِيلَ: فَمَا تَقُولُ فِي رَجُلٍ غَيْرِ مُوسِرٍ وَرَجُلٍ مُوسِرٍ تَدَاعَيَا يَاقُوتًا وَلُؤْلُؤًا؟
703 – For if you claim that you make it belong to the solvent man, while it is in the possession of both, together, you contradict the majority doctrine.	703 - فَإِنْ زَعَمْتَ أَنَّكَ تَجْعَلُهُ لِلْمُوسِرِ وَهُوَ بِأَيْدِيهِمَا مَعًا خَالَفْتَ مَذْهَبَ الْعَامَّةِ.
704 – But if you claim that you divide it between them, and don't make assumptions about them; then you should say [the same] regarding the goods of husband and wife.	704 - وَإِنْ زَعَمْتَ أَنَّكَ تَقْسِمُهُ بَيْنَهُمَا وَلاَ تَسْتَعْمِلُ عَلَيْهِمَا الظَّنَّ، فَهَكَذَا يَنْبَغِي لَك أَنْ تَقُولَ فِي مَتَاعِ الرَّجُلِ وَالْمَرْأَةِ.

This *mas'ala*-set exhibits a number of unique features, although it is typical enough in terms of presentation categories: §§686–7 (Abū Ḥanīfa, category F); §688 (Abū Yūsuf, category F); §689 (Ibn Abī Laylā, category G); §690 (Abū Ḥanīfa & Ibn Abī Laylā, category G); §§691 (al-Shāfiʿī, category D); §§692–704 (al-Shāfiʿī vs. anonymous opponent, category A). The *masāʾil* consider, for the most part, the question of how to distinguish household commodities (*matāʿ*) as belonging to husband or wife, when they must be divided for purposes of inheritance or divorce. Abū Ḥanīfa's stance is noteworthy; rather than present his own ruling for *mas'ala* #1—in §686, wherein the husband is survived by the wife—he simply transmits an *athar*-tradition of the famed Successor-jurist Ibrāhīm al-Nakhaʿī.[219] This latter ruled that goods of men belong to the husband; of women, to the wife; and of both, to whichever one is the survivor. Abū Ḥanīfa's position appears the most direct form of *taqlīd*; and it carries over into §687, where al-Nakhaʿī's doctrine is extended to *mas'ala* #2 (the husband unilaterally divorces the wife, and remains in the house). The adherence of both Abū Ḥanīfa and Abū Yūsuf to this two-*mas'ala* ruling is clearly stated at the end of §687; we are granted no insight as to further

---

[218] What appears between brackets differs in almost every edition consulted. I have preferred the Būlāq edition (*Umm*, vol. 7, p. 121): [وتركت الظاهر قيل لك ...], of which I can make better sense. Ḥassūn (*Umm*, vol. 9, p. 125) renders: [وتركت الظاهر؟ قيل ذلك]; while Maṭrajī has [وتركت الظاهر قيل ذلك، ...]; and ʿAbd al-Muṭṭalib (*Umm*, vol. 8, pp. 302–3) has [وتركت الظاهر قبل ذلك، ...]. Not one of the editions makes a note of their different renderings, nor of diverging manuscript witnesses.

[219] Matters of *taqlīd* or *istidlāl* from a Successor-jurist do not seem to be discussed in our lens-texts; I would mark this as a unique feature—and a frequent one, as we shall see—of proto-system juridical *jadal*. Bear in mind also that Ibrāhīm al-Nakhaʿī was famed as a proponent of "considered opinion" (*ra'y*), so long as it was twinned with reliable narrations (*riwāyāt*); see, among other sources, Lecomte's short article on al-Nakhaʿī in the *EI*², and Sezgin's references culled from Abū Naʿīm's *Ḥilyat al-Awliyāʾ* (*Tārīkh al-Turāth al-ʿArabī*, vol. 1, pt. 3, pp. 18 f.).

reasoning behind this position, although it is obvious a gender-based assumption for disputed possessions has efficiency in occasioning al-Nakhaʿī's rulings.[220]

Significantly, and by no means of rare occurrence, we next learn (in §688) that Abū Yūsuf recanted from this doctrine and proposed a different ruling for *masāʾil* ##1–2: the wife receives "only what her like would be provided with [as trousseau] (*mā yujahhazu bihi mithluhā*)."[221] He supports this with *ʿaql*—initiated with "because"—problematizing gender-based assumptions of ownership by appealing to three properties potentially born by the husband. These we might understand as efficient in occasioning his ownership: (1) if he is a merchant of feminine goods; (2) if he is an artisan [making feminine goods]; and (3) if there are [feminine] pledged-objects (*ruhūn*) in his keeping.

We may read these, collectively, as an objection to the doctrine of Ibrāhīm al-Nakhaʿī; in fact, they constitute three separate *masāʾil* for objections of "inconsistency" (*naqḍ*) or "breaking apart" (*kasr*)—each situation comprising a case wherein the property (*waṣf*) of "feminine goods" (*matāʿ al-nisāʾ*) is cancelled by another *waṣf*-property. We might say the efficiency of the 'object-property' of "the goods are feminine" is negated by the efficiency of the 'party-property' of "merchant of feminine goods" or "he is an artisan making feminine goods" as well as by the efficiency of the 'object-property' of "they are [feminine] pledged-objects (*ruhūn*) in his keeping." In this manner, mere reliance upon gender-relevancy is proven untrustworthy for occasioning a *ḥukm*, and we may classify Abū Yūsuf's new ruling as embodying—in broadest terms—a three-fold *iʿtirāḍ* of *naqḍ* or *kasr* (Shīr.VII.7 or VII.8; Bāj.IX.B.11.1 or Bāj.IX.B.12.2.1).[222]

In §689 we learn Ibn Abī Laylā's ruling for *masāʾil* ##1–2—all household goods belong to the husband, except for the obviously feminine (blouse, veil, etc.)—although, notably, neither *ʿaql* nor *naql* support is provided. Ibn Abī Laylā is careful to assert a proviso, however, whereby *bayyina*-evidence brought by the contender for ownership would override these general husband-favouring and gender-relevant assumptions. We may thus read his ruling as a more refined approach admitting the usual strength of claims backed by *bayyina*-evidence, as well as an implied *iʿtirāḍ* to both the rulings of Abū Ḥanīfa and Abū Yūsuf. We are impeded by

---

[220] Al-Afghānī (*Ikhtilāf Abī Ḥanīfa wa Ibn Abī Laylā*, p. 87, n. 1) cites al-Sarakhsī (*Mabsūṭ*, vol. 5, p. 213), who lists a host of opinions on *masāʾil* ##1–3 from prominent early jurists. Here, Abū Ḥanīfa's reasoning is portrayed as based upon conceptions of use (*istiʿmāl*) and the husband's "possession" of the wife. When the object comes under dispute, he ruled on the benefit of assumption, saying: "The [considered] claim is that of the user (*mustaʿmil*), for possession (*yad*) of the user in this case is stronger in terms of what is appropriate (*ṣāliḥ*) to one of the two; and as for what is appropriate for them both: the side of the husband is given preponderance in cases of *ṭalāq*-divorce, because he is the owner of the house, and she had been among the chattels (*matāʿ*) in his possession," etc.

[221] Again, we are provided indication of Abū Yūsuf's "following the *ḥujja*"—i.e., practicing the "good dialectic," not polemically defending a doctrine out of loyalty to region or teacher.

[222] al-Shīrāzī, *Maʿūna*, al-ʿUmayrīnī ed., pp. 104 ff. and 107 f.; al-Bājī, *Minhāj*, Turkī ed., p. 185, §413 and pp. 192 f., §436. Cf. Ibn ʿAqīl, *K. al-Jadal*, pp. 56 ff., §§276 ff. and pp. 65 f., §§305 ff. Bāj.IX.B.12.2.1 seems especially apt: "[Q] eliminates a property which is not efficient (*ghayr muʾaththir*) in occasioning the *ḥukm* which was made contingent upon the *ʿilla* [by R]."

not knowing the precise manner of Ibn Abī Laylā's *istidlāl*, but may see that the ruling itself implies an hierarchy of efficient properties: (1) "the claim of party X is backed by *bayyina*-evidence" (occasioning a *ḥukm* in favour of party X); followed by (2) "he is the owner of the dwelling" (occasioning a *ḥukm* in favour of the husband); and (3) "they are feminine goods" (occasioning a *ḥukm* in favour of the wife).

Though we are hindered from a specific identification, it is evident these properties, ordered in terms of efficiency, were seen by Ibn Abī Laylā to cancel those of opposing rulings. Note that al-Sarakhsī has neglected to mention the *bayyina*-evidence proviso in rendering Ibn Abī Laylā's ruling. He does, however, provide the argument for those who opine that all household goods belong to the husband—even if he resides in the wife's house (which appears to be Ibn Abī Laylā's position in §690): "because the wife is in the possession (*yad*) of the husband, and that which is in her house is also in the possession of the husband—don't you see/opine (*a-lā tarā*) that he is the owner (*ṣāḥib*) of the house, and the dwelling-place (*al-manzil*) is attributed to him (*yuḍāf ilayhi*)...?"[223] Note the persistence of the staple dialectical formula *a-lā tarā*—either as employed by al-Sarakhsī himself, or as forwarded from "historical" disputation, or both.[224] A final note: in §690 either Abū Yūsuf or al-Shaybānī reports the extension of the Abū Ḥanīfa and Ibn Abī Laylā rulings to *mas'ala* #3—wherein the husband divorces his wife in *her* house—i.e., she is the one remaining (*bāqī*). It is due to this I believe Ibn Abī Laylā maintained, as implicit to the second in his hierarchy of efficient properties, the "wife and her possessions are in the possession of the husband" argument, as related by al-Sarakhsī.

In §691 al-Shāfiʿī's refined approach to dealing with ongoing *masā'il* of this sort is once again displayed; and his ruling and arguments unfold in stages. First, he reformulates *masā'il* ##1–3 into a finer subset, detailing them one by one, as follows:

- when the spouses disagree regarding the goods of their shared house
  - before separation
  - after separation
  - when the house belongs to the husband
  - when the house belongs to the wife
- when both spouses die, and the heirs disagree as to who owned which of the goods
- when the husband/wife survives his/her spouse, and the heirs disagree with him/her regarding ownership of the goods

[223] Al-Afghānī (p. 87, n. 1), citing *Mabsūṭ*, vol. 5, p. 213.

[224] The *a-lā tarā* formula occurs, astonishingly, well over two thousand times in al-Sarakhsī's *Mabsūṭ*; it appears mostly employed by al-Sarakhsī himself, but at other times in arguments related from others. *A-ra'ayta*, though far less frequent, still enjoys some 150 occurrences.

Having thus detailed all variants of *masāʾil* within the broader area of *ikhtilāf*, al-Shāfiʿī declares: "that, all of it, is one and the same (*fa-sawāʾun dhālika kulluhu*)." I would pause here to note a hallmark method of proto-system legal argumentation: contended problem cases, ruled upon separately by other jurists, are often—via the affirmation of shared efficient properties, and the denial of efficiency for unshared properties—made to receive a singular set of rulings. This is similar to what I have termed "*manzila*-subsumption;" and, accordingly, I will label this species of argument "*taswiya*-subsumption." Just as *manzila*-subsumption is most often expressed with the formula "X is in the *manzila* of Y" and variants, *taswiya*-subsumption is most often expressed with the formula "*sawāʾun* X and Y [and Z, etc.]" and variants. In other words, whenever we find an expression employing *sawāʾun* and attributing a singular set of rulings to agents, objects, or acts which have received variant rulings elsewhere, we observe *taswiya*-subsumption at work. Note that the various "*taswiya*" formulae enjoy great currency in the subject text alone—with some 26 occurrences—not to mention in the *Umm* compendium as a whole—with some 700 additional occurrences. Like *manzila*-subsumption, *taswiya*-subsumption was evidently a common feature in the landscape of proto-system legal argumentation.

Returning to the current *masʾala*-set we learn that al-Shāfiʿī asserts a pair of rulings for these *masāʾil* tied through *taswiya*-subsumption: (1) if the contender brings *bayyina*-evidence for a thing, it belongs to him/her; (2) if neither has *bayyina*-evidence, the goods are considered to be in joint possession, and are divided between them half and half. Al-Shāfiʿī states his *istidlāl* for the latter ruling in no uncertain terms; in fact, it is as strong an assertion of *qiyās* as can be found in the subject-text. First, he says "no one, in my opinion, can ever be excused for neglecting it;" second, he confirms that its *aṣl* is sanctioned by *ijmāʿ*; and third, he provides for us that *aṣl*. This latter is introduced by the marker "just like (*kamā*)," and from its presentation we discern the following components: (1) the *aṣl* itself, being "two men disputing the goods in their collective possession"; and (2) the *ḥukm* of that *aṣl*: "[the goods] are [divided] between them in two halves after the oaths (*aymān*) [are taken]." The *ʿilla*, though never specifically designated, is easy to detect from the opening proviso, and might be formulated as a combination of two efficient properties: (1) relating to the parties: "neither brings *bayyina*-evidence;" and (2) relating to the object of contention: "it is [considered to be] in joint possession of the contending parties"—this latter being a consequence (if not a *ḥukm per se*) of the first. The whole constitutes a *qiyās al-ʿilla*, and may be diagramed as follows:

<u>*Aṣl*</u> two men dispute ownership of goods in their collective possession		<u>*Farʿ*</u> parties disagree as to husband's/wife's ownership of household goods
ʿIlla neither brings *bayyina*-evidence; the object is in joint possession	← SAME →	*ʿIlla* neither brings *bayyina*-evidence; the object is [considered] in joint possession
Ḥukm the goods are divided between them half and half, after the oaths are taken	SHOULD ALSO BE THE ← SAME →	*Ḥukm* [the goods (should also be) divided between them half and half, after the oaths are taken]

This is *qiyās al-ʿilla* of a sturdy construction, and bears the further *ḥujjiyya* of extension from an *aṣl* sanctioned by *ijmāʿ*.[225] Moreover, and considering its direct opposition to the doctrine of Ibrāhīm al-Nakhaʿī followed by Abū Ḥanīfa and Abū Yūsuf—and to the ruling of Ibn Abī Laylā as well—it most definitely constitutes a species of *iʿtirāḍ* against these positions. Once again, unfortunately, we are held back from a precise identification in the early *jadal*-theory works due to our lack of knowledge concerning the *istidlāl* of either al-Nakhaʿī or Ibn Abī Laylā. What is clear, however, is that al-Shāfiʿī has completely neutralized any gender-relevancy considerations, and denied the efficiency of such properties as "they are feminine/masculine goods," or "the house belongs to husband/wife." The only efficient properties for all of these cases linked by *taswiya*-subsumption, according to al-Shāfiʿī, are: (1) neither party has brought *bayyina*-evidence; and (2) the goods are jointly-possessed. These alone make up the *ʿilla*, which in turn occasions the *ḥukm* of half and half division.

Though we lack proper presentation of *istidlāl*, it is evident that certain opposing properties are being supplanted; and—considering the doctrines of al-Nakhaʿī and Ibn Abī Laylā as emanating from an inferior sort of *qiyās*—I would classify al-Shāfiʿī's *iʿtirāḍ* as either: (1) al-Baṣrī's *muʿāraḍa* of *qiyās* by way of *qiyās*;[226] or (2) the "Counter-Indication with a Self-Initiated Occasioning Factor (*al-Muʿāraḍa bi-ʿIlla Mubtada'a*)" of al-Shīrāzī and al-Bājī (Shīr.VII.15.2.1; Bāj.IX.B.15.2.1).[227] Al-Shāfiʿī's *qiyās* conforms particularly well to the pattern set by al-Bājī's example *mas'ala* (al-Shīrāzī does not present one in the *Maʿūna*). Like al-Shāfiʿī in §691, al-Bājī's Shāfiʿī Q disagrees with the Mālikī R's interpretation of what constitutes the efficient property in the *farʿ*, and instead proposes a new *ʿilla* in the *farʿ*, linking it back to a different *aṣl* with the same *ʿilla*, and thus justifying his counter-*ḥukm*.[228] The Shāfiʿī Q, like al-Shāfiʿī himself, brings a completely new *ʿilla*, counter-*aṣl*, and counter-*ḥukm*—a completely new *qiyās al-ʿilla*—and these are the hallmarks of *muʿāraḍa bi-ʿilla mubtada'a*.

Having thus set forth his own *istidlāl* for the various *masā'il*, al-Shāfiʿī initiates an "instructional" dialectical sequence. In §692, he begins immediately with a dialectical question from an anonymous Q (*fa-in qāla qā'il*), who challenges al-Shāfiʿī by asking: "How can there belong to a man [patently feminine objects A-D]; and [how can] there belong to a woman [patently masculine objects X-Z]?" It is evident from the start that al-Shāfiʿī's *qiyās* has been interpreted as cancelling the

---

[225] This *ijmāʿ*, as we shall see, is further alluded to as the claim of both the opponent and "the people (*al-nās*)" in §696, and of the "majority doctrine" (*madhhab al-ʿāmma*) in §703. These terms, linked with *ijmāʿ*, provide considerable data for al-Shāfiʿī's conception of consensus, which is sometimes disputed.

[226] *K. al-Qiyās al-Sharʿī*, Ḥamīd Allāh ed., p. 1044; Hallaq, "Treatise," p. 221.

[227] al-Shīrāzī, *Maʿūna*, Turkī ed., p. 262, §148 [missing from al-ʿUmayrīnī ed.]; al-Bājī, *Minhāj*, Turkī ed., p. 201, §455. Cf. Ibn ʿAqīl, *K. al-Jadal*, p. 71, §330.

[228] al-Bājī, op. cit.

efficiency of gender-based assumptions. Reading al-Shāfiʿī's *qiyās* as a *muʿāraḍa bi-ʿilla mubtadaʾa*, Q's question may again be construed as an objection to an objection. With the efficiency of gender-based assumptions at stake, I would label it a "demand for the mode of claiming lack of efficiency" (*muṭālaba bi-wajh iʿtirāḍ ʿadam al-taʾthīr*), or another such combination. On the other hand, in cases of *muʿāraḍa* the roles reverse; R becomes Q, with the full array of *qiyās*-oriented *iʿtirāḍāt* at his disposal. We may thus read Q's question—bearing in mind that al-Shāfiʿī is teaching his reader how to respond to a potential critique—as an original R's attempt to reassert a gender-based *ʿilla*. He might do this by leading al-Shāfiʿī (or any proponent of al-Shāfiʿī's *qiyās*) to concede premises by which he may rescue his argument; and, from this perspective, Q's question may simply constitute the first stage in an attempted charge of *naqḍ*, or *kasr*, etc.

Whatever Q's program, al-Shāfiʿī shows his audience how to nip it in the bud. In his *jawāb* in §693, he first asserts a premise which, as we will see, constitutes part of a larger strategy I would label a "*naqḍ*-dilemma." Flatly, he states: "Men might own the goods of women, and women the goods of men." Surprisingly, al-Shāfiʿī then usurps the role of Q in §694, pushing his opponent (now R) to concede to his premise with a dialectical question, as delivered through the familiar *a-raʾayta* formula. At first glance, this appears to be breaking the rules of later *jadal*-theory. However, we may consider that Q—by ostensibly reasserting his gender-based *ʿilla*, albeit in question form—has brought about his own reversion to the role of R.

Either way, al-Shāfiʿī commandeers the station of critique, and his *a-raʾayta* of §694 pushes R to concede the *endoxon* solution of a hypothetical case; he is asked: "Have you considered [what would happen] (*a-raʾayta*) if [1] a man furnishes *bayyina*-evidence for the goods of women, and [2] a woman [furnishes] *bayyina*-evidence for the goods of men—[3] would not each be judged favourably for what they furnished *bayyina*-evidence?" Thus al-Shāfiʿī pushes the first premise (*bayyina*-evidence establishes ownership over gender-assumptions) of his forthcoming charge of *naqḍ*;[229] and R—still notably in "instructional" mode, preceded by *fa-idhā qāla*—emphatically concedes in §695: "Of course (*balā*)!" Al-Shāfiʿī thus easily acquires his first *naqḍ* premise, and proceeds in §696 to a dialectical question in an even stronger formulation: "And have you not claimed—and the people claimed—that X is the case (*a-fa-laysa qad zaʿamta wa zaʿama al-nās* X)?" Note the double strength of this formulation; it points not only to *naqḍ*, with "have you not [elsewhere] claimed" (*qad zaʿamta*), but to a violation of a regional *ijmāʿ*, "[have not] 'the people' claimed" (*zaʿama al-nās* [meaning Iraqis]). As for the "X" of my rendering, it is the general ruling—asserted as doubly-*endoxon*— "that the existence (*kaynūna*) of a thing in the possession of two contenders confirms half for

[229] Al-Shāfiʿī's *a-raʾayta* in §694: dialogical, introducing a parallel *masʾalat al-naqḍ* to cancel the opponent's *ʿilla*, as a component in a larger strategy of *naqḍ*-dilemma, itself within a larger move of *muʿāraḍa*.

each of them."[230] This is al-Shāfiʿī's second *naqḍ* premise, and, as before, R emphatically concedes in §697 with: "Of course (*balā*)!"

In §698 al-Shāfiʿī now pushes for a final concession, drawing the first two conceded premises together in an effort to confirm the parity of efficiency between *bayyina*-backed claims and an object's status of being in joint-possession. R again concedes with "*balā*!" in §699, and al-Shāfiʿī acquires his third premise for *naqḍ*: joint-possession occasions half and half division between the two contending parties, just as *bayyina*-evidence occasions full ownership for the party furnishing it. All premises conceded, al-Shāfiʿī now springs his first charge of *naqḍ* in §700: "Then why don't you treat the two spouses like that, while it is in the possession of both?" This is classic *naqḍ*: R has conceded to ruling X and Y in general cases where the efficient properties of *bayyina*-backed claims (*naqḍ*-premise #1) and joint-possession (*naqḍ*-premise #2) are at work, and yet has ruled other than X and Y in the *masāʾil* at hand, wherein one or the other of those same efficient properties must be at work.[231] Al-Shāfiʿī's first *iʿtirāḍ* of *naqḍ* conforms well to the formulations of early *jadal*-theory, whereby R's conceded *ʿilla* is present (in the *masāʾil al-naqḍ*, being premises #1 and #2), but not his *ḥukm* (Shīr.VII.7; Bāj.IX.B.11.1).[232]

What is more, al-Shāfiʿī's *naqḍ*-conclusion flows naturally from the three premises he has garnered from R: (1) *bayyina*-evidence establishes ownership over gender-based considerations; (2) joint possession of a thing establishes half-ownership; and (3) joint possession is just as efficient in occasioning half-ownership as *bayyina*-evidence is in occasioning full-ownership. Thus, for the *masāʾil* at hand (linked through al-Shāfiʿī's *taswiya*-subsumption), R ought to have ruled either: (1) full-ownership with *bayyina*-evidence; or 2) half-ownership without *bayyina*-evidence. A contending party either has *bayyina*-evidence, or it does not; and if it does not, the goods are assumed to have been in joint possession. Al-Shāfiʿī might be considered to have achieved *elenchus* at this point, but he has a larger plan in mind. What follows—straight through to the end of this dialectical sequence—is a concise series of pre-emptive strikes whereby al-Shāfiʿī demonstrates how to block any potential counter-objections before R even has a chance to formulate them. R is overwhelmed by a thoroughly constructed "*naqḍ*-dilemma" in which every exit is closed, and we never again hear his voice.

---

[230] It is worth considering al-Shāfiʿī's use of the term existence (*kaynūna*), here. He employs *kaynūna* some fourteen times in the *Umm*, and almost always—as in §696—in combination with "possession" (*yad*). Thus, although *kaynūna* is cognate to the *kawn*, *kiyāna*, *kāʾin*, etc. of theological and philosophical discussions, it appears to bear, in al-Shāfiʿī's usage, a technical association with possession: as " the *kaynūna* of object X in the *yad* of party Y."

[231] As such, the "*naqḍ*-premises" ##1–2 constitute general *masāʾil al-naqḍ*, but I have chosen to present them as premises for the convenience of showing how they link together with *naqḍ*-premise #3, resulting in a thoroughly confounding conclusion of the opponent's inconsistency.

[232] al-Shīrāzī, *Maʿūna*, al-ʿUmayrīnī ed., pp. 104 ff.; al-Bājī, *Minhāj*, Turkī ed., p. 185, §§412–13. Cf. Ibn ʿAqīl, *K. al-Jadal*, pp. 56 f., §§276–7; and al-Baṣrī, *K. al-Qiyās al-Sharʿī*, Ḥamīd Allāh ed., pp. 1041 ff.; Hallaq, "Treatise," pp. 218 ff.

Still in §700, al-Shāfiʿī moves immediately to cover a potential counter-objection by setting up a third *mas'alat al-naqḍ*. He does this in case R prefers to "make assumptions about them [all] (*in istaʿmalta ʿalayhim al-ẓunūn*) and abandon what is manifest (*ẓāhir*)," and I would pause here to note the entry of a patently epistemological set of terms into the argument. *Ẓāhir* is employed here in the sense of a "sensory *status quo*": so far as anyone can tell from external indicants and contexts, the situation is X, and only *bayyina*-evidence can shift judgment in favour of one party over the other. Thus, in a sense, al-Shāfiʿī distinguishes the nature of—or, perhaps, the rationale (*ḥikma*) behind—the assumption inherent to the *ʿilla* of joint-possession: it is the "sensory *status quo*" to which any solution to the *mas'ala* must revert in absence of *bayyina*-evidence.[233] Note also that the term *ẓann* is treated in *uṣūl* and *jadal* literature—in introductory discussions of epistemological first principles—in the sense of "probability." Al-Juwaynī defines it thus in his *Waraqāt*: "The pairing of two matters, one of them being more evident than the other (*tajwīz amrayni aḥaduhumā aẓharu min al-ākhar*),"[234] and al-Bājī's definition in the *Minhāj* is almost the same.[235] Note that *ẓann* and *ẓāhir* are linked by this definition, and both occur here in §700. Their usage in a venue of dialectic is telling.

Returning to al-Shāfiʿī's *mas'alat al-naqḍ* in §700, preceded by this epistemological critique, al-Shāfiʿī now pushes R to abandon what I might, in broader terms, designate his "context-override." That is to say, R has already asserted a gender-based assumption we may consider an appeal to gender-context, and al-Shāfiʿī is now introducing a *mas'alat al-naqḍ* exhibiting a trade-context—and will soon introduce (in §702) another *mas'alat al-naqḍ* exhibiting a solvency-context.[236] As with his gender-based assumptions, R is expected to adhere to a principle of "overriding" the *endoxon* efficiency of *bayyina*-evidence/joint-possession with a special property-efficiency derived from the *mas'ala*'s context. Thus, I will label his property-efficiency arguments, in general, as "context-overrides."

Al-Shāfiʿī presents R with a third *mas'alat al-naqḍ* wherein perfume-maker (*ʿaṭṭār*) and tanner (*dabbāgh*), in joint possession of the goods of their individual trades, each claim possession of them against the other. Rhetorically, al-Shāfiʿī asks: "What do you say [about that]?" R has been pushed to abandon the sort of "context-override" by which he considered feminine goods as relevant to the wife, and masculine goods as relevant to the husband. Now, however, the

---

[233] Although *istiṣḥāb al-ḥāl* is conspicuously absent from al-Shāfiʿī's legal theory, we might conjecture as to whether or not this argument may be subsumed by what was later to become known as *istiṣḥāb al-ḥāl al-ʿaql*—or even, considering that al-Shāfiʿī's *aṣl* for *qiyās* enjoys the sanction of *ijmāʿ*, the highly-contended *istiṣḥāb ḥāl al-ijmāʿ*. I will revisit this question briefly in Chap. 7.

[234] *Waraqāt*, Qāsimī and Balkhī ed., p. 46.

[235] Turkī ed., p. 11, §14. "*tajwīz amrayni fa-zā'idan, aḥaduhumā aẓharu min al-ākhar.*"

[236] Ultimately, al-Shāfiʿī plays these various contexts against each other in order to lay bare the opponent's inconsistency and internal contradictions.

mas'ala setting has changed, and, for consistency's sake, we ought to expect he would override the joint-possession status of the goods of contention by a trade-relevancy consideration (perfume-trade goods to the perfume-maker; tanning-trade goods to the tanner). Al-Shāfiʿī does not pause for an answer, and his strategy becomes clear: if R persists in overriding the joint-possession *ʿilla* with context-based assumptions, then al-Shāfiʿī will simply produce another *mas'alat al-naqḍ*. If, however, he abandons his "context-overrides" for this or other *masā'il*, then he must do the same for the *masā'il* at hand. In such a manner al-Shāfiʿī marches R towards a larger *naqḍ*-dilemma.

In §701, al-Shāfiʿī pre-empts intransigence on the part of R, anticipating—due to R's insistence on context-override—that R would rule tanning-trade goods go to the tanner, and perfume-trade goods go to the perfume-maker—a context-override of trade-relevancy (as opposed to gender-relevancy). Al-Shāfiʿī builds the *naqḍ*-dilemma; assuming R would profess the above, he immediately produces yet another *mas'alat al-naqḍ* in §702. R is again (rhetorically) asked: "what do you say (*fa mā taqūlu fī*) as regards an insolvent man and a solvent man, who each claim against the other a ruby and a pearl?" I would pause again to note this as more than a clever strategy on the part of al-Shāfiʿī, a closing off of all exits before R has a chance to respond. It is also an excellent device for "instructional" dialectic. Al-Shāfiʿī is providing his student with a step-by-step elevating of *masā'il*; in so many words: "if R persists with his context-override, introduce the perfume-maker vs. tanner *mas'ala*. And if still he persists, introduce the solvent vs. insolvent *mas'ala*, the one with the pearl and ruby. And if still he persists..." (etc.)

Note that al-Shāfiʿī has also introduced small changes into the relationship between context and object of dispute; for "solvent" (*mūsir*) as a descriptor does not incite the same assumption for ownership of ruby or pearl as "tanner" (*dabbāgh*) does for the trade-tools of tanning, "perfume-maker" (*ʿaṭṭār*) for perfumes, "women" (*nisā'*) for feminine commodities, and "men" (*rijāl*) for masculine commodities. This only serves to underscore the inefficiency of context-based considerations. All of these contextual descriptors are equally negligible in terms of epistemic value, but the solvency example brings this to a new extreme. Being male has little enough to do with assumed right to ownership of a masculine commodity, being solvent even less with ownership of a valuable object.

Having problematized R's position to the maximum extent, al-Shāfiʿī finally springs his *naqḍ*-dilemma in the typically dichotomous form which dilemmas take: R is shown two exits, and in each lies a thorny patch he must balk to enter. Both refer back to the solvent vs. insolvent *mas'ala*, which encapsulates the whole of al-Shāfiʿī's preceding arguments. In §703, al-Shāfiʿī asserts: "if you claim that you make [ruby or pearl] belong to the solvent man, while it is in the possession of both, together, you contradict the majority doctrine (*madhhab al-ʿāmma*)." This course, if taken, would be charged as violation of the *ijmāʿ* al-Shāfiʿī has twice claimed for the efficiency of joint possession in occasioning a *ḥukm* of half and half division. In terms of early *jadal*-theory, al-Shāfiʿī is blocking R from this exit with *muʿāraḍa biʾl-nuṭq* (Shīr.VII.15.1; Bāj.IX.B.15.1), where the *nuṭq* is neither Kitāb nor Sunna, but *ijmāʿ*. That is to say, R's context-based *ʿilla*-interpretation would be exposed as contrary to a doctrine enjoying the epistemic sanction of consensus.[237]

Remember that *ijmāʿ*, as a general category of epistemic justification, provides one of the greatest areas of overlap in *uṣūl al-fiqh* with the Aristotelian conception of *endoxa* premises. This phrase "majority doctrine" (*madhhab al-ʿāmma*) is a particularly shining illustration, reminiscent of the "most of the people" *endoxa* set in Aristotle's hierarchy of "all the people, or most of them, or the wise—either all of them, most of them, or famous individual sages." It is difficult to tell whether al-Shāfiʿī's references to *al-nās* (as in §696) or *al-ʿāmma* (as here in §703) refer to the *Umma* at large, or to the community of jurists, or to some other subset (with *al-nās* very likely meaning the "Easterners" or "Iraqis"). Regardless, a conceptual overlap with Aristotle's *endoxa* hierarchy is evident; and R would be hard pressed to maintain such a stance against the *endoxon* "majority doctrine" without extraordinary justification. The first exit from al-Shāfiʿī's *naqḍ*-dilemma has been barred.

Finally, al-Shāfiʿī proceeds to the second component of dilemma, asserting: "But if you claim that you divide it between them, and don't make assumptions about them (*lā tastaʿmilu ʿalayhimā al-ẓann*); then you should say [the same] regarding the goods of husband and wife." This is the only viable exit for R, but it requires complete concession to the validity of al-Shāfiʿī's ruling for the *masāʾil* at hand, and the invalidity of R's own position—*ʿilla* and *ḥukm* both. The strategy of al-Shāfiʿī's *naqḍ*-dilemma is plain—and it corresponds to the ultimate aim of classical dialectical encounter: to collect from one's opponent the premises from which one's own conclusion must naturally flow. I would draw this analysis to a close by noting al-Shāfiʿī's *naqḍ*-dilemma shows not only the marks of a master-dialectician (and teacher of dialectic), but it belongs—at the present stage of research—solely to his unique style of argumentation. No hint of such larger strategies appears in the *jadal*-theory texts I have examined, and I have yet to uncover the like employed by another early jurist. That being said, there is a mountain of research and analyses undone, and every possibility this strategy will be found to be a more common feature of proto-system *jadal*.

[237] al-Shīrāzī, *Maʿūna*, Turkī ed., p. 262, §147 [Missing from al-ʿUmayrīnī ed.]; al-Bājī, *Minhāj*, Turkī ed., p. 201, §454. Cf. Ibn ʿAqīl (*K. al-Jadal*, p. 70, §327) who, unlike al-Shīrāzī, mentions only *qiyās* in conflict with Kitāb and Sunna. Al-Bājī directs us to earlier discussions, by which I assume he includes *ijmāʿ* along with Kitāb and Sunna.

Masāʾil-Set #6

§§744–773 from the *Chapter on Partnership, Manumission, Etc.* (*Bāb fiʾl-Sharika waʾl-ʿItq wa Ghayrihi*)[238]

744 – He [Abū Yūsuf] said: And if there is a slave [jointly owned] between two men, one of whom manumits his portion while he is solvent; the *khiyār*-option belongs to the other, according to the doctrine of Abū Ḥanīfa, may God be pleased with him. If he wishes, he manumits the slave just as his companion manumitted him. [Or] if he wishes, he enables the slave to earn his ransom, for half of his value, and the *walāʾ*-patronage is [divided] between them both. [Or] if he wishes, he makes his partner liable for half of [the slave's] value, and the partner claims what he was made liable for from the slave, and the *walāʾ*-patronage belongs to the partner, all of it. And [the slave] is a slave so long as some part of his ransom-earning remains.[239]	744 - قَالَ: وَلَوْ أَنَّ عَبْدًا بَيْنَ رَجُلَيْنِ أَعْتَقَ أَحَدُهُمَا نَصِيبَهُ وَهُوَ مُوسِرٌ، كَانَ الْخِيَارُ لِلآخَرِ فِي قَوْلِ أَبِي حَنِيفَةَ رضي الله عنه فَإِنْ شَاءَ أَعْتَقَ الْعَبْدَ كَمَا أَعْتَقَ صَاحِبُهُ، وَإِنْ شَاءَ اسْتَسْعَى الْعَبْدَ فِي نِصْفِ قِيمَتِهِ، فَيَكُونُ الْوَلاَءُ بَيْنَهُمَا، وَإِنْ شَاءَ ضَمَّنَ شَرِيكَهُ نِصْفَ قِيمَتِهِ وَيَرْجِعُ الشَّرِيكُ بِمَا ضُمِّنَ مِن ذَلِكَ عَلَى الْعَبْدِ، وَيَكُونُ الْوَلاَءُ لِلشَّرِيكِ كُلُّهُ، وَهُوَ عَبْدٌ مَا بَقِيَ عَلَيْهِ مِن السِّعَايَةِ شَيْءٌ.
745 – But Ibn Abī Laylā, may God Most High have mercy upon him, used to say: He is free, all of him, the day on which the first [partner] manumitted him. And this first is liable for half the value, though he does not claim it from the slave; and the *walāʾ*-patronage belongs to him. His companion is not granted *khiyār*-option[240] to manumit the slave or enable him to earn his ransom.	745 - وَكَانَ ابْنُ أَبِي لَيْلَى رَحِمَهُ اللّٰهُ تَعَالَى يَقُولُ: هُوَ حُرٌّ كُلُّهُ يَوْمَ أَعْتَقَهُ الأَوَّلُ، وَالأَوَّلُ ضَامِنٌ لِنِصْفِ الْقِيمَةِ، وَلاَ يَرْجِعُ بِهَا عَلَى الْعَبْدِ، وَلَهُ الْوَلاَءُ، وَلاَ يُخَيَّرُ صَاحِبُهُ فِي أَنْ يُعْتِقَ الْعَبْدَ أَوْ يَسْتَسْعِيَهُ.
746 – But if the one who manumits the slave is insolvent; *khiyār*-option—according to the doctrine of Abū Ḥanīfa—belongs to the other partner. If he wishes, he makes the slave liable for half his value, which [the slave] strives to earn, and the *walāʾ*-patronage is [divided] between them. [Or] if he wishes, he manumits him, just as his companion did, and the *walāʾ*-patronage is [divided] between them.	746 - وَلَوْ كَانَ الَّذِي أَعْتَقَ الْعَبْدَ مُعْسِرًا، كَانَ الْخِيَارُ فِي قَوْلِ أَبِي حَنِيفَةَ لِلشَّرِيكِ الآخَرِ؛ إِنْ شَاءَ ضَمَّنَ الْعَبْدَ نِصْفَ قِيمَتِهِ يَسْعَى فِيهَا وَالْوَلاَءُ بَيْنَهُمَا، وَإِنْ شَاءَ أَعْتَقَهُ كَمَا أَعْتَقَ صَاحِبُهُ، وَالْوَلاَءُ بَيْنَهُمَا.
747 – But Ibn Abī Laylā used to say: When [the manumitter] is insolvent; the slave earns his ransom for the partner who did not manumit, for half of his value—but the slave lays claim to that from the one who manumitted him—and the *walāʾ*-patronage, all of it, belongs to the manumitter. The other [partner] has no right to manumit any part of him.	747 - وَكَانَ ابْنُ أَبِي لَيْلَى يَقُولُ: إِذَا كَانَ مُعْسِرًا سَعَى الْعَبْدُ لِلشَّرِيكِ الَّذِي لَمْ يُعْتِقْ فِي نِصْفِ قِيمَتِهِ، وَيَرْجِعُ بِذَلِكَ الْعَبْدُ عَلَى الَّذِي أَعْتَقَهُ، وَالْوَلاَءُ كُلُّهُ لِلَّذِي أَعْتَقَهُ، وَلَيْسَ لِلآخَرِ أَنْ يُعْتِقَ مِنْهُ شَيْئًا.

(continued)

[238] Ḥassūn ed., vol. 9, pp. 132–5; ʿAbd al-Muṭṭalib ed., vol. 8, pp. 308–10.

[239] On full manumission (*ʿitq*), *walāʾ*-patronage, and related rulings, see *MF*, s.v. "عتق" (vol. 29, pp. 264–74) and "ولاء" (vol. 45, pp. 119–34); *EI*², s.v. "ʿAbd" (esp. §3.j-k) and "Mawlā" (esp. §II.5); and *DJP*, vol. 2, pp. 441–52 (esp. pp. 444–5, where the current *masʾala* is discussed).

[240] Here I have preferred the passive *wa-lā yukhayyaru ṣāḥibuhu*, rather than Ḥassūn's active voice (*Umm*, vol. 9, p. 132), as it is not the first partner who grants the second his *khiyār*-options, but an operation of law.

748 – And he used to say: When one manumits a portion in a slave, he has manumitted all of him—the slave is not divisible so that some of him be a slave and some of him a freeman. And he [Abū Yūsuf] embraced it. Have you considered what one manumitted; is it [still] a slave?	748 - وَكَانَ يَقُولُ: إِذَا أَعْتَقَ شِقْصًا فِي مَمْلُوكٍ فَقَدْ أَعْتَقَهُ كُلَّهُ، وَلاَ يَتَبَعَّضُ الْعَبْدُ فَيَكُونُ بَعْضُهُ رَقِيقًا وَبَعْضُهُ حُرًّا، وَبِهِ يَأْخُذُ. أَرَأَيْتَ مَا أَعْتَقَ مِنْهُ أَيَكُونُ رَقِيقًا؟
749 – And if it is the case that what one manumitted is [still] a slave, then he [the slave] has [nevertheless] been manumitted. So how can there combine in a single manumitted entity [both] ʿ*itq*-manumission and slavery?	749 - فَإِنْ كَانَ مَا أَعْتَقَ مِنْهُ يَكُونُ رَقِيقًا فَقَدْ عَتَقَ، فَكَيْفَ يَجْتَمِعُ فِي مُعْتَقٍ وَاحِدٍ عِتْقٌ وَرِقٌّ؟
750 – Don't you see/opine that "some of her is divorced" and "some of her is not divorced" and "some of her is the husband's wife" can never combine in a woman as she is?	750 - أَلاَ تَرَى أَنَّهُ لاَ يَجْتَمِعُ فِي امْرَأَةٍ بَعْضُهَا طَالِقٌ وَبَعْضُهَا غَيْرُ طَالِقٍ وَبَعْضُهَا امْرَأَةٌ لِلزَّوْجِ عَلَى حَالِهَا.
751 – Likewise with the slave. And he [Abū Yūsuf] embraced this [doctrine], except for a single practice: the slave does not claim what he earns [for ransom] from the one who manumitted him.	751 - وَكَذَلِكَ الرَّقِيقُ وَبِهَذَا يَأْخُذُ إِلاَّ خَصْلَةً لاَ يَرْجِعُ الْعَبْدُ بِمَا سَعَى فِيهِ عَلَى الَّذِي أَعْتَقَهُ.
752 – But Abū Ḥanīfa, may God Most High have mercy upon him, said: Some of him is not manumitted while some of him is a slave; but this one—all of him—is in the *manzila*-status of the slave, so long as some part of him is a slave, or he is working to earn his value.	752 - وَقَالَ أَبُو حَنِيفَةَ رَحِمَهُ اللهُ تَعَالَى: لاَ يُعْتَقُ بَعْضُهُ وَبَعْضُهُ رَقِيقٌ وَهَذَا كُلُّهُ بِمَنْزِلَةِ الْعَبْدِ مَا دَامَ مِنْهُ شَيْءٌ رَقِيقٌ أَوْ يَسْعَى فِي قِيمَتِهِ.
753 – Have you considered [what would happen] if the partner says: my partner's portion of him is free—but as for my portion: no. Is he manumitting of him what he does not own? And when he manumits of him what he *does* own, then how can he manumit of him what he does *not* own? Does ʿ*itq*-manumission occur in what a man does not own?	753 - أَرَأَيْتَ لَوْ أَنَّ الشَّرِيكَ قَالَ: نَصِيبُ شَرِيكِي مِنْهُ حُرٌّ وَأَمَّا نَصِيبِي فَلاَ، هَلْ كَانَ يُعْتِقُ مِنْهُ مَا لاَ يَمْلِكُ؟ وَإِذَا أَعْتَقَ مِنْهُ مَا يَمْلِكُ، فَكَيْفَ يُعْتِقُ مِنْهُ مَا لاَ يَمْلِكُ؟ وَهَلْ يَقَعُ عِتْقٌ فِيمَا لاَ يَمْلِكُ الرَّجُلُ؟
754 – Al-Shāfiʿī, may God have mercy upon him, said: When the slave is [jointly-owned] between two men, and one of them manumits his portion of him; if he is solvent so that he can pay out half his value, then the slave is free—all of him—and the *walāʾ*-patronage belongs to the first manumitter, and there belongs no *khiyār*-option to the other master of the slave. But if he is insolvent, then the first half is free, the second half belongs to its owner, and there is no ransom-earning enjoined upon him. And this is written in the *Book of Manumission*, with its arguments; except we have found in this [present] book[241] additional material we had not heard of, with regard to [the preceding jurists'] arguments.[242]	754 - قَالَ الشَّافِعِيُّ رحمه الله: وَإِذَا كَانَ الْعَبْدُ بَيْنَ الرَّجُلَيْنِ فَأَعْتَقَ أَحَدُهُمَا نَصِيبَهُ مِنْهُ، فَإِنْ كَانَ مُوسِرًا بِأَنْ يُؤَدِّيَ نِصْفَ قِيمَتِهِ فَالْعَبْدُ حُرٌّ كُلُّهُ، وَالْوَلاَءُ لِلْمُعْتِقِ الأَوَّلِ وَلاَ خِيَارَ لِسَيِّدِ الْعَبْدِ الآخَرِ. وَإِنْ كَانَ مُعْسِرًا فَالنِّصْفُ الأَوَّلُ حُرٌّ وَالنِّصْفُ الثَّانِي لِمَالِكِهِ وَلاَ سِعَايَةَ عَلَيْهِ. وَهَذَا مَكْتُوبٌ فِي كِتَابِ الْعِتْقِ بِحُجَجِهِ إِلاَّ أَنَّا وَجَدْنَا فِي هَذَا الْكِتَابِ زِيَادَةَ حَرْفٍ لَمْ نَسْمَعْ بِهِ فِي حُجَجِهِمْ.

(continued)

[241] I.e., the *Kitāb Ikhtilāf Abī Ḥanīfa wa Ibn Abī Laylā*, the Shaybānī Version, which is the object of al-Shāfiʿī's commentary.

[242] Meaning, the *a-lā tarā* argument in §750.

755 – There was, of what they argue in this book, that their proponent said: How is "a single entity is partly free and partly owned" not just like "the wife is not partly divorced and partly not divorced?"	755 - كَانَ مِمَّا احْتَجُّوا بِهِ فِي هَذَا الْكِتَابِ أَنْ قَالَ قَائِلُهُمْ: كَيْفَ تَكُونُ نَفْسٌ وَاحِدَةٌ بَعْضُهَا حُرٌّ وَبَعْضُهَا مَمْلُوكٌ لاَ يَكُونُ، كَمَا لاَ تَكُونُ الْمَرْأَةُ بَعْضُهَا طَالِقٍ وَبَعْضُهَا غَيْرُ طَالِقٍ؟
756 – And if he claims that the slave in whom [both] slavery and freedom exist is a correlational inference from the wife; it is said to him: Is a man allowed to marry part of a woman?	756 - فَإِنْ زَعَمَ أَنَّ الْعَبْدَ يَكُونُ فِيهِ الرِّقُّ وَالْحُرِّيَّةُ قِيَاسًا عَلَى الْمَرْأَةِ. قِيلَ لَهُ: أَيَجُوزُ لِلرَّجُلِ أَنْ يَنْكِحَ بَعْضَ امْرَأَةٍ؟
757 – And if he says: No. She is either married—all of her—or not married.	757 - فَإِنْ قَالَ: لاَ. لاَ تَكُونُ إلاَّ مَنْكُوحَةً كُلَّهَا أَوْ غَيْرَ مَنْكُوحَةٍ.
758 – It is said to him: And is it permitted that part of a slave be purchased?	758 - قِيلَ لَهُ: أَفَيَجُوزُ أَنْ يُشْتَرَى بَعْضُ عَبْدٍ؟
759 – And if he says: Yes.	759 - فَإِنْ قَالَ: نَعَمْ.
760 – It is said to him: So where is the slave in relation to the woman?	760 - قِيلَ لَهُ: فَأَيْنَ الْعَبْدُ مِنَ الْمَرْأَةِ؟
761 – And it is said to him: Is [a man] allowed to contract *kitāba*-ransom with his wife for a divorce, which is held back until she fully pays the *kitāba*-ransom, or defaults?[243]	761 - وَقِيلَ لَهُ: أَيَجُوزُ لَهُ أَنْ يُكَاتِبَ الْمَرْأَةَ عَلَى الطَّلاَقِ وَيَكُونَ مَمْنُوعًا حَتَّى تُؤَدِّيَ الْكِتَابَةَ أَوْ تَعْجَزَ؟
762 – And if he says: No.	762 - فَإِنْ قَالَ: لاَ.
763 – It is said: And is this permitted him regarding the slave?	763 - قِيلَ: أَفَيَجُوزُ هَذَا لَهُ فِي الْعَبْدِ؟
764 – And if he says: Yes.	764 - فَإِنْ قَالَ: نَعَمْ.
765 – It is said: Then why do you link them?	765 - قِيلَ: فَلِمَ تَجْمَعُ بَيْنَهُمَا؟
766 – And if he says: They are not linked [here].	766 - فَإِنْ قَالَ: لاَ يَجْتَمِعَانِ.
767 – It is said: Likewise, they are not linked wherever you have linked them.	767 – قِيلَ: وَكَذَلِكَ لاَ يَجْتَمِعَانِ حَيْثُ جَمَعْتَ بَيْنَهُمَا.
768 – And it is also said to him: Does a wife belong to two [men], like a slave is owned by two? And does the wife's husband have the right to gift her to a man—that she be his wife—just as a slave, when one gifts him, becomes the slave of the one to whom he was gifted?	768 - وَيُقَالُ لَهُ أَيْضًا: أَتَكُونُ الْمَرْأَةُ لِاثْنَيْنِ، كَمَا يَكُونُ الْعَبْدُ مَمْلُوكًا لِاثْنَيْنِ وَيَكُونُ لِزَوْجِ الْمَرْأَةِ أَنْ يَهَبَهَا لِلرَّجُلِ فَتَكُونَ زَوْجَةً لَهُ، كَمَا يَكُونُ الْعَبْدُ إِذَا وَهَبَهُ صَارَ عَبْدًا لِمَنْ وَهَبَهُ لَهُ؟
769 – And if he says: No.	769 - فَإِنْ قَالَ: لاَ.

(continued)

[243] *Kitāba* or *mukātaba* is a form of manumission contract by which, usually in regular installments, the slave (called a *mukātab*) purchases his freedom. In this case, it is asked if a man, whose wife seeks divorce, can contract a similar arrangement by which she gradually pays for a unilateral divorce (*ṭalāq*), which only he can pronounce (hence unilateral). For more on *kitāba*/*mukātaba* and related rulings, see *MF*, s.v. "مكاتبة" (vol. 38, pp. 360–3); and *DJP*, vol. 2, pp. 453–68.

770 – It is said: So why is it that the wife is correlated with the slave?	770 – قِيلَ: فَمَا بَالُ الْمَرْأَةِ تُقَاسُ عَلَى الْمَمْلُوكِ؟
771 – And it is said to him: Have you considered [what would happen] when the slave is manumitted once; does his master have the right to re-enslave him—as he enjoys, when he once divorces his wife, the right of her return?	771 - وَيُقَالُ لَهُ: أَرَأَيْتَ الْعَبْدَ إِذَا عَتَقَ مَرَّةً أَيَكُونُ لِسَيِّدِهِ أَنْ يَسْتَرِقَّهُ، كَمَا يَكُونُ لَهُ إِذَا طَلَّقَ الْمَرْأَةَ مَرَّةً أَنْ يَكُونَ لَهُ رَجْعَتُهَا؟
772 – And if he says: No.	772 - فَإِنْ قَالَ: لاَ.
773 – It is said: Then we don't know of anything more distant from it [manumission], than what he correlated it with [divorce].	773 – قِيلَ: فَمَا نَعْلَمُ شَيْئًا أَبْعَدَ مِمَّا قَاسَهُ بِهِ مِنْهُ.

In §744 Abū Ḥanīfa's three rulings for *mas'ala* #1—when the partner-manumitter is solvent (*mūsir*)—are neatly laid out. The non-manumitting partner has *khiyār*-option to either: (1) manumit the slave; (2) enable the slave to earn his ransom (half his value) with *walā'*-patronage divided between both partners; or (3) make his partner liable (for half the slave's value), who claims that from the slave, with *walā'*-patronage belonging only to the manumitting partner. The substantive principle underpinning these rulings is then plainly stated: "[the slave] is a slave so long as some part of his ransom-earning remains." I would mark this as reliance upon a general legal principle equating partial-manumission to full slave status in the eyes of the law.

Ibn Abī Laylā's three counter-rulings for *mas'ala* #1 are then laid out in §745: (1) the slave is entirely free the moment the first partner manumits him; (2) this first partner is liable for half the value to the non-manumitting partner and does not claim it from the slave, with *walā'*-patronage belonging entirely to the first; and (3) the non-manumitting partner is granted no *khiyār*-option for manumitting the slave or enabling him to earn his ransom. A substantive counter-principle to that of Abū Ḥanīfa, underpinning Ibn Abī Laylā's rulings, is implied here (and clearly stated in §748), and I would also mark this as reliance upon a general legal principle—this time equating partial-manumission to full manumission in the eyes of the law.

In §746 Abū Ḥanīfa's two rulings for *mas'ala* #2—when the partner-manumitter is insolvent (*muʿsir*)—are laid out. The non-manumitting partner has *khiyār*-option to either: (1) make the slave liable for half his value and enable him to earn it, with the *walā'*-patronage divided between both partners; or (2) manumit his portion, with the *walā'*-patronage divided between them. Ibn Abī Laylā's counter-rulings for *mas'ala* #2 are laid out in §747: (1) the slave earns his ransom (half of his value) from the non-manumitting partner and claims it from the manumitting partner, with *walā'*-patronage belonging entirely to the manumitting partner; and (2) the non-manumitting partner has no right to subsequently manumit his portion.

Evident in both sets of competing rulings for *mas'ala* #2 is a reliance upon the same counter-principles underpinning the competing rulings for *mas'ala* #1; and Ibn Abī Laylā's substantive counter-principle is now clearly stated at the start of §748: "When one manumits a portion in a slave, he has manumitted all of him—the slave is not divisible so that some of him be a slave and some of him a freeman."

Abū Yūsuf's adherence to this principle (and its associated rulings) is stated, and is followed by a rhetorical *a-ra'ayta* question—in whose voice, Abū Yūsuf's or al-Shaybānī's, it is not clear: "Have you considered what one manumitted; is it [still] a slave?" The effect of this is twofold: (1) it is a *reductio* argument confronting the opposing position with the untenable consequence of internal, logical contradiction (*tanāquḍ*); and (2) it pushes concession to the first premise of a larger justification (*istidlāl bi'l-qiyās*) and objection (*muʿāraḍa bi'l-ʿilla*).[244]

§749 is still governed by Abū Yūsuf's or al-Shaybānī's *a-ra'ayta*. The arguer first expands on the opposing position's inherent self-contradiction: "if it is the case that what one manumitted is [still] a slave, then [the slave] has [nevertheless] been manumitted," then follows through with a further rhetorical question (with *kayfa*): "how can there combine in a single manumitted entity [both] *ʿitq*-manumission and slavery?" This serves at once to: (1) underscore the opposing position's contradiction; (2) push concession to a second premise of the larger justification/objection which is coming; and (3) neatly conclude the current *reductio*. The whole stands as an objection to Abū Ḥanīfa's substantive principle, while confirming that *ʿitq*-manumission must extend from portion to whole, and that predicates X and ¬X cannot obtain in the same individual at the same time.[245]

The voice of Abū Yūsuf/al-Shaybānī continues in §750 with an *a-lā tarā* question which identifies an *aṣl* for *qiyās* (partly divorced and partly not-divorced cannot coexist in a wife at the same time) to the partially-manumitted = wholly manumitted principle. As this principle may be understood as occasioning or indicating the Ibn Abī Laylā/Abū Yūsuf/al-Shaybānī counter-rulings for both *masā'il*, the whole constitutes a simultaneous *istidlāl bi'l-qiyās* and *muʿāraḍa bi-ʿilla*.[246] That the case of the partially-divorced wife is meant to be an *aṣl* is confirmed by its being linked as an analogue to the *mas'ala* at hand in §751: "Likewise with the slave." Abū Yūsuf's adherence is then restated, with the exception of a single practice (*khaṣla*)[247]—his counter-ruling to Ibn Abī Laylā's ruling #2 for *mas'ala* #2.

---

[244] Abū Yūsuf's or al-Shaybānī's *a-ra'ayta* in §748: rhetorical, posing an untenable consequence in the form of a self-contradicting formulation, supporting a ruling with an analogous *aṣl* (identified in §750 via *a-lā tarā*) which avoids the contradiction inherent to the contrary opinion; constituting a justification/objection of *istidlāl bi'l-qiyās / tanāquḍ / muʿāraḍa bi-ʿilla* of the opposing *istidlāl bi'l-qiyās*.

[245] NB: at this stage, Abū Yūsuf's / al-Shaybānī's argument consists purely of *ʿaql*, from the basic logical principle of non-contradiction.

[246] Abū Yūsuf's or al-Shaybānī's *a-lā tarā* in §750: rhetorical, pushing concession to a parallel case with an established *ḥukm*, as an endoxon *aṣl* for *qiyās*, which *qiyās* avoids the internal, logical contradiction inherent to the contrary opinion; the whole constituting a justification/objection of *istidlāl bi'l-qiyās / muʿāraḍa bi-ʿilla* of opposing *istidlāl bi'l-qiyās*.

[247] NB: from this, and earlier references to *khaṣla/khiṣāl* in §§643 ff., it is evident that *khaṣla* is as likely to refer to a *ḥukm* re: an entity at hand, as it is to a property of that entity. In that sense, it is quite similar to the *khaṣīṣa* of al-Shīrāzī in his *qiyās al-dalāla* discussion.

In §752 Abū Ḥanīfa neatly sidesteps the problem of contradictory states by asserting they were never mixed in the first place: the slave is to be considered wholly a slave so long as any portion of him is a slave. This is basically a (re)statement that slavery (rather than manumission) extends from the portion to the whole; it stands as counter-thesis to Ibn Abī Laylā's ruling, which suggests manumission extends from the portion to the whole. Importantly, Abū Ḥanīfa asserts this with a formula of *manzila*-subsumption: "this one—all of him—is in the *manzila*-status of the slave, so long as some part of him is a slave, or he is working to earn his value." This complements his substantive principle of §744: "[the slave] is a slave so long as some part of his ransom-earning remains." In §753, Abū Ḥanīfa follows this reassertion with a triple *reductio* barrage against the Ibn Abī Laylā/Abū Yūsuf/al-Shaybānī position, delivered via *a-ra'ayta*, and posing three untenable consequences (non-*endoxon* rulings), contingent but possible, from derived cases[248]—thus pushing his opponents to concede the *endoxon* principle inherent to his counter-rulings.[249]

In §754 al-Shāfiʿī's rulings for *mas'ala* #1 and *mas'ala* #2 are presented. When the manumitting partner is solvent: (1) he pays his partner half-value, the slave is entirely free, with *walā'*-patronage only for the manumitting partner; and (2) the non-manumitting partner has no *khiyār*-option. When he is insolvent, however: (1) half of the slave is free, the other half still enslaved to the non-manumitting partner; and (2) the non-manumitting partner is not obliged to allow ransom-earning. His rulings for *mas'ala* #1 are thus in consonance with the Ibn Abī Laylā/Abū Yūsuf/al-Shaybānī position, but his rulings for *mas'ala* #2—though closer to the Abū Ḥanīfa position—are contrary to all. Note that al-Shāfiʿī holds to no *manzila*-subsumption principle, and his latter rulings require that part-free and part-enslaved can, in fact, coexist within an individual at the same time.

Al-Shāfiʿī presents no support here, but makes the following authorial comment: "And this is written in the *Book of Manumission*, with its arguments; except we have found in this [present] book additional material we had not heard of, with regard to [the preceding jurists'] arguments." This last observation refers back to the *a-lā tarā* argument in §750, above; and thus §§754–5 have significant bearing upon the problem of authorship and compilation of the *Umm*. Certainly there are multiple references in our subject-text to other "books" and chapters of the *Umm*,

[248] Abū Ḥanīfa's *a-ra'ayta* in §753: rhetorical, posing untenable consequences in the form of contingent-possible derived cases, as a triple-*reductio* supporting his rulings from an identified principle; the whole constituting a justification/objection of *istidlāl bi'l-qiyās* / *muʿāraḍa bi-ʿilla* of opposing *istidlāl bi'l-qiyās* (*aṣl* not stated).

[249] NB: all rulings from all positions are underpinned by a set of conflicting general principles: (1) Abū Ḥanīfa: if any portion remains enslaved, then the whole individual is in the *manzila* of the slave; and (2) Ibn Abī Laylā et al.: if any portion is manumitted, then the whole individual is in the *manzila* of the manumitted. In essence, this *ikhtilāf* is due to conflicting notions of efficiency in occasioning *manzila*-subsumption. For Abū Ḥanīfa, the portion enslaved occasions *manzila*-subsumption under the genus of slave; for Ibn Abī Laylā et al. the portion freed occasions *manzila*-subsumption under the genus of freed.

including, as here in §754, reference to a *Book of Manumission* (*Kitāb al-ʿItq*).[250] In the present instance, there is little doubt the book so referenced is the *Kitāb al-ʿItq* comprising the fourth "chapter" of the *Book of Juridical Disagreement of Mālik and al-Shāfiʿī* (*Kitāb Ikhtilāf Mālik wa'l-Shāfiʿī*).[251] However, "this book" (*hādhā al-kitāb*)—to which al-Shāfiʿī twice refers (once here, and again in §755)—is none other than our subject-text itself. More accurately, it is the Shaybānī Version of our subject-text upon which al-Shāfiʿī is presently expanding and commenting. In short, he claims sufficient argument for his position is made in his *K. al-ʿItq*, but that he has found something new here—in the Shaybānī Version of our subject-text—to debate; namely, the *qiyās*-comparison of manumission and divorce, delivered by Abū Yūsuf or al-Shaybānī via *a-lā tarā* in §750. The simplest explanation for the references in §§754–5 is this: having already authored the *K. al-ʿItq*, al-Shāfiʿī could merely direct his students/readers to a copy of that work and focus, instead, upon the new material—§750 of the Shaybānī Version of our subject-text—which he actually held in hand (or in memory) at the time of writing or dictating the *Umm* Version.

In §755, he continues his authorial comment, saying: "There was, of what they argue in this book [i.e., the Shaybānī Version], that their proponent said: How is 'a single entity is partly free and partly owned' not just like 'the wife is not partly divorced and partly not divorced?'"[252] And so al-Shāfiʿī—referring back to §750—summarizes the *problema* to be investigated. It appears (as we see more clearly in the following section) that "their proponent", Q, seeks to gain concession to *qiyās*. Al-Shāfiʿī's Q compares two propositions and demands to know how they *not* be deemed similar: "How can [proposition X] not be like [proposition Y]?" (*kayfa* [X] *lā yakūnu kamā* [Y]?) Following the preceding reference to a *Kitāb al-ʿItq*, we should expect *not* to find this sort of argument there; and, in fact, we do not—only the barest hint of *qiyās* may be discerned at all. The bulk of the debate in the *Kitāb al-ʿItq* centers upon what would later be known in *uṣūl* works as "conflict of

[250] See §681 of Ḥassūn's edition, vol. 9, p. 122; and the translation in my dissertation ("Dialectical Forge," pt. 2, p. 177).

[251] *Umm*, Ḥassūn ed., vol.9, pt.14, pp. 362–5.

[252] See §750, above. The problem is more felicitously worded as a statement in al-Muzanī's paraphrase, as follows: ... فإن قال قائل لا تكون نفس واحدة بعضها عبدا وبعضها حرا كما لا تكون امرأة بعضها طالقا وبعضها غير طالق, "And if one should say: A single individual is not part slave and part free, just like a wife is not part divorced and part not-divorced..." (see the editions of the *Mukhtaṣar*, and al-Māwardī's *Ḥāwī al-Kabīr*, Maʿʿūd, et al., eds., vol. 18, pp. 25–6). Al-Māwardī, commenting on al-Muzanī's paraphrase of this argument (and al-Shāfiʿī's dialectic with its proponent), attributes the manumission-divorce correlation to both Abū Ḥanīfa and Ibn Abī Laylā; perhaps "their proponent" (*qā'iluhum*) mentioned above refers to Abū Yūsuf. Al-Māwardī points out that those who prevent the combination of freedom and slavery in a single individual (Abū Ḥanīfa and Ibn Abī Laylā) oblige the slave to earn his remaining ransom, while those who allow such a combination (Mālik and al-Shāfiʿī) do not oblige the ransom-earning; he proceeds to a detailed and systematic rendering of al-Shāfiʿī's counter-arguments as we find them here in our subject-text (*al-Ḥāwī al-Kabīr*, op. cit.)

indicants" *taʿāruḍ al-adilla*—in this case, contradictory *ḥadīths*. Preliminary searches have revealed nothing on this model of manumission-divorce *qiyās* elsewhere in the *Umm*, leading me to conclude the *Kitāb al-ʿItq* referenced in §§754–5 is indeed that of the *Kitāb Ikhtilāf Mālik wa'l-Shāfiʿī*, as it appears in the *Umm* compendium.[253]

Thus in §755 al-Shāfiʿī sets the stage for an "instructional" dialectic against the argument he has just now discovered.[254] Having reformulated the problem into a dialectical *kayfa*-question, he proceeds in §756 to that "instructional" dialectic by relating the proper dialectical questions for debating the new claim. The formula is: "if he claims X... it is said to him Y" (*in zaʿama* X... *qīla lahu* Y), and al-Shāfiʿī says: "if he claims that the slave in whom [both] slavery and freedom exist is a correlational inference from the wife;[255] it is said to him: 'Is a man allowed to marry part of a woman?'"

Thus the parallel raised by *a-la tarā* in §750 is acknowledged as the opposing position's claimed basis for *qiyās*; and al-Shāfiʿī's first dialectical question introduces his first *mas'ala* for invalidating distinction (*farq*)—pitting partial ownership of a slave (allowed) against partial marriage of a woman (not allowed). He thus pushes his anonymous opponent R to concede premise #1 for *farq* #1. In §757, R concedes to the invalidating disjunction: "She is either married—all of her—or not married;"[256] and al-Shāfiʿī acquires premise #1 for *farq* #1. In §758, al-Shāfiʿī brings his second dialectical question: "is it permitted that part of a slave be purchased?"—pushing R's concession premise #2 for *farq* #1. In §759, R again concedes (with a simple "Yes"), and thus al-Shāfiʿī acquires premise #2. And so, in §760, al-Shāfiʿī confirms the first *qiyās*-invalidating *farq*-distinction with a rhetorical flourish: "So where is the slave in relation to the woman?"[257]

---

[253] I have, due to several features of interest, presented the whole of this *Kitāb al-ʿItq* in parallel translation in my dissertation ("Dialectical Forge," vol. 2, appendix II.§755, pp. 360–4).

[254] NB: This offers a fascinating window on proto-system *jadal* teaching and practice: al-Shāfiʿī initiates an "instructional" dialectic, against a (recently re-discovered) thesis from a "historical" dialectic, in order to prepare the student for an encounter with a proponent of the "historical" thesis.

[255] Meaning: if the proponent argues the impossibility of combining "freedom" and "slavery" in a single individual, by way of *qiyās* from the impossibility of combining "divorced" and "not-divorced" in a single woman—the objective being to prove impossible the freedom-slavery combination.

[256] This may be rendered as: $(x)[Wx \rightarrow (Mx \vee \neg Mx)]$; reading: "For any x, if x is a woman, then x is either entirely married (*mankūḥa*), or entirely not married."

[257] The exchange in §§756–60 is reminiscent of discussions found in later treatises on *qiyās*-invalidating inter-case distinctions (*furūq*)—though absent the common formula: "but there's a difference between them" (*wa'l-farq baynahumā*). Here, Q (al-Shāfiʿī) confronts the *qiyās*-proponent with the invalidating distinction (*farq*) between partial-purchase of a slave (permitted) vs. partial-marriage of a woman (not permitted). His *elenchus* is sealed with a rhetorical question (§760), asking, in so many words: "what does the slave have to do with the wife, that you correlate them in *qiyās*?" Notably, al-Māwardī identifies this (and al-Shāfiʿī's subsequent arguments) as the dialectical move of *farq* (*al-Ḥāwī al-Kabīr*, Maʿʿūd, et al., eds., vol. 18, p. 25).

Having proven the first *farq*, al-Shāfiʿī proceeds in §761 to his next dialectical question, introducing his second *mas'ala* for invalidating distinction (*farq*)—pitting *kitāba*-ransom for divorce (not allowed) against *kitāba*-ransom for manumission (allowed): "Is [a man] allowed to contract *kitāba*-ransom with his wife for a divorce, which is held back until she fully pays the *kitāba*-ransom, or defaults?"—and thus pushing R to concede premise #1 for *farq* #2. In §762, R again concedes (with a simple "No"), and thus al-Shāfiʿī acquires premise #1. Al-Shāfiʿī's dialectical question in §763 then ties the *mas'ala* of *farq* to the *mas'ala* at hand: "And is this permitted him regarding the slave?"—pushing R to concede premise #2 for *farq* #2. Again, R concedes in §764 (with a simple "Yes"), and thus al-Shāfiʿī acquires premise #2. And now (§765), as with the first, al-Shāfiʿī attempts to confirm the second *qiyās*-invalidating *farq*-distinction with a rhetorical question, asking: "Then why do you link them (*fa-lima tajmaʿu baynahumā*)?" R, however, has a response in §766: "They are not linked [here]." This is important, because he has opened himself to a new critique of method-*naqḍ*—inconsistent observance of manumission-divorce correspondence—and al-Shāfiʿī's quick retort in §767 confirms this: "Likewise, they are not linked wherever you have linked them." Thus, not only has al-Shāfiʿī (in §§761–767) gained concession to a second *farq*-distinction—there can be no correlation between a slave (whose *mukātaba* is permitted) and a wife (whose *kitāba*-ransom for divorce is not permitted)—but he has demonstrated R's method-*naqḍ*. R has conceded that he does not accept *qiyās* between woman and slave in this second *mas'alat al-farq*, but he does in the *mas'ala* at hand. I would consider this al-Shāfiʿī's first *elenchus*, for he has tied the conceded *masā'il* of *farq* (#1 and #2) to the *mas'ala* at hand, and charged R with method-*naqḍ*, saying, in so many words: "You do not do *qiyās* in the *masā'il al-farq*, nor should you do it here where the same invalidating distinctions prevent it."

But al-Shāfiʿī insists on driving the point further. In §768 he introduces another set of *masā'il al-furūq* (#3 and #4), simultaneously: "[3] Does a wife belong to two [men], like a slave is owned by two? And [4] does the wife's husband have the right to gift her to a man—that she be his wife—just as a slave, when one gifts him, becomes the slave of the one to whom he was gifted?"[258]—thus further pitting joint-ownership of a wife (not allowed) against joint-ownership of a slave (allowed), and gifting of a wife (not allowed) against gifting of a slave (allowed), and pushing R to concede all premises for *farq* #3 and *farq* #4. In §769, R concedes (with a simple "No"), and thus al-Shāfiʿī acquires his premises, and his second *elenchus* of both *farq* and method-*naqḍ*. He makes this plain in §770, again with rhetorical flourish:

[258] Note the didactic intent in al-Shāfiʿī's saying "and it is *also* said to him…" (*wa qīla lahu ayḍan*). We have moved, in other words, from the first *topos*—the first "location" of stored argument relevant to the opponent's thesis—to the second *topos*.

"So *why* is it that the wife is correlated with the slave?" (*fa-mā bālu al-marʾati tuqāsu ʿalā al-mamlūk?*) Not only does this confirm *farq* #3 and *farq* #4, but it is primarily a statement of *elenchus* (#2) due to method-*naqḍ*; in so many words: "you have no right, in view of these invalidating distinctions, to do *qiyās* between these, as you have done for the *masʾala* at hand."

That this question was meant rhetorically is confirmed by al-Shāfiʿī's proceeding directly to a dialogical *a-raʾayta* question in §771, introducing yet another *masʾala* of *farq* (#5): "when the slave is manumitted once; does his master have the right to re-enslave him—as he enjoys, when he once divorces his wife, the right of her return?"[259]—pitting re-enslavement of the manumitted (not allowed) against return to marriage after divorce (allowed), and pushing R to concede all premises for this *farq*. R concedes in §772 with a simple "No", and thus al-Shāfiʿī acquires acknowledgment of his fifth and final *qiyās*-invalidating distinction. His closing *elenchus* statement in §773 encapsulates the overwhelming, *qiyās*-destroying power of five *farq*-distinctions, in no uncertain terms: "Then we don't know of anything more distant from it [manumission], than what he correlated it with [divorce]" (*fa-mā naʿlamu shayʾan abʿada mimmā qāsahu bihi minhu*).[260] Al-Shāfiʿī has gained concession to five *furūq*—utterly destroying the *qiyās* of Abū Yūsuf/al-Shaybānī and "their proponent" R from the *aṣl* of partial marriage/divorce, and simultaneously accusing them of method-*naqḍ*.

[259] Al-Shāfiʿī's *a-raʾayta* in §771: dialogical, soliciting a ruling on a final derived *masʾala* [the last in a series of *masāʾil al-farq*], for an imminent charge of compound method-*naqḍ* (opponent observes a *farq*-distinction in the parallel *masāʾil*, but ignores it in the *masʾala*-at-hand).

[260] Again, the extended dialectic of §755–73 is a recognizable predecessor of the *furūq* literature; a clearer indication of the dialectical origins of this genre could hardly be found. Note the cases in the contended correlation do, in fact, appear quite similar—a woman cannot be both partly married and partly divorced, how then, can a slave be both partly enslaved and partly manumitted? But Q invalidates such a correlational inference by highlighting the critical differences between these cases (such as are announced, in the *furūq* literature, with: *waʾl farq baynahumā*). Al-Shāfiʿī here brings no less than five *furūq*; and these, as seen in §§760, 765, 767, and 770, are followed up with (mostly rhetorical) demands for *qiyās*-justifying bases of resemblance or occasioning elements. If not the properties exposed as different, then what is it that links these cases? Having cycled through a sufficiency of divergent elements, al-Shāfiʿī closes (§773) with a definitive pronouncement: nothing is further from manumission than the *qiyās*-proponent's alleged source-case of divorce.

Masāʾil-Set #7

§§1051–1061 from the *Chapter on Pilgrimage* (*Bāb fi'l-Ḥajj*)[261]

1051 – Abū Ḥanīfa, may God Most High have mercy upon him, was asked about the *muḥrim*-pilgrim who kills game, and for whom there is ruled, [as reparation] for this, an *ʿanāq*, or a *jafra*, or what passes for its like.[262] He said: there does not suffice [as reparation]—as pertains to the *hady al-ṣayd*—except what suffices for the *hady al-mutʿa*: the *jadhaʿ* of sheep, when it is large; or the *thaniyy* of goats, cows, and camels.[263] And what is above that does not recompense what is below that.	1051 - وَسُئِلَ أَبُو حَنِيفَةَ رَحِمَهُ اللّٰهُ تَعَالَى عَنِ الْمُحْرِمِ يُصِيبُ الصَّيْدَ، فَيُحْكَمُ عَلَيْهِ فِيهِ عَنَاقٌ أَوْ جَفْرَةٌ أَوْ شِبْهُ ذَلِكَ. فَقَالَ: لاَ يُجْزِئُ[264] فِي هَدْيِ الصَّيْدِ إِلاَّ مَا يُجْزِئُ فِي هَدْيِ الْمُتْعَةِ؛ الْجَذَعُ مِنَ الضَّأْنِ إِذَا كَانَ عَظِيمًا أَوْ الثَّنِيُّ مِن الْمَعْزِ وَالْبَقَرِ وَالإِبِلِ، فَمَا فَوْقَ ذَلِكَ لاَ يُجْزِئُ مَا دُونَ ذَلِكَ.
1052 – Don't you look to God's decree, to Him belong might and majesty, in His Book, on the reparation for [unlawful] game: «A *hady* brought to the *Kaʿba*» [Q.5:95]?	1052 - أَلاَ تَرَى إِلَى قَوْلِ اللّٰهِ عَزَّ وَجَلَّ فِي كِتَابِهِ فِي جَزَاءِ الصَّيْدِ: «هَدْيًا بَالِغَ الْكَعْبَةِ» [المائدة: 95].
1053 – And I asked Ibn Abī Laylā about that, and he said: It is sent [as sacrifice], even if it is [only] an *ʿanāq*, or a *ḥamal*.[265]	1053 - وَسَأَلْتُ ابْنَ أَبِي لَيْلَى عَن ذَلِكَ فَقَالَ: يُبْعَثُ بِهِ، وَإِنْ كَانَ عَنَاقًا أَوْ حَمَلاً.
1054 – Abū Yūsuf, may God have mercy upon him, said: He [Ibn Abī Laylā] embraced the *athar*-tradition regarding the *ʿanāq* and the *jafra*.[266]	1054 - قَالَ أَبُو يُوسُفَ رحمه الله: أَخَذَ بِالأَثَرِ فِي الْعَنَاقِ وَالْجَفْرَةِ.

(continued)

[261] Ḥassūn ed., vol. 9, pp. 178–80; ʿAbd al-Muṭṭalib ed., vol. 8, pp. 345–7.

[262] The *muḥrim* is a consecrated pilgrim, having entered a ritual state (*iḥrām*) for undertaking the greater pilgrimage (*ḥajj*), or the lesser (*ʿumra*). Among numerous norms pertaining to the *muḥrim* is a strict ban on hunting (*ṣayd*). The *ʿanāq* and *jafra* are usually understood to be goat kids or lambs, with the *jafra* having just been weaned and put to pasture and the *ʿanāq* somewhat older (though less than a year). For more on the ritual state of *iḥrām* and related rulings, see *MF*, s.v. "إحرام" (vol. 2, pp. 128–95; esp. §§160 ff., on hunting); *EI*², s.v. "Iḥrām"; *DJP*, vol. 1, pp. 381–90 (esp. 388–90, on hunting) and pp. 424–33 (on reparations for hunting); and Hallaq, *Sharīʿa*, p. 237.

[263] The *hady* is the animal offered to God, in the holy precinct (*ḥaram*), as expiatory sacrifice; the *hady al-ṣayd* is offered for breaking the ban on hunting, and the *hady al-mutʿa* is offered for incorporating the lesser into the greater pilgrimage. The *jadhaʿ* is usually understood to be a goat or sheep which has reached its second year, while *thaniyy* refers to similarly matured cows, camels, etc. For more on the *hady* see *MF*, s.v. "هدي" (vol. 42, pp. 231–52); and *EI*², s.v. "Hady".

[264] Here (and throughout) I have followed al-Afghānī in the Shaybānī version (يجزئ), rather than Ḥassūn and Maṭrajī (يجزي), or Būlāq, Najjār, and ʿAbd al-Muṭṭalib (يجزى).

[265] A *ḥamal* is a young ram.

[266] Referring to traditions (*āthār*) reported on certain Companions (see §1061, below; and al-Sarakhsī, *Mabsūṭ*, vol. 4, p. 93).

1055 – But Abū Ḥanīfa, may God have mercy upon him, said: Regarding that, all of it: its value. And he [Abū Yūsuf] embraced it.[267]	1055 - وَقَالَ أَبُو حَنِيفَةَ رحمه الله: فِي ذَلِكَ كُلِّهِ قِيمَتُهُ. وَبِهِ يَأْخُذُ.
1056 – Al-Shāfiʿī, may God Most High have mercy upon him, said: When a man kills small game, he redeems it through sacrificing a small sheep; because God, to Him belong might and majesty, says: «*mithlu*» [Q.5:95],[268] and the *mithlu* is the "like/equivalent" of what is redeemed through sacrifice. When it [the game] is large, then it [the sacrifice] is large. And when [game] redeemed through sacrifice is small, then it [the sacrifice] is small. And I do not know anyone who said: It is not allowed that small game be redeemed through sacrificing something small like it, of sheep—except that he has contradicted the Qur'ān, and the *āthār*-traditions, and the *qiyās*, and the *maʿqūl*-understanding.	1056 - قَالَ الشَّافِعِيُّ رَحِمَهُ اللّٰهُ تَعَالَى: وَإِذَا أَصَابَ الرَّجُلُ صَيْدًا صَغِيرًا فَدَاهُ بِشَاةٍ صَغِيرَةٍ؛ لأَنَّ اللّٰهَ عَزَّ وَجَلَّ يَقُولُ «مِثْلُ» [المائدة: 95] وَالْمِثْلُ مِثْلُ الَّذِي يُفْدَى. فَإِذَا كَانَ كَبِيرًا كَانَ كَبِيرًا. وَإِذَا كَانَ الَّذِي يُفْدَى صَغِيرًا كَانَ صَغِيرًا، وَلاَ أَعْلَمُ مَنْ قَالَ: لاَ يَجُوزُ أَنْ يُفْدَى الصَّيْدُ الصَّغِيرُ بِصَغِيرٍ مِثْلِهِ مِن الْغَنَمِ إلاَّ خَالَفَ الْقُرْآنَ وَالآثَارَ وَالْقِيَاسَ وَالْمَعْقُولَ.
1057 – And when he has claimed that game is forbidden, all of it; and claimed that the locust is redeemed through offering a dried date, or less than a dried date, due to its smallness and insignificance of value; and a feral cow is redeemed through the sacrifice of a cow, due to its largeness—how does he not claim that the small is redeemed through the sacrifice of the small, while he has offered a small thing in sacrifice for the small, and a large thing in sacrifice for the large; and God, to Him belong might and majesty, has said: «A compensation of the "like" of what he killed, from the grazing livestock» [Q.5:95]? On his part, he has done nothing but raise and lower according to the "like"—so how does he offer up a dried date, and not offer up an *ʿanāq*? And what do the sacrificial animals [for *ḥajj*-pilgrimage], and the *hady al-mutʿa*, and the compensation of game have to do with each other? Does he consider it the *qiyās* for the compensation of game, when the *muḥrim*-pilgrim kills a cow, to say: A sheep suffices him, just as it suffices one combining pilgrimages, or one sacrificing during *ḥajj*-pilgrimage? Or does he perform *qiyās* with it, when the *muḥrim*-pilgrim kills a locust, saying: nothing less than a sheep will suffice the *muḥrim*-pilgrim, just as nothing less than a sheep suffices one sacrificing during *ḥajj*-pilgrimage, or one combining pilgrimages?	1057 - وَإِذَا كَانَ يَزْعُمُ أَنَّ الصَّيْدَ مُحَرَّمٌ كُلُّهُ فَزَعَمَ أَنَّهُ تُفْدَى الْجَرَادَةُ بِتَمْرَةٍ أَوْ أَقَلَّ مِن تَمْرَةٍ؛ لِصِغَرِهَا وَقِلَّةِ قِيمَتِهَا. وَتُفْدَى بَقَرَةُ الْوَحْشِ بِبَقَرَةٍ لِكِبَرِهَا، فَكَيْفَ لَمْ يَزْعُمْ أَنَّهُ يُفْدَى الصَّغِيرُ بِالصَّغِيرِ وَقَدْ فَدَى الصَّغِيرَ بِصَغِيرٍ وَالْكَبِيرَ بِكَبِيرٍ. وَقَدْ قَالَ اللّٰهُ عَزَّ وَجَلَّ: «فَجَزَاءٌ مِّثْلُ مَا قَتَلَ مِن النَّعَمِ» [المائدة: 95] وَإِنَّمَا رَفَعَ وَخَفَضَ بِالْمِثْلِ عِنْدَهُ فَكَيْفَ يَفْدِي بِتَمْرَةٍ وَلاَ يَفْدِي بِعَنَاقٍ وَمَا لِلضَّحَايَا وَهَدْيِ الْمُتْعَةِ وَجَزَاءِ الصَّيْدِ، هَلْ رَآهُ قِيَاسَ جَزَاءِ الصَّيْدِ حِينَ أَصَابَ الْمُحْرِمُ الْبَقَرَةَ بِأَنْ قَالَ: يَكْفِيهِ شَاةٌ كَمَا يَكْفِي الْمُتَمَتِّعُ أَوْ الْمُضَحِّي. أَوْ قَاسَهُ حِينَ أَصَابَ الْمُحْرِمُ جَرَادَةً بِأَنْ قَالَ: لاَ يُجْزِي الْمُحْرِمَ إلاَّ شَاةٌ كَمَا لاَ يُجْزِي الْمُضَحِّيَ وَالْمُتَمَتِّعَ إلاَّ شَاةٌ.

(continued)

[267] Al-Afghānī (in Abū Yūsuf, *Ikhtilāf*, p. 141, n. 2) considers this instance of "and he embraced it" (or, as it appears in his Shaybānī Version, "and we embraced it") a mistake, since Abū Yūsuf (and al-Shaybānī) disagreed with Abū Ḥanīfa regarding the sacrifice of *ʿanāq* and *jafra*, agreeing with him only for such game as does not reach them in equivalence (explained in al-Sarakhsī, *Mabsūṭ*, op. cit.) That these doctrine-embracing formulae appear in both Shaybānī and *Umm* Versions may be interpreted as indicating the authenticity of the former. Should one argue that al-Afghānī's Shaybānī Version was extracted from the *Umm* Version by a later scholar, one would have to explain why this attribution of agreement with Abū Ḥanīfa—inconsistent with later reports on his companions—was not "corrected".

[268] Meaning "like" or "equivalent".

1058 – And if he says: No.	1058 - فَإِنْ قَالَ: لاَ.
1059 – It is said: Is it because the compensation of game—like God, Most Blessed, Most High, said—is «*mithlu*»; and the "like" is only small or large by the measure of what was killed?	1059 – قِيلَ: أَلأَنَّ جَزَاءَ الصَّيْدِ كَمَا قَالَ اللّٰهُ تَبَارَكَ وَتَعَالَى: «مِثْلُ» وَإِنَّمَا الْمِثْلُ صَغِيرًا أَوْ كَبِيرًا عَلَى قَدْرِ الْمُصَابِ.
1060 – And if he says: Yes.	1060 - فَإِنْ قَالَ: نَعَمْ.
1061 – It is said: Then what leads you away from the *jafra*, when it is "like" what was killed? And if you were following the doctrine of ʿUmar b. al-Khaṭṭāb—may God Most High be pleased with him—alone, regarding a case for no part of which you have any argument, apart from following his example—how have you come to contradict him, and, along with him, the Qur'ān, and the *qiyās*, and the *maʿqūl*-understanding, and others of the Prophet's Companions, may God bless and save him? For ʿUmar, may God be pleased with him, has ruled an *ʿanāq* [as reparation] for the hare; and a *jafra* [as reparation] for the jerboa. And [as reparation] for the lizard, he ruled a goat-kid [old enough to have] gathered water and shrubs.[269] And Ibn Masʿūd, may God be pleased with him, has ruled a *jafra* or *jafras* [as reparation] for the jerboa. And ʿUthmān, may God be pleased with him, ruled a *ḥullān* of the sheep—meaning a small ram—[as reparation] for a chameleon.	1061 - قِيلَ: فَمَا أَضَلَّكَ عَنِ الْجَفْرَةِ إِذَا كَانَتْ مِثْلَ مَا أُصِيبَ. وَإِنْ كُنْتَ تُقَلِّدُ عُمَرَ بْنَ الْخَطَّابِ رضي الله تعالى عنه وَحْدَهُ فِي أَقْضِيَةٍ لاَ حُجَّةَ لَكَ فِي شَيْءٍ مِنْهَا إِلاَّ تَقْلِيدَهُ فَكَيْفَ خَالَفْتَهُ وَمَعَهُ الْقُرْآنُ وَالْقِيَاسُ وَالْمَعْقُولُ وَغَيْرُهُ مِن أَصْحَابِ النَّبِيِّ - صَلَّى اللّٰهُ عَلَيْهِ وَسَلَّمَ؟ وَقَدْ قَضَى عُمَرُ رضي الله عنه فِي الأَرْنَبِ بِعَنَاقٍ، وَفِي الْيَرْبُوعِ بِجَفْرَةٍ، وَقَضَى فِي الضَّبِّ بِجَدْيٍ قَدْ جَمَعَ الْمَاءَ وَالشَّجَرَ. وَقَضَى ابْنُ مَسْعُودٍ رضي الله عنه فِي الْيَرْبُوعِ بِجَفْرَةٍ أَوْ جَفْرٍ. وَقَضَى عُثْمَانُ رضي الله عنه فِي أُمِّ حُبَيْنٍ بِحُلاَّنٍ مِن الْغَنَمِ، يَعْنِي حَمَلاً.

In §1051, Abū Yūsuf reports a past petition: "Abū Ḥanīfa... was asked about (*su'ila... ʿan*)..."—providing indication that this *mas'ala* (#1) was the object of a "historical" dialectic, and presenting Abū Ḥanīfa's ruling and general substantive principle for the same: (1a) the *hady al-ṣayd* must be equivalent to the *hady al-mutʿa* (being a large *jadhaʿ* or *thaniyy*);[270] and (1b) "what is above that does not recompense what is below that" (*mā fawqa dhālika lā yujzi'u mā dūna dhālika*). As explained by al-Sarakhsī,[271] Abū Ḥanīfa's meaning is that whatever does not suffice for the *hady al-mutʿa* cannot be allowed to suffice for the *hady al-ṣayd*. The *hady*, in other words, can only ever be a *jadhaʿ* or *thaniyy*—so if the hunted quarry is not equivalent to the *jadhaʿ* or the *thaniyy*, it is not to be recompensed by way of either ("what is above does not recompense what is below"). And, since nothing less than *jadhaʿ* or *thaniyy* can be sacrificed, if the hunted quarry (e.g., a hare) is equivalent to something less than *jadhaʿ* or *thaniyy*, a lesser animal (e.g., *ʿanāq* or *jafra*) cannot be offered as reparation—instead, the value of the game must be estimated (see §1055), and its equivalent in fasting or food-distribution performed as expiation.

[269] That is, a kid which has been weaned and started to drink and graze on its own (see al-Māwardī, *al-Ḥāwī al-Kabīr*, Maʿʿūd, et al., eds., vol. 4, p. 284).

[270] Note this as a kind of *taswiya*-subsumption, though neither Abū Ḥanīfa nor al-Sarakhsī after him employ the *sawā'un* formula.

[271] *Mabsūṭ*, vol. 4, p. 93; quoted by al-Afghānī in Abū Yūsuf, *Ikhtilāf*, pp. 141–2, nn. 1–2.

In §1052, this is supported by an *aṣl*, introduced by a rhetorical *a-lā tarā* question, consisting of the patently *endoxon dalīl*-indicant of Q.5:95:[272] "Don't you look to God's decree… in His Book, on the reparation for [unlawful] game: «A *hady* brought to the *Kaʿba*»?" Not only does this constitute the *aṣl* of Abū Ḥanīfa's *istidlāl bi'l-Kitāb*, but—as will become clear—it is an *iʿtirāḍ* against Ibn Abī Laylā's "drawing indication from the saying of a solitary Companion" (*istidlāl bi-qawl al-wāḥid min al-Ṣaḥāba*), and corresponds to Shīr.IV.2 "[Q] counter-indicates it (*yuʿāriḍuhu*) with the unambiguous text (*naṣṣ*) of Qur'ān or Sunna" (*an yuʿāriḍahu bi-naṣṣ Kitāb aw Sunna*).[273]

Abū Yūsuf continues to relate this "historical" dialectic in §1053, telling us: "And I asked Ibn Abī Laylā about that…" (*wa sa'altu Ibn Abī Laylā ʿan dhālika*), and presenting the latter's counter-ruling: "It is sent [as sacrifice], even if it is [only] an *ʿanāq*, or a *ḥamal*." Note this as a negation of Abū Ḥanīfa's principle, which appears to be a form of *taswiya*-subsumption; and Abū Yūsuf provides Ibn Abī Laylā's supporting *naql* in §1054: "[Ibn Abī Laylā] embraced the *athar*-tradition regarding the *ʿanāq* and the *jafra*"—a reference to ʿUmar's practice which we encounter in §1061. Interestingly, al-Sarakhsī explains the reasoning for all of Ibn Abī Laylā, Abū Yūsuf, and al-Shaybānī in his *Mabsūṭ*,[274] claiming it to be "juristic preference" (*istiḥsān*) based on: (1) *naql* from the *āthār*-traditions of Companions; (2) an *a fortiori* argument; (3) an *iʿtirāḍ* that Abū Ḥanīfa is actually doing *qiyās*, and that it is "correlational inference of something [already] textually decreed by way of something textually decreed" (*qiyās al-manṣūṣ bi'l-manṣūṣ*); and (4) an argument that "*hady*" can in fact include the *ʿanāq* and other lesser offerings. Ibn Abī Laylā's reliance upon *āthār*-traditions of ʿUmar, whether combined with al-Sarakhsī's reported cocktail of *istiḥsān* or alone, constitutes an *iʿtirāḍ* against Abū Ḥanīfa's position—but not one which appears to have a parallel in our lens-texts.

In §1055 we learn no more of Abū Ḥanīfa's response than his asserted ruling for all that does not correspond to the *hady al-mutʿa*: "Regarding that, all of it: its value (*qīma*)"—i.e., the unlawfully slaughtered game must be estimated and its expiatory equivalent in fasting or food-distribution be performed. Abū Yūsuf's adherence to this ruling is announced, though it is incongruent with what is reported in the *Mabsūṭ*.

Al-Shāfiʿī's rulings and arguments for the larger *mas'ala* are laid out in §1056. In brief, if the unlawfully slaughtered game (*ṣayd*) is small, the expiatory sacrifice (*hady*) is small; and if the former is large, the latter is large. Significantly, his justification (introduced with "because") is *istidlāl* from the same Qur'ānic verse (Q.5:95) employed by Abū Ḥanīfa, but his exegesis (*tafsīr*) focus on a different *lafẓ*-

[272] Abū Ḥanīfa's *a-lā tarā* in §1052: rhetorical, bringing supporting evidence by way of an epistemically-authoritative, primary *aṣl*, brought to bear directly; the whole constituting a justification/ objection of *istidlāl bi-naṣṣ al-Kitāb / iʿtirāḍ* against *istidlāl bi-qawl al-wāḥid min al-Ṣaḥāba*, type 2 (Shīr.IV.2).

[273] al-Shīrāzī, *Maʿūna*, al-ʿUmayrīnī ed., p. 82. Cf. Ibn ʿAqīl, *K. al-Jadal*, p. 39, §208.

[274] Vol. 4, p. 93.

expression: that of «like (*mithlu*)»; he says: "the *mithlu* is the 'like/equivalent' of what is redeemed through sacrifice. When [the game] is large, then [the sacrifice] is large. And when [game] redeemed through sacrifice is small, then [the sacrifice] is small." Then al-Shāfiʿī sets the stage for a "historical-instructional" dialectic, stating his objection to Abū Ḥanīfa's position in no uncertain terms: "I do not know anyone who said: 'It is not allowed that small game be redeemed through sacrificing something small like it, of sheep'—except that he has contradicted the Qur'ān, and the *āthār*-traditions, and the *qiyās*, and the *maʿqūl*-understanding." Note this reference to "the *maʿqūl*-understanding," and that it is listed among authoritative source indicants along with Qur'ān, *āthār*, and *qiyās*.[275]

Being that al-Shāfiʿī's *istidlāl* focuses upon a different component of Abū Ḥanīfa's *dalīl*-indicant in Q.5:95, his *iʿtirāḍ* may be identified in the lens-texts as "Sharing the Indicant (*al-mushāraka fi'l-dalīl*); with respect to [its] most apparent meaning (*min jihat al-ẓāhir*)" (Shīr.I.4[.1]; Bāj.I.3.1.2)[276]—as supported by *āthār*-traditions, *qiyās*, and "the *maʿqūl*-understanding." In fact, al-Shāfiʿī's *mushāraka fi'l-dalīl* matches al-Bājī's subtype exactly—and, remarkably, al-Bājī employs a very closely related *mas'ala*—employing even the same verse Q.5:95—as his example case.[277] This convergence of *masā'il* provides strong evidence for a theory promoted by this current project: that early *jadal*-theory consists in part of a study and analysis of past dialectic.

In §1057, al-Shāfiʿī continues setting the stage for a "historical-instructional" dialectic, introducing a pair of his opponent's (R's) rulings—(1) a date, or less, for the locust, because it is small/not valuable; (2) a cow for a feral cow, because it is large/valuable—quite evidently intending these as *masā'il al-naqḍ*, and following up with a rhetorical question: "how does he not claim that the small is redeemed through the sacrifice of the small, while he has offered a small thing in sacrifice for the small, and a large thing in sacrifice for the large; and God, to Him belong might and majesty, has said: «A compensation of the "like" of what he killed, from the

---

[275] Cf. the discussion about *ʿaql* and *maʿqūl* for §651, above; the further instances in §1061, and §1411, below; and my final assessment of what al-Shāfiʿī means by these terms in Sect. 8.2.

[276] al-Shīrāzī, *Maʿūna*, al-ʿUmayrīnī ed., p. 44.; al-Bājī, *Minhāj*, Turkī ed., pp. 59 f., §114. Cf. Ibn ʿAqīl, *K. al-Jadal*, p. 28, §148.

[277] Al-Bājī's more refined typology not only hits the mark exactly, but his example *mas'ala* is closely related to the very *mas'ala* under consideration in §1051–61, and employs the same Qur'ānic *aṣl*. First he defines this subtype of *Kitāb*-oriented *iʿtirāḍ*: "Each one of them [R&Q] links [the *ḥukm*] to the verse by way of a different *lafẓ*-expression from that to which the other links it, and he gives preponderance to his *lafẓ*-expression." Then, he presents his example *mas'ala*. In brief: (1) the Mālikī R draws upon Q.5:95 [*lafẓ* #1] to support his opinion re: the penance (*kaffāra*) for the one who unlawfully kills game (*qātil al-ṣayd*) (=feeding the poor); and (2) the Shāfiʿī Q objects, saying he draws *ḥujja* from the same verse [but *lafẓ* #2] for his opinion (=the *hady* is the compensation for the *ṣayd*, not *kaffāra*).

grazing livestock» [Q.5:95]?" This stands out as a rhetorical charge of method-*naqḍ*: R's method is to apply the Qur'ānic "by the *mithl*" principle elsewhere, but he denies it in the *mas'ala* at hand. His inconsistency is then drawn out further with another rhetorical question: "he has done nothing but raise and lower according to the 'like'—so how does he offer up a dried date, and not offer up an *ʿanāq*?" Thus al-Shāfiʿī again objects to R's method-*naqḍ*, his inconsistent application of the otherwise observed Qur'ānic principle.

Al-Shāfiʿī's questions now turn dialectical,[278] as he finally initiates a "historical-instructional" sequence, asking R: "[1] what do the sacrificial animals [for *ḥajj*-pilgrimage], and the *hady al-mutʿa*, and the compensation of game have to do with each other? [2] Does he consider it (*hal ra'āhu*) the *qiyās* for the compensation of game, when the *muḥrim*-pilgrim kills a cow, to say: 'A sheep suffices him, just as it suffices one combining pilgrimages, or one sacrificing during *ḥajj*-pilgrimage?' [3] Or does he perform *qiyās* with it (*aw qāsahu*), when the *muḥrim* pilgrim kills a locust, saying: 'nothing less than a sheep will suffice the *muḥrim*-pilgrim, just as nothing less than a sheep suffices one sacrificing during *ḥajj*-pilgrimage, or one combining pilgrimages?'" With the first question, he at once tries to determine if R is not in fact doing *qiyās* from the *uṣūl* of (a) the sacrifice for *ḥajj* and (b) the *hady al-mutʿa*; for which he shows obvious disapproval. This is similar to al-Bājī's third dialectical question "about the *dalīl*-indicant for the opinion" (*al-su'āl ʿan dalīl al-madhhab*), for al-Shāfiʿī is in fact asking: "Are you doing *qiyās* from these?" The second and third questions function as a *reductio* argument, exposing the untenable absurdity which would result from this *qiyās*, when the *muḥrim*-pilgrim would have to (a) compensate a more valuable cow with a less valuable sheep, and (b) compensate a mere locust with a far more valuable sheep.

It is evident from these dialectical questions, and the rhetorical questions that proceed them, that al-Shāfiʿī is moving towards a larger objection of method-*naqḍ*. Now, he has entered the phase of premise gathering from his opponent; and, in §1058, R concedes the first with a simple "No." We understand from this that R is *not* doing *qiyās* from these *uṣūl*, and concedes the absurdities consequent to its application in the contingent—but possible—cases which al-Shāfiʿī has raised. Al-Shāfiʿī thus acquires his first premise for method-*naqḍ*.

In §1059 al-Shāfiʿī shifts his query to the more appropriate *dalīl*-indicant by way of what may again, and more strongly, be identified as al-Bājī's "question about the *dalīl*-indicant for the opinion" (*al-su'āl ʿan dalīl al-madhhab*); he asks: "Is it because the compensation of game—like God, Most Blessed, Most High, said—is «*mithlu*»; and the 'like' is only small or large by the measure of what was killed?" Thus he presses for his second premise for method-*naqḍ*; and, in §1060, he acquires

[278] They are answered, collectively, by R in §1058.

it through R's simple concession: "Yes." From this we understand that R is indeed practicing *istidlāl* from Q.5:95's *lafẓ*-expression of «*mithl*».

Finally, with both premises securely in hand, al-Shāfiʿī seals his method-*naqḍ elenchus* with a series of rhetorical questions and supporting counter-transmissions in §1061. First, he rhetorically confirms R's inconsistency of method: "Then what leads you away from the *jafra*, when it is 'like' what was killed?" Note that, once again, al-Shāfiʿī's *naqḍ*-procedure conforms well to the Aristotelian dialectical program of Q's gathering from R such premises as naturally lead to: (1) exposure of R's inconsistency; and (2) a conclusion equivalent to Q's own thesis.

Al-Shāfiʿī does not leave it there, however, but shuts off R's only remaining retreat, which, as we may have expected from Ibn Abī Laylā's support in §1054, would consist in claiming adherence to certain *āthār*-traditions. "And if," al-Shāfiʿī says, "you were following the doctrine of ʿUmar b. al-Khaṭṭāb... alone, regarding a case for no part of which you have any argument, apart from following his example—how have you come to contradict him, and, along with him, the Qur'ān, and the *qiyās*, and the *maʿqūl*-understanding,[279] and others of the Prophet's Companions...?" Inherent to this biting critique are several implications: (1) that R's only remaining path is to claim *istidlāl* from "the saying of a solitary Companion" (*qawl al-wāḥid min al-Ṣaḥāba*); (2) that even so R has contradicted that Companion; and (3) along with the narrated deeds of ʿUmar b. al-Khaṭṭāb he has contradicted several more authoritative *uṣūl*. Having already proven Qur'ān, *qiyās*, and, presumably, the "*maʿqūl*-understanding," al-Shāfiʿī subsequently recites no less than three traditions about ʿUmar b. al-Khaṭṭāb—all of which expose R's inconsistent *taqlīd* of him—and follows this with additional traditions about Ibn Masʿūd and ʿUthmān—both of which show R contradicted other companions.

In the end, this may be the most powerful *elenchus* al-Shāfiʿī achieves in the subject-text—for he has shown that R has contradicted *all* the relevant *uṣūl*. His refutation thus consists, overall, of several *iʿtirāḍāt*. Against R's *qawl al-wāḥid min al-Ṣaḥāba*: (1) *muʿāraḍa bi-naṣṣ al-Kitāb* (Shīr.IV.2);[280] and (2) twofold conveyance of *khilāf* from other Companions (Shīr.IV.3; Bāj.V.2).[281] Against R's *istidlāl bi'l-Kitāb*: (1) *al-mushāraka fi'l-dalīl* (*min jihat al-ẓāhir*; Shīr.I.4[.1]; Bāj.I.3.1.2);[282] and (2) method-*naqḍ*. Ultimately, the dominant charge is method-*naqḍ*; for R has conceded his application of Q.5:95's *lafẓ*-expression of «*mithl*» elsewhere, but been shown to ignore it in the *mas'ala* at hand, where it is just as relevant (and where it confirms al-Shāfiʿī's rulings).

[279] NB: again, *maʿqūl* appears in a list of "sources," this time Qur'ān, *qiyās*, and *āthār*.

[280] al-Shīrāzī, *Maʿūna*, al-ʿUmayrīnī ed., p. 82. Cf. Ibn ʿAqīl, *K. al-Jadal*, p. 39, §208.

[281] al-Shīrāzī, *Maʿūna*, al-ʿUmayrīnī ed., p. 82; al-Bājī, *Minhāj*, Turkī ed., p. 144, §298. Cf. Ibn ʿAqīl, *K. al-Jadal*, p. 39, §209.

[282] al-Shīrāzī, *Maʿūna*, al-ʿUmayrīnī ed., 44.; al-Bājī, *Minhāj*, Turkī ed., 59 f., §114. Cf. Ibn ʿAqīl, *K. al-Jadal*, 28, §148. See previous note re: Al-Bājī's illustration by way of this very *mas'ala*.

Masāʾil-Set #8

§§1067–1080 from the *Chapter on Blood-Money* (*Bāb al-Diyāt*)[283]

1067 – Al-Shāfiʿī, may God Most High have mercy upon him, said: And when a man kills a man with deliberate intent, and the slain has heirs—[both] minors and majors; then indeed Abū Ḥanīfa, may God Most High have mercy upon him, used to say: The majors have the right to kill their man[284] [in retaliation], if they desire.[285]	1067 - قَالَ الشَّافِعِيُّ رَحِمَهُ اللّٰهُ تَعَالَى: وَإِذَا قَتَلَ الرَّجُلُ الرَّجُلَ عَمْدًا وَلِلْمَقْتُولِ وَرَثَةٌ صِغَارٌ وَكِبَارٌ، فَإِنَّ أَبَا حَنِيفَةَ رَحِمَهُ اللّٰهُ تَعَالَى كَانَ يَقُولُ: لِلْكِبَارِ أَنْ يَقْتُلُوا صَاحِبَهُمْ إِنْ شَاءُوا.
1068 – But Ibn Abī Laylā used to say: They have no right to kill until the minors come of age. And he [Abū Yūsuf] embraced it.	1068 - وَكَانَ ابْنُ أَبِي لَيْلَى يَقُولُ: لَيْسَ لَهُمْ أَنْ يَقْتُلُوا حَتَّى يَكْبُرَ الأَصَاغِرُ. وَبِهِ يَأْخُذُ.
1069 – Abū Yūsuf transmitted to us, on the authority of a man, on Abū Jaʿfar, that al-Ḥasan b. ʿAlī,[286] may God be pleased with them both, killed Ibn Muljam [in retaliation] for ʿAlī.	1069 - حَدَّثَنَا أَبُو يُوسُفَ عَن رَجُلٍ، عَن أَبِي جَعْفَرٍ؛ أَنَّ الْحَسَنَ بْنَ عَلِيٍّ - رضي الله عنهما - قَتَلَ ابْنَ مُلْجَمٍ بِعَلِيٍّ.
1070 – And Abū Yūsuf said: And ʿAlī, may God be pleased with him, had minor children [at the time].	1070 - وَقَالَ أَبُو يُوسُفَ: وَكَانَ لِعَلِيٍّ رضي الله عنه أَوْلَادٌ صِغَارٌ.

(continued)

[283] Ḥassūn ed., vol. 9, pp. 182–4; ʿAbd al-Muṭṭalib ed., vol. 8, pp. 348–9.

[284] No edition attempts to explain Abū Ḥanīfa's peculiar identification of a family-member's murderer as the heirs' "*ṣāḥib*". I have simply rendered it as "man", avoiding the more positive connotations usually associated with this word.

[285] On intentional homicide (*qatl ʿamd*), retaliation (*qiṣāṣ*), blood-money (*diya*), and related rulings, see *MF*, s.v. "قتل عمد" (vol. 32, pp. 336–43), "قصاص" (vol. 33, pp. 259–78), and "ديات" (vol. 21, pp. 44–95); *EI*[2], s.v. "Ḳatl," "Ḳiṣāṣ," and "Diya"; *DJP*, vol. 2, pp. 478–514; and Hallaq, *Sharīʿa*, pp. 320–2.

[286] Al-Ḥasan b. ʿAlī (d.49/669) was the Prophet's grandson, son of ʿAlī b. Abī Ṭālib (d.40/661), and second Shīʿī Imam.

1071 – Al-Shāfiʿī, may God Most High have mercy upon him, said: When a man kills a man with deliberate intent, and [the slain] has heirs—[both] minors and majors, or absent majors; not one of them has the right to kill [in retaliation] until the minors reach the age of majority, and those absent are present, and whoever has a share in his inheritance—be it wife, or mother, or grandmother—agrees to the killing. And when they unite in agreement, they have the right to kill. But when they do not unite in agreement, they have no right to kill. And when this [latter] is the case; then whichever of the present majors who wishes may take his share of the blood-money from the property of the perpetrator, to the measure of his inheritance from the slain. And when he does so, the *walī*-agents of those absent have the right to take their portions from the blood-money on their behalf. And the *walī*-guardians of the minors must [do the same], because the [retaliatory] killing has passed and become property, and the *walī*-guardian of the minor has no right to call for [retaliation], when his taking of [the blood-money] is possible.	1071 - قَالَ الشَّافِعِيُّ رَحِمَهُ اللهُ تَعالَى: وَإِذَا قَتَلَ الرَّجُلُ الرَّجُلَ عَمْدًا وَلَهُ وَرَثَةٌ؛ صِغَارٌ وَكِبَارٌ أَوْ كِبَارٌ غُيَّبٌ، فَلَيْسَ لأَحَدٍ مِنْهُمْ أَنْ يَقْتُلَ حَتَّى تَبْلُغَ الصِّغَارُ وَتَحْضُرَ الْغُيَّبُ وَيَجْتَمِعُ مَنْ لَهُ سَهْمٌ فِي مِيرَاثِهِ؛ مِن زَوْجَةٍ أَوْ أُمٍّ أَوْ جَدَّةٍ عَلَى الْقَتْلِ، فَإِذَا اجْتَمَعُوا كَانَ لَهُمْ أَنْ يَقْتُلُوا. فَإِذَا لَمْ يَجْتَمِعُوا لَمْ يَكُنْ لَهُمْ أَنْ يَقْتُلُوا. وَإِذَا كَانَ هَذَا هَكَذَا فَلأَيِّهِمْ شَاءَ مِن الْبَالِغِينَ الْحُضُورِ أَنْ يَأْخُذَ حِصَّتَهُ مِنَ الدِّيَةِ مِن مَالِ الْجَانِي بِقَدْرِ مِيرَاثِهِ مِنَ الْمَقْتُولِ، وَإِذَا فَعَلَ كَانَ لأَوْلِيَاءِ الْغُيَّبِ وَعَلَى أَوْلِيَاءِ الصِّغَارِ أَنْ يَأْخُذُوا لَهُمْ حِصَصَهُمْ مِنَ الدِّيَةِ؛ لأَنَّ الْقَتْلَ قَدْ حَالَ وَصَارَ مَالاً، فَلاَ يَكُونُ لِوَلِيِّ الصَّغِيرِ أَنْ يَدَعَهُ وَقَدْ أَمْكَنَهُ أَخْذُهُ.
1072 – And if one should say: How have you arrived at this opinion—to the exclusion of other doctrines—when one of the Ahl al-ʿIlm[287] has said: Any of the heirs to the slain who endorses [retaliation], kills—even if the others pardon; and he sets it in the *manzila*-status of the *ḥadd*-punishments?	1072 - فَإِنْ قَالَ قَائِلٌ: كَيْفَ ذَهَبْتَ إِلَى هَذَا دُونَ غَيْرِهِ مِنَ الأَقَاوِيلِ وَقَدْ قَالَ بَعْضُ أَهْلِ الْعِلْمِ: أَيُّ وُلاَةِ الدَّمِ قَامَ بِهِ قَتَلَ وَإِنْ عَفَا الآخَرُونَ. فَأَنْزَلَهُ بِمَنْزِلَةِ الْحَدِّ.
1073 – And another of the Ahl al-ʿIlm said: The majors kill, and they don't wait for the minors?[288]	1073 - وَقَالَ غَيْرُهُ مِن أَهْلِ الْعِلْمِ: يَقْتُلُ الْبَالِغُونَ وَلاَ يَنْتَظِرُونَ الصِّغَارَ.
1074 – And another said: The boy kills, and they don't wait for the wife?	1074 - وَقَالَ غَيْرُهُ: يَقْتُلُ الْوَلَدُ وَلاَ يَنْتَظِرُونَ الزَّوْجَةَ؟
1075 – It is said: We have arrived at this opinion because it is the Sunna which ought not to be contradicted—or shares the like *maʿnā*-intension of the Sunna—and [it is] the *qiyās* based upon *ijmāʿ*.	1075 - قِيلَ: ذَهَبْنَا إِلَيْهِ أَنَّهُ السُّنَّةُ الَّتِي لاَ يَنْبَغِي أَنْ تُخَالَفَ أَوْ فِي مِثْلِ مَعْنَى السُّنَّةِ وَالْقِيَاسِ عَلَى الإِجْمَاعِ.
1076 – And if he says: Then where is the Sunna for it?	1076 - فَإِنْ قَالَ: فَأَيْنَ السُّنَّةُ فِيهِ؟

(continued)

[287] The "Folk of Knowledge," meaning, presumably, the most highly respected scholars.
[288] Note this is the position of Abū Ḥanīfa in §1067.

1077 – It is said: The Messenger of God, may God bless and save him, said: «If someone is killed, his folk [must select] between two choices: If they prefer they take up retaliation; but if they prefer, [they take up] the blood-money.» And when such is a ruling of the Messenger of God, may God bless and save him—that the heirs of the slain have the right to kill, and they have the right to take property—and the *ijmāʿ* of the Muslims is that blood-money is inherited—it is not lawful for an heir, that one who inherits along with him should block the inheritance,[289] nor even that an heir block himself from the inheritance. And this is the *maʿnā*-intension of the Qur'ān, in the decree of God, to Him belong might and majesty: «And whoever is excused for it, by his brother, [owes] something: compliance with the well-honored custom, and payment to him in kindness» [Q.2:178]. And this is written in the *Book of Blood-Money*.[290]	1077 - قِيلَ: قَالَ رَسُولُ اللّٰهِ - صَلَّى اللّٰهُ عَلَيْهِ وَسَلَّمَ: «مَنْ قُتِلَ لَهُ قَتِيلٌ فَأَهْلُهُ بَيْنَ خِيرَتَيْنِ: إِنْ أَحَبُّوا أَخَذُوا الْقِصَاصَ، وَإِنْ أَحَبُّوا فَالدِّيَةُ» فَلَمَّا كَانَ مِن حُكْمِ رَسُولِ اللّٰهِ - صَلَّى اللّٰهُ عَلَيْهِ وَسَلَّمَ - أَنَّ لِوُلَاةِ الدَّمِ أَنْ يَقْتُلُوا وَلَهُمْ أَنْ يَأْخُذُوا الْمَالَ، وَكَانَ إِجْمَاعُ الْمُسْلِمِينَ أَنَّ الدِّيَةَ مَوْرُوثَةٌ لَمْ يَحِلَّ لِوَارِثٍ أَنْ يَمْنَعَ الْمِيرَاثَ مَنْ وَرِثَ مَعَهُ حَتَّى يَكُونَ الْوَارِثُ يَمْنَعُ نَفْسَهُ مِنَ الْمِيرَاثِ، وَهَذَا مَعْنَى الْقُرْآنِ فِي قَوْلِ اللّٰهِ عَزَّ وَجَلَّ: «فَمَنْ عُفِيَ لَهُ مِن أَخِيهِ شَيْءٌ فَاتِّبَاعٌ بِالْمَعْرُوفِ وَأَدَاءٌ إِلَيْهِ بِإِحْسَانٍ» [البقرة: 178]. وَهَذَا مَكْتُوبٌ فِي كِتَابِ الدِّيَاتِ.
1078 – And we found what contradicts it from among the doctrines to contain no sound argument, due to what I described of the Sunna opposing them.	1078 - وَوَجَدْنَا مَا خَالَفَهُ مِنَ الأَقَاوِيلِ لاَ حُجَّةَ فِيهِ لِمَا وَصَفْتُ مِن السُّنَّةِ بِخِلاَفِهِمْ.
1079 – Moreover, I found their doctrine self-contradicting: since they claim to refrain from taking blood-money from the killer, being that only blood is [incumbent] upon him, not property. So if they claim that, if one of the heirs pardons, the blood transforms into property, they have not adhered to their doctrine, but have contradicted it.	1079 - وَوَجَدْتُ مَعَ ذَلِكَ قَوْلَهُمْ مُتَنَاقِضًا إِذْ زَعَمُوا أَنَّهُمْ امْتَنَعُوا مِن أَنْ يَأْخُذُوا الدِّيَةَ مِن الْقَاتِلِ؛ لأَنَّهُ إِنَّمَا عَلَيْهِ دَمٌ لاَ مَالٌ. فَلَوْ زَعَمُوا أَنَّ وَاحِدًا مِنَ الْوَرَثَةِ لَوْ عَفَا حَالَ الدَّمُ مَالاً، مَا لَزِمُوا قَوْلَهُمْ وَلَقَدْ نَقَضُوهُ.

(continued)

[289] That is, by going ahead with the retaliatory killing regardless of the co-heir's wishes.

[290] Ibn al-Nadīm attributes no *Book of Blood-Money* (*Kitāb al-Diyāt*) to al-Shāfiʿī. In fact, there are only two such titles in the whole of the *Fihrist*—one of which, intriguingly, is attributed to Muḥammad b. al-Ḥasan (*Fihrist*, p. 345). A search through the *Umm* compendium also reveals no such title. There is, however—in addition to the *Chapter on Blood-Money* (*Bāb al-Diyāt*) in our subject-text—a *Bāb al-Diyāt* in the *Kitāb Ikhtilāf ʿAlī wa ʿAbd Allāh b. Masʿūd* (Ḥassūn ed., vol.9, pt.14, 287 ff.), and another in the *Kitāb al-Radd ʿalā Muḥammad b. al-Ḥassan* (Ḥassūn ed., vol.10, pt.15, 141–50). The first contains little of relevance to the *mas'ala* at hand; the second: nothing of relevance whatsoever (though replete with extensive and complex debate in dialectical format). Perhaps the discussion most relevant to this current *mas'ala* is found in the *Kitāb Jirāḥ al-ʿAmd* under the subheading of *Wulāt al-Qiṣāṣ* (Ḥassūn ed., vol.7, pt.12, 43 ff., §§20980 ff., especially at §§20985–9).

1080 – And as for whoever said: It is like the *ḥadd*-punishment:[291] any one of the heirs who wishes may execute it, even if another pardons—they have [themselves] distinguished between [retaliation] and the *ḥadd*-punishment, since they claim the heirs can waive the [retaliatory] killing, while they claim they cannot waive the *ḥadd*-punishment. And they claim their settling for blood-money over [retaliatory] killing is permitted; while they claim their settling for property over the *ḥadd*-punishment is not.[292]	1080 - فَأَمَّا الَّذِينَ قَالُوا: هُوَ كَالْحَدِّ يَقُومُ بِهِ أَيُّ الْوَرَثَةُ شَاءَ، وَإِنْ عَفَا غَيْرُهُ فَقَدْ خَالَفُوا بَيْنَهُ وَبَيْنَ الْحَدِّ، مِن أَجْلِ أَنَّهُمْ يَزْعُمُونَ أَنَّ لِلْوَرَثَةِ الْعَفْوَ عَنِ الْقَتْلِ، وَيَزْعُمُونَ أَنَّهُ لاَ عَفْوَ لَهُمْ عَنِ الْحَدِّ، وَيَزْعُمُونَ أَنَّهُمْ لَوْ اصْطَلَحُوا فِي الْقَتْلِ عَلَى الدِّيَةِ جَازَ ذَلِكَ، وَيَزْعُمُونَ أَنَّهُمْ لَوِ اصْطَلَحُوا عَلَى مَالٍ فِي الْحَدِّ لَمْ يَجْزِ.

In §1067, Abū Ḥanīfa's ruling for the *mas'ala* at hand is presented: majors have the right to retaliation, without waiting for the minors. Several things are implied here, and confirmed by what follows. The first is that Abū Ḥanīfa's ruling stems from an *athar*-tradition (presented and explained in §§1069–70), and constitutes "drawing indication from the saying of a solitary Companion" (*istidlāl bi-qawl al-wāḥid min al-Ṣaḥāba*).[293] Second, a more general principle is implied: majors don't wait for minors to mature and speak their right; and this in turn cancels any consideration that the only property efficient in allowing retaliation is "all heirs of the victim (*wulāt al-dam*) agree to retaliation." As we will see, this constitutes an objection to Ibn Abī Laylā's position and supporting reasoning.

In §1068 we learn Ibn Abī Laylā's counter-ruling for the *mas'ala* at hand: "They have no right to kill until the minors come of age," and that Abū Yūsuf adhered to this. Although no *istidlāl* or argument is provided, we can again discern a more general principle: majors must wait for minors to mature and speak their right; and this in turn fixes singular efficiency for the property "all heirs of the victim agree to retaliation."[294] Both principle and property are counter to Abū Ḥanīfa's. Unfortunately, neither Ibn Abī Laylā's nor Abū Yūsuf's *dalīl*-indicants are provided.

Abū Yūsuf, however, provides *naql* support for Abū Ḥanīfa's opposing ruling in §1069: nothing less than the case of al-Ḥasan b. ʿAlī's retaliation against his father's murderer, undertaken, as Abū Yūsuf explains in §1070, while some of ʿAlī's children were still minors.[295] Such a dramatic historical event employed as an *aṣl*—albeit one with a surprisingly ambiguous *isnād*, depending upon an anonymous

[291] Referencing the anonymous scholar of §1072.

[292] Note this not only as a double instance of self-inflicted *farq*-distinction, but also a charge of method-*naqḍ*; the opponents acknowledge these distinctions elsewhere but ignore them in the case at hand.

[293] This is confirmed by al-Sarakhsī (*Mabsūṭ*, vol. 26, p. 174; al-Afghānī [p. 143–4, n. 2] quotes a portion of the relevant material in full).

[294] Compare Abū Ḥanīfa and Ibn Abī Laylā in the current *mas'ala* with their rulings in *mas'ala*-set #2, §§236–8, above.

[295] Mark this as another example of Abū Yūsuf "following the *ḥujja*" and practicing the "good dialectic"; here, he has supplied material to help explain the opposing position.

"man"—can hardly pass without comment.[296] It is possible that the assassination of ʿAlī at the hands of the proto-Kharijite Ibn Muljam—an event that forever altered the Islamic political, cultural, theological, and legal landscape—here provides an empirical weight to the argument, overshadowing the questionable chain of transmission provided by Abū Yūsuf for the event of al-Ḥasan's retaliatory killing. Abū Ḥanīfa's ruling, however, can be understood as justified by *istidlāl bi-qawl al-wāḥid min al-Ṣaḥāba*, and we might conjecture that Ibn Abī Laylā's *istidlāl* would constitute an objection in that domain. Note, however, that Abū Ḥanīfa speaks (§1067) in terms of heirs (*waratha*), and, as al-Shāfiʿī shows us, the principles and rulings with regard to minors and inheritance may lie at the root of *ikhtilāf*.

In §1071 al-Shāfiʿī expands the *mas'ala* to include absent majors, then rules on both: (1a) no major heirs have the right to retaliation until all minor heirs mature and give consent; (1b) no major heirs have the right to retaliation until absent majors are present and grant the same; and (1c) *all* who lawfully share in the inheritance of the deceased must be in agreement with regard to retaliation, or there is no right to such. This clarifies al-Shāfiʿī's conception of efficiency in the *mas'ala* at hand: the *ʿilla* of unity in agreement of all heirs is firmly asserted as concomitant with the *ḥukm* of right to retaliation: "And when they unite in agreement, they have the right to kill. But when they do not unite in agreement, they have no right to kill." No *aṣl* is supplied at this point, but al-Shāfiʿī proceeds to a set of subsidiary rulings for the eventuality that unanimous agreement is not achieved when there are still minor heirs: (2a) present majors may take the measure of their inheritance share in blood-money from the property of the perpetrator; (2b) should they do so, the minors' *walī*-guardians must do the same. This latter ruling is supported by an *ʿaql* argument, introduced by "because," and pointing out: (1) the possibility for retaliation has passed, and the case converted to one of property (the blood-money); and (2) *walī*-guardians cannot demand retaliation when taking blood-money is possible.

In §1072–4, al-Shāfiʿī initiates an "instructional" dialectic, with himself in the role of R, by introducing a string of dialectical questions from an anonymous opponent. The questions open with the formula: "How have you arrived at this opinion, to the exclusion of other doctrines..." (*kayfa dhahabta ilā hādhā dūna ghayrihi min al-aqāwīl*)—thus resembling al-Bājī's third question "about the *dalīl*-indicant of the opinion" (*al-su'āl ʿan dalīl al-madhhab*)—and they incorporate three counter-opinions belonging to that *endoxa* set of "the wise" (Ahl al-ʿIlm). The first (§1072) belongs to one of the Ahl al-ʿIlm who applies *manzila*-subsumption with regard to intentional homicide, treating it in the same light as *ḥadd*-penalties (*fa-anzalahu bi-manzilat al-ḥadd*), and thus allowing any of the heirs of the deceased to exact retaliation even if another pardons. The second (§1073) belongs to another, who allows majors to exact retaliation without waiting for minor heirs (thus

[296] Note also that it is a markedly Shīʿī *isnād*, depending on Abū Jaʿfar (Muḥammad al-Bāqir; 5th Ithnā ʿAsharī Shīʿī Imām, d. btwn. 114–126/732–743). Perhaps this is why al-Sarakhsī goes a step further and claims the retaliation was in fact ʿAlī's dying decree to his son Ḥasan (*Mabsūṭ*, op. cit.)

asserting Abū Ḥanīfa's position in §1067, and possibly referring to Abū Ḥanīfa himself). The third (§1074) belongs to one who allows the boy to exact retaliation without waiting for the wife.

Clearly, Q is intent on exposing al-Shāfiʿī's rulings as non-*endoxa*, but al-Shāfiʿī's *jawāb* in §1075 draws upon three higher sources in the hierarchy of epistemic authority (and thus, in the larger *endoxa*-set). He claims: "We have arrived at this opinion (*dhahabnā ilayhi*) because [1] it is the Sunna which ought not to be contradicted (*al-Sunna allatī lā yanbaghī an tukhālafa*)—or [2] shares the like *maʿnā*-intension of the Sunna (*fī mithl maʿnā al-Sunna*)—and [3] [it is] the *qiyās* based upon *ijmāʿ*." Thus al-Shāfiʿī responds to the anonymous Q's *su'āl ʿan dalīl al-madhhab* with three separate species of *istidlāl*: (1) *istidlāl bi'l-Sunna*; (2) *istidlāl* from "the like *maʿnā*-intension of the Sunna"; and (3) *istidlāl bi-qiyās al-ʿilla*, of the *jalī* type, where the *ʿilla* is known by way of *ijmāʿ* (Bāj.4.1.1.2).[297]

The first and third forms of *istidlāl* need little explaining, but the second requires clarification in the light of the *ḥadīth* brought in §1077. In brief, al-Shāfiʿī's second mode of *istidlāl* resembles al-Shīrāzī's "[Restrictive] Indicant of the Instruction" (*dalīl al-khiṭāb*)—especially that sort promoted by Ibn Surayj, and which depends upon the "conditional expression" (*lafẓ al-sharṭ*).[298] As we see in §1077, al-Shāfiʿī's Sunnaic decree (*qawl*)—in the form of a disjunction—thrice incorporates a *lafẓ al-sharṭ*; the *mas'ala* opens with "who" (*man*), and the subsequent disjunction of rulings twice incorporates "if" (*in*). I would hesitate to label al-Shāfiʿī's *istidlāl* as *dalīl al-khiṭāb*, however, since the Sunnaic *qawl* itself internally suggests "either X or ¬X"—i.e., it does not require an additional hermeneutic. What is certain, however, is that it constitutes an *aṣl*, and that both *aṣl* and al-Shāfiʿī's ruling for the *mas'ala* at hand incorporate a disjunction; and perhaps this is what al-Shāfiʿī's claim that the latter "shares the like *maʿnā*-intension of the Sunna" refers to.

In §1076, Q proceeds to his second dialectical question: "Then where is the Sunna for it (*fa-ayna al-Sunna fīhi*)?" This could likely be the first stage of an intended "demand for validation of the reports" (*muṭālaba bi-taṣḥīḥ al-akhbār*), and thus be identified among the *muṭālabāt* subsumed by the first type of al-Bājī's fifth dialectical question.[299] Al-Shāfiʿī complies in §1077: "The Messenger of God... said: «If someone is killed, his folk [must select] between two choices: If they prefer they take up retaliation; but if they prefer, [they take up] the blood-money.»" The disjunction here is plain, and, when al-Shāfiʿī combines it with an *ijmāʿ*-sanctioned ruling, justification of his ruling is clarified: "when such is a ruling of the Messenger of God... that the heirs of the slain have the right to kill, and they have the right to take property—and the *ijmāʿ* of the Muslims is that blood-money is inherited—it is not lawful for an heir, that one who inherits along with him should block the inheritance, nor even that an heir block himself from the inheritance." The heirs must either retaliate or take blood-money; blood-money is inherited; no heir can

[297] al-Bājī, *Minhāj*, Turkī ed., p. 26, §47.

[298] *Lumaʿ*, Mustū ed., p. 106.

[299] al-Bājī, *Minhāj*, Turkī ed., p. 40, §78.

deny another (or even himself) their lawful inheritance share; therefore, no heir can deny blood-money (by unilaterally exacting retaliation) from another heir. Plainly, the heirs must *all* act in concert—as present majors—in exacting retaliation, or *all* settle for blood-money—majors and minors alike.

This, al-Shāfiʿī then asserts, "is the *maʿnā*-intension of the Qur'ān" in Q.2:178. Note that he did not open his argument with this Qur'ānic indicant, as one might have expected due to the Qur'ān's highest-tier authority. The ambiguity of the verse may indicate why. First establishing his solution on Sunna and *ijmāʿ*, al-Shāfiʿī brings this verse as a final seal to his argument—implying through the process that his combination of Sunna and *ijmāʿ* play the role of interpreter (*mufassir*) to the verse. Any opponent to his interpretation of Q.2:178 would be referred back to Sunna and *ijmāʿ*; the ambiguity of the verse, however, prevents it from serving as primary indicant. The overall effect, however, is to assert a consistency and consonance of al-Shāfiʿī's ruling in the *mas'ala* at hand vis-à-vis God's Law, as revealed through the most authoritative *adilla*-indicants of Qur'ān, Sunna, *ijmāʿ*, and *qiyās*. Al-Shāfiʿī closes the dialectic by directing his reader/student to his *Book of Blood-Money* (*Kitāb al-Diyāt*), and, presumably, the more complete arguments therein.

In §1078, al-Shāfiʿī turns to an *iʿtirāḍ* of positions opposed to his arguments in the *Kitāb al-Diyāt* (and, presumably, here); there is no *ḥujja* in them, he tells us, due to the fact that the Sunna opposes them. This may be understood as several types of *iʿtirāḍ* aimed at the doctrines of the Ahl al-ʿIlm raised by Q in §§1072–4. Against the first of them, it is "Counter-Indication with a Divinely-Sanctioned Decree (*al-Muʿāraḍa bi'l-Nuṭq*)," whereby that scholar's *manzila*-subsumption is supplanted by unambiguous text (*naṣṣ*) from the Sunna (Shīr.VII.15.1; Bāj.IX.B.15.1).[300] Against the second, which is Abū Ḥanīfa's position—and thus may be assumed *istidlāl bi-qawl al-wāḥid min al-Ṣaḥāba* (from the *athar*-tradition about al-Ḥasan b. ʿAlī and Ibn Muljam)—al-Shāfiʿī's *iʿtirāḍ* constitutes that sister form of *muʿāraḍa*, where "[Q] counter-indicates it (*yuʿāriḍuhu*) with the unambiguous text (*naṣṣ*) of Qur'ān or Sunna" (Shīr.IV.2).[301] As for the third, however, the *istidlāl* of its proponent is entirely unknown, and so must its corresponding rejection remain.

Apparently against another opposing argument, whose details are now revealed in §1079, al-Shāfiʿī brings a charge of *tanāquḍ*, saying: "Moreover, I found their doctrine self-contradicting" (*wajadtu maʿa dhālika qawlahum mutanāqiḍ*), and laying out their contradictory premises: "[1] they claim (*zaʿamū*) to refrain from taking blood-money from the killer, being that only blood is [incumbent] upon him, not property. So if [2] they claim that, if one of the heirs pardons, the blood transforms into property [i.e., blood-money becomes the only option], they have not adhered to their doctrine, but have contradicted it (*mā lazimū qawlahum wa laqad naqaḍūhu*)." This is plainly an *iʿtirāḍ* of *tanāquḍ*, a purely logical self-contradiction, and marks

[300] al-Shīrāzī, *Maʿūna*, Turkī ed., p. 262, §147 [missing from al-ʿUmayrīnī ed.]; al-Bājī, *Minhāj*, Turkī ed., p. 201, §454. Cf. Ibn ʿAqīl, *K. al-Jadal*, p. 70, §327.

[301] al-Shīrāzī, *Maʿūna*, al-ʿUmayrīnī ed., p. 82. Cf. Ibn ʿAqīl, *K. al-Jadal*, p. 39, §208.

the third and final charge of this kind—at least which openly employs the term *mutanāqiḍ*—appearing in the subject-text.[302]

This particular charge is of some import, especially considering the use of the verb *naqaḍa* at the close of the section, al-Shāfiʿī's usage of *khālafa* and *khilāf* in the previous section, and his use of *khālafa* in the following section. This is suggestive of a more precise or even technical application of these terms, whereby, for example, *mutanāqiḍ* and *naqaḍa* are reserved for internal, logical contradictions (as in self-contradicting arguments), while *khilāf* and *khālafa* are reserved for such claims as contradict presumed *endoxa* sources or opinions. A comparison of the usage of (1) *naqaḍūhu* (as R's claim X vs. his own doctrine ¬X) in §1079, with (2) *khālafahu* (as the doctrines of group G vs. the *ijtihād*-sources of al-Shāfiʿī) and (3) *khilāf* (as Sunna vs. the doctrines of group G) in §1078, and (4) *khālafū baynahu* (*mas'ala* X) *wa bayna* (legal category Y) in §1080, goes some way towards bearing this out.[303]

Finally, in §1080, al-Shāfiʿī returns to the doctrine of Q's first opponent from the Ahl al-ʿIlm (in §1072), exposing the inconsistency of his applied doctrine with a charge of method-*naqḍ*. Whoever makes such a claim, he says, "have [themselves] distinguished between [retaliation] and the *ḥadd*-punishment (*faqad khālafū baynahu wa bayna al-ḥadd*)"—meaning they have been inconsistent regarding the application of their own *manzila*-subsumption—being that (1) "they claim the heirs can waive the [the retaliatory] killing [*ḥukm* A], while they claim they cannot waive the *ḥadd*-punishment [*ḥukm* ¬A];" and (2) "they claim their settling for blood-money over [retaliatory] killing is permitted [*ḥukm* B]; while they claim their settling for property over the *ḥadd*-punishment is not [*ḥukm* ¬B]." Thus, by simultaneously claiming *ḥukm* A for the legal category of the *mas'ala* at hand (retaliation), but *ḥukm* ¬A for the subsuming legal category (*ḥadd*-punishment); and *ḥukm* B for the legal category of the *mas'ala* at hand, but *ḥukm* ¬B for the subsuming legal category; these anonymous opponents have in fact *themselves* proven the invalidating distinction disallowing *manzila*-subsumption of retaliation under *ḥadd*-punishment for the *mas'ala* at hand. It is nothing less than a self-inflicted charge of *farq*; and, by drawing attention to it, al-Shāfiʿī's overall charge against these first opponents from the Ahl al-ʿIlm is one of method-*naqḍ*: for they have observed the *farq* in these other cases he has just raised, but ignored it and gone ahead with their *manzila*-subsumption in the *mas'ala* at hand.

---

[302] Cf. §§102 and 469.

[303] It may even be that *mutanāqiḍ* and *naqaḍa* convey a sense of "being contradictory to," while *khilāf* and *khālafa* convey "being contrary to." Any confirmation or denial of this assertion, however, will require a great deal more of searching and comparison throughout the *Umm* and other works. For the present, I will note that all but two of the 28 occurrences of *mutanāqiḍ* in the *Umm* compendium are employed as descriptors of a doctrine (*qawl*), as in the basic formula: "and regarding this you have professed a self-contradicting doctrine" (*wa qulta fī hādhā qawlan mutanāqiḍan*). Interestingly, the term *mutanāqiḍ* does not appear in the *Risāla*, and so may have escaped the notice of previous *Risāla*-centered studies of al-Shāfiʿī's legal theory.

Masāʾil-Set #9

§§1125–1131 from the *Chapter on Theft* (*Bāb al-Sariqa*)[304]

1125 – Al-Shāfiʿī, may God Most High have mercy upon him, said: And when a man confesses to theft a single time, and the theft is equivalent to ten dirhams or more; then indeed Abū Ḥanīfa, may God Most High have mercy upon him, used to say: I cut him.[305] And he used to say: If I don't cut him, I make him owe it as a debt, and there is no cutting for a debt.[306]	1125 - قَالَ الشَّافِعِيُّ رَحِمَهُ اللّٰهُ تَعَالَى: وَإِذَا أَقَرَّ الرَّجُلُ بِالسَّرِقَةِ مَرَّةً وَاحِدَةً، وَالسَّرِقَةُ تُسَاوِي عَشَرَةَ دَرَاهِمَ فَصَاعِدًا، فَإِنَّ أَبَا حَنِيفَةَ رَحِمَهُ اللّٰهُ تَعَالَى كَانَ يَقُولُ: أَقْطَعُهُ. وَيَقُولُ: إِنْ لَمْ أَقْطَعْهُ جَعَلْتُهُ عَلَيْهِ دَيْنًا وَلَا قَطْعَ فِي الدَّيْنِ.
1126 – But Ibn Abī Laylā used to say: I don't cut him until he confesses twice. And he [Abū Yūsuf] embraced this [doctrine]. Then he reverted to the doctrine of Abū Ḥanīfa.	1126 - وَكَانَ ابْنُ أَبِي لَيْلَى يَقُولُ: لَا أَقْطَعُهُ حَتَّى يُقِرَّ مَرَّتَيْنِ. وَبِهَذَا يَأْخُذُ. ثُمَّ رَجَعَ إِلَى قَوْلِ أَبِي حَنِيفَةَ.
1127 – Al-Shāfiʿī, may God Most High have mercy upon him, said: And when a man confesses to theft a single time, and stands by the confession, and [the theft] is such as requires amputation of the hand; he is cut. And it is one and the same whether his confession was one time or more.	1127 - قَالَ الشَّافِعِيُّ رَحِمَهُ اللّٰهُ تَعَالَى: وَإِذَا أَقَرَّ الرَّجُلُ بِالسَّرِقَةِ مَرَّةً وَاحِدَةً وَثَبَتَ عَلَى الْإِقْرَارِ وَكَانَتْ مِمَّا تُقْطَعُ فِيهِ الْيَدُ قُطِعَ، وَسَوَاءٌ إِقْرَارُهُ مَرَّةً أَوْ أَكْثَرَ.
1128 – And if one should say: Just as I do not cut him except by way of two witnesses.	1128 - فَإِنْ قَالَ قَائِلٌ: كَمَا لَا أَقْطَعُهُ إِلَّا بِشَاهِدَيْنِ.
1129 – Then he, when two witnesses testify against him, cuts him, and pays no heed to his recanting if he has confessed. And yet—even if he confesses before him one hundred times, then recants—he does not cut him.	1129 - فَهُوَ إِذَا شَهِدَ عَلَيْهِ شَاهِدَانِ قَطَعَهُ وَلَمْ يَلْتَفِتْ إِلَى رُجُوعِهِ لَوْ كَانَ أَقَرَّ، وَهُوَ لَوْ أَقَرَّ عِنْدَهُ مِائَةَ مَرَّةٍ ثُمَّ رَجَعَ لَمْ يَقْطَعْهُ.
1130 – And if one should say: And in like fashion, if the witnesses recant, we do not cut him.	1130 - فَإِنْ قَالَ قَائِلٌ: فَهَكَذَا لَوْ رَجَعَتِ الشُّهُودُ لَمْ نَقْطَعْهُ.

(continued)

304 Ḥassūn ed., vol. 9, p. 191; ʿAbd al-Muṭṭalib ed., vol. 8, p. 354.

305 Meaning: he rules amputation of the thief's hand.

306 On the divinely-sanctioned punishment (*ḥadd*) for theft (*sariqa*), and related rulings, see *MF*, s.v. "سرقة" (vol. 24, pp. 292–347); *EI*², s.v. "Sariḳa"; *DJP*, vol. 2, pp. 536–46; and Hallaq, *Sharīʿa*, pp. 316–18.

1131 – It is said: If the witnesses recant from the *shahāda*-testimony against him, then they return and testify against him for [the same thing from which] they had recanted; their *shahāda*-testimony is not accepted. But if he confesses, then recants, then confesses; it is accepted from him—for confession is different from *shahāda*-testimonies from start to finish.[307]	1131 - قِيلَ: لَوْ رَجَعَ الشُّهُودُ عَنِ الشَّهَادَةِ عَلَيْهِ ثُمَّ عَادُوا فَشَهِدُوا عَلَيْهِ بِمَا رَجَعُوا عَنْهُ لَمْ تُقْبَلْ شَهَادَتُهُمْ، وَلَوْ أَقَرَّ ثُمَّ رَجَعَ ثُمَّ أَقَرَّ قُبِلَ مِنْهُ، فَالإِقْرَارُ مُخَالِفٌ لِلشَّهَادَاتِ فِي الْبَدْءِ وَالْمُتَعَقَّبِ.

In §1125, Abū Ḥanīfa's rulings for the *mas'ala* at hand are presented; when the stolen object reaches the operative minimum value (*niṣāb*) of ten dirhams and the thief confesses once, he amputates the hand of the thief; and, whether he amputates or not, he makes the stolen property a debt (*dayn*) in the thief's obligation, which thereafter disallows amputation. In either case, a second confession has no efficiency. Ibn Abī Laylā's counter-ruling appears in §1126: "I don't cut him until he confesses twice;" and this, we learn, was the doctrine of Abū Yūsuf until he recanted and ruled according to Abū Ḥanīfa's position.[308] From this we may infer a counter-*ʿilla* in which only double-confession has efficiency.[309]

The *Mabsūṭ* of al-Sarakhsī[310] supplies the purported history and reasoning behind these rulings, including the following: (1) al-Shaybānī adhered to Abū Ḥanīfa's doctrine; (2) the ruling of Ibn Abī Laylā and Abū Yūsuf (double-confession) was general in nature, applicable also to wine-drinking; (3) a certain man (*bashar*) mentioned Abū Yūsuf's reversion to Abū Ḥanīfa's doctrine; (4) "Their [Ibn Abī Laylā's and Abū Yūsuf's] proof is what was narrated concerning ʿAlī... that a man confessed to theft twice before him, so he cut his hand... because it is a *ḥadd*-punishment of God Most High, so the number of confessions for it is determined by the number of the *shahāda*-testimony, as with the *ḥadd*-punishment for illicit sex (*zinā*) [which requires four witnesses, thus four confessions]... and, due to this, it is narrated about Abū Yūsuf that he stipulated two confessions in two different sessions;" (5) "But Abū Ḥanīfa and Muḥammad b. al-Ḥasan... drew their indicant (*istadalla*) from what was narrated about the Prophet... that he came to a thief and

[307] Here, "[X] is different from [Y], from start to finish" (*fa-[X] mukhālifun li-[Y] fi'l-bad' wa'l-mutaʿaqqab*). And compare, in §288 above, "So [X] is not allowed to be a *qiyās* based upon [Y], while [X] is divergent from [Y] from start to finish" (*fa-lā yajūzu an yakūna qiyāsan ʿalayhā wa huwa mufāriqun fi'l-mubtada' wa'l-mutaʿaqqab*). These formulaic phrases appear to serve as "final word" statements, closing a *farq*-distinction refutation of *qiyās*. A search for this formula (in its current form, ending with *mutaʿaqqab*) has only produced one additional instance, however, in the *Umm*; and this instance, though preserving the same sense of "from start to finish", does not occur in a context of *qiyās*-refutation.

[308] Mark this as another example of his truth-seeking ethic.

[309] From al-Shāfiʿī's anonymous opponent in §1128 we might infer that Ibn Abī Laylā's *aṣl* for double-confession is the *endoxon* ruling requiring two witnesses for theft (*sariqa*). R's position in §1128 is that of Ibn Abī Laylā in §1126, and he amputates only for two confessions, by *qiyās* on the basis of the *aṣl* of cutting only for two witnesses. This *aṣl* is signalled by "just as" (*kamā*) at the start of R's profession in §1128.

[310] Vol. 9, p. 182; quoted by al-Afghānī in Abū Yūsuf, *Ikhtilāf*, pp. 152–3, n. 1.

said: 'Did you steal? I can't imagine he stole.' And he said: 'I stole it.' So he ordered his cutting, but did not stipulate the number of confessions regarding it. And because the *shahāda*-testimony of the two witnesses, as pertains to punishments (*ʿuqūbāt*) is confirmed by a singular confession, as with retaliation (*qiṣāṣ*)... and we have explained that illicit sex (*zinā*) is special (*makhṣūṣ*) among its parallel cases (*naẓā'irihi*);" (6) "And in the book (*kitāb*) he [Abū Ḥanīfa] established an occasioning factor (*ʿallala*), saying: 'If I don't cut him for the first time, I don't cut him for the second time, because the property became a debt owed by him from the first confession, and he, by the second confession, [probably] intends the elimination of liability from himself by the cutting of his hand [which punishment is deemed to expunge the debt], and is suspected of that... and if the property still remains as it was I return it after the first confession, before the second confession—so how is the cutting incumbent upon him by the confession, after the return of the property? Don't you see/opine (*a lā tarā*) that, by way of *shahāda*-testimony, the cutting is not imposed upon him after the return of the property? And by way of confession [this is] more appropriate (*awlā*)..." [etc.]

With regard to Abū Ḥanīfa's ruling, several items are of note. First and foremost, his primary justification appears to have been *istidlāl bi'l-Sunna*, with reference to the Prophet's deed (*fiʿl*). Second, this was further supported by *qiyās* or *manzila*-subsumption: amputation belongs to the category of punishments (*ʿuqūbāt*), and so has the same witness/confession procedure as retaliation (*qiṣāṣ*), wherein a single confession confirms two witnesses. Third, we encounter an *iʿtirāḍ* against Ibn Abī Laylā's position (which rests on *qiyās* or *manzila*-subsumption of amputation under the category of *ḥadd*-punishments): *zinā* (whose linked testimony-confession requirements are transferred to theft by Ibn Abī Laylā) is in fact unique (*makhṣūṣ*) among its *ḥadd*-punishment parallels (*naẓā'ir*)—and thus unsuitable as an *aṣl* in matters of confession. Fourth, Abū Ḥanīfa's conception that a second confession has no efficiency since the first makes the stolen property a debt is confirmed, and further confirmed by the return of the stolen property, when still intact, after the first confession. And fifth, a rhetorical *a-lā tarā*, introducing a *mas'alat al-naqḍ* (after the property is returned, two witnesses cannot occasion amputation) further confirms that a second confession has no efficiency; which, in turn, is bolstered by an *a fortiori* assumption that double-confession is even more appropriate (*awlā*) than testimony for non-efficiency in the post-return scenario. Overall, a number of objections to Ibn Abī Laylā's position may be identified, including: (1) "[Q] counter-indicates it (*yuʿāriḍuhu*) with the unambiguous text (*naṣṣ*) of Qur'ān or Sunna" (*an yuʿāriḍahu bi-naṣṣ Kitāb aw Sunna*) against Ibn Abī Laylā's *istidlāl bi-qawl al-wāḥid min al-Ṣaḥāba* (Shīr.IV.2);[311] (2) *muʿāraḍa* of *qiyās* by *qiyās* (al-Baṣrī), or *al-muʿāraḍa bi-ʿilla mubtada'a* against Ibn Abī Laylā's *istidlāl*

[311] al-Shīrāzī, *Maʿūna*, al-ʿUmayrīnī ed., p. 82. Cf. Ibn ʿAqīl, *K. al-Jadal*, p. 39, §208.

bi-qiyās al-ʿilla (Shīr.VII.15.2.1; Bāj.IX.B.15.2.1);[312] and (3) *naqḍ* against Ibn Abī Laylā's *istidlāl bi-qiyās al-ʿilla*: (Shīr.VII.7; Bāj.IX.B.11.1).[313]

As for Ibn Abī Laylā's position (and Abū Yūsuf's old position), the following is of note: (1) one of Ibn Abī Laylā's *dalīl*-indicants is an *athar*-tradition narrating a deed of ʿAlī (and thus constitutes *istidlāl bi-qawl al-wāḥid min al-Ṣaḥāba*); and (2) Ibn Abī Laylā also justified his ruling via counter-*qiyās* or *manzila*-subsumption, arguing that theft belongs to the category of *ḥadd*-punishments, so its witness/confession procedure parallels that of *zinā* in that the number of witnesses required equals the number of confessions required. Thus, certain objections against Abū Ḥanīfa's position may be identified: (1) either "abrogation by way of the contradictory doings of the Companions (*al-naskh bi-ʿamal al-Ṣaḥāba bi-khilāfihi*)" (Shīr.II.C.6.3; Bāj.II.2.5.3)[314] or *muʿāraḍat* [al-Sunna] *bi'l-ʿilla* (Shīr.II.C.8.2; Bāj.II.2.7.2)[315] against Abū Ḥanīfa's *istidlāl bi'l-Sunna*; and (2) *muʿāraḍa* of *qiyās* by *qiyās* (al-Baṣrī), or *al-muʿāraḍa bi-ʿilla mubtada'a* (Shīr.VII.15.2.1; Bāj.IX.B.15.2.1)[316] against Abū Ḥanīfa's *istidlāl bi-qiyās al-ʿilla*.

Al-Shāfiʿī's ruling for the *mas'ala* at hand is presented in §1127: the thief's hand is amputated for a single, un-retracted confession. This is followed by a statement of *taswiya*-subsumption: "And it is one and the same (*wa sawā'un*) whether his confession was one time or more." Al-Shāfiʿī immediately initiates an "instructional" dialectic with an anonymous opponent in §1128, leading off with the opponent's counter-doctrine *qiyās*—signalled by "just as X" (*kamā* X): "And if one should say: Just as I do not cut him except by way of two witnesses." In other words, the opponent justifies his ruling for double-confession by way of *qiyās* from the *aṣl* of witness requirements for theft, which compares favorably to the reported indicants and arguments of Ibn Abī Laylā (and pre-recanting Abū Yūsuf) above. Al-Shāfiʿī's opponent considers the evidentiary requirements of *ḥadd*-punishments as parallels (*naẓā'ir*, s. *naẓīr*), which should mirror each other (as in Type II *qiyās al-dalāla*). Thus, if *zinā* (requiring four witnesses) requires four confessions, then *sariqa* (requiring two witnesses) requires two confessions.

In §1129 al-Shāfiʿī's objection to the opponent's *qiyās* is flatly stated to the reader—without the signal "it is said to him" (*qīla lahu*) formula. He says: "Then he, when two witnesses testify against him, cuts him, and pays no heed to his recant-

---

[312] al-Baṣrī, *K. al-Qiyās al-Sharʿī*, Ḥamīd Allāh ed., p. 1044; Hallaq, "Treatise," p. 221; al-Shīrāzī, *Maʿūna*, Turkī ed., p. 262, §148 [missing from al-ʿUmayrīnī ed.]; al-Bājī, *Minhāj*, Turkī ed., p. 201, §455. Cf. Ibn ʿAqīl, *K. al-Jadal*, p. 71, §330.

[313] al-Shīrāzī, *Maʿūna*, al-ʿUmayrīnī ed., pp. 104 ff.; al-Bājī, *Minhāj*, Turkī ed., p. 185, §§412–13. Cf. Ibn ʿAqīl, *K. al-Jadal*, pp. 56 ff., §§276 ff. This is al-Bājī's first type of *naqḍ*, against an *ʿilla* which is "posited for the genus" (*wuḍiʿa li'l-jins*)—for Ibn Abī Laylā's *manzila*-subsumption treats the witness/confession requirements for theft under the genus of *ḥadd*-punishments.

[314] al-Shīrāzī, *Maʿūna*, al-ʿUmayrīnī ed., pp. 63 f.; al-Bājī, *Minhāj*, Turkī ed., pp. 112 f., §219. Cf. Ibn ʿAqīl, *K. al-Jadal*, p. 35, §185.

[315] al-Shīrāzī, *Maʿūna*, al-ʿUmayrīnī ed., pp. 67 f., n. 6; al-Bājī, *Minhāj*, Turkī ed., pp. 123 ff., §§244 ff.

[316] See note above for Abū Ḥanīfa's identical objection.

ing if he has confessed. And yet—even if he confesses before him one hundred times, then recants—he does not cut him." Al-Shāfiʿī's point is that his opponent pays no heed to the recanting of a confession when there are two witnesses testifying against the accused thief (case #1)—recanting, in case #1, simply does not occasion aversion of the *ḥadd*-punishment. In case #2, however, his opponent makes recanting efficient in averting the *ḥadd*-punishment—even after a hundred previous confessions. Al-Shāfiʿī thus appears to be levelling a charge of "lack of efficiency" (*ʿadam al-taʾthīr*) against his opponent, in stages: (1) neither confession nor recanting occasions anything when there are two witnesses (thus the number of confessions is irrelevant); (2) when there are no witnesses, whether confession is made once or a hundred times, all are cancelled by a single recanting (the number of confessions is again irrelevant); (3) the property of "twice" seems therefore to have no bearing upon the efficiency of confession as an occasioning factor; and (4) thus, as al-Shāfiʿī has stated (§1127), one confession and multiple confessions are one and the same (*sawāʾun*). This most resembles the *iʿtirāḍ* of *ʿadam al-taʾthīr* (Shīr.VII.6.2; Bāj.IX.B.14.2),[317] twice levelled, for the opponent's evidentiary property (double-confession) is proven irrelevant to the efficiency of the *ʿilla*.

Note that al-Shīrāzī describes his type 2 as "*ʿadam al-taʾthīr* for a *waṣf* which, when it is removed from the *ʿilla*, the *ʿilla* is not destroyed;" and al-Bājī describes his type 2 as "regarding a *waṣf* for which the *ʿilla* is not destroyed by its elimination; this *waṣf* being called a 'stuffing' [*ḥashw*];" and Ibn ʿAqīl describes his as "when he mentions, regarding the *ʿilla*, a *waṣf* of which the *ḥukm* stands independent, without it." The descriptors supplied by our *jadal*-theory authors correspond quite closely to my interpretation of al-Shāfiʿī's objection in §1129. Notably, the *ʿilla* of confession (*iqrār*)—accepted as efficient by all jurists in this *masʾala*-set—is not harmed by al-Shāfiʿī's critique. Rather, he denies that attaching a number to the confession bears any relevance to the efficiency of confession; i.e., the number-*waṣf* is a mere "stuffing" on the part of his opponent.[318]

In §1130 al-Shāfiʿī continues the "instructional" dialectic, this time leading off with the opponent's second counter-doctrine *qiyās*—signalled by "And in like fashion X" (*fa-hākadhā* X): "And if one should say: And in like fashion, if the witnesses recant, we do not cut him." Notably, the opponent has clung to his *qiyās* or *manzila*-subsumption argument for the efficiency of number, by stating another ruling which binds the evidentiary requirements of testimony and confession for theft. Al-Shāfiʿī's *jawāb*—properly signalled this time by "it is said" (*qīla*)—appears in §1131, and constitutes a charge of invalidating distinction (*farq*): "If the witnesses recant from the *shahāda*-testimony against him, then they return and testify against him for [the same thing from which] they had recanted; their

---

[317] al-Shīrāzī, *Maʿūna*, al-ʿUmayrīnī ed., pp. 102 f.; al-Bājī, *Minhāj*, Turkī ed., p. 200, §452. Cf. Ibn ʿAqīl, *K. al-Jadal*, 70, §274.

[318] Al-Shīrāzī's second mode of *jawāb* to this *iʿtirāḍ* (*Maʿūna*, al-ʿUmayrīnī ed., p. 102) is of some interest, for it shows us a good strategy by which al-Shāfiʿī's opponent might have benefited, and the example *masʾala* belongs to a domain similar to that of our subject-text's *masʾala*-set above.

shahāda-testimony is not accepted. But if he confesses, then recants, then confesses; it is accepted from him." In this fashion al-Shāfiʿī introduces a *mas'alat al-farq*: when recanting witnesses return to testify again, their testimony is not accepted. But this is simply not the case for the legal category of the *mas'ala* at hand—for when a recanting confessor confesses again, his confession is accepted. Al-Shāfiʿī seals his destruction of the opponent's *qiyās* with a *farq*-confirming formula we have seen before: "confession," he tells us, "is different from *shahāda*-testimonies from start to finish" (*mukhālifun li'l-shahādāt fi'l-bad'i wa'l-mutaʿaqqabi*).[319]

Note that al-Shāfiʿī's sole preoccupation in §1129 and §1131 is the destruction of his opponent's *qiyās* or *manzila*-subsumption—it is a wholly destructive, not constructive, critique, first by way of *ʿadam al-ta'thīr* and then by way of invalidating *farq*-distinction. Al-Shāfiʿī does not bring a counter-*qiyās*, nor—as we have seen earlier (in §288; §622 ff.)—does he argue by way of a "hypothetical" *qiyās*. We do not, in fact, even learn the *aṣl* of al-Shāfiʿī's own *istidlāl* here. However, I will presume it to be the same Sunnaic *dalīl* upon which Abū Ḥanīfa is said (by al-Sarakhsī) to have depended. Thus, we may identify al-Shāfiʿī's overall objection as *muʿāraḍa bi'l-nuṭq*—his opponent's *qiyās* is simply to be supplanted by al-Shāfiʿī's Sunnaic *dalīl*-indicant. Al-Shāfiʿī, however, has undertaken the additional task of laying bare the problems—lack of efficiency for any number attached to the *ʿilla* of *iqrār*-confession; and *farq* between the *aṣl* of *shahāda*-testimony and the *farʿ* of *iqrār*-confession—inherent to his opponent's *qiyās*. Considering that his larger objection may be identified as *muʿāraḍa bi'l-nuṭq*, and not *muʿāraḍa bi-ʿilla*—beneath which we find the varieties of *farq*-distinction in our lens-texts—I will treat this particular instance of *farq*-distinction as unique—either to proto-system *jadal* in general, or to al-Shāfiʿī's particular dialectical style.

Masā'il-Set #10

§§1217–1232 from the *Chapter on Marriage* (*Bāb al-Nikāḥ*)[320]

1217 – And when the man marries off his daughter, while she is a minor, to the son of his brother, while he is a minor and an orphan in his care; then indeed Abū Ḥanīfa, may God Most High have mercy upon him, used to say: The marriage is lawful, but he has the *khiyār*-option [to nullify it] when he attains sexual maturity. And he [Abū Yūsuf] embraced it.	1217 - وَإِذَا زَوَّجَ الرَّجُلُ ابْنَتَهُ وَهِيَ صَغِيرَةٌ ابْنَ أَخِيهِ وَهُوَ صَغِيرٌ يَتِيمٌ فِي حَجْرِهِ، فَإِنَّ أَبَا حَنِيفَةَ رَحِمَهُ اللهُ تَعَالَى كَانَ يَقُولُ: النِّكَاحُ جَائِزٌ وَلَهُ الْخِيَارُ إِذَا أَدْرَكَ. وَبِهِ يَأْخُذُ.

(continued)

[319] Cf. §288, above.

[320] Ḥassūn ed., vol. 9, pp. 205–7; ʿAbd al-Muṭṭalib ed., vol. 8, pp. 364–6.

1218[a] – But Ibn Abī Laylā used to say: That [marriage] is not allowed to be imposed on him until he attains sexual maturity.	1218[a] - وَكَانَ ابْنُ أَبِي لَيْلَى يَقُولُ: لاَ يَجُوزُ ذَلِكَ عَلَيْهِ حَتَّى يُدْرِكَ.
1218[b] – Then Abū Yūsuf recanted, and said: When the *walī*-guardian does the marrying off, there is no *khiyār*-option [to nullify]—he is like the father.[321]	1218[b] - ثُمَّ رَجَعَ أَبُو يُوسُفَ وَقَالَ: إِذَا زَوَّجَ الْوَلِيُّ فَلاَ خِيَارَ وَهُوَ مِثْلُ الأَبِ.
1219 – Al-Shāfiʿī, may God have mercy upon him, said: The marriage of male minors is not permitted, nor of female minors, unless fathers marry them [fem.] off—and grandfathers, when they [fem.] don't have fathers, for they [grandfathers] are fathers. And if anyone else marries them off, then the marriage is cancelled, and they do not mutually inherit in it—even if they matured [together]. And if he consummates, and has sexual relations with her; the *mahr*-dowry belongs to her, and they are separated. And if he pronounces *ṭalāq*-divorce before the marriage is cancelled; his *ṭalāq*-divorce is not effected—nor his *ẓihār*-oath, nor his *īlā'*-oath; because she was never a wife to begin with.[322]	1219 - قَالَ الشَّافِعِيُّ رحمه الله: وَلاَ يَجُوزُ نِكَاحُ الصِّغَارِ مِنَ الرِّجَالِ، وَلاَ مِنَ النِّسَاءِ إِلاَّ أَنْ يُزَوِّجَهُنَّ الآبَاءُ وَالأَجْدَادُ إِذَا لَمْ يَكُنْ لَهُنَّ آبَاءٌ، فَإِنَّهم آباءٌ، وَإِذَا زَوَّجَهُنَّ أَحَدٌ سِوَاهُمْ فَالنِّكَاحُ مَفْسُوخٌ وَلاَ يَتَوَارَثَانِ فِيهِ، وَإِنْ كَبُرَا، فَإِنْ دَخَلَ عَلَيْهَا فَأَصَابَهَا فَلَهَا الْمَهْرُ، وَيُفَرَّقُ بَيْنَهُمَا، وَلَوْ طَلَّقَهَا قَبْلَ أَنْ يُفْسَخَ النِّكَاحُ لَمْ يَقَعْ طَلاَقُهُ وَلاَ ظِهَارُهُ وَلاَ إِيلاَؤُهُ؛ لأَنَّهَا لَمْ تَكُنْ زَوْجَةً قَطُّ.
[§§1220–23 introduce variant rulings and arguments for another *mas'ala*, *viz.* whether a man can marry both a woman and her step-mother]	
1224 – Al-Shāfiʿī said: And if one should say: Why did you assert that fathers marry off minors?	1224 - قَالَ الشَّافِعِيُّ: فَإِنْ قَالَ قَائِلٌ: لِمَ زَعَمْتَ أَنَّ الآبَاءَ يُزَوِّجُونَ الصِّغَارَ؟
1225 – It is said: Abū Bakr married off ʿĀ'isha—to the Messenger of God, may God bless and save him—while she was a girl of six or seven. And the Prophet, may God bless and save him, consummated the marriage while she was a girl of nine. So the two states—within which marriage and consummation occurred—were while ʿĀ'isha was a minor: one having no authority over herself.	1225 - قِيلَ: زَوَّجَ أَبُو بَكْرٍ رَسُولَ اللهِ - صَلَّى اللهُ عَلَيْهِ وَسَلَّمَ - عَائِشَةَ وَهِيَ بِنْتُ سِتٍّ أَوْ سَبْعٍ وَبَنَى بِهَا النَّبِيُّ - صَلَّى اللهُ عَلَيْهِ وَسَلَّمَ - وَهِيَ بِنْتُ تِسْعٍ فَالْحَالاَنِ اللَّذَانِ كَانَ فِيهِمَا النِّكَاحُ وَالدُّخُولُ كَانَا وَعَائِشَةُ صَغِيرَةٌ مِمَّنْ لاَ أَمْرَ لَهَا فِي نَفْسِهَا.

(continued)

[321] For expositions on the role of the guardian (*walī*) in marriage (*nikāḥ*), and related rulings, see *MF*, s.v. "نكاح," esp. §§66–115 on the *walī* (vol. 41, pp. 247–94); *EI*², s.v. "Nikāḥ" (esp. §I.3); *DJP*, vol. 2, pp. 8–19; and Hallaq, *Sharīʿa*, pp. 274–6. Schacht summarizes certain elements from §1217 ff. in his *EI*² entry on "Nikāḥ": "The father or grandfather... has the right to marry his daughter or granddaughter against her will, so long as she is a virgin (he is therefore called *walī mudjbir, walī* with power of coercion); the exercise of this power is, however, very strictly regulated in the interests of the bride. As minors are not in a position to make a declaration of their wishes which is valid in law, they can only be married at all by a *walī mudjbir*. According to the Ḥanafīs, on the other hand, every blood relative acting as *walī* is entitled to give a virgin under age in marriage without her consent; but a woman married in this way by another than her ascendant is entitled on coming of age to demand that her marriage be declared void (*faskh*) by the *ḳāḍī* . A bridegroom who is a minor may also be married by his *walī mudjbir*."

[322] For expositions on these variant forms of marriage dissolution and their associated rulings, see *MF*, s.v. "طلاق" (vol. 29, pp. 5–77), "إيلاء" (vol. 7, pp. 221–40), and "ظهار" (vol. 29, pp. 189–210); *EI*², s.v. "Ṭalāḳ"; *DJP*, vol. 2, pp. 71–120 (*ṭalāq*), pp. 121–6 (*īlā'*), and pp. 127–39 (*ẓihār*); and Hallaq, *Sharīʿa*, pp. 280–3 (*ṭalāq*) and pp. 286–7 (*īlā'* and *ẓihār*).

1226 – And more than one of the Companions of the Messenger of God, may God bless and save him, married off his minor daughter.	1226 - وَزَوَّجَ غَيْرُ وَاحِدٍ مِن أَصْحَابِ رَسُولِ اللهِ - صَلَّى اللهُ عَلَيْهِ وَسَلَّمَ - ابْنَتَهُ صَغِيرَةً.
1227 – And if one should say: When you permit this for fathers, and pay no heed to the *qiyās*, [saying] that contracting marriage over [the wishes of] a free female minor then giving her the right to *khiyār*-option is *not* permitted—because [1] the base form of the *nikāḥ*-contract only allows *khiyār*-option for slave women when their status transforms, but the status of the free person does not transform; and [2] it is not allowed that one contract over [their wishes] something from which they have an escape, and then compel them [to it]—then why shouldn't you determine the [ruling for] *awliyā'*-guardians by way of *qiyās* from fathers?	1227 - فَإِنْ قَالَ قَائِلٌ: فَإِذَا أَجَزْتَ هَذَا لِلآبَاءِ، وَلَمْ تَلْتَفِتْ إِلَى الْقِيَاسِ فِي أَنَّهُ لاَ يَجُوزُ أَنْ يُعْقَدَ عَلَى حُرَّةٍ صَغِيرَةٍ نِكَاحٌ ثُمَّ يَكُونَ لَهَا الْخِيَارُ؛ لأَنَّ أَصْلَ النِّكَاحِ لاَ يَجُوزُ أَنْ يَكُونَ فِيهِ خِيَارٌ إِلاَّ فِي الإِمَاءِ إِذَا تَحَوَّلَتْ حَالُهُنَّ، وَالْحَرَائِرُ لاَ تُحَوَّلُ حَالُهُنَّ، وَلاَ يَجُوزُ أَنْ يُعْقَدَ عَلَيْهِنَّ مَا لَهُنَّ مِنْهُ بُدٌّ، ثُمَّ يُلْزِمُهُنَّ فَكَيْفَ لَمْ تَجْعَلِ الأَوْلِيَاءَ قِيَاسًا عَلَى الآبَاءِ؟
1228 – It is said: Due to the separation between fathers and *awliyā'*-guardians, and to the father owning of the contract over his child what none other besides him owns of it.[323]	1228 - قِيلَ: لاِفْتِرَاقِ الآبَاءِ وَالأَوْلِيَاءِ وَأَنَّ الأَبَ يَمْلِكُ مِن الْعَقْدِ عَلَى وَلَدِهِ مَا لاَ يَمْلِكُهُ مِنْهُ غَيْرُهُ.
1229 – Don't you see/opine that [the father] contracts [marriage] over the [wishes of the] virgin, as a major, and it is not held back from her even if she disapproves—and neither the paternal uncle, nor the brother, nor any *walī*-guardian besides him has that right?	1229 - أَلاَ تَرَى أَنَّهُ يَعْقِدُ عَلَى الْبِكْرِ بَالِغًا وَلاَ يُرَدُّ عَنْهَا وَإِنْ كَرِهَتْ، وَلاَ يَكُونُ ذَلِكَ لِلْعَمِّ وَلاَ لِلأَخِ وَلاَ وَلِيٍّ غَيْرِهِ.
1230 – And if one should say: In fact we do not allow the father to contract [marriage] over the [wishes of the] virgin, as a major; but we treat him—for [both virgin] and non-virgin—like others of the *awliyā'*-guardians.	1230 - فَإِنْ قَالَ قَائِلٌ: فَإِنَّا لاَ نُجِيزُ لِلأَبِ أَنْ يَعْقِدَ عَلَى الْبِكْرِ بَالِغًا، وَنَجْعَلُهُ فِيهَا وَفِي الثَّيِّبِ مِثْلَ غَيْرِهِ مِنَ الأَوْلِيَاءِ.
1231 – It is said: Yet you treat his taking-possession of the virgin's dowry as a [true] taking-possession, while not giving that right to any *walī*-guardian besides him—except an executor-guardian of property. And you make his [marriage] contract over her [wishes], as a minor, lawful—she having no *khiyār*-option in it; while giving her *khiyār*-option if another *walī*-guardian besides him contracts [marriage] over her [wishes].	1231 - قِيلَ: فَأَنْتَ تَجْعَلُ قَبْضَهُ لِمَهْرِ الْبِكْرِ قَبْضًا وَلاَ تَجْعَلُ ذَلِكَ لِوَلِيٍّ غَيْرِهِ إِلاَّ وَصِيٍّ بِمَالٍ، وَتَجْعَلُ عَقْدَهُ عَلَيْهَا صَغِيرَةً جَائِزًا لاَ خِيَارَ لَهَا فِيهِ، وَتَجْعَلُ لَهَا الْخِيَارَ إِنْ عَقَدَ عَلَيْهَا وَلِيٌّ غَيْرُهُ.
1232 – And if [the father] were like the rest of the *awliyā'*-guardians, I would have made no distinction between him and the *awliyā'*. This is written in the *Book of Marriage*.[324]	1232 - وَلَوْ كَانَ مِثْلُ سَائِرِ الأَوْلِيَاءِ مَا كُنْتُ قَدْ فَرَّقْتُ بَيْنَهُ وَبَيْنَ الأَوْلِيَاءِ. وَهَذَا مَكْتُوبٌ فِي كِتَابِ النِّكَاحِ.

(continued)

[323] Al-Shāfiʿī's response once again illustrates the move of *farq*-distinction; a critical difference between fathers and other *awliyā'*-guardians renders *qiyās* untenable in this *mas'ala*.

[324] Al-Shāfiʿī seals his *elenchus* with what might be read as a snappish remark, then refers us to the details of his argument in another "book" (*kitāb*). As with other such references, one should note we are directed to *written* material. If this is al-Shāfiʿī's genuine voice, then his discourses, explications, and didactic dialectics (whether dictated or written by his own hand) must have been available for reference in his own time. Even if this is the voice of a later compiler/editor, it may

In §1217, Abū Ḥanīfa's rulings for the *mas'ala* at hand (the *walī*-guardian of an orphaned nephew marries him to his daughter, while both are minors) are presented: (a) such a marriage is permitted (*jā'iz*); and (b) the minor orphan has *khiyār*-option to nullify when he becomes a major. Al-Sarakhsī's report in the *Mabsūṭ*[325] once again explains much of the purported reasoning behind Abū Ḥanīfa's position. Among other things, we learn: (1) the *ḥujja* of Abū Ḥanīfa and proponents is Qur'ānic, being Q.4:3 (which enjoins the marriage of two, three, or four women in order to care for orphans), and its *maʿnā*-intension is interpreted to include the marriage of orphans, since "this decree can only be realized when the marriage of the female orphan is allowed;" (2) a preponderating exegesis (*ta'wīl*) of this verse is narrated on ʿĀ'isha; (3) a *ta'wīl*-interpretation for Q.4:127 is also narrated on ʿĀ'isha, which provides an indicant for allowing *walī*-guardians to marry off female orphans in their care; (4) the Prophet married off Bint Ḥamza while she was a minor; and (5) "thc *āthār* traditions allowing that are widespread (*mashhūra*), [reported] on ʿUmar, ʿAlī, ʿAbd Allāh b. Masʿūd, Ibn ʿUmar, and Abū Hurayra." Following this list of *uṣūl*, al-Sarakhsī proceeds to rational inference from them: "The *maʿnā*-quality is that he is [the female orphan's] *walī*-guardian after maturity (*bulūgh*), so he is her *walī*-guardian during the state of minority (*ḥāl al-ṣighar*)—like the father and grandfather. This is due to the efficiency (*ta'thīr*) of maturity (*bulūgh*) in removing guardianship (*wilāya*); so when he is made her *walī*-guardian *after* her maturity—by way of this reason (*sabab*) we know he is her *walī*-guardian during the state of minority—through it he apportions property [upon the death of the parent];" etc. Other arguments and indicants follow these.

Abū Yūsuf's original adherence to Abū Ḥanīfa's doctrine (he changes to a variant in 1218[b]) is also stated; and again, we learn much from al-Sarakhsī,[326] including the following: (1) *khiyār*-option after maturity is also the doctrine of Muḥammad

yet refer to a treatise written or dictated by al-Shāfiʿī himself and published in his day—it need have no bearing on al-Shāfiʿī's genuine authorship of that *kitāb*, nor of its prior availability. Certainly the title is found in the *Umm* compendium (see Ḥassūn ed., vol. 5, pt. 10, pp. 7–192). Moreover, there is another internal cross-reference to a *Kitāb al-Nikāḥ* in the *Umm*: in the *Book of Judgments* (*Kitāb al-Aqḍiya*; see Ḥassūn ed., vol. 8, pt. 13, p. 181, §25252); and, most importantly, no less than four more references to a *Kitāb al-Nikāḥ* in this current *Chapter on Marriage* of our subject-text (at §§1241, 1253, 1257, and 1268; see pt. 2 of my dissertation for translations). Some of these are quite specific in reporting the indicants and arguments of this *kitāb*. Returning to our current *mas'ala* (the *farq*-distinction between fathers and other *awliyā'*), we find—as promised—a more detailed discussion in the *Umm* compendium's *Kitāb al-Nikāḥ*. This *mas'ala*, in fact, receives its own subheading: "What has Come Down to Us Regarding Marriage [Contracted by] Fathers" (*Mā Jā'a fī Nikāḥ al-Ābā'*; see Ḥassūn ed., vol. 5, pt. 10, pp. 57–61, §§15394–15414), under which al-Shāfiʿī's indicants and arguments are laid out in full. Interestingly, no *Kitāb al-Nikāḥ* is attributed to al-Shāfiʿī by Ibn al-Nadīm; though it could certainly have been among the (only partially-listed) contents of his *Mabsūṭ* (as transmitted by al-Rabīʿ and al-Zaʿfarānī; see *Fihrist*, p. 353). Finally, it may be noteworthy that he does attribute one to al-Shaybānī (*Fihrist*, p. 345).

325 Vol. 4, p. 214 [mistakenly cited as p. 215 by al-Afghānī in Abū Yūsuf, *Ikhtilāf*, p. 169, n. 2].

326 Ibid., p. 215; quoted by al-Afghānī, p. 170, n. 1.

b. al-Ḥasan [al-Shaybānī], Ibn ʿUmar, and Abū Hurayra; (2) the recanting of Abū Yūsuf from this doctrine (as we see in §1218) is again stated, and his new doctrine (they have no *khiyār*-option) is said to be that of ʿUrwa b. al-Zubayr; (3) the argument of this latter (an example of *qiyās al-ʿilla*) is reported: "this is an *ʿaqd*-contract for a *wilāya*-guardianship merited by family relationship (*qarāba*), so the *khiyār*-option of maturity is not confirmed for it—like the *ʿaqd*-contract of the father and the grandfather;" etc. (other arguments follow).[327] Abū Yūsuf's argument thus resembles *manzila*-subsumption: the *walī*-guardian is in the *manzila*-status of the father, with regard to the marrying off of minor wards. The ruling for the minor married off by the father (no *khiyār*-option upon maturity) is therefore the ruling of the minor married off by the *walī*-guardian.

In §1218[a], Ibn Abī Laylā's counter-ruling for the *mas'ala* at hand is presented: the *walī*-guardian of a minor, orphaned nephew *cannot* marry him off until he becomes a major. Note that at this point, multiple modes of justification and objection may be inferred from the rulings of Abū Ḥanīfa and Ibn Abī Laylā, and the reported *istidlāl* and reasoning of the former. Abū Ḥanīfa's position involves *istidlāl bi'l-Kitāb* (Q.4:3 and Q.4:127) accompanied by preponderating exegesis (*ta'wīl*) for the determination of *maʿnā*-intensions, such *ta'wīl* in turn being justified by ʿĀ'isha's explanations (hence: *istidlāl bi-qawl al-wāḥid min al-Ṣaḥāba*) and the Prophet's reported deed (*istidlāl bi'l-Sunna*), and all this in turn given epistemic weight by the plurality of Companions who practiced it (constituting *ijmāʿ* of the Companions, or a mode of *tarjīḥ*). Collectively, this delivers a *maʿnā*-quality for the case under consideration (he is her *walī*-guardian *after* majority), which occasions a *ḥukm* (he is her *walī*-guardian *before* majority), and that *ʿilla-ḥukm* pair is linked to an *aṣl* (the father and grandfather). In the end, Abū Ḥanīfa's justification is *istidlāl bi-qiyās al-ʿilla*, and his objection to an opposing position would most likely be some mode of *muʿāraḍa bi-ʿilla*. Ibn Abī Laylā's supporting arguments are unknown, however, though we may infer that he believed the efficiency of majority in cancelling all but the father's marriage-guardian function applied equally to all non-father *walī*-guardians, and thus to their marriage-guardian function in their wards' minorities as well. If this is correct, Ibn Abī Laylā's justification/objection would constitute a counter-*istidlāl bi-qiyās al-ʿilla / muʿāraḍa bi-ʿilla*.

In §1218[b], we learn that Abū Yūsuf recanted from his adherence to Abū Ḥanīfa's ruling (b) in §1217, and determined that no *khiyār*-option was to be granted the married-off minor ward upon his/her majority. From al-Sarakhsī we learn he had adopted a new *qiyās al-ʿilla*—from the shared efficient property of "it is an *ʿaqd*-contract for a *wilāya*-guardianship merited by *qarāba*," which occasions a *ḥukm* of no *khiyār*-option, as in the *aṣl* of the father/grandfather. In fact, it is a stricter *qiyās* from the father/grandfather than that of Abū Ḥanīfa, moving towards full *manzila*-subsumption of the non-father *walī*-guardian under the father in

[327] NB: the formulation of this last argument—"This (*farʿ*) is an (*ʿilla*-property), so (*ḥukm*), like (*aṣl*)"—is precisely the same as we find in most example-*masā'il* brought by *jadal*-theorists a generation or so after al-Sarakhsī.

terms of marriage-guardian functions. The minor married off by the *walī*-guardian is in the *manzila* of the minor married off by the father. This in turn implies an *iʿtirāḍ* against Abū Ḥanīfa's *qiyās al-ʿilla*. Note first that a new *ʿilla* has been brought, so it cannot be identified as *qalb*, though it appears similar at first. Rather it appears to be a form of *muʿāraḍat al-ʿilla bi'l-ʿilla* (Shīr.VII.15.2; Bāj.IX.B.15.2),[328] though of a subtype difficult to determine.

Al-Shāfiʿī's rulings for the *mas'ala* at hand expand considerably beyond those of the previous jurists, but all derive from a singular primary ruling: "The marriage of male minors is not permitted, nor of female minors, unless fathers marry them off, and grandfathers... And if anyone else marries them off, then the marriage is cancelled (*mafsūkh*)." In terms of marriage-guardian functions, al-Shāfiʿī has made it clear that fathers/grandfathers stand alone. This implies an *iʿtirāḍ* against the positions of Abū Ḥanīfa and Abū Yūsuf in all rulings; and, as we see in subsequent dialectic, it is best described as "Counter Indication with a Divinely Sanctioned Decree (*al-Muʿāraḍa bi'l-Nuṭq*)" (in §1225) supported by *farq*-distinction (§§1228 ff.)

In §1224, al-Shāfiʿī initiates an "instructional" dialectic with an anonymous Q, who asks: "Why did you assert (*lima zaʿamta*) that fathers marry off minors?" Note this as al-Bājī's third question: "about the indicant for the opinion" (*al-su'āl ʿan dalīl al-madhhab*). It is the first stage in Q's pushing concession to his *qiyās*—linking other *walī*-guardians with fathers—by attempting to secure al-Shāfiʿī's acceptance of his *aṣl* (presumably the same as that employed by Abū Yūsuf). Al-Shāfiʿī's response in §1225, however, introduces a new Sunnaic *aṣl*: the practice of the Prophet and Abū Bakr with regard to the marriage of ʿĀ'isha; thus, his justification may be qualified as *istidlāl bi'l-Sunna*. Al-Shāfiʿī accompanies his Sunnaic *dalīl*-indicant with *tafsīr*-exegesis clarifying certain efficient properties inherent to it: (1) both marriage and consummation occurred while ʿĀ'isha was a minor; and (2) the state/condition (*ḥāl*) of ʿĀ'isha's minority is described as when she had "no authority over herself" (*lā amra lahā nafsihā*). Continuing his response in §1226, al-Shāfiʿī lends weight to his *dalīl*-indicant with further reference to the practice of the Companions, saying: "And more than one of the Companions of the Messenger of God... married off his minor daughter." This might be identified as either an appeal to *ijmāʿ* of the Companions, or as a form of *tarjīḥ* (Shīr.IX.2.1).

The "instructional" dialectic continues in §1227 where Q launches a multi-premise *iʿtirāḍ* which resembles nothing so much as a charge of method-*naqḍ*, however difficult the details are to decipher. The overall pattern is relatively clear, however. According to Q, al-Shāfiʿī has disregarded (or refuted) the *qiyās* (from the *aṣl* of slave women) that minors, married off against their wishes, should have *khiyār*-option when they become majors, because: (1) there is a *qiyās*-invalidating *farq*-distinction between the *aṣl* of slave women and the *farʿ* of free minors: "the status of the free person does not transform;" and (2) there is an apparent absurdity in compelling someone to a contract against their wishes while including a

[328] al-Shīrāzī, *Maʿūna*, Turkī ed., pp. 262 ff., §§148 ff. [missing from al-ʿUmayrīnī ed.]; al-Bājī, *Minhāj*, Turkī ed., pp. 201 ff., §§455 ff. Cf. Ibn ʿAqīl, *K. al-Jadal*, p. 71, §§330.

stipulation that they can annul it. Thus, having reaffirmed that there is no *khiyār*-option for minors married off by their fathers against their wishes, why won't al-Shāfiʿī extend the same ruling to other *walī*-guardians by way of *qiyās*?

Al-Shāfiʿī's response in §1228 takes the following form: (1) he claims an invalidating difference (*iftirāq*) between fathers and other *walī*-guardians; and (2) he claims the special status of fathers in "owning of the contract over his child what none other besides him owns of it." This constitutes an *iʿtirāḍ* of *farq*-distinction, as part of a larger *muʿāraḍa bi'l-nuṭq*. Note that the lens-texts do not consider this combination. *Farq*-distinction falls only under *muʿāraḍa bi'l-ʿilla*, and we might have expected al-Shāfiʿī to be setting the stage for some species of *muʿāraḍa* by way of *qiyās*. Once again, however, we find al-Shāfiʿī's preoccupation is not so much in promoting his *istidlāl* as in destroying Q's *qiyās*—his exposing of *farq*-distinctions is a destructive, not constructive, critique. Moreover, as we have seen previously in §§1129 ff., he brings neither counter-*qiyās* nor "hypothetical" *muʿāraḍa-qiyās* (nor will he later in this sequence). We have already encountered the *aṣl* of his *istidlāl*: the Sunnaic deed and supporting *āthār*-traditions mentioned in §§1225–6; and, with some conviction, I would identify al-Shāfiʿī's overall objection as a *muʿāraḍa bi'l-nuṭq*, in which Q's *qiyās* is to be supplanted by al-Shāfiʿī's Sunnaic *dalīl*-indicant. As far as identifying his charges of *farq*, however, we are in the same position as before; i.e., the varieties of *farq*-objection fall under the heading of *muʿāraḍat al-ʿilla bi'l-ʿilla* in the *jadal*-theory texts. Here, however, al-Shāfiʿī brings no counter-*ʿilla*, only *nuṭq*. I will therefore, as before, treat his *farq*-objection in conjunction with *muʿāraḍa bi'l-nuṭq* as something unique—either to himself, or to proto-system *jadal*.

In §1229, al-Shāfiʿī usurps the role of Q with an *a-lā tarā* question: "Don't you see/opine that [the father] contracts [marriage] over the [wishes of the] virgin, as a major, and it is not held back from her even if she disapproves—and neither the paternal uncle, nor the brother, nor any *walī*-guardian besides him has that right?" The charge inherent to the question may be interpreted as a dual strategy of *farq* and method-*naqḍ*, as the *a-lā tarā* introduces a *mas'ala* exposing both. It at once supports al-Shāfiʿī's destruction of the opposing *qiyās* via *farq*-distinction, and charges the opposing position with method-*naqḍ*: inconsistent observance of that *farq*-distinction.[329]

Note that, from the context, it is plain al-Shāfiʿī's *a-lā tarā* In §1229 was meant to be rhetorical for proponents of a certain doctrine set. The response in §1230, launched by a new "And if one should say" (*fa-in qāla qā'il*), thus marks an additional mini-sequence to cover the possibility of an opponent who does not subscribe to that doctrine. The new R of §1230, in fact, rejects al-Shāfiʿī's *mas'alat al-naqḍ*—it does not create a contradiction for him, because R rules the opposite for that *mas'ala*: "In fact we do not allow the father to contract [marriage] over the [wishes of the] virgin, as a major; but we treat him—for [both virgin] and non-virgin—like others of the *awliyā'*-guardians." This corresponds well with al-Shīrāzī's

[329] Al-Shāfiʿī's *a-lā tarā* in §1229: rhetorical, delivering a *mas'ala* of both *farq* and method-*naqḍ*; all as components of a larger *muʿāraḍa bi'l-nuṭq*.

first mode of *jawāb* against a charge of *naqḍ*: "[R] does not concede to the *mas'alat al-naqḍ*," and al-Bājī's first method against the most relevant *naqḍ* subtype (11.2.1): "[R] denies (*an yamnaʿa*) the *mas'alat al-naqḍ*."[330]

Al-Shāfiʿī nevertheless proceeds to elenchus in §1231, via the introduction of two additional *masā'il al-naqḍ*: (1) "you treat his taking-possession of the virgin's dowry as a [true] taking-possession, while not giving that right to any *walī*-guardian besides him—except an executor-guardian of property;" and (2) "you make his [marriage] contract over her [wishes], as a minor, lawful—she having no *khiyār*-option in it; while giving her *khiyār*-option if another *walī*-guardian besides him contracts [marriage] over her [wishes]." In other words: R is exposed as ruling A for fathers, but ¬A for other *walī*-guardians (except the executor-guardian of property); and (2) R is exposed as ruling B for minors married off by fathers, but ¬B for minors married off by other *walī*-guardians.[331] This constitutes a double-charge of method *naqḍ*, for R is now firmly exposed as having observed the *farq*-distinction elsewhere, but not in the *mas'ala* at hand; he has been inconsistent with his *qiyās* method.

In §1232 al-Shāfiʿī seals his *elenchus*, saying: "if [the father] were like the rest of the *awliyā'*-guardians, I would have made no distinction between him and the *awliyā'*." Thus al-Shāfiʿī reasserts the *farq*-distinction as general: the father is different from other *awliyā'* across all relevant *masā'il*. Note that a charge of *farq*-distinction, as an objection to *qiyās*, is a potent tool against claims of *manzila*-subsumption. Although neither Abū Yūsuf nor al-Shāfiʿī's anonymous opponent(s) ever claim that other *awliyā'* are "in the *manzila* of the father," their reasoning appears to be pushing in this direction (note especially how Abū Yūsuf formulates his recanting in §1218). This concern expressed by al-Shāfiʿī—that a *farq*-distinction must be generally observed, across legal genera—is something I will refer to in following discussions as "*farq*-extension."[332] Finally, al-Shāfiʿī closes the sequence by directing his students/readers to another of his writings, the *Book of Marriage* (*Kitāb al-Nikāḥ*), where, presumably, his arguments are laid out in more detail.

---

[330] al-Shīrāzī, *Maʿūna*, al-ʿUmayrīnī ed., p. 104; al-Bājī, *Minhāj*, Turkī ed., p. 185, §415; p. 186, §419 (this *jawāb* is further subdivided depending upon whether or not R actually has a *madhhab* regarding the *mas'alat al-naqḍ*; see §§420–2). Bearing in mind this is an "instructional" dialectic, we can see that al-Shāfiʿī is "covering all the bases" which his pupil might encounter in course of a disputation on this *mas'ala*. This charge of *naqḍ* would have been sufficient had R professed the same *ḥukm* as al-Shāfiʿī for the *mas'alat al-naqḍ*.

[331] NB: R is thus shown to be a proponent of Abū Yūsuf's position (cf. §§1217 and 1218b).

[332] See my analysis of §78 in Chap. 6.

Masā'il-Set #11

§§1310–1326 from the *Chapter on Unilateral Divorce* (*Bāb al-Ṭalāq*)[333]

1310 – When the husband apostatizes from Islam and becomes an unbeliever; then indeed Abū Ḥanīfa, may God have mercy upon him, used to say: His wife is irrevocably separated from him when he apostatizes—there can be no *Muslima* beneath a *kāfir*. And he [Abū Yūsuf] embraced it.[334]	1310 - وَإِذَا ارْتَدَّ الزَّوْجُ عَنِ الإِسْلاَمِ وَكَفَرَ، فَإِنَّ أَبَا حَنِيفَةَ رحمه الله كَانَ يَقُولُ: بَانَتْ مِنْهُ امْرَأَتُهُ إِذَا ارْتَدَّ، لاَ تَكُونُ مُسْلِمَةٌ تَحْتَ كَافِرٍ. وَبِهِ يَأْخُذُ.
1311 – But Ibn Abī Laylā used to say: She is his wife as she was, until he is called upon to repent. And if he repents, then she is his wife; but if he refuses, he is killed, and she has her inheritance from him.	1311 - وَكَانَ ابْنُ أَبِي لَيْلَى يَقُولُ: هِيَ امْرَأَتُهُ عَلَى حَالِهَا حَتَّى يُسْتَتَابَ. فَإِنْ تَابَ فَهِيَ امْرَأَتُهُ، وَإِنْ أَبَى قُتِلَ وَكَانَ لَهَا مِيرَاثُهَا مِنْهُ.
1312 – Al-Shāfiʿī, may God have mercy upon him, said: When a man apostatizes from Islam, the marriage contract of his wife is suspended. And if he returns to Islam before her waiting period is completed, then they are bound by the first marriage contract. But if her waiting period is completed before his return to Islam, she has been irrevocably separated from him. And *baynūna*-separation is an annulment without *ṭalāq*-divorce; and if he returns to Islam, and becomes engaged to her, this is not *ṭalāq*-divorce. And this is written in the *Book on the Apostate*.[335]	1312 - قَالَ الشَّافِعِيُّ رحمه الله: وَإِذَا ارْتَدَّ الرَّجُلُ عَنِ الإِسْلاَمِ فَنِكَاحُ امْرَأَتِهِ مَوْقُوفٌ؛ فَإِنْ رَجَعَ إِلَى الإِسْلاَمِ قَبْلَ أَنْ تَنْقَضِيَ عِدَّتُهَا فَهُمَا عَلَى النِّكَاحِ الأَوَّلِ، وَإِنِ انْقَضَتْ عِدَّتُهَا قَبْلَ رُجُوعِهِ إِلَى الإِسْلاَمِ فَقَدْ بَانَتْ مِنْهُ، وَالْبَيْنُونَةُ فَسْخٌ بِلاَ طَلاَقٍ. وَإِنْ رَجَعَ إِلَى الإِسْلاَمِ فَخَطَبَهَا لَمْ يَكُنْ هَذَا طَلاَقًا. وَهَذَا مَكْتُوبٌ فِي كِتَابِ الْمُرْتَدِّ.

(continued)

[333] Ḥassūn ed., vol. 9, pp. 219–21; ʿAbd al-Muṭṭalib ed., vol. 8, pp. 377–9.

[334] On apostasy (*ridda/irtidād*) and related rulings, see *MF*, s.v. "ردة" (vol. 22, pp. 180–201; esp. §44 re: the effects of apostasy on marriage); *EI*², s.v. "Murtadd"; *DJP*, vol. 2, p. 552; and Hallaq, *Sharīʿa*, pp. 319–20.

[335] Ibn al-Nadīm (*Fihrist*, p. 353) lists both a *Small* and *Large Book on the Apostate* (*Kitāb al-Murtadd al-Ṣaghīr* and *Kitāb al-Murtadd al-Kabīr*) among works attributed to al-Shāfiʿī; and, significantly, we find a *Large Chapter on the Apostate* (*Bāb al-Murtadd al-Kabīr*) in the *Umm* compendium (see Ḥassūn ed., vol. 7, pt. 12, pp. 587 ff.) We also find another reference in the *Umm* to a *Kitāb al-Murtadd*, under the last subheading—"On the Apostate" (*Fi'l-Murtadd*)—of a long *Book on the Ruling for Fighting Polytheists and the Problem of the Resident of an Enemy Polity's Property* (*Kitāb al-Ḥukm fī Qitāl al-Mushrikīn wa Mas'alat Māl al-Ḥarbī*; Ḥassūn ed., vol. 5, pt. 9, p. 481, at §15126). As for the current *mas'ala* of our subject-text, it is treated in the *Bāb al-Murtadd al-Kabīr*, at the opening of a subheading entitled *Property of the Apostate and Wife of the Apostate* (*Māl al-Murtadd wa Zawjat al-Murtadd*; Ḥassūn ed., vol. 7, pt. 12, p. 601, §§23701 ff.)

1313 – He said: And when the woman recants from the Ahl al-Islām[336] to polytheism; this, and the first category [as in §§1310–11], are one and the same according to both their doctrines [Abū Ḥanīfa's and Ibn Abī Laylā's], together. Except that Abū Ḥanīfa used to say: Islam is strongly urged upon the woman, and if she submits to Islam, she is left alone. But if she refuses, she is detained in prison until she repents—but she is not to be killed. Such has reached us on the authority of Ibn ʿAbbās, may God be pleased with them both.	1313 - قَالَ: وَإِذَا رَجَعَتِ الْمَرْأَةُ مِن أَهْلِ الإِسْلاَمِ إِلَى الشِّرْكِ كَانَ هَذَا وَالْبَابُ الأَوَّلُ سَوَاءً فِي قَوْلِهِمَا جَمِيعًا، غَيْرَ أَنَّ أَبَا حَنِيفَةَ كَانَ يَقُولُ: يُعْرَضُ عَلَى الْمَرْأَةِ الإِسْلاَمُ؛ فَإِنْ أَسْلَمَتْ خُلِّيَ سَبِيلُهَا. وَإِنْ أَبَتْ حُبِسَتْ فِي السِّجْنِ حَتَّى تَتُوبَ وَلاَ تُقْتَلُ. بَلَغَنَا ذَلِكَ عَنِ ابْنِ عَبَّاسٍ رضي الله عنهما.
1314 – But Ibn Abī Laylā used to say: If she does not repent, she is killed. And he [Abū Yūsuf] embraced it.	1314 - وَكَانَ ابْنُ أَبِي لَيْلَى يَقُولُ: إِنْ لَمْ تَتُبْ قُتِلَتْ. وَبِهِ يَأْخُذُ.
1315 – Then he reverted to the doctrine of Abū Ḥanīfa.	1315 - ثُمَّ رَجَعَ إِلَى قَوْلِ أَبِي حَنِيفَةَ.
1316 – How is she to be killed, when the Messenger of God, may God bless and save him, has prohibited the killing of women in wars—as pertains to the Ahl al-Shirk[337]—and this one [fem.] is like them?	1316 - وَكَيْفَ تُقْتَلُ وَقَدْ نَهَى رَسُولُ اللهِ - صَلَّى اللهُ عَلَيْهِ وَسَلَّمَ - عَن قَتْلِ النِّسَاءِ فِي الْحُرُوبِ مِن أَهْلِ الشِّرْكِ، فَهَذِهِ مِثْلُهُمْ.
1317 – Al-Shāfiʿī, may God have mercy upon him, said: And when the woman apostatizes from Islam; there is no *farq*-distinction between her and the man: she is called upon to repent, and if she repents... [no consequence]. But if not; she is killed, just as is done with the man.	1317 - قَالَ الشَّافِعِيُّ رَحِمَهُ اللهُ: وَإِذَا ارْتَدَّتِ الْمَرْأَةُ عَنِ الإِسْلاَمِ فَلاَ فَرْقَ بَيْنَهَا وَبَيْنَ الرَّجُلِ، تُسْتَتَابُ، فَإِنْ تَابَتْ، وَإِلاَّ قُتِلَتْ كَمَا يُصْنَعُ بِالرَّجُلِ.
1318 – And "one of the people"[338] disagreed with us regarding this, and said: The man is killed when he apostatizes, but the woman is not killed. And he based his argument on something he narrated on the authority of Ibn ʿAbbās—the likes of which the Ahl al-Ḥadīth do not confirm.	1318 - فَخَالَفَنَا فِي هَذَا بَعْضُ النَّاسِ فَقَالَ: يُقْتَلُ الرَّجُلُ إِذَا ارْتَدَّ وَلاَ تُقْتَلُ الْمَرْأَةُ. وَاحْتَجَّ بِشَيْءٍ رَوَاهُ عَنِ ابْنِ عَبَّاسٍ لاَ يُثْبِتُ أَهْلُ الْحَدِيثِ مِثْلَهُ.
1319 – And something with the like quality of that chain of transmission has been narrated about Abū Bakr al-Ṣiddīq, may God be pleased with him—that he killed women who had apostatized from Islam—but we do not see fit to base our argument on it, when its chain of transmission is of the sort the Ahl al-Ḥadīth do not confirm.	1319 - وَقَدْ رُوِيَ شَبِيهٌ بِذَلِكَ الإِسْنَادِ عَن أَبِي بَكْرٍ الصِّدِّيقِ رضي الله عنه أَنَّهُ قَتَلَ نِسْوَةً ارْتَدَدْنَ عَنِ الإِسْلاَمِ، فَلَمْ نَرَ أَنْ نَحْتَجَّ بِهِ إِذَا كَانَ إِسْنَادُهُ مِمَّا لاَ يُثْبِتُهُ أَهْلُ الْحَدِيثِ.

(continued)

[336] The "Folk of Islam," or Muslims.

[337] That is, the "Folk of Polytheism," or polytheists.

[338] Once again, *baʿḍ al-nās* refers to a proponent of an Iraqi position; significantly, however, the position (she is not to be killed) is that of Abū Ḥanīfa (and, eventually, of Abū Yūsuf), but *not* of Ibn Abī Laylā (another Iraqi). We might infer from this that "*nās*" had both more general (Iraqi) and particular (proto-Ḥanafī) nuances for al-Shāfiʿī.

1320 – And the one who disagreed with us based his argument on the fact that the Prophet, may God bless and save him, forbade the killing of women in the Dār al-Ḥarb.[339] And he ["one of the people"] said: When the killing of female polytheists, who do not believe, is forbidden; then it is all the more appropriate that the female believer who apostatizes from Islam should not be killed.	1320 - وَاحْتَجَّ مَنْ خَالَفَنَا بِأَنَّ النَّبِيَّ - صَلَّى اللهُ عَلَيْهِ وَسَلَّمَ - نَهَى عَن قَتْلِ النِّسَاءِ فِي دَارِ الْحَرْبِ، وَقَالَ: إِذَا نُهِيَ عَن قَتْلِ الْمُشْرِكَاتِ اللاَتِي لَمْ يُؤْمِنَّ، فَالْمُؤْمِنَةُ الَّتِي ارْتَدَّتْ عَنِ الإِسْلاَمِ أَوْلَى أَنْ لاَ تُقْتَلَ.
1321 – It was said to one of those who profess this doctrine: You have [also] narrated that the Prophet, may God bless and save him, forbade the killing of the elderly, and the killing of the labourer. And you have [also] narrated that Abū Bakr al-Ṣiddīq forbade the killing of monks. So have you considered [what would happen] if an elderly *shaykh* apostatized, or a labourer—would you desist from killing them? Or if a monastic-type apostatized;[340] would you desist from killing him?	1321 - قِيلَ لِبَعْضِ مَنْ يَقُولُ هَذَا الْقَوْلَ: قَدْ رَوَيْتَ أَنَّ النَّبِيَّ - صَلَّى اللهُ عَلَيْهِ وَسَلَّمَ - نَهَى عَن قَتْلِ الْكَبِيرِ الْفَانِي، وَعَن قَتْلِ الأَجِيرِ، وَرَوَيْتَ أَنَّ أَبَا بَكْرٍ الصِّدِّيقَ نَهَى عَن قَتْلِ الرُّهْبَانِ. أَفَرَأَيْتَ إِنِ ارْتَدَّ شَيْخٌ فَانٍ أَوْ أَجِيرٌ أَتَدَعُ قَتْلَهُمَا؟ أَوِ ارْتَدَّ رَجُلٌ رَاهِبٌ أَتَدَعُ قَتْلَهُ؟
1322 – He said: No.	1322 - قَالَ: لاَ.
1323 – It was said: Why not? Is it because the rule of killing for apostasy is a rule of killing for a *ḥadd*-punishment—which the governing administrator may not obstruct—divergent to the rule of killing polytheists in the Dār al-Ḥarb?	1323 - قِيلَ: وَلِمَ؟ أَلأَنَّ حُكْمَ الْقَتْلِ عَلَى الرِّدَّةِ حُكْمُ قَتْلِ حَدٍّ لاَ يَسَعُ الْوَالِيَ تَعْطِيلَهُ مُخَالِفٌ لِحُكْمِ قَتْلِ الْمُشْرِكِينَ فِي دَارِ الْحَرْبِ؟
1324 – He said: Yes.	1324 - قَالَ: نَعَمْ.
1325 – I said: Then how have you based your argument on the ruling of the Dār al-Ḥarb for the killing of women, but did not see it as *ḥujja* for killing the elderly, the labourer, and the ascetic?	1325 - قُلْتُ: فَكَيْفَ احْتَجَجْتَ بِحُكْمِ دَارِ الْحَرْبِ فِي قَتْلِ الْمَرْأَةِ وَلَمْ تَرَهُ حُجَّةً فِي قَتْلِ الْكَبِيرِ الْفَانِي وَالأَجِيرِ وَالرَّاهِبِ.
1326 – Moreover, you have said: We have the right to desist from the Ahl al-Ḥarb[341] after mastering them, and we do not kill them. But we do not have the right to desist from an apostate. So how has their disparity escaped you as regards the woman? And indeed the woman is killed—wherever the man is killed—for adultery and homicide.	1326 - ثُمَّ قُلْتَ: لَنَا أَنْ نَدَعَ أَهْلَ الْحَرْبِ بَعْدَ الْقُدْرَةِ عَلَيْهِمْ وَلاَ نَقْتُلَهُمْ، وَلَيْسَ لَنَا أَنْ نَدَعَ مُرْتَدًّا، فَكَيْفَ ذَهَبَ عَلَيْكَ افْتِرَاقُهُمَا فِي الْمَرْأَةِ؟ فَإِنَّ الْمَرْأَةَ تُقْتَلُ حَيْثُ يُقْتَلُ الرَّجُلُ فِي الزِّنَا وَالْقَتْلِ.

Abū Ḥanīfa's ruling for the first *mas'ala* is presented in §1310: the wife of the Muslim who apostatizes is immediately and irrevocably separated from him; and Abū Yūsuf's adherence is stated. Then in §1310, Ibn Abī Laylā's counter-ruling is put forth: she remains his wife until he is called upon to repent; if he does, the marriage resumes; if he refuses, she inherits after he is executed. Al-Sarakhsī's

[339] The "Abode of War," meaning the lands of combatant, non-Muslim polities.

[340] Meaning, presumably, a Muslim ascetic.

[341] The "Folk of War," meaning resident combatants of the Dār al-Ḥarb.

report on the reasoning behind these rulings includes the following:[342] (1) Ibn Abī Laylā reached his ruling through *qiyās* from an authoritative source-case (*aṣl*) wherein one of the spouses converts to Islam; (2) the Ḥanafī position is that apostasy (*ridda*) is incompatible with marriage (*tunāfī al-nikāḥ*), and "the objection of the incompatible reason for marriage (*iʿtirāḍ sabab al-munāfī li'l-nikāḥ*) is itself a compelling agency for the separation (*mūjib li'l-furqa*), like the one prohibited due to forbidden degrees (*al-maḥramiyya*)... and as for being of different religions (*ikhtilāf al-dīn*), it is not incompatible with marriage, being that initiation of marriage is allowed between a Muslim [male] and a "woman of the Book" (*kitābiyya*); likewise becoming a Muslim is not incompatible with marriage—for indeed marriage is a blessing (*niʿma*), and through Islam one's blessings are preserved; and due to this separation (*furqa*) does not occur [in this case] except through the *qāḍī*'s judgment, after the other's rejection (*ibā'*) [of Islam];" etc.

Importantly, we learn that for Abū Ḥanīfa: (1) "the objection of the incompatible reason for marriage is itself a compelling agency for the separation (*mūjib li'l-furqa*)"—i.e., it is an *ʿilla* for his *ḥukm* of immediate separation; (2) this is "like the one prohibited due to forbidden degrees (*al-maḥramiyya*)"—i.e., this is the *aṣl* to which that *ʿilla-ḥukm* pair is referred; and (3) Abū Ḥanīfa's justification is thus *qiyās al-ʿilla* from the *aṣl* of the *maḥramiyya*. Abū Ḥanīfa's *iʿtirāḍ* against Ibn Abī Laylā's *qiyās al-ʿilla* is thus strongly indicated, and may be easily identified in the lens-texts as "Invalidating Distinction by way of Correlational Inference of the Occasioning Factor (*al-Farq bi-Qiyās al-ʿIlla*)" (Shīr.VII.15.2.2.1); and "Invalidating Distinction by way of the Occasioning Factor of the Ruling (*farq bi-ʿillat al-ḥukm*)," (Bāj. IX.B.15.2.2.1.1).[343] As for Ibn Abī Laylā, we learn that his justification rests on *istidlāl bi'l-qiyās* as well, from the *aṣl* of the non-Muslim spouse who converts to Islam. His *iʿtirāḍ* against Abū Ḥanīfa's ruling would most likely consist, therefore, of the same type as Abū Ḥanīfa's against his own.

---

[342] *Mabsūṭ*, vol. 5, p. 49; partially quoted [though incorrectly cited as p. 59] by al-Afghānī in Abū Yūsuf, *Ikhtilāf*, p. 199, n. 1.

[343] al-Shīrāzī, *Maʿūna*, al-ʿUmayrīnī ed., [initial section missing, remainder on p. 116]; Turkī ed., pp. 262–3 §§149; al-Bājī, *Minhāj*, Turkī ed., pp. 202 f. §§459 f. As we read in the *Mabsūṭ*, the objection to Ibn Abī Laylā's position rests upon a *farq* between his *aṣl* (wherein *ikhtilāf al-dīn* is not itself an immediate *mūjib* for *furqa*) and the *farʿ* (wherein objection to *ridda* is itself a *mūjib* for *furqa*). The Ḥanafī position thus brings another *aṣl* (the *maḥramiyya*), wherein the same *ʿilla* (i.e., "it is an obstacle to *nikāḥ*" [a property of forbidden degrees in the *aṣl*, and of *ridda* in the *farʿ*]) is found. Thus the same *ḥukm* of immediate separation may be transferred to the *farʿ* (i.e., to the *mas'ala* at hand). This corresponds perfectly to al-Shīrāzī's objection of *al-farq bi-qiyās al-ʿilla* and al-Bājī's *al-farq bi-ʿillat al-ḥukm*. Note that al-Bājī provides a finer subdivision, according to whether the *maʿnā* (of the *aṣl*) is agreed or disagreed upon (by R and Q). We can see that in Abū Ḥanīfa's *iʿtirāḍ* of Ibn Abī Laylā's position (as culled from statements in the *Mabsūṭ*), there is agreement as to the *maʿnā* of Ibn Abī Laylā's *aṣl* — the disagreement lies in the *maʿnā* of the *farʿ*; thus we may make a very precise identification (Bāj.IX.B.15.2.2.1.1).

In §1312, we learn al-Shāfiʿī's larger ruling and more detailed subsidiary rulings for the first *mas'ala*. In brief: (1) the marriage contract is suspended (*mawqūf*); (2) the wife begins her waiting period (*ʿidda*); (3) if he repents before the *ʿidda* is completed, the first contract resumes; (4) if not, there is *baynūna*-separation; and (5) this latter is not considered as *ṭalāq*-divorce.[344] Al-Shāfiʿī then refers us to his *Book on the Apostate* (*Kitāb al-Murtadd*).

In §1313, we proceed to a group of rulings on a second but closely related *mas'ala*. First, we learn that both Abū Ḥanīfa and Ibn Abī Laylā maintain the same rulings as above with regard to the woman who apostatizes from Islam: "this, and the first category [as in §§1310–11], are one and the same according to both their doctrines, together (*kāna hādhā wa'l-bāb al-awwal sawā'an fī qawlihimā jamīʿan*)." I would mark this as a case of *taswiya*-subsumption in typical formulation. Abū Ḥanīfa rules a singular exception, however, for the woman apostate. Like the man, if she repents she is thereafter left alone (ruling 2a), but in the case she refuses to return to Islam "she is detained in prison until she repents—but she is not to be killed" (ruling 2b). This latter ruling (2b)—the subsequent focus of *ikhtilāf* and disputation—receives *naql* support in the form of an *athar*-tradition: "Such has reached us on the authority of Ibn ʿAbbās." We may identify Abū Ḥanīfa's justification as "drawing indication from the saying of a solitary Companion" (*istidlāl bi-qawl al-wāḥid min al-Ṣaḥāba*).

In §1314, we learn Ibn Abī Laylā's counter-ruling to (2b): "If she does not repent, she is killed." No arguments or indicants are mentioned, but it is plain that Ibn Abī Laylā has determined the fate of the unrepentant female apostate by way of *qiyās* from the male: it is some form of *istidlāl bi'l-qiyās*. This ruling originally gained the adherence of Abū Yūsuf (§1314); but, as we learn in §1315: "Then he reverted to (*rajaʿa ilā*) the doctrine of Abū Ḥanīfa."[345] This reversion receives support in the form of a rhetorical "how" (*kayfa*) question in §1316, asked by either Abū Yūsuf or al-Shaybānī, which constitutes not only a justification of Abū Ḥanīfa's and Abū Yūsuf's ruling, but an objection to Ibn Abī Laylā's contradictory ruling: "How is she

[344] That is to say, their separation—effected by his apostasy—does not subject them to the same requirements as if it had been effected by a *ṭalāq*-divorce. We find al-Shāfiʿī's reasoning in the *Mabsūṭ* as well (vol. 5, p. 49; not quoted by al-Afghānī), but I find it difficult to reconcile with what al-Shāfiʿī says here in §1312. "Al-Shāfiʿī… said: If [the apostate] did not consummate the marriage, then it is [as in the Ḥanafī position: apostasy causes irrevocable separation]. But if [the apostasy] occurs after consummation of the marriage (*dukhūl*), the dissolution of marriage is not conditional upon the elapsing of three menstruations, building upon his [al-Shāfiʿī's] source-case (*aṣl*)—regarding the *farq*-distinction between confirmation (*ta'akkud*) of marriage by way of consummation, and its lack of confirmation—according to what we have explained regarding becoming a Muslim [i.e., the *mas'ala* brought to expose the *farq*-distinction, wherein the non-Muslim spouse converts to Islam]. For [the apostate], by way of apostasy, aims at secession from the religious community (*munābadhat al-milla*), not from the wife (*al-ḥalīla*), so such is not an efficient cause for separation (*mūjib li'l-furqa*) after its [the marriage's] confirmation [by way of consummation], so long as there is not combined with it another reason (*sabab*): like when one of them converts to Islam."

[345] Mark this as another sign of Abū Yūsuf's dialectical ethic.

to be killed, when the Messenger of God... has prohibited the killing of women in wars—as pertains to the Ahl al-Shirk—and this one [i.e., the female apostate] is like them?"

This clarifies Abū Yūsuf's justification as *istidlāl bi'l-qiyās* from an *aṣl* of Sunnaic prohibition, with the implication that there is a shared *ʿilla* between this *aṣl* and the *mas'ala* of the female apostate in (2b). At the same time, we might consider Abū Yūsuf as implying Abū Ḥanīfa had not gone far enough: in a sense, though supporting Abū Ḥanīfa's ruling, he is advancing his *istidlāl bi'l-qiyās* over the *istidlāl bi-qawl al-wāḥid min al-Ṣaḥāba* of his teacher; and this may be identified in the lens-texts as an *iʿtirāḍ* of *muʿāraḍa* (Bāj.V.1).[346] To be certain, it is a rhetorical *iʿtirāḍ* against Ibn Abī Laylā's position, and may be identified in the lens-texts as "Invalid Compatibility-Comparison (*Fasād al-iʿtibār*)," of the second type: "for what is known by way of the authoritative source-cases (*uṣūl*)" (Shīr.VII.12.2.2; Bāj. IX.B.10.2.2).[347]

Remarkably, we find the very *mas'ala* at hand presented by al-Shīrāzī and al-Bājī (and alluded to by Ibn ʿAqīl) as one of the example cases for this broad genus of objection.[348] In brief, both al-Shīrāzī and al-Bājī divide *fasād al-iʿtibār* into that which is known by way of univocal source-text (*naṣṣ*)—i.e., the objection to R's *istidlāl* is apparent in the same *naṣṣ* upon which R relies—and that which is known by the *uṣūl*—wherein R's *fasād al-iʿtibār* is made apparent through other *endoxa* rulings. As we can see, Abū Yūsuf or al-Shaybānī has implied an objection of the latter type by bringing the Prophet's prohibition for killing female polytheists (*mushrikāt*) in the abode of war (*dār al-ḥarb*). This type of *fasād al-iʿtibār* is further subdivided, however, and the most relevant subdivision (2.2) is that wherein R "considers a *farʿ* on the basis of an *aṣl*, while they differ with regard to a parallel (*naẓīr*) of the *ḥukm*."

Here al-Shīrāzī's second example-*mas'ala* is one and the same with al-Bājī's third (at §405), and, most importantly, with our *mas'ala* at hand. R has considered women on the basis of men with regard to killing for apostasy (this being Ibn Abī Laylā's position). Q, a Ḥanafī in al-Bājī's example, then objects, saying: "This is an invalid comparison (*iʿtibār fāsid*), because the *uṣūl* made distinction between them (*farraqat baynahumā*); don't you see/opine (*a-lā tarā*) that, as regards original state of unbelief (*al-kufr al-aṣlī*) [as with the born polytheist], the man is killed but the woman is not killed?"[349] This is remarkably similar to the objection of Abū Yūsuf/ al-Shaybānī in §1316, right down to the dialectical question—although Abū Yūsuf/ al-Shaybānī employs a *kayfa* question while al-Bājī's Ḥanafī Q employs *a-lā tarā*.

[346] It conforms particularly well to al-Bājī's first mode of *iʿtirāḍ* against this domain of *istidlāl*: "[Q] says: 'This is the saying of a solitary Companion, so *qiyās* is advanced over it.'" (*Minhāj*, Turkī ed., p. 144, §§296 f.)

[347] al-Shīrāzī, *Maʿūna*, al-ʿUmayrīnī ed., pp. 114 f.; al-Bājī, *Minhāj*, Turkī ed., pp. 181 f., §§402ff, especially at §405. Cf. Ibn ʿAqīl, *K. al-Jadal*, p. 64, §303.

[348] Indeed, in the middle of §405, al-Bājī asserts: "and this category is one of the broadest categories of objections" (*wa hādhā al-bāb min awsaʿ abwāb al-iʿtirāḍāt*).

[349] al-Bājī, op. cit.

This is important to our current project for a number of reasons, but here I will only mark that it supports my view that early *jadal*-theory was, in part, elaborated from an analysis of proto-system *jadal* teaching and practice.[350]

Al-Shāfiʿī's rulings in §1317 read almost as a direct response, and objection, to the *kayfa* question of §1316: "there is no *farq*-distinction between her and the man: she is called upon to repent, and if she repents… [no consequence]. But if not; she is killed, just as is done with the man." There are several points of interest here. First, al-Shāfiʿī's justification, on one level, is a form of *taswiya*-subsumption: "there is no *farq*-distinction between [X] and [Y]" (*lā farqa bayn* [X] *wa* [Y]). This corresponds closely to the response recommended for the same example *mas'ala* employed by al-Bājī:

> And the *jawāb* is that for original state of unbelief (*al-kufr al-aṣlī*) the woman is safeguarded against [being killed] while the man is not safeguarded against it; but, as regards our *mas'ala*, which is unbelief of apostasy (*kufr al-ridda*), neither the man nor the woman is safeguarded against it. They are equal (*istawayā*) as regards the obligation of execution, like in adultery (*zinā*) and homicide (*qatl*).[351]

Note that not only does al-Bājī's *jawāb* to the Ḥanafī Q's charge of *fasād al-iʿtibār* mirror al-Shāfiʿī's *taswiya*-subsumption (employing *istawayā*), but the examples used to confirm their *taswiya* (*zinā* and *qatl*) are precisely the two which al-Shāfiʿī employs—to the same end—in §1326. Again, there is remarkable convergence here, and support for a theory that later *jadal* theory stemmed, in part, from a study of proto-system disputation.

Returning to al-Shāfiʿī in §1317, we may easily identify his objection to Abū Ḥanīfa and Abū Yūsuf as *farq*-distinction—indeed, he uses the very term itself: "there is no distinction between her and the man" (*fa-lā farqa baynahā wa bayna al-rajul*). As we see in the ensuing dialectical sequence, however, there is a larger objection being made: non-observance of this *farq*-distinction, crystallizing into a charge of method-*naqḍ*. R is accused of ignoring a previously observed *farq* for the *mas'ala* at hand; and, with his method thus proven inconsistent, his overall *istidlāl* is destroyed.

In §1318, al-Shāfiʿī sets the stage for a "historical" dialectic, its narrative quality indicated by the formula "And 'one of the people' disagreed with us regarding this, and said…" (*fa-khālafanā fī hādhā baʿḍ al-nās fa-qāla…*).[352] First, the anonymous opponent's ruling is stated: "the man is killed when he apostatizes, but the woman is

---

[350] We will see below that al-Shāfiʿī's *jawāb* to his questioner in the ensuing dialectic (al-Shāfiʿī having taken up Ibn Abī Laylā's position) is also found in our lens-texts.

[351] *Minhāj*, Turkī ed., p. 182, §405.

[352] This is a common formula throughout the *Umm*. A preliminary search shows some 130 instances of *khālafanā… fa-qāla…*, and the subsequent dialectical sequence of our current *mas'ala*-set, or something like it, appears actually to have occurred. Al-Shāfiʿī persists in "historical" mode, employing past tenses (*qīla, qāla, qultu*)—to this, we may contrast the "instructional" dialectic, which employs conditionals (*fa-in qāla…, qīla….*) Note that al-Shāfiʿī never names his opponent, but we may assume he is a proto-Ḥanafī, since he draws upon the same *naql* and proposes the same rulings as Abū Ḥanīfa and Abū Yūsuf in previous sections.

not killed." Then, al-Shāfiʿī presents his opponent's *istidlāl*: "And he based his argument on something he narrated on the authority of Ibn ʿAbbās…," adding immediately his objection: "the likes of which the Ahl al-Ḥadīth do not confirm (*lā yuthbitu Ahl al-Ḥadīth mithlahu*)." Note that the opponent is arguing the same ruling, from the same *athar*-tradition of Ibn ʿAbbās supporting Abū Ḥanīfa in §1313. In §1320, we also see him reference the same Sunnaic *dalīl*-indicant employed by Abū Yūsuf/al-Shaybānī in the rhetorical *iʿtirāḍ* of §1316. As for al-Shāfiʿī's objection to that *athar*-tradition of Ibn ʿAbbās, it is patently transmission-oriented; it is against a *qawl al-wāḥid min al-Ṣaḥāba*, but oriented towards the *isnād*, and this combination is not found in our lens-texts. I will mark it, therefore, as peculiar to proto-system *jadal*.

This critique is deepened by al-Shāfiʿī in §1319, when he remarks: "And something with the like quality (*shabīh*) of that chain of transmission (*isnād*) has been narrated about Abū Bakr al-Ṣiddīq, may God be pleased with him—that he killed women who had apostatized from Islam [i.e., as al-Shāfiʿī rules]—but we do not see fit to base our argument on it, when its chain of transmission is of the sort the Ahl al-Ḥadīth do not confirm (*fa-lam nara an naḥtajja bihi idhā kāna isnāduhu mimmā lā yuthbituhu Ahl al-Ḥadīth*)." Not only is this a sign that al-Shāfiʿī is intent on (1) maintaining consistency in his methodology, and (2) pursuing a sincere dialectical ethic, but it constitutes a unique "hypothetical" *iʿtirāḍ* against the opposing *qawl al-wāḥid min al-Ṣaḥāba*. It conveys a methodological snub—in so many words: "I could have conveyed *khilāf* from another of the Companions (Shīr.IV.3; Bāj.V.2),[353] but I won't stoop to your level"—while maintaining a principle of *isnād*-critique.

As with al-Shāfiʿī's previous "hypothetical" *qiyās* for *muʿāraḍa* (in §§288 and 622 ff.)—while maintaining, on principle, that such a *qiyās* does not obtain in the *masʾala* at hand—we now witness a "hypothetical" *athar*-tradition for *khilāf*, while maintaining, on principle, that it cannot be used as an *aṣl*—for the same reason (problematic *isnād*) that his opponent's *athar*-tradition cannot be used. At this point, I would claim that this "hypothetical" argument style is a *common* strategy of al-Shāfiʿī. It is not discussed in our lens-texts; but again, it is broadly similar to Aristotelian arguments *per/ad impossibile* and the "procedure of hypothetical proof." Most importantly, it shows the fine-honing of legal theory in a dialectical venue. The essence of al-Shāfiʿī's objection is this: "Not only is your evidence of an inferior epistemic grade, but we can produce evidence for the opposite conclusion, of the same inferior epistemic grade. Thus, your evidence is not evidence at all, from two perspectives." A basic principle of *isnād*-theory is inseparably intertwined with a species of dialectical objection; this is proto-system legal theory acquiring the edge of *ḥujjiyya* in proto-system *jadal*.

In §1320, al-Shāfiʿī continues setting the stage for "historical" dialectic. He further references his opponent as "the one who disagreed with us" (*man khālafanā*), and presents his *ḥujja*, saying that he: "based his argument (*iḥtajja*) on the fact that

[353] al-Shīrāzī, *Maʿūna*, al-ʿUmayrīnī ed., pp. 82 f.; al-Bājī, *Minhāj*, Turkī ed., p. 144, §298. Cf. Ibn ʿAqīl, *K. al-Jadal*, pp. 39 f.

the Prophet... forbade the killing of women in the Dār al-Ḥarb." Here we recognize the same Sunnaic prohibition employed by Abū Yūsuf/al-Shaybānī as a supplanting *qiyās* and charge of *fasād al-iʿtibār* in §1316. But al-Shāfiʿī's opponent argues differently from this *aṣl*, saying: "When the killing of female polytheists, who do not believe, is forbidden; then it is all the more appropriate (*awlā*) that the female believer who apostatizes from Islam should not be killed." Note that the comparative *awlā min/an* (meaning "all the more so," or "it is more appropriate that," or "prior/superior in rank to," etc.) occurs in our subject-text on a great many occasions.[354] It is more than evident that so consistent a formula played an important role in the proto-system dialectician's toolbox. Here, an individual is ranked in terms of deserving punishment: "If [inferior X] is not to be killed, then all the more so should [superior Y] not be killed..." (the latter is *awlā* when it comes to not being killed). This particular instance of *a fortiori* reasoning is of the *a minore ad maius* mode—discussed, along with *a maiore ad minus*, in the *uṣūl* and *jadal* texts in chapters on *faḥwā al-khiṭāb*, *mafhūm al-khiṭāb*, *al-tanbīh*, *al-qiyās al-jalī*, and *al-istidlāl bi'l-awlā*. The opponent's justification may thus be identified as a form of "Drawing Indication from the *A Fortiori* Signification of the Instruction (*al-Istidlāl bi-Faḥwā al-Khiṭāb*)" or "clearly-disclosed correlational inference (*al-qiyās al-jalī*).[355] As an objection to al-Shāfiʿī's position, however, it may be read in the same light as the *fasād al-iʿtibār*, known by way of the *uṣūl* (Shīr.VII.12.2.2; Bāj.IX.B.10.2.2),[356] of Abū Yūsuf/al-Shaybānī in §1316.

In §1321, al-Shāfiʿī initiates the dialectical sequence, with himself in the role of Q, and his anonymous R identified only as "one of those who profess this doctrine (*baʿḍ man yaqūlu hādhā al-qawl*)." First, al-Shāfiʿī references two other authoritative *dalīl*-indicants which have been professed by R, saying: "You have [also] narrated [1] that the Prophet... forbade the killing of the elderly (*al-kabīr al-fānī*), and the killing of the labourer (*al-ajīr*). And you have [also] narrated [2] that Abū Bakr al-Ṣiddīq forbade the killing of monks (*al-ruhbān*)." These are clearly intended as components to a charge of method-*naqḍ*, and al-Shāfiʿī launches directly into a dialectical *a-ra'ayta* question, delivering the *masā'il al-naqḍ*: "So have you considered [what would happen] if an elderly *shaykh* apostatized, or a labourer—would you desist from killing them? Or if a monastic-type apostatized; would you desist from killing him?" The patent objective is to expose R's inconsistent method, and this dialectical *a-ra'ayta* pushes R to concede a first premise for method-*naqḍ*: that

[354] Note also that it occurs with great frequency in our lens-texts, especially in the modes of preponderance (*tarjīḥāt*); see the listings at the end of Appendices II and III.

[355] al-Shīrāzī, *Maʿūna*, al-ʿUmayrīnī ed., p. 35; al-Bājī, *Minhāj*, Turkī ed., p. 24, §45. Cf. Ibn ʿAqīl, *K. al-Jadal*, pp. 11–12, §§53–6 (*al-qiyās al-jalī*). As mentioned, this is of the *a minore ad maius* variety, or, in al-Bājī's formula: "[God, or the Prophet] clearly designates the lesser (*adnā*) and [thus] draws attention to the greater (*aʿlā*)" (al-Shīrāzī's is practically identical).

[356] See previous note for §1316, above. The opponent's position is one and the same, with the same implied *iʿtirāḍ*.

R has, indeed, ruled differently for these *masā'il al-naqḍ*.[357] At the same time, al-Shāfiʿī is building his case for *farq*-distinction between killing polytheists in war and killing Muslim apostates.[358]

In §1322, al-Shāfiʿī acquires his first premise for method-*naqḍ*; R concedes that he rules against killing in the *masā'il al-naqḍ*, with a simple "No." In §1323, the mark of a master-dialectician becomes plain when al-Shāfiʿī formulates his next dialectical question in such a way as incorporates R's expected reasoning in just the form he would like it to be delivered. "Why not (*wa lima*)?" he asks, "Is it because the rule (*ḥukm*) of killing for apostasy (*ridda*) is a rule of killing for a *ḥadd*-punishment—which the governing administrator (*wālī*) may not obstruct—divergent to (*mukhālifun li-*) the rule of killing polytheists (*mushrikīn*) in the Dār al-Ḥarb?" Al-Shāfiʿī has at once asked al-Bājī's third question: "about the indicant for the opinion" (*al-su'āl ʿan dalīl al-madhhab*) and pushed concession to his second premise for method-*naqḍ*: R's previous observation of the *farq*-distinction between his *aṣl* (killing polytheists in war) and the contended *farʿ* (killing Muslim apostates). And, in §1324, R concedes this previous recognition of the *farq*-distinction with a simple "Yes," and al-Shāfiʿī acquires his second premise.

In §1325, with both premises in hand, al-Shāfiʿī drives home his charge of method-*naqḍ* by way of a rhetorical "how" (*kayfa*) question attacking R's *istidlāl bi-faḥwā al-khiṭāb* or *al-qiyās al-jalī*: "how have you based your argument on the ruling of the Dār al-Ḥarb [R's *aṣl*] for the killing of women [the contended *farʿ*], but did not see it (*lam tarahu*) as *ḥujja* for killing the elderly, the labourer, and the ascetic [the *masā'il al-naqḍ*]?" The charge is clear: R has been inconsistent in his observance of the *farq*-distinction between his *aṣl* (killing polytheists in war) and the contended *farʿ* (killing Muslim apostates). It is a rhetorical charge of method-*naqḍ*, unique in depending upon R's *previous* observance of a critical *farq*. In essence, al-Shāfiʿī has asked: "Why did you observe the *farq*-distinction for those other cases, but not for the *mas'ala* at hand?" It is an attack upon R's methodology: he ought either to have employed his *faḥwā al-khiṭāb* in the *masā'il al-naqḍ*, or to *not* have employed it here. Hence: method-*naqḍ*.

Not content with this, al-Shāfiʿī seals his *elenchus* in §1326, saying: "Moreover, you have said: [1] We have the right to desist from the Ahl al-Ḥarb after mastering them, and we do not kill them. But [2] we do not have the right to desist from an apostate. So how has their disparity (*iftirāq*) escaped you as regards the woman?" In this manner R is again shown inconsistent in observing the *farq*-distinction between his *aṣl* (killing polytheists in war) and the contended *farʿ* (killing Muslim apostates). This constitutes a second charge of method-*naqḍ*. Finally, al-Shāfiʿī reaffirms his *taswiya*-subsumption of women and men for all capital infractions:

---

[357] Al-Shāfiʿī's *a-ra'ayta* in §1321: dialogical, soliciting R's ruling on parallel / derived *masā'il* (*masā'il al-farq*, for this species of method-*naqḍ*), for an eventual charge of method-*naqḍ* (R observes a *farq*-distinction in the parallel *masā'il*, but ignores it in the *mas'ala*-at-hand).

[358] This is mirrored, as we have seen, by the *jawāb* against *fasād al-iʿtibār* in al-Bājī's third *mas'ala* example. There, the distinction between original state of unbelief (*al-kufr al-aṣlī*) and unbelief of apostasy (*kufr al-ridda*) is underscored (see the discussion for §1317, above).

"And indeed the woman is killed—wherever the man is killed—for adultery (*zinā*) and homicide (*qatl*)."

Note how closely al-Shāfiʿī's closing statement resembles the one in al-Bājī's example response to *fasād al-iʿtibār*: "They are equal (*istawayā*) as regards the obligation of execution, like in adultery (*zinā*) and homicide (*qatl*)."[359] Although al-Shāfiʿī's opponent argued a form of "Drawing Indication from the *A Fortiori* Signification of the Instruction (*al-Istidlāl bi-Faḥwā al-Khiṭāb*)" or "clearly-disclosed correlational inference (*al-qiyās al-jalī*), we may also assess al-Shāfiʿī's final *elenchus* as a successful response (*jawāb*) to the *fasād al-iʿtibār* rhetorically levelled by Abū Yūsuf or al-Shaybānī in §1316—indeed, his argument, or contemporaneous arguments like it, may have provided the very model for our lens-texts themselves. Taken all together, the persistence of this *mas'ala* of *ikhtilāf* from before the time of al-Shāfiʿī, and its appearance as an example in our lens-texts some three hundred years later, speaks volumes regarding the continuity of proto-system *jadal* teaching and practice, through to the full-system theory literature. Persistent *ikhtilāf*, with persistent methods of objection and response, must have contributed analytical material and categories for later theorists; and the *masā'il*-set of §§1310–26 offers a prime illustration of this phenomenon.

Masā'il-Set #12

§§1402–1412 from the *Chapter on Unilateral Divorce* (*Bāb al-Ṭalāq*)[360]

1402 – When a man repudiates his wife with one *ṭalāq*-statement, and her waiting period concludes, and she marries a husband and he consummates the marriage then repudiates her, and the first [man] marries her [again]; then indeed Abū Ḥanīfa said: She is susceptible to all [3] of the *ṭalāq* [-statements].[361] And he [Abū Yūsuf] embraced it.	1402 - وَإِذَا طَلَّقَ الرَّجُلُ امْرَأَتَهُ وَاحِدَةً فَانْقَضَتْ عِدَّتُهَا، فَتَزَوَّجَتْ زَوْجًا وَدَخَلَ بِهَا ثُمَّ طَلَّقَهَا، ثُمَّ تَزَوَّجَهَا الأَوَّلُ، فَإِنَّ أَبَا حَنِيفَةَ قَالَ: هِيَ عَلَى الطَّلَاقِ كُلِّهِ. وَبِهِ يَأْخُذُ.

(continued)

[359] *Minhāj*, Turkī ed., p. 182, §405.

[360] Ḥassūn ed., vol. 9, pp. 231–2; ʿAbd al-Muṭṭalib ed., vol. 8, pp. 386–8.

[361] In other words, her second marriage to the first man begins with a clean slate of three possible *ṭalāq*-statements, rather than only two (which would be the case had she not married another in the meantime). On rulings related to the procedures and consequences of *ṭalāq*-divorce, see the references cited in the note for §1219, above. In the more accepted procedure of divorce (*ṭalāq sunnī*), the husband pronounces a single *ṭalāq*-statement (the first), then the wife enters her three-month waiting period (*ʿidda*), during which two things might occur which cause the

1403 – But Ibn Abī Laylā said: She is susceptible [only] to what remains [from the *ṭalāq*-statements].	1403 - وَقَالَ ابْنُ أَبِي لَيْلَى: هِيَ عَلَى مَا بَقِيَ.
1404 – Al-Shāfiʿī said: When a man repudiates his wife with one *ṭalāq*-statement, or with two, and her waiting period concludes, and she marries another husband, then [the new husband] has sexual intercourse with her, then he repudiates her, or dies on her, and her waiting period concludes, and she [re-] marries the first husband; she is, from his perspective, susceptible to [only] what remains from the *ṭalāq*-statements. The second husband eliminates the three *ṭalāq*-statements, but he does not eliminate the one, nor the two.[362]	1404 - قَالَ الشَّافِعِيُّ: وَإِذَا طَلَّقَ الرَّجُلُ امْرَأَتَهُ وَاحِدَةً أَوْ اثْنَتَيْنِ، فَانْقَضَتْ عِدَّتُهَا وَنَكَحَتْ زَوْجًا غَيْرَهُ، ثُمَّ أَصَابَهَا، ثُمَّ طَلَّقَهَا أَوْ مَاتَ عَنْهَا، فَانْقَضَتْ عِدَّتُهَا فَنَكَحَتْ الزَّوْجَ الأَوَّلَ، فَهِيَ عِنْدَهُ عَلَى مَا بَقِيَ مِنَ الطَّلاَقِ، يَهْدِمُ الزَّوْجُ الثَّانِي الثَّلاَثَ وَلاَ يَهْدِمُ الْوَاحِدَةَ وَلاَ الثِّنْتَيْنِ.
1405 – And this, our doctrine, is the doctrine of ʿUmar b. al-Khaṭṭāb, may God Most High be pleased with him, and a number of the chief/elder Companions of the Prophet, may God bless and save him.	1405 - وَقَوْلُنَا هَذَا قَوْلُ عُمَرَ بْنِ الْخَطَّابِ رضي الله تعالى عنه وَعَدَدٍ مِن كِبَارِ أَصْحَابِ النَّبِيِّ - صَلَّى اللهُ عَلَيْهِ وَسَلَّمَ.
1406 – But "one of the people" has disagreed with us on some of this, saying: If the [intervening] husband eliminates the three [*ṭalāq*-statements], he eliminates the one and the two. And he ["one of the people"] based his argument on the doctrine of Ibn ʿUmar and Ibn ʿAbbās, may God be pleased with them.	1406 - وَقَدْ خَالَفَنَا فِي بَعْضِ هَذَا بَعْضُ النَّاسِ فَقَالَ: إِذَا هَدَمَ الزَّوْجُ ثَلاَثًا هَدَمَ وَاحِدَةً وَاثْنَتَيْنِ. وَاحْتَجَّ بِقَوْلِ ابْنِ عُمَرَ وَابْنِ عَبَّاسٍ رضي الله عنهم.
1407 – And he questioned us, saying: From where do you claim that the [intervening] husband eliminates the three [*ṭalāq*-statements], but does not eliminate what is less?	1407 - وَسَأَلَنَا فَقَالَ: مِن أَيْنَ زَعَمْتُمْ أَنَّ الزَّوْجَ يَهْدِمُ الثَّلاَثَ وَلاَ يَهْدِمُ مَا هُوَ أَقَلُّ مِنْهَا؟
1408 – We said: We claimed it by way of the decree which no one may rightly reject.	1408 - قُلْنَا: زَعَمْنَاهُ بِالأَمْرِ الَّذِي لاَ يَنْبَغِي لأَحَدٍ أَنْ يَدْفَعَهُ.

(continued)

marriage to resume: (1) they might have sexual intercourse; and (2) the husband might recant his repudiation. If neither occurs before the end of the waiting period, the divorce is effected and their marriage contract is dissolved—no second or third *ṭalāq*-statement is required. However, they might remarry—under a new *nikāḥ*-contract—without the restriction of an intervening marriage with another man. If they do so, and the husband again pronounces a single *ṭalāq*-statement (the second), then the wife enters her three-month waiting period again, with the same conditions (1) and (2). If neither occurs and their second marriage is dissolved, then they might again remarry under a new contract without the intervening marriage restriction. If they do so, but the husband again pronounces a single *ṭalāq*-statement (the third), then the wife enters her three-month waiting period a final time—but the (third) marriage contract is dissolved immediately, there is no revoking the divorce and returning to the married state, and there is no remarrying with a new *nikāḥ*-contract until the wife has contracted, consummated, and dissolved an intervening marriage with another man. In the frowned-upon triple-*ṭalāq* (*ṭalāq bidʿī*)—whereby the husband makes all three *ṭalāq*-statements at once—this final set of consequences occurs immediately (i.e., no resumption of the marriage, and no remarrying until an intervening marriage with another is consummated and dissolved).

[362] Which is to say, an intervening marriage only wipes the slate clean of *ṭalāq*-statements if it occurs after the first husband's third *ṭalāq*-statement.

1409 – He said: And what is it?	1409 – قَالَ: وَمَا هُوَ؟
1410 – We said: God made her *ḥarām* after the three [*ṭalāq*-statements],[363] «until she marries another husband besides him.»[364] And the Messenger of God, may God bless and save him, explained [the decree of] God, to Him belong might and majesty: that the "*nikāḥ*" by means of which God made her lawful after the three [*ṭalāq*-statements] is the sexual intercourse of the [intervening] husband.[365] And she was forbidden before the [intervening] husband, not to be made lawful by any circumstance except through the [intervening] husband. So the rule for eliminating the three [*ṭalāq*-statements] was attached to the [intervening] husband, due to this *maʿnā*-intension. She was, [after] the one and the two, lawful [to the first husband]; so no rule attached to the [intervening] husband, in this case. And we claimed that he eliminates whenever she was not lawful for [the first husband] except by way of him—while his rule was in effect—and [that] he does not eliminate when no rule attaches to him, and when she was lawful to another [i.e., the first husband].	1410 - قُلْنَا: حَرَّمَهَا اللهُ بَعْدَ الثَّلاَثِ حَتَّى تَنْكِحَ زَوْجًا غَيْرَهُ. وَبَيَّنَ رَسُولُ اللهِ - صَلَّى اللهُ عَلَيْهِ وَسَلَّمَ - عَنِ اللهِ عَزَّ وَجَلَّ أَنَّ النِّكَاحَ الَّذِي أَحَلَّهَا اللهُ بِهِ بَعْدَ الثَّلاَثِ إِصَابَةُ الزَّوْجِ، وَكَانَتْ مُحَرَّمَةً قَبْلَ الزَّوْجِ لاَ تَحِلُّ بِحَالٍ إِلاَّ بِالزَّوْجِ، فَكَانَ لِلزَّوْجِ حُكْمُ هَدْمِ الثَّلاَثِ لِهَذَا الْمَعْنَى، وَكَانَتْ فِي الْوَاحِدَةِ وَالثِّنْتَيْنِ حَلاَلاً، فَلَمْ يَكُنْ لِلزَّوْجِ هَاهُنَا حُكْمٌ، فَزَعَمْنَا أَنَّهُ يَهْدِمُ حَيْثُ كَانَتْ لاَ تَحِلُّ لَهُ إِلاَّ بِهِ، وَكَانَ حُكْمُهُ قَائِمًا، وَلاَ يَهْدِمُ حَيْثُ لاَ حُكْمَ لَهُ وَحَيْثُ كَانَتْ حَلاَلاً بِغَيْرِهِ.
1411 – The *aṣl*-principle of what is rationally understood [of God's indicants, in general] was that nothing is made lawful for anyone through the action of another. So when God made lawful for him [the first husband] through the action of another [the intervening husband], we made lawful for him [only] when God made lawful for him.[366] But it was not permitted that we make correlational inference from this [exceptional case] for what diverges from it, if the *aṣl*-principle belongs to what is rationally understood [of God's indicants, in general].[367]	1411 - وَكَانَ أَصْلُ الْمَعْقُولِ أَنَّ أَحَدًا لاَ يَحِلُّ لَهُ بِفِعْلِ غَيْرِهِ شَيْءٌ، فَلَمَّا أَحَلَّ اللهُ لَهُ بِفِعْلِ غَيْرِهِ أَحْلَلْنَا لَهُ حَيْثُ أَحَلَّ اللهُ لَهُ، وَلَمْ يَجُزْ أَنْ نَقِيسَ عَلَيْهِ مَا خَالَفَهُ لَوْ كَانَ الأَصْلُ لِلْمَعْقُولِ فِيهِ.
1412 – And Muḥammad b. al-Ḥasan has reverted to this doctrine, after having professed the doctrine of Abū Ḥanīfa. And God knows best.	1412 - وَقَدْ رَجَعَ إِلَى هَذَا الْقَوْلِ مُحَمَّدُ بْنُ الْحَسَنِ بَعْدَمَا كَانَ يَقُولُ بِقَوْلِ أَبِي حَنِيفَةَ، وَاللَّهُ أَعْلَمُ.

In §1402, Abū Ḥanīfa's ruling on the *mas'ala* at hand is presented: "She is susceptible to all [3] of the *ṭalāq* [-statements] (*hiya ʿalā al-ṭalāq kullihi*);" and this in turn is followed by a statement of Abū Yūsuf's adherence to this ruling. Ibn Abī Laylā's

---

[363] *Ḥarrama*, "to make *ḥarām*," here delivers the same sense of "forbidden" which applies to a man's female relatives within the "forbidden degrees" of marriage.

[364] Al-Shāfiʿī partially quotes Q.2:230: «And if he unilaterally divorces her (*ṭallaqahā*), she is not lawful for him thereafter until she contracts marriage with another husband besides him (*ḥattā tankiḥa zawj*[an] *ghayrahu*).»

[365] It must be remembered that *nikāḥ*—besides the contract of marriage—has another meaning: "coitus."

[366] That is, in this one, exceptional case—after the first husband's third *ṭalāq*-statement—only.

[367] Again, see Sect. 8.2 for the meaning of *aṣl al-maʿqūl*.

counter-ruling: "She is susceptible [only] to what remains [from the *ṭalāq*-statements] (*hiya ʿalā mā baqiya*)" is briefly related in §1403.

Although no indicants or arguments are provided, we may infer at least that consummation with the second husband was understood by Abū Ḥanīfa as having the efficiency to occasion elimination of 1, 2, or 3 *ṭalāq*-statements—it is a full cleaning of the slate in every case—and that Ibn Abī Laylā understood it to be efficient only in cleaning the slate of 3. Al-Sarakhsī sheds more light on the terse pronouncements of §1402: "If he repudiates his wife with one *ṭalāq*-statement, or two, then he marries her after a husband has cohabited with her; she is, from his perspective, susceptible to three future statements of *ṭalāq* (*hiya ʿindahu ʿalā thalāthi taṭlīqātin mustaqbalātin*), according to the doctrine of Abū Ḥanīfa and Abū Yūsuf, may God Most High have mercy upon them both. And it is the doctrine of Ibn ʿAbbās, and Ibn ʿUmar, and Ibrāhīm, and the companions of ʿAbd Allāh b. Masʿūd, may God be pleased with them. But, according to Muḥammad [al-Shaybānī] and Zufar and al-Shāfiʿī, may God Most High have mercy upon them, she is, from his perspective, susceptible to [only] whatever remains of her *ṭalāq*-statements (*hiya ʿindahu bimā baqiya min ṭalāqihā*). And it is the doctrine of ʿUmar, and ʿAlī, and Ubayy b. Kaʿb, and ʿImrān b. al-Ḥuṣayn, and Abū Hurayra, may God be pleased with them."[368]

From this account, we may identify Abū Ḥanīfa's justification in similar fashion to the analysis for §§635 ff., in *mas'ala*-set #4. Even though incorporating more than four Companions (Ibn ʿAbbās, Ibn ʿUmar, Ibrāhīm, and the companions of ʿAbd Allāh b. Masʿūd), it may still be treated within the category of "the saying of a solitary Companion" (*qawl al-wāḥid min al-Ṣaḥāba*). It may also represent a possible attempt at "consensus of the Companions" (*ijmāʿ al-Ṣaḥāba*), and at numerical preponderance as a mode of *tarjīḥ*. Various modes of *iʿtirāḍ* are also implied, especially to the indicants brought forth by al-Shāfiʿī (whose ruling is in consonance with Ibn Abī Laylā's). If we were to presume that Ibn Abī Laylā drew from the same supporting *naql* presented by al-Shāfiʿī in §1405, then Abū Ḥanīfa's objection may have taken the form of: (1) *khilāf* of another Companion (Shīr.IV.3; Bāj.V.2) against the opposing *istidlāl bi-qawl al-wāḥid min al-Ṣaḥāba*; (2) *muṭālaba bi-taṣḥīḥ al-ijmāʿ* (Shīr.III.2; Bāj.III.1.1) or *khilāf* of another Companion (Shīr.III.3; Bāj.III.1.2) against the opposing *istidlāl bi-ijmāʿ al-Ṣaḥāba*; and (3) *tarjīḥ* of an *athar*-tradition due to more practitioners/narrators (similar to Shīr.IX.1.5; Bāj.XVI.1.1.3, but in the domain of *āthār*-traditions). Ibn Abī Laylā's objections would consist of the same.

---

[368] *Mabsūṭ*, vol. 6, p. 95; quoted by Afghānī in Abū Yūsuf, *Ikhtilāf*, p. 216, n. 2. NB: al-Sarakhsī's mention of al-Shāfiʿī corresponds with al-Shāfiʿī's opinion in §1404, and his authoritative transmissions in §1405. Interestingly, and although al-Shāfiʿī's opinion is referenced many hundreds of times in the *Mabsūṭ*, it appears only six times in al-Sarakhsī's commentary on the *Ikhtilāf Abī Ḥanīfa wa Ibn Abī Laylā* (in *Mabsūṭ*, vol. 30, pp. 128–67). Moreover, as we have seen above with regard to §1312, his reported reasoning does not always reconcile easily with what is found in the *Umm* Version. From this we might conclude that something like the Shaybānī Version—devoid of al-Shāfiʿī's arguments—was available and accessed by al-Sarakhsī for his commentary on the *Ikhtilāf Abī Ḥanīfa wa Ibn Abī Laylā*.

In §1404, after a retelling of the *mas'ala* at hand in typical detail, al-Shāfiʿī's ruling is presented: "she is, from [the first husband's] perspective, susceptible to [only] what remains from the *ṭalāq*-statements (*hiya ʿindahu ʿalā mā baqiya min al-ṭalāq*). The second husband eliminates the three *ṭalāq*-statements, but he does not eliminate the one, nor the two." The latter statement confirms his estimation of the efficiency of the second husband's consummation: it occasions the elimination only of 3 *ṭalāq*-statements, not of 1 or 2. We have seen al-Sarakhsī's report on al-Shāfiʿī's supporting *naql* (ʿUmar, ʿAlī, Ubayy b. Kaʿb, ʿImrān b. al-Ḥuṣayn, and Abū Hurayra), and might consider his justification, like those preceding, a form of *istidlāl bi-qawl al-wāḥid min al-Ṣaḥāba*, or of *ijmāʿ al-Ṣaḥāba*, or of *tarjīḥ*. Likewise, his objections to Abū Ḥanīfa's ruling (note that al-Shāfiʿī presents the same ruling as Ibn Abī Laylā) might have consisted of something similar to those listed above. In §1405, al-Shāfiʿī himself declares his own supporting *naql*—in less detail, but in consonance with what al-Sarakhsī reported: "And this, our doctrine, is the doctrine of ʿUmar b. al-Khaṭṭāb... and a number of the chief/elder Companions of the Prophet (*kibār Aṣḥāb al-Nabī*)...." Note this reference to the *kibār Aṣḥāb al-Nabī* may signal al-Shāfiʿī's push towards epistemic advantage via an *endoxon* sub-set of those closer to the Prophet (cf. Shīr.IX.1.3 and 1.6).[369]

In §1406, al-Shāfiʿī sets the stage for a "historical" dialectic, with the familiar formula "But 'one of the people' has disagreed with us on some of this, saying..." (*qad khālafanā fī baʿḍ hādhā baʿḍu al-nāsi fa-qāla...*), indicating that his opponent argues from the camp of Abū Ḥanīfa and Abū Yūsuf.[370] This is confirmed when al-Shāfiʿī relates his opponent's conception of the efficiency of the second husband's consummation: "if the [intervening] husband eliminates the three

[369] Importantly, al-Sarakhsī notes (*Mabsūṭ*, vol. 6, p. 95), as regards the *naql*-adherence of the opposing Abū Ḥanīfa/Abū Yūsuf vs. al-Shaybānī/al-Shāfiʿī positions: "So the younger set of the jurists (*al-shubbān min al-fuqahā'*) [al-Shaybānī, al-Shāfiʿī, Zufar] adhered to the doctrine of the elder set of the Companions (*al-mashā'ikh min al-Ṣaḥāba*) [ʿUmar, ʿAlī, et al.]... and the elder set of jurists [Abū Ḥanīfa, Abū Yūsuf] adhered to the doctrine of the younger set of Companions [Ibn ʿAbbās, Ibn ʿUmar, et al.]" Al-Shāfiʿī's reference to "other *kibār* of the *Aṣḥāb al-Nabī*" corresponds with this observation, and gives weight to the possibility that this "*shubbān* vs. *mashā'ikh* of the Companions" distinction may have played a role in his argument. Whether or not this is a question of design on the part of our jurists is difficult to confirm. It is possible, however, that when two opposing opinions were backed by comparable (in terms of number) sets of Companion *āthār*-traditions, a further epistemic consideration was put into effect for purposes of *tarjīḥ*. Those jurists adhering to the doctrine of the elder set of Companions might claim greater authority due to their having been closer to the Prophet. This finds a parallel in a different domain: the *isnād*-related *tarjīḥāt* of al-Shīrāzī. His third mode is: "That one of the two is closer (*aqrab*) to the Messenger of God; he is given precedence over [the other], because he is more perceptive/attentive (*awʿā*)" (Shīr.IX.1.3). Even more relevant is his sixth mode: "That one of the two is greater in terms of companionship [with the Prophet] (*ṣuḥba*); he is given precedence, because he is more knowing (*aʿraf*) of what persists of exemplary traditions (*sunan*)" (Shīr.IX.1.6). See the listings of *tarjīḥāt* at the end of Appendices II and III; and *Maʿūna*, al-ʿUmayrīnī ed., pp. 121–2.

[370] Cf. §1318, above, and §1377 in my dissertation ("Dialectical Forge," pt. 2, p. 337).

[*ṭalāq*-statements], he eliminates the one and the two;" and by al-Shāfiʿī's shorter account of his opponent's supporting *naql*: "he based his argument on the doctrine of Ibn ʿUmar and Ibn ʿAbbās…." By these statements we might infer that al-Shāfiʿī's opponent, who plays the role of Q in the ensuing dialectic, might attempt to supplant al-Shāfiʿī's supporting *āthār* traditions by way of a *qiyās* built upon, or even attributed to, his "younger set" of Companions—advancing his *istidlāl bi'l-qiyās* over al-Shāfiʿī's *istidlāl bi-qawl al-wāḥid min al-Ṣaḥāba* via that species of *muʿāraḍa* (Bāj.V.1) wherein "[Q] says: 'This is the saying of a solitary Companion, so *qiyās* is advanced over it.'"[371]

In §1407 the "historical" dialectic begins. Q asks: "From where do you claim (*min ayna zaʿamtum*) that the [intervening] husband eliminates the three [*ṭalāq*-statements], but does not eliminate what is less?" This bears a resemblance to both al-Bājī's third and fourth questions: "about the indicant of the opinion" (*al-suʾāl ʿan dalīl al-madhhab*) or "mode of the indicant" (*wajh al-dalīl*), or a combination thereof. Q seeks to problematize al-Shāfiʿī's *istidlāl*, but he must first come to know his *dalīl*-indicant and how he reasons from it, before gathering concessions to premises from which his own solution flows.

Al-Shāfiʿī's response in §1408 is not only parsimonious (as later theory texts would recommend), but borders on the abstruse: "We claimed it by way of the decree which no one may rightly reject." Alternately, one might consider such a formulation as having a dialectical function: it draws Q's attention to the *endoxa* hierarchies of epistemic authority shared by all in the realm of juristic debate, and alerts him to the fact that al-Shāfiʿī's forthcoming *dalīl*-indicant will occupy the highest rank. It is certainly an assertion that his justification is *endoxon*. In fact, this statement defines what is *endoxon* in the normative realm: it is "the *amr* which none may rightly reject."

Not surprisingly, when Q asks "what is it (*wa mā huwa*)?" in §1409, al-Shāfiʿī's response begins with the Qur'ān. It is a multilayered *jawāb*, leading in stages to *elenchus*, and in fact we do not hear from Q again. Al-Shāfiʿī begins: "God made her *ḥarām* after the three [*ṭalāq*-statements], «until she marries another husband besides him»"—this being a partial quoting of Q.2:230—"and the Messenger of God… explained [the decree of] God…: that the '*nikāḥ*' by means of which God made her lawful after the three [*ṭalāq*-statements] is the sexual intercourse of the [intervening] husband." The opening, of course, constitutes *istidlāl bi'l-Kitāb*; and what follows is not merely *istidlāl bi'l-Sunna*, but it is the merging of Qur'ān and Sunna in that fashion for which al-Shāfiʿī was especially renowned. The Prophet's Sunna is here, as in other arguments of the subject-text, brought as "interpreter" (*mufassir*) to the Qur'ān.[372] The Prophet clarifies (*bayyana*) God's speech: "*nikāḥ*" means the licit sexual intercourse of the intervening husband (*iṣābat al-zawj*). As before in

[371] *Minhāj*, Turkī ed., p. 144, §§296 f.

[372] See the references to Joseph Lowry, al-Shāfiʿī's *Risāla*, and other observations in the analysis of §255 above.

§255, where Sunna is *mufassir* to Sunna, I would stress that we are witnessing the assertion of a legal-theoretical principle in an early dialectical sequence. Al-Shāfiʿī's *mufassir*-theory is again being tested—and gaining the edge of argumentative conclusiveness (*ḥujjiyya*)—in the dialectical forge. At the very least, it is an appeal to a legal-theory principle: a Sunnaic hermeneutic is brought to bear upon a *lafẓ*-expression of the Qur'ān.

The next part of al-Shāfiʿī's response in §1410 consists of an *ʿaql* argument drawing forth the implications of his *adilla*-indicants, and is presented as distinct premises: "[1] she was forbidden (*muḥarrama*) before the [intervening] husband, [2] not to be made lawful by any circumstance except through the [intervening] husband. [3] So the rule (*ḥukm*) for eliminating the three [*ṭalāq*-statements] was attached to the [intervening] husband, due to this *maʿnā*-intension. [4] She was, [after] the one and the two, lawful [to the first husband]; [5] so no rule attached to the [intervening] husband, in this case." In other words: (1) before licit marriage and consummation with the intervening husband, the wife is unlawful to her divorcing husband; (2) she can *only* become lawful again to the divorcing husband through licit marriage and consummation with the intervening husband; (3) because of this *maʿnā*-intension (#1 and #2)—made plain by God and Prophet—the ruling (*ḥukm*) of cleaning the slate of three *ṭalāq*-statements was attached to the intervening husband; (4) but when she had only been divorced with one or two *ṭalāq*-statements, she was still lawful to her divorcing husband (i.e., they could remarry without the intervening husband); and (5) that is why, in that case, no ruling (*ḥukm*) of cleaning the slate of three *ṭalāq*-statements was attached to the intervening husband.

Al-Shāfiʿī succinctly summarizes and clarifies the norm resultant of this argument: "And we claimed that he eliminates [three *ṭalāq*-statements] whenever she was not lawful for [the first husband] except by way of him—while his rule (*ḥukm*) was in effect—and [that] he does not eliminate [three *ṭalāq*-statements] when no rule attaches to him, and when she was lawful to another [i.e., the first husband]." The equation is simple in the end: when the divorced wife may lawfully remarry her divorcing husband without the intervening husband, the special "*ḥukm* of elimination" is not attached to him; and when the divorced wife cannot lawfully remarry her divorcing husband without the intervening husband, the special "*ḥukm* of elimination" becomes attached to him. Thus, if the divorced wife marries the intervening husband after only one or two *ṭalāq*-statements from her divorcing husband, the special "*ḥukm* of elimination" is not attached to the intervening husband at the time they get married, so nothing at all is cleaned from the slate of *ṭalāq*-statements. The *only* time the intervening husband cleans the slate, is when there are three *ṭalāq*-statements on it.

Al-Shāfiʿī's argument, after further analysis, may best be described as *qiyās al-ʿaks*. The whole may be diagrammed as follows:

Aṣl wife divorced by 3 *ṭalāq*-statements		*Farʿ* wife divorced by 1 or 2 *ṭalāq*-statements
ʿIlla I she is unlawful to the divorcing husband; they cannot remarry	OPPOSITE/ CONTRADICTORY ← (*NAQĪḌ*) →	*ʿIlla* ¬I she is lawful to the divorcing husband; they can remarry
Ḥukm H intervening husband has *ḥukm* of elimination; marriage with H2 cleans the slate	THEREFORE ALSO OPPOSITE/ CONTRADICTORY ← (*NAQĪḌ*) →	*Ḥukm* ¬H intervening husband has no *ḥukm* of elimination; marriage with H2 cleans nothing

In §1411, al-Shāfiʿī proceeds to justify his arguments in broader terms of legal-theory. First, he says: "The *aṣl*-principle of what is rationally understood (*maʿqūl*) was that nothing is made lawful for anyone through the action of another." The opening term: "the *aṣl* of the *maʿqūl*" is of obvious import from a legal theoretical perspective. It appears to convey the same sense as the *qāʿida* of later legal theory—a usage of *aṣl* which corresponds well with what we see in the *Uṣūl* of al-Karkhī and elsewhere. It is as though al-Shāfiʿī has induced, from the Sharīʿa as a whole, the *aṣl* that "nothing is made lawful (*ḥalāl*) for party X by the action (*fiʿl*) of party Y;" and he next explains that God (in Q.2:230) has made an exception to this inductively-derived principle, this "*aṣl* of the *maʿqūl*," while maintaining that—*qua* exception—it cannot serve as the basis for *qiyās* (meaning: *qiyās al-ʿilla*).

I have, however, portrayed al-Shāfiʿī's argument as *qiyās al-ʿaks* from that very same exception-decree of Q.2:330. Drawing from al-Shāfiʿī's explanation here, it seems most likely he did not conceive of his argument as *qiyās* of any type—which is to say that the hermeneutic provided by Qur'ān-Sunna interplay was sufficient in solving the *mas'ala* at hand. Al-Shāfiʿī says: "when God made lawful for [the first husband] through the action of [the intervening husband], we made lawful for him [only] when God made lawful for him." That is to say, God's command regarding the intervening husband's "*ḥukm* of elimination" was for one scenario and one only: after the wife's triple divorce. There is no extending the "*ḥukm* of elimination," by way of *qiyās*, to any other scenario (of 1 or 2 *ṭalāq*-statements). Perhaps that is why the form of *qiyās al-ʿaks* makes sense of al-Shāfiʿī's argument. In the end, it does not extend the "*ḥukm* of elimination;" rather, it extends its opposite, and the same effect is achieved: God's exceptional command is observed only in its exceptional scenario, and nowhere else.

There are other items of import in §1411. It provides perhaps as detailed an indication of what al-Shāfiʿī means by *maʿqūl* as appears in the subject-text;[373] and note that this is the only instance of the phrase *aṣl al-maʿqūl* in all of the *Umm* and the *Risāla*—and, for that matter, all the *fiqh* works of the Shāfiʿī, Ḥanafī, and Mālikī *madhāhib* which I have been able to search electronically. Moreover, the *aṣl al-maʿqūl* which al-Shāfiʿī specifies: "nothing is made lawful for anyone through

[373] Cf. §§402, 633, 651, 929, and 1056.

the action of another" has every appearance, as earlier mentioned, of a "general principle" (*qāʿida*) derived inductively from the Sharīʿa as a whole. If this is indeed the case, we are witnessing in §1411 both: (1) a proto-system *qāʿida* raised in a dialectical sequence; and (2) a legal theory —"we may not use God's exception to the *aṣl al-maʿqūl* as a basis for *qiyās*"—also raised in a dialectical sequence.

Al-Shāfiʿī's justification here lays bare a critical principle of *qiyās* in his overall legal theory; mainly, when God goes against what appears to us as the *maʿqūl*, we must follow Him in that—but we must not build upon it with *qiyās*. In other words, we don't do *qiyās* with anything that is not consonant with the *maʿqūl*. I will tentatively conclude, therefore, that al-Shāfiʿī's argument is that *qiyās al-ʿilla* cannot be done from the *aṣl* of Q.2:230 because this particular *aṣl* constitutes the singular exception to a broader, inductively-corroborated *aṣl*. Al-Shāfiʿī did not conceive of his argument as any type of *qiyās*. Rather, he saw the *mas'ala* at hand (the wife divorced by one or two *ṭalāq*-statements) as being fully under the governance of the *aṣl al-maʿqūl*—she is, after all, *ḥalāl* to the first husband through no action on the part of the intervening husband. Therefore, according to al-Shāfiʿī, it would be wrong to claim that the "*ḥukm* of elimination" be attached to an intervening husband in the *mas'ala* at hand. This is because: (1) that intervening husband had nothing whatsoever to do with her being *ḥalāl* to the first husband; and (2) whenever the intervening husband does have something to do with her being *ḥalāl* to the first husband, it is God's singular exception, not the rule (i.e., not the *maʿqūl*).

Finally, the closing section (§1412) is also of some import to the current project. It appears to be an editorial comment in the voice of al-Rabīʿ, telling us: "Muḥammad b. al-Ḥasan [al-Shaybānī] has reverted to this doctrine, after having professed the doctrine of Abū Ḥanīfa. And God knows best." Note first that we have seen this recanting of Muḥammad b. al-Ḥasan confirmed by al-Sarakhsī (see the analysis of §1402, above). Intriguingly, however, these words do not appear in the Shaybānī Version as edited by al-Afghānī. This may provide indication that the Shaybānī Version—just as tradition would have it— is indeed older than the *Umm* Version. It would be easy to explain that al-Shāfiʿī or al-Rabīʿ added this comment to the urtext at hand; it is more difficult to explain why a later Ḥanafī editor—engaged in reconstructing a "lost" book of *ikhtilāf* by removing and altering parts of the *Umm* Version (e.g., leaving out al-Shāfiʿī's opinions, changing *ya'khudhu* to *na'khudhu*, etc.)—chose to excise a reference to al-Shaybānī which, left in, could only add credibility to his project.

Note that if all of al-Shāfiʿī's arguments are removed, the mention of al-Shaybānī in §1412 would follow logically, and accurately, from Ibn Abī Laylā's ruling (which is the same as al-Shāfiʿī's) in §1403. These textual details are hard to interpret in a way that goes against the "status quo" of our subject-text's redactional history (Abū Yūsuf to Muḥammad b. al-Ḥasan to al-Shāfiʿī to al-Rabīʿ); and, as they accumulate, a revisionist post-dating or re-ascription project becomes more difficult to maintain. Finally, one point is worthy of conjecture. Considering that some narratives have al-Shāfiʿī studying with Muḥammad b. al-Ḥasan, who encouraged him to engage him in *munāẓara*, might §1412 indicate that al-Shāfiʿī influenced his teacher to change his opinion? Could Muḥammad b. al-Ḥasan himself be the "one of the people" referenced in §1406? This must remain conjecture, of course; it is certainly possible that the doctrine mentioned in §1412 predates al-Shāfiʿī, and that al-Shaybānī came to it gradually, and by other means. One thing is for certain: his recanting illustrates that jurists were moved by strong argument more than "school" or "regional" loyalties in this early period. It may even be the case here that Muḥammad b. al-Ḥasan was moved to change his opinion via dialectic with a star pupil.

References

Abū Yūsuf, Yaʿqūb b. Ibrāhīm. *Ikhtilāf Abī Ḥanīfa wa Ibn Abī Laylā* [= Shaybānī Version]. Ed. Abū al-Wafā' al-Afghānī. Cairo: Maṭbaʿat al-Wafā', 1357/1939.

al-Aʿshā, Maymūn b. Qays, et al. *Kitāb Ṣubḥ al-Munīr fī Shiʿr Abī Baṣīr Maymūn b. Qays b. Jandal al-Aʿshā wa'l-Aʿshā'īn al-Ākhirīn* [*Gedichte von 'Abû Baṣîr Maimûn ibn Qais al-'A'šâ: nebst Sammlungen von Stücken anderer Dichter des gleichen Beinamens und von al-Musayyab ibn 'Alas*]. Ed. Rudolf Geyer. London: Printed for the trustees of the "E.J.W. Gibb Memorial" and published by Luzac & Co., 1928.

Badawī, ʿAbd al-Raḥmān, ed. *Manṭiq Arisṭū*. 3 Vols. Cairo: Maṭbaʿat Dār al-Kutub al-Miṣriyya, 1948.

al-Bājī, Abū al-Walīd Sulaymān. *Kitāb al-Minhāj fī Tartīb al-Ḥijāj* (*L'art de la Polémique: Édition Critique d'al-Minhāǧ de Bāǧī*). Ed. ʿAbd al-Majīd Turkī. Paris: Maisonneuve et Larose, 1978.

al-Baṣrī, Abū al-Ḥusayn Muḥammad. *Kitāb al-Qiyās al-Sharʿī*. In *idem*, *Kitāb al-Muʿtamad fī Uṣūl al-Fiqh*. Ed. Muḥammad Ḥamīd Allāh, Muḥammad Bakīr, and Ḥasan Ḥanafī. Damascus: al-Maʿhad al-ʿIlmī al-Faransī li'l-Dirāsāt al-ʿArabiyya bi-Dimashq, 1964–1965, vol. 2, pp. 1029–1050.

al-Baṣrī, Abū al-Ḥusayn Muḥammad. *Kitāb al-Qiyās al-Sharʿī*. In *idem*, *al-Muʿtamad fī Uṣūl al-Fiqh*. Ed. Khalīl al-Mays. Beirut: Dār al-Kutub al-ʿIlmiyya, 1983, vol. 2, pp. 443–62.

Crone, Patricia and Martin Hinds. *God's Caliph: Religious Authority in the First Centuries of Islam*. Cambridge; New York: Cambridge University Press, 1986.

DJP = Ibn Rushd. *The Distinguished Jurist's Primer* [= *Bidāyat al-Mujtahid wa Nihāyat al-Muqtaṣid*]. 2 vols. Trans. Imran Ahsan Khan Nyazee. Rev. Mohammad Abdul Rauf. Reading, UK: Centre for Muslim Contribution to Civilization: Garnet, 1994–1996.

EI[2] = *Encyclopaedia of Islam, Second Edition*. Ed. P. Bearman; Th. Bianquis; C.E. Bosworth; E. van Donzel; and W.P. Heinrichs. Brill Online, 2014 <http://referenceworks.brillonline.com/entries/encyclopaedia-of-islam-2>

Goichon, A.-M. *Vocabulaires Comparés d'Aristote et d'Ibn Sīnā*. Paris: Desclée de Brouwer, 1939.

Hallaq, Wael. *A History of Islamic Legal Theories: An Introduction to Sunnī Uṣūl al-Fiqh*. Cambridge; New York: Cambridge University Press, 1997.

Hallaq, Wael. *The Origins and Evolution of Islamic Law*. Cambridge; New York: Cambridge University Press, 2005.

Hallaq, Wael. *Sharīʿa: Theory, Practice, Transformations*. Cambridge; New York: Cambridge University Press, 2009.

Hallaq, Wael. "A Tenth-Eleventh Century Treatise on Juridical Dialectic." *Muslim World* 77 (1987): 197–228.

Ḥibshī, ʿAbd Allāh Muḥammad. *Jāmiʿ al-Shurūḥ wa'l-Ḥawāshī: Muʿjam Shāmil li-Asmā' al-Kutub al-Mashrūḥa fi'l-Turāth al-Islāmī wa-Bayān Shurūḥihā*. Abū Dhabī: al-Majmaʿ al-Thaqāfī, 2004.

Ibn ʿAqīl, Abū al-Wafā' ʿAlī. *Kitāb al-Jadal ʿalā Ṭarīqat al-Fuqahā'*. Al-Ẓāhir [Cairo]: Maktabat al-Thaqāfa al-Dīniyya, 1980. [An unattributed reproduction of George Makdisi, ed., *Le Livre de la Dialectique d'Ibn ʿAqīl*, minus his introduction and critical apparatus].

Ibn Baṭṭāl. *Sharḥ Ṣaḥīḥ al-Bukhārī*. Ed. Abū Tamīm Yāsir b. Ibrāhīm. Riyāḍ: Maktabat al-Rushd, 2003.
Ibn Ḥazm, Abū Muḥammad ʿAlī. *Al-Iḥkām fī Uṣūl al-Aḥkām*. 8 vols. Ed. Aḥmad Muḥammad Shākir. Beirut: Dār al-Āfāq al-Jadīda, n.d.
Ibn Khaldūn. *Muqaddima*. Ed. Khalīl Shaḥāda. Beirut: Dār al-Fikr, 2001. [Translation by Franz Rosenthal: *The Muqaddimah : an Introduction to History*. 2nd Ed. 3 vols. London: Routledge & Kegan Paul, 1967].
Ibn al-Muqaffaʿ, ʿAbd Allāh. *Al-Manṭiq li-Ibn al-Muqaffaʿ* [and the] *Ḥudūd al-Manṭiq li-Ibn Bihrīz*. Ed. Muḥammad Taqī Dānish'pazhūh. Tehran: Anjuman-i Shāhanshāhī-i Falsafa-i Īrān, 1357/1978.
Ibn al-Nadīm, Abū al-Faraj Muḥammad. *Al-Fihrist*. Ed. Yūsuf ʿAlī Ṭawīl. Beirut: Dār al-Kutub al-ʿIlmiyya, 1996.
al-Juwaynī, Imām al-Ḥaramayn. *Al-Kāfiya fi'l-Jadal*. Ed. Fawqiya Ḥusayn Maḥmūd. Cairo: Maṭbaʿat ʿĪsā al-Bābī al-Ḥalabī, 1979.
al-Juwaynī, Imām al-Ḥaramayn. *Al-Waraqāt fī Uṣūl al-Fiqh*. In *Arbaʿa Mutūn fī Uṣūl al-Fiqh ʿalā al-Madhāhib al-Arbaʿa*. Eds. Jamāl al-Dīn al-Qāsimī and Usāma al-Balkhī. Damascus: Dār al-Balkhī, 2005.
al-Khaṭīb al-Baghdādī, Abū Bakr Aḥmad b. ʿAlī. *Kitāb al-Faqīh wa'l-Mutafaqqih*. 2nd Ed. 2 Vols. Ed. Abū ʿAbd al-Raḥmān ʿĀdil b. Yūsuf al-ʿAzzāzī. Riyadh: Dār Ibn al-Jawzī, 1996.
Lane, Edward William. *An Arabic-English Lexicon*. Beirut: Librarie du Liban, 1968.
Lowry, Joseph. "The Legal Hermeneutics of al-Shāfiʿī and Ibn Qutayba." *Islamic Law and Society* 11:1 (2004): pp. 1–41.
al-Maktaba al-Shāmila [Electronic Library]. <http://shamela.ws/index.php/main>
al-Māwardī, Abū al-Ḥasan ʿAlī b. Muḥammad. *Al-Ḥāwī al-Kabīr: fī Fiqh Madhhab al-Imām al-Shāfiʿī, wa huwa Sharḥ Mukhtaṣar al-Muzanī*. Ed. ʿAlī Muḥammad Maʿʿūd, et al. 20 vols. Beirut: Dār al-Kutub al-ʿIlmiyya, 1999.
MF = *al-Mawsūʿa al-Fiqhiyya*. 45 Vols. Kuwait: Wizārat al-Awqāf wa'l-Shu'ūn al-Islāmiyya, 1990.
al-Muḥāmī, Aḥmad Bek b. Yūsuf b. Aḥmad al-Ḥusaynī. *Murshid al-Imām li-Birr Umm al-Imām*, 24 vols. MS Cairo, Dār al-Kutub al-Miṣriyya, nos. 1521–2.
al-Muzanī, Ismāʿīl b. Yaḥyā. *Mukhtaṣar al-Muzanī*.
- In Muḥammad b. Idrīs al-Shāfiʿī. *Al-Umm*. Ed. Maḥmūd Maṭrajī. Beirut: Dār al-Kutub al-ʿIlmiyya, 1993 (pt. IX, pp. 3–349).
- In Muḥammad b. Idrīs al-Shāfiʿī. *Al-Umm*. Ed. Muḥammad Zuhrī al-Najjār. Cairo: Maktabat al-Kulliyyāt al-Azhariyya, 1961 (pt. VIII, pp. 1–332).
- In Muḥammad b. Idrīs al-Shāfiʿī. *Al-Umm*. Ṭabʿa Muṣawwara ʿan Ṭabʿat Būlāq 1321 H. Cairo: al-Hay'a al-Miṣriyya al-ʿĀmma li'l-Kitāb, 1407/1987 (margins of pts. I-V).

Rodes, Robert E. and Howard Pospesel. *Premises and Conclusions: Symbolic Logic for Legal Analysis*. Upper Saddle River, NJ: Prentice Hall, 1997.
Sānū, Quṭb Muṣṭafā. *Muʿjam Muṣṭalaḥāt Uṣūl al-Fiqh, ʿArabī-Inkilīzī*. Beirut: Dār al-Fikr al-Muʿāṣir, 2000.
al-Sarakhsī, Muḥammad b. Aḥmad. *Kitāb al-Mabsūṭ*. Ed. Muḥammad Rāḍī, et al. 30 Vols. Cairo: Maṭbaʿat al-Saʿada, 1324-1331/1906-1913.
Schacht, Joseph. *The Origins of Muhammadan Jurisprudence*. Oxford: Oxford University Press, 1950.
Sezgin, Fuat. *Tārīkh al-Turāth al-ʿArabī*. [Vol. I, Pt. 3: "*al-Fiqh*"]. Trans. Maḥmūd Fahmī Ḥijāzī. Qum: Maktabat Āyat Allāh al-ʿUẓmā al-Marʿashī al-Najafī al-ʿĀmma, 1983-. [An Arabic translation of Sezgin's *Geschichte des Arabischen Schrifttums*, 12 vols. Leiden: E.J. Brill, 1967-].
al-Shāfiʿī, Muḥammad b. Idrīs. *Kitāb al-Umm*.
- ʿAbd al-Muṭṭalib = *Al-Umm*. 11 Pts. in 11 Vols. Ed. Rifʿat Fawzī ʿAbd al-Muṭṭalib. al-Manṣūra: Dār al-Wafā' li'l-Ṭibāʿa wa'l-Nashr wa'l-Tawzīʿ, 2001.
- Būlāq = *Al-Umm*. 7 Pts. in 3 Vols. [Pt. 1 is prefaced by al-Shāfiʿī's *Risāla*; with al-Muzanī's *Mukhtaṣar* on the margins of pts. 1–5; al-Shāfiʿī's *Musnad* on the margins of pt. 6; and al-Shāfiʿī's *Ikhtilāf al-Ḥadīth* on the margins of pt. 7]. Ṭabʿa Muṣawwara ʿan Ṭabʿat Būlāq 1321 H. Cairo: al-Hay'a al-Miṣriyya al-ʿĀmma li'l-Kitāb, 1407/1987.
- Ḥassūn = *Mawsūʿat al-Imām al-Shāfiʿī: al-Kitāb al-Umm*. 2nd ed. Ed. Aḥmad Badr al-Dīn Ḥassūn. 16 Pts. in 10 Vols. Beirut: Dār Qutayba, 2003.

- Maṭrajī = *Al-Umm*. Ed. Maḥmūd Maṭrajī. 9 Vols. [Vol. 9 contains the *Mukhtaṣar al-Muzanī ʿalā al-Umm*; the *Musnad al-Imām al-Shāfiʿī*, and the *Ikhtilāf al-Ḥadīth*]. Beirut: Dār al-Kutub al-ʿIlmiyya, 1993.
- Najjār = *Al-Umm*. Ed. Muḥammad Zuhrī al-Najjār. 8 Vols. [Vol. 8. includes al-Muzanī's *Mukhtaṣar*, and al-Shāfiʿī's *Musnad* and *Ikhtilāf al-Ḥadīth*]. Cairo: Maktabat al-Kulliyyāt al-Azhariyya, 1961.

al-Shāfiʿī, Muḥammad b. Idrīs. *Al-Risāla*. Ed. Aḥmad Muḥammad Shākir. Cairo: Maṭbaʿat Muṣṭafā al-Bābī al-Ḥalabī, 1940. [Translation 1: Lowry, Joseph. *The Epistle on Legal Theory*. New York: New York University Press, 2013. Translation 2: Khadduri, Majid. *Al-Shāfiʿī's Risāla: Treatise on the Foundations of Islamic Jurisprudence*. 2nd Ed. Cambridge, UK: Islamic Texts Society, 1999.]

al-Shāṭibī, Ibrāhīm b. Mūsā. *Al-Muwāfaqāt fī Uṣūl al-Sharīʿa*. Ed. Abū ʿUbayda Mashhūr b. Ḥasan Āl Salmān. Al-Khubar, KSA: Dār Ibn ʿAffān, 1997.

al-Shīrāzī, Abū Isḥāq Ibrāhīm. *Kitāb al-Maʿūna fi'l-Jadal*. Ed. ʿAbd al-Majīd Turkī. Beirut: Dār al-Gharb al-Islāmī, 1988.

al-Shīrāzī, Abū Isḥāq Ibrāhīm. *Al-Lumaʿ fī Uṣūl al-Fiqh*. Ed. Muḥyī al-Dīn Dīb Mustū and Yūsuf ʿAlī Badīwī. Damascus: Dār al-Kalam al-Ṭayyib; Dār Ibn Kathīr, 1995.

al-Shīrāzī, Abū Isḥāq Ibrāhīm. *Al-Maʿūna fi'l-Jadal*. Ed. ʿAlī b. ʿAbd al-ʿAzīz al-ʿUmayrīnī. Al-Ṣafāh, Kuwait: Manshūrāt Markaz al-Makhṭūṭāt wa'l-Turāth, 1987.

al-Shīrāzī, Abū Isḥāq Ibrāhīm. *Al-Tabṣira fī Uṣūl al-Fiqh*. Ed. Muḥammad Ḥasan Hītū. Damascus: Dār al-Fikr, 1983.

al-Ṭabarī, Abū Jaʿfar Muḥammad b. Jarīr. *Al-Aḥkām al-Fiqhiyya li'l-Imām al-Ṭabarī: Majmūʿa min Kitāb al-Tafsīr lahu*. Compiled and Edited by Muḥammad Ḥasan Muḥammad Ḥasan Ismāʿīl. Beirut: Dār al-Kutub al-ʿIlmiyya, 2000.

al-Ṭabarī, Abū Jaʿfar Muḥammad b. Jarīr. *Kitāb Ikhtilāf al-Fuqahā'*. Ed. Friedrich Kern. Beirut: Dār al-Kutub al-ʿIlmiyya, 1999.

Young, Walter Edward. "Uṣūl al-Fiqh." In *Oxford Islamic Studies Online. Oxford Islamic Studies Online*, http://www.oxfordislamicstudies.com/article/opr/t343/e0152

Young, Walter Edward. "The Dialectical Forge: Proto-System Juridical Disputation in the Kitāb Ikhtilāf al-ʿIrāqiyyīn." 2 vols. PhD diss., McGill University, 2012.

Zaman, Muhammad Qasim. *Religion and Politics under the Early ʿAbbāsids: the Emergence of the Proto-Sunnī Elite*. New York: E.J. Brill, 1997.

al-Zarkashī, Abū ʿAbd Allāh Badr al-Dīn Muḥammad. *Al-Baḥr al-Muḥīṭ fī Uṣūl al-Fiqh*. 8 Vols. [Edited by a Committee of Azharī ʿUlamā']. Cairo: Dār al-Kutubī, 1994.

Chapter 6
Short Dialectical Sequences and Independent Dialectical Formulae

6.1 Short Dialectical Sequences

Prefatory Notes

There are ten short dialectical sequences (presentation category B) in the subject-text. Unlike the preceding extended dialectical sequences, these will not be presented as *masāʾil*-sets with the rulings and arguments of Abū Ḥanīfa and company, but in isolation—treating only al-Shāfiʿī's additions to the Shaybānī Version.[1] I have, however, analyzed these sequences with full consideration to the relevant material which precedes them. As with the latter seven *masāʾil*-sets of Chap. 5, these short sequences will be followed by concise, play-by-play analyses, with additional observations restricted to footnotes. With regard to apparent didactic and justificatory intentions, the following fall somewhere between the longer instructional or historical sequences of category A and the more abbreviated arguments of categories C through E. All are of the instructional (*fa-in qāla*) variety between al-Shāfiʿī and an anticipated opponent. Al-Shāfiʿī's language thus makes his didactic intention plain, even while these short exchanges exhibit a justificatory role by strengthening key elements of his arguments.

[1] Please consult the Arabic editions and part 2 of my dissertation to situate the following sequences in their full argumentative contexts.

W.E. Young, *The Dialectical Forge*, Logic, Argumentation & Reasoning 9,
DOI 10.1007/978-3-319-25522-4_6

Short Sequence 1

§§35–37 from the *Chapter on Usurpation* (*Bāb al-Ghaṣb*)[2]

35 – Al-Shāfiʿī, may God Most High have mercy upon him, said: When a man [B] buys a female slave and has intercourse with her, then another man [O] lays rightful claim to her; [O] takes her and the dowry-of-her-like from [B]; and the dowry-of-her-like has no defined measure except what her like would [normally] marry by.[3] And the buyer [B] claims from the seller [S] the [same] price for which [B] took the female slave from [S]—but [B] does not claim [from S] the [cost of the] dowry which the owner of the female slave [O] took from [B], because it is like something that [B] himself consumed.[4]	35 - قَالَ الشَّافِعِيُّ رَحِمَهُ اللّٰهُ تَعَالَى: وَإِذَا اشْتَرَى الرَّجُلُ الْجَارِيَةَ فَوَطِئَهَا، ثُمَّ اسْتَحَقَّهَا رَجُلٌ أَخَذَهَا وَمَهْرَ مِثْلِهَا مِن الْوَاطِئِ وَلاَ وَقْتَ لِمَهْرِ مِثْلِهَا إلاَّ مَا يُنْكِحُ بِهِ مِثْلُهَا، وَيَرْجِعُ الْمُشْتَرِي عَلَى الْبَائِعِ بِثَمَنِ الْجَارِيَةِ الَّذِي قَبَضَ مِنْهُ ، وَلاَ يَرْجِعُ بِالْمَهْرِ الَّذِي أَخَذَهُ رَبُّ الْجَارِيَةِ مِنْهُ؛ لأَنَّهُ كَشَيْءٍ اسْتَهْلَكَهُ هُوَ.
36 – And if one should say: From where do you say this?[5]	36 - فَإِنْ قَالَ قَائِلٌ: مِن أَيْنَ قُلْتَ هَذَا؟
37 – It is said to him: When the Messenger of God, may God bless and save him, in the case of a woman married off without the permission of her *walī*-guardian, judged that her marriage was null and void and that—if subjected to sexual intercourse—the dowry was hers; the intercourse in *shubha*-ambiguity obliged the dowry. And the one who subjects to intercourse has no right to claim [anything] from the one who deceived him; because he himself was the "taker" in the sexual act. And if he did [have the right to] claim it from the one who deceived him, then he would owe the woman no dowry—because she might [herself] be his deceiver, and there cannot be obliged *for* her what he claims *from* her![6]	37 - قِيلَ لَهُ: لَمَّا قَضَى رَسُولُ اللّٰهِ -صَلَّى اللّٰهُ عَلَيْهِ وَسَلَّمَ- فِي الْمَرْأَةِ تُزَوَّجُ بِغَيْرِ إِذْنِ وَلِيِّهَا أَنَّ نِكَاحَهَا بَاطِلٌ، وَأَنَّ لَهَا إِنْ أُصِيبَتِ الْمَهْرَ، كَانَتِ الإِصَابَةُ بِشُبْهَةٍ تُوجِبُ الْمَهْرَ، وَلاَ يَكُونُ لِلْمُصِيبِ الرُّجُوعُ عَلَى مَنْ غَرَّهُ؛ لأَنَّهُ هُوَ الآخِذُ لِلإِصَابَةِ، وَلَوْ كَانَ يَرْجِعُ بِهِ عَلَى مَنْ غَرَّهُ لَمْ يَكُنْ لِلْمَرْأَةِ عَلَيْهِ مَهْرٌ؛ لأَنَّهَا قَدْ تَكُونُ غَارَّةً لَهُ فَلاَ يَجِبُ لَهَا مَا يَرْجِعُ بِهِ عَلَيْهَا.

In §35, al-Shāfiʿī's rulings for the *mas'ala* under consideration are meticulously laid out: (1) the rightful owner [O] takes the female slave and the "dowry-of-her-like" (*mahr mithlihā*) from the buyer [B]; (2) the dowry-of-her-like is neither to exceed nor fall short of what it would normally be; and (3) B claims from the

[2] Ḥassūn ed., vol. 9, p. 13; ʿAbd al-Muṭṭalib ed., vol. 8, p. 222.

[3] See Lane, *Lexicon*, s.v. "وقت". On the dowry (*mahr/ṣadāq*) and related rulings, see *MF*, s.v. "مهر" (vol. 39, pp. 151–209); *EI*[2], s.v. "Mahr"; *DJP*, vol. 2, pp. 20–36; and Hallaq, *Sharīʿa*, p. 277.

[4] For rulings related to the female slave (*jāriya*), see *MF*, s.v. "جارية" (vol. 15, pp. 86–7); and *EI*[2], s.v. "ʿAbd" (esp. §3.f).

[5] Meaning, presumably: "From where do you derive the authoritative indicant upon which you have based your claim?" This should be noted as the opponent's demand for a *dalīl*, which al-Shāfiʿī readily obliges in §37.

[6] Note this closing argument as an instance of reduction to an untenable consequence; in this case: perfectly-conflicting rulings. If the woman herself deceived the man, then—according to the logic of al-Shāfiʿī's opponent—he must at once pay her the dowry *and* claim it back from her.

seller [S] only the price by which he bought her, not the dowry.[7] Ruling (3) is then given *ʿaql*-support—signaled by the formula "because it is like X"—in which the efficient property occasioning ruling (3) is identified: "[the dowry] is like something that [B] himself consumed." In effect, al-Shāfiʿī has located the occasioning factor (*ʿilla*) in the contended branch-case (*farʿ*) which brings about his ruling (*ḥukm*), and—if called upon to do so—he needs only to produce the authoritative source-case (*aṣl*) in which this *ʿilla* and *ḥukm* are linked. The whole would correspond to "drawing indicant by way of correlational inference of the occasioning factor" (*al-istidlāl bi-qiyās al-ʿilla*).

In §36, al-Shāfiʿī initiates an "instructional" dialectic with the standard formula "if one should say" (*fa-in qāla qāʾil*); and his anticipated opponent there demands an authoritative basis for his argument. It is a request for a *dalīl*-indicant, and thus corresponds to al-Bājī's third question: "the question about the indicant for the *madhhab* opinion" (*al suʾāl ʿan dalīl al madhhab*).[8] In §37, we hear al-Shāfiʿī's response (*jawāb*)—signaled by the standard response formula "it is said to him" (*qīla lahu*)—and by which he readily supplies the requested *dalīl*: a Sunnaic decree (*qaḍā* Rasūl Allāh...) which, if all its elements identified with the contended case, would suffice as "drawing indicant by way of the Sunna" (*al-istidlāl biʾl-Sunna*). The cases, however, are parallel, not identical; al-Shāfiʿī has in fact provided the *aṣl* for his *qiyās*. He establishes this by pinpointing his source-case's efficient properties and legal effects: it is intercourse in *shubha*-ambiguity so the dowry is obliged; and the groom consumed sexual benefit so he cannot claim its price from the agent of invalid marriage. This latter *ʿilla-ḥukm* pair matches the contended case, and justifies his *qiyās* for ruling (3).

Again, this corresponds to *al-istidlāl bi-qiyās al-ʿilla*. At the same time, it constitutes an objection—and counter-thesis—to the position from which we assume the opponent to be arguing: Ibn Abī Laylā's assertion in §33 that B claims both price and dowry from S "because he had deceived him." In effect, al-Shāfiʿī has supplanted "deception"-occasions-"claims dowry" with "consumed sex"-occasions-"does not claim dowry;" Ibn Abī Laylā's *ʿilla* has been rejected, replaced by one that occasions the contradictory *ḥukm*, and the whole has been tied to a new *aṣl*. This corresponds to al-Baṣrī's second type of *al-muʿāraḍa bi-ʿilla* (*qiyās* supplanted by another *qiyās*);[9] and to the *muʿāraḍa bi-ʿilla mubtadaʾa* of al-Shīrāzī,

---

[7] The other jurists' rulings and arguments relevant to this *masʾala* are, by Ḥassūn's numbering system, §32 (Abū Ḥanīfa with Abū Yūsuf's adherence); §33 (Ibn Abī Laylā and a dialectical opponent—possibly al-Shaybānī); and §34 (that dialectical opponent's *a-raʾayta* question against Ibn Abī Laylā). Al-Shāfiʿī's rulings correspond, more or less, to Abū Ḥanīfa's in §32. Ibn Abī Laylā, however, ruled that B should claim both price *and dowry* from S, "because he had deceived him." This is attacked by an anonymous opponent who identifies (in §33) a property occasioning the opposite ruling (B, not S, committed the sex act), and follows (in §34) with an *a-raʾayta*-introduced *reductio* argument. Thus, al-Shāfiʿī's ruling (3)—conforming to Abū Ḥanīfa, Abū Yūsuf, and Ibn Abī Laylā's anonymous opponent—is to be the focus of dialectic; we may understand his opponent in the ensuing sequence as arguing from Ibn Abī Laylā's position.

[8] al-Bājī, *Minhāj*, Turkī ed., pp. 36–9, §§70–5.

[9] al-Baṣrī, *K. al-Qiyās al-Sharʿī*, Ḥamīd Allāh ed., p. 1044; Hallaq, "Treatise," p. 221.

al-Bājī, et al.[10] Finally, al-Shāfiʿī seals his argument with additional *ʿaql*-support—again signalled by "because"—by way of reduction to an untenable consequence. In short, this *reductio*—quite destructive of the opposing *ʿilla-ḥukm* pair—is contingent upon the possibility that the female slave herself is the "deceiver"; in such a case, B must simultaneously pay her dowry and claim it back, which is absurd.

Short Sequence 2

§§50–53 from the *Chapter on Disagreement Over Defects* (*Bāb al-Ikhtilāf fi'l-ʿAyb*)[11]

50 – Al-Shāfiʿī, may God Most High have mercy upon him, said: When a man buys a riding animal, or a garment, or whatever kind of *bayʿ*-commutation may be, and the buyer finds a defect in it, and the buyer and the seller disagree—the seller saying: It occurred in your keeping, but the buyer saying: Nay, in your keeping; if it is the kind of defect which could occur in [either] case, then the [accepted] declaration is that of the seller, along with his oath—of absolute certainty, by God—that he had sold it without this defect in it. Unless, that is, the buyer provides *bayyina*-evidence for his claim—for *bayyina*-evidence is superior to an oath. But if the seller abstains [from oath-taking], we revert the oath to the buyer—whether we suspect him or not—and if he swears, we send the commodity back to [the seller] due to the defect. But if [the buyer] abstains from the oath, we don't send it back to [the seller]—we don't reward [the buyer] due only to his associate's oath-abstention. Rather, we only reward him due to the oath-abstention when there is, along with the oath-abstention, his [own] oath.[12]	50 - قَالَ الشَّافِعِيُّ رَحِمَهُ اللّٰهُ تَعَالَى: وَإِذَا اشْتَرَى الرَّجُلُ الدَّابَّةَ أَوْ الثَّوْبَ أَوْ أَيَّ بَيْعٍ مَا كَانَ ، فَوَجَدَ الْمُشْتَرِي بِهِ عَيْبًا فَاخْتَلَفَ الْمُشْتَرِي وَالْبَائِعُ ، فَقَالَ الْبَائِعُ: حَدَثَ عِنْدَك. وَقَالَ الْمُشْتَرِي: بَلْ عِنْدَك. فَإِنْ كَانَ عَيْبًا يَحْدُثُ مِثْلُهُ بِحَالٍ فَالْقَوْلُ قَوْلُ الْبَائِعِ مَعَ يَمِينِهِ عَلَى الْبَتِّ بِاَللَّهِ لَقَدْ بَاعَهُ وَمَا هَذَا الْعَيْبُ بِهِ، إلاَّ أَنْ يَأْتِيَ الْمُشْتَرِي عَلَى دَعْوَاهُ بِبَيِّنَةٍ، فَتَكُونَ الْبَيِّنَةُ أَوْلَى مِن الْيَمِينِ، وَإِنْ نَكَلَ الْبَائِعُ رَدَدْنَا الْيَمِينَ عَلَى الْمُشْتَرِي، اتَّهَمْنَاهُ أَوْ لَمْ نَتَّهِمْهُ فَإِنْ حَلَفَ رَدَدْنَا عَلَيهِ السِّلْعَةَ بِالْعَيْبِ، وَإِنْ نَكَلَ عَن الْيَمِينِ لَمْ نَرْدُدْهَا عَلَيْهِ وَلَمْ نُعْطِهِ بِنُكُولِ صَاحِبِهِ فَقَطْ، إنَّمَا نُعْطِيهِ بِالنُّكُولِ إذَا كَانَ مَعَ النُّكُولِ يَمِينُهُ.

(continued)

[10] (Shīr.VII.15.2.1; Bāj.IX.B.15.2.1) al-Shīrāzī, *Maʿūna*, Turkī ed., p. 262, §148 [Missing from al-ʿUmayrīnī ed.]; al-Bājī, *Minhāj*, Turkī ed., p. 201, §455. Cf. Ibn ʿAqīl, *K. al-Jadal*, p. 71, §330.

[11] Ḥassūn ed., vol. 9, pp. 17–18; ʿAbd al-Muṭṭalib ed., vol. 8, p. 224.

[12] This particular *mas'ala* concerns burden of proof—more specifically, how a "benefit of assumption" is to be established; "*al-qawl qawl* X" means "party X receives the benefit of assumption." Similar discussions occur in the opening chapter of the subject-text, and at several other places—cf. §§1–2, 50, 133–4, 196–9, 359–61, 459, 860–1, and 1276–9. Note that similar formulaic expressions occur throughout most of these: "the *qawl* is the *qawl* of P; and upon Q is enjoined the X." For general expositions on the complex procedures of evidence (*bayyina*), oaths (*aymān*; s. *yamīn*), and related rulings, see *MF*, s.v. "أيمان" (vol. 7, pp. 245–314; esp. §19), "إثبات" (vol. 1, pp. 232–49; esp. §§28–9), "شهادة" (vol. 26, pp. 214–53; esp. §4), and "دعوى" (vol. 20, pp. 270–319); *EI*[2], s.v. "Yamīn" and "Bayyina"; *DJP*, vol. 2, pp. 556–66; and Hallaq, *Sharīʿa*, pp. 348–53.

51 – And if one should say: What provides indication for what you have stated?	51 - فَإِنْ قَالَ قَائِلٌ: مَا دَلَّ عَلَى مَا ذَكَرْتَ؟
52 – It is said: The Messenger of God, may God bless and save him, ruled, for the Helpers,[13] the [taking of] oaths, to merit retaliation for the blood of their companion.[14] They abstained, and he reverted the oaths onto the Jews, by which they exculpated themselves. Then ʿUmar b. al-Khaṭṭāb, may God be pleased with him, opined that oaths be demanded of those accused of bloodletting, by which they might exculpate themselves. They abstained, so he reverted [the oaths] to the claimants, and did not reward them anything on the basis of [the defendants'] oath-abstention, not even reversion of the oaths.[15] And the Sunna of the Messenger of God, may God bless and save him, is the interpreting *naṣṣ*-formulation providing indication for his general/non-specific Sunna.[16]	52 – قِيلَ: قَضَى رَسُولُ اللّٰهِ - صَلَّى اللّٰهُ عَلَيْهِ وَسَلَّمَ - لِلأَنْصَارِيِّينَ بِالأَيْمَانِ يَسْتَحِقُّونَ بِهَا دَمَ صَاحِبِهِمْ فَنَكَلُوا وَرَدَّ الأَيْمَانَ عَلَى يَهُودَ يَبْرَءُونَ بِهَا، ثُمَّ رَأَى عُمَرُ بْنُ الْخَطَّابِ رضي اللّٰه تَعَالَى عنه الأَيْمَانَ عَلَى الْمُدَّعَى عَلَيْهِمْ الدَّمَ يَبْرَءُونَ بِهَا فَنَكَلُوا، فَرَدَّهَا عَلَى الْمُدَّعِينَ وَلَمْ يُعْطِهِمْ بِالنُّكُولِ شَيْئًا حَتَّى رَدَّ الأَيْمَانَ، وَسُنَّةُ رَسُولِ اللّٰهِ - صَلَّى اللّٰهُ عَلَيْهِ وَسَلَّمَ - النَّصُّ الْمُفَسِّرَةُ تَدُلُّ عَلَى سُنَّتِهِ الْجُمْلَةِ.

(continued)

[13] The Anṣāriyyūn (s. Anṣārī), meaning those Medinans who leant full support to the Prophet and the early community of Muslims, and by which they are distinguished from the Muhājirūn ("Emigrants;" from Mecca) who were initially dependent upon their aid. See *EI*², s.v. "al-Anṣār" and "al-Muhād̲j̲irūn" for brief descriptions.

[14] See the *MF* (s.v. "دم", vol. 21, p. 25, §1), where the "one meriting blood" (*mustaḥiqq al-dam*) is equated with the "executor of a right to retaliation" (*walī al-qiṣāṣ*).

[15] That is, reversion of the oaths a second time, back to the accused. When the accused abstain from the oaths, the accusers must either take the oaths themselves, produce *bayyina*-evidence, or drop the case. Nothing is granted them simply because the accused would not take the oaths.

[16] Which is to say, what the Prophet did regarding the Anṣāriyyūn may be used to interpret his more general decree mentioned in §53. Cf. §255: "[your] *ḥadīth* is a general/non-specific type (*jumla*), while our *ḥadīth* is an interpreting type (*mufassir*)." Here at the end of §52, ʿAbd al-Muṭṭalib, without annotation, renders المجملة rather than الجملة, apparently substituting the standard technical term *mujmal* employed by full-system theorists to designate "ambiguous" *uṣūl* requiring additional, explanatory sources for intensional clarification (see, e.g., al-Bājī, *Minhāj*, Turkī ed., p. 12, §15).

53 – And likewise is the decree of ʿUmar b. al-Khaṭṭāb, may God Most High be pleased with him.[17] And the [more general] decree of the Prophet, may God bless and save him: «The *bayyina*-evidence is [obliged] for the claimant, and the oath is [obliged] for the accused;» then the [more specific] decree of ʿUmar b. al-Khaṭṭāb, may God Most High be pleased with him—that is a general/non-specific sense indicated by the *naṣṣ*-formulation of the ruling of each one of the two.[18] And whosoever said he does not exempt the accused from the oath; he contradicts this, and he augments and burdens the *ḥadīth* with what is not in it. We have set this down in the *Book of Judgments*.[19] And the oath is between those concluding a contract of commutation, [made] with absolute certainty with regard to what they have mutually contracted.	53 - وَكَذَلِكَ قَوْلُ عُمَرَ بْنِ الْخَطَّابِ رضي اللهُ تَعَالَى عنه وَقَوْلُ النَّبِيِّ -صَلَّى اللهُ عَلَيْهِ وَسَلَّمَ: «الْبَيِّنَةُ عَلَى الْمُدَّعِي، وَالْيَمِينُ عَلَى الْمُدَّعَى عَلَيْهِ» ثُمَّ قَوْلُ عُمَرَ بْنِ الْخطَّابِ رضي اللهُ تَعَالَى عنه ذَلِكَ جُمْلَةٌ دَلَّ عَلَيْهَا نَصُّ حُكم كُلِّ وَاحِدَةٍ مِنْهُمَا، وَالَّذِي قَالَ: لاَ يَعْدُو بِالْيَمِينِ الْمُدَّعَى عَلَيْهِمْ. يُخَالِفُ هَذَا فَيَكْثُرُ وَيُحَمِّلُ الْحَدِيثَ مَا لَيْسَ فِيهِ. وَقَدْ وَضَعْنَا هَذَا فِي كِتَابِ الأَقْضِيَةِ وَالْيَمِينِ بَيْنَ الْمُتَبَايِعَيْنِ عَلَى الْبَتِّ فِيمَا تَبَايَعَا فِيهِ.

In the initial part of §50, al-Shāfiʿī's rulings with regard to "benefit of assumption" are presented for the primary case in which the seller [S] is willing to swear the oath: (1) the declaration of S, with his oath, trumps the declaration of the buyer [B], and the commodity is not returned and refunded; and (2) the declaration of B, with *bayyina*-evidence, trumps the declaration and oath of S, so the commodity is returned and refunded. Rule (2) receives doctrinal support with a presumably

[17] Meaning, ʿUmar's decree also explains the Prophet's more general decree in §53.

[18] In other words, the more specific judgments of the Prophet and ʿUmar in §§52–3 not only provide details missing from the Prophet's general decree in §53, but they also serve as indicants for the general principle embodied by that decree: ultimately, in all cases, the burden of proof rests with the accusers. I have interpreted the conjunction *thumma* as indicating "a transition from the general to the more special"—as it is frequently employed in genealogies (Wright, *Arabic Grammar*, i. 293 B)—and which function is most appropriate to the *jumla-mufassir* distinction here described.

[19] There is a *Book of Judgments* (*Kitāb al-Aqḍiya*) in the *Umm* compendium (see Ḥassūn ed., vol. 8, pt. 13, pp. 7 ff., §§24360 ff.) In the opening (§24360) of this book, however, we find reference to a "*Book of Judgments* (*Kitāb al-Aqḍiya*), which is the *Book of the Witness and the Oath* (*Kitāb al-Shāhid wa'l-Yamīn*)." So there appears to have been another text called *Kitāb al-Aqḍiya*, and bearing an alternate title; and, although we do not find a chapter of the *Umm* with the exact title of *Kitāb al-Shāhid wa'l-Yamīn*, we do find references to such a book in other sources. Among them is the eulogy work (*manāqib*) of Ibn Ḥajar al-ʿAsqalānī (d.852/1449), the *Tawālī al-Ta'sīs*, which relates a highly relevant anecdote from one of al-Shāfiʿī's early ("Old Doctrine") students: "And al-Ābarī extracted [a report] (*akhraja*) from the transmission-chain (*ṭarīq*) of al-Zaʿfarānī [d.260/874]; who said: We were attending the disputation session (*majlis*) of Bishr al-Marīsī [d.218/833; eminent Murjiʾī and follower of Abū Yūsuf], but we were not capable of overcoming him in dialectical disputation (*kunnā lā naqdaru ʿalā munāẓaratihi*); then al-Shāfiʿī arrived and gave us the *Kitāb al-Shāhid wa'l-Yamīn*. I studied it in two nights, then I headed over to the teaching circle (*ḥalaqa*) of Bishr, engaged him in dialectic, and decisively refuted him (*nāẓartuhu fa-qaṭaʿtuhu*). And he said: This is no cleverness of yours (*laysa hādhā min kaysika*); this is from the arguments (*kalām*) of a man I saw in Mecca [i.e., al-Shāfiʿī]—and with him was half the intellect (*ʿaql*) of the world's people!" (*Tawālī*, p. 91, §41).

endoxon principle—the conclusion of some prior weighing of evidentiary genera against each other—suitably expressed with the comparative common to *tarjīḥ*: "the *bayyina*-evidence is superior to (*awlā min*) the oath." Efficient properties for both rulings are implied. For (1): absence of B's *bayyina* plus presence of S's oath occasions no return and refund; and for (2) presence of B's *bayyina* occasions return and refund.

In the latter part of §50, al-Shāfiʿī's rulings are presented for the subsidiary case in which S abstains from swearing the oath: (3) the oath reverts to B, he swears, and the commodity is returned and refunded; and (4) the oath reverts to B, he doesn't swear, so the commodity is not returned and refunded. Again, efficient properties for both are implied. For (3): the absence of S's oath plus the presence of B's oath occasions return and refund; and for (4) the absence of S's oath plus the absence of B's oath occasions no return and refund. Implicit to both sets is another principle—one of "reward"—by which B receives no special consideration due only to the oath-abstention (*nukūl*) of S; only when such is accompanied by B's oath is the case ruled in B's favor. Al-Shāfiʿī states this clearly at the close of §50; and so both his primary and subsidiary case rulings are supported by presumably *endoxa* principles.[20]

Again, al-Shāfiʿī has, in effect, located (or at least implied) the occasioning factors (*ʿilal*) which bring about his rulings (*aḥkām*) for the cases under consideration (*furūʿ*). In dialectic, we might anticipate the demand for a *dalīl*-indicant and, in response, al-Shāfiʿī's provision of the relevant *aṣl*—the whole of his justification again corresponding to his "drawing indicant by way of correlational inference of the occasioning factor" (*al-istidlāl bi-qiyās al-ʿilla*). This is precisely what occurs. In §51, al-Shāfiʿī again opens an "instructional" dialectic—focused on his ruling (4)—with the standard "if one should say" (*fa-in qāla qāʾil*); and his opponent demands his *dalīl*-indicant in even plainer fashion: "What provides indication for what you have stated (*mā dalla ʿalā mā dhakarta*)?" Again, this corresponds to al-Bājī's third question: "the question about the indicant for the *madhhab*-opinion" (*al-suʾāl ʿan dalīl al-madhhab*).[21] Al-Shāfiʿī's response—signalled by "it is said" (*qīla*)—is multifaceted, consisting of the anticipated *aṣl* (three *uṣūl*, in fact), a hermeneutical principle, an explanation of that principle, and an objection to the opposing ruling coupled with a charge of misinterpretation.

[20] By Ḥassūn's numbering system, the other jurists' relevant rulings and arguments are: §48 (Abū Ḥanīfa with Abū Yūsuf's adherence); and §49 (Ibn Abī Laylā). The locus of disagreement is whether or not the oath should revert to the accuser (B) upon the oath-abstention of the accused (S). Abū Ḥanīfa refuses to shift the burden from where the Prophet fixed it in his decree: "The *bayyina*-evidence is [obliged] for the claimant, and the oath is [obliged] for the accused" (cited by al-Shāfiʿī in §53). Ibn Abī Laylā, on the other hand, introduces a new efficient property—his own suspicion of B—which, if present, brings him not only to revert the oath to B, but to judge against him if he abstains. Thus al-Shāfiʿī's rulings (3) and (4) come closest to (though do not entirely identify with) Ibn Abī Laylā's position; and we might assume a dialectical opponent to be arguing from Abū Ḥanīfa's position.

[21] al-Bājī, *Minhāj*, Turkī ed., pp. 36–9, §70–5.

In §52 we learn al-Shāfiʿī's first two *dalīl*-indicants: a Sunnaic decree ("*qaḍā Rasūl Allāh…*") and an *athar*-tradition of ʿUmar. Again, these are parallels from another domain (homicide, not sale)—not identity-cases for *al-istidlāl bi'l-Sunna*. Rather, these are *uṣūl* for *qiyās*, and both share key elements with al-Shāfiʿī's rulings (3) and (4): not only was oath-abstention permitted, but its occurrence occasioned a reversion of the oath to the other party—from accusers to accused in the Sunnaic decree (the reverse of our current *mas'ala*), and from accused to accusers in the *athar*-tradition. This latter tradition shares a further element with al-Shāfiʿī's ruling (4): the accusers are granted nothing solely on the basis of the oath-abstention of the accused, but must themselves swear. The wording of al-Shāfiʿī's explanation of this *athar*-tradition ties it firmly to the "reward" principle by which he supports his ruling (4).

Al-Shāfiʿī then proceeds to explain the hermeneutical principle which ties his *uṣūl* together and produces the desired *ʿilla-ḥukm* pair for his *qiyās*. First he states the Prophet's decree for the Anṣāriyyūn is "the interpreting *naṣṣ*-formulation (*al-naṣṣ al-mufassira*) providing indication for (*tadullu ʿalā*) his general/non-specific Sunna (*sunnatihi al-jumla*)"; then, at the start of §53, he asserts the same of the *athar*-tradition of ʿUmar.[22] Both, in other words, interpret and expand upon the Prophet's more general decree—which is now quoted: «The *bayyina*-evidence is [obliged] for the claimant, and the oath is [obliged] for the accused»—and both, he explains, provide their own indication for this same "burden of proof" principle. Having knitted these traditions together in hermeneutical complementarity, he objects to the opposing ruling[23] by accusing its proponents of contradicting this hermeneutic and misinterpreting the "burden of proof" *ḥadīth*, then references his counter-argument in another writing.

---

[22] Cf. §255 and attached note, above. One cannot overstress the importance of al-Shāfiʿī incorporating an explicit reference to his legal theory within a dialectical sequence. This particular principle is familiar from his *Risāla*, where the terms *naṣṣ*, *mufassir*, and *jumla* all coincide when he explains the relationship between Qur'ān and Sunna. God has clarified (*abāna*) "that the Sunna is not an abrogator (*nāsikha*) to the *Kitāb*, rather it is subordinate (*tabaʿ*) to the *Kitāb*, relating to the like of what was revealed as *naṣṣ* (*bi-mithli mā nazala naṣṣan*), and an interpreter (*mufassira*) of the *maʿnā*-intension of what God revealed of [the *Kitāb*] in non-specific form (*jumalan*)" (*Risāla*, Shākir ed., p. 106, §314; cf. Joseph Lowry's translation [Epistle, p. 81, §127], and see his lucid discussions on al-Shāfiʿī's hermeneutic of *naṣṣ*, *mufassir*, and *jumla* in "Legal Hermeneutics of al-Shāfiʿī and Ibn Qutayba"). As regards *jumla*, Lowry notes: "*Jumla* is found in the *Risāla*, but in a very precise sense, meaning a 'general rule the details of which are found elsewhere'" (*op. cit.*, pp. 36–7). A similar discussion occurs in al-Shāfiʿī's *Kitāb Bayān Farāʾiḍ Allāh* (*Umm*, Ḥassūn ed., vol. 10, pt. 15, p. 90, §56). Here in §52, however, al-Shāfiʿī explains that what is univocal (*naṣṣ*) in the *Sunna* serves to interpret what is non-specific (*jumla*) in the *Sunna*; and the particular manner in which this precept obtains in the *mas'ala* at hand will be described in §53. This bears witness to the fine-honing of legal theory in a dialectical venue; and, of course, the hermeneutics of *naṣṣ*, *mujmal*, *mubayyan*, etc. receive full-chapter treatment in later, fully-systematized *uṣūl* works.

[23] Asserted by Abū Ḥanīfa in §48, and which does not allow oath-abstention of the accused without consequence: the oath does not revert to the accuser, and the case is ruled in his favor.

Al-Shāfiʿī's objection thus corresponds to the *jadal*-theorists' moves, in the domain of *istidlāl* from the Sunna, of "charge of overgeneralization" (*daʿwā al-ijmāl*)[24] and "interpretation" (*ta'wīl*) by way of "particularizing the general" (*takhṣīṣ al-ʿumūm*),[25] accompanied by a more unique variety of what we might call "hermeneutic-objection."[26] At the same time, he is supplanting this misapplication of general Sunna with his *qiyās* from a conglomeration of complementary traditions. Ultimately, therefore, his arguments and objections all correspond to that subtype of *muʿāraḍa bi'l-ʿilla*, in the domain of objections to *al-istidlāl bi'l-Sunna*, wherein "the Sunna is general (*ʿumūm*), allowing the possibility of particularization (*takhṣīṣ*)."[27] The section closes with a last subsidiary ruling (5): the oaths for both S and B must be sworn "with absolute certainty" (*ʿalā al-batti*).

Short Sequence 3

§§62–65 from the *Chapter on Disagreement Over Defects* (*Bāb al-Ikhtilāf fi'l-ʿAyb*)[28]

62 – Al-Shāfiʿī, may God Most High have mercy upon him, said: When a man buys a slave, or whatever commodity one may buy, with the understanding that the seller has *khiyār*-option—or the buyer, or both of them together—for a period they both described; if the period is three [days] or less, the *bay*ʿ-contract is lawful. But if it exceeds that by a mere instant or more, then the *bay*ʿ-contract is undone.[29]	62 - قَالَ الشَّافِعِيُّ رَحِمَهُ اللّٰهُ تَعَالَى : وَإِذَا اشْتَرَى الرَّجُلُ الْعَبْدَ أَوْ أَيَّ سِلْعَةٍ مَا اشْتَرَى عَلَى أَنَّ الْبَائِعَ بِالْخِيَارِ أَوْ الْمُشْتَرِي أَوْ هُمَا مَعًا إِلَى مُدَّةٍ يَصِفَانِهَا ؛ فَإِنْ كَانَت الْمُدَّةُ ثَلاَثًا أَوْ أَقَلَّ فَالْبَيْعُ جَائِزٌ ، وَإِنْ كَانَتْ أَكْثَرَ مِن ذَلِكَ بِطَرْفَةِ عَيْنٍ فَأَكْثَرَ فَالْبَيْعُ مُنْتَقَضٌ.

(continued)

[24] (Shīr.II.C.3.1; Bāj.II.2.2.3.2) al-Shīrāzī, *Maʿūna*, al-ʿUmayrīnī ed., p. 59; al-Bājī, *Minhāj*, Turkī ed., p. 102, §198. Cf. Ibn ʿAqīl, *K. al-Jadal*, p. 34, §179.

[25] (Shīr.II.C.7.2; Bāj.II.2.6.2) al-Shīrāzī, *Maʿūna*, al-ʿUmayrīnī ed., pp. 65–6; al-Bājī, *Minhāj*, Turkī ed., p. 118, §231. Cf. Ibn ʿAqīl, *K. al-Jadal*, p. 36, §§189.

[26] That is, his objection that the opposing position has "augmented and burdened the *ḥadīth* with what is not in it." I have not been able to find a match for this objection in our *jadal*-theory works; it seems as much a charge of misinterpretation due to not following his *mufassir*-to-*jumla* principle, as it is to "over-burdening" the *ḥadīth*. For the present, I will simply place it under a larger genus of "hermeneutic-objection."

[27] (Shīr.II.C.8.2.3; Bāj.II.2.7.2.3) al-Shīrāzī, *Maʿūna*, al-ʿUmayrīnī ed., pp. 67–8, n. 6 [the discussion, missing from the *Maʿūna*, is extracted from al-Shīrāzī's *Mulakhkhaṣ*]; al-Bājī, *Minhāj*, Turkī ed., p. 125, §247.

[28] Ḥassūn ed., vol. 9, pp. 20–1; ʿAbd al-Muṭṭalib ed., vol. 8, pp. 226–8.

[29] On the voluntary or conventionary (as opposed to automatic), time-limited, conditional *khiyār*-option, see *MF*, s.v. "خيار الشرط" (vol. 20, pp. 77–112; esp. §§15–16, which treat the current *mas'ala* of restricting *khiyār al-sharṭ* to three days); *EI*², s.v. "Khiyār" (esp. §1); *DJP*, vol. 2, pp. 250–1; and Hallaq, *Sharīʿa*, pp. 248–9. See also Schacht, *Origins*, pp. 326–7, where this short sequence of §§62–5 has been translated in full.

63 – And if one should say: How is it that *khiyār*-option is permitted for three, but not permitted for more than three [days]?	63 - فَإِنْ قَالَ قَائِلٌ: وَكَيْفَ جَازَ الْخِيَارُ ثَلاَثًا وَلَمْ يَجُزْ أَكْثَرُ مِن ثَلاَثٍ؟
64 – It is said: If not for the *khabar*-report on the Messenger of God, may God bless and save him, *khiyār*-option after separation of the contracting parties would not be permitted for an hour! [This is] because the Messenger of God, may God bless and save him, only gave them the right of *khiyār*-option up to the point that they part—which is to say: it is not permitted that a man turn over his property to the seller [as price], and the seller turn over his female slave to the buyer [as commodity], and that the seller not have the usufruct of the price of his commodity, nor the buyer enjoy the usufruct of his female slave. And if [1] we claim they both have the right to enjoy the usufruct [and] we claim that both are obliged to return if one of them wishes to return; and [2] when it is of the *aṣl*-principle of our *madhhab*-procedure[30] that I am not permitted to sell a female slave under condition that her [new] owner does not sell her—because, when I stipulate this for him, I have diminished something of [his] ownership, and it is not right that I transfer ownership to him, by way of compensation I take from him, except for something over which his ownership is complete—then [3] I will have deprived him—by way of *khiyār*-option stipulation—*of all ownership*, even to the extent of forbidding it to him! And the *aṣl*-principle of *bayʿ*-commutation with *khiyār*-option stipulation—if not for the *khabar*-report—ought necessarily to have been invalid, because we invalidate *bayʿ*-commutation for less than what I have mentioned. So when the Messenger of God, may God bless and save him, stipulated: «for the milking-animal whose milk has been held back in her udders:[31] *khiyār*-option of three [days] after the *bayʿ*-commutation»...	64 - قِيلَ لَوْلاَ الْخَبَرُ عَن رَسُولِ اللهِ -صَلَّى اللهُ عَلَيْهِ وَسَلَّمَ- مَا جَازَ أَنْ يَكُونَ الْخِيَارُ بَعْدَ تَفَرُّقِ الْمُتَبَايِعَيْنِ سَاعَةً؛ لأَنَّ رَسُولَ اللهِ -صَلَّى اللهُ عَلَيْهِ وَسَلَّمَ- إِنَّمَا جَعَلَ لَهُمَا الْخِيَارَ إِلَى أَنْ يَتَفَرَّقَا؛ وَذَلِكَ أَنَّ رَجُلاً لاَ يَجُوزُ أَنْ يَدْفَعَ مَالَهُ إِلَى الْبَائِعِ وَيَدْفَعَ الْبَائِعُ جَارِيَتَهُ لِلْمُشْتَرِي فَلاَ يَكُونُ لِلْبَائِعِ الاِنْتِفَاعُ بِثَمَنِ سِلْعَتِهِ وَلاَ لِلْمُشْتَرِي أَنْ يَنْتَفِعَ بِجَارِيَتِهِ، وَلَوْ زَعَمْنَا أَنَّ لَهُمَا أَنْ يَنْتَفِعَا زَعَمْنَا أَنَّ عَلَيْهِمَا إِنْ شَاءَ أَحَدُهُمَا أَنْ يَرُدَّ رَدَّ، فَإِذَا كَانَ مِن أَصْلِ مَذْهَبِنَا أَنَّهُ لاَ يَجُوزُ أَنْ أَبِيعَ الْجَارِيَةَ عَلَى أَنْ لاَ يَبِيعَهَا صَاحِبُهَا لأَنِّي إِذَا شَرَطْتُ عَلَيْهِ هَذَا فَقَدْ نَقَصْتُهُ مِن الْمِلْكِ شَيْئًا، وَلاَ يَصْلُحُ أَنْ أُمَلِّكَهُ بِعِوَضٍ آخُذُهُ مِنْهُ إِلاَّ مَا مِلْكُهُ عَلَيْهِ تَامٌّ فَقَدْ نَقَصْتُهُ بِشَرْطِ الْخِيَارِ كُلَّ الْمِلْكِ حَتَّى حَظَرْتُهُ عَلَيْهِ، وَأَصْلُ الْبَيْعِ عَلَى الْخِيَارِ لَوْلاَ الْخَبَرُ كَانَ يَنْبَغِي أَنْ يَكُونَ فَاسِدًا لأَنَّا نُفْسِدُ الْبَيْعَ بِأَقَلَّ مِنْهُ مِمَّا ذَكَرْتُ، فَلَمَّا شَرَطَ رَسُولُ اللهِ -صَلَّى اللهُ عَلَيْهِ وَسَلَّمَ-: «فِي الْمُصَرَّاةِ خِيَارَ ثَلاَثٍ بَعْدَ الْبَيْعِ».

(continued)

[30] Cf. al-Shāfiʿī's use of the term *aṣl* in §1411, to which this appears similar. Here, however, it is the *aṣl* of "our *madhhab*," meaning approximately "the base principle of our established way of doing things." The term *madhhab* was eventually to acquire a specific set of technical meanings, among them that of the doctrinal *madhhab*, or "school" (see Hallaq, *Sharīʿa*, pp. 60–3), but here in §65 al-Shāfiʿī seems to be appealing to an endoxic, general procedure.

[31] A reference to an apparently common practice of binding the udders of a milk-producing animal for some time before its sale, thus causing the milk to accumulate, and providing a false impression of the animal's productivity upon its first milking.

65 – ... and it was narrated about him,[32] upon him be blessings and peace, that he gave Ḥabbān b. Munqidh the right to *khiyār*-option of three [days] for what he purchased; we arrive ultimately at what the Messenger of God, may God bless and save him, commanded of *khiyār*-option. And we didn't exceed it, since the Messenger of God, may God bless and save him, did not exceed it. Which is to say:[33] his commanding it [in this manner] looks to be as the limit for its utmost extent,[34] since the udder-binding of the milking-animal might be realized after the first milking—in a day, or a night, or in two days—to the point [the buyer] does not doubt it of her. And if the *khiyār*-option was only so that he might come to clearly know of the udder-binding defect, it is more likely it be said: "*khiyār*-option[35] until he knows it is a bound animal—should that take a long time, or only a short time"—just as he [automatically] has the right to *khiyār*-option for a defect, when he discovers it, without a stipulated time period—whether after a long or short time. And even if the *khiyār*-option of Ḥabbān was only [to allow] for consulting another, it was possible that he consult him on the spot, or an hour later—and it was possible that he put off the consultation for a long while. So the *khabar*-report was providing indication that the *khiyār*-option of three [days] is the utmost limit for *khiyār*-option, and that we were not permitted to exceed it. Whoever exceeds it is, according to us, the stipulator of an invalid *bay*ʿ-contract.[36]

65 - وَرُوِيَ عَنْهُ عليه الصلاة والسلام أَنَّهُ جَعَلَ لِحَبَّانَ بْنِ مُنْقِذٍ خِيَارَ ثَلاَثٍ فِيمَا ابْتَاعَ، انْتَهَيْنَا إِلَى مَا أَمَرَ بِهِ رَسُولُ اللهِ -صَلَّى اللهُ عَلَيْهِ وَسَلَّمَ- مِن الْخِيَارِ وَلَمْ نُجَاوِزْهُ إذ لَمْ يُجَاوِزْهُ رَسُولُ اللهِ -صَلَّى اللهُ عَلَيْهِ وَسَلَّمَ- وَذَلِكَ أَنَّ أَمْرَهُ بِهِ يُشْبِهُ أَنْ يَكُونَ كَالْحَدِّ لِغَايَتِهِ مِن قِبَلِ أَنَّ الْمُصَرَّاةَ قَدْ تُعْرَفُ تَصْرِيَتُهَا بَعْدَ أَوَّلِ حَلْبَةٍ فِي يَوْمٍ وَلَيْلَةٍ وَفِي يَوْمَيْنِ حَتَّى لاَ يَشُكَّ فِيهَا، فَلَوْ كَانَ الْخِيَارُ إِنَّمَا هُوَ لِيَعْلَمَ اسْتِبَانَةَ عَيْبِ التَّصْرِيَةِ أَشْبَهَ أَنْ يُقَالَ: الْخِيَارُ حَتَّى يَعْلَمَ أَنَّهَا مُصَرَّاةٌ طَالَ ذَلِكَ أَوْ قَصُرَ، كَمَا يَكُونُ لَهُ الْخِيَارُ فِي الْعَيْبِ إِذَا عَلِمَهُ بِلاَ وَقْتٍ طَالَ ذَلِكَ أَوْ قَصُرَ، وَلَوْ كَانَ خِيَارُ حَبَّانَ إِنَّمَا كَانَ لِاسْتِشَارَةِ غَيْرِهِ أَمْكَنَهُ أَنْ يَسْتَشِيرَهُ فِي مقَامِهِ وَبَعْدَهُ بِسَاعَةٍ، وَأَمْكَنَ فِيهِ أَنْ يَدَعَ الِاسْتِشَارَةَ دَهْرًا، فَكَانَ الْخَبَرُ دَلَّ عَلَى أَنَّ خِيَارَ ثَلاَثٍ أَقْصَى غَايَةِ الْخِيَارِ، فَلَمْ يَجُزْ لَنَا أَنْ نُجَاوِزَهُ وَمَنْ جَاوَزَهُ كَانَ عِنْدَنَا مُشْتَرِطًا بَيْعًا فَاسِدًا.

[32] It is unclear why Ḥassūn chose to break off and begin a new section here, as al-Shāfiʿī moves fluidly from one supporting Sunnaic *dalīl* to another and ties them together as representing the sum-total of the Prophet's restrictions on *khiyār*-option.

[33] Here I have followed ʿAbd al-Muṭṭalib (Ḥassūn renders ولك).

[34] That is, the Prophet's decrees appear to limit *khiyār*-option to three days and no more.

[35] Again, I have followed ʿAbd al-Muṭṭalib over Ḥassūn, who renders له الخيار.

[36] See Schacht, *Origins*, pp. 326–7 (*Tr. I*, 12), where the whole of this sequence has been translated. Elsewhere (pp. 123–4), Schacht sees this argument as illustrating al-Shāfiʿī's "most important methodical rule regarding the use of *qiyās*... that a *qiyās* cannot be based on a special case which constitutes an exception from a general rule; in other words, that exceptions cannot be extended by analogy." He cites (p. 124, n. 1) not only the above as example but also (by his own numbering system) §§216 and 253—which, I believe, are the dialectical sequences ending in Ḥassūn §§1232 and §1412, respectively, of our subject-text. He also cites relevant discussions in al-Shāfiʿī's *Risāla*.

In §62 al-Shāfiʿī presents his ruling for the *mas'ala* at hand; in short: a *bay*ʿ-contract stipulating *khiyār*-option is lawful only when *khiyār*-option is stipulated for three days or less. We may understand this property ("it is for three days or less") as efficient in occasioning the ruling "it is lawful;" and we may anticipate this *ʿilla-ḥukm* pair as a focus for ensuing dialectic.[37] In §63 al-Shāfiʿī opens an "instructional" dialectic (*fa-in qāla qā'il*) with his opponent employing the question formula: "How is [X] lawful (*kayfa jāza*), and more than [X] not lawful (*lam yajuz*)?" This corresponds either to al-Bājī's fourth question: "the question about the mode of the *dalīl*-indicant" (*al-su'āl ʿan wajh al-dalīl*), or to a species of "demand-objection" (*muṭālaba*).[38]

Al-Shāfiʿī's response, heralded by "it is said" (*qīla*), begins in §64 and is multifaceted. In brief, it is an example of "drawing indicant by way of the Sunna" (*al-istidlāl bi'l-Sunna*) in which a particular *khabar*-report (allowing three days or less) makes an exception to the general Sunnaic rule (forbidding *khiyār*-option after the contract is concluded). His ensuing explanation (*tafsīr*) underscores the untenable consequence of the opposing "unlimited *khiyār*-option" position—the incompatibility of the claims of full ownership, full usufruct (*intifāʿ*), and full responsibility to return—and one of his objections may thus be classified as a species of *reductio*. The overall complex of objections includes an appeal to the "*aṣl*-principle of our *madhhab*-procedure," the effect of which is to clarify what the basis of *qiyās* would in fact be, if not for the *khabar*-report's exception.[39] Although

[37] By Ḥassūn's numbering system, the other jurists' relevant rulings and arguments are: §60 (Abū Ḥanīfa); and §61 (Ibn Abī Laylā with Abū Yūsuf's adherence). Abū Ḥanīfa rules against *bay*ʿ-contracts stipulating *khiyār*-option in excess of three days, and cites a Prophetic decree asserting a three-day limit for a particular case. Ibn Abī Laylā, however, judges it lawful even for a year. In this he is followed by Abū Yūsuf and—according to al-Sarakhsī (*Mabsūṭ*, vol. 13, p. 41)—by al-Shaybānī. Thus we find another instance of the "two companions" diverging from the master, and in full accord with his dialectical opponent. This is but one of many such instances—all indicate the "truth-seeking ethic" by which true dialectic is distinguished. Al-Shāfiʿī's ruling, however, clearly corresponds to Abū Ḥanīfa's position; we may presume his dialectical opponent argues from the position of Ibn Abī Laylā and company.

[38] The opponent's question may be more in the spirit of an objection than information-seeking; it becomes evident he shares al-Shāfiʿī's Sunnaic *dalīl*-indicant (by which three days is permitted), but will not concede to his restriction to *only* three days without further evidence and argument. We might therefore identify his question as belonging to the genus of "demand-objections" (the *muṭālabāt*, being al-Bājī's first type of *iʿtirāḍāt*; *Minhāj*, Turkī ed., pp. 40–1, §78).

[39] There is a parallel function here between "the *aṣl* of our *madhhab*" in §64 and "the *aṣl* of the *maʿqūl*" in §1411. Both phrases evince a general rule which *ought* to be the *aṣl* for *qiyās*, if al-Shāfiʿī at all believed that *qiyās* obtains for the *mas'ala* at hand. Both phrases, in other words, belong to an argument from al-Shāfiʿī's cardinal tenet (as noted by Schacht, *Origins*, pp. 123–4) that exceptions to general rules cannot serve as the basis for *qiyās*. The apparent difference between these two phrases is that "the *aṣl* of our *madhhab*" references a general rule belonging to a transmitted body of doctrine, while "the *aṣl* of the *maʿqūl*" references a general rule inductively derived from the Sharīʿa as a whole. Either way, the term *aṣl* is employed in the sense of a "general principle" (*qāʿida*)—the very meaning we find in the *Uṣūl al-Karkhī*.

al-Shāfiʿī's true *istidlāl* is directly from the Sunna, a "hypothetical" *muʿāraḍa* is thus evident, in the form of a "charge of invalidating distinction by way of correlational inference of the occasioning factor" (*farq bi-qiyās al-ʿilla*) or "by way of the occasioning factor of the norm" (*bi-ʿillat al-ḥukm*).[40] Also, at the end of this argument complex, we find a "hypothetical" *a fortiori* argument—heralded by the phrase "we invalidate *bay*ʿ-commutation for less than what I have mentioned," and meaning: when the "the *aṣl* of our *madhhab*" forbids *partial diminishment* of ownership, then all the more so should *full deprivation* of ownership be forbidden in the *mas'ala* at hand—were it not, of course, for the exception-making *khabar*-report. This report is at last quoted at the end of §64.[41]

In §65, al-Shāfiʿī's response continues with a second Sunnaic judgment (for Ḥabbān b. Munqidh) in support of his three-day restriction. This is followed by an assertion that his ruling is in full consonance with the Prophet's Sunna (he did not exceed three days, so neither do we). He proceeds to *tafsīr*-explanation establishing his *adilla*-indicants as representing the utmost time-limit for *khiyār*-option stipulation, and closes by ruling that stipulation beyond this limit renders the *bay*ʿ-contract invalid (*fāsid*). Thus, al-Shāfiʿī's overall justification remains firmly in the realm of *al-istidlāl bi'l-Sunna*, and is confidently tied to the *mas'ala* at hand. As an objection to the opposing position, it corresponds, overall, to an *iʿtirāḍ* of "supplanting [*qiyās*] by revelation-decree" (*muʿāraḍa bi'l-nuṭq*)[42]—the opponent's

---

[40] (Shīr.VII.15.2.2.1; Bāj.IX.B.15.2.2.1.1) al-Shīrāzī, *Maʿūna*, al-ʿUmayrīnī ed., [initial section missing, remainder on p. 116], and Turkī ed., pp. 262–3, §149; al-Bājī, *Minhāj*, Turkī ed., pp. 202 f. §§459 f. In short, al-Shāfiʿī is claiming that—were it not for the exception-making *khabar*-report—he would supplant his opponent's *ʿilla* with that derived from "the *aṣl* of our *madhhab*" (i.e., diminishment of ownership occasions a *ḥukm* of invalid contract). This is akin to problematizing the *ʿilla* of the opponent's *aṣl* with regard to the *far*ʿ (hence *farq*-distinction), but we recognize, in this case, that al-Shāfiʿī has problematized the opposing *aṣl* from a different perspective (it is an exception to the general rule). In any case, it is significant that he is once again employing a "hypothetical" objection.

[41] Al-Shāfiʿī's *tafsīr*-explanation and accompanying argument up to this point may be summarized as follows: (1) three days is an exception (indicated by a *khabar*-report) to a general rule (also derived from the Sunna) that there is no *khiyār*-option after separation of B and S; (2) it is not permitted that both B and S exchange property and female slave without having immediate usufruct (*intifā*ʿ) of female slave and property; (3) the opposing position claims they both have full usufruct *and* must both return when one of them desires it (which is contradictory); (4) if the "*aṣl* of our *madhhab*" (i.e., the *aṣl* which would serve for *qiyās*) forbids diminishment of full ownership, then unlimited *khiyār*-option (stripping B of all ownership) should be all the more strongly forbidden; and (5) the *aṣl* of sale with stipulated option (*bay*ʿ *ʿalā al-khiyār*) would be invalid if not for the exception report, because (ordinarily) we invalidate *bay*ʿ for less.

[42] (Shīr.VII.15.1; Bāj.IX.B.15.1) al-Shīrāzī, *Maʿūna*, Turkī ed., p. 262, §147 [missing from al-ʿUmayrīnī ed.]; al-Bājī, *Minhāj*, Turkī ed., p. 201, §454. Cf. Ibn ʿAqīl, *K. al-Jadal*, p. 70, §327.

attempted *qiyās* on the basis of the exception-making *khabar*-report is blocked by an argument direct from Sunnaic *adilla*-indicants.[43]

Short Sequence 4

§§78–80 from the *Chapter on Disagreement Over Defects* (*Bāb al-Ikhtilāf fi'l-'Ayb*)[44]

78 – Al-Shāfiʿī, may God Most High have mercy upon him, said: When a man sells a man a slave, with the understanding that he not sell him to so-and-so, or that he not put him to work, or that he provide such-and-such maintenance for him, or that he empower [the slave] to work independently while taking a portion of his earnings; the *bay*ʿ-contract for all of this is invalid—because [1] it is all something besides full ownership, and stipulating [less than full ownership] is not permitted except in a single place: ʿ*itq*-manumission in conformity to the Sunna; and because of [2] the dissimilarity of ʿ*itq*-manumission from everything else, for we say: If he buys [the slave] from him with the understanding that he manumit him; he manumits him, and the *bay*ʿ-contract is lawful.	78 - قَالَ الشَّافِعِيُّ رَحِمَهُ اللّٰهُ تَعَالَى: وَإِذَا بَاعَ الرَّجُلُ الرَّجُلَ الْعَبْدَ عَلَى أَنْ لاَ يَبِيعَهُ مِن فُلاَنٍ، أَوْ عَلَى أَنْ لاَ يَسْتَخْدِمَهُ، أَوْ عَلَى أَنْ يُنْفِقَ عَلَيْهِ كَذَا، أَوْ عَلَى أَنْ يُخَارِجَهُ، فَالْبَيْعُ فِيهِ كُلِّهِ فَاسِدٌ؛ لأَنَّ هَذَا كُلَّهُ غَيْرُ تَمَامِ مِلْكٍ، وَلاَ يَجُوزُ الشَّرْطُ فِي هَذَا إلاَّ فِي مَوْضِعٍ وَاحِدٍ؛ وَهُوَ الْعِتْقُ اتِّبَاعًا لِلسُّنَّةِ وَلِفِرَاقِ الْعِتْقِ لِمَا سِوَاهُ فَنَقُولُ: إِنِ اشْتَرَاهُ مِنْهُ عَلَى أَنْ يُعْتِقَهُ فَأَعْتَقَهُ فَالْبَيْعُ جَائِزٌ.
79 – And if a man should say: What occasions the *farq*-distinction between ʿ*itq*-manumission and everything else?	79 - فَإِنْ قَالَ رَجُلٌ: مَا فَرَّقَ بَيْنَ الْعِتْقِ وَغَيْرِهِ؟

(continued)

[43] Schacht devotes considerable attention to these sections of the subject-text (see above note at the end of §65). This, and two other sections, illustrate what he rightly observes to be a cardinal tenet of al-Shāfiʿī: "exceptions cannot be extended by analogy" (*Origins*, pp. 123–4). To this we might add another observation of import; mainly, the three examples cited by Schacht all occur as arguments within a dialectical sequence. The first is in the above category B sequence; the other two belong to the extended dialectical sequences we have previous analyzed in *masā'il*-sets #10 (§§1217–32) and #12 (§§1402–12). The significance is plain: at this stage in proto-system legal theory, this particular tenet of *qiyās*-extension had not gained general recognition. Thus he promotes it—and critiques opponents for not observing it—in no less than three separate instances within our subject-text. This is a fine illustration of a theory-principle gaining the edge of argumentative conclusiveness (*ḥujjiyya*) in the dialectical forge.

[44] Ḥassūn ed., vol. 9, pp. 23–4; ʿAbd al-Muṭṭalib ed., vol. 8, p. 229.

80 – It is said: There might belong to me half of a slave, and I gift it, and sell it, and do with it as I wish—besides ʿ*itq*-manumission—and the *ḍamān*-liability [to pay] for my partner's share in him is not incumbent upon me so long as my partner's share does not leave his possession. [This is] because each is an owner of what he owns. But if I manumit him while I am solvent, then [1] my partner's share—which I do not own, and which I did not manumit—is manumitted to my debit, and I become liable for his value, and he exits the possession of my partner without his say-so; and [2] the foetus [of our female slave] is manumitted [when] she gives birth in less than six months, so the ʿ*itq*-manumission falls upon [the child],[45] and if I sell him, the *bay*ʿ-contract is not allowed—along with [ʿ*itq*-manumission's] divergence from other things in this regard, and regarding the *umm al-walad*,[46] and the *mukātab*,[47] and others besides.	80 – قِيلَ: قَدْ يَكُونُ لِي نِصْفُ الْعَبْدِ فَأَهَبُهُ وَأَبِيعُهُ وَأَصْنَعُ فِيهِ مَا شِئْتُ غَيْرَ الْعِتْقِ فَلاَ يَلْزَمُنِي ضَمَانُ نَصِيبِ شَرِيكِي فِيهِ، وَلاَ يَخْرُجُ نَصِيبُ شَرِيكِي مِن يَدِهِ، لأَنَّ كُلًّا مَالِكٌ لِمَا مَلَكَ فَإِنْ أَعْتَقْتُهُ وَأَنَا مُوسِرٌ عَتَقَ عَلَيَّ نَصِيبُ شَرِيكِي الَّذِي لاَ أَمْلِكُ وَلَمْ أَعْتِقْ وَضَمِنْتُ قِيمَتَهُ، وَخَرَجَ مِن يَدَيْ شَرِيكِي بِغَيْرِ أَمْرِهِ وَأُعْتِقَ الْحَمْلُ فَتَلِدُهُ لأَقَلَّ [مِن][48] سِتَّةِ أَشْهُرٍ فَيَقَعُ عَلَيْهِ الْعِتْقُ وَلَوْ بِعْتُهُ لَمْ يَجُزِ الْبَيْعُ مَعَ خِلاَفِهِ لِغَيْرِهِ فِي هَذَا وَفِي أُمِّ الْوَلَدِ وَالْمُكَاتَبِ وَمَا سِوَاهُمَا.

In §78 al-Shāfiʿī judges a group of related stipulations—all detailing what a buyer must or must not do with a bought slave—with a single ruling: any *bay*ʿ-contract containing such a stipulation is invalid (*fāsid*). He proceeds immediately to ʿ*aql*-support—signalled by "because"—which identifies (1) the common efficient property (it is not full ownership) occasioning his collective ruling;[49] (2) the only exception to this general rule: Sunnaic ʿ*itq*-manumission; and (3) the dissimilarity (*firāq*) which sets ʿ*itq*-manumission apart from other transactions, and allows its lawful stipulation in a *bay*ʿ-contract.[50] In short, it is an appeal that the critical difference between ʿ*itq*-manumission and other matters be honored in the *mas'ala* at

---

[45] Meaning the paternity of one of the owners cannot be denied, so the child must be considered free; see *EI*², s.v. "ʿAbd" (at §3.f.)

[46] "Mother of the [master's] child;" a significant change in a female slave's legal status. For related rulings, see *MF*, s.v. "استيلاد" (vol. 4, pp. 164–9); *EI*², s.v. "Umm al-Walad"; and *DJP*, vol. 2, pp. 475–7.

[47] Meaning the slave under contract with his owner to ransom himself by means of regular payments. For related rulings, see *MF*, s.v. "مكاتبة" (vol. 38, pp. 360–3); *EI*², s.v. "ʿAbd" (at §3.j.); and *DJP*, vol. 2, pp. 453–68.

[48] Missing from Ḥassūn, but present in Būlāq, Maṭrajī, and ʿAbd al-Muṭṭalib editions.

[49] We encountered this same efficient property in the sequence of §§62–5.

[50] It is evident the ensuing debate will center on al-Shāfiʿī's insisting the dissimilarity (*firāq*) of ʿ*itq*-manumission be observed here, as elsewhere. The same methodological concern played a central role in al-Shāfiʿī's argument against *qiyās* from marriage/divorce to ownership/manumission in §§755 ff. Another instance of a primary dialectical "given", this is a concern that a critical *farq*-distinction be observed across substantive domains for the sake, presumably, of maintaining doctrinal consistency (and avoiding the charge of *naqḍ*). Nor is ʿ*itq*-manumission the only locus for this concern; something quite similar occurs in §§1321ff,. with al-Shāfiʿī's insistence that a *farq*-distinction be maintained between killing in war (*ḥarb*) and killing as a *ḥadd*-punishment. In that case, the opponent's non-observance of the *farq*-distinction in the contended *mas'ala*, juxtaposed with his observance of it elsewhere, led al-Shāfiʿī to charge him with method-*naqḍ*. With these examples in mind, a new label for this type of concern:

hand, as it is elsewhere—a dialectical consistency-concern which I have labeled "*farq*-extension". We may also guess at this point that an opponent justifying the validity of *bay*ʿ-contracts with such stipulations as al-Shāfiʿī disowns might do so by way of *qiyās* from the *endoxon* ruling allowing stipulations of *ʿitq*-manumission. In such a case, al-Shāfiʿī's argument compares favorably to that *iʿtirāḍ* known as "invalid compatibility-comparison" (*fasād al-iʿtibār*), as known by way of the *uṣūl*.[51]

In §79 al-Shāfiʿī opens an "instructional" dialectic—signalled by "if a man should say" (*fa-in qāla rajul*)—in which his opponent asks a unique, objection-oriented dialectical question: "What occasions the *farq*-distinction between [X] and other things (*mā farraqa bayna* [X] *wa ghayrihi*)?" Directed at an objection, and not a justification, this does not identify directly with al-Bājī's question types, though it shares obvious features with some; I would therefore propose the hybrid labels "question about the mode of the objection" (*su'āl ʿan wajh al-iʿtirāḍ*), or "demand for the *farq*-distinction" (*muṭālaba bi'l-farq*).[52]

Al-Shāfiʿī's response in §80, signalled by "it is said" (*qīla*), proposes a number of *masā'il* clearly illustrating the requested *furūq*-distinctions: (1) the *ʿitq*-manumission of a solvent man's share in a slave decisively impinges upon his partner's ownership of his share (which is manumitted and leaves his possession)—unlike in gifting, sale, etc.; (2) the foetus of a jointly-owned female slave is manumitted (once paternity of either of the partners is certain), and sale of

---

"*farq*-extension" might be proposed. In a manner similar to the way that "*manzila*-subsumption" describes a jurist's concern that X receive the *ḥukm* of Y across all relevant *masā'il* within a substantive legal domain, and "*taswiya*-subsumption" describes a jurist's concern that *masā'il* sharing the same efficient properties receive the same *ḥukm* (unless, of course, Kitāb and Sunna decree an exception), so too will "*farq*-extension" describe a jurist's concern that a critical difference between certain legal categories (ownership vs. marriage, *ʿitq* vs. divorce, *ḥarb*-killing vs. *ḥadd*-killing, *ʿitq* vs. all other *bay*ʿ stipulations) must be observed across all *masā'il* within relevant domains. And it is not unlikely the primary motive behind each of these similar preoccupations with consistency is the avoidance of being charged with *naqḍ*. These juridical concerns, and the formulae employed to convey them, all bear the forge-marks of dialectical disputation. Proto-system legal theory was directed by such consistency-concerns; and these, in turn, were driven by avoidance of a singular genus of *iʿtirāḍ*: *naqḍ*.

[51] See the final analysis for §80, below. By Ḥassūn's numbering system, the other jurists' relevant rulings and arguments are: §75 (Abū Ḥanīfa with Abū Yūsuf's adherence, and *naql*-support in §76); and §77 (Ibn Abī Laylā). Like al-Shāfiʿī after him, Abū Ḥanīfa rules that *bay*ʿ-contracts with such stipulations are invalid (*fāsid*). Ibn Abī Laylā, on the other hand, allows the *bay*ʿ-commutation while ruling the stipulation to be (automatically) null and void (*bāṭil*)—cf. Ibn Abī Laylā in §90[a], above, and attached note.

[52] Presumably the opponent entertains the viability of *qiyās* from the basis of *ʿitq*-stipulation, to other stipulations such as those mentioned at the start of §78. Due to this, one might read al-Shāfiʿī's *farq*-extension as an *iʿtirāḍ* of *fasād al-iʿtibār*, or *farq*, against such a *qiyās*; and the opponent's dialectical question—challenging al-Shāfiʿī to justify the difference as *qiyās*-invalidating—as an objection-oriented species of question (*su'āl*) or demand-objection (*muṭālaba*).

the child becomes invalid; and (3) allusions are made to other differences of *ʿitq*-manumission, and such as occur with the *umm al-walad*, *mukātab*, and others. The whole may of course be understood as a charge of *qiyās*-invalidating *farq*-distinction. However, the distinction is so general—as known by surveying the *uṣūl*—that the opponent's presumed basis for *qiyās* (the lawful stipulation of *ʿitq*-manumission in a *bayʿ*-contract) cannot possibly serve as a valid *aṣl*. For this reason, perhaps the most suitable identification for al-Shāfiʿī's objection is *fasād al-iʿtibār* known by way of the *uṣūl*.[53] Also implied, and again due to the general scope of the distinction, is a charge of method-*naqḍ*. In short, the opponent ought to recognize the *endoxic* quality of *ʿitq*-manumission's distinctive difference—he may in fact have observed it elsewhere, so most certainly should observe it in the *mas'ala* at hand.[54]

[53] (Shīr.VII.12.2.2; Bāj.IX.B.10.2.2) al-Shīrāzī, *Maʿūna*, al-ʿUmayrīnī ed., pp. 114 f.; al-Bājī, *Minhāj*, Turkī ed., pp. 181 f., §§402 ff. Cf. Ibn ʿAqīl, *K. al-Jadal*, p. 64, §§302–4. Of note here is the utility of *farq*-distinction as a tool for critique. We know, of course, that it is identified in the *jadal*-theory texts with the *muʿāraḍa* of an opponent's *ʿilla* by way of *qiyās al-ʿilla* and *qiyās al-dalāla*. We have also seen al-Shāfiʿī employ *farq* in his reply to an implied charge of *fasād al-iʿtibār* in the dialectical sequence of §§1320 ff. Now, however, we find him employing *farq*-distinction—in much the same manner as his opponent in §§1320 ff.—in order to press his own charge of *fasād al-iʿtibār*. Even as his opponent pushed him to accept the evidence of the *uṣūl* in establishing a *farq* between men and women (re: *ḥarb*-killing, to which he responded with his own *farq* between *ḥarb*-killing and *ḥadd*-killing), now we find that al-Shāfiʿī has pushed his opponent to concede the *farq* between *ʿitq*-manumission and other transactions, based upon the evidence of the *uṣūl* (the *masāʾil* in §80). This is the essence, and meaning, of *fasād al-iʿtibār*: the objector (*muʿtariḍ*) pushes the *ʿilla*-justifier (*muʿallil*) to concede that his *qiyās* is built upon an "invalid compatibility-comparison."

[54] Although not noted by Schacht in his *Origins*, this sequence again proves al-Shāfiʿī's adherence to that legal theorem by which an exception to a general rule cannot serve as the basis for *qiyās*. We may thus qualify his argument in three ways: (1) an appeal to this principle; (2) an *iʿtirāḍ* of *fasād al-iʿtibār* known by way of the *uṣūl*; and (3) an *iʿtirāḍ* of method-*naqḍ*. As for the first, it is equivalent to his claiming the opponent's *aṣl* may not be used as an *aṣl*, which links it to the charge of *fasād al-iʿtibār*. In fact, Schacht's principle tenet—no *qiyās*-extension from an exception to a general rule—is nothing less, once converted to objection-form, than a species of *fasād al-iʿtibār* known by way of the *uṣūl*. For al-Shāfiʿī, the Sharīʿa as a whole supplies evidence that the ruling his opponent employs as *aṣl* is an exception—it is critically different from others within the same domain of legal acts—and this *farq* must therefore be extended and observed across the *masāʾil* of that domain. His opponent's *qiyās* does not recognize this *farq*-extension—it is built upon an exception, an "invalid compatibility-comparison," which is the meaning of *fasād al-iʿtibār*. The resultant inconsistency of the opponent's doctrine allows us also to interpret al-Shāfiʿī's charge as method-*naqḍ*: the opponent observes these *furūq*-distinctions elsewhere, but not in the *masāʾil* at hand.

Short Sequence 5

§§155–157 from the *Chapter on Selling Unripe Fruit* (*Bāb Bayʿ al-Thimār Qabla an Yabdū Ṣalāḥuhā*)[55]

155 – Al-Shāfiʿī, may God Most High be pleased with him, said: And when a man [B] purchases a garment from a man [A] as *murābaḥa*[56] and then sells it [to C], then he finds that the first seller [A] who sold it to him as *murābaḥa* had cheated him regarding the price; it has been said: The cheated amount is subtracted from [A's price] by its portion from the profit, and [B] claims it from [A].[57] But even if the garment remains intact, [B] does not have the right to return it [to A]. And the only thing preventing us from invalidating the sale, and allowing [B] to return [the garment] when it remains intact, or granting him the value when not intact, is that the sale was not contracted for a thing forbidden to them both, together. Rather, it was contracted for a thing forbidden only to the deceiver [A] between them.[58]	155 - قَالَ الشَّافِعِيُّ رضي الله تعالى عنه: وَإِذَا ابْتَاعَ الرَّجُلُ مِن الرَّجُلِ ثَوْبًا مُرَابَحَةً فَبَاعَهُ، ثُمَّ وَجَدَ الْبَائِعَ الأَوَّلَ الَّذِي بَاعَهُ مُرَابَحَةً قَدْ خَانَهُ فِي الثَّمَنِ فَقَدْ قِيلَ: تُحَطُّ عَنْهُ الْخِيَانَةُ بِحِصَّتِهَا مِن الرِّبْحِ وَيَرْجِعُ عَلَيْهِ بِهِ، وَلَوْ كَانَ الثَّوْبُ قَائِمًا لَمْ يَكُنْ لَهُ أَنْ يَرُدَّهُ. وَإِنَّمَا مَنَعَنَا مِن إِفْسَادِ الْبَيْعِ وَأَنْ يَرُدَّهُ إِذَا كَانَ قَائِمًا، وَيَجْعَلَهُ بِالْقِيمَةِ إِذَا كَانَ فَائِتًا أَنَّ الْبَيْعَ لَمْ يَنْعَقِدْ عَلَى مُحَرَّمٍ عَلَيْهِمَا مَعًا وَإِنَّمَا انْعَقَدَ عَلَى مُحَرَّمٍ عَلَى الْخَائِنِ مِنْهُمَا.
156 – And if one should say: What resembles this, of the things for which *bay*ʿ-commutation is normally permitted, when the seller in [the contract] is a deceiver?	156 - فَإِنْ قَالَ قَائِلٌ: مَا يُشْبِهُ هَذَا مِمَّا يَجُوزُ فِيهِ الْبَيْعُ بِحَالٍ وَالْبَائِعُ فِيهِ غَارٌّ؟
157 – It is said: A man [X] fraudulently conceals a defect from a man [Y], and that fraud-sale is a thing forbidden to [X], and what [X] takes of its price is forbidden—just as what [A] took of the cheated amount was forbidden [to A]. But the [subsequent] sale of it [to Z] is not invalid, nor does the seller [Y] have *khiyār*-option regarding its return.[59] And it is said: The buyer [C] has the *khiyār*-option of [1] taking it by the price which is designated for it, or [2] cancellation of the sale; because the contract is not concluded except with a price designated. So when the buyer [C] discovers another [price], and does not consent to [the designated price], the sale is corrupted—because it reverts to a price unknown, in the mind of the buyer, which the seller [B] did not consent to.	157 – قِيلَ: يُدَلِّسُ الرَّجُلُ لِلرَّجُلِ الْعَيْبَ فَيَكُونُ التَّدْلِيسُ مُحَرَّمًا عَلَيْهِ وَمَا أَخَذَ مِن ثَمَنِهِ مُحَرَّمًا. كَمَا كَانَ مَا أَخَذَ مِن الْخِيَانَةِ مُحَرَّمًا، وَلاَ يَكُونُ الْبَيْعُ فَاسِدًا فِيهِ، وَلاَ يَكُونُ لِلْبَائِعِ الْخِيَارُ فِي رَدِّهِ، وَقِيلَ: لِلْمُشْتَرِي الْخِيَارُ فِي أَخْذِهِ بِالثَّمَنِ الَّذِي سُمِّيَ لَهُ أَوْ فَسْخُ الْبَيْعِ؛ لأَنَّهُ لَمْ يَنْعَقِدْ إِلاَّ بِثَمَنٍ مُسَمًّى، فَإِذَا وَجَدَ غَيْرَهُ فَلَمْ يَرْضَ بِهِ الْمُشْتَرِي فَسَدَ الْبَيْعُ؛ لأَنَّهُ يُرَدُّ إِلَى ثَمَنٍ مَجْهُولٍ عِنْدَ الْمُشْتَرِي لَمْ يَرْضَ بِهِ الْبَائِعُ.

[55] Ḥassūn ed., vol. 9, p. 37; ʿAbd al-Muṭṭalib ed., vol. 8, p. 238.

[56] On the *murābaḥa*-contract, by which a purchaser resells at a clearly-designated markup (the profit, or *ribḥ*) from the original purchase price, see *MF*, s.v. "مرابحة" (vol. 36, pp. 318–28); and *DJP*, vol. 2, pp. 256–9.

[57] Cf. Ibn Abī Laylā and Abū Yūsuf in §154 of Ḥassūn's edition. Al-Shāfiʿī appears to be referencing this ruling.

[58] Meaning: A's fraudulent *murābaḥa* sale to B was a forbidden thing for A; but B's subsequent sale to C was not a forbidden thing to B. Only A contracted something forbidden.

[59] On the concealment of defects (*tadlīs*) and related rulings, see *MF*, s.v. "تدليس" (vol. 11, pp. 126–30).

In §155 al-Shāfiʿī, having laid out the details of the *mas'ala*, appears to relate—with "it has been said" (*fa-qad qīla*)—the ruling of Ibn Abī Laylā and Abū Yūsuf in §154: (1) when B has sold the garment to C (before discovering he was duped by A), he reclaims only the cheated amount from A.[60] He then adds a second ruling, contradictory to that of Abū Ḥanīfa in §153: (2) even should the garment be intact, B has no right to return it to A. Since one might assume a fraudulent *murābaḥa* sale should be ruled invalid, or that B should have the right to cancel it for full return and refund when intact, al-Shāfiʿī proceeds to explain the only thing that prevents him from allowing this: of the two parties, only A has contracted something forbidden (the fraudulent price). Thus he at once implies, with regard to his ruling (2), the assumed efficient property for the opposing position (they have both contracted something forbidden: A with B, and B with C), and presents a "denial" or "obstruction" (*manʿ*) to that position by reassessing that property (only one of them has contracted something forbidden: A with B). This corresponds favorably to the *jadal* theorists' *iʿtirāḍ* called "denying the property in the branch-case" (*manʿ al-waṣf fi'l-farʿ*).[61] By objecting to the property (*waṣf*) interpretation of the opposing opinion, we might anticipate that al-Shāfiʿī will be asked by an opponent to prove his own interpretation by bringing a new *aṣl* which demonstrates it. By so doing, his final move will correspond to a type of *muʿāraḍa* by way of *qiyās*.

In §156 al-Shāfiʿī opens an "instructional" dialectic with the standard "if one should say" (*fa-in qāla qā'il*), in which his interlocutor asks a uniquely *qiyās*-oriented question in the form "What resembles this (*mā yushbihu hādhā*), of [*uṣūl* category X], when [same context]?" This objection-question challenges al-Shāfiʿī to produce a parallel among source-cases of permitted *bayʿ*-contracts in which the reassessed property is present (and thus indicative of a common *ʿilla*). There is no equivalent among al-Bājī's questions, though a similarity to *muṭālaba* is evident. For this reason, I propose the label of *muṭālaba* for *qiyās al-shabah*.

In §157 al-Shāfiʿī complies with an *aṣl* (sale with deliberately concealed defect [*tadlīs*]) in which the same properties and effects he attributes to the problem-case are evident. The result—bearing in mind that the properties are more indicating, than constituting, a shared occasioning factor—is a "correlational inference of resemblance" (*qiyās al-shabah*), which may be represented as follows:

---

[60] By Ḥassūn's numbering system, the other jurists' relevant rulings and arguments are: §153 (Abū Ḥanīfa); and §154 (Ibn Abī Laylā with Abū Yūsuf's adherence). For Abū Ḥanīfa, the original *murābaḥa* sale between A and B is not invalidated, because B has sold the garment (and, presumably, must suffer having been cheated); however, if B still has the garment in his possession, he can return it for a full refund of what he paid (thus cancelling the sale). For Abū Ḥanīfa, there is no case in which B is merely refunded the cheated amount. But Ibn Abī Laylā rules—whether B still possesses the garment or not, presumably—that B is refunded the cheated amount and its portion of the profit. Presumably for him, there is no case where B either must suffer having been cheated, or can return the garment for a full refund. Al-Shāfiʿī's ruling in §155 corresponds to Ibn Abī Laylā's position, and we might assume his opponent will argue from that of Abū Ḥanīfa. For further on these opinions, see al-Sarakhsī, *Mabsūṭ*, vol. 13, p. 86.

[61] (Shīr.VII.4; Bāj.IX.6.1.2) al-Shīrāzī, *Maʿūna*, al-ʿUmayrīnī ed., pp. 96–7; al-Bājī, *Minhāj*, Turkī ed., pp. 166–7, §359. Cf. Ibn ʿAqīl, *K. al-Jadal*, p. 50, §251.

Aṣl *bay*ʿ with concealed defect (*tadlīs*)		*Farʿ* *murābaḥa* with fraudulent price (*khiyāna*)
Waṣf-property *tadlīs* is a thing forbidden to X	← SAME →	*Waṣf*-property *khiyāna* is a thing forbidden to A
Waṣf-property the price is a thing forbidden to X	← SAME →	*Waṣf*-property the price is a thing forbidden to A
Ḥukm A Y's selling it to Z is not invalid	SHOULD BE [SAME] →	*Ḥukm* A [B's selling it to C is not invalid]
Ḥukm B Y has no *khiyār*-option	SHOULD BE [SAME] →	*Ḥukm* B [B has no *khiyār*-option]

Al-Shāfiʿī's response, as a justification of his rulings (1) and (2), thus constitutes "drawing indicant by way of correlational inference of resemblance" (*istidlāl bi-qiyās al-shabah*). Supposing that a proponent of the opposing position also drew indicant from *qiyās* (by way of an *aṣl* in which both parties contracted something forbidden), this response also corresponds to an *iʿtirāḍ* of *muʿāraḍa* by way of *qiyās al-shabah*.[62] Al-Shāfiʿī closes his argument by contrasting the position of the buyer of the garment in the fraudulent *murābaḥa* sale (B) with the buyer in his subsequent sale of the garment (C). Unlike B, when C discovers that A's original price was too high (and thus, presumably, B's subsequent selling price), he has recourse to *khiyār*-option and can cancel the sale. This ruling receives *ʿaql*-support—signalled by "because"—in the form of an *endoxon* principle of contract law: an unknown and/or unapproved price invalidates the *bay*ʿ-contract.

Short Sequence 6

§§534–536 from the *Chapter on Debt* (*Bāb fi'l-Dayn*)[63]

534 – Al-Shāfiʿī, may God have mercy upon him, said: When a man witnesses [something] while sighted, then contributes *shahāda*-testimony while blind; his *shahāda*-testimony is permitted, since the greater part of *shahāda*-testimony is hearing and sight, and both were [functioning] in him the day he witnessed.[64]	534 - قَالَ الشَّافِعِيُّ رحمه الله: وَإِذَا شَهِدَ الرَّجُلُ وَهُوَ بَصِيرٌ ثُمَّ أَدَّى الشَّهَادَةَ وَهُوَ أَعْمَى جَازَتْ شَهَادَتُهُ؛ مِن قِبَلِ أَنَّ أَكْثَرَ مَا فِي الشَّهَادَةِ السَّمْعُ وَالْبَصَرُ وَكِلاَهُمَا كَانَ فِيهِ يَوْمَ شَهِدَ.
535 – And if one should say: They are not both [functioning] in him on the day he testifies!	535 - فَإِنْ قَالَ قَائِلٌ: لَيْسَا فِيهِ يَوْمَ يَشْهَدُ.

(continued)

[62] (Shīr.VII.15.2.2.3; Bāj.IX.B.15.2.2.2.4) al-Shīrāzī, *Maʿūna*, al-ʿUmayrīnī ed., pp. 117–18; al-Bājī, *Minhāj*, Turkī ed., pp. 205–6, §466.

[63] Ḥassūn ed., vol. 9, p. 100; ʿAbd al-Muṭṭalib ed., vol. 8, p. 284.

[64] For general rulings related to *shahāda*-testimony, see *MF*, s.v. "شهادة" (vol. 26, pp. 214–53; esp. §19 for testimony of the blind); *EI*², s.v. "Shāhid"; *DJP*, vol. 2, pp. 556–60; and Hallaq, *Sharīʿa*, pp. 348–52.

536 – It is said: We require *shahāda* only for the day it *occurred*. As for the day on which it is *furnished*; it merely goes back to the judgment of something he had confirmed with full sight. And if we reject it when he is not sighted—because he does not see the object of testimony at the time he testifies—we are obliged not to allow the *shahāda*-testimony of the sighted for a deceased party, nor for an absent party; because the witness sees neither the deceased nor the absent. Yet the one who asserts he does not permit his *shahāda*-testimony after the onset of blindness—having affirmed it while fully sighted—permits *shahāda*-testimony of the sighted for the deceased and the absent.	536 – قِيلَ: إِنَّمَا احْتَجْنَا إِلَى الشَّهَادَةِ يَوْمَ كَانَتْ، فَأَمَّا يَوْمَ تُقَامُ فَإِنَّمَا هِيَ تُعَادُ بِحُكْمِ شَيْءٍ قَدْ أَثْبَتَهُ بَصِيرًا، وَلَوْ رَدَدْنَاهَا إِذَا لَمْ يَكُنْ بَصِيرًا؛ لأَنَّهُ لاَ يَرَى الْمَشْهُودَ عَلَيْهِ حِينَ يَشْهَدُ، لَزِمَنَا أَنْ لاَ نُجِيزَ شَهَادَةَ بَصِيرٍ عَلَى مَيِّتٍ وَلاَ عَلَى غَائِبٍ؛ لأَنَّ الشَّاهِدَ لاَ يَرَى الْمَيِّتَ وَلاَ الْغَائِبَ وَالَّذِي يَزْعُمُ أَنَّهُ لاَ يُجِيزُ شَهَادَتَهُ بَعْدَ الْعَمَى وَقَدْ أَثْبَتَهَا بَصِيرًا يُجِيزُ شَهَادَةَ الْبَصِيرِ عَلَى الْمَيِّتِ وَالْغَائِبِ.

In §534 al-Shāfiʿī's singular ruling—accepting the testimony of the one who becomes blind *after* witnessing—receives immediate *ʿaql*-support; this in turn clarifies his occasioning factor: hearing and sight were functioning at the time of the witnessed event.[65] If we assume an opposing ruling to be based—like Abū Ḥanīfa's in §§535–6—on an *athar*-tradition about ʿAlī b. Abī Ṭālib, this assertion of an occasioning factor by al-Shāfiʿī would resemble the move of *muʿāraḍa* of the Sunna by way of the *ʿilla*, wherein "the Sunna is general (*ʿumūm*), allowing the possibility of particularization (*takhṣīṣ*)."[66]

In §535 al-Shāfiʿī initiates an "instructional" dialectic with the standard "if one should say" (*fa-in qāla qāʾil*); and his opponent, atypically, asks no question, but asserts a potentially-efficient property believed to override al-Shāfiʿī's and produce the opposite *ḥukm*: hearing and sight are not *both* functioning at the time of testimony. Notably, the focus remains on occasioning factors, but no *aṣl* is demanded of al-Shāfiʿī (we might have anticipated he would be called upon to complete his *istidlāl* by way of *qiyās*).[67] Instead, his opponent levels an objection similar to that brought by al-Shāfiʿī in §155, above, corresponding to what the *jadal* theorists called "denying the property in the branch-case" (*manʿ al-waṣf fi'l-farʿ*).[68]

---

[65] By Ḥassūn's numbering system, the other jurists' relevant rulings and arguments are: §531 (Abū Ḥanīfa, with *naql*-support in §532); and §533 (Ibn Abī Laylā with Abū Yūsuf's conditional adherence). Abū Ḥanīfa does not accept the testimony of one who becomes blind after witnessing; this appears to be a straight application of ʿAlī's practice, as reported in the *athar*-tradition of §532. But Ibn Abī Laylā allows it; and Abū Yūsuf follows, but with a condition difficult to narrow to a single interpretation: *idhā kāna shay'un lā yaḥtāju an yaqifa ʿalayhi.* Al-Shāfiʿī's ruling corresponds to Ibn Abī Laylā's position; an opponent may be assumed to argue from Abū Ḥanīfa's.

[66] (Shīr.II.C.8.2.3; Bāj.II.2.7.2.3) al-Shīrāzī, *Maʿūna*, al-ʿUmayrīnī ed., pp. 67–8, n. 6 [the discussion, missing from the *Maʿūna*, is extracted from al-Shīrāzī's *Mulakhkhaṣ*]; al-Bājī, *Minhāj*, Turkī ed., p. 125, §247. The operative difference in this case, of course, is that he is supplanting an *athar*-tradition of ʿAlī, not a Prophetic *ḥadīth*.

[67] In this sequence, we never hear of a *dalīl*-indicant from among the authoritatively-sanctioned source-cases (*uṣūl*); nor does al-Shāfiʿī address the *athar*-tradition supporting the opposite ruling of Abū Ḥanīfa in §532. Significantly, the whole remains free of (named) textual indicants.

[68] (Shīr.VII.4; Bāj.IX.6.1.2) al-Shīrāzī, *Maʿūna*, al-ʿUmayrīnī ed., pp. 96–7; al-Bājī, *Minhāj*, Turkī ed., pp. 166–7, §359. Cf. Ibn ʿAqīl, *K. al-Jadal*, p. 50, §251.

Al-Shāfiʿī's response in §536 brings a number of premises tallying up to a double objection of *naqḍ*: (1) an appeal to *endoxa* principles: sight-witnessing is required only for the witnessed event, and furnished testimony merely references the sight-witnessed event; (2) a clarification of the opposing *ʿilla*: he does not see the object of testimony at the time he testifies; (3) a pair of problem-cases exposing the opposing position's inconsistency (*masāʾil al-naqḍ*): given the opposing *ʿilla*, one should (A) not permit testimony of the sighted about the deceased, nor (B) about the absent; (4) a confirmation of the opposing *ʿilla* as existing in these *masāʾil*: "because the witness sees neither the deceased nor the absent;" and (5) a confirmation that the opposing *ḥukm* does not exist in these *masāʾil*, for who denies the blind witness's testimony is known to allow testimony of the sighted about both deceased and absent parties. Al-Shāfiʿī's *iʿtirāḍ* is thus a model example of *naqḍ*[69]—he brings parallel cases, presumably *endoxa* to the opponent, in which the opponent's occasioning factor is present (*wujūd al-ʿilla*), but his ruling is not (*maʿa ʿadam al-ḥukm*)—exposing doctrinal inconsistency in the opposing position, and destroying its counter-*ʿilla*.

Short Sequence 7

§§540–544 from the *Chapter on Debt* (*Bāb fiʾl-Dayn*)[70]

540 – Al-Shāfiʿī, may God Most High have mercy upon him, said: When a man confesses to *zinā*,[71] and renders a description obliging the *ḥadd*-penalty, four times in a [single] session; he and the one who confesses to it in separate sessions are one and the same.[72] If we only require that he confess four times by way of *qiyās* from four witnesses, then whoever does not apply [the *ḥadd*-penalty] to him for four times in a single session, but applies it to him for four times in different sessions, has abandoned the *aṣl*-principle of his doctrine—because he claims that four witnesses are not admitted except in a single session.[73]	540 - قَالَ الشَّافِعِيُّ رَحِمَهُ اللّٰهُ تَعَالَى : وَإِذَا أَقَرَّ الرَّجُلُ بِالزِّنَا وَوَصَفَهُ الصِّفَةَ الَّتِي تُوجِبُ الْحَدَّ فِي مَجْلِسٍ أَرْبَعَ مَرَّاتٍ، فَسَوَاءٌ هُوَ وَالَّذِي أَقَرَّ بِهِ فِي مَجَالِسَ مُتَفَرِّقَةٍ، إِنْ كُنَّا إِنَّمَا احْتَجْنَا إِلَى أَنْ يُقِرَّ أَرْبَعَ مَرَّاتٍ قِيَاسًا عَلَى أَرْبَعَةِ شُهُودٍ، فَالَّذِي لَمْ يُقِمْ عَلَيْهِ فِي أَرْبَعِ مَرَّاتٍ فِي مَقَامٍ وَاحِدٍ وَأَقَامَهَا عَلَيْهِ فِي أَرْبَعِ مَرَّاتٍ فِي مَقَامَاتٍ مُخْتَلِفَةٍ تَرَكَ أَصْلَ قَوْلِهِ؛ لأَنَّهُ يَزْعُمُ أَنَّ الشُّهُودَ الأَرْبَعَةَ لاَ يُقْبَلُونَ إلاَّ فِي مَقَامٍ وَاحِدٍ.

(continued)

[69] (Shīr.VII.7; Bāj.IX.B.11) al-Shīrāzī, *Maʿūna*, al-ʿUmayrīnī ed., pp. 104 ff.; al-Bājī, *Minhāj*, Turkī ed., pp. 185 ff., §§412 ff. Cf. Ibn ʿAqīl, *K. al-Jadal*, p. 57, §278.

[70] Ḥassūn ed., vol. 9, pp. 101–2; ʿAbd al-Muṭṭalib ed., vol. 8, p. 285.

[71] *Zinā* (roughly: "fornication" or "adultery") denotes unlawful sexual intercourse, being outside a legal marriage, or concubinage, or its semblance. It is among the *ḥudūd*: offenses with divinely-sanctioned (Qurʾānic and Sunnaic) punishments and evidentiary requirements.

[72] On the divinely-sanctioned punishment (*ḥadd*) for unlawful sexual intercourse (*zinā*), its evidentiary requirements and related rulings, see *MF*, s.v. "زنى" (vol. 24, pp. 18–47; esp. §§37–8 re: confession); *EI*², s.v. "Zinā or Zināʾ"; *DJP*, vol. 2, pp. 521–30 (esp. pp. 528–9 for the current *masʾala* re: number of confessions); and Hallaq, *Sharīʿa*, pp. 312–15.

[73] See *MF*, s.v. "زنى" (vol. 24, pp. 38–9; §33) with regard to this requirement that all four witnesses present their testimony in a single session before the *qāḍī*.

541 – He said:[74] And if they are disunited [in their testimony], he inflicts them with the *ḥadd*-penalty [for false accusation of *zinā*].[75]	541 - قَالَ: وَلَوْ تَفَرَّقُوا حَدَّهُمْ.
542 – So it is right he should say: Fourfold confession in a [single] session is more established than in four sessions.	542 - فَكَانَ يَنْبَغِي لَهُ أَنْ يَقُولَ: الإِقْرَارُ أَرْبَعَ مَرَّاتٍ فِي مَقَامٍ أَثْبَتَ مِنْهُ فِي أَرْبَعَةِ مَقَامَاتٍ.
543 – And if he says: I have only embraced the *ḥadīth* of Māʿiz...[76]	543 - فَإِنْ قَالَ: إِنَّمَا أَخَذْتُ بِحَدِيثِ مَاعِزٍ.
544 – Then the *ḥadīth* of Māʿiz is not as he described. But even if it is as he described—that Māʿiz confessed in four separate situations, four times—the admittance of his confession in a [single] session, four times, is not contradictory to this; because we do not look to the sessions, we look only to the articulation [of the confessions]. Nor is the matter as either of them, together, have said,[77] when his confession *once* before the judge obliges the *ḥadd*-penalty—when established [as applicable to] him—until he is stoned. Don't you look to the decree of the Prophet, may God bless and save him: «Go, O Unays, to this woman, and if she confesses, then stone her»? And the *ḥadīth* of Māʿiz provides indication—when [the Prophet] asked: "is he possessed?"—that he turned him away four times because he denied his sanity.	544 - فَلَيْسَ حَدِيثُ مَاعِزٍ كَمَا وَصَفَ، وَلَوْ كَانَ كَمَا وَصَفَ أَنَّ مَاعِزًا أَقَرَّ فِي أَرْبَعَةِ أَمْكِنَةٍ مُتَفَرِّقَةٍ أَرْبَعَ مَرَّاتٍ مَا كَانَ قَبُولُ إِقْرَارِهِ فِي مَجْلِسٍ أَرْبَعَ مَرَّاتٍ خِلاَفًا لِهَذَا؛ لأَنَّا لَمْ نَنْظُرْ إِلَى الْمَجَالِسِ إِنَّمَا نَظَرْنَا إِلَى اللَّفْظِ، وَلَيْسَ الأَمْرُ كَمَا قَالاَ جَمِيعًا، وَإِقْرَارُهُ مَرَّةً عِنْدَ الْحَاكِمِ يُوجِبُ الْحَدَّ إِذَا ثَبَتَ عَلَيْهِ حَتَّى يُرْجَمَ. أَلاَ تَرَى إِلَى قَوْلِ النَّبِيِّ - صَلَّى اللّٰهُ عَلَيْهِ وَسَلَّمَ : «اُغْدُ يَا أُنَيْسُ إِلَى امْرَأَةِ هَذَا، فَإِنِ اعْتَرَفَتْ فَارْجُمْهَا» وَحَدِيثُ مَاعِزٍ يَدُلُّ حِينَ سَأَلَ أَبِهِ جِنَّةٌ؟ أَنَّهُ رَدَّهُ أَرْبَعَ مَرَّاتٍ لِإِنْكَارِ عَقْلِهِ.

In §540 al-Shāfiʿī provides a single ruling equating the legal effects of fourfold confessions in single or separate sessions; he applies the formula "[X] and [Y] are one and the same" (*fa-sawāʾun* [X] *wa* [Y])—evincing that categorical

[74] Here, I have followed Ḥassūn, though ʿAbd al-Muṭṭalib renders قال الشافعي رحمة الله عليه (referencing manuscripts ص and ظ).

[75] Also among the divinely-sanctioned *ḥudūd* is *qadhf*—false accusation of *zinā*. For full expositions and related rulings, see *MF*, s.v. "قذف" (vol. 33, pp. 5–26); *EI*², s.v. "Ḳadhf"; *DJP*, vol. 2, pp. 531–34; and Hallaq, *Sharīʿa*, p. 315.

[76] Related in §538: "It has reached us about the Messenger of God, may God bless and save him, that Māʿiz b. Mālik came to him and confessed before him to *zinā*, and he turned him away. Then he came to him a second time and confessed before him, and he turned him away. Then he came to him the third time and confessed before him, and he turned him away. Then he came to him the fourth time and confessed before him, so [the Prophet] asked [Māʿiz's] folk: Is there something wrong with his mind? They said: No. So he gave the order, and he was stoned (*rujima*). And he [Abū Yūsuf] embraced it."

[77] Meaning both Abū Ḥanīfa and Ibn Abī Laylā in §§537–9. The *masʾala* situates the confessor as standing before the *qāḍī*; Abū Ḥanīfa considers fourfold confession in a single session as a single confession (and does not impose the *ḥadd*-penalty), while Ibn Abī Laylā considers it sufficient for administering the *ḥadd*.

identity-claim I have labelled "*taswiya*-subsumption."[78] He then objects directly to the opposing position—first identifying a *qiyās*, then exposing its inconsistent application—as follows: (1) he identifies an opponent's *istidlāl*: "by way of *qiyās* from four witnesses;" (2) he identifies the opposing ruling: the *ḥadd*-penalty is imposed for four confessions in different sessions, but not four in one; (3) he asserts his opponent's inconsistency, saying he "has abandoned the *aṣl*-principle of his doctrine;" and (4) he produces that subverted *aṣl*-principle: "because he claims that four witnesses are not admitted except in a single session." The larger implication is this: the opponent must acknowledge that "*qiyās* from four witnesses" is the means by which he justifies fourfold confession in the first place. Thus, the same *aṣl* ought to serve as basis for *qiyās* in the *mas'ala* at hand (which concerns number of sessions)—but his opponent does not do this, or he must have ruled that *only* fourfold confession in a single session can be accepted. This is a charge of what I have labeled method-*naqḍ*: the opponent, relying only upon *qiyās*, will have been inconsistent in his *qiyās*-method for related *masā'il*—he will have "abandoned the *aṣl*-principle of his doctrine." Al-Shāfiʿī's demonstration of this takes the form of a "hypothetical" Type I *qiyās al-dalāla* which may be rendered as follows:

<u>*Aṣl*</u> witnesses to *zinā*		<u>*Far*ʿ</u> confessions to *zinā*
<u>*Ḥukm* A</u> must be four	← SAME →	<u>*Ḥukm* A</u> must be four
<u>*Ḥukm* B</u> must be in a single session	SHOULD BE [SAME] →	<u>*Ḥukm* B</u> [must be in a single session]

This style of argument has further implications with regard to a thesis of this monograph; namely, the dynamic symbiosis of *uṣūl* and *jadal* theory can be explained, in part, as due to the *mujtahid*'s anticipation of dialectical disputation during the course of his private *ijtihād*. In this case, the hypothetical *qiyās al-dalāla* employed by al-Shāfiʿī in critiquing the opposing view—at the start of a short dialectical sequence—may also have played a role in his private *ijtihād*. He certainly makes it clear that he does not rely upon this *qiyās al-dalāla*—he could not have ruled single and multiple sessions were "one and the same" otherwise—but he obviously considers it to bolster his final solution.

In §§541–2, al-Shāfiʿī adds further to this charge of method-*naqḍ* by intensifying the level of commitment shown by his opponent to the *aṣl* of four witnesses: not only must they testify in a single session before the *qāḍī*, but if their reports in

---

[78] By Ḥassūn's numbering system, the other jurists' relevant rulings and arguments are: §537 (Abū Ḥanīfa, with Abū Yūsuf's adherence and *naql*-support in §538); and §539 (Ibn Abī Laylā). Al-Shāfiʿī's ruling, though closer to Ibn Abī Laylā's, differs from them all. We may understand his dialectical opponent, however, to argue from Abū Ḥanīfa's position, relying upon the same *ḥadīth* about Māʿiz.

that session are not perfectly harmonious they are themselves inflicted with a *ḥadd*-punishment. With the *aṣl* thus weighted, the *farʿ* should be considered even more proven than before; al-Shāfiʿī not only identifies his opponent's inconsistency, but exaggerates his miscalculation.

Finally in §543 he begins an "instructional" dialectic with the standard formula; but his opponent merely claims adherence to the *ḥadīth* about Māʿiz (the same as supports Abū Ḥanīfa and Abū Yūsuf in §538). This is *istidlāl bi'l-Sunna*; we understand the efficient properties and effects of the opponent's ruling should derive from those of this *ḥadīth*. Al-Shāfiʿī's objections in §544 are multilayered: (1) he claims the *ḥadīth* of Māʿiz does not have the properties ascribed to it by his opponent; (2) he identifies the supposed properties: four times in four separate contexts; (3) he claims (for the sake of argument) that even were it so, his own argument (fourfold in a single session) is not contradicted; and (4) he explains that the articulation (*lafẓ*) (of the Prophet) should be the focus of examination, not the sessions (*majālis*).[79] The argument to this point constitutes a "hypothetical" *iʿtirāḍ* against the opponent's *istidlāl bi'l-Sunna* corresponding to what the theorists would call "sharing the indicant" (*al-mushāraka fi'l-dalīl*)[80]—it is "hypothetical" in that al-Shāfiʿī does not rely upon the *ḥadīth* about Māʿiz for his own ruling, he only "shares" this *dalīl* for the sake of arguing his opponent's misuse of it.

Al-Shāfiʿī now turns his critique on the rulings of *both* Abū Ḥanīfa *and* Ibn Abī Laylā, objecting to the more primary tenet they hold in common: the requirement of fourfold confession. In fact, only a single confession before the *qāḍī* is sufficient to oblige the *ḥadd*-punishment. Al-Shāfiʿī then justifies his own ruling—and simultaneously levels an *iʿtirāḍ*—via the dialectical "*a-lā tarā*" question; its function in this instance is to introduce the *ḥadīth* about Unays: at once his justificatory *dalīl*-indicant and his objection by *muʿāraḍa*.[81] Thus al-Shāfiʿī's penultimate objection

---

[79] Essentially, al-Shāfiʿī has claimed that this should not be so much *istidlāl* by way of Sunnaic act (*fiʿl*), as *istidlāl* by way of Sunnaic decree (*qawl*). Focus should remain, as we see at the very end of §544, on what the Prophet said—especially with regard to his asking if Māʿiz was *non compos mentis*. This is why I will consider his first *iʿtirāḍ* (*al-mushāraka fi'l-dalīl*) in the domain of Sunnaic *fiʿl*, but will place his second (*muʿāraḍa bi'l-nuṭq*) and third (*al-mushāraka fi'l-dalīl*) in the domain of Sunnaic *qawl*.

[80] (Shīr.II.E.4; Bāj.II.4.5) al-Shīrāzī, *Maʿūna*, al-ʿUmayrīnī ed., p. 74; al-Bājī, *Minhāj*, Turkī ed., p. 131, §263. Al-Bājī's larger genus of *al-mushāraka fi'l-istidlāl bi'l-Sunna* contains detailed subtypes. A precise identification is found under that type wherein both R and Q make their *ḥukm* conditional upon the most apparent intension (*ẓāhir*), then under that subtype wherein R and Q each focus upon a different articulation (*lafẓ*) of the *khabar*-report than the other (p. 105, §205; re: Sunnaic decree [*qawl*]). This matches al-Shāfiʿī's claim, when he says the opponent's *istidlāl*, if it were accurate, would not be the contradictory (*khilāf*) of his own, "because we do not look to the sessions, we look only to the articulation." In other words, both would be drawing indicant from the same *ḥadīth*, but focusing upon different formulations (*alfāẓ*) of that "shared" *dalīl*-indicant.

[81] Al-Shāfiʿī's *a-lā tarā* in §544: rhetorical, as a direct confrontation: pushing acknowledgement of an *endoxon* Prophetic *ḥadīth* (Unays) as directly solving the *mas'ala* at hand, supplanting opposing *qiyās* from another Prophetic *ḥadīth* (Māʿiz); also, the opposing position should have acknowledged the *ḥadīth* about Unays as a *bayān* for the *ḥadīth* about Māʿiz; for an overall justification/objection of *istidlāl bi'l-sunna* / *muʿāraḍa bi'l-nuṭq* and method-*naqḍ*.

corresponds to the theorists' "counter-indication [of Sunna] by [another] revelation-decree" (*muʿāraḍa bi'l-nuṭq*);[82] it also stands as another example of method-*naqḍ*.[83]

Finally, al-Shāfiʿī brings his critique to a close with one final objection—the seal of his *elenchus*—in the form of another "sharing the indicant" (*al-mushāraka fi'l-dalīl*).[84] In fact, it is a "reorientation of the indicant," for he introduces a different slant on the *ḥadīth* about Māʿiz: its four confessional episodes have more to do with the Prophet's doubting Māʿiz's sanity than anything else. There is a formulation (*lafẓ*), indicating a case-specific efficient property (the sanity of the confessor is suspect), which has been completely ignored by the opposing position, and which is actually the more significant (and perhaps more efficient) property. In effect, the *ḥadīth* about Māʿiz is distanced from the current *mas'ala* about sessions, and is made to seem more appropriate for *masā'il* in which the confessor's sanity is suspect. Al-Shāfiʿī, not content with supplanting the *ḥadīth* about Māʿiz with the *ḥadīth* about Unays, has also rendered it useless as an *aṣl* in the case at hand.

[82] (Shīr.II.C.8.1; Bāj.II.2.7.1) al-Shīrāzī, *Maʿūna*, al-ʿUmayrīnī ed., p. 67; al-Bājī, *Minhāj*, Turkī ed., pp. 119 ff., §§233 ff. Cf. Ibn ʿAqīl, *K. al-Jadal*, p. 36, §190. Note we are within the domain of *istidlāl bi'l-Sunna* (not *qiyās*), so al-Shāfiʿī's *muʿāraḍa* brings the sanctioned decree (*nuṭq*) of the *ḥadīth* about Unays to supplant Abū Ḥanīfa's, Abū Yūsuf's, and his opponent's *istidlāl* from the *ḥadīth* about Māʿiz (i.e., their interpretation of the *dalīl*-indicant it provides). This dovetails nicely with al-Shāfiʿī's subsequent and final *iʿtirāḍ*, as shall be seen.

[83] This is because his rhetorical *a-lā tarā* implies that Abū Ḥanīfa, Abū Yūsuf, and his opponent all concede the epistemic authority of the *ḥadīth* about Unays. This is akin to saying: "You acknowledge this *ḥadīth* elsewhere, but ignore it for the *mas'ala* at hand even though it is relevant." It is, in the modern parlance, a charge of "cherry picking." It may insinuate that opposing jurists have been knowingly selective in reviewing the Sunnaic evidence, choosing only such *adilla*-indicants as support their pre-determined solution.

[84] (Shīr.II.C.4; Bāj.II.2.3.1.2) al-Shīrāzī, *Maʿūna*, al-ʿUmayrīnī ed., pp. 60 f.; al-Bājī, *Minhāj*, Turkī ed., p. 105, §205. Cf. Ibn ʿAqīl, *K. al-Jadal*, p. 34, §181. Again, al-Shāfiʿī employs the same *ḥadīth* as a *dalīl*-indicant, but focuses upon a different *lafẓ*-articulation. Abū Ḥanīfa, Abū Yūsuf, and his opponent have considered only the overall number of confessions made by Māʿiz; al-Shāfiʿī turns focus on that *lafẓ*—"is he possessed (*a-bihi junna*)?"—which indicates the *reason* behind the Prophet's fourfold aversion of the *ḥadd*-punishment: he suspected his sanity. That Māʿiz eventually confessed four times now appears largely incidental; and the *ḥadīth* about Māʿiz loses immediacy as an *aṣl* for the *mas'ala* at hand—it is more for cases wherein the significant property (his sanity is suspect) is found.

Short Sequence 8

§§737–743 from the *Chapter on Partnership, Manumission, Etc.* (*Bāb fi'l-Sharika wa'l-ʿItq wa Ghayrihi*)[85]

737 – Al-Shāfiʿī, may God Most High have mercy upon him, said: *Mufāwaḍa*-partnership is null and void—I don't know anything in the world to be null and void, if *mufāwaḍa*-partnership is not null and void! Unless, that is, they are two partners who consider *mufāwaḍa* to be a mixing of property with property [as capital], and the work regarding it, and reciprocal distribution of the profit—for in this there is no harm. And this is the partnership which some of the Easterners[86] call *ʿinān*-partnership.[87]	737 - قَالَ الشَّافِعِيُّ رَحِمَهُ اللّٰهُ تَعَالَى: وَشَرِكَةُ الْمُفَاوَضَةِ بَاطِلَةٌ وَلاَ أَعْرِفُ شَيْئًا مِن الدُّنْيَا يَكُونُ بَاطِلاً إِنْ لَمْ تَكُنْ شَرِكَةُ الْمُفَاوَضَةِ بَاطِلَةً، إلاَّ أَنْ يَكُونَا شَرِيكَيْنِ يَعُدَّانِ الْمُفَاوَضَةَ خَلْطَ الْمَالِ بِالْمَالِ وَالْعَمَلَ فِيهِ وَاقْتِسَامَ الرِّبْحِ فَهَذَا لاَ بَأْسَ بِهِ، وَهَذِهِ الشَّرِكَةُ الَّتِي يَقُولُ بَعْضُ الْمشْرِقِيِّينَ لَهَا: شَرِكَةَ عِنَانٍ.
738 – So when two contract *mufāwaḍa*-partnership, and they mutually stipulate that the *mufāwaḍa* is, according to them both, of this *maʿnā*-intension; the partnership is valid. And whatever one of them happens to be endowed with—besides this property which they have, together, contracted [as capital]—from trade, rent, found-treasure, gift, or anything else; it belongs to him, to the exclusion of his companion.	738 - فَإِذَا اشْتَرَكَا مُفَاوَضَةً وَتَشَارَطَا أَنَّ الْمُفَاوَضَةَ عِنْدَهُمَا هَذَا الْمَعْنَى فَالشَّرِكَةُ صَحِيحَةٌ، وَمَا رُزِقَ أَحَدُهُمَا مِن غَيْرِ هَذَا الْمَالِ الَّذِي اشْتَرَكَا فِيهِ مَعًا مِن تِجَارَةٍ أَوْ إِجَارَةٍ أَوْ كَنْزٍ أَوْ هِبَةٍ أَوْ غَيْرِ ذَلِكَ فَهُوَ لَهُ دُونَ صَاحِبِهِ.
739 – But if they assert that the *mufāwaḍa*, according to them both, is that they are partners in all that they gain in one way or another, due to the [capital] property or otherwise; the partnership for this is invalid. And I don't know of gambling except in this, or in less than it: that two men contract partnership on two-hundred dirhams, then one of them finds a treasure and it is [divided] between them.	739 - وَإِنْ زَعَمَا بِأَنَّ الْمُفَاوَضَةَ عِنْدَهُمَا بِأَنْ يَكُونَا شَرِيكَيْنِ فِي كُلِّ مَا أَفَادَا بِوَجْهٍ مِنَ الْوُجُوهِ بِسَبَبِ الْمَالِ وَغَيْرِهِ، فَالشَّرِكَةُ فِيهِ فَاسِدَةٌ، وَلاَ أَعْرِفُ الْقِمَارَ إلاَّ فِي هَذَا أَوْ أَقَلَّ مِنْهُ؛ أَنْ يَشْتَرِكَ الرَّجُلاَنِ بِمِائَتَيْ دِرْهَمٍ فَيَجِدُ أَحَدُهُمَا كَنْزًا فَيَكُونَ بَيْنَهُمَا.

(continued)

[85] Ḥassūn ed., vol. 9, pp. 131–2; ʿAbd al-Muṭṭalib ed., vol. 8, p. 308.

[86] See the note for §252 re: the Mashriqiyyūn.

[87] Nyazee provides useful glossary definitions for *mufāwaḍa* (*DJP*, vol. 2, p. 587): "A kind of partnership in which the partners contribute their entire belongings, that is, they have unlimited liability. This is the meaning according to the Ḥanafites. The *mufāwaḍa* partnership approved by the Mālikites is more like the *ʿinān* form of partnership." And for *sharikat al-mufāwaḍa* (p. 593): "A partnership in which the partners contribute their entire belongings as capital along with their labour." And for *sharikat al-ʿinān* (ibid.): "A partnership in which the partners contribute capital and share profits and losses according to a determined ratio." As may be understood from the current *mas'ala* of §§737–43, the technical vocabulary was more fluid in al-Shāfiʿī's time. For more on the *mufāwaḍa* vs. *ʿinān* distinction, see *MF*, s.v. "شركة العقد" (vol. 26, pp. 38–9, §10); *EI*², s.v. "*Sharika*"; *DJP*, vol. 2, pp. 301–4 (esp. p. 304, where al-Shāfiʿī's argument against *mufāwaḍa* is explained); and Hallaq, *Sharīʿa*, pp. 252–3.

740 – Have you considered [what would happen] if they mutually stipulate this, without mixing any property—would it be permitted?[88]	740 - أَرَأَيْتَ لَوْ تَشَارَطَا عَلَى هَذَا مِن غَيْرِ أَنْ يَتَخَالَطَا بِمَالٍ كَانَ يَجُوزُ.
741 – And if he says: It is not permitted; because it is a giving of what belonged neither to the giver nor the receiver, and of something neither of the two knew about [at the time of contract]. So would you permit it with the two-hundred dirhams they contracted [as capital]?[89]	741 - فَإِنْ قَالَ: لاَ يَجُوزُ؛ لأَنَّهُ عَطِيَّةٌ مَا لَمْ يَكُنْ لِلْمُعْطِي وَلاَ لِلْمُعْطَى وَمَا لَمْ يَعْلَمْهُ وَاحِدٌ مِنْهُمَا، أَفَتُجِيزُهُ عَلَى مِائَتَيْ دِرْهَمٍ اشْتَرَكَا بِهَا؟
742 – And if they consider it a kind of *bay*ʿ-commutation; the *bay*ʿ-commutation of what does not exist [at the time of contract] is not permitted.	742 - فَإِنْ عَدُّوهُ بَيْعًا فَبَيْعُ مَا لَمْ يَكُنْ لاَ يَجُوزُ.
743 – Have you considered[90] a man who is given a gift, or who hires himself out for work, and who gains property from work or gift; is the other one a partner in it? They have rejected less than this.	743 - أَرَأَيْتَ رَجُلاً وُهِبَ لَهُ هِبَةٌ أَوْ أَجَرَ نَفْسَهُ فِي عَمَلٍ فَأَفَادَ مَالاً مِن عَمَلٍ أَوْ هِبَةٍ، أَيَكُونُ الآخَرُ فِيهَا شَرِيكًا؟ لَقَدْ أَنْكَرُوا أَقَلَّ مِن هَذَا.

In §§737–9 al-Shāfiʿī presents his rulings with regard to *mufāwaḍa*-partnership in a number of stages, as follows: (1) he emphatically rules as null and void (*bāṭil*) what is apparently the more common understanding of *mufāwaḍa*-partnership; (2) he rules a singular exception—with the common formula "in this there is no harm" (*lā ba'sa bihi*)[91]—regarding a very particular, well-defined understanding of *mufāwaḍa*, which serves to highlight the efficient properties which make it lawful: mixing of property with property (*khalṭ al-māl bi'l-māl*), plus mixing of contract-associated work (*al-ʿamal fīhi*), plus reciprocal distribution of profit (*iqtisām*

[88] Meaning, if two men contracted partnership for dividing whatever treasure either might find, without a prior mixing of capital.

[89] We may understand the closing question as al-Shāfiʿī's rhetorical *elenchus* (or retort).

[90] Schacht (*Origins*, p. 120, and n. 3) cites this occurrence of *a-ra'ayta* (and the one in §740) while discussing al-Shāfiʿī's expressions of considered opinion (*ra'y*). Schacht's language, however, is vague. Having indicated passages where he believes al-Shāfiʿī to "use *ra'y* in the same loose way as the ancient schools," and pointed out a preponderance of instances wherein al-Shāfiʿī "formulates his conclusions cautiously by giving them as his opinion in a non-technical sense;" Schacht adds: "He also uses *ara'aita* and *alā tarā* for introducing systematic arguments."

[91] The formula *lā ba'sa bi-/an* enjoys great currency among the jurists of our subject-text (with some eighteen instances, and well over 300 in the *Umm* compendium, overall). This is patently the language of normative assessment, in general, and in particular conveys that category more systematically termed *mubāḥ* ("permissible/indifferent"; normative neutrality) in later *uṣūl* literature. It may be compared over and against the formulae *aḥabba ilayya* and variants—conveying the later category of "recommended" (*mustaḥabb/mandūb*); and *akrahu/yakrahu* X *lahu* and variants—conveying the later category of "reprehensible" (*makrūh*). These latter formulae are also found in our subject-text, and plentifully throughout the *Umm* compendium.

al-ribḥ);[92] (3) he equates this permissible formulation of *mufāwaḍa*-partnership to what some of the Mashriqiyyūn call *sharikat ʿinān*.[93] He then continues in §738, ruling: (4) *mufāwaḍa* mutually contracted with this *maʿnā*-intension of the Mashriqiyyūn is valid (*ṣaḥīḥ*); and (5) a subsidiary ruling: income generated outside of—and by other means than—the contracted mixed-capital belongs only to its owner, not to his partner. Thus al-Shāfiʿī pinpoints the distinction between that property (*waṣf*) which occasions a valid contract (it stipulates *māl* generated from mixed capital) and that which occasions an invalid contract (it stipulates *māl* generated outside of mixed capital). He then continues in §739, ruling: (6) *mufāwaḍa* mutually-stipulating the incorrect *maʿnā*-intension (sharing of *all* income, including that generated outside the mixed-capital) is invalid (*fāsid*).[94]

Al-Shāfiʿī now brings an objection in the form of another virulent assertion: "I don't know of gambling (*qimār*) except in this, or in less than it: that two men contract partnership on two-hundred dirhams, then one of them finds a treasure

---

[92] The components forming al-Shāfiʿī's definition of this permissible (*mubāḥ*) form of *mufāwaḍa*-partnership also serve as the efficient properties occasioning his ruling of "there is no harm in it" (*lā baʾsa bihi*). Elsewhere, I have referenced one of al-Bājī's divisions of occasioning factors (*ʿilal*), for purposes of *naqḍ*, as "posited for the genus (*wuḍiʿa liʾl-jins*), being in the position (*manzila*) of the definition (*ḥadd*)." Here, al-Shāfiʿī's definition-*ʿilla* fits nicely within this category. As we shall see, his *elenchus* in this short sequence is a (multiple) charge of *naqḍ*; his defining of efficient properties here in §737 thus dovetails with his final refutation.

[93] §737 contains a number of important elements. It provides a window onto an era when contract typologies were more inchoate than in later times. There is testimony here to yet another dynamic of dialectic at work: the refinement and fixing of categories and technical terms within venues of disputation—we witness the ironing out of a technical definition for a specific contract type; and it is recorded in a book of *ikhtilāf*, at the head of a short dialectical sequence. Moreover, we again encounter the "Easterners" (cf. our analysis of §252, above); and al-Shāfiʿī's report of their distinct usage of *sharikat ʿinān* is telling. As already inferred—with the help of al-Rabīʿ—the Mashriqiyyūn include Abū Ḥanīfa but exclude Mālik; and, on the basis of the *ʿinān* distinction, it is now confirmed that this group comprised the jurists of a nascent Ḥanafism (in ʿIrāq and perhaps further east as well). The unique Ḥanafī treatment of *mufāwaḍa*, as distinct in most ways from the other three surviving Sunnī schools (see Hallaq, *Sharīʿa*, pp. 252–3) is evidence enough. We may also note a complete Ithnā ʿAsharī rejection of *mufāwaḍa*; comparing Shīʿī sources with §§737–9 is a worthy project, and might reveal *mufāwaḍa* as defined and critiqued in the same manner. Finally, it is worth considering the extent to which variant contract typologies reflect the separate evolution of pre- and early Islamic regional variants, eventually disputed in more systematized juridical-dialectical settings.

[94] By Ḥassūn's numbering system, the other jurists' relevant rulings and arguments are: §735 (Abū Ḥanīfa, with Abū Yūsuf's adherence); and §736 (Ibn Abī Laylā). The *masʾala* treated by them is formulated differently: it concerns a *mufāwaḍa*-partnership in which one partner contributes more capital than the other. Abū Ḥanīfa simply rules: "This is not *mufāwaḍa*;" while Ibn Abī Laylā rules: "this is a permitted *mufāwaḍa*-contract, and the [income] property is divided equally between them." Viewing these terse statements in the light of al-Shāfiʿī's generally anti-*mufāwaḍa* campaign, it becomes apparent that a divergence of contract definitions lies, in part, at the heart of *ikhtilāf*. Al-Shāfiʿī's objective becomes more clear: he is set on restricting the too-general scope of *mufāwaḍa* partnership to a strictly-defined set of valid stipulations—or, perhaps, subsuming these under *ʿinān*-partnership and abandoning *mufāwaḍa* altogether.

(*kanz*) and it is [divided] between them." This sets the stage for the ensuing "instructional" dialectic (and eventual charge of *naqḍ*) in several ways: first, he equates the invalid form of *mufāwaḍa* with the universally rejected transaction of gambling (*qimār*), and thus provides an authoritative *aṣl* for its invalidation; second, he introduces what is to serve as both a condemnable example of an invalid *mufāwaḍa*-contract and a problem case for exposing the opposing position's inconsistency (*mas'alat al-naqḍ*). Importantly, this *mas'alat al-naqḍ* contains the efficient properties (see §741) linking it to rejected *qimār*.

Al-Shāfiʿī now, in §740, initiates an "instructional" dialectic with himself in the role of questioner. His opening *a-ra'ayta* question pushes his opponent to rule on a derived form of the *mas'alat al-naqḍ* in §739, from which a singular property (stipulation of mixed capital) has been subtracted.[95] His opponent's response in §741—signalled by "and if he says" (*fa-in qāla*)—is a ruling in the negative (*lā yajūzu*), followed by *ʿaql*-support—signalled by "because"—detailing the properties which occasion its impermissibility ("it is [1] a giving of what belonged neither to the giver nor the receiver, and [2] of something neither of the two knew about [at the time of contract]"). Al-Shāfiʿī immediately interjects with a rhetorical question (or retort) by which he reinserts the subtracted property (stipulation of mixed capital) into the *mas'alat al-naqḍ* and challenges the opponent to rule differently: "So would you permit it (*a-fa-tujīzuhu?*) with the two-hundred dirhams they contracted [as capital]?" This is, effectively, a rhetorical *iʿtirāḍ* of *naqḍ*;[96] the same properties which occasioned the opponent's negative judgment in the reduced *mas'alat al-naqḍ* of §740 are present in the restored *mas'alat al-naqḍ* (and thus also in the invalid form of *mufāwaḍa*), but the opponent's same judgement is not. This fulfills the definition of *naqḍ* (presence of the *ʿilla* despite absence of the *ḥukm*), but at the same time involves a "subtraction-and-reinsertion" strategy which is uniquely al-Shāfiʿī's.[97] Presumably, his opponent is silenced.

In §742 al-Shāfiʿī leaps to close a last door of escape (if the partners reconsider the contract as *bayʿ*) by pointing out another efficient property in the *mas'alat al-naqḍ* (the treasure is not in existence at the time of contract) which occasions

[95] Al-Shāfiʿī's *a-ra'ayta* in §740: dialogical, soliciting a ruling for a derived sub-strategy *mas'alat al-naqḍ*, as part of a larger *naqḍ* objection with a unique subtraction-reinsertion strategy.

[96] (Shīr.VII.7; Bāj.IX.B.11.1) al-Shīrāzī, *Maʿūna*, al-ʿUmayrīnī ed., pp. 104 ff.; al-Bājī, *Minhāj*, Turkī ed., p. 185, §§412–13. Cf. Ibn ʿAqīl, *K. al-Jadal*, pp. 56 ff., §§276 ff. As foreshadowed by al-Shāfiʿī's definition-*ʿilla* in §737, his *naqḍ* corresponds to al-Bājī's first type; i.e., *naqḍ* of an *ʿilla* which is "posited for the genus (*wuḍiʿa li'l-jins*), being in the position of the definition (*bi-manzilat al-ḥadd*)." The "genus" in this case is the general contract category of *mufāwaḍa*.

[97] In sum, al-Shāfiʿī has: (1) taken a *mas'ala* the ruling for which, in his opponent's opinion, ought to be "permitted" (*jā'iz*); then (2) removed a property linking it to the *mas'ala* at hand; then (3) asked his opponent to rule on it (which he does, pronouncing it "not permitted" and stating the efficient properties himself); then (4) replaced the property linking the *mas'alat al-naqḍ* to the *mas'ala* at hand; then (5) rhetorically asked his opponent to rule on it again—forcing either his self-contradiction or silence. The particular genius of this strategy—in conformity with the classical aims of dialectic—is that the opponent has himself provided the efficient properties which (by linking invalid *mufāwaḍa* to *qimār*) occasion the questioner's own ruling. Al-Shāfiʿī's dialectical opponent has provided the premises by which al-Shāfiʿī at once refutes him and vindicates his own thesis.

the *ḥukm* of "not permitted" (*lā yajūzu*), and which *ʿilla-ḥukm* pair must be considered *endoxon* for *bayʿ*-contracts. (His opponent remains silent). Al-Shāfiʿī then proceeds to seal his *elenchus* in §743 with a rhetorical *a-ra'ayta* question introducing two more *masā'il al-naqḍ* (in which the *mufāwaḍa* partner receives a gift, or earns an outside wage); thus delivering a double *iʿtirāḍ* of *naqḍ*;[98] and, finally, concludes with what can only be described as an *a fortiori* punch: "They have rejected less than this" (*laqad ankarū aqall min hādhā*). In other words, his opponents have rejected less risky forms of contract—all the more so should they reject this gambling-equivalent *mufāwaḍa*.[99]

Short Sequence 9

§§785–788 from the *Chapter on Partnership, Manumission, Etc.* (*Bāb fi'l-Sharika wa'l-'Itq wa Ghayrihi*)[100]

785 – Al-Shāfiʿī, may God Most High have mercy upon him, said: And when the slave is [jointly-owned] between two men, and one of them contracts *tadbīr*-manumission with him; the other has the right to sell his portion—because the *tadbīr*-manumission, in my opinion, is a bequest. And likewise, the one who contracted *tadbīr*-manumission with him has the right to sell him.[101] And this is written in the *Book on the Slave Manumitted after the Owner's Death*.[102]	785 - قَالَ الشَّافِعِيُّ رَحِمَهُ اللّٰهُ تَعَالَى: وَإِذَا كَانَ الْعَبْدُ بَيْنَ رَجُلَيْنِ فَدَبَّرَهُ أَحَدُهُمَا فَلِلآخَرِ بَيْعُ نَصِيبِهِ؛ لأَنَّ التَّدْبِيرَ عِنْدِي وَصِيَّةٌ. وَكَذَلِكَ لِلَّذِي دَبَّرَهُ أَنْ يَبِيعَهُ. وَهَذَا مَكْتُوبٌ فِي كِتَابِ الْمُدَبَّرِ.

(continued)

[98] (Shīr.VII.7; Bāj.IX.B.11.1) See above note attached to the analysis of §741 for references. Al-Shāfiʿī's *a-ra'ayta* in §743: hypophoric, introducing additional *masā'il al-naqḍ* for a larger scheme of compound *naqḍ*.

[99] This argument is of the species *a minore ad maius*; and, although taking place within a larger framework of *naqḍ*, it finds no specific reference or example under *naqḍ* in our *jadal*-theory texts. I will consider it, therefore, as belonging either to al-Shāfiʿī's unique dialectical style, or to that of the jurists of his day, or merely to have been neglected by later theorists in their *naqḍ* discussions.

[100] Ḥassūn ed., vol. 9, pp. 136–7; ʿAbd al-Muṭṭalib ed., vol. 8, p. 311.

[101] On *tadbīr*—the contracted manumission of a slave (the *mudabbar*) upon the master's death—and related rulings, see *MF*, s.v. "تدبير" (vol. 11, pp. 124–5); *EI*², s.v. "Tadbīr," §2; and *DJP*, vol. 2, pp. 469–74.

[102] This is the only reference to a *Kitāb al-Mudabbar* made in the entire *Umm* compendium, and no such *Kitāb* appears among its many chapters and subheadings. There is, however, a *Kitāb al-Mudabbar* among the works attributed to al-Shāfiʿī by Ibn al-Nadīm (*Fihrist*, p. 354); and, in all likelihood, this *Kitāb* survives in the *Umm*, in either whole or piecemeal fashion. Certainly, another *dalīl*-indicant for al-Shāfiʿī's stance may be found in the *Kitāb Ikhtilāf Mālik wa'l-Shāfiʿī*, under the subheading *Chapter on the Sale of the Slave Manumitted on the Owner's Death* (*Bāb fī Bayʿ al-Mudabbar*; Ḥassūn ed., vol. 9, pt. 14, p. 523): ʿĀ'isha was reported to have sold a female slave (*jāriya*), with whom she had contracted *tadbīr*-manumission—as a punishment for having practiced sorcery against her. Al-Shāfiʿī and companions maintained this doctrine (*wa naḥnu naqūlu bi-qawl ʿĀ'isha wa ghayrihā*), while Mālik and companions maintained the *mudabbar*-slave cannot be sold.

786 – And whoever claims that the *mudabbir*-master has no right to sell the *mudabbar*-slave is obliged to claim that the *mudabbir*-master owes—if he is solvent—half the value to his partner, and that [the slave] is, all of him, a *mudabbar*—just as he is obliged to claim for ʿ*itq*-manumission.[103] When he treats this as ʿ*itq*-manumission, he must do so in every circumstance.[104]	786 - وَمَنْ زَعَمَ أَنَّهُ لَيْسَ لِلْمُدَبِّرِ أَنْ يَبِيعَ الْمُدَبَّرَ لَزِمَهُ أَنْ يَزْعُمَ أَنَّ عَلَى السَّيِّدِ الْمُدَبِّرِ نِصْفُ الْقِيمَةِ لِشَرِيكِهِ إِنْ كَانَ مُوسِرًا وَيَكُونُ مُدَبَّرًا كُلُّهُ، كَمَا يَلْزَمُهُ هَذَا فِي الْعِتْقِ إِذَا جَعَلَ هَذَا عِتْقًا يَكُونُ لَهُ بِكُلِّ حَالٍ.
787 – And if he says: The ʿ*itq*-manumission for which you have obliged half the value is a manumission which occurs on the spot.[105]	787 - فَإِنْ قَالَ: فَالْعِتْقُ الَّذِي أَلْزَمْتَهُ فِيهِ نِصْفَ الْقِيمَةِ عِتْقٌ وَاقِعٌ مَكَانَهُ.
788 – It is said: And you yourself claim, for the female slave [jointly-owned] between two men—[when] one of them has intercourse with her, and she gives birth—that she is an *umm walad*, and that he owes half the value [to his partner].[106] And this is a manumission which does *not* occur on the spot—it only occurs after a period of time, just as the manumission of the *mudabbar*-slave occurs after a period of time.	788 – قِيلَ: فَأَنْتَ تَزْعُمُ فِي الْجَارِيَةِ بَيْنَ الرَّجُلَيْنِ يَطَؤُهَا أَحَدُهُمَا فَتَلِدُ أَنَّهَا أُمُّ وَلَدٍ وَعَلَيْهِ نِصْفُ الْقِيمَةِ، وَهَذَا عِتْقٌ لَيْسَ بِوَاقِعٍ مَكَانَهُ، إِنَّمَا هُوَ وَاقِعٌ بَعْدَ مُدَّةٍ كَعِتْقِ الْمُدَبَّرِ يَقَعُ بَعْدَ مُدَّةٍ.

In §785, al-Shāfiʿī presents his rulings for the *mas'ala* at hand: (1) the non-manumitting partner may sell his portion; and (2) the manumitting partner may also sell his portion. These receive ʿ*aql*-support, heralded by "because;" al-Shāfiʿī subsumes *tadbīr*-manumission under the legal category of bequest (*waṣiyya*). Though without the signal formula (*fa-sawā'un* X and Y), this is an example of what I have labeled *taswiya*-subsumption; and it is thus also an example of *istidlāl bi-qiyās* (though the precise type of *qiyās* cannot be determined from his brief presentation).[107] For further support, al-Shāfiʿī directs us to a more complete argument in another of his writings.[108]

---

[103] Cf. §§744 ff., above, on ʿ*itq*-manumission.

[104] Note this as the clear expression of doctrinal and methodological consistency as a dialectical given.

[105] That is, as opposed to *tadbīr*-manumission, which occurs after the death of the master. The opponent is raising a *farq*-distinction.

[106] On the *umm al-walad*, see the references in the note attached to §80, above.

[107] Although we may assume the efficient property linking valid *tadbīr*-manumission to valid *waṣiyya*-bequest is something like: "it is a transfer of ownership which is effected upon the death of the legator," we learn neither the ʿ*illa* nor its indicants (shared properties or rulings) from the abbreviated presentation of §785. We might assume, however, it is type II *qiyās al-dalāla*, if we interpret al-Shāfiʿī as claiming that *tadbīr*-manumission and *waṣiyya*-bequest are "complementary parallels" (*naẓā'ir*).

[108] By Ḥassūn's numbering system, the other jurists' relevant rulings and arguments are: §781 (Abū Ḥanīfa, with Abū Yūsuf's adherence); and §782[a] (Ibn Abī Laylā). §782[b] through §784 is taken up by another *mas'ala*: a different problem relating to *mufāwaḍa*-partnership, which al-Shāfiʿī does not address (see my dissertation, Part II, p. 199, n. 14, for an attempted explanation). On the current problem of *tadbīr*, Abū Ḥanīfa rules that the non-manumitting partner may *not* sell his portion, with ʿ*aql*-support: due to what intervenes of ʿ*itq*-manumission. Ibn Abī Laylā simply rules that he has the right to sell his share. It becomes obvious from the short sequence of §§785–8 that al-Shāfiʿī's opponent is arguing from Abū Ḥanīfa's position.

He then, in §786, opens an "instructional" dialectic with "whoever claims [X]" (*wa man zaʿama* [X]), by presenting the opposing ruling as: "the *mudabbir*-master has no right to sell the *mudabbar*-slave" (the contradictory of his ruling [2]). Al-Shāfiʿī then proceeds immediately to an objection. First, he asserts—with "he is obliged to claim [Y]" (*lazimahu an yazʿuma* [Y])—that this opposing claim entails non-*endoxa* subsidiary claims: the solvent *mudabbir*-master must pay half-value to his partner, and the slave must be considered wholly *mudabbar*-manumitted. He then ties this to the opposing position's doctrine for *ʿitq*-manumission with "just as he is obliged to claim this for [Z]" (*kamā yalzamuhu hādhā fī* [Z]).[109] Al-Shāfiʿī, having already identified his own *aṣl* for *qiyās* in the *mas'ala* at hand (*waṣiyya*-bequest), has now insisted that another (*ʿitq*-manumission) be consistently observed by the opposing position.[110] His objection takes final shape with the formulaic norm: "When he treats this (*idhā jaʿala hādhā*) as *ʿitq*-manumission, he must do so in every circumstance (*yakūnu lahu bi-kulli ḥālin*)." This appeal to consistency plainly constitutes a charge of what I have labeled method-*naqḍ*: the opponent does not consistently observe the *taswiya*-subsumption of X and Y (*tadbīr* rulings) under Z (*ʿitq*-manumission), thus his *qiyās* (and resulting doctrine) are inconsistent.

In §787 the opponent's response, signaled by "and if he says" (*fa-in qāla*), is most easily interpreted as a counter-objection by way of *farq*-distinction. As an attempt to block al-Shāfiʿī's enforcement of *taswiya*-subsumption, his opponent identifies a distinct property of the imposed *aṣl* of *ʿitq*-manumission: it is "a manumission which occurs on the spot" (*ʿitqun wāqiʿun makānahu*)—this property, of course, is the contradictory of what is found in *tadbīr*-manumission (which occurs only after the *mudabbir*-master's death). In short, though not bringing another *aṣl*, the opponent has attempted to invalidate the *qiyās* which al-Shāfiʿī has imposed upon him.[111]

---

[109] The overall formula for this argument to consistency is thus: "whoever claims [X] is obliged to claim [Y] just as he is obliged to claim this for [Z]." It is an insistence upon strictly consistent *qiyās*.

[110] Recall that Abū Ḥanīfa cites the intervention of *ʿitq*-manumission in support of his ruling that the non-manumitting partner may not sell his portion; presumably the same was applied to the case of the manumitting partner, and this is the position which al-Shāfiʿī now attributes to his opponent.

[111] An alternate—and more hesitant—analysis is that he has attempted to parry al-Shāfiʿī's charge of method-*naqḍ* by justifying his "particularization of the occasioning factor" (*takhṣīṣ al-ʿilla*) for *ʿitq*-manumission. Sānū (*Muʿjam*, s.v. "تخصيص العلة") defines *takhṣīṣ al-ʿilla* as: "the absence (*takhalluf*) of the *ḥukm* from the property (*waṣf*) which is claimed to be an *ʿilla* in certain forms/modes (*fī baʿḍ al-ṣuwar*), due to the presence of an invalidating impediment (*mānīʿ*); and it is called *naqḍ*" (see also Hallaq, *History*, pp. 110–11, for an overview and detailed presentation of al-Sarakhsī's argument against *takhṣīṣ al-ʿilla*; and Zysow, "Economy of Certainty," pp. 403 ff. for a detailed historical and analytical overview). *Naqḍ* is indeed a *charge* of *takhṣīṣ al-ʿilla*, but only against those who do not subscribe to the theory that such a "specialization" of the *ʿilla* is allowed. Our *jadal*-theory texts make this plain; al-Shīrāzī, for example (*Maʿūna*, al-ʿUmayrīnī ed., p. 104),

In §788 al-Shāfiʿī blocks this move with another objection—a counter-counter-objection—by introducing a test-case (*mas'alat al-naqḍ*) exposing his opponent's inconsistency with the "it occurs on the spot" *farq*-distinction. Importantly, he draws from his opponent's own doctrine—"And you yourself claim" (*fa-anta tazʿumu*)—a ruling on the jointly-owned *umm al-walad*: the father-owner owes his partner half her value. We recall the opponent rejected *qiyās* for *tadbīr*-manumission (occurring only after the *mudabbir*-master's death) from the *aṣl* of *ʿitq*-manumission, due to the contradictory property of the latter (it occurs on the spot). Al-Shāfiʿī now shows his opponent nevertheless observes *qiyās* from the *aṣl* of *ʿitq*-manumission for the case of the *umm al-walad*—even though it is "a manumission which does *not* occur on the spot—it only occurs after a period of time, just as the manumission of the *mudabbar*-slave occurs after a period of time."[112] Thus al-Shāfiʿī seals his *elenchus*, and not only vindicates but doubles the strength of his original charge of method-*naqḍ*; for his opponent is doubly exposed: he is just as inconsistent with *farq*-distinctions as he is with *qiyās*.[113]

---

defines *naqḍ* as: "the presence of the *ʿilla*, and not a *ḥukm*, according to the doctrine of one who does not opine (*lā yarā*) *takhṣīṣ al-ʿilla*." It is not right, then, to say that *takhṣīṣ al-ʿilla* is called *naqḍ*, because the former is a theory, while the latter is a charge of practicing that theory (knowingly or otherwise) while disclaiming it. If this short sequence of §§785–8 may be interpreted as a dispute over *takhṣīṣ al-ʿilla*—though I am hesitant to assert this very strongly at this stage—it would acquire a new dimension of intellectual historical importance. It would provide testimony that this theory (in substance, if not name) was debated in the late second century H; and it would reveal what I have labelled *taswiya*-subsumption to be its *antidote*. If a jurist was not practicing *taswiya*-subsumption (as al-Shāfiʿī enjoins), then he might be accused of practicing *takhṣīṣ al-ʿilla* and charged with *naqḍ*. On the other hand, if he normally observes *taswiya*-subsumption, and it can be shown he has done so elsewhere but not in the disputed *mas'ala*, then he might be charged with method-*naqḍ*.

112 This finishing stroke may be rephrased as follows: (1) You claim that *ʿitq*-to-*tadbīr qiyās* in the problem at hand is impossible due to the *farq*-distinction between delayed *tadbīr* and immediate *ʿitq*; but (2) in the case of the jointly-owned *umm walad*, where you should be blocked by the same *farq*-distinction, you exercise *qiyās*; thus (3) my original charge of method-*naqḍ* stands: you ought to have observed *ʿitq*-to-*tadbīr qiyās* in the problem at hand, because there is no real impediment to your doing so, just as there was no impediment to your *ʿitq*-to-*umm walad qiyās*.

113 This is already an extraordinary, multi-layered argument, though further dimensions are apparent. First, it must be remembered that al-Shāfiʿī himself does not subscribe to *qiyās* from *ʿitq* to *tadbīr*. He has already told us he considers *tadbīr* to be a bequest (*waṣiyya*), and thus suggested his own *aṣl* for *qiyās*. When he argues for *ʿitq* as an *aṣl* for *qiyās* he is doing so "hypothetically"—to show his opponent *what he should have done* in the name of consistency. His argument style is, consequently, more "destructive" than "constructive." He is singularly focused on obliterating his opponent's claims, not on gaining concession to the premises from which his own thesis (*tadbīr*-as-*waṣiyya*) is constructed. The stages of the overall sequence, further abstracted, help us to understand better what a unique argument this is: In §786, al-Shāfiʿī claims his opponent *should* have extended his *qiyās* from *ʿitq* (though al-Shāfiʿī does not concede that *qiyās*) from the first to the second *tadbīr* ruling, but has not (method-*naqḍ* #1); in §787, his opponent claims *farq*-distinction against the hypothetical *qiyās* from *ʿitq*-to-*tadbīr*; and in §788, al-Shāfiʿī shows no

Short Sequence 10

§§1115–1119 from the *Chapter on Blood-Money* (*Bāb al-Diyāt*)[114]

1115 – Al-Shāfiʿī, may God Most High have mercy upon him, said: The one leading the mount,[115] and its driver, and its rider, are [all] liable for what it injured by foreleg, or mouth, or hind leg, or tail—and naught but this is allowed. But he is not liable for anything unless he induces it to trample something—then he is liable because its trampling derives from his action, and at that time [the mount] is like one of his implements, by which he inflicts harm.[116]	1115 - قَالَ الشَّافِعِيُّ رَحِمَهُ اللّٰهُ تَعَالَى: يَضْمَنُ قَائِدُ الدَّابَّةِ وَسَائِقُهَا وَرَاكِبُهَا مَا أَصَابَتْ بِيَدٍ أَوْ فَمٍ أَوْ رِجْلٍ أَوْ ذَنَبٍ، وَلاَ يَجُوزُ إلاَّ هَذَا، وَلاَ يَضْمَنُ شَيْئًا إلاَّ أَنْ يَحْمِلَهَا عَلَى أَنْ تطَأَ شَيْئًا فَيَضْمَنُ؛ لأَنَّ وَطْأَهَا مِن فِعْلِهِ فَتَكُونُ حِينَئِذٍ كَأَدَاةٍ مِن أَدَاتِهِ جَنَى بِهَا.
1116 – And should we say: He is liable for its foreleg, but he is not liable for its hind leg? This is arbitrariness!	1116 - فَأَمَّا أَنْ نَقُولَ: يَضْمَنُ عَن يَدِهَا وَلاَ يَضْمَنُ عَن رِجْلِهَا فَهَذَا تَحَكُّمٌ.
1117 – Then if he says: He does not see its back leg.[117]	1117 - فَإِنْ قَالَ: لاَ يَرَى رِجْلَهَا.
1118 – Then he—when he is driving—does not see its foreleg![118] Thus he should say for the driver: He is liable for the hind leg, but not liable for the foreleg. But there is no such doctrine.	1118 - فَهُوَ إذَا كَانَ سَائِقًا لاَ يَرَى يَدَهَا، فَيَنْبَغِي أَنْ يَقُولَ فِي السَّائِقِ: يَضْمَنُ عَنِ الرِّجْلِ، وَلاَ يَضْمَنُ عَنِ الْيَدِ. وَلَيْسَ هَكَذَا بِقَوْلٍ.

(continued)

farq-distinction was observed by his opponent in his *qiyās* from *ʿitq*-to-*umm walad*, where it *should* have been (method-*naqḍ* #2). In briefest paraphrase, al-Shāfiʿī has said: "The *aṣl* here is not *ʿitq*, it is *waṣiyya*. But even if it were *ʿitq*, you have neglected it where you should have subsequently observed it; and, if we accept your excusing distinction, you have observed it where you should have rejected it!"

[114] Ḥassūn ed., vol. 9, p. 189; ʿAbd al-Muṭṭalib ed., vol. 8, p. 353.

[115] The *dābba* (pl. *dawābb*) is usually understood, in *fiqh* works, to be a riding animal or a pack animal.

[116] On trampling mounts and related rulings, see *MF*, s.v. "حيوان" (vol. 18, p. 338, §9) and "إتلاف" (vol. 1, pp. 224–5, §§29–32); and *DJP*, vol. 2, pp. 503–4.

[117] That is, when leading (from in front) or riding the mount or pack animal.

[118] That is, when driving (from behind) the mount or pack animal.

1119 – And as for what was narrated about the Messenger of God, may God bless and save him—that «the hind leg is a *jubār*»[119]—it, and God Most High knows best, is a mistake; because the Ḥuffāẓ have not preserved anything of the sort.[120]	1119 - فَأَمَّا مَا رُوِيَ عَن رَسُولِ اللهِ - صَلَّى اللهُ عَلَيْهِ وَسَلَّمَ - مِن أَنَّ الرِّجْلَ جُبَارٌ، فَهُوَ - وَاللَّهُ تَعَالَى أَعْلَمُ – غَلَطٌ؛ لأَنَّ الْحُفَّاظَ لَمْ يَحْفَظُوا هَكَذَا.

In §1115, al-Shāfiʿī subsumes a spectrum of agents (leader, driver, rider) and injuring members (foreleg, mouth, hind leg, tail) under a singular ruling: (1) the agent is liable for the injury. This is paired with a critical stipulation, which also serves to identify the efficient property (he induced it to trample) occasioning this general ruling. Absence of this *ʿilla* occasions the opposite ruling: (2) he is not liable for anything. The *ʿilla-ḥukm* pair for ruling (1) receives *ʿaql*-support, heralded by "because", which identifies the underlying reason (*sabab* or *ḥikma*) of the *ʿilla*'s efficiency: the trampling derives from his action (i.e., his inducement), and the mount is his implement of harm.[121] Although al-Shāfiʿī brings no *aṣl*, it is evident he is justifying his rulings by *istidlāl bi-qiyās* from the general category of mulcts for intentional/unintentional injuries.[122]

In §1116, al-Shāfiʿī initiates an "instructional" dialectic in hypophoric fashion—with the formula "and should we say" (*fa-amma an naqūl*), followed by an opposing opinion (he is liable for the foreleg, but not the back leg),[123] and a swift objection: "this is arbitrariness (*fa-hādhā taḥakkum*)!" This charge of *taḥakkum*

[119] Ḥassūn equates *jubār* with *hadr* (meaning "waste"); then he explains: "And the meaning of the *ḥadīth*—and God Most High knows best—is that the dumb beast escapes and injures a person or something during its escape, but its wounding [in retaliation] is a waste" (vol. 9, p. 189, n. 1). Lane (*Lexicon*, s.v. "جبار") provides a somewhat clearer explanation. He first defines جبار as: "a thing of which no account, or for which no revenge or retaliation or mulct, is taken." Further on he explains جرح العجماء جبار [which is part of a Prophetic tradition on the authority of Abū Hurayra; see *DJP*, vol. 2, p. 503] as meaning: "The wound of the speechless beast, if it get loose or wound a man or other thing while loose, is a thing for which no retaliation or expiatory mulct is exacted." As for the narration mentioned in §1119—«the hind leg is a *jubār*»—it first appears in §1113, in support of Abū Ḥanīfa's ruling that the rider, driver, etc., are not liable for the mount's kicking out with its back leg. Ibn Rushd (*DJP*, vol. 2, p. 504) notes al-Shāfiʿī's rejection of this tradition.

[120] *Ḥuffāẓ* (s. *ḥāfiẓ*)—meaning those who preserve, or safeguard, through memorizing—usually applied to memorizers of the Qurʾān. It is possible al-Shāfiʿī here references another special class of scholars known in his day: those who were collecting narrations on the Prophet and the early community and committing them to memory.

[121] By Ḥassūn's numbering system, the other jurists' relevant rulings and arguments are: §1113 (Abū Ḥanīfa, with Abū Yūsuf's adherence); and §1114 (Ibn Abī Laylā). They treat only the case where the mount kicks out with its hind leg. Abū Ḥanīfa rules that the owner (*ṣāḥib*; and presumably including leader, driver, and rider) is not liable; *naql*-support is provided by quoting the Prophet's decree: «the hind leg is a *jubār*». Ibn Abī Laylā rules the opposite: he is liable for consequent injury. From this it is evident that al-Shāfiʿī differs from both, having highlighted the critical *ʿilla* of inducement to trample. It would appear from the short sequence that his opponent argues from Abū Ḥanīfa's position (or at least resorts to the same *naql*-support).

[122] This is confirmed in Ibn Rushd's discussion of this *masʾala* (*DJP*, vol. 2, pp. 503–4).

[123] Note this claim is made by neither Abū Ḥanīfa nor Ibn Abī Laylā in our subject-text.

may be unique to proto-system dialectic.[124] This position is nevertheless defended by an anonymous opponent in §1116, signaled by "then if he says" (*fa-in qāla*), with the argument that a leader or rider would not see its back leg (but would see its foreleg). This is a notably empirical premise—depending entirely upon the observed pragmatics (and angles of sight) inherent to leading or driving animals, with no authoritative textual reference. Al-Shāfiʿī's *ʿilla* (inducement to trample) occasions a *ḥukm* of liability for *all* injuring members. His opponent, however, has given additional efficiency to the property of sight, the effect of which is to limit liability to only *seen* injuring members: thus, induced plus seen renders liable, and induced plus not seen renders not liable. The opponent has appended an additional efficient property to al-Shāfiʿī's *ʿilla* and thus particularized its singular effect. This new conglomerate of properties constitutes a new *ʿilla*, and the opponent's objection—despite his not bringing a new *aṣl*—corresponds best with *muʿāraḍa* of *qiyās* by another *qiyās*,[125] or *muʿāraḍa bi-ʿilla mubtadaʾa*.[126]

Al-Shāfiʿī comes back with a charge of *naqḍ* in §1118, destroying the opponent's supplanting *ʿilla*: in the case of the driver, who does not see the beast's foreleg (the *masʾalat al-naqḍ*), the opponent should rule that he is liable for the hind leg but not the foreleg—but no one rules this. His conglomerate *ʿilla* is present, but his *ḥukm* is claimed by no one—or, rather, as al-Shāfiʿī says: "there is no such doctrine." This statement adds a new dimension to the objection, which might best be qualified as *naqḍ* via *e silentio*.[127] Finally, al-Shāfiʿī seals his *elenchus* by objecting to the Sunnaic decree submitted in support of Abū Ḥanīfa's ruling (and upon which his

---

[124] I have not yet encountered the term *taḥakkum* in our *jadal*-theory texts, although it occurs a number of times in the *Umm* compendium (in both verbal and *maṣdar* forms), and always as a charge of arbitrariness. As for the nature of this arbitrariness, one would assume that it stems from an opponent's lack of *dalīl*-indicant; i.e., the opponent stands accused of maintaining a position without having engaged in an accepted form of *istidlāl*. This is confirmed by an example in the *Chapter on What has Come Down to Us about Holy War* (*Bāb Mā Jāʾa fiʾl-Jihād*) of the *Kitāb Ikhtilāf Mālik waʾl-Shāfiʿī* (*Umm*, Ḥassūn ed., vol. 9, pt. 14, p. 467, §741): "... and as for the arbitrary proponent (*mutaḥakkim*) who proceeds arbitrarily (*yataḥakkama*), and claims of the two decrees of the Prophet... that one of them is a *ḥukm*, and the other *ijtihād*, without an indicant (*bi-lā dalālatin*); if this is allowed, the *sunan* will have departed from the hands of the people (*kharajat... min aydī al-nās*)." The key phrase is *bi-lā dalāla*; I would submit this as the very kernel of *taḥakkum*: it is reasoning rendered arbitrary via lack of *dalāla*-indication. As for the apparent lack of the term in *jadal*-theorists' discussions, this may be explained once we assume that arguing substantive rulings with no basis in accepted forms of *istidlāl* had long ago ceased to occur in both private *ijtihād* and public *jadal*. That is to say, the natural pursuit of argumentative conclusiveness (*ḥujjiyya*), fired by the dynamic of juridical *jadal*, disallowed later jurists from proposing solutions without first grounding their arguments in accepted modes of *istidlāl*. The age had passed in which charges of *taḥakkum* could be made.

[125] al-Baṣrī, *K. al-Qiyās al-Sharʿī*, Ḥamīd Allāh ed., p. 1044; Hallaq, "Treatise," p. 221.

[126] (Shīr.VII.15.2.1; Bāj.IX.B.15.2.1) al-Shīrāzī, *Maʿūna*, Turkī ed., p. 262, §148 [Missing from al-ʿUmayrīnī ed.]; al-Bājī, *Minhāj*, Turkī ed., p. 201, §455. Cf. Ibn ʿAqīl, *K. al-Jadal*, p. 71, §330.

[127] For the most part, this corresponds to that sub-species of *naqḍ* (Bāj.IX.B.11.2.1) which al-Bājī reserves for occasioning factors "posited to establish rulings for individuals [as opposed to genera]" (*wuḍiʿa li-ithbāt al-aḥkām fiʾl-aʿyān*), and "posited for obligation" (*mawḍūʿa liʾl-wujūb*) (*Minhāj*, Turkī ed., pp. 185 ff., §§415 ff.) The added dimension arises from al-Shāfiʿī's statement: "there is no such doctrine" (*wa laysa hākadhā bi-qawlin*). No one at all, in other words, has ever proposed

opponent might also draw for support). He proposes that it is an error (*ghalaṭ*) "because the Ḥuffāẓ have not preserved anything of the sort;" but, importantly, he mitigates this further *e silentio* assumption with "and God Most High knows best" (*wa Allāhu Taʿālā Aʿlam*).[128] This mitigated objection may be categorized as a transmission-oriented *iʿtirāḍ*.[129]

such a doctrine as entailed by the *mas'alat al-naqḍ* should the opponent's reasoning be extended to it. From one perspective, this stands as a powerful charge of non-*endoxic* reasoning. From another, however, it reads as an *e silentio* argument. Al-Shāfiʿī has argued: "You hold X_1 to be the case. But if X_1 is the case; then you should also have claimed that X_2 is the case. But no one at all has claimed that X_2 is the case." Read in this fashion, the argument is incomplete: it rests upon an *e silentio* assumption; and we cannot assume an opponent will not simply state "X_2 is also the case" in immediate reply. In the end, we might consider this a unique sub-species of *naqḍ*; al-Shāfiʿī has not so much pointed out an inconsistency as shown us an empty space in the opposing position's doctrine.

[128] We are reminded by this and other pious formulae throughout the subject-text, and in the literature of *fiqh* in general, that jurists in the main were attempting to operate within the greater normative controls of the "good dialectic" (*al-jadal al-ḥasan*). That is to say, such formulae provide indication that a sincere, truth-seeking dialectical ethic was recognized by disputants, and should be considered the *status quo* of normative practice. These formulae complement the sincerity apparent in, among other things, our jurists' marked obsession with authoritative indicants and consistency in the rational inferences made from them. The burden of proof therefore lies upon those who would claim that juridical *jadal* was a sophistical enterprise; and appeals to "human nature" are insufficient in light of the very demonstrable ethical dynamic of pre-modern Islamic scholarship (and societies). An exposition on this dynamic may be found in Hallaq's *Impossible State*, especially in Chap. 5, Sect. 5.2: "The Moral Technologies of the Self." Here we find an overview of the moral substrate presupposed, depended upon, and promoted by premodern *Sharīʿa*. My assertion that modern appeals to "human nature" lend insufficient support to claims of premodern juristic sophistry rests, in part, on our great remove from the *Sharʿī* moral dynamic explained by Hallaq. His rendering of Abū Ḥāmid al-Ghazālī's (d.505/1111) "theory of human nature," explained in the same section, stands in contradistinction to modern notions; and al-Ghazālī's theory captures a moral essence which fits hand-in-glove with the truth-seeking ethic of pre-modern juridical dialectic.

[129] As with other general transmission-oriented objections of al-Shāfiʿī, precise identification through the lens of the *jadal*-theory texts is difficult. Such *iʿtirāḍāt* as are directed against an opponent's *istidlāl bi'l-Sunna* "with respect to the chain of transmission" (*min jihat al-isnād*) are all quite specific. Any number of them might be implied by al-Shāfiʿī's general critique here. This particular charge also appears to be unique when compared to others al-Shāfiʿī has made, which usually take the form: "the Ahl al-Ḥadīth have not *confirmed* its like." Here, the Ḥuffāẓ—presumably designating the most trustworthy transmitters—"have not *preserved* anything of its like." Notably, Schacht—speaking of al-Shāfiʿī's "cautious" recognition of *ḥadīth* criticism in his *Risāla*—cites this *mas'ala*-set from our subject-text as an illustrative study case (*Tr. I*, §194 by Schacht's system, corresponding to Ḥassūn's §§1113–18). He translates the relevant passage of the *Risāla* (p. 55 of the Būlāq ed.) thus: "In most cases the truthfulness or lack of truthfulness of a tradition can only be known through the truthfulness or lack of truthfulness of the transmitter, except in a few special cases when he relates what cannot possibly be the case, or what is contradicted by better authenticated information" (*Origins*, pp. 37–8 and n. 1).

6.2 Independent Dialectical Formulae

Prefatory Notes

A great many arguments not situated in a dialectical sequence of our subject-text nevertheless employ the dialectical *ra'ā* formulae we have encountered in extended and short sequences—such are the parameters of presentation category C. Several of these have already been analyzed, as they belong to the larger *masā'il*-sets of Chap. 5, and the short sequences of the current chapter. As distinct from category A and B sequences, category C arguments either: (1) contain the familiar dialectical question/objection-formulae we have seen employed elsewhere—mostly the *ra'ā* formulae: *a-ra'ayta* and *a-lā tarā*; (2) provide some hint as to a "historical" dialectic—e.g., "one of the people said X" (*wa qāla ba'ḍ al-nās* X)—or a recurrent debate—e.g., "and whoever claims X" (*wa-alladhī yaz'umu* X); or (3) incorporate some other phrase which strongly indicates the *mas'ala* at hand was the subject of past or ongoing face-to-face or literary disputation. As such, category C arguments may emanate from any one of the featured jurists of the subject-text—*a-ra'ayta*, for example, issues not only from the mouths of Abū Ḥanīfa and Ibn Abī Laylā, but from the successor jurist Shurayḥ (§11), and even from the Prophet himself (§108).[130]

Due to the large number of category C presentations,[131] I cannot present full analyses here; instead, I will provide an overview of the roles played by various formulae, as induced from the larger arguments in which they occur. My basic assumption is that, despite abbreviated presentations, these arguments incorporating *a-ra'ayta*, etc., represent real moves and *elenchus* questions/statements from past or ongoing disputations. In other words, if Abū Yūsuf's argument closes with a rhetorical *a-lā tarā* question introducing a *mas'alat al-naqḍ*, I would assume that Abū Yūsuf truly: (1) silenced his opponent with it in the past; (2) presumes to silence, by means of it, contemporary opponents; or (3) wishes to convey to his student that key *topos* of objection which one should call forth in debate. Of course, all three intentions may be at work at the same time.

The following review of formulae is also meant to show that patently dialectical material need not be presented in Q&A sequential format, but may be buried within non-sequence arguments. A distinguishing feature of category C is that its argument formulations minimize the need to hypothesize (as in categories D through G) that such arguments actually unfolded, or were meant to unfold, in a dialectical venue. Rather, the stamp of dialectic is plainly upon them. More than this, what follows will draw attention to the discernibly formulaic style of proto-system juridical dialectic. A final note: in this section, I will start using abbreviations for the names of our disputant jurists, mostly when they appear in tables, as a space-saving device:

---

[130] See my dissertation for translations of the *masā'il* in which these occur ("Dialectical Forge," pt. 2, p. 3, §11; and p. 35, §108.)

[131] In terms of *ra'ā* formulae alone, there are nearly 60 instances of *a-ra'ayta* and *a-lā tarā*.

AH = Abū Ḥanīfa	AY = Abū Yūsuf
IAL = Ibn Abī Laylā	MIH = Muḥammad b. al-Ḥasan al-Shaybānī
SH = al-Shāfiʿī	RB = al-Rabīʿ
R = Respondent	Q = Questioner
SHAR = al-Shāfiʿī's Anonymous Respondent	SHAQ = al-Shāfiʿī's Anonymous Questioner

The Ra'ā *Formulae: Have You Considered* (A-ra'ayta)*? Don't You See/Opine* (A-lā tarā)*?*[132]

Overwhelmingly (though not entirely), the *ra'ā* formulae we have encountered in the subject-text are involved in some aspect of a *reductio* argument. Whether confronting R with some species of untenable consequence (the most common task of *a-ra'ayta*), or confronting him with some species of *endoxon* evidence or proof (the most common task of *a-lā tarā*), the *ra'ā* formulae perform a wide variety of specific tasks, but nearly all within *reductio* schemes. In nature they may be dialogical (meaning answered, and Q probably intended an answer), rhetorical (not usually answered, even in dialectical sequences, and probably intended by Q as the final word: the seal of an *elenchus*), or hypophoric (both asked and answered by Q); they may deliver direct and final objections (e.g., *naqḍ*), add to compounded forms of the same objection (e.g., double-*naqḍ*), or contribute elements to larger and composite argument schemes (e.g., *masā'il al-naqḍ* in a larger argument of *muʿāraḍa*). They may be aimed more at justifying Q's argument, or they may be aimed more at destroying R's; and they may bring parallel cases, supporting *dalīl*-indicants, or any of a variety of untenable consequences, be they inescapable contradictions or mere contingent possibilities stemming from derived scenarios.

In the analyses of Chap. 5 and in this chapter, we have encountered some eighteen instances of *ra'ā* formulae at work, fifteen of which were *a-ra'aytas* and three of which were *a-lā tarās*. There are many more scattered throughout our subject-text, however—nearly sixty in number—and I have grouped them all according to their larger, functional categories in the two lists below. Note that—as may be expected with dialectical premises and arguments in general—material introduced by *ra'ā* formulae questions may be interpreted as both justifying the questioner's position and undermining the opponent's. The function categories in the following lists—especially List 6.2—are sometimes approximate; they are based upon my estimation of whether Q intended them more in the way of attack or defense. This estimation was facilitated by the contexts and responses occurring in dialectical sequences (List 6.1); but it was far more difficult for formulae appearing in often quite terse monologue arguments (List 6.2), as will become apparent. We have encountered all of the instances recorded in List 6.1 in the extended sequences of Chap. 5 and the short sequences of this chapter. In List 6.2, instances that occurred in the *masā'il*-sets of Chap. 5 (but outside the dialectical sequences) have been highlighted.[133]

---

[132] Study of the *ra'ā* formulae of our subject-text is ongoing. See my forthcoming: "Have You Considered (*A-ra'ayta*)? Don't You See/Opine (*A-lā Tarā*)? A Working Typology of *Ra'ā* Formulae in Early Islamic Juridical Disputation."

[133] For parallel translations of all instances of *ra'ā* formulae we did not encounter in Chap. 5 and in this chapter, see part 2 of my dissertation.

List 6.1: Functions of *Ra'ā* Formulae Appearing in Dialectical Sequences: Confronting R with R's Self-Contradiction and Doctrinal Inconsistency

1.1. *Tanāquḍ* in Dialectical Sequence

- SH *a-ra'ayta* in §96: dialogical, pushing concession to premises for a final charge of *tanāquḍ*
- SH *a-lā tarā* in §249: rhetorical, pushing concession to an *endoxon dalīl* which contradicts the opposing opinion; followed by a *tanāquḍ*-like charge

1.2. *Naqḍ* in Dialectical Sequence

- SH *a-ra'ayta* in §740: dialogical, soliciting a ruling for a derived sub-strategy *mas'alat al-naqḍ*, as part of a larger *naqḍ* objection with a unique subtraction-reinsertion strategy
- SH *a-ra'ayta* in §694: dialogical, introducing a parallel *mas'alat al-naqḍ* to cancel the opponent's *ʿilla*, as a component in a larger strategy of *naqḍ*-dilemma
- SH *a-ra'ayta* in §1321: dialogical, soliciting R's ruling on parallel / derived *masā'il* (*masā'il al-farq*, for this species of method-*naqḍ*), for an eventual charge of method-*naqḍ* (R observes a *farq*-distinction in the parallel *masā'il*, but ignores it in the *mas'ala*-at-hand)
- SH *a-ra'ayta* in §647: rhetorical, soliciting a ruling for a parallel *mas'ala*, constituting a charge of method-*naqḍ* or *qiyās al-dalāla*-oriented *naqḍ*
- SH *a-ra'ayta* in §743: hypophoric, introducing additional *masā'il al-naqḍ* for a larger scheme of compound *naqḍ*
- SH *a-ra'ayta* in §771: dialogical, soliciting a ruling on a final derived *mas'ala* (the last in a series of *masā'il al-farq*), for an imminent charge of compound method-*naqḍ* (opponent observes a *farq*-distinction in the parallel *masā'il*, but ignores it in the *mas'ala*-at-hand)

1.3. *Muʿāraḍa bi'l-Nuṭq* in Dialectical Sequence

- SH *a-ra'ayta* in §653: dialogical, as part of a *reductio* sub-strategy: framing a disjunction of premises (the *endoxon* choice serving as a premise justifying his choice of *aṣl* for a "hypothetical" *muʿāraḍa-qiyās*, which is itself a *reductio* sub-strategy within a larger, non-reductio argument scheme (a "real" *muʿāraḍa bi'l-nuṭq*)
- SH *a-ra'ayta* in §663: dialogical, as a *reductio* sub-strategy drawing attention to an *endoxon dalīl* (from Qur'ān) for a "hypothetical" *muʿāraḍa-qiyās*, which is itself a *reductio* sub-strategy within a larger, non-reductio argument scheme (a "real" *muʿāraḍa bi'l-nuṭq*)

(continued)

- SH *a-lā tarā* in §544: rhetorical, as a direct confrontation (not sub-strategy): pushing acknowledgement of an *endoxon* Prophetic *ḥadīth* (Unays) as directly solving the *mas'ala* at hand, supplanting opposing *qiyās* from another Prophetic *ḥadīth* (Māʿiz); also, the opposing position should have acknowledged the *ḥadīth* about Unays as a *bayān* for the *ḥadīth* about Māʿiz; for an overall objection of *muʿāraḍa bi'l-nuṭq* and method-*naqḍ*
- SH *a-lā tarā* in §1229: rhetorical, delivering a *mas'ala* of both *farq* and method-*naqḍ*; all as components of a larger *muʿāraḍa bi'l-nuṭq*

List 6.2: Functions of *Ra'ā* Formulae Appearing in Monologue Arguments: Exposing Untenable Consequences and Introducing Supporting Evidence

2.1. *A-ra'ayta* in Monologue Arguments: Exposing Untenable Consequences

2.1.1. Untenable consequence: a self-contradicting formulation

- IAL/AY/ MIH *a-ra'ayta* in §748: rhetorical, constituting a justification/objection of *istidlāl bi'l-qiyās* / *tanāquḍ* / *muʿāraḍa bi-ʿilla* of the opposing *istidlāl bi'l-qiyās*; supporting a ruling with an analogous *aṣl* (identified in §750 via *a-lā tarā*) which avoids the contradiction inherent to the contrary opinion

2.1.2. Untenable consequence: in introduced parallel case(s) which are more logically necessary and immediate

- Shurayḥ *a-ra'ayta* in §11: rhetorical, Shurayḥ confronts a defendant with a *mas'alat al-naqḍ* in which the defendant's contradictory opinion is anticipated, for a probably rhetorical *naqḍ*
- AH/AY/MIH *a-ra'aytas* in §148 & §149: rhetorical, both solicit a ruling from a disjunctive pair (should we rule X or Y?); X is the (obvious) solution of AH/AY/MIH, Y is the (obviously untenable) solution of IAL; efficient properties are identified in §148 via *a-lā tarā*; supporting a ruling with efficient properties and *aṣl* (identified) for *istidlāl bi'l-qiyās* / *naqḍ*
- AH/AY/MIH *a-ra'ayta* in §150: hypophoric, instantiates a previous parallel case (§149): efficient properties were identified in §148 via *a-lā tarā*; supporting a ruling with efficient properties and *aṣl* (identified) for *istidlāl bi'l-qiyās* / *naqḍ*
- AH / AY *a-ra'ayta* in §836: rhetorical, efficient property identified in §831 by *a-lā tarā*, then confirmed by *athar*-tradition about ʿAlī in §832; preceded by four *a-lā tarās* in §831 and §§833–5; supporting a ruling with efficient properties and *aṣl* (identified) for *istidlāl bi'l-qiyās* / *naqḍ*

(continued)

- SH *a-ra'ayta* in §1195: rhetorical, two parallel cases (obvious *masā'il al-naqḍ*) act as a finishing stroke of *naqḍ* for type 2 *ta'līl bi'l-ism* in §§1193–4; efficient genus-identification is made in §1194, which is a continuation of *a-lā tarā* in §1193; supporting a ruling with efficient genus-identification (type 2 of al-Baṣrī's *al-ta'līl bi'l-ism* ["the *'illa* is established by genus"]), with a finishing stroke of *naqḍ*
- MIH (?) *a-ra'ayta* in §34: hypophoric, introduces an apparent *mas'alat al-naqḍ*, Q's follow up question is leading; an efficient property is identified in §33 via *kayfa...wa...*; supporting a ruling with an efficient property (identified), parallel case might act as an *aṣl* for *istidlāl bi'l-qiyās* / *naqḍ*

2.1.2.a. Variant: in introduced parallel case(s) probably entailing both an intra-doctrinal contradiction and a logical contradiction

- AH *a-ra'ayta* in §809: rhetorical, introduces a parallel case (an obvious *mas'alat al-naqḍ*) as a rhetorical *reductio*; parallel case is an *aṣl*, confirmed by *athar*-tradition about al-Nakha'ī, which identifies the *'illa*, in §810; supporting a ruling with *aṣl*, *athar*, and efficient property (all identified) for *istidlāl bi'l-qiyās* / *naqḍ* / *tanāquḍ*

2.1.3. Untenable consequence: in introduced derived case(s) which are more logically necessary and immediate, or contingent-possible

- The Prophet's *a-ra'ayta* in §108: The Prophet confronts his petitioner with a derived case which is contingent, but results in immediate injustice
- AH *a-ra'ayta* in §275: rhetorical, for an overall justification/objection of *istidlāl bi'l-qiyās*/*mu'āraḍa bi-'illa* of opposing *istidlāl bi'l-Sunna*; supporting a ruling with an efficient property (identified)
- AH *a-ra'ayta* in §753: rhetorical, as a triple-*reductio* supporting his rulings from an identified principle; the whole constituting a justification/objection of *istidlāl bi'l-qiyās* / *mu'āraḍa bi-'illa* of opposing *istidlāl bi'l-qiyās* (*aṣl* not stated).
- AH *a-ra'aytas* in §§817 and 818: rhetorical, together acting as a double *reductio*: a supporting efficient property is identified in §817 via *a-lā tarā*, but the *aṣl* is not; supporting a ruling with an efficient property (identified) for *istidlāl bi'l-qiyās* / *mu'āraḍa bi-'illa* of opposing *istidlāl* of unknown type
- AH *a-ra'ayta* in §320: rhetorical, an efficient property is identified in §319 via *a-lā tarā*, but the *aṣl* is not; supporting a ruling with an efficient property (identified) for *istidlāl bi'l-qiyās* / *mu'āraḍa bi-'illa* of opposing *istidlāl* of unknown type
- AH *a-ra'ayta* in §221: rhetorical, two untenable consequences, one framed as a disjunction: efficient genus is identified in §221 via *kayfa yakūnu*

(continued)

dhālika wa...; supporting a ruling with an efficient genus identification (type 2 of al-Baṣrī's *al-taʿlīl bi'l-ism* ["the *ʿilla* is established by genus"])

2.1.4. Untenable consequence: in introduced derived case(s) which are merely contingent-possible

- AH *a-ra'ayta* in §554: rhetorical, neither efficient property nor *aṣl* are evident; supporting ruling with an efficient "negative-potential" (?)
- AH *a-ra'ayta* in §1143: rhetorical, neither efficient property nor *aṣl* are evident; supporting ruling with an efficient "negative-potential" (?)

2.2. *A-lā tarā* in Monologue Arguments: Introducing Supporting Evidence

2.2.1. Supporting evidence: an epistemically-authoritative, primary *aṣl*, directly brought to bear

- AH *a-lā tarā* in §1052: rhetorical, the whole constituting a justification/objection of *istidlāl bi-naṣṣ al-Kitāb* / *iʿtirāḍ* against *istidlāl bi-qawl al-wāḥid min al-Ṣaḥāba*, type 2 (Shīr.IV.2).

2.2.2. Supporting evidence: a parallel case with an established *ḥukm*, sharing elements of the *mas'ala* at hand, identified (or obviously intended) as an *aṣl* for *qiyās*

- AY (supporting IAL) *a-lā tarā* in §277: rhetorical, for an overall justification/objection of *istidlāl bi'l-qiyās* / *muʿāraḍa bi'l-qiyās* of opposing *istidlāl bi'l-Sunna*; and as a *qiyās* in support of an *athar* (as a kind of *tarjīḥ*).
- IAL/AY/MIH *a-lā tarā* in §750: rhetorical, as an *endoxon aṣl* for *qiyās*, which *qiyās* avoids the internal, logical contradiction inherent to the contrary opinion; the whole constituting a justification/objection of *istidlāl bi'l-qiyās* / *muʿāraḍa bi-ʿilla* of opposing *istidlāl bi'l-qiyās*.
- SH *a-lā tarā* in §394: rhetorical, pushing concession to a parallel case with an established *ḥukm*, clearly identified as an endoxon *aṣl* for his *qiyās* at the end of §394; the efficient property is clearly explained throughout §394; against the apparent *taʿlīl bi'l-ism* of AH and AY, and IAL's unknown *istidlāl*; supporting a ruling with an efficient property and an *aṣl* for *qiyās* (both identified) for *istidlāl bi'l-qiyās* / *muʿāraḍa bi-ʿilla* of an opposing *taʿlīl bi'l-ism* (?) and opposing *istidlāl* of an unknown type / *naqḍ* (see §397)
- AH *a-lā tarā* in §460: rhetorical, pushing concession to a parallel case with an established *ḥukm*, clearly identified as an *endoxon aṣl* for his *qiyās* at the end of §460; supporting a ruling with an *aṣl* for *qiyās* (identified) for *istidlāl bi'l-qiyās* / *muʿāraḍa bi-ʿilla* of opposing *istidlāl* of unknown type

(continued)

- AH *a-lā tarā* in §723: rhetorical, pushing concession to the genus of the *mas'ala* as an efficient property (it is a ritual obligation [*farīḍa*]), and to a supporting parallel which is another species of genus *farīḍa*, from among the *uṣūl* (i.e., prayer); supporting a ruling with an efficient genus-property and an *aṣl* for *qiyās* (both obvious) for *al-ta'līl bi'l-ism*
- AY *a-lā tarā* in §995: rhetorical, pushing concession to a parallel case with an established *ḥukm*, clearly intended as an *endoxon aṣl* for his *qiyās*; the parallel case is the same as an *athar*-tradition about 'Umar supplied in §996; AY shows IAL's *'illa* (§994) occasions the opposite of what IAL says (*fasād al-waḍ'* ?); supporting a ruling with an *aṣl* for *qiyās* (identified) for *istidlāl bi'l-qiyās* / (*fasād al-waḍ'* ?)
- (probably AH) *a-lā tarā* in §103: rhetorical, pushing concession to a parallel *mas'ala* with a presumably *endoxon* ruling (sharing obvious properties with the *mas'ala* at hand), as support for his own ruling for the *mas'ala* at hand, and probably as an *aṣl* for *qiyās*; supporting a ruling via a parallel *mas'ala*, probably as an *aṣl* for *qiyās* (but not directly identified as such) for *istidlāl bi'l-qiyās* / *naqḍ*

2.2.3. Supporting evidence: a parallel case with a presumably established *ḥukm*, supporting Q, but clearly intended more as a *mas'alat al-naqḍ* than as an *aṣl* for *qiyās*

- AH *a-lā tarā* in §833: rhetorical, pushing concession to a parallel *mas'ala* with a presumably *endoxon* ruling, but which is clearly meant to be a *mas'alat al-naqḍ*, as (1) it follows direct confrontation with, and *athar*-tradition confirmation of, an efficient property (§§831–2), and (2) its parallel case articulates that property in its *lafẓ*-expression (part of §831–6 complex); supporting a ruling with an *athar*-tradition *aṣl* and efficient property (all identified) for *istidlāl bi'l-qiyās* (?)/ *naqḍ* / *mu'āraḍa bi-'illa* of opposing *'illa*
- AH *a-lā tarā* in §834: rhetorical, pushing concession to a parallel *mas'ala* with a presumably *endoxon* ruling, but which is clearly meant to be a *mas'alat al-naqḍ*, showing the presence of the opposing *'illa* (IAL in §827), but not the opposing *ḥukm*, support for AH's own ruling seems incidental (efficient property identified in §831 by *a-lā tarā*, then confirmed by an *athar*-tradition about 'Alī in §832); supporting a ruling with an *athar*-tradition *aṣl* and efficient property (all identified) for *istidlāl bi'l-qiyās* (?)/ *naqḍ* / *mu'āraḍa bi-'illa* of opposing *'illa*
- SH *a-lā tarā* in §397: rhetorical, pushing concession to a parallel *mas'ala* with presumably *endoxon* ruling, and equating it in the same question to the *mas'ala* at hand; that *endoxon* ruling is the efficient property which occasions SH's *ḥukm*; and the whole is clearly meant to show *naqḍ* of the opposing position (SH's efficient property is identified in §396); supporting a ruling with an efficient property and *aṣl* for *qiyās* (both identified

(continued)

earlier [see §394]) for *istidlāl bi'l-qiyās* / *muʿāraḍa bi-ʿilla* of opposing *taʿlīl bi'l-ism* (?) and opposing *istidlāl* of unknown type / *naqḍ*

- AH *a-lā tarā* in §54: rhetorical, pushing concession to a method-principle (absolution from genus entails absolution from its particular instances) inherent to 2 parallel *masā'il* with presumably *endoxa* rulings (opposing IAL position in §55 cannot concede them without method *naqḍ*); supporting a ruling by demonstrating consistent method-principle (method-*qiyās* (?) / method *naqḍ*)

2.2.4. Supporting evidence: a pair of contrasting parallel cases with presumably established rulings, meant solely to demonstrate *farq*-distinction

- RB *a-lā tarā* in §74: rhetorical, pushing concession to a *farq*-distinction demonstrated by a contrasting pair of *masā'il* with *endoxa* rulings, in order to support his particularization of the general rule which would usually apply to the *mas'ala* at hand (also supporting SH's ruling in §78–80); the *aṣl* of *ḥadīth* Barīra, though establishing the *farq*, does not act like an *aṣl* for *qiyās*; the overall argument is more like *al-taʿlīl bi'l-ism*: "it is of the genus *ʿitq*-manumission, thus incursion into partner's/buyer's ownership is allowed" (an exception to the general rule); supporting particularization of a general rule (*takhṣīṣ al-ʿāmm*) with a *farq*-distinction of the exception (identified), as established in an *aṣl* (identified) for *istidlāl bi'l-qiyās* / *al-taʿlīl bi'l-ism* (?)

2.2.5. Supporting evidence: a derived case with a patently *endoxon* ruling, presented as a vindicating consequence of Q's solution

- SH *a-lā tarā* in §235.a and §235.b: rhetorical, supporting a ruling with an efficient property (identified), but no *aṣl* for *istidlāl bi'l-qiyās* / *muʿāraḍa bi-ʿilla* of opposing *ʿilla*
  - §235.a (= part 1; followed by question in §235.b) pushing concession to (1) the presence of an efficient property occasioning his own *ḥukm* in the *mas'ala* at hand, and (2) a derived *mas'ala* with a patently *endoxon* ruling, which vindicates his own ruling for the *mas'ala* at hand—in effect, he first identifies the efficient property, then demonstrates its co-absence (*ʿaks*) with the *ḥukm*;
  - §235.b (= part 2 of his *a-lā tarā* in §235.a) pushing concession to a derived *mas'ala* with a patently *endoxon* ruling, which vindicates his own ruling for *mas'ala* at hand (efficient property is identified in §234 and §235.a, and is supplanting the time-oriented *ʿilla* of IAL in §233)
- AH *a-lā tarā* in §826: rhetorical, pushing concession to a derived *mas'ala* with a patently *endoxon* ruling, which vindicates his own ruling for the *mas'ala* at hand (efficient property is identified in §826, right before *a-lā tarā*, and is supplanting the time-oriented *ʿilla* of IAL in §827); supporting

(continued)

a ruling with an efficient property (identified), but no *aṣl* for *istidlāl bi'l-qiyās* / *mu'āraḍa bi-'illa* of opposing *'illa*

- AH *a-lā tarā* in §363: rhetorical, pushing concession to a derived *mas'ala* with a patently *endoxon* ruling, which vindicates his own ruling for the *mas'ala* at hand (efficient property is identified in §362 and §363; IAL's opposing efficient property is not made clear); supporting a ruling with an efficient property (identified), but no *aṣl* for *istidlāl bi'l-qiyās* / *mu'āraḍa bi-'illa* of opposing *istidlāl* of unknown type
- SH *a-lā tarā* in §151: rhetorical, pushing concession to a pair of derived *masā'il* with patently *endoxon* rulings, which vindicate his own ruling for the *mas'ala* at hand (efficient property is identified in §151; opposing efficient property is not made clear); supporting a ruling with an *aṣl* and an efficient property (both identified) for *istidlāl bi'l-qiyās* / *mu'āraḍa bi-'illa* of an opposing *istidlāl* of unknown type
- SH *a-lā tarā* in §1193: rhetorical, pushing concession to a derived *mas'ala* with a patently *endoxon* ruling, which vindicates his own ruling for the *mas'ala* at hand; the whole is *al-ta'līl bi'l-ism* (efficient genus-identification is made in §1194, which section fully explains "vindication" case of §1193; SH's *a-ra'ayta* in §1195 acts like a finishing stroke of *naqḍ*); supporting a ruling with an efficient genus-identification [type 2 of al-Baṣrī's *al-ta'līl bi'l-ism* ["the *'illa* is established by genus"]), with a finishing stroke of *naqḍ*
- AH *a-lā tarā* in §1243: rhetorical, pushing concession to a derived *mas'ala* with a patently *endoxon* ruling, which vindicates his own ruling for the *mas'ala* at hand; an efficient property is identified in §§1242–3, and argued to override the opposing property with a rhetorical *kayfa* question; the "vindicating" derived case is substantiated with an *athar*-tradition about 'Alī in §1244; supporting a ruling with an efficient property (identified), but no *aṣl* for *istidlāl bi'l-qiyās* / *mu'āraḍa bi-'illa* of opposing *istidlāl* of unknown type
- AH *a-lā tarā* in §1289: rhetorical, pushing concession to a derived *mas'ala* with a patently *endoxon* ruling, which vindicates his own ruling for the *mas'ala* at hand; an efficient property is firmly established in §1288 by *āthār*-traditions; supporting a ruling with an *aṣl* and an efficient property (both identified) for *istidlāl bi'l-qiyās* / *mu'āraḍa bi-'illa* of opposing *istidlāl* of unknown type

2.2.6. Supporting evidence: direct confrontation with the presence or absence of an efficient property, as part of *reductio* scheme (with no parallel or derived case)

- AH *a-lā tarā* in §319: rhetorical, pushing concession to the presence of an efficient property occasioning his own *ḥukm* in the *mas'ala* at hand; followed by a supporting *a-ra'ayta reductio* in §320; supporting a ruling with

(continued)

an efficient property (identified), but no *aṣl*, for *istidlāl bi'l-qiyās* / *mu'āraḍa bi-'illa* of opposing *istidlāl* of unknown type

- AH *a-lā tarā* in §817: rhetorical, pushing concession to the presence of an efficient property occasioning his own *ḥukm* in the *mas'ala* at hand; followed by AH *a-ra'aytas* in §§817 and 818, together a double *reductio*; supporting a ruling with an efficient property (identified), but no *aṣl*, for *istidlāl bi'l-qiyās* / *mu'āraḍa bi-'illa* of opposing *istidlāl* of unknown type
- AH *a-lā tarā* in §831: rhetorical, pushing concession to the presence of an efficient property occasioning his own *ḥukm* in the *mas'ala* at hand; the efficient property confirmed by an *athar*-tradition about 'Alī in §832; followed by three supporting *a-lā tarās* and one supporting *a-ra'ayta* reductio (§832–6); supporting a ruling with efficient properties and an *aṣl* (both identified) for *istidlāl bi'l-qiyās* / *naqḍ*
- AH *a-lā tarā* in §148: rhetorical, pushing concession to the presence of an efficient property occasioning his own *ḥukm* in the *mas'ala* at hand; it is the "obvious choice" of the previous *a-ra'ayta*-introduced disjunctive *mas'alat al-naqḍ* (first part of §148) [NB: this is part of a complex *reductio* (§§148–150)]; supporting a ruling with efficient properties and an *aṣl* (identified) for *istidlāl bi'l-qiyās* / *naqḍ*

2.2.7. Supporting evidence: direct confrontation with the presence or absence of an efficient property, not evidently part of a *reductio* scheme (with no parallel or derived case)

- AH *a-lā tarā* in §458: rhetorical, pushing concession to the presence of an efficient property occasioning his own *ḥukm* in the *mas'ala* at hand; followed by extension of that *ḥukm* to cover an entire genus of property (*māl*); IAL's opposing efficient property is in §457; supporting a ruling with an efficient property (identified), but no *aṣl*, for *istidlāl bi'l-qiyās* / *mu'āraḍa bi-'illa* of opposing *'illa*
- AH *a-lā tarā* in §1303: rhetorical, pushing concession to the absence of an efficient property which disallows the expected *ḥukm* in the *mas'ala* at hand; definition-*'illa* is provided in §1304; IAL's overriding efficient property is in §1305; supporting a ruling with an efficient property (identified), which is definitional of the transaction, for *istidlāl bi'l-qiyās* / *mu'āraḍa bi-'illa* of opposing *'illa*

2.2.8. Supporting evidence: direct confrontation with the rationale behind the efficient property (with no parallel or derived case)

- AH *a-lā tarā* in §876: rhetorical, pushing concession to the rationale (*ḥikma/sabab*) behind the efficient property (identified) occasioning his own *ḥukm* in the *mas'ala* at hand; an opposing efficient property or interpretation is not identified; supporting a ruling with an efficient property

(continued)

(identified), but no *aṣl*, for *istidlāl bi'l-qiyās* / *mu'āraḍa bi-'illa* of opposing *istidlāl* of unknown type

2.3. *A-lā tarā* Functions Which Are Anomalous or Difficult to Explain

2.3.1. Supporting evidence: a parallel case with a presumably established *ḥukm*, sharing efficient properties of both Q and R positions

- AH *a-lā tarā* in §835: rhetorical, pushing concession to a parallel *mas'ala* with a presumably *endoxon* ruling, but which appears to support the opposing *'illa* (IAL in §827) as well as AH's *'illa* (the efficient property is identified in §831 by *a-lā tarā*, then confirmed by an *athar*-tradition about 'Alī in §832); supporting a ruling with an *athar*-tradition as *aṣl* and an efficient property (all identified) for *istidlāl bi'l-qiyās* / *mu'āraḍa bi-'illa* of opposing *'illa* / *naqḍ*

2.3.2. Supporting evidence: an appeal to a common-sense possibility (with no parallel or derived case)

- AH *a-lā tarā* in §126: rhetorical, pushing concession to an (empirical?) possibility of a future status change: "Don't you see/opine that a man might become insolvent today, and obtain property (*māl*) tomorrow?"; supporting a ruling with an appeal to the possibility of a party's future change in status, neither *aṣl* nor efficient property identified

As earlier stated, the frequently terse presentations of monologue arguments create difficulties in determining the precise functions and supporting/attacking or constructive/destructive intentions of the *ra'ā* formulae of our subject-text. Regardless, and as I have attempted to show in the tables above, certain larger patterns appear after analysis. *Ra'ā* formulae, as should now be more than evident, are the ultimate vehicles for arguments falling under the genus *reductio*, or for components of *reductio* schemes, whether these are reductions to self-contradiction (*tanāquḍ*), to intra-doctrinal inconsistency (*naqḍ*), or to the violation of primary, divinely-sanctioned *uṣūl* (as in *mu'āraḍa bi'l-nuṭq*); or reductions to the untenable consequence of an opposing position's leading to a self-contradicting formulation, or of an opposing position's leading to impossibilities, injustices, or

[134] Again, for parallel translations of these instances, see part 2 of my dissertation.

absurdities; and whether these untenable consequences are exposed in introduced parallel cases (where they are more likely to be immediate and probable), or in introduced derived cases (where they are more likely to be contingent and merely possible); and whether Q confronts the opposing position with supporting evidence in the form of authoritative *uṣūl* for direct application, authoritative *uṣūl* for *qiyās*, established rulings in parallel cases, *farq*-distinctions in parallel cases, *endoxa* rulings as vindicating consequences of Q's ruling, the presence or absence of efficient properties, or the rationale behind them.

As for *a-ra'ayta* questions, on the whole they appear to act as vehicles by which Q confronts an opposing position with what Q believes to be the untenable consequence which that opposing position entails; *a-ra'ayta* thus conveys a *reductio* argument *more directly*. *A-lā tarā* questions, on the other hand, appear to act mostly as vehicles by which Q confronts the opposing position with compelling evidence which Q believes is at once supportive of his own position and contrary or contradictory to the opposing position; and Q further believes such *a-lā tarā* evidence will be difficult for the opposing position to deny. Denial, in fact, should itself entail an untenable consequence; and thus *a-lā tarā* may be said also to convey a *reductio* argument, albeit *less directly*.

Generally, we might say that *a-ra'ayta* has more to do with *iʿtirāḍ*. It is primarily the herald of objection and refutation, more closely tied to the advancing of objections and the declaration of *elenchi*. As for *a-lā tarā*, though it may deal with both *istidlāl* and *iʿtirāḍ*, it is primarily the herald of *endoxon* justification. It is more closely tied to the delivery of indicants, arguments, or parallel rulings in support of the arguing jurist's position, and to which an opponent is expected to concede. Put differently, we might say that *a-ra'ayta* is more often the vehicle by which R's thesis is problematized and refuted, while *a-lā tarā* is more often the vehicle by which Q's thesis is supported and justified. Notably, these constitute the two focal objectives of the questioner in the Aristotelian scheme of dialectic, and I would posit the persistence and abundant application of *ra'ā*-formulae—if not always systematic—is nevertheless linked to studied and transmitted procedural norms for dialectical debate which far predate Abū Ḥanīfa's time.

So when, and from where and whom, did our jurists learn, or inherit, or develop these formulaic modes of argument? I have not pursued the question to its fullest extent; but for the present I can say that we needn't look beyond the Qur'ān, and the *sunan* of Prophet, Companions, Imāms, and jurist-Successors—the disputational practices, in other words, of the founders of Islam, as bequeathed to and developed by the first generations of highly norm-conscious and actively-disputing Muslims.

The Qur'ān itself employs variants of *a-ra'ayta* and *a-lā tarā* a number of times, and a cursory review of these instances shows at least some with a similar pattern to the *ra'ā* formulae of our subject-treatise. For example, in Q.28:71–2, *a-ra'aytum* is employed to confront the polytheist with a contingent-possible scenario, forcing him to address the untenable consequence entailed by his inconsistent theology:

> «Say: *A-ra'aytum*? Have you considered what would happen? If Allāh made over you perpetual night until the Day of Judgment, what god *other than* Allāh could bring you light? Won't you listen? Say: *A-ra'aytum*? Have you considered what would happen? If Allāh made over you perpetual *day* until the Day of Judgment, what god *other than* Allāh could bring you the night in which to rest? Won't you see?»

As for the various *sunan* and *āthār*-traditions of the early community, our very own subject-treatise cites two instances wherein epistemic authority figures employ formulaic arguments on the same patterns. The Prophet, when asked about selling unripe fruit, says (§108): «*A-ra'ayta*? Have you considered what would happen? If God prevents the fruit [from becoming edible], then for what would you have taken the payment of your brother?» And the famed, early Successor-jurist Shurayḥ—having ruled that a laundryman was liable for a customer's clothes, destroyed when the laundryman's house burned down—was afterwards confronted by that laundryman, who said: "You make me liable, and my house has burned down?" So Shurayḥ said: "*A-ra'ayta*? Have you considered what *you* would do? If your customer's house had burned down; would *you* have relinquished your fee to *him*?"

Other Formulae Indicative of Past or Recurrent Dialectic

My purpose in examining the *a-ra'ayta* and *a-lā tarā* questions of our subject-treatise was not only to establish functional patterns. I also aimed to show that just as *ra'ā* formulae appear in extended and short sequences—and are thus confirmed as dialectical formulae occurring in real dialectic—they also appear in arguments outside of dialectical sequences—and are thus indicants of prior or recurrent dialectic. The point is that we do not always require the presentation of arguments in sequential Q&A format in order to make a strong claim that such arguments featured in, or were intended to feature in, real dialectical disputation. Such abbreviated presentations which employ these formulae (category C) very likely incorporate real dialectical arguments, even when the voice of an opponent is not heard. Nor are *a-ra'ayta* and *a-lā tarā* our only indicants; there are a host of other formulae which are every bit as revealing, and I will briefly review them here.

Primary among these are "how is it that [X is the case] while [Y is the case]?" (*kayfa... wa...*?) or "how is it that [X is the case] when/if [Y is the case]?" (*kayfa... idhā...*?) or other questions formulated with "how" (*kayfa*). We have seen these put to many and various uses, and—being that only the most general pattern seems to emerge—I will simply refer the reader to the sequences of Chap. 5, and of this current chapter, to gain a larger picture. Examples we have already encountered are: §§63 (SHAQ), 263 (SH), 660 (SH), 749 (AY/MIH/IAL), 753 (AH), 1057 (SH, *x*2), 1061 (SH), 1072 (SHAQ), 1227 (SHAQ), 1316 (AY/MIH), 1325 (SH), and 1326 (SH). All of these serve to problematize the opposing position in some manner or another, and the *kayfa* question is thus revealed as a tool for Q's advancing an objection and refutation against R's thesis (like the primary function of *a-ra'ayta*), as opposed to

Q's justification of his own thesis (as with the primary function of *a-lā tarā*). Additional instances of *kayfa* questions in category C presentations, outside the *masā'il*-sets I have analyzed, include: §§33 (MIH?), 221 (AH), 291 (AH), 387 (AH), 420 (AH), 1194 (SH), 1243 (AH), 1289 (AH), 1341 (AH), 1363 (AH), and 1367 (AH).[134] All of these instances of *kayfa* exhibit the same general function: R's position is problematized, and Q's objection or refutation is advanced. Lastly, note that all of these examples illustrate precisely how an objection (which is a kind of assertion) may be phrased as a question; for Q's *kayfa* question problematizes R's thesis in such a manner as either strongly implies Q's objection (which need not be asserted thereafter—this being a "rhetorical" *kayfa*), or in such a manner as sets the stage for Q's objection (which he thereafter asserts).

Asserted objections often also employ the verb *zaʿama/yazʿumu*, as when Q objects: "You have claimed X elsewhere, how is it that you now claim ¬X?" We have encountered numerous instances of *zaʿama* in dialectical sequences. Again, the presence of such formulae as "One who claims/claimed [opposing position X]" (*man / alladhī zaʿama / yazʿumu*) in non-sequence arguments provides obvious indication of prior or ongoing disputation. Examples of these latter include: §§467 (SH, relating three claims), 567–71 (SH, relating numerous claims), 729 (SH), 792 (SH), 824 (SH), and 1050 (SH).

In addition to *kayfa* questions and *zaʿama* assertions, there are a number of other signal formulae. In §10, for example, al-Shāfiʿī initiates his objection to an opposing opinion with: "One might interpose upon the one professing this, saying…" (*wa qad yadkhulu ʿalā qā'il hādhā an yuqāla lahu….*) Very similar expressions incorporating *dakhala* or *adkhala* (in the sense of interrupting and interposing) may be found in: §§33 (MIH?), 1032 (SH), and 1370 (SH). More obvious are the familiar references to "historical" dialectic we have encountered, although, of course, they are not followed in category C presentations by transcript-like sequences of Q&A. Al-Shāfiʿī begins his objection to an opposing position in §729 with "'one of the people' said [X]… and he drew argumentative support from [Y]" (*wa qāla baʿḍ al-nās* [X]… *wa iḥtajja bi-* [Y]….) In §§1377–83, al-Shāfiʿī raises a series of opposing opinions, then refutes them one after another. He begins by relating: "and 'some of the people' contradicted us in this matter with a number of statements" (*wa qad khālafanā fī hādhā baʿḍ al-nās bi-aqāwīl*); and then proceeds with "one of them said [X]" (*fa-qāla aḥaduhum* [X]), and "and another said [Y]" (*wa qāla ghayruhu* [Y]), and "and another said [Z]" (*wa qāla ghayruhu* [Z]). In §1417, on the other hand, al-Shāfiʿī concludes a justification of his ruling by noting: "but 'one of the people' contradicted this, and it is written in the *Book of Ḥadd-Punishments* with its supporting proofs" (*wa qad khālafa hādhā baʿḍ al-nās, wa hādhā maktūb fī Kitāb al-Ḥudūd bi-ḥujajihi*). Certainly no stronger indicants of past dialectical disputation may be found. Nor do such formulations as the following leave much to doubt: "and due to that we abandoned the doctrine of the one who said [X]" (*wa bi-dhālika taraknā qawl man qāla* [X]) (SH, in §1026); "and when they say [X]" (*idhā kānū yaqūlūna* [X]) (SH, in §1102); and, in most vigorous and thorough fashion, "I know neither source-case nor branch-case for the doctrine of the one who professes [X]" (*wa mā aʿrifu aṣlan wa lā farʿan li-qawl man qāla* [X]) (SH, in §1084).

I will close this discussion by suggesting we need not even rely upon such obvious formulae as the above for indications of past or recurrent dialectical disputation. Sometimes even the most abbreviated presentations, following directly on the heels of an opposing opinion, indicate the past occurrence of an argument in real disputation. Such is the case with Abū Ḥanīfa in §562, who, following Ibn Abī Laylā's ruling, is reported as saying: "the *qāḍī* need do no such thing, because he..." (*lā yanbaghī li'l-qāḍī an yafʿala dhālika, li-annahu*...); and, again following Ibn Abī Laylā's ruling [X], in §958: "Nay, rather [Y]" (*bal* [Y]). Our subject-text is, in all ways, a work of *ikhtilāf*; and every *mas'ala* within it had once formed—and continued to form—a focus for disputation. I have chosen to concentrate on presentation categories A, B, and C due only to the greater ease with which their overtly dialectical features may be identified, and the burdens of conjecture they tend to relieve.

6.3 A Note on Argumentative Material Which Is Not Overtly Dialectical

Presentation categories D, E, F, and G cannot be adequately treated in the current project, though I have already dealt with a number of them (with the exception of category E). These include: §§91–4, 280–1, and 691 (category D); §§239–41, 242–6, 634–41, 686–8, 1067, 1069–70, 1219, 1313b, 1317, and 1404–5 (category F); and §§89–90, 236–8, 689–90, 744–5, 1068, 1125–6, 1217–18, 1310–13a, and 1402–3 (category G). The analyses of Chap. 5, and of this current chapter, are testimony to what elements I have been able to distil from these presentations. A great deal more can be learned—especially from analyses of D and E arguments—but this must await further studies. Even so, a number of pertinent elements have manifested themselves through the cursory analyses corollary to the process of dividing up the subject-text by presentation category. The results of this surface analysis will be treated in Chap. 7.

As we have seen, a great deal can be gleaned from categories F and G as well—especially with the help of later *fiqh* and *ikhtilāf* works wherein the purported reasoning of arguing jurists is explained. Of course, as with categories D and E, they do not contain overtly dialectical formulae or Q&A sequences. My argument-identifications for categories F and G have thus been a far more conjectural enterprise than for other categories. I have considered opposing opinions as arising in a dialectical venue, and then inferred as best I could the types of *iʿtirāḍāt* most likely to have been employed. Importantly, however, and in addition to what one might harvest through so conjectural an activity, there are numerous elements of additional interest—in the form of technical terms, consistent formulae, modes of *istidlāl*, etc.—all of which contribute significantly to that small window on proto-system legal theory and juridical dialectic which our subject-text provides. These, at least, have been gleaned by my surface analyses of these categories, and are incorporated into the overall findings as well.

References

al-Bājī, Abū al-Walīd Sulaymān. *Kitāb al-Minhāj fī Tartīb al-Ḥijāj* (*L'art de la Polémique: Édition Critique d'al-Minhāǧ de Bāǧī*). Ed. ʿAbd al-Majīd Turkī. Paris: Maisonneuve et Larose, 1978.

al-Baṣrī, Abū al-Ḥusayn Muḥammad. *Kitāb al-Qiyās al-Sharʿī*. In *idem*, *Kitāb al-Muʿtamad fī Uṣūl al-Fiqh*. Ed. Muḥammad Ḥamīd Allāh, Muḥammad Bakīr, and Ḥasan Ḥanafī. Damascus: al-Maʿhad al-ʿIlmī al-Faransī li'l-Dirāsāt al-ʿArabiyya bi-Dimashq, 1964–1965, vol. 2, pp. 1029–1050.

al-Baṣrī, Abū al-Ḥusayn Muḥammad. *Kitāb al-Qiyās al-Sharʿī*. In *idem*, *al-Muʿtamad fī Uṣūl al-Fiqh*. Ed. Khalīl al-Mays. Beirut: Dār al-Kutub al-ʿIlmiyya, 1983, vol. 2, pp. 443–62.

DJP = Ibn Rushd. *The Distinguished Jurist's Primer* [= *Bidāyat al-Mujtahid wa Nihāyat al-Muqtaṣid*]. 2 vols. Trans. Imran Ahsan Khan Nyazee. Rev. Mohammad Abdul Rauf. Reading, UK: Centre for Muslim Contribution to Civilization: Garnet, 1994–1996.

EI² = *Encyclopaedia of Islam, Second Edition*. Ed. P. Bearman; Th. Bianquis; C.E. Bosworth; E. van Donzel; and W.P. Heinrichs. Brill Online, 2014 <http://referenceworks.brillonline.com/entries/encyclopaedia-of-islam-2>

Hallaq, Wael. *A History of Islamic Legal Theories: An Introduction to Sunnī Uṣūl al-Fiqh*. Cambridge; New York: Cambridge University Press, 1997.

Hallaq, Wael. *The Impossible State : Islam, Politics, and Modernity's Moral Predicament*. New York: Columbia University Press, 2013.

Hallaq, Wael. *Sharīʿa: Theory, Practice, Transformations*. Cambridge; New York: Cambridge University Press, 2009.

Hallaq, Wael. "A Tenth-Eleventh Century Treatise on Juridical Dialectic." *Muslim World* 77 (1987): 197–228.

Ibn ʿAqīl, Abū al-Wafāʾ ʿAlī. *Kitāb al-Jadal ʿalā Ṭarīqat al-Fuqahāʾ* (*Le Livre de la Dialectique d'Ibn ʿAqīl*). Ed. George Makdisi. *Bulletin d'Études Orientale* 20 (1967): 119–206.

Ibn ʿAqīl, Abū al-Wafāʾ ʿAlī. *Kitāb al-Jadal ʿalā Ṭarīqat al-Fuqahāʾ*. Al-Ẓāhir [Cairo]: Maktabat al-Thaqāfa al-Dīniyya, 1980. [An unattributed reproduction of George Makdisi, ed., *Le Livre de la Dialectique d'Ibn ʿAqīl*, minus his introduction and critical apparatus].

Ibn Ḥajar al-ʿAsqalānī. *Fī Manāqib al-Imām al-Shāfiʿī: Tawālī al-Taʾsīs li-Maʿālī Muḥammad b. Idrīs*. Ed. Abū al-Fidāʾ ʿAbd Allāh al-Qāḍī. Beirut: Dār al-Kutub al-ʿIlmiyya, 1986.

Ibn al-Nadīm, Abū al-Faraj Muḥammad. *Al-Fihrist*. Ed. Yūsuf ʿAlī Ṭawīl. Beirut: Dār al-Kutub al-ʿIlmiyya, 1996.

Lane, Edward William. *An Arabic-English Lexicon*. 8 vols. Beirut: Librarie du Liban, 1968.

Lowry, Joseph. "The Legal Hermeneutics of al-Shāfiʿī and Ibn Qutayba: A Reconsideration." *Islamic Law and Society* 11:1 (2004), pp. 1–41.

MF = *al-Mawsūʿa al-Fiqhiyya*. 45 Vols. Kuwait: Wizārat al-Awqāf wa'l-Shuʾūn al-Islāmiyya, 1990.

Sānū, Quṭb Muṣṭafā. *Muʿjam Muṣṭalaḥāt Uṣūl al-Fiqh, ʿArabī-Inkilīzī*. Beirut: Dār al-Fikr al-Muʿāṣir, 2000.

al-Sarakhsī, Muḥammad b. Aḥmad. *Kitāb al-Mabsūṭ*. Ed. Muḥammad Rāḍī, et al. 30 Vols. Cairo: Maṭbaʿat al-Saʿada, 1324-1331/1906-1913.

Schacht, Joseph. *The Origins of Muhammadan Jurisprudence*. Oxford: Oxford University Press, 1950.

al-Shāfiʿī, Muḥammad b. Idrīs. *Kitāb al-Umm*.

- ʿAbd al-Muṭṭalib = *Al-Umm*. 11 Pts. in 11 Vols. Ed. Rifʿat Fawzī ʿAbd al-Muṭṭalib. al-Manṣūra: Dār al-Wafāʾ li'l-Ṭibāʿa wa'l-Nashr wa'l-Tawzīʿ, 2001.

• Ḥassūn = *Mawsūʿat al-Imām al-Shāfiʿī: al-Kitāb al-Umm*. 2nd ed. Ed. Aḥmad Badr al-Dīn Ḥassūn. 16 Pts. in 10 Vols. Beirut: Dār Qutayba, 2003.

al-Shāfiʿī, Muḥammad b. Idrīs. *The Epistle on Legal Theory* [= *al-Risāla*]. Ed. and trans. Joseph E. Lowry. New York: New York University Press, 2013.

al-Shāfiʿī, Muḥammad b. Idrīs. *Al-Risāla*. Ed. Aḥmad Muḥammad Shākir. Cairo: Maṭbaʿat Muṣṭafā al-Bābī al-Ḥalabī, 1940.

al-Shīrāzī, Abū Isḥāq Ibrāhīm. *Kitāb al-Maʿūna fi'l-Jadal*. Ed. ʿAbd al-Majīd Turkī. Beirut: Dār al-Gharb al-Islāmī, 1988.

al-Shīrāzī, Abū Isḥāq Ibrāhīm. *Al-Maʿūna fi'l-Jadal*. Ed. ʿAlī b. ʿAbd al-ʿAzīz al-ʿUmayrīnī. Al-Ṣafāh, Kuwait: Manshūrāt Markaz al-Makhṭūṭāt wa'l-Turāth, 1987.

Wright, W. *Arabic Grammar* [Translated from the German of Caspari and Edited with Numerous Additions and Corrections by W. Wright]. Revised 3rd ed. by W. Robertson Smith and M.J. de Goeje. 2 vols. in 1. Mineola, N.Y.: Dover, 2005 [originally published: Cambridge: Cambridge University Press, 1896–1898, in 2 vols.]

Young, Walter Edward. "The Dialectical Forge: Proto-System Juridical Disputation in the Kitāb Ikhtilāf al-ʿIrāqiyyīn." 2 vols. PhD diss., McGill University, 2012.

Young, Walter Edward. "Have You Considered (*A-ra'ayta*)? Don't You See/Opine (*A-lā Tarā*)? A Working Typology of *Ra'ā* Formulae in Early Islamic Juridical Disputation." [In: Y. Papadogiannakis and B. Roggema (eds.), *Patterns of Argumentation and Exchange of Ideas in Late Antiquity and Early Islam*, (forthcoming).]

Zysow, Aron. *The Economy of Certainty: An Introduction to the Typology of Islamic Legal Theory*. PhD diss., Harvard University, 1984.

Chapter 7
A Picture of Proto-System *Jadal*

7.1 What is Common: Elements More Consonant with Full-System Theory

Introduction

Some of the questions, justifications, and objections of our subject-text have fallen easily, or relatively easily, into the categories of our lens-texts. Others have not, and may possibly (but not necessarily) represent dialectical phenomena unique to proto-system juridical *jadal*.[1] I will focus on the former in this section, and on the latter in the section following. Bear in mind that the findings reviewed in these sections are culled only from the analyses in Chaps. 5 and 6; and with regard to presentation category C, I have reviewed only the functions of its dialectical formulae. The bulk of arguments in category C, along with all the arguments of categories D through F, and the bare substantive rulings of category G, must await further (and considerably more difficult) study.

Bear in mind also that my lens-text identifications are not assertions that proto-system jurists would have recognized all the terms by which I have categorized their arguments—though they certainly would in many instances. I have examined proto-system material through a lens of *jadal*-theory fashioned at least two centuries later; and I have doubtless applied a more refined set of categories

[1] We must also allow that certain elements of dialectical practice in the era of full-system *jadal*-theory treatises were not discussed in our lens-texts. A ready example is the use of the *a-lā tarā* formula by all of our lens-text authors at various points, often while defending particular positions of *jadal*-theory itself. We do not find, however, any systematic treatment regarding where and to what purpose the *a-lā tarā* formula is to be used.

W.E. Young, *The Dialectical Forge*, Logic, Argumentation & Reasoning 9,
DOI 10.1007/978-3-319-25522-4_7

and definitions than existed in the proto-system era.[2] Nevertheless, my analytical categories are not an anachronistic back-projection of system and term; rather, I have endeavoured only to discover and categorize the theory and practice of an earlier time. If there is a key message to be read from the following presentation of findings, it is this: although elements of full-system theory were absent to a considerable extent from proto-system juridical dialectic, an extraordinary number were nevertheless *practiced*, and very evidently so. This obtains with regard to elements of full-system *uṣūl al-fiqh* and *jadal*-theory both.

The remarkable continuity from proto-system *jadal* teaching and practice to full-system *jadal*-theory treatises is what the findings of this first section should most impress. At the same time, one will recognize the extraordinary elaborations and refinements—the true, comprehensive *system*—which *jadal* theorists of the fourth/tenth through fifth/eleventh centuries achieved. They were the true Aristotles of Islamic juridical disputation praxis and legal theory. Their systems, however, were not created *ex nihilo*, nor were they taken over from other epistemic communities. Rather, they represent the analytical distillation of a continuous tradition of teaching and practice, increasingly refined over preceding centuries, and already marked by a high level of sophistication by the time of al-Shāfiʿī.

A final preparatory note: I will continue to abbreviate the names of disputing jurists throughout the summary tables of this chapter, and so present them again for reference:

AH = Abū Ḥanīfa	AY = Abū Yūsuf
IAL = Ibn Abī Laylā	MIH = Muḥammad b. al-Ḥasan al-Shaybānī
SH = al-Shāfiʿī	RB = al-Rabīʿ
R = Respondent	Q = Questioner
SHAR = al-Shāfiʿī's Anonymous Respondent	SHAQ = al-Shāfiʿī's Anonymous Questioner

[2] Many of the findings of this current project are fully consonant with a seminal study by Zafar Ishaq Ansari: his "Islamic Juristic Terminology Before al-Shāfiʿī." Ansari sheds light on early (second/eighth century) usages of the terms *ḥadīth*, *sunna*, *ijmāʿ*, *raʾy*, *qiyās*, etc. Moreover, he reaches a number of important, general conclusions (pp. 299–300). Among them are the following: (1) "there was a marked lag between the conceptual and terminological aspects of the development of *fiqh*," and "some of the fundamental concepts... are anterior to the period when they acquired standard technical terms for their expression;" (2) "if there is positive evidence about the existence of a concept as embodied by the term in use, we can confidently make an affirmative statement," but "if, on the contrary, positive terminological evidence is lacking in regard to some concept, this does not necessarily signify the non-existence of that concept;" (3) overall, there was a "trend towards an increasingly precise definition of terms... a more vivid *uṣūl*-consciousness reflected in the growing recognition of distinctions between the various sources of positive doctrines, and its corollary, an increasing formalism and finesse in technical legal thought;" and (4) "even though there was a semantic lag, yet the formulation of technical terms with accurate connotations was well on its way [by al-Shāfiʿī's time] and considerable progress seems to have been made in that respect."

Proto-System Dialectical Questions Within the Categories of the Lens-Texts

We should not be surprised by the absence of al-Bājī's questions #1 and #2 from the dialectical sequences of the *Kitāb Ikhtilāf al-ʿIrāqiyyayn/ʿIrāqiyyīn*. This may be explained by our subject-text's abbreviated nature; for each instance in which a dialectical sequence occurs, the *mas'ala* of contention had already been determined, and opposing solutions were already known. All that remained for al-Shāfiʿī, therefore, was to present such portions of his narrative or instruction wherein the *dalīl*-indicant was, or ought to be, elicited (*su'āl* #3); wherein the mode of the *dalīl*-indicant, if not clear, was, or ought to be, elicited (*su'āl* #4); and wherein the questioner proceeded, or ought to proceed, to critique (*su'āl* #5). Any assessment in terms of absences would only hold true if we understood al-Shāfiʿī and other proto-system jurists to have adhered to an ordered question-schema like that proffered by al-Bājī; there are, however, more than a few indications that they did not.

The following, therefore, is only a list of those questions which correspond to al-Bājī's schema, if not always a precise match. Identifications were often difficult to make: many questions appeared to combine information-seeking and refutational intentions. Many more were directed at an opponent's objection rather than his justification, and yet others simply found no easy classification in our lens-texts. For the most part, these latter will be treated in following sections as potentially unique to proto-system *jadal*.

Su'āl #3: The Question about the Indicant (*dalīl*) [of the *madhhab*-opinion]

- "Upon which thing did you (pl.) rely [for proof] (*ʿalā ayyi shay'in iʿtamadtum*)?"
  - §253 (SH)
- "Provide me an indicant for this (*fa-dlulnī ʿalā hādhā*)" (in the spirit of a *muṭālaba*)
  - §260 (SHAQ)
- "How have you arrived at this opinion, to the exclusion of other doctrines... (*kayfa dhahabta ilā hādhā dūna ghayrihi min al-aqāwīl...*)?"
  - §1072 (SHAQ; following up with three counter-doctrines)
- "Why did you assert X (*lima zaʿamta* X)?"
  - §1224 (SHAQ; as first stage in pushing concession to his *qiyās* [see SHAQ in §1227])
- "From where do you claim X (*min ayna zaʿamtum* X)?"
  - §1407, 1409 (SHAQ; [X = SH *ʿilla*-interpretation]; possibly *su'āl* #4; in §1409 he repeats his request for the *dalīl*-indicant: "what is it (*wa mā huwa*)?"

(continued)

- "From where do you say this (*min ayna qulta hādhā*)?"
    - §36 (SHAQ)
- "What provides indication for what you have stated (*mā dalla ʿalā mā dhakarta*)?"
    - §51 (SHAQ)
- *Su'āl* #3 as the means of eliciting premises for a charge of method-*naqḍ*
    - [in the way of a rhetorical *reductio*]
        - Q states the *uṣūl* and *farʿ* for R's *qiyās*, then asks: "Is X (which is absurd) the *qiyās*; or Y (which is absurd) the *qiyās*?"
            - §1057 (SH)
    - Q asks: "Did you rule as you did because of *dalīl*-indicant X? (*dalīl* X being that *dalīl* which R has not consistently applied, and which is also Q's *dalīl*)
        - §1059 (SH)
    - Q asks: "Why did you rule in the negative, is it because X is different from Y?" (this difference being the *farq*-distinction that R has not consistently observed)
        - §1323 (SH)

_Su'āl_ #4: The Question about the Mode (_wajh_) of the _Dalīl_-indicant

- "And how does [my *dalīl*-indicant] not contradict [your *dalīl*-indicant] (*kayfa lā yukhālifu...*)?"
    - §256 (SHAQ)
- "How does X resemble (*kayfa tushbihu*) Y?"
    - §285 (SHAQ; in the spirit of *muṭālaba bi-ithbāt al-waṣf fi'l-farʿ*)
- "And how is that" (*wa kayfa dhālika*)?"
    - §645 (SHAQ; in the spirit of a "*su'āl ʿan wajh al-iʿtirāḍ*" or "*su'āl ʿan wajh al-muʿāraḍa*")[3]
- "Then which of the two doctrines most resembles the *qiyās* (*fa-ayy al-qawlayn ashbahu al-qiyās*)?"
    - §650 (SHAQ; in the spirit of a "*su'āl ʿan wajh al-iʿtirāḍ*" or "*muṭālaba bi-taṣḥīḥ al-iʿtirāḍ*")
- "But how is the *qiyās* regarding this (*wa kayfa yakūnu al-qiyās fihi*)?"
    - §661 (SHAQ; in the spirit of a "*su'āl ʿan wajh al-muʿāraḍa*")
- "How is [X] lawful (*kayfa jāza*), and more than [X] not lawful (*lam yajuz*)?"
    - §63 (SHAQ; in the spirit of a *muṭālaba*)

[3] Such *muṭālabāt* as appear in quotes are not actual categories in the lens-texts. See the discussion below on question types which appear unique to proto-system *jadal*.

Su'āl #5: The Question According to the Mode of Critique (*'alā wajh al-qadḥ*) [against the *dalīl*-indicant][4]

Muṭālabāt (as setting the stage for *Mumānaʿāt*)

- Indeterminate Type
  - §§63 (SHAQ); 258 (SHAQ); 260 (SHAQ; in the form of *su'āl* #3, but in the spirit of a critical demand for a *dalīl*-indicant)
- *muṭālaba bi-ithbāt al-waṣf fi'l-farʿ*
  - (Bāj.IX.A.1.6)
    - §285 (SHAQ; setting stage for *manʿ al-waṣf fi'l-farʿ*)
- *muṭālaba bi-taṣḥīḥ al-akhbār*
  - §1076 (SHAQ: "Then where is the Sunna for it [*fa-ayna al-Sunna fihi*]?" likely the first stage of an intended [but never realized] *muṭālaba*)

Not many of the questions we encountered fit easily into al-Bājī's schema. Even such obvious candidates as "Provide me an indicant for this (*fa-dlulnī ʿalā hādhā*)" for question #3 were often uttered with a patently refutational design. Note this as an overall characteristic of our window on proto-system *jadal*: its dialectical questions do not conform well to the structured categories of later theory—at least, that is, with regard to those (##1–4, and the *muṭālabāt* of #5) which comprise the initial information-seeking stage of disputation. As for *iʿtirāḍāt* and *muʿāraḍāt*, however, there is a remarkable correspondence between proto-system practice and full-system theory. I will turn to these now, arranging identifications according to the organizing principle of our lens-texts.

Proto-System Istidlālāt *and* Iʿtirāḍāt *Within the* Adilla *Domains of the Lens-Texts*

Recall that our early *jadal* theorists organized the domains of *istidlāl* and *iʿtirāḍ* according to three supersets: *aṣl*, *maʿqūl aṣl*, and *istiṣḥāb ḥāl*. I will follow this arrangement in presenting the proto-system justifications and objections which conform to the categories of later theory. The immediate impression is that a remarkable amount of the arguments and dialectical moves of our subject-text would have been recognized and easily explained by later theorists. It is my thesis, of course, that this is no coincidence. It would appear that the system of al-Shīrāzī, for example, was not only formulated from the practice and pedagogy of his more immediate teachers (e.g., Abū al-Ṭayyib al-Ṭabarī [d.450/1058]) and teachers' teachers (in the line of Ibn Surayj and students), but by an analysis and structuring of the practice and teaching of such jurist-dialecticians as Abū Ḥanīfa, Abū Yūsuf, Muḥammad b. al-Ḥasan, and al-Shāfiʿī.

[4] Corresponding *iʿtirāḍāt* and *muʿāraḍāt* will be treated below in detail.

A few important caveats before the review. First of all, remember the abbreviated presentations of the subject-text—particularly in such categories as were not overtly dialectical—sometimes brought me to propose identifications of a more hypothetical nature. The juxtaposition of opposing rulings and arguments guided me in surmising the forms of objection they would represent in a venue of face-to-face dialectical debate. Of course, as a work of *ikhtilāf*, the contents of our subject-text were invariably the object of real-time dialectic at some point or another—they were rarely "transcripted" as such, however. I will therefore mark such objections identified by more conjectural means—inferred through the contrast of opinions—as "implied."

Recall also that abbreviated presentations—particularly for Abū Ḥanīfa, Ibn Abī Laylā, and Abū Yūsuf—often caused me to seek out later reports of background reasoning. These will also be labelled in what follows, as emanating either from the reports of al-Ṭabarī or al-Sarakhsī. As for all arguments and objections which do not bear the markers of "implied" or "reported," they may be considered as clearly indicated in our subject-text itself. Since we are dealing at present only with "overtly dialectical" material, this applies more to the copious dialectical moves which will follow.

A final important caveat, and one which applies to the whole of our analytical venture, and all of the discussions straight through to the end of this chapter: my analyses have been conducted with regard to portions of a single, early treatise of *ikhtilāf*, which itself constitutes less than a twentieth of the volume of the *Kitāb al-Umm*. Nor is the *Umm* the only early compendium in which patently dialectical material may be found in abundance. Our window onto proto-system *jadal* is thus a fraction of a fraction, and I am understandably reluctant to extend the picture we are provided beyond its borders to the whole of proto-system *jadal*. Bear this in mind as we proceed to assess this sliver of light cast onto the early juridical dialectical scene. Unless stated otherwise, my observations apply to our jurist-dialecticians only insofar as the *masā'il* of our subject text is concerned—they are not (necessarily) to be extended to their overall (and mostly unexamined) practice, and certainly not to the practice of their unnamed predecessors and peers. That being said, I will begin, by reviewing the superset of *aṣl*, and its subsets of *Kitāb*, *Sunna*, *Ijmāʿ*, and *Qawl al-Wāḥid min al-Ṣaḥāba*.

Kitāb ("the Book," i.e., the Qur'ān)

Incidents of Drawing Indication (*Istidlālāt*)

- §§1052 (AH; Q.5:95; implied [Qur'ānic *dalīl*-indicant is introduced by *a-lā tarā ilā*... i.e., presented by way of *muʿāraḍa*]); 1056 (SH; God's decree in Q.5:95; accompanied with SH *tafsīr*-explanation of «*mithlu*»); 1077 (SH; he claims his *istidlāl* from Sunna and *ijmāʿ* is "in the *maʿnā*-intension of" Q.2:178); 1410 (SH; Q.2:230; followed by *mufassir* Sunna)

(continued)

Incidents of Objection (*Iʿtirāḍāt*)

- sharing the indicant (*al-mushāraka fi'l-dalīl*); with respect to [its] most apparent meaning (*min jihat al-ẓāhir*)" (Shīr.I.4[.1]; Bāj.I.3.1.2)
  - §§1056 (SH; SH *istidlāl* focuses upon a different component of AH *dalīl*-indicant in Q.5:95; supported by *āthār*-traditions, *qiyās*, and *maʿqūl*);[5] 1061 (SH)

This seems a small representation of argument from the Qur'ān; it is not true of our subject-treatise as a whole, however. There are a dozen additional Qur'ānic justifications occurring outside of overtly dialectical material.[6] I would also propose that—with the Qur'ān occupying the uppermost rank of epistemic authority as it does—problem cases of *ikhtilāf* occurred more frequently in other domains of *istidlāl* which enjoyed less in the way of consistency and consensual interpretation in the proto-system era: particularly, the increasingly-important corpus of *sunan*.[7] The nascent science of the Ahl al-Ḥadīth (and its material) was newer to the Islamic intellectual landscape than that of the exegetes. Finally, bear in mind that we have examined but a single treatise of the *Kitāb al-Umm*; the whole of this compendium is replete with many hundreds of arguments from the Qur'ān.

The sole *iʿtirāḍ* from overtly dialectical presentations I have identified in this domain is "sharing the indicant" (*al-mushāraka fi'l-dalīl*). This might suggest that the relation of the rulings of the Qur'ān to various genera of the evolving *fiqh* of proto-Sunnism had already been well-argued and more or less delineated by the time of al-Shāfiʿī, but no positive confirmation can be made without a great deal more research. We may certainly observe, however, that the arguments of al-Shāfiʿī incorporate the complementary Qur'ān-Sunna relationship central to what Joseph Lowry has labelled al-Shāfiʿī's "concept of the *Bayān*," as formulated in his *Risāla*.[8] The role of Prophetic Sunna is indeed a large one in our dialectical sequences, and not only in the hands of al-Shāfiʿī, as we have seen.

[5] SH's *iʿtirāḍ* matches al-Bājī exactly, and al-Bājī uses this very *mas'ala* for his example (al-Bājī, *Minhāj*, Turkī ed., 59f., §114). The implications of this will be discussed in the following chapter.

[6] See Sect. 7.3, below.

[7] The normative materials of the Qur'ān are impressive in size and scope—not only by way of direct application to ritual and transaction, but as a source for *uṣūl* for extension, and for general principles. Its overall substantive corpus, however, is dwarfed by that of the *sunan*. This difference in substantive contribution may also have bearing on the relative infrequency of Qur'ān-oriented *istidlālāt* and *iʿtirāḍāt* in our subject-text.

[8] *Early Islamic Legal Theory*, pp. 23ff. and *passim*.

Sunna (The Prophet's Instruction and Exemplary Conduct)

Incidents of Drawing Indication (*Istidlālāt*)

- *Qawl* (Saying of the Prophet)
  - §§37 (SH; *qaḍā* Rasūl Allāh...; SH *tafsīr*-explanation links efficient properties to the *mas'ala* at hand); 52 (SH; *qaḍā* Rasūl Allāh...); 239 (AH); 247 (Ahl al-Baṣra); 254 (SHAR of the Mashriqiyyūn); 1075 (SH); 1077 (SH; combined with *ijmāʿ* and [ambiguous] *maʿnā*-intension of Q.2:178)
- *Fiʿl* (Deed of the Prophet)
  - §§64–5 (SH; 3x; accompanied by *tafsīr*-explanation of his hermeneutic); 261 (SH; *ḥadīth* is used incidentally as supporting *dalīl*-indicant to illustrate usage of *lafẓ*-expression contended by SHAQ); 276 (IAL); 543 (SHAR); 1125 (AH; reported by al-Sarakhsī); 1225 (SH; accompanied by SH *tafsīr-explanation*)
- undetermined type
  - §§78 (SH; general appeal to Sunna as witness to *farq*-distinction between *ʿitq*-manumission and all other transactions); 1410 (SH; as *mufassir* to Q.2:230)

Incidents of Objection (*Iʿtirāḍāt*)

With Reference to the Chain of Transmission (*Isnād*)

- Indeterminate: "a singular mode [of transmission] (*min wajhin wāḥidin*) which the Ahl al-Ḥadīth do not grant full confirmation (*lā yuthbituhu... kulla tathbīt*)."
  - §667 (SH; dismissing possible exception to his hypothetical *muʿāraḍa*)
- Indeterminate: it is an error (*ghalaṭ*) "because the Ḥuffāẓ have not preserved anything of the sort (*lam yaḥfaẓū hākadhā*)."
  - §1119 (SH)

With Reference to the Transmitted Text (*matn*) [as a Self-Initiated Saying of the Prophet (*qawl mubtada'*)]

- claim of ambiguity (*daʿwā al-ijmāl*)
  - *daʿwā al-ijmāl* regarding God's Law (*Sharʿ*)
    - (Shīr.II.C.3.1; Bāj.II.2.2.3.2)
      - §53 (SH)
  - *daʿwā al-ijmāl* regarding the Arabic Language (*lugha*); Contestation regarding the general scope (*al-munāzaʿa fī'l-ʿumūm*): [Q] claims ambiguity (*ijmāl*) regarding [the expression]
    - (Shīr.II.C.3.2; Bāj.II.2.2.3.2)
      - §247 (SH)
        - R's *ḥadīth* is *jumla*; Q's is *mufassir*: §255 (SH; supported by *adilla*-indicants: *āthār*-traditions of ʿUmar, Abān b. ʿUthmān, and al-Ḥakam, and later by other *āthār*-traditions)

(continued)

- sharing the indicant (*al-mushāraka fi'l-dalīl*)
    - (Shīr.II.C.4; Bāj.II.2.3.1.2)
        - §544 (SH employs the same *ḥadīth* as *dalīl*-indicant, but focuses upon a different *lafẓ*-expression)
- abrogation by way of the contradictory doings of the Companions (*al-naskh bi-ʿamal al-Ṣaḥāba bi-khilāfihi*)
    - (Shīr.II.C.6.3; Bāj.II.2.5.3)
        - §1126 (IAL/[old] AY; implied by al-Sarakhsī's report)
- counter-indication by way of divinely-sanctioned decree (*muʿāraḍa bi'l-nuṭq*)
    - (Shīr.II.C.8.1; Bāj.II.2.7.1)
        - §§248 (SH; *x*2); §544 (SH; counter-*ḥadīth* introduced by *a-lā tarā*)
- counter-indication by way of the occasioning factor (*muʿāraḍa bi'l-ʿilla*)
    - general
        - (Shīr.II.C.8.2; Bāj.II.2.7.2)
            - §1126 (IAL/[old] AY; implied)
    - when the Sunna is general (*ʿumūm*), allowing the possibility of particularization (*takhṣīṣ*)
        - (Shīr.II.C.8.2.3; Bāj.II.2.7.2.3)
            - §248 (SH); §257 (SH)
                - *Jawāb*: Shīr. and Bāj. recommend arguing against Q's *dalīl*-indicant so as to eliminate it, then persisting in *istidlāl* from the *ʿumūm*
                    - §258 (SHAR)

With Reference to the Transmitted Text (*matn*) [as the Prophet's deed (*fiʿl*)]

- sharing the indicant (*al-mushāraka fi'l-dalīl*)
    - (Shīr.II.E.4; Bāj.II.4.5)
        - §544 (SH; hypothetical; SH does not in fact concede that the concerned *ḥadīth* bears what SHAR has claimed of it, but if it did...)
- counter-indication by way of the occasioning factor (*muʿāraḍa bi'l-ʿilla*)
    - (Shīr.II.E.8.2; Bāj.II.4.9.3.2)
        - §274 (AH)

Modes of Preponderance (*Tarjīḥāt*)

- Regarding the Chain of Transmission (*Isnād*)
    - one of the two [*khabar*-reports] is more narrated; it is superior (*awlā*)
        - (Shīr.IX.1.5; Bāj.XVI.1.1.3)
            - §248 (SH)
- Regarding the Transmitted Text (*Matn*)
    - one of the two *khabar*-reports is consistent (*muwāfiq*) with another *dalīl*-indicant, from an authoritative source-case (*aṣl*), or what is rationally understood from one (*maʿqūl aṣl*)

(continued)

- (Shīr.IX.2.1)
    - §§276 (IAL; continuation of Prophet's transaction at Khaybar under the reigns of Abū Bakr and ʿUmar); 277 (IAL/AY; "And indeed, according to us, the *qiyās* for this concurs with the *athar*-tradition"); 1226 (SH; supports his *istidlāl* by way of Sunnaic deed with allusion to unnamed Companions)

This is a fine show of justifications and objections in the domain of Sunna. With regard to larger subcategories, only representatives of the Prophet's acknowledgment (*iqrār*), and *iʿtirāḍāt* oriented to the prompted saying of the Prophet (*qawl khārij ʿalā sabab*)—al-Bājī's Prompted Sunna (*Sunna wārida ʿalā al-sabab*)—are missing.[9] Of particular note with regard to proto-system *istidlāl bi'l-Sunna* is the following: (1) al-Shāfiʿī's *tafsīr*-explanation not only of the contents of a particular *khabar*-report, but of his own hermeneutic; (2) the support of his Sunna-interpretation via elements from other *uṣūl* (Qur'ān and *Ijmāʿ*); and (3) his employing Sunna as interpreter (*mufassir*) to Qur'ān, and as an incidental *dalīl*-indicant for *lafẓ*-expression interpretation with regard to another Sunnaic *aṣl*. These are legal theoretical elements which go beyond the mere claim of Sunnaic consonance for one's solution to the *mas'ala* at hand, and have all been brought forth in a dialectical venue.

As far as *iʿtirāḍāt* and *tarjīḥāt* in this domain, we are also provided a number of insights with regard to proto-system practice. First of all, note the vague form which al-Shāfiʿī's transmission-oriented objections often take; and this assessment applies to the greater part of our subject-treatise. This is certainly not to say that al-Shāfiʿī was not a master of (and contributor to) the transmission-theory of his time.[10] In the main, however, his objections are formulated as "the Ahl al-Ḥadīth do not confirm its like." Significantly, the other jurists of our treatise are quite silent with regard to transmission-oriented objections, although we must not assume that such did not play a role in the much abbreviated accounts of their arguments, or elsewhere in their dialectical encounters.

With regard to *matn*-oriented dialectical moves, I would highlight a number of features: (1) a concern with ambiguity/generality (*ijmāl*), and the appearance of al-Shāfiʿī's *jumla-mufassir* distinction in a Sunna-to-Sunna encounter; (2) the repeated practice of critiquing an opponent's interpretation of a particular *lafẓ*-expression; (3) the preponderating of one's Sunnaic *dalīl*-indicant by way of supporting *adilla*-indicants of a weaker epistemic value; (4) the *muʿāraḍa* of *ḥadīth* by *ḥadīth*; and (5) the supplanting of an opponent's conception of an efficient property with one's own conception (*al-muʿāraḍa bi'l-ʿilla*). Once again, all of these features depend upon legal-theoretical methods which go beyond a mere claim

---

[9] This is not to say, of course, that such did not occur in the abbreviated presentations of our subject-text, or elsewhere in the *Umm*.

[10] I will discuss incidences where elements of his theory arise in the course of objection in the following chapter.

that one's ruling is more in consonance with the Prophet's Sunna. There is a developed hermeneutic in place, and the fine-honing of epistemic justification through dialectical encounter is plain to see.

Ijmāʿ (Consensus)

Incidents of Drawing Indication (_Istidlālāt_)

- §1077 (SH; *ijmāʿ* on two substantive rulings is combined with a Sunnaic decree and claimed to be "in the *maʿnā* of" Q.2:178)
- [*ijmāʿ* as *aṣl* for *qiyās*][11]
  - §§274–5 (AH; *ijmāʿ* re: *aṣl* reported by al-Ṭabarī); 277 (IAL/AY; *ijmāʿ* re: *aṣl* reported by al-Ṭabarī); 691 (SH; *ijmāʿ* re: *aṣl* stated clearly); 1075 (SH; *al-qiyās ʿalā al-ijmāʿ*)
- [Q's general charge: R's violation of [what] 'the people claim' ([*mā*] *zaʿama al-nās*); and of the 'majority doctrine' (*madhhab al-ʿāmma*)][12]
  - §§696 (SH; twinned with *naqḍ* as component of "*naqḍ* dilemma"); 703 (SH; "If you rule X, you contradict the *madhhab* of the *ʿāmma*;" violation of *ijmāʿ* is the first option of "*naqḍ*-dilemma")

Incidents of Objection (_Iʿtirāḍāt_)

- against drawing indication by way of consensus of the Companions (*istidlāl bi-ijmāʿ al-Ṣaḥāba*): demand for validation of consensus (*muṭālaba bi-taṣḥīḥ al-ijmāʿ*)
  - (Shīr.III.2; Bāj.III.1.1)
    - §§635 (AH; implied); 636 (IAL; implied); 639 (SH; implied); 1402 (AH; implied by al-Sarakhsī's report); 1405 (SH; implied; *āthār*-tradition decrees of five of the Companions)
- against drawing indication by way of consensus of the Companions (*istidlāl bi-ijmāʿ al-Ṣaḥāba*): disagreement (*khilāf*) of another Companion
  - (Shīr.III.3; Bāj.III.1.2)
    - §§635 (AH; implied); 636 (IAL; implied); 637 (IAL; implied; *āthār*-traditions increased from one to three); 639 (SH; implied; *khilāf* of three *āthār*-tradition decrees [same as IAL]); 640–1 (SH; raises own *āthār*-traditions to four, AH *āthār*-traditions to five; then clearly indicates *khilāf* of Companions); 1402 (AH; implied by al-Sarakhsī's report); 1405 (SH; implied; *āthār*-tradition decrees of five of the Companions)

[11] Properly speaking, this is *istidlāl bi'l-qiyās*, not *istidlāl bi'l-ijmāʿ*; I have included *ijmāʿ* as the *aṣl* of *qiyās* in this domain simply to underscore that *ijmāʿ* appears to have been employed by our jurists as an *aṣl* with some frequency.

[12] Again, these instances properly belong to another domain—as components of a "*naqḍ* dilemma" (that unique argument strategy of al-Shāfiʿī's we will return to shortly). I have included it here, however, as the *ijmāʿ* which the opponent will appear to violate is also the *ijmāʿ* forming the basis of the questioner's *istidlāl*.

Although the samples of *ijmāʿ*-oriented *iʿtirāḍāt* are almost entirely of the "implied" sort, note that the *istidlālāt* are either reported by al-Ṭabarī or clearly stated in our subject-text. Moreover, there are a number of occurrences from other presentation categories awaiting further study. I would highlight the following features with regard to this small set of early *ijmāʿ*-oriented dialectical moves: (1) al-Shāfiʿī's skilful blending of *ijmāʿ* with Sunna and Qur'ān for the accretion of epistemic justification; (2) a common role for *ijmāʿ* in sanctioning an *aṣl* for *qiyās* with all key jurists of our subject-text; (3) al-Shāfiʿī's formulae of "[*mā*] *zaʿama al-nās*," and "*madhhab al-ʿāmma*" (both of which harmonize with Aristotle's *endoxa*-set); (4) the absence—so far as I can immediately discern—of reference to subcategories of *ijmāʿ*; and (5) the absence of demands for validation (*taṣḥīḥ*) of one's claim of *ijmāʿ* (beyond the domain of *ijmāʿ al-Ṣaḥāba*).[13]

As for the two objections against *ijmāʿ al-Ṣaḥāba*, these are mostly the result of my conjecture as to how our jurists might have employed their collections of supporting *āthār*-traditions when confronted with an opposing set. Though hesitant to generalize, I would submit our subject-text provides little indication that *ijmāʿ* was conceived of in anything like the more sophisticated manner of later *uṣūl* and *jadal*-theory systems. On the other hand, what little we have encountered in the way of *ijmāʿ*ic formulae and application corresponds well with the dialectic of Aristotle's *Topics*, from two perspectives: (1) appeals to *ijmāʿ*, to [*mā*] *zaʿama al-nās*, and to the *madhhab al-ʿāmma* (paralleling subsets within Aristotle's larger *endoxa* set); and (2) the employing of *ijmāʿ*-sanctioned rulings as *uṣūl* for *qiyās* (paralleling Aristotle's use of *endoxa* premises). Twinned with the hierarchy of epistemic authority inherent to our jurists' Islamic argumentation episteme (God, Sunna, *ijmāʿ*, *qiyās*, etc.), this latter parallel (the use of *endoxa* premises) may be said to extend to the full gamut of epistemic justifications in Islamic legal theory. Moreover, we may observe that it was juridical disputation that largely determined what these *endoxa* premises themselves would be. Thus, juridical *jadal* at once depended upon, and determined, what was *endoxon* for the Muslim jurist.[14]

[13] This may indicate nothing more than that such demands were unnecessary for the limited *masāʾil* of *ikhtilāf* with which our treatise is concerned.

[14] We will revisit this notion in Chap. 8 (Sect. 8.6).

Qawl al-Wāḥid min al-Ṣaḥāba (The Saying of a Solitary Companion)

Incidents of Drawing Indication (*Istidlālāt*)

- One Companion
  - §§52 (SH; *athar*-tradition judgment of ʿUmar, in support of Sunnaic judgment; SH *tafsīr*-explanation shows his *ʿilla* (and its rationale) at work in this *athar*-tradition *dalīl*-indicant); 89 (AH; *athar*-tradition decree of Ibn ʿAbbās; reported by al-Sarakhsī); 90[a] (IAL; *athar*-tradition of ʿĀʾisha; reported by al-Sarakhsī); 92–3 (RB relating SH; *athar*-tradition decree of Ibn ʿAbbās); 636 (IAL; *athar*-tradition decree of ʿAlī); 1061 (SHAR; *taqlīd* of ʿUmar b. al-Khaṭṭāb); 1067, 1069–70 (AH; *athar*-tradition deed of Ḥasan b. ʿAlī; al-Sarakhsī reports this was also ʿAlī's dying wish—i.e., it is also an *athar*-tradition decree of ʿAlī);[15] 1126 (IAL/[old] AY; reported by al-Sarakhsī; *athar*-tradition deed of ʿAlī); 1313[b] (AH; *athar*-tradition of Ibn ʿAbbās); 1318 (SHAR; same *athar*-tradition of Ibn ʿAbbās employed by AH in §1313[b])
- Two Companions
  - §§241 (IAL; enforced Caliphal decree is doctrine of Ḥijāzīs = *āthār*-tradition decrees of ʿAlī and Ibn ʿAbbās); 279 (IAL/AY; *āthār*-tradition deeds of Saʿd b. Abī Waqqāṣ and Ibn Masʿūd; used to support *ḥukm* extended by *qiyās*); 1406 (SHAQ; *āthār*-tradition decrees of Ibn ʿUmar and Ibn ʿAbbās)
- Multiple Companions (in the attempt to preponderate another *aṣl*, or show *ijmāʿ al-Ṣaḥāba*, or simply by way of *taqlīd*)
  - §§242–4 (SH; *āthār*-tradition decrees of ʿUmar, Abān b. ʿUthmān, and al-Ḥakam; used as *adilla*-indicants for *iʿtirāḍ* against *istidlāl bi'l-Sunna*); 267 (SH; ʿUmar I, ʿUthmān; and some Successors: ʿUmar II and others; used incidentally to support SH *ḥadīth* interpretation); 278 (IAL/AY; *āthār*-tradition deeds of ʿUmar, Ibn Masʿūd, and ʿUthmān; used to support *aṣl* for *qiyās*); 635 (AH; *āthār*-tradition decrees of Abū Bakr, Ibn ʿAbbās, ʿĀʾisha, Ibn al-Zubayr); 637 (IAL; *āthār*-traditions increased by addition of *āthār*-tradition decrees of Zayd b. Thābit and Ibn Masʿūd); 639 (SH; *āthār*-tradition decrees of Zayd b. Thābit, ʿAlī, and Ibn Masʿūd [same as IAL]); 640 (SH; *āthār*-traditions increased by addition of *athar*-tradition decree of ʿUthmān)
- Unstated Number of Companions
  - §§1054 (IAL; *taqlīd* of the *athar*-tradition re: *ʿanāq* and *jafra*; confirmed by al-Sarakhsī, with a host of other supports, all of which constitute *istiḥsān*); 1226 (SH; as support for his *istidlāl* by way of Sunnaic deed);

(continued)

[15] Note that our lens-texts do not treat the deeds (*afʿāl*) of Ṣaḥāba as a category for *istidlāl*.

1405 (SH; *athar*-tradition decree of ʿUmar, and other *kibār Aṣḥāb al-Nabī*; al-Sarakhsī reports: *āthār*-tradition decrees of ʿUmar, ʿAlī, Ubayy b. Kaʿb, ʿImrān b. al-Ḥuṣayn, and Abū Hurayra)

- Mixed: Companions and Successors (in attempt to show *ijmāʿ*, or to preponderate the *athar*-tradition decree of a Companion, or simply by way of *taqlīd*)
  - §1402 (AH; reported by al-Sarakhsī: *āthār*-tradition decrees of Ibn ʿAbbās, Ibn ʿUmar, Ibrāhīm, and the companions of ʿAbd Allāh b. Masʿūd)

Incidents of Objection (*Iʿtirāḍāt*)

- *qawl al-wāḥid min al-Ṣaḥāba idhā lam yaẓhar* is not a *ḥujja* (al-Bājī)
  - §§283 (SH; *matn* of opposing *āthār*-traditions is "not confirmed by its like")
- advancing *qiyās* over *qawl al-wāḥid min al-Ṣaḥāba*
  - (Bāj.V.1)
    - §1316 (AY/MIH)
- conveyance of *khilāf* from one of the Companions
  - (Shīr.IV.3; Bāj.V.2)
    - §§89 (AH; implied by al-Sarakhsī's report); 90[a] (IAL; implied by al-Sarakhsī's report); 635 (AH; *khilāf* of four Companions against IAL *athar*-tradition); 636 (IAL; *khilāf* of one); 637 (IAL; *āthār*-traditions increased from one to three); 639 (SH; *khilāf* of three *āthār*-tradition decrees [same as IAL]); 640 (SH; *āthār*-traditions increased from three to four); 1061 (SH; 2x); 1319 (SH; unique "hypothetical" *iʿtirāḍ*; he maintains the same principle of *isnād*-critique against the *khilāf*-proving *athar*-tradition he brings, as he does against the *athar*-tradition he opposes); 1402 (AH; implied by al-Sarakhsī's report: *āthār*-tradition decrees of Ibn ʿAbbās and several Successors); 1405 (SH; implied; *āthār*-tradition decrees of five of the Companions)
- [Q] counter-indicates it (*yuʿāriḍuhu*) with the unambiguous text (*naṣṣ*) of Qur'ān or Sunna
  - (Shīr.IV.2)
    - §§1052 (AH; the *nuṭq* is Q.5:95; introduced by *a-lā tarā ilā*); 1061 (SH; the *nuṭq* is Q.5:95); 1078 (SH; the *nuṭq* is a Sunnaic decree); 1125 (AH; reported by al-Sarakhsī; the *nuṭq* is a Sunnaic deed)

By far the most numerous subset of *aṣl*—as opposed to *maʿqūl aṣl*—employed for both *istidlāl* and *iʿtirāḍ* in the subject-text is *āthār*-traditions of the Companions. Adding to their important role in proto-system *jadal*, I would note that transmission-oriented objections with regard to them (treated below) enjoy a significant presence in our subject-text. Moreover, objections of this kind consist of the same arguments employed against faulty transmissions of Prophetic Sunna. Such a transmission-oriented mode of *iʿtirāḍ* was not treated by our lens-texts with specific regard to *āthār*-traditions, however.

Note also that our lens-texts are concerned only with decrees of singular Companions which bear no indicant of wide-spread adherence. The convention of categorizing by one, two, or multiple Companions is my own, and has been prompted by two considerations. First, I thought it likely that—just as the solitary report (*khabar al-wāḥid*) may have more than one transmitter at any, or all, stages of transmission, requiring only a falling-short of the conditions for "unbroken, consistent transmission with multiple transmitters at every stage" (*tawātur*) to be labelled solitary (*wāḥid*)—so too might the matching decrees of two, or even three Companions still be considered in the domain of *qawl al-wāḥid min al-Ṣaḥāba*, requiring only a falling-short of the conditions of *ijmāʿ al-Ṣaḥāba* to be labelled as *wāḥid*. Any positive claims as to this supposition on my regard must await a great deal more of research and comparison, however.

A second consideration was to see, by isolating references to one or two Companions from references to multiple Companions, if some sort of pattern would emerge. To a certain extent, we might say that one has, and may be described in the following terms. The singular *athar*-tradition of a Companion constituted a kind of lower-epistemic-grade glass weight which, in the absence of stronger *adilla*-indicants, could tip the scale in favour of a particular solution to the *mas'ala* at hand. As a source for *taqlīd*, of course, it could stand on its own, but would immediately be outweighed by a stronger *dalīl*-indicant from Kitāb, Sunna, or even *qiyās* (see, e.g., §§1052, 1061, 1125, and 1316). In consonance with another *dalīl*-indicant, however, the decree of a Companion would only add to that *dalīl*-indicant's utility for epistemic justification (witness, among others, §§52; 92; 278–9; 1054). Moreover, in sufficient numbers, matching decrees of Companions might provide indication for the reinterpretation (§§242–4) or even *naskh* (implied in §1126) of Prophetic Sunna itself.

Not surprisingly, we find *āthār*-traditions of Companions playing a number of roles in *iʿtirāḍāt* outside the domain of *qawl al-wāḥid min al-Ṣaḥāba* (i.e., besides against each other, as above in the numerous instances of "conveyance of *khilāf* from one of the Companions"). Within this domain, however, a few more points are worthy of highlighting: (1) al-Shāfiʿī's epistemic devaluation of opposing *āthār*-traditions because it is "not confirmed by its like," or it is "*waḥdahu*"—unaccompanied by another *dalīl*-indicant; (2) the apparent advancing of *qiyās* over *āthār*-traditions by both Ibn Abī Laylā and al-Shāfiʿī; (3) the balancing of one *āthār*-set against another *āthār*-set we witness in §§635ff., resulting in al-Shāfiʿī's observation that *khilāf* was split down the middle between opposing Companion-sets; and (4) al-Shāfiʿī's "hypothetical" *iʿtirāḍ*, whereby he critiques his opponent's *athar*-tradition by showing he can bring one of equally problematic transmission but conveying the opposite *ḥukm*. Once again, arguments such as these go beyond mere claims that one's ruling is consonant with the decree of a Companion; they draw deeper into argument axioms of preponderance, epistemology of *qiyās*, and epistemic valuation of conveyance-modes. This is proto-system legal theory wrought in the dialectical forge, and we will revisit some of these in the next chapter. At present, I will turn to the second superset of Indicants in Consonance with God's Law (*adillat Sharʿiyya*), the *maʿqūl aṣl* and its subsets of *faḥwā al-khiṭāb*, *dalīl al-khiṭāb*, *maʿnā al-khiṭāb*, etc.

Laḥn al-Khiṭāb *(the Unspoken Implication of the Instruction)*, Faḥwā al-Khiṭāb *(the* A Fortiori *Signification of the Instruction)*, Dalīl al-Khiṭāb *(the [Restrictive] Indicant of the Instruction)*, *and* al-Ḥaṣr *(Restriction)*

Nothing corresponding to *laḥn al-khiṭāb* or *al-ḥaṣr* was encountered in the course of analyses. This indicates nothing more than the absence of *adilla*-indicants with contended features relevant to these categories in the relatively few *masāʾil* of *ikhtilāf* fully explored in the current project. Nor are the merely singular occurrences of *faḥwā al-khiṭāb* and *dalīl al-khiṭāb*—and those only in the domain of *istidlāl*—particularly indicative of anything by their low representation.[16] As for the former, recall that al-Shāfiʿī's opponent was reported as arguing, from Sunnaic basis: "When the killing of female polytheists, who do not believe, is forbidden; then it is all the more appropriate (*awlā*) that the female believer who apostatizes from Islam should not be killed" (§1320). This is *faḥwā al-khiṭāb* of the species *a minore ad maius*, where the *khiṭāb* is the Prophet's, and he "cites the lesser (*adnā*) and [thus] draws attention to the greater (*aʿlā*)." And as for the latter, we have seen al-Shāfiʿī himself infer from the *naṣṣ* of Q.2:282—whereby God allows "debt [tied] to a 'designated' term (*dayn ilā ajal musamman*)"—that God does not allow debt tied to an *un*designated term (*dayn ilā ajal ghayr musamman*) (§91).[17] This is *dalīl al-khiṭāb*, and, as we recall, it bore the additional stamp of conforming to Ibn Surayj's stipulation that God's *khiṭāb* be expressed via a conditional expression (*lafẓ al-sharṭ*).

---

[16] There are further occurrences of each of these latter in other presentation categories, see the "additional elements" section below.

[17] Of note, too, is that al-Shāfiʿī further supported his argument with *tafsīr*-explanation via *dalāla*-indication from other verses: Q.2:189, 22:28, 2:233.

Maʿnā al-Khiṭāb, fa-huwa al-Qiyās (the Intension-Property of the Instruction—Meaning Correlational Inference)

Incidents of Drawing Indication (*Istidlālāt*)

- *Qiyās al-ʿIlla* (Correlational Inference of the Occasioning Factor)
  - *Jalī* (Clearly-Disclosed)
    - §§274–5 (AH; efficient property indicated; al-Ṭabarī reports *aṣl* and *ʿilla* and that *aṣl* enjoys sanction of *ijmāʿ al-kull*); 691 (SH; *ʿilla* of two efficient properties; *aṣl* is *ijmāʿ*); 1075 (SH; *al-qiyās ʿalā al-ijmāʿ*)
  - undetermined subtype
    - §§35 (SH; *ʿilla* and *aṣl* clearly indicated); 1310 (AH; *ʿilla* and *aṣl* reported by al-Sarakhsī); 1311 (IAL; *aṣl* reported by al-Sarakhsī)
- *Qiyās al-ʿAks* (Correlational Inference of The Opposite)
  - §1410 (SH; *ʿilla* and *aṣl* clearly indicated; *aṣl* is clarified by a *mufassir*-hermeneutic combining *istidlāl biʾl-Kitāb* with *istidlāl biʾl-Sunna*)
- Type I *Qiyās al-Dalāla* (Correlational Inference of Indication)
  - §§540 (SH; hypothetical; in context of method-*naqḍ*, showing what SHAR should have done to be consistent in his *qiyās*-method); 643 (SHAR of Ahl al-Kalām; via three *endoxa khiṣāl: ḥukm* A, *ḥukm* B, and "nominal" *waṣf*)[18]
- Type III *Qiyās al-Dalāla*: *Qiyās al-Shabah* (Correlational Inference of Resemblance)
  - §§157 (SH); 277 (IAL/AY; *aṣl* introduced via *a-lā tarā*; *aṣl* and *aḥkām* supported by *āthār*-traditions; al-Ṭabarī reports *aṣl* and *ʿilla* and that *aṣl* enjoys sanction of *ijmāʿ al-kull*); 286 (SHAQ; same as IAL/AY in §277)
- Indeterminate Type of *Qiyās*
  - §§785 (SH); 1125 (AH; reported by al-Sarakhsī); 1126 (IAL/[old] AY; reported by al-Sarakhsī); 1128 (SHAR); 1130 (SHAR); 1316 (AY/MIH; *aṣl* is Sunnaic prohibition)

Incidents of Objection (*Iʿtirāḍāt*)

- against *ʿilla*-justification by way of the name (*al-taʿlīl biʾl-ism*), Type 1 (al-Baṣrī)
  - §649 (SH; note that his opponent, who is doing *qiyās* based on the *ism al-ubuwwa*, is of the Ahl al-Kalām)
- Denying the Property (*manʿ al-waṣf/mumānaʿa fiʾl-waṣf*); in the branch-case (*farʿ*):
  - (Shīr.VII.4; Bāj.IX.6.1.2)
    - §§89 (AH; implied); 90[a] (IAL; implied); 155 (SH); 662 (SH; this *masʾala* cannot be a *farʿ*, because it shares no *maʿnā* with an *aṣl*)

(continued)

[18] Note the similarity between the anonymous opponent's usage of *khaṣla/khiṣāl* and al-Shīrāzī's usage of *khaṣīṣa*.

- *Jawāb*: *tafsīr*-explanation and *dalāla*-indication
    - §89 (AH; implied by al-Sarakhsī's report)
- Professing the compelling agency of the occasioning factor (*al-Qawl bi-mūjib al-ʿilla)*:
    - (Shīr.VII.9.2; Bāj.IX.8)
        - §90[a] (IAL; implied by al-Sarakhsī's report)
- Inconsistency (*Naqḍ*) (Shīr.VII.7)
    - when [R's] *ʿilla* is posited for the genus (*wuḍiʿa liʾl-jins*), being in the position (*manzila*) of the definition (*ḥadd*)
        - (Bāj.IX.B.11.1)
            - §§693–700 (SH); 700–703 (SH); 702 (SH) [sequence = components of "*naqḍ*-dilemma" which is sprung in §§703–4]; 740–1 (SH; rhetorical *elenchus* in §741; SHAR is silenced); 743 (SH; double *naqḍ*; *masāʾil al-naqḍ* delivered by *a-raʾayta*); 1125 (AH and/or al-Sarakhsī; *a-lā tarā* introduces *masʾalat al-naqḍ*)
    - when [R's] *ʿilla* is posited for the affirmation of rulings for individuals (*wuḍiʿa li-ithbāt al-aḥkām fiʾl-aʿyān*)
        - (Bāj.IX.B.11.2.1)
            - §§536 (SH; double charge of *naqḍ*)
                - *Jawāb*: "[R] does not concede to the *masʾalat al-naqḍ*"
                    - §1230 (SHAR)
- Reversal (*Qalb*)
    - (Shīr.VII.14.1) or (Bāj.IX.B.9.1.2)
        - Reversal by way of an intended ruling (*Qalb bi-Ḥukm Maqṣūd*) or Reversal of one/some of the properties of the occasioning factor (*qalb bi-baʿḍ awṣāf al-ʿilla*)
            - §651 (SH); 653 (SH; *a-raʾayta*); 655–60 (SH; hypothetical *qalb* in stages)
- Lack of Efficiency (*ʿAdam al-taʾthīr*)
    - for a property (*waṣf*) such as which the *ʿilla* is not destroyed by its removal; this is called "stuffing" (*ḥashw*)
        - (Shīr.VII.6.2; Bāj.IX.B.14.2)
            - §1129 (SH; SHAR's *waṣf* shown to have no relevance to efficiency of the *ʿilla*)
- Invalid Compatibility-Comparison (*Fasād al-iʿtibār*)
    - for what is known by way of the authoritative source-cases (*uṣūl*)
        - (Shīr.VII.12.2.2; Bāj.IX.B.10.2.2)
            - §§78 (SH; foreshadowed); 80 (SH; *aṣl* may not serve as an *aṣl* due to general *farq*-distinction demonstrated in a number of *masāʾil al-furūq*); 1316 (AY/MIH; NB: this is the very example we find in the *jadal*-theory texts); 1320 (SHAR; implied)
                - *Jawāb*: confirmation of *taswiya* between *aṣl* and *farʿ*
                    - §1326 (SH; NB: this is the very *jawāb* we find in al-Bājī)

(continued)

- Counter-Indication (*Muʿāraḍa*)
  - Counter-Indication with a Divinely-Sanctioned Decree (*al-Muʿāraḍa bi'l-Nuṭq*)
    - (Shīr.VII.15.1; Bāj.IX.B.15.1)
      - §§37 (SH; the *nuṭq* is Sunnaic judgment); 64–5 (SH; opponent's attempted *qiyās* from an exception-*khabar*-report is blocked by *tafsīr*-explanation and argument from Sunnaic *adilla*-indicants); 276 (IAL; implied; the *nuṭq* is Sunnaic deed); 282 (SH; the *nuṭq* [x2] is Sunnaic proscription and deed); 288 (SH; the *nuṭq* is Sunnaic proscription); 703 (SH; the *nuṭq* is *ijmāʿ*); 1219 (SH; implied); §1225 (SH; the *nuṭq* is Sunnaic deed)
  - Counter-Indication of *qiyās* by *qiyās* (al-Baṣrī); or Counter-Indication with a Self-Initiated Occasioning Factor (*al-Muʿāraḍa bi-ʿIlla Mubtada'a*)
    - (Shīr.VII.15.2.1; Bāj.IX.B.15.2.1)
      - §§155 and 157 (SH); 691 (SH; implied); 1125 (AH and/or al-Sarakhsī); 1126 (IAL/[old] AY; implied)
  - Counter-Indication with the Occasioning Factor of the Source-Case—which is Invalidating Distinction (*al-muʿāraḍa bi-ʿillat al-aṣl wa huwa al-farq*); by way of Correlational Inference of the Occasioning Factor (*al-Farq bi-Qiyās al-ʿIlla*); by way of the Occasioning Factor of the Ruling (*farq bi-ʿillat al-ḥukm*)
    - (Shīr.VII.15.2.2.1; Bāj.IX.B.15.2.2.1.1)
      - §§64 (SH; hypothetical; were it not for the exception-*khabar*-report, SH would supplant opponent's *ʿilla* with that derived from "the *aṣl* of our *madhhab*"); 277 (IAL/AY; *ʿilla* reported by al-Ṭabarī); 1310 (AH; strongly indicated by al-Sarakhsī's report); 1311 (IAL; suggested by al-Sarakhsī's report)
  - Invalidating Distinction by way of Correlational Inference of Indication (*al-Farq bi-Qiyās al-Dalāla*)
    - (Shīr.VII.15.2.2.2.1; Bāj.IX.B.15.2.2.2.1)
      - §§662–7 (SH; hypothetical)
  - Invalidating Distinction by way of Correlational Inference of Resemblance (*al-Farq bi-Qiyās al-Shabah*)
    - (Shīr.VII.15.2.2.3; Bāj.IX.B.15.2.2.2.4)
      - §288 (SH; hypothetical [he does not actually believe *qiyās* obtains here])
  - Indeterminate subtype of *muʿāraḍat al-ʿilla bi'l-ʿilla*
    - (Shīr.VII.15.2; Bāj.IX.B.15.2)
      - §§1218[b] (AY); 1406 (SHAQ; his *qiyās* having been performed by the "younger set" of Companions)
  - Indeterminate type of *farq*-distinction

(continued)

- §§1125 (AH and/or al-Sarakhsī; *zinā* is *makhṣūṣ* among its *naẓā'ir*); 1131 (SH; *farq-distinction* between SHAR's *aṣl* and *far'*; but SH's overall objection appears to be *mu'āraḍa bi'l-nuṭq*); 1219 (SH; implied); 1228ff. (SH; *farq-distinction* against SHAQ's *qiyās al-dalāla*; but SH's overall objection appears to be *mu'āraḍa bi'l-nuṭq*)

Modes of Preponderance (*Tarjīḥāt*)

- Indeterminate Preponderance of (Potentially-Efficient) Intension-Properties (*Tarjīḥ al-Ma'ānī*):
  - §§236 (AH; implied); 238 (IAL; implied); 245[a] (SH; implied)

This remarkable array of *qiyās*-oriented *istidlālāt* and *i'tirāḍāt* should impress upon the reader a number of important points, not least of which is a confirmation of Hallaq's observation: "*Qiyās*, the primary method of legal reasoning in Islamic law, is indeed the focal point of dialectic."[19] From what we see in the subject-text, this was just as true in the second/eighth century as it was in al-Baṣrī's day, and after. Even in the limited number of *masā'il* analyzed, nearly the full gamut of al-Shīrāzī's *qiyās* typology is represented, along with a significant number of *qiyās*-oriented *i'tirāḍāt*, including the full range of *mu'āraḍāt*. Such a showing speaks volumes for the sophistication of proto-system *jadal*, and demands further exploration of *qiyās*-oriented justifications and objections in the treatises of the *Umm*. The window has barely been cracked open in this regard.

Although expressed in a different language of *ma'nā*-intensions/qualities, or indirectly through markers such as "because it is X" (*li'annahu* X), and "just like Y" (*kamā* Y), etc., with the terms *'illa* and *waṣf* entirely absent,[20] and attribute (*ṣifa*) occurring only in a non-technical sense, and none of the language of *ṭard* and *'aks*, *jarayān* and *ta'thīr*; despite this, all of it, the proto-system method of *qiyās* revealed in our subject-text was very nearly as complex in *practice* as the full-system methods which theorists would formulate centuries later. What we may observe in the table above is ample evidence to support a premise which motivated the research and writing of this monograph: philological studies of legal-theoretical terms, and the comparison of these terms between earlier and later periods, are—though important ventures in a larger study—insufficient, by themselves, for the task of revealing the real nature of proto-system legal theory and disputation. We must also analyze the argumentation of early jurists in order to understand the relative sophistication and development of their methods. And nowhere is this more urgent than in the domains of *qiyās*-oriented justification and objection.

---

[19] "Treatise," p. 200.

[20] *'Illa* in fact does occur in §1045, but in the sense of "sickness" (*maraḍihim wa 'illatihim*). Note, however, that it is not entirely absent from the *Umm* in a technical, legal-theoretical sense; see Appendix II.§1417 in part 2 of my dissertation.

I will briefly highlight a number of features before moving on. As for *istidlāl* by way of *qiyās*, there are several items of note, including: (1) al-Shāfiʿī's frequent resort to "hypothetical" *qiyās*, when he does not believe *qiyās* to obtain in the *mas'ala* at hand, but nevertheless pursues a *qiyās*-method "for argument's sake" in order to problematize his opponent's reasoning; (2) an anonymous opponent from the Ahl al-Kalām employs the term *khaṣla/khiṣāl* in much the same way that al-Shīrāzī employs the term *khaṣīṣa/khaṣā'iṣ*, both in the domain of *qiyās al-dalāla*; and (3) the relevant frequency with which *uṣūl* for *qiyās* are sanctioned by *ijmāʿ*.

As for *iʿtirāḍāt*, first note that the opponent from the Ahl al-Kalām performs *qiyās* based, in part, on the *ism al-ubuwwa*, and that al-Shāfiʿī refutes him in a manner later suggested by al-Baṣrī. Considering that: (1) al-Baṣrī is our only *jadal*-theorist to treat *al-taʿlīl bi'l-ism* as a domain for *iʿtirāḍ*, and (2) he was also a significant figure in the history of the Muʿtazila, one might ask: was *al-taʿlīl bi'l-ism* a technique particularly employed by dialectical theologians from the second century through to al-Baṣrī's day? This question cannot be pursued in this study, but I would mark *al-taʿlīl bi'l-ism* as a site for potential (and early) cross-germination between speculative and normative epistemic projects. I would further note the astonishing frequency of charges of *naqḍ*, *qalb*, *fasād al-waḍʿ*, and *farq*-distinction, along with the numerous arguments by which *ʿilla* and *qiyās* are supplanted by way of *muʿāraḍa*. Many of these instances are accompanied by our familiar *ra'ā* formulae, and there is every reason to believe the frequent occurrences of *a-ra'ayta* and *a-lā tarā* among the earlier jurists (Abū Ḥanīfa, Ibn Abī Laylā, Abū Yūsuf, and al-Shaybānī)—blocked from deeper analysis by the terseness of the text—are nevertheless a sign that the general rubric of *reductio* arguments to which they are currently restricted was in fact populated by a number of distinctive and well-honed objection-types.

Istiṣḥāb al-Ḥāl *(Presumption of Continuity of the Legal* Status Quo Ante*)*

We have encountered little which may be claimed—and that only with hesitancy—by the domain of *Istiṣḥāb al-Ḥāl*. This is not surprising; it has been asserted, in the main, that the principle of *istiṣḥāb* is absent from the legal theory of al-Shāfiʿī.[21] In addition to this, a number of secondary works concerned with early

[21] See Y. Linant de Bellefonds in the *EI*[2] (s.v. "*Istiṣḥāb*"), who observes: "The s̲h̲āfiʿīs gave *istiṣḥāb* a much weightier significance than did the Ḥanafīs, which explains why this method of juridical reasoning has been generally, though erroneously, associated with s̲h̲āfiʿī teaching. The word *istiṣḥāb* does not even appear in the *Umm* of the Imām al-s̲h̲āfiʿī and he had recourse to the concept on one occasion only, without naming it (Schacht, *Origins*, 126)." Following this reference to Schacht's *Origins*, we read: "Shāfiʿī applies this principle in *Umm*, iv. 170 without, however, using the term *istiṣḥāb*; he obviously regards it as part of *qiyās* and 'reason' (*maʿqūl*)." After pursuing

legal theory do not appear to treat *istiṣḥāb* at all,[22] while more comprehensive histories do not treat of its origins, but only later manifestations.[23] Muṣṭafā al-Khinn, on the other hand, provides no less than five *masā'il*—claiming there are many more—in which the practice of *istiṣḥāb* by early *mujtahids* is supposedly made clear. Moreover, most of his examples begin with an argument by al-Shāfiʿī.[24] With a singular exception, however, I have not found al-Khinn's examples to support this claim.[25] The exception occurs in a *mas'ala* treating the inheritance of the missing party (*irth al-mafqūd*), and not only shows al-Shāfiʿī adhering to an *istiṣḥāb*-like principle, but is followed by an illuminating dialectical sequence.[26] Moreover, the same *mas'ala* has served as one of the more common illustrations for *istiṣḥāb*.[27]

Returning to our subject-text, I have discovered only one instance of something resembling *istiṣḥāb*: in §700, al-Shāfiʿī employs the term *ẓāhir* in a way which may be interpreted as a "sensory status quo." That is, in the absence of *bayyina*-evidence, one must assume the original state of a household object to be "jointly-possessed" between husband and wife. This might relate to an early conception of *istiṣḥāb al-ḥāl*; on the other hand, it occurs in a *qiyās*-oriented debate, and al-Shāfiʿī's own *qiyās* (stated in §691) is from an *aṣl* sanctioned by *ijmāʿ*. I would be hesitant—despite the *istiṣḥāb*-like qualities of al-Shāfiʿī's "*ẓāhir*" in this case—to locate his reasoning outside the domain of *istidlāl bi'l-qiyās*. At present, I think it more probable that *istiṣḥāb* has its real theoretical origins sometime in the century or two following al-Shāfiʿī, though it is very likely to have evolved from an analysis of *masā'il* of *ikhtilāf* such as that mentioned by al-Khinn above, which afterwards remained a key illustrative example.

---

this reference in the Būlāq edition of the *Umm*, I find it difficult to reconcile Schacht's note with the material therein. Al-Shāfiʿī's *istidlāl* throughout the cited passage is from Sunna and Qur'ān—*qiyās* and *maʿqūl* are not mentioned, and I am uncertain where this unnamed *istiṣḥāb* is thought to have occurred. On the other hand, recall that al-Bājī's discussion of *Istiṣḥāb al-Ḥāl* included a short section on related but erroneous modes of *istidlāl*. The third of these was attributed to al-Shāfiʿī himself: "*istidlāl*—by way of the absence of a *dalīl*-indicant for a thing—for the negation of that thing." Al-Bājī concludes that what al-Shāfiʿī is doing in such cases is actually presumption of continuity of a *status quo ante* for absolution from obligation (*istiṣḥāb al-ḥāl fī barā'at al-dhimma*).

[22] Among them, Hallaq, *Origins*; Hasan, *Early Development*; Lowry, *Early Islamic Legal History*; Vishanoff, *Formation* (with a single reference to *istiṣḥāb*, and only in a Ẓāhirī context).

[23] E.g., Schacht, *Introduction* (p. 21; saying only that it is "derived from Jewish law"); Coulson, *History*; Hallaq, *History*; Kamali, *Principles*.

[24] *Athar al-Ikhtilāf*, pp. 543–9.

[25] See my dissertation ("Dialectical Forge," pt. 1, p. 430–1) for an account.

[26] Khinn, *Athar al-Ikhtilāf*, pp. 546f.; referencing *Umm*, Būlāq ed., vol. 4, p.4.

[27] See, among others, Coulson, *History*, pp. 92–3; and Kamali, *Principles*, p. 389. Kamali treats the *mas'ala* under the category of "continuity of attributes" (*istiṣḥāb al-waṣf*).

Proto-System Istidlālāt *and* Iʿtirāḍāt *Expanded to Other Domains*

Certain objections we encountered in the subject-text corresponded well with lens-text categories, but enjoyed a broader range of application in proto-system *jadal* than in the discussions of later theorists; I will review these briefly before proceeding to the proto-system's unique dialectical moves. We have seen *naqḍ* and *manʿ* applied in the domain of *istidlāl bi'l-Sunna*, whereas they are both confined to the domain of *qiyās* in our lens-texts. We have also seen transmission-oriented objections employed against *istidlāl* from the *āthār*-traditions of Companions, whereas we do not find them within this domain of the *jadal*-theory works—there, they are restricted to the domain of *istidlāl bi'l-Sunna*. I will list these expanded-range objections here, along with modes of *istidlāl* which appear, as components of objection, outside their lens-text domains.

Naqḍ in Domains Besides Qiyās al-ʿIlla

- Against *al-istidlāl bi'l-Sunna*
  - cf. (Shīr.VII.7; Bāj.IX.B.11.2.1)
    - §263 (SH)
- Against Type I *qiyās al-dalāla*
  - §646–7 (SH; more likely a method-*naqḍ*; inconsistency pushed in §647 with *a-ra'ayta*)
- Against Type III *qiyās al-dalāla*
  - §649 (SH; 3x; the "nominal" *waṣf* is present in three *masā'il al-naqḍ*, but not the *ḥukm* of transfer; thus, the *waṣf* is not efficient)

Manʿ in the Domain of Istidlāl bi'l-Sunna

- denial of the ruling in the source-case (*manʿ al-ḥukm fi'l-aṣl; mumānaʿa fī ḥukm al-aṣl*)
  - cf. (Shīr.VII.3; Bāj.IX.B.5)
    - §248 (SH)

Transmission-Oriented Objections in the Domain of Qawl al-Wāḥid min al-Ṣaḥāba

- "its like is not confirmed by the Ahl al-Ḥadīth"
  - (indeterminate, but resembles: Shīr.II.B; Bāj.II.1 [against *isnād* for Sunna])
    - §§283 (SH); §1318 (SH)

Tarjīḥ in the Domain of _Qawl al-Wāḥid min al-Ṣaḥāba_

- *tarjīḥ* of an *athar*-tradition decree due to a Companion being closer to the Messenger of God
  - cf. (Shīr.IX.1.3)
    - §1405 (SH; implied)
- *tarjīḥ* of an *athar*-tradition decree due to more narrators
  - cf. (Shīr.IX.1.5; Bāj.XVI.1.1.3)
    - §§635 (AH; implied); 1402 (AH; implied by al-Sarakhsī's report); 1405 (SH; implied; *āthār*-tradition decrees of five Companions)
- *tarjīḥ* of an *athar*-tradition decree due to a Companion being greater in terms of companionship with the Prophet (*ṣuḥba*)
  - cf. (Shīr.IX.1.6)
    - §1405 (SH; implied)
- *tarjīḥ* of *āthār*-tradition decrees by showing they are the *qiyās*
  - cf. (Shīr.IX.2.1)
    - §§642 (Ahl al-Kalām); 651 (SH; hypothetical: if *qiyās* obtained [it doesn't], then the same properties for *qiyās* should produce a *ḥukm* closer to his own doctrine, derived from *āthār*-traditions)

These expanded categories may have several explanations. Among them is simply the possibility they were just as expanded in the practice of early *jadal* theorists, but for some reason it was not customary to treat, e.g., *naqḍ* outside the domain of *qiyās* in theoretical discourse. When we consider the systematic thoroughness of our authors, however, this explanation seems less likely than another: with far less choate and/or consensually-established legal-theoretical and dialectical bases to draw upon, it would only be natural had our proto-system jurists encountered *ikhtilāf* due to a greater variety of epistemic differences. As legal-theory grew more refined in dialectical debates, a role for *naqḍ* in the domain of Sunna may simply have disappeared. Similarly, a change in the theory and epistemic valuation of what was to become known as *qiyās al-dalāla* might have caused *naqḍ* charges to fall away. As for the use of *āthār*-traditions of the Companions in general, and the necessity for *tarjīḥ* and transmission-oriented objections regarding them, one can easily discern a decline of the whole domain over time. The role of *āthār*-traditions in full-system *jadal* and *uṣūl* theory is dwarfed by the expansive practice of our subject-text. One thing appears certain: the proto-system practice of the *Kitāb Ikhtilāf al-ʿIrāqiyyayn/ʿIrāqiyyīn*—though quite sophisticated—is less choate and in many ways dissimilar from the systems posited by early theorists. Gathering together the question types, justifications, and objections with no match in our lens-texts will make this plain.

7.2 What is Distinct: Elements More Unique to Proto-System Teaching and Practice

Proto-System Question Strategies Outside the Categories of the Lens-Texts

It was no easy task to match the question types and strategies of the subject-text to the strict procedural orderings of the lens-texts. Of particular note are objection-oriented questions, and the *Topics*-like strategy of Q's acquiring premises one at a time from R for eventual *elenchus.*

Objection-Oriented Questions (*As'ila*) and Demands (*Muṭālabāt*)[28]

- "*muṭālaba bi'l-farq*" (Q's demand for *farq*-distinction)
  - §§79 (SHAQ; "*mā farraqa bayna al-ʿitq wa ghayrihi?*"); 287 (SHAQ)
- "*muṭālaba bi'l-tarjīḥ*" (Q's demand for a decree from a Companion supporting R's *ḥadīth* interpretation: specifically, a demand for Shīr.IX.2.1)
  - §§264, 266 (SHAQ)
- "*su'āl ʿan/muṭālaba bi-wajh al-iʿtirāḍ*" (question about/demand for the mode of objection)
  - §§645 (SHAQ; eliciting the manner of SH's *iʿtirāḍ* [which is a kind of *muʿāraḍa*]); 651–2 (SHAQ; initial stages of *muṭālaba* [with SH's critique being *qalb*]); 692 (SHAQ; *muṭālaba* [with SH's critique being *ʿadam al-ta'thīr*])
- "*muṭālaba* for [*qiyās*] *al-shabah*" (Q's response to the rejection of his *aṣl*, consequent to a reinterpretation of the efficient property in the *farʿ*)
  - §156 (SHAQ challenges SH to produce a parallel among permitted *bayʿ*-contracts)

Q Procures Premise After Premise from R for *Elenchus* (in the Manner of the *Topics*)

- *elenchus* is via *tanāquḍ* (*reductio ad impossibile*):
  - sequence: §§96 (SH; via *a-ra'ayta*); 98 (SH; disjunctive question, one option absurd); 100 (SH)
  - sequence: §§249 (SH; *a-lā tarā* introduces *ḥadīth*); 250 (SHAR *jawāb* explains: this is not contradiction)

(continued)

[28] Again, categories in quotation marks, though combined from terms in the *jadal*-theory texts, are my own invention.

- *elenchus* is via *naqḍ*
  - sequence: §§693–702 (SH, 3x *naqḍ*; he subsequently springs "*naqḍ*-dilemma" in §§703–4 [NB: §694 pushes premise with *a-ra'ayta*; §696 pushes premise with "And have you not claimed—and the people claimed...?" (*a-fa-laysa qad zaʿamta wa zaʿama al-nās...?*)]
  - sequence: §§740 (SH *a-ra'ayta* pushes SHAR to rule on the *mas'alat al-naqḍ* minus a property of the *mas'ala* at hand); 741 (SH restores the property, rhetorically asks SHAR to rule again; elenchus: *naqḍ*); 742–3 (SH closes other exits with additional charges of *naqḍ*)
- *elenchus* is via hypothetical *qalb* (*qiyās* does not obtain here, but if it did...)
  - sequence: §§653 (SH; via *a-ra'ayta*); 655ff. (SH vs. SHAR); 658 (SH introduces *mas'alat al-qalb*); 660 (SH; elenchus via hypothetical *qalb*)
- *elenchus* is via hypothetical *muʿāraḍa* (*qiyās* does not obtain here, but if it did...)
  - sequence: §§662ff. (SH); 663 (SH; *a-ra'ayta* introduces Qur'ānic *aṣl*); 665 (SH; premise #2); 667 (SH; elenchus via hypothetical *muʿāraḍa*)
- *elenchus* is via *farq*-distinction and method-*naqḍ*
  - sequence: §§756–60 (SH; *farq*-distinction #1); §§761–7 (SH; *farq*-distinction #2 [NB: §§765–7 has additional charge of method-*naqḍ*]); §§768–70 (SH; *farq*-distinction #3 and #4; rhetorical elenchus via *farq*-distinction and method-*naqḍ*); §§771–3 (SH; *farq*-distinction #5; final SH elenchus via *farq*-distinction and method-*naqḍ*)
- *elenchus* is via method-*naqḍ*
  - sequence: §§1057 (SH; method-*naqḍ* premise #1); 1059 (SH; method-*naqḍ* premise #2); 1061 (SH seals method-*naqḍ* elenchus with series of rhetorical questions and supporting counter-*naql*)
  - sequence: §§1321 (SH; method-*naqḍ* premise #1 elicited by *a-ra'ayta*); 1323 (SH; method-*naqḍ* premise #2 elicited by al-Bājī's *su'āl* #3); 1325 (SH; rhetorical charge of method-*naqḍ*: inconsistent observance of the *farq*-distinction); 1326 (SH; second charge of method-*naqḍ* [for a related *mas'alat al-naqḍ*] by rhetorically bringing forth all premises as though pre-conceded by SHAR)
- SHAQ attempts *elenchus* via method-*naqḍ* (but SH succeeds in demonstrating *farq*-distinction)
  - sequence: §1224 (SHAQ; method-*naqḍ* premise #1); §1227 (SHAQ; multiple premises, then attempted elenchus: "how do you deny *qiyās* from X to Y?"); §§1228ff. (SH demonstrates *farq*-distinction between X and Y; then counters with his own charge of *naqḍ*)

As for the objection-oriented questions and demands, they would be natural to any dialectical engagement; I am uncertain why they do not enjoy independent treatment by theorists. One possible explanation is that al-Shīrāzī, et al., considered their thorough expositions on recommended responses (*ajwiba*) sufficient, without needing to elaborate a separate schema of counter-questions. In the end this genre of question and demand likely existed in the practice of theorists and their peers, but was not included in their systematizing discourse. Nevertheless, I will mark it as unique to proto-system *jadal*. Perhaps, as schemas like al-Bājī's were developed and imposed in real-time dialectical encounters, this older style of questioning the objection *qua* objection fell out of use. Once the roles of R and Q reversed due to *muʿāraḍa*, the new Q would simply proceed through the same, orderly schema his opponent had followed, testing his *muʿāraḍa* as a new, counter-*istidlāl*.

Q's *Topics*-like acquisition of premise after premise from R, then proceeding to a well-constructed *elenchus*, is a feature we might expect to find in the copious example-*masāʾil* provided by our *jadal* theorists. But we do not. Again, I suspect this was nevertheless a feature of full-system practice, but simply omitted from theory discourse. Its absence from the example-*masāʾil*, however, is difficult to explain. As a procedural style it is, of course, in full consonance with Aristotle's dialectical method. After some consideration, and picturing how a dialectical disputation following al-Bājī's procedure might appear if narrated/transcripted, I would conclude the following: the intentions and procedures of proto-system vs. full-system disputation signify—at times, but not always—distinctly different dialectical styles.

In other words, the aim and comportment of Q in questioning R was conspicuously different in al-Shāfiʿī's day than it was—assuming consistency of theory and practice—some two and a half centuries later. With regard to aim, there is a prominent proto-system concern with internal, logical contradiction—*tanāquḍ*—which simply does not figure into the theory and categories of our lens-texts.[29] In combination with the premise-gathering approach, however, it is in perfect consonance with the dialectical aims and methods of the *Topics*. In the systems of al-Shīrāzī and al-Bājī we witness something different at work. Programs for fashioning *elenchi* from R's conceded premises are not the focus; rather, Q follows an ordered procedure for probing and problematizing R's *istidlāl*, and, should R's *istidlāl* collapse, he supplants it via *muʿāraḍa*, the roles reverse, and the new Q submits him to the same program. But we also observe this in the dialectical sequences of the subject-text, with plentiful examples of *muʿāraḍa* and other features as witness.

Thus, the proto-system *jadal* of our subject-text at once incorporated *Topics* and *Minhāj* styles of dialectical method, whereas the full-system theory of our lens-texts treated only the latter. Proto-system *jadal* was, in this respect, broader with regard to method; and the significance of this for evolutionary narratives is

[29] We have seen discussions of *tanāquḍ* and "*an yanquḍa* X" among the categories terminating the debate (*aqsām al-inqiṭāʿ*) of al-Khaṭīb al-Baghdādī, al-Juwaynī, and Ibn Ḥazm. But *tanāquḍ* is not elaborated in these texts; and it finds no place (or even mention) in the core treatises of our *jadal*-theory lens.

clear. Recall the model of "common origins, parallel development, and cross-germination" proposed in Chap. 4. The "common origins" would have comprised a number of argumentation epistemes common to the pre-Islamic intellectual landscape of the Near East; some among them were patently Aristotelian, and indeed Aristotle and his commentators were directly studied and taught. With the rise of a Muslim intelligentsia, a host of Islamic axioms fused with various of these pre-existing epistemes, and new Islamic argumentation epistemes developed in numerous intellectual projects.

What we see in the dialectic of the *Ikhtilāf al-ʿIrāqiyyayn/ʿIrāqiyyīn* is an earlier stage in the development of epistemes which were eventually to become peculiar to *uṣūl al-fiqh* and juridical *jadal* theory. The broader scope of features—additional question types, strategies, objection-domains, and distinctive argument categories—exposes the proto-system as a wider collection of continually-evolving argumentation axioms, both prior and Islamic. Through the working of the dialectical forge, this wider collection became more refined, more precise, and consequently more narrow in terms of accepted and practiced axioms. Thus, although far more systematic, the full-system theory of al-Shīrāzī, al-Bājī, et al., was more restricted in terms of procedures and argument content. Among many other things, a focus on premise-by-premise construction of *elenchi* via *tanāquḍ* seems to have fallen away.

Proto-System Istidlālāt *and* Iʿtirāḍāt *Outside the* Adilla *Domains of the Lens-Texts*

Dialectical moves and strategies apparently unique to proto-system dialectic have appeared frequently. Divided into categories, they may be listed as follows:

Reported *Istiḥsān*

- §1054 (al-Sarakhsī reports IAL/AY/MIH reasoning = *istiḥsān* based on (1) *naql*: *āthār*-traditions of Companions; (2) *ʿaql*: *a fortiori* reasoning; (3) *iʿtirāḍ*: AH's *qiyās* = *qiyās al-manṣūṣ bi'l-manṣūṣ*; and (4) *ʿaql*: the *hady* can be an *ʿanāq*, etc.)

***Istidlāl/Taqlīd* of the Decree of a Successor**

- §§686–7 (AH & [old] AY; *athar*-tradition decree of Ibrāhīm al-Nakhaʿī); 1218[b] (AY; *taqlīd* of ʿUrwa b. al-Zubayr's *qiyās al-ʿilla/manzila*-subsumption; reported by al-Sarakhsī)

Objections Against *Istidlāl/Taqlīd* of the Decree of a Successor[30]

- *Naqḍ* or *Kasr*
  - cf. (Shīr.VII.7; Bāj.IX.B.11.1) and (Shīr.VII.8; Bāj.IX.B.12.2.1)
    - §688 (AY [new]; implied; 3x *naqḍ/kasr* against AH *athar*-tradition decree of Ibrāhīm)
- *Muʿāraḍa*
  - By way of *ʿilla mubtada'a*
    - cf. (Shīr.VII.15.2.1; Bāj.IX.B.15.2.1)
      - §691 (SH; implied; against the *qiyās* of Ibrāhīm and IAL)

Charges of Method-*Naqḍ*

- *endoxon qiyās*-method shown in parallel *mas'ala*, but R does not practice it in the *mas'ala* at hand; R is inconsistent with his *qiyās*-method
  - §§288 (SH); 540 (SH shows what SHAR should have done); 1227 (SHAQ; "how do you deny *qiyās* from X to Y?")
- against R's *manzila*-subsumption (same status consideration shown in parallel *mas'ala*, but R does not practice *manzila*-subsumption there)
  - §646–7 (SH; potentially a *qiyās al-dalāla*-oriented *naqḍ*; inconsistency pushed in §647 with *a-ra'ayta*)
- against R's *taswiya*-subsumption (R does not consistently observe *taswiya*-subsumption [X with Y], thus his rulings are inconsistent)
  - §§786–8 (SH; if SHAR treats X as Y, then X should belong to Y *bi-kulli ḥālin*)
    - *Jawāb*: §787 (SHAR attempts *farq*-distinction, or perhaps even *takhṣīṣ al-ʿilla*)
- against R's inconsistent observance of a *farq*-distinction
  - §§80 (SH; the opponent observes the demonstrated *farq*-distinctions elsewhere, but not in the four *masā'il* at hand); 761–7 (SH; along with *farq*-distinction #2, §§765–7 has additional charge of method-*naqḍ*; final SHAR concession is to both *farq*-distinction and method-*naqḍ*); 768–70 (SH; along with *farq*-distinction #3 and #4; rhetorical *elenchus* via *farq*-distinction and method-*naqḍ*); 771–3 (SH; *farq*-distinction #5; final SH *elenchus* via *furūq* and method-*naqḍ*); 1229 (SH; *a-lā tarā* introduces *endoxon mas'alat al-naqḍ* exposing the *farq*-distinction); §1231 (SH; double charge of method-*naqḍ* with two *masā'il al-naqḍ*); 1317ff.

(continued)

[30] The Shīrāzī and Bājī references in this and following categories are only for comparison. Equivalent chapters in the lens-texts do not exist.

(SH; SHAR is accused of ignoring a previously observed *farq*-distinction for the *mas'ala* at hand, and his *faḥwā al-khiṭāb* is thus destroyed; SHAR's methodology is attacked: he ought either to employ *faḥwā al-khiṭāb* in the *masā'il al-naqḍ*, or to *not* employ it in the *mas'ala* at hand); 1321–5 (SH gathers premises and delivers rhetorical charge of method-*naqḍ*); 1326 (SH; rhetorically states premises as though preconceded by SHAR, for second charge of method-*naqḍ*)

- R applies Qur'ānic principle elsewhere, but then ignores it for the *mas'ala* at hand
  - §§1057 (SH; multiple charges); 1057–61 (SH; collects method-*naqḍ* premises from SHAR; seals *elenchus* with rhetorical questions and counter-*naql*)
- R acknowledges *ḥadīth* elsewhere, but ignores it for the *mas'ala* at hand
  - §544 (SH; delivered via *a-lā tarā*)

"*Naqḍ* Dilemma" (Q Blocks all Exits with Multiple Charges)

- §§693–700 (SH; first charge of *naqḍ* from conceded premises); 700–703 (SH; second charge of *naqḍ* without R's response); 702 (SH; third charge of *naqḍ* without R's response); 703–4 (SH; "*naqḍ*-dilemma": if you rule X, you violate *ijmāʿ*; if you rule Y, you must do the same for the *mas'ala* at hand)

Method-*Muʿāraḍa*

- R violates a fundamental principle (by attempting *qiyās* where there is an established *khabar*-report); Q supplants R's *istidlāl bi'l-qiyās* with Q's *istidlāl bi'l-Sunna*
  - §644 (SH)

Linguistic Appeals

- Drawing a *dalīl*-indicant from Prophetic Era Poetry to determine usage of a *lafẓ*-expression
  - §262 (SH)
- Apparent argument to "customary linguistic usage" (*ʿurf al-lugha*) (= *endoxon* usage which R and Q share)
  - §647 (SH)

Modes of "Consistent Generalizing of the 'Illa"

In addition to these partly-unique modes of *istidlāl*, *iʿtirāḍ*, and multi-stage objection strategies, we have encountered a family of formulaic legal arguments evincing a marked concern for doctrinal consistency. I have called these *manzila*-subsumption, *taswiya*-subsumption, and *farq*-extension. They share many elements of the *qiyās*-oriented *istidlālāt* and *iʿtirāḍāt* of our lens-texts; but the relative uniformity with which these arguments were expressed, coupled with an absence of independent treatment by our theorists, suggests we should consider them unique to proto-system *jadal*. I have placed them all under a rubric of "Consistent Generalizing of the *ʿIlla*;" as they constitute a family of arguments sharing a singular concern.

General Arguments to *manzila*-subsumption

- §§634 (AH); 643 (SHAR); 752 (AH); 1072 (SHAQ reporting decree of one of the Ahl al-ʿIlm); 1051 (AH; clarified by report of al-Sarakhsī); 1125 (AH; reported by al-Sarakhsī); 1126 (IAL/[old] AY; reported by al-Sarakhsī); 1218 (AY; implied)

General Objections to *manzila*-subsumption

- via *muʿāraḍa bi'l-nuṭq*
    - cf. (Shīr.VII.15.1; Bāj.IX.B.15.1)
        - §1078 (SH; the *nuṭq* is a Sunnaic decree)
- via method-*naqḍ*
    - (Shīr.VII.7; Bāj.IX.B.11.1)
        - §1080 (SH; via exposing a self-inflicted "double-*farq-distinction*")
            - SH *mas'alat al-farq* #1: they claim *ḥukm* A for the legal category of the *mas'ala* at hand, but *ḥukm* ¬A for the subsuming legal category
            - SH *mas'alat al-farq* #2: they claim *ḥukm* B for the legal category of the *mas'ala* at hand, but *ḥukm* ¬B for the subsuming legal category
                - thus they are inconsistent in applying their *manzila*-subsumption to the *mas'ala* at hand
- via particularization
    - §1125 (AH and/or al-Sarakhsī; *zinā* is *makhṣūṣ* among its *naẓā'ir*)

Arguments from a Substantive Legal Principle for the Efficiency of a Quality for *manzila*-Subsumption

- from principles of legal status
  - §§744, 746 (AH; principle: partial manumission = slave in the eyes of the law)
  - §§745, 747ff. (IAL/AY/MIH; principle: partial manumission = entirely free in the eyes of the law)

Objections to a Substantive Legal Principle, or Against the Efficiency of a Quality for *manzila*-Subsumption

- against a principle of legal status
  - via *reductio* argument
    - §§748–9 (IAL/AY/MH *a-ra'ayta*; *reductio* to untenable consequence of *tanāquḍ*; and premise in larger objection of *muʿāraḍa*)
  - via *muʿāraḍa*
    - §§750–1 (AY/MIH/IAL *a-lā tarā*; delivers *aṣl* for *istidlāl bi'l-qiyās* and *muʿāraḍa*)
      - *Jawāb*: Objection to *muʿāraḍa qiyās*
        - §§755ff. (SH; *farq*-distinction employed; method-*naqḍ* employed)

Arguments to *Taswiya*-Subsumption

- §§540 (SH); 691 (SH); 1127 (SH); 1313[a] (AH & IAL, reported by AY/MIH); 1317 (SH); 1326 (SH)

Arguments to *Farq*-Extension

- §§78ff. (SH; *firāq* of *ʿitq*-manumission from all other transactions); 755ff. (SH); 1232 (SH; implied); 1321ff. (SH)

A final assessment regarding *manzila*-subsumption, *taswiya*-subsumption, and *farq*-extension: all of these categories constitute a sort of "super-*qiyās*" whereby the efficient properties relevant to the *mas'ala* at hand are brought into relationship with a larger genus of *masā'il*, or a category of substantive rulings. For *manzila*-subsumption, to say that X is in the *manzila* of Y for all Z is to say that X and Y share the relevant efficient properties occasioning the same *ḥukm* throughout the category of Z. For *taswiya*-subsumption, to say that "*hādhā kulluhu sawā'un*," is to claim that the stated set of *masā'il* share the same efficient properties necessary to constitute an *'illa* occasioning the same *ḥukm* for each *mas'ala* in that set. And as for *farq*-extension, to demand the *farq*-distinction between two types of legal entity be observed across relevant genera of substantive rulings is to simultaneously extend two sets of opposing *'illa*s occasioning opposing *ḥukms* across those genera. All three categories are marked by a concern with consistency and an aversion to intra-doctrinal contradiction; and I would claim that all three are prompted, in the end, by an anticipation of *naqḍ* and its avoidance.

Objections to Objections

I have presented objection-oriented questions and demands as a special feature of the dialectic of the *Ikhtilāf al-'Irāqiyyayn/'Irāqiyyīn*. Here I will review a similar category of objections to objections, of which there are two species. The samples for both belong to al-Shāfi'ī.

- Objection to an Objection Against a Substantive Principle for *Manzila*-Subsumption
  - via *Farq*-distinction between opponent's *qiyās* for *mu'āraḍa* and the *mas'ala* at hand
    - §§756–60 (SH; *farq*-distinction #1 [partial ownership vs. partial marriage] in stages, with rhetorical *elenchus*); 761–7 (SH; *farq*-distinction #2 [*kitāba* for divorce vs. *kitāba* for manumission] in stages, §§765–7 has additional charge of method-*naqḍ*; with final SHAR concession to *elenchus* via *farq*-distinction and method-*naqḍ*); 768–70 (SH; *farq*-distinction #3 [joint-ownership of wife vs. joint-ownership of slave] and *farq*-distinction #4 [gifting of wife vs. gifting of slave]; rhetorical *elenchus* via *farq*-distinction and method-*naqḍ*); 771–3 (SH; *farq*-distinction #5 [master re-enslaving slave vs. husband re-marrying wife; introduced by *a-ra'ayta*]; final SH statement seals *elenchus* via *furūq* and method-*naqḍ*: "we don't know of anything more distant from it, than what he correlated it with" [*fa-mā na'lamu shay'an ab'ada mimmā qāsahu bihi minhu*])
- Objection to a Charge of *Fasād al-I'tibār* Against *Qiyās*
  - via method-*naqḍ* (opponent who charged *fasād al-i'tibār* is accused of inconsistent observance of a *farq*-distinction)
    - §§1321ff. (SH)

Arguments of a More Ancient Tenor

I will now turn to arguments and features of our subject-text which appear most unique of all; and gathering them together has served to highlight the more antique character they exude. In this way, they draw closer to prior argumentation epistemes, infused with Islamic axioms, which lay at the root of juridical *jadal*'s long developmental history. Whatever their origins, if such could ever be traced, one thing is certain: the categories which follow receive no theoretical treatment by our *jadal* theorists. Nor have I yet detected them in the example-*masā'il* our lens-texts provide.

Tanāquḍ[31]

- Purely internal logical contradiction [R's solution asserts both X and ¬X]
  - "your doctrine is contradictory" (*fa qawluka mutanāqiḍ*):
    - §102 (SH; with demonstration of the *tanāquḍ*)
  - "...I found their doctrine self-contradicting" (*wajadtu ma'a dhālika qawlahum mutanāqiḍ*):
    - §1079 (SH; he clearly shows the two contradictory premises of the opposing solution, then announces the consequence: "they have not adhered to their doctrine, but have contradicted it [*mā lazimū qawlahum wa laqad naqaḍūhu*]")
- R's *istidlāl* from a *dalīl*-indicant contradicts the *ma'nā*-intension of that *dalīl-indicant* [He derives ¬X from X]
  - "no one who professes this doctrine finds a way out from [self-contradiction]" (*wa lā yajidu aḥadun qāla bi-hādhā al-qawl makhrajan min* [*tanāquḍ*])
    - §§249, 251 (SH)
  - "[*dalīl*-indicant X] does not possibly carry but one of two *ma'nā*-intensions, and you have contradicted them both together (*qad khālaftahumā ma'an*)" (while simultaneously claiming *dalīl*-indicant X)
    - §263 (SH; 2x)
- R's *istidlāl* contradicts *endoxa adilla*-indicants (which we assume R to have pre-conceded)
  - "I know not a single one of the people saved from contradicting the Prophet (*lam arā ba'ḍ al-nās salima min khilāf al-nabī*)... in either of the two matters—neither the one who sanctioned [X and Y], together, nor the one who proscribed [X and Y], together" (because the Prophet made X *ḥalāl* and Y *ḥarām*)
    - §282 (SH)

[31] We have seen *tanāquḍ* mentioned by al-Juwaynī and Ibn Ḥazm, but only as a "sign of defeat;" to my knowledge, *tanāquḍ* and "*qawl mutanāqiḍ*" receive no theoretical treatment.

General *Reductio* Arguments

- §§37 (SH; impossible result consequent to the application of IAL's ruling); 263 (SH; two consequences of opponent's solution combine to produce absurdity); 64 (SH; impossible result consequent to the application of SHAR's ruling); 275 (AH; delivered by *a-ra'ayta*; hypothetical); 748–9 (IAL/AY/MH; premises delivered with *a-ra'ayta*; conclusion with *kayfa*; rhetorical);[32] 753 (AH; *a-ra'ayta* introduces triple *reductio* barrage; rhetorical); 1057 (SH; two consequences of opponent's *qiyās* are absurd)
- plus, the relevant (in sequence) *ra'ā* formulae arguments reviewed at the end of Chap. 6

Argumentum ad Verecundiam **(Paralleling Appeals to Aristotle's *endoxa* Set of "the Wise")**

- Appeals to the Ahl al-Ḥadīth
  - §§283; 667; 1318–19 (SH)
- Appeals to the Ḥuffāẓ
  - §1119 (SH)
- Appeals to the method of the Ahl al-Fiqh
  - §284 (SH)
- Appeals to the Ahl al-ʿIlm
  - §§1072–4 (SHAQ, 3x)

Q's Objection to R's Affirming the Consequent (Aristotle's Fallacy of Consequent)

- §284 (SH; opponent implies that Companions' ruling X confirms that the Prophet ruled X)

Q's Objection to R's *Petitio Principii* or Mistaken Cause

- §284 (SH; using the verb *yaghlaṭu*, claims opponent has reversed *aṣl* X and *farʿ* Y, making Y the *aṣl* for X)

---

[32] NB: this is the logical axiom of non-contradiction extended into a question of legal status: status X and status ¬X cannot combine in a single individual. This constitute a "proof by contradiction" in legal argument.

a fortiori Argument (Outside the Domain of *faḥwā al-khiṭāb*)

- §64 (SH; hypothetical; the *aṣl madhhabinā* forbids partial X; all the more so should full X be forbidden in the *mas'ala* at hand [if not for the exception-making *khabar*-report])
- §743 (SH; sealing a triple-charge of *naqḍ* with an "*a fortiori* punch": "*laqad ankarū aqall min hādhā*" (i.e., SH's opponents have rejected less invalid contracts, all the more so should they reject invalid *mufāwaḍa*)

The Charge of *Taḥakkum*: R's Reasoning Rendered Arbitrary via Lack of *Dalāla*-Indication

- §1116 (SH; "And should we say: [opposing opinion X]? This is arbitrariness!" (*fa-amma an naqūl* [X], *fa-hādhā taḥakkum*!)
  - *naqḍ* via *e silentio*:
    - §1118 ("He should say [X] about [Y]. But there is no such doctrine." [*wa laysa hākadhā bi-qawlin*])

Empirical Inductive Argument

- §91 (SH; with *lā narā*; *ʿaṭā'*-distribution never comes but early or late)

Arguments to the Maʿqūl, *Appeals to Legal Theory, and Caliphal Imposition*

In addition to the many categories of questions, *istidlālāt*, and *iʿtirāḍāt* both within and without the domains of our lens-texts, there are three additional argument-categories worthy of note. The first has every appearance of an ancient category of "indicants of God's Law" (*adillat al-Sharʿ*), though its true nature has remained elusive thus far: it is the *maʿqūl* and the *ʿaql*, a combined source-category which seems to belong to al-Shāfiʿī alone. The second is what I have termed "open appeals to legal theory," all of which constitute a genus of dialectical argument, and all examples of which, once again, belong to al-Shāfiʿī. The third feature is not an argument, but must be included as an element of interest in proto-system *jadal*—for it brought a *mujtahid* and *qāḍī* to change his practice and profess a different opinion. The decree of the first ʿAbbāsid caliph shifted Ibn Abī Laylā from agreement (*ittifāq*) to disagreement (*ikhtilāf*) with Abū Ḥanīfa.

Arguments to *al-Maʿqūl* and *al-ʿAql*

- objection: the opponent has violated the *ʿaql* (among other sources)
  - §651 (SH)
- objection: the opponent has violated the *maʿqūl* (among other sources)
  - §1056 (SH)
- objection: "the *aṣl* of the *maʿqūl* was that nothing is made lawful for [party X] through the action of [party Y]"; and "it was not permitted that we do *qiyās* from [God's exception] for what diverges from it, if the *aṣl* belongs to what is rationally understood (*maʿqūl fīhi*)"
  - §1411 (SH)

Open Appeals to Legal Theory

- §52–3 (SH asserts hermeneutic: Sunna is *al-naṣṣ al-mufassira* providing indicant for (*tadullu ʿalā*) *jumla* Sunna; he then explains this hermeneutic at work in the *mas'ala* at hand)
- §248 (SH; "two [transmitters]—when they concur on the transmission on Jābir's authority, while the third is in concordance with them—are superior in affirming the *ḥadīth*, to when it diverges from the third")
- §257 (SH explains multiple applications of a focal *lafẓ*-expression; then acknowledges the need for a Prophetic *dalīl*-indicant to back his usage)
- §263 (SH criticizes SHAQ for not bringing *dalāla*-indication about the Prophet [i.e., SHAQ—unlike SH—brings no *dalīl*-indicant for his particularization of the focal *lafẓ*-expression])
- §265: (SH asserts: "Nor would it harm us, anyway—since it is confirmed on the authority of the Prophet...—if no one at all [among the Companions] professes it." The principle is that an established *ḥadīth* can stand alone; this is also a refutation of an *e silentio* argument.)
- §283 (SH; "And as for what was narrated concerning [Companions X and Y], that they [did Z]: it is neither confirmed by its like, nor by the Ahl al-Ḥadīth. But if anything is confirmed regarding someone with the Prophet...: [it is] decisive proof (*ḥujja*).")
- §284 (SH; *qiyās* is done for those beneath the Prophet, on the basis of what the Prophet did; not the reverse [i.e., we cannot presume to know the Prophet's commands based only upon *āthār*-traditions of the Companions])
- §§1410ff. (SH *istidlāl biʾl-Sunna* [as *mufassir* to Qur'ān] = Prophet clarifies [*bayyana*] God's *decree*: *nikāḥ* means the licit sexual intercourse of the intervening husband [*iṣābat al-zawj*])
- §1411 (SH; "it was not permitted that we do *qiyās* from [God's exception] for what diverges from it, if the *aṣl* belongs to what is rationally understood [*maʿqūl fīhi*]")

Caliphal Decree Alters *Mujtahid*'s Doctrine and/or Practice as *Qāḍī*

- §240 (IAL; forced to adhere to the doctrine of the Ḥijāzīs by al-Saffāḥ)

Formulae of Subsumption, Extension, and Objection

Having reviewed the genera and species of dialectical argument encountered during analyses of the subject-text's dialectical sequences, I would quickly note one last outstanding feature. With regard to several of the categories above—and noticeable throughout the whole of our subject-treatise—there is a remarkable formulaic consistency. The scripting of Q&A sequences, the presentation (and extension) of prior substantive rulings, and Abū Yūsuf's adherence to one doctrine or another require little in the way of comment—they speak for themselves, and provide insight to the nascent proto-system of the "science of disagreement" (*ʿilm al-khilāf*). But many families of argument also enjoy a considerable consistency of presentation, shedding light on a hidden *method*—the *ṭarīqa*—of proto-system *jadal* teaching and practice. Though far removed from the refinements of full-system *jadal*, the proto-system was a system nonetheless—with its own transmitted conventions. Nowhere is this more obvious than in recurrent argument formulae. Perhaps the most significant examples are the *ra'ā* formulae reviewed in Chap. 6. Here, however, I will review a select set of additional formulae we have encountered in the analyses, divided into two sets.

A. Formulae of Subsumption and Extension

***Manzila*-Subsumption**

- X is *bi-manzilat* Y *fī kull* Z: §634 (AH)
- X is *bi-manzilat* Y *idhā* Z: §635 (in the decrees of several Companions)
- *wa kadhālika qāla* [so-and-so] *fī hādhā al-manzila*: §637 (IAL)
- You rule A for party X, *wa kadhālika manzilat* party Y: §643 (SHAR; x2)
- Even if X corresponds to *manzilat* Y in this *mawḍiʿ*, neither you nor I rule Z: §646 (SH)
- X, all of it, is in the *manzila* of Y: §752 (AH)
- *fa-anzala* X *bi-manzilat* Y: §1072 (SHAQ reporting doctrine of one of the Ahl al-ʿIlm)

***Taswiya*-Subsumption**

- *fa-sawā'un dhālika kulluhu*: §691 (SH)
- *wa sawā'un* X and Y: §§540 (SH); 1127 (SH)

(continued)

- *kāna hādhā wa'l-bāb al-awwal sawā'an fī qawlihimā jamīʿan*: §1313[a] (AH & IAL, reported by AY/MIH)
- *lā farqa bayn* X and Y: §1317 (SH)
- for indeed A happens wherever B happens, with regard to substantive legal genera X and Y: §1326 (SH)

Extension of *ḥukm* to Relevant Genus of Substantive Law

- *fī qawlihimā jamīʿan*: §1313[a] (AH & IAL *taswiya*-subsumption reported by AY/MIH)
- *kadhālika qawluhumā fī kull* X: §90[b] (AY reporting AH vs. IAL)
- *wa kadhālika* X: §687 (AH & [old] AY)
- and in case Y, the *ḥukm* is *ʿalā mā waṣaftu fī qawlihimā* [re: case X] *jamīʿan*: §690 (re: AH & IAL)
- "Every X with *ʿilla* Y has *ḥukm* Z": §94 (SH)

***Maʿnā*-Sharing**

- X is *fī mithli maʿnā* Y: §§286 (SH); 1075 (SH; *fī mithli maʿnā al-Sunna*)
- X is in the *maʿnā* of Y: §1077 (SH; his *istidlāl* from Sunna and *ijmāʿ* is "in the *maʿnā* of" Q.2:178)

B. Formulae of Objection/Refutation[33]

Formulae with *Manaʿa*

- *innamā manaʿanā min* (*al-qawl bi-* [R's thesis/proof])
    - setting stage for *muʿāraḍa* of *qiyās* by *qiyās*, or *al-muʿāraḍa bi-ʿilla mubtada'a*
        - §155 (SH)
    - setting stage for *muʿāraḍa bi'l-nuṭq* against *istidlāl bi'l-Sunna*
        - §248 (SH)
- *al-maʿnā alladhī manaʿnā bihi* [*ḥukm* of R's *ḥadīth*] *qā'iman fī* [Q's *ḥadīth*]
    - setting stage for *muʿāraḍa bi'l-ʿilla* against *istidlāl bi'l-Sunna*
        - §248 (SH)

[33] In addition to the *ra'ā* formulae and others reviewed in Chap. 6.

Broad, Multiple Objection Formulae

- "*al-qawl alladhī akhtarta ab'ad min* [1] *al-qiyās* [2] *al-'aql*"
  - §651 (SH)
- "*wa lā a'lamu man qāla* X, *illā khālafa* [1] *al-Qur'ān*, [2] *al-āthār*, [3] *al-qiyās*, [4] *al-ma'qūl*"
  - §1056 (SH)
- "*kayfa khālaftahu* ['Umar b. al-Khaṭṭāb], *wa ma'ahu* [1] *al-Qur'ān*, [2] *al-qiyās*, [3] *al-ma'qūl*, [4] *ghayrahu min Aṣḥāb al-Nabī?*"
  - §1061 (SH)

Emphatic Expressions of *Farq*-Distinction

- it is not allowed that X be a *qiyās* on the basis of Y, while it is "*mufāriq lahā fi'l-mubtada' wa'l-muta'aqqab*"
  - §288 (SH)
- X is *mukhālif* to Y "*fi'l-bad' wa'l-muta'aqqab*"
  - §1131 (SH)

I have analyzed only twelve *masā'il*-sets concluding in category A extended dialectical sequences, and ten category B short dialectical sequences—a mere fraction of the contents of the subject-text, itself less than a twentieth of the pages of the *Umm* compendium. But an impressive array of dialectical elements—both consonant with, and diverging from, the contents of full-system *jadal* treatises—has been revealed. The larger implications will be discussed in the following chapter. Before this, however, I will add to the above an outline of the most salient elements manifesting themselves during my surface analysis of material outside overtly-dialectical presentation categories. The window on proto-system juridical *jadal* will than be as complete as the current study allows.

7.3 Additional Elements from Non-Sequence Arguments

What follows is far from a complete listing of features, nor is it a thorough analysis. It is designed only to exhibit what has arisen through my surface analysis of the remaining presentation categories, and to hint at the treasure of argument awaiting further study. For material familiar to our lens-texts, I will only employ general categories—combined justifications and objections for the familiar domains of *istidlāl*—with large groupings of examples. This will be followed by an inventory of more unique arguments and features culled from lists drawn at an earlier stage of research. In particular, the arguments of categories C through E remain open to exploration—as are the *ʿaql*-explanations of category F (largely absent from the below); while much may yet be distilled from the plain substantive statements of category G.[34] Much of what follows will be familiar from the categories above, but a number of new categories will also surface. This should provide an impression of how much more the subject-treatise may teach us about proto-system argumentation and legal theory.[35]

Istidlālāt and Iʿtirāḍāt Within the Adilla Domains of the Lens-Texts

Qur'ān

- §§565 (SH; Q.65:2; Q.2:282); 581 (AH & AY; Q.65:2); 583 (SH; support by interpretation of stipulation (*sharṭ*) of God in verses of §§565ff.); 1102 (SH); 604–5 (SH; Q.2:282 plus *athar*-tradition Ibn ʿAbbās); 677 (SH; with *tafsīr*-explanation, as *aṣl* for *qiyās*); 913–14 (AH; Q.4:102 [and *āthār*-traditions Ibn ʿAbbās and Ibrāhīm]); 955–6 (RB gives preponderance to a contrary SH solution over a previous SH solution via Qur'ānic *dalīl*-indicant); 1035 (SH; Q.5:96 and *tafsīr*-explanation of one of the Ahl al-ʿIlm); 1238 (SH; Q.4:23); 1257 (SH; Qur'ānic indicant for interpretation of Sunna); 1280 (SH; Q.66:1–2 as component of *aṣl* for *qiyās*); 1296 (AH; Q.65:6; "Why, when God has decreed X?" [*lima, wa qad qāla Allāhu* X?] = *muṭālaba bi'l-dalīl* plus *muʿāraḍa bi'l-nuṭq*])

Sunna

- §§31 (SH uses Sunnaic *Qāʿida* [*al-kharāj bi'l-ḍamān*] as basis for *Faḥwā al-Khiṭāb*); 42–3 (AH & AY); 48 (AH & AY); 60 (AH); 107–8 (SH; Prophet uses *a-ra'ayta*); 110–11 (AH & AY); 271–2 (AH & AY; x2); 378 (AH & AY; *Qāʿida* [*al-rahn bimā fīhi*]); 537–8 (AH & AY); 547 (SH); 609 (AH; *Qāʿida* [*al-bayyina ʿalā al-muddaʿī*]); 612 (SH; Sunnaic *Qāʿida* [*al-bayyina ʿalā al-muddaʿī*]; *muʿāraḍa bi'l-nuṭq* of opposing thesis); 705, 707–9 (AH & AY; Sunna supported by *āthār*-traditions of ʿUmar, Ibn Masʿūd, and al-Shaʿbī); 710–12 (SH; *tafsīr*-explanation of two *maʿnā*-intensions); 796 (SH; *wa hādhā maʿnā al-Sunnati naṣṣan*); 820 (SH); 901 (AH & AY; Sunna followed by comparison with multiple *āthār*-traditions); 911 (SH reasons from Prophet's Sunna and objects to a claim of *naskh*); 916 (IAL); 919 (SH; Prophet's Sunna was "in this *maʿnā*"); 922 (SH; with *tafsīr*-explanation); 928 (*khabar*-report of Prophet supports SH *taswiya*-subsumption); 981–2 (IAL & AY; with *tafsīr*-

(continued)

[34] Via the intermediary, that is, of later works of *ikhtilāf* and *fiqh*, with the arguments they attribute to our respective proto-system jurists.

[35] For parallel translations of the following material, see part 2 of my dissertation.

explanation); 991 (AY); 1010 (AY supplies AH *naql*: "something of that sort on the Prophet"); 1024 (SH); 1032 (SH & anon. opponent); 1039 (SH; with *tafsīr*-explanation including definition of a key *lafẓ*-expression); 1084 (SH *muʿāraḍa bi'l-nuṭq*; Sunna is the *khilāf* of opposing thesis); 1109 (AH & AY); 1111–12 (SH); 1113 (AH & AY); 1135 (AH); 1135–41 (SH *muʿāraḍa* of Sunna and *āthār*-traditions with better Sunna and *āthār*-traditions); 1147 (AH & AY; AY/MIH claims that AH confirmed *ḥadīth* as *marfūʿ*); 1199 (AH); 1213–16 (AH/AY/SH vs. IAL debate focused upon interpretation of single Sunnaic *lafẓ*-expression: "*nisā'uhā*"; each position is an *iʿtirāḍ* of the other); 1247 (SH); 1255 (AH & AY; application of principle via interpretation of *lafẓ*-expression ["consulted"]); 1257 (SH; Sunna interpreted by *tafsīr*-explanation, more Sunna, and Qur'ān); 1262–8 (AH vs. IAL & SH; *mushāraka fi'l-dalīl* [they interpret the *ḥadīth* Barīra differently]); 1269–73 (AH vs. IAL & AY & SH; *mushāraka fi'l-dalīl* [they interpret the Sunnaic *Qāʿida* (*al-walad li'l-firāsh...*) differently]); 1280 (SH; with Q.66:1–2; as *aṣl* for *qiyās*); 1415 (IAL; along with *āthār*-traditions); 1417 (SH; along with *āthār*-traditions); 1420 (IAL & AY); 1422 (AH & AY)

Ijmāʿ

- §§566–7 (SH reported by RB; *ijmāʿ* re: *maʿnā*-intension of Q.65:2/Q.2:282); 1383 (SH supports his ruling by fourfold citing of *ijmāʿ*)

***Ijmāʿ al-Ṣaḥāba* or *Tarjīḥ* by Accumulation of Companions (?)**

- §§330–1 (SH *taswiya*-subsumption supported by four Companions); 912 (SH; four Companions; *tafsīr*-explanation for ʿUthmān's practice); 1049 (SH supports ruling as "following upon" four Companions, four Successors, "and others"); 1417 (SH; four Companions plus Sunna)

Qawl al-Wāḥid min al-Ṣaḥāba

- §§3–4 (AH; ʿAlī); 24–6 (AH & AY; ʿAlī); 75–6 (AH & AY; ʿUmar); 120–2 (AH & AY; Ibn Masʿūd and ʿUmar [and Ibrāhīm]); 207–9 (AH & AY; ʿUmar, ʿUthmān, and Ibn Masʿūd); 212 (AH & AY; Ibn Masʿūd); 215 (SH; Ibn ʿAbbās); 340 (AH; Abū Bakr); 355 (AH; Ibn ʿAbbās); 454–5 (SH; ʿAlī and other Companions); 468 (SH reported by RB; ʿUmar); 496 (AH & AY; ʿAlī; *muʿāraḍa* of IAL *āthār*-traditions of Successors in §497); 506 (AH & AY; ʿUmar); 531–2 (AH; ʿAlī); 604–5 (SH; Ibn ʿAbbās; in support of *istidlāl* from Q.2:282); 620 (AH & AY; ʿUmar [and Shurayḥ]); 627 (AH & AY; Ibn Masʿūd [and Shurayḥ]); 705, 707–9 (AH & AY; ʿUmar, Ibn Masʿūd, and al-Shaʿbī [supporting Sunna]); 724 (SH; ʿUmar); 725 (SH; ʿĀ'isha); 727 (SH; ʿUmar); 798 (AH & AY; ʿAbd Allāh b. ʿUmar); 804–5 (SH; Ibn ʿUmar [and Shurayḥ]); 832 (AH; ʿAlī); 839 (AH; Ibn Masʿūd); 909 (IAL; ʿUmar [via Ibn ʿAbbās] and ʿAlī); 913–14 (AH; Ibn ʿAbbās [supporting Q.4:102; and supported by *athar*-tradition of Ibrāhīm]); 941 (SH; Ibn ʿUmar); 947 (IAL & AY; Ibn ʿAbbās); 959 (AH/AY; ʿAlī); 990 (AH; ʿUmar); 996 (AH/AY; ʿUmar); 1016 (IAL; Ibn ʿAbbās;

(continued)

muʿāraḍa of AH *athar*-tradition of Ibrāhīm); 1027 (anon. opponent; ʿUmar); 1028 (anon. opponent; Ibn ʿUmar); 1032 (SH & anon. opponent); 1041 (IAL/AY; Ibn ʿAbbās and Ibn ʿUmar); 1062–4 (IAL/AY; Ibn Masʿūd [and ʿĀmir (b. ʿAbd Allāh b. Masʿūd?) and ʿAṭāʾ b. Abī Rabāḥ]); 1099 (AH & AY; Ibrāhīm); 1135 (AH; ʿAlī and Ibn Masʿūd); 1140 (SH; Abū Bakr); 1141 (SH; ʿĀʾisha); 1181 (AH; Ibn ʿAbbās); 1234–5 (AH; two *āthār*-traditions of ʿUmar [supported by *athar*-tradition of Ibrāhīm]); 1238 (SH; support of Q.4:23 with ʿAbd Allāh b. Jaʿfar and ʿAbd Allāh b. Ṣafwān); 1244 (AH; ʿAlī); 1275 (AY; Ibn Masʿūd); 1288 (AH; ʿUmar, ʿAlī, Ibn Masʿūd, Zayd b. Thābit); 1297 (AH; ʿUmar supporting Q.65:6); 1300 (AH & AY; Ibn ʿAbbās); 1392 (SH; ʿAbd al-Raḥmān [b. ʿAwf]); 1393 (IAL; Ibn Masʿūd); 1413 (AH; ʿAlī); 1415 (IAL; Abū Bakr and ʿAlī; along with Sunna)

Faḥwā al-Khiṭāb

- §§30–1 (SH; *a maiore ad minus* from Sunnaic Qāʿida: *al-kharāj biʾl-ḍamān*)

Dalīl al-Khiṭāb

- §§734 (SH; "when we decree X, we do not permit the reverse of X" [*aṣl* not mentioned]); 1241 (SH; "God only made *ḥarām* through *ḥalāl*; and the *ḥarām* is the opposite of the *ḥalāl*")

Maʿnā al-Khiṭāb (Qiyās)

- §§8–9 (anon. opponent); 10 (SH; *farq*-distinction and *naqḍ*); 14 (anon. opponent); 19 (SH); 135–6 (SH); 167 (SH; *manʿ* of the *ʿilla* in the *farʿ*); 184 (SH; *farq*-distinction); 212 (AH & AY; reported by al-Sarakhsī); 292 (SH); 322 (SH ruling supported by *qiyās* [x3] = *muʿāraḍa* of AH *ʿilla*); 329 (SH ruling = *muʿāraḍa* of AH *ʿilla*); 337–8 (SH); 344–5 (SH; *qiyās* correlation between genera is underscored); 388 (SH; *qiyās* correlation between two genera of contracts is underscored); 389 (AH & AY; *qiyās* with another genus of contract); 391 (AY extends IAL ruling to related *masʾala* by way of *qiyās*); 417 (SH); 460 (AH/AY); 509 (SH; *aṣl* is from Qurʾān); 556 (SH supports parallel to AH §554 with *qiyās*); 633 (SH); 671–2 (SH; 2x *qiyās al-ʿilla*, with full explanation of efficient properties); 677 (SH; from Qurʾān; supported by *tafsīr*-explanation, and *athar*-tradition of ʿAṭāʾ); 726 (SH; *farq*-distinction); 729 (SH vs. anon. opponent); 960 (SH); 968 (SH); 987 (IAL; *muʿāraḍa* by *qiyās* with another genus of *zakāt*); 992 (*muʿāraḍa* of AH position via *a fortiori qiyās* and another *qiyās*); 997 (SH; *muʿāraḍa-qiyās* of AH & AY *ʿilla*); 1012 (SH); 1017–20 (SH *qiyās a maiore ad minus*; as X is in the *maʿnā* of Y, or *akhaffu minhu*); 1032 (SH); 1066 (SH; 2x *qiyās*); 1097 (SH); 1101 (SH); 1149 (SH; *aṣl* is Sunna); 1161 (AH & [new] AY; implied); 1195 (SH); 1233–5 (AH & AY; *muʿāraḍa* of IAL *ʿilla*, supported by *āthār*-traditions); 1243 (AH); 1280 (SH; *aṣl* consists of: Prophetic Sunna, Q.66:1–2); 1283 (SH); 1309 (SH); 1370 (SH; *naqḍ*); 1427–30 (AH/AY/SH vs. IAL; *ʿilla* of each implies *iʿtirāḍ* of the other's)

(continued)

Tarjīḥāt

- §§7ff. (SH; *qiyās* vs. *qiyās* via supporting *āthār*-traditions); 607 (SH; Ibn ʿAbbās vs. Ibn al-Zubayr; Ibn ʿAbbās closer to Qur'ān and *qiyās*); 796 (SH preponderates a *maʿnā*-intension as more appropriate [Schacht calls this: "*a potiori*" *qiyās*], supports with *ʿaql*: hypothetical situation in which one *maʿnā*-intension causes less harm)

***Istidlālāt* and *Iʿtirāḍāt* Outside the *Adilla* Domains/Categories of the Lens-Texts**

General Appeal's to God's Decrees (without mention of specific *adilla*-indicants); [= testimony of the primary source-cases (*shahādat al-uṣūl*)?]

- §308 (SH; re: testimony and procedure)

Reasoning from the Silence of the *Uṣūl*

- §931 (SH claims no Prophetic report has been preserved—*min wajhin yathbutu mithluhu*—contrary to his ruling; an anticipation of attempted *muʿāraḍa bi'l-nuṭq*?)

Argument from "Rights of God" vs. "Rights of People" Distinction

- §§509–10 (SH & RB); 1149–50 (SH; *qiyās* extended to "every *ḥadd* of God;" ruling for all *ḥuqūq al-ādamiyyīn* shows clear distinction of rights and consequences; subsidiary ruling combines both domains for theft)

***Tarjīḥ*-Oriented (?) Laying Out and Comparison of *Āthār*-traditions**

- §§900–8 (AH & AY; comparison of Prophetic Sunna and *āthār*-traditions of Abū Bakr, Ibn Masʿūd, ʿUmar, Ibn ʿAbbās, Ibn ʿUmar [with *tafsīr*-explanation of his decree], ʿAlī, and Muʿāwiya [with explanation of Kūfan vs. Syrian practices stemming from these latter two])

Transmission-Oriented Objections re: *Āthār*-traditions of Companions/Successors

- §§15–16 (anon. opponent; ʿAlī; SH claims as weak); 17 (anon. opponent; ʿUmar; SH claims as weak); 18 (anon. opponent; ʿAlī; SH claims as weak); 31 (SH against *athar*-tradition of ʿUmar; al-Bayḥaqī reports: because it is *mursal*; and against *athar*-tradition of ʿAlī); 1139 (SH); 1379 (SH)

Use of *Āthār*-traditions of Successors and Famed Jurists in Arguments

- §§11–12 (anon. opponent; Shurayḥ); 19 (SH; ʿAṭā' b. Abī Rabāḥ); 120–2 (AH & AY; Ibrāhīm [supporting Ibn Masʿūd and ʿUmar]); 123–4 (IAL; ʿUmar II);

(continued)

307 (SH; Shurayḥ); 340 (AH; Ibrāhīm); 356 (AH; Ibrāhīm); 374–6 (AH & AY; Ibrāhīm [x2], Abū Jaʿfar, ʿAṭāʾ); 465–6 (IAL & AY; Shurayḥ); 497 (IAL; Shurayḥ and Ibrāhīm; *muʿāraḍa* of AH/AY *athar*-tradition of ʿAlī in §496); 528 (AH & AY; Shurayḥ); 566 (SH reported by RB; Mujāhid; used for *tafsīr*-explanation of Qurʾānic *dalīl*-indicant); 571 (SH/RB; Shurayḥ); 585 (AH; Shurayḥ); 620 (AH & AY; Shurayḥ [supporting *athar*-tradition of ʿUmar]); 627 (AH & AY; Shurayḥ [and Ibn Masʿūd]); 677 (SH; ʿAṭāʾ; supporting *qiyās* from Qurʾān); 714 (AH & [old] AY; Ibrāhīm); 720 (AH; Ibrāhīm); 804–5 (SH; Shurayḥ [supporting Ibn ʿUmar]); 810 (AY/MIH; Ibrāhīm in support of AH ruling); 846[a] (IAL; Shurayḥ); 893–4 (IAL & AY; Ibrāhīm and ʿĀmir [b. ʿAbd Allāh b. Masʿūd?]); 898 (AH & AY; Ibrāhīm); 913–14 (AH; Ibrāhīm [supporting Q.4:102 and Ibn ʿAbbās]); 938 (IAL; Ibrāhīm); 939 (AH & AY; Ibrāhīm; *muʿāraḍa*: contrary *naql* from same Successor); 942 (IAL; Ibrāhīm); 948 (AH; Ibrāhīm); 971 (AH; Ibrāhīm); 979 (AH; Ibrāhīm; AY believes this to be AH's *naql*); 1014 (AH; Ibrāhīm); 1042 (AY; ʿAlī b. ʿAbd Allāh b. ʿAbbās; transmitted by anonymous *shaykh*); 1045 (SH; long, fully-quoted *athar*-tradition of ʿAbd al-Aʿlā b. ʿAbd Allāh b. ʿĀmir and his mother); 1048 (IAL/AY; ʿAṭāʾ b. Abī Rabāḥ); 1062–4 (IAL/AY; ʿĀmir [b. ʿAbd Allāh b. Masʿūd?] and ʿAṭāʾ b. Abī Rabāḥ [supporting Ibn Masʿūd]); 1233 (AH; Ibrāhīm [supporting two *āthār*-traditions of ʿUmar]); 1250–1 (IAL; ʿĀmir [b. ʿAbd Allāh b. Masʿūd?], Shurayḥ, and Ibrāhīm); 1286 (SH supports ruling with decree of Abū Bakr b. ʿAbd al-Raḥmān b. al-Ḥārith b. Hishām);[36] 1379 (anon. opponent; ʿUmar [II?]); 1381 (SH; Ibn al-Zubayr); 1396 (AH/AY; Ibrāhīm); 1399–1400[a] (AH; Ibrāhīm and ʿAṭāʾ b. Abī Rabāḥ)

Appeals to One, or Some, of the Ahl al-ʿIlm (Aristotle's *endoxa*-set of "the Wise"?)

- §§1035 (SH supports ruling with Q.5:96 and *tafsīr*-explanation of one of the Ahl al-ʿIlm); 1046 (SH supports ruling with doctrine of "more than one of the Ahl al-ʿIlm")[37]

Unique "Role-Reversal" *Qiyās*

- §1222 (IAL; cf. SH's strategy in §658)

"Limited *Qiyās*"

- §1261 (SH brings a parallel genus of contract, underscoring first the efficient property in the parallel which does not apply to the current *masʾala*, then he details the shared efficient property common to both contracts)

(continued)

[36] NB: this Abū Bakr is one of the *Fuqahāʾ al-Madīna al-Sabʿa* (d.94/712).

[37] Schacht (*Origins*, p. 89) references this as an example of consensus according to the ancient school usage. Note, however, that al-Shāfiʿī merely says "more than one of the Ahl al-ʿIlm."

Qiyās Based Upon Another Qiyās (?)

- §9 (anon. opponent)

Athar*-tradition to be Preferred Over *Qiyās

- §793 (SH attributes anon. opponent position to the Ahl al-Qiyās; [as we see from the main SH argument elsewhere in the *Umm* (from *naql*: *athar*-tradition of ʿĀ'isha), this is an accusatory charge for those who would prefer *qiyās* over an *athar*-tradition])

Argument to *al-maʿqūl*

- §§402 (SH; the *maʿqūl* of a contract type: *ḥawāla*); 633 (SH; the *maʿqūl* of a contract type: *waṣiyya*); 929 (SH; reasoning from a *maʿqūl* in a *khabar*-report of the Prophet: Prophet aimed at showing *farq*-distinction)

Argument to Custom or Convention

- §§481 (IAL; because it is "a manifest custom" (*ʿurf ẓāhir*) among the people);[38] 875 (SH efficient property occasioning *ḥukm* is "*idhā faʿala dhālika al-fiʿl alladhī yufʿalu bi-mithlihi fī dhālika al-waqt*"—i.e., the *ʿilla* is "his action was consonant with sea-faring convention")

Claimed/Reported *Istiḥsān*

- §§478 (IAL);[39] 484 (IAL);[40] 730 (AH);[41] 799 (IAL);[42] 801 (IAL);[43] 811 (AH);[44] 874 (IAL);[45] 1021 (AH)[46]

Precaution (*Iḥtiyāṭ*) as a Guiding Principle

- §§1018 (SH; "it is preferable to me" [*aḥabba ilayya*] ruling linked with *iḥtiyāṭ*)

---

[38] Considered *istiḥsān* by al-Sarakhsī (*Mabsūṭ*, vol. 30, p. 150); al-Afghānī (p. 64, n. 1). Noted as *istiḥsān* by Schacht (*Origins*, p. 112).

[39] *Mabsūṭ* vol. 7, p. 164; vol. 30, p. 150. Noted by Schacht (*Origins*, p. 112, and p. 273, n. 4).

[40] Noted by Schacht (*Origins*, p. 112).

[41] *Mabsūṭ* vol. 28, p. 34. Noted by Schacht (*Origins*, p. 112).

[42] *Mabsūṭ* vol. 7, p. 207. Noted by Schacht (*Origins*, pp. 111–12).

[43] *Mabsūṭ* vol. 7, p. 207. Noted by Schacht (*Origins*, pp. 111–12).

[44] Schacht (*Origins*, p. 112) claims: "Abū Ḥanīfa is systematically consistent, but still makes a very slight concession...."

[45] Schacht (*Origins*, p. 112) claims: "he [IAL] makes an inconsistent exception on account of *vis maior*, out of regard for material justice." After a comparison with SH's ruling (based upon sea-faring convention) in §875, I believe it is questionable to interpret IAL's exception as *istiḥsān*.

[46] As claimed by Schacht (*Origins*, p. 112), from his interpretation of al-Ṭaḥāwī's description of AH's decision as *ra'y*, recorded in the *Mabsūṭ* (vol. 4, p. 138). Notably, however, the *Mabsūṭ*—replete with references to *istiḥsān*—does not appear to employ the term with reference to AH's particular opinion on this *mas'ala*.

Unique Argument Types of a More Ancient Tenor

Charges of *tanāquḍ/qawl mutanāqiḍ*

- §469 (SH)

General *Reductio* Arguments

- §§13 (SH); 407 (IAL); 1194 (SH); 1289 (AH; *a-lā tarā*)
- plus, the relevant (non-sequence) *ra'ā* formulae arguments reviewed at the end of Chap. 6

***A Fortiori* Arguments (Outside the domain of *Faḥwā al-Khiṭāb*)**

- §§215 (SH; *a maiore ad minus*); 992 (SH; *qiyās; a minore ad maius*); 1017–20 (SH *qiyas a maiore ad minus*; as X is in the *maʿnā* of Y, or *akhaffu minhu*); 1084 (SH; *a minore ad maius*); 1102 (SH; *a maiore ad minus*); 1241 (SH overrides *ʿilla* concerns of previous sections by upgrading the *mas'ala* to full *zinā*—an "*a fortiori* strategy")[47]

Argument via Restrictive Disjunction

- §1395 (AH/AY; unlawful sex act must incur either *ṣadāq*-dowry or *ḥadd*-punishment—if not one, then it must be the other)

Schacht's "*a potiori*" *qiyās*:[48]

- §796 (SH preponderates a *maʿnā*-intension as more appropriate (*aḥrā*), supports with *ʿaql*: hypothetical situation in which one *maʿnā*-intension causes less harm)

***Ra'y*, According to Schacht:**

- §975 (AY; *lā arā* X);[49] §1044 (SH; *wa lā arā—wa Allāhu Taʿālā aʿlam*—that X is permitted)[50]

---

[47] §1241 is a terse presentation of a complex argument from another of al-Shāfiʿī's books. See my translation of the referenced argument in the appendices of my dissertation ("Dialectical Forge," pp. 371–3, Appendix II.§1241).

[48] *Origins*, p. 124 and n. 2: "A particular kind of *qiyās* is represented by conclusions *a potiori*..." A closer examination of SH in §796, however, shows something more like the *Tarjīḥ al-Maʿānī* of our *jadal*-theory texts.

[49] Schacht, *Origins*, p. 105: "an example of [Abū Yūsuf's] explicit use of *ra'y*...."

[50] Schacht, *Origins*, p. 120 and n. 1: "Shāfiʿī expresses his own *ra'y*." At the top of p. 120, Schacht reiterates that he considers our subject-treatise from al-Shāfiʿī's "earliest period," in which he uses *ra'y* "in the same loose way as the ancient schools."

Other Argument Categories/Elements

Open Appeals to Legal Theory

- §§56 (SH; several legal theoretical principles); 293 (SH; lack of *āthār*-traditions justifies use of *qiyās*); 609 (AH; "The oath is not transferred from the locus [*mawḍiʿ*] upon which the Prophet... placed it [*waḍaʿahā*]"); 1139 (SH; "*laysat fī aḥadin maʿa al-nabī... ḥujjatan*")

Appeal to Theological Principle

- §1425 (SH; "the ruling of God is one, it does not contradict [itself]" [*ḥukm Allāhi wāḥidun lā yakhtalifu*])

Practice of "precaution" (*Iḥtiyāṭ*)

- §503 (SH; in the context of "*Qāḍī* Instruction")

Apparent "public welfare considerations" (*Maṣlaḥa*) in *Āthār*-Traditions of Companions

- §15 (ʿAlī)

Apparent *Maṣlaḥa* in Reasoning/Practice? Al-Shāfiʿī Conceals His Real Solution, Out of Fear of Negative Societal Consequence

- §§20 (SH, reported by RB: fear of iniquitous artisans); 309 (SH, reported by RB: fear of iniquitous *qāḍīs*); 1179 (SH, reported by RB: fear of iniquitous *qāḍīs*)

Rulings Rendered According to Social Categories

- §590 (SH; "mosque folk" [*ahl al-masjid*] vs. "tribe folk" [*ahl al-qabīla*] vs. "market person" [*sūqī*])

Presumptions or Hypothetical Possibilities of Parties' Strategizing as Premises in Argument

- §§198 (SH); 273 (SH); 348–50 (SH); 590–1 (SH); 1175 (SH)

***Ra'ā* Formulae Appearing in Sunna/*Āthār*-Traditions of Successors**

- §§11 (Shurayḥ uses *a-ra'ayta*); 107–8 (SH; Prophet uses *a-ra'ayta*)

Al-Shaybānī Supplies a Later Doctrine of Abū Yūsuf

- §§514 ("my memory of Abū Yūsuf is that he professed X after that" [*wa ḥifẓī ʿan Abī Yūsuf annahu qāla baʿdu*: X]); 588 ("after that, Abū Yūsuf professed X" [*wa qāla Abū Yūsuf baʿda dhālika*: X])

Al-Rabīʿ Supplies Additional (More Clear/Correct) Doctrine of al-Shāfiʿī; or Alternate Ruling of al-Shāfiʿī

- §§199; 350; 439 ("my memory of al-Shāfiʿī is that he judged X" [*ḥifẓī ʿan al-Shāfiʿī... annahu yaqḍī* X]); 510; 843 (SH ruling lacking, so RB—in apparent

(continued)

reference to doctrine of AH & IAL—says: "al-Shāfiʿī had a response here" [*liʾl-Shāfiʿī... hāhunā jawābun*]); 955–6 (RB presents SH doctrine contrary to that presented by SH previously; preponderates the new doctrine with *ʿaql* and Qur'ānic *dalīl*-indicant); 1004 (RB supplies a contrary SH ruling he found "in another place [*mawḍiʿ*];" supports it with argument)

Al-Rabīʿ's *Tafsīr*-Explanation of al-Shāfiʿī's Ruling

- §499

Legal Theory Concepts and Terminology in Arguments[51]

***Naṣṣ* in the Sense of "univocal"**

- §796 (SH; *wa hādhā maʿnā al-Sunnati naṣṣan*)

***ʿĀmm/Khāṣṣ* Distinction**

- §§74 (RB uses *a-lā tarā* to show the distinction); 510 (RB; *khāṣṣ* distinction)

Qur'ānic and Sunnaic/Āthāric Hermeneutic, and Complementary Interplay

- §§566 (SH reported by RB; *athar*-tradition Mujāhid supports *tafsīr*-explanation of Qur'ānic *dalīl*-indicant); 570–1 (SH/RB; *athar*-tradition Shurayḥ conflicts with Qur'ān); 1213–16 (debate is focused upon interpretation of single *lafẓ*-expression: "*nisāʾuhā*"); 1257 (SH; Sunna interpreted by *tafsīr*-explanation, Sunna, and Qur'ān); 1425 (SH; Prophetic Sunna "is in the *maʿnā* of" Q.5:42 and Q.5:49)

Consistent Generalizing of the *ʿIlla* ("super-*qiyās*")

***Manzila*-Subsumption**

- §§201 (AH & AY); 202 (IAL); 346 (AH & AY); 391m (AH & AY); 474 (IAL); 537 (AH & AY); 987 (IAL); 1204 (IAL); 1341 (AH); 1348 (AH); 1350–2 (AH, AY, IAL); 1358–9 (AH, IAL)
    - §§1343–53: extensive *ikhtilāf* (IAL & AY vs. AH & SH [and new AY in §1350 (!)]) re: the *manzila* of a partially manumitted male slave

(continued)

[51] This is not a complete listing, more will be discussed in the following chapter. Also, see the additional epistemological terms under "Arguments and Rulings Bearing upon the Epistemology of Evidentiary Procedure," below.

- §§1354–60: extensive *ikhtilāf* (AH & SH vs. IAL & AY) re: the *manzila* of a partially manumitted female slave

***Taswiya*-Subsumption**

- §§7 (SH); 38 (SH); 69 (SH); 210 (SH); 329 (SH); 336 (AY); 380 (SH); 383 (SH); 461 (IAL); 462 (SH); 495 (SH); 525 (AY); 669 (AH & IAL); 928–9 (SH; *lā takhtalifu* X and Y, because each is *mawṣūla*); 970 (AH); 1097 (SH); 1110 (AH & IAL); 1149 (SH); 1163 (SH); 1178 (2x, SH); 1189 (AY); 1192 (SH); 1246 (AY); 1328 (AH & IAL); 1398 (AH)

Extension of *Ḥukm* to Relevant Genus/Genera (of transaction, parties, objects, etc.)

- §§332 (SH); 559 (SH); 671 (SH); 856 (SH); 891 (AH); 1000 (SH); 1149 (SH; *qiyās* extended to "every *ḥadd* of God"); 1277–8 (AH/AY)

Formulaic Modes of Objection

"all that prevents us from..." (*innamā manaʿnā*)

- §§68–9 (SH; x2); 394 (SH)

7.4 Elements of Wider Historical Interest

Elements of Additional Interest

The picture of proto-system dialectic and argument provided by our subject-treatise is almost complete. What follows is a listing of elements, mentions, etc. which—although incidental to the current project—will be of interest to the legal and social historian of early Islam. Without a doubt, and as will already be plain from the translated sequences in Chaps. 5 and 6, the *Ikhtilāf al-ʿIrāqiyyayn/ʿIrāqiyyīn* contains a treasure-trove of material for studying the legal status of women in the second/eighth century; the legal status of slaves (and the institution of slavery in general); the laws of contract and commerce; etc. Features relevant to these domains would be too numerous to list, so I will mention only narrower topics here, and refer the reader to the subject-text itself for these broader concerns. What follows is only a sampling, not a thorough survey.

Of Legal-Historical Import

- Reference to *Taqlīd*
  - §1061 (of ʿUmar)
- Caliphal Decree Alters *Mujtahid*'s Doctrine and/or Practice as *Qāḍī*
  - §240 (AY/MIH re: IAL)
- Mention of Iniquitous *Qāḍī*s
  - §§309 (SH, reported by RB); 1179 (SH, reported by RB)
- Reference to Community of Jurists (by Region)
  - Ahl al-Baṣra: §§247ff.
  - Mashriqiyyūn: §§252ff.; 737
  - Ahl al-Ḥijāz: §240
- Reference to Epistemic Community (by Project/Specialization)
  - Ahl al-Fiqh: §§284; 1429 (excluded from exemption from the *ḥadd*-punishment for ignorance of the law)
  - Ahl al-Ḥadīth: §§283; 667; 929; 1318–19; 1379 (Ahl al-ʿIlm bi'l-Ḥadīth)
  - Ahl al-Kalām: §§642ff.
  - Ahl al-Qiyās: §793 (with apparent accusation of preferring *qiyās* over an *athar*-tradition of ʿĀ'isha)
  - Ahl al-ʿIlm: §1046; 1072 (three separate doctrines mentioned)
  - The Ḥuffāẓ: §1119
- Different Rulings for Different Social Categories
  - Sūqī vs. ʿArab: §584
  - Ahl al-Masjid vs. Ahl al-Qabīla vs. Sūqī: §590
- Reference to Testimonial Subgroups, Evidentiary Specialists, and Court Functionaries
  - *dhawā ʿadlin*: §32
  - Ahl al-Maʿrifa al-Bāṭina: §§502–3
  - the *qā'if*: §680
  - Ahl al-Khibra bi'l-Mashhūd ʿalayhi: §685
  - the *jilwāz*: §1428 (in context of real Kūfan practice)
- Rulings re: Written Instruments
  - *kitāb al-qāḍī ilā al-qāḍī*: §§554ff.; 577ff.; 1161ff.
  - *dhikr ḥaqq*: §§477–86
  - *ʿuhda*: §§232–3
- Rulings re: the *Qāḍī*'s memory and the Epistemic Value of what is Registered in his *Dīwān*
  - §§1156ff.; 1176ff.
- Step-by-Step "*Qāḍī* Instruction" re: Procedural Concerns
  - §§129; 227; 437–8 (including what to write in the *qaḍā'*); 502–4; 1162–3 (re: verifying *kitāb al-qāḍī ilā al-qāḍī*)

(continued)

- Examples of a *Mujtahid-Qāḍī* Putting his Rulings into Practice
    - §§446 (AY, as reported [apparently] by MIH); 539 (IAL); 555 (IAL); 595 (IAL); 597 (IAL); 706 (IAL); 1165 (IAL); 1166 (AY); 1190 (IAL; x2); 1198 (IAL; x4); 1423 (IAL; firmly asserted by AY/MIH comment: *wa qad faʿala dhālika*); 1428 (IAL, as witnessed by AY)
- Regional Variations for Appellation of Contract
    - §202 (old Iraqi *muʿāmala* for Ḥijāzī *musāqāt*)
- Jurists Indicate Regional Variations of Practice Resultant of Different Customs of Different Companions
    - §§900–8 (AH/AY/MIH listing of *naql* and explanation shows, among other things, Kūfans taking up practice of ʿAlī and Syrians taking up practice of Muʿāwiya)

Of Other Historical Import

- References to (and Clarifications of) Weights and Measures
    - §§973–6 (*ṣāʿ*, *wasq*, *raṭl*, *mudd*, *makhtūm* by the Ḥajjājī standard, *makhtūm* by the Greater Hāshimī standard, the *ṣāʿ* of the Prophet); 985ff. (*mithqāl*, *dirham*, *dīnār*)
- Re: Canonization of the Qur'ān
    - §909 (IAL mentions ʿUmar as reading two "*sūras*" for *qunūt* [NB: these same *sūras* are found only in the non-canonical codex of Ubayy b. Kaʿb];[52] AY explains IAL transmitted [*yuḥaddithu*] this from Ibn ʿAbbās)
- Rulings with regard to the Kharijites
    - §§176–8

One last area of interest from our subject-text bears upon a tentative hypothesis raised in the next chapter: the possible interplay between the epistemologies of evidentiary procedure, of disputation procedure, and of *ijtihād*. Disputation between litigants in the *qāḍī*'s *majlis*, after all, shares certain features in common with disputation between jurist-dialecticians in a *majlis* of *jadal*; and the argumentation epistemes of this latter enterprise, as I hope will be plain, exerted a pressure dynamic on the epistemes of private *ijtihād*.

[52] See the note attached to §909 in my dissertation ("Dialectical Forge," pt. 2, p. 226, n. 6).

Arguments and Rulings Bearing Upon the Epistemology of Evidentiary Procedure

- Appeals to Sunnaic Qāʿida: «the burden of proof is on the claimant (*al-bayyina ʿalā al-muddaʿī*)...»
    - §§610–13
- Rulings regarding "the Benefit of Assumption"
    - §§1–2; 50; 133–4; 196–9; 359–61; 860–4; 1276–80
- "Evidentiary *Tarjīḥ*"
    - witness disqualification (*jarḥ*) is superior (*awlā*) to witness qualification (*taʿdīl*): §564
    - the Qāḍī's personal knowledge (*ʿilm*) [of a party/event] is superior (*awlā*) to witness testimony: §305
    - confession (*iqrār*) is superior (*awlā*) to witness-testimony (*shuhūd*): §479; 482
    - confession (*iqrār*) is superior (*awlā*) to *bayyina*-evidence: §477
    - Testimony and Oaths "according to one's knowledge" (*ʿalā ʿilm*) vs. "with categorical certainty" (*al-battata*):
        - §§504 (*al-shahāda ʿalā al-batti tu'awwalu ilā al-ʿilm*); 614–19; 685 (*maʿnā al-batt maʿnā al-ʿilm, wa maʿnā al-ʿilm maʿnā al-batt*)
- on the impossibility of determining which witnesses are lying/truthful: §590ff.
- Rulings re: the Qāḍī's knowledge of prior litigation
    - §§304–8 (epistemological concerns/terms include: *ʿilm, ẓāhir, shakk, yaqīn*)
    - §§1156ff., 1176ff. (the Qāḍī's memory and the epistemic value of his *dīwān*)
- "Qāḍī Instruction" guided by Epistemological Concerns
    - §§502–4 (epistemological concerns/terms include: *iḥtiyāṭ, maʿrifa, iḥāṭa, ʿilm, al-batt*); 682ff.; 1168–71 (epistemological concerns/terms include: *ẓāhir*)

7.5 Remarks on the Character of Proto-System Juridical *Jadal*

The wealth of information our relatively short subject-text is capable of providing, even to the limited extent I have analyzed it, is astonishing. The small window it provides opens onto a vista which ought not to surprise us at all, however: it is a juridical landscape blending prior Near Eastern argumentation epistemes (of which I have only pointed out the most Aristotelian) with those of early Islam, the whole of which—though broader in content, and in every way sophisticated—is not nearly as systematic and refined as its descendant-systems were to become over the following three centuries. As examples of the infusion of prior epistemes with Islamic axioms in the constitution of a new, and distinct, argumentation episteme, I would cite the evident differences between: (1) the Aristotelian *endoxa* set vs. the early Islamic *endoxa* hierarchy; and (2) the organizing principle of the *Topics* vs. that of our lens-texts.

As for the first, we observe in proto-system *jadal* an Islamic hierarchy of epistemic authority at a relatively advanced stage, along with plentiful evidence that the ranking of *uṣūl* was still being wrought in the dialectical forge. Parallels with the Aristotelian "everyone" (*ijmāʿ al-kull*) and "the wise" (*ijmāʿ* of the Companions, or *ʿulamāʾ*) and "the famous of the wise" (the Sunna of the Prophet, *qawl al-wāḥid min al-Ṣaḥāba, taqlīd* of a venerated *mujtahid*) are still quite evident, and may be witnessed in the full heat of a dialectically-motivated epistemic valuation. By the era of our *jadal*-theory texts, much more had been resolved in this regard—at least within the nascent Sunnism to which our lens-texts belong—and again through the venue of dialectical encounter. Contention remained in a number of areas, however, as all our theorists report.

As for organizing principles, note that Aristotle's *topoi* of predicables are not at all easy to distinguish in either our subject-text or lens-texts. Overtly syllogistic formulations are absent from both as well. The general aims and procedures of "good dialectic" are evident, but our lens-text organizing principles are in accordance with the axioms of Islamic epistemic valuation (the hierarchy of *uṣūl*). In the proto-system *Ikhtilāf al-ʿIrāqiyyayn/ʿIrāqiyyīn*, we also see these features at a relatively advanced stage in practice, although elements which appear quite Aristotelian (especially premise-gathering for reduction to *tanāquḍ*, absurdity, etc.) are far more evident than in any of the theory texts, if not in fact entirely particular to our proto-system.

I believe these observations justify referring to the *jadal* teaching and practice of the subject-text as belonging to a proto-system. It is "proto" in the sense that it is a less-refined precursor to such as evolved over the following centuries; and it is a "system" with respect to all its transmitted conventions—especially with regard to the formulae of subsumption and extension and other justifications, reduction to untenable consequences and other objections, question and response, and statements of substantive rulings. To this I would add a remarkable consistency of both substantive and legal-theoretical technical terms, though this latter set in particular would continue to evolve (e.g., from *maʿnā* to *waṣf* and *ʿilla*, from *qiyās* to *qiyās al-ṭard, qiyās al-ʿaks, qiyās al-ʿilla, qiyās al-dalāla*, etc.)

But I also must reiterate an earlier caveat: these analyses, categories, and assessments can only be said, at this point, to belong to the subject-text, and to the comportment of its dialectician-jurists only insofar as its contended *masāʾil* are concerned. Nevertheless, although at a very early stage of exploration, and understandably hesitant to abstract findings into broader strokes of the legal-historian's brush, I will attempt to distil certain dynamics from these findings and incorporate them into larger themes of legal-historical development.

References

Abū Yūsuf, Ya'qūb b. Ibrāhīm. *Ikhtilāf Abī Ḥanīfa wa Ibn Abī Laylā* [= Shaybānī Version]. Ed. Abū al-Wafā' al-Afghānī. Cairo: Maṭba'at al-Wafā', 1357/1939.

Ansari, Zafar Ishaq. "Islamic Juristic Terminology Before Šāfi'ī: A Semantic Analysis with Special Reference to Kūfa." *Arabica* 19:3 (1972): pp. 255–300.

al Bājī, Abū al Walīd Sulaymān. *Kitāb al-Minhāj fī Tartīb al-Ḥijāj (L'art de la Polémique: Édition Critique d'al-Minhāǧ de Bāǧī)*. Ed. 'Abd al-Majīd Turkī. Paris: Maisonneuve et Larose, 1978.

Coulson, N. J. *A History of Islamic Law*. Edinburgh: University Press, 1964.

EI² = *Encyclopaedia of Islam, Second Edition*. Ed. P. Bearman; Th. Bianquis; C.E. Bosworth; E. van Donzel; and W.P. Heinrichs. Brill Online, 2014 <http://referenceworks.brillonline.com/entries/encyclopaedia-of-islam-2>

Hallaq, Wael. *A History of Islamic Legal Theories: An Introduction to Sunnī Uṣūl al-Fiqh*. Cambridge; New York: Cambridge University Press, 1997.

Hallaq, Wael. *The Origins and Evolution of Islamic Law*. Cambridge; New York: Cambridge University Press, 2005.

Hallaq, Wael. "A Tenth-Eleventh Century Treatise on Juridical Dialectic." *Muslim World* 77 (1987): 197–228.

Hasan, Ahmad. *The Early Development of Islamic Jurisprudence*. Islamabad: Islamic Research Institute, 1988.

Kamali, Mohammad Hashim. *Principles of Islamic Jurisprudence*. 3rd Edition. Cambridge, UK: The Islamic Texts Society, 2003.

al-Khinn, Muṣṭafā Sa'īd. *Athar al-Ikhtilāf fi'l-Qawā'id al-Uṣūliyya fī Ikhtilāf al-Fuqahā'*. Beirut: Mu'assasat al-Risāla, 1972.

Lowry, Joseph. *Early Islamic Legal Theory : the Risāla of Muḥammad ibn Idrīs al-Shāfi'ī*. Leiden; Boston: Brill, 2007.

al-Sarakhsī, Muḥammad b. Aḥmad. *Kitāb al-Mabsūṭ*. Ed. Muḥammad Rāḍī, et al. 30 Vols. Cairo: Maṭba'at al-Sa'ada, 1324-1331/1906-1913.

Schacht, Joseph. *An Introduction to Islamic Law*. Oxford: Clarendon Press, 1964.

Schacht, Joseph. *The Origins of Muhammadan Jurisprudence*. Oxford: Oxford University Press, 1950.

al-Shāfi'ī, Muḥammad b. Idrīs. *Kitāb Ikhtilāf Abī Ḥanīfa wa Ibn Abī Laylā* [= *Umm* Version]. In *idem*, *Mawsū'at al-Imām al-Shāfi'ī: al-Kitāb al-Umm* (2nd ed.) Ed. Aḥmad Badr al-Dīn Ḥassūn. Beirut: Dār Qutayba, 2003, vol. 9, pt. 14, pp. 7–235.

al-Shāfi'ī, Muḥammad b. Idrīs. *Mawsū'at al-Imām al-Shāfi'ī: al-Kitāb al-Umm*. 2nd ed. Ed. Aḥmad Badr al-Dīn Ḥassūn. 16 Pts. in 10 Vols. Beirut: Dār Qutayba, 2003.

Vishanoff, David R. *The Formation of Islamic Hermeneutics: How Sunni Legal Theorists Imagined a Revealed Law*. New Haven, Conn: American Oriental Society, 2011.

Young, Walter Edward. "The Dialectical Forge: Proto-System Juridical Disputation in the Kitāb Ikhtilāf al-'Irāqiyyīn." 2 vols. PhD diss., McGill University, 2012.

Chapter 8
Uṣūl al-Fiqh and *Jadal*-Theory in the Dialectical Forge

8.1 Introducing the Dialectical Forge Model

I will now turn to the implications of what we have surveyed, analyzed, and concluded in preceding chapters. In so doing, I will proceed from more particular observations and their implications to the more general and abstract. First I will briefly sketch the overall Dialectical Forge model, and then, as we proceed through subsequent discussions I will attach various component processes as they arise, and the whole will be recapped at the end. In one sense, I will construct the engine frame first, then plug in its powering mechanisms as they are induced.

As a metaphor, "the dialectical forge" aims to describe. It is meant to evoke the intense and animated venue of disputation as it was practiced throughout large swathes of Islamicate civilization since the earliest times, the sometimes heated but usually scholarly (and increasingly systematic) workspace in which substantive doctrines—and the theoretical, methodological, and argumentative tools which built and sustained them—were produced, reshaped, and refined. In this sense, "the dialectical forge" was at work in any number of particular projects, although I will maintain focus on its influence in the endeavor of discovering God's Law. As a theoretical model, on the other hand, the Dialectical Forge aims to explain. It seeks to account for the formative dynamic of dialectical debate: its compelling agency, motives, influences, and inter-relationships with regard to the epistemic systems which frequently engage in it. In the current study, my particular concern has been to explain the relationship between dialectical debate and the juridical sciences of *uṣūl al-fiqh* and *jadal*. "The dialectical forge," then, is the venue in which these sciences were shaped; but the Dialectical Forge was the engine which powered that venue and ensured—so long as wholly operational—that its *uṣūl* and *jadal*-theory products were continually tested and refined, and working towards increasing systematization.

The various mechanisms of the engine were derived from the analyses and assembled in the discussions which follow. These focus on: (1) commonalities

W.E. Young, *The Dialectical Forge*, Logic, Argumentation & Reasoning 9,
DOI 10.1007/978-3-319-25522-4_8

between proto-system dialectic and full-system *jadal*-theory, (2) commonalities between proto-system legal theory and full-system *uṣūl al-fiqh*, (3) differences between these systems, (4) how legal-theory was employed in disputation, and (5) how *jadal*-theory itself developed from its self-refining practice. The engine itself has two simultaneously-functioning engine-compartments: one for dialectic and legal theory, the other for dialectic and *jadal*-theory. Like pistons, the mechanisms of this chapter's discussions will be located in their compartments, and seen to contribute to the functioning of the engine as a whole. In the first compartment (dialectic and legal theory), the following processes—each of which I have named, and explained, in its place—will be found at work: (1) the "three-stage cycle"; (2) dynamic symbiosis and co-evolution; (3) the bequeathing of dialectical axioms; (4) the *ijtihādic* anticipation of *jadal*; and (5) the "first principles parallel." As for the second compartment (dialectic and *jadal*-theory), its working mechanisms are: (1) *jadal* practice shaping *jadal*-theory; (2) dialectic defining what is *endoxon*; and (3) transmission and analysis of past *jadal*.

The remaining sections of this chapter will address the differences between proto-system and full-system legal theory and *jadal*-theory, review select instances of elements from both theories "gaining the edge of argumentative conclusiveness (*ḥujjiyya*)" in the dialectical forge, compare the Dialectical Forge model with select evolutionary paradigms for *uṣūl al-fiqh* (with an eye towards integration), and, finally, return to a brief outline of the model in its current form.

8.2 Proto-System *Jadal* and the Development of *Uṣūl*-Theory

Differences Between Proto-System Legal Theory and Full-System Uṣūl al-Fiqh

In previous chapters we have encountered numerous elements of proto-system legal theory—al-Shāfiʿī's, in the main—manifesting themselves, with some frequency, in the subject-text. Occasionally, I noted differences between this manifest theory and the more refined, fully-systematized theories we find in the works of early *uṣūl* theorists—among them, of course, the *uṣūl* and *jadal* treatises of our lens-text authors. We will now give primary focus to this endeavour, with the objective of exploring further implications. Bear in mind that—due to the very content and arrangement of our lens-texts—the survey of elements in the subject-text was as much legal-theoretical as it was dialectical. The focus of the lens-texts, after all, is the justification and critique of *istidlāl*—and the language and method of *istidlāl* is propounded in terms of the *ʿilm uṣūl al-fiqh*. Thus I will propose that differences between proto-system and full-system legal theory have already manifested themselves in two significant ways, in the preceding chapter: (1) via elements from our subject-text which did not match categories in our lens-texts;

and (2) via elements from our lens-texts which one would have expected to find in relevant discussions of our subject-text, but were absent.

Among many examples I may cite is the comparatively less developed manner in which the *qiyās*-method of our subject-text is expressed. Although the term *qiyās* occurs some two dozen times in the *Ikhtilāf al-ʿIrāqiyyayn/ʿIrāqiyyīn* (along with a half dozen or more incidents of the verb *qāsa/yaqīsu*), nowhere is the *mode* of *qiyās* technically expressed. Invariably we only encounter phrases such as "*qiyāsan ʿalā*" and "*qāsahu ʿalā.*" Entirely absent, in other words, are technical references to *qiyās al-ṭard*, *qiyās al-ʿaks*, *qiyās al-ʿilla* (with *jalī*, *wāḍiḥ*, and *khafī* subtypes), *qiyās al-dalāla*, and *qiyās al-shabah*; although we have seen that many such species of *qiyās* were there in practice. Moreover, although some of the discussions of *qiyās*-relationship in our lens-texts are conducted in terms of *maʿnā/maʿānī*, the technical language of *waṣf* and *ʿilla* dominates full-system *jadal* theory. The *qiyās*-relationships of the subject-text, on the other hand, are conducted entirely in terms of *maʿānī*, with the notable exception of a reported claim of the Ahl al-Kalām, which employs *khiṣāl*. So, not only are the terms *ʿilla* and *waṣf* entirely absent from our subject-text, but so too are any technical references to *ṭard*, *ʿaks*, *jarayān*, and *taʾthīr*.

In a similar fashion, al-Shāfiʿī's *ḥadīth* justifications and transmission-oriented objections appear only in the vaguest terms in our subject-text; the latter are invariably some version of: "its like is not confirmed by the Ahl al-Ḥadīth," and absent are any technical references to *āḥād* and *mutawātir*, *mursal* and *musnad*, etc. We have seen that there are, however, indications of the less refined *ḥadīth* science then in place—signs, in other words, of another proto-system. As for the domain of hermeneutic, other differences are manifest. Certainly we have seen the hermeneutics of *lafẓ*-expressions, *bayān*, *jumla/mufassir*, and *ʿāmm/khāṣṣ* (among others) at work; but absent from our subject-text—and indeed, from the *Umm* and the *Risāla* as a whole—are the technical hermeneutics of absolute (*muṭlaq*) vs. restricted (*muqayyad*), and literal (*ḥaqīqa*) vs. tropical (*majāz*).

Even more significantly, there are differences with regard to the presence and absence of entire categories of *istidlāl*. The term *khiṭāb*, for example, appears nowhere at all in either *Umm* or *Risāla*, much less *laḥn al-khiṭāb*, *faḥwā al-khiṭāb*, *dalīl al-khiṭāb*, and *maʿnā al-khiṭāb*. Although we have found, in our subject-text alone, nearly the full gamut of *istidlāl* and *iʿtirāḍ* in the domain of *maʿnā al-khiṭāb* in practice, and a few instances of *faḥwā al-khiṭāb* and *dalīl al-khiṭāb* in practice, technical references to these and other categories of *maʿqūl aṣl* are simply missing from al-Shāfiʿī's legal theory as a whole. So, too, is any acknowledgement of *istiṣḥāb*; the term and its cognates are absent from both *Umm* and *Risāla*. On the other hand, we find indicants of guiding principles at work in proto-system legal theory—and not just al-Shāfiʿī's—which simply receive no theoretical treatment in our (juridical) *jadal* theory texts. Among these are: (1) a concern with internal, logical consistency (manifest in charges of *tanāquḍ*); (2) concerns which mirror the principle of public welfare considerations (*maṣlaḥa*)—surprisingly absent from al-Bājī (it is a staple of later Mālikī *uṣūl*); (3) demonstrated concerns with juristic precaution (*iḥtiyāṭ*), accompanied by the term itself; and (4) reported juristic preference (*istiḥsān*).[1]

This brings us to that most interesting "source" in al-Shāfiʿī's legal theory which we have come across several times, and whose true equivalent I have yet to identify in the early *jadal* theory texts. I am speaking, of course, of his arguments to the *ʿaql* and the *maʿqūl*, and I will pause now to offer my final assessment as to what al-Shāfiʿī might have intended by these terms.[2] Notably, references to the *maʿqūl* occur some seventy times throughout the *Umm*, and seven of these occur in the subject-text: at §§402, 633, 929, 1056, 1061, and 1411 (2x); and we have also encountered al-Shāfiʿī's argument to the *ʿaql* in §651. Before proceeding to my own assessment, however, note that Schacht has contributed to this topic:[3]

> Shāfiʿī often refers to *ʿaql* 'reason' or *maʿqūl* 'what is reasonable', sometimes as a synonym of *qiyās* [citing *Tr. I*, 160, which is Ḥassūn's §929], and in the numerous cases where he speaks of *qiyās* and *ʿaql* or *qiyās* and *maʿqūl*, sometimes in a broader meaning, implying that a doctrine is consistent and stands to reason [citing *Tr. I*, 73, which is Ḥassūn's §402].[4] So *maʿqūl* can be opposed to *qiyās* proper [citing *Tr. I*, 121, which is Ḥassūn's §633], or be used to show that there is no place for *qiyās* [citing *Tr. I*, 253, which is Ḥassūn's §1411].[5]

As for Ḥassūn's §402, we find that al-Shāfiʿī argues from the *maʿqūl* in a contract type (*ḥawāla*); he does so again in §633, with reference to the *maʿqūl* in *waṣiyya*-bequest, using the term in a consistent fashion in both cases. Schacht, as we see, interprets the first as *maʿqūl* "in a broader meaning, implying that a doctrine is consistent and stands to reason," and the second as "*maʿqūl*... opposed to *qiyās* proper." In §929, however, we find that al-Shāfiʿī argues from the *maʿqūl* in a *khabar*-report of the Prophet, specifically asserting that the Prophet "aimed at (*arāda*) the *farq*-distinction between the obligatory ritual act (*farīḍa*) and the supererogatory (*nāfila*)." Schacht interprets this, as we have seen, "as a synonym of *qiyās*." I find it unlikely that al-Shāfiʿī, remarkably consistent in all respects, would employ *maʿqūl* both as a "synonym for *qiyās*" and as "opposed to *qiyās* proper." Unless, that is, by "opposed to *qiyās* proper" Schacht meant that al-Shāfiʿī's *maʿqūl* is broader than just *qiyās* proper; in which case, and with an eye to the *maʿqūl* of the *jadal*-theorists, I would entirely agree.

In all of §§651, 1056 and 1061, we find that al-Shāfiʿī lists *ʿaql* and *maʿqūl* as a distinct "source" among "sources"—as though it were an *aṣl* among *uṣūl*:

---

[1] *Istiḥsān*, of course, was a hotly debated principle in proto-system legal theory, and thus itself the object of proto-system juridical dialectic. A key witness is al-Shāfiʿī's *Book on the Nullification of Juristic Preference* (*Kitāb Ibṭāl al-Istiḥsān*).

[2] In the end, I believe *maʿqūl* does not have equivalents so much as descendants in the lens-texts: the domains within the larger category of *Maʿqūl Aṣl* and the *Adillat al-Maʿqūl*.

[3] *Origins*, p. 126.

[4] Here, Schacht also cites numerous other instances from treatises of the *Umm*, the *Risāla*, and the *Ikhtilāf al-Ḥadīth*.

[5] Schacht continues: "*Ijtihād* must be exercised by *ʿaql*...; Allah has endowed mankind with *ʿaql* and guides them either by an explicit text or by indications on which to base their *ijtihād*...;" twice citing the *Risāla* (*Origins*, p. 126).

- §651: "the doctrine (*qawl*) you have chosen is furthest from (*abʿad min*) [1] *al-qiyās* [2] *al-ʿaql*"
- §1056: "and I don't know anyone who says X without contradicting (*khālafa*) [1] *al-Qur'ān*, [2] *al-āthār*, [3] *al-qiyās*, [4] *al-maʿqūl*"
- §1061: "then how have you contradicted [ʿUmar b. al-Khaṭṭāb] (*khālaftahu*), and with him [1] *al-Qur'ān*, [2] *al-qiyās*, [3] *al-maʿqūl*, [4] and others of the Companions of the Prophet (*ghayrahu min Aṣḥāb al-Nabī*)?"

Not only may we observe the hallmarks of consistent usage in the above examples, but three characteristics of *ʿaql/maʿqūl* make themselves plain here: (1) they are listed separately from *qiyās*—i.e., they are *distinct* from *qiyās*; (2) they may be paired with other *adilla*-indicants as a super-authoritative epistemic conglomeration; and (3) they are something that an opponent can violate through faulty reasoning.

This brings us back to the intriguing "*aṣl al-maʿqūl*" of §1411. Here we found al-Shāfiʿī arguing:

- "the *aṣl al-maʿqūl* was that nothing is made lawful for party X by the action of party Y"
- "it was not permitted that we do *qiyās* from [God's exception] for what diverges from it, if the *aṣl* belongs to what is rationally understood (*li'l-maʿqūl fīhi*)"

Schacht has interpreted these two instances as *maʿqūl* "used to show that there is no place for *qiyās*." Although I would agree that he is correct in judging the context to be one in which "there is no place for *qiyās*," I would argue that it is in fact the term *aṣl* which shows it, not the term *maʿqūl*. *Aṣl* in §1411, though qualified by *al-maʿqūl* and *li'l-maʿqūl fīhi*, seems to refer to God's "original" ruling(s) with regard to the key quality (lawful for party X via action of party Y) inherent to the *mas'ala* at hand. In other words, it is God's *aṣl*-principle that this arrangement should never be the case, and this *aṣl*-principle bears the further epistemic advantage of "belonging to the *maʿqūl fīhi*." God's explicit ruling in the *mas'ala* at hand is therefore God's own exception to God's *aṣl*-principle (which is for us, in hermeneutical terms, *maʿqūl fīhi*); thus, according to al-Shāfiʿī's legal-theoretical teaching, it must never be allowed to serve as the basis of *qiyās* when the end-solution would contradict God's "original" *aṣl*-principle. In other words, "belongs to what is rationally understood (*li'l-maʿqūl fīhi*)" is merely a descriptor for God's *aṣl*-principle, reminding the opponent that this principle is perfectly apparent to the discerning intellect; and its belonging to the *maʿqūl fīhi* is not what prevents *qiyās*.

Before my final assessment as to what al-Shāfiʿī means by *ʿaql* and *maʿqūl*—which terms now seem very consistent in his usage—I would shift focus to the second subset of the "indicants of God's Law" (*adillat al-Sharʿ*) according to our lens-texts: the *maʿqūl aṣl*. More specifically, I would draw attention to the fact that—although one might suspect *maʿqūl aṣl* to mean something like "rational principle"—we must take into consideration the following fact: every form of *maʿqūl aṣl* in the *jadal*-theory literature is bound to a textual *dalīl*-indicant. That is to say, no form of *maʿqūl aṣl* (such as *faḥwā al-khiṭāb*, or *maʿnā al-khiṭāb*, etc.) exists in isolation from Qur'ān or Sunna—they are all hermeneutically linked to the instruction (*khiṭāb*). This is the source of epistemic strength for the modes of reasoning grouped under this rubric, and the reason for their superiority over *istiṣḥāb al-ḥāl* and other principles operating in the absence of specific textual *adilla*-indicants.

Moreover, all of the categories of *maʿqūl aṣl* may be described in the following manner: they are modes of discovering or bringing to the surface God's intensions (*maʿānī*) with regard to His decrees and rulings, when such intensions are not plainly stated in the textual *dalīl*-indicant. This applies to all of *laḥn al-khiṭāb*, *faḥwā al-khiṭāb*, *dalīl al-khiṭāb*, and *maʿnā al-khiṭāb*. By way of each of these modes, a solution for the *mas'ala* at hand is subsumed beneath what is *understood* to be God's fuller normative intention. I have italicized "understood" in the previous sentence because I believe this to be the crux of the matter: *maʿqūl* is synonymous with *mafhūm*, but with the added nuance of "understood" via varying degrees of rational effort. The "varying degrees of rational effort" also explains the hierarchical ranking of these modes of *istidlāl* in our *jadal*-theory texts, with *laḥn al-khiṭāb* requiring the least rational effort, and *maʿnā al-khiṭāb* requiring the most. And the lesser the degree to which humankind must exercise its rational faculty in comprehending the full range of God's command, the lesser the degree to which human error can creep in, and the greater the epistemic authority of the command thus "understood".

Returning to al-Shāfiʿī, I will offer my final assessment as to what he means by *maʿqūl* and *ʿaql*, taking all of the above into account. None of the instances in which al-Shāfiʿī employs these terms prevent us from defining the *maʿqūl* as "that which is understood (*mafhūm*) of God's command via rational effort (to lesser or greater degrees), when it is not plainly stated in a textual *dalīl*-indicant." In other words, al-Shāfiʿī's conception of *maʿqūl* and *ʿaql* is in consonance with our lens-texts' conception of *maʿqūl aṣl*, despite two obvious differences: (1) al-Shāfiʿī never once makes technical reference to *khiṭāb* throughout his legal theory (i.e., he formulates no typology for *maʿqūl aṣl*); and (2) al-Shāfiʿī consistently references *ʿaql* and *maʿqūl* independently of *qiyās*. As for this latter, it is not to suggest he did not see a relationship between *maʿqūl* and *qiyās*, but only that he did not subsume *qiyās* beneath *maʿqūl* as our *jadal*-theorists subsumed it beneath *maʿqūl aṣl*.

So, when al-Shāfiʿī argues to the *maʿqūl*, he is arguing to that "rational understanding" which would later be expressed in terms of *laḥn al-khiṭāb*, *faḥwā al-khiṭāb*, and *dalīl al-khiṭāb*—but not *maʿnā al-khiṭāb*, which he maintains separately as *qiyās*.

If this is correct,[6] then there are two very important implications for the current project, each of which may again be expressed in terms of difference and similarity with full-system *jadal* and *uṣūl* theory. First, al-Shāfiʿī's *maʿqūl* and *ʿaql* are different in that he developed no refined typology of subtypes as later theorists did for *maʿqūl aṣl*—even if he in fact practiced modes of reasoning which may be qualified in terms of these subtypes. Thus, once again, proto-system legal theory appears just as we would expect: less choate, less refined, less comprehensive. As with other areas, some of the base material is there, but without the categories and refined definitions it would receive with our *jadal* and *uṣūl* theorists. Second, the very fact that we find a parallel consideration sharing the technical term *maʿqūl* speaks volumes with regard to the continuity and perpetual development and refinement of certain proto-system concepts. *Uṣūl al-Fiqh* did not emerge in the fourth century from a vacuum, but neither was al-Shāfiʿī the Aristotle of this

---

[6] A confirming reference may be found in Éric Chaumont's *EI*[2] entry on al-Shāfiʿī. Under section (2) "Doctrine," subsection (b), "*uṣūl al-fiqh*," Chaumont explains, with regard to al-Shāfiʿī's modes of derivation of *aḥkām*:

> This legal statute is either presented as such in the scriptural sources (the Ḳurʾān and the Sunna), which al-S͟hāfiʿī calls "the foundation" (*al-aṣl*), or is it possible, by means of analogical reasoning (*ḳiyās* [*q.v.*]) to infer it from the *aṣl*, the latter being the bearer of a latent "rationally deducible content", the *maʿḳūl al-aṣl* ? All the efforts of al-S͟hāfiʿī–and herein lies his originality in comparison with his predecessors–were subsequently to be applied to defining with precision, establishing critically and ranking in order of priority these different sources (*aṣl* and *maʿḳūl al- aṣl*) and to determining the modalities of their usage.

Chaumont's translation of *maʿqūl al-aṣl* as "rationally deducible content" is in perfect consonance with not only the *ʿaql* and *maʿqūl* we have found in the *Umm*, but with the arch-category of *maʿqūl aṣl* as we find it in our *jadal*-theory texts. Also of note is Joseph Lowry's extensive discussion on the topic of *maʿqūl* and *ʿaql* in his *Early Islamic Legal Theory*, which I may briefly summarize as follows. First, he notes that al-Shāfiʿī refers to *ʿaql* in three different ways in his *Risāla*: (1) with seeming disapproval, in reference to the Ahl al-ʿUqūl; (2) positively, as "a tool furnished by God so that His servants can do what is most important: perform legal reasoning; and (3) by referring to *mas'ala* solutions as *maʿqūl* (pp. 313–14). With regard to the passages cited for (2), Lowry observes: "Shāfiʿī seems less overtly hostile to *ʿaql*, but also unwilling to let it operate unconstrained by revelation" (p. 314). With regard to the specific sense of *maʿqūl* in two examples, Lowry describes the term: (1) as corresponding to "the most obvious implication of the [Qur'ānic] passages in question (*ashbahuhumā bi'l-maʿqūl al-ẓāhir*)," and as bearing a similarity to "the identification of the *maʿnā* in *maʿnā*-based *qiyās*;" and (2) as corresponding to "simply a sensible [solution], apparently unanchored in a revealed text." As for Lowry's final analysis: "it can be said that Shāfiʿī disapproves of reason as a substitute for revelation but recognizes the necessity of using reason as a tool for interpreting revelation" (pp. 315–17). Importantly, Lowry's discussion of *ʿaql* and *maʿqūl* is taking place within a larger chapter entitled: "Internal Evidence for the *Risāla*'s Polemical Content." In other words, he is well-aware of the *Risāla*'s dialectical features.

science. He was indeed an eminent contributor to proto-system legal theory; but he was not alone in making early contributions, and the real systematizing Aristotles came later.

This is supported by all the parallels and divergences we have noted between the proto-system legal theory of the subject-text and the full-system theory of fourth/tenth and fifth/eleventh century theorists. Certain core elements of later *uṣūl al-fiqh* are present, but in reduced number and with less refinement. Certain elements are missing entirely, and apparently fashioned at a later date. Technical terms are generally scarce, and of broader scope—though consistently applied; and certain of those terms in vogue in proto-system theory would eventually take on different nuances and gain additional subcategories. Most importantly of all, and as both our subject-text and lens-texts stand witness, all of these elaborations and refinements were resultant of continual epistemic pressures brought to bear in venues of juridical disputation. *Uṣūl al-Fiqh* as we know it was born and refined in the dialectical forge.

Legal Theory in the Dialectical Forge

Being that: (1) our *jadal*-theory lens for analyzing the subject-text was also an *uṣūl*-theory lens; and (2) most of the material analyzed was overtly dialectical, appearing in transcript-like Q&A sequences replete with argument and counter-argument; it is not an exaggeration to say: these arguments, so long as they depended upon a lens-text domain of *istidlāl*, constitute examples of legal-theoretical axioms—be they epistemological, hermeneutical, or rational-inferential—gaining, sustaining, or losing the edge of *ḥujjiyya* in the dialectical forge. Certain examples, however, were more noticeably of a legal-theoretical bent, and I have pointed them out as we progressed through Chaps. 5, 6, and 7. Primary among these were the "open appeals to legal theory" mentioned once in the review of category A-B material (nine examples), and again for the C-G material (five examples).[7] And in addition to these were many other instances wherein it was quite clear that a legal-theoretical axiom was employed—sometimes accompanied by a plainly technical vocabulary. In the following table, I have recorded a number of instances according to general legal-theoretical domains as I understand them, though this should not be considered a complete listing.

[7] I will try to avoid repetition here; please see the tables in Chap. 7, and accompanying notes.

Epistemology (Having to Do with Knowledge, Certainty, Doubt, etc.)[8]

- §§700 (with "doubt/assumption" [*ẓann*] and "most apparent" [*ẓāhir*]); 504, 614–19, 685 (with "according to knowledge" [*ʿalā ʿilm*] vs. "with categorical certainty" [*al-battata*]); 304–8 (with "knowledge" [*ʿilm*], *ẓāhir*, "doubt" [*shakk*], "certainty" [*yaqīn*]); 502–4 ("intellection" [*maʿrifa*], *ʿilm*, "definitive" [*al-batt*]); 1168–71 (with *ẓāhir*); 1273 (with *ẓāhir*)

Transmission Theory (Having to Do with *Isnāds*, Conveyance of *Akhbār*)

- §§248 (with *awlā*, *ijtamaʿa*, *wāfaqa*, and *tathabbut*); 283; 667 (critique: it is *min wajhin wāḥidin lā yuthbituhu Ahl al-Ḥadīth kulla al-tathbīt*); 1138 (critique: *laysat min wajh yathbutu mithluhu law infarada*); 1139 (critique: *laysat fī aḥadin maʿa al-nabī... ḥujjatan*; and *lā aʿlamuhu thābitan ʿan wāḥidin minhumā*); 1147 (with *marfūʿ*)

Hermeneutical Theory (Having to Do with *Lafẓ*-Expressions, General/ Particular [*ʿāmm/khāṣṣ*], Ambiguous/Clarified [*mujmal/mufassar*], etc.)

- §§52 (Sunna is *al-naṣṣ al-mufassira* providing indicant for [*tadullu ʿalā*] *jumla* Sunna); 64–5; 87–8 (with *mawḍūʿ* and *waḍʿ*); 247 (with *jumla*, *maʿnā*, *shabīh*, *khilāf*, and *iḥtamala*); 255 (SH *ḥadīth* is *mufassir* to SHAR's *jumla ḥadīth*); 257 ff. (with *sammā*, *dalāla*, and *jumla*); 263 (with *khāṣṣ*, *dalāla*, *ism*, *yaḥtamilu*, *maʿnā*, *khālafa*); 265; 1056 ff.; 1077; 1255; 1271; 1410 ff.

Primary Rational-Inferential Theory (Having to Do with *Qiyās*-Theory)

- every instance where *maʿnā* is evoked (e.g., §248, where SH claims the *maʿnā* of his *ḥadīth* is present [*qāʾim*] in the *masʾala* at hand)[9]
- §§282 ff. (*qiyās* cannot trump established Sunna); 284; 293 (lack of *āthār* justifies use of *qiyās*); 787 (*takhṣīṣ al-ʿilla*?); 1071 (concomitance?); 1261; 1411

Secondary Rational-Inferential Theory (Having to Do with *Iḥtiyāṭ*, *Maṣlaḥa*, *Adilla ʿAqliyya*, etc.)

- all arguments to *ʿaql* and *maʿqūl*; all instances of reported *istiḥsān*; and all instances of apparent appeals to *ʿurf*, *iḥtiyāṭ*, *maṣlaḥa*

---

[8] See also, in Chap. 7, the table: "Arguments and Rulings Bearing upon the Epistemology of Evidentiary Procedure."

[9] Note that al-Shāfiʿī employs *qāʾim*, and not some cognate of *ithbāt* as we usually find in the later *uṣūl* literature.

And there are other cases where a legal-theoretical principle is brought to the fore, such as: §984, where al-Shāfiʿī appears to allude to the rationale behind the occasioning factor of a ruling; and §§1023–8, wherein he explains clearly why he abandons the *athar*-tradition of a Companion for a Prophetic *ḥadīth*. And to all of the above, we might add a host of substantive legal definitional concerns:

- §§301 (*maʿnā* of *ikrāh*-compulsion); 735 ff. (definition of *mufāwaḍa*-partnership); 864 (definition/properties of "cancelled [contract]" [*mafsūkh*]); 1299–1306 (definitions of *īlā'*-divorce); 1307–9 (definitions of *ẓihār*-divorce); 1124 (the *maʿānī*-qualities of slaves [properties (*amwāl*) or persons (*nufūs*)? SH discussion is framed by a *maʿnā*-quality as "separating" [*mufāriq*] from one genus (*amwāl*), and "uniting" [*mujāmiʿ*] with another genus (*nufūs*)])[10]

I have also pointed out a number of examples wherein legal theory and method were the objects of dialectical critique itself—a theory-oriented genus of objections. Although treatises such as al-Shāfiʿī's *Book on the Nullification of Juristic Preference* (*Kitāb Ibṭāl al-Istiḥsān*) make it abundantly clear that legal theory was often the object of proto-system *jadal*, we are fortunate to have encountered several examples within the dialectical sequences of our own subject-text. Primary among these are the many instances of method-*naqḍ*, and several examples from the "open appeals to legal theory" reviewed in the previous chapter.

My objective in compiling these examples is to support a primary thesis of the current study: juridical dialectic was the major dynamic in the formation and epistemic advancement of Islamic legal-theoretical principles. It was a sifting of good argument from bad, sound method from problematic, irrefutable from refutable; all according to the pressures exerted by juridical *jadal*'s continually evolving argumentation episteme. This is the basic principle of the Dialectical Forge model; and I would claim that until this critical dynamic in the evolution of legal theory is recognized and explained, and its implications fully explored, no legal-historical paradigm for the origins and evolution of *uṣūl al-fiqh* will be complete.

8.3 The Dialectical Forge and Current Paradigms for the Evolution of *Uṣūl al-Fiqh*

My objective in this section is not to supplant current paradigms—all of which offer interpretations important in their own right, and several of which are replete with accurate observations and insightful assessments of various stages in

[10] NB: This mirrors the Aristotelian notion whereby a complete definition is properly including (*jāmiʿ*) all that should fall under its rubric, and excluding (*māniʿ*) all that should not.

the development of *uṣūl al-fiqh*.[11] But I have encountered no paradigm which incorporates juridical dialectic to the extent required, nor adequately accounts for its formative dynamic—that is, if dialectic is mentioned at all, and it most often is not. The present aim, therefore, is to determine if more current paradigms are consonant with the Dialectical Forge model in its basic outline, or if they allow integration with minimal conflict. I will begin with the more comprehensive evolutionary paradigms with which I am familiar, then proceed through successively less comprehensive paradigms. Along the way, the Dialectical Forge model will be enhanced by a number of important observations by leading scholars.

There are a great many more historical overviews of the evolution of *uṣūl al-fiqh* in current secondary literature than I will present here. What follows represents what I am most familiar with, what is relatively comprehensive, and what does not rely extensively on other secondary sources. Mohammad Hashim Kamali's brief historical discussion,[12] for example, does not appear in the following simply because he does not pursue the history of *uṣūl* after al-Shāfiʿī, and his comments are drawn, in the main, from Muḥammad Abū Zahra's *Uṣūl al-Fiqh* (whose historical trajectory I will treat in some detail). The same applies to the trajectory of Muḥammad al-Khuḍarī in his *Uṣūl al-Fiqh*; the greater part of his observations find their parallels in Abū Zahra's text. So too, do those of Aḥmad Badr al-Dīn Ḥassūn (whose edition of the *Kitāb al-Umm* I have mostly relied upon for my translation).[13] Finally, the important contributions of Éric Chaumont are not being neglected here;[14] his discussions regarding the evolution of *uṣūl al-fiqh*, however, are in the main subsumed by those of Hallaq, Calder, and Muḥammad Abū Zahra.

Wael Hallaq

As we have seen, Hallaq is one of the few contributors to the modern study of juridical dialectic, and I will briefly revisit some of his observations regarding *jadal* in following sections. With regard to the legal history of Islam as a whole he has advanced several trajectories of particular concern to this current project.

[11] A disclaimer: due to constraints of space, this section is inevitably reductive; many of the paradigms reviewed are quite complex, but will here be abbreviated to outline form. Though I have avoided problematic distortions to the best of my ability, a full grasp of the trajectories and historical models which follow—with all their important details and implications—may only be gained through consulting their authors' full expositions.

[12] Pages 4–6 of his *Principles of Islamic Jurisprudence*.

[13] See in particular the overview of al-Shāfiʿī's contributions in his lengthy introduction (*Mawsūʿa*, vol. 1, pp. 151 ff.)

[14] See the introduction to his translation of al-Shīrāzī's *Kitāb al-Lumaʿ*, esp. at pp. 3–16.

These are elaborated in detail in a number of books and articles; fortunately they have been gathered together and summarized in a more recent publication. Here we observe how particular narratives integrate to form a larger, comprehensive paradigm for the formative period of Islamic legal conceptions, doctrinal schools, and institutions.[15] The following outlines, though necessarily abbreviated, still hope to capture the essence of decisive trends and evolutionary stages as Hallaq presents them. I will begin with the earliest developments of concern—corresponding to the proto-system of legal theory, through to the age of al-Shāfiʿī—and then proceed to subsequent developments—roughly from al-Shāfiʿī's time through to the first, full-system treatments of *uṣūl al-fiqh*.

On the Rise of "Legal Specialists"[16]

- [1] 80–120 H: private scholars studying law for pious reasons contribute *sunan*-based, positive opinions and Qur'ānic interpretations; some become judges
- [2] Study circles (*ḥalaqāt*) form in important cities and regions (Medina, Mecca, Kūfa, Baṣra, Damascus, Fusṭāṭ, Yemen, Khurāsān; mostly in the Ḥijāz and Iraq): some are exclusively juridical; specializations evolve in Qur'ānic inheritance law, ritual law, *sunan*, etc.
- [3] "The activities of the legal specialists initiated what was to become a fundamental principle of Islamic law, namely, that legal knowledge as an *epistemic* quality was to be the final arbiter in law-making;"
  - "...those men in possession of a greater store of knowledge grew more influential than others less learned, gaining in the process—by sheer virtuousness of their knowledge—exclusive authority as legists. [....] This epistemic and moral authority became a defining feature of Islamic law."

The early tradition of scholarly *ḥalaqāt* is of key importance here; they undoubtedly were as much venues for dialectical disputation in the first half of the second century H (the era of Abū Ḥanīfa and Ibn Abī Laylā) as they were in the latter half

[15] I will focus only on those which bear most upon the Dialectical Forge model—some of which, in fact, were essential to my understanding of developments from proto-system to full-system legal theory. My approach, in this regard, is therefore doubly-reductive; for I am forced to set aside certain important narratives (e.g., the evolution from proto-*qāḍī* to full-fledged judiciary, the formation of doctrinal *madhāhib*, the creation of "axes of authority," etc.) which integrate into Hallaq's larger paradigm for the concerned period, as well as reduce such narratives as I do address to outline form.

[16] Hallaq, *Sharīʿa*, pp. 43–5. For a more detailed rendering, see Hallaq, *Origins*, pp. 63–6.

(the era of Abū Yūsuf, al-Shaybānī, and al-Shāfiʿī). Hallaq's observation (#3) with regard to legal knowledge and "epistemic and moral authority" is of even greater import, for these critical elements were gaining weight through a discourse which had started even earlier—at least by the time of the Successors (Tābiʿūn), several of whom—such as Ibrāhīm al-Nakhaʿī (d. ca. 96/717)—survived into the beginning of this period of early *ḥalaqāt*.[17] The discourse of this generation, and of those prior, was replete with novel and problematic cases requiring carefully considered solutions; these in turn required modes of epistemic justification, and early justifications took the form of references to Qur'ān and *sunan*, coupled with the exercise of "considered opinion" (*ra'y*).

In these former two sources we find not only authoritative rulings, but the new argumentation axioms of early Islam.[18] As for *ra'y*, we would undoubtedly find the axioms of prior Near Eastern argumentation epistemes—if indeed they are not also to be found in the Qur'ān and *sunan*. As I have mentioned earlier, it was the infusion of Islamic axioms into prior epistemes that forms the stem from which both theological and juridical *jadal* flourished; and, most importantly, it was in such venues as were provided by early *ḥalaqāt* that the early development of distinctively Islamic argumentation epistemes took place. The dialectical forge was lit from the earliest times.

---

[17] Our subject-text is filled with references to Ibrāhīm in particular, and we will note that he was (like Ibn Abī Laylā, Abū Ḥanīfa, and Abū Yūsuf after him) a Kūfan. What is more, he was famed for his cautious recourse to *ra'y* in conjunction with *sunan* (see Lecomte's *EI*² entry, s.v. "al-Nakhaʿī").

[18] Besides the conception of epistemic authority residing in the Qur'ān and the *sunan*, there are the argumentation axioms expressed in these sources themselves. With regard to the Qur'ān, see pp. 93–209 of Heinrich's edition of al-Ṭūfī's *ʿAlam al-Jadhal fī ʿIlm al-Jadal*, where the author presents an analysis of the *jadal* of the Qur'ān, *sūra* by *sūra*. In Chap. 6, I mentioned that *ra'ā* formulae appear in the Qur'ān; I would note here that variants of *a-ra'ayta* occur some twenty times (most often as *a-ra'aytum*), and with the very same syntax (interrogative alif with conditional) as we find in our subject-text (see, e.g., Q.6:40–1, 46–7; 10:50, 59; etc.) *A-lā tarā* enjoys at least one occurrence (Q.12:59; as *a-lā tarawn*), and so far as I have investigated these they appear to exhibit similar rhetorical functions as when employed by Abū Ḥanīfa and the other jurists of the subject-text. Also with regard to the argumentation of the Qur'ān, see Gwynne's *Logic, Rhetoric, and Legal Reasoning in the Qur'ān*. Analyzing the arguments of our subject-text, and of the *Umm* as a whole, through the argumentation methods of the Qur'ān is an important study yet to be done. With regard to the argument axioms of the *sunan*, we have encountered in our analyses references to the *qiyās* of the Ṣaḥāba, and will see a relevant observation in the next paradigm (Hallaq on the evolution of Sunnaic epistemic authority).

On the Evolution of Sunnaic Epistemic Authority: From a Larger Pool of Exemplary *Sunan* to the Primacy of Prophetic Sunna[19]

- [1] There was an ancient, pre-Islamic Arabian concept of *sunna* as exemplary conduct: "a normative practice to be emulated"
- [2] The Prophet's *sīra* overlapped with *sunna* from the beginning; his Sunna was thus most important (but not primary) immediately after his death; still, the Prophet's Sunna was one among many *sunan*
- [3] Early transmission: *qāḍīs* and others begin transmitting Prophetic *ḥadīth*; there were new and more strident epistemic and pedagogical pressures; Prophetic Sunna was recognized to play a special role in Qur'ānic hermeneutics; still, reference to non-Prophetic *sunan* continues on the same level
- [4] Post-Prophetic *sunan* are projected back onto the Prophet; this was a natural phenomenon, as the *sunan* and *ra'y* of Companions were regarded as an extension of the Prophet's (i.e., they were understood to have been emulating him)
- [5] The proliferation of *ḥadīth* (including many fabrications); *ḥadīth* began to compete and conflict with practice-based *sunan*: in the Ḥijāz, "The literary narrative of *ḥadīth* acquired validity only to the extent that it was supported by this local usage;" also in Iraq, "living tradition" was the measure; this is "*ḥadīth* vs. *sunna*ic practice"
- [6] Due to the efforts of "a mobile class of traditionists," the literary *ḥadīth* eventually overtook *sunna*ic practice in terms of epistemic authority
- [7] Al-Shāfiʿī asserts that only formal *ḥadīth* can determine Prophetic Sunna, though this principle did not catch on immediately

A background dynamic of proto-system *jadal* integrates well with all of these stages and trends. We can even see some of them, in the heat of transformation, in the dialectical sequences of the *Ikhtilāf al-ʿIrāqiyyayn/ʿIrāqiyyīn*. Among other things, a substantial showing of non-Prophetic *sunan* is plain to see, although the *āthār*-traditions of Companions (and Successors) already appear most useful either in the absence of more authoritative *adilla*-indicants, or as glass weights adding epistemic mass to *istidlāl* from another *dalīl*-indicant. Regarding #4, we have seen references to *āthār*-traditions of the Companions as continuations of the Prophet's decrees and transactions, just as we have seen references to the *qiyās* of the Companions. Moreover, we have seen al-Shāfiʿī problematize his opponent's attempt to assume the Prophet's ruling on the basis of *āthār*-traditions (cf. #7 above). As Prophetic Sunna proliferated and/or was back-projected, the

[19] Hallaq, *Sharīʿa*, pp. 40–8. In more detail: Hallaq, *Origins*, pp. 69–78, 102–9, 117–20.

jurist-dialectician had an ever-growing store of more epistemically-authoritative *dalīl*-indicants with which to justify his *ijtihād* and critique his opponent's. In fact, no finer presentation of a source for *istidlāl* and *iʿtirāḍ* gaining primacy of *ḥujjiyya* in the dialectical forge—no finer example of the advancement of a distinctly Islamic and juridical argumentation episteme—can be provided than what we find in Hallaq's *sunan*-to-Sunna evolutionary paradigm.

On the Evolution of Authoritative Rational-Inferential Method: From a Less Choate *ra'y* to al-Shāfiʿī's More Refined Conception of *qiyās*[20]

- [1] From early on *ra'y* was closely associated with *sunna* and consensus, as exemplified by the method of the "people of *ra'y*;" a large range of types of reasoning were subsumed by *ra'y*: from the more informal to the "strictly logical"
- [2] A new generation of scholars (in the latter half of the second century H) participated in a juridical landscape marked by an increased authority for Prophetic *ḥadīth*, and a shrinking arena for "discretionary opinion;" *ra'y* began to acquire a "negative connotation"
  - "Non-textual *ra'y* obviously was no match for the Sunna"
- [3] There is a gradual process of terminological refinement into three categories: (1) *ijtihād*; (2) *qiyās*; (3) *istiḥsān*
- [4] Al-Shāfiʿī rejects "arbitrary" *ra'y* and *istiḥsān*, and incorporates *qiyās/ijtihād* into his legal theory; eventually *qiyās* "was to become the basis of all later legal theories, elaborated under the rubric of *uṣūl al-fiqh*"

We are again privileged to have seen these trends playing out in our subject-text. The rational-inferential methods revealed through our analyses extended far beyond the refined (and more disciplined)[21] typology of *maʿqūl aṣl* expounded in later theory; perhaps these argument types and strategies which I have marked as potentially unique to proto-system *jadal*—including those practiced by al-Shāfiʿī himself—may be subsumed beneath the later "negative" rubric of *ra'y*. If such is the case, then this current study will have revealed something of just what *ra'y* was—which arguments, specifically, were employed by early proponents of *ra'y* and did not make the epistemic grade established by later generations of

[20] Hallaq, *Sharīʿa*, pp. 48–51. In more detail: Hallaq, *Origins*, pp. 113–21.

[21] I have borrowed this apt descriptor from Hallaq; see #6 in the following paradigm of the "Great Synthesis."

theorists.[22] Moreover, I would even suggest that several of the argument axioms of al-Shāfiʿī's early legal theory—despite his later rejection of *ra'y* and *istiḥsān*—would themselves have been identified as *ra'y* by later theorists, and even by himself, in the "New Doctrine" legal theory of the *Risāla*.[23]

Whatever the case may be, I hope to have shown that this gradual refinement of *endoxon* argumentation-method came about in dialectical contexts, and I will pause here to propose what the wider implications of this might be. In short: just as natural selection—dictated by environmental change—is the ultimate determinant of speciation—for the extinction or survival (and, ultimately, evolution) of species—so too is the heat of dialectical encounter for species of argument. Regulated by an ever-advancing argumentation episteme, the exigencies of dialectic are equally a determinant for the extinction, survival, and evolution of species of argument.[24] Perhaps the most critical environmental factor of all in this respect was the gradually crystallizing Islamic hierarchy of epistemic authority; such prior species of argument as could adapt to this determining grade were to survive in enhanced forms (e.g., the more technically advanced species of *qiyās*, and the reformulated species of *istiḥsān*), while those which could not adapt disappeared gradually from the juridical dialectical landscape. Such is the evolution of legal theory's rational-inferential methodology as we see it described in the narrative above. The *Ikhtilāf al-ʿIrāqiyyayn/ʿIrāqiyyīn* provides a snapshot of the middle stage in the proto-system's evolution, with the final steps towards full-system legal theory to be taken in the following century, as Hallaq's next narrative will show.

On "The Great Rationalist-Traditionalist Synthesis" (As the True Cradle of *Uṣūl al-Fiqh*)[25]

- [1] After the end of the second century H there was a clear distinction between "rationalist" and "traditionalist" approaches to law
  - "exclusive affiliation to one or the other camp became the general rule"

(continued)

[22] I have avoided speaking of *ra'y* throughout my analyses and reviews, with the explicit intention of moving beyond this nebulous category, and getting at the true substance of proto-system argumentation outside of later "canon" domains of *istidlāl*. Perhaps now that we have seen which argument types lay outside of this later canon, and which lay within, we might consider subsuming the former set under the later "negative connotation" of *ra'y*.

[23] This topic is more than worthy of pursuit, and remains an open door for future study.

[24] Note that this ever-advancing argumentation episteme itself had a determinant: the generally pious, truth-seeking comportment of jurist-dialecticians as we have seen it time and again. This is an important point, for argumentation epistemes in a more sophistical environment cannot advance in the same manner as those in an environment of "good" truth-seeking dialectic, if they advance at all.

[25] Hallaq, *Sharīʿa*, pp. 55–9. In more detail: Hallaq, *Origins*, pp. 122–7.

- [2] The *Miḥna* (218–34 H)[26] marks a culmination in the rationalist (Caliphs, Muʿtazila, many Ḥanafīs) vs. traditionalist (proto-Ḥanbalīs) conflict
- [3] The third century H sees a growth in traditionists and traditionalists, a mostly unidirectional "migration" or "conversion" from the rationalist to the traditionalist "camp," and before the end of the century six law-oriented "canonical" *ḥadīth* collections had been compiled
- [4] *Ḥadīth* as "a textual entity" acquired an epistemic advantage of consistency:
    - "A universally transmitted *ḥadīth*... proved more appealing as a material and textual source of law than the living, *sunna*ic practice as defined by a specific city or legal community, since the latter had developed their own judicial and juristic peculiarities in keeping with their own particular environment."
- [5] By the end of the third century H "most jurists are reported to have combined the two [rationalist and traditionalist approaches] in some way;" this is the "Great Synthesis," as recorded by historians and biographers
    - "It was the midpoint between the two movements that constituted the normative position of the majority; and it was from this centrist position that Sunnism... was to emerge."
- [6] "...it was not the defeat of rationalism or the absolute victory of traditionalism that underpinned the emergence of *uṣūl al-fiqh*, but rather a redefinition and methodical disciplining of the former and the rise and dramatic increase of the latter."
- [7] "The Ḥanafites had to accommodate this new genre no later than in the third/ninth century..."
- [8] "Ibn Ḥanbal's jurisprudence—restrictive in its ways of reasoning—was soon abandoned by his immediate and later followers," the latter eventually accepted not only *qiyās* (abhorred by Ibn Ḥanbal), but even *istiḥsān* (abhorred by al-Shāfiʿī)
- [9] The Great Synthesis was the phenomenon from which full-system *uṣūl al-fiqh* was born:
    - "It was with this development that *uṣūl al-fiqh*... was at last defined. [...] legal theory emerged as a result of this Synthesis, which itself embodied, and was reflected by, this theory."

---

[26] See *EI*², s.v. "Miḥna," for an introduction to this period of "trial" initiated by the Caliph al-Ma'mūn (r. 198-218/813-833), who sought to impose—in inquisitional fashion, and to multiple political, theological, and juristic ends—a doctrine of the Qur'ān's createdness.

A potent—if not lasting—effect of the *Miḥna* period was the admixture of political dynamics into the evolving Islamic argumentation episteme. A new axiom was introduced into the set: the *argumentum ad baculum*.[27] Although disputational sessions (*majālis*) held before Caliphs prior to this period may have been tainted by a looming political presence, the *Miḥna* was something else entirely: a real and oft-administered threat to opponents of a thesis whose potential to achieve *endoxon* status was engulfed by the political sanction it enjoyed. As Hallaq notes, however, the *Miḥna* merely marks the "climax" of a disputational trend which had been ongoing for some time prior, and was to resolve itself sometime afterward in the "Great Synthesis."

The evolutionary processes leading to the "Great Synthesis"—in both speculative and normative projects—matured in the dialectical forge. In this case, it would benefit our understand to shift the definition of "dialectic" from its Aristotelian definition to its derived Hegelian definition, whereby *thesis* (the theories and methods of the "rationalist camp") meets *antithesis* (the theories and methods of the "traditionalist camp"), and resolves into *synthesis*: a new theoretical and methodological episteme comprising axioms of both. As Hallaq's narrative portrays, the epistemic quality of Sunnaic practice confirmed via *endoxa* methods simply could not be ignored by participants in an argumentation episteme infused with Islamic axioms of hierarchical authority. Hence the "migration" to the traditionalist camp. On the other hand, the undeniable necessity for human rational assessment in the testing and confirmation of the conveyance of potential *adilla*-indicants (i.e., transmission-oriented concerns), the interpretation of established *adilla*-indicants (i.e., hermeneutical concerns), and the derivation and extension of norms from established *adilla*-indicants (i.e., rational-inferential concerns) also could not be ignored. Hence the "disciplining" of proto-system legal theory's hermeneutical and rational-inferential modes, and the eventual extinction, as Hallaq shows us, of such argumentation epistemes which did not adopt these modes in their enhanced forms.[28]

With the exception of the *Miḥna* interlude, we are witness to a rationally evolving legal theory, dictated not so much by politics and factional loyalties (though they were at times a powerful factor) as by the exigencies of dialectical exchange. Hallaq exposes a Hegelian process of rationalist thesis conflicting with tradition-

[27] Although we have seen an earlier case of Caliphal imposition in our subject-text, outside of the *Miḥna* period such occurrences were rare and had no programmatic, inquisitional qualities. Caliphal interference—before or after the *Miḥna*—was not a decisive factor in the evolving argumentation episteme of Islamic law and legal theory. Which is not to say Caliphs were not keenly interested in the juristic enterprise; but they were, rather, participants within an established, scholarly practice—not imposers of self-formulated decrees. This is true of both al-Saffāḥ and al-Ma'mūn as well; the substance of their decrees—though imposed—was not self-formulated, but the provenance of particularly favored epistemic communities (e.g., Ḥijāzī jurists and the Muʿtazila).

[28] Besides the transformation of proto-Ḥanbalism (#8 in the above outline), Hallaq points to the eventual extinction of Ẓāhirism due to its strict stance against rational-inferential methods which had become *endoxa* within the remainder of the Sunni sphere (*Sharīʿa*, p. 59).

alist antithesis and resolving in a "Great Synthesis," which, in turn "embodied, and was reflected by" *uṣūl al-fiqh*. I would only add that this progression unfurled through the medium of *jadal*, whose participants were morally committed to "following the *ḥujja*." To claim that *uṣūl al-fiqh* was born from the Great Synthesis is to presuppose it was born in the dialectical forge.

On the Early Systematization of *Uṣūl al-Fiqh*[29]

(1) "One of the first groups to begin propounding legal theory in its organic and comprehensive form was a circle of Baghdadian Shāfiʿites, headed by the distinguished jurist Ibn Surayj (d. 306/918)."
(2) "This group was to contextualize legal theory as a synthesis between rationality and the textual tradition..."
(3) "...the first and foremost Shāfiʿite authors to write works on *uṣūl al-fiqh* (as a full-fledged methodology) were [Ibn Surayj's] students, such as Abū Bakr al-Fārisī (fl. c. 350/960), Ibn al-Qāṣṣ (d. 335/946), Abū Bakr al-Ṣayrafī (d. 330/942) and al-Qaffāl al-Shāshī (d. 336/947)."
(4) "However, it must be emphasized that the legal theory produced by this circle of scholars was not the product of an ongoing process of elaboration based on an established tradition, as later theory came to be. Instead, it was largely the product of the specific historical process that had begun a century or so earlier, and that had culminated under the influence of the Synthesis formed at the close of the third/ninth century and the first half of the fourth/tenth. Their theory can thus be characterized as the child of its environment, and it owed little more to al-Shāfiʿī than partial or nominal affiliation. The Ḥanafites, for instance, did not lag far behind in elaborating their own theory of law."
(5) "In fact, Shāfiʿī had little to do with the elaboration of *uṣūl al-fiqh*, since he advocated the synthesis in a rudimentary and incomplete form. And there were others, during the decades after his death, who discoursed on certain aspects of legal methodology and reasoning, usually advocating or refuting one specific position or another. Thus Shāfiʿī's theory was not accepted as standard by the community of third/ninth century jurists...."
(6) "By the middle of the fourth/tenth century, therefore, an elaborate and comprehensive theory of *uṣūl* had emerged. The next century and a half witnessed a phase in the history of this theory that produced the standard works on which later expositions so heavily depended, but the essential developments had already occurred by 350/960 or thereabouts."

[29] Hallaq, *Sharīʿa*, pp. 59–60. In more detail: *idem*, *Origins*, pp. 127–8; *idem*, *History*, pp. 30–5; *idem*, "Was al-Shāfiʿī the Master Architect."

With the Great Synthesis we arrive at the beginning of full-system *uṣūl al-fiqh*; and, with regard to its *literary* beginnings, we should not be surprised that—with a few important exceptions—legal theory itself had not been the focus of systematic treatises up to this point. It was only in the course of the preceding three-quarters of a century that: (1) the Great Synthesis was achieved; and (2) legal theory itself had become a singular object of frequent and critical dialectical debate—indeed, theory-oriented dialectic reached a boiling point.

Full expositions on a comprehensive and systematic science for *ijtihād* became a necessity, and it would appear that Ibn Surayj was among the first to provide one.[30] In addition to the Baghdādian Shāfiʿī affiliation of Ibn Surayj and his prolific students, Hallaq also notes they embodied the by-then-normative combination of traditionalist, jurist, and speculative theologian.[31] To this I will add another area of expertise: dialectician (also noted by Hallaq).[32] Ibn Surayj was famed as the vindicator of the Shāfiʿī *madhhab*, with numerous disputational sessions (*munāẓarāt*) with famed opponent contemporaries (such as Abū Bakr Muḥammad b. Dāwūd [al-Ẓāhirī]).[33] Among his many compositions several argumentative treatises against opponent-jurists, past and present, are listed, and his name has even been attached to a famed puzzle of juridical dialectic: the *mas'ala al-Surayjiyya*, or *dawr al-ṭalāq*.[34] Abū Bakr Muḥammad b. ʿAbd Allāh al-Ṣayrafī was also an author on *uṣūl al-fiqh*, and noted for his *munāẓara* with none other than the prominent dialectical theologian (*mutakallim*) Abū al-Ḥasan al-Ashʿarī (d.324/935-6).[35] Abū Bakr al-Qaffāl al-Shāshī was "the first among jurists to compose [a treatise on] the 'good dialectic' (*al-jadal al-ḥasan*)—not to mention a *Kitāb fī Uṣūl al-Fiqh* and a commentary on al-Shāfiʿī's *Risāla*.[36]

Beginning with this period, *uṣūl al-fiqh* and *jadal*-theory were to know many systematizing Aristotles. I would pause, however, to reflect upon the important combination of elements embodied by Abū Bakr al-Qaffāl al-Shāshī in particular. United in this scholar are a number of indicants providing support for certain claims of this current project. Regarding the "dynamic symbiosis" of juridical *jadal* and *uṣūl al-fiqh*, and the simultaneous development and literary fluorescence

[30] It is possible that he even composed one (or several) in literary form, as he is credited with some 400 works (al-Shīrāzī, *Ṭabaqāt*, al-Mays ed., p. 118).

[31] *Sharīʿa*, p. 59.

[32] See "Was al-Shāfiʿī the Master Architect," p. 596, where he notes: "...Qaffal was the author of both a commentary on the *Risāla* and a treatise on legal theory, as well as the first to have written on juridical dialectic [citing Ibn Khallikān's *Wafayāt*]. That both [al-Ṣayrafī and Qaffāl] were distinguished *uṣūlīs*, *muḥaddiths*, speculative theologians, and dialecticians betrays their debt to Ibn Surayj who mastered all these sciences and placed them in the service of the law."

[33] al-Shīrāzī, *Ṭabaqāt*, al-Mays ed., p. 118.

[34] See Schacht's *EI*[2] entry on Ibn Surayj for a complete rendering of the *mas'ala*.

[35] al-Shīrāzī, *Ṭabaqāt*, al-Mays ed., p. 118; Ibn Qāḍī Shuhba, *Ṭabaqāt*, ʿAbd al-ʿAlīm Khān ed., vol. 1, pp. 113, 116–7.

[36] al-Shīrāzī, *Ṭabaqāt*, al-Mays ed., p. 118.

of both as comprehensive systems (themes which I will shortly elaborate in more detail), we have in our purported first author of a systematized *jadal*-theory treatise a scholar who was also among the very first authors of systematized *uṣūl al-fiqh*. These full genre treatises emerged, in other words, not only simultaneously, but frequently by the same hand—as proven also by our later lens-text authors—and they did so from the start of the full-system era.

I have also asserted there was a marked continuity from proto-system *jadal* teaching and practice through to full-system *jadal* theory, and would now call attention to al-Qaffāl al-Shāshī's commentary on the *Risāla*. Although what I perceive of continuity has most to do with the significant overlap of al-Shāfiʿī's dialectical practice with the modes of *istidlāl* and *iʿtirāḍ* found in the lens-texts, I find al-Qaffāl al-Shāshī's looking back to al-Shāfiʿī's proto-system legal theory to be indicative of a singular aspect of overall continuity; mainly, that the formulation of full-system theory depended, in part, upon an analysis of the teaching and practice of proto-system *mujtahids*. Among other things, note the *Risāla*, like the *Umm*, is replete with dialectical sequences—although, significantly, they are of a much more Socratic-pedagogical type (Q&A between teacher and student), than they are of an Aristotelian-disputational type (Q&A between proponents of opposing positions).[37] Still, al-Qaffāl al-Shāshī's conversance with the *Risāla* suggests his conversance with the *Umm*, and it is quite possible he was just as interested in al-Shāfiʿī's dialectical practice as he was with his more "rudimentary and incomplete" legal theory.[38]

Nevertheless, this assertion of continuity on my part appears at odds with Hallaq's quoted statements in #4 and #5 of the above outline. On closer inspection, however, it is not. Hallaq's clear intention is to show that the first formulators of comprehensive *uṣūl al-fiqh* were not elaborating upon "an established tradition" founded by al-Shāfiʿī. Al-Shāfiʿī was no founder in the real sense of the word (my analyses and observations in preceding chapters confirm this), and the relationship between the students of Ibn Surayj and al-Shāfiʿī's legal theory was clearly not the same as the relationship between al-Shīrāzī, al-Bājī, al-Juwaynī, et al. with the legal theory of Ibn Surayj and students. It was the dialectical trends which played out in the four or five generations after al-Shāfiʿī's death which inspired the full systematization of the *ʿilm uṣūl al-fiqh*; and this newly-systematized *ʿilm* "owed little more to al-Shāfiʿī than partial or nominal affiliation."

The only additions entailed by my assertion of "continuity" from proto-system to full-system may be summarized by the following statement: there are a num-

---

[37] A comparison of dialectical styles between *Risāla* and *Umm* constitutes another worthy research project.

[38] As has been pointed out to me by Hallaq himself, we must bear in mind that al-Qaffāl al-Shāshī would have approached both *Umm* and *Risāla* at a significant developmental remove from the era of their authorship. That is to say, the nascent sciences of *uṣūl* and *jadal* (of which al-Shāshī would be among the first, if not *the* first, to systematize in comprehensive fashion) had developed significant refinements in the intervening century. Among other things, al-Shāshī would have read these texts from a perspective of more advanced hermeneutics.

ber of elements (though less refined, and far less numerous than those of full-system theory) which were practiced and sometimes expounded by al-Shāfiʿī, many—if not all—of which preceded him (i.e., he did not "found" them), and which continued to be refined in the dialectical forge after his death, through to the Great Synthesis and the first comprehensive formulations of *uṣūl al-fiqh* and juridical *jadal*. These include "rudimentary" hermeneutical conceptions of *ʿāmm* and *khāṣṣ*, *jumla* and *mufassir*, etc., and the less-developed modes of *istidlāl* as we have seen them in the analyses.

Al-Shāfiʿī, in other words, was merely a participant—albeit a significant one—in a continually-evolving argumentation episteme which did not culminate into full systematization until a century or more after his death. His *Risāla* may best be described as the distillation and organizing of principles from a "rudimentary and incomplete" proto-system somewhere in its middle stage, its third-century latter stage merging with the first stage of full-system *uṣūl al-fiqh*, somewhere at the heart of the Great Synthesis. My assertion of proto-system to full-system continuity—for dialectical and legal-theoretical elements shared by both—supports, rather than conflicts with, Hallaq's claims as quoted above.

Hallaq has also stated: "The next century and a half [after the treatises of Ibn Surayj's students] witnessed a phase in the history of this theory [*uṣūl al-fiqh*] that produced the standard works on which later expositions so heavily depended...." I would further note that some of the most important of these "standard works" of *uṣūl* were composed by the very authors of our *jadal*-theory lens-texts;[39] and, just as Hallaq observes, they constitute a continuation and elaboration upon the full-system theory of Ibn Surayj's circle (often referencing Ibn Surayj himself).

Muḥammad Abū Zahra

In the following tables I have attempted to outline the prolific Muḥammad Abū Zahra's "formation (*nash'at*) of the *ʿilm uṣūl al-fiqh*," from the opening pages of his introductory volume entitled, simply, *Uṣūl al-Fiqh*. Overall, he makes a number of significant points underscoring various elements of the Dialectical Forge model—especially with regard to al-Shāfiʿī's legal theory and *jadal*. I may even claim the model integrates well with his overall account. An added bonus of citing Abū Zahra on such matters is that we benefit from his full immersion in the relevant pre-modern literature, and may bring the current project into comparison with a modern, Muslim-Traditionalist narrative.

[39] They are the *Lumaʿ*, *Sharḥ al-Lumaʿ*, and *Tabṣira* of al-Shīrāzī; the *Iḥkām al-Fuṣūl fī Aḥkām al-Uṣūl* and *Kitāb al-Ishāra fī Maʿrifat al-Uṣūl wa-l-Wajāza fī Maʿnā al-Dalīl* of al-Bājī; the *Kitāb al-Wāḍiḥ fī Uṣūl al-Fiqh* of Ibn ʿAqīl; and the *Burhān fī Uṣūl al-Fiqh* and *Waraqāt* of al-Juwaynī. All of these have been edited and appear in print.

On *Uṣūl al-Fiqh* Before al-Shāfiʿī[40]

- [1] "The *ʿilm uṣūl al-fiqh* was conceived along with the science of derived law (*ʿilm al-fiqh*), even if the *fiqh* had been set down in writing before it."
- [2] **In the era of the Companions (Ṣaḥāba)**: The rational inference (*istinbāṭ*) of *fiqh* began immediately after the passing of the Prophet. Abū Zahra supplies examples of *istinbāṭ*, *istidlāl*, and *manāhij* (systematic programs) for legal solutions, as reported of ʿAlī (a kind of primitive *qiyās* and 'closing the way to wrongdoing/harm' [*sadd al-dharāʾiʿ*]), and ʿAbd Allāh b. Masʿūd (who observed *naskh*)
    - "Thus we must acknowledge that the Companions in their *ijtihād* adhered to systematic programs, even if they did not announce them in every circumstance."
- [3] **In the era of the Successors (Tābiʿūn)**: "rational inference (*istinbāṭ*) broadens due to the multiplication of novel cases (*ḥawādith*) and the concern of a group of the Successors with [issuing] *fatwās*...."[41] Such were in possession of Qur'ān, Sunna, and the *fatwās* of the Companions, "and among them were such as pursued the systematic programs of *maṣlaḥa* (public welfare considerations) when there was no *naṣṣ* ([unambiguous] text)... and of *qiyās*; and the *tafrīʿāt* (derivations) deduced by Ibrāhīm al-Nakhaʿī and others of the jurists of Iraq were directed towards the extraction (*istikhrāj*) of occasioning factors for *qiyās* (*ʿilal al-aqyisa*), and their regulation (*ḍabtihā*), and the derivation [of new rulings] from them by the application of those occasioning factors to various branch-cases (*furūʿ*)."
    - "Here we find that systematic programs became clearer than before, and whenever the 'legal schools' (*madāris fiqhiyya*) disagreed, this *ikhtilāf* was a cause for distinction between the systematic programs of rational inference for each 'school'."
- [4] **In the era of the Mujtahid Imams**: "we find that systematic programs were even more clear in form, and with the distinction of systematic programs the rules (*qawānīn*) of rational inference were clarified; their teaching spread, and manifested on the tongues of the imams in unambiguous expressions, clear and refined..."
    - **Abū Ḥanīfa**: "defines the foundational systematic programs for his rational inference by way of Qur'ān, then Sunna, then *fatwās* of the Companions (*fatāwā al-Ṣaḥāba*)—taking up what they formed consensus upon, and choosing from among their opinions with regard to what they disagreed upon, and not going beyond them. But he did not

(continued)

[40] Abū Zahra, *Uṣūl al-Fiqh*, pp. 13–14.

[41] He names Saʿīd b. al-Musayyab in Medina, and ʿAlqama and Ibrāhīm al-Nakhaʿī in Iraq.

take up the *ra'y* of the Successors because they were men like him. And one finds that he pursued *qiyās* and *istiḥsān* according to a systematic program (*minhāj*), to the point that his pupil Muḥammad b. al-Ḥasan al-Shaybānī said of him: His companions used to dispute with him (*yunāziʿūnahu*) with regard to his *qiyās*, and when he said: 'I prefer...' (*astaḥsinu*), no one adhered to him (*lam yalḥaq bihi aḥadun*)."

- **Mālik**: "used to pursue clear, *uṣūl*-theory programs in his drawing argumentative support (*iḥtijāj*) by way of the Practice of the Medinese (*ʿAmal Ahl al-Madīna*), and his declaration of such in his books and treatises, and in his stipulation of such with regard to the narration of *ḥadīth*. In his critique (*naqdihi*) of *ḥadīths* he criticized with all adroitness, and in his rejection of some of the *āthār*-traditions attributed to the Prophet due to their contradicting what is unambiguous (*naṣṣ*) in the Qur'ān, or the well-known and acknowledged of the general principles of religion (*qawāʿid al-dīn*)..."
- **Abū Yūsuf**: "And like this, too, was Abū Yūsuf in his *Book on Land Tax* (*Kitāb al-Kharāj*), and in his *Refutation of al-Awzāʿī's Laws of War* (*Radd ʿalā Siyar al-Awzāʿī*); he pursued a clear and unambiguous program (*minhāj*): the program of his *ijtihād*."

I have consciously avoided employing the term *uṣūl al-fiqh* with regard to legal theory predating the full-system era of Ibn Surayj's circle and afterwards (i.e., before the fourth/tenth century). For the proto-system I have preferred the more general "legal theory," simply due to the conception of a less choate and less refined body of principles which the ambiguity of the term allows. If we read Abū Zahra's *uṣūl al-fiqh* in the above quotations and paraphrases in the same spirit—and he makes it quite plain we may do so in following discussions—then nothing prevents an easy integration of the Dialectical Forge model into Abū Zahra's pre-Shāfiʿī history of proto-system legal theory. In fact, almost all of his assertions harmonize with claims I have made with regard to the proto-system (a notable exception being a supposed lack of engagement with the *ra'y* of the Successors).

Importantly, Abū Zahra acknowledges that legal theory was not invented by al-Shāfiʿī, but that it was an ongoing process from the dawn of Islam and had reached a level of sophistication by al-Shāfiʿī's time. This corresponds well with my placement of al-Shāfiʿī somewhere in the middle of the proto-system's trajectory; certainly the likes of the *manāhij* Abū Zahra attributes to Abū Ḥanīfa, Mālik, and Abū Yūsuf are plentifully indicated by the arguments of our subject-text alone, and thoroughly vindicated by the other treatises and arguments in the *Umm* compendium, and other early compendia. Of even greater significance, however, is his observation that "whenever the 'legal schools' (*madāris fiqhiyya*) disagreed, this *ikhtilāf* was a cause for distinction between the systematic programs of rational inference for each 'school'."[42]

In so many words, Abū Zahra has himself acknowledged the dialectical forge; the venue in which *ikhtilāf* between opposing positions sought resolution was that of juridical *jadal*, as our subject-text stands witness, and a consequence was the formation and refinement of distinctive legal theoretical and dialectical "toolboxes" for various juristic "schools." In this manner we can speak of projects within a greater project, as distinctive sets of argument axioms were employed by distinct groupings of jurists in the early proto-system of legal theory. These were variant argumentation epistemes within a larger, constantly evolving episteme—and all of this before the arrival of al-Shāfiʿī.

"Al-Shāfiʿī Sets Down in Writing the *ʿIlm Uṣūl al-Fiqh*"[43]

- [1] "Al-Shāfiʿī came along and found the wealth of *fiqh* which had been transmitted from the Companions and Successors and 'Imams of Fiqh' who had preceded him, and he found the *jadal* between the proponents of various positions, and he found the current disputational sessions (*munāẓarāt*) between the *fiqh* of Medina and the *fiqh* of Iraq...;"
  - in short, al-Shāfiʿī's genius, coupled with his knowledge of Medinan *fiqh* learned from Mālik, and Iraqi *fiqh* learned from Muḥammad b. al-Ḥasan, and of the *fiqh* of Mecca, allowed him to posit "scales by which wrong might be distinguished from right; and these scales are the *uṣūl al-fiqh*."
- [2] "It is not at all strange that research (*baḥth*) into the derived laws (*furūʿ*) of *fiqh*, and its putting down in writing (*tadwīn*), should precede the putting down in writing of *uṣūl al-fiqh*; because when the *ʿilm uṣūl al-fiqh* consists of scales for the regulation (*ḍabṭ*) of rational inference (*istinbāṭ*) and the intellection (*maʿrifa*) of wrong from right, then it is a regulating science (*ʿilm*), and the material (*mādda*) is *fiqh*. And such is the nature of all the regulating sciences; for grammar (*al-naḥw*) arrived subsequent to classical literary form (*al-nuṭq biʾl-fuṣḥā*), and the poets used to utter poetry in meter (*mawzūnan*) before Khalīl b. Aḥmad set down in writing the rules of prosody (*ḍawābiṭ al-ʿarūḍ*), and the people used to debate each other (*yatajādalūn*) and speculate before Aristotle set down in writing the science of logic (*ʿilm al-manṭiq*)."

(continued)

[42] Note also that in the following descriptions of *manāhij* for Abū Ḥanīfa, Mālik, and Abū Yūsuf, all three are discretely tied to juridical disputation, whether in the form of contentious students (an illustration of the 'study circle' [*ḥalaqa*] as a site for *jadal*), or published critical rejections of *ḥadīth*, or in disputational treatises and epistles.

[43] Abū Zahra, *Uṣūl al-Fiqh*, pp. 13–18.

- [3] Al-Shāfiʿī was especially suited to the task of setting down in writing the rules of rational inference (*ḍawābiṭ al-istinbāṭ*), due to his scholarly accomplishments and wide scope of experience in: (1) the Arabic language (*al-lugha*); (2) *ḥadīth*; (3) the *fiqh* of his era; and (4) the *ikhtilāf* of the Companions and current scholars
    - "And he spared no effort to come to know the causes of divergence (*khilāf*), and the various positions proffered in the theories of the disputants (*anẓār al-mukhtalifīn*)."
- [4] Al-Shāfiʿī's special training in the Qur'ānic science of Ibn ʿAbbās, and his vast knowledge of Sunna, allowed him to assess "the station (*maqām*) of Sunna with regard to the Qur'ān, and its status (*ḥāl*) in case of the opposition (*muʿāraḍa*) of some of its apparent meanings (*ẓawāhir*) to those of the Qur'ān. His study of the *fiqh* of considered opinion (*ra'y*), and the transmitted considered opinions from the Companions, was a foundation for the regulations (*ḍawābiṭ*) for *qiyās* which he set down."
- [5] "And thus did al-Shāfiʿī set down in writing the general principles (*qawāʿid*) for rational inference; but they were not, on the whole, an innovation of his manufacture. Rather, they are a detailed noting down of what the jurists who were guided by them followed, from among the systematic programs for their rational inference which they did not set down in writing. For he did not originate the systematic programs of rational inference, but he has precedence insofar as he gathered together the various threads of those systematic programs which he selected, and set them down in writing in a science of interconnected parts; his equivalent in that is the example of Aristotle in his putting down in writing (*tadwīn*) for the logic (*manṭiq*) of the Peripatetics—for he [Aristotle] made no innovation with regard to the original material (*aṣl*) of the systematic program; rather, his innovation was in the regulating (*ḍabṭ*) of the systematic program. This is the opinion of the majority (*jumhūr*) of the jurists in their prior assessment of al-Shāfiʿī with regard to the putting down in writing of that science, and not one of them disagrees about that."[44]
- [6] "And we do not say that al-Shāfiʿī brought the science in a complete state, according to all its modes (*wujūh*), so that nothing remained for the efforts of those who followed him; rather, there came after him those who elaborated and augmented, and revised numerous *masā'il* with

(continued)

[44] After this point, Abū Zahra gently debates an Imāmī Shīʿī claim that the Imām Muḥammad al-Bāqir was the first to set down in writing the *ʿilm uṣūl al-fiqh* and to regulate it. In brief, he reiterates the claim that al-Shāfiʿī's precedence arises only from his compilation and systematization; it is acknowledged that his predecessors possessed and elaborated programs of their own and transmitted them, but not that they produced written systematizations (*Uṣūl*, pp. 16–18).

regard to this science, just as those who came after Aristotle did in the East and West, as relates to the science of logic (*ʿilm al-manṭiq*). For they revised it and augmented it, even if the origin with regard to its being treated as an established science of well-ordered parts goes back to Aristotle."

- [7] Al-Shāfiʿī's *ʿilm al-uṣūl* may be found in his *Risāla*, *K. Jimāʿ al-ʿIlm*, and *K. Ibṭāl al-Istiḥsān*; Abū Zahra sees al-Shāfiʿī as considering his science as universal laws and guiding principles for rational inference of rulings (*aḥkām*) across the ages; and that he employed this systematic program in debating (*munāqasha*) the considered opinions of current jurists, and of Mālik, the Iraqis, Abū Yūsuf and al-Awzāʿī (mentioning the *ikhtilāf* treatises in the *Umm*). In short, he did not much depart from this systematic program which he had regulated. Al-Shafiʿi's *uṣul al-fiqh* was thus not only theoretical, but practical.

From the start (#1 above) Abū Zahra makes it plain that al-Shāfiʿī entered into a dialectical world; indeed it was the *jadal* of his predecessors and peers that prompted his own early attempt at systematization (and we see some reference to his own *jadal* in #7—the application of his program [*minhāj*] in debate [*munāqasha*]). Equally important is Abū Zahra's nod towards a natural explanation of *fiqh* preceding *uṣūl al-fiqh*: a regulating science indeed must be preceded by the subject material whose elaboration it seeks to regulate, and a similar notion will come into play in my expansion upon the Dialectical Forge model. His assessment of the role of al-Shāfiʿī, however, also marks a minor point of conflict with my narrative: I have asserted on more than one occasion that the true Aristotles of *uṣūl al-fiqh* came a century and more after the death of al-Shāfiʿī, and that al-Shāfiʿī, indeed, was no Aristotle.

Hallaq's research vindicates my adherence to this statement, and for additional support one need only make a set of comparisons: first, between: (1) the limited scope of the contents of al-Shāfiʿī's *Risāla*, *Jimāʿ al-ʿIlm*, *Ibṭāl al-Istiḥsān*, along with whatever might be gleaned (as I have attempted in the subject-text) from other treatises; and (2) the far-more comprehensive, detailed, and refined treatments of even the earliest extant *uṣūl al-fiqh* treatises (the *Fuṣūl* of al-Jaṣṣāṣ and the *Muʿtamad* of al-Baṣrī). This is more than sufficient; and I am further confirmed in my conclusion by Joseph Lowry.[45]

[45] See the concluding chapter of his *Early Islamic Legal History* entitled: "The *Risāla* and its Relationship to Mature *Uṣūl al-Fiqh*." In a brief but comprehensive review, Lowry narrows the loci of major differences (and markers of elaboration and advancement) from al-Shāfiʿī's legal theory to that of full-system *uṣūl al-fiqh*: (1) the relationship between *uṣūl* and *furūʿ*; (2) "the capacity for abstraction;" (3) epistemological tools; (4) linguistic argument; and (5) theoretical vs. functional aims (*Early Legal Theory*, pp. 359–68).

Second, one might compare both of the above sets with Aristotle's *Organon*, by criteria of: (1) systematic categorization, (2) refinement of definition, and (3) comprehensiveness of scope. Al-Shāfiʿī's collected expressions of legal theory barely attain the level of Aristotle's *Categories* and *De Interpretatione*, much less the sophisticated contributions of the *Prior* and *Posterior Analytics*, *Topics*, etc. Later *uṣūl*ist polymaths, on the other hand, have in fact gone further in terms of comprehensive systematizing than Aristotle himself ever did for logic. And if al-Shāfiʿī falls far short, while later *uṣūl*ists exceed, then we might expect the "Aristotle of *uṣūl al-fiqh*" to fall somewhere in between.[46] *Uṣūl al-fiqh* in truth had many systematizing Aristotles; but if we must choose a first set, that honour would most probably go to the circle of Ibn Surayj, his students, and their students. Lacking copies of their works, we would perforce extend the honour to al-Jaṣṣāṣ and al-Baṣrī; and, with greater enthusiasm, to al-Shīrāzī, his students, and his peers.

At the same time, we must never neglect the fact that al-Shāfiʿī's *Risāla* and other treatises are indeed expressions of a system, and that he was a masterful systematizer in his own right. This is well-expressed by Abū Zahra above; and, if read against the background of the dialectical forge, we understand al-Shāfiʿī's legal theory, in both earlier and later stages, to be a distillation of observations, analyses, selections, and refinements, which had fermented throughout a long career of dialectical interaction with teachers and peers in a number of scholarly centers. In short, it is the most refined formulation, demonstrating the greatest temper of epistemic justification, as the dialectical forge produced by the middle stage of proto-system developments. But it was not the singular foundation for what came later, nor was it anything like as comprehensive.

On *Uṣūl al-Fiqh* After al-Shāfiʿī[47]

- [1] Following generations of jurists turned to commenting upon and refining his system, others accepted it in broad outline but disagreed on the greater part of details and added *uṣūl* (many of which al-Shāfiʿī had disagreed with):
    - Ḥanafīs: added juristic preference (*istiḥsān*) and custom (*ʿurf*)

(continued)

[46] Admittedly, this line of inquiry is of dubious benefit; but focus on the three mentioned criteria (systematic categorization, refinement of definition, and comprehensiveness of scope), with regard to all that we know of Aristotle's and al-Shāfiʿī's respective systematization projects, is telling. Al-Shāfiʿī's project—at a level of genius in its own right—still falls far short, in a quantitative and qualitative sense, of Aristotle's. Nor, we might add, did al-Shāfiʿī's *Risāla* and other treatises ever play, in subsequent centuries of the *ʿilm uṣūl al-fiqh*, anything like the role which Aristotle's *Organon* played in the subsequent millennium and more of logic studies. Contributions on a par with Aristotle in terms of our three criteria and subsequent influence belong to later systematizers of *uṣūl al-fiqh*, and not likely to a single individual at that.

[47] Abū Zahra, *Uṣūl al-Fiqh*, pp. 18–25.

    - Mālikīs: added consensus of the Medinese (*ijmāʿ Ahl al-Madīna*), juristic preference (*istiḥsān*), non-textually regulated public welfare considerations (*maṣlaḥa al-mursala*), and pre-emptive 'closing off the way' to potential injustice/harm (*sadd bāb al-dharāʾiʿ*)
- [2] Such additions constitute the only real sites of *khilāf*; the four *uṣūl* of Qur'ān, Sunna, *ijmāʿ*, and *qiyās* are subject to consensus (*majmaʿ ʿalayhā*)
- [3] Though many closed the 'gate of *ijtihād*' on themselves, *uṣūl al-fiqh* (which remained very much alive) did not lose its value in the age of following a qualified *mujtahid* (*taqlīd*), and was further elaborated without threatening the boundaries of the *madhhab* doctrine as it had been developed: its new role was as a tool in *jadal* and *munāẓara*, with reference to the *ikhtilāf* of the age.
- [4] After doctrinal-*madhāhib* were established, *uṣūl* studies split into two branches:[48]
    - The *Uṣūl al-Shāfiʿiyya* or *Ṭarīqat al-Mutakallimīn*: remained purely theoretical, unattached to the derived laws (*furūʿ*) of any particular doctrinal-*madhhab*; it was not concerned with doctrinal justification, only with the most certain methods.[49]
    - The *Uṣūl al-Ḥanafiyya*: turned towards justifying the doctrine of a particular *madhhab* and establishing the correctness of its *ijtihād*, past and present, as well as the general principles (*qawāʿid*) that supported their *madhhab*; this style of *uṣūl* fixed the particular methods of the *madhhab*, and allowed for 'derivation of rules in the manner of eponymic *mujtahids*' (*takhrīj*)—thus it developed and expanded the *madhhab*.[50]

(continued)

[48] As Abū Zahra makes plain, despite the Shāfiʿī/Ḥanafī appellations, scholars from all doctrinal-*madhāhib* engaged in and wrote *uṣūl* works, in both trends.

[49] Abū Zahra delves into the Shāfiʿī *ṭarīqa* in much greater detail in pages 20–2 of his *Uṣūl al-Fiqh*. He stresses, among other things, the prescriptive role of this branch of the *ʿilm al-uṣūl*. He names the three greatest works of the Shāfiʿī/*Mutakallimūn ṭarīqa* as follows: (1) the *Muʿtamad* of al-Baṣrī; (2) the *Burhān* of al-Juwaynī; and (3) the *Mustaṣfā* of al-Ghazālī. These spawned many commentaries, abridgments, and glosses. The *Maḥṣūl* of Fakhr al-Dīn al-Rāzī and the *Iḥkām* of al-Āmidī both built upon these great works, and were in turn the objects of abridgement and commentary.

[50] Abū Zahra also turns to a more detailed discussion of the Ḥanafī *ṭarīqa* in pages 22–5. He stresses how their method measured *furūʿ* against the *qawāʿid* of the *uṣūl*, and how their *istinbāṭ* was thus verified, and that by means of it they were equipped for undertaking *jadal* and *munāẓara*. Whereas the *uṣūl al-Shāfiʿiyya* were a program for rational inference (*minhāj li'l-istinbāṭ*) and prescriptive (*ḥākima ʿalayhi*), the Ḥanafī *ṭarīqa* was not prescriptive with regard to derived rules (*ḥākim ʿalā al-furūʿ*) after they had been set down in writing—i.e., they derived the *qawāʿid* that aided their doctrinal-*madhhab*, and they defended them (cf. Hallaq vs. Calder with regard to the prescriptive vs. descriptive function of *uṣūl al-fiqh*). Several contributions of this *ṭarīqa* to jurisprudence in general are mentioned, and then Abū Zahra begins to list the most important works,

- Finally, scholars came along attempting to reunite the two tendencies: (a) developing abstract *uṣūl*; (b) applying them, beyond even the Ḥanafī method.[51]

With regard to #1 and #2 above, there is again a point of conflict with my model (and with Hallaq's overall narrative); for it does not appear that jurists in the main referred back to and built upon al-Shāfiʿī's particular distillation of proto-system legal theories in the ensuing century. I believe, rather, that latter stages in the development of proto-system legal theory may best be described as follows: the *ijtihādic* and dialectical principles and methods which had been debated in al-Shāfiʿī's day (and before) continued to be debated in increasingly refined terms (with tighter definitions, the expansion of categories, and the recognition of subtypes within categories) while the seminal intellectual-historical events of Hallaq's narrative (crystallization of "camps," subsequent "migrations" and "disciplining," and eventual synthesis) unfolded. What we have in al-Shāfiʿī's *Risāla* and other treatises was not a foundation upon which later jurists built; rather, it is more of a snapshot of select mid-proto-system developments provided by one legal theorist's and master dialectician's *minhāj* (not to mention his critique of other *manāhij*).

As for the hierarchy of Qurʾān, Sunna, *ijmāʿ*, and *qiyās* being common to subsequent systems, I would note the following: (1) as Abū Zahra himself avows, this was not an invention of al-Shāfiʿī's, nor was it even his objective, as is confirmed by the research of Joseph Lowry;[52] (2) the "four sources" were not common to all subsequent systems within proto-Sunnism (witness the Ẓāhirīs and proto-Ḥanbalīs); and (3) the precise modes of confirming epistemic authority (in matters of conveyance, *naskh*, interpretation, etc.) and giving preponderance to

as follows: (1) the *Uṣūl* of al-Karkhī (being the oldest book of this type); (2) the *uṣūl* work of al-Jaṣṣāṣ ("broader and more detailed" than al-Karkhī's); (3) the *Taʾsīs al-Naẓar* of al-Dabbūsī; (4) the *Uṣūl* of al-Bazdawī (the clearest and most straightforward work of the Ḥanafī *ṭarīqa*); and (5) the *uṣūl* work of al-Sarakhsī (like al-Bazdawī's, but broader and more detailed). These spawned commentaries, etc., and works in the *ṭarīqa* by authors of other *madhāhib* are mentioned, with reference even to the Imāmī Shīʿa and Zaydīs. Note that I have considered al-Karkhī and al-Dabbūsī as authors in the proto-system of the *ʿilm al-khilāf*, in Chap. 3; and a review of their named treatises will show how different was the enterprise in which they were engaged, as compared to al-Jaṣṣāṣ and al-Bazdawī.

[51] Abū Zahra first mentions the *Badīʿ al-Niẓām* of Ibn al-Sāʿātī (combining the works of al-Bazdawī and al-Āmidī), then proceeds to list other important works from this synthetic genre.

[52] See his "Does Shāfiʿī Have a Theory of 'Four Sources' of Law?;" and pp. 11f. of his *Early Islamic Legal Theory*. The whole of Lowry's *Risāla* research constitutes a thorough antidote to previous "four sources" hierarchy readings of the *Risāla*, and provides a comprehensive exposition as to its true theoretical thrust: *Bayān* theory.

adilla-indicants continued to be debated well into al-Shīrāzī's day and beyond. In short, the "four source" hierarchy was not the object of consensus (*majmaʿ ʿalayhi*)—neither generally, nor with regard to subsidiary concerns—and elaborations of *istiḥsān*, *maṣlaḥa*, etc. do not constitute mere additions to an established hierarchy.

With regard to #3 above, it is certainly true that *uṣūl al-fiqh* played a role in *jadal* and *munāẓara* in the age(s) of established doctrinal *madhāhib*. I would expand upon this conception, of course, and will do so shortly by developing further mechanisms for the Dialectical Forge model. At this point, suffice it to say that legal theory played a role in juridical *jadal* throughout the evolutionary history of both legal theory and *jadal*-theory—long before doctrinal *madhāhib* and long after—and this is but one facet of what I have termed their "dynamic symbiosis."

Finally, with regard to #4, these oft-referenced legal-literary trends—potentially originating with the intellectual-historical analysis of Ibn Khaldūn (see the sections following)—offer yet another point for integration of the Dialectical Forge model of *jadal-uṣūl* dynamics. In short, the notable development of distinctly "pure-theoretical" vs. "*furūʿ*-oriented" *ṭarīqa*-methods may be attributed to organic sub-projects developing within the co-evolving argumentation epistemes of *jadal* and *uṣūl al-fiqh*. In other words, and as we have already seen in proto-system *jadal*, legal theory itself was often the object of dialectical disputation—i.e., as distinct from the object of justifying and critiquing substantive rulings. There seems always to have been, in this sense, (1) a *fiqh*-oriented *jadal*; and (2) an *uṣūl al-fiqh*-oriented *jadal*.

In subsequent eras dominated by *madhhab*ic affiliation (itself partly the end-product of distinct methodological "toolboxes" forged and refined in dialectical disputation—the *uṣūl al-madhāhib*), it is only natural that these prior *jadal* orientations would morph into *ṭarīqa*-methods which (1) distil the methodology of past *mujtahids* associated with the *madhhab*, and by which distillation the doctrinal "core" of that *madhhab* may continue to be justified and expanded upon (the Ḥanafī *ṭarīqa*); and (2) continue to pursue an ideal, "universal" answer to the question: "What are the most epistemically sound theoretical principles and practical methods by which we might 'discover' God's *Sharīʿa*?"

I must stress that these *ṭarīqa*-methods of *uṣūl al-fiqh* literature are permutations of organic dialectical agendas—*furūʿ*-oriented vs. *uṣūl*-oriented; justificatory vs. exploratory; "descriptive" vs. "prescriptive"—already noticeable in proto-system *jadal*. What is more, the synthetic project of combining *uṣūl al-fiqh ṭarīqa*-methods, beginning with Ibn al-Sāʿātī (al-Baʿlabakī al-Baghdādī; d.694/1294), coincides chronologically with another synthetic project—this time in the realm of *jadal*-theory. I am speaking, of course, of the first formulation of the *Ādāb al-Baḥth* by Shams al-Dīn Muḥammad al-Samarqandī (d. 722/1322).[53]

[53] See Miller, "Islamic Disputation Theory," pp. 196 ff. There may be more than a chronological coincidence between synthetic projects, of course, and this is worthy of further exploration.

Between Hallaq and Abū Zahra, we have already acquired a relatively thorough outline of key developments in the evolution of *uṣūl al-fiqh*. The differences between these and other narratives, as far as I have encountered them, are usually the result of variant interpretations (regarding, e.g., the status of al-Shāfiʿī's contribution, the earlier and later functions of *uṣūl al-fiqh*, etc.) of otherwise agreed-upon developments, and we will see something of a variant interpretation in Calder's narrative, following. I have been able so far to highlight the threads of dialectic running through these narratives, and to weave a conception of the dialectical forge among them with considerable ease. It is significant that the Dialectical Forge model—whereby formative primacy in the evolution of *uṣūl al-fiqh* is given to juridical *jadal* and its co-evolving axioms of argumentation—has found no real conflict with current legal-historical narratives. I believe this is sufficient evidence that it is a workable model; the two remaining narratives will largely confirm this, though further points of conflict will be highlighted.

Norman Calder

Perhaps the best source from which we can distil Calder's historical narrative for legal theory is his entry on *uṣūl al-fiqh* in the *Encyclopaedia of Islam*. Despite certain conceptions with which I disagree (and only some of which will be addressed in the following notes), this is an informative article consisting of a combination of observations, chronological considerations, and authorial theses. Notably, much of Calder's account depends upon Ibn Khaldūn and al-Ghazālī, but his overall assessment—especially with regard to the origins and function of *uṣūl al-fiqh*—exhibits a decidedly Ḥanafī *ṭarīqa*, "defence of the *madhhab*," orientation.[54]

On the Origins and Evolution of *Uṣūl al-Fiqh*

- [1] Ibn Khaldūn, regarding "the relatively late development of *uṣūl al-fiḳh* as a comprehensive science," believed that "for the earliest generations, the relevant skills were intuitive and innate (in respect of language and its use) or based on personal experience (in respect of assessing transmitters of *ḥadīth*, etc.)"[55]

(continued)

[54] Due to the structure of Calder's article, a number of his observations and theses will not appear in the same order in my summaries. I have attempted as chronological an arrangement here as possible. A more complete conception of Calder's view on *uṣūl al-fiqh*—its literature, origins, development, nature, and function—may only be obtained through referencing the *EI*² article and other works, such as his *Studies*.

[55] Calder, "Uṣūl al-Fiḳh," *EI*², ¶6.

- [2] Ibn Khaldūn considered the *Risāla* to be the first work of *uṣūl al-fiqh*;[56] but the influence and early date of al-Shāfiʿī's *Risāla* has been questioned by modern scholars.[57]
- [3] As a literary genre, *uṣūl al-fiqh* enjoys an unbroken span from its apparent origins in the 4th/10th c. to the 13th/19th c.
- [4] The early *uṣūl al-fiqh* literature is already quite "developed;" Calder suggests "there was a prior tradition of teaching and study, a gradually emerging system for the classification and presentation of problems, and, at least, informal notebooks."
- [5] Notable representations of *uṣūl al-fiqh*—at its birth as a literary genre—are the works of the Ḥanafī scholars Aḥmad b. Muḥammad al-Shāshī (d.344/955) and Aḥmad b. ʿAlī Abū Bakr al-Jaṣṣāṣ (d.370/980).[58]
- [6] Calder notes Ibn Khaldūn's "famous distinction" between: (1) "the *uṣūl* of the theologians;" and (2) "that of the jurists."[59]
- [7] Ibn Khaldūn, with regard to the "early landmarks of the theologians' tradition," believes this *ṭarīqa* begins with Muʿtazilīs, is then developed by Shafiʿī-Ashʿarīs, and later elaborated (in summary and commentary) by scholars of the other three surviving Sunni schools.[60]
- [8] Ibn Khaldūn's representatives of the Ḥanafī *ṭarīqa* are: (1) ʿAbd Allāh b. ʿUmar al-Dabbūsī (d.430/1038), who was seen to be the "most important early writer in this tradition;" (2) ʿAlī b. Muḥammad al-Bazdawī (d.484/1089), who continued al-Dabbūsī's work, and that of other early figures.[61]

(continued)

[56] Ibid.

[57] Ibid., ¶1. Citing Hallaq, "Was al-Shāfiʿī the Master Architect;" and his own *Studies* (Chap. 9).

[58] NB: Calder does not mention the Shāfiʿī predecessors Ibn Surayj (d.306/918) and his students. As we have seen, it is this circle of scholars which Hallaq observes to be "the first and foremost Shāfiʿite authors who [wrote] on *uṣūl al-fiqh*" (*History*, p. 33; and see, in more detail, "Was al-Shāfiʿī the Master Architect," pp. 595–6). This marks, in my opinion, something of a Ḥanafī-method bias on Calder's part, and others will follow. Note also that attribution of the *Uṣūl al-Shāshī* to Aḥmad b. Muḥammad al-Shāshī (d.344/955) should very likely be discounted, as I have mentioned briefly at the end of Sect. 4.1 (see also my dissertation [pt. 1, pp. 93–7] for a more complete argument).

[59] Calder, "Uṣūl al-Fiḳh," *EI*², ¶7. The distinguishing factor is named as *tajrīd* (abstraction), following which Calder says only "the theologians abstracted the principles and the rules of the science from their normative exemplification." Here, as elsewhere (see, especially, "*Al-Nawawī's Typology of Muftīs*"), he maintains a strict priority for the "descriptive" over the "prescriptive" function of *uṣūl al-fiqh*.

[60] Calder, "Uṣūl al-Fiḳh," *EI*², ¶7. The following authors and works are listed: (1) Qāḍī ʿAbd al-Jabbār (Muʿtazilī, d.415/1025): *K. al-ʿUmda*; (2) the commentary on this by Abū al-Ḥusayn al-Baṣrī (d.436/1044): *al-Muʿtamad*; (3) Imām al-Ḥaramayn al-Juwaynī (Shāfiʿī, d.478/1085): *K. al-Burhān*; (4) al-Ghazālī (Shāfiʿī, d.505/1111): *al-Mustaṣfā*; (5) Fakhr al-Dīn al-Rāzī (Shāfiʿī, d.606/1209): *al-Maḥṣūl*; and (6) Sayf al-Dīn al-Āmidī (Shāfiʿī, d.631/1233): *al-Iḥkām*. Then Calder names the "two standard textbooks of Ibn Khaldūn's time": (1) Ibn Ḥājib (Mālikī, d.646/1249): *al-Mukhtaṣar*; (2) al-Bayḍāwī (Shāfiʿī, d. 685/1286 or 692/1293): *al-Minhāj*.

[61] Ibid., ¶8.

- [9] Ibn Khaldūn mentions the *K. al-Badīʿ* of Ibn al-Sāʿātī (d.694/1295), which "combined... the Ḥanafī (jurists') tradition with the tradition derived from al-Āmidī, thereby ensuring considerable convergence of the two traditions in the subsequent period."[62]

Calder's assertions in #4 and #8 are important to the current project. As for the first, it confirms that *uṣūl al-fiqh* did not emerge from an intellectual vacuum, and that indeed there was a "prior tradition of teaching and study." This is our proto-system of legal theories, throughout its pre-Shāfiʿī, middle, and final stages, continually shaped and honed by the pressure of the dialectical forge. And as for the second, the fact that al-Dabbūsī was seen to be the "most important writer in [the Ḥanafī] tradition" is important; we have examined his *Taʾsīs al-Naẓar* at some length in Chap. 3, and its dialectical agenda has been made plain. In this we are provided further indication that the *ṭarīqa*-methods of post-*madhhab* legal theory originated from nothing more than the natural concerns of variant dialectical projects, whose threads may be discerned throughout the full gamut of co-evolving *jadal-uṣūl* theory.

On the Shāfiʿī/Mutakallimūn vs. Ḥanafī/Fuqahāʾ *Ṭarīqas*; and the (Primary) Function of *Uṣūl al-Fiqh* as Preservation and Defence of the *Madhhab*

- [1] Calder begins to address the Shāfiʿī vs. Ḥanafī approaches[63] by suggesting that an ideal *uṣūl al-fiqh* may be seen as "a pure science presented in radical abstraction from normative detail."
- [2] As for al-Ghazālī (in his *Mustaṣfā*): (1) *uṣūl al-fiqh* is set apart from *ʿilm al-khilāf*, since only *khilāf* works "dealt with specific examples of norms and their relationship to revealed texts;" (2) the function of *uṣūl al-fiqh* is "to identify the sources of the law and the general hermeneutical principles which permitted extrapolation of norms from texts."[64]

(continued)

[62] Ibid. Calder points out that Ibn Khaldūn's "survey" of *uṣūl al-fiqh* tradition represents only "his assessment of highlights" (Ibid., ¶9).

[63] Noting: "Ibn K̲h̲aldūn identified these tendencies as that of the theologians and that of the jurists respectively" (ibid., ¶2).

[64] Ibid. Note that Calder sees the *Mustaṣfā* as exemplary of: (1) the standard contents of an *uṣūl al-fiqh* book; (2) a high point in the Shāfiʿī tradition ("a peak of organisation and expression"). He observes it had much influence on later works (ibid., ¶4).

- [3] The Shāfiʿī tradition of *uṣūl al-fiqh* "owed much to the Muʿtazila and to the Mālikī Abū Bakr al-Bāḳillānī (d. 403/1014)."[65]
- [4] As for the early Ḥanafīs: their work was "much less purist" and "more focused on the defence of acknowledged norms." He suggests, however, that over time the Ḥanafī approach was influenced by "the more abstract tradition" and came into closer conformity with it.
- [5] As for Ḥanafī *ṭarīqa*-method: "This tradition should be seen as prior to and productive of the theologians' tradition. It is more focused on the rules of the law and the discovery of principles that justify the rules than on the abstract analysis of hermeneutical principles. This is probably how the discipline developed, emerging out of polemical defence of known rules."[66]
- [6] As for the nature and function of *uṣūl al-fiqh*:[67]
    - some modern scholars (mainly Hallaq), and some pre-modern "indigenous" scholars (e.g., al-Ghazālī) have misrepresented *uṣūl al-fiqh* "as an ongoing method for the discovery and the development of rules, implying that it points to a capacity for change and evolution in the juristic tradition"
    - the "historical reality" (in both "broad terms" and "details") is that: "the norms of the law were known prior to and independent of the tradition of *uṣūl*;" and most Muslims ("by virtue of family or geography") adhered to one of the *madhāhib* "by a loyalty that was ultimately acknowledged and termed *taḳlīd*"[68]
    - "Chaumont (*Ijtihād et histoire*) has shown that the theory of *idjtihād* is not developmental: it is concerned with the discovery of the law as an eternal and enduring truth"[69]
    - Ibn Khaldūn's "illuminating comment on the real situation," in his discussion of *jadal* ("which he perceived as a sub-genre within the science of *uṣūl*"), is summarized as follows: (1) *uṣūl al-fiqh* was only "deductive (*li'l-istinbāṭ*)" for the *mujtahids* (meaning only the *madhhab* founders), (2) "Later jurists used the hermeneutical skills and

(continued)

[65] He cites Chaumont's *Bāqillānī*, and Ibn K͟haldūn (Ibid., ¶4).

[66] Ibid., ¶8. Note this being "more focused on the rules of the law and the discovery of principles that justify the rules" is reminiscent of Abū Zahra's description of the Ḥanafī *ṭarīqa*.

[67] All of the following assertions are in ibid., ¶11.

[68] Calder rightly notes that "caveats" surround use of this term.

[69] It is not clear how this is meant to support claims of a "defence of the *madhhab*" primary orientation for *uṣūl al-fiqh*. Moreover, Hallaq has shown quite plainly how the machinery of development and change was built into the very structure of the Islamic jurisprudential enterprise, largely through the activities of *muftīs* and author-jurists (*muṣannifs*); see his *Authority, Continuity and Change*, especially Chaps. 5 and 6.

arguments of *uṣūl* in order to *preserve and defend* norms that had already been deduced and were accepted through *taḳlīd*" [italics are Calder's]

- "Re-creation, re-discovery, re-experience: it is concern with repetition and defence of the known law, not concern with development, that most characterises—and most reveals the profound religious and cultural values of the legal sciences of Islam, both *furūʿ* and *uṣūl*."[70]

As for #1 above, Calder's conception of the Shāfiʿī/Mutakallimūn *ṭarīqa*-method is drawn mostly from al-Ghazālī, as his citations suggest. It is difficult to reconcile Calder's description: "presented in radical abstraction from normative detail" with the works of such as al-Baṣrī which, like those of our other *jadal* theory authors, are replete with substantive examples from the full range of *adilla*-indicants and *masāʾil* of *ikhtilāf*. In particular, one wonders to which *ṭarīqa*-method the *uṣūl* works of al-Shīrāzī, al-Bājī, al-Juwaynī, and Ibn ʿAqīl ought to be assigned, considering the very obvious interconnectedness between the principles of *uṣūl al-fiqh* and "normative detail" demonstrated by the many hundreds of example-*masāʾil* in their *jadal* texts. Either way, assuming a strict dichotomy between the two *ṭarīqa*-methods on the basis of derivation from/justification of *furūʿ* vs. "abstraction" from *furūʿ* may be misleading; and a certain ambiguity of nature and function seems further confirmed by Calder's observation in #4.

As for #5, it is not clear why Calder concludes the Ḥanafī *ṭarīqa*-method must precede the Shāfiʿī; I would suggest instead that both evolved as sub-projects from a pair of co-evolving orientations within a larger dialectical episteme. It is also here in #5, however, that Calder provides a telling allusion to the dialectal forge: "This is probably how the discipline developed, emerging out of polemical defence of known rules." The key term is "polemical," and the proof is written large in compendia such as the *K. al-Umm*. My amendment would be to substitute "dialectical" for "polemical," to change "defence" to "justification and critique," and "known rules" to "*ijtihād*ic solutions;" I would also broaden the scope. In other words, I would say: this is probably how the discipline [of *uṣūl al-fiqh*, as a whole] developed, emerging out of dialectical justification and critique of *ijtihād*ic solutions. Calder's allusion is another sign the Dialectical Forge model may be integrated with minimal adjustment.

Finally, with regard to the insistence that the true nature and primary function of *uṣūl al-fiqh* is descriptive and unconcerned with development, I have suggested something of a Ḥanafī *ṭarīqa* bias lurks in Calder's developmental narrative. Hallaq has more recently dissolved the "descriptive" vs. "prescriptive" dichotomy by showing, *inter alia*, how the former "meshes into" the latter.[71] As to Chaumont's

[70] Calder, "Uṣūl al-Fiḳh," *EI*², ¶12.

[71] *Sharīʿa*, pp. 72 ff.; on "The function of legal theory."

"non-developmental" assertion, this is adequately dealt with by Hallaq—in the chapter of *Sharīʿa: Theory, Practice, Transformations* just referenced, and in the latter chapters of *Authority, Continuity and Change*. I would only add that it is difficult to reconcile a non-developmental legal theory with a legal system which flourished, in practice, across Islamicate societies—from Andalusia to Indonesia, for a millennium and more—unless one were to suggest that these societies themselves were utterly static. Novel situations demand novel legal solutions, and legal specialists provided them within a larger *uṣūl*ist episteme, as the *fatwā* literature clearly demonstrates. As to how *fatāwā* were cycled into a *madhhab*'s doctrinal corpus, thus promoting development within *madhāhib*, see Hallaq's *Authority, Continuity and Change*.

On the whole, I would posit that "descriptive" and "prescriptive" functions were never so much on the minds of jurists engaged in dialectical disputation; the objective remained the testing of *ijtihād*ic solutions and the refinement of *ijtihād*ic method, no matter whether the *mas'ala* at hand was completely novel, or a long-standing *mas'ala* of *ikhtilāf*. Perhaps these twin concerns (*furū*ʿ-oriented and *uṣūl*-oriented *jadal*) may best account for perceived "descriptive" vs. "prescriptive" functions for *uṣūl al-fiqh*. Then again, we might place the whole dichotomy at Ibn Khaldūn's doorstep, and attribute modern championing of the "descriptive" function to an over-reliance on his somewhat reductive narratives for *uṣūl* theory and *jadal* theory development.

Khalīl al-Mays

In the introduction to his edition of the *Uṣūl al-Shāshī*,[72] al-Mays sets forth a brief historical narrative for *uṣūl al-fiqh*, paying much more attention to variant traditions than Nadwī does in the introduction to his edition of the same work.[73] It is found under the subheading "Programs of the Authors" (*Manāhij al-Mu'allifīn*). As is the norm, al-Mays begins with al-Shāfiʿī, but tells us that, among the *ʿulamā'*

[72] Pp. 8–11.

[73] I have not treated Nadwī's narrative here for several reasons. Besides offering no additions to the narratives included thus far, it seems never to have been intended to provide a comprehensive overview. At first, he paints with broad strokes, whereby al-Shāfiʿī's *Risāla* (as our first extant *uṣūl* work) is followed by *ʿulamā'* writing on this art, until al-Shāṭibī wrote his *Muwaffaqāt*, which "rose above all [works] ancient and modern, as regards the *bayān*-explanation of the induced aims of God's Law (*maqāṣid al-Sharīʿa*) and its universal principles (*qawāʿid al-kulliyya*)." He then narrows focus to Ḥanafī scholars, citing the most famed works on the subject to be: (1) the *Uṣūl* of al-Karkhī; (2) the *Ta'sīs al-Naẓar* of al-Dabbūsī; and (3) the *Uṣūl* of al-Bazdawī. Then he presents the *Uṣūl al-Shāshī* as "one of the most important *Mukhtaṣar*s belonging to the Ḥanafī's for this noble art," it being much studied, relied upon, commented upon, etc., all over the Islamic world (*Uṣūl al-Shāshī*, pp. 5–6).

who followed him, "the *manāhij* [of authorship] multiplied, and their *ṭarīqa*-method diverged (*ikhtalafat*) into three: (1) the *Ṭarīqat al-Mutakallimīn*, or *Uṣūl al-Shāfiʿiyya*; (2) the *Ṭarīqat al-Aḥnāf* [Ḥanafīs]; and (3) the *Ṭarīqat al-Muta'akhkhirīn* ['post-classical' scholars]."[74] He then proceeds to briefly describe each *ṭarīqa*-method, and then to list the more notable works for each. As we have already covered the developmental areas mentioned in his quick synopsis, I will simply summarize his account of the major characteristics of the three *ṭarīqa*-methods, in parallel with their major works, in the following tables:

Ṭarīqat al-Mutakallimīn	
Characteristics:	**Most important works:**
• Distinguished by verification (*taḥqīq*) of *masā'il*; accurate rendering (*taqrīr*) of general principles (*qawāʿid*); testing and rectification (*tamḥīṣ*) of contended solutions (*khilāfāt*), with rational drawing of indication (*istidlāl ʿaqlī*), and increased *jadal* • Like the scholarship of *Kalām*; a purely theoretical orientation; almost in isolation from the building and testing of substantive legal elaborations (*furūʿ*), with little concern for application • It is a program (*minhāj*) for rational inference (*istinbāṭ*), prescriptive with regard to the *furūʿ* (*ḥākima ʿalayhi*)	• The pillars (*arkān*) of this *technē* (*fann*) and its general principles (*qawāʿid*): ○ *al-ʿUmda* of Ibn ʿAbd al-Jabbār (Muʿtazilī, d.415) ○ (its commentary) *al-Muʿtamad* of Abū Ḥusayn al-Baṣrī (Muʿtazilī, d.473 [*sic*]) ○ *K. al-Burhān* of al-Juwaynī (d.478) ○ *al-Mustaṣfā* of al-Ghazālī (d.505) • Most important work of the later tradition: ○ *al-Iḥkām* of al-Āmidī

Ṭarīqat al-Aḥnāf	
Characteristics:	**Most important works:**
• Distinguished by accurate rendering (*taqrīr*) of general legal-theoretical principles (*qawāʿid uṣūliyya*) according to the requirements conveyed from the [Ḥanafī] imams; verification (*taḥqīq*) and application (*taṭbīq*) of the *furūʿ* according to those *qawāʿid* • An *uṣūl al-fiqh* derived from the *furūʿ* and *masā'il* of *fiqh*, on the authority of the Ḥanafī imams • It is not prescriptive with regard to the *furūʿ* after they were established	• Oldest: the *Uṣūl* of al-Karkhī (d.340) • Broader and more detailed: the *Uṣūl* of al-Jaṣṣāṣ (d.370) • Between these two works: the *Khamsīn* of Abū ʿAlī al-Shāshī (d.344)[75] • After writing continued to progress: ○ the *Ta'sīs al-Naẓar* of al-Dabbūsī (d.430) ○ the *Uṣūl* of al-Bazdawī (d.483); the most lucid book of the early *madhhab* ○ (writings continue to this day)

[74] *Uṣūl al-Shāshī*, al-Mays ed., p. 8.

[75] The so-called *Uṣūl al-Shāshī*. Most likely an incorrect attribution, due to the anachronistic references pointed out by Nadwī in his edition.

Ṭarīqat al-Muta'akhkhirīn	
Characteristics:	**Most important works:**

• A combination of the two *ṭarīqa*-methods
• Distinguished by verification (*taḥqīq*) of the *qawāʿid uṣūliyya* and furnishing proof (*burhān*) for them, and by application (*taṭbīq*) and linking (*rabṭ*) of these *qawāʿid* to the *furūʿ* of *fiqh*
	• The *Badīʿ al-Niẓām* of Ibn al-Sāʿātī (d.694); combines the Ḥanafī *Uṣūl al-Bazdawī* and the Shāfiʿī *Iḥkām* of al-Āmidī
	• The *Tanqīḥ al-Uṣūl* and its *sharḥ*, of al-Bukhārī al-Ḥanafī (d.747); still used in al-Azhar and elsewhere
	• The combination of both *ṭarīqas* progressed:
	  ○ the *Jamʿ al-Jawāmiʿ* of al-Subkī (Shāfiʿī, d.771)
	  ○ the *Taḥrīr* of Ibn al-Himām al-Ḥanafī (d.861)
	• Among the last, and most detailed:
	  ○ the *Musallam al-Thubūt* of Ibn ʿAbd al-Shakūr (d.1119)

Again, the listing of al-Karkhī's *Uṣūl* and al-Dabbūsī's *Ta'sīs* among the early works of the Ḥanafī *ṭarīqa*-method is important for what it suggests of the interrelated literary projects of the *ʿilm al-khilāf*, *ʿilm al-jadal*, and *ʿilm uṣūl al-fiqh*. The great difference in contents and agenda between these two works, however, and, e.g., the *uṣūl* of al-Jaṣṣāṣ or (the unidentified) al-Shāshī, continues to cast a certain ambiguity over the *ṭarīqa* distinction in the first place. Between the listing of works and the salient characteristics noted by al-Mays we hear strong echoes of Abū Zahra's and Calder's accounts. All three may derive ultimately from Ibn Khaldūn.

References to Jadal *in Secondary Works on Islamic Legal Theory*

I have reviewed Wael Hallaq's discourses on juridical *jadal* in Chap. 2. Apart from this, mentions of *jadal* in current scholarship on Islamic legal theory are rare. I must briefly review two more instances, however, before closing this section on developmental narratives for *uṣūl al-fiqh*. The first belongs to Joseph Lowry, who dedicates an entire chapter of his *Early Islamic Legal Theory* to "Internal Evidence for the *Risāla*'s Polemical Contexts."[76] Among other things, he explores the various epistemic groups mentioned by al-Shāfiʿī in appeals and critiques (the Ahl al-ʿIlm/Fiqh/Ḥadīth/etc.), and the largely overlooked reading of "The *Risāla* as a Theological Polemic" (including the discussion of al-Shāfiʿī's *ʿaql* and *maʿqūl* I have noted earlier). Again, the significance of *jadal* as a formative dynamic in legal

[76] Chap. 6, pp. 275–318.

theory is hinted at by Lowry's discourse; and the findings of this current project augment his observations with regard to the overall character and intent of al-Shāfiʿī's *Risāla.*

The second belongs to Bernard Weiss, who provides, in his monumental *Search for God's Law*, a number of beneficial notes on juridical dialectic. He cites Miller's dissertation, and firmly grounds al-Āmidī's (d.631/1233) *Iḥkām* in its dialectical contexts. Among other things, the following observations are of import to the themes of this current project: (1) "A scholar could adhere to an opinion only so long as he was confident that it could be shown, in the context of debate, to be at least as worthy as that of other scholars, if not superior;" (2) "One often gets the feeling in reading [al-Āmidī's] works that they constitute, at least in part, records of debates in which he himself participated, memoirs of a master dialectician;" and (3) "Āmidī clearly wrote largely to meet the practical needs of scholars... who wished to prove their mettle in scholarly debate," and "his shorter works... were probably intended as manuals to be used by students in memorizing the essentials of arguments that could be useful in debate." As for (1) it is an acknowledgement of the scholarly ethic of "good dialectic" as we have seen it described elsewhere; and as for (2) it is reminiscent of the style we find in the *Umm* compendium, and the marker of a long-standing contextual continuity; and as for (3) these are clear echoes of the didactic intent plainly visible in al-Shāfiʿī's "instructional" dialectical sequences, and in the ordered schemas of our lens-texts.[77]

8.4 *Uṣūl*-Theory Components of the Dialectical Forge Model

On the Three-Stage Cycle, the Bequeathing of Dialectical Axioms, and Dynamic Symbiosis and Co-Evolution

The role of dialectic in the evolution of *uṣūl al-fiqh* has received little in the way of focused study. More than likely this is due, overall, to the fact that "dialectic is a grossly understudied genre in Islamic thought."[78] A primary objective of the

[77] Weiss also provides: (1) a discourse on the nature of the *mas'ala*, mentioning (with regard to *uṣūl al-fiqh* in general): "its entire range of issues is determined by a long history of debate;" (2) a discussion of al-Āmidī's dialectical presentation of material (with statement of the *mas'ala*, various opinions, invalid arguments, objections, etc.); and (3) a useful overview of the interplay between objection and counter-argument (Weiss, *Search*, pp. 46–50; see also his "Medieval Islamic legal education as reflected in the works of Sayf al-Dīn al-Āmidī").

[78] I am quoting Robert Wisnovsky, from a class lecture on "Dialectic and *Ādāb al-Baḥth*." With particular regard to the vital relationship between dialectic and *uṣūl al-fiqh*, the trend continues. At the time of writing, the latest, relevant secondary publication of which I am aware is David Vishanoff's *Formation of Islamic Hermeneutics*. This is an exceedingly thorough work in terms of both the secondary literature on *uṣūl al-fiqh* and its primary sources. There is no treatment of

current project has been to elevate juridical *jadal* to its proper place in *uṣūl al-fiqh* studies—to a leading position it more than deserves as the most potent dynamic in the evolution of legal theory. As we have seen, however, there have been a few exceptions to the rule of relative neglect; I will now return briefly to one of the more significant of these.

In charting the introduction to al-Baṣrī's *K. al-Qiyās al-Sharʿī*, Wael Hallaq mentions he will take up "[*jadal*'s] relationship to legal theory which *provided the premises and points of departure for dialectic.*"[79] In a subsequent section he expands upon this relationship between juridical dialectic and the concerns of *uṣūl al-fiqh*.[80]

> Dialectic, whose aim it is to reach the truth about a judgment of a case of law, presupposes the existence of the case and at least one *ẓannī* judgment. The process by which a judgment is derived belongs to the realm of legal theory. But establishing the validity of the material evidence for the judgment and the particular methods by which the judgment was reached is the task of dialectic. Thus, logically as well as procedurally the role of legal theory precedes that of dialectic. The latter comes to confirm or refute a conclusion reached by a legal theoretician (*uṣūlī*). Following the Aristotelian tradition, Muslim jurists held that dialectic takes its start from views or opinions rather than from textual premises. *Uṣūl al-fiqh*, on the other hand, departs from such premises to yield a conclusion which, being only inferred, in turn becomes the premise for the arguments of dialectic. But Muslim jurists went slightly beyond the Aristotelian conception to give dialectic a more important and expanded role. Juridical dialectic, though unequipped to provide new cases with legal solutions, could reconsider the premises and methods the 'uṣūlists' employ in reaching these solutions, and could thus declare them either valid or void.

This passage heralds one of the key mechanisms of the Dialectical Forge model. First, note that the bulk of utterances in a typical *uṣūl al-fiqh* text are in fact theoretical and methodological propositions. As such, they may—and do—constitute the building blocks of argument (i.e., premises). In some cases they are apodeictic (generally, or within specific contexts of the Islamic argumentation episteme), in others they are assertoric, and in others they are markedly dialectical (i.e., they are *endoxa*: either generally, or within a *madhhab*'s theoretical teachings). And, of course, such propositions as are most directly concerned with *istidlāl* (i.e., methodological propositions) are also normative; for they are statements of how one *ought to* analyze the textual *dalīl*-indicant, or establish the *ʿilla* in the *aṣl*, or establish *jarayān*, or preponderate conflicting *adilla*-indicants, etc.

One component of the Dialectical Forge model may thus be presented in simplest terms as a "three-stage cycle": (1) *uṣūl al-fiqh* premises are forged and refined in dialectical encounter; (2) tested and confirmed, these same premises are employed in *ijtihād*; and (3) when this *ijtihād* is itself tested in disputation, these

juridical dialectic, however, despite a significant exposition on al-Shāfiʿī, and frequent reference to *uṣūl*ists who were famed dialecticians and/or authors of *jadal*-treatises. This is not so much an oversight of the author's as a by-product of dialectic's continuing low visibility in legal-theoretical—and, indeed, in historical-intellectual—studies.

[79] "Treatise," p. 197. Italics are mine.

[80] Ibid., pp. 199–200.

same premises (and others, also forged in previous dialectic) are brought to bear in both the justification of the respondent's *istidlāl*, and in the questioner's critique. Thus, *jadal* employs premises of *uṣūl al-fiqh* which were themselves produced by *jadal*. With regard to the evolution of systems for both *uṣūl al-fiqh* and *jadal*, the augmented effect of this three-stage cycle is what I have previously spoken of in terms of "co-evolution" and "dynamic symbiosis;" for, ultimately, as *uṣūl* premises are refined, so too is *jadal* refined, and the effect is cumulative up to whatever point of development participating jurists can sustain.

Importantly, there is another facet to this cycle: the premises particular to *uṣūl al-fiqh* are in fact distillations from larger principles and methods hammered out in venues of juridical dialectic, from the very beginning of the proto-system era and continually thereafter. They are impregnated with the axioms inherent to formal, dialectical encounters. In other words, we may read in the premises of *uṣūl al-fiqh* certain dialectical "givens" (non-contradiction, consistency, adherence to the *endoxa*) and "motives" (avoidance and detection of self-contradiction, avoidance of the non-*endoxa*, or of amphiboly, circularity, accident, mistaken cause, etc.)[81] This is the phenomenon I have earlier suggested in terms of the "bequeathing of axioms" from the argumentation episteme of juridical *jadal* to the argumentation episteme of *uṣūl al-fiqh*.

In sum, these are the first three mechanisms in the model's *uṣūl* and *jadal* theory compartment: (1) the "three-stage cycle," whereby *uṣūl* premises are forged in dialectic, then used in *ijtihād*, then employed in the dialectical testing of that *ijtihād* (in both R's justification of *istidlāl*, and in Q's *iʿtirāḍ*); (2) a consequence of this cycle: the "bequeathing of dialectical axioms" (both "givens" and "motives") from the *jadal* argumentation episteme to the *uṣūl al-fiqh* argumentation episteme; and (3) the augmented effect: the "dynamic symbiosis and co-evolution" of *jadal* and *uṣūl al-fiqh* systems towards greater and greater degrees of refinement. If the dialectical forge concept is consonant with the historical evolution of these systems—and the relative ease with which it integrates with current narratives is a positive sign that it is—then I would claim: (1) legal theory and dialectic are inseparable; (2) they have been inseparable since the start of the greater Islamic jurisprudential project; and (3) they have remained inseparable through all subsequent phases of development in which disputation was both active and truly dialectical.

I have already suggested a reason as to why this most powerful dynamic has been, for the most part, overlooked: the relatively small amount of study which has been dedicated to juridical *jadal*, as opposed to a much larger amount for *uṣūl al-fiqh*. I would add that the role of *uṣūl* propositions as premises in argument may not be immediately perceptible in their contexts of *ijtihād*—a private process whose premises may remain unspoken, unrecorded, or in other ways inaccessible to the researcher. Obviously, this is not the case with *jadal*, where: (1) legal theo-

[81] A very brief, preliminary exploration of dialectical "givens" and "motives" will be presented in Sect. 9.2.

retical propositions are indeed spoken as premises of an argument (as we see a number of times in our subject-text); (2) they receive much more obvious attention as argument premises in *jadal*-theory texts than they do in *uṣūl* texts—with the exception, of course, of *uṣūl*-text chapters on *iʿtirāḍāt*, *tarjīḥāt*, etc.;[82] and (3) their use as argument is thrown into bold relief by *masāʾil* of *ikhtilāf.*

I would now quickly revisit a pair of "subsidiary theories" introduced in earlier discussions. The first of these is what was called "*ijtihād*ic anticipation of *jadal*;" the second concerns an important Aristotelian parallel with regard to the role of "scientific" premises in dialectic.

On the Three-Stage Cycle and Ijtihādic *Anticipation*

The three-stage cycle, as formulated above, is related to another theory earlier suggested; mainly, that the public procedure of *jadal* may be said to intrude into the private procedure of *ijtihād*, insofar as we assume the *mujtahid* to anticipate the publication and subsequent debate of his *ijtihād*ic solution, whether face-to-face, or through a literary medium. The anticipated directives of *jadal*, in this fashion, may be said to influence the jurist *qua mujtahid*, not only *qua mustadill/mujīb*.[83] This finds confirmation in the *uṣūl* texts themselves; and, to a certain extent (and in a different sense of the word), this theory of *ijtihād*ic anticipation has itself been anticipated by Hallaq.[84] During his discourse on the role of dialectic in testing a jurist's *ijtihād*, drawing from al-Ghazālī and al-Bājī, he notes that: "to safeguard the *ratio legis* [*ʿilla*] against the critique of the opponent, the jurisconsult must take into account a number of considerations...." These he proceeds to list, and they are five in number: (1) that the *ḥukm* at which the proponent aims has not already been plainly revealed in an authoritative text (for, "He would be an easy prey if the opponent could produce a revealed text in which the rule for the case in question is explicitly stated"); (2) that the source-text for *qiyās* is not abrogated, is unambiguous, not subject to *ikhtilāf*, and has a transferable *ḥukm*; (3) the proponent must be able to prove *taʾthīr*; (4) the proponent must avoid *naqḍ* and *takhṣīṣ al-ʿilla*; and (5) he must be certain that his *ʿilla* cannot occasion a different *ḥukm*. Each of these concerns comprises an *ijtihād*ic anticipation of *jadal*.

The importance of this mechanism is plain: in this *ijtihād*ic anticipation of *jadal* we find yet another crossing of currents between the argumentation epistemes of *jadal* and *uṣūl al-fiqh*—another entry point for the argument axioms of dialectic.

---

[82] As Weiss shows, detailed works such as al-Āmidī's *Iḥkām* are also exceptions; the place of dialectic as a formative dynamic is made quite plain by the author's treatment of each legal theoretical premise.

[83] That is, not only as "the one doing *istidlāl*," or "the respondent."

[84] *History*, pp. 94 f., citing al-Ghazālī (*Mustaṣfā*) and al-Bājī (*Iḥkām*).

And, once again, these axioms would consist of the "givens"—and particularly the "motives"—of dialectic. The *mujtahid*, in other words, during the course of *ijtihād*, might anticipate charges of inconsistency, non-*endoxon istidlāl*, mistaken cause, etc.; and this anticipation of dialectical charges would influence the current course of his private *ijtihād*.[85]

On the First Principles Parallel: "Scientific" Premises and Aristotelian Dialectic

Returning to Hallaq's summation above, his statement that "logically as well as procedurally the role of legal theory precedes that of dialectic" is a particular departure point for the current study. For, in combination with what we have witnessed of a formative role for dialectic in premise-forging, it constitutes the very impetus of the three-stage cycle. Importantly, one finds a striking—if not entirely unexpected—parallel for this in the role of Aristotelian dialectic with regard to the demonstrative sciences. In short, as indicated by Aristotle in the *Topics*, it is through dialectic that the *archai*—the self-evident "first principles" upon which any syllogistic argument must ultimately depend within a demonstrative system—are discussed and (re-)defined:

> Further, [dialectic] is useful in connexion with the ultimate bases of each science; for it is impossible to discuss them at all on the basis of the principles peculiar to the science in question, since the principles are primary in relation to everything else, and it is necessary to deal with them through the generally accepted opinions on each point. This process belongs peculiarly, or most appropriately to dialectic; for, being of the nature of an investigation, it lies along the path to the principles of all methods of inquiry.[86]

As Aristotelian dialectic is to the demonstrative sciences, so might *jadal* be to the *ʿilm uṣūl al-fiqh*. It is in this very direction which Hallaq appears to point when he observes the "expanded role" for dialectic among Muslim jurists, whereby they "reconsider the premises and methods the 'uṣūlists' employ in reaching these solutions, and could thus declare them either valid or void." A major thrust of this current project is merely to expand upon this model, and to argue that the premises and methods of *uṣūl al-fiqh* were *originally* considered and *first* developed in

---

[85] Anticipation of this sort may best be considered a "natural" consequence of pre-knowledge of a forthcoming examination or debate. In the rhetorical realm of political debate, the politician will attempt to anticipate the justifications and objections of his/her opponent, along with the attitudes of his/her audience. In the presumably "good" dialectic of academia, the researcher will attempt to anticipate the criticism of colleagues in the presentation of his/her research, and in the construction of supporting arguments from empirically sound or *endoxon* premises.

[86] *Top*. I.2, 101a36-101b4.; trans. Forster. See also the variant views on the role of dialectic as regards *archai* and the demonstrative sciences set forth by G.E.L. Owen, "*Tithenai ta phainomena*;" Robin Smith, "Dialectic and Method in Aristotle;" and Robert Bolton, "The Epistemological Basis of Aristotelian Dialectic."

the venue of dialectic, as well as *re*-considered (and subsequently refined) time and again throughout the long course of evolution. Of course, the *ʿilm uṣūl al-fiqh* is not a demonstrative science like geometry (Aristotle's favorite example); but it nevertheless has its first principles and foundational premises, and these were determined, tested, and reshaped when necessary in dialectical venues.

At this point, we have therefore located—in the *jadal* and *uṣūl* theory compartment of the Dialectical Forge model—a collection of interrelated mechanisms acting as pistons driving their half of the overall engine: (1) the three-stage cycle; (2) the bequeathing of dialectical axioms; (3) dynamic symbiosis and co-evolution; (4) *ijtihādic* anticipation of *jadal*; and (5) the first principles parallel. I will now turn to the other half of the engine and explore its other compartment, locating the mechanisms behind the formative dynamic of juridical dialectic as pertains to its own theory: the *ʿilm al-jadal*.

8.5 Proto-System *Jadal* and the Development of *Jadal*-Theory

Differences Between Proto-System Jadal *Teaching and Practice and Full-System* Jadal*-Theory*

Throughout the analyses of the subject-text in Chaps. 5 and 6, and the subsequent review and categorization of elements in Chap. 7, we encountered dialectical moves which did not correspond well with the schemas and categories of our *jadal*-theory lens-texts; and some of these fell into larger categories. With regard to "expanded range" objections, for example, I discussed certain implications for *jadal*-system evolution. In sum, I concluded they present a picture of proto-system *jadal* in its middle stage, before the refining processes of the latter stage led to a more narrowed field of operation for certain modes of *istidlāl* and *iʿtirāḍ*. Combining this with the half-developed model of the Dialectical Forge above, I would now suggest that dynamic symbiosis and co-evolution led to such refinements in both *jadal* and *uṣūl* that the need for—or appropriateness of—these objections outside of certain domains simply fell away over time.

In fact, I would propose the same for other categories of difference, besides "expanded range" objections: the question strategies, *istidlālāt*, and *iʿtirāḍāt* outside the categories of our *jadal*-theory texts might all be understood as having fallen away over time due to the ceaseless working of the dialectical forge. Concerns which might have lessened and disappeared over time, as a result of continual refinements in legal theory, would include these primary examples: (1) *istidlāl* by way of the decree of a Successor (and objections to it); (2) such arguments as I have subsumed beneath the heading: "Consistent Generalizing of the *ʿIlla*" or "super-*qiyās*;" and (3) certain species of objection-oriented *muṭālabāt*, and "strategies" such as *naqḍ*-dilemma, and objections to objections. Each of these might have disappeared due to refinements—and restrictions—in respective areas of: (1) the epistemic weight and ranking of *adilla*-indicants; (2) *endoxa qiyās*-methods; and (3) the order and typology of acceptable questions—i.e., the tightening of Q&A procedure.

So, too, might arguments to *ʿaql* and *maʿqūl* have fallen away over time, as a continually-refined legal theory developed specific categories of *laḥn al-khiṭāb*, *faḥwā al-khiṭāb*, *dalīl al-khiṭāb*, etc. (the domain of *maʿqūl aṣl*). Charges of *taḥakkum*, I argued, might simply have no longer been necessary; there were no longer jurists in the latter stages of the Great Synthesis whose *ijtihād* was not grounded to some extent or another in accepted *adilla*-indicants—even the reformulated *istiḥsān* was eventually cleansed of traces of "arbitrariness." In the end, all of these "disappearances" may be explained, or potentially so, as the workings of the dialectical forge, with specific regard to dynamic symbiosis and co-evolution of *jadal* and legal theory systems. More important for my present concern, however, is that they provide examples of *jadal shaping itself*. That is, these proto-system elements, absent from full-system *jadal*, serve as indicants that the dialectical forge was just as important a dynamic in the shaping of *jadal*-theory as it was for the shaping of *uṣūl al-fiqh*. This is the primary thesis of concern in this section.

Returning to the question of what marks the proto-system dialectic of our subject-text as "different," there were other types of arguments which captured our attention. These were not only absent from later *jadal*-theory discourse, but had certain characteristics prompting me to describe them as more "ancient in tenor." Besides—or, perhaps, included among—what might, retrospectively, be labelled as "considered opinion" (*ra'y*), were a number of elements to which I sometimes attached the descriptor "Aristotelian," or which I rendered in the names accorded them by Latin scholasticism. These included: (1) Q's procuring premise-after-premise for *elenchus*, in the manner of the *Topics*; (2) charges of *tanāquḍ*; (3) *reductio* arguments, and arguments *ad verecundiam*, *a fortiori* (without a textual *dalīl*), and *a potiori*; and (4) apparent objections to sophistical *elenchi*, such as affirming the consequent, *petitio principii*, or mistaken cause.

These arguments are important not only for their apparent falling away from discourse and/or practice due to the workings of the dialectical forge, but in the picture they provide for us of the "prior argumentation epistemes" which featured in the early Islamic dialectical landscape. These, as I have suggested, were infused by the new axioms of Islam, and a new episteme of distinctly Islamic argumentation continued to evolve and transform. An ideal illustration of this process may be found in the fusion of a prior argument axiom (the assumption that the *a fortiori* argument is epistemically sound) with a new Islamic axiom (the assumption that argument must be grounded in an authoritative textual *dalīl*-indicant to be considered sound) to produce two features of the more evolved *jadal*/*uṣūl al-fiqh* argumentation episteme: (1) the "*A Fortiori* Signification of the Instruction" (*Faḥwā al-Khiṭāb*); and (2) "Drawing Indication by way of *A Fortiori* Valuation" (*al-Istidlāl bi'l-Awlā*). The fact that we find *a fortiori* arguments which are *not* based in textual *adilla*-indicants—as well as those which are—in the dialectic of the subject-text, coupled with the fact that we do not find the former receiving theoretical treatment in our *jadal*-theory texts, is just that sort of indicant which allows us to consider al-Shāfiʿī's era as somewhere in the middle of proto-system development.

The presence of these more "ancient" argument axioms alongside distinctly Islamic axioms also encourages us to ponder how best to qualify the "ancient" set; in short, we are tempted to ask: "Just how 'Aristotelian' is the dialectic of the *Ikhtilāf al-ʿIrāqiyyayn/ʿIrāqiyyīn*?" I have put forward numerous caveats with regard to genetic projects of this sort, and will stand by them here.[87] However, no one could rightly deny the presence of distinctly Aristotelian epistemes in the early Islamic landscape—even before the Translation Movement—as there is a preponderance of evidence it was there. Before turning to the question of how 'Aristotelian' our subject-text's prior axioms appear to be, however, I will pause to examine that prime candidate, and most interesting feature, we have come across: al-Shāfiʿī's charges of *tanāquḍ*.

Arguments to Tanāquḍ *and the Meaning of* Mutanāqiḍ

One means of pursuing this question further would be to: (1) search for instances of *mutanāqiḍ*, *naqaḍa*, *khilāf*, etc. throughout the whole of the *Kitāb al-Umm* and *Risāla*; and (2) compare the contexts in which all such terms are employed. A larger undertaking of this sort must await future studies, but a preliminary search for *mutanāqiḍ* has revealed some 28 instances in the *Umm*—yet none whatsoever in the *Risāla*.[88] Of particular note is this: of the 28 instances in the *Umm*, all but two are expressly employed as descriptors of a professed opinion or doctrine (*qawl*) in

[87] Primary among these is that parallels alone do not indicate probability of genetic relation, but only possibility; and possibilities do not accumulate to produce probability. That is to say, even if I have gathered as many parallels as I seem to have done, this does not make it probable that our early jurists were reading Aristotle; only some other indicant of a greater epistemic weight (e.g., direct in-text references to the *Organon*, or confirmed accounts of a jurist's studying Aristotle, etc.) can shift our parallels into the realm of probability or certainty. Nor does the cynical stance that a pathetic monolith of "Islamic Tradition" conspired to hide or disguise traces of "Greek logic" in its earlier history constitute any sort of argument at all; the burden of proof lies with the claimant, and one who makes such a claim as this must bring strong evidence of conspiratorial erasure and/or camouflage. Incidentally, it may be considered an added benefit of the Dialectical Forge model—with regard to the gradual disappearance of prior axioms from various evolving Islamic epistemes—that it offers an alternative explanation to claims of a "denaturalized Hellenism."

[88] Of course, this does not preclude the existence of cognates and verbal forms. Should the term and cognates prove entirely absent from the *Risāla*, then such would provide indicant for a conclusion certain scholars (e.g., Ḥassūn and Schacht) reached with regard to our subject-text; namely, that its contents are representative of al-Shāfiʿī's "Old Doctrine," whereas the *Risāla* is representative of his "New." The implications are interesting in two ways: (1) my analyses might not only have uncovered a picture of proto-system *jadal*, but a very specific snapshot of al-Shāfiʿī's "Old Doctrine" legal theory and method; and (2) the mechanisms of the Dialectical Forge model, as I have described them, may be seen as working not only within the general argumentation episteme of the community of jurists, but within a single jurist throughout his career. This latter should not be viewed as surprising. It is already documented—a recognition of al-Shāfiʿī's evolution from Old to New Doctrines, in the legal literature, biographies, etc.

a dialectical context—as with the basic formula: "you have professed a contradictory doctrine for this" (*wa qulta [fī hādhā] qawlan mutanāqiḍan*), and variants such as: "you were contradictory of doctrine with regard to it" (*kunta mutanāqiḍa al-qawli fīhi*).[89] A search for the term *tanāquḍ* in the *Umm* yields nearly a dozen more instances, most of which are also descriptively tied to a *qawl*. A particularly illuminating example of *qawl mutanāqiḍ* may be found at the end of §11635 of the *Bāb Man Qāla Lā Yūrathu Aḥadun ḥattā Yamūta*:[90]

And he professes, regarding it, a *qawl mutanāqiḍ* (contradictory doctrine) outside the pale, all of it, of the *aqāwīl al-nās* (doctrines of 'the people'), and the *qiyās*, and the *maʿqūl*.	فَيَقُولُ فِيهِ قَوْلاً مُتَنَاقِضًا خَارِجًا كُلَّهُ مِن أَقَاوِيلِ النَّاسِ وَالْقِيَاسِ وَالْمَعْقُولِ.

There could be no more effective description of what is non-*endoxon* than: "outside the pale, all of it, of the doctrines of 'the people', the *qiyās*, and what is rationally understood." Note also another instance wherein *al-maʿqūl* is listed among *endoxa* sources.

Another example combining these elements is in §1331 of the *Bāb fī Bayʿ al-Ḥayawān* of the *Kitāb Ikhtilāf Mālik wa'l-Shāfiʿī*:[91]

And you [pl.] professed, regarding it, a *qawl mutanāqiḍ* (contradictory doctrine) outside the pale of the Sunna, and the *āthār*-traditions, and the *qiyās*, and the *maʿqūl*.	وَقُلْتُمْ فِيهِ قَوْلاً مُتَنَاقِضًا خَارِجًا مِن السُّنَّةِ وَالْآثَارِ وَالْقِيَاسِ وَالْمَعْقُولِ.

Certainly, when reading through the 28 instances of *mutanāqiḍ* in the *Umm*, a remarkable formulaic consistency may be observed; this is the mark of an established dialectical art, as practiced by a master dialectician, and speaks volumes about the level of sophistication of proto-system *jadal*. But perhaps what we gain most from these two examples above is that a *qawl mutanāqiḍ* is "outside the pale" of *endoxa* premises; that is to say, al-Shāfiʿī's legal theory at this stage in his career incorporated specific *endoxa* sets which he may easily list when he perceives his opponent's *qawl* to fall outside of them. They are, at least in the above examples: the *aqāwīl al-nās*; *qiyās*; *maʿqūl*; Sunna; and *āthār*-traditions. Whatever we determine *mutanāqiḍ* to mean, we may be certain of this much: it is subsumed by the non-*endoxa*.

There is another way to interpret these passages; mainly: "not only is *qawl* X *mutanāqiḍ*, but it is outside the pale of (*khārijan min*) *endoxa* sets A, B, and C." There may not be much of a difference either way, but I wish to point out that the key

[89] The two instances which appear in the *K. Jimāʿ al-ʿIlm* call for particular scrutiny; there is a great deal to be learned from an analysis of this treatise.

[90] *Umm*, Ḥassūn ed., vol. 4, pt. 8, p. 195.

[91] *Umm*, Ḥassūn ed., vol. 9, pt. 14, p. 575.

meaning of *mutanāqiḍ*, as my analyses have shown (and the term itself implies), has to do with contradiction. In this sense, *mutanāqiḍ* is a particular non-*endoxon* quality of the opponent's *qawl* ("it is contradictory"), among other non-*endoxa* qualities ("it is *khārijan min* A, B, C"); that is to say: *mutanāqiḍ* does not simply mean "non-*endoxon*," although it certainly *is* non-*endoxon*.

My final analysis, having examined the instances we encountered in our subject-text, is this: *tanāquḍ* refers to either (1) "internal," or (2) "wider-doctrine," logical contradictions. That is to say: Q accuses R of *tanāquḍ* when R claims "X is the case" *and* "¬X is the case," either (1) within the same argument (as closely juxtaposed premises), or (2) between arguments made in different instances of his wider doctrine. As for this latter manifestation—i.e., when R argues "X is the case" regarding the same sort of *mas'ala* for which he elsewhere argues "¬X is the case," this is remarkably similar to *naqḍ* (and of course, *tanāquḍ* and *naqḍ* are cognates). The difference is that, to qualify as *naqḍ*, the opponent must have caused the same *ʿilla* to occasion a different *ḥukm* in a parallel *mas'ala*. In "wider-doctrine *tanāquḍ*," however, the contradiction may manifest itself outside this strictly *ʿilla-ḥukm* relational concern.

Either way, R might be brought to concede a past claim that "X is the case" during the course of investigating his current claim that "¬X is the case." Thus, the *tanāquḍ* would be made "immediate" through the dialectical process (i.e., Q may cause R to juxtapose the two contradictories [*naqīḍayn*] in such a way as the contradiction becomes "internal" as opposed to "wider doctrine"). Again, there is an ambiguous overlapping of *tanāquḍ* with the *naqḍ* of our *jadal*-theory texts, but this should not surprise us at all. Indeed, the cognate relationship of the terms, against the backdrop of our dialectical forge, may provide indicant for a certain continuity from proto-system *jadal* teaching and practice to full-system treatises. Certainly, we have seen plentiful indicants elsewhere, and I might hesitantly propose that *tanāquḍ* is, in one way or another, a precursor to the eventual full-system category of *naqḍ*. Should such be the case, we would have yet another example of *jadal*-theory shaped in its own dialectical forge.

So how 'Aristotelian' are arguments to *tanāquḍ*, and other apparently prior argument axioms? Rather than repeat material from the *Topics* and *Sophistical Elenchi* presented at the end of Chap. 4—much of which offered suggestive parallels—I will turn instead to al-Fārābī's definition of *jadal*. The benefit is this: we may see in this definition an overall account of what Aristotelian dialectic is, as expressed in Arabic terms, by a renowned Baghdadian contemporary of the students of Ibn Surayj.[92] In fact, one would have difficulty finding a better measure for determining how "Aristotelian dialectical" a particular disputational style might be. Of major concern, as we shall see, are al-Fārābī's (and Aristotle's)

[92] Al-Fārābī (d.339/950) spent most of his life in Baghdād, and did not leave for Syria until 330/942.

emphases on destroying/defending theses with universal subjects, and on exposing/avoiding contradiction. Here is my translation:[93]

The *technē* of *jadal* is the *technē* by means of which one obtains: [1] the capability to fashion—from *endoxa* premises—a *qiyās*-syllogism for the nullification of every thesis whose subject is universal, acquiring it through concession, by way of questioning a respondent responsible for its preservation, whichever of the two parts of the *naqīḍ*-contradictory it may be. And [2] [the capability to] preserve every thesis whose subject is universal, held in opposition to the questioner entrusted with its nullification—whichever of the two parts of the *naqīḍ*-contradictory that may be.	صناعة الجدل هي الصناعة التي بها يحصل للإنسان القوة على أن يعمل من مقدمات مشهورة، قياساً في إبطال [كلّ][94] وضع موضوعه كلّي يتسلّمه بالسؤال عن مجيب يتضمن حفظه، أي جزء من جزئي النقيض اتفق، وعلى حفظ كلّ وضع موضوعه كلّي يعرضه لسائل يتضمن إبطاله، أي جزئين من جزئي النقيض اتفق ذلك.
And Aristotle treats this *technē* as a *ṭarīq*-method when he defines it, saying: "It is a *ṭarīq*-method by means of which we are prepared to fashion—from *endoxa* premises—a *qiyās*-syllogism for every considered *mas'ala*-problem; and that it be such that, when we respond with a *jawāb*-response, we don't bring anything contrary [*muḍādd*] in its regard." And his saying "*muḍādd*": he uses it in place of "*muqābil*" [opposite], and indicates "*munāqiḍ*" [contradictory] by way of it. And our saying "we don't bring anything contradictory [*munāqiḍ*] in its regard:" we mean "we don't concede anything by which we are bound to the *naqīḍ*-contradictory of the thesis we are responsible for preserving." And his saying "for every considered *mas'ala*-problem": he means "for every thesis acquired through concession via questioning." And he intends by it "whichever part may be from the two parts of the *naqīḍ*-contradictory," that the questioner obtain it as a concession from the respondent.	وأرسطوطاليس يجعل هذا الصناعة عند تحديده لها أنّها طريق، ويقول إنّها طريق، يتهيّأ لنا بها أن نعمل من مقدمات مشهورة قياساً في كلّ مسألة تُقْصَدْ، وأن يكون إذا أجبنا جواباً لم نأتِ فيه بشيء مضاد. فقوله مضاد استعمله مكان المقابل وأشار به الى المناقض. وقولنا، لم نأتِ فيه بشيء مناقِض نعني لم نسلّم شيئاً يلزمنا عنه نقيض الوضع الذي تضمّنا حفظه. وقوله في كل مسألة تُقْصَدْ، يعني في كل وضع تسلّم بالسؤال وأراد به أي جزء اتفق من جزئي النقيض أن يتسلّمه السائل عن المجيب.

[93] I have preferred my own translation, but should note that Miller ("Disputation Theory," pp. 54–5 and n. 10) also translates the first part of this same definition, as follows: "The art (ṣināʿa) of dialectic is the art through which a man acquires the capacity to (1) fashion from commonly accepted premises a syllogism that destroys a thesis whose subject is universal, and that he obtains through questioning a respondent who was entrusted with defending either part of a contradictory alternation, whatever that happens to be; and (2) to defend any proposition with a universal premise by opposing himself to a questioner entrusted with destroying either part of a contradictory alternation, whatever that happens to be" (Miller cites a typescript of a MS, but I have located this passage in Rafīq al-ʿAjam's ed. [al-Fārābī, *Al-Manṭiq ʿinda al-Fārābī: al-Juzʾ al-Thālith: Kitāb al-Jadal*, p. 13], which apparently relies upon the same MS, as the folio numbers in the margins coincide perfectly). Compare this also with DiPasquale's translation in *Alfarabi and the Starting Point of Islamic Philosophy*, Appendix 1.

[94] The editor finds this "*kull*" in one of his MSS, but has not included it in his transcription (al-ʿAjam ed., p. 13, n. 2).

Between al-Fārābī's rendering of Aristotle and al-Shāfiʿī's *tanāquḍ* practice as we have seen it, both similarities and differences are plain. With regard to his strategy of premise-gathering for *elenchus* by *tanāquḍ*, with certain recurrent terms (*mutanāqiḍ*, *tanāquḍ*, *naqaḍa*, etc.), coupled with the formulaic consistency with which he uses them, the *tanāquḍ* dialectic employed by al-Shāfiʿī in the subject-text appears very Aristotelian indeed. At the same time, however, we must note the differences. Primary among them is that the Q of the above passage does not bring a counter-thesis, whereas al-Shāfiʿī—and all jurist-dialecticians for that matter—are engaged in a contest whose ultimate aim is *muʿāraḍa*: the supplantation of the opponent's ruling with one's own counter-ruling. Al-Shāfiʿī's charge "your *qawl* is *mutanāqiḍ*" is the means by which opposition to his own posited ruling is removed. Also, al-Shāfiʿī says *mutanāqiḍ*, not *munāqiḍ*; and, importantly, the terms *naqīḍ* or *naqīḍān/naqīḍayn* do not appear anywhere in the whole of the *Umm* or the *Risāla*—and neither, for that matter, does *munāqiḍ*. Nor does the term *muqaddimāt* appear anywhere in *Umm* or *Risāla*, while *muqaddima* only occurs in other meanings besides "premise." And completely absent from al-Shāfiʿī's works, too, are both *muḍādd* and *muqābil*.[95] If certain of al-Shāfiʿī's argument strategies ultimately derive from an Aristotelian teaching, that teaching appears not to have been expressed in the same Arabic terms by which Aristotelian dialectic was rendered in al-Fārābī's time (or in his particular Baghdadian tradition).

Already the question is growing more difficult, and this difficulty is significantly compounded by the following: *munāqiḍ*, as employed by al-Fārābī, is the active participle of the third form *nāqaḍa*, whose *maṣdar* is *munāqaḍa*; and *munāqaḍa*, as we have seen it employed by al-Juwaynī, is largely synonymous with *naqḍ*. Nor is this all. If we search for the terms of root *n-q-ḍ* with which we have been most concerned to this point, then we will find the following occurrences in some of our earliest full-system *uṣūl al-fiqh* treatises:[96]

Source	*tanāquḍ / mutanāqiḍ*	*munāqiḍ*	*munāqaḍa*	*naqīḍ*
The *Fuṣūl* of al-Jaṣṣāṣ	20	7	9	1
The *Muʿtamad* of al-Baṣrī	24	1	23	64
The *Tabṣira* of al-Shīrāzī	10	0	7	1
The *Lumaʿ* of al-Shīrāzī	0	0	0	2
The *Burhān* of al-Juwaynī	35	21	34	44
The *Uṣūl* of al-Sarakhsī	14	3	13	0

[95] On the other hand, the term *muḍādd* occurs at least once in the *Fuṣūl* of al-Jaṣṣāṣ, twice in the *Muʿtamad* of al-Baṣrī, and twice in the *Burhān* of al-Juwaynī; while the term *muḍādda(t)* is found six times in the *Uṣūl* of al-Sarakhsī, and eight times in the *Burhān* of al-Juwaynī. As for the terms *muqābil* and *muqābala*, they enjoy great frequency in all of these texts; *muqābala* may also be found four or five times in the *Tabṣira* of al-Shīrāzī.

[96] All of the numerals in this table (excepting zero, of course) should be qualified by the descriptor "at least;" e.g., there are at least 64 occurrences of the term *naqīḍ* in the *Muʿtamad* of al-Baṣrī.

Insofar as I can tell from a brief review of the above, wherever the terms *tanāquḍ* or *mutanāqiḍ* occur, they do so with the same meanings and in the same contexts as we find in the subject text (although, significantly, not in the same formulaic patterns). On the other hand, *munāqiḍ* and *naqīḍ* occur in the same way that al-Fārābī employs them, and *munāqaḍa* appears to maintain its synonymy with *naqḍ*. Yet these latter terms appear nowhere in the *Umm* or *Risāla*.

Pursuit of this question must await further study; in the main, my objective has been to demonstrate how complicated the tracing of terms can quickly become.[97] My objective was also to further problematize any assumptions one might draw from al-Shāfiʿī's usage of *tanāquḍ* and *mutanāqiḍ* in dialectical contexts. Accordingly, my own final assumptions will be stated only with hesitation, and in general terms: (1) there are a number of reasons to believe that certain elements of al-Shāfiʿī's dialectic derive, ultimately, from Aristotelian tradition(s); (2) it will be a difficult, if not impossible, task to pinpoint the core transmitted doctrine of the "source" tradition(s), the path of transmission, and the chronology of that transmission; and (3) it will be just as difficult to trace these (and other) prior argument axioms *after* al-Shāfiʿī's era (bearing in mind that we do not assume "post-Shāfiʿī" to mean "derived from al-Shāfiʿī").

One thing is certain, however. Despite the fact that *tanāquḍ* and *mutanāqiḍ* appear in the arguments of early full-system *uṣūl al-fiqh* works, and they seem to bear the same sense (if not formulaic presentation) by which al-Shāfiʿī employs them, "*al-tanāquḍ*" and "*qawl mutanāqiḍ*" do not constitute distinct categories of analysis in our earliest *jadal*-theory texts.[98] On the other hand, "*naqḍ/munāqaḍa*" do constitute distinct categories of analysis; yet these latter terms are absent from the dialectic of both *Umm* and *Risāla*.[99] Although we may never untangle the web of terminological relationships and associated paths of transmission, these differences between the dialectic of al-Shāfiʿī and that of full-system treatises still provide indicant for a complex reworking of dialectical tools in the dialectical

[97] I am certainly not implying this is not a worthwhile pursuit—there is a great deal to be learned yet from a terminological comparison between our earliest legal theoretical and dialectical texts. These are complex undertakings, however, and demand a far more careful study than can be undertaken in the current project.

[98] In a similar fashion, note that the formula *a-lā tarā*—a staple of proto-system dialectic—also enjoys great currency in these same *uṣūl* texts we have treated (at least 180 occurrences in the *Fuṣūl* of al-Jaṣṣāṣ, 170 in the *Muʿtamad* of al-Baṣrī, 120 in the *Tabṣira* of al-Shīrāzī and 17 in his *Lumaʿ*, and 190 in the *Uṣūl* of al-Sarakhsī; intriguingly, it is entirely absent from al-Juwaynī's *Burhān*). At the same time, this formula receives no independent treatment in our *jadal*-theory texts; at the very least, we might expect to find it as a distinct question-category, or fully treated in connection to certain objection types. This reminds us of the possibility that certain elements of proto-system *jadal* may indeed have continued *in practice* in subsequent eras, and yet found no place for discussion in the theory-texts.

[99] As noted earlier, *naqḍ*—though absent from the *Risāla*—occurs plentifully in the *Umm*; however, it appears—so far as I have seen—only in substantive contexts (relating mostly to the termination of contractual agreements). In other words, "*naqḍ*" in any relation to a dialectical move does not occur.

forge. *Jadal*, as confirmed by the still-debated application and objection-value of *naqḍ* reported in our lens-texts, continued to be a dynamic in the shaping of *jadal*-theory.

There is one last area of difference we have noted between al-Shāfiʿī's argument strategies and the discussions we find in full-system *jadal*-theory treatises; namely: (1) his many "hypothetical" objections (wherein, e.g., he states that *qiyās* does not obtain, then demonstrates that even if it did his opponent's *qiyās*-method is faulty); (2) his *naqḍ*-dilemma strategy (§§693–704); and (3) his unique "remove then replace a property" strategy (§§740–1). Such strategies—and there are doubtless others I have missed, and many more to be discovered in other treatises of the *Umm*—raise a number of important questions; among them: Where and from whom did al-Shāfiʿī learn to argue in this fashion? Or are these his own innovations, a unique contribution to dialectical strategy? And if learned through teachers or peers, to what prior argumentation epistemes do they belong? These questions are intriguing ones, and deserve detailed studies all their own.[100] At present, I can only say this much: discussions of dialectical strategies, *per se*, do not occur in the early theoretical literature of juridical *jadal*. Why this is so remains something of a mystery; but it is my suspicion that—as a corollary development in *jadal*'s evolving argumentation episteme—a gradually expanding discourse on the "good" dialectical ethic (wherein such strategies may have appeared detrimental to the truth seeking enterprise) led to a corresponding decrease in their use.[101]

8.6 *Jadal*-Theory Components of the Dialectical Forge Model

On Jadal *Practice Shaping* Jadal-*Theory*

Any one of the features which seem to have "disappeared" between proto-system *jadal* teaching and practice and the theory propounded by our full-system treatises may be considered a candidate example for the following notion: dialectical theory was itself shaped through dialectical exchange. In the main, the strongest evidence we have for this phenomenon is written quite plainly in our fifth/

[100] In particular, one might begin by scouring the arguments of works attributed to Muḥammad b. al-Ḥasan, and any arguments attributed to him in later sources. How similar was al-Shaybānī's dialectical method to al-Shāfiʿī's?

[101] This is not to suggest, of course, that al-Shāfiʿī did not pursue the "good" dialectical ethic. As we have seen, there is plentiful evidence that he did, not the least of which is the very existence of an Old and New Doctrine. Rather, I am merely pointing out—as with so many other elements of proto-system dialectic—certain strategies may have fallen away due to more stringent (not to mention systematized) standards of later generations.

eleventh century *jadal*-theory texts. Our authors quite frequently draw attention to persistent areas of *ikhtilāf* with regard to the validity of procedures, dialectical question types, and various objections and responses. In particular, I would draw attention to al-Juwaynī's discourse on the number and types of dialectical questions, with frequent reference to variant opinions: "among them are those who say X" (*wa minhum man qāla*: X); "and among them are those who say Y" (*wa minhum man qāla*: Y); etc.; interspersed with his own arguments as to what is valid and what is not.[102] In fact, this is a salient procedure of al-Juwaynī's throughout the entirety of his *Kāfiya*, and it is not infrequent that he employs the familiar *a-lā tarā* formula in his justifications, and/or fully-transcripted "instructional" dialectical sequences.[103]

On further consideration, one realizes that the earliest extant treatises upon which I have relied are as much examples of *jadal* as they are attempts at systematization. Witness al-Bājī's *Minhāj*, where practically every other category of *iʿtirāḍ* and *jawāb*, throughout the whole gamut of "indicants of God's Law" (*adillat al-Sharʿ*), is followed by a thorough discussion (and refutation) of "what is subjoined to [objection type X] but is not of it" (*mā yulḥaqu bi-*[X] *wa laysa minhu*).[104] Al-Shīrāzī, too, is quite fond of appending "Additional modes of the Ḥanafīs" to his ordered lists of *iʿtirāḍāt*, and, upon occasion, debating them.[105] When our authors composed their treatises, they were quite consciously promoting their received, reformulated, or innovative program (*minhāj*) of acceptable *jadal* procedure and moves—over and against other programs. This is precisely the picture of dialectical theory shaped through dialectical exchange which I believe we should consider an important mechanism of the Dialectical Forge model.

It is almost too obvious to need mentioning with regard to full-system theoretical developments, and I have already suggested the disappearance of proto-system elements provides another indicant of *jadal*-theory shaped through *jadal* practice. To these previous examples, I would add al-Shāfiʿī's occasional habit of usurping the role of Q (§653; §694; §1229)—a practice which was definitely frowned upon in later *jadal*-theory. But what of specific instances in our subject-text of overtly *jadal*-oriented dispute; can we, after all, witness the shaping of a *jadal* proto-theory in the act? I would hesitantly claim a potential site for this in the subject-text; namely, those questions and arguments I have labelled "objection-oriented," and "objections to objections." Here, the focus of debate has shifted from *istidlāl* to *iʿtirāḍ*, and in a very real sense that *iʿtirāḍ* is under pressure of scrutiny just as much as Q's (potentially invalid) usage of it. In particular, such exam-

---

102 *Kāfiya*, Maḥmūd ed., pp. 77 ff., §§190 ff.

103 See, for example, ibid., pp. 3 ff., §§10 ff. Other examples of dialectical sequences may be found throughout.

104 *Minhāj*, Turkī ed., *passim*.

105 More typically, he simply illustrates them with examples. Plainly, he is attempting to ensure that the dialectician-in-training is prepared to face modes of justification and critique which he himself does not advocate.

ples as I have subsumed under the hybrid category "*su'āl ʿan wajh al-iʿtirāḍ/muṭālaba bi-wajh al-qadḥ*" provide a locus for this phenomenon: by way of challenging Q to clarify and support his objection, R is in fact preparing to measure Q's *iʿtirāḍ* against his own standard of what constitutes a valid *iʿtirāḍ*.

On somewhat stronger footing, I would draw attention to al-Shāfiʿī's exchange in §§1227 ff. Notably, he is in the role of R, and responding to his opponent's critique, who, after arguing the removal of *qiyās* invalidating barriers asks: "why shouldn't you determine the [ruling for] *awliyā'*-guardians by way of *qiyās* from fathers?" Note that the *qiyās* which Q is pushing is his own *qiyās*—it is evident he seeks to supplant al-Shāfiʿī's *istidlāl* with it, and is attempting to compel his concession to this *qiyās* by asking him to explain the unexplainable. Al-Shāfiʿī's response is a unique combination of *farq*-distinction in support of *muʿāraḍa bi'l-nuṭq*. From one perspective, he succeeds in showing that in a disputation governed by the hierarchy of authoritative *dalīl*-indicants, Q cannot compel R to concede to *qiyās* when R draws directly from unambiguous Sunna. Although the legal-theoretical aspects of al-Shāfiʿī's argument overshadow the strictly *jadal*-procedure aspects, I would still mark this as an instance where something like a critique of Q's *jadal* practice is being played out. The same might be true in §1411, where al-Shāfiʿī is again in the role of R, and his opponent again seems to be imposing a *qiyās* upon him, then al-Shāfiʿī makes his elegant argument to the effect that one simply cannot base *qiyās* on God's singular exception to His own "rationally understood general principle" (*aṣl al-maʿqūl*). It is in specific points of conflict such as this where I believe we may locate *jadal* practice shaping a proto-theory of *jadal*.

More in the line of the "disappearance" indicant, I would also consider those examples of "expanded range" objections. §248, in which *manaʿa* is twice employed in a sense similar to that conveyed in the *jadal* literature, but outside its typical *jadal*-theory domain, stands as an example. More intriguingly, however, al-Shāfiʿī employs—in this same section—a species of *tarjīḥ al-ẓawāhir* for which al-Shīrāzī references *ikhtilāf* in his day.[106] Doubtless there are other examples of this sort which may be found in our subject-text, and certainly they will be found when the whole of the *Umm*'s dialectical sequences have been explored (the work, I imagine, of a decade or more.) I would also suggest a project with intriguing possibilities; mainly, that all "benefit of assumption" rulings ("and the considered claim is the claim of party X" [*fa'l-qawlu qawlu* X]), as well as rulings and arguments in the evidentiary domain of oath-taking and *bayyina*-evidence, should be explored. There is an obvious overlap between certain epistemological concerns of evidentiary procedure and of *jadal*-theory, and every possibility that a thorough examination of dialectical sequences in surviving juridical and theological literature

[106] *Maʿūna*, al-ʿUmayrīnī ed., pp. 121–2: "And among our [Shāfiʿī] companions are those who say: [the *ḥadīth*] is not preponderated [in terms of numbers of transmitters], like testimony (*shahāda*). But the first [opinion, which allows this] is more valid." In other words, al-Shīrāzī sanctions a *tarjīḥ*-method which we find al-Shāfiʿī employing in §248 nearly 300 years earlier.

will uncover a complementary dynamic between court disputation-procedure and that of *jadal* sessions.

In the end, though it is easy to see our subject-text jurists were engaging in a studied and transmitted, formal and formulaic, tradition of *jadal* teaching and practice, it is not easy to see them dispute (or even discourse) upon that teaching and practice. There is plentiful evidence, in other words, that a proto-theory was in the making, but our subject-text reveals no instances of *jadal* targeting that proto-theory in the same, open way that our lens-text theorists discourse on the right and wrong procedures and dialectical moves. On the other hand, our *jadal* theorists *did* debate *jadal*-theory itself, and frequently reached back as far as Ibn Surayj with their comments. If we have not caught al-Shāfiʿī and company "in the act" of debating *jadal* itself in the subject-text, it is nevertheless likely such exchanges occurred, and most certain that they did in subsequent generations. *Jadal* about *jadal* is far older than the era of our lens-texts.

A final note with regard to *jadal* practice shaping *jadal*-theory in the dialectical forge: although engendering no specific indications of the dialectical forge *per se*, Miller's quite thorough examination of variant opinions among *jadal* theorists with regard to accepted procedures, question types, and objections—across all projects: theological, philosophical, juridical, and synthetic—constitutes an excellent secondary source for the study of dialectical theory being shaped through dialectical debate. In fact, it is the supposed "expansions" and revisions of juridical dialectic with regard to the older and outstanding problems raised by theological *jadal* upon which Miller hinges certain of his juridical take over claims.

In the previous section, I located the mechanisms at work in the "*jadal* and *uṣūl*-theory compartment" of the Dialectical Forge model. Now, and considering what was discussed above in this current section, I would place the first component in the "*jadal* and *jadal*-theory compartment": "the forging of dialectical theory via the medium of dialectical exchange"—or, more simply, "*jadal* practice shaping *jadal*-theory." This mechanism, of course, is also intertwined with co-evolution and dynamic symbiosis, but is unique in that *jadal*-theory itself becomes the object of *jadal*. This component also comes with a pair of subsidiary processes, to the first of which I will now turn.

On Dialectic Defining What is Endoxon

This particular mechanism is corollary to the "first principles parallel" I proposed with regard to *jadal* and *uṣūl al-fiqh*. To explain, we must first return to an earlier discussion in Chap. 7. Instances of *ijmāʿ* in the subject-text were reviewed, then compared to Aristotle's dialectical premises—i.e., such as are found within his greater *endoxa*-set; and I noted certain parallels between the two conceptions. What is important at present is that the following was also noted: thanks to the hierarchy of epistemic authority which gradually developed in the juridical argumentation epistemes of proto-Sunnism (God, then Sunna, then *ijmāʿ*, *qiyās*, etc.), the parallel of Aristotle's dialectical premises might be said to stretch across the full gamut of epistemic justifications in Islamic legal theory (i.e., not just *ijmāʿ*). In other words, the premises employed in juridical *jadal* were not delimited by: (1) what everyone believes; or (2) what most of the people believe; or (3) what most of the wise believe; etc. Rather, the Proto-Sunnī juridical *endoxa*-set became: (1) what God said; *then* (2) what God's Messenger said/did/acknowledged; *then* (3) what the Community of Muslims has formed consensus on; *then* (4) what may be rationally understood from #1 and #2, with minimal hermeneutical effort; *then* (5) what may be rationally understood with greater hermeneutical effort, *then* (6)... etc. In other words, it became an *endoxa*-set of *hierarchical epistemic authority*, not a sets-within-the-superset model of Aristotelian dialectic (even though this model has great consonance with *ijmāʿ* theory).

I also noted briefly that it was juridical disputation that determined what this hierarchical—and distinctly Islamic—*endoxa*-set would be. Juridical *jadal*, I concluded, at once depended upon *and determined* what was *endoxon* for the Muslim jurist. It is this theory of "dialectic defining the *endoxon*" which I would now like to locate within the Dialectical Forge model; and, like the "first principles" theory discussed earlier—which demonstrates an obviously correspondent concern for [re-]defining *archai*—this "defining the *endoxon*" mechanism also finds its parallel in the *Topics*. Near the end of his introduction to dialectical propositions, and before turning to dialectical problems, Aristotle says the following:[107]

> It is also obvious that all opinions which accord with the arts are dialectical propositions; for one would accept the opinions of those who have examined the subjects in question. For example, on questions of medicine one would think as the doctor thinks and in matters of geometry as the geometrician thinks,[108] and so too with the other arts.

We have seen the role which dialectic may play in (re-)defining the first principles (*archai*) of the demonstrative sciences. Here, Aristotle confirms—as common sense would also dictate—that the "opinions" (*doxai*) of the demonstrative sciences are obviously within the larger *endoxa*-set of dialectical propositions (presumably concentrated in the subset of "the wise"). Of course these *doxai* of the demonstrative sciences ultimately depend upon *archai* which are themselves indemonstrable (but may be [re-]defined via dialectic). Thus we begin to see the parallel roles of Aristotelian dialectic (in both defining the *archai* of the demonstrative sciences, and depending upon their *doxai*) and juridical *jadal* (in both defining the premises of *uṣūl al-fiqh*, and depending upon them): in the end, both species of dialectic play a role in determining what is *endoxon*. Juridical *jadal*, I would claim, has determined what is *endoxon* for the Muslim jurist (i.e., hierarchies of epistemic authority and all of their subsidiary theories and methods: the very premises of *uṣūl al-fiqh* and *jadal*-theory) throughout the many stages of its development as a system.

---

[107] *Top.* I.10, 104a34ff. (trans. Forster).

[108] Geometry was one of Aristotle's favourite examples of a demonstrative science. See the *Cambridge Companion to Aristotle*, pp. 25 f., 47.

This mechanism may now be added to the *jadal* and *jadal*-theory compartment of the Dialectical Forge model. Happily, it also highlights the great advantage afforded us in being able to study Islamic juridical *ikhtilāf* and *jadal* in such detail, in so many sources, across so many genres, geographical regions, and eras: this wealth of material provides an illustration of what may be a far more universal paradigm for intellectual-historical evolution. Dialectic, in a very palpable manner, both expands and refines the premises of the *endoxa*-set. As a result, *all* of the theory-systems born and developed in the larger dialectical forges of world intellectual projects—including theory-systems of dialectic itself—grow increasingly sophisticated over time. So long as the dialectical forge is fully staffed and cleanly managed, intellectual projects utilizing formal dialectic are limited only by the rational capabilities of studied practitioners and theorists, or by whatever constraints which state, society, or historical accident may impose.

On the Transmission, Study, and Analysis of Past Jadal *by* Jadal *Theorists*

In previous discussions, we have also encountered clear signs that two additional processes were at work in the development of *jadal*-theory. The first I described in terms of the transmission of often quite particular (even *mas'ala*-specific) dialectical methods from teacher to student. The second, and clearly related process, was *jadal* theorists looking back to the past and incorporating analyses of the *jadal*-practice of venerated exemplar *mujtahids* into their discussions. I would now briefly revisit these processes, and locate them as final mechanisms at work in the *jadal* and *jadal*-theory compartment of the Dialectical Forge model.

During the course of analyses, it became abundantly clear that the *Ikhtilāf al-ʿIrāqiyyayn/ʿIrāqiyyīn* was a treatise compiled, transmitted, and commented upon with a patently didactic intent. In short, our subject-text constitutes a *manual* of argument and strategy for the practicing jurist-dialectician, just as much as it constitutes a storehouse of past and recurrent *masā'il* of *ikhtilāf*. The import here lies in the continuity (and forward-looking consistency) at which such pedagogical features appear to aim. I would hypothesize as to this aim and its fruition: the eventual culmination of teachings in comprehensive systems, with the aid of certain indicants we have already encountered.

Primary among these is the very nature and intention of both "historical" and "instructional" dialectical sequences in the subject-text. With regard to the "instructional," the didactic intent of "and if one should say... it is said to him..." (*fa-in qāla qā'il... qīla lahu...*) is so plain as to have earned this label from the start. But the "historical" sequence, though equally important in the didactic project, provides proof of another vital phenomenon; namely, the transmission of past *jadal* sequences as a base template for current and future *jadal*. Al-Shāfiʿī evoked "historical" sequences from past encounters in order to prepare his auditor/reader for future dialectical exchanges over continuing *masā'il* of *ikhtilāf*.

This is important for what it shows of a marked and intentional continuity between generations of middle proto-system jurists (i.e., from the jurists of Abū Ḥanīfa's era to those of al-Rabīʿ's). The transmission of the subject-text itself (Ibn Abī Laylā & Abū Ḥanīfa → Abū Yūsuf → al-Shaybānī → al-Shāfiʿī → al-Rabīʿ), and the accretions of variant opinions and arguments it gained along the way, are an eloquent testimony to this. Perhaps the most startling example by which continuity is brought into sharp focus, however, is what we witnessed in §§755 ff. There, we will recall, al-Shāfiʿī discovers "in this book" (i.e., in the Shaybānī Version of our subject-text) an opposing argument from the past which he had not personally encountered in his own dialectical exchanges. He then proceeds to refute it in "instructional" format in order to prepare his auditor/reader for any future encounter with a proponent of this "historical" argument. In a very real way, then, he *revived* a past argument for the sake of maintaining the comprehensiveness of an ongoing (and *mas'ala*-specific) set of counter-arguments. Nor is this all that we saw of continuity within the middle proto-system; for we found that al-Muzanī, in his own dialectical sequence in the *Mukhtaṣar*, imitates al-Shāfiʿī's dialectic from §262. Not only do we have indicants for the *intention* of didactic continuity, but we have evidence of its *success*.

With regard to this sort of *jadal*-specific continuity from middle to late proto-system and onwards into the eras of full-system *jadal* theory, we have moved beyond the scope of the current study's analyses. In terms of providing a more complete picture for the evolution of juridical *jadal* theory, the extant textual material from the third and early fourth centuries H remains a very significant open door—there is a great deal which will be learned from this material once it has been subjected to the kind of analysis I have attempted for the *Ikhtilāf al-ʿIrāqiyyayn/ʿIrāqiyyīn.*[109] All the same, we still have plentiful indications that a marked continuity (and, of course, elaboration and refinement) of past *jadal* teaching and practice will be revealed. The dialectical *ra'ā* formulae of *a-ra'ayta* and *a-lā tarā*, along with their associated functions, are a clear marker of a certain level of continuity throughout the long evolution of juridical *jadal*. I have pointed out their frequency in both the roots and branches of the developmental tree.

More important yet are certain indicants of "analyses of the past" which we found in our lens-texts. The authors of our earlier extant theory-works looked back to the arguments and methods of venerated exemplar *mujtahid*s (eponymic founders and companions). We noted, for example, that al-Bājī opens his chapter on the modes of *Tarjīḥāt* with: "Know that *tarjīḥ* is a method (*ṭarīq*) for the advancing of one of the two *dalīl*-indicants over the other; and the ancients (Qudamā') used to make use of it in intellectual investigation (*al-naẓar*), and they did so frequently…."[110] So, too, did they look back for paradigms of *uṣūl* and *furūʿ* oriented arguments. While attempting to identify al-Shāfiʿī's *Kitāb*-oriented *iʿtirāḍ* in §1056,

---

[109] And, as we have seen, even such condensed collections of abstracted substantive rulings as al-Muzanī's *Mukhtaṣar* may yield the occasional dialectical sequence for analysis.

[110] *Minhāj*, Turkī ed., p. 221, §504.

we discovered that al-Bājī not only appeared to describe the very same dialectical move, but that his example *mas'ala* consisted of the very same *mas'ala* under consideration in §1051–61, with the same Qur'ānic *dalīl*-indicant and variant *lafẓ*-expression interpretations.

And again, we found the dialectical move of Abū Yūsuf and/or Muḥammad b. al-Ḥasan in §1316 exactly described in our lens-texts (as a species of *fasād al-iʿtibār*), then illustrated by the very same *mas'ala* of *ikhtilāf*, with the very same supporting *dalīl*-indicant (introduced, no less, by *a-lā tarā*).[111] What is more, with regard to the ensuing dialectic of §§1321 ff., we also discovered a description matching al-Shāfiʿī's *jawāb* to a charge of *fasād al-iʿtibār* (in §1326, having himself taken up Ibn Abī Laylā's position)—again, not only in relation to the very same *mas'ala*, but responding by the very *taswiya*-subsumption (al-Bājī employs *istawayā*) advanced by al-Shāfiʿī, and with the very same confirmatory rulings (re: *zinā* and *qatl*).[112] Thus both the charge of al-Shāfiʿī's opponent, and al-Shāfiʿī's *jawāb*, are echoed in the prescriptions and example *mas'ala* of al-Bājī some 250 years later. Moreover, the *mas'ala* of *ikhtilāf* itself precedes al-Shāfiʿī by at least another 50 years; thus, the full span of continuity (from Abū Ḥanīfa and Ibn Abī Laylā to al-Bājī) is more in the line of 300 years.[113]

In sum, two theories of continuity find support in our subject-text and lens texts: (1) the forward-looking transmission of dialectical methods from teacher to student; and (2) the backward-looking research of *jadal* theorists seeking to incorporate analyses of the dialectical teachings and practices of venerated exemplars into their discussions. The relationship between these two processes is self-evident, and perhaps they would best be combined and rendered as a single process under the general rubric "transmission and analysis of past *jadal*." This is the last mechanism I would locate in the *jadal* and *jadal*-theory compartment of the Dialectical Forge model, and—at this current stage of research—in the model as a whole.

8.7 The Dialectical Forge Model in its Current Form

The Dialectical Forge model, aimed at explaining and illustrating the powerful formative dynamic of dialectical disputation in the evolution of Islamic legal and juridical-dialectical theory systems, is now as complete as the current

[111] al-Shīrāzī, *Maʿūna*, al-ʿUmayrīnī ed., pp. 114 f.; al-Bājī, *Minhāj*, Turkī ed., pp. 181 f., §§402ff.—especially at §405. Cf. Ibn ʿAqīl, *K. al-Jadal*, p. 64, §303.

[112] al-Bājī, *Minhāj*, Turkī ed., p. 182, §405.

[113] Nor are these the only indicants of continuity and analysis of past *jadal*. All instances in which al-Shāfiʿī makes his opponent's method the object of critique, show that method-oriented dialectic in practice precedes any distinction between *fiqh*-oriented and *uṣūl al-fiqh*-oriented juridical dialectic. Such examples illustrating the sub-projects of proto-system *jadal* are what allows us to seek the roots of "Ḥanafī vs. Shāfiʿī" *ṭarīqa*s long before the full systematization of *uṣūl al-fiqh*. These projects are the continuity of, and elaboration upon, older tendencies, and both derived many a principle from proto-system *jadal* practice.

micro-study allows. With its various mechanisms located in their relevant compartments, the model in its current form would appear, in outline, as follows:

The Dialectical Forge Model	
Dialectic and *Uṣūl*-Theory	**Dialectic and *Jadal*-Theory**
• the three-stage cycle	• *jadal* practice shaping *jadal*-theory
• the bequeathing of dialectical axioms	• dialectic defining what is *endoxon*
• dynamic symbiosis and co-evolution	• transmission and analysis of past *jadal*
• *ijtihādic* anticipation of *jadal*	
• the first principles parallel	

This is a preliminary model, and is expected to expand and contract as new mechanisms are discovered and incorporated, and if older ones are problematized, altered, or eliminated. In the meantime, it serves to draw together key themes of the current project, and to explain the complex relationship between *jadal* and *uṣūl al-fiqh*. It is a starting point, a template, and a tool for sharpening focus on key processes. Most importantly, however, it demonstrates the critical importance of dialectical disputation in the Islamic legal enterprise as a whole. With the model as complete as can be for the time being, I will turn towards two subsidiary schemes in a brief final chapter, before drawing the current project to a close.

References

Abū Zahra, Muḥammad. *Uṣūl al-Fiqh*. Cairo: Dār al-Fikr al-ʿArabī, 1424/2004.

Aristotle. *Posterior Analytics* (Ed. and Transl. Hugh Tredennick); *Topica* (Ed. and Transl. E.S. Forster). Aristotle II; Loeb Classical Library #391. Cambridge, Mass: Harvard University Press, 1960.

al-Bājī, Abū al-Walīd Sulaymān. *Kitāb al-Minhāj fī Tartīb al-Ḥijāj* (*L'art de la Polémique: Édition Critique d'al-Minhāǧ de Bāǧī*). Ed. ʿAbd al-Majīd Turkī. Paris: Maisonneuve et Larose, 1978.

Barnes, Jonathon, ed. *The Cambridge Companion to Aristotle*. New York: Cambridge University Press, 1995.

Bolton, Robert. "The Epistemological Basis of Aristotelian Dialectic." In Sim, ed., *Puzzles to Principles? Essays on Aristotle's Dialectic* (Lanham, MD: 1999): pp. 57–105.

Calder, Norman. "Al-Nawawī's Typology of Muftīs and its Significance for a General Theory of Islamic Law." *Islamic Law and Society* 4 (1996): pp. 137–64.

Calder, Norman. *Studies in Early Muslim Jurisprudence*. Oxford: Clarendon Press, 1993.

DiPasquale, David Michael. "Alfarabi and the Starting Point of Islamic Philosophy: A Study of the *Kitāb Al-Jadal* (*Book of Dialectic*)." PhD diss., Harvard University, 2002.

EI^2 = *Encyclopaedia of Islam, Second Edition*. Ed. P. Bearman; Th. Bianquis; C.E. Bosworth; E. van Donzel; and W.P. Heinrichs. Brill Online, 2014 <http://referenceworks.brillonline.com/entries/encyclopaedia-of-islam-2>

al-Fārābī, Abū Naṣr. *Al-Manṭiq ʿinda al-Fārābī: al-Juzʾ al-Thālith: Kitāb al-Jadal*. Ed. Rafīq al-ʿAjam. Beirut: Dār al-Mashriq, 1986.

Gwynne, Rosalind Ward. *Logic, Rhetoric, and Legal Reasoning in the Qurʾān: God's Arguments*. London: Routledge Curzon, 2004.

Hallaq, Wael. *Authority, Continuity and Change in Islamic Law*. Cambridge: Cambridge University Press, 2001.

Hallaq, Wael. *A History of Islamic Legal Theories: An Introduction to Sunnī Uṣūl al-Fiqh*. Cambridge; New York: Cambridge University Press, 1997.

Hallaq, Wael. *The Origins and Evolution of Islamic Law*. Cambridge; New York: Cambridge University Press, 2005.
Hallaq, Wael. *Sharīʿa: Theory, Practice, Transformations*. Cambridge; New York: Cambridge University Press, 2009.
Hallaq, Wael. "A Tenth-Eleventh Century Treatise on Juridical Dialectic." *Muslim World* 77 (1987): pp. 197–228.
Hallaq, Wael. "Was al-Shāfiʿī the Master Architect of Islamic Jurisprudence?" International Journal of Middle East Studies 25 (1993), pp. 587–605.
Ibn ʿAqīl, Abū al-Wafā' ʿAlī. *Kitāb al-Jadal ʿalā Ṭarīqat al-Fuqahā'*. Al-Ẓāhir [Cairo]: Maktabat al-Thaqāfa al-Dīniyya, 1980. [An unattributed reproduction of George Makdisi, ed., *Le Livre de la Dialectique d'Ibn ʿAqīl*, minus his introduction and critical apparatus].
Ibn Qāḍī Shuhba, Abū Bakr b. Aḥmad. *Ṭabaqāt al-Shāfiʿiyya*. 4 vols. Ed. ʿAbd al-ʿAlīm Khān. Hyderabad (India): Maṭbaʿat Majlis Dā'irat al-Maʿārif al-ʿUthmāniyya, 1978–1980.
Kamali, Mohammad Hashim. *Principles of Islamic Jurisprudence*. 3rd Edition. Cambridge, UK: The Islamic Texts Society, 2003.
al-Khuḍarī, Muḥammad. *Uṣūl al-Fiqh*. Cairo: Dār al-Ḥadīth, 1424/2003.
Lowry, Joseph. "Does Shāfiʿī have a Theory of Four Sources of Law?" In Bernard Weiss, ed. *Studies in Islamic Legal Theory* (Leiden: Brill, 2001): pp. 24–51.
Lowry, Joseph. *Early Islamic Legal Theory : the Risāla of Muḥammad ibn Idrīs al-Shāfiʿī*. Leiden; Boston: Brill, 2007.
Miller, Larry Benjamin. "Islamic Disputation Theory: A Study of the Development of Dialectic in Islam from the Tenth Through Fourteenth Centuries." PhD diss., Princeton University, 1984.
Owen, G.E.L. "*Tithenai ta phainomena*." In Nussbaum, ed., *Logic, Science and Dialectic* (Ithaca, NY: 1986): pp. 239–51.
Sānū, Quṭb Muṣṭafā. *Muʿjam Muṣṭalaḥāt Uṣūl al-Fiqh, ʿArabī-Inkilīzī*. Beirut: Dār al-Fikr al-Muʿāṣir, 2000.
Schacht, Joseph. *The Origins of Muhammadan Jurisprudence*. Oxford: Oxford University Press, 1950.
al-Shāfiʿī, Muḥammad b. Idrīs. *Kitāb Ikhtilāf Abī Ḥanīfa wa Ibn Abī Laylā* [= *Umm* Version]. In *idem*, *Mawsūʿat al-Imām al-Shāfiʿī: al-Kitāb al-Umm* (2nd ed.) Ed. Aḥmad Badr al-Dīn Ḥassūn. Beirut: Dār Qutayba, 2003, vol. 9, pt. 14, pp. 7–235.
al-Shāfiʿī, Muḥammad b. Idrīs. *Mawsūʿat al-Imām al-Shāfiʿī: al-Kitāb al-Umm*. 2nd ed. Ed. Aḥmad Badr al-Dīn Ḥassūn. 16 Pts. in 10 Vols. Beirut: Dār Qutayba, 2003.
al-Shāshī [?]. *Uṣūl al-Shāshī: Mukhtaṣar fī Uṣūl al-Fiqh al-Islāmī, ta'līf Niẓām al-Dīn al-Shāshī, min Rijāl al-Qarn al-Sābiʿ al-Hijrī*. Ed. Muḥammad Akram al-Nadwī, with introduction by Yūsuf al-Qaraḍāwī. Beirut: Dār al-Gharb al-Islāmī, 2000.
al-Shāshī [?]. *Uṣūl al-Shāshī, li-Abī ʿAlī al-Shāshī; wa bi-Hāmishihi ʿUmdat al-Ḥawāshī li'l-Mawlā Muḥammad Fayḍ al-Ḥasan al-Kankūhī*. Ed. Khalīl al-Mays. Beirut: Dār al-Kitāb al-ʿArabī, 1982.
al-Shīrāzī, Abū Isḥāq Ibrāhīm. *Kitāb al-Lumaʿ fī Uṣūl al-Fiqh* (*Traité de Théorie Légale Musulmane*). Introduction, traduction annotée et index par Éric Chaumont. Berkeley, CA: Robbins Collection, 1999.
al-Shīrāzī, Abū Isḥāq Ibrāhīm. *Al-Maʿūna fi'l-Jadal*. Ed. ʿAlī b. ʿAbd al-ʿAzīz al-ʿUmayrīnī. Al-Ṣafāh, Kuwait: Manshūrāt Markaz al-Makhṭūṭāt wa'l-Turāth, 1987.
al-Shīrāzī, Abū Isḥāq Ibrāhīm. *Ṭabaqāt al-Fuqahā'*. Ed. Khalīl al-Mays. Beirut: Dār al-Qalam, n.d.
Smith, Robin. "Dialectic and Method in Aristotle." In Sim, ed., *From Puzzles to Principles? Essays on Aristotle's Dialectic* (Lanham, MD: 1999): pp. 39–55.
al-Ṭūfī, Sulaymān b. ʿAbd al-Qawī. *ʿAlam al-Jadhal fī ʿIlm al-Jadal*. Ed. Wolfhart Heinrichs. Wiesbaden: F. Steiner Verlag, 1987.
Vishanoff, David R. *The Formation of Islamic Hermeneutics: How Sunni Legal Theorists Imagined a Revealed Law*. New Haven, Conn: American Oriental Society, 2011.
Weiss, Bernard. "Medieval Islamic legal education as reflected in the works of Sayf al-Dīn al-Āmidī." In Joseph E. Lowry, Devin J. Stewart, and Shawkat M. Toorawa, eds. *Law and Education in Medieval Islam: Studies in Memory of Professor George Makdisi* (Cambridge: E.J.W. Gibb Memorial Trust, 2004): pp. 110–27.

Weiss, Bernard. *The Search for God's Law: Islamic Jurisprudence in the Writings of Sayf al-Din al-Āmidī.* Salt Lake City: University of Utah Press, 1992.

Wisnovsky, Robert. "Dialectic and *Ādāb al-Baḥth.*" Class Lecture, Islamic Logic. McGill University, Institute of Islamic Studies, 08 Jan. 2007.

Young, Walter Edward. "The Dialectical Forge: Proto-System Juridical Disputation in the Kitāb Ikhtilāf al-ʿIrāqiyyīn." 2 vols. PhD diss., McGill University, 2012.

Chapter 9
Supplementary Paradigms and Open Doors

9.1 Towards a Background Narrative for the Early Evolution of Juridical Dialectic and Legal Theory

The Dialectical Forge model has assumed a level of abstraction and generality that may not seem prudent on the basis of an analytical, purely intellectual-historical micro-study.[1] I would therefore reiterate that it is only intended as a preliminary model. By this I mean that it is proffered as a flexible template, a general pointing of the way and reminder of the mechanisms and processes I have deemed significant in the overall formative dynamic—the engine driving towards increasing refinement and systematization—of the dialectical forge, and that it is open and, I believe, amenable, to alteration on the basis of further analytical studies of proto-system argumentative and dialectical material.

At the same time, I would point out the following: (1) a sophisticated juridical dialectic has played a role in Islamic legal evolution since the earliest times, as our subject-text, the whole of the *Umm*, and other early compendia stand witness; (2) with regard to proto-system legal theory, the role of juridical dialectic was indeed a formative one, a thesis which I believe my analyses and discussions strongly support; (3) with regard to *jadal*-theory (proto-system and full-system both), the role of juridical dialectic was also formative—the full-system itself built upon *jadal* axioms debated, dialectically, in venues practicing that system—as our lens-texts strongly attest (and our subject-text potentially suggests); and (4) the Dialectical Forge model integrates well with current paradigms for the evolution of Islamic legal theory, throughout all early stages. My goal, in the end, has been to raise

[1] As mentioned at the start of Chap. 2, the current project has not ventured into the domain of social history, where relevant studies like El Shamsy's *Canonization of Early Islamic Law* have offered compelling paradigms of early social and intellectual dynamics alike. The focus of the current project has remained on the formative dynamic of dialectical disputation, with the general aims of revealing its critical importance for the evolution of Islamic law and legal theory, and of promoting its study.

W.E. Young, *The Dialectical Forge*, Logic, Argumentation & Reasoning 9,
DOI 10.1007/978-3-319-25522-4_9

juridical dialectic to the forefront of Islamic legal-historical considerations; and my claim, in the end, is that dialectic and its progressivley self-refining argumentation axioms constituted the major dynamic—within the larger set of cultural norms—powering the evolution of both *uṣūl* and *jadal* theory.

On this basis, I would now take the first steps towards a background layer for developmental narratives, current and future, for *uṣūl al-fiqh* and *jadal* theory—incorporating and highlighting a role for the Dialectical Forge model in its current form, and pointing out areas where a great deal of caution should be exercised, or a significant amount of research and analysis remains to be done. A true, comprehensive layer of underlying dynamics cannot be proposed at this stage; what follows is expressed in only the most general terms, and is intended more in the way of suggesting areas for future concentration.

The Confluence of Argumentation Epistemes and the Early Development of Epistemic Justification and Objection in Islamic Law

Even from the most general overview of early Islamic intellectual projects, developments, and debates, in the domains of philosophy, theology, and law—considered along with the backdrop and continuity of pre-Islamic intellectual-historical developments in the lands which formed the nucleus of early Islamicate civilization—it is sensible to propose that numerous sets, or bodies, of argumentation epistemes blanketed the early Islamic intellectual landscape. As for delineating these bodies of argumentation epistemes—marking out where one begins, and another ends, and which may have incorporated parts of another—that is a different matter entirely, and one which I have more or less abandoned in the current project. Nevertheless, when we narrow our focus especially to the teaching and practice of proto-system *jadal* in Islam, we might at least posit the existence of certain argumentation epistemes, and hypothesize as to their interaction, confluence of axioms, and overall genetic role in the evolution of juridical dialectic.

Regarding what was on the scene during various stages in the evolution of *jadal* and *uṣūl* systems, one could posit quite a large number of argumentation epistemes, of larger and smaller sets. The difficulty of attributing "origins" and "influences" has been plain from the outset, even with the inclusion of a rough (and, in some respects arbitrary) pre-Islamic vs. early Islamic chronological divide. Beginning from the pre-Islamic, for example, and from a cultural and/or ethnic perspective, one could posit argumentation epistemes which may be more antique Mesopotamian, more Aramaic, or more Persianate (axioms of which might be culled, e.g., from their respective wisdom literatures); or more Indic (culled, e.g., from the *Nyāya Sūtras*, and other texts of Hindu philosophy and logic); or more Arabian (culled, e.g., from accounts of pre-Islamic disputes and arbitration, and from the argument style of the Qur'ān itself); or more Hellenic (culled, e.g., from the Aristotelian corpus and commentaries, and other philosophical traditions).

Then again, from the perspective of religious communities, one might draw axioms of argumentation from a vast body of Zoroastrian, Judaic, Hindu, Buddhist, Sabaean, Christian, and other confessional community literatures—each in turn comprising different sets of argumentation epistemes, with regional and theological variants. Moreover, and shifting to a legal perspective, what host of argumentation epistemes might one derive from an examination of the vast legal records of ancient Mesopotamia, from Syro-Roman law books, Byzantine manuals, Sasānid Zoroastrian law books, the Palestinian and Babylonian Talmuds, and countless other source of ancient and late antique law?

The argumentation epistemes of the pre-Islamic Near East were plainly manifold, and must be sought in a bewildering number and variety of sources, even when broken down into these reductive categories (which are incomplete in scope, and problematic in terms of overlap). And as far as tracing "origins" and "influence" between one episteme and the next, we are faced with incredible difficulties; for parallels in argument or substance are hardly proofs of influence to begin with—and even if they were, an absolute priority would be impossible to ascertain in the great majority of instances. We can say with certainty, however, that a great many argumentation epistemes were on the scene at the dawning of Islam, and that they continued into early Islam, whatever their relationship to each other, and whatever their relationship to the nascent argumentation epistemes of early Islamic intellectual traditions.

As for the argumentation epistemes of the first two centuries of Islam, we have an imposing body of literature to examine in the realms of theology and law alone. That being said, we may identify with certainty the appearance of a new, distinctly Islamic argumentation episteme from the outset—from the era of the Prophet himself[2]—and expanding through various projects into a wide variety of intellectual proto-systems and schools, each with variant argumentation epistemes, but all with patently Islamic axioms. The religio-political and legal events of the 1st/7th century contributed this basic set of Islamic axioms—primary among them: the epistemic authority of God's Qur'ān, and His arguments and decrees recorded therein; and the epistemic authority of the *sunan* of the Prophet and his Companions and/or Family members and/or community, and their recorded arguments and decrees—to a thereafter distinctly Islamic set of argumentation epistemes across legal, theological, and philosophical domains.

Muslim scholars who engaged in speculative and normative projects were building, from the start, upon foundational epistemes incorporating Islamic axioms, along with whatever axioms may have been inherited from pre-Islamic times, whatever axioms new generations of scholars brought with them, and whatever axioms were spontaneously generated, reinvented, formulated afresh, or refined. In short, the intellectual landscape within which Islamic juridical dialectic first evolved was populated with numerous argumentation epistemes, old

[2] As evidenced, primarily, by the argumentation of the Qur'ān; and, secondarily, by the argumentation in such passages of historical and Sunnaic works which survive the tests of critical scrutiny.

and new, overlapping and mutually influencing; and the primacy of one episteme over another—in terms of chronology or influence—is almost impossible to divine. It is here, however, that we may begin to consider in earnest the working of the dialectical forge in its specifically Islamicate context.

The developmental model I proposed in Chap. 4 portrayed the evolutionary stages of theological and juridical *jadal* in terms of common origins, parallel development, and cross-germination. We are now at the base of that model—the "common origins" are the complicated web-works of epistemes and axioms I have just described. But it is important to recognize that the variant aims and agendas of speculative (theological) and normative (juridical) projects are the real and immediate causes behind the subsequent branching and distinctive trajectories of theological and juridical argumentation epistemes. Even though a great many, perhaps even a majority, of scholars throughout the full range of developmental history were polymaths engaged in both of these projects (and others), the natures of the projects themselves were essentially different, and the accompanying axioms of argumentation evolved accordingly (and, of course, in dialectical venues).[3]

In one sense, there was no real branching in terms of the projects themselves, for their directives were always different. What I attempted to show in the model of Chap. 4, however, was a branching of the distinctly Islamic argumentation epistemes associated with these projects, for the argument axioms of both were initially drawn from a common pool. Once these projects began in earnest, however—whether in the era of Successors, Companions, of even the Prophet himself—the transformative dynamic of the dialectical forge was immediately at work. And as for the spark which lit the forge: it is *ikhtilāf*, and we may date the true beginnings of Islamic theological and juridical projects, along with their evolving sets of argumentation epistemes, from the very first instances of speculative and normative disagreement, and the epistemic justifications which were put forward in support of variant opinions.

With special regard to the evolution of legal theory and juridical dialectical theory, such mechanisms of the Dialectical Forge model as do not presuppose a longer interval of development may be considered to provide explanation for underlying intellectual dynamics from the very beginning—that is to say, from the first juridically-themed disputations onwards. As for the details of these disputations and their participants, they must be culled from the earliest extant legal materials we possess; and—although so much more is yet to be done for the earliest periods—I believe that the model will integrate well with more detailed

[3] Witness, for example, the "drawing indication for the absent/unseen by way of the present/seen" (*istidlāl bi'l-shāhid ʿalā al-ghā'ib*) of theological discourse over and against the various modes of *istidlāl* we find in juridical *jadal* and legal theory. Note, too, the *qiyās* of philosophical and theological discourse over and against the *qiyās* of juridical discourse. The similarities between these modes of reasoning stem from a common pot of argumentation epistemes at the shared base of the evolutionary tree, and were sustained through subsequent cross-germination. The differences between them may be explained by divergent but parallel development, as driven by variant speculative vs. normative aims, and in differently-evolving dialectical venues.

narratives as they emerge, as it already appears to do with the more general narratives of current scholarship.

Progressing to the era of venerated *mujtahids* like Abū Ḥanīfa, Ibn Abī Laylā, Abū Yūsuf, Mālik, al-Awzāʿī, Muḥammad b. al-Ḥasan, al-Shāfiʿī, et al., further analyses of arguments and dialectical sequences in the *Umm* compendium and other sources will not only widen our window on proto-system *jadal*, but contribute to the expansion and refinement of the Dialectical Forge model. As this model was largely derived from proto-system elements culled from the dialectic of the *Ikhtilāf al-ʿIrāqiyyayn/ʿIrāqiyyīn*, it is not untoward to suggest that the Dialectical Forge will prove useful in examining other treatises of the *Umm*, explaining more familiar elements, and expanding to incorporate the new phenomena which emerge through analysis.

As we move past the middle of our proto-system into the third or ninth century, we can only acknowledge an even greater corpus awaiting argument analysis. Still, I am assured by the relative consonance of the Dialectical Forge model with current developmental narratives that it will continue to account for or incorporate phenomena as they emerge. And, finally, as we reach the fourth or tenth and fifth or eleventh centuries, where so much recent scholarship has been done (and so much more awaits exploration and analysis), narratives of legal-historical development are, on the whole, in full consonance with the current form of the Dialectical Forge model. The culmination of dynamics which the model hopes to account for is plainly writ in the earliest extant, full-system, comprehensive treatises of juridical *jadal* and *uṣūl al-fiqh*. Perhaps one of the more important challenges with regard to the evolution of these systems still remains, however: the backwards tracing of dialectical styles and *uṣūl*ist premises to the first half of the fourth or tenth century, and a cautious reconstruction of the systems formulated by the first Aristotles of juridical dialectic and legal theory.

9.2 Towards a Motive Model for the Bequeathing of Dialectical Axioms

Of all the mechanisms of the Dialectical Forge model, perhaps the most important is that which I have labeled "the bequeathing of dialectical axioms" to legal theory; for if there is a base metal which has been hammered into the premises of *uṣūl al-fiqh* through countless dialectical exchanges, strengthening their *ḥujjiyya* and allowing them to hold their edge, then it is surely composed of dialectical axioms. The *mujtahid*-dialectician is the blacksmith at the anvil, and we have seen two activities wherein he is prompted to harden the steel of legal theoretical and methodological premises. The first is his private *ijtihād*, where anticipation of dialectical objection prompts a careful search for the most sound, most epistemically-superior base materials, a careful analysis and interpretation of the same, and a thorough tightening of rational inference to the *mas'ala* at hand. The second is in the fire of dialectical disputation itself, where the *ijtihād*ic solution is put to the test, and carefully forged premises—if at all tenable—may be reworked and refined to the necessary extent.

My focus here is the first forging which occurs through *ijtihād*ic anticipation; and, in a first attempt to illustrate how the anticipation of dialectical encounter might contribute dialectical axioms to the formation of argumentation epistemes, I have composed the following (preliminary) table.[4] The particular axioms under consideration are those of the species I have labelled "motive;" and what follows is meant to suggest how, in anticipation of dialectic, the transference of dialectical "motive" axioms might contribute to the formation of systematic subprojects within larger argumentation epistemes. For each "motive" I have suggested in the following table, recipient subprojects will be listed for: (1) prior argumentation epistemes;[5] (2) proto-system legal theory; and (3) full-system *uṣūl al-fiqh*.

Dialectical Motive: Avoiding Charges of Epistemic Insufficiency in Premises and Signs

- Prior Argument Epistemes (Aristotelian)
  - epistemic authority of demonstrative premises (theory of *archai*)
  - epistemic authority of dialectical premises (theory of *endoxa*)
- Proto-System Legal Theory
  - gradually evolving hierarchical epistemic authority: God, Prophet, [Companions/Imāms/Successors], *ijmāʿ*, *qiyās/al-maʿqūl*, etc.
    - theories of abrogation: *naskh* (preponderating epistemic values within Qur'ān and Sunna)
    - theories of transmission: early *ḥadīth* theory (preponderating epistemic values for modes of transmission)
    - proto-system practices of *tarjīḥ*
- Full-System Legal Theory
  - development and refinement of epistemically authoritative ranks: *Kitāb, Sunna, Ijmāʿ, Qawl al-Wāḥid min al-Ṣaḥāba, faḥwā al-khiṭāb, dalīl al-khiṭāb, maʿnā al-khiṭāb*, etc.
    - refined categories within epistemically authoritative ranks (e.g., *Kitāb: naṣṣ*, then *ẓāhir* and *ʿāmm*, then *mujmal*)

(continued)

[4] This is a first attempt; my objective is mainly to suggest a way in which we may begin to think about and categorize these critical processes. The "recipient" subprojects are hardly comprehensive, but further reflection will doubtless produce many more. Also, as mentioned in the previous chapter, a listing of dialectical motives influencing a jurist's *ijtihād* may be culled from Hallaq's discussion in *History*, p. 94f.

[5] As it is the only prior argumentation episteme I have explored to any extent in the current project, the Aristotelian will be our main representative. Many more sources for prior argumentation epistemes may be added to this preliminary outline, but will have to await further studies.

        - refined conceptions of *nāsikh* and *mansūkh*
        - refined conceptions of *tawātur*, *āḥād*, *mursal*, *musnad*, etc.
        - further development of principles in the absence of textual *adilla*-indicants (e.g., *istiṣḥāb*, *maṣlaḥa*)
    - refined conceptions of *ʿilm*, *istidlāl*, *ẓann*, *shakk*, etc.

Dialectical Motive: Avoiding Charges of Intensional and Semantic Misinterpretation

- Prior Argument Epistemes (Aristotelian)
    - theory of "categories" and typologies of predicables
    - theory of definitions, and other hermeneutical theories
- Proto-System Legal Theory
    - proto-system hermeneutic: *ʿāmm* and *khāṣṣ* distinctions, *jumla* and *mufassir* distinctions, *naṣṣ* and *ẓāhir* distinctions, etc.
- Full-System Legal Theory
    - refinements in categories of *amr* and *nahy*, *ʿāmm* and *khāṣṣ*, *mujmal* and *mubayyan*, *muṭlaq* and *muqayyad*, *naṣṣ* and *ẓāhir*, etc.

Dialectical Motive: Avoiding Charges of Invalid Inference and Internal/Doctrinal Inconsistency

- Prior Argument Epistemes (Aristotelian/Stoic)
    - development of formal syllogistic axioms
        - valid and invalid moods of categorical syllogistic
        - "indemonstrables" of hypothetical conditional syllogistic
    - strategies for dialectical method
    - guidelines for fallacy identification
- Proto-System Legal Theory
    - development of general, proto-system *qiyās*
        - *maʿnā* theory
    - *manzila*-subsumption
    - *taswiya*-subsumption
    - *farq*-extension
    - debate over *istiḥsān*
- Full-System Legal Theory
    - refined categories of *qiyās al-ṭard* and *qiyās al-ʿaks*
    - refined tripartite typologies for *qiyās al-ʿilla* and *qiyās al-dalāla*
    - refinements in definition: *waṣf* vs. *ʿilla*
    - refined relational conceptions: *ta'thīr*, *jarayān*, *ṭard*, *ʿaks*, etc.
    - refined categories of *tarjīḥ al-maʿānī*
    - debate over *takhṣīṣ al-ʿilla*

Though reductive to an extreme, such a model allows us to conceive—at least in broad strokes—the manner by which dialectical motives may produce and/or shape logical and legal-theoretical sub-projects and their axioms. This leads to perhaps the most general theory the current study will put forward. In short, I would claim that the major dynamic behind the systematization of argument epistemes is the practice of formal, argumentative dialogue; i.e., it is dialectical disputation which forges and hones theories of epistemology, of hermeneutics, of rational inference, and of dialectic itself—ultimately prompting the structuring of refined categories and elements into a *system*. It was the dialogical argumentation practiced in Aristotle's day—be it the "good" Socratic and Platonic dialectic of the Academy, or the "bad" disputation of the Sophists—which prompted him to his extraordinary systematization of syllogistic logic and its *technēs*. In a similar fashion, it was prior and current dialogical argumentation which prompted al-Shāfiʿī's "rudimentary" system of legal theory. And it was prior and current dialectical disputation which, eventually, prompted the comprehensive systematization of *uṣūl al-fiqh* by Islamic legal theory's first real Aristotles.

9.3 Open Doors

I hope to have succeeded in adequately introducing the categorical systems of the lens-texts and, with their aid, opening a small window onto the vista of proto-system juridical dialectic as we find it in the subject-text. The sophistication of juridical *jadal*, even at an early stage, should be plain; and the lens-texts speak for themselves in terms of detail, intricacy, high-level organization, and comprehensive scope. As for my investigatory procedure—analyzing the *Ikhtilāf al-ʿIrāqiyyayn/ʿIrāqiyyīn* through the lens of full-system *jadal* theory—I am hopeful it may prove a useful method, with the necessary corrections and refinements, and will be taken up for analyzing material in other subject-texts. With respect to the Dialectical Forge model: its components and mechanisms are still fledgling theories—untried in the main, and no doubt requiring much in the way of correction and refinement (assuming they survive the modern, and presumably dialectical, forge of Islamic legal studies). Even at this provisional stage, however, they may be of some utility for those who wish to explore early Islamic juridical argument.

Whatever the final assessment, this much is certain: for any window the current project may have opened onto the vista of proto-system juridical *jadal* and the formative dynamics of dialectical disputation, it has opened many more doors to unexplored territory. Innumerable questions have perforce been set aside, and an enormous amount of material remains to be analyzed, even in the subject-text, which still has more to teach us. This being so, what is unexplored of the *Umm* appears daunting, though I believe it should be eagerly and methodically analyzed, argument by argument, for the untold riches it surely contains, and the additional vistas of proto-system *jadal* and legal theory it will reveal. Having just scratched the surface of the *Ikhtilāf al-ʿIrāqiyyayn/ʿIrāqiyyīn* with our *jadal*-theory lens, it is hard to imagine what treasury of elements might be revealed when that lens—or additional lenses, compiled from additional sources—is turned on the remainder of the *Umm*.

Shifting to a larger perspective, Islamic law with its theoretical sciences constitutes a major intellectual-historical event. But more sophisticated studies of juridical *jadal* are required before we can truly discover and accurately describe its complex inner workings as an integrated, dialectical whole. What is revealed in the course of this endeavor, if pursued, will have repercussions in more general domains and disciplines outside of Islamic studies. Waiting here is an enormous and untapped wealth of contributions to Legal Argumentation and Normative Ethics.

My most strident hope, however, is that the critical importance of dialectic for Islamic intellectual history in general will be realized by a greater and ever increasing cadre of scholars in the field. The study of Islamic dialectical disputation as a whole must be promoted; it is more than a key for unlocking the argumentation of Islam's many outstanding scholar-dialecticians, and it is more than a means to comprehending the systems they built. It is the study of a distinguished contribution to the intellectual history of the world.

Appendices

Appendix I: al-Baṣrī's Modes of *Qiyās*-Oriented Dialectic[1]

Section (*faṣl*): On the Definition (*ḥadd*) of Qiyās[2]

Section: On Argument (*kalām*) Regarding the *Ḥukm*[3]

- 1) The *ḥukm*'s relation to the *aṣl*
  - Is the *ḥukm* present or not?[4]
  - If present, is it present for the whole of the *aṣl*, or not?[5]
  - Is the *ḥukm* established in the *aṣl* via *qiyās* on the basis of another *aṣl*, or not?[6]

---

[1] al-Baṣrī, *K. al-Qiyās al-Sharʿī*, Ḥamīd Allāh ed., pp. 1032–50; Hallaq, "Treatise," pp. 207–28. Most of al-Baṣrī's explanations, variant views, answers for the respondent (*mujīb*), etc., are omitted from this outline. The following notes mix paraphrase and translation.

[2] Ḥamīd Allāh ed., pp. 1032–3; Hallaq, "Treatise," pp. 207–9. Here al-Baṣrī provides definitions for "correlational inference of co-presence" (*qiyās al-ṭard*) and "correlational inference of the opposite"(*qiyās al-ʿaks*), with further discourse on components, variant conceptions, and examples. Importantly, he tells us "argument regarding correlational inference" (*al-kalām fi'l-qiyās*) is directed at either: (A) the *ḥukm*—either (1) the *ḥukm* itself, (2) its relation to (*taʿalluq bi-*) the *aṣl*, (3) its relation to the *farʿ*, or (4) its relation to both—or (B) the *ʿilla*—either (1) its presence/absence (in *aṣl* and *farʿ*), or (2) its validity/invalidity.

[3] Ḥamīd Allāh ed., pp. 1033–5; Hallaq, "Treatise," pp. 209–12. What follows is a methodical sequence for examination of one's own *qiyās*, or one's opponent's *qiyās*.

[4] The reasoning behind the question: there may be consensus that the *aṣl* cannot be used for *qiyās*. One might disagree re: the presence of the *ḥukm*, and, as questioner (*sā'il*), obstruct (*tamnaʿu*) the one doing *qiyās* (*qā'is*) from his *qiyās*, or as respondent (*mas'ūl*), transfer dialectic to the *aṣl*.

[5] One might critique the one doing *qiyās* (*qā'is*) if he attempts *qiyās* on the basis of the whole, while the *ḥukm* is present only in the part.

[6] Perhaps the *qā'is* referred the *farʿ* to the *aṣl* by a certain *ʿilla*; but the *ḥukm* of that other *aṣl* is occasioned by another *ʿilla*.

W.E. Young, *The Dialectical Forge*, Logic, Argumentation & Reasoning 9,
DOI 10.1007/978-3-319-25522-4

- 2) The *ḥukm*'s relation to the *far*ʿ, alone
    - Is the presence of the *ḥukm* possible in the *far*ʿ, or not?[7]
    - Is it possible to establish the *ḥukm* in the *far*ʿ via *qiyās*, or not?[8]
    - If established, is the *ḥukm* present in the whole *far*ʿ, or only part of it?[9]
- 3) The *ḥukm*'s relation to both *aṣl* and *far*ʿ, together
    - Is it possible that the *ḥukm* of that *far*ʿ be derived from that *aṣl*, or not?[10]
        - This is: "disparity of the object of the source-case and the branch-case" (*ikhtilāf mawḍūʿ al-aṣl wa'l-far*ʿ)[11]
- 4) The *ḥukm* in isolation from *aṣl* and *far*ʿ
    - Is it possible for you yourself [as questioner] to profess the *ḥukm* which the *qā'is* linked to the ʿ*illa*?[12]
        - This is: "professing the compelling agency of the occasioning factor" (*al-qawl bi-mūjib al-ʿilla*)[13]

Section: On Argument (*kalām*) Regarding the *ʿIlla*[14]

- 1) The ʿ*illa*'s presence in the *aṣl*:
    - Is it present in the whole of the *aṣl*, or part of it?[15]

---

[7] The reasoning behind the question: there may be univocal, divine text (*naṣṣ*) or consensus (*ijmā*ʿ) which prevents its presence in the *far*ʿ.

[8] The reasoning behind the question: the *ḥukm* may be of the types for which *qiyās* is not allowed, such as for ritual atonement (*kaffāra*), divinely-sanctioned punishment (*ḥadd*), etc. If Q subscribes to one of these no-*qiyās* views, he can halt the dispute.

[9] One might critique the *qā'is* if he attempts *qiyās* to the whole of the *far*ʿ, while the *ḥukm* may be present only in the part.

[10] The reasoning behind the question: perhaps the object of the *aṣl* is intensifying (*taghlīẓ*), while the object of the *far*ʿ is lightening (*takhfīf*), and its *ḥukm* should be for lightening. One may object that this disparity (*ikhtilāf*) is a sign (*amāra*) that the *ḥukm* of one is distinct from the other.

[11] Cf. the *qiyās*-oriented objections in the *i*ʿ*tirāḍ* tables for al-Shīrāzī and al-Bājī: this corresponds to "invalidity of occasioned status" (*fasād al-waḍ*ʿ) (Shīr.VII.11; Bāj.IX.B.10).

[12] The reasoning behind the question: maybe it is an over-general/ambiguous (*mujmal*) *ḥukm* which R has made conditional upon his ʿ*illa*, and it is possible that Q can also profess it. If Q can also claim it, then the *qā'is* has failed to provide indicant for the locus of disagreement (*mawḍi*ʿ *al-khilāf*); Q can insist on the *ḥukm*, according to a potentially-efficient intension-property (*ma*ʿ*nā*), if the *qā'is* has not yet distinguished one.

[13] Cf. Shīr.VII.9; Bāj.IX.B.8.

[14] Ḥamīd Allāh ed., p. 1035; Hallaq, "Treatise," pp. 212–13. What follows is a methodical sequence for examination of the opponent's ʿ*illa*.

[15] The reasoning behind the question: (1) the one justifying the ʿ*illa* (*mu*ʿ*allil*) might refer the *far*ʿ to the whole of the *aṣl*, when the ʿ*illa* is only in part of the *aṣl*—this nullifies his *qiyās*; and (2) if he refers the *far*ʿ to the object in which you yourself (as Q) find the ʿ*illa* of the *aṣl*, you must investigate: Is it permissible that part of the *aṣl* be endowed with an ʿ*illa* without [another] part? If so, you (as Q) permit what he did. If you don't accept that part of the *aṣl* may have an ʿ*illa*, or that the ʿ*illa* can be allowed unless it is for the whole *aṣl*, then R's *qiyās* is nullified.

- 2) The *ʿilla*'s presence in the *farʿ*:
  - Is the *ʿilla* present in the *farʿ*, according to you?
  - If so, is it present in the whole of the *farʿ*, or part of it?[16]

Section: On What Provides Indicant for the Validity (*ṣiḥḥa*) of the *ʿIlla*[17]

- Indicant for the validity of the *ʿilla* is provided by either:
  - 1) Univocal, Divinely-Sanctioned Text (*Naṣṣ*)[18]
  - 2) Rational Inference (*Istinbāṭ*)[19]
  - 3) [a certain group draws indication for validity of the *ʿilla* by other modes][20]

Section: On What Distinguishes the *ʿIlla* as Pertains to Modes which Invalidate It (*al-wujūh al-mufsida lahā*)[21]

- [Either Muslim Communal Doctrine (*Qawl al-Umma*) or Rational Inference (*Istinbāṭ*); the latter has several modes]:
- Mode 1: "*ʿIlla*-Justification by way of the Name" (*al-Taʿlīl bi'l-Ism*)[22]

---

[16] The *qā'is* might ascribe a property (*ṣifa*) to the *farʿ* which is not permitted according to his opponent (*khaṣm*); or there might be consensus that the *ḥukm* for that *farʿ* cannot be confirmed except by a single *ʿilla*, which nullifies *ʿilla*-justification (*taʿlīl*) for a single *ʿilla* which is not in the whole of the *farʿ*.

[17] Ḥamīd Allāh ed., pp. 1036–8; Hallaq, "Treatise," pp. 213–16.

[18] Al-Baṣrī explains that *naṣṣ* provides indicant for the validity of the *ʿilla* by either: (1) unambiguous expression (*ṣarīḥ*), or (2) a type of self-evident appeal (*tanbīh*).

[19] Al-Baṣrī explains that *istinbāṭ* provides indicant for the validity of the *ʿilla* by different modes: (1) the *qiyās* scholars (*qā'isūn*) agree on a limited number of properties in the *aṣl*, there is no allowance for more, and all but one *ʿilla* is invalidated, so we know it is the *ʿilla* (it must be, or the agreed-upon premise of a limited number of properties is wrong); (2) there is co-presence and co-absence of the *ʿilla* and *ḥukm* in the *aṣl*, with no allowance for another efficient property in the *ʿilla* of the *aṣl* (this establishes probability for the efficiency of the *ʿilla*); and (3) the *ʿilla* must have efficiency (*ta'thīr*) in both genus (*jins*) and species (*qabīl*)—so it is probable that this *ʿilla* is superior (*awlā*) to others.

[20] Al-Baṣrī argues against each one of these other modes: (1) the *ʿilla* is valid if it is safeguarded from invalidating factors; (2) if the opponent fails to invalidate the *ʿilla*, this provides indicant for its validity; and (3) the concomitance (*jarayān*) of the occasioning factor (*ʿilla*) in the occasioned thing (*maʿlūl*) provides indicant for its validity.

[21] Ḥamīd Allāh ed., pp. 1039–45; Hallaq, "Treatise," pp. 216–23. Al-Baṣrī begins by observing: The following provide indicant for the invalidity of the *ʿilla*: (1) Muslim Communal Doctrine (*Qawl al-Umma*), and (2) Rational Inference (*Istinbāṭ*); the latter consists of several modes. He proceeds to list them, and most find their match in the *qiyās*-oriented objections of al-Shīrāzī and al-Bājī.

[22] No equivalent for this category exists among the *qiyās*-oriented objections of al-Shīrāzī and al-Bājī.

  - Type 1: [the name has no efficiency][23]
  - Type 2: the *ʿilla* is established by genus[24]
- Mode 2: "Divergence of Occasioned Status" (*Ikhtilāf al-Waḍʿ*)
  - [no definition][25]
- Mode 3: "Lack of Efficiency" (*ʿAdam al-Taʾthīr*)[26]
  - [Definition]: the one justifying the *ʿilla* (*muʿallil*) mentions, among the collective properties of the *ʿilla*, such a property that, if it is absent in the *aṣl*, the *ḥukm* yet remains[27]
- Mode 4: "Reversal of the Correlational Inference" (*Qalb al-Qiyās*)[28]
  - [Definition]: the contradictory (*naqīḍ*) of the *ḥukm* stated in the *qiyās* [of R] is made conditional upon the *ʿilla* [by Q], and the *farʿ* is referred, by means of that *ʿilla*, to the [same] *aṣl* to which the *farʿ* of [R's] *qiyās* is referred.[29]
  - Type 1: one of the two *ḥukm*s made conditional on the *ʿilla* is general (*mujmal*) and the other particular (*mufaṣṣal*)[30]

---

[23] In al-Baṣrī's example *mas'ala*, the one justifying the *ʿilla* (*muʿallil*) fixes the *ʿilla* for proscription of grape-wine (*taḥrīm al-khamr*) on the fact that the Arabs called it *khamr*. This is invalid (*fāsid*), because the Arab designation has no efficiency (*ta'thīr*).

[24] In al-Baṣrī's example *mas'ala*, the *ʿilla* that a beverage is of the genus of grape-wine (*khamr*) occasions the *ḥukm* of proscription (*taḥrīm*). This is *not* invalid; "being of the genus" may have efficiency. He proceeds to explain that the following are also allowed: (1) *ʿilla*-justification (*taʿlīl*) by way of an attribute (*ṣifa*) among attributes, or (2) *taʿlīl* by way of a ruling (*ḥukm*) among rulings (i.e., one divinely-sanctioned *ḥukm* may be used to establish another). NB: the first corresponds to the *qiyās al-shabah* of al-Shīrāzī, and the second corresponds to his Type I and II *qiyās al-dalāla*.

[25] As mentioned earlier, this is the "invalidity of occasioned status" (*fasād al-waḍʿ*) of al-Shīrāzī and al-Bājī (Shīr.VII.11; Bāj.IX.B.10). Al-Baṣrī's example is: *ʿilla*-justification (*taʿlīl*) from a clearly intensification (*taghlīẓ*)-oriented *ḥukm* to a clearly lightening (*takhfīf*)-oriented *ḥukm*; this divergence may constitute a sign (*amāra*) that one can't do *qiyās*. It may, however, be done if a *dalīl* provides indicant for it, or if a combination of associated rulings (*aḥkām*) comprises an *ʿilla* indicating its validity. If, however, the opponent says no to this, the dispute shifts focus to indication (*dalāla*) of the *ʿilla*'s validity.

[26] This species of objection finds its match with al-Shīrāzī and al-Bājī (Shīr.VII.6; Bāj.IX.B.14).

[27] Al-Baṣrī explains: If we allow this to be, then we must allow any of an infinite number of [non co-present] properties to be attached to the *ʿilla*—so we know that the *ʿilla* can't be that collective, as we must reject that one property; and the destruction (*intiqāḍ*) of that property provides indicant for the invalidity of the *ʿilla*. He proceeds to warn against possible trickery on the part of an opponent: It is not allowed to attach a property (*waṣf*) to an *ʿilla* [merely] to save it from inconsistency (*naqḍ*)—we must know first that the *ḥukm* of the *aṣl* is conditional upon it (*yuʿalliqu bihā*). If the property is not efficient in the *ḥukm*, it cannot be allowed to be part of the *ʿilla*. If, after that property is removed, the remaining properties are proven inconsistent (*muntaqaḍ*), we know the invalidity of the *ʿilla*.

[28] Cf. Shīr.VII.14; Bāj.IX.B.9.

[29] In other words, Q counters with the same *qiyās* as R, after causing his *ʿilla* to occasion the contradictory (*naqīḍ*) of R's *ḥukm*.

[30] Al-Baṣrī explains: This does not invalidate the *ʿilla*, because it may induce a particular *ḥukm* while still having a general *ḥukm* attached to it; general does not contradict particular, and only incompatible *ḥukm*s invalidate the same *ʿilla*. Contradictory, particular *ḥukm*s, on the other hand, invalidate—as one must be true, the other false.

  - Type 2: "Reversal of Equalization" (*Qalb al-Taswiya*)—the one doing reversal (*qālib*) says: "It must be that such-and-such is equal to such-and-such," when their equality re: the *ḥukm* is confirmed. While one of them is prohibited (*maḥẓūr*), the other must be like it [i.e., also prohibited].[31]
- Mode 5: "Inconsistency" (*al-Naqḍ*)[32]
  - [Definition]: the presence of the *ʿilla* in a locus (*mawḍiʿ*) from which its *ḥukm* is absent[33]
- Mode 6: "Breaking Apart" (*al-Kasr*)[34]
  - [Definition]: inconsistency (*naqḍ*) of the *ʿilla* on account of its *maʿnā*-quality, not its formulation (*lafẓ*)[35]
- Mode 7: "Counter-Indication by way of an Occasioning Factor" (*al-Muʿāraḍa bi-ʿIlla*)[36]
  - Type 1: the *muʿāraḍa* falls upon the *ʿilla* of the *aṣl*, in that the one objecting (*muʿtariḍ*) establishes another *ʿilla* for the *aṣl*[37]
  - Type 2: the *qiyās* is opposed by another *qiyās*[38]

---

[31] Cf. Shīr.VII.14.2; Bāj.IX.B.9.3.

[32] Cf. Shīr.VII.7; Bāj.IX.B.11.

[33] Al-Baṣrī explains: When the one justifying the *ʿilla* (*muʿallil*) establishes his *ʿilla* for the general (*jumla*), then it is "contradicted" by particularization (*tafṣīl*); it is not *naqḍ*, because the *ḥukm* of the *ʿilla* itself is general, and this is not absent from the locus in which the *ʿilla* is found. Rather, only the particularized *ḥukm* is absent, and the particularized *ḥukm* is not that which is made conditional upon [the *ʿilla*]. He then concludes: If the *muʿallil* establishes his *ʿilla* for the particularized, then he is contradicted by the general; this is valid *naqḍ*.

[34] Cf. Shīr.VII.8; Bāj.IX.B.12.

[35] As al-Baṣrī explains: Q rejects one of the properties of the *ʿilla* because he does not consider it to be efficient, and allows that the *ḥukm* be made conditional upon another property, then replaces the rejected property with a more general one, then eliminates all but that one property. If the *muʿallil* objects to this breaking apart (*kasr*), he must prove the discarded property has efficiency in the *ḥukm*, so that it must be included. NB: Q has "broken apart" the properties of R's proposed *ʿilla* [hence: *kasr*], discarded one, replaced it, then eliminated all others. Note that this differs somewhat from the definitions and explanations of al-Shīrāzī and al-Bājī. Al-Baṣrī also notes that *kasr* has been called *ʿaks*, but that this *ʿaks* is different from the "co-absence of the occasioning factor" (*ʿaks al-ʿilla*) which is opposite to (*muqābil*) "co-presence" (*al-ṭard*). He then proceeds to a detailed discussion of this.

[36] Cf. Shīr.VII.15.2; Bāj.IX.B.15.2.

[37] Al-Baṣrī explains: If the one doing *qiyās* (*qāʾis*) is not one of those who profess "two *ʿillas*", he cannot profess them both [i.e., both his and his opponent's]. If, however, profession of "two *ʿillas*" is of his doctrinal *madhhab*, he still cannot profess them both in this [single] locus (*mawḍiʿ*) except after he validates his *ʿilla*. [This is] because the one doing *muʿāraḍa* (*muʿāriḍ*) did not concede to him—rather, he is contending with him as regards [the *ʿilla* of the *qāʾis*], and says to him: The *ʿilla* in the *aṣl* is not what you have stated, rather, it is what I myself have stated.

[38] Al-Baṣrī claims: If it is [like] this, then discourse on it has preceded. I have been unable to locate, however, just where such a discussion has taken place in the *K. al-Qiyās al-Sharʿī*. This category appears to correspond to the *muʿāraḍa* by way of a "self-initiated occasioning factor" (*ʿilla mubtadaʾa*) of al-Shīrāzī and al-Bājī (Shīr.VII.15.2.1; Bāj.IX.B.15.2.1), which entails Q's bringing an entirely new *ʿilla*, *aṣl*, and *ḥukm*—i.e., a whole new *qiyās*—to supplant that of R.

Section: On *Tarjīḥ* of the *'Illa* of the *Aṣl* Over Another *'Illa*, and *Tarjīḥ* of a *Qiyās* Over a *Qiyās*[39]

- [part 1] *tarjīḥ* of one *ʿilla* over the other, when *muʿāraḍa* occurs to the *ʿilla* of the *aṣl*, and the two *ʿilla*s are equal
  - Mode 1: [the *tarjīḥ*] refers back to the strength of the method (*ṭarīq*) of validating the *ʿilla*
    - [1.1] one *ʿilla* is subject to consensus, and the other is not
    - [1.2] one is unambiguously designated in divinely-sanctioned text (*manṣūṣ ʿalayhā*), and the other is known via patent understanding of divinely-sanctioned text (*mafhūm al-naṣṣ*)
    - [1.3] the method (*ṭarīq*) for one is patent understanding of divinely-sanctioned text (*mafhūm al-naṣṣ*), and for the other it is rational inference (*istinbāṭ*)
- Mode 2: [the *tarjīḥ* refers back] to the transitiveness (*taʿaddī*) of the *ʿilla*
  - [2.1] one *ʿilla* is transitive (*mutaʿaddiya*), but not the other
  - [2.2] one *ʿilla* has more branch-cases (*furūʿ*) than the other[40]

[Section: On the *Tarjīḥ* of *Qiyās* Over *Qiyās*][41]

- [part 2] when they are equal, then one of them is brought to preponderate over the other...[42]
  - [Mode 1]: ... by what refers back to its *aṣl*
    - [1.1] the method (*ṭarīq*) of confirming the *ḥukm* in one of the two is stronger than the method of confirming it in the other
    - [1.2] the method of *ʿilla*-justification (*taʿlīl*) for one of the two *aṣl*s is stronger than the method of *ʿilla*-justification for the other
    - [1.3] when the *ḥukm* of the *aṣl*, from which the *ḥukm* of the *farʿ* is derived, is stronger in one of the two
      - then one of the two *qiyās*es must be stronger
      - likewise when the method of validating the *ʿilla* for one of them is stronger
  - [Mode 2]: ... by what refers back to its *ḥukm*

---

[39] Ḥamīd Allāh ed., p. 1046; Hallaq, "Treatise," p. 223. *Tarjīḥ* is a procedure by which one *dalīl*-indicant or element is weighed against another and brought to preponderate in terms of epistemic conclusiveness. The second type of *tarjīḥ* (*qiyās* over *qiyās*), though mentioned here, is discussed in the following section (*faṣl*).

[40] Al-Baṣrī concludes: The majority doctrine is that the *ʿilla* is not invalidated if it is not transitive (*mutaʿaddiya*).

[41] Ḥamīd Allāh ed., p. 1046; Hallaq, "Treatise," pp. 223–4.

[42] Before this, al-Baṣrī notes: When *qiyās* is opposed by *qiyās*, its *ʿilla* reverts to the discourse regarding its validity or invalidity, as has preceded.

  - [2.1] one of the two *ḥukm*s is more comprehensive/precautionary (*aḥwaṭ*)[43]
  - [2.2] we have recommended the elimination (*isqāṭ*) of one of the two *ḥukm*s due to doubt (*shubha*)[44]
- [Mode 3]: by what refers back to its *ʿilla*[45]

[Additional *Tarjīḥ*-Related Discussion][46]

- the *ʿilla* might be brought to preponderate because it is supported by a "most apparent" (*ẓāhir*) [textual designation]—such necessitates that it be superior (*awlā*) to one which is not [so designated]
- *Tarjīḥ* and invalidation (*ifsād*) of the *ʿilla* do not go outside of the categories we have discussed; because undermining the *ʿilla* itself must be either via a mode separated from [the *ʿilla*] or by a mode which refers back to it[47]

---

[43] Al-Baṣrī's examples: Like when one of them is obligation (*wujūb*), and the other recommendation (*nadb*); or one is proscription (*ḥaẓr*) and the other neutral permissibility (*mubāḥ*).

[44] Al-Baṣrī's example: Like the divinely-sanctioned punishments (*ḥudūd*)—some of the scholars (*baʿḍ al-nās*) hold to the opinion of *tarjīḥ* by means of that, while some don't.

[45] Al-Baṣrī explains: We have already discussed this; except: *tarjīḥ* by transitiveness (*al-taʿaddī*) is not possible here—it is a *qiyās*, so transitiveness must already have been proven.

[46] Ḥamīd Allāh ed., p. 1047; Hallaq, "Treatise," p. 224.

[47] Intriguingly, al-Baṣrī here engages in what we might call a "meta-logical" concern; he systematically outlines the relationship between categories of objection earlier discussed (*naqḍ*, *kasr*, etc.) and the modes of preponderance (*tarjīḥāt*). He first defines two categories of undermining the *ʿilla*: [I] by a mode separated from the *ʿilla*; and [II] by a mode which connects to the *ʿilla*. To the first category [I] belongs *muʿāraḍa* of the *ʿilla* by way of another *ʿilla*. To the second category [II] belongs a list of dialectical moves, separated into two further sub-categories: Type 1 [II.1], in which the mode entails a conditional dependence (*taʿalluq*) on something else besides the *ʿilla*; and Type 2 [II.2], in which the mode does not entail this. To this second Type [II.2] belongs al-Baṣrī's *taʿlīl bi'l-ism*. As for the first Type [II.1], it is further subdivided into two more divisions: [II.1.1] in which the "something else" [of II.1] is the locus (*makān*) of the *ʿilla*'s existence (*wujūd*)—i.e., it has no *farʿ* to which it is extended; and [II.1.2] in which the "something else" is the *ʿilla*'s *ḥukm*. Finally, this latter division [II.1.2] is further divided into: [II.1.2.1] in which the mode undermining the *ʿilla* upon which the *ḥukm* is conditionally dependent refers to the generality (*jumla*) of the *ʿilla*; and [II.1.2.2] in which such a mode refers to a one of [the *ʿilla*'s] parts (*ajzāʾ*). Of the former subcategory [II.1.2.1], we are told it includes what is conditionally dependent upon [the *ʿilla*'s] indication (*dalāla*) of the *ḥukm*—herein are located all of: *ikhtilāf al-waḍʿ* (the *ʿilla* is not fit to provide indicant for the *ḥukm*); *al-qawl bi-mūjib al-ʿilla* (allowed by the *ḥukm* not being explicit in the *dalāla*-indication); *al-qalb* (the *ʿilla* provides indicant for the *ḥukm* and for its *naqīḍ*-contradictory); *al-naqḍ* (the *ḥukm*'s *ʿilla* provides indication in one locus, but not in another, yet is still found in it); and *al-kasr* (which also comprises concerns of absence [*ʿadam*], efficiency [*ta'thīr*], and inconsistency [*naqḍ*]). As for the latter subcategory [II.1.2.2], here we find that case wherein one of the *ʿilla*'s properties (*awṣāf*) does not have efficiency in the *ḥukm*; this we understand to correspond to al-Baṣrī's definition of *ʿadam al-ta'thīr*.

A Supplement (*ḍamīma*) on *Qalb*[48]

- Definition of *qalb al-qiyās*: the one doing *qalb* (*qālib*) to the *qiyās* makes the contradictory (*naqīḍ*) of the *ḥukm* stated in the *qiyās* dependent upon the *ʿilla*, and he refers the *farʿ* back to that same, exact *aṣl*. In terms of conditional dependence upon the *ʿilla*, one of the two *ḥukms* is not superior (*awlā*) to the other; nor is it valid that they both, together, be dependent upon it, due to their mutual negation (*tanāfīhimā*).
- [Three objections to *qalb*; followed by al-Baṣrī's refutation of all three]
- [Conclusion]: So it is clarified *qalb* exists in three modes (*wujūh*):
  - Mode 1: one of the two *ḥukms* is general/ambiguous (*mujmal*), with no mention of equalization (*taswiya*), and the other particular (*mufaṣṣal*)
  - Mode 2: the two *ḥukms* are both particular (*mufaṣṣal*), without being mutually contradictory, in that the *ḥukm* in the *farʿ* has two orientations (*jihatayn*), and both the one doing *qalb* (*qālib*) and the one doing *qiyās* (*qāʾis*) aim at one of the two orientations, while they don't mutually contradict in the *aṣl*, but they mutually contradict in the *farʿ*, due to consensus (*ijmāʿ*)
  - Mode 3: one of the two *ḥukms* is particular and the other general/ambiguous, and its generality/ambiguity comes from the orientation of equalization (*taswiya*)

[48] Ḥamīd Allāh ed., pp. 1048–50; Hallaq, "Treatise," pp. 224–8.

Appendix II: al-Shīrāzī's Modes of *I'tirāḍ*[49]

*[Disputing the Authoritative Source-Case (*Aṣl*)]*

I. Modes of Argument Against Drawing Indication from the Qur'ān (*Wujūh al-Kalām 'alā al-Istidlāl bi'l-Kitāb*)[50]

- *I'tirāḍ* 1: "you, yourself, do not advocate it" (*annaka lā taqūlu bihi*)
  - Mode 1: [R] draws indication from the Qur'ān by a method (*ṭarīq*) of legal theory (*uṣūl*) which he does not advocate
  - Mode 2: [R] does not profess [his *ḥukm*] in the locus which he is treating
- *I'tirāḍ* 2: [Q] professes [the verse's] compelling agency (*mūjibihā*)
  - Type 1: [R] draws argumentative support from (*yaḥtajju min*) the verse by one of two objects, and [Q] asserts [the verse's] compelling agency by linking it to the other object (*waḍ'*)
  - Type 2: [Q] asserts [the verse's] compelling agency in the locus from which [R] draws argumentative support
- *I'tirāḍ* 3: the ambiguity (*ijmāl*) of the verse is claimed, by measure of either God's decrees (*Shar'*) or the customary usage (*al-lugha*)
  - [1] by measure of God's decrees
  - [2] by measure of the customary usage
- *I'tirāḍ* 4: Sharing the Indicant (*al-mushāraka fi'l-dalīl*)[51]
- *I'tirāḍ* 5: Variant Reading [of the Qur'ān] (*ikhtilāf al-qirā'a*)
- *I'tirāḍ* 6: Abrogation (*naskh*)
  - Mode 1: that the abrogation be clarified unambiguously (*ṣarīḥan*)
  - Mode 2: that [Q] claim [the verse's] abrogation by a later verse
  - Mode 3: that [Q] claim [the verse's] abrogation because it references God's law for past communities (*shar' man qablanā*)
- *I'tirāḍ* 7: Preponderating Exegesis (*Ta'wīl*)
  - Type 1: preponderating exegesis of the most apparent meaning (*ta'wīl al-ẓāhir*)[52]
  - Type 2: particularization of the general (*takhṣīṣ al-'umūm*)

---

[49] This outline is derived from al-Shīrāzī's *Ma'ūna fi'l-Jadal*; his example *masā'il* and suggested responses have been omitted, though some are provided in the notes by way of clarification.

[50] *Ma'ūna*, al-'Umayrīnī ed., pp. 48–78.

[51] Al-'Umayrīnī provides al-Shīrāzī's explanation from his *Mulakhkhaṣ*: "He treats that by which the one doing *istidlāl* (*mustadill*) draws indication as a *dalīl*-indicant in the *mas'ala*.... Type 1: each of them draws indication by the *dalīl*-indicant with respect to its most apparent meaning (*min jihat al-ẓāhir*), and there is no distinctive priority (*mīza*) for one over the other as regards what he claims of the most apparent meaning. Type 2: each of them draws indication by the *dalīl*-indicant with respect to generality (*min jihat al-'umūm*), there being no distinctive priority for one over the other" (p. 44, n. 1).

[52] al-'Umayrīnī provides more from al-Shīrāzī's *Mulakhkhaṣ*, wherein the *ta'wīl al-ẓāhir* is further subdivided into: Type 1 (*ta'wīl*-exegesis of the *lafẓ*-formulation according to the frequently used *ma'nā*-intension); and Type 2 (according to the infrequently used *ma'nā*-intension).

- *Iʿtirāḍ* 8: Counter-Indication (*Muʿāraḍa*)
  - Type 1: counter-indication by way of divinely-sanctioned decree (*muʿāraḍa bi'l-nuṭq*)
  - Type 2: counter-indication by way of the occasioning factor (*muʿāraḍa bi'l-ʿilla*)

II. Argument Against Drawing Indication from the Sunna (*al-Kalām ʿalā al-Istidlāl bi'l-Sunna*)[53]

- (A) *Iʿtirāḍ* against the Sunna as Outright Rejection (*Radd*) [on the basis of legal-theoretical principles]
  - Mode 1: the rejection of the Shīʿa (*Rāfiḍa*) [of solitary reports (*akhbār āḥād*)]
  - Mode 2: the rejection of the Ḥanafīs [of solitary reports, when they go against] common knowledge (*mā yaʿummu bihi al-balwā*)
  - Mode 3: the rejection of the Mālikīs [of reports] which contradict (*khālafa*) the *qiyās*
  - Mode 4: the rejection of the Ḥanafīs [of reports] which contradict *qiyās* of the *uṣūl*
  - Mode 5: the rejection of the Ḥanafīs [of reports] necessitating addition to the unambiguous text (*naṣṣ*) of the Qur'ān, and that such constitutes abrogation[54]
- (B) *Iʿtirāḍ* against the Sunna with reference to the Chain of Transmission (*Isnād*)
  - Mode 1: Demand for [the *isnād*'s] Confirmation (*al-Muṭālaba bi-ithbātihi*); for *akhbār*-reports which are not consistent with the exemplary traditions (*sunan*), and are not audited except by dissenters (*mukhālifīn*)
  - Mode 2: Degrading the Chain of Transmission (*al-Qadḥ fi'l-Isnād*)
    - Mode 2.1: [Q] states a reason (*sabab*) regarding the narrator (*rāwī*) which obliges rejection (*radd*); saying: "[the narrator] is a liar, or innovator (*mubtadiʿ*), or careless"
    - Mode 2.2: [Q] states that [the narrator] is unknown (*majhūl*)
    - Mode 2.3: [Q] states that [the *isnād*] is interrupted (*mursal*)[55]
  - (3) Other Modes of the Ḥanafīs:
    - Mode (3.1): the noble predecessors (*salaf*) rejected it[56]

---

[53] al-ʿUmayrīnī ed., pp. 40–8.

[54] By way of example, al-Shīrāzī mentions the *khabar*-report drawn upon by Shāfiʿīs in justification of their ruling banishment (*taghrīb*) for the fornicator (*zānī*). This *mas'ala* of banishment is debated in full dialectic in the *Umm* compendium, but without reference to *naskh* of the Qur'ān. The Prophet's practice of banishing is mentioned in §1417 of our subject-text, and a complete argument is there referenced in another of al-Shāfiʿī's writings (see the parallel translations of both in my dissertation, Part II, p. 345, §1417 and pp. 374–9 [appendix II.§1417]).

[55] Meaning, "its chain of transmission does not reach entirely back to the Prophet: whether one or more narrators are missing, or that a narrator is missing from beginning, middle, or end; this is considered one of the types of "weak" (*ḍaʿīf*) *ḥadīth*-reports by the majority of scholars" (Sānū, *Muʿjam*, s.v. "المرسل").

[56] Al-Shīrāzī's example: "like the report on the oath of expurgation (*ḥadīth al-qasāma*): ʿAmr b. Shuʿayb said: By God, the *ḥadīth* is not as Sahl transmitted."

    - Mode (3.2): the narrator [himself] denies the *ḥadīth*[57]
    - Mode (3.3): its narrator did not act upon it[58]
    - Mode (3.4): "This is an augmentation not conveyed by the more reliable transmission"[59]
- (C) *Iʿtirāḍ* against the Sunna with reference to the transmitted text (*matn*) [as a self-initiated saying of the Prophet (*qawl mubtada'*)]:[60]
  - *Iʿtirāḍ* 1: [R] draws indication by way of something he does not profess
    - Mode 1: [R] draws indication by a *ḥadīth* the sort of which he himself does not accept[61]
    - Mode 2: [the Ḥanafī] draws indication from [the *khabar*-report] by a method (*ṭarīq*) he does not profess[62]
    - Mode 3: [R] doesn't profess it in the locus in which it is found/ mentioned
  - *Iʿtirāḍ* 2: [Q] professes [the transmitted text's] compelling agency (*yaqūlu bi-mūjibihi*)
    - Mode 1: [R] draws argumentative support (*yaḥtajju*) by one of two objects; and [Q] asserts [the transmitted text's] compelling agency (*mūjib*) by linking it with the other object (*waḍʿ*)
    - Mode 2: [Q] professes [the transmitted text's] compelling agency (*mūjib*) in the locus from which [R] draws argumentative support
  - *Iʿtirāḍ* 3: [Q] claims ambiguity (*ijmāl*), by measure of either God's decrees (*Sharʿ*) or the customary usage (*al-lugha*)
    - (1) by measure of God's Law
    - (2) by measure of customary usage[63]

---

[57] Al-Shīrāzī's example: "like they say regarding the Prophet's saying [...]—transmitted by al-Zuhrī, who had said: I don't know it."

[58] Al-Shīrāzī's example: "like the *ḥadīth* about ritual washing (*ghasl*)—seven times, for the licking of a dog—that its narrator is Abū Hurayra, but he had given a *fatwā* that it is three times."

[59] Al-Shīrāzī's example: "like the Prophet's saying: "[...], when it attains five *awsaq* [in weight]"—[the Ḥanafīs] say: this *ḥadīth* was transmitted by a group, and they mentioned nothing but a [single] *wasq*, which indicates that it is not an authoritative *aṣl* for them."

[60] al-Shīrāzī explains: "As for transmitted text (*matn*), there are three [types]: [the Prophet's] saying (*qawl*), deed (*fiʿl*), and acknowledgment (*iqrār*). As for [the Prophet's] saying (*qawl*), it is of two types: self-initiated (*mubtada'*) and prompted (*khārij ʿalā al-sabab*). And the self-initiated is like the Qur'ān—one directs to it [in terms of debate] what one directs to the Qur'ān. And we have explained it [in the section re: the Qur'ān, above], but I will repeat the doctrine as regards the Sunna, because it is more clear in terms of example, and maybe there will occur something additional regarding it which was not mentioned about the Qur'ān" (*Maʿūna*, al-ʿUmayrīnī ed., pp. 55–6; the same is repeated, nearly verbatim, by Ibn ʿAqīl, *K. al-Jadal*, p. 32). First, al-Shīrāzī deals with the *iʿtirāḍāt* to the Prophet's *qawl* as self-initiated (pp. 56–67), then the *qawl* as prompted (pp. 68–70), then to the Prophet's act (pp. 71–7), and then to his acknowledgment (p. 78).

[61] al-Shīrāzī explains: "like [the Ḥanafī's] *istidlāl* by a solitary report (*khabar al-wāḥid*) against something which is common knowledge, or [the Mālikī's *istidlāl*] regarding something which contradicts the *qiyās*, and for which like they do not make assertion based on a solitary report."

[62] al-Shīrāzī explains: "like his drawing indication by way of '[restrictive] indicant of the instruction' (*dalīl al-khiṭāb*), though he doesn't advocate [this method]."

[63] Al-Shīrāzī's example problem, treating pledge/security (*rahn*), and its transmitted maxim ("the security is for what it was pledged for" [*al-rahn bimā fīhi*]), appear in a number of places in

- *I'tirāḍ* 4: Sharing the Indicant (*al-mushāraka fi'l-dalīl*)
- *I'tirāḍ* 5: Variant Narration (*ikhtilāf al-riwāya*)
- *I'tirāḍ* 6: Abrogation (*naskh*)
  - Mode 1: abrogation by unambiguous declaration (*al-naskh bi-taṣrīḥ*); [the Prophet] conveys [the *khabar*-report's] abrogation unambiguously (*yanqulu naskhahu ṣarīḥan*)
  - Mode 2: abrogation by conveying a later transmission (*al-naskh bi-naql al-muta'akhkhir*); [Q] conveys what negates [the *khabar*-report] (*yunāfīhi*), as coming later, and claims abrogation by means of it
  - Mode 3: abrogation by way of the contradictory doings of the Companions (*al-naskh bi-'amal al-Ṣaḥāba bi-khilāfihi*); [Q] conveys, about the Companions [of the Prophet], such doings as contradict [the *khabar*-report], in order to indicate its abrogation
  - Mode 4: abrogation because it is God's law for past communities (*al-naskh bi-annahu shar' man qablanā*); [Q] claims its abrogation, because it is God's law for past communities (*shar' man qablanā*), and its abrogation is our Law (*Shar'*)
  - Another Mode of the Ḥanafīs: abrogation by way of cessation of the occasioning factor (*al-naskh bi-zawāl al-'illa*)
- *I'tirāḍ* 7: Preponderating Exegesis (*Ta'wīl*)
  - Type 1: preponderating exegesis of the most apparent meaning (*ta'wīl al-ẓāhir*)[64]
  - Type 2: particularization of the general (*takhṣīṣ al-'umūm*)
- *I'tirāḍ* 8: Counter-Indication (*Mu'āraḍa*)
  - Type 1: counter-indication by way of divinely-sanctioned decree (*mu'āraḍa bi'l-nuṭq*)
  - Type 2: counter-indication by way of the occasioning factor (*mu'āraḍa bi'l-'illa*)[65]
    - (1) When the Sunna is univocal (*naṣṣ*), not allowing the possibility of preponderating exegesis (*ta'wīl*)
    - (2) When the Sunna is most apparent (*ẓāhir*), allowing the possibility of preponderating exegesis (*ta'wīl*)
    - (3) When the Sunna is general (*'umūm*), allowing the possibility of particularization (*takhṣīṣ*)

---

the *Umm* compendium. See, e.g., §378 of our subject-text (in my dissertation, Part II, p. 106 and n. 2, and related references in the appendices).

[64] Al-'Umayrīnī (p. 66, n. 2) adds a note from al-Shīrāzī's *Mulakhkhaṣ*: "*Ta'wīl al-Ẓāhir* is of two types: (1) [Q] does *ta'wīl*-exegesis for the *lafẓ*-formulation, about a matter in which the *lafẓ*-formulation is frequently employed; (2) he does *ta'wīl*-exegesis for it, about a *ma'nā*-intension in which the *lafẓ*-formulation is rarely employed."

[65] Though we anticipate it from al-Shīrāzī's typology of the 8th *i'tirāḍ* (al-'Umayrīnī ed., p.66) further discussion of *mu'āraḍa bi'l-'illa* is lacking. Noting this, al-'Umayrīnī supplies the relevant discussion from his manuscript of al-Shīrāzī's *Mulakhkhaṣ fi'l-Jadal* (in n. 6, starting on p. 67 and continuing to p. 68). The above is compiled from this footnote. The same material is also lacking from the Turkī ed., but has not been supplemented.

- (D) *Iʿtirāḍ* against the Sunna with reference to the transmitted text (*matn*) [as prompted saying of the Prophet (*qawl khārij ʿalā sabab*)]:[66]
  - Type 1: The *lafẓ*-expression stands alone, by itself (*bi-nafsihi*), without the reason (*sabab*) [which prompted it], and argument against it (*al-kalām ʿalayhi*) is like arguing against the self-initiated (*mubtada'*) Sunna
    - [1.2] Additional *iʿtirāḍ* of the Mālikīs against [a stand-alone *lafẓ*-expression]: "This has indeed been revealed (*warada*) for a reason (*sabab*), and must be restricted to it (*yaqtaṣira ʿalayhi*)"
  - Type 2: What does not stand alone, by itself, without the reason [which prompted it]; and what distinguishes it from the [other] *iʿtirāḍ* is a claim of ambiguity (*daʿwā al-ijmāl*)
- (E) *Iʿtirāḍ* against the Sunna with reference to the transmitted text (*matn*) [as the Prophet's deed (*fiʿl*)]:[67]
  - *Iʿtirāḍ* 1: [R] does not profess it (*lā yaqūlu bihi*)
  - *Iʿtirāḍ* 2: [Q] disputes with [R] (*yunāziʿuhu*) regarding [the deed's] obligation (*muqtaḍāhu*)
    - *Ṭarīq* 1: [Q] contends with [R] regarding what [the Prophet] did
    - *Ṭarīq* 2: [Q concedes] what he did, but contends with [R] regarding the obligation (*muqtaḍā*) of his deed
  - *Iʿtirāḍ* 3: Claim of Ambiguity (*Daʿwā al-Ijmāl*)
  - *Iʿtirāḍ* 4: Sharing the Indicant (*al-Mushāraka fiʾl-Dalīl*)
  - *Iʿtirāḍ* 5: Variant Narration (*Ikhtilāf al-Riwāya*)
  - *Iʿtirāḍ* 6: Claim of Abrogation (*Daʿwā al-Naskh*)
  - *Iʿtirāḍ* 7: Preponderating Exegesis (*Ta'wīl*)
  - *Iʿtirāḍ* 8: Counter-Indication (*Muʿāraḍa*)
    - [1] By the most apparent meaning (*ẓāhir*)
    - [2] By the occasioning factor (*ʿilla*)
- (F) *Iʿtirāḍ* against the Sunna with reference to the transmitted text (*matn*) [as the Prophet's acknowledgment (*iqrār*)]:
  - Type 1: [the Prophet's] acknowledgment of [another's] saying (*iqrār ʿalā al-qawl*)[68]
  - Type 2: [the Prophet's] acknowledgment of [another's] deed (*iqrār ʿalā al-fiʿl*)[69]

---

[66] Referring back to al-Shīrāzī's typology (al-ʿUmayrīnī ed., pp. 55–6), the *matn* of the Sunna has three categories (*qawl*, *fiʿl*, and *iqrār*), and *qawl* is further subdivided into self-initiated (*mubtada'*) and prompted (*khārij ʿalā sabab*). The preceding section treats the former type of decree—hence its relation to dialectical moves against *istidlāl* from the Qur'ān—and we now proceed to the latter type.

[67] Al-Shīrāzī explains: "As for the [Prophet's] deed (*fiʿl*), one directs against it from among the *iʿtirāḍāt* what one directs against the [Prophet's] saying (*qawl*)" (*Maʿūna*, al-ʿUmayrīnī ed., p. 71). We may observe there are now eight categories of *iʿtirāḍāt* common to arguing against: (1) *istidlāl* from the Qur'ān; (2) *istidlāl* from Sunnaic *qawl*; and (3) *istidlāl* from Sunnaic *fiʿl*.

[68] Al-Shīrāzī explains: "it is like [the Prophet's] decree, with regard to both *iʿtirāḍ* and response (*jawāb*)."

[69] Al-Shīrāzī explains: "it is like [the Prophet's] decree, with regard to both *iʿtirāḍ* and response (*jawāb*), and we have explained the lot."

III. *I'tirāḍ* Against Drawing Indication from Consensus (*al-I'tirāḍ 'alā al-Istidlāl bi'l-Ijmā'*)[70]

- *I'tirāḍ* 1: Outright Rejection (*Radd*) [on the basis of legal-theoretical principles]
  - Mode 1: the rejection of the Shī'a (*Rāfiḍa*); for indeed, according to them, consensus is not a proof (*ḥujja*) for any rulings (*aḥkām*)
  - Mode 2: the rejection of the Ẓāhirīs of the consensus of other than the Companions [of the Prophet]
  - Mode 3: the rejection of the Ẓāhirīs, also, of that for which the decree of one of [the Companions] appears, but the rest are silent. For indeed, according to them, that is not a proof (*ḥujja*)[71]
- *I'tirāḍ* 2: Demand for Validation of the Consensus (*al-muṭālaba bi-taṣḥīḥ al-ijmā'*)
- *I'tirāḍ* 3: [Q] conveys disagreement (*khilāf*) from one of [the Companions]
- *I'tirāḍ* 4: [Q] debates it as he does the transmitted text (*matn*) of the Sunna

IV. Argument Against the Saying of a Solitary Companion (*al-Kalām 'alā Qawl al-Wāḥid min al-Ṣaḥāba*)[72]

- *I'tirāḍ* 1: [Q] says: the saying of a solitary Companion is not a proof (*ḥujja*)
- *I'tirāḍ* 2: [Q] counter-indicates it (*yu'āriḍuhu*) with the unambiguous text (*naṣṣ*) of Qur'ān or Sunna
- *I'tirāḍ* 3: [Q] conveys disagreement (*khilāf*) from another Companion, in order to make of the *mas'ala* a disagreement (*khilāf*) between the Companions

[Disputing What Is Rationally Understood from the Authoritative Source-Case (Ma'qūl al-Aṣl)]

V. Argument Against the *A Fortiori* Signification of the Instruction (*al-Kalām 'alā Faḥwā al-Khiṭāb*)[73]

- *I'tirāḍ* 1: [Q] demands validation (*taṣḥīḥ*) of the *ma'nā*-intension which necessitates intensification (*ta'kīd*) of the *far'* over the *aṣl*
- *I'tirāḍ* 2: [Q] professes the compelling agency of the intensification (*yaqūla bi-mūjib al-ta'kīd*)

---

[70] al-'Umayrīnī ed., pp. 79–81.

[71] Cf. Ibn 'Aqīl, *K. al-Jadal*, p. 38. His description of how to deal with Ẓāhirīs is more detailed; he adds: "Another *i'tirāḍ* is denial (*man'*) of the silence of the Companions (*sukūt al-Ṣaḥāba*) [as being proof], due to the doctrine of some [Ẓāhirīs] that it constitutes *ijmā'*. And such a one provides indication for this by claiming that the [Companions], if they opposed, would have spoken up (*law khālafū la-naṭaqū*); and if they had spoken up, it would have been conveyed (*law naṭaqū la-nuqila*). [....] So their consensus is confirmed by way of their silence." (This constitutes, of course, an *argumentum ex silentio*.)

[72] al-'Umayrīnī ed., pp. 82–3.

[73] al-'Umayrīnī ed., pp. 84–6.

- *Iʿtirāḍ* 3: Nullification (*ibṭāl*)[74]
- *Iʿtirāḍ* 4: [Q] demands [R's] ruling for the intensification (*ḥukm al-ta'kīd*)[75]
- *Iʿtirāḍ* 5: [Q] makes the intensification (*ta'kīd*) into a proof against [R][76]
- *Iʿtirāḍ* 6: [Q] opposes the intensification with what eliminates it (*bimā yusqiṭuhu*)[77]

VI. Argument Against the [Restrictive] Indicant of the Instruction (*al-Kalām ʿalā Dalīl al-Khiṭāb*)[78]

- *Iʿtirāḍ* 1: Outright Rejection (*Radd*) [of the method itself]
- *Iʿtirāḍ* 2: That [Q] counter-indicates it with a divinely-sanctioned decree (*nuṭq*) or by the *a fortiori* signification of a divinely-sanctioned decree (*faḥwā al-nuṭq*)—which is [also called] "self-evident appeal" (*tanbīh*)—or with correlational inference (*qiyās*)
- *Iʿtirāḍ* 3: That [Q] debates it by way of preponderating exegesis (*ta'wīl*), explaining the lesson inherent to the singling out [of the object of the decree] (*fā'idat al-takhṣīṣ*)
    - [3.1] [Q] says: "This context is only specified by mention because it is a locus of ambiguity (*ishkāl*)"[79]
    - [3.2] [Q] says: "It is specified by mention because it usually only occurs in this context"[80]

---

[74] From al-Shīrāzī's example, it may be seen that *ibṭāl*-nullification is achieved in the same manner as *naqḍ* in the domain of *qiyās*. The efficient property (sin) said to be more intense in the *farʿ* (intentional homicide) than the *aṣl* (unintentional homicide), and thus all the stronger in occasioning the *ḥukm* of penitence, is nullified by bringing a parallel case (apostasy) in which the efficient property (sin) is even more intense than it is in the *farʿ* (intentional homicide), but does not occasion the *ḥukm* of penitence. In both *ibṭāl* and *naqḍ*, R's efficient property is destroyed when Q brings a parallel case in which R's *ʿilla-ḥukm* pair is proven inconsistent.

[75] In al-Shīrāzī's example case, Q argues from the basis of R's *a fortiori* ruling to another ruling which contradicts R's doctrine (if you say that vinegar is all the more permissible for cleansing filth because it is more purging than water, then you should say vinegar is preferred over water for cleansing filth—but you don't, you say water is preferred).

[76] In al-Shīrāzī's example case, Q accepts R's identification of the intensified efficient property, but shows it occasions another effect which he wields as a proof (*ḥujja*) against R's ruling.

[77] In al-Shīrāzī's example case, Q reverses the direction of the *a fortiori* assumption by showing the efficient property to be more intense in R's *aṣl* than it is in R's *farʿ*.

[78] al-ʿUmayrīnī ed., pp. 87–9.

[79] In al-Shīrāzī's example case, R argues that, since God specifically mentions unintentional homicide as requiring penitence, it must not be required for intentional homicide. Q explains: He only singled out unintentional homicide for mention because it is a locus for ambiguity—so that no one would doubt, due to its being an accident, that penitence is obliged.

[80] In the example, R argues that, since God specifically mentions dry ablution as permitted during travel, it must not be permitted when not traveling. Q explains: He only specifically mentions travel because water is usually lacking only during travel.

VII. Argument Against the Intension-Property of the Instruction—Meaning Against Correlational Inference (*al-Kalām ʿalā Maʿnā al-Khiṭāb wa huwa al-Qiyās*)[81]

- *Iʿtirāḍ* 1: Outright Rejection (*Radd*) [on the basis of legal-theoretical principles]
  - Mode 1: With reference to deniers of *qiyās* for all rulings[82]
  - Mode 2: With reference to maintainers of *qiyās*—being the Ḥanafīs—for they forbid *qiyās* in certain places[83]
- *Iʿtirāḍ* 2: [Q] says: "You don't advocate *qiyās* for this ruling"[84]
- *Iʿtirāḍ* 3: Denial (*manʿ*) of the *ḥukm* in the *aṣl*
  - [1] [responses with examples]
  - [2] Additional objection of the Ḥanafīs: Denial (*manʿ*) of the *aṣl* with respect to *qiyās*[85]
- *Iʿtirāḍ* 4: Denial (*manʿ*) of the property (*waṣf*) in the *aṣl*, or in the *farʿ*, or in both
  - [1] Against the *aṣl* of [R]
  - [2] Against the *aṣl* of [Q]
- *Iʿtirāḍ* 5: Demand for Validation of the Occasioning Factor (*al-Muṭālaba bi-taṣḥīḥ al-ʿilla*)[86]
  - [response with methods (*ṭuruq*)]
    - [1] Method of its Validation: context of the *lafẓ*-expressions (*siyāq al-alfāẓ*)
      - its indication is from the mode of univocal text (*dalālatuhā min wajh al-naṣṣ*)

[81] al-ʿUmayrīnī ed., pp. 90–118; Turkī ed., pp. 225–65. There are two major problems in al-ʿUmayrīnī's edition for this chapter. First, two pages of printed material, which ought to have appeared between pp. 91–2, have somehow been transposed to pp. 94-5—a printer's error, as I have confirmed via comparison with Princeton's manuscript of the *Maʿūna* (MS. 867; Garrett no. 447H). Second, there is a large lacuna in the Gotha manuscript upon which al-ʿUmayrīnī relied for his diplomatic edition; consequently, there are several pages of material missing (the point of the lacuna occurs at the bottom of p. 115). The Princeton manuscript does not suffer this problem, and al-Turkī's critical edition contains the missing material along with his notes marking the start and end of the Gotha lacuna (p. 256 [and n. 10] to p. 263 [and n. 1]).

[82] For such an opponent, al-Shīrāzī tells us: "The response is that it be said: 'This is one of the Base-Principles of Islam (*uṣūl al-dīn*);' and if he does not concede, you provide authoritative indication for it."

[83] Al-Shīrāzī lists the categories for which Ḥanafī's forbid correlational inference (establishing linguistic usages, *ḥadd*-punishments, modes of ritual expiation, etc.) and provides advice for debating each one.

[84] Partially transposed to p. 95 in al-ʿUmayrīnī's ed.; the remainder is on p. 92.

[85] As al-Shīrāzī shows, this results from the Ḥanafī practice of mitigating strict *qiyās* by way of "juristic preference" (*istiḥsān*) from other textual indicants. Should a Ḥanafī Q consider R's source-case the result of *istiḥsān*, he will attempt to block its use (hence: *manʿ*) as an *aṣl* for *qiyās*, saying: "*Qiyās* upon an object of *istiḥsān* is not permitted."

[86] Cf. Ibn ʿAqīl, *K. al-Jadal*, pp. 50–1; his approach is quite different. He breaks down *taṣḥīḥ al-ʿilla* according to the *dalīl*-indicant upon which R relies: divinely-sanctioned decree (*nuṭq*), *a fortiori* signification of the divinely-sanctioned decree (*faḥwā al-nuṭq*), and rational inference (*istinbāṭ*), treating each of these separately.

        - its indication is from the mode of most apparent meaning (*dalālatuhā min wajh al-ẓāhir*)
            - The most apparent meaning (*ẓāhir*) is a divinely-sanctioned decree (*nuṭq*)
            - The most apparent meaning (*ẓāhir*) is a reason (*sabab*) conveyed with the *ḥukm*
    - [2] Method of its Validation: rational inference (*istinbāṭ*)
        - Type 1: efficiency (*ta'thīr*)[87]
        - Type 2: testimony of the authoritative source-cases (*shahādat al-uṣūl*)[88]
- *Iʿtirāḍ* 6: Lack of Efficiency (*ʿAdam al-ta'thīr*), which is the presence of the *ḥukm* despite the absence of the *ʿilla*[89]
    - Type 1: Lack of Efficiency for a property (*waṣf*), which, when it is removed from the *ʿilla*, the *ʿilla* is destroyed[90]
    - Type 2: Lack of Efficiency for such as which the *ʿilla* is not destroyed by its removal[91]
- *Iʿtirāḍ* 7: Inconsistency (*Naqḍ*); which is the presence of the *ʿilla*, but not the *ḥukm*, according to the doctrine of one who does not opine (*lā yarā*) [the theory of] "particularization of the occasioning factor" (*takhṣīṣ al-ʿilla*)[92]

---

[87] Al-ʿUmayrīnī provides (p. 99, n. 3) an additional explanation from al-Shīrāzī (he does not cite the source): "*al-Ta'thīr* is that the *ḥukm* is present with the existence of a *maʿnā*-quality, and it becomes most probable that it is due to [this *maʿnā*-quality] that [the *ḥukm*] is established; and that [the *maʿnā*-quality] is an occasioning factor (*ʿilla*) for that *ḥukm*. And it is distinguished by validation (*taṣḥīḥ*) of the occasioning factors (*ʿilal*) upon which the *ḥukm* is contingent in God's Law (*Sharʿ*). Such is in two modes (*wajhayn*): (1) "Negation and Presence" (*al-Salb wa'l-Wujūd*), which is that the *ḥukm* is present with the existence of a *maʿnā*-quality, and [the *ḥukm*] is negated by [the *maʿnā*-quality's] removal in one of the *uṣūl*; (2) "Collation and Division" (*al-Muqābala wa'l-Taqsīm*): which is that one mention [a number of] *maʿānī*-qualities in the *aṣl*, and all but one of them are nullified, so we know that the valid one (*al-ṣaḥīḥ*) is that one, and what is not that one is null (*bāṭil*)." (Note this latter corresponds to the method of "examination and division" [*al-sabr wa'l-taqsīm*] in later *uṣūl* works [see Hallaq, *History*, pp. 92].)

[88] Al-ʿUmayrīnī (p. 99, n. 4) provides explanation from al-Shīrāzī's *Sharḥ al-Lumaʿ*: "*Shahādat al-Uṣūl* is what distinguishes correlational inference of indication (*qiyās al-dalāla*); it is that the *ʿilla* is testified to by the *uṣūl* in that category (*bāb*), in terms of both co-presence and co-absence (*ṭardan wa ʿaksan*)."

[89] Ibn ʿAqīl devotes a number of detailed and enlightening discussions to this type of *iʿtirāḍ* in a *Bāb al-Iʿtirāḍ bi-ʿAdam al-Ta'thīr* (*K. al-Jadal*, pp. 54–6).

[90] As al-ʿUmayrīnī notes (p. 100, n. 2): "al-Shīrāzī divided this mode, in the *Mulakhkhaṣ*, into two types: (1) the property (*waṣf*) has efficiency (*ta'thīr*) according to the *madhhab*-doctrine of [R] (*al-muʿallil*) [al-ʿUmayrīnī has *madhhab al-ʿilal*, which appears to be a typo], and the *ḥukm* is dependent upon it according to him, but it has no *ta'thīr*-efficiency in the *uṣūl*; and (2) it has no *ta'thīr*-efficiency according to the *madhhab*-doctrine of [R] (*al-muʿallil*), nor in anything of the *uṣūl*."

[91] As originally listed on p. 100 of al-ʿUmayrīnī's edition of the *Maʿūna*, this category reads: "*ʿAdam al-ta'thīr* for a *waṣf* which, when it is removed from the *ʿilla*, the *ʿilla* is not destroyed."

[92] The opening (§276) of Ibn ʿAqīl's *Bāb al-Naqḍ* begins: "*al-Naqḍ* is presence of the occasioning factor despite absence of the ruling (*wujūd al-ʿilla maʿa ʿadam al-ḥukm*), and that is the opposite (*ḍidd*) of *ta'thīr*-efficiency, because *ta'thīr*-efficiency is presence of the ruling without the occa-

- *Iʿtirāḍ* 8: Breaking Apart (*Kasr*); which is the presence of the *maʿnā*-quality of the *ʿilla*, but not the *ḥukm*[93]
- *Iʿtirāḍ* 9: Professing the compelling agency of the occasioning factor (*al-Qawl bi-mūjib al-ʿilla*)
  - Type 1: regarding an *ʿilla* by which [Q] provides indication for the nullification (*ibṭāl*) of the reason (*sabab*) of the *ḥukm*
  - Type 2: regarding an *ʿilla* by which [Q] provides indication for nominating the [same] *ḥukm*[94]
- *Iʿtirāḍ* 10: That the *ʿilla* does not oblige its rulings (*aḥkām*); which is that [R's] *ʿilla* obliges two rulings, but [R only] makes one of them conditional upon it, without the other
- *Iʿtirāḍ* 11: Invalidity of Occasioned Status (*Fasād al-waḍʿ*); which is that [R] makes conditional upon the *ʿilla* the opposite (*ḍidd*) of what it necessitates
  - [1] what is known with respect to the Messenger [of God] (*min jihat al-Rasūl*)[95]
  - [2] what is known with reference to the authoritative source-cases (*min jihat al-uṣūl*)[96]
- *Iʿtirāḍ* 12: Invalid Compatibility-Comparison (*Fasād al-iʿtibār*)
  - [1] for what is known by way of unambiguous text (*naṣṣ*) [from Qur'ān and Sunna]; which is that [R] considers (*an yaʿtabira*) a *ḥukm* on the basis of another *ḥukm*, although *naṣṣ*-text has revealed the dividing difference (*tafriqa*) between them
    - [1.2] Additional objection of the Ḥanafīs: Linking the unrestricted (*muṭlaq*) [ruling] to the restricted (*muqayyad*)

---

sioning factor (*wujūd al-ḥukm bi-ghayr al-ʿilla*). And that is a valid question according to the doctrine of one who does not profess "particularization of the occasioning factor" (*takhṣīṣ al-ʿilla*), and such are our [Ḥanbalī] companions" (*K. al-Jadal*, p. 56).

[93] Al-ʿUmayrīnī explains (p. 107, n. 4): "*al-Kasr* is a valid question for the invalidation (*ifsād*) of the *ʿilla* when it is situated in its conditions (*shurūṭ*). And most of the scholars have agreed as to its validity and the invalidation of the *ʿilla* by means of it. They call it 'Inconsistency by way of the Intension-Property' (*al-Naqḍ min Ṭarīq al-Maʿnā*), and 'Elenchus by way of Derived Law' (*al-Ilzām min Ṭarīq al-Fiqh*). But some of the legal theorists hold the opinion that *al-Kasr* is not a question which objects to the *ʿilla*, and [thus] does not oblige a response (*jawāb*)." He cites al-Shīrāzī's *Sharḥ al-Lumaʿ* and *Mulakhkhaṣ*, and Ibn ʿAqīl, *K. al-Jadal*, p. 65. As for Ibn ʿAqīl, he opens his *Bāb fi'l-Kasr* saying it is accepted by most, with the exception of some Shāfiʿī's.

[94] Al-Shīrāzī's example cases are instructive. In one of them, R claims standing in prayer is obliged while on a ship, because it is an individual duty (*farḍ*) on land, so it is obligatory on board just like the rest of the individual duties. Q says: "I profess [your *ʿilla*'s] compelling agency; for indeed standing in prayer is obliged while on a ship—when it is not moving!" Thus we see that Q has accepted the efficiency of R's *ʿilla* (it is a *farḍ* on land) in occasioning R's *ḥukm* (it is obligatory on board), but has restricted its general scope to a very particular situation (when the ship is motionless).

[95] In the example case, Q invalidates R's *qiyās* by relating an action of the Prophet, later explained by the Prophet himself, which indicates R has caused an efficient property of his *ʿilla* to occasion the opposite *ḥukm* it should.

[96] Q claims, in the example case, that R has caused his *ʿilla* (it obliges capital punishment) to occasion a lightening of severity (no ritual penance is required) when it should—based, presumably, on a survey of relevant source-cases—occasion an intensification of severity (and thus oblige ritual penance).

- [2] for what is known by way of the authoritative source-cases (*uṣūl*)
  - Mode 1: [R] considers a *ḥukm* on the basis of another *ḥukm*, but one of them is founded upon expansion (*tawsiʿa*), while the other is [founded] upon restriction (*taḍyīq*); or [R] considers incipience (*ibtidāʾ*) on the basis of persistence (*istidāma*); or [R] considers slavery (*riqq*) on the basis of *ʿitq*-manumission, or *ʿitq*-manumission on the basis of *bayʿ*-commutation, while one is founded upon weakness (*ḍuʿf*) and the other upon strength (*quwwa*); and the consideration (*iʿtibār*) of one on the basis of the other is not permitted
  - Mode 2: [R] considers a *farʿ* on the basis of an *aṣl*, but they are divergent (*mukhtalifān*) with regard to parallel cases (*naẓāʾir*) of the *ḥukm*[97]
- [3.1] Additional Mode of the Ḥanafīs: consideration (*iʿtibār*) of the advanced (*mutaqaddim*) on the basis of the delayed (*mutaʾakhkhir*) is not permitted
- [3.2] Additional Mode of the Ḥanafīs: [R] is not allowed to draw indication from the prohibition of *ṭalāq*-divorce in a suspended marriage (*al-nikāḥ* [***][98] *al-mawqūf*), for the nullity of suspended marriage, because [R] is not allowed to draw indication by way of an unintended subsidiary effect for establishing nullity of contract.
- [3.3] Additional Mode of the Ḥanafīs: [R] is not allowed to make the *ḥukm* dependent upon some newly thought up *maʿnā*-quality[99]

• *Iʿtirāḍ* 13: [R's] *ʿilla* is opposed to its *aṣl*
  - Mode 1: its *aṣl* is eliminated [by it][100]
  - Mode 2: its *aṣl* is particularized [by it][101]

• *Iʿtirāḍ* 14: Reversal (*Qalb*)
  - Type 1: Reversal by way of an intended ruling (*Qalb bi-Ḥukm Maqṣūd*)
  - Type 2: Reversal of Equalization (*Qalb al-Taswiya*)
  - Type 3: [Q] makes the occasioned effect (*maʿlūl*) an occasioning factor (*ʿilla*), and the occasioning factor an occasioned effect

---

[97] The example cases are: (1) the comparison of minors with majors in determining the obligation of alms tax (*zakāt*), despite the fact that their rulings diverge in the parallel categories (*naẓāʾir*) of prayer (*ṣalāt*), fasting (*ṣawm*), and pilgrimage (*ḥajj*); and (2) the comparison of women with men in determining their killing (*qatl*) for apostasy (*ridda*), despite the fact that their rulings diverge in the parallel category of their killing in an original state of unbelief (*kufr*; i.e., as members of a non-Islamic, enemy polity).

[98] Here begins the lacuna in al-ʿUmayrīnī's diplomatic edition. Missing material is supplied from al-Turkī's critical edition.

[99] That is, R cannot invent new categories of properties upon which to hang his ruling, but must reason from those which have some precedence or are considered *endoxa*.

[100] In the example case, Q argues that R's proposed *ʿilla* has the untenable effect of nullifying a *ḥukm* patently inherent to the *aṣl*.

[101] In the example case, Q argues that R's proposed *ʿilla* has the untenable effect of particularizing the patently general *ḥukm* of the *aṣl*. That is, it is plain to Q that the *aṣl*-decree was intended to be general in scope, but R's proposed *ʿilla* restricts it to something unintended.

- *I'tirāḍ* 15: Counter-Indication (*Mu'āraḍa*)
  - (1) Counter-Indication with a Divinely-Sanctioned Decree (*al-Mu'āraḍa bi'l-Nuṭq*); [*al-Nuṭq*] being Qur'ān, Sunna, and Ijmā'
  - (2) Counter-Indication with the Occasioning Factor (*al-Mu'āraḍa bi'l-'Illa*)
    - Type 1: Counter-Indication with a Self-Initiated Occasioning Factor (*al-Mu'āraḍa bi-'Illa Mubtada'a*)
    - Type 2: Counter-Indication regarding the *Aṣl*, which is Invalidating Distinction (*Farq*)
      - [2.1] Invalidating Distinction by way of Correlational Inference of the Occasioning Factor (*al-Farq bi-Qiyās al-'Illa*) (***)[102]
        - Type I: Q's *'illa* is an object of agreement (*muttafaq 'alayhi*)
        - Type 2: Q's *'illa* is an object of disagreement (*mukhtalaf 'alayhi*)
      - [2.2] Invalidating Distinction by way of Correlational Inference of Indication (*al-Farq bi-Qiyās al-Dalāla*)
        - Type 1: That [Q] make distinction by way of one of the rulings of the branch-case (*ḥukm min aḥkām al-far'*)[103]
        - Type 2: That [Q] make distinction by way of one of the parallel cases of the ruling (*naẓīr min naẓā'ir al-ḥukm*)
      - [2.3] Invalidating Distinction by way of Correlational Inference of Resemblance (*al-Farq bi-Qiyās al-Shabah*)

[Disputing Presumption of Continuity (Istiṣḥāb Ḥāl)]

VIII. Argument Against Presumption of Continuity of the Legal *Status Quo Ante* (*al-Kalām 'alā Istiṣḥāb al-Ḥāl*)[104]

- [1] [Against] Presumption of Continuity of a *Status Quo Ante* of Rational Intellection for Absolution from Obligation (*Istiṣḥāb Ḥāl al-'Aql fī Barā'at al-Dhimma*)
  - Mode 1: Counter-Indication by way of its Like (*al-Mu'āraḍa bi-mithlihā*)
  - Mode 2: [Q] conveys [the ruling] away from the original state (*aṣl*) [i.e., away from the *status quo ante*] by way of a *dalīl*-indicant
- [2] [Against] Presumption of Continuity of a *Status Quo Ante* of Consensus (*Istiṣḥāb Ḥāl al-Ijmā'*)[105]

---

[102] Turkī ed., pp. 262–3, §149. It is in this section that al-'Umayrīnī's edition resumes after the preceding lacuna.

[103] I have followed Turkī here; al-'Umayrīnī renders "one of the rulings of God's Law" (*ḥukm min aḥkām al-Shar'*).

[104] al-'Umayrīnī ed., pp. 119–20.

[105] This type of *istiṣḥāb*, as listed on page p. 119 of al-'Umayrīnī's edition, reads: "Presumption of Continuity of a *Status Quo Ante* of Consensus regarding something about which disagreement has been preserved" (*Istiṣḥāb Ḥāl al-Ijmā' fīmā Ḥufiẓa 'alayhi al-Ikhtilāf*). Here (p. 120, n. 2) al-'Umayrīnī explains: "The scholars (*'ulamā'*) have disagreed as to the validity of conditionality on *istiṣḥāb ḥāl*

[Modes of Preponderance]

IX. Preponderance of Expressions Whose Intensions Are Most Apparent (*Tarjīḥ al-Ẓawāhir*)[106]

[1]: Regarding the Chain of Transmission (*Isnād*); specifically concerned are solitary reports (*akhbār al-āḥād*)

- Mode 1: That one of the two narrators is older/more eminent (*kabīr*), and the other younger/less eminent (*ṣaghīr*); the narration of the *kabīr* is advanced (*taqaddama*), because he is more accurate (*aḍbaṭ*).
- Mode 2: That one of the two is more knowledgeable (*aʿlam*); his narration is advanced, because he is more knowledgeable of what he narrates.
- Mode 3: That one of the two is closer (*aqrab*) to the Messenger of God; he is given precedence over [the other], because he is more perceptive/attentive (*awʿā*).
- Mode 4: That one of the two is a direct-contact propagator of the anecdote (*mubāshiran li'l-qiṣṣa*), which is dependent upon him; he is given precedence because he is more knowing (*aʿraf*).
- Mode 5: That one of the two [*khabar*-reports] is more narrated; it is superior (*awlā*), because the Law is better preserved (*aḥfaẓ*) in a group than it is among a small number. Due to this the Prophet said: «al-Shayṭān is with one, but he is further from two.»
  - And among our [Shāfiʿī] companions are those who say: [the *khabar*-report] is not given preponderance [in terms of numbers] like testimony (*shahāda*). But the first [opinion] is more valid.
- Mode 6: That one of the two is greater in terms of companionship [with the Prophet] (*ṣuḥba*); he is given precedence, because he is more knowing (*aʿraf*) of what persists of exemplary traditions (*sunan*).
- Mode 7: That one of the two is better in terms of [transmitting an] overall context (*aḥsan siyāqan*) for the *ḥadīth*; he is given precedence due to his diligence.
- Mode 8: That one of the two is later; he is given precedence because he narrated the latter of two decrees.
- Mode 9: That one of the two did not muddle his expression [of the report], but the other did; the one who did not is given precedence, because he is more accurate (*aḍbaṭ*).
- Mode 10: That one of the two is more pious (*awraʿ*), or more confirmed as prudent (*athbata iḥtiyāṭan*), with regard to the *ḥadīth*; he is given precedence, because he is more trustworthy (*awthaq*).
- Mode 11: That one of the two [reports] belongs to narrators of the Folk of Mecca and Medina (*Ahl al-Ḥaramayn*); it is given precedence over the narration of others, because they are more knowledgeable (*aʿraf*) of what persists of

---

al-ijmāʿ; and among them are those who say: 'It is valid (*ṣaḥīḥ*)'—and such is the *madhhab*-doctrine of Abū Bakr al-Ṣayrafī; and al-Muzanī and Abū Thawr chose it; and it is the *madhhab*-doctrine of Dāwūd. But among them are those who say: 'It is null (*bāṭil*),' and al-Shīrāzī thought this more likely (*rajjaḥahu*)."

[106] al-ʿUmayrīnī ed., pp. 121–4.

exemplary traditions (*sunan*). Zayd b. Thābit said: "If you find the Ahl al-Madīna [doing] something, then it is *sunna*."

- Mode 12: That the narration does not diverge from one of the two, but it does from the other;[107] regarding it there are two opinions:
  - Among our [Shāfiʿī] companions are those who say: The two narrations are opposed to each other and cancel each other, and there remains the narration of the one from whom it did not diverge.
  - And among our companions are those who say: One of the two narrations on the authority of the one from whom the narration diverges is made to preponderate over [his] other narration, by way of support from the narration of the one from whom the narration did not diverge.

[2]: Regarding the Transmitted Text (*Matn*)

- Mode 1: That one of the two *khabar*-reports is consistent (*muwāfiq*) with another *dalīl*-indicant, from an authoritative source-case (*aṣl*), or what is rationally understood from one (*maʿqūl aṣl*); it is given precedence, because it is accompanied by something which facilitates understanding of it.
- Mode 2: That one of the two [*khabar*-reports] was used by the Imams; it is superior (*awlā*), because it is the latest of what came down concerning [the Prophet] from among the exemplary traditions (*sunan*).
- Mode 3: That one of the two [*khabar*-reports] is an authoritative decree (*nuṭq*), and the other an indicant (*dalīl*); the decree is superior (*awlā*), because it is an object of consensus (*majmaʿ ʿalayhi*), while the *dalīl* is an object of disagreement (*mukhtalaf fīhi*).
- Mode 4: That one of the two [*khabar*-reports] is a saying (*qawl*), and the other a deed (*fiʿl*); regarding it there are three opinions:
  - 1) that they are both equal
  - 2) the deed is superior (*awlā*)
  - 3) the saying is superior (*awlā*), because it has a form (*ṣīgha*) which extends [a norm] by its *lafẓ*-expression.
- Mode 5: That the *ḥukm* is intended in one of the two [*khabar*-reports]; it is superior (*awlā*) to that in which the *ḥukm* is not intended, because it goes further towards the intention (*maqṣūd*).
- Mode 6: That one of the two [*khabar*-reports] is more obvious (*aẓhar*) in indicating the *ḥukm*; it is given precedence, because it is stronger (*aqwā*).
- Mode 7: That there is, accompanying one of the two [*khabar*-reports], the exegesis (*tafsīr*) of the narrator; [that one is superior], because the narrator is more knowledgeable (*aʿraf*) of what is intended (*murād*).
- Mode 8: That one of the two [*khabar*-reports] is cited without a [prompting] reason (*sabab*); it is superior (*awlā*) to that which is cited with a reason, because what is cited with a reason is an object of disagreement with regard to its general scope [of application] (*ʿumūm*), while what is cited without a reason is an object of consensus with regard to its general scope.

---

[107] Meaning, conflicting reports [both X and ¬X] are attributed to one but not the other.

- Mode 9: That one of the two [*khabar*-reports] is a conveyor [of consensus] (*nāqil*); it is superior (*awlā*), because it conveys a completely understood legal norm (*ḥukm sharʿī*).
- Mode 10: That one of the two [*khabar*-reports] is an affirmation (*ithbāt*), and the other a denial (*nafy*); the affirmation is superior (*awlā*), because along with what is affirmed comes an augmentation of knowledge.
- Mode 11: That one of the two *khabar*-reports is later (*muta'akhkhar*); it is superior (*awlā*), because it is the latter of the two commands. Ibn ʿAbbās said: "We used to take up newer and newer commands of the Messenger of God."
- Mode 12: That one of the two [*khabar*-reports] is more prudent (*aḥwaṭ*); it is superior (*awlā*), because it is more prudent (*aḥwaṭ*).
- Mode 13: That one of the two [*khabar*-reports] is proscribing (*ḥāẓir*), and the other permitting (*mubīḥ*); regarding it there are two approaches:
  - Among our [Shāfiʿī] companions are those who say: "They are both equal."
  - And among them are those who say: "The proscribing is superior (*awlā*), because it is more prudent (*aḥwaṭ*)."[108]

X. Preponderance of (Potentially-Efficient) Intension-Properties (*Tarjīḥ al-Maʿānī*)[109]

- Mode 1: That the *aṣl* of one of the two [*maʿnā*-qualities] is authoritatively and textually fixed (*manṣūṣ ʿalayhi*); it is superior (*awlā*), because it is stronger (*aqwā*).
- Mode 2: That the *aṣl* of one of the two [*maʿnā*-qualities] is confirmed by a *dalīl*-indicant which is decisively settled (*maqṭūʿ bihi*); it is given precedence over that which is confirmed by a *dalīl*-indicant which is not.
- Mode 3: That one of the two [*maʿnā*-qualities] has authoritative source-cases (*uṣūl*); it is superior (*awlā*), because it is stronger in probability (*aqwā fi'l-ẓann*).
- Mode 4: That one of the two [*maʿnā*-qualities] is derived from the basis of an *aṣl* authoritatively and textually fixed as a basis for *qiyās*; it is superior (*awlā*), because it is the *qiyās* of God's Law.
- Mode 5: That one of the two [*maʿnā*-qualities] is the standard for *qiyās* for its genus; it is superior (*awlā*), because it is more probable for it (*aqrab ilayhi*).
- Mode 6: That one of the two *ʿilla*s is authoritatively and textually fixed (*manṣūṣ ʿalayhā*); [it is superior, because] it is stronger (*aqwā*).
- Mode 7: That the property (*waṣf*) of one is perceptible by the senses (*maḥsūs*), and the property of the other is a judgment (*ḥukm*); regarding it, there are two approaches:
  - Among our [Shāfiʿī] companions are those who say: "The *maḥsūs* is superior (*awlā*), because it is more firmly established (*athbat*)."

[108] Al-ʿUmayrīnī explains (124, n.3): "This last the author (*muṣannif*) preponderated (*rajjaḥahu*) in [his] *Sharḥ al-Lumaʿ* and in [his] *Lumaʿ*."

[109] *Maʿūna*, al-ʿUmayrīnī ed., pp. 125–7.

- ○ And among them are those who say: "The *ḥukm* is superior (*awlā*), because the *ḥukm* is of greater indicative power (*adall*) for the *ḥukm*."
- Mode 8: That one of the two [*maʿnā*-qualities] is an affirmation (*ithbāt*), and the other a denial (*nafy*); the affirmation is superior (*awlā*), because its allowance is an object of consensus (*majmaʿ ʿalā jawāzihi*), while the denial is an object of disagreement (*mukhtalaf fīhi*).
- Mode 9: That the property (*waṣf*) of one of the two is a name (*ism*), and the property of the other an attribute (*ṣifa*); the attribute is superior (*awlā*), because it is an object of consensus (*majmaʿ ʿalayhā*), while the allowance of the name is an object of disagreement (*mukhtalaf fī jawāzihi*).
- Mode 10: That one of the two [*maʿnā*-qualities] has less properties (*aqalla awṣāfan*); regarding it, there are two approaches:
  - ○ [1] The lesser of properties is superior (*awlā*), because it is more general (*aʿamm*) and safer (*aslam*).
  - ○ [2] The greater of properties is superior (*awlā*), because it is stronger in resemblance to the *farʿ*.
- Mode 11: That one of the two [*maʿnā*-qualities] exhibits co-presence and co-absence [with the *ḥukm*], while the other exhibits co-presence, but not co-absence; the one which exhibits co-presence and co-absence is superior (*awlā*), because its validity is indicated by [both] co-presence and co-absence.
- Mode 12: That one of the two [*maʿnā*-qualities] obliges prudence (*iḥtiyāṭ*); it is superior (*awlā*), because it safer (*aslam*).
- Mode 13: That one of the two [*ʿilla*s] obliges proscription (*ḥaẓr*), while the other obliges permission (*ibāḥa*); regarding it, there are two approaches—just as we mentioned for the *akhbār*-reports.
- Mode 14: That one of the two [*ʿilla*s] is a conveyor [away from the *status quo ante*] (*nāqila*), and the other a maintainer [of the *status quo ante*] (*mubqiya*); the conveyor is superior (*awlā*).
- Mode 15: That one of the two [*ʿilla*s] causes the *ḥadd*-punishment to fall away, while the other obliges it, or one of the two [*ʿilla*s] obliges the non-Muslim poll tax (*jizya*), while the other causes it to fall away; regarding it, there are two approaches:
  - ○ Among our [Shāfiʿī] companions are those who say: "They are equal."
  - ○ And among them are those who say: "That which causes the *ḥadd*-punishment to fall away or obliges the poll tax is superior (*awlā*)."
- Mode 16: That one of the two [*ʿilla*s] is consistent with another *dalīl*-indicant, from an authoritative source-case (*aṣl*), or what is rationally understood from one (*maʿqūl aṣl*); it is superior (*awlā*), because it is stronger (*aqwā*).

Appendix III: al-Bājī's Modes of *I'tirāḍ*[110]

[Disputing the Authoritative Source-Case (Aṣl)*]*

I. Explanation of the Modes of Objection Against Drawing Indication from the Qur'ān (*Bayān Wujūh al-I'tirāḍ 'alā al-Istidlāl bi'l-Kitāb*)[111]

- 1) [Objection] that [R] does not advocate it (*lā yaqūlu bihi*)
    - 1.1) regarding one of the principles of legal theory (*aṣl min al-uṣūl*)
    - 1.2) regarding one of the derived branch-cases (*far' min al-furū'*)
    - 1.3) [related but fallacious modes]
- 2) Profession of the compelling agency of the indicant (*al-qawl bi-mūjib al-dalīl*) from the Qur'ān, and contestation (*munāza'a*) regarding what the *lafẓ*-expression necessitates
    - 2.1) [Disputation] about the univocal (*naṣṣ*)
        - 2.1.1) Denial (*man'*) of the univocal by way of claiming ambiguity (*da'wā al-ijmāl*)
        - 2.1.2) Denial (*man'*) by way of claiming equivocality (*da'wā al-iḥtimāl*)
    - 2.2) Contestation regarding the most apparent meaning (*al-munāza'a fi'l-ẓāhir*)
        - 2.2.1) most apparent via posited intension (*ẓāhir bi'l-waḍ'*)
            - 2.2.1.1) [Denial by way of] linking to customary usage (*al-ḥaml 'alā 'urf*) [two subtypes]
            - 2.2.1.2) Denial (*man'*) by way of [Q's] linking [the expression] to another *ma'nā*-intension than what [R] links it to, in Arabic linguistic usage (*fi'l-lugha*) [three subtypes]
        - 2.2.2) most apparent via customary usage (*ẓāhir bi'l-'urf*)
            - 2.2.2.1) most apparent via customary linguistic usage (*ẓāhir bi-'urf al-lugha*) [two subtypes]
            - 2.2.2.2) most apparent via customary legal usage (*ẓāhir bi-'urf al-shar'*)
        - 2.2.3) most apparent via indication (*ẓāhir bi'l-dalāla*) [two subtypes]
    - 2.3) Contestation regarding the general scope (*al-munāza'a fi'l-'umūm*)
        - 2.3.1) by claiming ambiguity (*da'wā al-ijmāl*)
        - 2.3.2) [Q] concedes [the expression] is general (*'āmm*), but denies that it treats the locus of disagreement (*mawḍi' al-khilāf*)
    - 2.4) Contestation regarding the ambiguous expression (*al-munāza'a fi'l-mujmal*)
        - 2.4.1) [Q] denies the ambiguity of the verse (*ijmāl al-āya*)
        - 2.4.2) [Q] denies that [R's] *khabar*-report is an explanation (*bayān*) of the verse

---

[110] This outline is derived from al-Bājī's *Kitāb al-Minhāj fi Tartīb al-Ḥijāj*; his example *masā'il* and suggested responses have been omitted.

[111] *Minhāj*, Turkī ed., pp. 42 ff.

- 3) Claim of Sharing [R's] Drawing of Indication from the Qur'ān (*daʿwā al-mushāraka bi'l-istidlāl bi'l-Kitāb*)
    - 3.1) with respect to the most apparent meaning (*min jihat al-ẓāhir*)
        - 3.1.1) [R and Q use the same *lafẓ*-expression of the verse, but it has two *maʿnā*-intensions, and they each link to a different one]
        - 3.1.2) [R and Q use two different *lafẓ*-expressions in the verse, and each attempts to give his preponderance over the other's]
    - 3.2) with respect to the general in scope (*min jihat al-ʿumūm*)
    - 3.3) [related but fallacious modes]
- 4) Variant Readings [of the Qur'ān] (*ikhtilāf al-qirā'āt*)
    - 4.1) [R] draws indication from a reading (*qirā'a*), and [Q] opposes him with another reading in order to modify [R's] reading
    - 4.2) [R] draws indication from a reading, and [Q] opposes him with another reading in order to stop [R's] drawing indication from that reading
    - 4.3) [related but fallacious modes]
- 5) Claim of Abrogation (*daʿwā al-naskh*)
    - 5.1) [Q] conveys an unambiguous transmission (*naql ṣarīḥ*) about the abrogation of a verse by another verse
    - 5.2) [Q] claims abrogation of an earlier verse by a later verse
    - 5.3) [Q] claims its abrogation because it references God's law for past communities (*sharʿ man qablanā*)
    - 5.4) [Q] claims abrogation of all the rulings of the verse by the abrogation of one of its rulings
- 6) [Objection] with reference to Preponderating Exegesis (*min jihat al-ta'wīl*)
    - 6.1) preponderating exegesis of the most apparent meaning (*ta'wīl al-ẓāhir*)
        - 6.1.1) [Q] employs the *lafẓ*-expression according to its most common usage
        - 6.1.2) [Q] gives preponderance to the *lafẓ*-expression, and links it to what is not its most common usage
        - 6.1.3) [related but fallacious modes]
    - 6.2) particularization of the general (*takhṣīṣ al-ʿumūm*)
- 7) Counter-Indication (*Muʿāraḍa*)
    - 7.1) by way of divinely-sanctioned decree (*nuṭq*)
        - 7.1.1) [Q's *nuṭq*] is more particular (*akhaṣṣ*) than [R's verse]
        - 7.1.2) [Q's *nuṭq*] is more general (*aʿamm*) than [R's verse]
        - 7.1.3) [Q's *nuṭq*] is like [R's verse] in general scope (*mithlahu fi'l-ʿumūm*)
            - 7.1.3.1) both are general (*ʿāmm*)
            - 7.1.3.2) both are particular (*khāṣṣ*)
            - 7.1.3.3) both are particular from one perspective, general from another (*khāṣṣ min wajh, ʿāmm min wajh*)
    - 7.2) by way of an occasioning factor (*ʿilla*)
        - 7.2.1) [R's] verse is univocal (*naṣṣ*), not susceptible of preponderating exegesis (*ta'wīl*)

    - 7.2.2) [R's] verse is most apparent of meaning (*ẓāhir*), susceptible of preponderating exegesis (*ta'wīl*)
    - 7.2.3) [R's] verse is general in scope (*ʿumūm*), susceptible of particularization (*takhṣīṣ*)
- 8) [related but fallacious modes]

II. Objection Against Drawing Indication from the Sunna (*al-Iʿtirāḍ ʿalā al-Istidlāl bi'l-Sunna*)[112]

- 1) [Objection] with respect to the Chain of Transmission (*min jihat al-isnād*)
  - 1.1) [an opponent to the category of "multiple-party transmission of a *maʿnā*-intension" (*al-tawātur ʿalā al-maʿnā*) says]: "these are solitary reports (*akhbār āḥād*) and we don't profess such"
  - 1.2) Objection to the Chains of Transmission for Reports Relied upon for Argument
    - 1.2.1) with reference to Demand and Validation (*al-muṭālaba wa'l-taṣḥīḥ*) [two subtypes]
    - 1.2.2) with reference to Degrading and Defaming (*min jihat al-qadḥ wa'l-tajrīḥ*)
      - 1.2.2.1) [Q] degrades the narrator with an accusation which obliges rejection of his *ḥadīth*
      - 1.2.2.2) [Q] states that [the narrator] is unknown (*majhūl*)
      - [numerous related but fallacious modes]
- 2) Modes of Objection to the Transmitted Text of the Sunna (*wujūh al-iʿtirāḍ ʿalā matn al-Sunna*); [for Sunna which came about for no particular individual (*wārida fī ghayr muʿayyan*)]
  - 2.1) Because [R] does not profess it (*al-mustadill lā yaqūlu bihi*)
    - 2.1.1) regarding one of the principles of legal theory (*aṣl min al-uṣūl*)
    - 2.1.2) regarding one of the derived branch-cases (*farʿ min al-furūʿ*)
    - 2.1.3) [related but fallacious modes]
  - 2.2) Contestation regarding what the *lafẓ*-expression of the Sunna necessitates, and profession of its compelling agency (*al-munāzaʿa fī muqtaḍā lafẓ al-Sunna wa'l-qawl bi-mūjibihā*)
    - 2.2.1) Contestation regarding univocal text (*al-munāzaʿa fi'l-naṣṣ*)
      - 2.2.1.1) [Q] claims its ambiguity (*ijmāl*)
      - 2.2.1.2) [Q] claims its susceptibility (*iḥtimāl*) to a *maʿnā*-intension other than that from which [R] draws indication
    - 2.2.2) Contestation regarding the most apparent meaning (*al-munāzaʿa fi'l-ẓāhir*)
      - 2.2.2.1) most apparent via posited intension (*ẓāhir bi'l-waḍʿ*)

[112] *Minhāj*, Turkī ed., pp. 76 ff.

- 2.2.2.1.1) [Denial by way of] linking to customary usage (*al-ḥaml ʿalā ʿurf*) [two subtypes]
- 2.2.2.1.2) Denial (*manʿ*) by way of [Q's] linking [the expression] to another *maʿnā*-intension than what [R] links it to, in Arabic linguistic usage (*fiʾl-lugha*) [three subtypes]
- 2.2.2.2) most apparent via customary usage (*ẓāhir biʾl-ʿurf*)
  - 2.2.2.2.1) most apparent via customary legal usage (*ẓāhir bi-ʿurf al-sharʿ*)
  - 2.2.2.2.2) most apparent via customary linguistic usage (*ẓāhir bi-ʿurf al-lugha*) [two subtypes]
- 2.2.2.3) most apparent via indication (*ẓāhir biʾl-dalāla*) [two subtypes]
- 2.2.3) Contestation regarding the general scope (*al-munāzaʿa fiʾl-ʿumūm*)
  - 2.2.3.1) [Q] concedes [the expression] is general (*ʿāmm*), but denies that it treats the locus of disagreement (*mawḍiʿ al-khilāf*)
  - 2.2.3.2) [Q] claims ambiguity (*ijmāl*) regarding [the expression]
  - 2.2.3.3) [related but fallacious modes]
- 2.2.4) Contestation regarding the ambiguous expression (*al-munāzaʿa fiʾl-mujmal*)
- 2.3) Sharing [R's] Drawing of Indication from the Sunna (*al-mushāraka fiʾl-istidlāl biʾl-Sunna*)
  - 2.3.1) with respect to the most apparent meaning (*min jihat al-ẓāhir*)
    - 2.3.1.1) [R and Q use the same *lafẓ*-expression, but it has two *maʿnā*-intensions, and they each link to a different one]
    - 2.3.1.2) [R and Q use two different *lafẓ*-expressions in the same *khabar*-report]
  - 2.3.2) with respect to the general in scope (*min jihat al-ʿumūm*)
  - 2.3.3) [related but fallacious modes]
- 2.4) Variant Narration (*ikhtilāf al-riwāya*)
  - 2.4.1) substituting one *lafẓ*-expression in place of another [two subtypes]
  - 2.4.2) substituting one vowel (*ḥaraka*) in place of another
  - 2.4.3) [related but fallacious modes]
- 2.5) Claim of Abrogation (*daʿwā al-naskh*)
  - 2.5.1) [Q] conveys an unambiguous abrogation (*naskh ṣarīḥ*)
  - 2.5.2) [Q] conveys a later *khabar*-report about the Prophet, which contradicts the *khabar*-report of [R]
  - 2.5.3) [Q] conveys contradictory doings of the Companions which provide indicant for its abrogation
  - 2.5.4) [several related but fallacious modes]
- 2.6) [Objection] with reference to Preponderating Exegesis (*min jihat al-taʾwīl*)
  - 2.6.1) preponderating exegesis of the most apparent meaning (*taʾwīl al-ẓāhir*)
    - 2.6.1.1) [Q] links the *lafẓ*-expression to its most common usage

            - 2.6.1.2) [Q] links [the *lafẓ*-expression] to a mode which is used rarely (*nādiran*) and metaphorically (*majāzan*)
            - 2.6.1.3) [related but fallacious modes]
        - 2.6.2) particularization of the general (*takhṣīṣ al-ʿumūm*)
    - 2.7) Counter-Indication (*Muʿāraḍa*)
        - 2.7.1) by way of divinely-sanctioned decree (*nuṭq*)
            - 2.7.1.1) [Q's] *nuṭq* is known by reason of the Qur'ān or an unbroken, consistent transmission with multiple transmitters at every stage (*khabar al-tawātur*)
                - 2.7.1.1.1) [Q's] *nuṭq* is more general (*aʿamm*) than [R's] *dalīl*-indicant
                - 2.7.1.1.2) [Q's] *nuṭq* is more particular (*akhaṣṣ*) than [R's] *dalīl*-indicant
                - 2.7.1.1.3) [Q's] *nuṭq* is like [R's *dalīl*-indicant] in general scope and particularity (*mithlahu fi'l-ʿumūm wa'l-khuṣūṣ*)
            - 2.7.1.2) [Q's] *nuṭq* is merely more probable (*maẓnūn*), as a solitary report (*khabar al-āḥād*)
                - 2.7.1.2.1) [Q's] *nuṭq* is more general (*aʿamm*) than [R's] *dalīl*-indicant
                - 2.7.1.2.2) [Q's] *nuṭq* is more particular (*akhaṣṣ*) than [R's] *dalīl*-indicant
                - 2.7.1.2.3) [Q's] *nuṭq* is like [R's *dalīl*-indicant] in general scope and particularity (*mithlahu fi'l-ʿumūm wa'l-khuṣūṣ*)
                    - 2.7.1.2.3.1) both are general (*ʿāmm*)
                    - 2.7.1.2.3.2) both are particular (*khāṣṣ*)
                    - 2.7.1.2.3.3) both are particular from one perspective, general from another (*khāṣṣ min wajh, ʿāmm min wajh*)
        - 2.7.2) by way of an occasioning factor (*ʿilla*)
            - 2.7.2.1) [R's] Sunna is univocal (*naṣṣ*), not susceptible of preponderating exegesis (*ta'wīl*)
            - 2.7.2.2) [R's] Sunna is most apparent of meaning (*ẓāhir*), susceptible of preponderating exegesis (*ta'wīl*)
            - 2.7.2.3) [R's] Sunna is general in scope (*ʿumūm*), susceptible of particularization (*takhṣīṣ*)
- 3) Objection against Drawing Indication from Prompted Sunna (*al-iʿtirāḍ ʿalā al-istidlāl bi'l-Sunna al-wārida ʿalā al-sabab*)
    - 3.1) Sunna which came about for a particular individual (*wārida fī muʿayyan*); the ruling of the Prophet may be transmitted with respect to a particular individual (*qad yunqal ḥukm al-Nabī fī ʿayn*)
        - 3.1.1) no reason (*sabab*) is conveyed with the ruling (*ḥukm*)
            - [Q] says: "This is a case individuated, for an individual (*ʿayn*), and the context is susceptible of interpretation (*muḥtamala*); and it is not valid to make the *ḥukm* dependent on one context without the other except by way of a *dalīl*-indicant"

    - 3.1.2) a reason (*sabab*) is conveyed with the ruling (*ḥukm*); the *ḥukm* came with regard to a particular individual for a specific reason (*muʿayyan bi-sabab*) [several modes]
- 4) Objection against Drawing Indication from the Deeds of the Prophet (*al-iʿtirāḍ ʿalā al-istidlāl bi-afʿāl al-Nabī*)
  - 4.1) Denial that one can draw argumentative support by way of it (*al-manʿ min al-iḥtijāj bihi*)
  - 4.2) [R] does not profess it
  - 4.3) Contestation regarding [the deed's] obligation (*munāzaʿa fī muqtaḍāhi*)
    - 4.3.1) [Q] contends with [R] regarding what [the Prophet] did
    - 4.3.2) [Q] contends with [R] regarding the obligation (*muqtaḍā*) of the deed
  - 4.4) Claim of Ambiguity (*Daʿwā al-Ijmāl*)
    - 4.4.1) [related but fallacious objection]
  - 4.5) Sharing the Indicant (*al-Mushāraka fī'l-Dalīl*)
  - 4.6) Variant Narration (*Ikhtilāf al-Riwāya*)
  - 4.7) Claim of Abrogation (*Daʿwā al-Naskh*)
  - 4.8) Preponderating Exegesis (*Ta'wīl*)
    - 4.8.1) about the *lafẓ*-expression by which the deed is told
    - 4.8.2) about the context in which the deed occurred
  - 4.9) Counter-Indication (*Muʿāraḍa*)
    - 4.9.1) the *muʿāraḍa* is by way of a deed (*fiʿl*)
    - 4.9.2) the *muʿāraḍa* is by way of a saying (*qawl*)
    - 4.9.3) the *muʿāraḍa* is by way of an occasioning factor (*ʿilla*)
      - 4.9.3.1) the deed is susceptible of interpretation (*muḥtamal*)
      - 4.9.3.2) the deed is not susceptible of interpretation
  - 4.10) [related but fallacious objections]
- 5) Objection against Drawing Indication from the Acknowledgment of the Prophet (*al-iʿtirāḍ ʿalā al-istidlāl bi'l-iqrār*)
  - 5.1) [the Prophet] saw something and acknowledged it
  - 5.2) something was done in [the Prophet's] time in such a manner as could not be hidden from him

III. Explanation of the Modes of Objection Against Drawing Indication from Consensus (*Bayān Wujūh al-Iʿtirāḍ ʿalā al-Istidlāl bi'l-Ijmāʿ*)[113]

- 1) Drawing indication from Consensus of a type known by agreement (*ittifāq*)
  - 1.1) Demand for Validation of the Consensus and its Conspicuousness (*al-muṭālaba bi-taṣḥīḥ al-ijmāʿ wa ẓuhūrihi*) [three subtypes]
  - 1.2) Conveyance of Disagreement (*naql al-khilāf*)
    - 1.2.1) [related but fallacious objections]

---

[113] *Minhāj*, Turkī ed., pp. 138 ff.

- 1.3) [Q] discusses what is conveyed [of the consensus], of decree (*qawl*), deed (*fiʿl*), and acknowledgment (*iqrār*); just as with Sunna
- 2) Drawing indication from Consensus of a type known by disagreement (*ikhtilāf*); [when the *ikhtilāf* is split evenly in two camps, disallowing a third opinion]
- 3) [related but fallacious modes]

IV. Objection Against Drawing Indication from the Consensus of the Folk of Medina (*al-Iʿtirāḍ ʿalā al-Istidlāl bi-Ijmāʿ Ahl al-Madīna*)[114]

- [al-Bājī points out that the method (*ṭarīq*) by which we know the consensus of the Medinese is by way of transmission (*naql*); it is in fact a drawing of argumentative support (*iḥtijāj*) by way of a *khabar*-report]
- 1) Medinese consensus that attains the degree of an unbroken, consistent transmission with multiple transmitters at every stage (*ḥadd al-tawātur*)
  - this does not allow *iʿtirāḍ*, because it occasions necessary knowledge (*ʿilm ḍarūrī*)
- 2) [Medinese consensus that] falls short of *tawātur*
- 3) what enjoys consensus with reference to considered opinion and correlational inference (*min jihat al-ra'y wa'l-qiyās*)

V. Objection Against Drawing Indication from the Saying of a Solitary Companion When It Is Not Conspicuous (*al-Iʿtirāḍ ʿalā al-Istidlāl bi-Qawl al-Wāḥid min al-Ṣaḥāba idhā lam yaẓhar*)[115]

- [al-Bājī reiterates an earlier stance that the non-conspicuous saying of a solitary Companion does not constitute authoritative proof (*ḥujja*), this being the prominent opinion (*ẓāhir*) of the Mālikī doctrinal school (*madhhab*)]
- 1) [Q] says: "This is the saying of a solitary Companion, so *qiyās* is advanced over it."
- 2) [Q] conveys disagreement (*khilāf*) [among the Companions] as regards the contended case (*mas'ala*)
- 3) [Q] debates the transmitted material (*manqūl*) in the same way he debates [R's supporting] Sunna

[114] *Minhāj*, Turkī ed., pp. 142 f.

[115] *Minhāj*, Turkī ed., pp. 143 f.

[Disputing What Is Rationally Understood from the Authoritative Source-Case (Maʿqūl al-Aṣl)]

VI. Objection Against Drawing Indication from the Unspoken Implication of the Instruction (*al-Iʿtirāḍ ʿalā al-Istidlāl bi-Laḥn al-Khiṭāb*)[116]

- [al-Bājī explains: *Laḥn al-khiṭāb* is not something by which drawing indication (*istidlāl*) is intended; rather, it anticipates (*yuqaddiru*) the discourse (*kalām*), so that *istidlāl* by means of it may be completed.]
- 1) [objection when] the unspoken implication is added to the words (*kalām*) so that they be completed by it
- 2) [objection when] the unspoken implication is added so that its preponderating exegesis (*taʾwīl*) be validated

VII. Objection Against Drawing Indication from the *A Fortiori* Signification of the Instruction (*al-Iʿtirāḍ ʿalā al-Istidlāl bi-Faḥwā al-Khiṭāb*)[117]

- 1) [objection when] the *a fortiori* signification of the instruction is clearly-disclosed (*jalī*)—it being in the *maʿnā*-intension of what is authoritatively and textually fixed (*manṣūṣ ʿalayhi*)
- 2) [objection when] the *a fortiori* signification is latent (*khafī*)
    - 2.1) [Q] denies the object of agreement's sharing (*mushāraka*) with the object of disagreement in the occasioning factor of the ruling (*ʿillat al-ḥukm*)
    - 2.2) [Q] makes the *ḥukm* contingent upon another *ʿilla* besides that upon which [R] made it contingent

---

[116] *Minhāj*, Turkī ed., pp. 145 f. Al-Bājī provides three definitions for *laḥn al-khiṭāb* in his introductory glossary (p. 12): "[1] What is understood of the intention (*qaṣd*) of the speaker which his *lafẓ*-expression does not posit; and it is said: [2] The restriction (*qaṣr*) of the *ḥukm* of what is enunciated (*manṭūq bihi*) to some of what it treats, and the *ḥukm* of what is not enunciated (*maskūt ʿanhu*) to its contradictory; and it is said: [3] It is the concealed element (*ḍamīr*) without which the discourse (*kalām*) is not completed." The second definition is close to al-Shīrāzī's definition for *dalīl al-khiṭāb*, except al-Bājī defines *dalīl al-khiṭāb* as: "Making the *ḥukm* contingent on a *maʿnā*-quality for some of the genus (*jins*), whether name (*ism*) or attribute (*ṣifa*)" (op. cit.) Note, however, that al-Bājī does not treat *dalīl al-khiṭāb*, as al-Shīrāzī does, nor does al-Shīrāzī treat *laḥn al-khiṭāb* in his *Maʿūna*. In his *Lumaʿ*, however (Mustū ed., pp. 104 f.), we find that al-Shīrāzī includes *laḥn al-khiṭāb* under the general category of "what is understood of the instruction" (*mafhūm al-khiṭāb*), between *faḥwā al-khiṭāb* and *dalīl al-khiṭāb*, and he defines it twice: first, as we see in al-Bājī's third definition; then as: "omission (*ḥadhf*) of the governing noun [of a genitive construct] (*muḍāf*), and standing the governed noun (*muḍāf ilayhi*) in its place." He accompanies this definition with a Qur'ānic paradigm: «ask the village!» (*wa isʾal al-qarya*), by which God means "the people of the village" (*ahl al-qarya*). This same definition and Qur'ānic paradigm may be found in the first example al-Bājī provides (*Minhāj*, Turkī ed., pp. 146) for *laḥn al-khiṭāb*. Al-Shīrāzī accompanies his first definition with a Qur'ānic paradigm as well, and both definitions, with the same Qur'ānic paradigms, may be found—verbatim—in al-Khaṭīb al-Baghdādī's *al-Faqīh wa'l-Mutafaqqih* (al-ʿAzzāzī ed., vol. 1, p. 233).

[117] *Minhāj*, Turkī ed., pp. 146 f.

VIII. Objection Against Drawing Indication by Way of Restriction (*al-Iʿtirāḍ ʿalā al-Istidlāl bi'l-Ḥaṣr*)[118]

- 1) [Q] says: "this is drawing indication by way of the [restrictive] indicant of the instruction (*dalīl al-khiṭāb*), and you do not advocate [this method]."[119]
- 2) counter-indication (*muʿāraḍa*) of his *dalīl*-indicant by way of divinely-sanctioned decree (*nuṭq*)

IX. Objection Against Drawing Indication by Way of the Intension-Property of the Instruction—Meaning Against Correlational Inference (*al-Iʿtirāḍ ʿalā al-Istidlāl bi-Maʿnā al-Khiṭāb, wa huwa al-Qiyās*)[120]

- A) [Explanation of the logical sequence for these objections][121]
  - 1) Demand (*Muṭālaba*)
    - 1.1) [Q] demands [R's] validation (*taṣḥīḥ*) that this kind of *ḥukm* may be affirmed by way of *qiyās*
    - 1.2) Demand for [R's] *dalīl*-indicant that what he made a source-case (*aṣl*) is allowed to serve as an *aṣl*
    - 1.3) Demand for [R's] *dalīl*-indicant that what he made a ruling (*ḥukm*) is allowed to be a *ḥukm*
    - 1.4) Demand for [R's] *dalīl*-indicant that what he made an occasioning factor (*ʿilla*) is allowed to be an *ʿilla*
    - 1.5) Demand for [R's] confirmation of the property (*waṣf*) in the *aṣl*
    - 1.6) Demand for [R's] confirmation of the property (*waṣf*) in the contended branch-case (*farʿ*)
    - 1.7) Demand for [R's] validation of the occasioning factor (*taṣḥīḥ al-ʿilla*)
  - 2) Objection (*Iʿtirāḍ*)
    - 2.1) Profession of the Compelling Agency of the Occasioning Factor (*al-qawl bi-mūjib al-ʿilla*)
    - 2.2) Reversal of the Occasioning Factor (*qalb al-ʿilla*)
    - 2.3) Objection by Invalidity of Occasioned Status (*al-iʿtirāḍ bi-fasād al-waḍʿ*)
    - 2.4) Inconsistency (*al-naqḍ*)
    - 2.5) Breaking Apart (*al-kasr*)

---

[118] *Minhāj*, Turkī ed., pp. 147 f.

[119] In al-Bājī's example, Q is a Ḥanafī and R is a Mālikī. After the Ḥanafī Q's critique: "you don't profess the method of *dalīl al-khiṭāb*," the Mālikī R says: "this is not *dalīl al-khiṭāb*, rather, it is only *istidlāl bi'l-ḥaṣr*." This serves to explain why al-Bājī does not have a section treating *dalīl al-khiṭāb* in his *Minhāj*, as al-Shīrāzī does in his *jadal* and *uṣūl* works.

[120] *Minhāj*, Turkī ed., pp. 148 ff.

[121] In this section we gain clear insight into al-Bājī's ordering principles and procedure, and an explanation of the higher-tier categories (*muṭālaba*, *iʿtirāḍ*, and *muʿāraḍa*) into which each species of dialectical objection falls.

        - 2.6) Demand for Concomitance of the Occasioning Factor in What it Occasions (*al-muṭālaba bi-ijrā' al-ʿilla fī maʿlūlātihā*); [Demand (*sic*) that the Occasioning Factor is not Concomitant in What it Occasions (*al-muṭālaba bi-an al-ʿilla lā tajrī fī maʿlūlātihā*)]
        - 2.7) Objection to the Occasioning Factor by Lack of Efficiency (*al-iʿtirāḍ ʿalā al-ʿilla bi-ʿadam al-ta'thīr*); [Demand (*sic*) by Lack of Efficiency (*al-muṭālaba bi-ʿadam al-ta'thīr*)]
    - 3) Counter-Indication (*Muʿāraḍa*)
- B) [al-Bājī's Fifteen Modes of Objection to *Qiyās*]
    - 1) Objection that the object of disagreement is not allowed to be confirmed by way of *qiyās* (*al-mukhtalaf fīhi lā yajūzu ithbātihi bi'l-qiyās*)
        - 1.1) With reference to deniers of *qiyās*
        - 1.2) With reference to maintainers of *qiyās* [eight sub-types]
    - 2) Objection that what serves as a basis for [R's] *qiyās* is not allowed to be made an *aṣl*
        - 2.1) [Q] claims that [R's] *aṣl* is abrogated (*mansūkh*)
        - 2.2) [Q] claims it is not valid that the *ʿilla* of the *aṣl* be known
        - 2.3) [five related but fallacious modes]
    - 3) Objection that what he made an occasioning factor (*ʿilla*) is not allowed to be an *ʿilla*
        - 3.1) [Q] objects that [R] makes [an object of] agreement (*al-ittifāq*) an *ʿilla*
        - 3.2) [Q] objects that [R] makes [an object of] disagreement (*al-ikhtilāf*) an *ʿilla*
        - 3.3) [five related but fallacious modes]
    - 4) Objection that what he made a ruling (*ḥukm*) is not allowed to be a *ḥukm*
        - 4.1) [when] [R] says about the *ḥukm* of the *ʿilla*: "so it resembles such and such;" but he does not clarify [the presence of] the contended *ḥukm* [in the *aṣl*]
        - 4.2) and for justifying the *ʿilla* of equalization (*al-taʿlīl li'l-taswiya*), [R] says: "And such and such is equal to it;" but he does not make explicit the *ḥukm* for which the two are equal
    - 5) Denying the Source-Case (*manʿ al-aṣl*); Objection by Denial regarding the Ruling of the Source-Case (*mumānaʿa fī ḥukm al-aṣl*)
        - 5.1) [R] follows a designated doctrine (*madhhab manṣūṣ*) for the denial (*manʿ*) which does not contradict [that of Q]; [R's] *madhhab*-doctrine does not disagree regarding its denial
        - 5.2) [R's] doctrine contradicts [that of Q]; [R's] *madhhab*-doctrine disagrees
        - 5.3) it is entirely unknown if [R] has a doctrine regarding it
        - 5.4) [two related but fallacious modes]
    - 6) Denying the Property (*manʿ al-waṣf/mumānaʿa fi'l-waṣf*)
        - 6.1) against [Q's] source-case (*aṣl*)
            - 6.1.1) denying the property in the *aṣl*
            - 6.1.2) denying the property in the branch-case (*farʿ*)

- 6.1.3) denying the property in both [*aṣl* and *far*ʿ]
- 6.2) against [R's] source-case (*aṣl*)
- 7) Demand for Validation of the Occasioning Factor (*al-muṭālaba bi-taṣḥīḥ al-*ʿ*illa*)
  - 7.1) [Q] begins by critique of [R's] ʿ*illa*
  - 7.2) [Q] begins by demanding [R's] validation (*taṣḥīḥ*) of it
    - 7.2.1) with reference to divinely-sanctioned decree (*nuṭq*)
      - 7.2.1.1) the Qur'ān's indication (*dalāla*) of the ʿ*illa* [three modes]
      - 7.2.1.2) the Sunna's indication [three modes]
    - 7.2.2) with reference to rational inference (*istinbāṭ*)
      - 7.2.2.1) method 1: efficiency (*ta'thīr*)
        - 7.2.2.1.1) Negation and Presence (*al-salb wa'l-wujūd*)
        - 7.2.2.1.2) Division and Collation (*al-taqsīm wa'l-muqābala*)
      - 7.2.2.2) method 2: testimony of the authoritative source-cases (*shahādat al-uṣūl*)
    - 7.2.3) [three related but fallacious modes]
- 8) Professing the compelling agency of the occasioning factor (*al-Qawl bi-mūjib al-*ʿ*illa*)
  - 8.1) when [R's] *qiyās* is posited for obligation (*wuḍi*ʿ*a li'l-wujūb*)
  - 8.2) when [R's] *qiyās* is posited for permission (*wuḍi*ʿ*a li'l-jawāz*)
- 9) Reversal (*Qalb*)
  - 9.1) [Q] makes the reversal explicit with decisive argument/proof (*an yuṣarriḥa al-qalb bi'l-ḥujaj*)
    - 9.1.1) Reversal of all the properties of the occasioning factor (*qalb bi-jamī*ʿ *awṣāf al-*ʿ*illa*)
    - 9.1.2) Reversal of one/some of the properties of the occasioning factor (*qalb bi-ba*ʿ*ḍ awṣāf al-*ʿ*illa*)
  - 9.3) Reversal of Equalization (*qalb al-taswiya*)
  - 9.4) [three related but fallacious modes]
- 10) Invalidity of Occasioned Status (*Fasād al-Waḍ*ʿ)
  - 10.1) when [R] makes contingent upon the ʿ*illa* the opposite (*ḍidd*) of what it necessitates
    - 10.1.1) when this is known by way of divinely-sanctioned decree (*nuṭq*)
    - 10.1.2) when this is known by way of authoritative source-cases (*uṣūl*)
    - 10.1.3) [related but fallacious objection]
  - 10.2) Invalid Compatibility-Comparison (*Fasād al-i*ʿ*tibār*)
    - 10.2.1) it is known by way of divinely-sanctioned decree (*nuṭq*)
    - 10.2.2) it is known by way of authoritative source-cases (*uṣūl*) [several subtypes]
    - 10.2.3) [several related but fallacious modes]
- 11) Inconsistency (*Naqḍ*)
  - 11.1) when [R's] ʿ*illa* is posited for the genus (*wuḍi*ʿ*a li'l-jins*), being in the position (*manzila*) of the definition (*ḥadd*)

    - 11.2) when [R's] *ʿilla* is posited for the affirmation of rulings for individuals (*wuḍiʿa li-ithbāt al-aḥkām fi'l-aʿyān*)
      - 11.2.1) [R's] *ʿilla* is posited for obligation (*mawḍūʿa li'l-wujūb*)
      - 11.2.2) [R's] *ʿilla* is posited for permission (*mawḍūʿa li'l-jawāz*)
      - 11.2.3) [several related but fallacious modes]
  - 12) Breaking Apart (*Kasr*); which is called inconsistency (*naqḍ*) with respect to the intension-property (*min jihat al-maʿnā*)
    - 12.1) [Q] replaces one of the properties (*awṣāf*) of the *ʿilla* by something in its [same] *maʿnā*-intension
      - 12.1.1) [related but fallacious mode]
    - 12.2) [Q] eliminates one of the properties (*awṣāf*) of the *ʿilla*
      - 12.2.1) [Q] eliminates a property which is not efficient (*ghayr mu'aththir*) in occasioning the *ḥukm* which was made contingent upon the *ʿilla* [by R]
      - 12.2.2) [Q] eliminates an efficient property[122]
  - 13) Demand for Demonstrating Concomitance of the Occasioning Factor with What it Occasions (*al-muṭālaba bi-ijrā' al-ʿilla fī maʿlūlātihā*)[123]
    - 13.1) [R] makes some *ḥukm* or other contingent upon the *ʿilla*, then [Q] demands that he make a similar *ḥukm* contingent upon the same *ʿilla*, saying: "if it is an *ʿilla* for one of the two *ḥukms*, it should be so for the other"
    - 13.2) [related but fallacious objection]
  - 14) Lack of Efficiency (*ʿAdam al-ta'thīr*), meaning the *ḥukm* is not absent when the *ʿilla* is absent in some locus or another
    - 14.1) for a property (*waṣf*), which, when it is removed from the *ʿilla*, the *ʿilla* is destroyed
      - 14.1.1) the property has efficiency according to [R's] *madhhab*-opinion, and according to him the *ḥukm* is contingent upon it; however it has no efficiency in the authoritative source-cases (*uṣūl*)
      - 14.1.2) it has no efficiency according to [R's] *madhhab*-opinion, nor in any of the *uṣūl*
    - 14.2) for a property (*waṣf*) such as which the *ʿilla* is not destroyed by its removal; this is called "stuffing" (*ḥashw*)
      - 14.2.1) [related but fallacious objection]
  - 15) Counter-Indication (*Muʿāraḍa*)
    - 15.1) Counter-Indication of the Occasioning Factor with Divinely-Sanctioned Decree (*muʿāraḍat al-ʿilla bi'l-nuṭq*)
    - 15.2) Counter-Indication of the Occasioning Factor with [another] Occasioning Factor (*muʿāraḍat al-ʿilla bi'l-ʿilla*)
      - 15.2.1) Counter-Indication with a Self-Initiated Occasioning Factor (*al-muʿāraḍa bi-ʿilla mubtada'a*)

[122] Al-Bājī argues that this is an invalid mode of objection.

[123] Al-Bājī notes this mode of objection is very similar to the preceding mode: *kasr*.

- 15.2.2) Counter-Indication with the Occasioning Factor of the Source-Case—which is Invalidating Distinction (*al-muʿāraḍa bi-ʿillat al-aṣl wa huwa al-farq*)
    - 15.2.2.1) Invalidating Distinction by way of the Occasioning Factor of the Ruling (*farq bi-ʿillat al-ḥukm*); the *maʿnā*-quality upon which the *ḥukm* is made contingent in God's Law (*fi'l-Sharʿ*) is in the *aṣl*, but the opposite (*ʿaks*) is true of the *farʿ*
        - 15.2.2.1.1) the *maʿnā*-quality is an object of agreement (*muttafaq ʿalayhi*)
        - 15.2.2.1.2) the *maʿnā*-quality is an object of disagreement (*mukhtalaf ʿalayhi*)
    - 15.2.2.2) Invalidating Distinction by way of Indication of the Ruling (*farq bi-dalālat al-ḥukm*)
        - 15.2.2.2.1) [Q] makes distinction between the *farʿ* and the *aṣl* by way of a *ḥukm* peculiar to the *farʿ*, without leaving [the example of the *farʿ*]
        - 15.2.2.2.2) [Q] makes distinction by way of the same *ḥukm*, in other loci of disagreement (*mawāḍiʿ al-khilāf*)
        - 15.2.2.2.3) [Q] makes distinction by way of a *ḥukm* which resembles the contended *ḥukm*
        - 15.2.2.2.4) [Q] makes distinction by way of a type of property resemblance (*shabah*)

X. Argument Against Drawing Indication by Way of *A Fortiori* Valuation (*al-Kalām ʿalā al-Istidlāl bi'l-Awlā*)[124]

- [Definition of *al-istidlāl bi'l-awlā*]: [R] links the *farʿ* to the *aṣl* by way of a *maʿnā*-quality which obliges their connection (*jamʿ*), then he clarifies in the *farʿ* an augmentation (*ziyāda*) which obliges the intensification (*ta'kīd*) of the *ḥukm* of the *farʿ* over the *aṣl*.
- 1) *iʿtirāḍ* by way of demand (*muṭālaba*) of validation (*taṣḥīḥ*) for the *maʿnā*-quality necessitating intensification (*ta'kīd*) of the *ḥukm* of the *farʿ* over the *ḥukm* of the *aṣl*
- 2) *iʿtirāḍ* by way of inconsistency (*naqḍ*)
- 3) *iʿtirāḍ* by way of breaking apart (*kasr*)
- 4) *iʿtirāḍ* by way of [Q's] making the intensification (*ta'kīd*) into a decisive argument (*ḥujja*) against [R]
- 5) *iʿtirāḍ* by way of opposition (*muqābala*) of the intensification (*ta'kīd*) of the *farʿ* with a *maʿnā*-quality which eliminates it
- 6) *iʿtirāḍ* by way of invalidating distinction (*farq*)

[124] *Minhāj*, Turkī ed., pp. 207 ff. Cf. al-Bājī's first definition for this method of *istidlāl* (ibid., p. 27).

XI. Argument Against Drawing Indication by Way of Analytical Disjunction (*al-Kalām 'alā al-Istidlāl bi'l-Taqsīm*)[125]

- 1) Against Type 1, in which "[R] states the divisions (*aqsām*) of things upon which the opponent (*khaṣm*) can possibly make the *ḥukm* contingent, then clarifies the invalidity of all of them, and so establishes that truth (*ḥaqq*) lies in their contradictory (*khilāf*)"
    - 1.1) *i'tirāḍ* by way of inconsistency (*naqḍ*)
    - 1.2) *i'tirāḍ* by way of breaking apart (*kasr*)
    - 1.3) [Q] clarifies another division (*qism*) which [R] neglected, then makes the *ḥukm* contingent upon it
    - 1.4) [Q] claims the contingency (*ta'līq*) of the *ḥukm* upon one of the aspects for which [R] has provided indication of its nullification (*ibṭāl*), then he validates it
- 2) Against Type 2, in which "[R] states the divisions (*aqsām*) of things upon which contingency (*ta'līq*) of the *ḥukm* is possible, then clarifies the invalidity of all but one, and so establishes that truth (*ḥaqq*) lies in that one"
    - 2.1) [Q] makes the *ḥukm* contingent upon one of the divisions for which [R] has provided indication of its nullification (*ibṭāl*), then he validates it

XII. Argument Against Drawing Indication by Way of the Opposite (*al-Kalām 'alā al-Istidlāl bi'l-'Aks*)[126]

- 1) *i'tirāḍ* by way of inconsistency (*naqḍ*)
- 2) *i'tirāḍ* by way of breaking apart (*kasr*)
- 3) *i'tirāḍ* by way of invalidating distinction (*farq*)

XIII. Argument Against Drawing Indication by Way of Clarifying the Occasioning Factor (*al-Kalām 'alā al-Istidlāl bi-Bayān al-'Illa*)[127]

- 1) Against Type 1, in which "[R] clarifies the *'illa* of the *ḥukm*, then draws indication—from its presence in the locus of disagreement (*mawḍi' al-khilāf*)—for confirmation of the *ḥukm* [therein]"
    - 1.1) Denial (*Man'*); when [R] has begun his *istidlāl*
        - 1.1.1) [Q] denies what [R] stated to be the *'illa* of the *ḥukm*, or [the *ḥukm*'s] efficient property (*waṣf mu'aththir fīhi*).
        - 1.1.2) [Q] denies that what [R] stated is the whole *'illa*.
    - 1.2) Inconsistency (*Naqḍ*); when [R] has begun his *istidlāl*

---

[125] *Minhāj*, Turkī ed., pp. 210 ff. Cf. al-Bājī's first definition for this method and its two types (pp. 27–8).

[126] *Minhāj*, Turkī ed., pp. 212 ff. See al-Bājī's introductory example for this method (p. 29).

[127] *Minhāj*, Turkī ed., pp. 214 ff. Cf. al-Bājī's first definition for this method and its two types (pp. 28–9).

    - 1.2.1) the *ʿilla* is present despite the absence of the *ḥukm*
    - 1.2.2) the *ḥukm* is present despite the absence of the *ʿilla*
- 2) Against Type 2, in which "[R] clarifies the *ʿilla*, and draws indication from its absence [in the locus of disagreement] for the negation of the *ḥukm* [therein]"
  - 2.1) [same as 1.1 above]
  - 2.2) [same as 1.2 above]

XIV. Argument Against Drawing Indication by Way of Testimony of the Authoritative Source-Cases (*al-Kalām ʿalā al-Istidlāl bi-[Shahādat] al-Uṣūl*)[128]

- 1) Inconsistency (*Naqḍ*): [Q] clarifies for [R], in the *uṣūl*, the contradictory (*khilāf*) of what [R] claims; and such constitutes a denial (*manʿ*) of what [R] claims of the *uṣūl*, and a destruction [by inconsistency] (*naqḍ*) of what [R] brings in terms of a *dalīl*-indicant
- 2) Invalidating Distinction (*Farq*): [Q] clarifies that this particular case (*mawḍiʿ*) is contradictory (*mukhālif*) to the rest of the *uṣūl* with respect to the *maʿnā*-quality, and due to this it contradicts them with regard to the *ḥukm*

[Disputing Presumption of Continuity (Istiṣḥāb Ḥāl)]

XV. Argument Against Presumption of Continuity of the Legal *Status Quo Ante* (*al-Kalām ʿalā Istiṣḥāb al-Ḥāl*)[129]

- 1) [Against] Presumption of Continuity of a *Status Quo Ante* of Rational Intellection (*Istiṣḥāb Ḥāl al-ʿAql*)
  - 1.1) Counter-Indication (*Muʿāraḍa*); [Q] counter-indicates it with its like [in epistemic strength]
  - 1.2) Conveyance by way of Indicant (*al-naql biʾl-dalīl*); [Q] conveys [the ruling] away from the *status quo ante* by way of a *dalīl*-indicant, saying: "Indeed, the original state (*aṣl*) is absolution from obligation by way of rational intellection (*barāʾat al-dhimma biʾl-ʿaql*); however, God's Law (*al-Sharʿ*) has provided an indicant for the involvement of his obligation (*ishtighāl dhimmatihi*)"
- 2) [Against] [Fallacious Mode] Presumption of Continuity of a *Status Quo Ante* of Consensus (*Istiṣḥāb Ḥāl al-Ijmāʿ*)
  - 2.1) Comprehensive denial (*manʿ*) that one may draw indication by this mode of presumption
  - 2.2) Counter-Indication (*Muʿāraḍa*) [as in 1.1]
  - 2.3) Conveyance by way of Indicant (*al-naql biʾl-dalīl*) [as in 1.2]

[128] *Minhāj*, Turkī ed., pp. 217 f. See al-Bājī's introductory example for this method (p. 29).
[129] *Minhāj*, Turkī ed., pp. 219 f.

[Modes of Preponderance]

XVI. Argument on the Modes of Preponderance (*al-Kalām ʿalā al-Tarjīḥāt*)[130]

[A]: Preponderance of Expressions whose Intensions are Most Apparent (*Tarjīḥ al-Ẓawāhir*)

[1]: Regarding the Chain of Transmission (*Isnād*)

- 1.1) One of the two *khabar*-reports includes an anecdote which is widespread, well-circulated and well-known to the Scholars of Transmission (*qiṣṣa mashhūra mutadāwala maʿrūfa ʿinda Ahl al-Naql*), but the opposing [*khabar*-report] deviates from [that anecdote]; [the first is superior]
- 1.2) The narrator of one of the two *khabar*-reports is more accurate (*aḍbaṭ*) and has a better memory (*aḥfaẓ*), but the narrator of the opposing [*khabar*-report] is less so; [the first is superior]
- 1.3) The [independent, initial] narrators of one of the two *khabar*-reports are more [numerous] than the narrators of the other; [the first is superior]
- 1.4) One of the narrators says: "I audited the Messenger of God," but the other says: "The Messenger of God... wrote this to me;" the one who audited is superior (*awlā*)
- 1.5) The validity of one of the two *khabar*-reports is an object of agreement (*muttafaqan ʿalā ṣiḥḥatihi*)—firmly attributed to the Messenger of God—while that of the other is an object of disagreement (*mukhtalif fīhi*)—some saying: "It [is a *ḥadīth* which] terminates at a Companion (*mawqūf ʿalā al-Ṣaḥābī*)," but others saying: "It [is a *ḥadīth* whose] *isnād* reaches the Prophet (*musnad*);"[131] [the first is superior]
- 1.6) One of the two *khabar*-reports is ascribed (*mansūban*) to the Messenger of God by unambiguous text (*naṣṣ*) or deed (*fiʿl*), while the other is [ascribed] by reliance on an indicant (*istidlāl*); [the first is superior]
- 1.7) [For one of the two *khabar*-reports] [later] narrators have diverged from what [the first] narrated about the Prophet—some of them transmit that he narrated affirmation of the [contended] ruling (*ithbāt al-ḥukm*), and some of them transmit that he narrated denial of it (*nafīhi*); [the chain which is less confused is superior]

---

[130] *Minhāj*, Turkī ed., pp. 221 ff.

[131] Al-Bājī's opening glossary treats terms from the domain of *ḥadīth* science (Turkī ed., p. 13, §17). Among them we find his short definitions for: (1) *al-mursal*: "whose *isnād* is severed (*inqaṭaʿa*);" (2) *al-mawqūf*: "what terminates (*waqafa*) at a Companion or Successor, and [its *isnād*] does not reach the Messenger;" and (3) *al-musnad*: "whose *isnād* connects (*ittaṣala*) [to the Prophet]. The term *marfūʿ*, "attributed to the Prophet," is not mentioned; it is a category of origin, not validity.

- 1.8) The narrator of one of the two *khabar*-reports is the author of the anecdote and was involved in it (*ṣāḥib al-qiṣṣa wa'l-mutalabbis bihā*), and the other is not; the *khabar*-report of the direct-contact propagator (*mubāshir*) is superior (*awlā*)
- 1.9) The customary practice (*ʿamal*) of the Medinese is in agreement (*iṭbāq*) with what one of the two *khabar*-reports compels; it is superior (*awlā*) to the *khabar*-report which contradicts the *ʿamal* of the Medinese
- 1.10) One of the two narrators is more thorough in investigation (*ashadda taqaṣṣiyan*) of the *ḥadīth*, and more systematic (*aḥsana nasaqan*) with regard to it, than the other; his *ḥadīth* is advanced over the other's
- 1.11) One of the two *isnāds* is free of disorder (*iḍṭirāb*), while the other is disordered (*muḍṭaraban*); the one free of disorder is superior (*awlā*)
- 1.12) [Fallacious *tarjīḥ* of the Ḥanafīs]: The narrator of one of the two *khabar*-reports is a specialist regarding the *ḥukm*, while the narrator of its opposite is not

[2]: Regarding the Transmitted Text (*Matn*)

- 2.1) The transmitted text of one of the two *ḥadīths* is free of disagreement (*ikhtilāf*) and disorder (*iḍṭirāb*), but such obtains in the other; the one whose *lafẓ*-expression is unanimous, and whose preservation from confusion is certain, is advanced [over the other]
- 2.2) The *ḥukm* of one of the two *khabar*-reports is unambiguously decreed (*manṭūqan bihi*), while that of the other is equivocal (*muḥtamalan*); the one whose *ḥukm* is unambiguously decreed is advanced [over the other]
- 2.3) One of the two [*khabar*-reports] stands alone, not requiring [explanation of] a concealed element (*mustaghnīyan ʿan al-ḍamīr fīhi*), while the other requires it; the former is superior (*awlā*)
- 2.4) The two *khabar*-reports are employed [together] in a locus of disagreement (*mawḍiʿ al-khilāf*); it is superior (*awlā*) to the use (*istiʿmāl*) of one and discarding (*iṭṭirāḥ*) of the other
- 2.5) The particularization (*takhṣīṣ*) of one of the two general [reports] is disputed, while that of the other is agreed upon; the making contingent [of the *ḥukm*] on the general [report] whose particularization is not the object of consensus (*lam yajmaʿ ʿalā takhṣīṣihi*) is superior (*awlā*)
- 2.6) One of the two *khabar*-reports is intended as an explanation of the ruling (*bayān al-ḥukm*), while the other is not intended for that; adherence to the one intended as an explanation of the ruling is superior (*awlā*)
- 2.7) One of the *khabar*-reports is efficient regarding the ruling (*mu'aththir fī'l-ḥukm*), while the other is not efficient; the efficient is superior (*awlā*)[132]

[132] Turkī's source manuscript reads: "One of the *khabar*-reports is unbroken, consistent, with multiple transmitters at every stage (*mutawātir*), as regards the ruling (*ḥukm*), while the other is not *mutawātir*; the *mutawātir* is superior (*awlā*)." His correction (which I have followed, above) is drawn from al-Bājī's *uṣūl* work, the *Iḥkām al-Fuṣūl*. The preference of *mu'aththir* over *mutawātir* makes sense when compared to al-Bājī's example *mas'ala*, which disputes the former quality and makes no mention of the latter.

- 2.8) One of [the *khabar*-reports] was prompted by a reason (*warada ʿalā sabab*), while the other was not prompted by a reason; the one which was not prompted is advanced over the prompted *khabar*-report for everything but what is made contingent [from the prompted report] by way of the reason (*sabab*) for which it was revealed; a group of legal specialists profess: "Whatever was revealed for a reason is restricted to its reason."
- 2.9) One of the two *khabar*-reports has been used to pass judgment against the other (*qad qaḍā bihi ʿalā al-ākhar*) in a certain locus; it is superior (*awlā*) to it in the rest of the loci
- 2.10) One of the two *khabar*-reports is transmitted with various expressions (*manqūl bi-alfāẓ mutaghāyira*) and by different paths (*ṭuruq mukhtalifa*); it is superior (*awlā*)
- 2.11) One of the two *khabar*-reports negates a shortcoming (*naqṣ*) of the Companions of the Messenger of God, while the second attributes it to them; the former is superior (*awlā*)
- 2.12) [Fallacious *tarjīḥ*]: One of the two *khabar*-reports affirms a ruling (*muthbitan li-ḥukm*), while the other denies it (*nāfiyan lahu*)
    - al-Ḥasan b. al-Qaṣṣār, and Our Shaykh Abū Isḥāq [al-Shīrāzī]: the one affirming is superior (*awlā*) to the one denying
    - al-Qāḍī Abū Bakr [al-Bāqillānī], and Our Qāḍī Abū Jaʿfar: they are equal (*humā sawā'un*)[133]
- 2.13) [Fallacious *tarjīḥ*]: One of the two *khabar*-reports is proscribing (*ḥāẓiran*) and the other permitting (*mubīḥan*)
    - Ibn al-Qaṣṣār, and Our Shaykh Abū Isḥāq: proscription is advanced over permission
    - al-Qāḍī Abū Bakr, and al-Qāḍī Abū Jaʿfar: they are equal (*humā sawā'un*)[134]

[B]: Preponderance of (Potentially-Efficient) Intension-Properties (*Tarjīḥ al-Maʿānī*)

- 1) One of the two *ʿillas* is authoritatively and textually fixed (*manṣūṣan ʿalayhā*), while the other is not; [the first is superior]
- 2) One of the two *ʿillas* does not entail particularization (*takhṣīṣ*) for its *aṣl*, while the second does; the one which does not entail particularization for its *aṣl* is superior (*awlā*) and more appropriate (*aḥrā*)
- 3) One of the two [*ʿillas*] is consonant with the *lafẓ*-expression of the *aṣl*, while the other is not; the consonant one is advanced [over the other]
- 4) One of the two *ʿillas* is concomitant [with its ruling] (*muṭarrada munʿakisa*), while the other shows co-presence but not co-absence (*muṭarrada ghayr munʿakisa*); the one showing co-absence (*munʿakisa*) is made to preponderate
- 5) One of two *ʿillas* finds testimony in many *uṣūl*, while the other finds testimony in only one; the former is superior (*awlā*)

---

[133] Al-Bājī agrees, saying: "This is the correct view" (*wa huwa al-ṣaḥīḥ*).

[134] Again, al-Bājī agrees that this is the correct view.

- 6) One of the two doing *qiyās* refers the *far'* to an *aṣl* of its genus, while the other refers the *far'* to an *aṣl* which is not of its genus; the *qiyās* of the one who refers the *far'* to its genus is superior (*awlā*)
- 7) One of the two *'illas* is intransitive (*wāqifa*), while the other is transitive (*muta'addiya*); the transitive is superior (*awlā*) to the intransitive
- 8) One of the two [*'illas*] does not generally encompass its branch-cases (*furū'*), while the other generally encompasses its (*furū'*); the general (*'āmma*) is superior (*awlā*)
- 9) One of the two *'illas* is general (*'āmma*) and the other is particular (*khāṣṣa*); the general (*'āmma*) is superior (*awlā*)
- 10) One of the two *'illas* is drawn from an *aṣl* which is authoritatively and textually fixed (*manṣūṣ 'alayhi*), while the other is drawn from an *aṣl* which is not; the one drawn from an *aṣl* which is authoritatively and textually fixed is superior (*awlā*)
- 11) One of the two *'illas* has few properties (*aqall awṣāfan*), while the other has many properties (*kathīrat al-awṣāf*); the one with few properties is advanced [over the other]
  - This is the *qawl* of Abū Isḥāq al-Shīrāzī
  - Some Shāfi'īs say: they are equal (*humā sawā'un*)
  - Some Shāfi'īs say: the one of many properties is superior (*awlā*)
  - Ibn al-Qaṣṣār has wavered regarding it (*qad iḍṭaraba fī dhālika*)
- 12) One of the two *'illas* is a conveyor [away from the *status quo ante*] (*nāqila*), while the other is a maintainer [of the *status quo ante*] (*mubqiya 'alā ḥukm al-aṣl*); the maintainer is superior (*awlā*)
  - Our Shaykh Abū Isḥāq, and a group of Legal Theorists, like Ibn al-Qaṣṣār and others: the conveyor is superior (*awlā*)
- 13) [Common and recurrent mode of the Theorists of Intellectual Investigation (Ahl al-Naẓar)]: One of the two *'illas* is proscribing (*ḥāẓira*), while the other is permitting (*mubīḥa*); they are equal (*humā sawā'un*)
  - Ibn al-Qaṣṣār, Abū Isḥāq [al-Shīrāzī], Abū al-Ḥasan al-Karkhī: proscription is advanced over permission
- 14) [Common and recurrent mode of the Disputation Theorists]: One of the two *'illas* obliges the *ḥadd*-punishment, while the other causes it to fall away; they are equal (*humā sawā'un*)
  - This is the doctrine of Abū Isḥāq al-Shīrāzī
  - Some Shāfi'īs say: what causes the *ḥadd*-punishment to fall away is superior (*awlā*)
- 15) [Common and recurrent mode of the Disputation Theorists]: One of the two *'illas* is a compelling agent for manumission (*mūjiba li'l-'itq*), while the other is not; they are equal (*humā sawā'un*)
  - This is the doctrine of Abū Isḥāq al-Shīrāzī
  - Some of the Dialectical Theologians (Mutakallimūn) say: the one which is a compelling agent for manumission is advanced [over the one which is not]

References for the Appendices

al-Bājī, Abū al-Walīd Sulaymān. *Kitāb al-Minhāj fī Tartīb al-Ḥijāj* (*L'art de la Polémique: Édition Critique d'al-Minhāǧ de Bāǧī*). Ed. ʿAbd al-Majīd Turkī. Paris: Maisonneuve et Larose, 1978.

al-Baṣrī, Abū al-Ḥusayn Muḥammad. *Kitāb al-Qiyās al-Sharʿī*. In *idem*, *Kitāb al-Muʿtamad fī Uṣūl al-Fiqh*. Ed. Muḥammad Ḥamīd Allāh, Muḥammad Bakīr, and Ḥasan Ḥanafī. Damascus: al-Maʿhad al-ʿIlmī al-Faransī li'l-Dirāsāt al-ʿArabiyya bi-Dimashq, 1964–1965, vol. 2, pp. 1029–1050.

Hallaq, Wael. *A History of Islamic Legal Theories: An Introduction to Sunnī Uṣūl al-Fiqh*. Cambridge; New York: Cambridge University Press, 1997.

Hallaq, Wael. "A Tenth-Eleventh Century Treatise on Juridical Dialectic." *Muslim World* 77 (1987): 197–228.

Ibn ʿAqīl, Abū al-Wafāʾ ʿAlī. *Kitāb al-Jadal ʿalā Ṭarīqat al-Fuqahāʾ*. Al-Ẓāhir [Cairo]: Maktabat al-Thaqāfa al-Dīniyya, 1980. [An unattributed reproduction of George Makdisi, ed., *Le Livre de la Dialectique d'Ibn ʿAqīl*, minus his introduction and critical apparatus].

al-Khaṭīb al-Baghdādī, Abū Bakr Aḥmad b. ʿAlī. *Kitāb al-Faqīh wa'l-Mutafaqqih*. 2nd Ed. 2 Vols. Ed. Abū ʿAbd al-Raḥmān ʿĀdil b. Yūsuf al-ʿAzzāzī. Riyadh: Dār Ibn al-Jawzī, 1996.

Sānū, Quṭb Muṣṭafā. *Muʿjam Muṣṭalaḥāt Uṣūl al-Fiqh, ʿArabī-Inkilīzī*. Beirut: Dār al-Fikr al-Muʿāṣir, 2000.

al-Shīrāzī, Abū Isḥāq Ibrāhīm. *Kitāb al-Maʿūna fī'l-Jadal*. Ed. ʿAbd al-Majīd Turkī. Beirut: Dār al-Gharb al-Islāmī, 1988.

al-Shīrāzī, Abū Isḥāq Ibrāhīm. *Al-Lumaʿ fī Uṣūl al-Fiqh*. Ed. Muḥyī al-Dīn Dīb Mustū and Yūsuf ʿAlī Badīwī. Damascus: Dār al-Kalam al-Ṭayyib; Dār Ibn Kathīr, 1995.

al-Shīrāzī, Abū Isḥāq Ibrāhīm. *Al-Maʿūna*. Princeton University Library; Manuscripts Collection (Islamic Manuscripts); MS. 867; Garrett no. 447H. Available at: http://pudl.princeton.edu/objects/2f75r807h

al-Shīrāzī, Abū Isḥāq Ibrāhīm. *Al-Maʿūna fī'l-Jadal*. Ed. ʿAlī b. ʿAbd al-ʿAzīz al-ʿUmayrīnī. Al-Ṣafāh, Kuwait: Manshūrāt Markaz al-Makhṭūṭāt wa'l-Turāth, 1987.

Young, Walter Edward. "The Dialectical Forge: Proto-System Juridical Disputation in the *Kitāb Ikhtilāf al-ʿIrāqiyyīn*." 2 vols. PhD diss., McGill University, 2012.

Glossary: Select Technical Terms of Islamic Legal Theory and Dialectic

adab*, pl. *ādāb proper comportment and its guidelines
ʿadam al-taʾthīr lack of efficiency (of the *ʿilla*, in occasioning the *ḥukm*)
adillat al-Sharʿ the indicants of God's Law
adillat al-maʿqūl the indicants of what is rationally understood [of the *aṣl*]
ʿaks opposite; co-absence (of *ʿilla* and *ḥukm*) [as opposed to *ṭard*]
ʿāmm*, *ʿumūm general (sense) [as opposed to *khāṣṣ*]
amr command, injunction
ʿaql rational intellect; rational intellection; self-made rational inference [as opposed to *naql*]
aṣl*, pl. *uṣūl lit. "root/stem/trunk"; [in *qiyās*] the authoritative, non-derived source-case whose *ḥukm* is known, and with which the *farʿ* is correlated; root-case; source-case; authoritative, divinely-sanctioned (or inspired) source-case; premise-principle [cf. *qāʿida*]; *status quo ante*
athar*, pl. *āthār reported/transmitted tradition; effect
awlā superior; more appropriate; prior in consideration
baḥth [dialectical] inquiry and investigation
barāʾat al-dhimma exemption from obligation
bāṭil null and void
bayān explanation, explication, clarification; explanatory capability
burhān*, pl. *barāhīn demonstration, (demonstrative) proof
dalāla indication
dalīl*, pl. *adilla indicant drawn from an epistemically authoritative source
dalīl al-khiṭāb (restrictive) indication of the instruction
daʿwā claim, allegation
dawarān concomitance; co-presence and co-absence of *ʿilla* and *ḥukm* [cf. *jarayān*; *al-ṭard waʾl-ʿaks*]
faḥwā al-khiṭāb *a fortiori* signification of the instruction
fann *technē*, art
faqīh*, pl. *fuqahāʾ jurist competent in *fiqh*

W.E. Young, *The Dialectical Forge*, Logic, Argumentation & Reasoning 9,
DOI 10.1007/978-3-319-25522-4

***far*ʿ, pl. *furū*ʿ** lit. "branch"; [in *qiyās*] the derivative case whose *ḥukm* is determined by correlation with the *aṣl*; branch-case, derived case; substantive ruling determined via *ijtihād*
farq*, pl. *furūq invalidating distinction, *qiyās*-invalidating difference
fasād invalidity [as opposed to *ṣiḥḥa*]
fasād al-iʿtibār invalid compatibility-comparison
fasād al-waḍʿ invalidity of occasioned status
fāsid invalid [as opposed to *ṣaḥīḥ*]
fiʿl*, pl. *afʿāl deed, act, action, performance; [in the Sunna] a deed of the Prophet
fiqh the jurist's "understanding" of God's Law, the fruit of *ijtihād*; a corpus of derived substantive law
furūq *qiyās*-invalidating inter-case distinctions [a genre of legal literature]
ḥadīth*, pl. *aḥādīth Prophetic report, conveying a unit of Sunna with *isnād* and *matn*
al-ḥaṣr restriction (of the *khiṭāb*, to a particular object)
ḥujja*, pl. *ḥujaj decisive argument; proof
ḥujjiyya argumentative conclusiveness
ḥukm*, pl. *aḥkām ruling, norm (substantive, procedural, or methodological); [in *qiyās*] the ruling of the *aṣl* which the proponent seeks to transfer to the *far*ʿ
ibṭāl nullification
ifḥām the silencing of a dialectical opponent
iḥtijāj drawing argumentative support
***ijmā*ʿ** consensus; Muslim communal and/or scholarly consensus on a particular *ḥukm*
ijmā*ʿ *Ahl al-Madīna the consensus of the Medinese
ijmāl ambiguity
ijtihād the attempted discovery of God's Law via exhaustive research and rational application of legal theoretical rules and methods; the cultivation of *furū*ʿ from *uṣūl* via the principles developed in *uṣūl al-fiqh*
ikhtilāf disagreement; plurality of opinion; divergence [synonym: *khilāf*]; juridical disagreement [a genre of legal literature]
ikhtilāf al-qirā'a variant readings of the Qur'ān
ikhtilāf al-riwāya variant narrations of a report
ʿ*illa*, pl. ʿ*ilal* [in *qiyās*] the occasioning factor which gives rise to the *ḥukm*
ʿ*ilm*, pl. ʿ*ulūm* knowledge; knowledge system; science
ʿ*ilm al-jadal* the science of juridical dialectic
ʿ*ilm al-khilāf* the science of juridical disagreement
ʿ*ilm uṣūl al-fiqh* the science of legal theory and method
ilzām the inexorable concession of a dialectical opponent
intiqāl shifting ground (to a different topic)
iqrār [in the Sunna] the Prophet's acknowledgment of another's saying or deed
isnād [in *ḥadīth*] the chain of transmission [as opposed to the *matn*]
istidlāl drawing indication; drawing forth a *dalīl*-indicant, as epistemic justification for the argued solution to the *mas'ala*; mode of argument from authoritative indicants

al-istidlāl bi'l-'aks drawing indication by way of the opposite
al-istidlāl bi'l-awlā drawing indication by way of *a fortiori* valuation
al-istidlāl bi-bayān al-'illa drawing indication by way of clarifying the occasioning factor
al-istidlāl bi'l-taqsīm drawing indication by way of analytical disjunction
al-istidlāl bi'l-uṣūl drawing indication by way of the collective testimony of divinely-sanctioned source-cases
istinbāṭ rational inference
istiṣḥāb ḥāl presumption of continuity of a legal *status quo ante*
istiṣḥāb ḥāl al-'aql presumption of continuity of a *status quo ante* of rational intellection
istiṣḥāb ḥāl al-ijmā' presumption of continuity of a *status quo ante* of consensus
istiṣḥāb ḥāl al-'umūm presumption of continuity of the generality
istiṣḥāb ḥāl barā'at al-dhimma presumption of continuity of a *status quo ante* of absolution from obligation
ithbāt confirmation, affirmation
i'tirāḍ*, pl. *i'tirāḍāt dialectical objection, critique
jadal dialectic; theory and practice of (juridical) dialectical disputation
al-jadal al-ḥasan the "good" (truth-seeking, non-sophistical) dialectic
jā'iz allowed, permitted
jalī clearly disclosed, perspicuous
jarayān concomitance; co-presence and co-absence of *'illa* and *ḥukm* [cf. *dawarān*; *al-ṭard wa'l-'aks*]
jawāb*, pl. *ajwiba (proper) response, reply, or rebuttal to an objection
jawāz allowance, permission
jumla*, pl. *jumal general or non-specific [as opposed to *mufassir*]
kalām speech, discourse; argument, argumentative discourse; dialectical theology
kasr breaking apart (the properties composing the *'illa*)
khabar transmission, transmitted report
khafī latent, hidden
khārij 'alā sabab proceeding from a reason; prompted [as opposed to *mubtada'*]
khaṣīṣa*, pl. *khaṣā'iṣ special characteristic
khaṣm opponent (in disputation)
khāṣṣ particular (sense) [as opposed to *'āmm*, *'umūm*]
khilāf (juridical) disagreement [synonym: *ikhtilāf*]; the contrary or contradictory
khiṭāb speech, discourse; instruction from an epistemically authoritative source (in Qur'ān or Sunna)
al-Kitāb lit. "the Book," meaning: the Qur'ān
lafẓ*, pl. *alfāẓ expression; vocable
laḥn al-khiṭāb the unspoken implication of the instruction
mabda'*, pl. *mabādi' first principle
madhhab*, pl. *madhāhib doctrinal opinion; doctrinal school (e.g., Ḥanafī, Shāfi'ī, etc.); predominant opinion on a point of law within a doctrinal school
maḥall*, pl. *maḥāll locus, place in which something is situated

māhiyya quiddity; essence
man' denial; prevention, blocking [synonym: *mumānaʿa*]
ma'nā*, pl. *ma'ānī intension-property of a legal object or context, potentially efficient in occasioning its *ḥukm*; intension; meaning; property; intrinsic quality
ma'nā al-khiṭāb intension-property of the instruction [= *qiyās*]
manzila status
maqṣid*, pl. *maqāṣid aim, objective
maqāṣid al-Sharī'a induced objectives of God's Law [genre of legal literature]
ma'qūl aṣl what is rationally understood from an *aṣl*
mas'ala*, pl. *masā'il *problēma*; contended problem-case for which a solution is sought
mas'alat al-naqḍ the parallel case brought by Q to expose R's intra-doctrinal inconsistency
mas'ūl the respondent (R) [as opposed to the *sā'il*]
matn [in *ḥadīth*] the transmitted text [as opposed to the *isnād*]
mawḍi'*, pl. *mawāḍi' locus; topos; case; passage (in a book)
mu'allil the respondent (R), when engaged in *taʿlīl* [as opposed to the *sā'il*]
mu'āraḍa counter-indication (Q's bringing a counter-*dalīl* to oppose and supplant R's *dalīl*)
al-mu'āraḍa bi-'illa counter-indication by way of an occasioning factor
al-mu'āraḍa bi-nuṭq counter-indication by way of divinely-sanctioned decree
mubayyan clear, unambiguous
mubtada' self-initiated; unprompted [as opposed to *khārij ʿalā sabab*]
mufaṣṣal unambiguous [as opposed to *mujmal*]
mufassir interpreting, specifying [as opposed to *jumla*]
muḥāl absurd, impossible; absurdity, impossibility
muḥtamal equivocal; 'possibly bearing' or 'susceptible of' another *maʿnā*-intension
mūjib compelling agency
mujmal ambiguous [as opposed to *mufaṣṣal*]
mujtahid jurist qualified to perform *ijtihād*
mukābara obstinate contentiousness; contending to prove oneself superior
mumāna'a denial; prevention, blocking [synonym: *manʿ*]
munāza'a contestation
munāẓara dialectical disputation; theory and practice of investigation via dialectical disputation
mushāraka sharing
al-mushāraka fi'l-dalīl sharing the indicant
mustadill the respondent (R), when engaged in *istidlāl* [as opposed to the *sā'il*]
muṭālaba evidential demand; a demand for verification, justification, etc.
naqḍ a dialectical charge of intra-doctrinal inconsistency
naqīḍ the logical contradictory
naql transmission of textual support from a prior authority [as opposed to *ʿaql*]
naskh abrogation
naṣṣ univocal source-text; unambiguous text; univocal formulation

naẓar intellectual investigation, speculation, or analytical insight
naẓīr*, pl. *naẓā'ir parallel case; one of two legal objects or categories whose corresponding rulings mirror each other
nizāʿ contention, dispute
nuṭq divinely-sanctioned decree (as found in Qur'ān or Sunna)
qadḥ critiquing, degrading (the narrator of a report)
qāʿida*, pl. *qawāʿid general legal principle [cf. *aṣl*]
qalb reversal (of the *qiyās*, to produce the contradictory *ḥukm*)
qaṭʿī decisive, certain [as opposed to *ẓannī*]
qawāʿid fiqhiyya the induced general principles of derived law [a genre of legal literature]
qawl*, pl. *aqwāl profession; assertion; doctrine; [in the Sunna] a saying of the Prophet
al-qawl bi-mūjib al-ʿilla professing the compelling agency of the occasioning factor
qawl al-wāḥid min al-Ṣaḥāba decree of a solitary Companion; an asserted doctrine of one of the Companions of the Prophet
qirā'a reading (of the Qur'ān)
qism*, pl. *aqsām division, category
qiyās correlational inference [= *maʿnā al-khiṭāb*]
qiyās al-ʿaks correlational inference of the opposite
qiyās al-dalāla correlational inference of indication
qiyās al-ʿilla correlational inference of the occasioning factor
al-qiyās al-jalī clearly-disclosed correlational inference
qiyās al-shabah correlational inference of resemblance
qiyās al-ṭard correlational inference of co-presence
ra'y considered opinion
riwāya narration (of a report)
sabab reason, cause
ṣaḥīḥ valid [as opposed to *fāsid*]
sā'il the questioner (Q) [as opposed to the *mas'ūl*, *mustadill*, or *muʿallil* (R)]
shabah*, pl. *ashbāh resemblance
Sharʿ/Sharīʿa God's Law
ṣifa attribute
ṣiḥḥa validity [as opposed to *fasād*]
su'āl*, pl. *as'ila (dialectical) question
sunna*, pl. *sunan traditions of past authority figures' exemplary conduct
Sunna the Sunna; the Prophet's instruction, exemplary conduct, and acknowledgment
taḥakkum arbitrariness
taḥqīq verification
tajrīḥ defaming (the narrator of a report)
takhṣīṣ particularization
takhṣīṣ al-ʿilla particularization of the occasioning factor; the theory that an *ʿilla* occasioning *ḥukm* X, in general circumstances, can be "particularized" by a

certain preventative factor (*māniʿ*) in order to occasion *ḥukm* Y, in particular circumstances

ta'kīd intensification (of a *ḥukm*, as occurs in *a fortiori* arguments)

taʿlīl justifying the occasioning factor; *ʿilla*-justification

al-taʿlīl bi'l-ism *ʿilla*-justification by way of the name

tanāquḍ intra-argument, logical contradiction

tanbīh appeal to the self-evident

taqsīm analytical disjunction

ṭard co-presence (of *ʿilla* and *ḥukm*) [as opposed to *ʿaks*]

al-ṭard wa'l-ʿaks concomitance; co-presence and co-absence of *ʿilla* and *ḥukm* [cf. *jarayān*; *dawarān*]

ṭarīqa*, pl. *ṭuruq systematic method

tarjīḥ preponderance; the bringing of one *dalīl*-indicant to preponderate over another in terms of epistemic strength

taṣḥīḥ validation

ta'thīr efficiency (in causing or occasioning something)

tawātur unbroken, consistent transmission (of a report), with multiple transmitters at every stage

ta'wīl preponderating exegesis

ʿumūm see *ʿāmm*

ʿurf custom; customary usage

al-uṣūl the divinely-sanctioned root-cases of Qur'ān, Sunna, and Ijmāʿ

uṣūl al-fiqh fully systematized legal theory and methodology, the science of *ijtihād*; the epistemological, hermeneutical, and rational-inferential tools and methods employed by the *mujtahid* to discover God's Law

waḍʿ posited linguistic intension; thesis; occasioned status

wāḍiḥ plainly-evident

wajh*, pl. *wujūh mode

waṣf*, pl. *awṣāf property, quality

ẓāhir most apparent meaning, sense, or interpretation

ẓannī probable [as opposed to *qaṭʿī*]

Index

W.E. Young, *The Dialectical Forge*, Logic, Argumentation & Reasoning 9,
DOI 10.1007/978-3-319-25522-4

D

G

I

T

Kolibri 360 GmbH
Ferdinand-Jühlke-Straße 7
99095 Erfurt, Deutschland
produktsicherheit@kolibri360.de